What's New in D

IDE Improved

The most obvious change to the Integrated Development Environment (IDE) is the introduction of the Internet Explorer look-and-feel, with those fancy cursor-highlighted buttons. The following additions, if not as stylish, are a little more practical:

- DLL Debugging Support
- Code Editor Enhancements

  * Gutters
  * Evaluation hints
  * Code templates
  * Multi-byte character support
  * Component templates

VCL and Runtime Library Improved

A huge number of additions and changes were made to the Visual Component Library (VCL) and Runtime Library. The following list details the new components:

  * TAnimate
  * TToolbar
  * TSplitter
  * TCoolBar
  * Internet Components
  * TSpeedButton
  * TOpenPictureDialog and TSavePictureDialog

Compiler Revised

Apart from the changes required to support the new VCL and RTL features, the compiler was also revised to implement the following functionality:

- Assert Procedure Included
- Package Support
- WideString added for multi-byte character support

OLE Support Undergoes Serious Development

OLE support now includes Component Object Model (COM) and ActiveX functionality. The new Delphi ActiveX framework (DAX) allows you to easily build COM servers, ActiveX controls, ActiveForms ActiveX property pages, and OLE automation servers. These objects then can be used in applications such as Internet Explorer 3, Delphi, C++ Builder 4 & 5, Visual Basic, and IntraBuilder.

Database Support Revised, Enhanced

Version 3 revises the structure of database support and provides several enhancements:

- Distributed Datasets
- TDataSet Changes
- Database Explorer Enhancements

Special Edition

USING
DELPHI 3™

Special Edition

USING
DELPHI 3™

Written by Todd Miller and David Powell with

Roland Bouchereau • Julian Bucknall • Bill Curtis • Scott Frolich
Joe C. Hecht • Chaim Krause • Mark Pritchard • Noel Rice
J.W. Rider • Quentin Sarafinchan • Stephen A. Schafer • Eric Uber

Special Edition Using Delphi 3

Library of Congress Catalog No.: 97-65019

ISBN: 0-7897-1118-4

99 98 97   6   5   4   3   2   1

Interpretation of the printing code: the rightmost double-digit number is the year of the book's printing; the rightmost single-digit number, the number of the book's printing. For example, a printing code of 97-1 shows that the first printing of the book occurred in 1997.

Screen reproductions in this book were created using Collage Plus from Inner Media, Inc., Hollis, NH.

Contents at a Glance

Table of Contents

III | Database Development

9 Working with Local Databases 323

IV | Component Development

15   Working with Packages   445

VI | Advanced Topics

Credits

PRESIDENT
Roland Elgey

PUBLISHER
Stacy Hiquet

SENIOR TITLE MANAGER
Bryan Gambrel

EDITORIAL SERVICES DIRECTOR
Elizabeth Keaffaber

STRATEGIC MARKETING MANAGER
Barry Pruett

ACQUISITIONS EDITOR
Jeff Riley

PRODUCTION EDITOR
Don Eamon

COPY EDITOR
Chris Haidri

PRODUCT MARKETING MANAGER
Kristine Ankney

ASSISTANT PRODUCT MARKETING MANAGERS
Karen Hagen
Christy M. Miller

TECHNICAL EDITORS
David Rippy
Alain Tadros

TECHNICAL SUPPORT SPECIALIST
Nadeem Muhammed

ACQUISITIONS COORDINATOR
Carmen Krikorian

SOFTWARE RELATIONS COORDINATOR
Susan D. Gallagher

EDITORIAL ASSISTANT
Andrea Duvall

BOOK DESIGNER
Ruth Harvey

COVER DESIGNER
Dan Armstrong

PRODUCTION TEAM
Maribeth Echard
Kay Hoskin
Darlena Murray
Nicole Ruessler

INDEXER
Chris Barrick

Composed in *Century Old Style* and *ITC Franklin Gothic* by Que Corporation.

About the Authors

Lead Authors

Todd Miller has been a professional software engineer for over four years. After getting his Bachelor's degree in Computer Science from California State University, Long Beach, Todd started working at Borland International as an Associate Engineer in the dBASE Developer Support Department. Todd currently is a Senior Advisor in the Delphi Developer Support Department. He also is Delphi Client/Server certified and has been working with the Delphi product since the early beta of Delphi 1. Todd lives in Scott's Valley, California, with his wife Joyce, and his two children Troy and Heather. Todd's favorite things to do are playing computer games with his kids and going for walks on the beach with his wife. He can be reached on CompuServe at **71333,2144**.

David Powell is a Senior Delphi Support Engineer for Borland International and is Delphi Client/Server certified. He has a B.S. in Computer Engineering from San José State University and has been using Pascal since Turbo Pascal 3. David's programming background ranges from graphical marketing software for life insurance companies to real-time embedded code systems for military aircraft. David lives in Scott's Valley, California, with his wife Karina, two sons Daniel and Jonathan, 200 African cichlids, two chameleons, one iguana, and a rabbit. David can be reached at **76711.1441@compuserve.com**.

Contributing Authors

Roland Bouchereau is a Consulting Engineer at Borland International. He is a computer professional of 14 years and specializes in Client/Server DBMS programming. Prior to joining Borland, Roland worked as a network administrator and as a developer in A/R and A/P systems. He lives in Campbell, CA, with his wife Michelle, and daughters Shanelle and Kesi. Roland can be reached on CompuServe at **75300,1734**.

Julian M. Bucknall has been a programmer for longer than he can remember, and has reputedly been earning money at it for at least 18 years. He is the Director of Tools Development at TurboPower Software and has been known to contribute design ideas, components, code, documentation, and debugging time for their range of Delphi products, including Orpheus, Async Professional for Delphi, SysTools, and FlashFiler. He has even been known to code in his spare time—of which he has none, as he is also an amateur actor. Julian wishes to thank Jeff Riley for bearing with him as he got further behind schedule with his chapter, Orpheus (the cat this time), who slept on his mousepad whilst he wrote it, and Donna for reading the thing after he finished it (and not understanding a word). He can be reached on CompuServe at **100116,1572**.

Bill Curtis is a Senior Engineer in Borland International's SQL Links/Connectivity Technical Support Department. His areas of focus at Borland are: Borland's BDE and SQL Links, database programming and design, and C/S software and platform features and requirements. Bill is hooked on computers and technology. While waiting for the next big thing in tech toys, you might catch him gardening, taking in a new (or old favorite) film or video, or planning a relaxing "getaway." Bill lives in Santa Cruz, California, with his partner and future wife Melinda.

Scott Frolich is a Consulting Engineer for Borland International, currently working in the Delphi Developer Support Department. Areas of specialization are: Delphi Database Components, Borland Database Engine (BDE), BDE API, InterBase, and SQL. Scott has worked with the Delphi product since its conception in mid-1994. Scott graduated from California State University, Chico, with a Computer Science B.S. degree. In his free time, Scott enjoys bicycling, running, and video games. He can be reached on CompuServe at **74431,257**.

Joe C. Hecht has been involved in the printing, typography, and publishing industry since 1976, and has been the chief architect for many graphics engines and print drivers for both the DOS and Windows environments over the last 12 years. Joe is currently employed as Field Engineer at Borland's Delphi Developer Support Group and can be reached through the Internet at **joehecht@gte.net** or through CompuServe at **70714,1353**.

Mark Pritchard has been writing GUI-based applications from a young age, leading to expertise in interface design and object-oriented, event-driven programming. He currently heads a software company specializing in the design and creation of custom software solutions using languages such as Delphi, C++, C, and VB. He can be reached on the Internet at **pritchma@ozemail.com.au**.

Chaim Krause is an Engineer for Borland International. He works on the Delphi Developer Support Team. Most of Chaim's interests revolve around computers, games, and military history. Most of his time is spent in front of the computer, and most of his conversations are through e-mail. Next to his dog, an American eskimo named after General George Washington (it was the white hair), his most trusted companion is his spell checker. Chaim can be reached on the Internet at **chaim@chaim.com**.

Noel Rice is a recovering AS/400 programmer who works as a senior engineer in Borland International's Delphi Developer Support Department. He enjoys playing guitar and synthesizer, sailing, and spending time with his significant other, Dee. Noel lives in Aptos, California, and can be reached at **nrice@ix.netcom** or **pw1.netcom.com/~nrice/home.html**.

J. W. Rider is a senior programmer/analyst at Pragmatics, Inc., McLean, VA, where he has been developing medical bibliographic software for the National Library of Medicine (NLM) in a Delphi client/server environment. Prior to joining Pragmatics, he developed systems at several sites across the country, in a variety of programming languages. In his spare time, J. W. also teaches information system technology in the Northern Virginia Community College system, and tackles electronic technical queries concerning Delphi as a member of Team Borland. J. W. lives with his wife Maradee, son Jim, and daughter Heather in Herndon, VA. He can be reached at **70007.4652@compuserve.com**.

At the time of this writing, **Quentin Sarafinchan** worked for Borland in Delphi Developer Support. Although he's a jack-of-all-computing areas, Quentin's primary interests lie in the areas of telecommunication and graphics/animation. He now is contracting and spending time on the ski slopes in Canada, where he lives in Edmonton, Alberta, with his wife, a gorgeous six-month-old little girl named Quenndelynn, and a pug named Chausy.

Steve Schafer is currently an Assistant Professor in the Department of Physics at Oklahoma State University. He teaches courses in lasers, optics, and general physics and is involved in research investigating the interaction of light with biological materials. Prior to joining the OSU faculty, he worked in the medical imaging industry. Steve wrote his first computer program (in Fortran II) at age 11. It crashed the school district's IBM mainframe. Buoyed by feelings of power, he has been involved with computers ever since. Steve has been using Turbo/Borland Pascal (and now Delphi) since 1985, and in 1991 joined Team Borland. He can be found hanging out on the DELPHI and BDELPHI32 forums on CompuServe, and can be reached by e-mail at **76711.522@compuserve.com** or **pandeng@telepath.com**.

Eric Uber is a Quality Assurance engineer on Borland's core Delphi development team. Previously, he was a senior technical engineer on Borland's Delphi Developer support team where he served a dual role, acting as a liaison for Borland's C++ Builder Developer support team. Previous experience includes a senior developer position at Ellipsys Technologies, developing Expert Systems for the Telephony industry. Eric has coauthored three other books for Que and does consulting on the side. In his spare time, he rides his RM250 and 1982 IT250 dirt bikes and hangs out with his wife Dawn, and year-and-a-half-old son Tyler. Eric can be reached at **ezee@compuserve.com**.

About the Technical Editors

David Rippy is a manager with Ensemble Corporation, specializing in the design and development of client/server and Internet applications. He also is a contributing writer to Delphi Informant magazine and is frequently a guest speaker at various industry conferences. He can be reached on CompuServe at **74444,415**.

Alain Tadros is a Senior Quality Assurance Engineer for the Delphi development team, specializing in the COM, OLE, and ActiveX arena. Alain had the opportunity to write some of the code during the development of ActiveX Framework in Delphi 3.0. Alain worked on several teams at Borland, including C++ and Delphi developer support, and also on the C++ development team. Alain has written for several major magazines and has produced several Borland Web sites with OLE, COM, ActiveX, and Development using C++ and Delphi together. Alain lives in Scott's Valley, California, with his wife Jessica, and Delphi the cat. He can be reached on the Internet at **atadros@wpo.borland.com**.

We'd Like to Hear from You!

As part of our continuing effort to produce books of the highest possible quality, Que would like to hear your comments. To stay competitive, we *really* want you to let us know what you like or dislike most about this book or other Que products.

Please send your comments, ideas, and suggestions for improvement to:

The Expert User Team
E-mail: **euteam@que.mcp.com**
CompuServe: **72410,2077**
Fax: (317) 581-4663

Our mailing address is:

Expert User Team
Que Corporation
201 West 103rd Street
Indianapolis, IN 46290-1097

You can also visit our Team's home page on the World Wide Web at:

http://www.mcp.com/que/developer_expert

Thank you in advance. Your comments will help us to continue publishing the best books available in today's market.

Thank you,

The Expert User Team

Essentials

What's New in Delphi 3

by Mark Pritchard

Congratulations! By opening *Special Edition Using Delphi 3*, you have taken the first step into the latest, and most amazing, incarnation of Delphi—version 3. Delphi 3 is simply the most powerful and flexible application development tool available today. It combines visual interface design with a greatly enhanced, object-oriented version of the Pascal language. With Delphi 3, you can build fast, intuitive, and robust Win32-compliant applications in a remarkably short time.

Unlike other development environments, Delphi actually delivers what its hype promises. We can guarantee that when you install Delphi 3 and start playing with its remarkable features, you will feel an involuntary grin creep across your face. Life was never so easy! From its new code templates and fly-over variable watches to the blindingly quick native code compiler and linker, Delphi 3 is the development environment you have been waiting for.

Delphi's features

This book takes you through Delphi's many features to give you an idea of the considerable resources at your disposal.

What's new in Delphi

This covers the innovations introduced with Delphi 3. When developing Delphi, Borland consistently did what the rest of the market considers unthinkable—it listened to its customers. The result of this is a host of great features and changes that make the product even more exciting.

What you'll learn in this book

This section takes you through the topics covered in this book. If you are hunting for a particular piece of information, or just want to get a feel for the material contained within a chapter, this is the stuff to read.

Now, the skeptics among you will think, "Sure, you need to promote the product to sell the book." Well, Delphi doesn't really need promotion from our side—industry experts and people just like you have given the previous versions of Delphi some impressive accolades. *PC Magazine* tagged Delphi with their stamp of Technical Excellence in the Development Tools category. *ComputerWorld* reports that Delphi is the Highest Ranking Product on their Buyers' Satisfaction Scorecard. Even publications devoted to Delphi's competitors think highly of the product—Delphi received the Editor's Choice award in the *Visual Basic Programmers Journal*. If you have Internet access, take a look at Delphi's many decorations at **http:// www.borland.com/delphi/delaward.html**.

You are probably asking why you should use this book to come to grips with Delphi 3. If so, you have definitely skipped the authors' biographies. The caliber of the author team is the most compelling reason for choosing this book. The two lead authors are Todd Miller and David Powell—Senior Advisors in the Delphi Developer Support Department. The remaining members of the author team are not fly-by-night gurus either. All are accomplished Delphi practitioners, whose quite extensive skills are detailed in their biographies. ■

CAUTION

This book doesn't teach you programming fundamentals. It teaches Delphi 3, and assumes knowledge of core programming concepts such as variables, functions, and loops. If you have experience in another language such as C++ or Visual Basic, the introductory chapters give you a sound basis in Delphi programming. If you are an old hand at Pascal or a user of a previous version of Delphi, you will have no trouble following this book.

Delphi's Main Features

Delphi isn't just an editor and compiler, it's a development environment packed full of neat features that make your development life easier. To cover all the features would require this entire book, so we only cover the most commonly used and beneficial items.

Customizable Development Environment

For several years, we have enjoyed the integration of traditional programming tools—the editor, compiler, and debugger. Windows development environments added the capability to visually create your program's interface and automatically generate supporting code. Delphi takes these features and goes a step further. The Open Tools API allows you to write utilities, such as an auto-save expert, which plug into Delphi's Integrated Development Environment (IDE). The Open Tools API is covered further in Chapter 29, "Working with Delphi's Open Tools API."

Object Orientation

Languages such as Visual Basic are pseudo-object oriented—they use objects and methods, but they do not support the basic object-oriented concepts of encapsulation, inheritance, and polymorphism. Delphi is truly object-oriented—it allows you to combine data and code into a class (encapsulation), create new descendant classes (inheritance), and treat a descendant class as a parent class (polymorphism).

Component Library

You probably have noticed that the screen elements that make up Windows applications are quite similar. Take the standard button as an example—it usually is represented as a raised, gray rectangle with some function-specific text on its surface. Delphi takes the functionality of the button—its capability to respond to a mouse click and to display text, and wraps it into an object known as a *component*. This component is stored in the *component library*. Delphi ships with a heavily populated component library, containing all the objects you need to create a full-fledged Win32 program.

The object-oriented nature of Delphi adds a neat twist to the component library. If you require additional functionality or want to modify the behavior of a component, simply derive a new component from that stored in the library and start coding!

OCX and ActiveX Support

Delphi also supports objects that are created with other languages, such as C++, and are distributed using the OCX standard. OCX objects are generally supplied by third-party software companies, and provide a wide range of functionality from a Web browser to a whiz-bang spreadsheet and mundane spell checking. ActiveX is a redevelopment of the OCX model and is emerging as a standard for plug-in objects, especially for Internet browsers. With Delphi's capability to create and manipulate ActiveX objects, you'll have that Internet domination you dreamed of by lunchtime!

Templates

Just when you thought your programming talents were about to be reduced to merely manipulating components and OCX objects, along come templates that make even this task trivial! Delphi recognizes four types of templates: form, application, component, and code. The form, application, and component templates allow you to reuse customized collections of objects in separate programs, or as the basis for a new program. A code template is a new feature, which greatly reduces the repetitive typing associated with programming. It's covered later in this chapter in the section, "New Features in Delphi 3."

True Compilation

Many Windows development environments generate semi-compiled or p-code executables. Because p-code is not machine executable, it must be translated at runtime—a massive performance penalty. Imagine the wasted CPU time as an image conversion routine is executed! Delphi uses a true compiler and linker and produces a 100-percent native machine code executable. This executable has no performance overhead, a welcome feature in these days of bloatware—programs so over-engineered, they require a high-end system just to load the title screen!

Using a true compiler provides another advantage—the ability to create DLLs that may contain any of the components from the component library. These DLLs can then be used to extend your Delphi application or they can be used as service providers to programs developed with less sophisticated tools.

Robust Applications

If you have coded in any other language, you have come across the need for error checking and resource protection. The old way of handling this was to execute a function and then check its result. If it was successful, do something else and check its status. You would continue this process until your source code was indented to the point where 99 percent of it was white space. Delphi neatly solves this problem of error detection with the concept of an *exception*. Rather than working on the assumption that each step will fail and having to test accordingly, Delphi enables you to code as if your statements will succeed. If a statement fails, Delphi raises an exception, which can be trapped with a single exception handler. This allows your program to recover from an error gracefully, with minimal effort on your part, and is much easier on your Tab key.

Data Access

Hands up, those of you who have never written a program that accesses a database. Never. Not even once. Not many, are there? Borland recognized that most of your applications are data-centric; after all, this is what computers are really good at anyway—collecting, processing, and reporting data. This data obviously must be stored somewhere and developers usually choose a database. Delphi provides objects and components that greatly reduce the effort involved in creating database-enabled applications. With Delphi, it is possible to write a simple data-enabled program without a scrap of code!

New Features in Delphi 3

The latest release of Delphi brings an incredible array of new features, which could fill a separate book or a hard disk of five years ago. Hold on to your seat while we leap into the wondrous world of Delphi 3.

What's New in the IDE

The most obvious change to the Integrated Development Environment (IDE) is the introduction of the Internet Explorer look-and-feel with those fancy cursor-highlighted buttons. The following additions, if not as stylish, are a little more practical.

DLL Debugging Support   Previous versions of Delphi did not support integrated debugging of DLLs because DLLs are not stand-alone executables—they are loaded at the request of an application. In Delphi 3, you can specify an executable that uses your new DLL, which allows Delphi to trap calls to the routines in the DLL and route them through the integrated debugger. Chapter 27, "Testing and Debugging," covers debugging DLLs in more detail.

Code Editor Enhancements   The Code Editor has undergone revisions in Delphi 3 that are covered in the following paragraphs.

Gutter   The Code Editor window now supports a *gutter*, a rectangular region that contains descriptive symbols, such as breakpoints and procedure bodies. The gutter allows the editor to handle character positions correctly rather than reserving the first column for symbol display.

Evaluation Hints   One of those really simple things that it took Delphi to implement is *evaluation hints*. By now, every application worth using provides fly-over hints—those little help windows that pop up when you rest the mouse cursor on an object. The Code Editor uses this concept to display the runtime value of any variable or property when you place the mouse cursor over it.

Code Templates   The advent of *code templates* is worth celebrating. How many times have you typed in the same code constructs such as if...then...else or for...do? Code templates now automate this task, saving you time and frustration, especially if you are a typist of the "hunt-and-peck" variety. The use of code templates is covered further in Chapter 2, "Working with Delphi's IDE."

Multi-Byte Character Support   With the veritable explosion of Internet use, global distribution of your application is no longer a far-fetched idea. To assist you with deployment of multi-language enabled programs, the Code Editor now supports *multi-byte characters* in comments and string constants.

Component Templates   Previous versions of Delphi provided form and application templates, which allow you to reuse collections of forms and components in new projects. Delphi 3 adds the concept of a *component template*—a customized group of components that you configure once, add to the repository, and reuse. Component templates simplify the process of creating standard collections of components to a single mouse operation and are covered later in Chapter 16, "Creating Components."

What's New in the VCL and RTL

A huge number of additions and changes were made to the Visual Component Library (VCL) and Runtime Library. The following sections cover the most useful items.

New Components   The following components are new to the Delphi 3 VCL, and documented further in Chapters 6 and 7, "Using Delphi Components" and "Using Win32 Common Controls."

TSplitter   The TSplitter component allows you to define rectangular regions of your forms that are able to be resized at runtime. The Windows Explorer provides an example of this functionality: You can drag the center divider to the left or right to alter the size of the folder tree and file list.

TAnimate   This component is like a cut-down version of TMediaPlayer—it plays Audio Video Interleaved (AVI) files within its display area.

TImageList   The TImageList component included in previous versions of Delphi, is now publicly available in the component library. This component allows you to efficiently store a large collection of images.

TToolBar   Applications created with previous versions of Delphi used a TPanel component to create a toolbar. In Delphi 3, TToolBar takes the place of TPanel and adds some useful toolbar-specific functionality.

TCoolBar   If you have admired the toolbars of Internet Explorer from afar, you will love the TCoolBar component. It gives you Internet Explorer toolbars in a component, which is easily included in your Delphi application.

TOpenPictureDialog and TSavePictureDialog   These components present a file open or save dialog box with a picture preview—useful when loading or saving image files.

Internet Components   There are too many components to cover individually here. The set of Internet components makes developing Internet-aware applications an absolute breeze. High-level protocol programming is effortless with component-level support for the HTTP, HTML, FTP, NNTP, POP, SMTP, TCP, and UDP protocols. If you are reeling from this list, try adding client and server socket components, and the capability to create Internet server applications! Chapter 28, "Creating Web Server Applications," covers the Internet components in more detail.

Modified Components   Several commonly used objects have been modified in Delphi 3.

TSpeedButton   A new property named Flat has been added. If True, the TSpeedButton behaves like the buttons in Microsoft's Internet Explorer.

TFont   As part of multi-byte character support, the TFont object gains a property called Charset, which specifies the font's character set.

TCanvas   Programming graphics in a multithreaded application used to be tricky—you had to use the TThread.Synchronize method to draw on a TCanvas object. Delphi 3 adds two methods, Lock and Unlock, to the TCanvas object to make this task easier. The Lock method grants exclusive access to a TCanvas drawing surface, and Unlock releases it.

What's New in the Compiler

Apart from the changes required to support the new VCL and RTL features, the compiler was also revised to implement the following functionality.

Assert   The inclusion of the Assert procedure is a perfect case of "Ask and ye shall receive." Assert raises an exception when a Boolean expression is False. It is primarily used when developing your application to ensure that a particular condition exists before executing a segment of code.

Package Support   One of the benefits of using Delphi is its capability to create a stand-alone executable file, requiring no runtime DLLs. The downside is that each application includes its own copy of the VCL. Delphi 3 introduces the notion of a *package*—a collection of components and objects compiled into a sharable DLL. Sharing the component library reduces memory usage and load times. There is one caveat: You must include the DLL package when distributing your program.

Visual Basic Logical Compatibility   With Delphi's capability to create DLLs and ActiveX controls, you may find yourself needing to interface with Visual Basic (VB) programs. To bring Delphi's logical data types of ByteBool, WordBool, and LongBool in line with VB, their representation of True has changed from 1 to –1. False remains 0. The basic logical data type, Boolean, is unchanged and continues to represent True as 1 and False as 0.

WideString   The WideString type was introduced as part of multi-byte character support. A WideString stores Unicode (16-bit) characters and is similar to the standard String type—it is dynamically allocated and null-terminated.

What's New in OLE

OLE support has undergone some serious development work for Delphi 3. OLE support now includes Component Object Model (COM) and ActiveX functionality. The new ActiveX class framework allows you to easily build COM servers, ActiveX controls, ActiveX property pages, and non-visual OLE automation servers. These objects then can be used in applications such as Internet Explorer, Delphi, C++, Visual Basic, and IntraBuilder.

What's New in Database Development

Delphi has always had powerful database capabilities. Version 3 revises the structure of database support and provides many enhancements.

Distributed Datasets   The dataset model in previous versions of Delphi linked the client application directly to the database through the BDE, which meant the application included code to interface to the entire BDE, even if it required only a small part of BDE functionality. Delphi 3 introduces the concept of a distributed dataset, which treats all database types as client/server—the client (application) keeps a local copy of the table and simply sends modifications to the server. With this simplification, your executable needs to support only a single client object, encapsulated into the new TMemoryDataSet object. All other engine-specific code is housed in the BDE and shared by concurrently executing applications. Just in case you are terrified over having to modify all your code, don't worry—the internals of TTable, TQuery, and so on have already been updated to reflect the new structure and are completely compatible with existing code.

TDataSet Changes   The TDataSet object and its associated units, DB and DBTABLES, were revised to support the new distributed dataset structure. BDE-specific functionality has moved from TDataSet to TBDEDataSet and from the DB unit to DBTABLES.

Additional Format Support   The new Borland Database Engine (BDE) includes drivers for FoxPro and Access databases. OLE database providers automatically appear as individual BDE drivers.

Database Explorer Enhancements   The Database Explorer now supports DB2 and Informix. You may also edit certain SQL objects such as views and stored procedures, Oracle packages and Interbase generators, and exceptions. If you execute Database Explorer from within Delphi, you can use the Code Editor to edit SQL statements. Delphi now supports stored procedures as a drag-and-drop source—you can simply drag the stored procedure from Database Explorer and drop it onto a form displayed in the Form Designer, creating a TStoredProc component automatically. The many features of the Database Explorer are covered in more detail in Chapter 12, "Using Quick Reports."

What You Will Learn in This Book

This book is divided into the following sections, some of which span several chapters.

The Delphi Development Environment

Chapter 2, "Working with Delphi's IDE," introduces you to the Integrated Development Environment (IDE). We walk you through the huge array of menu options so that you grasp the scope of the environment. You learn about the three most commonly used tools when developing an application: the Object Inspector, Code Editor, and Form Designer. After you understand these tools, we take you through your first Delphi application, step-by-step, to put the theory into practice. The chapter finishes by discussing the Project Manager and Object Repository—two tools that will increase your productivity.

The Object Pascal Language

This section covers the Object Pascal language, the foundation of any Delphi program. It is split into the following two chapters:

- Chapter 3—"Object Pascal: A Fundamental Approach." This chapter shows how the rapid development cycle of Delphi goes all the way to the core with the structure, scope, and simplicity of the underlying Object Pascal language. You learn how to take simple pieces of information and store them as varied data types, combine them together with operators to form expressions, control execution of the expressions with structured statements, and make your programs modular using functions, procedures, and units.

- Chapter 4—"Object Pascal: Advanced Concepts." Having covered the basics, we extend your initial view of Object Pascal to include object-oriented concepts. You learn how to combine fields, methods, and properties to create useful classes, and you learn how to use some of the most valuable pieces of the libraries that ship with Delphi.

Error Handling and Resource Protection

Chapter 5, "Exception Handling," covers Delphi's powerful error-detection and -correction constructs. It details the `try...except` and `try...finally` statements and where you should use them. Because it would be hypocritical if we didn't follow our own programming guidelines, many examples in this book will use the material covered in this chapter.

Components and Controls

The Component Library is one of the most innovative and flexible tools in Delphi's repertoire. The following two chapters cover the components and controls that form the component library:

- Chapter 6—"Using Delphi Components." In this chapter, you learn that all components in the Component Library descend from two basic types—visual and non-visual. We first cover each type's standard properties and events and then move on to discuss each component's specific functionality.

- Chapter 7—"Using Win32 Common Controls." This chapter covers the new common controls introduced by Windows 95 such as iconic lists and segmented progress bars. It also covers some great new controls such as `TCoolBar`, `TToolBar`, and `TAnimate`. You learn about key properties and methods through numerous small code examples as well as some larger examples that integrate the latest look-and-feel design issues.

Creating Applications

Chapter 8, "Creating Applications" covers the issues that relate to developing applications in Delphi. It details the properties and events of the TForm class—the basic building blocks for any graphical application. After you understand the fundamentals, we continue by discussing the three types of applications—Single Document Interface, Multiple Document Interface, and Console. Along the way, you learn about project and compiler options, and you are introduced to a little API programming. We round out this chapter with some advanced coding techniques: tricks and classes you can use to implement common functionality.

Database Programming

Delphi provides a gold mine of data-aware components that make database programming with the Borland Database Engine (BDE) an almost trivial task. The following chapters cover the various aspects of database programming:

- Chapter 9—"Working with Local Databases." This chapter introduces you to the concept of a database and defines the jargon associated with database programming such as table, record, and field. We move on to cover the file structure of the two native local database formats of Paradox and dBASE. After you understand just what a database is and what it looks like, you learn about Delphi's component interface to the Borland Database Engine. We round out the chapter with a discussion of several advanced BDE features, such as cached updates and transactions.

- Chapter 10—"Working with SQL Databases." In this chapter, we build on what you learned in Chapter 9. We introduce the concepts of SQL, SQL databases, and SQL servers and cover the advantages and disadvantages of using SQL. You learn about the SQL-specific components found in the VCL such as TStoredProc and TUpdateSQL. The final section of the chapter covers BDE configuration settings, which you can use to increase the performance of your SQL server.

- Chapter 11—"Using Delphi's Database Tools." This chapter examines the database management tools that ship with Delphi. You will discover features of the Database Explorer, Data Dictionary, and SQL Monitor, and you learn how to use each of these tools in the development process of your database-aware applications.

- Chapter 12—"Using Quick Reports." Delphi 3 includes version 2.0 of Quick Reports. This chapter discusses the important properties and events of each component in this collection. You learn how to use the QuickReport Wizard and Report Templates to construct simple list, master/detail, and mailing label reports.

- Chapter 13—"Creating Custom Datasets." This chapter starts by discussing the benefits of Delphi's new virtual dataset, TDataSet. The TDataset class is not new to Delphi, but it has been changed to allow the creation of custom datasets. We discuss the essential methods that must be overridden to create a custom dataset and illustrate these concepts by building a dataset that knows how to access fixed-length ASCII text files without using the BDE.

■ Chapter 14—"Building Multi-Tier Applications." Delphi 3 introduces a new remote dataset technology. This chapter describes the many features and uses of remote datasets and finishes with a discussion of how to employ remote datasets within Web applications.

Extending Components

Delphi's component framework is incredibly powerful: You can take any object and modify or enhance its behavior. This section is divided into the following chapters, which cover the techniques you use to extend your component usage:

■ Chapter 15—"Working with Packages." In this chapter, we cover the concept of a package—a new feature in Delphi. You learn what packages are and when and how to use them. You learn how to install packages and create new packages of components.

■ Chapter 16—"Creating Components." This chapter examines the basics of creating custom components. You learn what custom components are, if you need to create one, how to choose the correct ancestor class, how to debug your component, and how to specify the icon used in the Component Palette. We walk you through the creation and use of a custom component, step-by-step.

■ Chapter 17—"Writing Advanced Components." This chapter builds on Chapter 16 and covers some advanced aspects of component writing. You learn how to determine the state of your component, create custom property and component editors, respond to custom messages, and create data-aware controls.

OLE and ActiveX

Microsoft's Object Linking and Embedding (OLE) technology is generally accepted as an industry standard for the distribution and sharing of object-based functionality. ActiveX is a revision of the OLE standard and has been popularized by increasingly heavy Internet usage. This section details Delphi's OLE and ActiveX support, which allows your program to exist in the increasingly object-oriented world of commercial software. Sound boring? Well, you can also create gratuitously fancy Web pages! The material is segmented into the following chapters:

■ Chapter 18—"Working with OLE, Document Servers, and ActiveX Controls." This chapter covers how to create, load, and save OLE objects at design-time and runtime, and how to stream them to and from databases. It describes the commands provided by the OLE Automation Server, and the variety of parameter-passing methods it supports. The chapter then discusses ActiveX and its similarities to OLE programming.

■ Chapter 19—"Working with COM Interfaces." This chapter begins with a discussion of Component Object Model (COM) fundamentals. Next you see an example COM Server to give you an understanding of just what goes on behind the scenes.

We then go back through the example, using the new Delphi interface extensions and Delphi ActiveX (DAX) framework, which greatly simplifies the development of COM Servers. We round out the chapter with an example that uses the DAX framework to create a COM Server that contains a Windows 95 and NT 4 Context Menu Shell Extension object.

■ Chapter 20—"Working with OLE Automation." In this chapter, you learn how to access and manipulate an existing OLE Automation object. After you have this down pat, we cover the creation of automation objects, both in-process and local. We also discuss how to create type library information for OLE-automated objects so that other environments such as Microsoft's Visual Basic can use Delphi-created OLE automation objects.

■ Chapter 21—"Creating ActiveX Controls." This chapter discusses how to create ActiveX controls and Active forms with the new Delphi ActiveX (DAX) framework. This chapter also explores the use of DAX within Web pages displayed by Microsoft's Internet Explorer.

Graphics and Printing

Delphi provides several classes that simplify the complexity of the Windows Graphic Device Interface (GDI). These classes allow you to draw shapes and text on-screen or on a nominated printer. The following chapters are dedicated to these topics:

■ Chapter 22—"Working with Graphics." This chapter covers everything from Delphi's high-level drawing objects such as TCanvas, TPen, and TBrush, to low-level GDI function calls, metafiles, and regions.

■ Chapter 23—"Printing in Delphi." Chapter 22 introduces the GDI and Delphi's range of classes, which make handling graphics remarkably easy. This chapter extends this topic into the realm of printers and covers a multitude of topics. Among other topics, you learn how printer drivers work, common problems when dealing with printed output, how screens and printers represent colors, and tricks for printing fonts. We finalize the chapter by delving into the magic of the TPrinter class and how to configure your printer programmatically.

Multithreaded Applications

One marvelous addition to the Win32 operating system is the thread. In Chapter 24, "Working with Threads," you learn what a thread is, how threads are created, how they run, and how they are stopped. We discuss when they should, and when they must not, be used. You learn how to make your threads work together through several synchronization methods—critical sections, events, mutexes, and semaphores. We move on to discuss global data and how to make global data specific to each thread. Having given you a firm grasp of thread theory and its implementation in Win32, we complete the chapter with an investigation into Delphi's encapsulation of threads—the TThread class.

DLL Programming

The Dynamic Link Library (or DLL) has been a part of Windows applications for years. It provides functionality that is used on demand, allowing your application to make efficient use of its host machine's resources. The following two chapters cover DLL programming:

- Chapter 25—"DLL Programming: An Introduction." This chapter introduces you to DLL programming and presents just enough code to get your feet wet. After reading this chapter, you will appreciate the issues involved in moving from a Win16 operating system to the new Win32 environment. You learn how DLLs are loaded, how routines are both imported and exported, and Delphi's implementation of the DLLMain function.

- Chapter 26—"DLL Programming: Advanced Concepts." Using Chapter 25 as a basis, we look at some advanced DLL programming techniques. This chapter teaches you how to declare a class in a DLL and how to use an instance of the class in the host application. We discuss interface units, the Turbo Dump utility, portions of the PE file format, and how to break the process boundaries for the sharing of data.

Testing and Debugging

Unfortunately, none of us can write bug-free code. As such, testing and debugging is a critical part of application development, but often is not performed adequately. Chapter 27, "Testing and Debugging," describes the built-in testing and debugging capabilities of Delphi, which make this cycle of development almost enjoyable. The testing features covered in this chapter include conditional compilation and assertions, both of which simplify your task of testing. We discuss Delphi's Integrated Debugger, explaining how to set breakpoints, trace through your code, set watches, and use the remainder of debugging tools. We complete the chapter with a section on "brute-force" debugging, and what to do when all else fails.

Internet Programming

Chapter 28, "Creating Web Server Applications," shows how to expand your realm to include the world of the Net. It defines the buzzwords of Internet development and introduces you to core technologies used in the creation of Web server applications. You learn the areas of Web-server programming that Delphi can handle and follow a step-by-step example of creating a server-side extension using the ISAPI standard. We cover how to test and debug your extension, and close the chapter with a discussion of the multitude of Internet-specific components found in the Delphi VCL.

Extending the IDE

Delphi's Integrated Development Environment (IDE) is not a static set of tools. It can be extended in limitless directions through the use of the Open Tools API. Chapter 29, "Working with Delphi's Open Tools API," discusses the various services that the API provides, and how to create and register the four types of IDE Experts. We cover this material by demonstrating how to manipulate projects (load, save, include, and remove files), build an advanced expert that affects the Code Editor, and perform advanced grep type searches on your source files.

Sharing Code with C++

The Delphi compiler is capable of generating binary object (OBJ) files, which can be linked into other environments such as C++. Chapter 30, "Delphi and C++ Synergy," covers this method of integration and moves on to document the preferred method of connecting C++ and Delphi—the DLL. You learn the correct method of declaring and exporting your functions and how to convert data types between C++ and Delphi.

Advanced Function Calls

The previous chapters used calls into the standard Delphi libraries. Two other sets of functions are available to your applications—the Win32 API and 16-bit function libraries. These topics are covered in the following chapters:

- Chapter 31—"Working with the Windows API." This chapter covers a wide range of API programming topics, including interfacing to the Windows API, dynamic linking, and function prototyping. We detail everything from patching Delphi's WINDOWS.PAS file, to code for working with unsigned 32-bit integers. Finally, we present an example that employs Windows system hooks and callback functions to implement PlayKeys. This powerful addition to your programming toolbox will allow you to easily send messages to any Windows control.

- Chapter 32—"Thunking in Delphi." This chapter examines a technique called thunking, which is used to call API functions written for a different operating system architecture. You learn about the three types of thunking and see a full example of flat thunking with an undocumented Win32 thunking method called `QT_Thunk`.

Conventions

As you read this book, you will notice different text styles. These are quite intentional and are meant to communicate contextual information. The styles are:

- Fixed Width Font—The `fixed width font` (also known as `monospace`) is used to highlight Delphi-specific words such as variable, property, or function names. This text style stops you from reading a paragraph with a glazed look in your eyes and missing what we are talking about, or confusing it with a word from the English language.

- Underscore—To indicate an accelerator key for a menu option or screen element, we underscore the appropriate letter. For example, opening the File menu is accomplished by holding down the Alt key and pressing F.

- Italics—Italics are used when a *new term* is introduced.

Examples

We want this book to teach you Delphi, so we relate our blocks of theoretical mumbo-jumbo to real-world practicalities. When we discuss self-contained coding topics, and the real world doesn't apply to such a small scope, we introduce a code example. These code examples are easy to pick out; they look like this:

```
{ This is a comment for the code below }
if VisualBasicIsInstalled and DelphiHasNotBeenUsed then
    ShowMessage('The men in white coats will be along shortly');
```

On the CD

This book's companion CD-ROM contains the larger examples mentioned through the book, so if the example you created ended up formatting your hard drive, you can always look at what we originally intended (after restoring your system, of course). As a visual notice that you should look to the CD-ROM, a special icon appears in the margin beside the related text.

Putting It All Together

The "Putting It All Together" sections and the "Summary" sections act as mini-refresher courses, and take you back through the material covered in the chapter. This helps you take control of the chaotic whirl of information and turn on that proverbial light bulb. Let's take a look at what this chapter covered.

We started by familiarizing ourselves with Delphi's considerable features—powerful Integrated Development Environment (IDE), object-oriented nature, Component Library, OLE and ActiveX support, templates, true compilation, robust applications, and data access.

We then zeroed in on the features provided by Delphi 3: Its enhanced IDE, Visual Component Library (VCL), Runtime Library (RTL), and compiler. This topic introduced the new distributed dataset and the heavily extended Borland Database Engine (BDE).

After you began to appreciate what Delphi can do, we presented a topic overview, which gave you a feel for the information the book covers.

This section completes the chapter and gives us the opportunity to wish you well in your ventures through the wonderful world of Delphi 3. ●

CHAPTER 2

Working with Delphi's IDE

by Mark Pritchard

The creation of an application in the dark ages of visual programming was a mind-numbing task. To design the interface, you were required to individually set each property of an on-screen element, right down to the top-left corner of a button. You accomplished this by typing line after line of code into an editor, saving the text, then running a compiler, which turned these hundreds of lines of code into an executable program. After compilation, you looked at the resulting interface, decided on a couple of changes, and hit the editor again to modify the appropriate code (providing you could find it again!). Satisfied with the interface, you started coding the application logic and then used another tool to debug the application. Not only was this process a time-consuming, laborious task, it also was incredibly boring, repetitive, and error-prone.

To neatly solve these issues, you enter the haven that is Delphi's IDE, or Integrated Development Environment. This swish-sounding title encompasses the group of windows, menus, and programs that allows you to design your interface visually, connect code to each screen element, and debug the application entirely *within* Delphi.

The Main Window/Control Center

This section describes the main window, which is central to the IDE. It allows you to do all kinds of useful things, such as loading and saving files, searching for text and using components.

Interface development tools

This section describes two tools—the Object Inspector and the Form Designer. These tools let you design the Graphic User Interface (GUI) presented to your user in a remarkably quick and painless fashion.

Code Editor window

This section covers the portion of the IDE devoted to making the intuitive interface you just designed do something useful.

Project management with the IDE

This section describes a tool named the Project Manager that assists with the management of your project.

Object reuse with the Object Repository

Save time and money with the Object Repository. The Object Repository lets you use a project as a basis for another application or to use a previously designed form in another project.

For those of you who have never used Delphi, this chapter will prove quite useful because it describes each major component of the IDE and walks you through the myriad of available tools, screens, and options. The gung-ho code cutters who can't wait to hit the keyboard also should take time out to familiarize themselves with the powerful interface Delphi provides, if only to find out where to start typing! ■

N O T E This book makes extensive reference to an object termed a *form*. A form is simply a window displayed by your application. An Open File dialog is a form, as is a window that displays a text file. ■

Using the Main Window

The main window acts as the control center for your development process. It controls the files included in your application and handles their maintenance, compilation, and debugging.

When you load Delphi for the first time, the main window appears at the top of your display and should resemble Figure 2.1.

FIG. 2.1

The main window, or control center, of the IDE.

The main window is divided into the following three sections:

- **Menubar**—The Menubar is the most common element of Windows applications. In Delphi, the Menubar gives you access to all the functionality provided by the IDE, such as installing components, setting environment and compiler options, viewing debugging and informational windows, or creating new forms and units. The Menubar appears immediately under the title bar of the main window.

- **Speedbar**—The Speedbar provides shortcuts to most of the commands available via the Menubar. The Speedbar can be totally customized, allowing you to tailor the environment to your development style. The Speedbar is located on the left side of the main window, below the Menubar.

- **Component Palette**—The Component Palette is a fantastic resource that is essential to rapid application development. It provides a central repository for components such as edit boxes and labels, which can be dropped onto forms to create your application's interface. The Component Palette is located toward the right side of the main window, below the Menubar.

The Menubar

The Menubar divides the Delphi IDE's large feature set into several logical groups.

N O T E The Delphi Menubar behaves strangely for an application with different types of windows—it is not altered when the active window changes. This behavior is due to the fact that Delphi is a Single Document Interface (SDI) application, rather than Multiple Document Interface (MDI). The differences between SDI and MDI applications are covered in greater detail in Chapter 8, "Creating Applications." ■

 T I P Context-sensitive help is available for each item in the Menubar. Highlight the item with the cursor keys and press F1.

 T I P Frequently used commands in the Menubar have shortcut keys. These keys are listed to the right of the command name.

File Menu In addition to the standard Open, Save, and Close commands, the File menu provides individual commands to create a new application, form, or data module.

Clicking New invokes the New Items dialog box, which allows you to create an object of a different type such as an MDI application, thread, or component. This dialog box displays the objects stored in the Object Repository, which is covered in greater detail in a later section, "Using the Object Repository."

 T I P Use the Reopen command to open a recently used file or project.

 T I P Delphi uses the project name as the file name for the compiled executable or dynamic link library.

Using Another Unit or Form To add another unit to the uses clause of the currently open form, use the Use Unit command. This command displays the Use Unit dialog box, shown in Figure 2.2. For information on why you would actually want to do this, see the section on Delphi units and the uses clause in Chapter 3, "Object Pascal: A Fundamental Approach."

FIG. 2.2
The Use Unit dialog box
adds another unit to
the uses clause.

Project Management Commands   The two project management commands, Add to Project and Remove from Project, are covered in greater detail in a following section, "Using the Project Manager."

Printing Forms and Units   The Print command is used to print the active form or unit. You probably will be using the Print Selection dialog box shown in Figure 2.3, to set printing options, as follows:

- Header/page number—When selected, Delphi prints the name of the unit, the current date, and the page number at the top of each page.
- Line numbers—Makes a Delphi printout look like a program written in an old version of BASIC. It prints line numbers on the left side of the page.
- Syntax print—Emulates the colored syntax highlighting displayed in the Code Editor by using bold, underline, and italics.
- Use color—Uses color to print syntax highlights. If you have a black-and-white printer, this option is disabled.
- Wrap lines—This option causes long Code Editor lines to be split over several printed lines. A lot more useful than the default option of truncation!
- Left margin—The left margin allows you to specify the number of characters to use as the left margin. Use of characters as a measuring system is satisfactory because this is monospaced output (useful if you want to leave some room to scribble comments about sections of code.)

FIG. 2.3

The Print Selection dialog box lets you customize printing.

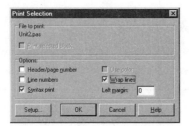

Exiting Delphi   Finally, the File menu provides an Exit command, which exits the Delphi IDE. It is doubtful you will ever voluntarily use this command.

Edit Menu   The Edit menu contains common editing commands such as Redo, Cut, and Paste. These commands apply to both components on the Form Designer and text in the Code Editor.

The Select All command selects all components on the form currently displayed in the Form Designer.

If you dislike using the right mouse button, you will find the Form Designer's Speedmenu is duplicated here under the Edit menu.

If it worked, the Object command would allow you to edit the object housed in the OLE container component. It also didn't work in previous versions of Delphi. If you are interested in OLE programming, read Chapter 18, "Working with OLE, Document Servers, and ActiveX Controls," and Chapter 20, "Working with OLE Automation."

Search Menu   The Search menu contains the common text manipulation commands such as find, replace, and go to line "x", which are useful only in the Code Editor. If you try to trick Delphi by using them with a form active, the Code Editor is automatically activated.

Finding Code Responsible for a Runtime Error   If your application displays a runtime error and an address that generated it, you can use the Find Error command to find the source code responsible. You enter the address of the last runtime error into the Find Error dialog box, shown in Figure 2.4, and upon clicking OK, Delphi transports you to responsible code.

FIG. 2.4

The Find Error dialog box allows you to quickly jump to the source code represented by an address.

Browse Symbol and the Object Browser   The Object Browser is an excellent tool that shows you the properties, methods, and variables for each object used by your application. Object Browser orders this information by the object hierarchy, as shown in Figure 2.5.

FIG. 2.5

The Object Browser shows all objects in your application.

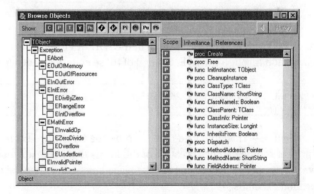

The Object Browser, although useful, is quite complex and it can take some time to find the object for which you are looking. This is where the Browse Symbol command is useful—it filters the display of the Object Browser to display only the symbol or object you specify. To use this command, follow these steps:

Part
I
Ch
2

1. Open the Search menu and click Browse Symbol. The Browse Symbol dialog box, shown in Figure 2.6, is displayed.

FIG. 2.6

The Browse Symbol dialog box allows you to filter the display of the Object Browser.

2. Enter the name of the symbol or object for which you want to search, such as TForm.
3. Click the OK button. The Object Browser is displayed, filtered to TForm, as shown in Figure 2.7.

FIG. 2.7

The Object Browser with a filter of TForm.

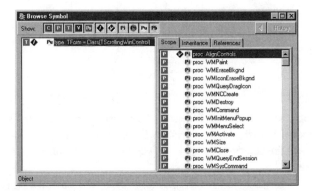

View Menu   The View menu affects which of the IDE windows is currently displayed, and aids your navigation through the IDE. Several of these commands deserve individual attention:

 To close a window with the keyboard, press Alt+F4.

■ Project Source—This item loads the source code for the project into the Code Editor. The project source handles creation of the forms that make up your application, and allows you to specify processing to take place before and after the GUI portion of your application executes.

CAUTION

Be careful making changes to the project source. Delphi relies on it to maintain critical project information, such as which forms it can automatically create and the files that actually make up your project!

■ Window List—The Window List command displays the Window List dialog box, which helps you navigate through the IDE. This is useful when you get carried away and display every single window available. The Window List dialog box is shown in Figure 2.8.

FIG. 2.8

The Window List dialog box aids your navigation through the IDE.

- Toggle Form/Unit—This command switches between the Code Editor and the Form Designer. You will use this command frequently, so make use of the shortcut key (F12).

- Units and Forms—The Units and Forms commands present a dialog box that allows you to choose a unit or form to display. Delphi will open the form or unit if it isn't currently open.

- New Edit Window—If you can write several sections of a program simultaneously, Delphi allows you to display more than one Code Editor window. Actually, a practical example of its use is viewing declarations in the interface section of a unit, while coding in the implementation section, as shown in Figure 2.9.

FIG. 2.9

Delphi allows you to open multiple Code Editor windows.

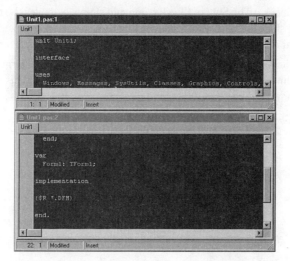

- Speedbar and Component Palette

  The Speedbar and Component Palette commands toggle the visibility of these sections of the main window. Useful if you have a lot of components and don't mind losing speed button functionality, or if you want to use all the speed buttons and using the Component List command doesn't bother you.

N O T E   You can add the CPU Window command to the View menu. This command displays a window titled Disassembly View and shows details such as register contents and a hexadecimal dump of the program. You need to edit your registry. Under the key "HKEY_CURRENT_USER\SOFTWARE\BORLAND\DELPHI3\DEBUGGING," add the string value `EnableCPU`. Set this string value to 1 to enable the option in the View menu, and set the string value to 0 to disable it. ■

Project Menu   The Project menu groups together project-oriented commands. Add to Project and Remove from Project are covered in a following section, "Using the Project Manager." The Add To Repository command is discussed in "Using the Object Repository."

Compilation Commands   The Project menu provides several compilation commands, each with slightly differing functionality:

- ▣ Compile—This command compiles files that have changed since the last compilation. It then links together these compiled files to form the executable program or Dynamic Link Library (DLL).

- ▣ Build All—Performs exactly as the Compile command, with one exception. It compiles all files used by the project, even those unmodified since the last compilation.

- ▣ Syntax Check—The Syntax Check command simply compiles the files that were modified since the last build. It doesn't link them to create the executable or DLL. This command is useful to establish whether your code has syntax errors.

- ▣ Information—Displays interesting information about the final target of your build, such as the number of lines of source compiled and the stack size. This Information dialog box is shown in Figure 2.10.

FIG. 2.10
The Information dialog box provides informa-tion on the compilation target.

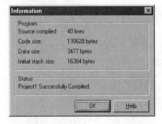

Project Options   The Options command allows you to set project-specific options, covered in greater detail in Chapter 8, "Creating Applications."

Run Menu   The Run (F9) command executes your program. The compiler is invoked auto-matically if any units contributing to the project were modified.

   Your source files and desktop layout can be saved automatically before Run executes. Use the Autosave options discussed later in this chapter, in "Using the Environment to Build an Application."

The Parameters command displays the Run parameters dialog box, which allows you to do two things:

- **Specify the host application**—Testing a DLL in the previous versions of Delphi used to be a nightmare because you couldn't use the integrated debugger. The Host application edit allows you to specify an executable that launches your DLL, allowing the integrated debugger to kick in and make debugging a breeze. Chapter 27, "Testing and Debugging," covers the debugging of DLLs in greater detail.

- **Specify command-line parameters**—Command-line parameters still have their place in Windows applications. If a user executes a file type registered to your application, Windows launches your program to manipulate the file. Windows may pass you the file name in two ways—by DDE or as a command-line argument. If you don't want to mess around with DDE, which is understandable, command-line arguments are the simple way out. The Run parameters combo allows you to set the command line passed to your program at runtime by the IDE. It is useful for testing purposes.

The remaining commands under the Run menu, such as Step Over, Add Watch, and Evaluate/Modify are discussed in Chapter 27, "Testing and Debugging."

Component Menu   The Component menu allows you to create new components (New), install them into the component library (Install), and add a component template to the Component Palette (Add Component Template). For details on these commands, see Chapter 16, "Creating Components."

The Create Component Template command allows you to create a customized set of components, such as a TLabel and TButton, and then add this set to the component library. This lets you build a collection of reusable component sets, reducing your interface development time. For more information on component templates, see Chapter 16, "Creating Components."

Configure Palette lets you customize the Component Palette. This command is covered in a later section, "The Component Palette."

Database Menu   The Explore command invokes the Database Explorer, covered in Chapter 12, "Using Quick Reports."

The SQL Monitor command executes the SQL Monitor application. SQL and the monitor application are detailed in Chapter 10, "Working with SQL Databases."

The Form Expert walks you through the process of creating a data-aware form. Data-aware components and forms are covered in greater detail in Chapter 9, "Working with Local Databases."

Tools Menu   The Options command invokes the Environment Options dialog box, discussed in greater detail under "Using the Environment to Build an Application."

The Repository command displays the Object Repository, which is covered in "Using the Object Repository."

Part
I

Ch
2

The Tools command allows you to customize the list of programs displayed under the Tools menu. To add an item to your tool list, follow these steps:

1. Open the Tools menu and click the Configure Tools item. The Tool Options dialog box, shown in Figure 2.11, is displayed.

FIG. 2.11

The Tool Options dialog box lets you create shortcuts to frequently used tools.

2. Click the Add button. The Tool Properties dialog box, shown in Figure 2.12, is displayed.

FIG. 2.12

Use the Tool Properties dialog box to set properties for items under the Tools menu.

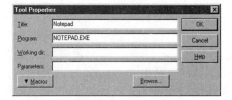

3. Enter the text to appear in the Tools menu in the Title edit (such as **Notepad**).

4. Enter the command to execute when selecting this item using the Program edit (such as **NOTEPAD.EXE**).

5. Click the OK button. The Tool Properties dialog box closes, and the new tool now appears in the Tool Options dialog box.

6. Click Close. The Tool Options dialog box closes, and the new tool appears under the Tools menu.

The Speedbar

The Speedbar is a group of buttons that provide an alternative means of accessing functions contained in the Menubar. The Speedbar may be customized to suit your usage patterns. To illustrate, if you frequently print files by opening the File menu and clicking Print, you may add this command to the Speedbar by following these steps:

1. Right-click anywhere on the Speedbar. A pop-up menu appears.

2. Choose Properties from the pop-up menu. The Speedbar Editor dialog box, shown in Figure 2.13, is displayed.

FIG. 2.13

Use the Speedbar Editor to customize the Speedbar.

3. Select the File item in the list of Categories. The list of available Commands displays file-related commands.

4. Scroll down the Commands list to locate Print active form or unit.

5. Drag the Print active form or unit command from the Speedbar Editor dialog box, and drop it on the Speedbar. The icon that represents the Print command is now displayed in the Speedbar.

6. Click Close to close the Speedbar Editor dialog box.

N O T E You can:

- Alter the size of the Speedbar by dragging the separator between the Speedbar and Component Palette.

- Move buttons on the Speedbar by dragging them to a new location while the Speedbar Editor dialog box is displayed.

- Remove buttons from the Speedbar by dragging them off the Speedbar while the Speedbar Editor dialog box is displayed.

- Reset the Speedbar to the default layout by clicking the Reset button on the Speedbar Editor dialog box. ■

The Component Palette

The Component Palette displays the set of components present in the component library. The component library is simply a collection of components you can use when building the interface for your application, and when you are coding its logic.

The concept of a *component* is a remarkable feature of the Delphi environment. Think of a component as a set of functionality neatly bundled together in a reusable package. A button that a user may click to trigger a function is a component, as is an edit into which your user enters some text.

The object-oriented nature of Delphi adds a powerful twist to the concept of components. Because each component is essentially an object, a component may be used as a base for a new component that exhibits additional or modified behavior. This new component may then be added to the component library, and used in as many applications as you desire. Using components in applications is documented further in Chapter 6, "Using Delphi Components," and Chapter 7, "Using Win32 Common Controls." Components development is covered in Chapter 16, "Creating Components."

The Component Palette groups components according to functionality, and displays each of these groups on separate pages.

N O T E   You can access any component in the component library by opening the <u>V</u>iew menu and clicking the Component <u>L</u>ist command. This action displays the Components dialog box, shown in Figure 2.14, which allows you to select a component and add it to the currently active form. ▓

FIG. 2.14
The Components dialog box provides access to all components in the component library.

The default configuration of the Component Palette pages is as follows:

- **Standard**—The Standard page holds basic components that have been present since the early versions of Windows, such as TMainMenu, TButton, TListbox, and TLabel.

- **Additional**—This page contains more specialized components, introduced in more recent software such as TSpeedButton, TStringGrid, and TImage. The TSplitter component is worthy of individual attention—it lets you design an interface with sizable sections, just like the Delphi main window with its Speedbar and Component Palette sections. TChart is also a new addition to this page. TChart allows you to easily incorporate professional-looking graphs into your Delphi programs.

- **System**—The System page contains components that rely on the operating system to provide most of their functionality. The TTimer component is an example—it executes a function at a programmer-defined interval. Determination of these intervals is handled by the operating system.

- **CommCtrl**—This page holds the new components introduced with the redesigned interface found in Windows 95 and the latest versions of Windows NT. Examples are the TTreeView and TListView components.

- **Dialogs**—This page contains components that encapsulate the functionality of the dialogs provided by Windows, such as TOpenDialog and TSaveDialog. You should use these components in your program to conform to the standard Windows "look and feel."

- **Data Access**—The Data Access page provides components that simplify your use of dataset-based information. Examples are the TTable and TSession components. These components are non-visual—they do not display themselves at runtime.

- **Data Controls**—This page contains components known as data-aware controls. These components provide a visual interface to the non-visual data set components contained in the Data Access page. Examples are TDBGrid, TDBChart, and TDBCheckBox.

- **Win3.1**—The Win3.1 page provides components present in Delphi version 1 that have been superseded by the advent of Win32 and the new Windows 95 style interface. To illustrate, the TTabbedNotebook found in Delphi 1 was replaced with the TPageControl component.

- **Internet**—This page contains components that streamline the production of Internet- and intranet-enabled applications. Examples are the TSMTP, THTML, and TClientSocket components.

- **Samples**—The Samples page provides examples of custom-designed components. The TGauge component on this page should be used for compatibility purposes only. The CommCtrl page contains a progress bar that conforms to the new Windows interface.

- **ActiveX**—This page contains a number of components that demonstrate Delphi's capability to use OLE and ActiveX controls.

- **QReport**—The QReport page provides a suite of components that you use to create reports, without the overhead of ReportSmith.

> **TIP** Context-sensitive help is available for each component in the Component Palette. To display help, select the component of interest, and press F1.

Customizing Component Palette Pages   If you prefer an alternative grouping of components, you may create and delete pages, move components between pages, and even remove components from the palette completely.

To display the dialog box used to customize the Component Palette, follow these steps:

1. Right-click the Component Palette. A pop-up menu appears.

2. Select Properties from the pop-up menu. The Environment Options dialog box appears and displays the palette configuration page, as shown in Figure 2.15.

FIG. 2.15
The palette page of the Environment Options dialog box lets you customize the grouping of components on the Component Palette.

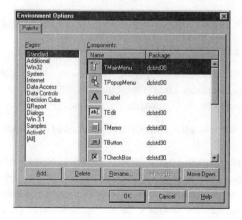

You can customize the palette in the following ways:

- **Modify Page or Component Order**—You can alter the page or component order by selecting an item from the Pages or Components list, and then clicking the Move Up or Move Down buttons.

 T I P   You also may alter the item order by dragging an item to a new position in the list.

- **Add a Page**—You can add a page to the Component Palette by clicking the Add button and entering a new page name.
- **Rename a Page**—You can rename a page by selecting a page from the Pages list, clicking the Rename button dialog, and entering a different page name.

N O T E   If you select an item in the Components list, the Add and Rename buttons are disabled. To enable them, select an item in the Pages list. ■

- **Delete a Page**—You may delete a page by selecting it from the Pages list, and clicking the Delete button. You must hide all components on the page before it is deleted. Note that Delete appears only when you select an item from the Pages list.
- **Hide a Component**—If you no longer use a component, you can hide it by selecting the component from the Components list and clicking Hide. Note that Hide appears only when an item in the Components list is selected.

 Adding New Components to the Component Palette   Although the component library is an amazing beast, it really comes into its own when you add new components, either developed by you or by a third party. Third-party components can be found on any of the huge number of Internet sites devoted to Delphi, and questions may be posted to several Delphi-specific newsgroups, such as **news://comp.lang.pascal.delphi.components.misc**.

With the advent of component packages, installation of components is now split into two steps—creating a component package and installing the component package.

For more information about component packages and their use, see Chapter 15, "Working with Packages."

Using the Object Inspector

The Object Inspector, shown in Figure 2.16, is one of three valuable tools at your disposal when designing the application's interface. The remaining tools, the Form Designer and Code Editor, are discussed later in this chapter, in "Using the Form Designer and Code Editor."

You use the Object Inspector to set the published properties of a component or form.

N O T E   Properties are items of data that belong to, and describe, an object. The color of a car is a property of the object "car". Delphi objects and components also possess properties, such as the width of a TButton component, or the text displayed by a TLabel component. For more information on objects and properties, see Chapter 4, "Object Pascal: Advanced Concepts." ■

FIG. 2.16

The Object Inspector lets you set properties of components displayed on a form.

The Object Inspector contains a drop-down list, located at the top of the window, which lists all components on the form you are currently designing. You may select a component from this drop-down list, or use your mouse to select a component on the form.

NOTE The form object defines published properties that may be altered with the Object Inspector. To select the form, you may do one of the following:

- Click a non-occupied section of the form.
- Select the form from the drop-down list at the top of the Object Inspector.
- If a component on the form is highlighted, press the Escape key repetitively until the form is selected. The Form Designer must be active.
- Press Ctrl+Shift and click the currently selected component. ■

The remainder of the Object Inspector window lists properties for the currently selected component, and is split into two pages:

- **Properties**—The Properties page lists published properties of the component, such as the width of the component or the font it uses to display text.
- **Events**—The Events page lists a special type of published property, the event. An event property does not contain a piece of information about the component; rather, it contains a link to a segment of Object Pascal code that is executed when the event is triggered. For more information on events, see the following discussion under "Event Properties," and Chapter 6, "Using Delphi Components."

Each page of the property list is split into two columns. The left column lists the property names and the right column lists the property values.

Modifying Properties

A well-written component initializes its properties when it is created, ensuring that the component always will be in a valid state. Imagine a TButton component that did not set its background color property. How would it be displayed?

The Object Inspector allows you to change these initial settings. These changes are recorded in the form's DFM (Delphi ForM) file, and used by the compiler to automatically generate code to set your new property values at runtime.

There are basically four types of property editor:

- **Text**—The text property editor presents the property value as editable text. It is used for numeric properties such as Width, and string properties such as Caption.

- **Enumerated**—This type of property may take one value from a predefined set. The Object Inspector displays a drop-down list of possible values. The Cursor property is an enumerated value—a component may display only one cursor at a time, which must be chosen from those made available to the application.

- **Set**—A property of this type may take any number of values from a predefined set. The Object Inspector displays this type of property as an expandable list of True/False pairs for each element in the set. The BorderIcons property of a TForm is an example of this type of property—you may include or exclude any of the icons capable of appearing in the border of a window.

- **Object**—This type of property is itself an object and is displayed as an expandable list of properties, each of which may be edited individually. Some objects register their own property editors, which are dialog boxes that allow you to edit the entire object property in one hit. These custom property editors are activated by either double-clicking the property value, or clicking the button labeled with an ellipsis. The Font property is an example of both edit methods—it can be expanded into a list, and provides its own custom editor.

To illustrate the process of changing a property, set the title of the main form in an application to something tacky, such as "Isn't Delphi wonderful?". Follow these steps:

1. Open the File menu and select the New Application command. A nice, fresh application appears.

N O T E   The Object Inspector automatically selects the main form when you create a new application. ▓

2. Press the F9 key to compile and run the application. The main form is displayed, as shown in Figure 2.17. Note the caption of the form; it should be "Form1."

N O T E   If you have automatic saving enabled, Delphi prompts you to save the currently open files before it compiles and executes the application. ▓

FIG. 2.17
An unmodified Delphi
application.

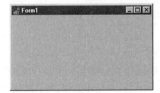

3. Close the application. The Delphi IDE will be displayed.

4. In the Object Inspector, click the `Caption` property value. The edit cursor appears in the property value box, ready for you to alter.

TIP If you click the property name, the entire property value is selected. This selection makes it easy to delete the entire value in one step.

5. Change the current value, Form1, to "Isn't Delphi wonderful". Notice how the title of the form changes as you modify the property value.

N O T E Most properties do not update their contents as you alter their value. To signify the end of an alteration and set the new value, press the Enter key or click another part of the Object Inspector. ▓

6. Press the F9 key to compile and run the application. The main form reappears, with your new caption, as shown in Figure 2.18.

FIG. 2.18
The Object Inspector lets you make changes to component properties without a single line of code!

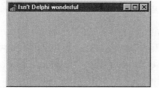

7. Close the application. The Delphi IDE reappears.

The Name Property

Quite often, you will want to update component properties at runtime. Perhaps you want to display the name of the file currently displayed in your application. As the preceding example shows, the `Caption` property of a form may be modified with the Object Inspector, which is known as a design-time change. In our example, the name of the displayed file is only accessible at runtime. You must write Object Pascal code to assign the new value to the `Caption` property of the form.

The property name tells the compiler which property you want to alter, but how do you reference the form? Through its `Name` property. Using the preceding example again, the `Name` of the form was "Form1." To alter the `Caption` property, you write the following:

```
Form1.Caption := 'AFileName';
```

This Object Pascal statement assigns the text "AFileName" to the `Caption` property of the form named "Form1." For more information on Object Pascal, see Chapter 3, "Object Pascal: A Fundamental Approach," and Chapter 4, "Object Pascal: Advanced Concepts."

NOTE Delphi assigns a unique value to a component's Name property as you add it to your application. This value, while following a nice mathematical progression, is effectively meaningless. You should change Name to a value that reflects the component's use, such as "edtPassword" for an edit used to retrieve a password. ▪

Event Properties

Programs written for operating systems such as MS-DOS are known as procedural—the execution of the application proceeds sequentially. For example, if you were to enter a new customer record into an MS-DOS program, you would do something like the following:

1. Enter name.
2. Enter address.
3. Enter contact phone number.
4. Save customer to the database.

If the customer didn't have a contact phone number, you would have to enter a blank just to get to the point where you could save the record.

Windows changes this. Windows applications are event-driven—segments of the application execute in response to a particular situation having arisen. This is known as *event handling*. Most components already provide basic event handling, such as a button depressing when clicked or an edit adding a character to its display when the user presses a key. Although this functionality saves you work, it is not the stuff applications are made of!

NOTE Because the user may choose to trigger virtually any event, in any order, event-driven programs cannot rely on the state of an application to the extent a procedural program can. An event-driven program, for example, must check that all required data was entered before it can save a record. ▪

If you were entering a customer record into a Windows-based application, you may enter the customer's name and address, and then save the record by clicking a button labeled Save. This act of clicking a button triggers an event that you can trap and use to execute some Object Pascal code, which saves the record.

Trapping an event is accomplished by setting an *event property* to the name of an Object Pascal procedure. When the component detects an event, such as a mouse click, it calls the procedure referenced by the event property.

NOTE The event property uses the enumerated property editor. The event may execute only one procedure, from a set of procedures that already exists in the unit associated with the form. ▪

The argument list of the event procedure must conform exactly to the template laid down by the event.

You can let Delphi take care of the following: generating a procedure name; the correct argument list; and setting the event property to the procedure name. The following example illustrates setting the Caption of the form to the name of the program's executable, when you click the form's surface:

1. Open the File menu. Select New Application. A blank application appears.
2. Click the Events tab of the Object Inspector property list. The Events page appears.
3. Double-click the OnClick property value. The Code Editor appears, with a new procedure, FormClick, neatly typed for you. Delphi has generated the argument list for the procedure, and set the OnClick event property to the name of this new procedure.
4. Press the Tab key to signify one indent level, and type the following code (your screen now should resemble Figure 2.19):

   ```
   Caption := Application.EXEName;
   ```

FIG. 2.19
Delphi can generate procedure skeletons and connect them to events automatically.

NOTE The preceding code does not specify which form owns the Caption property. Because the event-handling code belongs to the form object, the compiler is intelligent enough to add the form reference automatically. This intelligence extends to all objects—the default scope is the object itself.

5. Press F9 to compile and run the application. The application appears, with the title currently set to "Form1."
6. Click anywhere on the form. The title changes to the file name of the project's executable.
7. Close the application. The Delphi IDE reappears.

TIP If you double-click a component, Delphi will create the default event handler, such as OnClick for a button or OnChange for an edit box.

N O T E   If you change a component's Name property, Delphi automatically renames all of its event
procedures. ■

Those of you who have escaped from the Visual Basic camp and are familiar with the concept
of controls arrays may be thinking that you can use a common event handler to service multiple
components. You're right! This trick is discussed further in Chapter 8, "Creating Applications."

Locating Event Procedures

Because event handlers are listed in creation order, they can be difficult to find in a complex
form that contains several components. You can jump directly to an event handler by double-
clicking its property value on the Events page, as the following steps illustrate:

1. Open the File menu. Select New Application. A new application appears.

2. Double-click the form. The Code Editor displays the automatically generated OnCreate
    event handler, a procedure named FormCreate.

3. Drag the scroll bar on the right side of the Code Editor window to the top. Your display
    should look similar to Figure 2.20.

FIG. 2.20

Delphi automatically
generates the code that
supports your interface
and events.

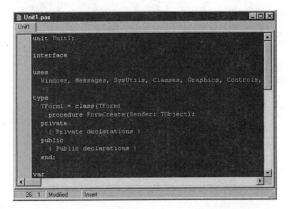

4. Select the Events tab in the Object Inspector. The Events page is displayed.

5. Double-click the OnCreate property value. The Code Editor jumps to the OnCreate event
    handler, the procedure named FormCreate.

Using the Form Designer and Code Editor

The Form Designer and Code Editor are tightly linked and round out the set of tools that you
will use most frequently to create applications.

You may recall that Delphi uses a DFM file to store component properties. This DFM file is displayed by the Form Designer. The code associated with the form, such as the form definition and event procedures, is stored in a Delphi unit or PAS (object PAScal) file. The PAS file is displayed by the Code Editor. For more information on Delphi units, see Chapter 3, "Object Pascal: A Fundamental Approach."

Form Designer

The Form Designer is not really a separate program grafted into the IDE. It actually refers to the view of a form at design-time as opposed to runtime. Non-visual components such as TTable and TTimer are displayed in the Form Designer at design-time, so they may be selected and manipulated with the Object Inspector. You can display multiple forms at design-time, but only one of them may be active. Partnered with the Object Inspector, the Form Designer lets you do the following:

- Add components to the form
- Modify properties of the form and its components
- Connect component event handlers to Object Pascal code contained in the Code Editor

Adding Components to a Form   The process of adding components to a form is really the core of the rapid development cycle. Unlike the old visual programming environments, this process of visual design lets you design and test an interface in minutes rather than days.

Adding a component to a form is a simple task, usually involving only two clicks. The following steps illustrate:

1. Open the File menu. Select the New Application command. A blank application appears.
2. Select a component from the Component Palette. Any one will do.
3. Click anywhere on the form. The component is displayed with its top-left point located under your mouse click. Figure 2.21 shows the form after dropping a TButton component near the center of the form.

FIG. 2.21
Two clicks and you have
a component on a form.
Hello, speed!

 To move a component, simply drag it to its new location.

 You can create a component at any size by selecting it from the palette, and then dragging out its size on the form.

T I P   To add multiple components of the same type, hold down Shift while selecting the component from the Component Palette. You may now left-click madly all over the form to create new instances of the component. To get back to selection mode, click the mouse-cursor icon to the left of the Component Palette.

Some components may act as component containers. The component acting as the container is known as the *parent*, and the component subject to containment is known as the *child*. The TGroupBox is an example of this relationship:

1. Open the File menu. Select the New Application command. A blank application appears.

2. Select a TGroupBox component from the Component Palette. It is located on the Standard page, third from the right.

3. Click the form. The TGroupBox component appears on the form, named "GroupBox1".

4. Select a TButton component from the Component Palette. It is located on the Standard page, sixth from the left.

5. Click inside the TGroupBox component you just dropped on the form. The TButton is displayed inside the group box, as shown in Figure 2.22.

CAUTION
If you click outside the TGroupBox component, the button will be a child of the form. Doing so defeats the purpose of this example—you want the TButton to be a child of the TGroupBox.

FIG. 2.22
Certain components
may act as parents for
other components.

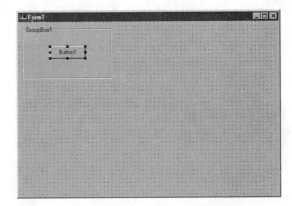

6. Drag the group to another location. Note the button moves with it.

N O T E   Positional properties such as Left and Top are relative to the coordinates of the component's parent. ■

If you already placed a component on a form and want to make it a child of another, use Edit, Cut to move the child component to the clipboard, select the parent component, and then issue the Edit, Paste command.

 To select the parent of a child control, select the child, and then press Escape while the Form Designer is active.

Manipulating Groups of Components   You may recall the example that demonstrated how to set the Caption property of a form. The Form Designer allows you to select multiple components and modify their properties simultaneously.

You may select a group of components either by dragging out a selection rectangle with the mouse, or by pressing and holding Shift while selecting several components.

 If you are really dexterous, you can combine both selection methods.

As you select components, the Object Inspector displays only properties common to each component type. For example, if you select a TButton and TEdit, the Caption property is not listed because it is not provided by all components in the group.

N O T E   The Name property is an exception to this rule. All components have a Name property, but they must be unique—allowing Name to be set as a group will cause duplicates. ■

Form Designer Speedmenu   A right-click on the Form Designer displays a Speedmenu with the following commands:

- Align To Grid—The Form Designer overlays a grid on the form. Align to Grid modifies the Left and Top properties of a component to ensure that it is placed on a grid line. This command is useful if you want all your components to be in straight lines.

 The grid spacing can be changed by using the Environment Options dialog box.

- Bring To Front and Send To Back—The Left, Top, Width, and Height properties describe the two-dimensional aspects of a component. Delphi allows you to overlap components, which introduces the third dimension, depth, or Z. Bring To Front makes the component(s) first in the Z-order, while Send To Back makes them last.
- Revert to inherited—If this form was derived from another, this command removes all your changes, taking the form back to its original state.
- Align—Displays the Alignment dialog box, which allows you to position a group of components relative to itself instead of the form grid. For example, if you choose to Space equally, the Form Designer moves the components so that an equal amount of space exists between each component.

The Alignment Palette window contains speed buttons for each of the alignment commands. Open the View menu and select Alignment Palette.

- ■ Size—Displays the Size dialog box, used to adjust the Width and Height properties of a group of components. An example of its use would be to set the Width of each component to the largest in the group.

- ■ Scale—Allows you to enter a scaling factor, which the Form Designer uses to modify the Left, Top, Width, and Height properties of each component on the form. A scaling factor of 50% would halve the coordinates and sizes of each component on the form.

- ■ Tab Order—One of the original design criteria of Windows was that an application must be able to be used without a mouse. To allow this, the application must permit the user to navigate through the components of a form with the Tab key. The TabStop property of a component indicates its position in the tab sequence. The Tab Order command presents you with the Edit Tab Order dialog, shown in Figure 2.23, which assists you in the task of modifying the tab sequence.

FIG. 2.23
The Edit Tab Order dialog box lets you easily adjust the tab sequence for components.

 If you manually change the TabStop property, Delphi automatically renumbers the tabstops for other components.

- ■ Creation Order—This allows you to change the order in which non-visual components are created.

CAUTION
Code that relies on creation order is generally not a good idea. Having to continually adjust the creation order when adding and removing components is remarkably inefficient, and poor programming style.

- ■ Add To Repository—Yet another way of adding a form to the Object Repository. Has it sunk in how useful the Object Repository is?

■ View as Text—You may recall the discussion on the old style of visual programming, where each property of an object was set manually. This command gives you an appreciation of all the work Delphi is doing behind the scenes by displaying the DFM file as text. To go back to the much more appealing form view, right-click again, and select View as Form.

Code Editor

The Code Editor, shown in Figure 2.20, is where you produce the nuts and bolts of your application. You can produce all kinds of fancy parts with the Form Designer and Object Inspector, but without Object Pascal code to connect the parts, your interface is precisely that, an interface.

The Code Editor can be customized heavily through the Environment Options dialog box, covered in a following section, "Using the Environment to Build an Application."

Code Editor Speedmenu   The Code Editor provides a Speedmenu with the following commands:

 You can open the Speedmenu by pressing Alt+F10.

■ Close Page—Closes the active page. Prompts you to save, if required.

 You can save the current page in the Code Editor by pressing Ctrl+S.

■ Open File at Cursor—Loads the file referenced at the current cursor position. Delphi looks in the current directory for the file, then scans the project search path.

 You can switch to the next page in the Code Editor by pressing Ctrl+Tab. To move to the previous page, press Shift+Ctrl+Tab.

■ New Edit Window—Displays the current file in another Code Editor window.

■ Browse Symbol at Cursor—Equivalent to the View, Browse Symbol command discussed previously, in "Browse Symbol and the Object Browser," with one neat twist—it types the symbol name into the Browse Symbol dialog box.

■ Topic Search—Searches the online help system for the text at the cursor.

■ Debugging Commands—Toggle Breakpoint, Run to Cursor, Evaluate/Modify, and Add Watch at Cursor are discussed in Chapter 27, "Testing and Debugging."

■ View As Form—Displays the current page as a form. Enabled only if the current page is a form that has been displayed as text.

- Read <u>O</u>nly—Toggles your rights to change the current file.

- <u>M</u>essage View—Toggles the visibility of the compiler message window. This window appears at the bottom of the Code Editor window.

- P<u>r</u>operties—Displays the Environment Options dialog box, filtered to pages concerned with the Code Editor.

Code Insight   Code Insight provides several welcome additions to the Code Editor that reduce your syntax errors, cut down on typing, and hopefully introduce some standard coding styles. These features are enabled through the Environment Options dialog box.

Code Completion   This feature analyzes the code at the current cursor position and presents you with a list of properties, methods, and events that are applicable at that point. Imagine that you have a form variable named `frmMain`. Typing **frmMain.** (with the period) into the Code Editor and pressing Ctrl+Space to activate Code Completion will cause Delphi to display a list of properties, methods, and events that are available to the `frmMain` object.

Code Parameters   Code Parameters are a godsend if you find yourself continually referring to the online help system to remember the parameter list of a function or method. Simply typing the function name, and the opening bracket, such as **Format(**, will cause Delphi to display the required argument structure.

Code Templates   A Code Template automatically completes standard code constructs such as `if...then` and `for...do`. To use it, type in the first characters of a construct, such as `case`, and press Ctrl+J. The Code Editor displays the Code Templates list, shown in Figure 2.24 (it's the list box sitting unceremoniously below and to the right of the `case` statement).

FIG. 2.24
The Code Templates list dramatically reduces your typing overhead.

You then can use the directional cursor keys to highlight a particular code template, and press Enter to select it. If you decide not to use a template, press Escape to clear the list box.

Adding Your Own Code Templates Almost everything in Delphi is customizable, even code templates. If you find yourself typing in a particular block of code repeatedly, follow these steps to add it to the available set of templates:

1. Select Tools, Environment Options. Select the Code Insight tab. The Code Insight page, shown in Figure 2.25, is displayed.

FIG. 2.25

The Code Insight page lets you customize the behavior of the enhancements to the Code Editor.

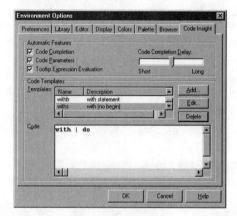

2. Click Add. The Add Code Template dialog box, shown in Figure 2.26, is displayed.

FIG. 2.26

The Add Code Template dialog box lets you add a new code template.

3. Type a brief name for this code template in the Shortcut Name edit box.
4. Use the Description edit to specify a detailed description of this template.
5. Click OK. The Add Code Template dialog box disappears, and the new template is added to the Templates list, ready for you to edit.
6. Enter the code for this template in the Code edit box.
7. Click OK to save the code template.

 To leave the Code Templates dialog box open and still save the new template, simply click another item in the Templates list. Although Delphi remembers the changes while the dialog box is open, you must click OK when closing the dialog box to apply the changes to the environment.

> **CAUTION**
>
> Your changes are discarded if you click Add without closing the Code Templates dialog box or selecting another item from the Templates list.

Using the Environment to Build an Application

The Delphi IDE is incredibly flexible. Before you begin to develop your first application, take some time to examine the different environment options that allow you to tailor the IDE to your development style.

Environment Options

To display the Environment Options dialog box shown in Figure 2.27, select Tools, Options.

FIG. 2.27
The Environment Options dialog box allows you to customize the IDE to your liking.

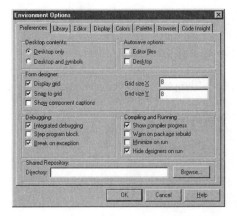

The Environment Options dialog box is divided into several pages:

- **Preferences**—The Preferences page lets you set several categories of options. Two noteworthy categories are:

    Autosave options—Determines which elements of the environment Delphi saves before executing your project. Checking Editor files forces you to save forms and units before execution. Desktop automatically saves the size and position of each IDE window.

    Shared Repository—Allows you to specify a directory that contains a shared repository of form, data module, and application templates. The Shared Repository is covered further in Chapter 8, "Creating Applications."

■ **Library**—The Library page contains settings used by the compiler when building the component library.

■ **Editor**—Alters the feature set of the Code Editor window to emulate a development environment such as Object Pascal for DOS.

 If you will be sharing code with others, turn off the Use tab character setting. Code formatted with different tab settings is displayed as a complete mess.

■ **Display**—Allows you to modify the look-and-feel of the Code Editor window. You can change the font size and type, keystroke mapping, whether the gutter is visible, and so on.

 The gutter displays several symbols useful for debugging, such as breakpoints, function calls, and function boundaries.

■ **Colors**—The Colors page lets you alter the colors used to highlight the code in the Code Editor.

 Syntax highlighting is a wonderful thing. It reduces typographical errors and makes your code easier to read.

■ **Palette**—The Palette page allows you to add and remove components from the Component Palette. It was discussed previously in the section, "Customizing Component Palette Pages."

■ **Browser**—This page allows you to alter the settings for the Object Browser, detailed previously in "Browse Symbol and the Object Browser."

■ **Code Insight**—This page lets you enable, disable, and modify the behavior of the enhancements to the Code Editor.

Building Your First Application

Now that you are familiar with the Delphi IDE, we can put all this newfound knowledge into practice with a good old demonstration program—temperature conversion. Suppress those groans; Delphi can make even this old classic fun. This program converts Celsius to Fahrenheit. The development process is split into two steps:

■ Interface design

■ Interface functionality

Interface Design   The first step to creating a GUI-based application is creating the interface. Follow these steps:

1. Open the File menu. Click New Application.

2. Place a TLabel component at the top-left corner of the form, and alter its Caption property to **Temperature**.

3. Place a TEdit component to the right of the TLabel component. Change its Name property to **edtTemperature**, Width to **65**, and make Text completely empty (Null).

4. Place another TLabel component on the form, underneath the "Temperature" TLabel. Change its Caption property to **Result**.

5. Place a TPanel component next to the "Result" TLabel. Set its Name property to **pnlResult**, Caption to Null, and BevelOuter to bvLowered.

6. Select the TPanel and TEdit components.

7. Click the right mouse button to display the Form Designer Speedmenu. Select the Size command.

8. Under the Width group, select Shrink to smallest. In the Height group, select Shrink to smallest. Click OK.

9. Select the form. Change its Height property to **96**, Width to **161**, Caption to **Temp Convert**, and BorderStyle to bsSingle. Remove biMaximize and biMinimize from the BorderIcons property.

After these steps, your form should resemble Figure 2.28.

FIG. 2.28

The interface for your first application.

Considering what you have just accomplished, that process was remarkably painless. To look at what Delphi has done behind the scenes, right-click the form and select View as Text. You should see about 45 lines, detailing each property modification. Imagine writing that yourself! To go back to form view, right-click all that code and select View as Form.

Now is a good time to save the project. Follow these steps:

1. Open the File menu, and select the Save Project As command.

   Delphi prompts you to save each form and unit before saving the project. Because the project file contains the file names of each form and unit in the project, this is logical.

2. Select the directory in which to save this file. Enter **F_MAIN** as the file name for Unit1.

   This action saves two files—F_MAIN.PAS, which is the Object Pascal code for the form, and F_MAIN.DFM, which is the form.

3. Enter **TEMPCONVERT** as the file name for Project1.

Interface Functionality   Having built the interface, you can write the code to make the program convert temperatures.

You may have noticed there is no "convert" button to trigger the conversion process. The TEdit component triggers an event named OnChange when you alter the text it displays. This updated value is accessible through the Text property. The program will trap the OnChange event, and convert the current value into Fahrenheit.

Follow these steps:

1. Select the edtTemperature edit and click the Events page in the Object Inspector.

2. Double-click the property value for OnChange. The Code Editor appears, and Delphi automatically generates an event handler named edtTemperatureChange.

3. Add the following code between the procedure header (the line starting with procedure), and the line containing begin:

```
var
    iCelsius : Integer;
```

This code declares an integer variable, iCelsius, which is used to store the Celsius value entered into the TEdit component. Variables and types are covered in greater detail in Chapter 3, "Object Pascal: A Fundamental Approach."

4. Add the following code to the body of edtTemperatureChange procedure:

```
iCelsius := StrToIntDef(edtTemperature.Text,0);
```

This line retrieves the value entered into the edtTemperature component. Because iCelsius is an integer variable, you need to convert the string type returned by the Text property into an integer by using the StrToIntDef function.

N O T E The StrToIntDef function allows you to specify a default return value if the string is not a valid integer. The StrToInt function, which also converts a string to an integer, raises an EConvertError exception when converting an invalid integer. Exceptions are covered in greater detail in Chapter 5, "Exception Handling."

5. Place the following line beneath the code entered in Step 4:

```
pnlResult.Caption := FloatToStr(iCelsius * 1.8 + 32);
```

This line converts the value stored in the iCelsius variable to Fahrenheit. Because the conversion results in a floating point number, you must use the FloatToStr function to convert it into the string value required by the Caption property of the TPanel.

Your code for the edtTemperatureChange procedure should look like the following:

```
procedure TForm1.edtTemperatureChange(Sender:Tobject);
var
    iCelsius : Integer;
begin
    iCelsius          := StrToIntDef(edtTemperature.Text,0);
    pnlResult.Caption := FloatToStr(iCelsius * 1.8 + 32);
end;
```

Automatically Generated Code   Now that you have entered a mere four lines of code, take some time to look at the other code Delphi has automatically generated. Scroll to the top of the unit. The first three lines are:

```
unit F_Main;
interface
uses
```

The first line is used by the compiler to check that this text file is indeed a Delphi unit, and that this unit is the one specified by the file name. The second line indicates that the `interface` section of the unit is to follow. The third line marks the beginning of the `uses` clause for the `interface` section of this unit. The structure of a unit is discussed further in Chapter 3, "Object Pascal: A Fundamental Approach."

The ninth line starts a type declaration block, which looks like this:

```
type
  TForm1 = class(TForm)
    Label1: TLabel;
    edtTemperature: TEdit;
    Label2: TLabel;
    pnlResult: TPanel;
    procedure edtTemperatureChange(Sender: TObject);
  private
    { Private declarations }
  public
    { Public declarations }
  end;
```

This block defines the class `TForm1`, which is the template for the form you designed earlier. Note that each component you placed on the form is listed. The event-handling procedure, `edtTemperatureChange`, is listed as a method of the object declared in this block.

The remaining lines are as follows:

```
var
  Form1: TForm1;
implementation
{$R *.DFM}
```

The first two lines in this snippet declare an object variable named Form1, of type `TForm1`.

> **CAUTION**
>
> Referencing the object variable for a form that has not been created causes an Access Violation. The Project Options dialog lets you define which forms are automatically created at runtime. For a project that manually creates forms at runtime, see "Creating MDI Applications," in Chapter 8, "Creating Applications."

The next line indicates the start of the `implementation` section of the unit.

The last line is an example of a statement intended specifically for the compiler, known as a *compiler directive*. The `$R FileName` statement is resource file directive and tells the compiler to include all resources found in files matching `FileName`. This line is automatically generated for units that define `TForm` descendants, allowing the compiler to locate component resource definitions.

Using the Project Manager

Now that you created your first application, we can cover some additional features of the IDE. The Project Manager, shown in Figure 2.29, provides assistance with several project-related tasks. You may access the Project Manager by opening the View menu and selecting the Project Manager command.

FIG. 2.29
The Project Manager helps you manage the forms and units in your project.

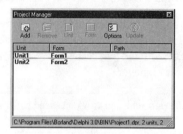

Part
I

Ch
2

Adding and Removing Files

The uses clause in a unit lets you access routines and objects in other units. The compiler will locate a unit, provided that it is in the search path. Adding a file to the project can make your development work easier in two ways:

■ The compiler knows which files to check for modifications before compilation.

■ You can quickly open forms and units associated with the project.

To add a file to your project using the Project Manager, follow these steps:

1. Open the View menu. Select the Project Manager command. The Project Manager is displayed.

2. Click the Add unit speed button, located first from the left on the Speedbar. The Add to project dialog box appears.

3. Select a file to add to your project. The selected file appears in the Project Manager window.

To remove a file from your project, select it in the Project Manager, and click the Remove unit speed button, located second from the left on the Speedbar.

Creating and Opening Forms and Units

Many applications, such as word processors, contain at least two form types—a main form that contains the menu and Speedbar and a minor form that displays a document.

You will probably find that multiple forms share common functionality, such as a routine to check access to a particular record in a table. This common functionality can be placed in a separate unit, which is not related to a specific form. Each form requiring the services of that unit simply adds the unit's name to its uses clause.

You can use the Project Manager to create a new form or unit by:

1. Right-clicking the Project Manager window. A Speedmenu appears.
2. Selecting the New Unit or New Form command. A new unit or form appears.

 TIP You can create new units and forms with the speed buttons located on the main window.

In an application with multiple forms and units, it would be time-consuming to open each file manually, especially if it were located in a different directory. The View Unit and View Form speed buttons, located third and fourth from the left, respectively, allow you to quickly open the file currently selected in the Project Manager.

 TIP Forms and units can also be opened with the View Form and View Unit speed buttons located on the main window.

Project Options

The Project Options speed button, located second from the right, displays the Project Options dialog box, which allows you to modify several project-wide settings. Project options are covered in more detail in Chapter 8, "Creating Applications."

Updating the Project File

The project file stores the units and forms that contribute to your application in a file ending with the extension DPR (Delphi PRoject). Recall that this file may be displayed by opening the View menu, and selecting the Project Source command. If you alter this file manually, the information shown in the Project Manager may be incorrect.

The Update speed button, located rightmost on the Speedbar, forces the Project Manager to scan the project file and rebuild its list of included files.

Using the Object Repository

The Object Repository lets you store forms and projects to use as templates for future development. Figure 2.30 shows the New Items dialog box, invoked when you open the File menu and select the New command. This dialog box displays the contents of the Object Repository.

The Object Repository may also contain a link to an expert or IDE add-on, which assists you in performing a certain task. An example of this is the Application Expert object, contained on the Projects page of the New Items dialog box. Chapter 29, "Working with Delphi's Open Tools API," covers the creation of experts in greater detail.

FIG. 2.30
The New Items dialog box displays items in the Object Repository.

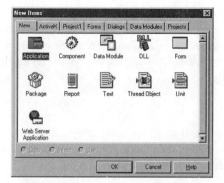

Object Repository Building Blocks

Delphi supplies several basic object templates, each of which can be used as a foundation for another, more complex object. These templates are located in the New Items dialog box, on the page titled New. The Form template provides a useful example of a basic template—it can be customized by the addition of components and Object Pascal code, and then added to the repository on either the Forms or Dialogs page.

Object Reuse Across Projects

Objects on the Forms, Dialogs, or Data Modules pages may be used across several projects in three ways:

- **Copy**—This adds an exact duplicate of the object to your project. Changes to either the project or repository objects will not affect the other.

- **Inherit**—Derives a new object from the one stored in the repository, and adds it to your project. Changes to the project object will not affect the object stored in the repository. Alterations to the repository object will affect the copy in your project. If the same portion of an object has changed in both the repository and project, the project version takes precedence. An About form with your company's logo is a good case for inheritance.

- **Use**—Includes the object from the repository as if it were just another file in your project. Changes made to the object in your project are immediately reflected in the repository, and in all other projects using that object.

Object Reuse Within a Project

Delphi also allows you to reuse an object within a project. This lets you define a base object and build on its functionality without storing it in the global Object Repository.

N O T E Object reuse within a project is logically restricted to inheritance only. Making an exact duplicate (Copy) of a project object serves no purpose—why not use the copy already present? Including the project object as if it were part of the project (Use) is redundant—it is already present. ■

A candidate for object reuse within an application is a program that displays multiple types of files, such as images, tables, and text. You could create a base form that provides common functionality, such as opening, saving, and printing. From this base form object, you can derive a form that handles file-type specific behavior such as zooming for an image or editing for a table.

Project Reuse

Projects may also be added to the Object Repository and used as templates for new applications. Delphi provides several project templates, such as an MDI Application, and stores them on the Projects page of the New Items dialog box.

You could create a project that defines a standard look-and-feel for your company and use it for all new development.

Putting It All Together

So now you are familiar with the Delphi IDE, its power and its flexibility, and you have built a small application to put this newfound knowledge into practice. Now, let's quickly restate what this chapter covered in order to really drive it home.

The Main Window

This section discussed the three segments of the window central to the IDE—the Menubar, the Speedbar, and the Component Palette.

The Menubar provides a central location from which you can access all the features of the Delphi IDE, such as the Object Browser, Project Options, and various compilation commands.

The Speedbar is an easily modifiable collection of shortcuts to the Menubar commands you find yourself frequently using.

The Component Palette contains an array of visual and non-visual components that assist you in the rapid development of your application. You may customize the grouping of components, and install third-party components into your library.

Designing the Application Interface

The application interface is primarily designed with two tools—the Object Inspector and the Form Designer. These tools allow you to completely define the "look" portion of an application's "look-and-feel."

The Object Inspector lets you alter the properties of components placed on the Form Designer.

The Form Designer helps you build forms quickly by providing a visual representation of the form as you design it.

Object Pascal: A Fundamental Approach

by J.W. Rider

Modern technology has gone to considerable lengths to make many aspects of our daily lives simpler. All you have to do is sit behind the steering wheel of a high-performance automobile, and you will note how carefully every single accessory and control is located within easy reach for convenient operation. However, the apparent simplicity only hides a complexity that still must exist beneath the dashboard. The complexity is there, and you can see it every time you open the hood to check the oil. Every cable, every hose, every connection that runs from place to place has a function. It may seem a little intimidating, and you don't really need to understand automotive mechanics in order to drive a car. It can be made understandable, however, and after you understand what goes on under the hood, it's even easier to interpret all of the indicators that you see on the dashboard. ■

An introduction to Object Pascal

See firsthand the underlying Object Pascal language that makes Delphi such a rapid application development tool.

Working with data types

You learn about the variety of ways in which Object Pascal can store your application's data internally and how to create customized containers for information.

Working with operators and expressions

You learn how to combine elementary data components to create complex expressions.

Using statements to control application execution

You learn the elementary statements that are constructed to modify or display information.

Creating procedures and functions

You learn how to combine groups of statements in an efficient, reusable, and modular fashion.

Building units

You learn how to put together collections of data types, procedures, and functions to create stand-alone library routines that can be shared between applications.

An Introduction to Object Pascal

In Delphi, you don't have to go too far to peek under the hood. Create a new project. Double-click the form. Suddenly, you are staring into the raw power of the engine that makes Delphi work, the Object Pascal language:

```
procedure TForm1.FormCreate(Sender: TObject);
begin

end;
```

So now, what do you do? Well, you really have no limits. However, this doesn't quite mean that anything goes. You are still constrained to use legal Pascal. You are constrained by the "syntax" of the language on how you can state what you want to do. You are constrained by "scope" that limits what is proper for you to reference and what you can modify. You are constrained by the principles of "structured" programming to put machine instruction in an order that makes sense for proper program execution.

Despite all the constraints, what you want to do here is up to you; only, don't make your choices so complex that you cannot understand them. Although you are perfectly capable of invoking a rash of complex and esoteric directives to the compiler, the Object Pascal language also makes it possible for you to do simple things.

At the core of all programming languages, the elementary executable action is the *assignment statement*. In Object Pascal, the assignment statement takes the following form:

```
Target := Expression
```

Here, the assignment statement assigns the value returned from the expression to the target, a location in your program for holding such values. For example, you can insert the following Object Pascal statement between the words `begin` and `end` of procedure `TForm1.FormCreate`:

```
Caption := 'Hello, world!'
```

Here, you identify that the target to which you want to assign a value has the name `Caption`, and the expression that you want to assign to the target is the constant string, `Hello, world!` This is all the customization that you need to generate a real Delphi application. You can compile your program, run it, and watch what it does. At the moment all it does is present an empty form with a caption bar that has `Hello, world!` in it. However, you will be able to elaborate on your application as you become more familiar with the features of Delphi.

The preceding example was not selected by accident. The choice of displaying `Hello, world!` was a deliberate decision. Getting programs to display `Hello, world!` is one thing that developers have done for years whenever they happen to run across a new programming language or development environment. Usually, it's a simple task. However, some programming languages can make the process seem unnecessarily cumbersome. In Delphi, all you need to get a program to display "`Hello, world!`" is a simple assignment statement.

This simplicity doesn't arise by accident; it results from a consistent design of the Object Pascal programming language. Sure, you're looking under the hood, but Delphi has focused your attention to the part of the program that you're interested in customizing. There are plenty of other cables and hoses running to and fro, but in Object Pascal, you can break large programs up into many smaller pieces, and each piece works in almost complete independence from one another. The "independence" is important. It keeps two pieces of your program from invariably interfering with each other. The fact that Object Pascal allows smaller pieces to work almost completely independent of one another is also important because it allows you to specify how your very small pieces interact. You combine the smallest pieces to form larger pieces; combine larger pieces together to form even larger pieces; and, eventually, you put together the largest pieces to form your application, perhaps making some substitutions at the lowest scale.

Delphi puts you on your course here. The previous TForm1.FormCreate procedure is one of the smaller pieces. The dot between the TForm1 and FormCreate indicates that this piece is a part of a larger piece named TForm1. For every application, Delphi automatically creates a new form and puts it into a still larger piece known as a *unit*. If you scroll up and down in the code window where you found TForm1.FormCreate, you can see that the little "Hello, world!" assignment statement that you added is just a small part of a bigger piece, as follows:

```
unit Unit1;
interface
uses
  Windows, Messages, SysUtils, Classes, Graphics, Controls,
  Forms, Dialogs;
type
  TForm1 = class(TForm)
    procedure FormCreate(Sender: TObject);
  private
    { Private declarations }
  public
    { Public declarations }
  end;
var
  Form1: TForm1;
implementation
{$R *.DFM}
procedure TForm1.FormCreate(Sender: TObject);
begin
  Caption := 'Hello, world!'
end;
end.
```

From this example, you can see that the piece of the program named TForm1 is a special kind of type declaration known as a *class*. After the declaration of the type TForm1, the example goes on to declare a variable named Form1 of the type TForm1. However, despite all of the statements and frameworks in the example, the unit shows at best "potential." The declarations are just lying around, waiting to be used, which is where the project comes into play. For every program, Delphi automatically defines a new project, and if you looked at the source code hidden in the file PROJECT1.DPR, you see even further under the hood at the pieces that make your application buzz:

```
program Project1;
uses
  Forms,
  Unit1 in 'Unit1.pas' {Form1};
```

```
{$R *.RES}
begin
  Application.Initialize;
  Application.CreateForm(TForm1, Form1);
  Application.Run;
end.
```

Sometimes things can be surprisingly simple. Every word, every phrase, every sequence of characters in the preceding code has a purpose, and every line is a perfectly valid Object Pascal statement, ready-made to make your killer application suitable to the compiler. However, what Delphi generates for you automatically is, in itself, only a small piece of what you can make the program do. The preceding project code is a simple example of the kinds of things that could be put into a program. A more thorough (but still incomplete) picture of what a program can do is shown in the following skeleton:

```
program programid;
uses
    unitid,unitid2,unitid3;
labels
    label1,label2,label3;
const
    constid = constant_expression;
type
    typeid = type_definition;
var
    var1: type_definition;
procedure proc1;
procedure_definition;
function func1:typeid;
function_definition;
begin
    statements;
end.
```

Or, you could look at the program module as being a simpler format, as follows:

```
program header
program block
```

The notion of a piece of Object Pascal having a *header* followed by a *block* (sometimes called a "body") recurs again and again in the syntax of the language. At a minimum, a block consists of local declarations and a single executable statement. In the case of the program block, the block consists of the following:

```
program uses clause
program declarations
program executable statement
```

The uses clause is optional, but it must occur before any declarations or the executable statement. Declarations include labels, constants, type definitions, variables, procedures, and functions, which generally can be declared in any desired order. However, an identifier (a sequence of alphanumeric characters with or without embedded underscores that doesn't start with a digit) must be declared in a declaration somewhere before it can be used. The executable statement is always a *compound statement* that consists of `begin`, followed by any number of other kinds of executables statements, and ending with `end`, followed by a period.

NOTE If Object Pascal is the first programming language you learned, you will find it easiest to just accept the way programs are organized at face value. If you've already mastered several other programming languages, you're already aware that language features that appear to be similar between languages just don't work the same for all of them. If you are familiar with development in just one other programming language, you may need to readjust how you think about program organization and the meaning of several terms so that you can develop successfully in Delphi.

For example, C/C++ programmers are accustomed to partitioning applications into multiple functions. All C/C++ applications must start with a single function named `main()` or `Winmain()`. Delphi applications have no similar named routine that gets called. Rather, the Delphi program starts execution at the `begin....end.` compound statement that occurs at the end of the `program` block. There can be only one `program` module in a Delphi application, just like there can be only one `main()` function in a C/C++ application. ▒

Part
I
Ch
3

This approach is repeated again and again in the definition of the Object Pascal language: All programming problems are given a name, and then viewed as declarations of ways to store information internally and to manipulate the information after it is stored. Everything then gets tied together with a single executable statement.

So, for the rest of this chapter you look at ways the Object Pascal language allows you to do the following:

- Store information into variables of various data types
- Combine information together with appropriate operators to form expressions
- Control the evaluation of expressions at runtime with statements
- Group statements together in procedures and functions
- Associate logically related components and make them accessible to multiple programs in units

This still isn't the whole story of either Delphi or Object Pascal. It's just a start, and you will assimilate additional features of the development environment or programming language throughout the rest of this book.

Data Types

Data types are the way the programmer explains to the compiler how to store information in the program. Whenever you declare a variable, you also must state its data type. Some data types are already defined in the language; others you can define on your own. In early programming languages, only a limited number of data types were permitted. Pascal was one of the first programming languages that permitted the programmer to define new data types to be manipulated within the program.

User-defined data types usually are declared in a type declaration part of a program or unit, but they also are permitted within the context of procedure or function block. The scope of a type declaration is limited to the block in which it is declared. Outside of that block, the type declaration will not be visible and cannot be referenced. Inside the block, the type declaration will override any declaration of the same identifier outside of the block. The new declared data type can be used almost anywhere within the scope except that its own definition cannot reference itself (with one exception, mentioned under "Pointer Types," a following section of this chapter).

Pascal type declarations are blueprints for the compiler to remember just in case it happens to run across a reference to the type later in the program. Nothing happens in your program simply because you define a new type.

Pascal var declarations, however, are where you tell the compiler to do something with a type you defined earlier. A variable's data type constrains both values that the variable can represent and the operations that can be performed on those values.

Both type and var declarations can occur at several distinct places with the components of the program. Whenever they occur, the declarations are formed as follows:

```
type                            // New data types are declared in a "type"
   type1 = type_definition1;    // section. Every new type is given a name
                                // and then defined in terms of earlier
                                // type definitions.
   type2 = type_definition2;    // More than one type can be declared in
                                // a single type section.
   type3 = type1;               // A type definition can be as simple as
                                // a single type name.
var                             // New variables are declared in a
   var1 : type_definition3;     // "var" section. Every new variable
                                // is given a name and then
                                // defined in terms of earlier type
                                // definitions.
   var2, var3 : type_definition4; // More than one variable can be
                                // declared in a single var section.
                                // Multiple variables can share the
                                // same type definition.
   var4 : type1;                // You'll find it easier to follow
                                // your programs if you define new
                                // variables in terms of existing types.
```

The syntax of Object Pascal permits you to define extremely complicated type definitions at the same time that you declare a variable. However, you will find it easier to share the type information with other parts of your programs if you limit type definitions to a type section of any particular Pascal block. You should define your types from the following categories:

- Simple types, which allow you to store information in the form of numbers and other "ordered" values

- String types, which allow you to store character information in sequences

- Structured types define a nestable mechanism for combining more than one kind of information simultaneously

- Pointer types define system-specific ways to reference indirectly variables of a specified type

- Procedural types allow references to procedures and functions to be treated as data

- Variant types allow a single variable to store values of different types

Usually, type identifiers can be used only in the context of new type definitions or variable declarations. A few routines, however, do permit type names to be used as part of an executable statement. For example, `SizeOf(T)` returns the number of bytes occupied by the argument type, T.

The `SizeOf` function plays an important role in writing robust programs. Many of the predefined Object Pascal types occur in a variety of flavors, and the flavors can occupy a variety of bytes of memory to represent its values. Some of the flavors of data types are designed deliberately to represent values in a logical fashion rather than in some preconceived notion of how big a chunk of memory the microprocessor and operating environment can handle. The `SizeOf` function eliminates the need for you to assume that any data type is a particular size.

Simple Data Types

Every real-world data type, however complicated it may seem upon first examination, eventually can be reduced into small components that are easily represented and manipulated by a microprocessor. In Object Pascal, such simple data types are conveniently separated into two groups—ordinal types, which represent information in the variously sized pieces that microprocessors can easily manipulate, and real types, which approximate information that can be represented by mathematical real numbers. The division between ordinals and reals is slightly arbitrary. You also can think of partitioning simple data types into numbers and non-numbers. The Object Pascal language, however, treats ordinals and reals in different ways, and the distinction is useful.

Ordinal Types   Of the simple data types, ordinal types are the simplest. *Ordinal types* represent information as discrete elements. The connection between the discrete elements and how they are represented in memory provides a natural ordering relation between the elements. Hence, the term *ordinal*.

Object Pascal has three predefined ordinal type groups and two user-defined types. The predefined type groups are *integers*, *characters,* and *Booleans*. The user-defined ordinal type groups are *enumerations* and *subranges*.

All of the values of any ordinal type form an ordered sequence, and the "ordinal value" of each ordinal type value is determined by the position of the value within the ordered sequence. Except for integer type values, which can be both positive and negative, the first element of an ordinal type has the position index 0, the next is 1, and so on. The position index of an integer type value *is* the value. Because of the underlying ordering relationship, all ordinal types share some common operations that can be used to manipulate their values up and down, along the whole order. Several standard routines are built into Object Pascal for manipulating ordinal data types, as shown in Table 3.1.

Table 3.1 Ordinal Routines

Routine	Returns (or Description)
Low(T)	The minimum value in the range of the given ordinal type T.
High(T)	The maximum value in the range of the given ordinal type T.
Ord(X)	The ordinal expression's numerical ordering within the host ordinal type. For integer expressions, this simply is the value of the expression. For other ordinal types, the Ord function returns the physical representation of the expression interpreted as if it were an integer ordinal type. The result of Ord is always some integer type.
Pred(X)	The predecessor of the value. For integer expressions, equivalent to "X–1."
Succ(X)	The successor of the value. For integer expressions, equivalent to "X+1."
Dec(V)	Decrements a variable. Equivalent to "V := Pred(V)."
Inc(V)	Increments a variable. Equivalent to "V := Succ(V)."

For all ordinal types, Object Pascal provides a *value typecast* method for converting integer values into the corresponding ordinal value. If "T" is the name of an ordinal type and "X" is an integer expression, then "T(X)" returns a value of type "T" whose ordinal value is "X."

N O T E C/C++ programmers are accustomed to using the operators "++" and "−−" to combine the effect of incrementing and decrementing a variable and returning its value before or after the adjustment. Delphi programmers always break this kind of operation into its simplest components by using Pred, Succ, Dec, and Inc. ▪

Integer Types *Integer types* represent information as whole numbers, with absolutely no fractional part. Object Pascal's predefined integer types are divided into *physical* (fundamental) and *logical* (generic) types. You usually are better off using the logical integer types where possible as variables within your applications, because the logical types are sized to get the best performance for the specific microprocessor and operating environment for which your program executes. The physical integer formats should be specified only when the actual range or size of the type makes a difference. Within Object Pascal, integer types may go by several different names, as follows:

```
Integer
Shortint
SmallInt
LongInt
Byte
Word
Cardinal
```

Note that one of these integer types is itself named "integer." This can cause some confusion, especially when the only immediately available distinction is where you put the qualifying word "type." Because the distinction is important for many Object Pascal data types, this chapter puts "type" after the name when referencing one or more types of a group. When a specific pre-defined identifier that is a type, "type" is placed before the identifier. Consequently, the type Integer is one of seven predefined "integer types."

The physical integer types can hold different ranges of integer values, depending upon exactly how many physical bytes of memory they occupy (which is the same as the SizeOf that physical type). Table 3.2 shows the range of values that can be stored into each physical data type.

Table 3.2   Physical Integer Formats

Type	Range	Physical Format
ShortInt	–128 .. 127	Signed 8-bit
SmallInt	–32,768 .. 32,767	Signed 16-bit
LongInt	–2,147,483,648 .. 2,147,483,647	Signed 32-bit
Byte	0 .. 255	Unsigned 8-bit
Word	0 .. 65,535	Unsigned 16-bit

The range and format of the physical integer types are independent of the underlying micro-processor and operating environment. It doesn't (or, at least, shouldn't) change across different implementations or different versions of Object Pascal.

The logical integer types (Integer and Cardinal) are completely dependent upon the underlying physical integer types to control the range of values that they can represent. Table 3.3 shows that the range of values that can be stored in a logical type is dependent upon the underlying physical data type that is represented. In Delphi, the 32-bit representation is always the default.

Table 3.3   Logical Integer Types

Type	Range	Physical Format (Type)
Integer	–32,768 .. 32,767	Signed 16-bit (SmallInt)
Integer	–2,147,483,648 .. 2,147,483,647	Signed 32-bit (LongInt)
Cardinal	0 .. 65,535	Unsigned 16-bit (Word)
Cardinal	0 .. 2,147,483,647	Unsigned 32-bit (LongInt)

NOTE   C/C++ hold integer values in types known as int, short int (or just "short"), and long int (or just "long"). The C/C++ int corresponds to the Delphi Integer, and the C/C++ long corresponds to the Delphi LongInt. However, the C/C++ ShortInt corresponds to the Delphi SmallInt rather than to the Delphi ShortInt. The equivalent to the Delphi ShortInt in C/C++ is signed char. The C/C++ unsigned char would be equivalent to the Delphi Byte. C/C++ also has an unsigned long, which has no direct equivalent in Delphi.

Integer data types share all the same operations with other ordinal types, but you are likely to want to use them as numbers rather than "non-numeric ordinals" on occasion. As numbers, you'll be able to add integers (+), subtract(–),and multiply them (*) as well as you can "real" numbers. However, some numerical operations and functions take on slightly different meanings when applied to integers, as follows:

Operation	Result
Abs(X)	Returns the absolute integer value of X
X Div Y	Returns the number of times that Y divides X
X Mod Y	Returns the remainder that is left after Y divides X
Odd(X)	Returns a Boolean True if X is an odd integer, or False if the integer is even
Sqr(X)	Returns the integer square of X. That is, "X * X"

N O T E   Always exercise caution in moving numerical expressions between languages. Basic uses the SQR function for computing square roots. ■

N O T E   C/C++ programmers denote integer division with a single slash (/). In Delphi, if you use a slash between two integers, a floating-point division results. ■

Character Types   Although the meaning of a character data type value is often obvious when displayed on-screen or written to printer, defining *character data types* seems to depend on what you think a character is. Usually, character data types provide a scheme or relationship between various-sized pieces of memory and some kind of standard encoding/decoding for character-information interchange. In classic Pascal, no specific scheme was dictated, and implementations made use of what everyone else may have been using on the same computer.

Early microprocessor implementations of Pascal in the United States used a seven-bit scheme named *ASCII* (*American Standard Code for Information Interchange*). The seven-bit ASCII encoding still has a widespread following today, but the information has almost always been stored in eight-bit pieces of memory. The extra bit doubles the number of possible character representations, and implementations that extended the ASCII character sets have sometimes been far from standard. The current definition of Delphi refers to the eight-bit character set as being *extended ANSI* (*American National Standards Institute*). Giving the scheme a different name is slightly arbitrary. The old-style ASCII codes are still there, and they are all that the compiler actually uses outside of quoted strings. For everything else, you get whatever coding scheme happens to be used by the operating system. For Microsoft windowing operating systems, this scheme is ANSI and includes a limited number of international characters for display. For a more extensive set of international characters, most of the world is heading in the direction of a 16-bit scheme named *UNICODE*, which is defined in a way that the lowest 256 entries correspond directly with the 256 characters defined in ANSI.

To accommodate these different kinds of representations, Object Pascal defines two physical character data types and one generic or logical character data type.

The physical character types are as follows:

AnsiChar	Byte-sized characters, ordered according to the extended ANSI character set.
WideChar	Word-sized characters, ordered according to the internationalized UNICODE character set. The first 256 UNICODE characters are designed to correspond to the ANSI characters.

There is no double-word, 32-bit sized character data type.

The generic character type is named simply char. In classic Pascal, only the type char existed. In Delphi, char always corresponds to the physical data type AnsiChar. For American programmers, the association of a single character with a byte-sized piece of memory has been around for so long that it's sometimes easy to forget that other encoding schemes are possible. Future considerations about internationalization of applications on the Internet or World Wide Web conceivably could force fundamental changes in the way that programmers think about character sizes. If you use the generic char type, make implementations for other microprocessors and operating environments that might define char to be WideChar. When writing code that might need to handle characters of either size, use the standard function SizeOf rather than a hard-coded constant for character size.

The function call Ord(C), where C is any character data type value, returns the integer type value that is used to represent the character C in the microprocessor's memory.

Chr(X)	Converts an integer into a char with the same ordinal value. In Delphi, equivalent to Char(X).
UpCase	Converts a single character to uppercase.

NOTE From the CPU's point of view, Delphi and C/C++ represent the type char in exactly the same way. Operationally, the languages treat the type char in very different ways. In C/C++, the type char is an integer type that is assignment-compatible with all other integer types. You can assign character data to an int and numeric data to a char with a simple expression. In Delphi, character data is handled as if it were different from numeric data. If you want to move a char value to an integer in Delphi, you need to explicitly use the Ord function. ■

NOTE Basic represents single character values as a string. The Delphi Chr function is equivalent to the Basic CHR$. The Delphi Ord function, which returns the ANSI code in the case of character data, is comparable to the Basic ASC function when a one-character string is used as an argument. ■

Boolean Types   Early in their education, programmers learn the concept of a two-state "bit" that can be used to store information that is either one thing or another. The bit can be 0 or 1, YES or NO, ON or OFF, UP or DOWN, STOP or GO. In Object Pascal, information about something that can be represented as either True or False is stored in a *Boolean type*. There are four predefined Boolean types, of various sizes, as shown in Table 3.4.

Table 3.4   Boolean Type Sizes

Type	Size
Boolean	1 byte
ByteBool	1 byte
WordBool	2 bytes (size of 1 word)
LongBool	4 bytes (size of 1 longint)

In keeping with the integer and character type notions of separating data types into physical and generic types, you might expect that the types ByteBool, WordBool, and LongBool denote the physical types and that the type Boolean denotes the generic type. No, not quite, this time. All four types are distinct. The type Boolean is preferred by Object Pascal programmers. The other Boolean types are provided for compatibility with other computer programming languages and the operating environment.

Variables of the type Boolean can assume only the values False or True. Variables of type ByteBool, WordBool, and LongBool can assume other ordinal values that are usually interpreted by the convention where 0 is False and any non-zero value is True.

N O T E   The Delphi Boolean types are comparable to the FORTRAN type LOGICAL. Neither Basic nor C/C++ has a Boolean type as such. Boolean expressions are just as intrinsic to Basic and C/C++ just as they are in other programming languages, but the results of such expressions are interpreted as if they were numbers rather than a separate type. In both Basic and C/C++, the Boolean expressions yield numeric results such that 0 is evaluated as False and non-zero values are evaluated as True. These results are consistent with the ordinal value of the Boolean expressions within Delphi.

N O T E   In C/C++, simple comparisons result in integer values of 1 for True and 0 for False. This representation is equivalent to how Delphi stores Boolean values. Delphi just types the comparison as "Boolean" result rather than any integer result. The Delphi Boolean will be translated as a C/C++ char in most cases.

N O T E   Basic has reserved words named TRUE (equivalent to the constant –1) and FALSE (equivalent to the constant 0). In Basic, TRUE is less than FALSE; in Delphi, True is greater than False.

Enumerated Types

```
Type enum_type = ( first_value, value2,  value3, last_value);
```

Usually, an *enumerated data type* is capable of representing discrete values that have names rather than numeric values. The type `Boolean` is a predefined example of an Object Pascal enumeration. Boolean has two such names—True and False, and the type `Boolean` is predefined in Object Pascal as if you had declared it on your own as follows:

Type Boolean = (False, True);

Of course, the `Boolean` type is intrinsic to how Object Pascal handles comparisons. Most enumerated types are simply a list of unique names or identifiers that you decide that you want reserved for a specific purpose. For example, you might want to create a `MyColor` enumeration type and associate the values `myRed`, `myGreen`, and `myBlue` with the type. This can be done simply with the following:

Type MyColor = (myRed, myGreen, myBlue);

This line declares four new identifiers: `MyColor`, `myRed`, `myGreen`, and `myBlue`. The identifier `MyColor` is defined as an ordinal type, which means you can use the identifier anywhere in the syntax of the Object Pascal language where an ordinal type is permitted. The other three identifiers are defined as *values* of the type `MyColor`.

Like character and Boolean data types, enumerations aren't numeric and it usually doesn't make sense to use them as if they were numbers. However, because enumerations are ordinal types, an ordering does exist for any enumerated type that you define. The identifiers in the list of unique names get assigned sequential numbers as their ordinal values. The first name gets an ordinal value of 0; the second name gets an ordinal value of 1, and so on.

> **N O T E** C/C++ has an enum type that is similar to the Delphi enumerated type. In C/C++, the programmer can modify the assignment of constant values to identifiers. In Delphi, the values are assigned so that the first identifier gets an ordinal value of 0, and every subsequent identifier has the ordinal value incremented by one. In C, an enum usually is treated like a shorthand notation to quickly assign sequential numbers to a group of integer constants. In C++, the identifiers declared in an enumeration can only be assigned to variables of the same enumeration type. ∎

Subrange Types A *subrange type* represents information that can fit within some specific range of values for a single "host" type, which can be any other ordinal type but not a subrange type. The following line shows the syntax for subrange types:

Type subrange_type = low_value .. high_value;

Variables of a subrange type share all characteristics of the "host" type. The only difference between a variable type host type and a variable of the subrange type is that the variable of the subrange type can be assigned values only within the specified subrange. The range-checking directive controls this checking of the proper subrange upon assignment.

Most programmers seldom need to define a subrange type explicitly. However, all programmers use the subrange type construction implicitly whenever they create an array. The low and high dimension of an array defines a subrange type.

Real Types   *Real types* represent numeric information that may have both whole or integer parts and fractional parts. Object Pascal has six kinds of real types. They all can represent the numerical value 0. However, they differ in terms of threshold (the smallest positive number that the type can represent), the maximum value that be represented, the significance or precision of values, and the size that its variables occupy in memory, as shown in Table 3.5.

Table 3.5   Real Types

Type	Threshold	Maximum	Significant Digits	*SizeOf* (Bytes)
Real	2.9E-39	1.7E38	11-12	6
Single	1.5E-45	3.4E38	7-8	4
Double	5.0E-324	1.7E308	15-16	8
Extended	3.4E-4932	1.1E4932	19-20	10
Comp	1.0	9.2E18	19-20	8
Currency	0.0001	9.2E14	19-20	8

N O T E   The type Real is provided for backward compatibility with earlier versions of Delphi and Borland Pascal. Because the storage format of the type Real isn't native to the Intel CPU family, operations on values of type Real are sometimes slower than the other floating-point types.

Integer types represent whole numbers; that is, a number with a fractional part of zero. No matter how close you try to get them, two different whole numbers are always going to be at least one "1" apart. It's a feature that makes integer types useful for distinguishing between discrete values, whether or not the real-world feature has anything to do with numbers. Real types are used to represent numbers that might have non-zero fractional parts, which make real types useful for representing quantities that may be closer together, even almost "continuous."

But only *almost* continuous. Even though Object Pascal calls them "real," the real types are not the same thing as mathematical real numbers. An *Object Pascal* real type is a strict subset of real numbers that you can represent in floating-point notation with a fixed number of digits. What complicates the issue even further for unwary developers is that the standard *IEEE (Institute of Electrical and Electronic Engineers)* floating-point formats used by Delphi applications and most other Windows programs only can represent exactly numbers with a fixed number of "bits" in the fractional part. Surprisingly, data as apparently simple as "0.1" cannot be stored in the IEEE extended format without some error, albeit a very small difference, which makes the floating-point notation a tad inconvenient for applications that need to maintain and display a fixed number of decimal places for numerical values. This includes any application that tracks "real" money.

In addition to the floating-point formats, Object Pascal includes two fixed-point formats to partially relieve this problem.

The type Comp (computational) holds only whole numbers within the range of $-2^{63}+1$ to $2^{63}-1$, which is approximately -9.2×10^{18} to 9.2×10^{18}. With American currency, developers usually seek the "natural" way of storing money as dollars and cents in terms of whole dollars and fractions. If you store the values in a variable of type Comp, you need to adjust the units implied by this approach and store the whole value in terms of whole cents. You just need to be careful to divide by 100 when converting the number of cents to dollars and to multiply by 100 when converting dollars to cents.

Alternatively, you can use the type Currency and let the compiler keep track of the scaling automatically. Currency values are stored physically as whole numbers in the same memory as a Comp variable. However, the compiler knows to divide by 10,000 (not just by 100) to convert the value into its proper units, and to multiply by 10,000 when storing the value to memory. This gives the type Currency an explicit precision of four decimal places to the right of the decimal point.

The Delphi System unit includes a number of routines for manipulating real data types. The most common ones are listed in Table 3.6. Additional routines are available in the SysUtils and Math units.

Part

I

Ch

3

Table 3.6 Real Functions

Function	Returns
Abs(x)	Absolute value of x.
ArcTan(x)	Inverse tangent of x.
Cos(x)	Cosine of x (an angle, measured in radians, not in degrees).
Exp(x)	The "exponential" of x.
Frac(x)	Fractional part of x.
Int(x)	Integral part of x. Despite the name, Int returns a real type (floating point) value rather than an integer type value. Int does set the fractional part of x to zero.
Ln(x)	Natural logarithm of x.
Pi	Pi. (3.1416....).
Round(x)	The whole number closest to x. The result of Round is an integer type rather than a real type. "Closest to x" is ambiguous when x has a fractional part of exactly 0.5 and is located at the midpoint between two whole numbers. Delphi lets the operating system decide how to round these halfway values at runtime. Usual behavior with Intel CPUs is the IEEE recommendation to "round to the nearest even" whole number. This behavior is sometimes referred to as "banker's rounding."
Sin(x)	Sine of x.

continues

Table 3.6 Continued

Function	Returns
Sqr(x)	Square of x. That is, x*x.
Sqrt(x)	Square root of x.
Trunc(x)	Integral part of x. Unlike Int, which returns a real type value, Trunc returns an integer type value.

N O T E Always exercise caution in moving numerical expressions between languages. Basic uses the SQR function for computing square roots. In Delphi, the function Sqr computes the square of a number; the function Sqrt computes the square root. ◼

String Types

In expressions, Delphi supports three kinds of physical string formats: *short* (ShortString), *long* (AnsiString), and *wide* (WideString). AnsiStrings, ShortStrings, and WideStrings can be mixed in assignments and expressions, and Delphi performs the needed conversions automatically.

Both of the types AnsiString and WideString store their characters in a dynamically allocated array, with a maximum length limited only by available memory. The difference between these two types is that the AnsiString stores its characters in an array of char, and the WideString stores its characters in an array of WideChar. Usually, the only kind of string that you ever want to use is the AnsiString, but the WideString will be more useful to you if you deal with international character sets such as UNICODE.

Physically, the type ShortString is stored as an array [0..255] of char. The first position in the array denotes the dynamic length of the string, which can vary between 0 and 255 characters. The characters composing the string occupy positions 1 to 255. The type ShortString primarily exists to be compatible with earlier versions of Delphi and Borland Pascal.

The generic string type is known as simply String. Whether the type String refers to a ShortString or an AnsiString is controlled by a compiler directive, $H. In the default state, {$H+}, String indicates an AnsiString. In the {$H-} state, String indicates ShortString with a maximum length of 255 characters.

To be compatible with other programming languages, Delphi also supports a class of character strings called *null-terminated strings*. No special reserved words or identifiers indicate the use of a null-terminated string.

Null-terminated strings are composed of non-null characters followed by a null (#0) character. Unlike Object Pascal AnsiString, ShortString, and WideString, null-terminated strings have no separate length indicator. The null character always indicates the end of a null-terminated string.

Physically, null-terminated strings behave as if they are stored in arrays of characters with a zero-based integer index type, like `array[0..X] of char` where X is some positive non-zero integer, although you usually will not declare null-terminated strings like this. Instead, you declare a pointer variable of type `Pchar`, and allocate the memory on your own. For convenience, the Delphi `AnsiString` may be value typecast to a `Pchar`.

Table 3.7 shows several of the routines available to you for manipulating string data types.

> **N O T E** C programmers are accustomed to storing all strings in null-terminated arrays. They don't really use the value of the strings, the character sequence, in expressions. Rather, strings are passed from one part of the program to another as pointers. Basic programmers are accustomed to using the characters in the string as a whole. The Delphi `AnsiString` is suitable to both of these viewpoints. ■

Table 3.7 String Functions

Function	Description
Concat(s1,s2,s3)	Returns the concatenation of a sequence of strings. Equivalent to s1+s2+s3.
Copy(s,pos,len)	Returns a substring that is at most `len` characters in length starting at position `pos` of string s. Comparable to the MID$ function in Basic.
Delete(s,pos,len)	Deletes at most `len` characters from string s, starting at position `pos`.
Insert(source, target,pos)	Inserts the string `source` into the string variable `target` starting at position `pos`.
Length(s)	Returns the dynamic length of a string. Comparable to the LEN function in Basic and to the `strlen()` function in C/C++.
Pos(substring,s)	Returns the location of the first instance of a substring in string s. Comparable to the SUBSTR function in Basic and to the `strstr()` function in C/C++.
SetLength(s,newlen)	Sets the dynamic length of a string variable
SetString	Sets the contents and length of a given string.
Str(x, s)	Converts a numeric expression into a string variable.
StringOfCharS	Returns a string of a given number of characters.
UniqueString	Makes a given string unique, with a reference count of one.
Val(s, v, code)	Converts a string s to its corresponding numerical representation.

Structured Data Types

At an elementary level, the most useful data types are those that can hold numbers and those that hold strings (or character) information. From these elementary types, additional useful data types can be created by combining more than one instance of the elementary types.

The *structured data types* provide ways to create new data types by extending the definition of previously defined data types to hold more than one value. The components of structured types can be manipulated, individually or as a whole, and can themselves be structured types. No limit is placed on the number of such nested structures.

Delphi's structured types are shown in the following list:

- Record types
- Array types
- Set types
- File types
- Class types
- Class reference types

Usually, the preceding items aren't data types all by themselves, they are structured methods to complement existing data types.

The structured class types and class reference types are discussed in Chapter 4, "Object Pascal: Advanced Concepts."

Records   The record reserved word permits you to group different kinds of information in a single type. The general syntax of this type declaration will look like the following:

```
record
    fieldname1: fieldtype1;
    fieldname2, fieldname3: fieldtype2;
    case optional_tagfield: required_ordinal_type of
    1: variantname1: varianttype3;
    2,3: variantname2: varianttype4;
end
```

The declaration consists of both a fixed part and a variant part. However, you don't need to include both parts in a single record type declaration. You usually will find it simpler to work with the two parts separately.

Fixed Records   The fixed part of a record type defines one or more independent fields. You always have to give a name and type for each field.

```
record
    fieldname1: fieldtype1;
    fieldname2, fieldname3: fieldtype2;
end
```

When you can access information in the record, you can deal with the whole record (you can handle all the fields at the same time) or with an individual field. To reference an individual field, type the record name, a period, and then the field identifier. For example,

MyRec.Fieldname1

To access an entire record, just use the name of the record.

N O T E The C struct type is the equivalent of a Delphi fixed record type. C++ also uses a struct type that is syntactically compatible with the C struct type. However, the C++ struct has additional features that also make it resemble the Delphi class type. ◼

Variant Records   The variant part of a record type provides different ways to interpret memory shared by each of the named variants.

```
record
     case optional_tagfield: required_ordinal_type of
     1: variantname1: varianttype3;
     2,3: variantname2: varianttype4;
end
```

N O T E The use of the term *variant* in connection with records has nothing to do with the pre-defined type Variant discussed in a following section of this chapter. Although each field within a variant record is referred to as a "variant," they never have the type Variant. In fact, the type Variant is prohibited within any part of the variant record definition. ◼

Each variant overlays the same space in memory. Each variant is distinguished by a constant. If you are so inclined, you can access all fields of all variants at all times. However, this is not generally meaningful except in a very simple example, where you know exactly how the information for each variant's type is stored in memory.

Each variant is identified by at least one constant. All constants must be unique and of an ordinal type compatible with the tagfield's type.

The optional tag field is an identifier for an additional field in the fixed part of the record. This means that even in what would otherwise be a pure variant record, the tag field is a common part within each of the variant definitions. Ordinarily, you will use the tag field in order to determine which of the variants makes sense to access at any one time.

You don't have to use a tag field, but you still need to have a required ordinal type. Without a tag field, your application is going to have to select which variant makes sense by some other means.

It doesn't make sense to interpret some data types in multiple ways. The Object Pascal language enforces this limitation for some critical types. Consequently, fields in the variant part of a record cannot be of a long string type or of the type Variant. Likewise, fields in the variant part of a record cannot be of a structured type that contains a long string or Variant components.

N O T E   The C/C++ `union` type is the equivalent of the Delphi variant record type. ▪

Arrays   *Arrays* can exist in either one-dimensional or multidimensional varieties, as follows:

```
array [ ordinal_type ] of type_definition;
array [ ordinal_type1, ordinal_type2 ] of type_definition;
```

Each array holds multiple instances of information, all of which must have the same type. Each instance of the information is referenced by the array name and by an index value, which is enclosed in square brackets.

Note that the syntax specifies some kind of `ordinal_type` is used to determine how many places, the number of elements, are allocated to each dimension of the array. You can just use a named type, such as `Boolean` or `AnsiChar`. However, the usual practice is to use an explicit subrange of integers.

The number of elements in a multidimensional array is the product of the number of values in each index type.

To access the elements of the array, add brackets and an index value to the array identifier. For instance, suppose you define a variable as follows:

```
var MyArray: Array [ 1..10] of Integer;
```

Then you can access the third element of the array as `MyArray[3]` and can treat references to this element as if the element had been declared an `Integer` all by itself.

N O T E   Most programming languages include an array concept. However, syntax sometimes differs. Both Basic and FORTRAN use parentheses instead of brackets. C/C++ numbers the array indices starting from 0. FORTRAN numbers the array indices starting from 1. Basic can number array indices from either 0 or 1, depending on the value of the last executed `OPTION BASE` statement. Some versions of Basic can specify the lower and upper limits in a manner similar to Delphi. ▪

N O T E   In C/C++, references to an array variable identifier in an expression returns the address of the first ("0") element of the array. In Delphi, a reference to an array variable identifier references the *entire* array variable, not a single element. ▪

***set* Types**   The reserved word `set` defines an ordered collection of no more than 256 possible ordinal values.

```
set of ordinal_type
```

The ordinal values of the upper and lower bounds of the set's base ordinal type must be between 0 and 255, inclusively. A variable of the `set` type must then include or exclude all the possible values of the base ordinal type. A value within the range is either in the set or it is not. Consider the following example:

```
type CharSet = set of AnsiChar; // a set type that contains ANSI characters
var MyAlphaSet: CharSet;         // a variable of type CharSet
```

A variable of a set type can hold none or all of the values of the set. In expressions, you can specify set membership by listing the ordinal values within brackets, as in the following example:

```
MyAlphaSet := [ 'A', 'E', 'I', 'O', 'U', 'Y'];  // all upper case vowels
```

The notation [ ] denotes the empty set, which has no elements included. It is compatible with all set types.

N O T E   Many languages don't include a set structured type. From the point of view of another language, a set may look like some kind of "bitmap" or "bitfield." ■

The *file* Type   A file type controls access to a linear sequence of elements that can be of any type except those that contain file type or class types. The basic declaration is similar to the declaration of array, except that the number of elements is not set by the file-type declaration.

```
file of type1 // a "typed" file or one composed of "fixed length" records
file          // also know as an "untyped" or "block" file
textfile      // file of variable length records separated by CR/LF
```

N O T E   More than any other aspect of programming languages, the mechanisms for moving information into and out of an application varies from implementation to implementation and from language to language. In most instances, the application programmer is supposed to ignore the underlying structure of the input/output control variable and rely entirely on the associated routines to accomplish the movement of information. The implementation is supposed to be considered black magic. In Basic, files are characterized by file numbers or handles. In C/C++, the programmer manipulates pointers to a FILE structure. Only in Delphi does the programmer have the whole file structure declared as a variable. ■

Pointer Types

A *pointer type* is a value that points to variables of a base type. A pointer-type variable contains the memory address of a variable (see Table 3.8).

```
pointer    // an "untyped" pointer
^type1     // a "typed" pointer
```

If the base type is an undeclared identifier, you must declare it in the same type section as the pointer type.

A data type's scope doesn't include itself with the exception of pointer types.

Table 3.8   Pointer Routines

Routine	Description
New	Allocates a new memory area in the application heap for a dynamic variable and stores the address of this area in the pointer variable.

continues

Table 3.8   Continued

Routine	Description
@ operator	Directs the pointer variable to the memory area containing any existing variable or procedure or function entry point, including variables that already have identifiers.
GetMem	Creates a new dynamic variable of a specified size, and puts the address of the block in the pointer variable.

Pointer and Address Routines   The kind of value that is stored in a pointer variable is a machine memory address. These kinds of values are internal to your applications and can change every time your application runs. The following functions provide you with a way of accessing address information within your program and testing pointer variables.

Function	Description
Addr	Returns the address of a specified object
Assigned	Tests to determine if a function or procedural variable is Nil
Ptr	Converts a given address to a pointer

The reserved word Nil denotes a constant pointer-value that isn't actually supposed to point to anything. Pointers that are assigned a value of Nil are said to be "unassigned."

Pointer type definitions are the only exception to the general practice in Object Pascal to require identifiers, including types, to be declared before they can be used. Object Pascal lets you use the name of a type that you haven't gotten around to declaring quite yet, as in the following example:

```
type
    PointerType = ^NotYetDefinedType;
```

However, the language requires that you define the unknown type nearby, later in the same type-declaration block.

The predefined type Pointer is an untyped pointer. You cannot dereference variables of type Pointer; writing the pointer symbol ^ after such a variable is an error. However, you can dereference generic pointers through typecasting.

Values of type Pointer are compatible with all other pointer types.

N O T E   Many languages don't offer a separate pointer data type. However, C/C++ does, and in C/C++, pointer types are indicated with an asterisk prior to the type or variable declaration. Beyond this, C/C++ pointers are treated as if they were almost like integers. Delphi programmers tend not to manipulate pointers this way nearly as often. ■

Procedural Types

Although pointers are useful for storing typed information and dereferencing variables, storing addresses of named procedures and functions was quickly demonstrated to be an extremely dangerous practice. Early Turbo Pascal programmers had to be well-versed in exactly how procedures and functions were stored and called in memory. *Procedural types* simplify the problem considerably and enable you to treat procedures and functions as if they were values that can be assigned to variables and passed around as parameters being other parts of a program.

A procedural type declaration looks similar to the declaration of a procedure or function header (discussed under the heading "Procedures and Functions" later in this chapter). The obvious difference is that the name of the routine that would ordinarily occur after the procedure or function keyword is omitted.

Outside of a class type, Object Pascal only permits *global* procedural types. That is, the procedure or function that can be assigned to a procedural type cannot be assigned within the scope of another procedure or function.

Delphi also enables you to use procedural types that are methods. This capability enables you to call particular methods of particular object instances at runtime. The main advantage to method procedural types is that you then can adjust the behavior of an instance of a class without deriving a new class type and overriding the associated methods.

Internally, Delphi uses method procedure pointers to associate events with your customized code as needed. For example, this mechanism is used in the introduction of this chapter to specify that TForm1.Form1Create method was called when the form was created.

Syntax-wise, the only appreciable difference between a method procedural type and a global procedural type is the phrase, "of object" that follows the function or procedure prototype for the method procedural type.

The type pointer value Nil is used in a special way in connection with procedural types. Variables of a specific procedural type may be assigned Nil, but no other pointer values. After Nil has been assigned to the procedure variable, the variable is deemed to be *unassigned*. You can test for this condition using the function Assigned.

Global procedural types and method procedural types are mutually incompatible. You cannot assign one to the other.

NOTE Physically, Delphi procedural types seem to be stored as pointer values, but you never explicitly dereference the pointer because procedural types are not syntactically pointer types. Rather, the dereference of the pointer value is implied whenever the procedural variable is referenced.

In C/C++, a variable can have a data type of *pointer to function*. To call the associated function in "pre-ANSI" C, you had to deliberately dereference the pointer. Because of the preexisting usage, ANSI C will let the programmer use both explicit and implicit dereference of the pointer variable. If you are familiar with the ANSI style, you're better off in Delphi.

Variants

The type Variant can represent values that change type dynamically. While a variable of any other type is statically bound to that type, a variable of the type Variant can assume values of differing types at runtime. The type Variant is most commonly used in situations where the actual type to be operated on varies or is unknown at compile-time.

Variant Values   In the description of record types, you read how a record may have a variant part where you can store information of varying types in the same place in memory. Except for the simplest of data type formats, this usually is not very meaningful. It just doesn't do you any good to be able to look at how a single floating-point variable is stored in memory and interpret the results as if it were an integer. The type Variant (the name has nothing to do with the variant part of a record) is smarter about being able to handle these different kinds of values in a way that is useful. Variables of the type Variant can be assigned any integer values, any real values, any string, and any Boolean values. For compatibility with other programming languages, date-and-time values and OLE Automation objects can also be assigned. Variants also can contain arrays of varying size and dimension whose elements are any of these types.

All integer, real, string, character, and Boolean types are assignment-compatible with the Variant type. You can combine variants with other variants, integers, reals, strings, and Booleans in expressions, and Delphi performs all necessary conversions automatically. You can force expressions of these types to be explicitly type Variant by using a value typecast of the form Variant(X).

Two special variant type values are predefined. The value Unassigned is used to indicate that a variant has not yet been assigned a value of any kind. The value Null is used to indicate unknown or missing data. The distinction between these two values is subtle. Variant variables are assigned Unassigned automatically when they are created, regardless of whether the variant is global, local, or part of some other structured data type such as a record or array. Unassigned means that the variant is not in use. On the other hand, Null means that the variant was used, only there was no information to place into it. The Null is then a marker that is applied deliberately to indicate that the variant has not somehow been overlooked. In this way, Null value could not be used to indicate the value of Variant was "Not applicable" or "Not available."

Variants offer considerable flexibility in how you can combine expressions of differing types. However, the penalty is that they also consume more memory than statically typed variables. Operations on variants take longer than the corresponding operations on statically typed values.

One interesting aspect of the variant is making the variant an array. The elements of a variant array must be all of the same type, which may seem a considerable limitation at first. However, you can always set the element type to Variant. Then, each individual element can contain different types of information, including other variant arrays. The usual way to create variant arrays is through the VarArrayCreate routine.

Variant arrays with an element type of varByte are the usual way of passing binary data between OLE Automation controllers and servers. Variant arrays of varByte are not subject to any conversion or other translation of the information contained in the binary data. They can be efficiently accessed using the VarArrayLock and VarArrayUnlock routines.

N O T E The element type of a variant array cannot be varString. To create variant arrays of strings, you must use the varOleStr type code. ■

Manipulate Variants with System Routines Table 3.9 lists the variant array standard procedures and functions that are all defined in the System unit.

Table 3.9 Variant Support Routines

Routine	Description
VarArrayCreate	Creates a variant array of given bounds and type
VarArrayDimCount	Returns the number of dimensions of a given variant
VarArrayHighBound	Returns the high bound of a given dimension of a given variant array
VarArrayLock	Locks a given variant array
VarArrayLowBound	Returns the low bound of a given dimension of a given variant array
VarArrayOf	Returns a given variant array with specified elements
VarArrayRedim	Resizes a given variant array by changing the high bound
VarArrayUnLock	Unlocks a given variant array
VarAsType	Converts a variant to a specified type
VarCast	Converts a variant to a specified type and stores it
VarClear	Clears a given variant
VarCopy	Copies a given variant into a specified variant
VarFromDateTime	Returns a variant that contains a given date and time
VarIsArray	Returns whether a given variant is an array
VarIsEmpty	Returns whether a given variant is Unassigned
VarIsNull	Returns whether a given variant is Null
VarToDateTime	Converts a given variant to a date and time value
VarType	Converts a variant to a specified type and stores it

Table 3.10 lists the types that can be assigned to a variant, and the resulting variant type codes.

Table 3.10   Variant Type Codes

Expression Type	Variant Type Code
Integer types	`varInteger`
Real types except `Currency`	`varDouble`
Type `Currency`	`varCurrency`
String and character types	`varString`
Boolean types	`varBoolean`

Variants are assignment-compatible with the elementary Object Pascal data types `integer`, `real`, `string`, and `Boolean`. Delphi takes care of these conversions for you. If you want to specifically ensure that a variant value be interpreted as an integer, real, string, or Boolean type, use a value typecast of the form `TypeName(V)`, where `TypeName` is an integer, real, string, or Boolean type identifier and `V` is an expression of type `Variant`. The value typecast only changes the value as it is read from the `Variant`. It doesn't change how the `Variant` stores the value internally. To force a change in the internal representation, use the `VarAsType` or `VarCast` routines.

OLE Automation   When assigned an OLE Automation object, variants are useful in accessing and modifying properties of the OLE Automation object, and to call methods within the OLE Automation object. You enable this functionality by using the `OleAuto` unit.

The syntax of an OLE Automation object method call or property access is similar to how you can call methods and access properties of the classes that you create. A few differences are important. For one thing, OLE Automation object method calling is *late bound*, which means that the compiler doesn't double-check to ensure that the method exists and that the parameters are properly typed. Any method identifier and any number and type of parameters are perfectly acceptable to the compiler. On the other hand, it also means that it's possible for the method call to fail when it is executed at runtime.

For the identifiers used to specify OLE Automation object methods, properties, and named parameters, all alphabetical characters from an international character set—such as á, ü, and Ø—are permitted.

Operators and Expressions

Simply being able to represent information in memory in various ways doesn't make a program. Useful programs modify the information in a variety of ways in order to carry out the computations for which computers get their name. The lowest level of syntactical elements of Object Pascal that carry out these operations are known as *operators*. Operators and variables and constant values can be joined together in logical groupings that are known generically as *expressions*. The actual order evaluation of expressions at runtime depends on the relative precedence of the operators involved.

The precedence of the Object Pascal operators is shown in Table 3.11.

Table 3.11   Operators by Precedence Category

Operators	Category
. ^	Fielding, pointer dereferencing (High precedence)
@ not	Unary operators
* / div mod as and shl shr	Multiplicative and typecasting operators
+ – or xor	Conjunctive (additive) operators
= <> < > <= >= in is	Comparison operators (Relational, set membership, and type comparisons) (Low precedence)

Some of these operators wind up having different meanings, depending on how they are used in an expression. For example, the "+" finds itself in the unique position of not only denoting arithmetical addition of two numbers but also of concatenating two strings together and doing a union of two set expressions. Similarly the, "–" operator denotes both arithmetic subtraction and set differences.

Otherwise, the operators are put together as you might view any algebraic statement. Depending on the kinds of expressions that you are creating, Object Pascal has several options.

For example, if you work with numbers, you may use any of the following numerical arithmetic operators (return either integer or real values, depending on the operands):

> + (addition), – (subtraction), * (multiplication)
>
> / (floating-point division)
>
> div (integer division), mod (integer remainder)

If you deal with strings, only a single operator is available for string operations (return string values):

> + (concatenation)

If you are trying to compare either numbers or strings or any ordinal type, use the following operators for elementary comparisons (return Boolean values):

> = (equals), <> (is not equal to)
>
> < (is less than), > (is greater than)
>
> <= (is less than or equal to), >= (is greater than or equal to)

N O T E   The comparison operators compare the format of values as they are stored in memory. Although you can use the comparison operators to make comparisons between floating-point values, it often makes no sense. Because of the inexactness of how numbers are represented in floating-point formats, erroneous results occur if the comparison operators are used blindly. Rather than asking if two real numbers are stored in memory in exactly the same way, you should ask if the two real numbers are sufficiently close together that it doesn't make any practical difference that they are not exactly the same. ■

There are additional operators, but all use names rather than a punctuation mark. Some of the other operators with names have two uses: as *bitwise operators* and as Boolean operators. The bitwise operators change the bit values for an integer type variable.

Bitwise Operator	Description
not	Reverses bit values. For example, if the bit is 1; if not, it changes to a 0.
and	Bitwise and. I and J returns a result where the only bits that are 1 were those that both I and J have set.
or	Bitwise or. I or J returns a result where the only bits are 0.
xor	Bitwise xor. I xor J returns a result where the bits that are 1 were those where both I and J matched. (Both 1 or both 0.)
shl	Bitwise shift left. I shl J shifts the value of I to the left by J bits. Similar to multiplying I by 2, J times.
shr	Bitwise shift right. I shr J shifts the value of I to the right by J bits. Similar to dividing I by 2, J times.

The bitwise operators not, and, or, and xor also are Boolean operators.

N O T E　Developers coming from other programming languages need to be careful how they interpret some operators. C/C++ uses pre-* to indicate pointer dereferencing, and / may imply integer division (the Delphi "div") . Basic uses ^ to raise a number to a power. ■

Statements

As important as the evaluation of expressions is in the execution of your program, expressions alone cannot give you control over when the various components of your program will execute. The Object Pascal *statement* controls whether your expression gets evaluated, the order in which your expressions get evaluated, and how many times they get evaluated. Statements describe all the algorithmic actions that your program can execute.

If you are the kind of programmer who divides everything into two groups, you might view all of the statements as being one of two basic types:

> Simple statements
>
> Structured statements

As with most divisions of complex problems, this division is arbitrary, but it does yield some important results.

Simple Statements

Simple statements modify memory, assign a value, activate a procedure or function, or transfer the running program to another statement in the code.

The simple statements that Object Pascal supports are as follows:

Assignment (:=) statements

Procedure statements

Goto statements

There's an even simpler statement than these that is sometimes known as the "null statement" or "empty statement." It doesn't actually do anything, but it is a legal statement from the point of view of the syntax of the Object Pascal language. You usually find out about it when you use it accidentally in a loop.

The Goto statement is a bit of a nuisance. It's there; it's always been there. However, its use has always been discouraged, and many professional programmers have never used a single one in a Pascal program. The Goto statement completely alters the structured flow of your source code. If you've never before used a Goto in a program, you're just as well off not learning how it works. Your time is better spent concentrating on the other two kinds of simple statements.

The other two kinds of simple statements (*assignment* and *procedure call*) are fundamental to what a useful program should do. At the lowest level of your program, nothing happens unless you are modifying a variable in some way. You can do so directly in an assignment statement, or indirectly by calling a procedure. Although all the "structured" statements can evaluate expressions that are arbitrarily complex, your program will do nothing if the structured statement doesn't have an assignment statement or procedure call nested somewhere down the structure.

Assignment In a practical sense, assignment statements are the only kind of statements that actually modify memory within your program. Assignment statements take the value of the expression on the right side of the assignment operator (:=) and apply it to the target on the left. The assignment operator always separates the two sides, as in the following syntax example:

```
target := expression ;
```

The expression usually is evaluated independently from the size or type of the target, but for the assignment to be valid, the target and expression must be assignment-compatible. The rules of assignment compatibility tend to be complex. Two variables of the same type usually are assignment-compatible, but file variables and any structures that include a file field or element never are assignment-compatible. Integer values always can be assigned to real variables, but real values can never be assigned to an integer variable. Both long and short string types are compatibles. A character always can be assigned to a string, but not the other way around. An array of characters (a *packed string*) can be assigned to a string, but not the other way around. A null-terminated string can be assigned to an AnsiString (long string), but not the other way around. A string constant can be assigned to a Pchar, but it makes no sense to assign a Pchar to a constant. A zero-based character array can be assigned to a Pchar; the other way still doesn't work. However, Variant variables or expressions are mutually assignment-compatible with variables or expressions of integer, real, string, or Boolean types.

N O T E In C/C++, assignments are a part of expressions rather than a statement by itself, and you can do an assignment wherever an expression may be permitted. Delphi prohibits you from trying to put assignments in places where C/C++ says that it's okay, as in the predicate of an if...then... statement or attempting to do multiple assignments with a single expression. ▪

Procedure Statement   *Procedure statements* (or "procedure calls") transfer control to a procedure or method and execute that procedure's "block" before returning and continuing execution with the statement that follows the procedure statement.

```
procname(parm1,parm2);
```

If the corresponding procedure heading contains formal parameters, then the procedure statement must match those with actual parameters. The actual parameters are passed to the formal parameters as part of the call. The actual mechanism used in passing the parameters depends on the nature of the formal parameters and is discussed in the following section, "Procedures and Functions."

It's usually not obvious from a procedure statement whether any variables are changed as a result of the procedure call.

The *Goto* Statement   The goto statement transfers program execution to the statement marked by the specified label. In classic Pascal, a label was a digit sequence in the range 0 to 9999 (leading zeroes are not significant). Object Pascal also allows identifiers to function as labels.

```
goto label1;
```

Labels must be declared in a "label section" for the block where you want to use the goto. The labeled statement must be in the same block as the goto statement. You cannot use a goto to jump from one procedure to another.

Proper programming practices should promote you to perform gotos as little as possible. In structured programming languages, the goto was never required. With the advent of early loop termination (break) and procedure termination (exit), the goto is not even convenient to use any more in Object Pascal.

N O T E Most programming languages do have a goto statement. Both Basic and C/C++ do. It's discouraged in all of them. Object Pascal just makes it more inconvenient to use than the others. ▪

Structured Statements

Structured statements are constructs composed of other statements that are to be executed in a sequence, on some condition, multiple times while or until some criterion is satisfied repeatedly, or that modify the scope of identifiers while the statements are executing. Analogously with structured types, structured statements are not in themselves statements. Structured statements are used to control how other statements are executed.

The structured statements that Object Pascal supports can be grouped into the following categories:

Compound statement

Conditional statements

Loops

With statement

Compound Statement (*begin...end*)   Compound statements specify an order in which the statements that it contains are to be executed. When the sequence of statements is grouped together between a begin and an end, the whole sequence is treated as if it were a single statement and can be used wherever the syntax of Object Pascal calls for a single statement.

Part I

Ch 3

```
begin
    statement1;
    statement2;
end
```

The reserved words begin marks the beginning of the sequence, and end marks the end. Each statement is separated by a semicolon. The semicolon before end is optional. Syntactically, if a semicolon is placed before end, the compiler assumes that the semicolon separates the last written statement from an "empty" statement.

N O T E   C/C++ uses semicolons to terminate statements rather than the Object Pascal approach to use the semicolons as separators. In a compound statement, the distinction is not too important because the final semicolon would be optional. The distinction is more of an issue in an if statement, where Object Pascal doesn't permit a semicolon to be located in front of the alternative else part. ∎

N O T E   In C/C++, left and right curly braces ({})are often used to group together sequences of statements. Consequently, when moving between languages, there is some motivation to try to equate the C left brace with the Object Pascal "begin" and the right brace with "end." However, the symbols are not quite equivalent. In Object Pascal, only executable statements can appear within the begin...end pair; no other declarations are permitted. In C/C++, both data declarations and executable statements are permitted within the braces. This makes the C/C++ statement grouping more like what Object Pascal refers to as a syntactic "block," which permits data declarations at the beginning and is terminated by a single compound statement. C/C++ happens to refer to the braces as being used to form "block statements." ∎

Conditional Statements   *Conditional statements* let you control whether or not certain statements are ever executed. They test if a specific condition (often referred to as the "predicate") is met before executing the statement that follows the test.

Object Pascal has two kinds of conditional statements—the `if` statement and the `case` statements. The `if` statement is used to select between two possible situations. The `case` statement is used to select among several situations.

The If...Then *Statement* The Boolean expression (or predicate) specifies the condition under which a statement will execute.

```
if boolean_expression then
    statement1;               // do statement1 optionally

if boolean_expression then
    statement1
else
    statement2; // do either statement1 or statement2
```

If the Boolean expression after the `if` is True, the statement after the `then` is executed. Otherwise, if the Boolean expression after the `if` is False, and an `else` part is present, the statement after the `else` is executed. If there is no `else` part, execution continues with the statement following the `if` statement.

A semicolon is never allowed immediately before an `else` clause.

Boolean and Functional Conditions The Boolean expressions used in predicates always evaluate to True or False. Boolean expressions can consist of the values True, False, a reference to a Boolean variable or function, or a comparison between two other kinds of operands as described in the section on operators and expressions.

Boolean Logic Four of the bitwise operators mentioned previously have related, but special meaning when applied to Boolean expressions.

Those Boolean operators are as follows:

Operator	Operation
not	Negation takes a Boolean value and reverses the meaning. `not` True is False. `not` is a Unary operator.
and	Logical and. X `and` Y returns True only if both X and Y are True.
or	Logical or. X `or` Y returns True if either X or Y or both are True.
xor	Logical xor. X `xor` Y returns True only if X or Y, but not both, are True. Equivalent to X `<>` Y.

case...of *Statements* *Case statements* are used to execute one of several statements depending on some kind of ordinal state the code encounters. The statement consists of a case expression (the selector) and the statements to be executed, each prefixed with one or more constants (known as *case constants*), and an optional statement to be executed, prefixed with the word `else`, in case no other case constants are equal to the selector.

```
case ordinal_expression of       // case selector of
  1: statement1;                  // constant(s): statement;
  2,3: statement2;                // constant(s): statement;
```

```
    else catchallstatement;                 // else statement;
end;                                         // end
```

The selector can only be of an ordinal expression. Real expressions and strings are not valid selectors.

The case constants must be of the same ordinal type as the selector and must be unique from one another. When the case statement executes, only the statement prefixed by the constant that is equal to the selector will be performed. If no constants equal the selector and an `else` part is present then the `else` statement is performed. If there is no else part, program execution continues with the next statement following the `case` statement.

N O T E The C/C++ "switch" statement is similar to the Delphi `case` statement. An important difference is that C/C++ sees the `switch` as being alternative entry points into a sequence of statements rather than alternative statements, only one of which is to be executed. C/C++ uses the `break` statement to separate the `switch` statements into alternatives. ▨

N O T E The Basic SELECT CASE statement is comparable to the Delphi `Case` statement. ▨

Looping Constructs   Loops enable you to execute statements zero or more times. Object Pascal supports three kinds:

```
for..to/downto..do
while...do
repeat..until
```

Each of these loops:

Break   Terminates a `for`, `while`, or `repeat` statement early by jumping the statement immediately following the loop.

Continue   Executes a `for`, `while`, or `repeat` statement part again by starting at the test.

N O T E The C/C++ break statement is similar to the Delphi `Break` procedure. In C/C++, `break` also terminates a branch in a `switch` statement. ▨

N O T E In Basic, the EXIT FOR or EXIT DO statements are comparable to the Delphi `Break` procedure. ▨

The For ... Do Loop   The `For` statement causes the statement after `do` to be executed once for each value between the initial value of the range and final value, inclusive. `For` loops are useful if you know beforehand exactly how many times you want the loop to execute.

```
For control_variable := initial_value To final_value Do statement;
For control_variable := initial_value Downto final_value Do statement;
```

The control variable always starts off at an initial value. In the To loop, the control variable must be less than the final value to execute the statement, and the control variable is incremented by 1 after every execution of the statement. In the Downto loop, the control variable must be greater than the final value to execute the statement, and the control variable is decremented by 1 after every execution of the statement.

Not just any control variable will do. The control variable must be of ordinal type and declared within the block containing the loop. Obviously, the loop makes sense only if the initial and final values are assignment-compatible with the control variable.

Do not expect the value of the control variable to have any specific value after the For statement is executed.

A common programmer error with this loop is to put a semicolon between the Do and the intended statement.

N O T E In Delphi, the For... Do loop is designed to be fast. Many of the limitations on the loop control variable arise from that consideration. Other languages take a more flexible approach. The FORTRAN DO, the Basic FOR, and the C/C++ for statements are often better translated into a Delphi While... Do loop. ▓

The Repeat ... Until Loop   The statements between Repeat and Until are executed in sequence while the Boolean expression in the until statement evaluates to True.

```
Repeat
    statement1;
    statement2;
Until boolean_expression;
```

This construction is unusual from other Object Pascal construction because it permits a sequence of statements to be executed and does not require them to be inside a compound statement (begin...end).

The sequence of statements between the Repeat and Until is always executed at least once. The Boolean expression is not evaluated until after the execution of the sequence.

N O T E C/C++ has a do...while(...) loop statement similar to the Delphi Repeat...Until statement. The primary difference is that the predicates have exactly the opposite meanings. ▓

While ... Do ...   A While statement also can control the repeated execution of a statement.

While boolean_expression **Do** statement;

In the While statement, the statement after Do executes only as long as the Boolean expression evaluates to True. The Boolean expression is evaluated before the statement is ever executed. If the expression is False at the beginning, the statement is not executed at all.

N O T E The C/C++ while(...)... loop statement is equivalent to the Delphi While...Do loop statement. ■

N O T E The Basic WHILE... WEND syntax is equivalent to the Delphi While... Do loop statement. ■

The *With... Do* Loop The With statement provides a convenient shorthand method for referencing the fields of a specific record, and the members of an object.

With record_variable Do statement;

Within the with statement, the fields of a record variable can be referenced using only the field's identifiers, without directly writing the name of the record variable in the dot notation. For instance, if you've declared a record variable

var arecord = **record** field1:integer; field2:integer; **end;**

you can set the fields of this variable by writing either of the following two examples:

arecord.field1:=1; arecord.field2:=2;   // using dot notation

with arecord **do begin** field1:=1; field2:=2; **end;**   // same same assignments

A little precaution is required. The with statement is an abbreviated way of specifying which record a field references. However, it is not expanded, as a macro directive might be. If the record variable reference involves indexing an array or dereferencing a pointer, the array will be indexed and the pointer dereferenced only once. On the inside of the with statement, a field identifier can only be associated with a single, specific record.

N O T E The explicit With... Do statement is a unique feature of Delphi in comparison with other programming languages. ■

Procedures and Functions

In the introduction of the chapter, you read that programs consisted of a heading and a block. Procedures let you nest additional blocks within the program block. Analogous to the program, a procedure declaration consists of a procedure heading followed by a procedure block.

The procedure heading consists of the reserved word Procedure, the name of the procedure for the procedure and, optionally, the formal parameters (listed in parentheses).

A procedure is activated by a procedure statement, which states the procedure's identifiers and actual parameters.

The procedure block consists of the following:

> A *declaration* part that declares local constants, types, variables, procedures and functions.

A *compound statement* (`begin ... end`). When the procedure is activated by a procedure statement, the statements between the `begin` and `end` are executed sequentially.

Like procedures, functions are also used to nest additional blocks within the main program block. However, functions are used to indicate blocks that execute statements and then return some value which will be used in evaluating an expression from where the function was called. Function declarations consist of a *function heading* and a *function block*. The function header consists of the reserved word `function`, the name of the function, any optional formal parameters, and the function result type. The function result type can be any time except a file type or a structured type that includes a file field or elements embedded at any depth within the structure.

The function block consists of declarations of local labels, constants, types, variables, procedures or functions, and a single compound statement (`begin...end`) that groups the statements to be executed when the function is referenced in an expression.

The statement part of the function block must contain at least one statement that assigns a value to the function identifier or to the identifier `result`. The identifier `result` is implicitly defined within the statement part of every function to be of the same type as the function's return value. Assigning to `Result` is equivalent to assigning to the name of the function. However, you cannot determine what is the last value assigned by referencing the name of the function. (Referencing the name of a function in an expression tells the compiler to attempt to *call* the function.) The advantage to having `result` is that it gives you a convenient identifier that you can reference to retrieve the current value assigned within an expression while you are still inside the function. When the function completes execution the last value so assigned is the value returned to the expression.

Functions are activated when the function is referenced during the evaluation of an expression. Such function calls denote the function by name and the actual parameters—if any are required—inside parentheses that follows the name of the function, as in the following syntactical example:

```
function funcid(parameters):typeid;    // "function heading"
const constid = constant_expression;   // everything after the function
type typeid=type_definition;           // heading is the "function block"
var var1,var2:type_definition;
                                       // "local" constants, types, variables,
                                       // procedures, and functions can be
                                       // declared in any order.

procedure proc1;
procedure_definition;
function func1:typeid;
function_definition;
begin
   statements;
   result:=typeid_expression;
end;
```

Identifier Scoping

At first glance, the primary advantage to using procedures and functions is to group together several statements that must be executed in sequence and then to call those statements as a group from several places elsewhere in the program. However, the nesting of procedures inside one another has considerable control over being able to structure which identifiers mean what at specific locations in the program—the *identifier's scope*.

In Object Pascal, scope can be very complex. Local identifiers are visible only to the declarations contained within the block, which declares the identifier. However, there can be many levels of "locality" within a program or unit. The only way to get something that can be termed a "global identifier" would be to declare it in the interface section of a unit. Such global identifiers are still visible to all declarations within that unit. However, when the identifiers are declared in the interface of Unit A, the identifiers become visible to declarations in the program or another unit that includes Unit A in a uses clause.

An identifier is not visible anywhere before it is declared, then only in the same block in which it has been declared.

Inside a block, you can re-declare any identifier that was declared outside of the block. The new declaration defines the meaning of the identifier from that point until the end of the block.

Parameter Passing

Parameters may be used to pass information from a calling block to a procedure or function elsewhere.

When a routine (either a procedure or a function) is declared, the heading part of the declaration specifies the *formal parameters*. Each of the formal parameters is an identifier that is local to the procedure or function being declared. Within the routine, the formal parameters behave like variables and can be referenced to by name in the routine's compound statement. There are different flavors of formal parameters, and each constrains the kinds of actual parameters that may be passed to the routine by a procedure statement or function call.

Passing By Value   A formal parameter passed by value acts like a variable declared local to the declaring routine.

```
parm1, parm2: atype;                // value parameters of same type
```

When the routine is activated, the actual parameter indicated in the call does an assignment of the actual parameter to the formal parameter.

As a local variable, the called routine can make any changes made to a formal parameter identifier, and the changes will be not reflected anywhere outside the routine.

Because the value is assigned during the call, the actual parameter must be something that is assignment-compatible with the formal parameter type. For example, it's never legal to pass a file as a value parameter.

Passing by Reference A `Var` formal parameter requires that a variable be passed as the actual parameter. Physically, all that is really passed is the address of parameter, but in the called routine, the formal parameter is accessed as if it were the actual parameter. Changes made to the formal parameter are immediately applied to the actual parameter; they're really the same variable.

```
Var parm1, parm2: atype;          // reference parameters of  same type
```

File types can be passed only as variable parameters.

Assignment compatibility is not sufficient for passing arguments by reference. The types of the actual parameter and the formal parameter must be equivalent.

Const A *constant formal parameter* (or const) is a local read-only variable that gets its value from the corresponding actual parameter.

```
const parm1, parm2: atype;        // constant parameters of same type
```

Inside the called routine, you cannot directly modify a `const` formal parameter. Nor can you pass a `const` parameter as an actual `var` parameter to another routine.

The corresponding actual parameter for a `const` parameter must be an expression and, therefore, assignment-compatible with `const` parameter types.

For simple types, passing by value is just as economical as passing as a `const`. For structured and string variables as the actual parameters, the compiler will generate more efficient code with `const` formal parameters than with value parameters.

Untyped Parameters When the formal parameter is an *untyped parameter*, the corresponding actual parameter can be either a variable or constant reference, of any type. The only difference between the two styles is that `Var` parameters can be modified by the called routine, and `const` parameters are read-only.

```
var parm1, parm2;    // untyped variable reference
```

```
const parm1,parm2;    // untyped constant reference
```

You will have to do, however, a variable (as opposed to a value) typecast with the formal parameter. Within the called routine, untyped formal parameters are truly without type, and completely incompatible with variables of any other types.

Consequently, untyped formal parameters can give you greater freedom in interpreting passed variables. The freedom comes with a price. The compiler can no longer verify valid operations with the type, and the burden is placed upon you, the programmer.

Open Arrays *Open-array formal parameters* allow arrays of different sizes to be passed as actual parameters to the same routine.

```
var parm1: array of atype;            // open array of a type
```

Open-array parameters can be value parameters, constant parameters, or variable parameters, and the same restrictions for those parameters hold. Within the routine, the formal parameter behaves as if it had been declared as follows:

```
var parm1: array[0..N - 1] of atype;
```

Here, N is the number of elements in the actual parameter. That is, the index range of the actual parameter is mapped into the integer subrange 0 to N - 1. The original dimensions of the array are immaterial to the mapping. As a bonus, if the actual parameter is a simple variable of type atype, it is treated as an array with one element of type atype.

There is one important exception to the parameter behaving as if the type had been declared directly. Formal open-array parameters can be accessed only on an element-by-element basis. Assignments dealing with the whole array are invalid.

N O T E For an open-array value parameter, the compiler creates a local copy of the actual parameter within the procedure or function's stack frame. Therefore, be careful not to overflow the stack when passing large arrays as open-array value parameters. To ensure that the stack doesn't overflow, use var or const when passing open-array value parameters. ■

In the calling block, you can construct an open-array parameter immediately, with no intervening variable or constant. Just enclosing the desired array elements, separated by commas, between brackets.

```
AverageThese([18.3, 19.8, 122.133, 3.4309874]);
```

The syntax looks much like a set construction, but the compiler recognizes that an open-array parameter is what is needed at this point.

The standard functions shown in Table 3.12 can be applied to an open-array parameter.

Table 3.12   Open Array Function Results

Function	Returns
Low(A)	Zero
High(A)	The index of the last element in the actual array parameter
SizeOf(A)	The size of the actual array parameter

The array of const Open Array   The syntactic construction array of const allows an open array of values of more than one type to be passed to a routine in relatively type-safety.

```
const parm1: array of const;          //  pass almost anything
```

This is the kind of feature that makes it possible to declare a routine that accepts any number of items of varying types. The compiler always treats the construct array of const as equivalent to an array of TVarRec. TVarRec is a special record type defined in the System unit.

Inside the called routine, you would use the TVarRec type to access the individual elements of an array of const. The TVarRec.VType field would tell the simple type of each parameter passed in the array.

Delphi Units

Unit skeleton:

```
unit unitid;      // "Unit heading"
interface         // "Unit interface"
uses
    unitid2,unitid3;
const
    constid = constant_expression;
type
    typeid = type_definition;
var
    var1: type_definition;
procedure proc1;              // Interfaced procedures and functions
function func1:typeid;       // have only their headings in a
                             // unit interface.
implementation    // "Unit implementation"
uses
    unitid,unitid2,unitid3;
const
    constid = constant_expression;
type
    typeid = type_definition;
var
    var1,var2: type_definition;
procedure proc1;
procedure_block;
function func1:typeid;
function_block;
initialization    // "Unit initialization"
    statements;   //      statements to be executed before
                  //      program starts; startup code.
finalization      // "Unit finalization"
    statements;   //      statements to be executed after
                  //      program ends; shutdown code.
end.      // End of unit
```

Interface

A unit's interface specifies what unit identifiers are to be given global scope.

The interface part of a unit starts at the reserved word interface, which appears after the unit header, and ends before the reserved word implementation.

Inside the unit interface declares constants, types, variables, and the headings of procedures and functions that are supposed to have global scope. That is, the identifiers will be visible to other programs or units that can then use them.

Only the heading of a routine is declared in the interface. The block of the procedure or function will be in the unit implementation.

If a uses clause appears in the unit interface, it must come immediately after the reserved word interface and before any other interface declarations.

Implementation

A unit's *implementation* can declare any constants, types, variables, procedures, and functions that are going to be local to the unit. The implementation also needs to define the block of all global procedures and functions whose headings had been declared in the unit interface.

All of the identifiers declared in the unit interface part are visible in the implementation. (A unit's implementation always uses the unit itself.) Declarations made in the implementation part of a unit are entirely local to the unit.

The order in which identifiers are declared in the interface makes no difference in the implementation. Routine declarations can be completed in any order.

If a uses clause is in the implementation, it must come immediately after the reserved word `implementation` and before any other declarations. The implementation part ends with the reserved word `initialization`, or `end.` (with a period).

Initialization

Unit *initializations* are optional. The part consists of the reserved word `initialization` followed by a sequence of statements to be executed when the program is started. The initialization parts of all the units used by a program will be executed in the same order that the units appear in the uses clause of the program module.

Some care should be exercised in making assumptions about what other units may or may not have been already initialized when the initialization part of a unit is executed. Other units may be in a state of only having been partially initialized. References to global pointer variables may not yet be valid.

Finalization

The *finalization* part is optional, but can only be used if you've added an initialization part to the unit. The part consists of the reserved word `finalization`, followed by a list of statements that are executed when the program shuts down. Any resources (memory, files, and so on) allocated or opened by a unit in its initialization part are typically released or closed in the finalization part. The finalization part can also release any resources acquired by normal unit execution.

Unit finalization parts execute in the opposite order of initializations, in the reverse order of the way the units are listed in the program module.

After a unit's initialization code starts to execute, the corresponding finalization part will execute when the program terminates. Exercise some caution here also. The finalization part must therefore be able to handle incompletely initialized data because, if an exception is raised during initialization, the initialization code may not have executed completely.

Putting It All Together

The Object Pascal language exercised by Delphi was designed to create sophisticated applications based upon extending simple concepts. Object Pascal programs can declare their own data, their own procedures and functions, and have a single compound statement that controls execution of everything that happens when the program is run.

Data types are the fundamental building blocks of an Object Pascal program. At the simplest level, data can be numbers or strings, or your own ordinal types. You can create your own compound data types by using the records. You can store multiple instances of data in an array. You can reference your data indirectly by using a pointer.

You combine and manipulate data within expressions. Object Pascal includes elementary binary operators for numerical arithmetic, string concatenation, and Boolean comparisons.

You control the evaluation of expressions by using statements in a structured manner. The simplest kinds of statements are the assignment and the procedure call. You define the order in which statements execute by sequencing them in a compound (begin...end) statement. You can execute a statement conditionally by using the if...then or case...end statements. You can execute a statement iteratively by using for, while, or repeat...until statements.

Logically related statements can be combined together to create procedures and functions. In many respects, procedures and functions behave as if they were just small programs that can have their own data. They can be a compound statement executed when they are called. They can even define their own internal procedures and functions that cannot be referenced from outside (in the rest of the program).

Logically related data types, procedures, and functions can be combined to create units, which can be shared between applications. Units are like small programs, but their organization is defined in terms of an interface part (which controls what unit components can be accessed by another unit or by the program module), an implementation part, an initialization part, and a finalization part.

Certainly, the picture of the Object Pascal language in this chapter is not a complete definition of what has evolved into Delphi. This chapter provided a view of some of the "classic" elements of the language, emphasizing the Pascal part of the Object Pascal name. Object-oriented aspects are covered in Chapter 4, "Object Pascal: Advanced Concepts." ●

CHAPTER 4

Object Pascal: Advanced Concepts

by J.W. Rider

When Niklaus Wirth first designed the Pascal programming language, it was an object lesson in the elegance of the principle of parsimony. Every effort was made to stream-line the assorted syntactic elements to such an extent that only a mere handful of reserved words, operators and standard identifiers were all that was left of the language definition. From the viewpoint of a dialogue between computers and humans, having too many ways to do things just didn't make much sense, and redundant approaches were eliminated. Yes, the language had its critics. Missing were many of the features of other lan-guages favored by programmers. All that was left seemed merely the essence of the structured programming para-digm. There was data, and there was code, and there were just so many ways in which you could put them together in a single program.

They tried, too. The language did not provide for a large number of readily available standardized routines. Conse-quently, Pascal programmers trained themselves to be-come very adept at solving problems based entirely upon their own talents. Some third-party routines did exist in shared libraries, but programmers didn't waste a lot of time trying to force-fit generalized solutions before com-ing to grips with the real-world problems. Nor did they spend extra effort trying to achieve elaborate and

Classes

You learn the syntactic features behind the elements of object-oriented programming in Delphi.

Typecasting

You learn both safe and dangerous ways of making one data type look like some other data type.

Class-reference types

You learn both safe and dangerous ways of making one data type look like some other data type.

Runtime library

You learn to reuse the routines that already come with Delphi.

Putting it all together

You learn how well advanced fea-tures of Object Pascal have been put into Delphi.

complicated solutions. Minimalistic programming was the name of the game. You found one way that worked and stuck to it, but you did find a way. The next time you tried to solve a similar problem, you adapted the way that worked before to the new problem and went on.

The language also changed to allow programmers more opportunity for capturing the ways in which they solved problems and reused them again and again. In the original definition of the language, you dealt with ways of structuring data and organizing the code to manipulate the structures. Then, the notion of a unit was introduced, and Pascal programmers found themselves doing things the same way that they had always done them. In each unit, they structured data and organized the code to manipulate it. Only this time, the language supported their efforts to share their solutions between programs. Rather than concentrating on the whole program, programmers now could focus their attention on smaller pieces of the picture. Then, Object Pascal was introduced, and programmers could focus their creative endeavors on even smaller pieces of the whole program. There was still data; there was still code; and there was still only a certain number of ways that you could put them together. Structured programming had evolved into object-oriented programming. This revolution did not occur overnight. It was "merely" a logical extension of the way Pascal programmers had been solving real-world problems all along. The language changed in very subtle ways, but at the core, it was still Pascal.

In Delphi, the visual components are the obvious result of the way in which Object Pascal evolved to allow easier design and development of reusable elements.

At the same time, more standardized routines were provided in string and utility libraries. As in the original Pascal, minimalist is still the rule. It just doesn't make sense to solve problems in multiple ways if there is already a perfectly good way.

The language still makes it easy to adapt your code to solve problems. You can use the runtime library routines. However, you usually are better off encapsulating your ideas in the form of a *class* first. ■

Classes

The Object Pascal class is a fundamental building block for software development in Delphi. Sure, smaller, lower-level elements are defined within the language, but none of these elements fully captures the wholeness of the ways in which the "class" brings together both data and code into a single integrated component.

Like the structured types mentioned in Chapter 3, "Object Pascal: A Fundamental Approach," a class is not a type all by itself. Like a *record type*, a *class type* is composed of a number of smaller pieces or elements. The class is the aggregate of these components. Classes are also known as "object types." Either of these two terms can be used. A specific instance of a class is an "object." However, because of the object reference model, this is not quite the same thing as a "variable of class type."

You can look at the possible components in different ways. Operationally, you will deal with members as one of the components described in the following table:

Component	Description
Fields	Similar to the fields of a record type, but classes cannot have variant parts.
Methods	Routines that perform operations on the object's fields.
Properties	Which you would use as if they were fields, but are implemented as methods.

Unlike other types, the only place that you can declare a class type is in a `type` declaration at the global level of a program or unit. As a practical matter, the only place that you are going to want to declare your reusable classes is in the interface of a unit. The Object Pascal language, however, prevents you from trying to declare the class at an inappropriate point. Specifically, you cannot declare a class type in connection with a `var` declaration part or locally within a procedure or function block.

Syntax

```
type TMyClass = class                              // class type name
  (THeritage)                                      // ancestor class
  public {or private, protected, published}        // scope
  afield: atype;                                   // field
  procedure AMethod(Parm: Atype);                  // method
    {"static," virtual, dynamic, message, abstract, override}
  property Aproperty: atype read afield write amethod;   // property
  class procedure AClassMethod;                    // class method
  end;
```

You declare a class type by using the reserved word `class`, and then listing its member components or just "members."

Class types are different from other types. Besides being able to declare class types only globally, you cannot declare a file type with a component type of a class. One reason for this is that the variables of a class type don't physically represent an instance of the class (an "object"). Objects are created only at runtime. Variables of class type point to the objects that they represent. This paradigm is sometimes called the *object reference model*. Physically, variables of class type are stored as if they were pointers. However, the Object Pascal language allows you to treat the members of an object as if they were directly embedded in the variable. The primary difference is that you can have multiple variables, all of which reference a single object rather than having multiple objects with the same value.

You don't have to list all the class type's components when you declare it. A class type also inherits members from a base class type. The inheriting class is referred to as a *descendant*, and the base class is the *ancestor*. A descendant class implicitly contains all the members defined for all of its ancestral classes. When a descendant inherits its members from an ancestor, and the ancestor inherits its members from a "grandparent," then the descendant also inherits the members from the grandparent. This makes inheritance transitive. The collection of all classes that inherit from a single ancestor is known as the "domain" of the ancestor.

The list of members associated with descendants can only get bigger. You can add new members to a class when you declare it. You cannot eliminate a member previously defined for any of the ancestor classes.

Object Pascal uses a predefined class type, TObject, to denote the original ancestor for all other class types. If you don't specify an ancestor, the declaration of a class type doesn't specify an ancestor type (that is, if you omit the heritage clause from the class declaration), the class type inherits directly from TObject and is a descendant of TObject. TObject is declared in the System unit, and that declaration lists several members that then will permeate throughout the TObject domain. These members, therefore, are available to all classes that you might define.

Your class types will be assignment-compatible with any of their ancestral types. During program execution, a variable of a class type may well be referencing an instance of another type anywhere within the domain of the type. The actual type of the instance could match exactly the type of the variable, or the variable may refer to an instance of any descendant type. Consider the following class type declarations:

```
type
  TThing = class
     :
  end;
  TAnimal = class(TThing)
     :
  end;
  TMammal = class(TAnimal)
     :
  end;
  TVegetable = class(TThing)
     :
  end;
  TTree = class(TVegetable)
     :
  end;
```

An instance of type TAnimal can be assigned to variables of type TAnimal, TThing, and TObject. During execution of a program, a variable of type TThing might reference an instance of TThing, TAnimal, TMammal, TPlant, TTree, or any other instance of a descendant of TThing. However, you are not able to assign a value of type TTree to a variable of type TMammal, and because a TThing may be TTree, you cannot assign a value of ancestral type TThing to a variable of type TMammal.

Scope

The list of members of a class acts like an interface into instances of the class. The members of class can have different *scoping* directives applied to the interface: private, protected, public, and published. These directives only restrict the visibility of the members as far as other units can access them. Within the unit where the class is declared, all members are visible.

Unlike many of the identifiers used in declaring types, these directives are not reserved words outside the context of class type declarations. However, it's good practice to treat them as if they really were reserved words and not redefine them to mean something different.

The scoping directive for a member need not be explicitly mentioned for each individual member. After a directive is cited, the associated scope is applied to all members listed in the class type declaration until another scoping directive is cited. Multiple members placed adjacent to another after the directive all will have the same scope. This collection of members is referred to as a "part" when analyzing class type declarations.

N O T E C++ class members also have scoping qualifiers of public, protected, and private. The terms used in Object Pascal are similar but not identical. Specifically, in Object Pascal, the scope of a member in the unit in which it is declared is always public. ▪

Private   The most restrictive of these class scoping directives is private. Outside the unit in which the class is declared, its private members are simply not visible.

You probably want to reserve private for members whose values are critical to the behavior of an object or whose members must be carefully synchronized with other aspects of the object and you don't want to modify inadvertently. If you want to create two classes who can access each other's private members, declare the two class types in the same unit. The implementation details of the member are completely hidden from the end user.

Protected   The protected directive relaxes the restriction on visibility for a special purpose. Outside the unit in which the class is declared, members declared as "protected" are visible only to descendants of the class, the class domain. If you don't create a descendant, you cannot access a protected member, just as if it were private.

Unless you create such a descendant, the implementation details remain hidden. However, protected members remain available to programmers who want to descend new classes from your classes without making it necessary for the class type declarations to exist all in a single unit.

Public   Public members are visible wherever the class itself is visible. No special restrictions are applied to a class type's public members.

Published   Declaring a member as published generates *runtime type information* (RTTI) for member, including the field, method, or property within the application's published interface. The runtime type information permits a program to determine what the fields, methods, and properties are of an otherwise indeterminate object at runtime.

At runtime, internal to the program, a published member behaves identically to that of a public member. All published members are visible to any unit where the class itself is visible. The difference between published and public members is that external applications get information about the published members through a published interface.

The Delphi Object Inspector, for example, uses the published interface of objects in the Component palette to determine which properties and events are displayed at design time. The Delphi Visual Class Library uses run-time type information to manipulate a visual component's properties when writing the component to and reading the component from external files.

There are a number of restrictions on the use of the published directive that keep you from using the directive too freely.

Part
I
Ch
4

1. A class type cannot have published members of any kind unless it is compiled in a state that the generates run-time type information, or is a descendant of such a class. The $M compiler directive controls this RTTI generation.

2. Any fields defined in a published part must be of a class type. Fields of any other types must be put into a public, protected, and private part.

3. Published properties are restricted by types. They cannot be array properties, but they can be an ordinal type, a real type (Single, Double, Extended, or Comp, but not the type Real), a string type, a small set type, a class type, or a method pointer type (and not a global procedural type). The small set type is simply a set type whose base type has lower and upper bounds with ordinal values between zero and fifteen. Physically, a small set is represented by the bits of a single byte or a word of memory.

At the top of the listing of the members of a class, no scoping directive is needed. If omitted, the scope for the members is presumed to be published. However, because this "unnamed part" is used in a special way by Delphi in connection with visual components, you probably should get into the habit of not depending on it. Always explicitly list your scope for the members that you define.

Methods

For a class, *methods* bind code with the data types that the code is intended to manipulate. To accomplish this, methods are allowed to access an object's fields without having the fields passed to the method explicitly as parameters.

Methods usually have two parts. The declaration part inside the class type declaration (usually, in the interface of a unit) informs the compiler of your intention to have this method. This is similar to how a "forward" declaration works with procedures and functions. The body of the method is defined outside the class type declaration but within the implementation of the same unit. On the inside, the body of the method looks similar to an ordinary function or procedure. However, the method body header must contain the name of the class type where the method was declared previously, as in the following:

```
procedure TMyClass.AMethod(Parm1: AType);
begin
...
end;   { AMethod }
```

Within a method body, a function call or procedure statement allows a qualified method designator to activate a specific method. This type of call is known as a *qualified method activation*.

The reserved word inherited denotes the ancestor of the enclosing method's object type.

Within the block of a method procedure, scoping rules are a little different than for other procedures. There is an identifier, Self, that represents an implied local variable of the same type as the class. When a method is invoked, the Self variable is assigned the instance of the class type associated with the call. You never have to pass Self as a separate parameter; the compiler takes care of the connection for you.

By default, methods are *static*, which means that a reference to a method denotes a call to a specific procedure. However, methods also may take any of the forms listed in Table 4.1.

Table 4.1   Method Effects from Directives

Directive	Effect
Virtual	Procedure called is determined by *virtual method table*
Dynamic	Procedure called is determined by *dynamic method table*
Message	Procedure called is determined by a *message dispatch mechanism*
Abstract	Procedure doesn't exist for this class and must be overridden
Override	Change *virtual* or *dynamic* method for objects of this class
Class	Calls method without using the implicit Self variable

Methods also may be *constructors* or *destructors*. These specialized methods control how objects are created prior to use and disposed when no longer needed. The constructor ensures, besides all the other things that constructors might do, that the virtual methods appropriate for a specific object are called.

Static   Methods declared in an object type are by default *static*. No special identifier is used to denote such methods. When a static method is called, the type of the variable itself is what determines which procedure method starts to execute. The type of the referenced object is not even considered. When the compiler comes across a reference to AnObject.AStaticMethod, and AnObject is a variable of class AClassType, code is generated to call the procedure AClassType.AStaticMethod or, possibly, some AStaticMethod inherited by AClassType. Of course, AnObject could be referencing an object of any descendant class of AClassType, and the descendant could have redefined AStaticMethod to be something else. However, the actual class of the object isn't used by the compiler in determining which static method to call. The only possible target would be AClassType.AStaticMethod.

Virtual   In contrast to static method calls, *virtual* method calls are not resolved immediately by the compiler. The actual procedure method to be executed is determined at runtime, through a process known as *late binding*. You can make any method virtual by including a virtual directive at the end of the method definition in the class type member listing.

When a virtual method is referenced, the actual class type of the object referenced by the variable is used to determine which procedure will be called. The reason that this makes a difference is because a descendant class type may override any of the virtual methods that descendant class type had inherited from its parent class type. This change in the virtual method also will be inherited. The scope of an override method extends over all the descendants of the class with the override, or until you redefine the method identifier.

An override of a virtual method must match exactly any procedure formal parameters passed. If the virtual method is a function, both the formal parameters and the return type must match. The override must include the override directive in place of virtual.

The override directive is the only way to override a virtual method. If a method declaration in a descendant class specifies the same method identifier as an inherited method, but doesn't specify an override directive, the new method declaration hides, but doesn't override, the inherited declaration.

When the compiler encounters a reference to AnObject.AVirtualMethod, the compiler is aware that AVirtualMethod may have been overridden after the AClassType was declared. Rather than generate code to call AClassType.AVirtualMethod directly, the compiler generates code that looks up the address of the AVirtualMethod by examining the actual object type rather than the declared type of the variable.

Dynamic A similar dispatching mechanism to virtual is used in the dynamic directive. Both dynamic and virtual methods involve looking up the address of the method procedure, based upon the actual type of the object. From the point of view of your program, you won't be able to see much difference.

The code generated also will be only slightly different. Calls to virtual methods are slightly faster but their use causes your program to be slightly larger. Calls to dynamic methods are a little slower, but their use doesn't cause the slight increase in program size that the virtual method does.

Usually, you will find that virtual methods are the favorite way to create *polymorphic procedures* (procedures that can handle arguments of multiple types). On the other hand, if you have to create a base class with dozens of descendants and only override a handful of methods in each inheritance, you may want to consider making the methods dynamic.

Message A specialized form of the dynamic method is a *message-handling method.* The compiler generates code to call methods declared with the message directive by using a mechanism almost identical to the dynamic method call. However, you don't really need to be aware of this. You will not use message-handling methods in the same way as dynamic methods.

When you create message-handling methods, you need to keep in mind the following three features:

- How the handler is declared
- How messages are sent to the handler
- How to call an inherited handler

Message-handling methods are more limited in how you can declare other methods. Unlike virtual and dynamic methods, which can be either procedures or functions, message-handlers are always procedures. Following the message directive, there must be an integer constant (which is used as the index in the same table that is searched for dynamic methods). Moreover, only a single var argument can be passed as the formal parameter.

Message-handlers are crucial to the way in which the Windows operating system is ultimately processed by Delphi visual components. Many of the index numbers are already reserved for specific Windows messages. Inside of a class declaration, a message-handling method might be defined as the following:

```
procedure Handle_WM_Paint_Message(var MsgInfo); message WM_PAINT;
```

The name that you give to the message-handler method is not important to the compiler, and not knowing the name doesn't prevent you from invoking the correct method at runtime. Only the integer constant after message is considered. Likewise, the declaration of the argument is completely up to you, as long as there is only one, and it's a var parameter (either typed or untyped). In a descendant of the class that defined `Handle_WM_Paint_Message`, you could decide that you don't want to use the default handler for `WM_PAINT` messages. You just redeclare a message handler with the same dynamic index number, as follows:

```
procedure Paint_It_This_Way(var AMessage: TWMPaint); message WM_PAINT;
```

However, the contents of the actual var parameter are important in determining what method actually gets called. When the time comes to actually handle the message, the invocation of the proper method is determined in a call inherited by all objects from `TObject` called `Dispatch(var Message)`.

`TObject.Dispatch` calls a message-handling method for the object, based upon the first two bytes of the actual, untyped argument. These bytes are interpreted as an integer value, which is then used as the dynamic index. Any kind of data can be passed to `Dispatch`, but most of the Windows-triggered messages are specific about the kind of information that will be in the message.

Every class that defines dynamic or message-handling methods has these methods listed in a *dynamic dispatch table*. Message-handling methods are included along with their associated message index. Inside `TObject.Dispatch`, a list of message-handling methods defined for the class of the actual object is searched to see if the message index is present. If the actual class of the object never defined a message handler for a specific index, `TObject.Dispatch` follows a pointer to the dynamic dispatch table of the class' ancestor type, and so on.

`TObject.Dispatch` doesn't really know ahead of time if your object can actually handle any given message. For example, you might design your class so that only a limited number of message indices are handled. If your object has no message-handling method assigned for that particular message index, `TObject.Dispatch` calls your object's `DefaultHandler` method instead.

Often, you discover that when modifying inherited methods, you don't want to completely replace the inherited method. You may want to take a few extra steps before the default method is executed, and perhaps a couple of steps afterwards. Within a message-handler method, calling the inherited method is particularly easy, even if you don't know the name of the method or the type of the argument. You just use the directive `inherited` by itself.

As an example, the `Paint_It_This_Way` message handler might be implemented as follows:

```
procedure TMyClass.Paint_It_This_Way(var AMessage: TWMPaint);
begin
  with AMessage do begin
    ... // get ready to call real message handler
    inherited;  // calls "TMyAncestor.Handle_WM_Paint_Message(AMessage)"
    ... // do something after real message handler has been called.
  end;
end;
```

The same dispatch mechanism is used to invoke the inherited message handler, except that the search for inherited handler begins with the ancestor's dynamic dispatch table. If no ancestor has a message handler defined for `WM_PAINT`, then `DefaultHandler` is still called.

Abstract   Ordinarily, when you define a method in a class declaration, the compiler expects to find a method procedure somewhere in the implementation of the unit. When you define a method in the base class, the method establishes a default behavior for all descendants of the base. To change the behavior in a descendant, you override the behavior with a new method in the descendant. If no default behavior makes sense, use the `abstract` directive to tell the compiler that no default method will be implemented.

```
type
   TMyParent = class
       procedure AMethod; virtual; abstract;
       end;
   TMyClass = class (TMyParent)
       procedure AMethod; override;
       end;

procedure TMyClass.AMethod;
begin
   ... // do something
end;
```

When you define an `abstract` method, you tell the compiler that the method has to be over-ridden in descendant classes. The compiler will generate the correct code to look up the actual implementation, but if someone has forgotten to override the method in a descendant, a runtime library routine named `Abstract` is called that generates an error or exception.

Because overriding is always required for `abstract` methods, only `virtual` and `dynamic` methods can be declared `abstract`, never `static` methods. Otherwise, `abstract` methods have all the same characteristics as other methods. With one almost-obvious exception: There is no inherited method that the overriding method may call.

Override   The `override` directive redefines `virtual` and `dynamic` methods. Consider the following:

```
type
  TMyParent = class
    procedure AMethod; virtual;
  end;
  TMyClass = class(TMyParent)
    procedure AMethod; override;
  end;
```

The preceding code defines two classes (`TMyParent` and `TMyClass`) and two methods. Elsewhere in the implementation, procedures named `TMyParent.AMethod` and `TMyClass.AMethod` must be defined. Variables of type `TMyParent` (see the following line of code) can be assigned an object that could be either an instance of `TMyParent` or `TMyClass`:

```
var AnObject:TMyParent;
```

References to `AnObject.AMethod` calls either `TMyParent.AMethod` or `TMyClass.AMethod` depending on the actual type of the object that `AnObject` references.

The override directive accomplishes this change by substituting the new method for the old one. The overriding method must exactly match any formal parameters by order and type. For an overridden function method, the result type also must be the same.

Either virtual or dynamic methods may be overridden. However, you need to ensure that you use override rather than inadvertently using virtual or dynamic. The distinction is subtle. Consider the following:

```
type
   TMyOtherClass = class(TMyParent)
      procedure AMethod; virtual;
      end;
```

In this case, the compiler considers AMethod to be a second, and different, method that just happens to have the same name as one defined in an ancestor. For variables of class TMyOtherClass (and its descendants), the first meaning of AMethod is ignored, and AMethod refers only to the second method. For variables of class TMyParent, the second AMethod is unknown, and AMethod always refers to the virtual method of TMyParent. If an instance of the class TMyOtherClass is assigned to a variable of type TMyParent, a reference of AMethod will always call TMyParent.AMethod.

Class Methods   Ordinarily, methods define behavior for instances of the classes. Sometimes, the behavior you want to define for a class doesn't depend on an instance of the class existing at all. *Class methods* define behavior for the class type as if the type were a value rather than one of its instances. However, there may not be any object involved at all. So, you need to implement class methods in such a way that at runtime, the methods do not rely on whatever values may have been in an object's fields or its properties.

To declare a class method, you only have to put the reserved word class in front of the procedure or function keyword that starts the method definition. From this moment, the compiler treats the method a little differently than it treats methods that intended to define behavior for class instances ("objects").

In other methods, the identifier Self is implicitly used as a local variable of the same type as the class in which the method is defined. The actual instance of the associated object is assigned to this variable. For class methods, Self has another meaning altogether. Rather than being a variable of a class type, Self becomes a variable of a class reference type. The specific type still depends on the class type in which the method is defined. You can use Self to call constructors and other class methods.

Just because the object isn't required to exist doesn't mean that you cannot call its class methods. You can invoke class methods through either class type references (such as TMyClass.AClassMethod) or object references (such as AnObject.AClassMethod). When you use the object reference, the actual class of the object is passed as the Self value.

Part

I

Ch

4

Typecasting

When you declare a variable of any type, the compiler usually limits you to invoking only operations pertinent to the type of the variable that you declared. Occasionally, the compiler automatically handles a few type conversions, as in the case where you assign an integer value to a real variable. Usually, you're limited to the declared type, even in the instances where you are absolutely certain of the actual type of a referenced value and want to take advantage of some of the features of the actual type.

Delphi provides a number of ways to let you have your way with these variables. The Is and As operators use run-time type information and are relatively safe. However, with the explicit typecasting mechanism, the compiler takes you at your word and depends on your assurances that everything will turn out for the best.

Is and As

The operator is determines whether a given object is of a given class type or one of its descendants.

The expression like the following example returns true if AnObject references an instance of class type TMyClass or one of its descendants:

```
AnObject is TMyClass
```

Obviously, if the expression were true, then AnObject is assignment-compatible with variables of type TMyClass.

Is does nothing related to typecasting by itself. The operator simply checks to see if the object instance is compatible. To accomplish a safe typecasting of an object, you use the As operator, as follows:

```
With AnObject as TMyClass do ....
```

This operator is equivalent to the explicit, and otherwise dangerous, typecast:

```
With TMyClass(AnObject) do ....
```

except that first the As operator checks to see if AnObject really Is TMyClass. If not, the As raises an EInvalidCast exception. The preceding As expression wraps the explicit typecast in a type-safe container. The expression could be better translated as follows:

```
if AnObject is TObjectType then
    with TObjectType(AnObject) do ...
else
    raise EInvalidCast.Create('Invalid typecast');
```

Explicit

Explicit typecasting is a feature that you can use to change the type of an expression or variable. Misused, this can be dangerous. Used correctly, the feature can keep you from having to go to pains to convert information from one type to another. Explicit typecasting occurs in two flavors—value typecasting and variable typecasting.

Value typecasting allows you to change the type of an expression to another type. However, not all expressions can be typecast to just any type. The expression type and the target type must be either an ordinal or a pointer type. Classic Pascal defined two functions that did the equivalent of value typecasting: Ord(X) and Chr(X). Ord(X) took any ordinal expression and converted it into a value of type Integer. Chr(X) took any integer expression and converted it into type Char. Value typecasting extends what happened with Ord and Chr to other ordinal types and adds pointer types to boot. No special function name is required. The name of the type *is* the name of the function. Integer(X) takes any ordinal or pointer expression and converts it into an integer. Char(X) takes any ordinal or pointer expression and converts it into a char.

The value and target type don't have to be exactly the same size. The result of the value typecast depends on whether the target size is the same, smaller, or larger than the original value type. If the sizes are the same, the value is not physically altered at all; the compiler merely interprets the value as if it were the target type. If the target type is smaller than the value type, the excess high-order bytes of the value are simply eliminated. If the target type is larger than the value type, the value is sign extended to a type of the same size.

On the other hand, no change in size is permitted for variable typecasting, which changes the type of variable reference. Only the type is changed; nothing happens to the physical representation of the variable referenced. The compiler simply interprets the variable as if it were a different type. The size of the variable must be the same as the size of the target type.

Class-Reference Types

In classic Pascal, the *type* of a variable existed only during the compilation of a program. After the program was compiled, the *type* was fixed and was never changed during program execution. Object Pascal provides a structured mechanism for handling class types in the form of a *class-reference type* declared in the following format:

```
Class Of TMyClass
```

Class-reference types allow you to reference class types at runtime. A class-reference type is not the same as a class type, which allows you to define fields, methods, and property pertinent to instances of the class. From the viewpoint of the class-reference type, the class type is a *value* that can be stored in variables of a class-reference type.

At runtime, a class-reference type can be assigned a number of class types at various points during program execution. At each point, you then may reference the assigned class type, almost as if the type had been statically declared. Of course, "almost" is not the same as actually having the class type specified. However, class-reference types still are useful in a number of relatively common situations. Class-reference types usually are employed to invoke the virtual constructor of an unknown class in order to create instances of the unknown class. If you defined class methods for a class, you invoke the method through the class-reference without knowing what the actual underlying class is. Also, the right-hand operand of an Is or As operation is syntactically a class-reference value, which is the same thing as a class type.

Part

I

Ch

4

Consider the following declaration:

```
type
  TParent = class
    :
  end;
  TParentClass = class of TParent;
  TChild = class(TParent)
    :
  end;
  TChildClass = class of TChild;
var
  AParent, AParent2: TParent;
  AChild, AChild2: TChild;
  AParentClass: TParentClass;
  AChildClass: TChildClass;
```

This code declares TParentClass as a type that can reference class TParent (or any class that descends from TParent), and TChildClass as a type that can reference class TChild (or any class that descends from TChild).

Class-type identifiers function as constant values of their corresponding class-reference types. For example, besides its other uses, the TParent identifier functions as a value of type TParentClass, and the TChild identifier functions as a value of type TChildClass.

A class-reference type value is assignment-compatible with any ancestor class-reference type. Therefore, during program execution, a class-reference type variable can reference the class for which it was defined or any descendant class of the class for which it was defined. Referring to the previous declarations, the following assignments are all reasonable:

```
AParentClass := TParent; // type TParent may be assigned to a class of TParent
AParentClass := TChild; // a descendant of TParent may be assigned to class of
➥TParent
AChildClass := TChild; // the type TChild may be assigned to a class of TChild
```

However, this assignment would be invalid:

```
AChildClass := TParent; // error, TParent not a valid value for a class of TChild
```

This last assignment will cause an error because TParent isn't a descendant of TChild and, therefore, not a legal value that can be stored in a variable of type TChildClass.

In comparison with the corresponding class types, the assignments of a class reference type to a class reference variable for the same or for a descendant class will be valid. The only common problem is trying to assign a class type to a class reference variable of a descendant class, as shown in the following example:

```
AParent := AParent2;      // OK
Aparent := Achild;        // OK
Achild := Achild2;        // OK
Achild := Aparent;        // Fails, but AChild:=AParent as Tchild would
                          // work if the instance assigned to Aparent was
                          // of class type Tchild or its descendants
```

All classes have a method function called ClassType, which is inherited from TObject. The result of TObject.ClassType is a class-reference type TClass, which is declared to be class of TObject. However, as the preceding example shows, you cannot store TClass values into variables of type other than TClass. You may need to do a typecast to a more specific class-reference type, as follows:

```
if AParent is TChild then
  AChildClass := TChildClass(AParent.ClassType)
else
  AChildClass := nil;
```

Runtime Library

The visual components are the most obvious feature of the product Delphi when someone first sees its interface. Although the visual components are absolutely essential for rapidly developing applications, it occasionally surprises new programmers to learn that the visual components are not an intrinsic part of the underlying Object Pascal language. You learn more about the visual components in the rest of the book. Here, you will learn about the non-visual routines that are at the core of Delphi.

Most of the routines in the runtime library are not an intrinsic part of the Object Pascal language, either. The routines defined in the Delphi runtime library, however, are far more elaborate today than when Wirth first defined Pascal with its Spartan set of standard functions and procedures. Some routines were already discussed in these two chapters. Even the remaining routines are far more numerous than can be adequately described in just a few pages. However, there does seem to be a number of routines that first-time Delphi developers seem to miss. Even long-term Delphi developers have been known to miss a few.

The runtime library (RTL) of Delphi consists of three separately compiled units: System, SysUtils, and Math. As with units that you might create, these units declare a combination of constants, types, variables, and routines that may be called on demand from other units that list these in a uses clause.

System Unit

The *System unit* is the most fundamental part of the Delphi runtime library. It implements the low-level routines expected by the compiler for all its "predefined" features, including file input and output, long- and short-string handling, fundamental floating-point numerical routines, and dynamic memory allocation and management.

The System unit is so intrinsic to the way in which Object Pascal works that you never actually need to list it in a uses clause. It is automatically used.

Selected Types   The System unit defines some data types that may be used in a number of places in your program. One of the simplest of these is TDateTime, which is just declared as a special kind of floating-point type, as follows:

```
Type TDateTime = Double;
```

This kind of redeclaration of the type Double gives you a way to distinguish floating-point variables that are intended to hold date/time values from floating-point variables used for other purposes.

More complex data types are used to provide low-level access into the data types that you might use more casually. For example, the low-level type TVarData declares the internal structure of the predefined type "Variant." The low-level type TVarRec declares the internal structure of variables that are passed to routines as formal arguments of type "array of const."

Selected Variables   The System unit defines a number of "global variables" used in various ways by other routines. Sometimes, these variables are declared as var; sometimes, they are declared as typed constants.

```
CmdLine:    Pchar=nil;     // Command line pointer
CmdShow:    Integer=0;     // ShowWindow parameter
FileMode:   Byte=2;        // Default File open mode (read/write)
Hinstance:  Longint=0;     // Handle of this instance in the Windows
                           // environment
InOutRes:   Integer=0;     // I/O result buffer
Input:      Text;          // Standard input file.
IsConsole:  Boolean;       // Returns whether or not a module is a console
                           // application.
Null:       Variant=nil;   // Indicates that a variant has no value.
Output:     Text;          // Output standard file.
RandSeed:   LongInt=0;     // Random seed
Unassigned: Variant;       // Indicates if a variant has not been assigned a
                           // value.
```

Ordinarily, you will not access these variables outside of calling the library routines that are designed to manipulate them. However, on occasion, you may find yourself referencing the variable directly. For example, the variable InOutRes is used indirectly by calling the function IOResult. On the other hand, the file variables Input and Output may often be referenced directly.

Selected Routines   Besides the standard routines mentioned in the previous chapter, the System unit also defined a number of routines that you can call directly, such as the following:

Routine	Result
BlockRead(F,Buffer, Count,Res);	Reads count or fewer records from untyped file F into variable Buffer. The type of Buffer is unimportant, but it should certainly be large enough to hold count records. The actual number of records read is stored in Res, an integer variable.
BlockWrite(F,Buffer, Count,Res);	Writes count or more records to untyped file F from variable Buffer. The actual number of records written is stored in Res, an integer variable.
ChDir(S);	Changes the current directory to S.
GetDir(N,S);	If N=0, stores the current directory name in the string variable S. For N=1..26, stores the current working

Routine	Result
	subdirectory of drive "A:" to drive "Z:." If a drive is invalid, returns the root directory.
MkDir(S);	Creates a new subdirectory with path S.
ParamCount	Returns the number of parameters passed to the program on the command line.
ParamStr(N)	Returns the Nth command-line parameter. If N>ParamCount, returns an empty string. If N=0, returns the path and file name of the executing program.
Random	Returns a random number. By itself, Random returns a real value that represents a random number uniformly distributed between 0 and 1. When used with an argument Random(N), where N is an integer value, returns an integer value uniformly distributed between 0 and N-1.
Randomize	Initializes the built-in random number generator with an arbitrary value. The value is usually acquired for the system clock. There is never any need to call Randomize more than once in a program. Calling Randomize too often can result in Random results that are not as random as desired.
RmDir(S)	Remove/delete the subdirectory named S.

SysUtils Unit

While the System unit declares the core identifiers used within Delphi, the SysUtils unit extends the definition with declarations for things such as exception classes, additional string routines, date and time routines, and miscellaneous utility routines.

In the Delphi development environment, when you create a new form, the SysUtils unit is automatically placed into the uses clause. However, you may need to add the unit manually to a uses clause in formless units.

Constants1 The SysUtils unit declares a number of constants that allow you to use mnemonics rather than remembering arbitrary values.

File Attribute Constants File attributes constants are used when a file attribute parameter is passed as a formal parameter to a routine.

```
faReadOnly    = $00000001; // Read-only files
faHidden      = $00000002; // Hidden files
faSysFile     = $00000004; // System files
faVolumeID    = $00000008; // Volume ID files
faDirectory   = $00000010; // Directory files
faArchive     = $00000020; // Archive files
faAnyFile     = $0000003F; // Matches attributes of any file
```

File attributes usually are combined together by using Or operator to set selected bits in the actual file attribute parameter. Note that `faAnyFile` is defined in a way that sets all the bits in any previously declared attributes. An equivalent way to have declared this value is as follows:

```
faAnyFile = faReadOnly Or faHidden Or faSysFile Or faVolumeID
➡          Or faDirectory Or faArchive;
```

File Open Mode Constants   The *file open mode* constants are used to control the sharability of a file or stream when you open it. The class `TFileStream`, for example, has a method named `Create` that includes a `Mode` parameter that you can set to one of the following constants:

```
fmOpenRead       = $0000; // Read access only
fmOpenWrite      = $0001; // Write access only
fmOpenReadWrite  = $0002; // Read and write access
fmShareCompat    = $0000; // Compatible with FCB open
fmShareExclusive = $0010; // No others may read nor write
fmShareDenyWrite = $0020; // No others may write
fmShareDenyRead  = $0030; // No others may read
fmShareDenyNone  = $0040; // Others may access simultaneously
```

Only the first three modes are applicable when opening typed and untyped file variables. This is controlled by assigning one of the values to the `FileMode` variable declared in the System unit.

Other File Mode Constants   The `SysUtils` unit even defines a couple of the "magic" constants that are used internally by your program to keep track of the status of file variables, as follows:

```
fmClosed = $D7B0;
fmInput  = $D7B1;
fmOutput = $D7B2;
fmInOut  = $D7B3;
```

Types   The `SysUtils` unit declares a number of types that may be used as needed. Some of these types are simple redeclarations, such as:

```
TFileName=string;
```

Some of the types provide for an enumerated list of values that may be passed to routines expecting such parameters, as follows:

```
TFloatFormat=(ffGeneral, ffExponent,ffFixed,ffNumber,ffCurrency);
TFloatValue=(fvExtended,fvCurrency);
```

Some of the types provide low-level definitions of predefined types. You can use the predefined types without knowing the low-level definition, but the information is there if you want to look more closely at how the type is being used:

TFileRec	Internal structure of a typed or untyped `File` variable
TTextRec	Internal structure of a `TextFile` variable
LongRec	
TFloatRec	
THeapStatus	

```
TMethod

WordRec

TSearchRec
```

Of the preceding types, the one you are most likely to use in your routines is the TSearchRec. You do so by declaring variables of type TSearchRec when searching for named files in a subdirectory.

All of these last type declarations are generally record types of some kind, and define various fields for the underlying variables. For example, the types TFileRec and TTextRec possess a Mode field that will contain one of the "magic" file mode constant values. Any other value indicates that the file variable has not been initialized with an Assign or AssignFile call.

Objects   The SysUtil unit declares the base type "Exception" and a number of predefined descendants. Exceptions are covered more thoroughly in Chapter 5, "Exception Handling."

Variables   The most extensive set of global variables defined in the SysUtil unit deal with the formatting of date and time values. Initially, the variables are assigned values based on the contents of the system registry by using the Win32 API routine GetLocaleInfo. You can change these values on your own. They also can be changed in response to the WM_WININICHANGE message. For Delphi non-console applications, whether or not the values are automatically updated depends on the status of the Application.UpdateFormatSettings property.

The description of each of the following variables specifies the LOCALE constant used to fetch the initial value by using the GetLocaleInfo function in the Win32 API:

Variable	Contains
CurrencyString	The currency symbol (or characters) used in floating-point to string conversions. LOCALE_SCURRENCY is the locale constant used to fetch the information from the system registry. For U.S. dollars, this will be '$'.
CurrencyFormat	The currency symbol placement and separation used in floating-point to string conversions. The four possible values are: 0 = '\$1' 2 = '\$ 1' 1 = '1\$' 3 = '1 \$' LOCALE_ICURRENCY is used to fetch the information.
NegCurrFormat	The currency format used in floating-point to string conversions of negative amounts. The sixteen possible values are: 0 = (\$1) 8 = –1 \$ 1 = –\$1 9 = –\$ 1 2 = \$–1 10 = 1 \$– 3 = \$1– 11 = \$ 1–

continues

Part

I

Ch

4

continued

Variable	Contains
	4 = (1\$) 12 = \$ −1
	5 = −1\$ 13 = 1− \$
	6 = 1−\$ 14 = (\$ 1)
	7 = 1\$− 15 = (1 \$)
	LOCALE_INEGCURR is the locale constant used to fetch the information initially.
ThousandSeparator	The character used to separate thousands in amounts with more than three digits to the left of the decimal separator. LOCALE_STHOUSAND. For U.S. users, this is generally a comma (','). For European users, this is generally a period ('.').
DecimalSeparator	The character used to separate the whole part of a number from its fractional part. LOCALE_SDECIMAL. For U.S. users, this usually is a "decimal point" or period ('.'). For European users, a comma (',') is used. Just the reverse of the ThousandSeparator.
CurrencyDecimals	The number of digits to the right of the decimal point in a currency amount. LOCALE_ICURRDIGITS. For U.S. users, this is conventionally 2 to indicate two decimal places to hold "cents" as hundredths of dollars.
DateSeparator	The character used to separate the year, month, and day parts of a date value. LOCALE_SDATE. The forward slash ('/') is used widely in the U.S. International standards specify that this should be a hyphen ('-').
ShortDateFormat	The format string used to convert a date value to a short string suitable for editing. The short date format should only use the date separator character and the *m,mm,d,dd,yy*, and *yyyy* format specifiers of the FormatDateString routine. LOCALE_SSHORTDATE.
LongDateFormat	The format string used to convert a date value to a long string suitable for display. LOCALE_SLONGDATE.
TimeSeparator	The character used to separate the hour, minute, and second parts of a time value. LOCALE_STIME. The colon (':') is usually used.
TimeAMString	The suffix string used for time values between 00:00 and 11:59 in 12-hour clock format. LOCALE_S1159. Some common choices are 'am,' 'AM,' or 'A.M.'
TimePMString	The suffix string used for time values between 12:00 and 23:59 in 12-hour clock format. LOCALE_S2359. Some common choices are 'pm,' 'PM,' or 'P.M.'

Variable	Contains
ShortTimeFormat	The format string used to convert a time value to a short string with only hours and minutes. The default value depends upon both LOCALE_ITIME and LOCALE_ITLZERO. Typical values include 'hhnn' or 'hh:nn' or 'hh:nn ampm.'
LongTimeFormat	The format string used to convert a time value to a long string with hours, minutes, and seconds. This also depends upon both LOCALE_ITIME and LOCALE_ITLZERO.
ShortMonthNames	An array of strings containing shortened or abbreviated month names. Items from this array are used when an 'mmm' format specifier is passed in a format string to FormatDateTime. LOCALE_SABBREVMONTHNAME. A typical set of values includes 'Jan,' 'Feb,' 'Mar,' through 'Dec.'
LongMonthNames	An array of strings containing month full names. Items from this array are used when an 'mmmm' format specifier is passed in a format string to FormatDateTime. LOCALE_SMONTHNAME. A typical set of values includes 'January,' 'February,' through 'December.'
ShortDayNames	An array of strings containing shortened or abbreviated day-of-week names. Items from this array are used when a 'ddd' format specifier is passed in a format string to FormatDateTime. LOCALE_SABBREVDAYNAME. A typical set of values includes 'Sun,' 'Mon,' 'Tue,'... 'Sat.'
LongDayNames	An array of strings containing day-of-week full names. Items from this array are used when a 'dddd' format specifier is passed in a format string to FormatDateTime. LOCALE_SDAYNAME. A typical set of values includes 'Sunday,' 'Monday,' through 'Saturday.'

Routines   Routines declared in the SysUtils unit are used for a variety of purposes. Some routines are extremely simple, like "Beep," which causes a simple sound. The following functions are a sampling of the kinds of routines available in SysUtils.

String Type Functions   Some of the functions in the following table are filters, returning a string value based upon the contents of a string argument:

Routine	Result
AdjustLineBreaks(S)	Returns string with CR/LF used rather than just CR, just LF, or LF/CR
AnsiLowerCase(S)	Returns a lowercase string, based on the installed language driver
AnsiUpperCase(S)	Returns an uppercase string, based on the installed language driver

Part

I

Ch

4

continues

continued

Routine	Result
LowerCase(S)	Returns a string with all uppercase letters lowered
Trim(S)	Returns a string with both leading and trailing blanks and control characters removed
TrimLeft(S)	Returns a string with leading blanks and control characters removed
TrimRight(S)	Returns a string with trailing blanks and control characters removed
UpperCase(S)	Returns a string with all lowercase letters raised

The following functions compare two strings, S1 and S2, returning –1 if S1<S2, 0 if S1=S2, and 1 if S1>S2:

Routine	Result
AnsiCompareStr (S1,S2)	Returns comparison by installed language driver with case sensitivity
AnsiCompareText (S1,S2)	Returns comparison by installed language driver without case sensitivity
CompareStr (S1,S2)	Case-sensitive comparison
CompareText (S1,S2)	Non-case-sensitive comparison

Directory Routines   Some of the directory routines are used to create or remove directories in a manner that is easier to use than MkDir and RmDir, as in the following list:

- ▪ CreateDir(Dirname)—Returns True if new directory was created successfully, else False.
- ▪ RemoveDir(Dirname)—Returns True if directory removed successfully, else False.

Date/Time Routines   Some of the date/time routines return the current date and/or time, as follows:

Date—Returns the current date

Now—Returns the current date and time

Time—Returns the current time

However, most date/time routines deal with the problem of converting a date and time into other forms, particularly strings, and vice versa. All the Date/Time routines use the Currency and Date/Time formatting variables of the SysUtils unit.

The following routines take a date or time and generate a string:

Routine	Result
DateTimeToStr(DT)	Converts a value from time format to a string
DateTimeToString(ResultStr, FormatStr,DT)	Converts a value from time format to a string
DateToStr(DT)	Converts a value from date format to a string
FormatDateTime	Formats a date and time using the specified format
TimeToStr	Converts a time format to a string

The following routines convert a string that contains a valid value to a value of type TDateTime:

Routine	Result
StrToDate(S)	Converts a string to a date format
StrToDateTime(S)	Converts a string to a date/time format
StrToTime(S)	Converts a string to a time format

The following routines accomplish miscellaneous conversions:

Routine	Result
DayOfWeek(DT)	Returns an integer value representing the day of the week of the given TDateTime parameter: 1=Sunday, 2=Monday, through 7=Saturday
DecodeDate	Decodes the specified date
DecodeTime	Decodes the specified time
DateTimeToFileDate	Converts the Delphi date format to the DOS date format
EncodeDate (Yyyy,Mm,Dd)	Returns TDateTime value
EncodeTime(Hour,Min,Sec,MSec)	Returns TDateTime value
FileDateToDateTime (Filedate)	Converts a DOS date format to the Delphi date format

File and Drive Management Routines The following routines manipulate named files that are not currently open:

Routine	Result
DeleteFile(Filename)	Returns True if named file is successfully deleted, else False
FileAge(Filename)	Returns the age of a file

continues

continued

Routine	Result
FileCreate(Filename)	Creates a file with the specified name
FileGetAttr(Filename)	Returns file attributes
FileSetAttr(Filename, NewAttr)	Sets file attributes
RenameFile(OldName,NewName)	Renames a file

The following routines determine whether or not a named file exists:

Routine	Result
FileExists(Filename)	Returns True if file exists
FileSearch(FileName,DirList)	Searches through the directories for a specific file
FindClose(SearchRec)	Terminates a FindFirst/FindNext sequence
FindFirst(FileSpec,Attr, SearchRec)	Searches a directory for a specified file name and set of attributes
FindNext(SearchRec)	Returns the next entry that matches the name and attributes

The following routines are string filters, returning file names or their components. It usually doesn't matter whether or not the file actually exists:

Routine	Result
ChangeFileExt(FileName, FileExt)	Changes the file extension.
ExpandFileName(Filename)	Returns a string that contains a fully qualified path name and file name.
ExpandUNCFileName(Filename)	Returns a string that contains a fully qualified network path name and file name.
ExtractFileDir(Filename)	Returns only the drive and directory parts of the file name.
ExtractFileDrive(Filename)	Returns only the drive portion of a fully qualified path name.
ExtractFileExt(Filename)	Returns only the file extension.
ExtractFileName(Filename)	Returns only the file name proper. That is, not the drive or name of the directory where the file is located. However, it does include the file extension.
ExtractFilePath(Filename)	Returns the path to the specified file.

The following routines deal with files at the operating system level rather than as file variables of Object Pascal. It's important not to mix these different ways of dealing with files on the same opened file:

Routine	Result
FileClose(Filehandle)	Closes a specific file
FileGetDate(Filehandle)	Returns the DOS date-and-time stamp of the file
FileOpen(Filename,Mode)	Opens a specific file using specified access mode. Returns a "file handle" that will be used as an argument, or –1 on failure
FileRead(Filehandle, Buffer,NumBytes)	Reads from a specific file
FileSeek(Filehandle, Offset,Origin)	Changes the current position of the file
FileSetDate(Filehandle, NewAge)	Sets the DOS date-and-time stamp of the file
FileWrite(Filehandle, Buffer,NumBytes)	Writes to a specific file

The following routines return drive capacity information:

- DiskFree(Drive)—Returns the amount of free disk space. Drive=0 for current, logged-in drive, 1 for drive A:, 2 for drive B:, and so on.
- DiskSize(Drive)—Returns the size of the specified disk. Drive=0 for current, logged-in drive; 1 for drive A:, 2 for drive B:, and so on.

Floating-Point Conversion Routines   The following routines deal with conversions of floating-point values to other forms. Some of the arguments can get complicated, as follows:

Routine	Result
FloatToDecimal	Converts a floating-point value to a decimal representation
FloatToStrF	Converts the floating-point value to its string representation
FloatToStr(X)	Converts the floating-point value to its string representation
FloatToText	Converts the given floating-point value to its decimal representation
FloatToTextFmt	Converts the given floating-point value to its decimal representation

continues

Part
I

Ch
4

continued

Routine	Result
`FormatFloat`	Formats the floating-point value using the format string given by Format
`StrToFloat(S)`	Converts the given string to a floating-point value
`TextToFloat`	Converts the null-terminated string to a floating-point value
`IntToStr(X)`	Converts integer values into a string
`StrToInt(S)`	Converts a string into an integer value

String Formatting Routines The `SysUtils` unit includes routines that can format strings in very general ways. Most of the special-purpose string formatting routines actually call these routines to accomplish their formatting:

Routine	Result
`FmtStr`	Formats a series of arguments
`Format`	Formats a series of arguments and returns the result as a Pascal string
`FormatBuf`	Formats a series of arguments
`StrFmt`	Formats a series of arguments
`StrLFmt`	Formats a series of arguments and the result contains a pointer to the destination buffer

String-Handling Routines (Nulls Terminated) The `SysUtils` unit declares a number of routines that deal exclusively with null-terminated strings. The string arguments are of type `Pchar` rather than type `String`. Most of these routines are provided for compatibility with other languages:

Routine	Result
`StrAlloc(Size)`	Allocates a buffer for a null-terminated string with a maximum length of one less than `Size`
`StrBufSize(S)`	Returns the maximum number of characters that may be stored in a string buffer allocated by `StrAlloc`
`StrCat(S1,S2)`	Appends string `S2` to the end of string `S1` and returns a pointer to the concatenated string (`S2`)
`StrComp(S1,S2)`	Compares two strings
`StrCopy(S1,S2)`	Copies string `S2` to string `S1`
`StrDispose(S)`	Disposes a string on a heap
`StrECopy(S1,S2)`	Copies one string to another and returns a pointer to the end of the resulting string

Routine	Result
StrEnd(S)	Returns a pointer to the end of a string
StrIComp(S1,S2)	Compares two strings without case sensitivity
StrLCat(S1,S2)	Appends characters from string S2 to the end of S2 and returns a pointer to the concatenated string (S2)
StrLComp(S1,S2)	Compares two strings, up to a maximum length
StrLCopy(S1,S2)	Copies characters from one string to another
StrLen(S)	Returns the number of characters in null-terminated string S
StrLIComp(S1,S2)	Compares two strings, up to a maximum length, without case sensitivity
StrLower(S)	Converts a string to lowercase
StrMove(S1,S2)	Copies characters from one string to another
StrNew(S)	Allocates a string on a heap, returning the address of the new string
StrPas(S)	Converts a null-terminated string to a Pascal-style string. Returns a value of type String
StrPCopy(S1,S2)	Copies a Pascal-style string S2 to a null-terminated string S1
StrPLCopy(S1,S2,MaxLen)	Copies a maximum of MaxLen characters from the Pascal style string S1 into the null-terminated string S2
StrPos(S1,S2)	Returns a pointer to the first occurrence of string S2 in string S1
StrRScan(S,C)	Returns a pointer to the last occurrence of a character in a string
StrScan(S,C)	Returns a pointer to the first occurrence of a character in a string
StrUpper(S)	Converts a string to uppercase

Math Unit

The *Math unit* provides a common place to find numerical routines that are at times provided in other languages. The unit does define a new exception, EInvalidArgument, and a new type TPaymentTime that is used in some of the financial routines, but the principal feature of the Math unit is the vast declaration of functions that accomplish useful numerical calculations.

Elementary Functions   Many of the functions that inspired the creation of the Math unit are relatively simple mathematical functions that most programmers could have easily created on their own with a little help from a textbook on algebra. Placing the functions in the math unit has provided you with a conventional approach for using these functions in your own code.

Routine	Result
Ceil(X)	Whole number greater than or equal to X
Floor(X)	Whole number less than or equal to X
Hypot(X,Y)	Hypotenuse of right triangle with sides X and Y. The implementation is designed to be more numerically accurate than you may achieve if you just pulled the Pythagorean formula out of a textbook
Log2(X)	The logarithm base two of X
Log10(X)	The common logarithm (base ten) of X
LogN(X)	The natural logarithm (base "e") of X
Power(X,Y)	X raised to the Y power
RandG(Mean, Variance)	A normally distributed random value with given mean and variance

Trigonometric Routines   Classic Pascal defined three trigonometric routines (routines that arise in solving geometric problems associated with right triangles) for programmers: Sin, Cos, and ArcTan. For mathematically astute programmers, these functions were all that were needed in order to compute related trigonometric values. The Math unit provides built-in functions for computing a wider variety of trigonometric values that includes inverses, complements, hyperbolic trigonometric values, and conversions between different units for measuring angles (radians, degrees, gradients, cycles).

Routine	Result
ArcCos(X)	Angle in radians whose cosine is X
ArcCosh(X)	Inverse hyperbolic cosine of X
ArcSin(X)	Angle in radians whose sine is X
ArcSinh(X)	Inverse hyperbolic sine of X
ArcTan2(Y,X)	Angle in radians whose tangent is Y/X, adjusted for quadrant
ArcTanh(X)	Inverse hyperbolic tangent of X
Cosh(X)	Hyperbolic cosine of X
Cotan(X)	Cotangent of X radians
CycleToRad(X)	Number of radians in X revolutions
DegToRad(X)	Number of radians in X degrees
GradToRad(X)	Number of radians in X gradients (400 gradients in a circle)
RadToCycle(X)	The number of revolutions in X radians
RadToDeg(X)	The number of degrees in X radians

Routine	Result
RadToGrad(X)	The number of gradients in X radians (400 gradients in a circle)
Sinh(X)	The hyperbolic sine of X
Tan(X)	The tangent of X radians
Tanh(X)	The hyperbolic tangent of X

Financial Routines   The set of financial functions in Delphi either solves the cash-flow equation for specific values or handles depreciation. The routines should not be used too casually. It is very easy to forget sign changes:

DoubleDecliningBalance	NumberOfPeriods
FutureValue	Payment
InterestPayment	PeriodPayment
InterestRate	PresentValue
InternalRateOfReturn	SLNDepreciation
NetPresentValue	SYDDepreciation

Statistical Routines   The set of statistical routines includes an argument that is an array of floating-point values.

MaxValue	PopnVariance
Mean	StdDev
MeanAndStdDev	Sum
MinValue	SumOfSquares
MomentSkewKurtosis	SumsAndSquares
Norm	TotalVariance
PopnStdDev	Variance

Miscellaneous Math Routines   The following routines are also available. Some of these routines are provided for compatibility with other languages or are called internally within the unit and considered to be worth calling globally:

Routine	Result
Frexp	Converts a floating-point value into its component parts
IntPower(X,N)	Computes the value of X raised to integer power N
Ldexp	Creates a floating-point value based upon specific component parts
LnXP1(X)	Computes the natural logarithm of X+1
SinCos	Computes both the sine and cosine of a value simultaneously

Putting It All Together

The visual components in Delphi are reasonably straightforward applications of the elements of the Object Pascal language presented in the last two chapters.

In the integrated development environment, when you are presented with a blank form, you're dealing with a blank form *type*. Delphi will define the skeleton for your type automatically and make it a descendant of the TForm class. You can see this quickly in the interface of the unit declaring the form (initially called Unit1):

```
Type TForm1 = class(TForm)
```

As a descendant of the TForm class, your blank form inherits all the fields, methods, and properties of the class. The TForm type is defined initially in a unit named Forms. As in the case of any other unit, you cannot reference a type definition in Forms until you place the name of the unit in a uses clause. Delphi automatically adds Forms whenever you create a new blank form, and you can see it in the interface of your unit:

```
Uses ...,Forms,...;
```

In the interface of the Forms unit, TForm is defined as the descendant of yet another class, TScrollingWinControl. TForm inherits all of the fields, methods and properties of TScrollingWinControl. TForm also defines a large number of these on its own. Only a very small, demonstrative subset is shown in the following declaration:

```
Type TForm = class(TScrollingWinControl)
     private
          FOnCreate: TNotifyEvent;
          function IsForm: Boolean;
     published
          property Caption stored IsForm;
          property OnCreate: TNotifyEvent
              read FOnCreate write FOnCreate stored IsForm;
```

This declaration shows a FOnCreate *field* with a type of TNotifyEvent and a static Boolean method called IsForm, which is used in the storage of information to the application resource file. Both of these members are private, which means that you cannot reference them directly. What you can reference are the two published properties, Caption and OnCreate.

TScrollingWinControl also has a definition of its own, and you can follow the ancestry of the definitions all the way back to the base class, TObject:

```
TScrollingWinControl = class(TWinControl) // in unit Forms
TWinControl = class(TControl)             // in unit Controls
TControl = class(TComponent)              // in unit Controls
TComponent = class(TPersistent)           // in unit Classes
TPersistent = class(TObject)              // in unit Classes
TObject = class                           // in unit System
```

The ancestors of your form are not the only type definitions with which you are going to be concerned. Also in the Classes unit, two other types are defined that will make your simple form work correctly—TNotifyEvent and TComponentClass.

```
Type
    TNotifyEvent = procedure(Sender: TObject) of object;
    TComponentClass = class of Tcomponent;
```

This makes TNotifyEvent an indirect reference to the method of some class, and TComponentClass a class reference type. You will use the TNotifyEvent type directly in association with the OnCreate property. The TComponentClass type gets used in a slightly different way.

It's important to keep in mind that your blank form (initially named TForm1) is a *type* all by itself and not a specific instance of a type, a *variable*. As a type, TForm1 represents a lot of potential, but it doesn't do anything particularly useful within your application at runtime, until you create a variable of the type. Delphi automatically will declare an appropriate variable of the type for you. In the unit interface, it occurs immediately after the type definition:

```
var Form1: TForm1;
```

This is an improvement, but it is still incomplete because it doesn't properly initialize the variable. Fortunately, Delphi also handles this for you automatically. In the application project file (initially named PROJECT1.DPR), you will find the following statement:

```
Application.CreateForm(TForm1,Form1);
```

Application is a variable defined in the interface of the Forms unit. You will see the Forms unit referenced in the project Uses clause. In the Forms unit, the Application variable is declared as an instance of the type TApplication:

```
var Application: TApplication;
```

The TApplication is defined in the Forms unit as a class, which inherits from Tcomponent, and then defines a large number of fields, methods, and properties of its own, including the one directly referenced when initializing your form:

```
type TApplication = class(TComponent)
    procedure CreateForm(
        InstanceClass: TComponentClass; var Reference);
```

The ancestry of the TComponent here is the same as ancestry of the TComponent for the TForm class. It's the same TComponent class. So, this makes the Application variable an instance of the TPersistent class as well as the TObject class.

The TApplication.CreateForm method is used to initialize any instance of the TComponent class. The method takes two arguments: a value of type TComponentClass and a variable of arbitrary type. Your newly created form never existed before you created it. Yet, the Application variable knows how to create an instance of your newly created form because the type of your form's class gets passed as an argument.

Of course, so far, you really haven't done anything that makes your form different from any other TForm. You could add any field, method, or property to your form that you desire. However, the simplest approach is to make your form respond to some predefined event differently from the default TForm. For example, when you double-click the form in design mode, Delphi automatically adds a new method to your form definition like the following:

```
procedure FormCreate(Sender: TObject);
```

Delphi then places you in the edit window at a skeleton method implementation for your method:

```
procedure TForm1.FormCreate(Sender: TObject);
begin

end;
```

Note that the structure of this method is exactly what is necessary to satisfy the definition of a TNotifyEvent value. That's not a coincidence. Behind the scenes, Delphi already has assigned this method to your form's OnCreate property. This sets up everything you need to define what happens whenever your form gets created. For example, you could take advantage of the nature of the Caption property and assign a new string to your form's caption:

```
Caption:='Hello, world!';
```

Of course, you don't need to write a whole method like TForm1.FormCreate in order to change the form's caption when the program starts. Because Caption is a published property with a storage specifier, you could just modify the form's Caption property in the Delphi object inspector directly. However, the example does demonstrate how simple it is to make your own event handlers.

In fact, the event-driven nature of Windows programming means that most of the time, you'll be doing just that: creating new methods that handle events in the environment. You will be carefully setting up your applications to respond to situations that may arise, and until the situation arises, your code waits patiently to be executed. The Application variable will initialize your components, and then pass control to you with the simple statement:

```
Application.Run;
```

Then you'll be off and running. ●

CHAPTER 5

Exception Handling

Support for exception handling has existed in Delphi since version 1.0. The entire VCL makes use of Delphi's exception-handling syntax. This support provides you with the advantage of a working model for using exception-handling techniques in your code.

This chapter focuses on errors that occur at runtime, specifically exceptions and how to handle them. ■

Learn about runtime errors

About runtime errors and how they are converted into exceptions.

Exceptions

How to program with exceptions at the global level as well as where they occur.

Exceptions classes

About exception classes, including defining your own.

Runtime Errors

You probably are already familiar with compile-time errors and logic errors. This chapter deals with *Runtime errors.*

Runtime errors are a result of failed execution of functions, procedures, and methods that operate within the RunTime Library (RTL), Visual Component Library (VCL), and even within the Operating System (OS). Code that can potentially trigger the error must handle and take into consideration all variants in processing.

Historically, a language's RTL routines would return a predefined value if the routine failed in execution. In some cases, a global variable would be set with a code that could be used to define the error. If an operation that corrupted memory or accessed an invalid device was performed, the OS in some cases will display a rather unpleasant error message and, in other cases, blow you out of the program altogether.

The following code shows the traditional yet defensive programming style required to trap runtime errors in code:

```
procedure UseFunctions;
var cVal: char;
    sStrVal: string;
begin
  sStrVal := 'Delphi Rock ';
  cVal := CharFromString(sStrVal,12);
  if cVal <> #0 then
  begin
    if cVal <> 's' then
      if InsertChar('s',sStrVal,12) then
        ShowMessage(sStrVal)
      else
        Exit;
  end
  else
    Exit;
end;
```

The UseFunctions routine employs a couple of hypothetical functions. CharFromString returns a character from the specified position in a string or 0 if the position is out of range. InsertChar returns True if the function can successfully insert the specified character into the given var string at the specified position, otherwise InsertChar returns False. In the example, complete runtime error-checking requires the code to check the return value of both functions for failures. If a failure occurs, the UseFunctions procedure terminates. If an error does not occur, processing continues, resulting in a message dialog box. The message dialog box displays the text "Delphi Rocks."

Consider if CharFromString and InsertChar raised exceptions upon failure, rather than providing return values for you to evaluate. This would allow you to move the error-checking out of the main flow of the program code. This method would also make the code more readable. Consider the following modifications to UseFunctions:

```
procedure UseFunctions;
var cVal: char;
    sStrVal: string;
begin
  try
    sStrVal := 'Delphi Rock ';
    cVal := CharFromString(sStrVal,12);
    if cVal <> 's' then
      InsertChar('s',sStrVal,12);
    ShowMessage(sStrVal);
  except
    Exit;
  end;
end;
```

Because `CharFromString` and `InsertChar` now make use of exceptions, you can write your code assuming that all will proceed without error in a top-down fashion. If an error does occur, program execution jumps directly to the exit statement. Note that most of Delphi's RTL uses exceptions instead of magic codes in the return values. Given this, it's nearly impossible to write a rock-solid application with Delphi without providing some form of exception handling.

Even routines in Delphi that internally call Application Programming Interface (API) functions in the OS convert failures into exceptions. Delphi also makes use of the built-in Windows 95 and NT exception architecture to allow you to capture errors that occur in the OS itself or by devices used by the OS. The remainder of this chapter discusses exceptions and exception handling in detail.

Understanding Exceptions

An *exception* is a change in processing conditions that causes an application to interrupt or even stop processing. The exception can conceivably occur at any time in your application. There can be any number of sources of the exception, all of which are directly or indirectly interacting with your code. The possibilities include the following:

- Components you include in your application
- Database drivers, such as any of the SQL Links, BDE, or ODBC
- The operating system
- Device drivers, such as the video driver or Unimodem communications drivers
- Network DLLs, Version control systems, and Antivirus programs
- Delphi's own RTL or VCL

When an exception occurs, whatever its source, your application is notified. The compiler generates code that knows how to interrupt your code's processing. From the point of interruption, the call stack begins to unwind. Passed parameters and local variables allocated on the stack are popped off, therefore free from memory.

Part I
Ch 5

N O T E Only local variables and parameters passed to a function exist on the stack. If the default-calling convention Fast-Call (or Register) is in use, some of the parameters are passed on the extended CPU registers.

If a function has a local variable of type pointer whose memory is allocated off the heap, using New( ), GetMem( ), or HeapAlloc( ), only the 4 bytes allocated on the stack for the pointer variable itself are freed as the stack unwinds. Given this, you must have an error-handling scheme in place that will free heap-allocated memory when exceptions occur. ■

The unwinding process continues up the call stack tree until one of two things happens:

1. A try...except construct is encountered.
2. A global exception-handler is encountered.

Both of these result in what is known as *handling the exception*. When you build your application, the compiler generates a certain amount of code. This code results in what is often termed "Compiler Magic." Part of the Compiler Magic is to generate code that deals with exceptions as they occur. Part of this includes stack maintenance. Another thing that happens is an error object is created which stays in memory until it is freed. The freeing of this error object is referred to as "handling the exception." The object itself is what is referred to as the "exception object instance."

N O T E If you're already familiar with the existence of try...except, you also may be familiar with try...finally. Note that the try...finally construct doesn't free the exception object instance, which thus doesn't "handle the exception." The contrast between these two constructs is discussed in greater detail in following sections of this chapter. ■

Defining a Default Exception-Handler

Each VCL-based project in Delphi has a global variable named Application available to it. Application is an instance of the TApplication class defined in the FORMS unit. The Application object instance encapsulates all the autocreated forms in your program. As with almost all classes in Delphi, TApplication has an assortment of methods and properties available to you at runtime.

N O T E When a project uses the FORMS unit, the CONTROLS unit is indirectly used, and it is referenced in the uses clause of FORMS. The initialization code in CONTROLS calls the procedure InitControls. InitControls is responsible for the instantiation of the Application object instance. Given this, it is not necessary for you to manually create the Application instance or to free it. This work is handled for you when the FORMS unit is used in your project. ■

The Application object serves many purposes, one of which is to provide a global, default exception-handling mechanism. When the Application object is notified that an exception occurred, it fires an event called OnException.

The *OnException* Event

You probably have seen the Application object used in the DPR file's initialization section. In a new default project, a call is made to the Initialize method. Initialize is used to automatically register or unregister an OLE automation object if your application happens to be OLE-enabled (see Chapter 18, "Working with OLE, Document Servers, and ActiveX Controls," for more information about OLE and Automation). If it is not, the call can be deleted. After the call to Initialize, CreateForm is called, which creates an instance of your main form and associates it with the Application object instance. But how does Application apply to exception handling? Simple, the TApplication class has a property named OnException.

When an exception is raised at any level in your application, where no handling is otherwise provided, the Application object executes its HandleException method. HandleException in turn executes all code attached to the OnException property. If no code is assigned to the OnException property, another method called ShowException is called. ShowException provides the default handling when the OnException event occurs.

If code is assigned to the OnException property, it must be contained within a method. The method format must be exactly the same as the TExceptionEvent type. The FORMS unit declares TExceptionEvent as follows:

```
TExceptionEvent = procedure (Sender: TObject; EInstance: Exception) of object;
```

TExceptionEvent is declared as a procedure type that must be a method of an object.

Assigning Your Own Handler to *Application.OnException*

On the CD

To assign your own handler to the OnException property of the Application object, several steps are required. The first step is to create a new project. Fortunately, all the code for your custom exception-handler can be placed in the projects DPR file. The DPR file is accessible from the Pro&ject Source command in the &View menu. You can find the code in Listing 5.1 (and in listings throughout this chapter) on this book's companion CD-ROM, in the Chapter 5 directory.

Part
I

Ch

5

Listing 5.1   \UDELPHI3\CHP5\PROJECT1.DPR—Assigning a Custom Global Exception-Handler to *OnException* in the DPR File

```
program Project1;

uses
  SysUtils,
  Forms,
  Unit1 in 'Unit1.pas' {Form1};

type
  TGlobalExHandler = class
  public
    procedure HandlerProc(Sender: TObject; EInstance: Exception);
  end;
```

continues

Listing 5.1 Continued

```
procedure TGlobalExHandler.HandlerProc(Sender: TObject; EInstance: Exception);
begin
  ... {Statments to respond to exceptions here}
end;

var
  GlobalExHandler: TGlobalExHandler;

{$R *.RES}

begin
  GlobalExHandler := TGlobalExHandler.Create;
  Application.OnException := GlobalExHandler.HandlerProc;
  Application.Initialize;
  Application.CreateForm(TForm1, Form1);
  Application.Run;
end.
```

Listing 5.1 begins with the insertion of the SYSUTILS unit into the uses clause. SYSUTILS contains the declaration of the EXCEPTION class type. The `type` section of the unit declares a new class named `TGlobalExHandler`. `TGlobalExHandler` has a single method named `HandlerProc`. Ultimately, `HandlerProc` will be assigned to the `OnException` property. `HandlerProc`, as shown, does pretty much nothing. However, you can insert whatever code is applicable for your application. Suppose that your code in `HandlerProc` determines the error is fatal. A routine can be called to free any globally allocated memory, close files, warn the user, and otherwise gracefully terminate the program.

After `HandlerProc` is defined, a global variable named `GlobalExHandler` of type `TGlobalExHandler` is declared. `GlobalExHandler` is instantiated in the initialization code of the DPR file. After instantiation, `HandlerProc` is assigned to `Application.OnException`.

When the application runs, if an exception were to occur that is not otherwise handled, an exception object instance will be raised and remain in memory until it reaches the call to the `Application` object's `HandleException` method. This method in turn executes the code assigned to `Application.OnException`. In the previous example, `GlobalExHandler.HandlerProc` is assigned to `Application.OnException` and therefore will be executed.

N O T E The OnException property requires that the method assigned to it is of the same format
as the TExceptionEvent type:

```
TExceptionEvent = procedure (Sender: TObject;
➡        Einstance:Exception) of object;
```

The second parameter is the exception object instance and will be of type `Exception` or of a type which descends from `Exception`. You can use the passed parameter `EInstance` to access the public and published members of the exception object. These members can provide more information about the source of the exception itself. The best example is the `Message` property. You can use it to retrieve the error string associated with the exception. For example:

```
procedure TGlobalExHandler. HandlerProc(Sender: Tobject;
    EInstance: Exception);
begin
  MessageDlg(EInstance.Message, mtInformation,[mbOK],0);
  {requires "Dialogs" in the uses section }
end;
```

Delphi provides two `try` constructs that allow you to handle exceptions where and when they occur. They also provide mechanisms to determine the source of the error, its exact type, and to obtain an actual reference to the instance of the raised exception object.

Programming with Exceptions

The built-in handling of exceptions in the call to `ShowException` consists of the display of a dialog box that contains the text assigned to the `Message` property of whatever exception type is raised. Whenever possible, programmatic handling of exceptions should be used to close files, release heap-allocated memory, and call any deinitialization routines your program provides.

Programmatic handling of exceptions can be accomplished by providing a new default handler. Delphi also provides two `try` constructs for dealing with exceptions when and where they occur. If the constructs are used and an exception is raised that is of a type with which your program code doesn't know how to deal, you have the option to re-raise the exception to the default handler.

Debugging Exception-Handling Code in the IDE

Delphi's Integrated Development Environment (IDE) provides a rather robust set of debugging features. It gives you the ability to turn integrated debugging off or on again, include debug and symbol information in the project, step trace, set breakpoints, watch variables, and evaluate expressions. By default, when an exception occurs while running in the IDE, the execution of your program stops on the line that triggered the error.

Sometimes, when exceptions are raised, the integrated debugger is unable to determine what line of code triggered the error. The program will still pause, but the offending line will not be selected. You usually can get around this by turning off Optimizations and turning on Stack Frames. These options are accessible from the Compiler page of the Project Options dialog box. The Project Options dialog box is accessible from Project, Options.

Part

I

Ch

5

N O T E Delphi's default calling convention is *Fast-Call* (or *Register*). This calling convention is optimal as it uses the extended CPU registers whenever possible for passing parameters to a routine. This method is faster and more efficient than use of stack-based-only protocols such as StdCall and Pascal. With Fast-Call in place, it isn't always necessary to generate a stack frame for every routine called. Stack frame generation slightly denigrates performance. The Integrated Debugger relies on the generation of stack frames that can be unwound to the source of the error. If no stack frame is in place, Delphi cannot tell you where the error occurred.

The stopping of execution of your program on the line of code that triggers an exception is a great debugging feature during the development phase of your project. However, it slows the process of debugging your actual exception-handling code. If you included a new global handler and an exception is raised, the Integrated Debugger kicks in and stops the execution of your program, therefore never arriving to the global handler whose functionality you want to test. After the program breaks, pressing F9 to continue results in the penalty of the pause in execution and the extra keystroke. When debugging your exception-handling code, you can turn off the Break On Exception feature.

To turn off this feature:

1. In the IDE, choose Tools, Options. The Environment Options dialog box appears.

2. Choose the Preferences page.

3. Uncheck the Break on Exception box.

The *try* Constructs

Delphi provides two constructs for dealing with exceptions as soon as they occur. The constructs are `try...finally` and `try...except`. The syntax for their use is similar, but their purposes are much different. Start by looking at the following syntax for `try...finally`:

```
try
   {statements go here}
finally
   {more statements go here}
end;
```

If an exception occurs as a result of any statements that execute following the `try` directive but before the `finally` directive, program execution jumps to the first statement that follows the `finally` directive. All statements are executed between the `finally` directive and closing `end;`. The `try...except` construct behaves similarly. The simplest syntax for `try...except` is:

```
try
   {statements go here}
except
   {more statements go here}
end;
```

Like the `try...finally` construct, if an exception occurs between the `try` and `except` directives, execution jumps to the statements between the `except` directive and closing `end;`.

Using the *try...finally* Construct   The try...finally construct is used to trap an exception long enough to execute any cleanup code before the exception gets raised to the global exception-handler or next level of error-checking. The try...finally construct doesn't free the exception object instance, and thus doesn't "handle" the error.

Consider the case of dynamic memory allocation from the heap. You allocate a block of memory to a pointer inside a routine, and then operate on the pointer variable. Suppose that one of the operations results in memory overwrite. An exception will be raised that breaks you out of the current line of execution. The routine that owns the pointer is unwound; therefore, stack variables are freed. Because the pointer was a local variable, its 4 bytes were allocated on the stack and are now gone. Therefore, your reference to the memory block is gone. Now you have no way to release the memory allocated on the heap. The result is a memory leak in your program. The following lines show how a try...finally construct solves this scenario:

```
procedure TForm1.Button1Click(Sender: TObject);
var pVar: PChar;
begin
  GetMem(pVar,10);
  try
    StrCopy(pVar,'This string is longer than 10 characters!');
  finally
    FreeMem(pVar,10);
  end;
end;
```

First, the pointer variable pVar is declared. Then a 10-byte block of memory is allocated to it from the heap by using the GetMem RTL function. After the try directive, the RTL function StrCopy is called to copy a string into the memory block associated with pVar. The string is clearly longer than 10 characters, which results in memory overwrite. In this case, an exception is raised from the RTL. The specific exception instance raised is of type EAccessViolation which descends from the Exception class. When the exception occurs, processing jumps to the call to FreeMem that releases the memory allocated to pVar from the heap. After FreeMem, the exception continues to raise up the call stack, stopping at any encapsulating try...finally constructs until finally it reaches the global handler or an encapsulating try...except construct (which handles the exception).

Using the *try...except* Construct   The try...except construct is used to trap an exception, and then optionally "handle" this exception, which frees the exception object instance and continues processing normally. The try...except construct has an optional extension to its syntax that allows you to determine the specific type of exception that occurred. This optional syntax takes the form of on...do (discussed in the following section).

Suppose that you're writing a program that uses the RTL function ChDir. By default, ChDir raises an exception of type EInOutError if the drive/directory passed is invalid. You can use ChDir in conjunction with a try...except construct to determine on what drive a particular directory exists, as in the following example:

```
procedure TForm1.Button1Click(Sender: TObject);
var iCtr: integer;
begin
  for iCtr := Ord('A') to Ord('Z') do
    try
      ChDir(Char(iCtr)+':\DUKE3D');
      MessageDlg('Found \DUKE3D on drive '+Char(iCtr),
                 mtInformation,[mbOK],0);
      Break;
    except
      MessageDlg('\DUKE3D not found on drive '+Char(iCtr),
                 mtError,[mbOK],0);
    end;
end;
```

Here, the `Button1Click` method uses a `for...do` construct to iterate through the drive letters A to Z. Each pass calls the RTL function `ChDir`, passing the drive letter plus a directory named DUKE3D. When `ChDir` is called, if the drive/directory is invalid, an exception of type `EInOutError` is raised. Program execution jumps to the first line of code following the `except` directive. In this example, a message is displayed to the user, stating that the drive/directory is invalid. The call to `MessageDlg` and `Break` that immediately follow `ChDir` never will get executed if `ChDir` always fails. However, if the drive/directory is found, they execute, resulting in a break out of the loop and normal termination of the method.

The act of catching the error in the `except` statements causes the compiler to resolve the exception. The exception will not continue to raise unless you specifically tell it to. This is the main contrast between `try...except` and `try...finally`. `try...finally` allows the exception to continue to raise up the call stack until it reaches the first level of encapsulating `except` statements or the global handler.

Using the *on...do* Construct   The `try...except` construct contains an optional syntax that allows you to determine exactly what type of exception occurred as well as to retrieve a reference to the exception object instance. With this instance, you can access the public and published members of the object. The optional syntax comes in the form of another construct. This construct is `on...do`.

The `on...do` construct is valid only between the `except` directive and terminating `end;` of a `try...except` construct. The following shows its syntax:

```
try
  {statements go here}
except
  on E: Exception do
    {Statement or begin..statements..end }
  else
    {Statement or begin..statements..end }
end;
```

Use `on...do` when your exception processing should branch depending on the type of exception that is raised. Alternatively, use it to handle expected exceptions and re-raise unexpected exceptions. Consider the following:

```
procedure TForm1.Button2Click(Sender: TObject);
var pVal: PChar;
begin
  try
    GetMem(pVal,sizeof(Stream.Memory^));
    StrLCopy(pVal,Stream.Memory,sizeof(Stream.Memory^)+1);
  except
    On E: EOutOfMemory do
      LowMemTerminate;
    On E: EAccessViolation do
    begin
      if MessageDlg(E.Message+': Terminate the program?',
                    mtError,[mbYes,mbNo],0) = mrYes then
        Application.Terminate
    end
    else
        Raise;
  end;
end;
```

Here, enough memory is allocated to pVal to store a copy of the memory in the hypothetical global TMemoryStream variable Stream. Then, the memory in Stream is copied by using StrLCopy. There are two places here that may result in an exception being raised. If Stream is too big, GetMem may fail and raise an exception of type EOutOfMemory. If GetMem is successful, then StrLCopy will fail anyway because the Size parameter is 1 byte more than was allocated by using GetMem. In this case, an exception of type EAccessViolation will be raised. Whichever exception occurs, this code handles it.

The example uses two on...do constructs in a fashion similar to a case...of construct. When the exception occurs, the type is checked against EOutOfMemory. If the raised exception object instance is not of that type, it's checked to see if it's of type EAccessViolation. If it is not, the statement following the else executes. Then the exception is re-raised by calling the Raise statement, in which case the exception continues to raise up the call stack, ultimately to the Application object's global handler.

The E after On is a reference to the exception object instance and can be used to access any of the object's public or published members. This is shown in the call to the MessageDlg function. Do not call the Free method for the instance because this is done automatically.

Rather than using a series of on...dos, you can write basically the same code by using a single on...do in conjunction with a dynamic-type check. Consider the following example:

```
procedure TForm1.Button3Click(Sender: TObject);
var pVal: PChar;
begin
  try
    GetMem(pVal,sizeof(Stream.Memory^));
    StrLCopy(pVal,Stream.Memory,sizeof(Stream.Memory^)+1);
  except
    On E: Exception do
    begin
      if E is EOutOfMemory then
        LowMemTerminate;
```

Part

I

Ch

5

```
      if E is EAccessViolation then
      begin
        if MessageDlg(E.Message+': Terminate the program?',
                      mtError,[mbYes,mbNo],0) = mrYes then
          Application.Terminate;
      end
      else
        Raise;
    end;
  end;
end;
```

In this example, On E:Exception is used once, which translates to "give me all exceptions of any type." The reference E then is type-checked by using the is operator against the two types of exceptions expected. If the exception is neither of these types and is not a descendant of at least one of these types, the statement that follows the else directive executes. The single statement Raise is called, which causes the exception to re-raise to the next level of handling.

Nesting *try* Blocks   Delphi allows you to logically nest the try constructs. The try...finally construct can be nested within a try...except construct and the try...except construct can be similarly nested within the try...finally construct. The restriction is that the inner construct must be completely encapsulated between the try directive and closing finally or except directive. The following syntax is completely valid:

```
try
  {statements}
  try
    {statements}
  finally
    {statements}
  end;
  {statements}
except
  {statements}
end;
```

The reverse of this syntax also is valid:

```
try
  {statements}
  try
    {statements}
  except
    {statements}
  end;
  {statements}
finally
  {statements}
end;
```

The preceding two examples are valid because each construct is completely nested within the correct area of the other. The following example is not valid:

```
try
  {statements}
  try
    {statements}
  except
    {statements}
finally
  {statements}
end;
  {statements}
  end;
```

If you really understand each construct, it is clear why this example is not valid even if the compiler allows it. Listing 5.2 shows a common use of nesting try blocks.

Listing 5.2 is an example of nesting a try...finally within a try...except.

Listing 5.2   \UDELPHI3\CHP5\UNIT1.PAS—Nesting a *try...finally* in a *try...except*

```
procedure TForm1.Button4Click(Sender: TObject);
var sVar: string;
    pVar: PChar;
begin
  try
    GetMem(pVar,10);
    try
      StrCopy(pVar,'ListBox');
      with ListBox1.Items do
      begin
        Add('Line1 - index 0');
        Add('Line2 - index 1');
      end;
      sVar := ListBox1.Items[2];
      {some more statements that use sVar and pVar}
    finally
      FreeMem(pVar,10);
    end;
  except
    on EStringListError do
      MessageDlg('List index out of bounds', mtError, [mbOk], 0);
    on EAccessViolation do
      MessageDlg('Memory Overwrite', mtError, [mbOk], 0);
    else
      Raise;
  end;
end;
```

Part
I
Ch
5

Listing 5.2 allocates 10 bytes of memory to pVar. The string 'ListBox' is copied to the pVar buffer using StrCopy. Next, two strings are added to ListBox1. The items property of TListBox is used to retrieve one of the strings now in the list. The problem is this code forgets that indexing begins at 0 and ends at 1. The code passes a 2 to the items array, which attempts to return the third (nonexistent) element:

```
sVar := ListBox1.Items[2];
```

The result is an EStringList exception. Because the exception occurs within a try...finally construct, the call to FreeMem executes despite the exception. This call releases the memory allocated to pVar. Because try...finally does not actually "handle" (or resolve) the exception, it raises to the next level of handling—in this case try...except. The on...do specifically looks for the EStringListError exception type, and then executes its call to MessageDlg.

The example includes checking for EAccessViolation in addition to EStringList. If the following call were actually valid, any statements you insert after this line that manipulate pVal could potentially result in an EAccessViolation:

```
sVar := ListBox1.Items[2];
```

Wherever GetMem is used, you should automatically include checking for the EAccessViolation exception type. But what if an exception occurs within the handling of an exception? What if both GetMem and FreeMem fail? If the call to GetMem failed due to lack of resources, an EOutOfMemory error would occur. The finally would execute with the call to FreeMem. This execution potentially results in yet another type of error (EInvalidPointerOperation or still maybe EAccessViolation) because FreeMem would try to free a pointer that was never successfully allocated. In this scenario, EAccessViolation is the only type of exception that will be raised. If the exception is EOutOfResources, you probably are going to bail out of the application, anyway. Given this, the else portion of the on...do executes, which calls Raise explicitly, which re-raises the exception to the next level of handling. In this case, it would be the global handler.

In contrast to the previous example, you can position a try...except within a try...finally construct, as shown in Listing 5.3.

Listing 5.3   \UDELPHI3\CHP5\EXCEPTU1.PAS— Nesting a *try...except* in a *try...finally*

```
procedure TForm1.Button5Click(Sender: TObject);
var sVar: string;
    pVar: PChar;
begin
  GetMem(pVar,10);
  try
    StrCopy(pVar,'ListBox');
    {Statements that manipulate pVar here}
    try
      sVar := ListBox1.Items[0];
      {Statements that manipulate sVar or pVar here}
    except
```

```
      on EStringListError do
      begin
        ListBox1.Items.Add('Item1');
        sVar := ListBox1.Items[0];
      end
      else Raise;
    end;
    {Statements that manipulate sVar here}
  finally
    FreeMem(pVar,10);
  end;
end;
```

Listing 5.3 allocates 10 bytes of memory to the buffer pVar. This example is different than Listing 5.2 in that all memory allocation errors are excepted to be raised to the global handler. The call to StrCopy attempts to copy a string into pVar. If the copy fails, the execution jumps to the line following the finally directive, thus executing FreeMem. The exception then continues to raise. If StrCopy is successful, an attempt is made to extract the first item in ListBox1. If ListBox1 is empty, an exception of type EStringListError is raised. The on...do code captures this error, appends an item into the listbox, and then retrieves the value. Processing continues to the call to FreeMem.

If the following statement happens to be valid, and you had inserted more code after this statement, potentially more exception types could be raised:

```
sVar := ListBox1.Items[0];
```

This is why we look specifically for EStringListError. If the exception were of another type, it would be re-raised and captured by the outer try...finally construct. This causes the FreeMem statement to execute, and thereby releases the heap-allocated memory. The exception continues to raise to the next level of handling or the global exception-handler.

Raising Exceptions

Throughout this chapter, you saw the term "Raise" used frequently. *Raise* is a directive and a special part of Delphi's exception-based syntax. Raise is used to create an instance of the Exception class or of a class that descends from the Exception class type.

Raise is useful in many situations. Previously in this chapter, the authors made use of a hypothetical function named InsertChar. Here is what InsertChar might have looked like with the use of the raise syntax:

```
function InsertChar(cVal: char; var sVal: string; iPos: integer): boolean;
begin
  Result := False;
  if iPos <= Length(sVal) then
  begin
    sVal[iPos] := cVal;
    Result := True;
  end;
end;
```

Here, `InsertChar` is a function that returns `True` on success and `False` on failure, requiring any code that uses it to validate the call by checking the return value. `InsertChar` can be converted to use exceptions, so that the caller can use the `try` constructs if the functions fail. Consider the following modifications:

```
procedure InsertChar(cVal: char; var sVal: string; iPos: integer);
begin
  if iPos > Length(sVal) then
    Raise Exception.Create('Out of Range');
  sVal[iPos] := cVal;
end;
```

Both examples perform length checking on the var string `sVal`. In the first example, the function returns `False` if length checking fails. In the second example, `InsertChar` is converted to a procedure as an exception is raised if the function fails. The execution of code stops at the point the exception is raised. The following statement never gets called if the length checking fails:

```
sVal[iPos] := cVal;
```

What is interesting about this is it provides a mechanism to simulate an early return without making a call to the RTL Exit procedure (which has no way to inform you that the call failed). Use of early returns is historically a questionable programming style but is quite useful in some instances. This is true in the execution of certain VCL events like `OnBeforePost`, which stops the posting of a record if it is invalid. Early returns are also necessary in the implementation of State logic in State Machine code such as that used in Expert Analysis systems.

The `Raise` syntax is as follows:

```
Raise <Instance>;
```

`Raise` acts like the variable that receives a dynamic instantiation but directs the compiler to break the flow of execution and unwind the call stack. Consider the following:

```
Button1 := TButton.Create(Self);
```

The preceding example shows the dynamic instantiation of a `Button` object. Compare it to the following:

```
Raise Exception.Create('An Error Has Occurred');
```

The two statements appear very similar. The most noticeable difference syntactically is that the `Raise` syntax doesn't use the `:=` operator. Of course, the most important difference is in how they behave. The authors certainly wouldn't expect instantiation of a button to cause an early return and its instance be raised up through the call stack to the global exception-handler. Of course, if the instantiation of a button failed, an exception object instance would be created that may give this appearance.

The Silent Exception

Delphi provides yet another feature in its exception-handling architecture—the use of *silent exceptions*. Silent exceptions are any exception object instances that are instantiated from the

EAbort class or from a class descending from EAbort. Use of the EAbort exception prevents an exception from being raised beyond the first level of its use. You can use EAbort to instigate an early return to avoid redundant processing. Consider the following:

```
var Delphi: string;

procedure SetDelphiVariable(sValue: string);
begin
  if Delphi = sValue then
    Raise EAbort.Create('');

  if (Length(sValue) > 0) and (Length(sValue) < 50) then
    Delphi := sValue;
end;

procedure TForm1.Button6Click(Sender: TObject);
begin
  SetDelphiVariable('Anders Hejlsberg');
end;
```

The Button6Click method calls a function SetDelphiVariable passing a string. The purpose of SetDelphiVariable is to do some validation on the received variable sValue before assigning it to the global variable Delphi. If the validation is successful, the Delphi variable is set to the value of sValue. However, if the variable Delphi is already the same value as sValue, the validation and assignment results in redundant processing if no checking is performed. SetDelphiVariable remedies this situation by checking sValue up front for a string equal to what is currently stored in the Delphi variable. If the Delphi variable is in fact equal to sValue, an exception of type EAbort is raised, thus returning immediately without the extra processing.

Notice that the call to SetDelphiVariable in the Button6Click method is not wrapped in a try construct. You may expect the exception to be raised to the global handler assigned to Application.OnException. With EAbort, this is not the case, because EAbort is the "Silent Exception." If you decided to wrap the call in a try construct, the except or finally statements execute as excepted. Additionally, you could re-raise the exception to the next level.

The Exception Base Class

This chapter has talked a lot about the Exception class defined in the SYSUTILS unit. Now it is time to look at it. If you recall from previously in this chapter, the on...do construct allows you to use E: to retrieve a reference to the exception instance. With a new global handler assigned to Application.OnException, the TExceptionEvent type gives you a variable EInstance in the second parameter, which is also the exception instance. But what good is a reference to an instance of an Exception object? Because an object is an instance, or instantiation, of a class, when you have a reference to it you can access any public or published members. Listing 5.4 shows the interface portion of the Exception class, as currently declared in the SYSUTILS unit.

> **Listing 5.4   \UDELPHI3\CHP5\SYSUTILS.PAS—All Other Exceptions Descend from the *Exception* Class Type**

```
{ Exceptions }

  Exception = class(TObject)
  private
    FMessage: string;
    FHelpContext: Integer;
  public
    constructor Create(const Msg: string);
    constructor CreateFmt(const Msg: string; const Args: array of const);
    constructor CreateRes(Ident: Integer);
    constructor CreateResFmt(Ident: Integer; const Args: array of const);
    constructor CreateHelp(const Msg: string; AHelpContext: Integer);
    constructor CreateFmtHelp(const Msg: string; const Args: array of const;
      AHelpContext: Integer);
    constructor CreateResHelp(Ident: Integer; AHelpContext: Integer);
    constructor CreateResFmtHelp(Ident: Integer; const Args: array of const;
      AHelpContext: Integer);
    property HelpContext: Integer read FHelpContext write FHelpContext;
    property Message: string read FMessage write FMessage;
  end;
```

The Exception class is a base class to all of the other exception types. EAbort, EAccessViolation, EInvalidPointerOperation, and many others descend from it. Exception contains the base functionality for any exception class by providing a series of useful constructors. It also can hold a message string retrievable from the public Message property. If an exception is raised while debugging and a help context ID is assigned to the HelpContext property, the IDE will seek out the appropriate topic for the user to view.

Exception Class Constructors

The Exception class makes eight different static constructors available to use. These constructors are useful when your code needs to raise an exception of any type. Each constructor is different in the parameters it accepts, but all result in achieving the same purpose—to instantiate the instance and store a string that describes the nature of the exception. It is this string that can be retrieved via the Message property. This is the same string the IDE shows when it breaks if an exception occurs in debugging mode. And finally, you see this string if no exception handling is in place forcing the Application object to call it ShowException method.

The Create constructor is used most often while developing your application. It takes a single string in its only parameter. This is the constructor shown thus far in this chapter. The CreateFmt constructor also takes a string, but it expects the string to contain a format specifier and an open array of arguments to assign to each specifier (search Delphi's online help for "format strings" for more information on format specifiers). The CreateRes constructor requires an ID in its parameter. The ID is used internally to retrieve a string from the string resource table compiled into the executable (see the `LoadStr` function in the online help for more information). This is handy when it's time to localize your application. The remaining constructors combine, in variation, each of the constructs discussed.

Creating New Exception Types

All exceptions descend from the `Exception` base class. Because exceptions come in the form of classes, new exception classes can be easily created and raised in your applications. There are two reasons you may want to descend from the `Exception` class:

- Add functionality to the `Exception` class
- Provide a mechanism to do specific dynamic type checking.

I think each constructor in the `Exception` class should have provided an `ErrorCode` parameter by default. In this way, when a reference to the exception object instance is retrieved, it can be checked for a specific indication of the error without having to use dynamic type checking, as you would otherwise have to in any code you attach to `Application.OnException`. To avoid the rather inefficient use of dynamic type checking, some people do a string comparison using the `Message` property, as follows:

```
procedure TGlobalExHandler.HandlerProc(Sender: TObject; EInstance: Exception);
begin
  if pos('EOutOfResource',EInstance.Message) > 0 then
    {an EOutOfResource error occurred - response code goes here}
end;
```

If an error code was provided, the numeric values for each exception can be declared as constants. In this way, a case statement can be used to determine the type of exception that occurred. Consider the following example:

```
procedure TGlobalExHandler.HandlerProc(Sender: TObject; EInstance: Exception);
begin
  if Sender is EMyComponentError then
    case (Sender as TComponent).Tag of
      cInvalidValue: {statements for appropriate action here};
      cRangeError  : {statements for appropriate action here};
    else
      begin
        ShowMessage('Fatal Error - Terminating program');
        Application.Terminate;
      end;
    end;
end;
```

In this example, a single dynamic type check determines if the exception is of the custom `EMyComponentException` type or a descendant of it. If so, it uses a `case...of` construct to determine what course of action to take, depending on the value of the `ErrorCode` property. If the `ErrorCode` is unknown, a message is displayed to the user, and then the application terminates. Listing 5.5 shows what the custom exception descendant class `EMyComponentError` might look like.

Part I

Ch 5

Listing 5.5   \UDELPHI3\CHP5\PROJECT1.DPR—Adding Functionality to the Base *Exception* Class by Creating a New Type

```
type
  EMyComponentError = class(Exception)
  private
    FErrorCode: integer;
  public
    property ErrorCode: integer read FErrorCode write FErrorCode;
    constructor Create(const Msg: string; ErrCode: integer);
  end;
...
implementation
...
constructor EMyComponentError.Create(const Msg: string; ErrCode: integer);
begin
  Inherited Create(Msg);
  FErrorCode := ErrCode;
end;
...
end.
```

Listing 5.5 creates a new exception type named EMyComponentError, which descends directly from the Exception class. It adds a property named ErrorCode that directly reads and writes FErrorCode. A new static constructor, Create, is created that has one more parameter than the ancestor Create. This parameter is an error code that ultimately will be accessible via the ErrorCode property. The code to raise this new exception type will look like the following:

```
...
Raise EMyComponentError.Create('Value is out of range', cRangeError);
...
```

You may want to create a new exception class so that you can better identify the cause of the error by using dynamic type checking. Consider the following:

```
procedure TGlobalExHandler.HandlerProc(Sender: TObject; EInstance: Exception);
begin
  if Sender is EMyComponentError then
  begin
    if Sender is EMyCompoRangeError then
      {statements for appropriate action here}
    else
    if Sender is EMyCompoInvalidValue then
      {statements for appropriate action here};
  end
  else
    begin
      ShowMessage('Fatal Error - Terminating program');
      Application.Terminate;
    end;
end;
```

This code first checks for `EMyComponentError`. If the error is of type `EMyComponentError`, more type checking is used to determine exactly what type of error occurred. The second level of checking is against two more custom types:

```
type
  EMyCompoRangeError = class(EMyComponentError);
  EMyCompoInvalidValue = class(EMyComponentError);
```

Unlike `EMyComponentError`, `EMyCompoRangeError` and `EMyCompoInvalidValue` do not descend directly from the `Exception` class. Rather, they descend from `EMyComponentError`, which allows you to first check if the raise exception could logically be of either type by looking for the hierarchical ancestor `EMyComponent`. If the this test evaluates to False, there is no reason to look for the more specific `EMyCompoRangeError` or `EMyCompoInvalidValue`.

Summary

This chapter discussed Delphi's implementation of exception handling, its constructs, their use, and the overall importance of this topic. Exception handling will come into play in many areas of this book as well as when using Delphi for each project you create. More often than not, you will use the discussed `try...except` and `try...finally` constructs. The creation of custom exception types will be used mostly when you create custom components. No matter what your implementation, the implementation of a custom global exception-handler should be incorporated into all your projects. ●

Part
I

Ch
5

Application Development

CHAPTER 6

Using Delphi Components

by Mark Pritchard

The *component* is an integral part of application development with Delphi. Components form the basis of your application's user interface, and allow you to build intuitive and complex programs quickly, with minimal effort. ■

Common properties and events

Due to Delphi's superb object-oriented structure, most visual components derive their basic functionality from several objects—`TControl`, `TWinControl`, and `TGraphicControl`. This section covers the properties and events provided by these objects.

Interface design components

Many visual components add properties and events to the set inherited from `TControl`, `TWinControl`, and `TGraphicControl`. This section discusses these additions and shows you the common uses for each of the components in the Component Palette.

System components

Generally classed as non-visual or wrapper components, system components allow you to rapidly build an application's logic. This section covers which aspects of the system these components wrap, and how to use them.

N O T E Your Delphi box should contain a pictorial view of the major players in the object hierarchy. It makes a wonderful wall hanging that doesn't just look good—it's also extremely informative. ▨

Interface design and system components are also respectively known as visual and non-visual components. The distinction is as follows:

■ **Interface design/Visual**—These components are visible both at design-time and run-time. They may display data and accept input from the mouse. More complex visual components allow you to enter text, select an item from a list, or provide advanced mouse handling. These components are documented further in this chapter, under "Visual Components."

N O T E Visual components from Delphi's component palette are commonly called "controls," presumably because they are used to control an application. As with most things, there is an exception—an OLE/ActiveX control may be invisible and not respond to keyboard or mouse input! OLE/ActiveX controls are covered in more detail in Chapters 18 through 21. ▨

■ **System/Non-visual**—These components are visible at design-time, and invisible at runtime. Generally, non-visual components act as abstractions for a large set of related functionality, and are known as "wrappers." They present system-level callback functions as events of a component, and shoehorn complex record formats into component properties. Non-visual components are covered in greater detail in the section, "Non-Visual Components."

N O T E Strangely, a non-visual component may display something on-screen, such as a dialog box. The "non-visual" description simply means the component itself is invisible at runtime. ▨

Several pages of the component palette are not covered in this chapter, and can be found elsewhere in the book:

Page	Chapter
CommCtrl	7, "Using Win32 Common Controls"
Data Access	9, "Working with Local Databases"
	10, "Working with SQL Databases"
Data Controls	9, "Working with Local Databases"

The Win3.1 page of the component palette contains several components supplied with the first version of Delphi. These components were superseded by the subsequent releases of Delphi, and should not be used in new projects. *Special Edition Using Delphi 1* documents these components, should you need to convert an old project to Delphi 3.

Chapters 18 through 21 cover the components located on the ActiveX page, and Chapter 28, "Creating Web Server Applications," documents the components found on the Internet page.

Visual Components

For some time, Graphic User Interfaces (GUIs) used basic screen elements such as buttons, edit boxes, and lists. The continual refinement of application interfaces added screen elements such as Speedbars, status bars, and multipage dialogs to Windows-based programs. Operating systems such as Windows 95 contributed to interface design by popularizing pop-up menus and the three-dimensional look.

The Delphi component library neatly wraps up these screen elements into controls, allowing you to include them in your application with minimal fuss. You only have to worry about making your interface both intuitive and functional.

Common Properties and Events

As you may have guessed, Delphi is object-oriented. Object orientation allows controls to share basic sets of functionality and to introduce new behavior or customize features of their parent control type. With this in mind, all controls such as TListBox, TEdit, and TButton share the functionality of their common ancestor, TControl.

N O T E   Don't expect every TControl descendant to make all properties, methods, and events available. Controls such as TShape do not publish the Font property because they do not display text. ■

TControl **Properties**   The TControl object provides many properties useful to all controls.

Align   The Align property is an enumerated value which determines the control's position and size within its parent control (or form). It is useful to maintain a constant relative position for a control when its parent changes size. The status panel at the bottom of the Code Editor window has its Align property set to alBottom, and fills the bottom of the window, no matter what its size or position.

Caption   The Caption property contains a string, used to determine the control's label. To illustrate, consider a TButton control. Rather than being a featureless, beveled square, you may set its Caption property to indicate its function. Figure 6.1 shows a standard open file dialog box, with several buttons. The Open button's caption is, not surprisingly, "Open".

N O T E   Underlined letters in captions indicate an accelerator key combination. Holding the Alt key down and pressing the indicated letter is equivalent to clicking the control with the mouse. To specify an accelerator key, simply include an ampersand (&) character before your chosen letter. To illustrate, the Caption property of an Open button will be set to "&Open." ■

Color   The Color integer property determines the basic color of the control. Although you can create some incredibly gaudy color schemes, Color is best left alone for standard controls and forms. If you decide to alter a control's color, consider the fact that you may change the desktop color scheme with the Control Panel. Objects of non-standard color will not reflect the new color scheme in a consistent manner. If you simply must change a Color property, try to use one of the enumerated values for various system colors, such as clBtnHighlight.

FIG. 6.1

The standard open file dialog box uses several visual components.

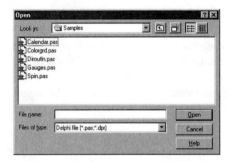

> **N O T E**   If you set the Color property to a value unavailable in the current palette, Windows approximates the color by dithering, which usually looks terrible. Try to avoid custom colors unless you know the target machine supports a large palette. ▪

DragCursor *and* DragMode   These enumerated properties are useful for programming drag-and-drop operations. The DragCursor property allows you to specify the shape of the mouse cursor when it passes over a control that will accept the dragged object. The DragMode property determines how Delphi handles the beginning of a drag operation. If it's set to dmAutomatic, the control may be dragged at any time. If you set it to dmManual, you must manually begin and end the drag process. The following code provides an example:

```
procedure TForm1.ListBox1Click(Sender: TObject);
begin
    if ListBox1.SelCount >= 2 then
        ListBox1.BeginDrag(False);
end;
```

In this code fragment, the TListBox object named ListBox1 has its DragMode property set to dmManual and its MultiSelect property set to True. When the user clicks the control, the OnClick event handler checks whether at least two items were selected from the list before beginning the drag operation. The argument passed to the BeginDrag method determines whether dragging begins immediately (True) or waits until the mouse cursor has moved at least five pixels (False).

Font   The Font object property specifies the font used to display the control's Caption or Text properties.

Because Font is an object property, you should use the Assign method to set it to a new value. This example assigns a new font to the form on which the TFontDialog component named fntdlgFont resides:

```
Font.Assign(fntdlgSelect.Font);
```

ParentColor, ParentFont, *and* ParentShowHint   These Boolean properties indicate that the control should take its values for Color, Font, and ShowHint from its parent control. This practice gives your interface a consistent, uniform look.

PopupMenu   A feature popularized by Windows 95, a pop-up menu is a small, topic-sensitive menu that allows you to quickly select a commonly used command. The PopupMenu property simply specifies the TPopupMenu component activated when you right-click a control.

Text   The Text property is similar to Caption in that it stores a string that specifies the text displayed by the control. Text differs from Caption in that Text represents a string that you may directly modify, such as that found in the TEdit control, while Caption cannot be altered.

***TControl* Events**   Remember that events are notifications of a particular situation having arisen, which you trap to provide your interface functionality.

Because a TControl is a visual object, you expect to use a mouse to interact with it. To accommodate this, TControl provides the following three types of mouse events:

- Selection
- Movement
- Drag and Drop

Selection *Events*   A selection event is triggered when you use a mouse button while the mouse cursor is over a control. The selection events are shown in the following list:

- OnClick—The OnClick event is triggered when you press the left mouse button.

N O T E   Controls may define additional situations in which OnClick is triggered. An example for the TButton control is pressing the spacebar while it has focus. ▪

- OnDblClick—The OnDblClick event is generated when you click a control with the left mouse button twice within the "double-click" interval. The double-click interval defines the time period in which the second click must occur to be interpreted as a double-click, rather than as two separate single clicks.

N O T E   Certain controls allow you to connect event handlers to both OnClick and OnDblClick. Try to resist the temptation to do this! An object that performs two different tasks depending on how quickly you press the mouse button is a poor choice in interface design. Use two controls instead. ▪

- OnMouseDown and OnMouseUp—These events allow more complex mouse handling to take place. OnMouseDown is fired as soon as you press either mouse button, and OnMouseUp is triggered when you release it.

You may expect the above events to occur in the predictable order of an OnMouseDown and OnMouseUp pair that precedes either an OnClick or OnDblClick event. This is not the case. The order, for a double-click, is as follows:

1. OnMouseDown
2. OnClick
3. OnMouseUp

4. OnDblClick

5. OnMouseDown

6. OnMouseUp

N O T E   A single click simply generates events 1 to 3, in the listed order. ■

As much as you may scratch your head, this order really is logical. An OnMouseDown event is always followed by an OnMouseUp event (you eventually must either release the button or walk around with the mouse stuck to your hand). With this in mind, Delphi is free to order events by priority rather than by detection sequence. The OnClick event is more important than OnMouseUp, and should be processed first. OnDblClick is of higher priority than both OnMouseDown and OnMouseUp.

Delphi also allows you to generate selection and movement events manually, in any desired order. This is useful when you want to artificially produce a situation, such as clicking a TButton control. You may call the event handler just as you call any other method. The following code demonstrates this:

```
btnLoad.Click(Self);
```

This statement executes the OnClick event for the TButton control named btnLoad. The OnClick event is of type TNotifyEvent and requires a Sender parameter. Here, you can just pass the Self object, which points to the TForm that owns btnLoad. If you were calling another type of event handler, such as TKeyEvent, you must provide the arguments it expects.

Movement   Controls trigger an event named OnMouseMove when the mouse cursor moves while in their display area. The event handler is passed the coordinates of the mouse cursor. Many image manipulation programs, such as Paint, use the OnMouseMove event to display the coordinates of the mouse cursor in an image. The following code provides an example of this:

```
procedure TForm1.Image1MouseMove(Sender: TObject; Shift: TShiftState;
➥                               X, Y: Integer);
begin
   Panel1.Caption := '('+IntToStr(X)+','+IntToStr(Y)+')';
end;
```

This code fragment uses the OnMouseMove event of a TImage control. It sets the Caption property of a TPanel control named Panel1 to the coordinates of the mouse cursor. These coordinates are relative to the upper left corner of the TImage control.

N O T E   Delphi sends two additional movement messages to a control—CM_MOUSEENTER and CM_MOUSELEAVE. These messages indicate when the mouse enters and leaves the display area of a control, and must be manually trapped. This process is covered further in Chapter 4, "Object Pascal: Advanced Concepts," and Chapter 16, "Creating Components." ■

Drag-and-Drop Basics   The concept of drag and drop allows you to drag an object to another location on a form or even into a different application. Usually, the following two controls are involved in a drag-and-drop operation:

■ **Source**—The source control holds the item being dragged. Your application may define the drag item as either the whole control, such as an image, or just a selected portion, such as the currently selected line in a TListBox.

■ **Destination**—The destination control is the location onto which the source item will be dropped.

The entire operation may be handled with the following three events:

■ OnDragOver—The OnDragOver event is triggered by the destination control when you drag an object over it. Arguments passed to the event handler are: the source object, the current location of the mouse cursor, and the drag state. This allows the destination control to either accept or reject the source item. The drag state indicates whether the dragged object has entered the control, is being moved around in the control's area, or has just left the control's area without being dropped.

■ OnDragDrop—The OnDragDrop event is triggered by the destination control when you drop an object on it. To allow your application to process the drag and drop easily, the event handler is passed the source object and the current mouse location.

■ OnEndDrag—The OnEndDrag event is generated by the source control when you complete a drag-and-drop operation. The event handler is passed the destination object, and the location at which the object was dropped.

TIP Some controls define an additional event, OnStartDrag, fired by the source control when a drag-and-drop operation commences.

The events occur in the following order:

1. OnStartDrag for the source control
2. OnDragOver for the destination control
3. OnDragDrop for the destination control
4. OnEndDrag for the source control

Programming Drag-and-Drop Operations   Drag-and-drop operations can be programmed by writing two event handlers and setting a single property. Imagine that you have two TListBox controls—ListBox1 and ListBox2. Ensure that the DragMode property for ListBox1 is set to dmAutomatic, which reduces your work—you don't need to worry about calling BeginDrag.

Now, to write those event handlers. The first event handler determines whether the drag operation is accepted by ListBox2. The following event handler takes care of this:

```
procedure TForm1.ListBox2DragOver(Sender, Source: TObject;
 X, Y: Integer; State: TDragState; var Accept: Boolean);
begin
   if Source = ListBox1 then
      Accept := True;
end;
```

This code fragment checks whether the Source object is ListBox1, and if so, sets the Accept argument to True.

Now that ListBox2 accepts the drop, it's a good idea to do something with the dropped items. This event handler simply adds the selected/dragged item from ListBox1 to ListBox2:

```
procedure TForm1.ListBox2DragDrop(Sender, Source: TObject;
 X, Y: Integer);
begin
   with Source as TListBox do
       ListBox2.Items.Add(Items[ItemIndex]);
end;
```

TWinControl and TGraphicControl

Although the set of objects deriving from TControl is quite large, they may all be classified into one of two groups—windowed controls, documented in "TWinControl," and non-windowed controls, covered further in "TGraphicControl."

TWinControl   TWinControl provides basic functionality for those components who want to receive input focus, or keyboard input. An excellent example is the TEdit component, which provides a window into which you may type text. The TListBox component, displayed as a scrolling list of strings, also can receive focus because the selection bar may be moved with the directional cursor keys.

N O T E   A component may indicate it has input focus in two ways:

- **Edit cursor**—For text-based components, the current text insertion point is marked by an application defined bitmap, known as the edit cursor. This cursor may be moved with the directional cursor keys. The default edit cursor is a flashing vertical line.

- **Focus rectangle**—This component draws a dotted line, the focus rectangle, around currently selected text. For example, a TButton surrounds its caption with a focus rectangle, while a TListBox highlights the currently selected row in the list. ▪

N O T E   In a component with multiple items, such as a TListBox, the focus rectangle is often supplemented by drawing the selected item in a different color. ▪

So why is this type of control called TWinControl and not TFocusControl or something similar? Remember that a *form* is just a Delphi encapsulation of a standard window. Components able to receive input focus also are windows—a TButton control is simply a button-style window wrapped up in a Delphi component. These components are known as "windowed controls," giving the "Win" in TWinControl.

Another advantage to windowed controls is that they can contain other windows or controls. You have already seen this in practice when you drop components on a form—the form acts as the parent window for the components.

TWinControl *Properties*   TWinControl adds the following properties to TControl:

- Ctl3D and ParentCtl3D—This Boolean property determines whether the control will "look" two- or three-dimensional. Three-dimensional interfaces have become very popular for two simple reasons—they look great, and they are used extensively in Windows 95. Two-dimensional interfaces are "out"—the third dimension is "in." ParentCtl3D indicates the control is to use the Ctl3D value of its parent control.

- Enabled—The Enabled property uses a Boolean to determine whether the control accepts input from the mouse and keyboard. A disabled control will not trigger mouse or keyboard events, and generally appears dimmed or grayed.

- Handle—The Handle property is basically an integer that represents the window handle of a control. A window handle is used to provide each window with a unique identifier. The operating system notifies a window of an event, such as a mouse click or key press, by sending the window a message, via its handle. Many low-level Windows API functions require a control's window handle.

- HelpContext—This property specifies the control's help context number, which links the control to a specific screen in a help file. The help system is activated when you press the F1 key while the control has focus.

- TabOrder and TabStop—The TabOrder property is an integer used to determine the control's numerical position in the tab sequence. TabStop is a Boolean that determines whether the control should honor its position in the tab sequence or to just pass focus to the next control.

TWinControl *Events*   The TWinControl object adds the following two types of events to TControl:

- **Focus change**—*Focus change events* notify the control of a change in its possession of input focus. OnEnter is triggered when the control gains focus, through a mouse click on its surface, or being next in the tab sequence. OnExit is generated when the control loses focus, through a mouse click on another control, or when the Tab key is pressed (indicating a jump to the next control in the tab sequence).

- **Keyboard**—Delphi provides notification of three keyboard events:

  OnKeyDown—A control generates an OnKeyDown event when you press a key while the control has focus. The event handler is passed the virtual key code of the key. A virtual key code represents a constant numeric identifier for each key, kindly translated by Windows from the shifting values returned by each type of keyboard.

  OnKeyUp—The OnKeyUp event is generated when you release a key. The event handler is passed the virtual key code and the current state of the keyboard.

TIP Virtual key codes for alphanumeric keys are equal to the key's ASCII value.

Part
II

Ch
6

> **N O T E**   A control continually triggers `OnKeyDown` and `OnKeyUp` alternately while the key is held down. ■

`OnKeyPress`—The `OnKeyPress` is triggered when a key is pressed and released. Just to make things different, the event handler is passed the ASCII value of the pressed key. You may change this value by modifying the `Key` argument passed to the event handler. This really is useful only in one special case—if the current key press is not in a desired set, you may set the `Key` argument to character zero, which deletes the key press. The following `OnKeyPress` event handler ensures that the user cannot enter a capital `'Z'` into a `TEdit` control named `Edit1`:

```
procedure TForm1.Edit1KeyPress(Sender: TObject; var Key: Char);
begin
    if Key = 'Z' then
        Key := #0;
end;
```

The keyboard events for a single key press occur in the following order:

1. `OnKeyDown`
2. `OnKeyPress`
3. `OnKeyUp`

The keyboard events share the same priority-based ordering scheme as the mouse selection events discussed in a previous section, "Selection Events." Because you eventually must release a key, Delphi is free to generate an `OnKeyPress` event as soon as the key is pressed, rather than waiting for it to be detected.

TGraphicControl   Like `TWinControl`, `TGraphicControl` objects also descend from `TControl`. A `TGraphicControl` component doesn't require the services of the keyboard, and does away with the Windows-imposed overhead associated with `TWinControl` derivatives. The `TImage` component, which displays images, is an example of a `TGraphicControl`. The `TSpeedButton` component descends from `TGraphicControl` because it never needs to receive input from the keyboard. Its sole purpose is to provide quick mouse access to commonly used commands.

> **N O T E**   A `TGraphicControl` descendant cannot be selected with the Tab key. This is logical—the component has no way of processing the Tab key to transfer focus to the next component. With this in mind, it is important to provide a keyboard shortcut for every command in your application, if only to appease the power users. ■

`TGraphicControl` adds the `Canvas` property and `Paint` method to its `TControl` ancestor.

Canvas *Property*   The `Canvas` property encapsulates a Windows device context, which really is just a collection of nasty, low-level drawing functions. Using the methods of the `Canvas` property, you can easily draw lines, arcs, rectangles, and ellipses. You may specify the foreground and background colors, and write text onto the surface.

Paint *Method* TGraphicControl provides a virtual Paint method, which is called whenever the surface of the control needs to be drawn. Chapter 4, "Object Pascal: Advanced Concepts," covers virtual methods in greater detail.

The Paint method usually employs the Canvas property of the control to ease the drawing process.

N O T E Both TGraphicControl and Canvas define their own brush, font, and pen objects. The Paint method doesn't automatically copy the TGraphicControl objects to the Canvas—you must do this manually. ■

Chapter 22, "Working with Graphics," covers the Canvas property and Paint method in more detail.

Standard Controls

Delphi provides several controls that can be termed "standard," because they have become common fixtures in applications. These controls may be separated into the groups discussed in the following sections.

Text Display Simple text display is handled by the TLabel control, primarily used to describe the function of another control which does not supply its own Caption property. The standard open file dialog box (refer to Figure 6.1) provides an example. The Look in text, found in the top left corner, indicates the function of the drop-down TComboBox to its right.

You may control the alignment of the text, such as left, center, and right, with the Alignment property. The AutoSize property is useful to automatically adjust the Height and Width properties of the control when you change the Caption or Font. The WordWrap property is handy where you have a long Caption and want it to break at the width of your TLabel, and then continue on the next line.

Alignment and WordWrap have no effect if AutoSize is set to True.

The TLabel control also may be used to set focus to a TWinControl derivative. You accomplish this by setting the FocusControl property to the desired TWinControl descendant, and defining an accelerator key in the Caption. In the standard open file dialog (again, refer to Figure 6.1), the Look in TLabel defines the accelerator key "i." The FocusControl property is set to the TComboBox on its right. The ShowAccelChar property determines whether ampersands in the Caption property are used to specify accelerator keys, or merely displayed as ampersand symbols.

You can display an ampersand in a Caption when ShowAccelChar is True by prefixing it with another ampersand symbol. To display "Delphi & Windows," you set Caption to **Delphi && Windows**.

T I P If `ShowAccelChar` is set to `False`, `FocusControl` has no effect.

The `Transparent` property indicates the `Caption` is to be drawn with a transparent background, rather than filled with the color specified by the `Color` property. This is useful when you want to identify sections of an image, such as a map, and do not want the `TLabel` to obscure rectangular regions.

Text Entry   Virtually every application supports some type of keyboard input, true even for applications which only display a file dialog—you still may type in the name of the file. The text entry controls are `TEdit` and `TMemo`, discussed in the following sections, and `TRichEdit`, discussed in Chapter 7, "Using Win32 Common Controls."

`TEdit` Control   The `TEdit` control is a standard Windows edit box which allows you to display and alter text. Figure 6.1 (which you have now bookmarked!) shows the standard open file dialog, which uses a `TEdit` control to allow you to type the file name.

The `AutoSelect` property determines whether all text in the control is selected automatically when you use Tab to activate it. Because selected text is replaced as you type, this capability is useful where the entire text will be discarded and not simply modified.

You may force upper- or lowercase text by setting the `CharCase` property to either `ecUpperCase` or `ecLowerCase`.

The `PasswordChar` property lets you specify a single character to be displayed rather than the character you actually typed. This feature allows you to provide additional security, for example, when entering passwords. The Windows 95 login screen, shown in Figure 6.2, uses a `TEdit` control with its `PasswordChar` set to "*".

FIG. 6.2

The `PasswordChar` property provides additional security when entering sensitive information.

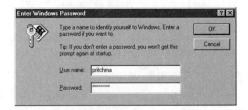

`TMemo` Control   The `TMemo` control is basically a standard edit control that allows you to enter multiple lines of text, each of which is accessible through the `Lines` string array property. The following code displays the second line of a `TMemo` control named `memComments` (remember that array properties are zero-based):

```
ShowMessage(memComments.Lines[1]);
```

The `ScrollBars` property determines whether the `TMemo` control displays horizontal or vertical scroll bars, when the amount of text is too large to completely display at its current size.

The `WantReturns` and `WantTabs` properties control whether the `TMemo` captures the Enter and Tab keys.

TIP Returns and tabs can be entered into a TMemo that isn't trapping these keys, by holding down the Control key while you press Enter or Tab.

Common Properties and Events   The text entry controls share several properties and events. The MaxLength property controls the maximum number of characters which may be entered into the control.

Your program is notified of changes to the text in the following two ways:

- **OnChange Event**—The OnChange event is triggered when the text of the control is changed. OnChange occurs after OnKeyDown and OnKeyPress but before OnKeyUp.
- **Modified Property**—This Boolean property is True if the text was modified since the last time it was set to False.

Although the main function of an edit box is to allow you to modify text, you can make it display only by setting the ReadOnly property to True. This approach isn't usually recommended for TEdit and TMemo controls because you still may click the control and move the edit cursor, which gives the appearance that you can edit the text. Setting the Enabled property to False is a better solution.

Text in an edit control may be selected with the mouse or keyboard. You can interrogate or modify the selection range and the selected text, with the following three properties:

- SelLength—Specifies the length of the selection, in characters
- SelStart—Determines the offset of the selection from the first character
- SelText—Holds a string that contains the currently selected text

Figure 6.3 shows a TEdit box which has its SelStart property set to 1 and SelLength set to 2. SelText returns el.

FIG. 6.3

Text entry controls allow you to select portions of text.

Command   An extremely common element in Windows applications is the *command button*, used to initiate a specific task. The TButton control encapsulates the standard Windows button, and provides several useful properties.

If the Cancel property is set to True, the OnClick event will trigger when you press Escape. This usually is associated with buttons indicating a lack of desire to perform an action. An example is the "Cancel" button on a file open dialog box, which indicates that you decided not to open a file.

Setting the Default property to True causes the OnClick event to be generated when you press the Enter key. The Enter key usually is associated with buttons that indicate a desire to perform an action. One example is typing a file name into a file open dialog box and pressing

Enter, which automatically selects the default button, Open. The border of a button with `Default` set to `True` is drawn in bold.

> **N O T E**   Any button that currently has focus becomes the default button temporarily, and pressing Enter activates its `OnClick` event. When a nonbutton control receives focus, the first button in the tab order with its `Default` property set to True once again becomes the default button. ■

Setting the `ModalResult` property of a modal form to anything other than `mrNone` causes the form to close. When you click a `TButton`, it sets the `ModalResult` property of its owner form to the value specified in its `ModalResult` property. This neatly avoids the trouble of writing a one-line `OnClick` event handler to close the form.

Set   The three set controls, `TCheckBox`, `TRadioButton`, and `TRadioGroup` let you quickly choose a value from a predefined set. Examples of these controls may be found in Delphi's Replace Text dialog box, as shown in Figure 6.4.

FIG. 6.4
The Replace Text dialog box uses TCheckBox and TRadioButton components.

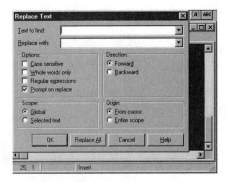

TCheckBox *Control*   The `TCheckBox` control presents an option which may either be selected or unselected. Selection is represented by the presence of a tick mark in the box next to the control's `Caption`. The Case sensitive option in the Replace Text dialog box uses a `TCheckBox` to indicate whether the search for text should be case-sensitive, or case-insensitive.

The `AllowGrayed` option adds a third state, *"checked and grayed,"* to the two states of checked and unchecked. The Add/Remove Programs dialog box, shown in Figure 6.5, uses this additional state. The unchecked items indicate that no subitems are installed, grayed items indicate some of the subitems are installed, and checked items indicate all subitems are installed.

Your program is notified of changes to the selection state through the `OnClick` event. The current selection state is reflected in the `Checked` and `State` properties. The following code checks whether a `TCheckBox` control named `chkPrintPlain` is selected:

```
if chkPrintPlain.Checked then
    PrintPlainList
else
    PrintFancyList;
```

FIG. 6.5
The AllowGrayed
provides a three-state
TCheckBox.

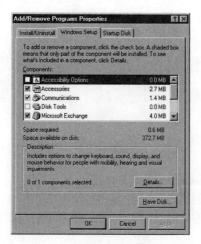

TRadioButton *Control*   The TRadioButton control is used when the alternative state for a two-choice option is not evident, such as those shown in Figure 6.4, or when you want to make a choice between more than two states. Groups of TRadioButton objects indicate choices that are mutually exclusive—only one value from the set may be chosen. Like the TCheckBox, the TRadioButton object's selection state is returned by the Checked property.

N O T E   The OnClick event for a TRadioButton is triggered when only it is checked. The TCheckBox control, however, triggers its OnClick event when it is either checked or unchecked. ■

TRadioGroup *Control*   The TRadioGroup control provides an alternative to creating each TRadioButton manually and placing it in the form. A TRadioButton is created for each item listed in the Items property and is arranged in the number of columns specified by the Columns property. ItemIndex returns the currently selected TRadioButton.

List   The two list controls, TListBox and TComboBox, let you display and select an item from a predefined list.

TListBox *Control*   The TListBox presents a scrolling list of objects, from which you may select one or more items. The Delphi Components dialog box shown in Figure 6.6 presents the component library in a TListBox.

The Columns property indicates the number of columns the TListBox should use when displaying its items. Setting the Columns property to zero causes the TListBox to scroll the list vertically. A non-zero value makes the TListBox scroll horizontally, with the list divided up into the number of columns specified by the Columns property. An example of a list with 0, 1, and 2 columns is shown in Figure 6.7.

Part
II

Ch
6

FIG. 6.6

The Components dialog box makes use of an owner draw TListBox.

FIG. 6.7

You can specify the number of columns for a TListBox with the Columns property.

The TListBox control supports the selection of multiple items with two Boolean properties—ExtendedSelect and MultiSelect. The MultiSelect property determines whether the list is to support multiple selections. If ExtendedSelect is True, you must use Shift or Control in combination with the mouse to select multiple items. If ExtendedSelect is False, you must use the mouse to select multiple items. The SelCount property returns the number of currently selected items. Selected list items may be identified by iterating through the Selected Boolean array property. The following code converts all selected list items in a TListBox control named ListBox1 to uppercase:

```
var
    iCount : Integer;
begin
    with ListBox1 do
        for iCount := 0 to Items.Count-1 do
            if Selected[iCount] then
                Items[iCount] := UpperCase(Items[iCount]);
end;
```

The TopIndex property lets you ensure that a particular line is visible in the TListBox. This code fragment forces the TListBox to display the line that contains "Delphi":

```
with ListBox1 do
    TopIndex := Items.IndexOf('Delphi');
```

TComboBox *Control*   A TComboBox is similar to a collapsed TListBox. You may either enter a new value or select an item from the drop-down list. The Delphi Find Text dialog box, shown in Figure 6.8, contains a TComboBox with its drop-down list displayed.

The number of items displayed in the drop-down list is controlled by the DropDownCount property.

FIGURE 6.8

The TComboBox allows you to enter text or select it from a drop-down list.

Common Properties and Events   The items displayed in a TListBox and the drop-down list of a TComboBox are accessible through the Items property. The items can be displayed alphabetically by setting the Sorted property to True. The ItemIndex property returns the index of the currently selected item, and is -1 if no items are selected.

A list control is not limited to simple text—you can draw each item, a process known as *owner drawing*. You draw the list in the OnDrawItem event, triggered for each item that requires painting. The Style property specifies whether the height of each item in the list is fixed or variable. For fixed height lists, use the ItemHeight property to specify the height of each item. For variable height lists, the TListBox generates the OnMeasureItem event, allowing you to indicate the height of the item before it is drawn in OnDrawItem. The Delphi Components dialog (refer to Figure 6.6) contains a fixed height owner draw TListBox.

Grouping   Grouping controls act as containers for other standard controls. Each contained control is a child window of the parent grouping control.

TPanel Control   The TPanel provides a beveled rectangle that can contain several controls. The most common use for a TPanel is in grouping several TSpeedButton controls to form a Speedbar. TPanel may be seen in the MDI Application created by Delphi's Project Expert shown in Figure 6.9.

TGroupBox Control   The TGroupBox control is mainly used to visually indicate a group of functionally related controls. This may be seen in the standard print dialog shown in Figure 6.10, which uses a TGroupBox to indicate that the Number of copies and Collate controls are related to each other functionally.

Positional   The TScrollBar is used to specify a value in a predefined range. Although its use is similar to the TTrackBar component (see Chapter 7, "Using Win32 Common Controls"), TTrackBar usually is used to control the current position in a window or list. Figures 6.6 and 6.7 demonstrate the use of a TTrackBar in a TTrackBar control.

The current value of the TScrollBar is returned by the Position property, and is constrained to the range bounded by the Min and Max properties. You can specify the magnitude of both a small and large change by using the SmallChange and LargeChange properties, respectively.

The OnScroll event is triggered when you alter the position of the slider.

FIG. 6.9

TPanel controls are commonly used to create Speedbars.

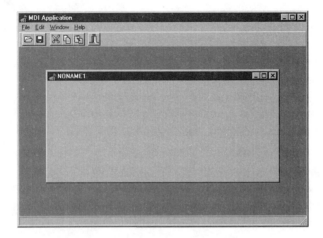

FIG. 6.10

The standard Print dialog box uses the TGroupBox and TRadioGroup controls.

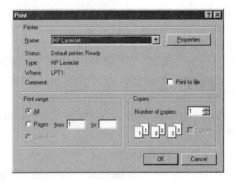

Additional Controls

Ongoing refinement of application interfaces has led to several new kinds of controls. Delphi provides these new controls on the Additional page of the component palette.

Enhanced Command   The standard TButton command control was extended in two directions—TBitBtn and TSpeedButton.

TBitBtn *Control*   The TBitBtn control descends from TButton and basically adds the capability to display a descriptive image on the button surface.

The Kind property allows you to quickly set several properties such as such as Default, Cancel, and Caption in one operation.

TSpeedButton *Component*   Commonly found in Speedbars for applications such as Delphi, the TSpeedButton component provides a button-style control that usually displays an image and an optional Caption.

TSpeedButton components add two elements of functionality to the TBitBtn control—they may be grouped, and they may indicate one of two states.

Grouping is accomplished by setting the GroupIndex property to the same non-zero value for all TSpeedButtons in the group. A group of TSpeedButtons presents a mutually exclusive choice, similar to that provided by a TRadioButton group.

The Down property indicates the state of the TSpeedButton, and is only effective when the GroupIndex property is non-zero. When Down is True, the TSpeedButton is considered selected. Delphi's Component Palette is an example of a set of grouped TSpeedButton controls.

Common Properties   Both TBitBtn and TSpeedButton define the Glyph property, used to specify the image displayed by the component. You may choose to provide more images to represent the four states of the button—Up, Disabled, Down, and Stay Down. This is accomplished by setting Glyph to a single image, which contains the separate state images stored next to one another horizontally. Each state image must be the same size. The NumGlyphs property indicates the number of state images contained in the Glyph property.

The positions of Caption and Glyph are controlled with the following three properties:

- Layout—The Layout property determines whether the Glyph is located to the left, right, top, or bottom of the button. The Caption, if specified, originates from the edge opposite the Glyph.

- Margin—This property specifies the number of pixels between the edge of the button and the edge of the Glyph.

- Spacing—The Spacing property controls the number of pixels between the Caption and Glyph.

Enhanced Edit   When the basic TEdit control isn't enough, turn to the TMaskedEdit, TDrawGrid, and TStringGrid controls for that little bit extra.

TMaskedEdit *Control*   The TMaskedEdit control adds some extensive validation and formatting functionality to the basic TEdit control. The EditMask property defines the mask to which the data entered into the control must conform. Restrictions are applied on a per-character basis and, for example, may force numeric, alphabetic, or specific case for a particular character position.

Literals such as date and time delimiters may be introduced into the EditMask property to enforce a particular display format. The EditMask controls whether these literals are returned in the Text property. The EditText property returns the text as displayed in the control.

If you attempt to move to another control while the text doesn't conform to the mask, an exception is raised and focus is returned to the TMaskedEdit control.

TDrawGrid *Control*   The TDrawGrid control allows you to present data in column and row format. The TCalendar component shown in Figure 6.11 is a grid control.

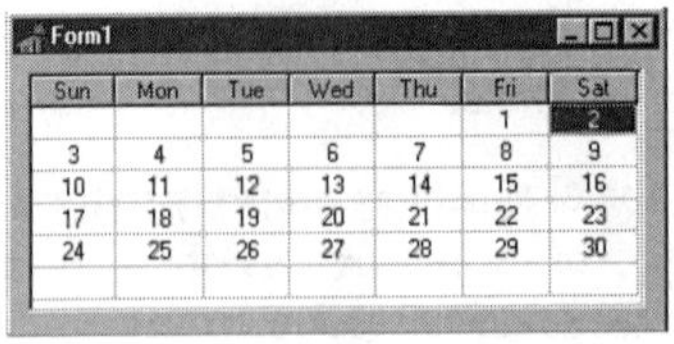

FIG. 6.11

Grids have a large
number of uses, such as
the TCalendar control.

You may specify the number of columns and rows with the ColCount and RowCount properties. The Col and Row properties indicate which cell currently has input focus. If you select a range of cells, the bounding rectangle is returned in the Selection property.

The DefaultColWidth property sets the default column size for each column in the grid, with DefaultRowHeight performing the same function for each row. You may change a column's width or a row's height with ColWidths and RowHeights. The following code changes the width of column 2 for a TDrawGrid named DrawGrid1 to 20 pixels:

```
DrawGrid1.ColWidths[1] := 20;
```

FixedRows and FixedCols determine the number of locked rows, useful for grid headings. You may specify which cell appears in the top left corner of the grid with TopRow and LeftCol. The number of fully visible rows and columns are returned by the VisibleColCount and VisibleRowCount properties. The following code displays the bottom right set of cells in a TDrawGrid named DrawGrid1:

```
with DrawGrid1 do
    begin
        TopRow := RowCount - VisibleRowCount;
        LeftCol := ColCount - VisibleColCount;
    end;
```

The Options property allows you to modify the behavior of the grid, such as turning grid lines off or allowing the resizing of columns and rows at runtime.

The OnColumnMoved and OnRowMoved events are triggered when you drag a column or row to a new position. The OnTopLeftChanged event is generated when you scroll the grid to display hidden cells. OnSelectCell is triggered when you move the input focus to another cell.

The TDrawGrid essentially is owner draw—the default drawing mode simply blanks the cell and sets the font of the cell to that specified by the Font property. You provide drawing code in the OnDrawCell event, triggered for each cell that needs drawing.

Because a cell can contain basically anything you want, you must manually maintain your data. When you begin to edit a cell, the TDrawGrid triggers the OnGetEditText event, allowing you to set the text to edit. The OnGetEditMask event allows you to provide an edit mask for the data entry. The OnSetEditText event is generated as you alter the contents of the cell.

TStringGrid *Control* If you possess the sensible aversion to writing unnecessary code, you will find the TStringGrid useful—it takes all the functionality of the TDrawGrid and automates the storage and retrieval of the strings used as data for the grid.

The Cells property gives you access to the string connected to each cell in the grid. The Cols and Rows property provide the set of strings for each column and row, respectively.

The default drawing process is extended to draw the text specified for the cell in the Cells property. You still may provide an OnDrawCell event handler if you want to customize the drawing process.

Graphic   The graphic set of components primarily displays some form of visual shape, be it a complex bitmap or simple square.

TImage Control   The TImage control allows you to display an image on your form. You specify the image with the Picture property. If the image is larger than the control, it's cropped at the border. You may set AutoSize to True to automatically expand or shrink the TImage control as the image size changes. Alternatively, you can keep the size of the control constant, and then stretch or compress the image by setting the Stretch property to True. You may center the image in the control's bounding rectangle by setting the Center property to True. This has no effect if AutoSize or Stretch are set to True.

TShape Control   The TShape control displays a geometric shape on the form, saving you the trouble of drawing it with TCanvas methods and the OnPaint event.

The basic shape of the control is set with the Style property, which allows you to draw an ellipse, rectangle, square, or circle.

The Brush property determines the TShape object's fill color and pattern. The border's style, width, and color are specified by the Pen property.

TBevel Control   The TBevel control simply displays a beveled line, box, or frame on the form. TBevel is useful to provide three-dimensional shading to segments of your forms.

The Shape property determines whether the TBevel displays a line, box, or frame. The Style property is used to specify whether the bevel is raised or lowered.

Runtime Control Manipulation   This group of components allows you to control the size or position of controls placed on a form at runtime.

TScrollBox Control   The TScrollBox allows you to create a scrolling section of the form, which may contain any other type of controls. This is useful when you want to fix portions of the screen in place, while scrolling others. The Paint program installed with Windows and shown in Figure 6.12 provides an example of this—you can scroll the image contained in the TScrollBox while the toolbar and status bar remain in place.

TSplitter Control   The TSplitter control allows you to dynamically size controls at runtime. The Windows Explorer shown in Figure 6.13 provides an example of this control, used to adjust the size of the Folders window.

FIG. 6.12

Scroll boxes are useful to create independently scrolling sections of a form.

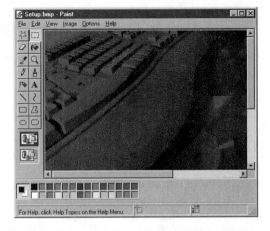

FIG. 6.13

The `TSplitter` control enables you to resize controls at runtime.

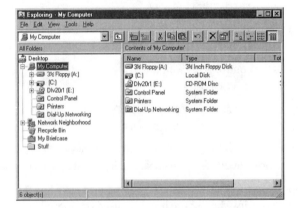

To make use of the `TSplitter` control, you must set the `Align` property of your controls to something other than `alNone`. In Figure 6.13, the Folders window has its `Align` property set to `alLeft`. The `TSplitter` is placed to the right of the Folders window, with its `Align` property also set to `alLeft`. The Contents window has its `Align` property set to `alClient`, which causes it to resize to fill the remaining client area.

You may specify the minimum size for a resizable window with the `MinSize` property of the `TSplitter` control.

System Controls

Visual system controls wrap complex system functionality into easy-to-use Delphi components.

TOleContainer Control   The `TOleContainer` control lets you easily add OLE 2.0 objects to your Delphi application. Chapter 18, "Using OLE Objects in Delphi," is devoted to this topic.

***TPaintBox* Control**   A TPaintBox provides a surface which automatically clips drawing operations to its boundary. This is useful when you perform custom drawing on the form and do not want to continually check whether you are outside a particular region.

The TPaintBox generates an OnPaint event when its surface requires redrawing and provides a Canvas property to ease the drawing process. See Chapter 22, "Working with Graphics," for more information on drawing.

***TMediaPlayer* Control**   The TMediaPlayer encapsulates the painful record formats and API calls that make up the Media Control Interface (MCI). Figure 6.14 provides an example of the TMediaPlayer playing an AVI movie from the Delphi CD-ROM.

FIG. 6.14
TMediaPlayer gives
you TV-dinner style
multimedia—just heat
and serve!

You specify the type of media with the DeviceType property. The start and end positions for playing or recording are specified with the StartPos and EndPos properties. The current position is returned in the Position property.

Each button on the control can be hidden or disabled with the VisibleButtons and EnabledButtons properties.

If you set the Wait property to True, control isn't returned to your application until the MCI function completes. To illustrate, if you start to Play an audio track on a CD and Wait is set to True, control will not return to your application until the track finishes playing.

The control generates the OnClick event when you click a button. You may choose to perform the default action associated with this button, such as Play or Eject, or provide your own processing. The OnPostClick event occurs after the OnClick event was called. If you choose to perform the default action associated with a button, and Wait is set to False, OnPostClick may be called before the OnClick event finishes.

The Notify property determines whether an OnNotify event is generated when a media control function has completed. The OnNotify event is useful when a media control function is expected to take a long time to complete and you want to perform other processing.

By default, TMediaPlayer opens a separate window to display video-based media. If this is undesirable, you can specify a TWinControl descendant in the Display property, and the TMediaPlayer will direct its output to this control.

Part
II

Ch
6

N O T E   The video MCI requires its display to be aligned on a four-pixel grid. To comply,
TMediaPlayer shifts the form slightly—an amateurish effect in a professional application.
When calculating your form's coordinates, remember that horizontal positioning is zero-based, while
vertical positioning is based at 1. ▧

Sample Controls

Delphi provides several components installed on the Samples page of the component palette.
These components provide superb examples of the flexibility and extensibility found in the
Visual Component Library. The sample components are as follows:

- TGauge—A TGraphicControl descendant, TGauge displays a colored bar indicating a
  position between two points. Commonly used to mark progress in a lengthy operation,
  the TGauge has been replaced by the TProgressBar control, covered further in Chapter 7,
  "Using Win32 Common Controls."

- TColorGrid—The TColorGrid descends from TCustomControl, and presents you with a
  grid from which you may select a color.

- TSpinButton—This component inherits from TWinControl. It provides two buttons,
  which generally increment or decrement a value.

- TSpinEdit—The TSpinEdit control inherits from TCustomEdit. Input into the TSpinEdit
  is restricted to numerics only, and it provides a TSpinButton control to increment and
  decrement the value.

- TDirectoryOutline—This component descends from TCustomOutline and lists the
  directory structure for a given drive.

- TCalender—The TCalender is a TCustomGrid descendant, and displays a particular
  calendar month in a grid format.

Non-Visual Components

Non-visual components wrap complex system functions into Delphi components, speeding
your development process.

Dialog Components

Windows provides several standard dialog boxes, termed *common dialogs*, used for opening
and saving files, specifying fonts, and printing. Delphi streamlines the use of the common
dialogs into several simple components, which may be grouped according to functionality.

File   The File group of dialogs allows you to select files for use in your application and comes
in two basic flavors—TOpenDialog, to open files, and TSaveDialog, to save files.

TOpenDialog *Component*   The TOpenDialog component provides the standard open file
dialog (refer to Figure 6.1).

The caption of the dialog is determined by the `Title` property. The `InitialDir` property specifies the directory displayed when the dialog is first activated.

You may filter the files displayed in the dialog with the `Filter` property. The `FilterIndex` property determines the default filter used when the dialog first appears.

The `FileName` property returns the fully qualified path for the selected file. The `DefaultExt` property is used to specify a default file extension for a file name typed into the File name edit box on the dialog. The `Files` property holds a list of selected files for dialogs which support multiple selection.

The `Options` property lets you specify several options for the dialog, such as displaying a Help button or hiding the Network button.

The following code displays the file age for a file selected via a `TOpenDialog` named `opndlgFile`:

```
var
    iAge : Integer;
begin
    if opndlgFile.Execute then
    begin
        iAge := FileAge(opndlgFile.FileName);
        ShowMessage(DateToStr(FileDateToDateTime(iAge)));
    end;
end;
```

TSaveDialog *Component*   The `TSaveDialog` simply changes the buttons and labels found on a `TOpenDialog` to indicate saving as opposed to opening files. The `TSaveDialog` is shown in Figure 6.15.

FIG. 6.15

The TSaveDialog makes retrieving file names remarkably easy.

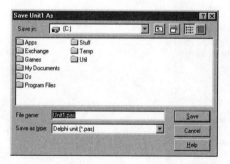

Part

II

Ch

6

Font   The `TFontDialog` component encapsulates the standard font selection dialog, and is shown in Figure 6.16.

FIG. 6.16
The TFontDialog
allows you to specify
screen and printer fonts.

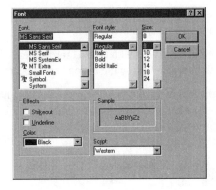

The selected font is returned in the Font property.

You may restrict the font list displayed in the dialog to either Screen or Printer fonts (or both), with the Device property. The MaxFontSize and MinFontSize properties provide a restriction to the range of available font sizes.

The Options property allows you to set many options for the dialog, such as fixed pitch or whether effects such as strikeout and underline are available.

The OnApply event is triggered when you click the Apply button.

Color   The TColorDialog presents the standard color selection dialog box, shown below in Figure 6.17.

FIG. 6.17
With the
TColorDialog, you
can select a color from
the palette.

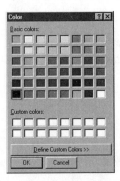

The color selected in the dialog is returned in the Color property.

The CustomColors property allows you to specify a set of custom colors, which are added to the set displayed in the dialog.

Printer   This set of dialogs provide access to two dialogs used to control printing—TPrintDialog and TPrinterSetupDialog.

TPrintDialog Component   The TPrintDialog encapsulates the standard print options dialog, (refer to Figure 6.10).

The dialog presents three options for specifying a print range—all, page range, or selection. The PrintRange property determines which option is selected by default.

If you choose a page range, it is returned in the FromPage and ToPage properties. You can restrict the range of these values with the MinPage and MaxPage properties.

The number of copies is returned in the Copies property. The Collate property indicates whether the printing will be collated.

The PrintToFile property indicates that you want to send the output to a file rather than a printer.

The Options property lets you customize the behavior of the print dialog. It can inhibit actions such as printing to files or entering a page range.

TPrinterSetupDialog *Component*   The TPrinterSetupDialog allows you to configure your printer before the print job is issued, which is shown in Figure 6.18.

FIG. 6.18

You use the TPrinterSetupDialog to set up your printer before a print job.

Text   Text dialogs are used to search for and replace text maintained by your application.

TFindDialog *Component*   The TFindDialog presents the standard text search dialog, as shown in Figure 6.19.

FIG. 6.19

The TFindDialog allows you to search for text.

Part

II

Ch

6

The FindText property contains the string for which your application will search. The OnFind property is triggered when you click the Find Next button.

The Position property determines the screen location at which the dialog appears.

You can refine the behavior of the dialog with the Options property, which allows you to disable features such as case-sensitive matching or whole-word searches.

TReplaceDialog *Component*   The TReplaceDialog encapsulates the standard find-and-replace dialog box, shown in Figure 6.20.

The TReplaceDialog provides all the capabilities of the TFindDialog.

The ReplaceText property contains the text your application will use as a replacement for text specified in FindText.

The OnReplace event is generated when you click either the Replace or Replace All buttons. The Options property allows you to differentiate between the two types of replacement.

System Components

System components usually are unrelated because they deal with separate sets of system functionality.

TMainMenu *and* **TPopupMenu**   The TMainMenu component encapsulates the menu bar found at the top of most applications. TPopupMenu provides a localized or task-specific menu, usually displayed by right-clicking an object once.

The Items property contains a list of TMenuItem objects that comprise the menu.

The Menu Designer, shown below in Figure 6.21, assists with the creation of your menu structure.

TMenuItem *Component*   The sole event for a TMenuItem, OnClick, is triggered when you left-click the menu item or press Enter while the item is highlighted.

The TMenuItem object also provides an Items property, allowing you to create submenus.

The Shortcut property specifies a keyboard shortcut used to activate the menu item. An example may be found in the Delphi menu system. The File, Save menu item uses "S" for its shortcut key, allowing you to execute the save operation by holding down Control and pressing "S."

A TMenuItem may act like a TCheckBox through the use of its Checked property. The RadioItem property enables you to emulate the functionality of a TRadioButton set.

***TTimer* Component**   The TTimer component generates the OnTimer event when a predetermined time has passed. The Date/Time Properties dialog box shown in Figure 6.22 uses a TTimer component to continually update the clock.

FIG. 6.22

The TTimer component triggers an event repetitively.

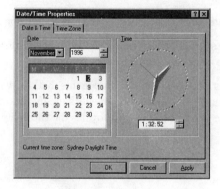

The Interval property defines the interval, in milliseconds, between each OnTimer event.

Putting It All Together

Now that you have been introduced to the structure of the component library and have studied several components useful in building applications, take a moment to reflect on what this chapter covered.

Visual Components

This section introduced the Delphi object hierarchy, discussed common properties and events, and then covered groups of controls and their uses.

The Delphi object hierarchy allows objects to inherit common properties and events, modify existing behavior, or add new functionality. The basic control ancestor, TControl, provides standard properties, such as Caption and Color, and standard events, such as OnMouseDown and OnMouseMove.

Controls then split in two directions—those that descend from TWinControl, and those that inherit from TGraphicControl.

Part
II
Ch
6

TWinControl descendants are able to receive input focus, or input from the keyboard. They provide a window handle, useful for low-level API calls. TWinControl descendants trigger several new events, such as OnEnter and OnKeyDown.

TGraphicControl descendants are used mainly for displaying images and drawing shapes. They do not supply a window handle and, therefore, cannot receive input focus.

The chapter then moved on to discuss the groups that exist in the Visual Component Library (VCL), such as the Set group that contains the TCheckBox, TRadioButton, and TRadioGroup controls.

Non-Visual Components

This section discussed two categories of non-visual components—dialog and system.

The dialog category provides streamlined access to the common dialogs found in Windows, such as the standard open file dialog or color selection dialog.

The system category provides a catch-all for the components that deal with sets of unrelated functionality. The TMainMenu and TPopupMenu components simplify the often-complex production of application menus. The TTimer component provides the capability to trigger an event repetitively. ●

Using Win32 Common Controls

by Noel Rice

Creating an application with substance is well and good, but you really need a slick interface. Fractiousness aside, the presentation of data in a clean, understandable format is largely a job made easier with Common Controls. Common Controls provide the Windows 95 look-and-feel, and also drive rapid application development by automating design tasks.

This chapter provides a tour of each component, key properties and methods, brief code examples, a description of common uses, and possible new applications of Common Controls. ■

Simple Common Controls

You start with simple controls that do not contain child objects or manage lists, but instead are intended to display or set single property values. including the Track Bar, Up-Down Control, Hot Key, and Progress Bar controls.

New for Delphi 3

Next you look at capabilities and operations of the latest controls to debut on the palette: `TToolBar`, `TCoolBar`, `TDateTimePicker`, and `TAnimate` controls.

Complex Common Controls

Most of this exploration takes place by using Common Controls that either manage string lists or contain multiple child objects, including the Status Bar Control, Header Control, Image List, Tab Control, Page Control, Rich Edit, List View, and Tree View.

Putting it all together

You learn how to use Windows messages and functions directly to extend past the functionality surfaced by Delphi. For example, you learn the process used to create enhanced versions of `TTabControl` and `TPageControl` with hot tracking and the ability to display the tabs along any side of the control.

Simple Common Controls

The controls in this first group are used to display or set single values or ranges of values.

Track Bar

When your user wants to quickly set a whole number value within a range, the TTrackBar component allows adjustment of whole number values by sliding a pointer along a bar. The Position property sets the location of the TTrackBar pointer or *thumb* at design or runtime. Tick marks along the side of the bar mark intervals within a range controlled by Min, Max, and Frequency properties.

To dictate the exact position of each tick mark programmatically, set the TickStyle property to tsManual, and then call the SetTick method. Here's a quick example of setting the ticks manually by using program code:

1. Start with a default project by selecting File, New Application.
2. From the Win32 page of the component palette, place a TTrackBar, TUpdown on the form.
3. From the Standard page of the component palette, place a TEdit and TButton on the form.
4. In the Object Inspector, set the TTrackBar TickStyle property to tsManual.
5. In the Object Inspector, set the TUpDown Associate property to Edit1 (more on the TUpdown component in following sections of this chapter).
6. In the Object Inspector Events tab, Create an OnClick event handler for the TButton component. Enter the following code into the OnClick event handler.

```
procedure TForm1.Button1Click(Sender: TObject);
begin
  TrackBar1.SetTick(StrToInt(Edit1.Text));
end;
```

For a slightly more complex use of the TTrackBar control, you can use the SetTick method to graphically display the frequency of certain kinds of data, and allow the user to navigate the data using the TTrackBar control. You can also hijack the TApplication OnShowHint to give your users the benefit of a text description for the current position on the TTrackBar.

The next example will display shares, stock symbols, and prices from the Holdings demo table in a grid. TTrackBar allows the user to navigate to records where the number of shares corresponds to the Position property of the TTrackBar.

In Figure 7.1, ticks along the left side of the TTrackBar mark each instance of a Shares value. As a secondary benefit to the user, the interval of ticks shows the distribution of the amount of shares. As the user moves the TTrackBar thumb vertically, the table cursor jumps to the nearest matching Shares value.

Before running the example shown in Listing 7.1, create an index on the Shares column named ByShares in Database Desktop, and set the IndexName property of Table1 to your new index. You find the SETTKC2.PAS file on this book's companion CD-ROM.

FIG. 7.1
The TrackBar Shares
Selector example.

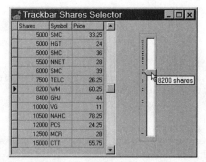

**Listing 7.1   \UDELPHI3\CHP7\TRACKBAR\SETTCK2.PAS—File that
Contains the *TrackBar* Shares Selector**

```
unit settck2;

interface

uses
  Windows, Messages, SysUtils, Classes, Graphics, Controls, Forms, Dialogs,
  DB, DBTables, Grids, DBGrids, ComCtrls, StdCtrls;

type
  TForm1 = class(TForm)
    DBGrid1: TDBGrid;
    TrackBar1: TTrackBar;
    Table1: TTable;
    DataSource1: TDataSource;
    Table1SYMBOL: TStringField;
    Table1SHARES: TFloatField;
    Table1PUR_PRICE: TFloatField;
    procedure FormCreate(Sender: TObject);
    procedure FormShow(Sender: TObject);
    procedure TrackBar1Change(Sender: TObject);
  private
    procedure AppShowHint(var HintStr: string; var CanShow: Boolean;
      var HintInfo: THintInfo);
  end;

var
  Form1: TForm1;

implementation

{$R *.DFM}

uses CommCtrl;

(*
```

continues

Part

II

Ch

7

Listing 7.1 Continued

```
  TBM_GETTHUMBRECT
  wParam = 0;
  lParam = (LPARAM) (LPRECT) lprc;
  The TBM_GETTHUMBRECT message retrieves the size and position
  of the bounding rectangle for the slider in a trackbar.
*)

// Position the hint next to the trackbar thumb.
procedure TForm1.AppShowHint(var HintStr: string; var CanShow: Boolean;
  var HintInfo: THintInfo);
var
  TrackBarThumbRect: TRect;
begin
  SendMessage(TrackBar1.Handle, TBM_GETTHUMBRECT, 0,
    LongInt(@TrackBarThumbRect));
  HintInfo.HintPos :=
    TrackBar1.ClientToScreen(TrackBarThumbRect.BottomRight);
end;


// note: make sure table is closed in design mode --
// avoid the dreaded "table is busy" error.
procedure TForm1.FormCreate(Sender: TObject);
begin
  with Application do
  begin
    OnShowHint := AppShowHint;
    HintPause := 0;
    HintShortPause := 0;
  end;
end;

procedure TForm1.FormShow(Sender: TObject);
begin
  with Table1 do
  begin
    Open;
    Last;

    TrackBar1.Max := Table1['Shares'];
    First;
    TrackBar1.Min := Table1['Shares'];
    TrackBar1.LineSize := TrackBar1.Max div 20;
    TrackBar1.PageSize := TrackBar1.Max div 4;
    while not EOF do
    begin
      TrackBar1.SetTick(Table1['Shares']);
      Next;
    end;
  end;
end;

procedure TForm1.TrackBar1Change(Sender: TObject);
```

```
begin
  if Table1.State in [dsBrowse] then
  begin
    Table1.FindNearest([TrackBar1.Position]);
    TrackBar1.Hint := Table1.FieldByName('Shares').AsString +
      'shares';
  end;
end;

end.
```

Up-Down Control

An Up-Down control increments or decrements a whole numeric value displayed in an attached edit control.

N O T E   You can actually use a TMemo or TRichEdit rather than a TEdit, and the TUpdown still will operate correctly, although you probably will never have an occasion for using resources in this manner. ■

Attach the Up-Down control by selecting an edit control from the drop-down list in the Associate property. The TUpdown control repositions itself to the right or left of the associated component, based on an AlignButton property of udLeft or udRight. Orientation may be udVertical or udHorizontal.

You don't have to associate an edit control to use the TUpDown. The OnClick event notifies you of user changes to the next or previous position, which allows your program to react in a flexible way. For example, a calendar form with TUpDown associated to the current month displayed in a TEdit limits you to a numeric display of that month. By leaving the Associate property nil and using the OnClick event handler, you can display the month written out in full (see Figure 7.2).

On the CD

Before the OnClick event fires, the OnChanging event gives you a chance to block the change from occurring by setting the AllowChange parameter. Unfortunately, there is no way to know within the OnChanging event handler if the user hit the btPrev or btNext button. Missing this information hampers tasks such as preventing future dates within the handler. You find the UDCAL1.PAS file shown in Listing 7.2 on this book's companion CD-ROM.

Part

II

Ch

7

FIG. 7.2

Using TUpdown in conjunction with TCalendar.

Listing 7.2 \UDELPHI3\CHP7\UPDOWN\UDCAL1.PAS—*TUpdown* with *TCalendar*

```
unit UDCal1;

interface

uses
  Windows, Messages, SysUtils, Classes, Graphics, Controls, Forms,
  Dialogs, ExtCtrls, ComCtrls, StdCtrls, Grids, Calendar, Buttons,
   CommCtrl;

type
  TfrmDate = class(TForm)
    Calendar1: TCalendar;
    StatusBar1: TStatusBar;
    Panel2: TPanel;
    Panel1: TPanel;
    Edit1: TEdit;
    Edit2: TEdit;
    UpDown1: TUpdown;
    UpDown2: TUpdown;
    Button1: TButton;
    cbAllowChange: TCheckBox;
    procedure FormCreate(Sender: TObject);
    procedure UpDown1Click(Sender: TObject; Button: TUDBtnType);
    procedure UpDown2Click(Sender: TObject; Button: TUDBtnType);
    procedure Calendar1Change(Sender: TObject);
    procedure Button1Click(Sender: TObject);
    procedure UpDown1Changing(Sender: TObject;
      var AllowChange: Boolean);
  end;

const
  Months: array [1..12] of ShortString = (
  'January', 'February', 'March', 'April', 'May', 'June', 'July',
  'August', 'September', 'October', 'November', 'December'
  );

var
  frmDate: TfrmDate;
```

```
implementation

{$R *.DFM}

procedure TfrmDate.FormCreate(Sender: TObject);
begin
  Edit1.ReadOnly := True;
  Edit1.Text := Months[Calendar1.Month];
  Edit2.ReadOnly := True;
  Edit2.Text := IntToStr(Calendar1.Year);
  UpDown1.Position := Calendar1.Month;
  with UpDown2 do
  begin
    Min := 1900;
    Max := 3000; // That should hold 'em (famous last words..)
    Position := Calendar1.Year;
    Thousands := False;
  end;
end;

procedure TfrmDate.UpDown1Click(Sender: TObject; Button: TUDBtnType);
begin
  with Calendar1 do
  begin
    if (Button = btNext) then
      Month := Month + 1
    else // Button = btPrev
      Month := Month - 1;
    Edit1.Text := Months[Month];
  end;
end;

procedure TfrmDate.UpDown2Click(Sender: TObject; Button: TUDBtnType);
begin
  Calendar1.Year := UpDown2.Position
end;

procedure TfrmDate.Calendar1Change(Sender: TObject);
begin
  with Calendar1 do
    StatusBar1.SimpleText := Months[Month] + ' ' +
      IntToStr(Day) + ', ' + IntToStr(Year);
end;

procedure TfrmDate.Button1Click(Sender: TObject);
begin
  Close;
end;

procedure TfrmDate.UpDown1Changing(Sender: TObject;
  var AllowChange: Boolean);
begin
  AllowChange := cbAllowChange.Checked;
end;

end.
```

Part

II

Ch

7

HotKey Control

In a situation where you want the user to define his or her own shortcut keys and assign them to menu items at runtime, we can use a HotKey control. The main property of THotKey is, predictably, "HotKey" of type TShortCut, which can be manipulated with ShortCutToText and TextToShortCut functions of the Menus unit.

To control which modifier keys (hkShift, hkCtrl, hkAlt, hkExt) are considered default when the user presses only a character or function key, specify the Modifiers set property. For example, if the Modifiers property reads "[hkShift, hkCtrl]" and the user keys "A," the THotKey control reads "Ctrl + Shift + A." The modifiers are displayed in the order specified in the Modifiers set.

You can prevent specific modifiers from being keyed with the InvalidKeys set property. For example, an InvalidKeys property of [hcNone] prevents an unmodified key combination. If Modifiers and InvalidKeys both specify the same key, the Modifiers property wins out.

You can create a sample that allows the user to define hot keys to a menu during runtime. You need two forms. Listing 7.3 shows the first form containing a TBitBtn and a TMainMenu (although a TPopUpMenu also should do). You will use the second form (see Listing 7.4) to list menu items and to perform the actual assigning of new hot keys. This second form will contain a TListView and a THotKey control. You read more about TListView later in the chapter, so please take the sample code referring to TListView on faith for now.

The code for the first form's TBitBtn click creates the second form and loads the TListView items from the list of menu items and their associated shortcuts. The user may select menu items represented in the TListView and assign new shortcuts in the THotKey control (see Figure 7.3). When the second form closes, the main menu is updated from the contents of the List View control (see Figure 7.4). You find the HKEY1.PAS (see Listing 7.3) and HKEY2.PAS (see Listing 7.4) on this book's companion CD-ROM.

FIG. 7.3

Defining a new HotKey at runtime.

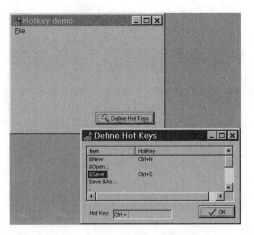

FIG. 7.4
Newly assigned HotKey,
shown in main menu.

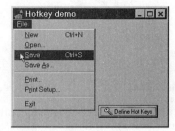

Listing 7.3   \UDELPHI3\CHP7\HOTKEY\HKEY1.PAS—Form that Contains Main Menu

```
unit HKey1;

interface

uses
  Windows, Messages, SysUtils, Classes, Graphics, Controls, Forms,
  Dialogs, Menus, StdCtrls, Buttons;

type
  TForm1 = class(TForm)
    MainMenu1: TMainMenu;
    BitBtn1: TBitBtn;
    File1: TMenuItem;
    Exit2: TMenuItem;
    N3: TMenuItem;
    PrintSetup2: TMenuItem;
    Print2: TMenuItem;
    N4: TMenuItem;
    SaveAs2: TMenuItem;
    Save2: TMenuItem;
    Open2: TMenuItem;
    New2: TMenuItem;
    procedure BitBtn1Click(Sender: TObject);
    procedure Exit1Click(Sender: TObject);
  end;

var
  Form1: TForm1;

implementation

{$R *.DFM}

uses ComCtrls, HKey2;

procedure TForm1.BitBtn1Click(Sender: TObject);
var
  i: integer;
  NewItem : TListItem;
  ShortCutStr: string;
begin
```

continues

Part

II

Ch

7

Listing 7.3   Continued

```
  with TfrmDefineMenu.Create(self) do
    try
      for i := 0 to File1.Count - 1 do
      begin
        NewItem := ListView1.Items.Add;
        NewItem.Caption := File1.Items[i].Caption;
        ShortCutStr := ShortCutToText(File1.Items[i].ShortCut);
        NewItem.SubItems.Add(ShortCutStr);
      end;
      ShowModal;
      for i := 0 to ListView1.Items.Count - 1 do
        File1.Items[i].ShortCut :=
          TextToShortCut(ListView1.Items[i].SubItems[0]);
    finally
      Free;
    end;
end;

procedure TForm1.Exit1Click(Sender: TObject);
begin
  Close;
end;

end.
```

Listing 7.4   HKEY2.PAS—Form Containing *THotKey*

```
unit HKey2;

interface

uses
  Windows, Messages, SysUtils, Classes, Graphics, Controls, Forms,
  Dialogs, StdCtrls, Buttons, ComCtrls;

type
  TfrmDefineMenu = class(TForm)
    HotKey1: THotKey;
    BitBtn1: TBitBtn;
    Label1: TLabel;
    ListView1: TListView;
    procedure ListView1Click(Sender: TObject);
    procedure FormKeyPress(Sender: TObject; var Key: Char);
    procedure FormCreate(Sender: TObject);
  end;

var
  frmDefineMenu: TfrmDefineMenu;

implementation

{$R *.DFM}
```

```
uses Menus;

procedure TfrmDefineMenu.ListView1Click(Sender: TObject);
begin
  with ListView1 do
    if (Assigned(Selected) and (Selected.Caption <> '-')) then
      HotKey1.HotKey := TextToShortCut(Listview1.Selected.SubItems[0]);
  HotKey1.SetFocus;
end;

procedure TfrmDefineMenu.FormKeyPress(Sender: TObject; var Key: Char);
begin
  with ListView1 do
  begin
    Selected.SubItems[0] := ShortCutToText(HotKey1.HotKey);
    UpdateItems(Selected.Index, Selected.Index);
  end;
end;

procedure TfrmDefineMenu.FormCreate(Sender: TObject);
var
  NewColumn: TListColumn;
begin
  // These properties may be set in the Object Inspector
  // but are included here for clarity.
  KeyPreview := True;
  with ListView1 do
  begin
    ReadOnly := True;
    ViewStyle := vsReport;
    NewColumn := ListView1.Columns.Add;
    NewColumn.Caption := 'Item';
    NewColumn.Width := 100;
    NewColumn := ListView1.Columns.Add;
    NewColumn.Caption := 'HotKey';
    NewColumn.Width := 200;
  end;
end;

end.
```

Progress Bar Control

The Progress Bar control makes life easier for your users by letting them gauge the approximate status of lengthy operations, such as loading forms and disk-intensive procedures such as file copying. To use the TProgressBar control, set the Min, Max properties, and then set the Position property in code as your operation progresses.

This following example demonstrates updating the progress bar on a splash screen while loading forms into memory. To create this project, take these steps:

1. From the File menu, select New Application.

Part

II

Ch

7

2. From the File menu, select New, Forms, About Box.

3. Remove the OK button from the AboutBox form.

4. Add a TProgressBar to the AboutBox form and set the Align property to alBottom.

5. From the File menu, select New Form. Repeat this step two more times. You now should have units 1 through 5 in your project.

6. Select View, Project Source and edit the source to match the source shown in Listing 7.5 (which can be found on this book's companion CD-ROM).

Listing 7.5   \UDELPHI3\CHP7\PROGRESSBAR\PRGBAR1 \PROJECT1.DPR—Displaying Progress of Loading Forms

```
program Project1;

uses
  Forms,
  Unit1 in 'Unit1.pas'    {Form1},
  Unit2 in 'Unit2.pas'    {AboutBox},
  Unit3 in 'Unit3.pas'    {Form3},
  Unit4 in 'Unit4.pas'    {Form4},
  Unit5 in 'Unit5.pas'    {Form5};

{$R *.RES}

begin
  Application.Initialize;
  with TAboutbox.Create(Application) do
  try
    Show;
    Update;
    Application.CreateForm(TForm1, Form1);
    ProgressBar1.Position := 25;
    Application.CreateForm(TForm3, Form3);
    ProgressBar1.Position := 50;
    Application.CreateForm(TForm4, Form4);
    ProgressBar1.Position := 75;
    Application.CreateForm(TForm5, Form5);
    ProgressBar1.Position := 100;
  finally
    Free;
  end;
  Application.Run;
end.
```

Besides Min, Max, and Position, you may set the Step property and call the StepIt method to increment Position by the Step amount. If you want to move Position by a specified amount in a single method call, use the StepBy method.

The following example (see Figure 7.5 and Listing 7.6) uses file streams to make a binary copy of a file. The Max, Min, and Step properties are set to proportions of the source-file size. The number of bytes copied with every call of TFileStream.CopyFrom is small for the sake of illustration. In your production projects, allow larger chunks to be copied for best performance. The example also employs the TStatusBar control slightly ahead of schedule. The status bar is used here merely to house the TProgressBar control. You find the STSPRG1.PAS file on this book's companion CD-ROM.

FIG. 7.5

Copy file streams with Progress Bar.

Listing 7.6 \UDELPHI3\CHP7\PROGRESSBAR\PRGBAR2\ STSPRG1.PAS—Displaying File Copy Progress

```
unit StsPrg1;

interface

uses
  Windows, Messages, SysUtils, Classes, Graphics, Controls, Forms,
  Dialogs, StdCtrls, ComCtrls;type
  TForm1 = class(TForm)
    Button1: TButton;
    Edit1: TEdit;
    Edit2: TEdit;
    Label1: TLabel;
    Label2: TLabel;
    StatusBar1: TStatusBar;
    lblStep: TLabel;
    lblMin: TLabel;
    lblMax: TLabel;
    lblSize: TLabel;
    procedure Button1Click(Sender: TObject);
  end;

var
  Form1: TForm1;

implementation

{$R *.DFM}


procedure TForm1.Button1Click(Sender: TObject);
var
  FromStream, ToStream: TFileStream;
  BytesToCopy: LongInt;
begin
  FromStream := TFileStream.Create(Edit1.Text, fmOpenRead);
```

continues

Part

II

Ch

7

Listing 7.6 Continued

```
ToStream := TFileStream.Create(Edit2.Text, fmCreate or fmOpenWrite);
{ Set up Statusbar control }
StatusBar1.SimplePanel := True;
StatusBar1.SizeGrip := False;
StatusBar1.SimpleText := 'Saving to ' + Edit2.Text;
StatusBar1.Refresh; // ensure the text is displayed
try
  with TProgressBar.Create(Self) do
  try
    { Position the progress bar within the
      status bar on the right side. }
    Top := Top + 3;
    Left := StatusBar1.Width - Width;
    Height := Height - 3;
    Parent := StatusBar1;
    { Set small portions for the copy steps. }
    Step := FromStream.Size div 1000;
    Max := FromStream.Size;
    BytesToCopy := Step;
    { Display statistics. }
    lblStep.Caption := 'Step: ' + InttoStr(Step);

    lblSize.Caption := 'From Stream size: ' +
      InttoStr(FromStream.Size);
    lblMin.Caption := 'Min: ' + InttoStr(Min);
    lblMax.Caption := 'Max: ' + InttoStr(Max);
    { Perform the stream copy. }
    while (ToStream.Position + BytesToCopy <= FromStream.Size) do
    begin
      ToStream.CopyFrom(FromStream, BytesToCopy);
      StepIt;
    end;
    { Copy remaining bytes }
    ToStream.CopyFrom(FromStream, FromStream.Size - ToStream.Size);
    Position := ToStream.Size;
  finally
    StatusBar1.SimpleText := '';
    Free;
  end;
finally
  ToStream.Free;
  FromStream.Free;
end;
end;

end.
```

New for Delphi 3

Delphi 3 surfaces the latest controls from COMCTL32.DLL. The Tool Bar and Cool Bar controls in particular boost your capability to rapidly build applications with a consistent user interface.

Tool Bar

Now that TToolBar is on my palette, I'm not sure how programmers got along without it. The new TToolBar is a windowed control that assists rapid application development by allowing quick creation and management of same sized buttons. The buttons within a Tool Bar are called TToolButtons, lightweight descendants of TControl that do not consume Windows handles. TToolBar can also contain windowed controls such as TEdit or TComboBox.

Features of *TToolBar* at Design Time   To create TToolButtons at design time, right-click the Tool Bar and select New Button or New Separator from the context menu. These buttons can be dragged around in the Tool Bar control, resized, and supplied with captions. The Tool Bar maintains identical dimensions for each of its buttons, so if you resize one button, all buttons resize to match.

Use TImageList to supply graphics to TToolButtons through the Images property. Drop a TImageList on your form and load it with several bitmaps from \Images\Buttons. Now right-click the Tool Bar control and add a few buttons. Finally, set the Images property of the Tool Bar control and view the result (see Figure 7.6). Each TToolButton is supplied a graphic from the ImageList. TToolButton has an ImageIndex property that is automatically incremented along the bar and can be changed at design or runtime.

FIG. 7.6
The TToolBar at design time.

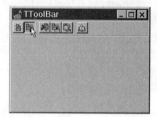

To get a flat button look similar to the MS Internet Explorer 3 toolbar, set the Flat property to True. If you want to display a second set of images as the user's mouse passes over each button, add another TImageList and assign it to the HotImages property.

If the form is resized smaller than the area that contains the TToolBar and Wrapable is True, buttons automatically move down. Also, each TToolButton has a Wrap property that forces the buttons to the right to move to the following line.

Working with *TToolBar* Programmatically   To add a TToolButton to the Tool Bar control, first create a TToolButton instance, and then set the Parent property, as follows:

```
with TToolButton.Create(Self) do
    Parent := ToolBar1;
```

To delete all TToolButtons on the bar, use the ClearButtons method. ClearButtons acts only on TToolButtons and doesn't delete any windowed controls placed on the bar. To delete a particular button on the tool bar, send the TB_DELETEBUTTON Windows message. The following example deletes the second button on ToolBar1 (the index is zero-based).

```
procedure TForm1.Button1Click(Sender: TObject);
var
  ButtonIndex: LongInt;
begin
  ButtonIndex := 1;
  SendMessage(ToolBar1.Handle, TB_DELETEBUTTON, ButtonIndex, 0);
end;
```

You can create a Tool Box that allows the user to customize a tool palette while running your application.

To create a framework application that demonstrates user-customizable tool bars, you need two forms. You load the first Tool Box form with a TToolBar, several predefined TToolButtons, and an Image List control. Populate the Tool Bar control with several new buttons, and the Image List with enough bitmaps from \Delphi 3.0\Images\Buttons to match the available buttons. Set the DragMode property of the buttons to dmAutomatic and the BorderStyle property of the TToolBar to bsSingle.

The ToolBox unit needs only an event handler defined for a single button-click for demonstration purposes. Assign this handler to all the buttons on the TToolBar, as follows:

```
procedure TfrmToolBar.CameraClick(Sender: TObject);
begin
  MessageDlg('You clicked on the ' + (Sender as TToolButton).Name +
    ' Button.', mtInformation, [mbOk], 0);end;
```

The second form also will contain a TToolBar for the user to drop new buttons onto. Set the form's Visible property to True so that when you run the project, both forms will appear at once. The unit contains more code to accept the DragDrop, to copy the buttons onto the user form, and to assign new OnClick event handlers for them.

You find the USRDEF1 and USRDEF2.PAS files (see Listing 7.7) on this book's companion CD-ROM.

Listing 7.7   \UDELPHI3\CHP7\TOOLBAR\USRDEF\USRDEF2.PAS—Creating User-Definable Tool Bars

```
unit UsrDef2;

interface

uses
  Windows, Messages, SysUtils, Classes, Graphics, Controls, Forms, Dialogs,
  ToolWin, ComCtrls;

type
  TfrmUserForm = class(TForm)
    tbUserDefined: TToolBar;
    procedure tbUserDefinedDragOver(Sender, Source: TObject; X, Y: Integer;
      State: TDragState; var Accept: Boolean);
    procedure tbUserDefinedDragDrop(Sender, Source: TObject; X, Y: Integer);
  end;
```

```
var
  frmUserForm: TfrmUserForm;

implementation

uses UsrDef1;

{$R *.DFM}

procedure TfrmUserForm.tbUserDefinedDragOver(Sender,
➥Source: TObject; X, Y: Integer;
  State: TDragState; var Accept: Boolean);
begin
  Accept := ((Sender <> Source) and (Source is TToolButton));
end;

procedure TfrmUserForm.tbUserDefinedDragDrop(Sender,
➥Source: TObject; X, Y: Integer);
const
  Count: SmallInt = 0;
begin
  with TToolButton.Create(Self) do
  begin
    // Place the button on the surface of the toolbar.
    Parent := tbUserDefined;
    // Assign button images.
    // Backtrack from the source button, get it's parent, cast to TToolBar,
    // then use the TToolBar's Images property.
    tbUserDefined.Images := TToolBar((Source as TToolButton).Parent).Images;
    ImageIndex := (Source as TToolButton).ImageIndex;
    // Give the button a new unique name.
    Name := 'New' + (Source as TToolButton).Name +
      IntToStr(Count);
    // Assign the OnClick handler
    OnClick := (Source as TToolButton).OnClick;
    Inc(Count);
  end;
end;

end.
```

Cool Bar—What's So Cool About It?

It's easy to get the idea that the Cool Bar is a gadget that acts like the Internet Explorer 3 tool bar. In fact, it's really more of a backdrop or manager for buttons and other controls. TCoolBar contains multiple TCoolBands that each contains a control that your users can dynamically position and size. TCoolBar and each of its bands can each display a single bitmap that covers only a band or the entire TCoolBar area. Additionally, the Images property associated with a TImage provides a small graphic to the left of each TCoolBand.

Cool Bands at Design Time The first task in working with TCoolBar is to create a series of Bands, one for each control to be managed by the Cool Bar. There are two ways to create Bands. You can click the ellipses on the Bands property, add a control to the form, then select

Part

II

Ch

7

the Control property of the band to associate that control with that band. For a shorter route, drop the control directly on the Cool Bar and the band automatically is created and associated to the band's Control property.

Adding Bands at Runtime   To add a TCoolBand at runtime, declare a variable of type TCollectionItem. Use the TCoolBar Add method to return a TCollectionItem instance. To use the TCollectionItem instance, you cast it to type TCoolBand. This method of creation is not quite like any we have looked at until now, is not intuitive, and may change by the time the product ships:

```
procedure TForm1.Button1Click(Sender: TObject);
var
  CoolBand: TCollectionItem;
begin
  CoolBar1.Images := ImageList1;
  CoolBand := CoolBar1.Bands.Add;
  with CoolBand as TCoolBand do
  begin
    Control := Edit1;
    Text := Edit1.Text;
    Bitmap := Image1.Picture.Bitmap;
  end;
end;
```

TDateTimePicker

TDateTimePicker provides a validated method for choosing dates and times. Initially, the TDateTimePicker looks like a combo box that contains a date but when clicked, a calendar drops down, allowing the user to browse through months or years, return to "Today," and finally to select a date. By changing the Kind property from dtDate to dtTime, TDateTimePicker becomes a time-editing control that looks somewhat like a TUpDown control. The actual value selected by the user is stored in the control's Date and Time properties of type TDate and TTime, respectively.

Although TDateTimePicker handles tedious date and time validation, you may want to interpret user input typed directly to the control. To do so, set the ParseInput property to True and check the input in the OnUserInput event handler. OnUserInput passes you the raw string as entered by the user and expects a TDateTime back. Also, you can prevent any change from occurring by setting AllowChange to False. If you want to prevent the user from picking a date through the drop-down portion of the control, set DateMode from dmComboBox (the default) to dmUpDown.

TAnimate

TAnimate plays movie clips (.AVI files) in the background while the main thread continues processing. The control can load .AVI files through the FileName or ResourceID properties, but can play only files without sound or compression. The control is designed to accept only plain-vanilla sequences of .BMP files packed into a single AVI. To play a silent AVI at design time, set the FileName property and set the Active property to True. If the "Cannot Open AVI" exception appears, the AVI probably has compression or sound, so you need to use TMediaPlayer to handle these files. Right-clicking the TAnimate component at design time allows you to execute the context menu for Next Frame and Previous Frame. The Repetitions property sets the number of times the clip loops. The default for Repetitions is –1, which causes the movie clip to cycle endlessly.

Runtime methods are Open, Close, Play, Seek, and Stop. The Play method takes parameters for the zero-based index of the starting frame, ending frame, and frame to display. A starting frame of zero causes the clip to start at the first frame. An ending frame of –1 indicates to play until the last frame in the clip. Seek positions the clip at a given frame.

TAnimate's most useful feature is the Common AVI. In Windows 95 Explorer, copying files displays a Common AVI of paper floating from one folder to another. Test this new control by dropping it onto a form, select from the CommonAVI property drop-down list, and set the Active property to True.

Complex Common Controls

As you explore the functionality of the next group of controls, notice that each has the ability to add to itself in some way. Some controls use arrays or lists; others create child objects or have Add methods. With TTabControl and TPageControl, the same underlying Windows control is surfaced along two different lines. TTabControl manages itself by employing a Tabs[] array; the TPageControl uses separate TTabSheet objects as children.

Status Bar Control

The status bar essentially allows you, as programmer, to hold a conversation with the user. With the status-bar control, you can keep the user apprised of database states, progress of operations, hints, and just about any written or painted information. You can treat the status bar as a single "simple panel" or as multiple panels with control over each panel's text alignment, style, text, bevel, and capability to owner-draw.

The *SimplePanel* Property   To use the Status Bar in its most elementary form, set the SimplePanel property to True, and assign a string to the SimpleText property, as follows:

```
StatusBar1.SimplePanel := True;
StatusBar1.SimpleText := 'a simple example';
```

Taking the simple text idea further, you can assign the application's OnHint event handler to update the TStatusBar text so that, as the user passes the mouse cursor over various controls, the hints appear in the status bar. To test this capability, provide strings for the Hint property of several controls on your form. Then set up an OnHint event handler and assign the handler in the form's OnCreate, as follows:

```
type
  TForm1 = class(TForm)
  .
  .
```

```
.
  private
    procedure StatusHint(Sender: TObject);
  end;
.
.
.
procedure TForm1.StatusHint(Sender: TObject);
begin
  StatusBar1.SimpleText := Application.Hint;
end;

procedure TForm1.FormCreate(Sender: TObject);
begin
  StatusBar1.SimplePanel := True;
  Application.OnHint := StatusHint;
end;
```

Multiple Panels   In the following sections, you learn how to create multiple panels program-matically and how to manipulate each panel. These sections work with these panels as surfaces for drawing and as containers for windowed controls.

Creating Panels On-the-Fly   To create a new panel in a `TStatusBar` where `SimplePanel` is false, use the `Add` method of the `TStatusBar` Panels object. Now that you have a `TStatusPanel` reference passed back from the `Add` method, you can set properties of the panel.

```
Procedure MyProc;
var
  Panel: TStatusPanel;
begin
  Panel := StatusBar1.Panels.Add;
  with Panel do
  begin
    Text := 'New Panel';
    Bevel := pbLowered;
    Alignment := taCenter;
    Width := 100;
  end;
end;
```

For a better feel of how you can manipulate the panel settings programmatically, the next project (see Listing 7.8) mimics the functionality of the `Panels` property editor. To create the project shown in Figure 7.7, you need an edit component to supply the panel text, a second edit component associated with a `TUpdown` control for panel width, two `TRadioGroup` controls to manage the `Alignment` and `Bevel` properties, and a `TButton` to kick off the creation of the panel. You find the STSBAR1.PAS file on this book's companion CD-ROM.

FIG. 7.7
Creating panels
"on-the-fly."

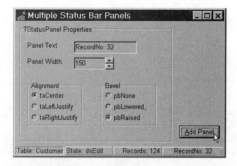

Listing 7.8 \UDELPHI3\CHP7\STATUSBAR\STSBAR1\STS1.PAS—Exploring Panel Properties

```pascal
unit Sts1;

interface

uses
  Windows, Messages, SysUtils, Classes, Graphics, Controls, Forms, Dialogs,
  ComCtrls, StdCtrls, ExtCtrls, Buttons;

type
  TForm1 = class(TForm)
    StatusBar1: TStatusBar;
    Button1: TButton;
    GroupBox1: TGroupBox;
    rgAlignment: TRadioGroup;
    edPanelText: TEdit;
    Label1: TLabel;
    rgBevel: TRadioGroup;
    edPanelWidth: TEdit;
    Label2: TLabel;
    UpDown1: TUpdown;
    procedure Button1Click(Sender: TObject);
  end;

var
  Form1: TForm1;

implementation

{$R *.DFM}

//-------------------------------------------------------------------
// Add a new panel and set panel attributes
//-------------------------------------------------------------------
procedure TForm1.Button1Click(Sender: TObject);
const
  BevelSettings: array[0..2] of TStatusPanelBevel =
    (pbNone, pbLowered, pbRaised);
  AlignmentSettings: array[0..2] of TAlignment =
    (taCenter, taLeftJustify, taRightJustify);
```

continues

Part
II

Ch

7

Listing 7.8   Continued

```
var
  Panel: TStatusPanel;
begin
  Panel := StatusBar1.Panels.Add;
  with Panel do
  begin
    Text := edPanelText.Text;
    Bevel := BevelSettings[rgBevel.ItemIndex];
    Alignment := AlignmentSettings[rgAlignment.ItemIndex];
    Width := StrToInt(edPanelWidth.Text);
  end;
end;

end.
```

Drawing on the Panel   You may have noticed the Style property was left out from the previous example. The Style property gives you control over drawing any panel. The default style is psText. If the panel style is psOwnerDraw, you are free to use the TStatusBar OnDrawPanel event. The OnDrawPanel event supplies you with references to the TStatusBar component as a whole, the specific panel that is being drawn, and the rectangle of the drawing area.

For example, Listing 7.9 demonstrates that you can paint three-dimensional text, raised or lowered, directly on the status bar canvas (see Figure 7.8). The source for STS2.PAS is located on the companion CD-ROM.

FIG. 7.8

Drawing 3-D text to the status panel.

Listing 7.9   \UDELPHI3\CHP7\STATUSBAR\STSBAR2\STS2.PAS—Drawing 3-D Text to the Status Panel

```
unit Sts2;

interface

uses
  Windows, Messages, SysUtils, Classes, Graphics, Controls, Forms,
  ComCtrls, ExtCtrls, StdCtrls, Buttons;
```

```
type

  TTextStyle = (spTextRaised, spTextLowered);

  TForm1 = class(TForm)
    StatusBar1: TStatusBar;
    edPanelText: TEdit;
    Label1: TLabel;
    rgTextStyle: TRadioGroup;
    procedure StatusBar1DrawPanel(StatusBar: TStatusBar;
      Panel: TStatusPanel; const Rect: TRect);
    procedure FormCreate(Sender: TObject);
    procedure edPanelTextChange(Sender: TObject);
    procedure Draw3DText(Canvas: TCanvas;
      PanelRect: TRect; Text: String;  TextStyle: TTextStyle);
  end;

var
  Form1: TForm1;

implementation

{$R *.DFM}

procedure TForm1.Draw3DText(Canvas: TCanvas;
  PanelRect: TRect; Text: String; TextStyle: TTextStyle);
begin
  with Canvas do
  begin
    // paint only the text, not the background
    Brush.Style := bsClear;
    Font.Color := clHighlightText;
    DrawText(Handle, PChar(Text), -1, PanelRect,
      DT_VCENTER and DT_SINGLELINE);
    if (TextStyle = spTextRaised) then
    begin
      Inc(PanelRect.Left);
      Inc(PanelRect.Top);
    end
    else
    begin
      Dec(PanelRect.Left);
      Dec(PanelRect.Top);
    end;
    Font.Color := clWindowText;
    DrawText(Handle, PChar(Text), -1, PanelRect,
      DT_VCENTER and DT_SINGLELINE);
  end;
end;

procedure TForm1.StatusBar1DrawPanel(StatusBar: TStatusBar;
  Panel: TStatusPanel; const Rect: TRect);
var
  PanelRect: TRect;
begin
```

continues

Listing 7.9   Continued

```
  Panel.text := edPanelText.Text;
  PanelRect := Rect;
  with PanelRect do
    Left := Left + Canvas.TextWidth('W');
  if rgTextStyle.ItemIndex = 0 then
    Draw3DText(StatusBar.Canvas, PanelRect, Panel.Text, spTextRaised)
  else
    Draw3DText(StatusBar.Canvas, PanelRect, Panel.Text, spTextLowered)
end;

procedure TForm1.FormCreate(Sender: TObject);
var
  Panel: TStatusPanel;
begin
  Panel := StatusBar1.Panels.Add;
  Panel.Style := psOwnerDraw;
end;

procedure TForm1.edPanelTextChange(Sender: TObject);
begin
  StatusBar1.Refresh;
end;

end.
```

Using the OnDrawPanel method, you're not limited to text, or where you can draw within the TStatusBar control. Having access to the TStatusBar Canvas, you can animate a stock ticker moving along the length of the status bar or display a bitmap along with text.

Because the status bar is a windowed control, it can house other controls. For example, you can populate the status bar with TImage components, load the image Picture property with a representation of a program icon, create an "Actionable" status bar, much like the system tray in Windows 95, or the smaller icons of Microsoft Word 7.0 found at the bottom of the screen that initiate spell checking or change the keyboard state.

The project shown in Figure 7.9 contains a status bar with miniature application icons that, when clicked, will run a corresponding program.

The action takes place during the form creation (see Listing 7.10). A list of application executable names are loaded into a TStringList, and in the same loop, an ImageList is loaded with a series of images using the Imagelist_AddIcon API call (supported by COMMCTRL.PAS). Imagelist_AddIcon requires the ImageList handle, and an icon derived from another API call, ExtractIcon. (The function header for ExtractIcon is located in SHELLAPI.PAS.) ExtractIcon takes an instance handle, the name of the file containing an icon, and the index of the icon, as follows:

```
Imagelist_AddIcon(ImageList.Handle, ExtractIcon(Handle, PChar(ExeList[i]), 0));
```

Load the TImageList and TStringList and pass them to the DisplayIconImages procedure, along with an instance of a windowed control used to parent a series of TImages. Within

`DisplayIconImages`, you loop through the `ImageList`, creating `TImage` components on the status bar as you go. Each `TImage` canvas is painted with the status bar color and a scaled-down representation of the program icon, given a `Hint` property from the `TStringList` containing the executable name, and hooked up to an `OnClick` handler that takes care of executing the associated application.

The actionable status bar concept could be expanded to include a user-configured list of applications. Or it could display icons for a series of actions taken within your application, such as navigating a table, spell checking a rich-text document, or sending an e-mail by using SMTP. You find the ACTBAR1.PAS file on this book's companion CD-ROM.

FIG. 7.9
An "actionable" status bar.

Listing 7.10 \UDELPHI3\CHP7\STATUSBAR\ACTBAR1\ACTBAR1.PAS—Creating an "Actionable" Status Bar

```
unit ActBar1;

interface

uses
  Windows, Messages, SysUtils, Classes, Graphics, Controls, Forms,
  Dialogs, ComCtrls, ExtCtrls, StdCtrls, Buttons;

type
  TForm1 = class(TForm)
    StatusBar1: TStatusBar;
    procedure FormCreate(Sender: TObject);
  private
    procedure StatusIconClick(Sender: TObject);
    procedure DisplayIconImages(ImageList: TImageList;
      ExeNameList: TStringList; WinControl: TWinControl);
  end;

var
```

continues

Listing 7.10 Continued

```
  Form1: TForm1;

implementation

{$R *.DFM}

uses ShellAPI, CommCtrl;

procedure TForm1.StatusIconClick(Sender: TObject);
begin
  WinExec(PChar((Sender as TImage).Hint), SW_ShowNormal);
end;

procedure TForm1.DisplayIconImages(ImageList: TImageList;
  ExeNameList: TStringList; WinControl: TWinControl);
var
  IconLeft: integer;
  i: integer;
begin
  IconLeft := ImageList.Width div 2;
  for i := 0 to ImageList.Count - 1 do
    with TImage.Create(Self) do
    begin
      Parent := WinControl;
      Hint := ExeNameList.Strings[i];
      ShowHint := True;
      OnClick := StatusIconClick;
      Top := (WinControl.Height - ImageList.Height) div 2;
      Left := IconLeft;
      Width := ImageList.Width;
      Height := ImageList.Height;
      IconLeft := IconLeft + Width + 5;
      Canvas.Brush.color := StatusBar1.Brush.Color;
      Canvas.FillRect(Canvas.ClipRect);
      ImageList.Draw(Canvas, 0, 0, i);
    end;
end;

procedure TForm1.FormCreate(Sender: TObject);
const
  ExeList: array[0..9] of String = (
    'CALC.EXE',
    'CLIPBRD.EXE',
    'NOTEPAD.EXE',
    'REGEDIT.EXE',
    'PBRUSH.EXE',
    'SYSMON.EXE',
    'DEFRAG.EXE',
    'EXPLORER.EXE',
    'TELNET.EXE',
    'TERMINAL.EXE'
  );
var
  StringList: TStringList;
```

```
    ImageList: TImageList;
    i: integer;
begin
  StringList := TStringList.Create;
  ImageList := TImageList.Create(Self);
  try
    for i := 0 to 9 do
    begin
      Imagelist_AddIcon(ImageList.Handle,
        ExtractIcon(Handle, PChar(ExeList[i]), 0));
      StringList.Add(ExeList[i]);
    end;
    DisplayIconImages(ImageList, StringList, StatusBar1);
  finally
    StringList.Free;
    ImageList.Free;
  end;
end;


end.
```

Header Control

The Header Control is a general-purpose panel aligned to the top of the form that can be treated much like the TStatusBar. Similar techniques can be used to add sections and to handle owner draw events. Unlike TStatusBar, THeaderControl contains Sections instead of Panels. To find out what's happening in your Sections, use the THeaderControl OnSectionClick, OnSectionResize, and OnSectionTrack events.

You can create new sections during design time by clicking the ellipses for the Sections property and clicking the property editor Add button. By selecting a THeaderSection within the property editor, you can set text or specify width.

To create Sections programmatically, use the Sections Add method and assign the result to a THeaderSection (see Listing 7.11). You can find SECCRT1.PAS on this book's companion CD-ROM.

**Listing 7.11 \UDELPHI3\CHP7\HEADERCONTROL\SECTIONCREATE
\SECCRT1.PAS—Creating Header Sections Programmatically**

```
procedure CreateSections(HeaderControl: THeaderControl;
  SectionText: array of string);
var
  I: integer;
  HS: THeaderSection;
begin
  for I := Low(SectionText) to High(SectionText) do
  begin
    HS := HeaderControl.Sections.Add;
    HS.Text := SectionText[I];
```

Part
II

Ch
7

continues

Listing 7.11 Continued

```
    end;
  end;

procedure TForm1.FormCreate(Sender: TObject);
begin
  CreateSections(HeaderControl1, ['one', 'two', 'three', 'four']);

end;
```

Each section can be owner drawn or drawn by the control. If you specify a Style property of hsOwnerDraw for the section, you need to write code for the OnDrawSection event handler. The short example shown in Figure 7.10 demonstrates drawing an ImageList graphic in response to pressing a section (see Listing 7.12). The color of the font also changes to highlight the current text. You find SECDRW1.PAS on this book's companion CD-ROM .

FIG. 7.10

Owner draw of header sections.

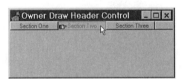

Listing 7.12 \UDELPHI3\CHP7\HEADERCONTROL\ONSECTIONDRAW\ SECDRW1.PAS—Taking Control of Drawing Header Sections

```
procedure TForm1.HeaderControl1DrawSection(HeaderControl: THeaderControl;
  Section: THeaderSection; const Rect: TRect; Pressed: Boolean);
begin
  with HeaderControl.Canvas do
    if Pressed then
    begin
      Font.Color := clRed;
      ImageList1.Draw(HeaderControl.Canvas, Rect.Left + 2, Rect.Top + 2, 0);
      TextOut(Rect.Left + ImageList1.Width + 4, Rect.Top + 2, Section.Text);
    end
    else
    begin
      Font.Color := clBlue;
      TextOut(Rect.Left + ImageList1.Width + 4, Rect.Top + 2, Section.Text);
    end;
end;
```

THeaderControl contains two unique events OnSectionTrack and OnSectionResize. OnSectionTrack triggers when the user drags the divider. When the divider is released, the OnSectionResize event fires. You might use these two event handlers to keep the widths for other controls, such as TListBoxes, in sync with respective sections.

Image List

The Image List is a non-visual control, indirectly descended from TComponent whose entire purpose is to store a series of same-size images. It doesn't look like much, but many of the Win32 components use TImageList as a source for visual distinction.

A list of images can be easily defined at design time in the TImageList component editor, and then assigned to various image properties of controls such as TTreeView, TListView, TToolBar, and TCoolBar. For example, TListView has both SmallImages and LargeImages properties that point to separate TImageLists that supply graphics for small and full-size icons. TImageList also has its own drawing methods, methods for displaying images during dragging of a window control, and support for masks and overlay images.

> **N O T E** The latest Common Controls DLL (4.0) that come with Internet Explorer 3.0 expand the role of Image List. The Image List, for example, is used in conjunction with an enhanced Header Control that automates the process of displaying images in the header, obviating the need for obtaining a canvas and drawing directly. ■

The *ImageList* in Design Mode   You can get a feel for the ImageList basics without writing code. In a new project, add a TTreeView to your form. Set the TTreeView Images property to ImageList1. Then find the Items property and click the ellipses to initiate the TTreeView Items Editor.

Click the New Item button and fill in any text (see Figure 7.11). Leave the image selected, and state index properties at their defaults for now. Repeat the New Item option a few times and enter any text. When you reach the last item, click the New SubItem button and fill in the text. For the SubItem, set the Image Index to 1. To finish, click OK to exit the Items Editor.

FIG. 7.11
The TTreeView Items
Editor.

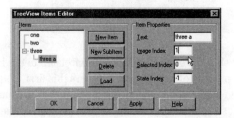

Now double-click the TImageList component to display the ImageList Editor. The editor displays four cells along the bottom of the dialog box to contain your series of images. Horizontal scrollbars appear when a fifth image is added to the series. Click Add and point the directory to \DELPHI3\IMAGES\BUTTONS and double-click the first file in the list ABORT.BMP and repeat this step with ALARM.BMP. In response to the dialog box request to "separate into 2 separate bitmaps?", click No. Select the Options radio button to Crop. Click OK on the ImageList Editor to view the TTreeView control and run the project (see Figure 7.12). The first level of items display the ABORT.BMP image, and the subitems show ALARM.BMP. Changing the Image Index of a node results in displaying the corresponding entry in the Image List.

Part
II
Ch
7

FIG. 7.12

`TTreeView` and associated images.

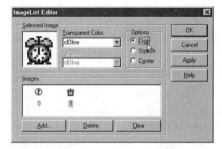

You will see more of `TImageList` supporting roles as you explore other Win32 controls that depend on the Image List. For now, see what `TImageList` is capable of on its own.

***TImageList* Screen Capture**   Image sizes default to 16×16 pixels, but really can be quite a bit larger, even as large as the entire screen. Call the `CreateSize` constructor with new width and height parameters to carve out a new chunk of image-storing real estate. With `CreateSize` and the `GetBitmap` method, you can implement a rudimentary screen-capture utility that captures the desktop as a whole, saves, and loads the bitmap image from the file (see Figure 7.13).

FIG. 7.13

Image List screen capture utility.

Drawing and saving the desktop as one giant canvas is unrelated to the Image List specifically, but fundamental to a screen capture, so this section covers this first. You need to obtain a handle to a Device context for the entire desktop, and assign it as the handle to a `TCanvas`. In the private section of the form-type declaration, place a variable to contain the desktop canvas.

```
type
  TForm1 = class(TForm)
  .
  .
  .
private
  DeskTopCanvas: TCanvas;
end;
```

Also, in the form `OnCreate` handler, place the assignment of the desktop device context to the handle of the new canvas.

```
// Get device context of the desktop window.
procedure TForm1.FormCreate(Sender: TObject);
begin
  DeskTopCanvas := TCanvas.Create;
  DeskTopCanvas.Handle := GetDC(Hwnd_Desktop);
end;
```

N O T E Hwnd_Desktop is a special constant defined in WINDOWS.PAS that identifies the desktop. Hwnd_Desktop is currently defined as merely being equal to zero, but the constant is included for compatibility and readability. ■

Now that you have access to TCanvas methods and properties, you can save the desktop as a bitmap for later insertion into the TImageList. To test the validity of the steps so far, place a button on the form with code to draw text to the upper left corner of the desktop.

```
procedure TForm1.Button1Click(Sender: TObject);
begin
  DeskTopCanvas.TextOut(0,0,'   howdy world'   );
end;
```

After testing this, get rid of the test code, and delete the button from the form. In the remainder of this section, you see through an example how to:

- Capture the image of the desktop to the Image List
- Keep track of and display the Image List bitmap
- Drag the displayed image within the viewer

Dragging the image within the viewer takes a disproportionate amount of code, so this is deferred to a later addition and added on then.

The project requires a panel that covers most of the form except for a strip on the bottom, with Align set to alTop and BevelOuter to bvLowered. Drop a TImage control onto the panel and set Align to alClient. At the bottom of the form place a Speed Button, Image List, Edit control, and TUpdown control. Set the Associate property of the TUpdown to Edit1 and the Max property to zero. Load VIDEO.BMP as the graphic for the speed button.

This takes care of roughing in the user interface. Because the Image List defaults to only a 16×16 pixel image, now you need to run the constructor CreateSize to allow the large screen-size bitmaps that need to be stored there. You do this by passing the screen width and height parameter so that the form OnCreate handler now looks like:

```
procedure TForm1.FormCreate(Sender: TObject);
begin
    // Get device context of the desktop window.
  DeskTopCanvas := TCanvas.Create;
    // Reconstruct the Imagelist with larger dimensions
  ImageList1.CreateSize(Screen.Width, Screen.Height);
end;
```

Part
II

Ch
7

I place the code for redrawing the Image control in a single routine that takes the upper-left coordinates of the area to be painted. This helps out later when trying to drag the image around within the viewer.

```
procedure TForm1.RefreshImage(X, Y: SmallInt);
begin
    Image1.Canvas.FillRect(Image1.Canvas.ClipRect);
    ImageList1.Draw(Image1.Canvas, X, Y, UpDown1.Position);
    Image1.Refresh;
end;
```

The button click handler for the speed button causes a temporary bitmap to be created that allows you to perform a `CopyRect` method of the `DeskTopCanvas`. Next, the temporary bitmap is used to add to the Image List control, and then the `TUpDown` is updated to reflect the new number of images contained by the Image List. Finally, the image is redrawn via `RefreshImage`.

```
procedure TForm1.SpeedButton1Click(Sender: TObject);
begin
  BitMap := TBitMap.Create;
  DeskTopCanvas.Handle := GetDC(Hwnd_Desktop);
    try
    // Size the bitmap to dimensions of the screen
    // and draw screen canvas to it.
    BitMap.Width := Screen.Width;
    BitMap.Height := Screen.Height;
    Bitmap.Canvas.CopyRect(Bitmap.Canvas.ClipRect,
    DeskTopCanvas, DeskTopCanvas.ClipRect);
    // Add the new bitmap to the Image List
    ImageList1.Add(BitMap, nil);
    // Update the TUpdown control to reflect number of images
    UpDown1.Max := ImageList1.Count - 1;
    UpDown1.Position := UpDown1.Max;
    Updown1.Invalidate;
    // Repaint the current Image List bitmap onto the Image control
    RefreshImage(0, 0);
    finally
    ReleaseDC(Handle, Hwnd_Desktop);
    BitMap.Free;
    end;
end;
```

There are two other one-liner routines—one for the `TUpDown` control `OnClick` that causes a `RefreshImage`, and a second routine that frees the `DeskTopCanvas` object during form destruction.

To restrict the bitmap redrawing to occur only when the mouse button is pressed and the mouse is moving, you need to add a `MouseIsDown` Boolean to the form type declaration to check during the `OnMouseMove` event handler. You also need to add variables `ImgX` and `ImgY` to track the upper-left corner of the bitmap as it's dragged within the Image control.

You can assign an open-hand cursor to the `TImage` control, indicating the capability to drag.

```
type
  TForm1 = class(TForm)
  .
  .
  .
private
    DeskTopCanvas: TCanvas;
```

```
    BitMap: TBitMap;
  ImgX, ImgY: SmallInt;
  MouseIsDown: Boolean;
  procedure RefreshImage(X, Y: SmallInt);
end;

implementation

{$R *.DFM}

const
  crHandOpen = 1;
```

Add code to the form OnCreate handler to initialize the hand cursor, as follows:

```
// Use an open hand cursor to indicate the bitmap can be dragged
Screen.Cursors[crHandOpen] := LoadCursorFromFile('HandFlat.cur');
Image1.Cursor := crHandOpen;
```

The remaining code in Listing 7.13 calculates distance and direction of the image drag and redraws in the new location. You find the SCRCAP1.PAS file on this book's companion CD-ROM.

Listing 7.13 \UDELPHI3\CHP7\IMAGELIST\SCRCAP\SCRCAP1.PAS—ImageList Screen Capture

```
unit ScrCap1;

interface

uses
  Windows, Messages, SysUtils, Classes, Graphics, Controls, Forms,
  Dialogs, ExtCtrls, StdCtrls, Buttons, ComCtrls;

type
  TForm1 = class(TForm)
    ImageList1: TImageList;
    SpeedButton1: TSpeedButton;
    Edit1: TEdit;
    UpDown1: TUpDown;
    Panel1: TPanel;
    Image1: TImage;
    Label1: TLabel;
    procedure FormCreate(Sender: TObject);
    procedure FormDestroy(Sender: TObject);
    procedure SpeedButton1Click(Sender: TObject);
    procedure UpDown1Click(Sender: TObject; Button: TUDBtnType);
    procedure Image1MouseMove(Sender: TObject; Shift: TShiftState; X,
      Y: Integer);
    procedure Image1MouseUp(Sender: TObject; Button: TMouseButton;
      Shift: TShiftState; X, Y: Integer);
    procedure Image1MouseDown(Sender: TObject; Button: TMouseButton;
      Shift: TShiftState; X, Y: Integer);
  private
    DeskTopCanvas: TCanvas;
```

continues

Part II
Ch 7

Listing 7.13   Continued

```pascal
    BitMap: TBitMap;
    ImgX, ImgY: SmallInt;
    MouseIsDown: Boolean;
    procedure RefreshImage(X, Y: SmallInt);
  end;

var
  Form1: TForm1;

implementation

{$R *.DFM}

const
  crHandOpen = 1;

// Clear old bitmap, draw new bitmap on the Image control
// force a repaint.
procedure TForm1.RefreshImage(X, Y: SmallInt);
begin
  Image1.Canvas.FillRect(Image1.Canvas.ClipRect);
  ImageList1.Draw(Image1.Canvas, X, Y, UpDown1.Position);
  Image1.Refresh;
end;

procedure TForm1.FormCreate(Sender: TObject);
begin
  // Get device context of the desktop window.
  DeskTopCanvas := TCanvas.Create;
  // Reconstruct the Imagelist with larger dimensions
  ImageList1.CreateSize(Screen.Width, Screen.Height);

  Screen.Cursors[crHandOpen] := LoadCursorFromFile('HandFlat.cur');
  Image1.Cursor := crHandOpen;
end;

procedure TForm1.FormDestroy(Sender: TObject);
begin
  DeskTopCanvas.Free;
end;

procedure TForm1.SpeedButton1Click(Sender: TObject);
begin
  Visible := False;
  BitMap := TBitMap.Create;
  DeskTopCanvas.Handle := GetDC(Hwnd_Desktop);
  try
    // Size the bitmap to dimensions of the screen
    // and draw screen canvas to it.
    BitMap.Width := Screen.Width;
    BitMap.Height := Screen.Height;
    Bitmap.Canvas.CopyRect(Bitmap.Canvas.ClipRect,
      DeskTopCanvas, DeskTopCanvas.ClipRect);
    // Add the new bitmap to the Image List
```

```
      ImageList1.Add(BitMap, nil);
      // Update the UpDown control to reflect number of images
      UpDown1.Max := ImageList1.Count - 1;
      UpDown1.Position := UpDown1.Max;
      Updown1.Invalidate;
      // Repaint the current Image List bitmap onto the Image control
      ImgX := 0;
      ImgY := 0;
      RefreshImage(0, 0);
    finally
      ReleaseDC(Handle, Hwnd_Desktop);
      BitMap.Free;
      Visible := True;
    end;
end;

procedure TForm1.UpDown1Click(Sender: TObject; Button: TUDBtnType);
begin
  RefreshImage(0, 0);
end;

procedure TForm1.Image1MouseMove(Sender: TObject; Shift: TShiftState;
  X, Y: Integer);const
  LastX: SmallInt = 0;
  LastY: SmallInt = 0;
begin
  if MouseIsDown and (ImageList1.Count > 0) then
  begin
    if X > LastX then
      ImgX := ImgX + (X - LastX)
    else
    if X < LastX then
      ImgX := ImgX - (LastX - X);
    if Y > LastY then
      ImgY := ImgY + (Y - LastY)
    else
    if Y < LastY then
      ImgY := ImgY - (LastY - Y);
    RefreshImage(ImgX, ImgY);
  end;
  LastX := X;
  LastY := Y;
end;

procedure TForm1.Image1MouseUp(Sender: TObject; Button: TMouseButton;
  Shift: TShiftState; X, Y: Integer);
begin
  MouseIsDown := False;
end;

procedure TForm1.Image1MouseDown(Sender: TObject; Button: TMouseButton;
  Shift: TShiftState; X, Y: Integer);
begin
  MouseIsDown := True;
end;

end.
```

Part

II

Ch

7

Tab Control

The Tab Control, such as `TPageControl`, is a descendant of `TCustomTabControl`. `TTabControl` displays tabs across the top of the control, but has no built-in pages. Use the Tab Control where you want a notebook metaphor, without the overhead of maintaining additional windowed controls, as is the case for `TPageControl`. Although the `TTabControl` is lighter weight than the `TPageControl`, choosing `TTabControl` also means having to programmatically respond to new tab selection by the user.

Managing Tabs   Creating new tabs is performed by using the `Tabs` property. Use the `Tabs` property editor during design time to set new tabs. Because the `Tabs` property is of type `TStrings`, you also can add, delete, and insert tabs at runtime. The `TabIndex` property tracks the currently selected tab.

> **CAUTION**
>
> A TabIndex setting of –1 indicates no tab was selected, so test for this and avoid the "EList error...tab control access error." You may think this condition will never arise, but just after deleting a tab programmatically, no tab is selected.

On the CD   You can test managing the `Tabs` property programmatically with minimal code (see Figure 7.14). In a new project, drop a `TTabControl`, an Edit control, and three Bit Buttons. Label the Bit Buttons "Add," "Insert," and "Delete," and assign names as bbAdd, bbInsert, and bbDelete. Create `OnClick` event handlers for all three buttons and insert the code found in Listing 7.14. The complete listing for TC1.PAS is located on this book's companion CD-ROM.

FIG. 7.14

Adding, inserting, and deleting tabs at runtime.

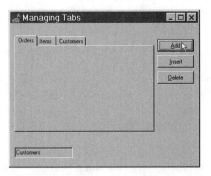

Listing 7.14   \UDELPHI3\CHP7\TABCONTROL\ADDINSRT\TC1.PAS—
Adding, Inserting, and Deleting Tabs at Runtime

```
procedure TForm1.bbAddClick(Sender: TObject);
begin
  TabControl1.Tabs.Add(Edit1.Text);
end;

procedure TForm1.bbInsertClick(Sender: TObject);
```

```
begin
  if (TabControl1.TabIndex <> -1) then
    TabControl1.Tabs.Insert(TabControl1.TabIndex, Edit1.Text);
end;

procedure TForm1.bbDeleteClick(Sender: TObject);
begin
  if (TabControl1.TabIndex <> -1) then
    TabControl1.Tabs.Delete(TabControl1.TabIndex);
end;
```

Tab Dimensions and Placement   `TabWidth` and `TabHeight` indicate the size of the dimension in pixels. Sizing tab width and height is done by the control when `TabHeight` and `TabWidth` are left at the default of zero. After you set `TabWidth` or `TabHeight` to a non-zero value, these dimensions become fixed.

`MultiLine` is a Boolean property that controls the behavior of tabs that exceed the width of the Tab Control. With `MultiLine` false, a set of arrows appears that allow the user to scroll to tabs not visible on the control. If `MultiLine` is true, the tabs stack up vertically within the visible area of the Tab Control (see Figure 7.15).

FIG. 7.15

Tab Control with
`MultiLine`,
`TabWidth`,
`TabHeight` settings.

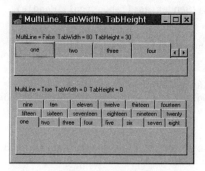

Tab Control Events   The Tab Control has two notable events. The first, in the order that the events are fired, is the `OnChanging` event. You can use the `OnChanging` event's `AllowChange` parameter to prevent the user from moving to another tab before meeting validation criteria. For example, you may want them to fill out an edit control before allowing a change to the new tab.

```
procedure TForm1.TabControl1Changing(Sender: TObject;
  var AllowChange: Boolean);
begin
  AllowChange := (Edit1.Text <> '');
end;
```

The `OnChange` event occurs next, after the tab change takes place. Use this event handler to house code that refreshes data, or displays controls based on the current `TabIndex` property.

Drawing Directly to the Tab Control   You can draw directly to the client or tab areas of the Tab Control, as the following two sections demonstrate.

Part

II

Ch

7

Drawing to the Tab Control Client Area The Tab Control has a tantalizing set of properties, such as `DisplayRect`, that would seem to indicate that you can draw on it, if only you had a canvas. On the other hand, you cannot draw to the form's canvas because the Tab Control obscures the view. You could, of course, throw a `TImage` control onto the Tab Control and draw on the `TImage` `Canvas`.

On the CD

Fortunately, an extra control is unnecessary. The `TTabControl` has a `Handle` property that can be used in a call to `GetDC`. All you need to do is create a `TCanvas`, and assign the handle returned from `GetDC` to the `Canvas` `Handle` property (see Listing 7.15). You find the TCDRAW1.PAS file on this book's companion CD-ROM.

**Listing 7.15   \UDELPHI3\CHP7\TABCONTROL\PAINT\TCDRAW1.PAS—
Painting to the TabControl**

```
procedure TForm1.TabControl1Change(Sender: TObject);
var
  Canvas: TCanvas;
begin
  Canvas := TCanvas.Create;
  try
    Canvas.Handle := GetDC((Sender as TTabControl).Handle);
    try
      Canvas.Font.Color := clRed;
      with (Sender as TTabControl), DisplayRect do
      begin
       Canvas.Brush.Color := clWhite;
       Canvas.FillRect(DisplayRect);
       Canvas.TextOut((Right - Canvas.TextWidth(Tabs[TabIndex]))
         div 2, Bottom div 2, Tabs[TabIndex]);
      end;
    finally
      ReleaseDC((Sender as TTabControl).Handle, Canvas.Handle);
    end;
  finally
    Canvas.Free;
  end;
end;
```

N O T E The technique used to draw on the Tab Control client area can be used in a number of circumstances, where a specific OnDraw event handler or `Canvas` property is not provided. Remember that if you have a window handle, you can derive the device context through `GetDC` and assign it to a `Handle` property of a canvas that you create. ■

Drawing on the Tab What about drawing to the tab area of a `TTabControl`? Perhaps you want to draw a graphic in one of the tabs, or change the color of the text in the tab. The same general technique works here, with one addition. You need the rectangle of the currently selected tab. Browsing through the `TTabControl` properties, you have `BoundsRect`, `ClientRect`, and `DisplayRect`. These `TRect` properties don't do much good because all refer to the `TTabControl` as a whole.

Delphi doesn't always supply every property you may want, but it often allows you access to the tools to provide for yourself. In this case, you can send the Windows API message `TCM_GETITEMRECT` directly to the control and receive the bounding rectangle for a particular tab. The basic syntax for the call is shown in the following line:

```
SendMessage(TabControl1.Handle, TCM_GETITEMRECT, TabIndex, LongInt(@TCRect));
```

The `SendMessage` requires the handle to the control, the message constant `TCM_GETITEMRECT` (defined in COMMCTRL.PAS), the index of the tab in question, and the address of a `TRect` variable. After you have the `TRect` variable loaded with the dimensions of the tab, you can use the same set of techniques to paint on the tab area.

To demonstrate the technique, I've written an enhanced a Tab Control called `THilightTabControl` that highlights the current tab index in a red font by overwriting the original text (see Listing 7.17). I will not delve into component creation or installation here; other parts of this book address these issues. Do notice that we're trapping the `WM_PAINT` Windows message here rather than, say, trapping the `OnChange` event. Trapping at this level will give us correct repainting behavior even when the control is first shown or when covered and then revealed by another window. Listing 7.16 (HLTABC1.PAS) is on this book's companion CD-ROM.

Listing 7.16 \UDELPHI3\CHP7\TABCONTROL\HILITE\HLTABC1.PAS—The
***THIlightTabControl* Component Listing**

```
unit HLTabC1;

interface

uses
  Windows, Messages, SysUtils, Classes, Graphics, Controls, Forms,
  Dialogs, ComCtrls;

type

  THilightTabControl = class(TTabControl)
  private
    procedure WMPaint(var Message: TWMPaint); message WM_PAINT;
  end;

procedure Register;

implementation

uses CommCtrl;

procedure THilightTabControl.WMPaint(var Message: TWMPaint);
var
  InnerRect, TCRect: TRect;
  Canvas: TCanvas;
begin
  inherited;
  SendMessage(Handle, TCM_GETITEMRECT, TabIndex, LongInt(@TCRect));
```

continues

Part

II

Ch

7

Listing 7.16   Continued

```
  Canvas := TCanvas.Create;
  try
    with TCRect do
      InnerRect := Rect(Left + 6, Top + 2, Right - 6, Bottom - 2);
    Canvas.Handle := GetDC(Handle);
    Canvas.Font.Color := clRed;
    Canvas.Brush.Color := clBtnFace;
    Canvas.TextOut(InnerRect.Left, InnerRect.Top, Tabs[TabIndex]);
  finally
    Canvas.Free;
  end;
end;

procedure Register;
begin
  RegisterComponents('UDelphi3', [THilightTabControl]);
end;

end.
```

Page Control

TPageControl and TTabControl descend from a common ancestor—TCustomTabControl—and share similar properties and events. MultiLine, TabHeight, TabWidth, OnChange, and OnChanging are identical between the two controls. TPageControl, however, contains Tab Sheets that can in turn contain other visual controls, and the methods used to manage the tabs also are handled differently from the Tab Control.

Creating Tab Sheets at Design Time   There isn't an editor in TPageControl that allows editing a string list of tabs, as is the case with TTabControl. Rather, Tab Sheets (or *Pages*) are separate controls created and associated with the Page Control through the Tab Sheet PageControl property. Adding Tab Sheets to a Page Control actually adds to an array of TTabSheet known as the *Pages property*. Each time Pages acquires a new Tab Sheet, a PageCount property is incremented.

To add a Tab Sheet at design time, right-click the Page Control and select New Page from the context menu. The context menu also provides for navigating to previous and next pages during design time.

Creating Tab Sheets at Runtime   To add a Tab Sheet to a Page Control programmatically, first create the TTabSheet control, and then assign its PageControl property.

```
// Create 5 Tab Sheets on PageControl1
procedure TForm1.FormCreate(Sender: TObject);
var
  i: integer;
begin
  for i := 0 to 4 do
    with TTabSheet.Create(Self) do
```

```
    begin
      PageControl := PageControl1;
      Caption := 'TabSheet' + IntToStr(i);
    end;
end;
```

Listing 7.17 contains a small example that creates a tab for every table found in a data module (see Figure 7.16). Start a new project, place a Page Control on Form1, and set the Align property to alClient. From File, New, Data Modules, add CustomerData to the project. Double-click Form1 and add the code shown in the listing to the OnCreate event handler. Be sure that you add DB, DBTables, and DBGrids to the uses clause, as well as the data module unit name.

Finally, in Project, Options, make CustomerData the first unit on the Auto-Create list, above Form1. Failing to set the order here causes an access violation when you try to reference objects in a data module that hasn't been created.

FIG. 7.16

Creating tab sheets for tables in a data module.

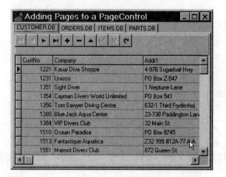

**Listing 7.17 \UDELPHI3\CHP7\PAGECONTROL\PC1\PCART1.PAS—
Creating a Tab Sheet per Table**

```
unit PCCrt1;

interface

uses
  Windows, Messages, SysUtils, Classes, Graphics, Controls, Forms,
  Dialogs, ComCtrls;

type
  TForm1 = class(TForm)
    PageControl1: TPageControl;
    procedure FormCreate(Sender: TObject);
  private
    { Private declarations }
  public
    { Public declarations }
  end;
```

continues

Part

II

Ch

7

Listing 7.17   Continued

```
var
  Form1: TForm1;

implementation

{$R *.DFM}

uses
  PCCrt2, // CustomerData data module
  DB, DBTables, DBGrids, DBCtrls, ExtCtrls;

procedure TForm1.FormCreate(Sender: TObject);
var
  i: integer;
  CurrentDataSrc: TDataSource;
  CurrentTab: TTabSheet;
  CurrentPanel: TPanel;
  CurrentCount: LongInt;
begin
  // Get number of components available before adding more
  CurrentCount := CustomerData.ComponentCount - 1;
  // Search the data modules components for data sources.
  for i := 0 to CurrentCount do
  // If we find a data source, create a tab.
  if (CustomerData.Components[i] is TDataSource) then
  begin
    // Assign the datasource to a temporary variable.
    CurrentDataSrc := TDataSource(CustomerData.Components[i]);
    with TTabSheet.Create(Self) do
      // Add the tab to the PageControl Pages array
      PageControl := PageControl1;
    // Assign the tab a temporary variable
    CurrentTab := PageControl1.Pages[PageControl1.PageCount - 1];
    // If the data comes through a TTable, use the table name for the tab
    if (CurrentDataSrc.DataSet is TTable) then
      CurrentTab.Caption := TTable(CurrentDataSrc.DataSet).TableName;
    with TPanel.Create(Self) do
    begin
      Parent := CurrentTab;
      Align := alTop;
      Caption := '';
      CurrentPanel := Form1.Components[Form1.ComponentCount - 1] as TPanel;
      with TDBNavigator.Create(Self) do
      begin
        Parent := CurrentPanel;
        DataSource := CurrentDataSrc;
      end;
    end;
    // Show the data in a new DBGrid
    with TDBGrid.Create(Self) do
    begin
      Parent := CurrentTab;
      Align := alClient;
```

```
        DataSource := CurrentDataSrc;
        CurrentDataSrc.DataSet.Open;
      end;
    end;
  end;

  end.
```

TROUBLESHOOTING

When creating multiple objects dynamically, and the object properties are interdependent, how can we get references to these objects? By using a technique of loading temporary object instance pointers, such as CurrentPanel, with the pointer to the last component added to the components array, you have a convenient reference to use in assigning properties, as in the following example:

```
CurrentPanel := Form1.Components[Form1.ComponentCount - 1] as TPanel;
with TDBNavigator.Create(Self) do
begin
  Parent := CurrentPanel;
  DataSource := CurrentDataSrc;
end;
```

If you didn't just add the component, you may have to cycle through the entire components array looking for the object instance. In other cases, there may be a more specific array that contains the object instance, as is the case with CurrentTab being assigned the last entry of the Pages[] array in the PageControl.

Navigating Pages The ActivePage property, of type TTabSheet, sets the selected page at both design and runtime. ActivePage is an object of type TTabSheet. If you just want to programmatically move to the next or preceding page, use the SelectNextPage method. To get a reference of a particular page in relation to a current page without moving focus to it, use the FindNextPage method.

On the CD

The example in Listing 7.18 demonstrates navigating pages in a number of ways, as well as allowing you to observe the effect of PageIndex, TabIndex and Visible properties (see Figure 7.17). You find the ACTPAG1.PAS file on this book's companion CD-ROM.

PageIndex controls where a TTabSheet appears within the Pages[] array.

You could go crazy trying to get the Visible property to work the way you expect, or you may just think it's broken. To save you a little time, understand that there are two properties—Visible and *TabVisible*. Visible controls the visibility of items within the client area of a Tab Sheet. TabVisible allows display of the Tab Sheet as a whole. TabIndex is an index value into an array of *visible* Tab Sheets.

Part

II

Ch

7

FIG. 7.17

Navigating pages.

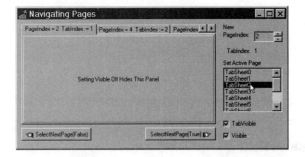

**Listing 7.18   \UDELPHI3\CHP7\PAGECONTROL\ACTPAGE\
ACTPAG1.PAS—Navigating Pages**

```pascal
unit ActPag1;

interface

uses
  Windows, Messages, SysUtils, Classes, Graphics, Controls, Forms,
  Dialogs StdCtrls, Buttons, ComCtrls;

type
  TForm1 = class(TForm)
    Edit1: TEdit;
    UpDown1: TUpdown;
    Label1: TLabel;
    ListBox1: TListBox;
    Label2: TLabel;
    BitBtn1: TBitBtn;
    BitBtn2: TBitBtn;
    Label4: TLabel;
    PageControl1: TPageControl;
    CheckBox1: TCheckBox;
    CheckBox2: TCheckBox;
    Label3: TLabel;
    lblTabIndex: TLabel;
    procedure PageControl1Change(Sender: TObject);
    procedure UpDown1Click(Sender: TObject; Button: TUDBtnType);
    procedure FormCreate(Sender: TObject);
    procedure ListBox1Click(Sender: TObject);
    procedure BitBtn1Click(Sender: TObject);
    procedure BitBtn2Click(Sender: TObject);
    procedure CheckBox1Click(Sender: TObject);
    procedure CheckBox2Click(Sender: TObject);
  end;

var
  Form1: TForm1;

implementation

{$R *.DFM}
```

```
Uses ExtCtrls;

procedure TForm1.PageControl1Change(Sender: TObject);
begin
  Updown1.Position := PageControl1.ActivePage.PageIndex;
  lblTabIndex.Caption := IntToStr(PageControl1.ActivePage.TabIndex);
  CheckBox1.Checked := PageControl1.ActivePage.TabVisible;
  CheckBox2.Checked := PageControl1.ActivePage.Visible;
end;

procedure TForm1.UpDown1Click(Sender: TObject; Button: TUDBtnType);
begin
  PageControl1.ActivePage.PageIndex := Updown1.Position;
end;

procedure TForm1.FormCreate(Sender: TObject);
var
  i: integer;
begin
  for i := 0 to 9 do
    with TTabSheet.Create(Self) do
    begin
      PageControl := PageControl1;
      TabVisible := i mod 2 = 0;

      Name := 'TabSheet' + IntToStr(i);
      Caption := 'PageIndex = ' + IntToStr(PageIndex) +
        ' TabIndex := ' + IntToStr(TabIndex);
      with TPanel.Create(Self) do
      begin
        Parent := PageControl.Pages[PageControl.PageCount - 1];
        Align := alClient;
        Caption := 'Setting Visible Off Hides This Panel';
      end;
    end;

  with PageControl1 do
  begin
    UpDown1.Max := PageCount - 1;
    for i := 0 to PageCount - 1 do
      ListBox1.Items.AddObject(Pages[i].Name, TObject(Pages[i]));
  end;
end;

procedure TForm1.ListBox1Click(Sender: TObject);
begin
  with ListBox1 do
    if ItemIndex <> -1 then
      PageControl1.ActivePage := Items.Objects[ItemIndex] as TTabSheet;
  PageControl1Change(Sender);
end;

procedure TForm1.BitBtn1Click(Sender: TObject);
begin
```

continues

Listing 7.18   Continued

```
    PageControl1.SelectNextPage(False);
end;

procedure TForm1.BitBtn2Click(Sender: TObject);
begin
    PageControl1.SelectNextPage(True)
end;

procedure TForm1.CheckBox1Click(Sender: TObject);
begin
    PageControl1.ActivePage.TabVisible := CheckBox1.Checked;
    PageControl1Change(Sender);
end;

procedure TForm1.CheckBox2Click(Sender: TObject);
begin
    PageControl1.ActivePage.Visible := CheckBox2.Checked;
    PageControl1Change(Sender);
end;

end.
```

Tab Sheet Drag and Drop   You can drag and drop sheets between Page Controls, although you have to choose the application for this technique carefully. Examples such as the following work well only with small tables.

An additional gotcha is that the PageControl doesn't pick up on DragOver events when there is no TTabSheet left on the control. So you need to leave at least one page on the PageControl.

To create a number of Tab Sheets that each have drag-and-drop capability, each sheet must have the OnMouseDown, OnDragOver, and OnDragDrop event handlers assigned. In fact, all objects on the surface of the Tab Sheet also must be assigned handlers, and the logic within the handlers must take into account the class type of these objects.

The example demonstrates loading a series of Tab Sheets, each based on a record from PARTS.DB. (see Figure 7.18). To create the application, you need a TTable component with DataBaseName set to DBDemos, Table name to PARTS.DB, and Active to True. Also, place two TPageControl components side-by-side on the form. You need three event handlers and a CreateDragTabSheet function within the forms declaration, as follows:

```
procedure TabSheetMouseDown(Sender: TObject; Button: TMouseButton;
    Shift: TShiftState; X, Y: Integer);
procedure TabSheetDragOver(Sender, Source: TObject; X, Y: Integer;
    State: TDragState; var Accept: Boolean);
procedure TabSheetDragDrop(Sender, Source: TObject; X, Y: Integer);
function CreateDragTabSheet(APageControl: TPageControl): TTabSheet;
```

The form's OnCreate handler takes care of tab sheet and label creation and assignment of event handlers (see Listing 7.19). You find the DRAG1.PAS file on this book's CD-ROM.

FIG. 7.18

Dragging tab sheets.

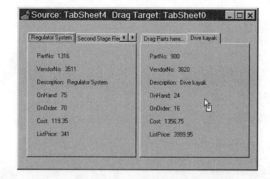

Listing 7.19   \UDELPHI3\CHP7\PAGECONTROL\PC2\ DRAG1.PAS—
Dragging Tab Sheets Between Page Controls

```
unit Drag1;

interface

uses
  Windows, Messages, SysUtils, Classes, Graphics, Controls, Forms,
  Dialogs, ComCtrls, StdCtrls, Mask, DBCtrls, Db, DBTables;

type
  TForm1 = class(TForm)
    PageControl1: TPageControl;
    PageControl2: TPageControl;
    Table1: TTable;
    Table1PartNo: TFloatField;
    Table1VendorNo: TFloatField;
    Table1Description: TStringField;
    Table1OnHand: TFloatField;
    Table1OnOrder: TFloatField;
    Table1Cost: TCurrencyField;
    Table1ListPrice: TCurrencyField;
    procedure FormCreate(Sender: TObject);
  public
    procedure TabSheetMouseDown(Sender: TObject; Button: TMouseButton;
      Shift: TShiftState; X, Y: Integer);
    procedure TabSheetDragOver(Sender, Source: TObject; X, Y: Integer;
      State: TDragState; var Accept: Boolean);
    procedure TabSheetDragDrop(Sender, Source: TObject; X, Y: Integer);
    function CreateDragTabSheet(APageControl: TPageControl): TTabSheet;
  end;

var
  Form1: TForm1;

implementation

{$R *.DFM}
```

continues

Part
II

Ch
7

Listing 7.19   Continued

```
// Determine if the object is valid to drag.
// If the object is a child of a TTabSheet,
// drag the parent object.
procedure TForm1.TabSheetMouseDown(Sender: TObject; Button: TMouseButton;
  Shift: TShiftState; X, Y: Integer);
var
  CurrentTab: TTabSheet;
begin
  if Button = mbLeft then
  begin
    if (Sender is TTabSheet) then
      CurrentTab := (Sender as TTabSheet)
    else
      CurrentTab := (Sender as TLabel).Parent as TTabSheet;
    if CurrentTab.PageControl.PageCount > 1 then
      CurrentTab.BeginDrag(True);
  end;
end;

// We're only dragging a TTabSheet here, so
// we only need to check that we're not dragging
// back on top of the source object.
procedure TForm1.TabSheetDragOver(Sender, Source: TObject; X, Y: Integer;
  State: TDragState; var Accept: Boolean);
begin
    Caption := 'Source: ' + (Source as TComponent).Name +
      ' Drag Target: ' + (Sender as TComponent).Name;
    if Sender <> Source then Accept := true;
end;

procedure TForm1.TabSheetDragDrop(Sender, Source: TObject; X, Y: Integer);
var
  PCSource, PCTarget: TPageControl;
  DraggedPage: TTabSheet;
begin
  // Set up some temporary object instance pointers
  // for more readable code.
  if (Sender is TTabSheet) then
    PCTarget := (Sender as TTabSheet).PageControl
  else
    PCTarget := ((Sender as TLabel).Parent as TTabSheet).PageControl;
  DraggedPage := (Source as TTabSheet);
  PCSource := DraggedPage.PageControl;
  // reassign the Tab Sheet parent
  DraggedPage.PageControl := PCTarget;
  // set an active page for source and target
  PCTarget.ActivePage := DraggedPage;
  PCSource.ActivePage := PCSource.Pages[0];
end;

function TForm1.CreateDragTabSheet(APageControl: TPageControl): TTabSheet;
```

```
begin
  Result := TTabSheet.Create(Self);
  with Result do
  begin
    PageControl := APageControl;
    OnMouseDown := TabSheetMouseDown;
    OnDragOver := TabSheetDragOver;
    OnDragDrop := TabSheetDragDrop;
  end;
end;

procedure TForm1.FormCreate(Sender: TObject);
var
  Flds, Indent, i: integer;
  CurrentTab: TTabSheet;
begin
  i := 0;
  Indent := PageControl1.Font.Size * 2;
  with Table1 do
  begin
    First;
    while not EOF do
    begin
      CurrentTab := CreateDragTabSheet(PageControl1);

      CurrentTab.Name := 'TabSheet' + IntToStr(i);
      Inc(i);

      CurrentTab.Caption := FieldByName('Description').AsString;
      for Flds := 0 to FieldCount - 1 do
        with TLabel.Create(CurrentTab) do
        begin
          Parent := CurrentTab;

          Name := 'Label' + IntToStr(i) + IntToStr(Flds);

          Caption := Fields[Flds].FieldName + ':  ' +
            Fields[Flds].AsString;
          Left := Indent;
          Top := Indent + (Flds * Height * 2);
          OnMouseDown := TabSheetMouseDown;
          OnDragOver := TabSheetDragOver;
          OnDragDrop := TabSheetDragDrop;
        end;
      Next;
    end;
  end;
  CurrentTab := CreateDragTabSheet(PageControl2);

CurrentTab.Caption := 'Drag Parts here...';end;

end.
```

Rich Edit

Rich Text Format (RTF) is a specification that encodes text formatting within the printable ASCII character set. If you're interested in learning more about Rich Text Format internals, you might try **www.microsoft.com** or **www.wotsit.demon.co.uk** which, at the time of this writing, was stuffed with a myriad of file-format specifications, including Rich Text Format. TRichEdit is intended to encapsulate much of the complexity of RTF, but the underlying control is cantankerous.

> **N O T E** Some improvements were made since Delphi 2.0. When printing in the NT 4.0 environment, a divide-by-zero error used to occur in Delphi 2.0; this has been fixed. The Rich Edit control had a 64K limit in Delphi 2.0, due to the way in which messaging was handled. The encapsulation of the control was redesigned to lift this limit. ■

You can find a complete Rich Edit demo found in \Delphi 3.0\Demos\RichText that ships with Delphi, so rather than duplicating this application, let's break down some of the Rich Edit control functionality.

Text Attributes   TRichEdit has text attribute properties that control things such as font name, color, style, size, and pitch, which can be set for default or selected text. The SelAttributes property controls all text within SelStart to SelLength characters. All other text is controlled by the DefAttributes property. Both SelAttributes and DefAttributes are of type TTextAttributes.

The project in Listing 7.20 has a dual purpose. First, it streams out the RTF text and displays the same data in a second Rich Edit control, where the PlainText property is true, which allows you to see the Rich Text in its raw state. Second, the project demonstrates some TTextAttributes properties for selected text. When you run this project, try selecting some text, and then changing the font, font color, and size. As you observe the result in the second Rich Edit control, you will begin to see the work being done behind the scenes to maintain the rich text format. Notice, for example, a section labeled "colortbl" that's referenced later in the rich text by an index into the table, like "C1" just prior to the affected text string (see Figure 7.19). You find the SELATR1.PAS file on this book's companion CD-ROM.

FIG. 7.19
Exploring
SelAttributes
and rich text.

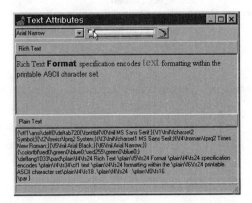

**Listing 7.20 \UDELPHI3\CHP7\RICHEDIT\SELATR\SELATR1.PAS—
Exploring *SelAttributes* and Rich Text**

```
unit SelAtr1;

interface

uses
  Windows, Messages, SysUtils, Classes, Graphics, Controls, Forms,
  Dialogs, StdCtrls, ComCtrls, ExtCtrls, ToolWin;

type
  TForm1 = class(TForm)
    RichEdit1: TRichEdit;
    RichEdit2: TRichEdit;
    ToolBar1: TToolBar;
    ComboBox1: TComboBox;
    StatusBar1: TStatusBar;
    Panel1: TPanel;
    Panel2: TPanel;
    TrackBar1: TTrackBar;
    ToolButton1: TToolButton;
    ColorDialog1: TColorDialog;
    ImageList1: TImageList;
    procedure RichEdit1Change(Sender: TObject);
    procedure FormCreate(Sender: TObject);
    procedure ComboBox1Click(Sender: TObject);
    procedure RichEdit1SelectionChange(Sender: TObject);
    procedure TrackBar1Change(Sender: TObject);
    procedure ToolButton1Click(Sender: TObject);
  end;

var
  Form1: TForm1;
  InStream: TMemoryStream;

implementation

{$R *.DFM}

procedure TForm1.RichEdit1Change(Sender: TObject);
begin
  InStream.Clear;
  RichEdit1.Lines.SaveToStream(InStream);
  InStream.Position := 0;
  RichEdit2.Lines.LoadFromStream(InStream);
end;

procedure TForm1.FormCreate(Sender: TObject);
var
  I: integer;
begin
  RichEdit2.PlainText := True;
  Combobox1.Items.Clear;
```

Part
II

Ch
7

continues

Listing 7.20   Continued

```
  with Screen do
    for I := 0 to Fonts.Count - 1 do
      if (Combobox1.Items.IndexOf(Screen.Fonts[I]) = -1) then
        ComboBox1.Items.Add(Screen.Fonts[I]);
  ComboBox1.ItemIndex := 0;
end;

procedure TForm1.ComboBox1Click(Sender: TObject);
begin
  RichEdit1.SelAttributes.Name := ComboBox1.Items[ComboBox1.ItemIndex];
end;

procedure TForm1.RichEdit1SelectionChange(Sender: TObject);
begin
  TrackBar1.Position := RichEdit1.SelAttributes.Size;
end;

procedure TForm1.TrackBar1Change(Sender: TObject);
begin
  RichEdit1.SelAttributes.Size := TrackBar1.Position;
end;

procedure TForm1.ToolButton1Click(Sender: TObject);
begin
  ColorDialog1.Options := [cdSolidColor, cdPreventFullOpen];
  if ColorDialog1.Execute then
    RichEdit1.SelAttributes.Color := ColorDialog1.Color;
end;

initialization
  InStream := TMemoryStream.Create;
finalization
  InStream.Free;
end.
```

Formatting Paragraphs   Indentation, tabbing, and alignment are controlled by the `Paragraph` property. `FirstIndent`, `LeftIndent`, and `RightIndent` properties define the indentation of the first line, left paragraph margins, and right paragraph margin, respectively. You can set a series of tab stops for the currently selected paragraph by initializing `TabCount` equal to the number of tabs you want to set and each element of the `Tab[]` array to new tab locations. Here's an example procedure that handles setting tab stops:

```
procedure SetTabStops(RichEdit: TRichEdit; TabStops: array of integer);
var
  I: integer;
begin
  with RichEdit.Paragraph do
  begin
    TabCount := High(TabStops) + 1;
    for I := 0 to TabCount do
    Tab[I] := TabStops[I];
```

```
  end;
end;
```

By passing the Rich Edit control an array of integers, all tab stops are set at one time, as follows:

```
SetTabStops(RichEdit1, [20, 120, 200]);
```

You could conceivably align a Track Bar control across the top of the form and use the `SetTick` method to illustrate the placement of tabs. The Header Control that uses owner draw also may be a good candidate for a horizontal ruler used to control `Paragraph` attributes.

I suppose that it's old-fashioned, but I sometimes like to have a printed listing of a table's fields, along with their types and sizes. Neither DataBase Desktop nor the DB Explorer seem to handle this task. To fill the bill, you can list field information in a Rich Edit control with the Tab property set to align the columns (see Figure 7.20). Listing 7.21 demonstrates how to use the `SelAttributes` property to bold and underline the column titles, and the `Paragraph` property to center the title called "Index." You find TBLPRT1.PAS on this book's companion CD-ROM.

CAUTION

As I mentioned previously, the underlying control on which `TRichEdit` is based has flaws. Where possible, the Delphi development team worked around them, or left the offending portions unsurfaced. In some cases, particularly with `TRichEdit`, the flaws were insurmountable. You will find, for example, that `TRichEdit` `Paragraph` handled programmatically doesn't format properly when text extends off the visible area of the control. Likewise, `TTextAttributes` handled programmatically do not always behave in a predictable manner. Test this control before counting on particular functionality.

FIG. 7.20

Listing table field structures.

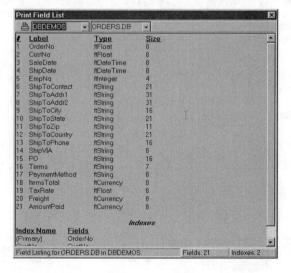

Part

II

Ch

7

**Listing 7.21   \UDELPHI\CHP7\RICHEDIT\TABLEPRINT\TBLPRT1.PAS—
Print Field List**

```
unit TblPrt1;

interface

uses
  Windows, Messages, SysUtils, Classes, Graphics, Controls, Forms,
  Dialogs, StdCtrls, ComCtrls, ToolWin, DBTables, Db;

type
  TForm1 = class(TForm)
    StatusBar1: TStatusBar;
    ToolBar1: TToolBar;
    RichEdit1: TRichEdit;
    ToolButton1: TToolButton;
    ImageList1: TImageList;
    cbDatabaseName: TComboBox;
    cbTableName: TComboBox;
    Table1: TTable;
    procedure FormCreate(Sender: TObject);
    procedure cbDatabaseNameChange(Sender: TObject);
    procedure cbTableNameChange(Sender: TObject);
    procedure ToolButton1Click(Sender: TObject);
  end;

const
  FldTyps: array[ftUnknown..ftTypedBinary] of string = (
    'ftUnknown', 'ftString', 'ftSmallint', 'ftInteger', 'ftWord',
    'ftBoolean', 'ftFloat', 'ftCurrency', 'ftBCD', 'ftDate', 'ftTime',
    'ftDateTime', 'ftBytes', 'ftVarBytes', 'ftAutoInc', 'ftBlob',
    'ftMemo', 'ftGraphic', 'ftFmtMemo', 'ftParadoxOle', 'ftDBaseOle',
    'ftTypedBinary'
  );
  TABCHAR = #9;

var
  Form1: TForm1;

implementation

{$R *.DFM}

procedure SetTabStops(RichEdit: TRichEdit; TabStops: array of integer);
var
  I: integer;
begin
  with RichEdit.Paragraph do
  begin
    TabCount := High(TabStops) + 1;
    for I := 0 to TabCount do
     Tab[I] := TabStops[I];
  end;
end;
```

```
procedure WriteIndexDescription(Table: TTable; RichEdit: TRichEdit);
var
  I: integer;
begin
  with Table do
  begin
    SetTabStops(RichEdit, [80]);
    IndexDefs.Update;
    if IndexDefs.Count > 0 then
    begin
      with RichEdit, SelAttributes do
      begin
        Paragraph.Alignment := taCenter;
        Style := Style + [fsBold, fsItalic];
        Lines.Add('');
        Lines.Add('Indexes');
        Paragraph.Alignment := taLeftJustify;
        Style := Style - [fsItalic] + [fsUnderline];
        Lines.Add('Index Name' + TABCHAR + 'Fields');
        Style := Style - [fsBold, fsUnderline];
        for I := 0 to IndexDefs.Count - 1 do
          if ixPrimary in IndexDefs[I].Options then
            Lines.Add('(Primary)' + TABCHAR + IndexDefs[I].Fields)
          else
            Lines.Add(IndexDefs[I].Name + TABCHAR +
              IndexDefs[I].Fields);
      end;
    end;
  end;
end;

procedure WriteTableDescription(Table: TTable; RichEdit: TRichEdit);
var
  I: integer;
begin
  with Table, RichEdit, SelAttributes do
  begin
    SetTabStops(RichEdit, [20, 120, 200]);
    Style := Style + [fsUnderline, fsBold];
    Lines.Add('#' + TABCHAR + 'Label' + TABCHAR + 'Type' + TABCHAR +
      'Size');
    Style := Style - [fsUnderline, fsBold];
    for I := 0 to FieldCount - 1 do
      with Fields[I] do
        Lines.Add(IntToStr(FieldNo) + TABCHAR + DisplayLabel + TABCHAR
        + FldTyps[DataType] + TABCHAR + IntToStr(DataSize));
  end;
end;

procedure TForm1.FormCreate(Sender: TObject);
begin
  Session.GetDatabaseNames(cbDatabaseName.Items);
  cbDatabaseName.ItemIndex := 0;
  cbDatabaseNameChange(Sender);
```

Part

II

Ch

7

continues

Listing 7.21   Continued

```
end;

procedure TForm1.cbDatabaseNameChange(Sender: TObject);
begin
  with cbDatabaseName do
    Session.GetTableNames(Items[ItemIndex], '', True, False,
      cbTableName.Items);
  cbTableName.ItemIndex := 0;
  cbTableNameChange(Sender);
end;

procedure TForm1.cbTableNameChange(Sender: TObject);
begin
  if cbTableName.ItemIndex <> -1 then
  begin
    with Table1 do
    try
      DatabaseName := cbDatabaseName.Items[cbDatabaseName.ItemIndex];
      TableName := cbTableName.Items[cbTableName.ItemIndex];
      Open;
      RichEdit1.Lines.Clear;
      WriteTableDescription(Table1, RichEdit1);
      WriteIndexDescription(Table1, RichEdit1);
      StatusBar1.Panels[0].Text := 'Field Listing for ' + TableName +
        ' in ' + DatabaseName + '.';
      StatusBar1.Panels[1].Text := 'Fields: ' + IntToStr(FieldCount);
      StatusBar1.Panels[2].Text := 'Indexes: ' +
        IntToStr(IndexDefs.Count);
    finally
      Close;
    end;
  end;
end;

procedure TForm1.ToolButton1Click(Sender: TObject);
begin
  RichEdit1.Print(StatusBar1.Panels[0].Text);
end;

end.
```

Displaying Line and Column   The Rich Edit control, like TEdit and TMemo, is a descendant of TCustomMemo, and so can be sent the same "EM_" edit controls messages that allow you to exceed the bounds of the VCL. You can use these messages to supply statistics on the current column and line.

`EM_LINEFROMCHAR` provides the row number, based on the current character position. To get the column, you need to subtract the number of characters that lead up to the current line from the current cursor position. Use the `OnSelectionChange` event of the Rich Edit control to check for the new row and column (see Figure 7.21).

```
procedure GetRTRowCol(RichEdit: TRichEdit; var Row, Col: LongInt;
begin
  with RichEdit do
  begin
    Row := SendMessage(Handle, EM_LINEFROMCHAR, SelStart, 0);
    Col := SelStart - SendMessage(Handle, EM_LINEINDEX, Row, 0);
  end;
end;

procedure TForm1.RichEdit1SelectiOnChange(Sender: TObject);
var
  RTRow, RTCol: LongInt;
begin
  GetRTRowAndColumn(RichEdit1, RTRow, RTCol);
  StatusBar1.Panels[0].Text := 'Ln ' + IntToStr(RTRow) +
          ' Col ' + IntToStr(RTCol);
end;
```

Text Search   Searching for text in a RichEdit control involves two operations—executing the `TFindDialog` and handling the `OnFind` event. Even before this, set `HideSelection` on the `RichEdit` to False so that you can view the found text, even when focus is not on the Rich Edit control.

```
procedure TForm1.FormCreate(Sender: TObject);
begin
  RichEdit1.HideSelection := False;
end;
```

If you want the Find Dialog to display near the text cursor, set the `TFindDialog` Position property by using the `EM_POSFROMCHAR` message to get the pixel location of the text cursor. Also before executing the dialog, you should preload the `FindText` property with any user-selected text, as follows:

```
procedure TForm1.tbFindClick(Sender: TObject);
var
  TempPoint: TPoint;
begin
  with RichEdit1, FindDialog1 do
  begin
    Perform(EM_POSFROMCHAR, LongInt(@TempPoint), SelStart + SelLength + 2);
    Position := ClientToScreen(TempPoint);
    FindText := Copy(Text, SelStart + 1, SelLength);
    Execute;
  end;
end;
```

> **CAUTION**
>
> Microsoft documentation used in Delphi 2.0 contains an incorrect definition for EM_POSFROMCHAR. First, the EM_POSFROMCHAR constant is defined incorrectly in RICHEDIT.PAS. ComCtrls has the correct definition and also pulls other definitions from RICHEDIT.PAS as needed, so you shouldn't need to include RICHEDIT.PAS yourself.
>
> Also, EM_POSFROMCHAR and EM_CHARFROMPOS syntax is incorrectly defined as taking a character index for the wParam, and returning the coordinates of the character. Actually, the message should look something like
>
> SendMessage(Handle, EM_POSFROMCHAR, LongInt(@RTPos), SelStart);
>
> where RTPos is passed as an address of a TPoint.

When the user clicks the Find Next button, the OnFind event handler fires. The Copy function reselects the text to search, based on the current location of the text cursor. Then the Pos function locates the FindText within the text to be searched. If Pos locates the search criteria, SelStart and SelLength are set to highlight the found text, as follows:

```
procedure TForm1.FindDialog1Find(Sender: TObject);
var
  SearchToken: string;
  FoundAt: LongInt;
begin
  if FindDialog1.FindText <> '' then
    with RichEdit1 do
    begin
      SearchToken := Copy(Text, SelStart + SelLength + 1,
        Length(Text) - SelStart);
      FoundAt := Pos(UpperCase(FindDialog1.FindText),
        UpperCase(SearchToken));
      if (FoundAt <> 0) then
      begin
        SelStart := SelStart + SelLength + FoundAt - 1;
        SelLength := Length(FindDialog1.FindText);
      end;
    end;
end;
```

Besides setting SelStart and SelLength, you also can change the SelAttributes to mark the found text as underlined or a distinctive color. You can use this same idea within a new reader program to highlight strings beginning with "http//" to indicate a hotlink to a Web browser.

List View

The List View control displays a list in a way that matches the style with which your user is most comfortable. The list of items, for example, can be displayed as large icons or in a columnar report. You can find the List View control nearly everywhere in Windows 95. For example, the Windows Explorer client area is a List View control.

FIG. 7.21
"Edit" found at Line 4,
Column 10.

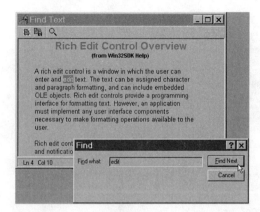

List View Design Time Characteristics   The principal properties that determine how
TListView displays visually are as follows:

- The Items property, of type TListItems, is a collection of TListItem that forms the
  content of the list. Items has a property editor you can use to create and set each Item's
  Caption, ImageIndex, and StateIndex properties. ImageIndex and StateIndex are used
  to point to entries in an Image List.

- TListItem also has a TStrings property named SubItems. When looking at the List View
  in Details mode, SubItems form the text listed under columns to the right of the initial
  Caption property.

- ViewStyle that corresponds to the rightmost four buttons on the Windows Explorer—
  Large Icons, Small Icons, List, and Details. These correspond to vsIcon, vsSmallIcon,
  vsList, and vsReport.

- If ViewStyle is vsReport (Details), you need to create TListColumn within the Columns
  property.

Working with List View at Runtime   Creating items in a List View follows the pattern of
Common Controls: Call the parent object Add method, get a reference, and assign properties
using the reference.

```
var
  ListItem: TListItem;
begin
  ListItem := ListView1.Items.Add;
  ListItem.Caption := Edit1.Text;
```

When the ViewStyle property is vsReport, the List View control becomes a series of columns
with Items taking the leftmost column (see Figure 7.22). Each Item has SubItems listed to the
right.

Part

II

Ch

7

FIG. 7.22

TListView with
ViewStyle of
vsReport.

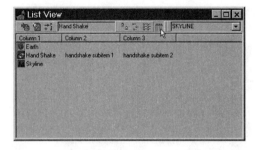

Before you can see the SubItems, you must create Columns, as follows:

```
var
  ListColumn: TListColumn;
begin
  ListColumn := ListView1.Columns.Add;
  ListColumn.Caption := Edit1.Text;
  ListColumn.Width := Length(Edit1.Text) * Font.Size;
```

Then you can load an Item's SubItems property. SubItems is a TStrings with each array element belonging to a column, as follows:

```
ListView1.Selected.SubItems.Add('This sub item displays to the right
 of the selecteditem text.');
```

The example program in Listing 7.22 allows you to test the capabilities of the List View to create Items, SubItems, and Columns on-the-fly. During the form create, load one Image List with 16 × 16 pixel bitmaps, a second Image List with 32 × 32 icon images, and a Combo Box with the names of each icon (note the call to the CreateSize method to override the 16 × 16 default size). When the user clicks the Add List Item tool bar button, the current index of the Combo Box is used to supply the ImageIndex property. You find the LVADD1.PAS file on this book's companion CD-ROM.

**Listing 7.22 \UDELPHI3\CHP7\LISTVIEW\ADDITEMS\LVADD1.PAS—
Working with List View at Runtime**

```
unit LVAdd1;

interface

uses
  Windows, Messages, SysUtils, Classes, Graphics, Controls, Forms,
  Dialogs, StdCtrls, ComCtrls, ToolWin;

type
  TfrmMain = class(TForm)
    ListView1: TListView;
    ImageList1: TImageList;
    ToolBar1: TToolBar;
    ToolButton1: TToolButton;
    ToolButton2: TToolButton;
```

```
      ToolButton3: TToolButton;
      ToolButton4: TToolButton;
      tbAddListItem: TToolButton;
      ToolButton6: TToolButton;
      Edit1: TEdit;
      ToolButton7: TToolButton;
      il16: TImageList;
      il32: TImageList;
      ComboBox1: TComboBox;
      ToolButton8: TToolButton;
      tbAddColumn: TToolButton;
      tbAddSubItem: TToolButton;
      procedure tbAddListItemClick(Sender: TObject);
      procedure ToolButton1Click(Sender: TObject);
      procedure ToolButton2Click(Sender: TObject);
      procedure ToolButton3Click(Sender: TObject);
      procedure ToolButton4Click(Sender: TObject);
      procedure FormCreate(Sender: TObject);
      procedure tbAddColumnClick(Sender: TObject);
      procedure tbAddSubItemClick(Sender: TObject);
   end;

var
   frmMain: TfrmMain;

implementation

Uses CommCtrl, ShellAPI, LVAdd2;

{$R *.DFM}

procedure TfrmMain.tbAddListItemClick(Sender: TObject);
var
   ListItem: TListItem;
begin
   ListItem := ListView1.Items.Add;
   ListItem.Caption := Edit1.Text;
   ListItem.ImageIndex := Combobox1.ItemIndex;
end;

procedure TfrmMain.ToolButton1Click(Sender: TObject);
begin
   ListView1.ViewStyle := vsIcon;
end;

procedure TfrmMain.ToolButton2Click(Sender: TObject);
begin
   ListView1.ViewStyle := vsSmallIcon;
end;

procedure TfrmMain.ToolButton3Click(Sender: TObject);
begin
   ListView1.ViewStyle := vsList;
end;
```

continues

Part
II

Ch
7

Listing 7.22 Continued

```
procedure TfrmMain.ToolButton4Click(Sender: TObject);
begin
  ListView1.ViewStyle := vsReport;
end;

procedure TfrmMain.FormCreate(Sender: TObject);
const
  DirPath = 'C:\Program Files\Borland\Delphi 3.0\Images\Icons\';
var
  SearchRec: TSearchRec;
begin
  il32.CreateSize(32, 32);
  if (FindFirst(DirPath + '*.BMP', faAnyFile, SearchRec) = 0) then
  begin
    try
      while (FindNext(SearchRec) = 0) do
        il16.FileLoad(rtBitmap, DirPath + SearchRec.Name, clNone);
    finally
      FindClose(SearchRec);
    end;
  end;

  if (FindFirst(DirPath + '*.ICO', faAnyFile, SearchRec) = 0) then
  begin
    try
      while (FindNext(SearchRec) = 0) do
      begin
        Imagelist_AddIcon(il32.Handle, ExtractIcon(Handle,
          PChar(DirPath + SearchRec.Name), 0));
        ComboBox1.Items.Add(Copy(SearchRec.Name, 0,
          Pos('.', SearchRec.Name) - 1));
      end;
    finally
      FindClose(SearchRec);
    end;
  end;

  ComboBox1.ItemIndex := 0;
end;

procedure TfrmMain.tbAddColumnClick(Sender: TObject);
var
  ListColumn: TListColumn;
begin
  ListColumn := ListView1.Columns.Add;
  ListColumn.Caption := Edit1.Text;
  ListColumn.Width := Length(Edit1.Text) * Font.Size;
  tbAddSubItem.Enabled := True;
end;

procedure TfrmMain.tbAddSubItemClick(Sender: TObject);
begin
  if Assigned(ListView1.Selected) then
```

```
  begin
    frmAddSubItems.ShowModal;
    ListView1.Selected.SubItems.Assign(frmAddSubItems.Memo1.Lines);
  end
  else
    ShowMessage('To add SubItems, first select an item.');
end;

end.
```

Tree View

The `TTreeView` control contains text, graphics, and data in an outlined list. Each entry in the list is a `TTreeNode` object. The list as a whole is a `TTreeNodes` object, represented by the `Items` property. When you want to manipulate the list of items, for example to add a node, look to the `Items` property.

> **N O T E** It's not that the `TTreeView` is a complicated beast, but the terms used to identify properties are easy to confuse.
>
> For example, the property `Item` is of type `TTreeNode` and the two terms tend to be used interchangeably. Similarly, "Items," the property that represents an array of Item, is of type `TTreeNodes`. So again, the term "Items" might be used in place of "TTreeNodes." ▪

Assigning Items at Design Time   Now, do a quick run-through of loading a `TTreeView` with items at design time and also supply images for each item. You need two Image Lists as well as a `TTreeView` on the form. Add any two images from the \Images\Buttons directory to ImageList1 to correspond to the `ItemIndex` and `SelectedIndex` properties. Add only one image from \Images\Buttons to ImageList2. This second `TImageList` supplies `StateImages`, which display as an extra graphic to the left of the item. `StateImages` are useful for marking an item as part of a group. If you had an invoice listing, for example, you can place check boxes next to the paid invoices.

Use the Object Inspector to select ImageList1 for the Tree View's `Images` property. For the `StateImages` property, select ImageList2.

To create a list of items for the `TTreeView` at design time, click the ellipses next to the `TTreeView` Items property to display the `TTreeView` Items Editor. Click the New Item button and supply some test text in the properties section of the dialog. Leave Image Index equal to zero, but change the Selected Index to 1.

You also will want to set a `StateIndex` property for the item. A state image is an extra graphic that displays to the far left of the item. It can be used to denote open mail, paid invoices, and so on. The `StateIndex` property default of –1 indicates that no state image is selected. Changing this value to zero will display the first image in ImageList2. Add several more items and sub-items. Before running the example, add the following two lines of code to the `TTreeView` `OnDblClick` handler.

```
procedure TForm1.TreeView1DblClick(Sender: TObject);
begin
  TreeView1.Selected.StateIndex := 1;
  TreeView1.Invalidate;
end;
```

Run the example and observe that the state images from ImageList2 are positioned to the far left next to the item (see Figure 7.23). The image displayed between the state image and the text corresponds to the graphic in ImageList1 specified by the `ImageIndex`. Click any item to display the second graphic in ImageList1 pointed at by `SelectedIndex`.

FIG. 7.23

TTreeView with images.

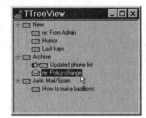

Assigning Items at Runtime   The code for adding a new item to the TTreeView may seem familiar. Use the Add method of the Item's TTreeNodes object.

```
var
  Node: TTreeNode;
begin
  Node := TreeView1.Items.Add(TreeView1.Selected, Edit1.Text);
```

The new node will be added to the end of the same level as the node specified in the first parameter. If the parameter is nil, the addition always occurs at the root level. The second parameter is the text to display.

There are several flavors of methods that add and insert TTreeNodes. These methods tend to fall into the following two categories:

- Methods that add TTreeNodes at the same level as TTreeNode passed as a parameter. These include Add, AddFirst, Insert, InsertObject AddObject, and AddObjectFirst.

- Methods that add TTreeNodes indented to the next level down such as AddChild, AddChildFirst, AddChildObject, and AddChildObjectFirst.

N O T E   The methods that refer to objects include a pointer parameter that can be used to store any 4-byte value. You can store a LongInt, a pointer to a record, or an object instance (which is just a 4-byte pointer). You need to allocate and free any memory needed beyond the 4 bytes for the pointer. ■

Example: Loading from a Database Table   Loading the Tree View control from a table involves setting up a While loop to cycle through the table records, and placing an Items.Add method inside the loop, as follows:

```
Customers.Open;
while not Customers.EOF do
begin
  CustomerNode := Items.Add(Nil, Customers['Company']);
  Next;
end;
```

You also may want to represent master/detail relationships where the detail records display as children indented from the master records. The general steps are shown in the following list:

- Save the reference returned from the Items.Add method call. For example, in the preceding code snippet, CustomerNode contains the return value from Items.Add. You need CustomerNode later when adding child items.

- After the Items.Add call and before the call to the Next method, place code to subset the detail records. (You can filter the records or use a TQuery against the detail data.)

- Replicate the While loop call for the detail level data and place this code just before the call to Next for the master data. Change all table-specific identifiers from the master table name to the detail table name. Change the Items.Add to Items.AddChild, and pass the saved TTreeNode object from earlier as the first parameter.

The following example uses the CustomerData DataModule to supply table data. For just one master and one detail, the minimal code would look something like the following example:

```
procedure TForm1.ToolButton1Click(Sender: TObject);
var
  CustomerNode: TTreeNode;
begin
  with Treeview1, CustomerData do
  begin
    Orders.Filtered := True;
    // Add all customer names to TreeNodes
    while not Customers.EOF do
    begin
      CustomerNode := Items.Add(Nil, Customers['Company']);
      // Add all orders for the last customer record to TreeNodes
      with Orders do
      begin
        Filter := 'CustNo = ' +
          Customers.FieldByName('CustNo').AsString;
        Refresh;
        while not EOF do
        begin
          Items.AddChild(CustomerNode, '#' +
            FieldByName('OrderNo').AsString + ' ' +
            FieldByName('SaleDate').AsString);
          Next;
        end;
      end; // Orders
      Customers.Next;
    end;
    // Set focus to first item in the Tree View
    Items.GetFirstNode.Selected := True;
  end; // TreeView1, CustomerData
end;
```

The next example project performs these steps three levels deep, from Customers to Orders to Line Items (see Figure 7.24). Additionally, if a customer has an ItemTotal greater than a given amount, a check mark is placed next to the customer's name by specifying an Image List in the StateImages property, and if the condition arises, setting the Node's StateIndex equal to the index of a graphic in the Image List. A Progress Bar keeps the user apprised of the percentage of records loaded. Also note the BeginUpdate and EndUpdate methods of TTreeNodes. BeginUpdate prevents TTreeView from drawing until EndUpdate is called (see Listing 7.23). You find the LOADTBL1.PAS file on this book's companion CD-ROM.

FIG. 7.24

Loading TreeView from a database table.

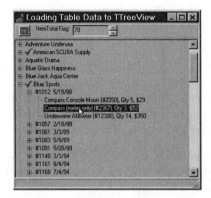

Listing 7.23   \UDELPHI3\CHP7\TREEVIEW\LOADTABLE \LOADTBL1.PAS—Loading *TreeView* from a Database Table

```
unit LoadTbl1;

interface

uses
  Windows, Messages, SysUtils, Classes, Graphics, Controls, Forms,
  Dialogs, ComCtrls, ToolWin, StdCtrls;

type
  TForm1 = class(TForm)
    StatusBar1: TStatusBar;
    ToolBar1: TToolBar;
    TreeView1: TTreeView;
    ToolButton1: TToolButton;
    ImageList1: TImageList;
    ProgressBar1: TProgressBar;
    ImageList2: TImageList;
    Edit1: TEdit;
    UpDown1: TUpDown;
    Label1: TLabel;
    procedure ToolButton1Click(Sender: TObject);
  end;

var
  Form1: TForm1;
```

```
implementation

uses OrderExp2;

{$R *.DFM}

procedure TForm1.ToolButton1Click(Sender: TObject);
var
  LineItemsNode, OrdersNode, CustomerNode: TTreeNode;
begin
  with Treeview1, CustomerData do
  begin
    // Initialize Tables
    LineItems.Filtered := True;
    LineItems.Open;
    Orders.Filtered := True;
    Orders.Open;
    Customers.Close;
    Customers.IndexName := 'ByCompany';
    Customers.Open;
    // Setup Progress Bar on surface of StatusBar1
    with ProgressBar1 do
    begin
      Max := Customers.RecordCount;
      Parent := StatusBar1;
      StatusBar1.SimplePanel := True;
      Left := StatusBar1.Canvas.TextWidth('W') * 4;
      Top := 4;
      Height := StatusBar1.Height - (StatusBar1.Height div 3);
      Visible := True;
    end;
    Items.Clear;
    // Defer drawing TreeView until EndUpdate
    Items.BeginUpdate;
    // Add all customer names to TreeNodes
    while not Customers.EOF do
    begin
      CustomerNode := Items.Add(Nil, Customers['Company']);
      // Add all orders for the last customer record to TreeNodes
      with Orders do
      begin
        Filter := 'CustNo = ' +
          Customers.FieldByName('CustNo').AsString;
        Refresh;
        while not EOF do
        begin
          OrdersNode := Items.AddChild(CustomerNode, '#' +
            FieldByName('OrderNo').AsString + ' ' +
            FieldByName('SaleDate').AsString);
          // Flag customers with large item total
          if (FieldbyName('ItemsTotal').AsInteger >
            (UpDown1.Position * 1000)) then
            CustomerNode.StateIndex := 1;
          // Add all items for the last order record to TreeNodes
```

continues

Listing 7.23   Continued

```
            with LineItems do
            begin
              Filter := 'OrderNo = ' +
                Orders.FieldByName('OrderNo').AsString;
              Refresh;
              while not EOF do
              begin
                LineItemsNode := Items.AddChild(OrdersNode,
                  FieldByName('PartName').AsString +  ' (#' +
                  FieldByName('PartNo').AsString + '), Qty ' +
                  FieldByName('Qty').AsString +  ', $' +
                  FieldByName('Price').AsString);
                Next;
              end;
            end; // LineItems
            Next;
          end;
        end; // Orders
        Customers.Next;
        // Update Status
        ProgressBar1.Position := Customers.RecNo;
        StatusBar1.SimpleText := ' % ' + IntToStr((Customers.RecNo * 100)
          div Customers.RecordCount);
        // Allow Status Bar text and Progress Bar to be painted
        Application.ProcessMessages;
      end;
      // Now Draw the TTreeView now that all items are loaded
      Items.EndUpdate;
      // Set focus to first item in the Tree View
      Items.GetFirstNode.Selected := True;
      ProgressBar1.Visible := False;
      StatusBar1.SimpleText := '';
    end; // TreeView1, CustomerData
  end;

end.
```

Climbing the Inheritance Tree   What if you want to load items in reverse order? If you wanted to list an object inheritance hierarchy, starting with a particular object, such as TForm1 for example, and listing ancestors going all the way back to TObject, how can you display this same list in a TTreeView starting with TObject at the top (see Figure 7.25)?

Now, to cut this task to smaller pieces. Never mind the display details, how do you create this list in the first place? First, you need to declare a temporary variable of type TClass that you can call Cls and assign it the class TForm1. Then set up a While loop using the ClassName function to supply class names to a list box, and finally reassign Cls by using ClassParent. You exit the loop when you assign Cls the ClassParent of TObject—TObject is the root of the inheritance tree and has no parent, so Cls now becomes Nil, as follows:

```
procedure TForm1.FormCreate(Sender: TObject);
var
  Cls: TClass;
begin
  Cls := TForm1;
  while Assigned(Cls) do
  begin
    ListBox1.Items.Add(Cls.ClassName);
    Cls := Cls.ClassParent;
  end;
```

Now that you can extract a list that represents an inheritance hierarchy, you can concentrate on ordering the list within a Tree View control, with TObject at the top, and each descendant indented below its ancestor. You know how to add to the Items property, but how do you insert an item at the top of the list, and reassign the items below it as children of that new item? Remember when an Items.Add method was performed previously, that the method returned a TTreeNode to variable Node, but nothing was done with the reference?

```
var
  Node: TTreeNode;
begin
  Node := TreeView1.Items.Add(TreeView1.Selected, Edit1.Text);
```

You can use this reference as a parameter to the TTreeNodes MoveTo method, so that you can move an existing TTreeNode under a newly added item.

```
procedure TForm1.FormCreate(Sender: TObject);
var
  Cls: TClass;
  Node: TTreeNode;
begin

  Cls := TForm1;
  while Assigned(Cls) do
  begin
    with TreeView1 do
    begin
      Node := Items.Add(Nil, Cls.ClassName);
      if (Node <> Items[0]) then
        Items[0].MoveTo(Node, naAddChild);
    end;
    Cls := Cls.ClassParent;
  end;
  TreeView1.FullExpand;
end;
```

Now, step through the logic of this loop, as follows:

1. The variable Cls is assigned TForm1.

2. You enter the loop checking that Cls is not Nil.

3. You add your first node containing the "TForm1" text.

4. This is the first iteration, so there are no previous nodes to move, Items[0] and Node are equal, and the MoveTo method is not executed.

5. Cls is assigned its ClassParent, TForm.

6. You add a new node with the "TForm" text.

7. At this point, your TTreeView would list "TForm" as Items[0], and then "TForm1" as Items[1], both displayed at the root level of the TTreeView. You have a previous item, so now, the MoveTo method is executed and the old Items[0] is added as a child to the newly added node.

8. The loop continues until Cls is of type TObject, each time the old item becomes a child of a newly added node.

FIG. 7.25

Displaying Object Hierarchy. A TListBox shown on the left, and a reverse-order listing is shown in a TTreeView on the right.

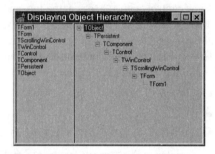

Exploring TTreeView   The Tree View control has a bewildering number of properties and methods beyond just populating the list. Now review a few of the significant methods that operate on the control as a whole, and to TTreeNode objects in specific.

The next example project uses a TToolBar, a TTreeView below left, and a TPageControl below right (see Figure 7.26). The Tool Bar control executes TTreeView level methods and properties that govern expanding and collapsing all items, and graphic features such as indenting and the appearance of lines and buttons to the left of the items. Also on the Tool Bar is a set of buttons that programmatically control item editing.

FIG. 7.26

Exploring TTreeView.

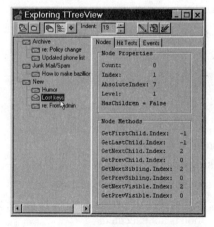

The Page Control section "Nodes" will give you a chance to play with and analyze the position and relationship of nodes within the list. "Hit Tests" graphically represents the return values of the `GetHitTestInfoAt` method. "Events" displays a running list of the last 50 events particular to `TTreeView`.

Due to the amount of code involved, we won't walk through this entire example. Instead, I'd like to explain some of the techniques used that are not readily apparent from reading code or comments. You find the full project on this book's companion CD-ROM, in the \UDELPHI3\CHP7\TREEVIEW\TVPROPS\ folder.

Nodes The output for the "Nodes" page is managed entirely through the TTreeView's `OnChange` event. The event conveniently passes the changed `TTreeNode` so you need to set up a 'with Node do...' and format a caption for each property or method result.

```
procedure TForm1.TreeView1Change(Sender: TObject; Node: TTreeNode);
begin
  with Node do
  begin
    lblCount.Caption   := Format('Count:      %s', [IntToStr(Count)]);
    lblIndex.Caption   := Format('Index:      %s', [IntToStr(Index)]);.
```

You can use methods of `TTreeNode` that provide information on the relationship between nodes, like `GetFirstChild`, in routines where you want to move a group of related items within a Tree View. Drag-and-drop operations and outlines allowing promotion or demotion of groups are two likely candidates where you may need these methods.

Hit Tests The problem I tried to solve in the Hit Tests page was displaying the results of the `GetHitTestInfoAt` method (see Figure 7.27). `GetHitTestInfoAt` takes the mouse coordinates from, for example, an `OnMouseDown` event, and returns a `THitTests`.

FIG. 7.27
Hit tests.

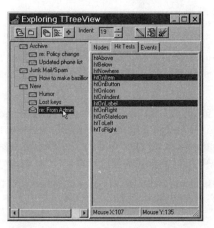

Part
II

Ch
7

```
function GetHitTestInfoAt(X, Y: Integer): THitTests;
THitTest = (htAbove, htBelow, htNowhere, htOnItem, htOnButton,
  htOnIcon, htOnIndent, htOnLabel, htOnRight, htOnStateIcon,
  htToLeft, htToRight);
THitTests = set of THitTest;
```

So how do you then steer clear of a horrendous If/Then statement, and also represent a Pascal Set graphically where multiple items might be part of the set?

First you have to represent the possible values present in the set. You can load a TListBox using an array of string that exactly matches the set type.

```
. const
  HTest: array[htAbove..htToRight] of String = (
    'htAbove',
    'htBelow',
    'htNowhere',
    'htOnItem',
    'htOnButton',
    'htOnIcon',
    'htOnIndent',
    'htOnLabel',
    'htOnRight',
    'htOnStateIcon',
    'htToLeft',
    'htToRight'
  );
```

N O T E Using this technique, you can map nearly any set of values to any other set of values. Rather than strings, you could list a series of class reference types, for example, that allow you to create a series of objects dynamically. ■

With the array HTest defined in the preceding lines, loading the ListBox lbHitTest becomes straightforward, as follows:

```
var
  HT: THitTest;
begin
  for HT := htAbove to htToRight do
    lbHitTest.Items.Add(HTest[HT]);
```

Using a counter variable HT, you can roll through the possible values of THitTest and access the corresponding descriptive strings in the "HTest" array, using the counter to index into the array.

When an OnMouseDown occurs for the Tree View control, you need to show the entries in the TListBox that apply as selected. At design time, set the list box MultiSelect property to True. Again roll through THitTest values and for each node in the TreeView, set the Selected property to true if GetHitTestInfoAt returns a matching THitTest, as follows:

```
procedure TForm1.TreeView1MouseDown(Sender: TObject; Button: TMouseButton;
  Shift: TShiftState; X, Y: Integer);
var
  HT: THitTest;
begin
  for HT := htAbove to htToRight do
    // Select the list box item if there was a corresponding hit
    // returned from GetHitTestInfoAt.
    lbHitTest.Selected[Ord(HT)] := HT in TreeView1.GetHitTestInfoAt(X, Y)
end;
```

Events   The "Events" page demonstrates a brute force, but helpful technique used as a diagnostic and for getting familiar with event order (see Figure 7.28). The basic approach is to create a method that adds a given string to a `TListBox`, then sprinkle the method call to event handlers in which you have an interest, supplying a description for each call. The only twist here is in limiting the number of entries to 50 by deleting the first item as new items are added on.

```
procedure TForm1.LogEvents(EventStr: ShortString);
begin
  // create rolling list by killing the first entry in the list
  if lbEvents.Items.Count > 50 then
    lbEvents.Items.Delete(0);
  lbEvents.Items.Add(EventStr);
  // Set focus to our new entry
  lbEvents.ItemIndex := lbEvents.Items.Count - 1;
end;
```

and the call...

```
procedure TForm1.TreeView1Collapsed(Sender: TObject; Node: TTreeNode);
begin
  LogEvents('    OnCollapsed'   );
end;
```

FIG. 7.28

Event Listing for `TTreeView`.

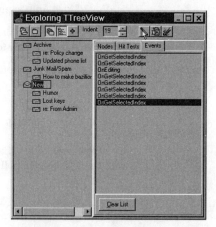

Putting It All Together

In this chapter, you explored how Common Controls work at both design time and runtime to create a polished interface. In the process, you saw how to add objects to Common Controls that have arrays with `Add` methods or contain child objects. And you glimpsed at using API calls and Windows messaging to extend Common Control capability.

Part
II

Ch
7

Adding and Creating with Common Controls

Table 7.1 summarizes some of the add and create methods for Common Controls.

Table 7.1   Common Controls Methods for Adding

Object	Child Object or Array	Sample Syntax
TTabControl	Tabs[]	TabControl1.Tabs.Add('sample text');
TPageControl	TTabSheet	MySheet := TTabSheet.Create(Self); MySheet.PageControl := PageControl1; MySheet.Caption := 'sample text';
TTreeView	TTreeNode	MyNode := TreeView1.Items.Add (Nil, 'sample text');
TListView	TListItem	MyItem := ListView1.Items.Add; MyItem.Caption := 'sample text';
THeaderControl	THeaderSection	MySection := HeaderControl1.Sections.Add; MySection.Text := 'sample text';
TRichEdit	Lines[]	RichEdit1.Lines.Add('sample text');
TStatusBar	TStatusPanel	MyStatusPanel := StatusBar1.Panels.Add; MyPanel.Text := 'sample text';
TToolBar	TToolButton	with TToolButton.Create(Self) do Parent := ToolBar1;

TCoolBar	TcollectionItem;
	 TCoolBand
		var
		 CoolBand: TcollectionItem;
		 begin
		 CoolBand := CoolBar1.Bands.Add;
		 with CoolBand as TCoolBand do
		 Control := Edit1;
		 end;

Down to the Metal

Although the Common Controls eliminates complexity of working with the Common Controls API directly, there are disadvantages. The VCL may "surface" problems latent in the original control or introduce new problems. Also, some functions and features may not be present in the VCL encapsulation of the control. Fortunately, Delphi gives you a way around its own limitations by allowing you access to the Windows API. So, if a method doesn't exist, a message directly to the control can do the trick.

You need to research the Windows API reference for Windows messages and API calls in some cases to find functionality not surfaced by Delphi. This was done in the "Drawing on the Tab" example by sending a `TCM_GETITEMRECT` message to the Tab Control. Check the online help by using the initials of the control where, for example, "SB" bags you `SB_GETBORDERS` through `SB_SIMPLE`.

If the feature or function is new, search the Microsoft Developers Network CD-ROM (MSDN) for "C" header files that must be translated to Pascal.

To get past the obvious functionality of the Common Controls, you need to become familiar with the source. Common Controls are referred to in a number of files, but be sure to review COMMCTRL.PAS and COMMCTRLS.PAS, which give the following help:

- COMMCTRL.PAS found in \source\rtl\win provides the low-level constants, macros, and function headers to the Windows API housed in comctl32.dll.
- COMTRLS.PAS in \source\vcl\ contains Delphi objects that build off the work done in COMMTRL.PAS.

Surfacing New Window Styles The example featuring `THilightTabControl` is made obsolete by the new `TCS_HOTTRACK` style that highlights tab text as the cursor passes over. You can place tabs on any border of the `TTabControl` by using the `TCS_BOTTOM`, `TCS_VERTICAL`, and `TCS_RIGHT` styles in the `CreateParams` method.

N O T E Late in the production of Delphi 3, the new window styles were added to TCustomTabControl. I include the following to explain the *process* of surfacing new functionality from the Microsoft DLLs. Not all the new DLL functionality has surfaced yet, so there is still plenty to play with. ■

My favorite enhancement is `TCS_SCROLLOPPOSITE` (see Figure 7.29). Have you ever clicked a tabbed control where the relative positions for the tabs shifted relative to the clicked tab? `TCS_SCROLLOPPOSITE` leaves everything in order by acting like an old style Rolodex "flip-file."

FIG. 7.29
The Enhanced Tab Control.

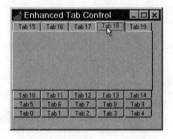

To surface new window styles, override the `CreateParams` method. Delphi initializes a window's style and passes it in the "Params" structure of the `CreateParams` method. `CreateParams` gives a hook into the process just before the window handle is created. It may seem counterintuitive, but to add a style you use "or" and, to subtract a style use "and."

```
Params.Style := Params.Style or TCS_HOTTRACK;
```

This next brief example in Listing 7.24 shows the effect of TCS_HOTTRACK and TCS_SCROLLOPPOSITE window styles. Source for IE31.PAS is available on this book's companion CD-ROM.

Listing 7.24   \UDELPHI3\CHP7\TABCONTROL\IE3\IE31.PAS—The Enhanced Tab Control

```
unit IE31;

interface

uses
  Windows, Messages, SysUtils, Classes, Graphics, Controls, Forms, Dialogs,
  ComCtrls;

type
  THotTabControl = Class(TTabControl)
  private
    procedure CreateParams(var Params: TCreateParams); override;
  end;

  TForm1 = class(TForm)
    procedure FormCreate(Sender: TObject);
  end;

var
  Form1: TForm1;

implementation

{$R *.DFM}

const
  TCS_SCROLLOPPOSITE    = $0001;   // assumes MultiLine tab
  TCS_BOTTOM            = $0002;
  TCS_RIGHT             = $0002;   // used with TCS_VERTICAL
  TCS_HOTTRACK          = $0040;
  TCS_VERTICAL          = $0080;   // only valid with MultiLine mode

procedure THotTabControl.CreateParams(var Params: TCreateParams);
begin
  inherited CreateParams(Params);
  with Params do Style := Style or
    TCS_HOTTRACK or
    TCS_SCROLLOPPOSITE;
end;

procedure TForm1.FormCreate(Sender: TObject);
var
  i: integer;
begin
  with THotTabControl.Create(Self) do
  begin
```

```
      Parent := Self;
      for i := 0 to 19 do
        Tabs.Add('Tab ' + IntToStr(i));
    end;
  end;

  end.
```

Listing 7.25 demonstrates a database application using the Tab Control, employing several of the properties and methods discussed so far (see Figure 7.30). This example simply loads phone extensions and names from the Employee table to an enhanced TTabControl, where each letter of the alphabet is represented by a tab. The source for TC1.PAS is located on the companion CD-ROM.

FIG. 7.30

The Tab Control phone list.

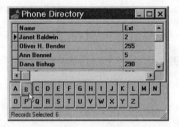

Listing 7.25   \UDELPHI3\CHP7\TABCONTROL\PHONELIST\TC1.PAS—The Tab Control Phone List

```
unit TC1;

interface

uses
  Windows, Messages, SysUtils, Classes, Graphics, Controls, Forms,
  Dialogs, ExtCtrls, DBCtrls, Grids, DBGrids, DB, DBTables, ComCtrls,
  StdCtrls;

type
  THotTabControl = Class(TTabControl)
  private
    procedure CreateParams(var Params: TCreateParams); override;
  end;

  TForm1 = class(TForm)

    procedure FormCreate(Sender: TObject);
    procedure TabControl1Change(Sender: TObject);
    procedure Query1FilterRecord(DataSet: TDataSet;
      var Accept: Boolean);
    procedure Query1AfterOpen(DataSet: TDataSet);
  public
    Query1: TQuery;
```

Part

II

Ch

7

continues

Listing 7.25   Continued

```
    DataSource1: TDataSource;
    DBGrid1: TDBGrid;
    HotTabControl1: THotTabControl;
    StatusBar1: TStatusBar;
  end;

var
  Form1: TForm1;

implementation

{$R *.DFM}

const
  TCS_SCROLLOPPOSITE      = $0001;    // assumes multiline tab
  TCS_BOTTOM              = $0002;
  TCS_RIGHT               = $0002;    // used with TCS_VERTICAL
  TCS_HOTTRACK            = $0040;
  TCS_VERTICAL            = $0080;    // only valid with multiline mode

procedure THotTabControl.CreateParams(var Params: TCreateParams);
begin
  inherited CreateParams(Params);
  with Params do Style := Style or
    TCS_HOTTRACK or
    TCS_BOTTOM;
end;

procedure TForm1.FormCreate(Sender: TObject);
var
  i: integer;
begin
  Query1 := TQuery.Create(Self);
  with Query1, SQL do
  begin
    OnFilterRecord := Query1FilterRecord;
    AfterOpen := Query1AfterOpen;
    DataBaseName := 'DBDEMOS';
    Filtered := True;
    Add('SELECT FIRSTNAME || " " || LASTNAME AS Name, ');
    Add('PHONEEXT as Ext, LASTNAME ');
    Add('FROM EMPLOYEE');
    Add('ORDER BY LASTNAME');
  end;

  DataSource1 := TDataSource.Create(Self);
  DataSource1.DataSet := Query1;

  StatusBar1 := TStatusBar.Create(Self);
  StatusBar1.Parent := Self;
  StatusBar1.SimplePanel := True;

  HotTabControl1 := THotTabControl.Create(Self);
  with HotTabControl1 do
```

```
  begin
    OnChange := TabControl1Change;
    Parent := Self;
    Align := alClient;
    Font.Style := [fsBold];
    TabWidth := Canvas.TextWidth('W') * 2;
    TabHeight := Canvas.TextHeight('W') * 2;
    MultiLine := True;
    for i := Ord('A') to Ord('Z') do
      Tabs.Add(Chr(i));
  end;

  DBGrid1 := TDBGrid.Create(Self);
  with DBGrid1 do
  begin
    Parent := HotTabControl1;
    Align := alClient;
    DataSource := DataSource1;
  end;
  TabControl1Change(Self);
end;

procedure TForm1.TabControl1Change(Sender: TObject);
begin
  Query1.Close;
  Query1.Open;
  { This check avoids an "EInvalidOperation
    'control 'Tabcontrol1' has no parent window'
    which occurs when the application is closing
    and the filter hasn't allowed any records in
    the grid.
  }
  if (Query1.RecordCount = 0) then
  begin
    Query1.Close;
    StatusBar1.SimpleText := 'No Records Selected.';
  end
  else
    StatusBar1.SimpleText := 'Records Selected: ' +
      IntToStr(Query1.RecordCount);
end;

// Allow records where the first letter of the last name
// is equal to the letter on the tab.
procedure TForm1.Query1FilterRecord(DataSet: TDataSet;
  var Accept: Boolean);
begin
  with (DataSet as TQuery) do
    Accept := (Copy(FieldByName('LASTNAME').AsString,1,1) =
      HotTabControl1.Tabs[HotTabControl1.TabIndex]);
end;

// Set column display attributes using TField properties
procedure TForm1.Query1AfterOpen(DataSet: TDataSet);
begin
  with (DataSet as TQuery) do
```

Part

II

Ch

7

continues

Listing 7.25   Continued

```
begin
  FieldByName('LastName').Visible := false;
  FieldByName('Name').DisplayWidth := 30;
  FieldByName('Ext').DisplayWidth := 15;
end;
end;

end.
```

Encapsulating the Enhanced *TPageControl*   You don't want to declare and create a new control for every combination of window style, but how can you change styles on-the-fly if the styles are only implemented during window creation? In the VCL, you find a method of TWinControl called RecreateWnd that destroys and reestablishes the window handle. You can store window styles in properties of your object class so that, when a property such as HotTrack changes, you can fire the RecreateWnd method, and add or subtract styles during CreateParams.

Tab and Page Controls are different implementations of the same Window class, WC_TABCONTROL (as set in the CreateParams method of their common ancestor, TCustomTabControl), and so the new styles that worked for TTabControl also work for TPageControl.

The following example (see Figure 7.31 and Listing 7.26) encapsulates the new features within a new descendant of the TPageControl component that introduces new properties ScrollOpposite, HotTrack, and TabAlign. Component writing is discussed in more detail later in this book, but I include the component listing for later reference.

Tabs aligned to the left or right may not draw correctly in Windows 95. TCustomTabControl simply avoids this problem by not using styles to align tabs to the right and left sides.

On the CD

The source for NEWTAB.PAS (see Listing 7.26) is located on the companion CD-ROM.

FIG. 7.31
Enhanced
TPageControl.

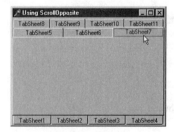

Listing 7.26 \UDELPHI3\CHP7\PAGECONTROL\IE3\NEWTAB.PAS—
Enhanced Page Control

```
unit Newtab;

interface

uses
  Windows, Messages, SysUtils, Classes, Graphics, Controls, Forms,
  Dialogs, ComCtrls;

const
  TCS_SCROLLOPPOSITE     = $0001;    // assumes MultiLine tab
  TCS_BOTTOM             = $0002;
  TCS_RIGHT              = $0002;    // used with TCS_VERTICAL
  TCS_HOTTRACK           = $0040;
  TCS_VERTICAL           = $0080;    // only valid with MultiLine mode

type
  TabAlignments = (pcaTop, pcaBottom, pcaLeft, pcaRight);

  THotPageControl = class(TPageControl)
  private
    FScrollOpposite: Boolean;
    FHotTrack: Boolean;
    FTabAlign: TabAlignments;
    procedure CreateParams(var Params: TCreateParams); override;
    procedure SetScrollOpposite(Value: Boolean);
    procedure SetHotTrack(Value: Boolean);
    procedure SetTabAlign(Value: TabAlignments);
  published
    property ScrollOpposite: Boolean
      read FScrollOpposite
      write SetScrollOpposite;
    property HotTrack: Boolean
      read FHotTrack
      write SetHotTrack;
    property TabAlign: TabAlignments
      read FTabAlign
      write SetTabAlign;
  end;

procedure Register;

implementation

procedure THotPageControl.CreateParams(var Params: TCreateParams);
begin
  inherited CreateParams(Params);
  with Params do
  begin
    if FHotTrack then Style := Style or TCS_HOTTRACK;
    if FScrollOpposite then Style := Style or TCS_SCROLLOPPOSITE;
    case FTabAlign of
```

continues

Part
II
Ch
7

Listing 7.25   Continued

```
      pcaBottom: Style := Style or TCS_BOTTOM;
      pcaLeft:   Style := Style or TCS_VERTICAL;
      pcaRight:  Style := Style or TCS_VERTICAL or TCS_RIGHT ;
    end;
  end;
end;

procedure THotPageControl.SetScrollOpposite(Value: Boolean);
begin
  if (FScrollOpposite <> Value) then
  begin
    FScrollOpposite := Value;
    // RecreateWnd method descends from TWinControl
    // and allows changing window styles on the fly.
    RecreateWnd;
  end;
end;

procedure THotPageControl.setHotTrack(Value: Boolean);
begin
  if (FHotTrack <> Value) then
  begin
    FHotTrack := Value;
    RecreateWnd;
  end;
end;

procedure THotPageControl.SetTabAlign(Value: TabAlignments);
begin
  if (FTabAlign <> Value) then
  begin
    FTabAlign := Value;
    RecreateWnd;
  end;
end;

procedure Register;
begin
  RegisterComponents(UDELPHI3', [THotPageControl]);
end;

end.
```

Creating Applications

The most typical use for Delphi is creating applications. You may create any type of application with Delphi—a command-line utility, an electronic mail program or a multiuser financial database.

Chapters 6 and 7, "Using Delphi Components" and "Using Win32 Common Controls," covered components—the basic building blocks of applications. This chapter takes this knowledge and extends it by detailing the fundamentals of application development, and the three basic types of application. As a bonus, we cover some advanced material that will speed your development cycle and increase the professionalism of your programs. ■

Learn how to use forms

A form is a prerequisite of almost every Windows application. This section documents the properties and events specific to Delphi forms, and moves on to cover form reuse through templates and inheritance.

Learn about application types

This section details the three basic types of application: Single Document Interface (SDI), Multiple Document Interface (MDI), and Console.

Learn the features of two key runtime components

This segment covers the useful features provided by two runtime only components: TApplication and TScreen.

Learn some tricks of the trade

This section presents a neat trick which you may use to reduce the complexity of your program, and shows you how to implement one of the most common programming tasks.

Working with Forms

Much like the foundation of a building locks down its structure, a form locks down the components you place on it. The form provides a central location for the interaction between your program and its user. Your application may use several forms, each dedicated to a particular purpose, such as a dialog box or data entry form.

Delphi encapsulates the concept of a form into a class named TForm. Each form you design with the Form Designer and Object Inspector derives basic properties, methods, and events from this class.

N O T E The TForm class is an indirect descendant of TWinControl. The properties, methods, and events provided by the TWinControl class are documented further in Chapter 6, "Using Delphi Components." ▦

TForm Properties

The TForm class provides several properties that allow you to modify the behavior and look of your forms.

Active   The Active property reflects whether the form currently has input focus. It returns True if the form currently has focus, and False if it doesn't. Windows indicates which form is currently active by drawing the form's title bar in a different color.

N O T E Inactive windows continue to receive mouse-selection and mouse-movement messages. ▦

Regardless of the application's type, only one form has its Active property set to True at any time. You may notice that the title bar of an MDI parent form will be drawn in the "active" color. Don't be fooled—the Active property of an MDI parent form will never be True.

T I P The ActiveForm property of the TScreen class, documented in a following section, "TScreen Component," returns the form which currently has input focus.

ActiveControl   The ActiveControl property indicates the TWinControl descendant that currently has input focus. You may set this value at design-time to nominate which control will have input focus when the form initially becomes active. A common use for the ActiveControl property, at runtime, is to force focus to an invalid field on a data entry screen. The following code ensures you entered text into the edtCustName control before the form is closed:

```
procedure TDataEntryForm.FormCloseQuery(Sender: TObject;
➥  var CanClose: Boolean);
begin
    { Check whether the user has entered text into the control }
    if edtCustName.Text = '' then
    begin
        { Abort the form close }
```

```
        CanClose := False;
        { Set the focus to the invalid field }
        ActiveControl := edtCustName;
    end;
end;
```

TIP The SetFocus method of a TWinControl descendant sets input focus to the control and updates the ActiveControl property.

N O T E Most events pass a parameter named Sender to their handlers. Sender identifies which control detected the event and triggered the event handler. Sender is covered in greater detail in "Shared Event Handlers."

AutoScroll, HorzScrollBar, and VertScrollBar   The AutoScroll property manages the automatic appearance of scroll bars on a form too small to display its set of controls. If AutoScroll is set to True, and you resize the form so that a control is hidden, scroll bars automatically appear. If AutoScroll is False, the control is just cropped at the form's border.

TIP The TScrollBox component, covered in Chapter 6, "Using Delphi Components," allows you to scroll sections of the form independently.

You may manually control the scroll bars with the HorzScrollBar and VertScrollBar properties. This technique is quite useful in a drawing program that implements a zoom feature. Because the diagram may be larger than the form, and you are drawing manually, the AutoScroll property is not activated by a control outside the form's area. To implement a 200 percent zoom feature, use the following code, which allows you to scroll around an area twice the current size of the form:

```
{ Expand the range of the vertical scrollbar }
VertScrollBar.Range   := Height * 2;
{ Show the vertical scrollbar }
VertScrollBar.Visible := True;

{ Expand the range of the horizontal scrollbar }
HorzScrollBar.Range   := Width * 2;
{ Show the horizontal scrollbar }
HorzScrollBar.Visible := True;
```

You may wonder how to check the current position in the scrollable area. Remember from Chapter 6, "Using Delphi Components," that the Position property of a TScrollBar control returns the scroll bar's current location.

BorderIcons   The BorderIcons property is a set of Boolean values, used to determine which icons appear in the title bar of the form.

The biMinimize and biMaximize values create icons at the right edge of the title bar, allowing you to minimize or maximize the form with a single click.

N O T E   The BorderStyle property must be set to bsSizeable or bsSizeToolWin for
biMinimize and biMaximize to have an effect. ■

The biHelp value displays a question mark icon to the right of the title bar. This icon causes
context-sensitive help to be displayed in the same style as Hint text, rather than launching the
Windows Help program. The Display Properties applet under Control Panel, shown in Figure
8.1, demonstrates this style of context-sensitive help.

FIG. 8.1

Context-sensitive help
may be accessed
through the Help border
icon.

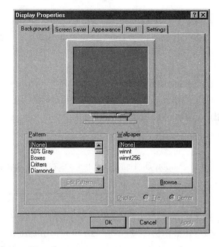

The biSystemMenu value creates an icon positioned to the left of the title bar. If you click this
icon with either mouse button, Windows displays the "system" or "control" menu shown in
Figure 8.2.

FIG. 8.2

The system menu allows
you to move, close, and
resize a form.

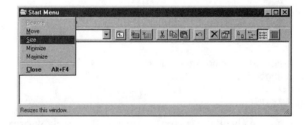

N O T E   For biMinimize, biMaximize, and biHelp to take effect, BorderIcons must contain
the biSystemMenu value. ■

Altering the BorderIcons set at runtime usually is not recommended—it modifies basic behavior of a form and may confuse the user of your application.

BorderStyle   The BorderStyle property is an enumerated type that determines the following:

- The look of the form's title bar
- The available border icons
- The visibility of the menu bar
- The behavior of the form's border

Figure 8.3 shows the six values for BorderStyle. Each form is 200 × 200 pixels at design-time.

FIG. 8.3
The BorderStyle property affects basic form behavior. Clockwise from top left: bsSizeable, bsDialog, bsSingle, bsSizeToolWin, bsToolWindow, and bsNone.

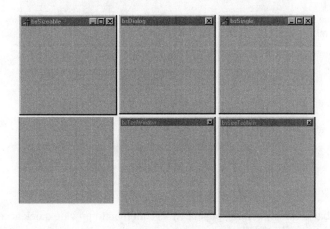

BorderStyle defaults to bsSizeable, which creates a generic, resizable window. This window has a standard height title bar, and doesn't limit the available set of border icons. You usually find the BorderStyle property of an application's main form set to bsSizeable. Examples are the main windows of programs such as Explorer and Notepad.

The bsDialog value creates a dialog window. Dialog windows are used when your program requires a specific response to continue an operation, or needs to display a particular set of information. The now-unfashionable, 16-bit versions of Windows, display bsDialog style windows with a wide border, drawn in the same color as the dialog's title bar. Surprisingly, if you follow the new gray-scale 3-D interface, bsDialog borders look exactly the same as bsSizeable borders! Because dialog forms may not be resized, the only visible difference between these two window styles is that your mouse cursor doesn't change shape as you move it over the border of a bsDialog form.

N O T E   The biMinimize and biMaximize values of the BorderIcons property have no effect on forms with BorderStyle set to bsDialog. ■

Third in popularity is bsSingle—it creates a form that may not be resized at runtime. Unlike bsDialog, bsSingle doesn't restrict the BorderIcons set in any way. With this in mind, the maximize button (biMaximize) usually isn't enabled in a bsSingle-style window—you probably designed the form with the assumption that it will not change size. Examples of programs that use bsSingle-style windows are the Calculator program supplied with Windows, and the BDE Configuration Utility, shown in Figure 8.4. Note that the maximize button is disabled.

FIG. 8.4

The bsSingle border style is useful when the user doesn't need to re-size a form.

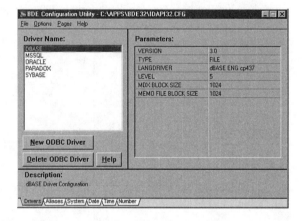

The toolbar is rapidly gaining popularity as a method to provide quick access to groups of related functionality. Toolbar windows are recognizable by their reduced height title bar and "thin" title font. You can construct a toolbar in Delphi by placing groups of TSpeedButton components on a form that has the border style set to bsSizeToolWin or bsToolWindow. The bsSizeToolWin border style creates a manually resizable toolbar window. It doesn't support the biMinimize, biMaximize, or biHelp border icons. The bsToolWindow border style is exactly the same as bsSizeToolWin, with one extra limitation—it cannot be manually resized.

The bsNone border style creates a window without a border or title bar. This isn't recommended for standard forms or dialogs, but it's handy when you create screen savers or splash screens. Figure 8.5 shows the borderless splash screen for Microsoft Exchange.

N O T E   If you select a value for BorderStyle that creates a resizable window, such as
bsSizeable or bsSizeToolWin, Delphi automatically sets AutoScroll to True.
AutoScroll is set to False if you select bsNone, bsDialog, bsToolWindow, or bsSingle. ▪

N O T E   Forms with border styles of bsDialog and bsNone are incapable of displaying menu
bars. ▪

FIG. 8.5
Screen savers and splash screens usually use the bsNone border style.

Height **and** *Width*   The Width and Height properties specify the width and height of a form in pixels. You commonly use these to adjust the dimensions of a form when your program executes in environments that use different display resolutions. The following code resizes the form so that it occupies the entire screen area:

```
{ Move the form to the top left corner of the screen }
Left := 0;
Top  := 0;

{ Adjust the width and height of the form }
Width  := Screen.Width;
Height := Screen.Height;
```

The TScreen class, and the Screen object, provide the width and height of the screen. These are discussed in the following section, "TScreen Component."

Although this code works, it's quite inefficient—the form display is refreshed four times. The SetBounds method, available to all TWinControl descendants, takes four parameters—Left, Top, Width, and Height. SetBounds sets the four relevant properties, and then refreshes the form once. The preceding code, rewritten to use SetBounds, looks like the following example:

```
SetBounds(0, 0, Screen.Width, Screen.Height);
```

ClientHeight **and** *ClientWidth*   A window is simply a display surface created by an application, and maintained by Windows. It's divided into two areas—client and non-client. Applications usually draw in the client area, the size of which is returned by the ClientWidth and ClientHeight properties. Controls and components placed on a form also draw themselves in the client area. A common use for ClientWidth and ClientHeight is to ensure that the form can completely display an object of a specific size. The following code resizes the client area of a form to the width and height of an image contained in a TImage component named imgPicture:

```
with imgPicture.Picture do
begin
    { Resize the client area }
    ClientWidth  := Width;
    ClientHeight := Height;
end;
```

The non-client area is usually drawn by Windows and encompasses the title bar, menu bar, and window border. You can draw in the non-client areas by trapping the WM_NCPAINT message. This process is covered further in Chapter 4, "Object Pascal: Advanced Concepts." Programs such as Microsoft Word use this technique to draw fancy, color-graduated title bars.

FormStyle   The FormStyle property is an enumerated type that determines how the form interacts with your application and Windows. There are two basic styles of forms—MDI style and non-MDI style.

The two MDI form styles are fsMDIForm and fsMDIChild. These styles are discussed in the following section, "Creating MDI Applications."

Non-MDI forms come in two flavors—fsNormal and fsStayOnTop. The fsNormal style is the most popular. It creates the standard, meat-and-potatoes style form used for dialogs, toolbars, and SDI applications. Basically, anything that isn't fsMDIForm or fsMDIChild is fsNormal.

The least used form style is fsStayOnTop. It creates a form that remains on top of all other forms and applications. This is useful for programs that display system information such as resource usage. If your computer is connected to a network, you probably used the exemplary work-group productivity tool, Chat. Shown in Figure 8.6, Chat provides an Always on Top item in the system menu, which keeps the program in front of all your unimportant work.

FIG. 8.6

The fsStayOnTop form style keeps the form on top of all other forms and applications.

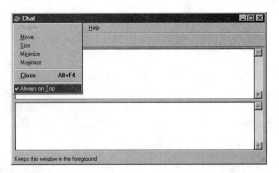

Like Chat, the convention for controlling the fsStayOnTop option is a toggled menu item. The following code implements this option:

```
procedure TForm1.mnuAlwaysOnTopClick(Sender: TObject);
begin
    with mnuAlwaysOnTop do
    begin
        { Toggle the check mark on the menu item }
        Checked := not Checked;

        { Test whether the menu item is checked }
        if Checked then
            { Make the form fsStayOnTop style }
            FormStyle := fsStayOnTop
```

```
        else
            { Revert to fsNormal style }
            FormStyle := fsNormal;
    end;
end;
```

N O T E Changing the `FormStyle` property at runtime re-triggers the `OnShow` event. ■

Icon The `Icon` property determines the icon displayed when your form is minimized. In the new Win95-style interface, this icon is drawn in the biSystemMenu control box that appears in the top left corner of your form. If you don't specify a value for this property, the form uses the `Icon` property of the global `Application` object. The `Application` object is discussed in "TApplication Component."

KeyPreview `TForm` descendants publish the `OnKeyDown`, `OnKeyUp`, and `OnKeyPress` events, as provided by the `TWinControl` class. The `KeyPreview` property controls the situations in which these events are triggered.

When `KeyPreview` is `False`, keyboard events are sent only to the control that currently has focus. In the unusual event that your form doesn't contain controls, the keyboard event is sent to the form. When `KeyPreview` is `True`, keyboard events are first sent to the form, and then to the active control—the form effectively "previews" the keystroke.

N O T E Because the Tab key is used to transfer focus to another control, it doesn't trigger an event. ■

A common use for `KeyPreview` is to handle function keys, which must be detected regardless of which control has focus.

Without `KeyPreview`, you would have to write a one-line event handler for each control's `OnKeyDown` event, which simply passed the `Key` parameter to a routine that checked for a function key. Using this technique is messy—if you had twenty controls, you would have twenty single-line event handlers. When modifying the form, you would need to remove the event-handling code when you deleted the control, and add it to newly created controls. Shared event handlers, detailed in a following section of this chapter, "Shared Event Handlers," are another, slightly more elegant solution. However, for keyboard events, `KeyPreview` provides a better way.

Enabling `KeyPreview` sends all keystrokes to the `OnKeyDown`, `OnKeyUp`, and `OnKeyPress` events of the form automatically. To trap a function key, simply write one event handler for the form's `OnKeyDown` event handler. The advantage of this technique is that it's easy to implement and requires no ongoing maintenance—just set `KeyPreview` to `True` and write the event handler. Hey-presto, function key detection for the entire form. As an example, the following code closes the form when you press the F2 key:

```
procedure TForm1.FormKeyDown(Sender : TObject; var Key : Word;
Shift : TShiftState);
begin
   { Check if Key pressed was function key 2 }
   if Key = VK_F2 then
       { Close the form }
       Close;
end;
```

N O T E When trying this example, make sure that you set KeyPreview to True, or it will not
work! ▇

Remember from Chapter 6, "Using Delphi Components," that the OnKeyDown and OnKeyUp
events use virtual key codes. The VK_F2 identifier in the preceding example is a constant defined by Delphi, representing the virtual key value for function key two. It is certainly easier to
remember than its ordinal value of 113! The WINDOWS.PAS unit, located in your SOURCE\RTL\WIN
folder, contains a list of available virtual key codes.

Menu The Menu property identifies a TMainMenu component that provides the form's main
menu bar. This property allows you to make the application's menu context-sensitive, and is
often used in OLE-enabled applications, where your original menu and speedbar are replaced
by those of the server application. Figure 8.7 shows a Wordpad document with an embedded
Media Clip object. Note the menu and toolbar are those of Media Player, not Wordpad.

FIG. 8.7

You can create context-
sensitive main menus
with the Menu property.

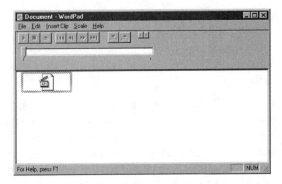

To alter the Menu property, simply assign it a new TMainMenu descendant, as in this example:

```
Menu := mnuNewMainMenu;
```

Position The Position property is an enumerated type, which determines the position of the
form when you run the application.

The default value of Position is poDesigned, which causes the form to display at the same size
and position you set at design time. The size and position are taken from the Left, Top, Width,
and Height properties. Because you cannot rely on the resolution of the target system, this
value is not user-friendly—the form may be only partially displayed on low-resolution screens.

The poScreenCenter value is more useful. It uses design-time Width and Height to determine the form's size, and adjusts Left and Top to ensure that the form displays in the center of the screen.

If you set Position to poDefault, Windows automatically sets Left, Top, Width, and Height. Using this value relinquishes all control over your form's size and placement. If you design your form as a 300-by-300-pixel square, it may be displayed with a Width of 640 pixels, and a Height of 480 pixels. For this reason, poDefault usually is restricted to MDI style forms, where initial size and positioning is not an issue.

The poDefaultPosOnly value uses the Width and Height properties to determine the size of the form, and automatically sets Left and Top. This value is useful in MDI applications where you require a specific size for an MDI child form.

The final value is poDefaultSizeOnly. It uses the Left and Top properties to determine the position of the form, and sets Width and Height automatically. Again, this value is useful primarily in MDI applications, where you must display a form in a specific location, but the form's size is of no concern.

Although the Position property allows you to easily specify the location and size of your form, professional applications of today "remember" the display properties of a form. This generally is accomplished by writing the Left, Top, Width, and Height properties to the Registry, or an INI file. Which location you choose is a matter of preference. One view is to avoid cluttering the Registry, and store application-specific data in an INI file located in the same folder as your program's executable file.

Storing the display properties is quite easy, and usually is performed in the form's OnDestroy event. The following code illustrates this:

```
procedure TForm1.FormDestroy(Sender: TObject);
var
    sAppPath : String;
    iniSettings : TINIFile;
begin

    { Retrieve the path to the program's executable }
    sAppPath := ExtractFilePath(Application.EXEName);

    { Create the TINIFile object }
    iniSettings := TINIFile.Create(sAppPath + 'SETTINGS.INI');
    try
        { Write the display properties to the INI file }
        iniSettings.WriteInteger(Name,'Left',Left);
        iniSettings.WriteInteger(Name,'Top',Top);
        iniSettings.WriteInteger(Name,'Width',Width);
        iniSettings.WriteInteger(Name,'Height',Height);
    finally
        iniSettings.Free;
    end;

end;
```

N O T E   You need to include the INIFiles unit in your uses clause for this example to
compile. ▓

After executing the preceding code, your INI file looks something like this:

```
[Form1]
Left=108
Top=174
Width=540
Height=165
```

Note the use of the form's Name property for the section line. This practice avoids conflicts
when storing display information for multiple forms.

Restoring the display properties requires a little more work, because the INI file may not exist
when the application is executed. The following code, placed in the OnCreate event of a form,
reads the display properties from the INI file:

```
procedure TForm1.FormCreate(Sender: TObject);
const
    cNOTFOUND = -1;
var
    sAppPath : String;
    iniSettings : TINIFile;
    liValue : LongInt;
begin

    { Retrieve the path to the program's executable }
    sAppPath := ExtractFilePath(Application.EXEName);

    { Create the TINIFile object }
    iniSettings := TINIFile.Create(sAppPath + 'SETTINGS.INI');
    try
        { Attempt to read the Left value }
        liValue := iniSettings.ReadInteger(Name,'Left',cNOTFOUND);

        { Check whether the value was present }
        if liValue = cNOTFOUND then
        begin
            { No properties have been stored. Centre the form. }
            Left := (Screen.Width - Width) div 2;
            Top  := (Screen.Height - Height) div 2;
        end
        else
        begin
            { Read the display properties from the INI file }
            Left   := iniSettings.ReadInteger(Name,'Left',Left);
            Top    := iniSettings.ReadInteger(Name,'Top',Top);
            Height := iniSettings.ReadInteger(Name,'Height',Height);
            Width  := iniSettings.ReadInteger(Name,'Width',Width);
        end;
    finally
        iniSettings.Free;
    end;

end;
```

WindowState   The WindowState property is an enumerated type which controls whether the form is minimized, maximized, or normal. WindowState defaults to wsNormal, which displays the window at its default size, as determined by the Position, Left, Top, Width, and Height properties. Setting WindowState to wsMaximize maximizes the form, while wsMinimize minimizes the form.

> **N O T E**   See the "Minimize and Maximize" section under the "TApplication Methods" topic for a tip on minimizing forms. ▪

TForm Events

The TForm class adds several events to TWinControl. These events allow you to customize your form's behavior by performing tasks such as loading and saving state information or allocating and releasing additional resources.

When a form is created and shown, it triggers five events, in the following order:

1. OnCreate—This event is triggered when the form is created. This event allows you to allocate resources and initialize the form. The Position property, documented in the preceding code, contains an example of initializing a form's display properties in the OnCreate event.

2. OnShow—This event occurs just prior to the form being displayed. All controls and components are created and initialized at this time.

> **N O T E**   Although the form isn't yet visible while OnShow is executing, the Visible property is True. ▪

3. OnResize—This event is generated when you resize the form at runtime. You usually place code in the OnResize event handler to change the size and position of controls that don't support the Align property. OnResize is generated once at form creation, when Delphi sets the form's initial size.

> **N O T E**   OnResize is triggered repeatedly during the resizing operation. ▪

4. OnActivate—This event occurs when the form gains input focus. OnActivate is triggered only when focus is transferred from one form to another in the same application. If you switch to your application from another, Delphi generates the OnActivate event of the global Application object.

5. OnPaint—This event is triggered when the form needs to be drawn. This may occur when the form has just been made visible, partially uncovered or increased in size. This event is useful when you are manually drawing information onto the form's surface.

> **N O T E**   The OnCreate event occurs only once during the lifetime of a form instance. OnShow, OnResize, OnActive, and OnPaint may occur multiple times. ▪

When a form is closed and destroyed, it also generates five events, in this order:

1. OnCloseQuery—This event is trigged in response to an action which will close the form. The event handler is passed a Boolean variable, CanClose, which determines whether the form may continue to close. If you set CanClose to False, the form remains open. CanClose defaults to True. You generally use the CanClose event to check whether to save an unsaved file or check whether you really want to exit an application. The following code confirms a request to close the current form:

```
procedure TForm1.FormCloseQuery(Sender: TObject;
var CanClose: Boolean);
begin
    CanClose := MessageDlg('Close form?',mtConfirmation,
                           [mbYes,mbNo],0) = mrYes;
end;
```

2. OnClose—This event is generated just prior to a form closing. This event usually is used when you want to change the default behavior when a form closes. To accomplish this, Delphi passes the OnClose event handler a variable named Action. This variable may take one of four values: caHide, caMinimize, caNone, or caFree. The default action for a non-MDI form is caHide, which hides the form. For an MDI child form, Action defaults to caMinimize, which minimizes the form. If you set Action to caNone, no close action is taken—the form remains open. If Action is caFree, Delphi closes the form, and frees all associated memory. Referencing the form instance after caFree causes an exception.

N O T E OnClose is triggered only when a form is closed explicitly by clicking its close button, or executing its Close method. If you close the main form of an application, all other open forms are closed implicitly, and their OnClose events are not triggered. OnCloseQuery always occurs—whether the form is closed explicitly or implicitly. ■

3. OnDeactivate—This event occurs when the form loses focus, and follows the same rules as the OnActivate event.

4. OnHide—This event is triggered just prior to the form being made invisible.

N O T E Although the form is still visible when OnHide is generated, the Visible property is False. ■

5. OnDestroy—This event is generated just before a form is destroyed. You usually use the OnDestroy event handler to free any resources allocated in OnCreate.

N O T E The OnDestroy event is generated only once during the lifetime of a form. OnCloseQuery, OnClose, OnDeactivate, and OnHide may be triggered more than once. ■

Reusing Forms

By now, you should be familiar with the object-oriented nature of Delphi. Because a TForm is itself a class, it also may be reused, extended, and customized. Form reuse is supported in two ways—Form Templates and Form Inheritance. Both of these methods use the Object Repository, which was introduced in Chapter 2, "Working with Delphi's IDE."

Form Templates   Form Templates provide the basic structure for a new form. They are similar to a cast or die in manufacturing—you may create many items from the one pattern. Delphi ships with a populated Object Repository, which contains several form, dialog, and project templates.

Using Form Templates   Form Templates may be used in the following two ways:

- **Copy**. The Copy option adds a duplicate of the form template to your project. Changes to the object stored in the project or repository do not affect the other.
- **Use**. The Use option links the form template directly into your project. Changes to the object in your project affect the repository object, and vice versa.

To illustrate the use of a form template, let's add a new form based on the About box template to a fresh project. Follow these steps:

1. Select File, New Application. A blank application appears.
2. Select File, New. The New Items dialog appears.
3. Click the Forms tab at the top of the dialog. Delphi displays the available form templates, as shown in Figure 8.8.

FIG. 8.8
Form templates allow you to save and reuse common forms.

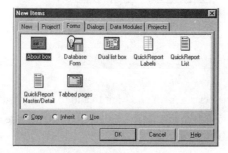

4. Ensure that either Copy or Use is selected.
5. Click OK. A new About box form is added to your project.

If you selected Copy, the About box form is a duplicate of the template. Further changes to the form in your project will not affect the object stored in the repository.

If you selected Use, Delphi simply connects the About box form's source files to the current project. Changes to this form are therefore propagated through all other projects that Use the About box template.

Adding Your Own Templates   Although the default templates are useful, modifications are required each time they are used to make the new form comply with your specifications. To eliminate this repetitive work, you may create form templates and add them to the Object Repository. This process is quite simple, as the following example shows:

1. Create your new form, adding components and code as you desire. You can, of course, base it on another form template.

2. Save your form in the OBJREPOS folder, located under your Delphi installation folder.

N O T E   The Object Repository doesn't store a copy of the form template. Rather, it stores a link to the location of its .DFM and .PAS files. If you delete either of the form's files, the template becomes unusable. Deleting repository objects is covered under "Maintaining the Object Repository." ▆

3. Right-click the form and click Add to Repository. Delphi displays the Add To Repository dialog box, shown in Figure 8.9.

FIG. 8.9

You use the Add To Repository dialog box to add your form templates to the Object Repository.

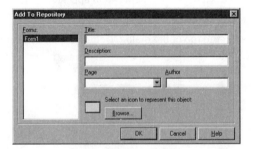

4. From the Forms list, select the form you want to add to the repository.

5. Enter the title for the form template in the Title edit box. This title appears beneath the template's icon in the New Items dialog box.

6. From the Page combo-box, select the page on which you want the template to appear.

7. Click OK. Your form is added to the Object Repository.

N O T E   Delphi automatically includes newly created forms in the current project. These forms are connected to the project, just as if you had selected the Use option from the New Items dialog box. If you are satisfied with the form template, remove it from your project and add a new form, based on the template. ▆

Shared Repository You may not find the idea appealing of storing your form templates under the OBJREPOS folder. If you choose to uninstall Delphi, you must remember to copy your templates out of the Object Repository folder before it is deleted. Alternatively, you may develop in a network environment, and want all programmers to use the same set of templates. The concept of a shared repository solves both these problems.

The shared repository is simply a folder that contains two files, used to store locations of templates stored in the Object Repository. You may set the location of the shared repository by following these steps:

1. Select Tools, Options. The Environment Options dialog box, shown in Figure 8.10, is displayed.

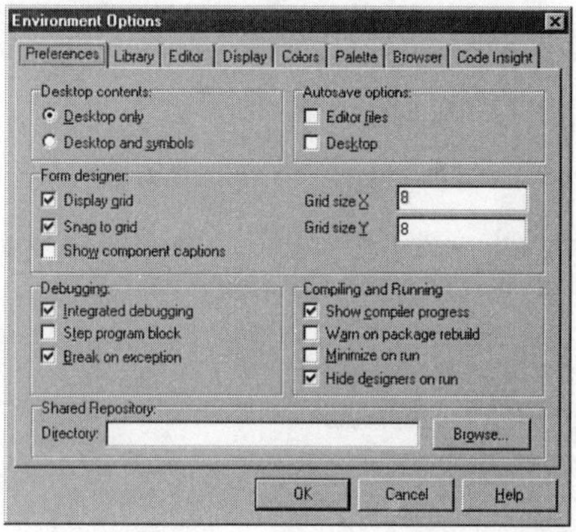

FIG. 8.10
The Shared Repository option allows you to specify a shared location for templates.

2. Click the Preferences tab at the top of the Environment Options dialog box.
3. In the Directory edit box at the bottom right of the dialog box, enter the path to the folder you want to use for the shared repository.
4. Click OK. Delphi now scans the shared repository for templates when the New Items dialog box is invoked.

After the shared repository has been configured, you are free to store templates in any folder.

Maintaining the Object Repository When you add your own templates to the Object Repository, you may find yourself wanting to delete or edit templates. You accomplish this by using the Object Repository dialog box, shown in Figure 8.11. To invoke this dialog, select Tools, Repository.

The Pages list box to the left of the dialog box lists the pages displayed in the New Items dialog box. This set of pages is maintained by the Add Page, Delete Page, and Rename Page buttons.

FIG. 8.11

Use the Object Repository dialog box to maintain your templates.

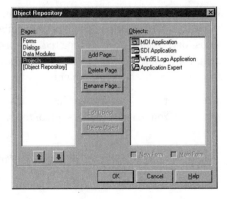

Selecting a page from this list fills the Objects list box with the objects contained on that page. If you select the [Object Repository] item, Objects lists the entire contents of the repository. You can move an object between pages by dragging it from the Objects list to a new page in the Pages list.

The Edit Object button displays the Edit Object Info dialog box, shown in Figure 8.12. This dialog allows you to edit the properties of the object at any time.

FIG. 8.12

You may edit the properties of an object in the repository with the Edit Object Info dialog box.

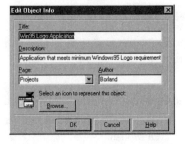

The Delete Object button removes the object from the Registry, but doesn't delete the associated files from your disk.

The check box controls located at the bottom of the dialog box perform two powerful tricks. The first control, New Form, allows you to specify the template used when you create a new form. The second, Main Form, indicates the template used to build the main form when you create a new application. To indicate the new default template for either New Form or Main Form, simply select the template object from the Objects list, and click the appropriate check box.

If you select a project rather than a form, the dialog replaces the New Form and Main Form check boxes with a New Project check box. This allows you to indicate which project template is used by default when creating a new application.

Form Inheritance   Form Inheritance combines the best features of the two form reuse options of Copy and Use. With Copy, you can create duplicates of a form template, and add components and code to the new forms. The disadvantage is that changes made to the repository object are not propagated through the new forms. The Use method implements this propagation, but because your project links to a single form object, all instances of the form are exactly the same.

The Inherit option allows you to create multiple instances of a template, all of which may be different, just like Copy. Inherit also automatically distributes changes made to the repository object, just like Use.

Using Form Inheritance   The Object Repository contains several examples of form inheritance. Follow these steps to create a new dialog box that descends from another form:

1. Select File, New Application. A blank application appears.
2. Select File, New. The New Items dialog box appears.
3. Click the Dialogs tab. The dialogs page is displayed.
4. Select the dialog with Help icon that has the buttons arranged vertically along the right side of the form.
5. Select the Inherit option.
6. Click OK. Delphi displays the new dialog form.

The caption of the new dialog box is OKHelpRightDlg2. Why didn't Delphi create this dialog box as OKHelpRightDlg? The answer lies in form inheritance. Your project's form list contains four items—Form1, OKHelpRightDlg, OKHelpRightDlg2, and OKRightDlg. Because you derived your new form from OKHelpRightDlg, Delphi included OKHelpRightDlg in your project to compile your program. This forces your new form to be named OKHelpRightDlg2 to avoid naming conflicts. In turn, OKHelpRightDlg is derived from OKRightDlg, so OKRightDlg must also be included.

> **CAUTION**
>
> The two ancestral forms, OKHelpRightDlg and OKRightDlg, are linked into your project just as if you selected the Use option from the New Items dialog box. If you modify these forms, you modify the objects stored in the repository.

The inheritance chain is reflected in the automatically generated code. The class declaration for OKHelpRightDlg2 shows that it descends from OKHelpRightDlg, as follows:

```
TOKHelpRightDlg2 = class(TOKHelpRightDlg)
private
   { Private declarations }
public
   { Public declarations }
end;
```

NOTE   By convention, class declarations or types, are prefixed with the letter T. ■

This declaration is not terribly informative—because you added no new components or code, OKHelpRightDlg2 doesn't define any new properties, methods, or events. The class definition for OKHelpRightDlg is a little more interesting:

```
TOKHelpRightDlg = class(TOKRightDlg)
   HelpBtn: TButton;
   procedure HelpBtnClick(Sender: TObject);
private
   { Private declarations }
public
   { Public declarations }
end;
```

As you can see from the preceding code, OKHelpRightDlg takes the components and code from OKRightDlg, and adds a TButton named HelpBtn, and an event handler named HelpBtnClick.

The Power of Form Inheritance   As mentioned previously, the power of form inheritance lies in its capability to add new components and code to an object, and still maintain a link back the original template. If you change the template, the descendant objects are automatically updated. Prepare an example with these steps:

1. Select File, New Application. A blank application appears.
2. Close the main form, which is the window titled Form1.
3. Select File, New. The New Items dialog appears.
4. Click the Dialogs tab at the top of the dialog. The Dialogs page is displayed.
5. Select the Standard dialog with the buttons arranged vertically on the right side of the form.
6. Click the Inherit option.
7. Click OK. Delphi displays a new form, titled OKRightDlg2.
8. Select View, Forms. The View Form dialog is displayed.
9. Select the template form, OKRightDlg. Click OK. Delphi displays the template form, titled Dialog, positioned exactly over the new form.

Now for the demonstration. Move the template form to just beneath the Delphi main window. Did you notice the new form, OKRightDlg2, was not uncovered? This is because Delphi updates OKRightDlg2's Left and Top properties as its parent's properties are modified—instant propagation of the changes made to an ancestor object.

The other side of the modification coin is a direct change to the descendant object. Direct modifications of the descendant object take precedence over changes flowing from the ancestor object, and are not propagated back up the inheritance chain. Now prepare the current example for the next demonstration:

1. Select View, Forms. The View Forms dialog is displayed.

2. Select OKRightDlg2, and click OK. OKRightDlg2 appears.

3. Move OKRightDlg2 to the bottom of the screen.

Your screen should now look like Figure 8.13.

FIG. 8.13
Change distribution
flows in only one
direction, ancestor to
descendant.

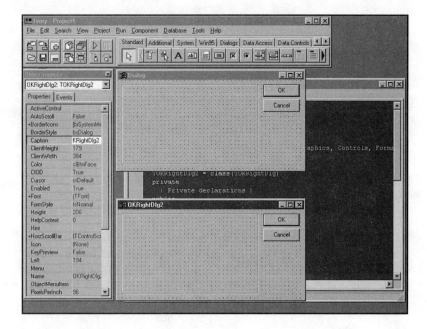

If you move OKRightDlg2 to the right side of the screen, the template form remains stationary. This demonstrates the fact that change propagation occurs in only one direction—from ancestor to descendant.

For more information on object inheritance, see Chapter 4, "Object Pascal: Advanced Concepts."

Creating SDI Applications

SDI stands for Single Document Interface, and describes an application which allows you to load a single document at a time. Notepad, shown in Figure 8.14, is a perfect example of the SDI application—it allows you to load and work on only one text file at a time.

The term "document" is becoming a little outdated. Applications are becoming more object-centric—they work with a central object, into which you may embed external objects. These external objects are generally maintained by another application. Wordpad (refer to Figure 8.7) is an example of an object-centric application. It allows you to embed any type of OLE object into a Wordpad file. It is still known as an SDI application because you may load only one Wordpad object, or document, at a time.

FIG. 8.14

Notepad is a typical SDI application.

The capability to work on a single object at a time does not prevent the application using additional forms, such as dialogs, toolbars, and status windows. Figure 8.15 shows the toolbars of Wordpad in their window state. To implement this in Delphi, simply add another form to your application, and sets its `FormStyle` to `fsSizeToolWin` or `fsToolWindow`.

FIG. 8.15

Wordpad is a multi-form, SDI application.

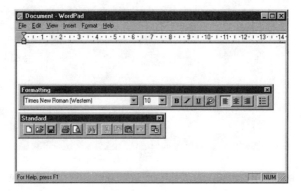

Applications such as Delphi make heavy use of the capability to display multiple forms. Delphi uses the main form to display the menu bar, toolbar, and component library. Forms such as the Object Inspector and Code Editor coexist in a peer-to-peer environment. An application such as Notepad doesn't exploit this capability, and limits itself to forms that just cannot exist without the main window, such as the File Open dialog box. Although Delphi may display virtually any window at any time, it still conforms to the SDI model—you may load only one project at a time.

An SDI Example

To demonstrate SDI functionality, let's create a simple image viewer.

This project may be found on this book's accompanying CD-ROM, under the folder named EgSDIApp.

Building the Interface for the SDI Example   Usually, the first step to building a Delphi program is designing the interface. To build the image viewer's interface for yourself, follow these steps:

1. Open the File menu. Click New Application. A blank application appears.

N O T E   Delphi creates a basic SDI application by default. The Object Repository dialog box, invoked by selecting Tools, Repository, allows you to set a new default project template.

2. Set the following properties of the form:

Property Name	Property Value
Caption	Image Viewer
Name	frmMain
ShowHint	True

3. Place a `TPanel` component on the form. Set its properties to the following values:

Property Name	Property Value
Align	alTop
Caption	-No value-

4. Place three `TSpeedButton` components in the `TPanel` and name them `spbtnLoad`, `spbtnStretch`, and `spbtnCenter`. Set the following properties:

Property Name	Property Value
spbtnLoad.Hint	Load
spbtnLoad.Left	8
spbtnLoad.Top	8
spbtnStretch.AllowAllUp	True
spbtnStretch.GroupIndex	1
spbtnStretch.Hint	Stretch
spbtnStretch.Left	48
spbtnStretch.Top	8
spbtnCenter.AllowAllUp	True
spbtnCenter.GroupIndex	2
spbtnCenter.Hint	Center
spbtnCenter.Left	80
spbtnCenter.Top	8

5. Place another TPanel component on the form. Set the following properties:

Property Name	Property Value
Align	alClient
Caption	- No value -

6. Place a TImage component in the newly created TPanel. Set the properties of the TImage to the following:

Property Name	Property Value
Align	alClient
Name	imgMain

7. Add a TOpenDialog to the form. Set the following properties:

Property Name	Property Value
Filter	Bitmaps (*.bmp)|*.bmp
Name	opndlgLoad
Options	[ofPathMustExist,ofFileMustExist]

Delphi provides a number of glyphs you can use for TSpeedButton components. These are stored in the IMAGES\BUTTONS folder, located under your Delphi installation folder. For this example, the Glyph properties were set to:

Property Name	Property Value
spbtnLoad.Glyph	FLDROPEN.BMP
spbtnStretch.Glyph	FONTSIZE.BMP
spbtnCenter.Glyph	PICTURE.BMP

Now is a good time to save your project—select File, Save Project As. Save Unit1 as Main, and the project as EgSDIApp.

Your main form should now look like Figure 8.16.

FIG. 8.16
SDI applications generally consist of one main form.

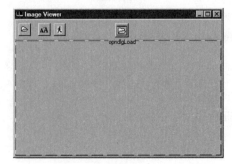

Writing Code for the SDI Example   Now that you created the interface, move on to writing the code that controls your application.

The first stage is to load the image. Follow these steps:

1. Double-click the `spbtnLoad` component. Delphi displays the Code Editor, and automatically creates the `OnClick` event handler.

2. Type the following code:

```
if opndlgLoad.Execute then
    imgMain.Picture.LoadFromFile(opndlgLoad.FileName);
```

The `Execute` method of `opndlgLoad` invokes the standard file open dialog. If you click OK, `Execute` returns `True` and sets the `FileName` property to the path of your selected file. If you click Cancel, or press the Esc key, `Execute` returns `False`.

The `TImage` component provides a `Picture` property, which is an instance of the `TPicture` class. The `TPicture` class provides properties and methods to manage bitmaps, icons and metafiles. One of the methods is `LoadFromFile`, which loads the image file specified by the string argument.

Select <u>R</u>un, <u>R</u>un to compile and execute your application. Try opening a bitmap. See how easy life can be?

Now, add the stretch functionality. Follow these steps:

1. Double-click the `spbtnStretch` component. The Code Editor and newly created `OnClick` event handler appear.

2. Add the following code:

```
imgMain.Stretch := spbtnStretch.Down;
```

The `TSpeedButton` component provides a property named `Down`, which is `True` when the `TSpeedButton` is depressed and `False` when it is not. The `Stretch` property of a `TImage` component is set to `True` when you want to be able to stretch the image, and `False` when you do not.

Centering works in the same way. Add the following code to the `spbtnCenter` component's `OnClick` event:

```
imgMain.Center := spbtnCenter.Down;
```

Compile and run your program. It now stretches, and centers.

Creating MDI Applications

An MDI, or Multiple Document Interface, application lets you load more than one document, or object, at a time. The File Manager program, since replaced by various incarnations of Explorer, is an MDI application, and is shown in Figure 8.17.

FIG. 8.17

File Manager is an MDI application.

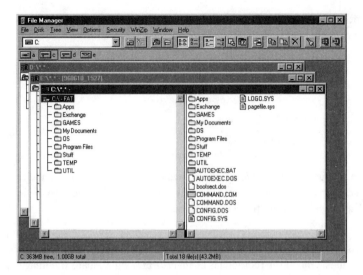

MDI projects usually consist of at least two forms—the MDI parent and an MDI child. MDI parent forms have their `FormStyle` property set to `fsMDIForm`. Set the `FormStyle` property to `fsMDIChild` to create an MDI child window.

The MDI parent acts as a container for multiple child windows. These child windows are restricted to the client area of the MDI parent and may be moved, resized, minimized, or maximized. You may have several types of MDI child in the one application, such as one type that displays images, and another type which handles text.

Creating Forms

In MDI applications, you usually need to display multiple instances of a form class. Because each form is an object, it must be created before it is used, and freed when no longer needed. Delphi may handle this automatically, or you can create forms manually as required.

Automatic Form Creation By default, when you execute your application, Delphi automatically creates one instance of each form class in your project, and frees each instance when your application terminates. Automatic creation is handled with Delphi-generated code in three places.

The first place is the interface section of the form's unit file:

```
type
  TForm1 = class(TForm)
  private
    { Private declarations }
  public
    { Public declarations }
  end;
```

This code declares the TForm1 class. Chapter 4, "Object Pascal: Advanced Concepts," covers class declarations in more detail.

The second place is just beneath the TForm1 class declaration:

```
var
  Form1: TForm1;
```

This code declares an object variable, Form1, which points to an instance of a TForm1 object. This object variable is accessible to any unit in your project and usually is used at runtime to manipulate the form.

The third place is the project source code, accessible by opening the View menu and clicking Project Source. The code worthy of attention is as follows:

```
Application.CreateForm(TForm1, Form1);
```

This statement creates an instance of the form class TForm1, and assigns it to the automatically declared object variable named Form1.

Destruction is handled through the concept of an owner object. When an object is destroyed, it automatically destroys all objects it owns. The form created by the CreateForm method is owned by the Application object, and destroyed when the application is terminated.

Dynamic Form Creation   Although automatic form creation is useful in SDI applications, it doesn't apply in MDI programs that may display multiple instances of a form class—for example, a program that displays multiple images at a time would open several MDI child windows, one for each image.

To implement dynamic creation, you use the Create constructor of the form class to create a new instance. The following code creates a new instance of TForm1 at runtime and sets its Caption property to NewForm:

```
Form1 := TForm1.Create(Application);
Form1.Caption := 'NewForm';
```

The Create constructor expects you to pass a TComponent descendant as a parameter. This TComponent acts as the owner for the form. By convention, Application is usually passed as the owner so that the form instance is automatically destroyed when the application terminates. You could pass Nil as the parameter, to create an ownerless form, but then would have to ensure that you destroyed the object manually. In the event of an unhandled error, not destroying a form instance would cause a memory leak, and is generally poor programming.

With the preceding code example, Form1 will point only to the last created instance. Because this isn't terribly useful, you may not want to store the instance in an object variable. The following code acts as a replacement:

```
with TForm1.Create(Application) do
    Caption := 'NewForm';
```

N O T E   In an MDI application, the Show method is unnecessary—Delphi automatically shows a
newly created MDI child form. An SDI application requires you to Show the new form. ∎

Even with dynamic creation, Delphi still will create and display a single instance of each form.
You must remove the form class from the auto-create list with the Project Options dialog box,
shown in Figure 8.18. An example of this process may be found in a following section, "Building the Interface for the MDI Example."

FIG. 8.18

The Project Options
dialog box allows you to
set project-specific
options.

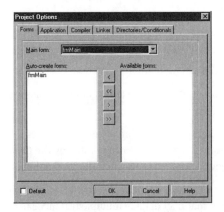

If you want to access a particular MDI child instance of a form class, you can use the
MDIChildren property discussed in the following section, "MDI Specific TForm Properties."
The TScreen object provides a Forms property that allows you to access any form instance. The
Forms property is discussed in the following section, "TScreen Component."

MDI-Specific *TForm* Properties

The TForm object provides several properties specific to MDI applications.

ActiveMDIChild   The ActiveMDIChild property returns a TForm object, indicating which MDI
child form currently has focus. This property is useful when your parent form contains a
toolbar or main menu that provides commands that act on the open MDI child forms.

As an example, imagine that your project uses an MDI child form, which contains a TMemo
control named memDailyNotes. The class name for this child form is TfrmMDIChild. The MDI
parent form provides a Clear button on its toolbar, which empties the contents of the
memDailyNotes control found on the currently active MDI child form. The following code
implements this functionality:

```
procedure TfrmMDIParent.spbtnClearClick(Sender:TObject);
begin
    if not (ActiveMDIChild = Nil) then
        if ActiveMDIChild is TfrmMDIChild then
            TfrmMDIChild(ActiveMDIChild).memDailyNotes.Clear;
end;
```

The first line ensures that ActiveMDIChild is not Nil, because referencing a Nil object will raise an exception.

N O T E ActiveMDIChild is Nil when there are no MDI children open, or the FormStyle property is not fsMDIForm.

Because ActiveMDIChild returns a TForm object, the compiler has no way of accessing memDailyNotes—it is only provided by TfrmMDIChild instances. The second line checks whether ActiveMDIChild points to a TfrmMDIChild class.

By the third line, you have established that ActiveMDIChild is both valid, and points to the required class. You are now free to typecast ActiveMDIChild into a TfrmMDIChild object, and call the Clear method of its memDailyNotes component.

MDIChildren and MDIChildCount   The MDIChildren property is an array of TForm objects which give you access to the set of currently created MDI child forms. The array lists the child forms in tab sequence order. MDIChildCount returns the number of elements in the MDIChildren array.

These properties are commonly used to perform an action on all open child forms. To illustrate, imagine a Minimize All command. To implement this, you need to set the WindowState property of each child form to wsMinimized. The following code performs this function:

```
procedure TForm1.mnuMinimiseAllClick(Sender : TObject);
var
    iCount : Integer;
begin
    for iCount := MDIChildCount-1 downto 0 do
        MDIChildren[iCount].WindowState := wsMinimized;
end;
```

If you iterate forward through the MDIChildren array (from index zero to index MDIChildCount-1), the loop will not work correctly. When you minimize the first form in the MDIChildren array, the array is re-sorted in creation order, and the loop may not hit each array element. Iterating in reverse order solves this problem by minimizing the form at index zero last.

TileMode   The TileMode property is an enumerated set that controls how the MDI parent arranges its child forms when you call the Tile method. If TileMode is set to tbHorizontal, which is the default value, the child forms are arranged horizontally. Setting TileMode to tbVertical arranges the children vertically. These modes are shown in Figure 8.19.

FIG. 8.19

The TileMode property controls the arrangement of MDI child windows.

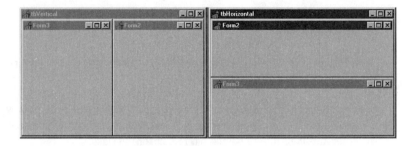

WindowMenu   Professional MDI applications allow you to activate an MDI child by selecting it from a list in the menu bar. The WindowMenu property nominates a TMenuItem object that Delphi will use to provide a list of available MDI children.

For the list to display, the TMenuItem must be a top-level menu. By convention, this menu has its Caption property set to &Window. Figure 8.20 shows a three-item MDI child list, appended to the Window menu.

FIG. 8.20

The WindowMenu property is used to provide an MDI child form list.

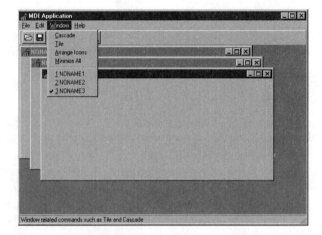

MDI-Specific *TForm* Events

In an MDI application, the OnActivate event is triggered only when switching from one MDI child to another. If focus is transferred from a non-MDI form to an MDI child, the OnActivate event of the MDI parent is generated, although the parent's Active property is never set to True. This strange process is actually logical—if OnActivate were always triggered for an MDI child, there would be no way of knowing whether the MDI group of forms had received focus from a non-MDI source or just another MDI child.

MDI-Specific *TForm* Methods

The TForm object provides several methods useful in MDI applications:

- ArrangeIcons—Organizes the icons of minimized child forms in a nice pattern along the bottom of the MDI parent form.

- Cascade—Staggers the child forms so that their title bars are visible.

- Next and Previous—Moves through the child form array in tab sequence, just as if you had used Ctrl+Tab or Ctrl+Shift+Tab.

- Tile—Arranges the child forms so they don't overlap. The preceding Figure 8.19 shows the two tiling options.

An MDI Example

This section demonstrates an MDI application by extending the image viewer that was built in the preceding section, "An SDI Example." This example project may be found on this book's companion CD-ROM, in the EgMDIApp folder.

TIP The MDI application template, available from the New Items dialog box, streamlines the process of creating MDI style programs.

Building the Interface for the MDI Example   The interface for the MDI version of the image viewer program is similar to the SDI version. The basic difference is that each image now will be displayed on a separate form, rather than on the main form.

Follow these steps to create the MDI parent form:

1. Select File, New Application. A blank application appears.

2. Set the following properties:

Property Name	Property Value
Caption	Image Viewer
FormStyle	fsMDIForm
Name	frmMDIParent
ShowHint	True

3. Place a TPanel control on the form. Set the following properties:

Property Name	Property Value
Align	alTop
Caption	- No value -

4. Place three TSpeedButton components in the TPanel, and name them spbtnLoad, spbtnStretch, and spbtnCenter. Set the following properties:

Property Name	Property Value
spbtnLoad.Hint	Load
spbtnLoad.Left	8
spbtnLoad.Top	8
spbtnStretch.AllowAllUp	True
spbtnStretch.GroupIndex	1
spbtnStretch.Hint	Stretch
spbtnStretch.Left	48
spbtnStretch.Top	8
spbtnCenter.AllowAllUp	True
spbtnCenter.GroupIndex	2
spbtnCenter.Hint	Center
spbtnCenter.Left	80
spbtnCenter.Top	8

For this MDI project, the Glyph properties were set to the same values as the SDI example.

5. Add a TOpenDialog to the form. Set the following properties:

Property Name	Property Value
Filter	Bitmaps (*.bmp)|*.bmp
Name	opndlgLoad
Options	[ofPathMustExist,ofFileMustExist]

Now for the child form:

1. Select File, New Form. A blank form appears.

2. Set the following properties:

Property Name	Property Value
FormStyle	fsMDIChild
Name	frmMDIChild
Position	poDefaultPosOnly

3. Place a TImage component on the form. Set its properties to the following:

Property Name	Property Value
Align	alClient
Name	imgMain

The final step is to remove the MDI child form from the auto-create form list. Follow these steps:

1. Select Project, Options. The Project Options dialog (refer to Figure 8.18) is displayed.
2. Select frmMDIChild from the Auto-create forms list.
3. Click the button labeled ">." The frmMDIChild item moves from the Auto-create forms list to the Available forms list.
4. Click OK.

Now that the interface is created, save the project. Select File, Save Project As. Save Unit1 as MDIParent, Unit2 as MDIChild, and the project as EgMDIApp.

Writing Code for the MDI Example   The code for the MDI application is similar to the code in the example SDI application.

The first step is to load the image. Enter the following code into the OnClick event of the spbtnLoad component:

```
procedure TfrmMDIParent.spbtnLoadClick(Sender: TObject);
begin
   if opndlgLoad.Execute then
      with TfrmMDIChild.Create(Application) do
      begin
          Caption := opndlgLoad.FileName;

          imgMain.Picture.LoadFromFile(opndlgLoad.FileName);

          ClientWidth  := imgMain.Picture.Width;
          ClientHeight := imgMain.Picture.Height;
      end;
end;
```

After executing the dialog, the code creates a new instance of the MDI child class. The Caption property of this new form instance is set to the file name of the image, and we then load the image. After the image is loaded, the client area of the form is resized to ensure that the entire image is displayed.

One thing remains before this example will work. This unit references the TfrmMDIChild type, which is contained in the MDIChild unit. Add the following code under the implementation line:

```
uses
    MDIChild;
```

Compile and run the application. Try opening the bitmap files in the IMAGES\SPLASH\16COLOR folder. Notice how the MDI child forms are minimized when you click the Close button. To force the forms to close, quit the application and add the following code to the OnClose event of the TfrmMDIChild class:

```
Action := caFree;
```

This line changes the default value of the Action variable from caMinimize to caFree—closing the form, and releasing its resources.

The Stretch and Center TSpeedButton components perform the same function as those found in the SDI example, with a slight difference in implementation. Here is the code for the spbtnStretch component's OnClick event:

```
if not (ActiveMDIChild = Nil) then
    if ActiveMDIChild is TfrmMDIChild then
        TfrmMDIChild(ActiveMDIChild).imgMain.Stretch := spbtnStretch.Down;
```

You should recognize this code from the discussion on the ActiveMDIChild property, found in the previous section, "ActiveMDIChild."

The code for the spbtnCenter component's OnClick event is similar:

```
if not (ActiveMDIChild = Nil) then
    if ActiveMDIChild is TfrmMDIChild then
        TfrmMDIChild(ActiveMDIChild).imgMain.Center := spbtnCenter.Down;
```

Compile and run the application. You can stretch and center the images. However, one problem remains—the state of the Stretch and Center TSpeedButton components isn't updated when you switch between child forms. To solve this problem, add the following code to the OnActivate event of the TfrmMDIChild class:

```
frmMDIParent.spbtnStretch.Down := imgMain.Stretch;
frmMDIParent.spbtnCenter.Down  := imgMain.Center;
```

To compile the program, you need to add the MDIParent unit to the uses clause in the MDIChild unit. Add the following code below the implementation line:

```
uses
    MDIParent;
```

Compile and run the application. Load several images, and play with the Stretch and Center TSpeedButton components. Notice that the state is automatically updated when you activate a new child form.

CAUTION

In this example, assigning a new value to the Down property of a TSpeedButton generates its OnClick event. Be careful writing code in an event handler that generates an event through setting a property—it may cause infinite recursion.

Creating Console Applications

Forget all that bunk about intuitive interfaces, icons, and buttons—real users want text-mode applications back. Seriously, although DOS-style applications are definitely out of vogue, and for good reason, there are still situations in which text-mode programs are useful.

Command-line utilities such as Edit and PkZip are the most prevalent examples of text-mode interfaces. The problem in the past has been that these utilities must run in an MS-DOS environment, and therefore have no access to the Windows API, or resources such as printers and memory management. With the advent of Console application support in Delphi, you can write a text-mode program that executes as a native 32-bit task. This Console program may call Windows API functions and use resources. Most important, the Delphi Console application uses the flat memory model and object library of standard Delphi applications.

You usually use a Console-style application when your interface requirements are simple, perhaps just single-line status messages. With these kinds of programs, the overhead of the graphic environment of Windows is substantial. An ancient tool used to teach a programming language was the "Hello World" application, a simple program which uses the language's editor and compiler to display a "Hello World" message. In Delphi, this program is easily created by placing a TLabel component on a form, and setting its Caption property to "Hello World." This simple program compiles to over 150K! Written as a console application, the executable is under 10K.

A Console Example

On the CD

The best way to cover console applications is to create the "Hello World" example. This project is included on this book's companion CD-ROM, in the EgConsoleHello folder. If you want to create it manually, follow these steps to set up the project:

1. Select File, New Application. A blank application appears.
2. Select File, Remove From Project. The Remove From Project dialog appears, shown in Figure 8.21.
3. The project contains only one form unit. Ensure that it is selected and click OK. A "Save changes to Unit1.pas?" confirmation dialog appears.
4. Click No. The form is removed from the project.

Take a moment to save the project as EgConsoleHello.

FIG. 8.21

The Remove From Project dialog box allows you to remove units and forms from your project.

Although this has now created a formless application, it remains GUI-based and includes a lot of unused resources. If you were to compile it now, it would still be over 150K. To make the compiler generate a pure, text-based application, you must edit the project source. Select View, Project Source. The Code Editor displays the following source code for the project:

```
program EgConsoleHello;

uses
  Forms;

{$R *.RES}

begin
  Application.Initialize;
  Application.Run;
end.
```

The uses clause includes the Forms unit, which provides routines to manage the forms of an application. Because this program uses no forms, delete the entire uses clause.

The {$R *.RES} statement is a compiler directive. It tells the compiler and linker to include all resource files that may contain icons or string resources. You use another compiler directive later to make the compiler generate a console-mode program.

The next two statements of interest are Application.Initialize and Application.Run. The first is used to initialize external OLE servers. The second basically shows the main form of the application, and waits until it closes. Because the console application has no use for either OLE or forms, delete both lines.

The final step is to switch the program into Console mode by using the $APPTYPE compiler directive. This directive has one parameter, which may take one of two values—CONSOLE or GUI. If you use the GUI value, Delphi generates its standard graphic-based application. This mode is the default. The CONSOLE value tells the compiler to generate a Console mode application. Add the following code under the program EgConsoleHello line:

```
{$APPTYPE CONSOLE}
```

The project source should now look like this:

```
program EgConsoleHello;

{$APPTYPE CONSOLE}

{$R *.RES}

begin
end.
```

Congratulations! You now have a full-fledged console application. It doesn't actually do anything yet, so add the "Hello World" functionality. Place the following line between the begin and end statements:

```
WriteLn('Hello World');
```

Save the project, compile, and run it. You should notice a DOS-style window briefly displayed with the text "Hello World" located at the top-left corner.

This behavior is not unusual—if you run the DIR command from an icon, it creates a console window, displays its output, and then closes. If you run a console application from an MS-DOS box, it uses the MS-DOS window for its display. Test this by executing your program from the command line.

For the programmers among you who are old hands at Pascal, Console programs associate their standard input and output text streams with the text window, which means you can use the Read, ReadLn, Write, and WriteLn functions to retrieve and output text. For the C programmers, Console programs connect their stdin, stdout, and stderr channels to the text window.

Windows API Functions for Consoles

If you want to do anything more advanced than reading or writing text, you need to delve into the Windows API. There are approximately 40 functions that deal with areas such as changing the display attributes of text, controlling the console's size and position, and monitoring mouse activity.

On the CD

The example in Listing 8.1 changes the text displayed in the title bar of the console window. You can find this example on this book's companion CD-ROM, in the EgConsoleTitle folder.

Listing 8.1 Sample Console Application—Changes the Title Bar of a Console Window

```
program EgConsoleTitle;

{$APPTYPE CONSOLE}

uses
   Windows, SysUtils;

{$R *.RES}

var
   sNewTitle, sErrMsg : String;

begin

   sNewTitle  := 'Welcome to Console World';
   if not SetConsoleTitle(PChar(sNewTitle)) then
   begin
      sErrMsg := 'Unable to set caption - '+SysErrorMessage(GetLastError);
      MessageBox(0,PChar(sErrMsg),'Error',MB_ICONEXCLAMATION+MB_OK);
   end;

   ReadLn;

end.
```

A brief explanation of the code is warranted. The SetConsoleTitle API function returns False if it cannot set the new title. GetLastError returns a numeric identifier, indicating the last API error, which SysErrorMessage converts into a string for display. The MessageBox function displays a dialog box with the error message, an exclamation point, and an OK button. Finally, ReadLn waits for you to press enter before the application terminates and destroys the console window.

N O T E The Win32 help file supplied with Delphi covers Console API functions. To access this information, display the Console Reference topic, and then click the >> button. ■

Reusing Applications

The Object Repository is not limited to housing forms, units, and dialogs—entire projects may be stored as templates. A project template may contain forms, units, and custom-written code and is used as a starting point for new projects.

Using Project Templates

Delphi ships with the following three project templates:

- **MDI Application**—This template creates a fully functional MDI project. The MDI parent form includes menu, speed, and status bars. This project contains substantial code that implements the menu functions, and manages the messages displayed on the status bar.

- **SDI Application**—The SDI Application template provides a simple SDI project. The main form, like the preceding MDI parent form, contains menu, speed, and status bars. This project also includes a simple About box dialog, and code which implements the functionality of its interface.

- **Win95 Logo Application**—This template creates a project which is modeled on the guidelines set down by Microsoft for their Win95 Logo certification program. Conforming to these style guidelines and receiving certification from Microsoft allows your program to display the "Designed for Win95" logo.

To create a new SDI application by using the SDI Application template, follow these steps:

1. Select File, New. The New Items dialog box (refer to Figure 8.8) is displayed.

2. Click the Projects tab. The Projects page is displayed.

3. Select the SDI Application icon. Click OK. The Select Directory dialog box, shown in Figure 8.22, is displayed.

FIG. 8.22
The Select Directory dialog box allows you to specify the directory in which Delphi will create the new project.

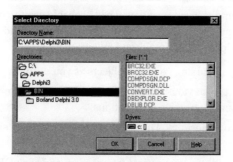

4. Nominate the directory for the new project.

 TIP If you select a non-existent directory, Delphi creates it for you.

5. Click OK. The new project is created.

N O T E Copy is the only option available when creating a new project from the Object Repository. The template's files are copied from the Object Repository into the directory you nominate in step 4. Further changes to the project in the Object Repository have no effect on previously created projects. ■

The Projects page contains one other icon—Application Expert. The Application Expert (see Figure 8.23) walks you through the process of creating a new application step by step. It automates tasks such as building your menu and speedbar and setting default file extensions for the open and save dialog boxes.

FIG. 8.23

The Application Expert automates much of the project creation process.

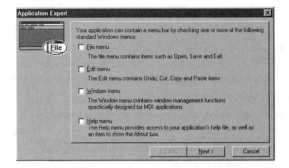

N O T E   The application templates, and the projects generated by the Application Expert, are worth studying in detail. They provide many insights into the methodology and design style of Windows programs. ■

Adding Your Own Project Templates

Although the application templates are useful, you will probably want to customize and enhance them. To avoid continually making the same changes, you may add a project template to the Object Repository. This process is simple, and follows these steps:

1. Create your new project, adding code and objects as you desire.

2. Save the project. See the previous section, "Shared Repository," for a discussion on the OBJREPOS directory, and alternative file locations.

3. Select Project, Add To Repository. The Add to Repository dialog, shown in Figure 8.24, is displayed.

4. Fill in the edit boxes with the appropriate information, and click OK. The project is added to the Object Repository.

Project templates are maintained in exactly the same fashion as form and dialog templates. This topic was covered in the preceding section, "Maintaining the Object Repository."

FIG. 8.24
The Add to Repository dialog box allows you to add a project to the Object Repository.

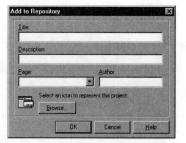

Project Options

There is a vast set of options you may modify when building your project. The Project Options dialog box (refer to Figure 8.18) allows you to set these options, and groups them across several pages.

N O T E You can set the default project configuration by checking the Default check box, located in the lower left corner of the Project Options dialog box. This configuration is then used for all new projects. ▓

Forms

The Main form drop-down list determines the main form of your application. Delphi displays the main form first, and terminates the application when this form is closed.

The two list boxes, Auto-create forms and Available forms, allow you to determine which forms are automatically created at runtime. Form creation is discussed further in "Creating Forms."

Application

The Title edit box is used to set the text your application displays in the task bar and task manager. Delphi, for example, sets this property to the name of the currently open project. If you don't specify a title, it defaults to the project name, which may be something quite obscure. With Delphi, it would be DELPHI32.

You use the Help file edit box to connect a help file to your application. This assists with the implementation of context-sensitive help.

The Load Icon button lets you set your application's icon, which is used as the default icon for shortcuts and is displayed in the task bar and task manager.

The last item on this page is Target file extension. This option lets you modify the file extension of the final executable, such as OCX for an ActiveX control, or DLL for a Dynamic Link Library. You generally leave this option alone—the standard-issue file extension assigned by Delphi is usually quite satisfactory.

Compiler

The compiler tab contains a number of check boxes allowing you to modify the huge array of compiler options. Two useful options are Show hints and Show warnings. Turning on these options causes the compiler to generate messages identifying things such as unused and uninitialized variables.

Linker

The Map file options are useful to those hotshot programmers who read long lists of technical information such as segment addresses, public symbols, and the program start address. If you don't know or don't care what these are, leave the Map file setting Off.

Linker output controls whether the compiler produces a Delphi Compiled Unit (DCU), or an Object (OBJ) file when compiling your source code. OBJ files are useful if you share Delphi code with another language such as C++. For more information on this topic, see Chapter 30, "Delphi and C++ Synergy."

EXE and DLL options allow you to create a console application, documented further in "Creating Console Applications," or include Turbo Debugger for Windows debug information, covered further in Chapter 27, "Testing and Debugging."

Memory sizes determine the minimum and maximum stack size for your application, and set the preferred base address for your DLL. If your program uses a lot of recursion, perhaps in a Quick Sort routine, or uses large local variables, you may need to increase the stack size. The base address should be left as its default value, unless you know what you are doing when you modify it.

The EXE Description allows you to provide a string, included in the executable or DLL, which describes your application. An example could be "My Cool Delphi Application, Version 1, Copyright Me."

Directories/Conditionals

The Output and Unit output settings control where the compiler places the executable or DLL and compiled units. These settings are useful if you don't like to clutter your source folder with extra files. If you leave them blank, compiled units are placed in the same folder as their source code, and the executable or DLL is placed in the project folder.

Conditional defines are used to establish flags to be tested during compilation, and are commonly used to include or exclude blocks of code when compiling your project.

Unit Aliases exist to provide backward compatibility. In the first version of Delphi, the `Windows` unit was split into two files—`WinTypes` and `WinProcs`. By assigning the `Windows` alias to both `WinTypes` and `WinProcs`, code from previous versions may be compiled without modification.

VersionInfo

The VersionInfo page lets you tag your executable or DLL with version information such as Major Version, Minor Version, and FileDescription.

A really useful feature is Auto-increment build number—it causes Delphi to increment the build number automatically whenever you compile the program.

The Module Attributes section lets you include flags such as Debug Build in your executable. Selecting an option from this set has no effect on compilation—it is for informational purposes only.

The grid to the bottom of this page provides standard version information keys. You are free to supply values as you desire.

Packages

The Packages page lets you decide which packages are to be available for use at design time, and linked into your application at build time.

The Design packages group presents a list of registered packages. Selecting a package from this list makes it available at design-time, and allows the linker to use the package when building the application's executable.

The Runtime packages group lets you define which packages the linker will use when building the executable. By default, Build with runtime packages is turned off, which means that all objects from the VCL will be linked into your executable. Turning this option on means that your application will share a single copy of each package with any other Delphi application currently executing. For more information on packages, see Chapter 15, "Working with Packages."

Advanced Coding Techniques

Now that you are familiar with the three types of application, and understand the concept of form and application reuse, it is time to detail two extremely useful components—`TApplication` and `TScreen`. These components provide information on the environment in which your program is executing, and allow you to enhance the professionalism of your application.

TApplication Component

The `TApplication` component encapsulates the runtime state of your application. Delphi automatically creates an instance of the `TApplication` class at runtime, named `Application`. To use the `Application` object, you must include the `Forms` unit in your uses clause.

***TApplication* Properties**   TApplication exposes several properties which allow you to monitor the status of your application and control several basic aspects of its look and behavior.

Active   The Active property returns True when your application currently has input focus, and False when it doesn't. If Active is True for the Application object, it also must be True for one form in your application. The Active property is commonly used when you want to determine whether your application has focus before displaying a status message, or drawing on a TCanvas object. If Active is False, another program has focus, and there is little point in altering your application's display.

N O T E   Your application will receive mouse-movement messages while inactive. ▨

EXEName   The EXEName property returns a string that contains the fully qualified path of your application's executable file. In C, this is argv[0]. This property usually is used to determine the folder in which the executable is stored—useful when you want to store application-specific settings and don't want to clutter your Windows folder.

T I P   To extract the folder from a fully qualified path, use the ExtractFilePath or ExtractFileDir functions, located in the SysUtils unit.

Hint *and* ShowHint   The Hint property contains the text that will be displayed when the OnHint event is triggered. For more information on Hint and OnHint, see "OnActivate and OnDeactivate" in "TApplication Events."

The ShowHint property is used to determine whether fly-over hints are displayed. Setting it to False disables the hint system for all controls in the entire application, regardless of whether their individual ShowHint properties are True. This property is commonly used in conjunction with a TMenuItem that is checked when hints are to display and unchecked when they are to be disabled. The following code implements this functionality using a TMenuItem named mnuToggleHints:

```
procedure TForm1.mnuToggleHintsClick(Sender : TObject);
begin
    { Toggle the current display state }
    mnuToggleHints.Checked := not mnuToggleHints.Checked;

    { Update the Application's ShowHint property }
    Application.ShowHint   := mnuToggleHints.Checked;
end;
```

HintColor, HintPause, HintHidePause, *and* HintShortPause   The HintColor property determines the color of the fly-over hint windows. The following code changes the HintColor to a lovely shade of green:

```
Application.HintColor := clLime;
```

The `HintPause` and `HintHidePause` properties control the timing for the display of fly-over hints and are used in the following simple sequence:

1. The mouse cursor is placed over a `TControl` descendant.

N O T E The OnHint event is triggered as soon as the mouse cursor enters the `TControl`. ■

2. Delphi waits `HintPause` milliseconds before displaying the hint window.
3. The cursor remains over the `TControl`.
4. Delphi waits `HintHidePause` milliseconds before hiding the hint window.

The `HintShortPause` property determines the delay before displaying the hint of the control if another control's hint is already visible. It's useful when you want to avoid displaying each hint as you move the mouse cursor across several objects, such as a set of `TSpeedButton` controls.

Icon   The `Icon` property lets you alter the icon that represents your application in the task bar or task manager at runtime. Modifying this property is useful when you want to indicate your application has changed state. The following code sets the application's `Icon` property to the icon found in the INACTIVE.ICO file:

```
Application.Icon.LoadFromFile('INACTIVE.ICO');
```

Title   The `Title` property specifies the text displayed for your application in the task bar or task manager. Delphi sets its title to the name of the currently open project. The following code implements this change, using the project name stored in the string variable `sPrjName`:

```
Application.Title := 'Delphi 3.0 ' + sPrjName;
```

TApplication Methods   The `TApplication` class provides several methods that act on the application as a whole.

Minimize _and_ Maximize   The `Minimize` and `Maximize` methods cause the application as a whole to be minimized or maximized, respectively. You may wonder why this is necessary, when setting the `WindowState` property for a `TForm` object has the same effect. If you set the main form's `WindowState` to `wsMinimized`, Delphi will minimize the form to the desktop, and not the taskbar. Calling the `Minimize` method minimizes it correctly.

ProcessMessages   The `ProcessMessages` method forces your application's main process or task to process awaiting messages. This is useful when you are executing a long loop and want your application to remain responsive. Take the following example, which continually loops while the application has not been terminated:

```
while not Application.Terminated do
    ;
```

If you execute this code, your application will be totally unresponsive—you cannot move or resize the form, interact with any of its controls, or close the program. The main thread of your application is devoted to executing this loop, and does not have the opportunity to process mouse, keyboard, or system messages. These messages are not discarded—they are queued for later processing.

The `ProcessMessages` interrupts the loop and processes these queued messages. Modifying the code to the following allows the loop to continue operating, and your application remains responsive.

```
while not Application.Terminated do
    Application.ProcessMessages;
```

> **N O T E**   It is often preferable to use the `TThread` object to implement background processing. The
> `TThread` object is covered further in Chapter 24, "Working with Threads." ■

Terminate   The `Terminate` method is the preferred way of closing an application. It sets the `Terminated` property of the `TApplication` object to `True`. `Terminate` doesn't close the application immediately—it waits for event handlers and other processing to complete. The `Terminate` method is commonly used in a File, Exit menu item. The following code implements this function:

```
procedure TForm1.mnuFileExitClick(Sender : TObject);
begin
    Application.Terminate;
end;
```

TApplication Events   The `TApplication` class provides several events, which are triggered when application-specific situations arise.

Handling `TApplication` _Events_   Because `TApplication` is unavailable at design-time, installing a `TApplication` event handler is slightly more complex—you cannot use the Object Inspector to automate the process.

Remember from Chapter 2 that an event property is a pointer to the procedure which executes when the event is triggered. The Object Inspector automatically handles the declaration and definition of an empty event handler, and sets the event property to the new handler. If you use events of the `TApplication` object, you must do this manually. This process has three steps. The following text illustrates with the `OnActivate` event, covered in the following section, "OnActivate and `OnDeactivate`."

The first step is to declare your event handler. Because objects detect and trigger events, an event handler must be a method of an object—it cannot exist as a separate function in a unit. The event handler also must conform to the event's calling convention, which may be determined from the online help system. From the help files, the `OnActivate` event is of type `TNotifyEvent`—the most common event type. The declaration for the `TNotifyEvent` type is as follows:

```
TNotifyEvent = procedure (Sender: TObject) of object;
```

This declaration indicates that your event handler must take a `TObject` parameter. This parameter allows you to determine which object is detected and sent this event, and is covered in more detail in "Shared Event Handlers."

Now, to continue with the example. Create a new application, and use the Code Editor to modify the type declaration for TForm1 to the following:

```
type
  TForm1 = class(TForm)
  private
    { Private declarations }
    procedure OnActivateHandler(Sender:TObject);
  public
    { Public declarations }
  end;
```

N O T E Declaring the OnActivateHandler procedure as private is a matter of convention only. You may declare it as private, protected, or public. The only proviso is that it must be a method of an object. ▪

Now that you have declared the event handler, the second step is to define it. Add the following code to the implementation section of your unit:

```
procedure TForm1.OnActivateHandler;
begin
    { Your event handler code goes here }
end;
```

N O T E The definition of a procedure or function doesn't require the parameter list to be restated. You are free to restate the parameters for your own documentation purposes. ▪

The third and final step is to connect your event handler to the event. This usually is performed in the OnCreate event of the main form. Modify the OnCreate event handler of the TForm1 class to the following:

```
procedure TForm1.FormCreate(Sender: TObject);
begin
    Application.OnActivate := OnActivateHandler;
end;
```

This statement assigns the address of the OnActivateHandler procedure to the OnActivate event property of the Application object.

OnActivate *and* OnDeactivate   These events notify your program of a change to the Application object's Active property. OnActivate occurs after Active is set to True, or after the application has gained focus. OnDeactivate is triggered after Active is set to False.

OnException   The OnException event is triggered when an unhandled exception occurs. Chapter 5, "Exception Handling," covers exceptions in detail.

OnHint   The OnHint event is generated when you move the mouse cursor over a TControl descendant that has its Hint property set to something other than a null string. It is commonly used to display the hint message in the status bar, and is especially useful for TMenuItem objects, which do not activate the fly-over tip windows. The text for this hint is returned in the Hint property of the Application object.

This example assumes that you are using a TPanel named pnlStatus as the status bar:

```
procedure TForm1.OnHintHandler(Sender:TObject);
begin
    pnlStatus.Caption := Application.Hint;
end;
```

OnIdle   The OnIdle event is triggered when your application is waiting for an event such as a mouse movement, and is not executing an event handler. It is commonly used to perform background tasks, such as loading database information or processing images.

The event handler is passed a Boolean parameter named Done, which is True by default. If Done is True when the event handler completes, the event is not triggered until the application has processed another message, and its message queue is again empty. If you set Done to False, the event is triggered continually, while your application is waiting for a message.

> **N O T E**   Because the application is unresponsive while the OnIdle event handler is executing, keep the routine short or use plenty of ProcessMessage calls. ▨

Many programs display the current time in a status panel at the bottom of their window. The following event handler implements this functionality using a TPanel control named pnlTime:

```
procedure OnIdleHandler(Sender:TObject; var Done:Boolean);
begin
    pnlTime.Caption := TimeToStr(Now);
end;
```

TScreen Component

The TScreen class encapsulates the state of the screen or display area. Delphi automatically creates an instance of the TScreen class at runtime, named Screen. To use the TScreen class, you must include Forms in your unit's uses clause.

TScreen Properties   The TScreen class publishes several properties that are remarkably useful when developing your application.

ActiveControl   The ActiveControl property returns the TWinControl object that currently has input focus. It's commonly used to implement the Copy, Cut, and Paste commands for text-based controls. The following code, placed in a TMenuItem object's OnClick event performs the Copy function:

```
procedure TForm1.mnuEditCopyClick(Sender:TObject);
begin
    Screen.ActiveControl.Perform(WM_COPY,0,0);
end;
```

Remember that virtually everything that occurs in Windows and Delphi is the result of a message received by an object. A form paints its surface when it receives the WM_PAINT message, and closes when it receives the WM_CLOSE message. The Perform method of a TWinControl sends the message passed as the first parameter to itself. In the preceding example, the WM_COPY message causes the TWinControl to copy the current selection to the clipboard. The other relevant messages are WM_CUT, which causes the control to cut its selected contents to the clipboard, and WM_PASTE, which pastes the clipboard contents into the TWinControl.

ActiveForm   The ActiveForm property returns a TForm object, which indicates which form currently has focus. If the application is inactive, this property indicates which form will have focus when control is switched to it from another application. An example of its use is to flash the active form's title bar when the application wants to gain your attention. The following example uses the Windows API function FlashWindow, which requires the handle of the window whose title bar you want to flash:

```
FlashWindow(Screen.ActiveForm.Handle,False);
```

If you pass False as the second parameter, the title bar flashes and returns to its original state. Passing True toggles the state of the title bar for each successive call to FlashWindow.

Cursor   The Cursor property specifies the mouse cursor's shape for the entire application. It is commonly used to announce that the application is engaged in a lengthy process. The following code provides an example of its use:

```
{ Set the mouse cursor to an hourglass }
Screen.Cursor := crHourglass;

try

    { Perform a long process }
    for iCount := 1 to 1000000000 do
        ;

finally
    { Reset the mouse cursor to default state }
    Screen.Cursor := crDefault;
end;
```

Delphi provides many cursor shapes—look up the DragCursor topic in the online help for more details.

N O T E   You also may set the Cursor property for individual TControl descendants, including TForm classes.

Forms* and *FormCount   The Forms property returns an array of TForm objects. The elements of this array point to each form owned by the application, including MDI parent and MDI child forms. The FormCount property returns the number of elements in the Forms array. The "MDIChildren and MDIChildCount" section provides an example of iterating through a TForm array.

Height *and* **Width**   The most useful properties of the TScreen class. Height and Width return the height and width of the screen in pixels. These properties are useful in a wide variety of situations, especially when determining where to position a form. The following code will center the form:

```
Left := (Screen.Width - Width) div 2;
Top  := (Screen.Height - Height) div 2;
```

TScreen Events   The TScreen class provides two events which notify your program of a change in focus. Like the TApplication class, the services of the TScreen class are available only at runtime. To connect an event handler to a TScreen event, you must follow the same process covered in the "Handling TApplication Events" section.

OnActiveControlChange   The OnActiveControlChange event occurs when you transfer focus from one control to another. The ActiveControl property is updated prior to this event being triggered. You can use this event to display the control's hint text in a status bar, without relying on the positioning of the mouse cursor. The following event handler sets the Caption property of a TPanel control to the active control's Hint property:

```
procedure TForm1.ActiveControlChangeHandler(Sender:TObject);
begin
    if (not Application.Terminated) then
        pnlStatus.Caption := ActiveControl.Hint;
end;
```

Delphi generates an OnActiveControlChange event as the application terminates. At this time, referencing pnlStatus causes an exception, because it was destroyed.

OnActiveFormChange   The OnActiveFormChange event is triggered when you either create a new form or transfer focus from one form to another. This event is commonly used in MDI applications to update available menu functions and speed buttons. The following code fragment from the MDI Application template shows this:

```
procedure TMainForm.UpdateMenuItems(Sender: TObject);
begin
    FileCloseItem.Enabled := MDIChildCount > 0;
    FileSaveItem.Enabled := MDIChildCount > 0;
    FileSaveAsItem.Enabled := MDIChildCount > 0;
```

The UpdateMenuItems procedure was connected to the OnActiveFormChange event on the form's OnCreate event handler:

```
procedure TMainForm.FormCreate(Sender: TObject);
begin
    Application.OnHint := ShowHint;
    Screen.OnActiveFormChange := UpdateMenuItems;
end;
```

Shared Event Handlers

By now, you know that each class is capable of publishing its own events. Each of these events has a specific type, such as TNotifyEvent for OnClick or TCloseEvent for OnClose. Delphi allows you to write an event handler and connect it to multiple events of the same type—effectively sharing the event handler.

Imagine a TEdit control, which provides the OnKeyDown and OnKeyUp events. Because both events are of the same type, TKeyEvent, you could write one procedure and connect it to both events. This procedure then will be called twice for each key press—once when OnKeyDown is triggered and once when OnKeyUp is triggered. Alternatively, you can use one procedure for both the OnCreate and OnClick events of a TForm—they both are of type TNotifyEvent.

Although these examples illustrate a point, a more common use of shared event handlers is connecting an event provided by two separate controls. These controls do not have to be of the same class. Follow these steps to create a shared OnClick handler between a TButton control and a TEdit control:

1. Select File, New Application. A blank application appears.
2. Place a TButton control on the form. Enter the following code into its OnClick handler:

```
procedure TForm1.Button1Click(Sender: TObject);
begin
    Edit1.SetFocus;
    Edit1.SelectAll;
end;
```

3. Place a TEdit control on the form. In the Object Inspector, drop down the list next to the TEdit control's OnClick event. Select Button1Click.

If you click the TButton control, focus is transferred to the TEdit control, and its text is completely selected. If you click the TEdit control, the shared event handler sets focus to the TEdit, and selects its text.

The *Sender* Parameter   Because multiple objects may share the same event handler, how do you tell which object generated the event? Each event handler is passed a parameter named Sender, which points to the object that detected the event and triggers the event handler. It is often used to perform custom processing that depends on the type or instance of the Sender object.

Creating Single-Instance Applications

One common task when writing an application is restricting it to a single instance only. By default, if you double-click the icon for your Delphi program five times, Windows creates five discrete instances of your application. The Windows Explorer is an example of an application that allows multiple instances to execute simultaneously. The easiest and cleanest way to implement a single-instance application is by searching for a window title.

Searching for a Window Title   When an instance of a window is created, Windows requires it to register a *window class name*. Delphi uses the form's class as the window class name. For example, when Delphi creates the Form1 instance of the TForm1 class, it registers TForm1 as the window class name for Form1. Further, each form provides a Caption property, which is known as the window's *title*. The FindWindow API function returns the handle of the window that matches the class name and title. The following code stores the handle for the Form1 window in a variable named hwndForm1:

```
hwndForm1 := FindWindow('TForm1','Form1');
```

The first parameter is the window class name, and the second, is the window's title. If FindWindow cannot locate a matching form, it returns zero.

The FindWindow call cannot be placed in the TForm1 class because an instance of the form must be created for the code to execute. This causes your application to detect itself and terminate, thinking it is already running. The code therefore must be placed in the project source. Modify your project source to the following:

```
begin
    Application.Initialize;

    if FindWindow('TForm1','Form1') <> 0 then
        Application.Terminate;

    Application.CreateForm(TForm1, Form1);
    Application.Run;
end.
```

Because you are using an API function, you must include the Windows unit in your uses clause.

The FindWindow function searches for the form and if located, terminates the application. If the form isn't located, it's created, and the application continues to execute.

N O T E   If Delphi is loaded, the Form Designer already created a window that matches the FindWindow search. Your application will detect the Object Inspector's window and terminate. Close Delphi and run this test program from the command line. ■

The problem with this method is that it relies on the window class name and title to be fixed and known before the form is created at runtime. If you change the Caption or Name properties of the form with the Object Inspector, you also must update the project source.

Activating the Previous Instance   Retrieving the window handle is useful—you can automatically activate the previous instance of the application. This is more professional than simply terminating or displaying a "Sorry, go and find the other instance" message. To achieve this, you need to drag out another API function, SetForegroundWindow. This function takes a single parameter—the handle of the window that you want to activate. Modify the project source as follows:

```
var
   hwndPrev : HWND;

begin
   Application.Initialize;

   hwndPrev := FindWindow('TForm1','Form1');
   if hwndPrev <> 0 then
   begin
       SetForegroundWindow(hwndPrev);
       Application.Terminate;
   end;

   Application.CreateForm(TForm1, Form1);
   Application.Run;
end.
```

Putting It All Together

This chapter covered quite a few topics. This section is a recap to hammer home the material.

The first section covered the most common element of a Delphi program—the TForm class. It discussed the properties and events provided by the TForm class, and mentioned the fact that as an indirect descendant of TWinControl, TForm classes also share properties and events with the remainder of the VCL. The chapter then moved on to discuss form reuse with the Object Repository, and the three options when reusing form templates: Copy, Use, and Inherit.

The second segment detailed the three types of application: SDI, MDI, and Console. It covered the TForm properties, methods, and events specific to MDI applications, and the Windows API functions used when developing Console applications. You learned about application templates, and application reuse with the Object repository.

The chapter then documented the TApplication and TScreen classes, which provide properties, methods, and events that reflect the state of your application at runtime. You covered the process required to connect event handlers to the Application and Screen objects.

This chapter concluded with a discussion on shared event handlers, and creating single-instance applications by using the Windows API. ●

Database Development

CHAPTER 9

Working with Local Databases

by Mark Pritchard and Noel Rice

The previous chapters showed you how to build applications in Delphi that accept input from the user, process it, and return a result. You learned about the various types of applications, and the multitude of components supplied with Delphi's Visual Component Library (VCL).

These skills will help you join the growing market for utilities and Web browser plug-ins, but the largest market still is the provision of robust data-centric applications. Demand for data-centric applications also must grow as the marketplace stampedes toward concepts such as client satisfaction and quality control. Where do you store information on the client's preferences, purchases, and localities? How do you control the internal data flow that stems from the day-to-day operation of your business? How do you store this data in a safe, easily accessible form? The answer to these questions is remarkably easy—use a database.

However, just how to implement this simplistic answer has been a thorny question for decades and has provided the basis for many doctorates in computing. We couldn't treat the topic of databases in ten books, much less in a couple of chapters in *Special Edition Using Delphi 3*. With this in mind, we will only introduce the two types of databases—*local* and *remote* (or *SQL*)—and then cover the database support offered by Delphi. ■

An introduction to local databases

An overview of local database concepts (tables, fields, and records). Also covered: the two native table formats supported by the Borland Database Engine (BDE)—Paradox and dBASE.

Delphi component interface to the BDE

You learn how Delphi encapsulates commonly used BDE functionality into two simple components—TTable and TQuery.

Interface controls for data-centric applications

You learn about the VCL controls that automate the process of transferring data between the dataset (TTable or TQuery) and application interface.

Advanced topics

After mastering the basics of database programming, you will tackle some advanced material. This section details topics such as cached updates, transactions, and exception handling.

N O T E   For more information on database theory and design, visit your local bookstore.   ▪

Delphi's BDE support is superbly structured—you can develop an application using a local database, such as Paradox, and then scale it up to your corporate database server once it works reliably. Chapter 10, "Working with SQL Databases," covers the additional complexities of interacting with SQL servers and how Delphi supports the extra functionality.

What Are Local Databases?

Let's start with a couple of definitions to ensure that we understand each other.

A *database* is a collection of data that describes a system, such as the classic example of stock or inventory management. The database stores information on stock levels, customers, orders, and shipping details. A well-designed database consists of several *tables*, each of which holds information about instances of a single type of object in the system. The customer object is a prime example for its own table. What are some of the properties of a customer? Account number and billing address spring to mind. These properties translate to columns in the table and are known in database parlance as *fields*. Each instance of a customer in the system is represented as a separate row in the customer table, known as a *record*. Figure 9.1 shows the CUSTOMER.DB table, located in the DEMOS\DATA folder under your Delphi installation folder.

FIG. 9.1

A simple customer table.

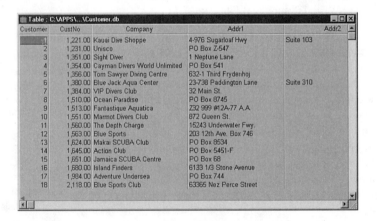

Each table in a local database is like a document or spreadsheet. Local tables are saved on your computer's hard disk or stored centrally on a network drive. You can move them around with Explorer and back them up with standard backup software. The difference is that local tables, unlike documents or spreadsheets, are meant to be used by more than one application simultaneously (they support concurrent access).

To manage this simultaneous use, a set of procedures must be in place to control and protect access to records and tables, such as where two people try to gain access to a single record for editing purposes. There is no set method for this control—each type of database (local or remote/SQL) implements locking protocols in its own way.

Types of Local Databases

The Borland Database Engine (BDE) natively supports two types of local tables—Paradox and dBASE. Each table type has advantages and disadvantages.

Advantages of the Paradox Table   Paradox tables have been in constant evolution since their original design and have many features.

Numerous Field Types   Paradox tables support around 15 field types, ranging from numeric fields through fixed and variable-length text fields to fields capable of storing raw binary data. This large array of field types adds flexibility to your database design options and allows you to more accurately represent the information you are storing.

Suppose that you want to store a Yes/No or True/False value. You can use a single-character text field (Y for Yes and N for No), or you can use a small integer field (zero for No and non-zero for Yes). The problem with these options is that you are free to store Z, y, or # in the field. A better choice is the Paradox Boolean field type—provided for this purpose.

For more information on the available field types, see the "field types, Paradox" topic in the DBDDESK.HLP file, located in the folder in which you installed Database Desktop.

Referential Integrity   The concept of *referential integrity* ensures that references between tables are valid. Using the stock-management application as an example, imagine a case where a customer places an order. Each customer is tagged with a unique number. This number is stored in the customer table (naturally) and in the orders table (to identify which customer placed the order). If you delete the customer record from the customer table, you would have a record in the orders table that references a non-existent customer. This situation is quite undesirable.

You could manually code what is known as a *cascading delete*—deleting all references to that customer from each table in the database, but why bother? For Paradox tables, the BDE can do it for you, saving you needless development time.

Password Security   If you are writing an application that deals with sensitive data, you probably will manually encrypt it before storing it in the database. Although this is fine for small tables, imagine the additional maintenance required for 10 tables with 20 fields in each table! How do you implement security on a field-by-field basis? Again, Paradox does the job. With a Paradox table, you can supply a master password that may perform any type of operation on the table, such as editing data in any field or restructuring the table. Auxiliary passwords provide additional flexibility, such as limited access to a subset of fields, or allowing the user to insert only records.

Simple Data Validity   Most field values are constrained by a *range*, such as a field that stores a person's age. Clearly, any value below zero is invalid, as is any value over about 130. Like referential integrity, this business rule can be manually coded, but in a system composed of more than one program, adherence to this rule can become a nightmare. Paradox tables let you move the database logic out of the program and into the database where it belongs.

You may define a minimum, maximum, and default value for each field. Minimum and maximum values constrain the contents of the field to a particular range. If you try to store a value outside the range, Delphi raises an exception and ignores the invalid value. Default values are automatically assigned to fields when you insert a new record.

Disadvantages of the Paradox Table   You may be thinking that Paradox tables are simply the bees knees of local tables. Well, life is never this easy, and there are two caveats regarding their use.

Large Number of Physical Files   A Paradox table is stored as several files, with each file using a different extension that indicates its function, as shown in Table 9.1.

Table 9.1   Paradox Table File Extensions

Extension	Function
.DB	Table data. This is the file you really want to restore when your computer crashes.
.MB	Binary Large Object (BLOB) data. Used for memo, formatted memo, graphic, binary, and OLE field types.
.PX	Primary index. This file controls the primary sort and search order for your table.
.XG?, .YG?	Secondary indexes. These files manage alternative sort and search orders for your table.
.VAL	Stores settings for validity checks and referential integrity.
.TV	Stores the manner in which a table is displayed in Database Desktop, such as column order and width.
.FAM	Used in conjunction with the .TV file.

If you want to move a table from one folder to another without using the BDE, you must move all these files, which may or may not be a problem.

N O T E   Don't panic if your table doesn't use all these files—they are created only when necessary. ■

The .NET File   The .NET file controls access to Paradox databases and has always been a bugbear in developing applications that use Paradox tables. If you want users to share a table, they all must use the same .NET file. On a small network with one file server, this usually isn't an issue—simply create a separate folder to store the .NET file and give everyone full access to it. On a larger network with multiple file servers, Paradox adds a small administrative overhead—all database users must have access to the server hosting the .NET file.

N O T E The global `Session` object (an automatically created instance of the `TSession` class) lets you specify a different .NET file location for each application. For more information, look up the `NetFileDir` property of the `TSession` class. ■

dBASE tables do not require the services of the .NET file used by Paradox.

> **CAUTION**
>
> If you try to access a database controlled by a different .NET file, Delphi generates an exception. Database-oriented exception handling is covered in the "Handling Exceptions" section.

Paradox Specifics   When creating your Paradox table, there are several settings you may want to adjust. These are modified by the BDE Administrator program, shown in Figure 9.2. BDE Administrator is named BDEADMIN.EXE and is found under the folder into which you installed the BDE.

FIG. 9.2

The BDE Administrator lets you configure the BDE.

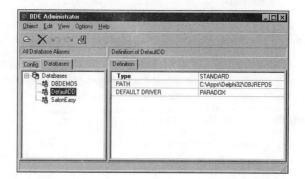

Settings of interest are

- **Block Size**—The maximum physical file size (in megabytes) for a Paradox table is calculated from the block size setting. Block size must be a multiple of 1,024 bytes. A block size may be as large as 32,768. The relationship is

  `PhysicalFileSize = BlockSize / 1024 * 64`

- **Fill Factor**—This setting determines the percentage of the current index block that must be used before the BDE allocates another block. Reducing this setting increases the performance of the table, at the expense of disk space.

- **Strict Integrity**—This option is useful when dealing with applications that don't recognize referential integrity (perhaps they use an older version of the BDE). If Strict Integrity is set to False, these applications may read from and write to the database, potentially compromising referential integrity. If set to True, these applications can only read from the table.

Advantages of the dBASE Table The dBASE table is one of the original PC table formats, and as such, is supported by virtually every application that deals with data in row-and-column format. The dBASE file format brings several additional benefits, which we cover in the following sections.

Small Number of Physical Files Compared to Paradox, the set of dBASE physical files is positively anemic. The Table 9.2 indicates the function of each physical dBASE file:

Table 9.2   dBASE Table File Extensions

Extension	Function
.DBF	The table's data
.DBT	BLOB data (memo, binary, and OLE)
.MDX	Manages the set of maintained indexes
.NDX	Stores the set of non-maintained indexes

This reduced number of files leads to easier backup administration and file maintenance.

Enhanced Index Functionality As previously mentioned, an index maintains a sort order for the table. If you want to search on a customer's name, you should place an index on the customer name field to speed the search process.

dBASE supports the following two advanced indexing options:

- **Expression Indexes**—An *expression index* lets you create an index based on the combination of several fields. Imagine a customer table with FIRSTNAME and SUR-NAME fields. An expression index of SURNAME+FIRSTNAME creates a new field, which holds the concatenation of the record's values for the two fields. This new field forms the basis of the expression index. The advantage of using an expression index is that you need to search only a single field when looking for a SURNAME and FIRSTNAME pair. The disadvantage is that the field values are combined, so locating and iterating through all records that contain a particular SURNAME is more difficult.

- **Subset Index**—A *subset index* is really just a filter. It defines a set of records that match given criteria. Using the customer table again, you could create a subset index of SURNAME=Blogs. Using this index automatically filters out all records whose SUR-NAME field does not equal Blogs. The advantage of a subset index is that your application logic is simpler when dealing with a particular subset of records in the table—to iterate through the set of Blogs records, simply apply the subset index to the table, and then loop through the records. Without a subset index, you have to check whether you are still processing records that meet your search requirements. The disadvantage is that you have to create a subset index for each filter you want to use.

Soft Deletes When you delete a record from a dBASE table, it is simply marked as deleted and is not physically removed from the table. Records marked as deleted do not match searches and are not included when iterating through records of the table.

To undelete the record, you use the BDE `DbiUndeleteRecord` API function. To physically remove all deleted records from a table, you call `DbiPackTable`. For more information on these API calls, see the BDE32.HLP file, located in the folder in which you installed the BDE.

Disadvantages of the dBASE Table   Apart from the lack of support for referential integrity, data validation, and security, dBASE tables also suffer two additional disadvantages:

- **Short Field Names**—Field names are limited to eight characters, with no spaces. If you were a DOS or Windows 3.x user, you will appreciate this limitation—it's difficult to determine the field's use simply by its name.

- **Limited Field Types**—dBASE supports only eight field types—character, float, number, date, logical, memo, OLE, and binary. This reduced set means you cannot take advantage of the automatic formatting of field values when retrieving data from the table. An example is the lack of a currency type—your application must specifically format a dBASE number field type as a currency value, while the Paradox currency type handles this automatically.

Paradox versus dBASE: Which to Use?   So which table format should you use? Apart from the advantages and disadvantages discussed previously, there are two more points:

- **Ease of Migration**—Referential integrity, validity checks, default values, and password security are all supported in Paradox and SQL databases. These common attributes simplify the move from a local Paradox database to a SQL server.

- **Performance**—Paradox has a slight performance edge when compared to dBASE. Insertion and updates of records is quicker in Paradox, as is searching on both indexed and non-indexed fields.

Generally, you should use the Paradox table type for application development, unless you find (or know) that you cannot resolve the problems associated with the .NET files.

Data Access Components

Now that you have decided on the table type, you can read this section to learn more about the components that streamline BDE usage.

TTable and *TQuery*

The `TTable` class lets you access logical tables, while the `TQuery` class allows you to generate an answer table based on a SQL query. Both logical tables and SQL query answer tables are known as *datasets*. Because of this commonality, `TTable` and `TQuery` share many properties, events, and methods.

Properties   The `TTable` and `TQuery` classes publish several properties that reflect the state of the underlying dataset.

The* Active *Property The Active property uses a Boolean value to determine whether the dataset is open or closed. If Active is True, the dataset is open and available for use. The Open and Close methods perform the same function as modifying the Active property and are easier to understand. The following code demonstrates this process with a TTable object named tblCust:

```
{ Open the customer table by setting the Active property }
tblCust.Active := True;
{ Close the customer table }
tblCust.Active := False;

{ Open the customer table with the Open method }
tblCust.Open;
{ Close the customer table }
tblCust.Close;
```

> **CAUTION**
>
> Closing a dataset doesn't automatically save the current record. Use the Post method to save changes before calling Close or setting Active to False.

BOF *and* EOF These properties indicate whether your current position in the dataset is at the beginning (BOF) or the end (EOF). BOF is True in the following situations:

- You open the table for the first time in this session.
- You call the First method.
- You called Prior when you were already at the first record.

Alternatively, EOF is True in the following circumstances:

- You open an empty table.
- You call the Last method.
- You called Next when you were already at the last record.

The most common use for EOF is to iterate through all records in a table. The following code calculates the sum of an integer field named Age, located in a TQuery dataset named qryResult:

```
var
    iSum : Integer;
begin
    { Initialize the sum }
    iSum := 0;

    { Jump to the first record }
    qryResult.First;

    { Iterate through the dataset }
    while not qryResult.Eof do
    begin
```

```
        { Increment the sum variable }
        Inc(iSum, qryResult.FieldByName('Age').AsInteger);

        { Move to the next record }
        qryResult.Next;
    end;
end;
```

The DatabaseName Property   The DatabaseName property indicates the database that this dataset is to access. It may be a BDE alias, such as DBDEMOS, or a folder path for Paradox and dBASE databases. You usually assign this value during design mode.

DBHandle and Handle   These properties let you make direct calls to the BDE API, to implement functionality not supported by the supplied Delphi components.

DBHandle returns the internal BDE identifier for the table's parent database, while Handle returns the internal identifier for the dataset. The following code assumes that a TTable object named tblCust exists and was correctly initialized. It calls the DbiPackTable API to rebuild the table, reclaiming wasted storage space, as follows:

```
Check(DbiPackTable(tblCust.DBHandle,tblCust.Handle,Nil,Nil,True));
```

Fields and FieldCount   The Fields property returns an array of TField objects that allow you to reference each field by its index value. FieldCount returns the number of TField objects in the array. The following code adds a list of field names from a TTable object named tblStock to a TListBox control named lbFieldList, as follows:

```
var
    iCount : Integer;
begin
    { Clear the items in the TListBox }
    lbFieldList.Clear;

    { Iterate through the Fields array }
    for iCount := 0 to tblStock.FieldCount -1 do
        { Add the field name for this field to the TListBox }
        lbFieldList.Items.Add(tblStock.Fields[iCount].FieldName);
end;
```

The Modified Property   The Modified property uses a Boolean value to indicate whether the current record has changed and hasn't been written to the dataset. The following code checks whether a record in a TQuery object named qryResult has been saved and asks whether you want to save it:

```
if qryResult.Modified then
    if MessageDlg('Save record?',mtConfirmation,[mbYes,mbNo],0)
            = mrYes then
        qryResult.Post;
```

The RecordCount Property   The RecordCount property returns the number of records in the dataset and is useful when you want to indicate the progress of processing a set of records. The following code iterates through all records in a TTable object named tblCust and updates a TPanel control named pnlProgress to reflect the progress in terms of percentage complete:

```
var
    iRecNo, iRecCount : Integer;
begin
    { Retrieve the number of records in the table }
    iRecCount := tblCust.RecordCount;

    { Move to the first record }
    iRecNo := 1;
    tblCust.First;

    { Iterate through the table }
    while not tblCust.EOF do
    begin
        { Update the progress panel }
        pnlProgress.Caption := IntToStr(100 * iRecNo div iRecCount)
                                  + '%';

        { Record processing goes here }

        { Move to the next record }
        tblCust.Next;
        Inc(iRecNo);
    end;
end;
```

Methods   The TTable and TQuery classes publish a huge number of methods that allow you to manipulate the dataset at runtime. The most commonly used methods are discussed in this section, with the online help providing extensive coverage of the remaining methods.

The FieldByName *Method*   The FieldByName method lets you access a field in a table by its field name, rather than its index in the Fields array. This means that your code doesn't rely on the underlying structure of the table, and is much more readable. The following code demonstrates the use of FieldByName and assumes that the CustNo field is the first field in the table (has an index of zero in the Fields array).

```
{ Place dataset into edit mode }
tblCust.Edit;

{ Set the CustNo field to 100 with FieldByName }
tblCust.FieldByName('CustNo').AsInteger := 100;

{ Set the CustNo field to 100 with Fields[0] }
tblCust.Fields[0].AsInteger := 100;
```

If you are a speed freak, expect a performance penalty when using FieldByName. However, the negligible loss in performance is far outweighed by the increases in code maintainability.

Edit, Insert, Post, *and* Cancel   These methods give you control over the insertion and editing of records and whether changes are to be discarded or kept.

The Edit method locks the current record for editing. If you try to write data to a record that isn't in edit mode, Delphi generates an exception and ignores the change. If your call to the `edit` method succeeds, and another application tries to edit this record, it will receive an error message, and its edit request will be ignored.

The `Insert` method creates a blank record in the dataset and automatically places the record in edit mode.

After you finish editing the record, you can either call the `Post` method to write the record to the dataset or the `Cancel` method to discard the changes.

The following code inserts a new record into a `TTable` named `tblCust` and then asks whether you want to save or discard it:

```
{ Insert the new record }
tblCust.Insert;

{ Check if you want to save or discard it }
if MessageDlg('Save record',mtConfirmation,[mbYes,mbNo],0) = mrYes then
    { Save the record }
    tblCust.Post
else
    { Discard the record }
    tblCust.Cancel;
```

First, Last, Prior, Next, *and* **MoveBy**   These methods let you programmatically navigate through the dataset. `First`, `Last`, `Prior`, and `Next` should be self-explanatory.

The `MoveBy` method allows you to jump several records at a time—unlike `Next` and `Prior`, which move only a single record at each call. `MoveBy` returns the number of records actually traversed, so you can check whether you hit the beginning or end of the table during the move. The following code displays a message when you try to jump past the last record of a table:

```
tblCust.Last;
if tblCust.MoveBy(5) <> 5 then
    MessageDlg('Unable to move forward five records');
```

The `Locate` **Method**   The `Locate` method finds the first record in the dataset that matches the search criteria, and takes three arguments in the following order:

1. The name of the field to search.
2. The value for which you are searching. This may be any type—integer, string, double, and so on.
3. A set of type `TLocateOptions`, which is used to customize the search. The `loCaseInsensitive` member makes the search case-insensitive (it is case-sensitive by default). `loPartialKey` means that the BDE will match John when searching for Jo and Doe when searching for Do.

N O T E   Searches that use `loPartialKey` are case-insensitive, even if you don't include the `loCaseInsensitive` member. ▪

Locate has the following advantages over FindKey (a TTable specific method):

- Locate doesn't require you to change indexes to search on a different field. FindKey requires the index you are searching on to be the current sort order for the table.

- Searching with Locate means that you can forget about creating composite indexes (made up of more than one field) for each possible search type. Rather, you can simply create single-field indexes for the fields that you want to search—the BDE is smart enough to use all available indexes when possible.

- You can use Locate on both TQuery and TTable datasets. FindKey may only be used on TTable datasets.

Events   The TTable and TQuery classes share the same set of events, which notify you of changes in the state of the dataset. This section documents the most commonly used events. For more information on dataset specific events, see the TTable and TQuery topics in the online help.

***The* BeforeXXX *Event*—**The BeforeXXX set of events is composed of BeforeCancel, BeforeClose, BeforeDelete, BeforeEdit, BeforeInsert, BeforeOpen, BeforePost, and BeforeScroll. Not surprisingly, each of these events takes place before the specific action they reference occurs.

If you attach an event handler to the BeforeDelete event, it will be triggered by a call to the Delete method but executed *before* the BDE actually deleted the record. If you raise an exception in a BeforeXXX event handler, the action doesn't take place. The following code demonstrates this process:

```
procedure TForm1.tblCustBeforeDelete(DataSet: TDataSet);
begin
    { Check if customer has placed an order }
    if tblOrders.FindKey([DataSet.FieldByName('CustNo').AsInteger]) then
        { Raise an exception to abort the delete operation }
        raise Exception.Create('Unable to delete customer.');
end;
```

This code fragment is an implementation of simple referential integrity. It checks whether a customer has an order in the orders table and, if so, disallows the deletion of the customer.

Remember that event handlers may be shared across multiple objects. Therefore, the event handler is passed the TDataSet (TTable or TQuery) that triggered the event, allowing you to easily manipulate the appropriate TDataSet.

***The* AfterXXX *Event*   **The AfterXXX set of events consists of AfterCancel, AfterClose, AfterDelete, AfterEdit, AfterInsert, AfterOpen, AfterPost, and AfterScroll. These events are similar to the BeforeXXX set, in that they notify you of a specific change in the dataset. The difference is that these events are triggered after the change occurs. A common use for these events is the display of status messages. The following code updates a TPanel control, used as a status panel, when a record was successfully posted to the table:

```
procedure TForm1.tblCustAfterPost(DataSet: TDataSet);
begin
    { Update the TPanel }
```

```
    pnlStatus.Caption := 'Record saved successfully';
end;
```

The `OnCalcFields` Event   Delphi allows you to define *calculated fields*, or fields that are not present physically in the table, but are created and assigned values at runtime. The `OnCalcFields` event gives you the opportunity to generate the values for calculated fields.

Before you can determine the value for a calculated field, you first must define it. Follow these steps to define a calculated field:

1. Right-click your `TDataSet` derivative (`TTable` or `TQuery`).
2. Select Fields Editor from the pop-up menu. The Field Editor window appears, as shown in Figure 9.3.

Part
III

Ch
9

FIG. 9.3
Use the Field Editor to define a custom set of fields for a dataset.

3. Right-click the Field Editor and select <u>N</u>ew Field. The New Field dialog box appears, as shown in Figure 9.4.

FIG. 9.4
The New Field dialog box lets you define a custom field for your dataset.

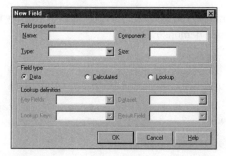

4. Fill the dialog box with the appropriate information. Don't forget to select <u>C</u>alculated from the Field Type group. Click OK, and the new field is added to your dataset.

Now, assume that you created a field named UpperName, which holds the uppercase value of a field titled Name. To specify the value for UpperName, you would write the following event handler:

```
procedure TForm1.tblCustCalcFields(DataSet: TDataSet);
begin
```

```
    { Calculate the UpperName field value }
    with DataSet do
        FieldByName('UpperName').AsString :=
            UpperCase(FieldByName('Name').AsString);
end;
```

> **N O T E** By default, OnCalcFields is triggered only when you move to a new record. If you set the
> AutoCalcFields property to True, OnCalcFields also will be generated whenever a
> field value is modified, which ensures that the calculated fields are always valid. ■

TTable **Specifics**

The TTable class provides several properties and methods that are not supported by TQuery.

Properties   This section covers the several commonly used properties which are unique to the TTable class.

The TableName *Property*   One of the most important properties for an object of class TTable is the TableName property—it specifies the underlying table for the object. If you try to Open a TTable which doesn't have its TableName property set to a valid table, the BDE generates an error. You usually set TableName at design-time by using the Object Inspector.

The Exclusive *Property*   The Exclusive property uses a Boolean value to determine whether to open the underlying table in exclusive mode. If your application has exclusive access to a table, no other application can access the table for reading or writing. This setting is useful when your application must perform some critical data processing and requires the dataset to remain in a constant state.

To open a table in exclusive mode, you must set the Exclusive property to True while the table is inactive, as the following code demonstrates:

```
with tblCust do
begin
    { Close the table }
    Close;

    { Set up exclusive mode }
    tblCust.Exclusive := True;

    { Reopen the table in exclusive mode }
    tblCust.Open;
end;
```

The IndexName *Property*   The IndexName property specifies the current sort order for the table. By default, IndexName is set to null, meaning the BDE will use the primary index to sort the table. You may switch to alternative sort orders by setting IndexName to the name of a secondary index. For example, imagine the good old customer table once again. Each customer has a unique identifier, which is used as the primary key for the table. Because you also may want to search the table by customer name, you decide to create a secondary index on the Name field, which you title NameIndex. The following code switches to the NameIndex

index, locates the record for a customer named Do, and changes it to Doe. It then switches back to the primary index, as follows:

```
with tblCust do
begin
    try

        { Change to NameIndex order }
        tblCust.IndexName := 'NameIndex';

        { Search for record Do }
        if tblCust.FindKey(['Do']) then
        begin

            { Edit the customer record }
            Edit;

            { Modify the field }
            FieldByName('Name').AsString := 'Doe';

            { Post the record to the table }
            Post;

        end;

    finally

        { Switch back to the primary index }
        tblCust.IndexName := '';

    end;
end;
```

Methods   The TTable class publishes several methods that are useful when dealing with tables. The more obscure methods are documented in the online help; the more commonly used methods are explained in this section.

The LockTable Method   The LockTable method limits the level of table access granted to other applications. You may place two types of lock on a table:

■ **Read**—The BDE doesn't allow another process to place a write lock on the table while a read lock is in place. This is useful when you want to guarantee read-and-write access to a table and want to deny access to any process that wants to exclusively write to the table. A read lock is specified by the ltReadLock constant.

■ **Write**—A write lock doesn't allow another process to place any type of lock on the table. This is not the same as exclusive mode. Exclusive mode denies access to a table, whereas a write lock simply means an application may not place a read or write lock on the table. This is useful when you want to guarantee that your application is the only one writing to the table but do not want to deny concurrent access while your processing is in progress. You specify a write lock with the ltWriteLock constant.

The following code places a write lock on the stock table, while it increases all prices by ten percent:

```
with tblStock do
begin
    { Lock the table }
    LockTable(ltWriteLock);

    try
        { Jump to the first record in the table }
        First;

        { Iterate through all records of the stock table }
        while not EOF do
        begin
            { Increase the price by 10% }
            FieldByName('Price').AsFloat :=
                FieldByName('Price').AsFloat * 1.1;

            { Move to the next record }
            Next;
        end;

    finally

        { Remove the write lock from the table }
        UnlockTable(ltWriteLock);

    end;
end;
```

The SetRange Method   The SetRange method is used to apply a filter to the table and is used when you want to deal with a subset of records in the table.

N O T E   For local tables, such as Paradox and dBASE, the field on which you are filtering must be indexed. ▪

The following example switches the index for a table to PurchaseDateIndex, and then applies a filter of 1/1/1997 to 31/12/1997:

```
with tblOrder do
begin
    { Set the current index to Purchase Date }
    IndexName := 'PurchaseDateIndex';

    try

        { Apply the date range filter }
        SetRange([EncodeDate(1997,1,1)], [EncodeDate(1997,12,31)]);

        { Perform processing on subset here }

    finally
```

```
            { Reset index to primary }
            IndexName := '';

    end;
end;
```

TQuery Specifics

The TQuery class lets you use SQL statements to access local or remote datasets and exposes several new properties and methods.

Properties   The TQuery class exposes several properties that you can use to manipulate the object at runtime.

Params *and* ParamCount   SQL statements allow you to specify *parameters* to be used when evaluating and executing the SQL statement. The Params property array holds the set of parameters for the query, with ParamCount indicating the number of elements in the array. These properties are covered in greater detail in Chapter 10, "Working with SQL Databases," under "Additional Topics."

RequestLive *and* CanModify   The RequestLive property uses a Boolean value to determine whether to return a live or read-only result set. If you set RequestLive to True and execute the query, the BDE returns a dataset that can be edited. RequestLive is False by default. The CanModify property is True if the returned dataset is live, and False if it is read-only.

N O T E   Setting RequestLive to True doesn't guarantee that you will be able to modify the returned dataset. For a SQL statement to be live, it must conform to a set of requirements—among other things, it may not use summation operators or calculated fields. ■

The* UniDirectional *Property   Another Boolean property, UniDirectional is used when you want to decrease the memory usage of your application. If you set UniDirectional to True, you may navigate only forward through your TQuery dataset, from beginning to end. By default, UniDirectional is set to False, allowing you to navigate both backward and forward.

Methods   The TQuery class provides a large number of methods that allow you to manage the object at runtime. Of particular interest is the ExecSQL method. ExecSQL is used in place of Open when your SQL statement will not return a result set. An example is the DELETE statement, which simply deletes records matching the criteria specified in the WHERE clause. The following example uses ExecSQL to run a query that deletes all records from a table named TempStorage:

```
with qryEmpty do
begin
    { Remove current SQL }
    SQL.Clear;

    { Add our statement }
    SQL.Add('delete * from TempStorage');

    { Execute the statement }
    ExecSQL;
end;
```

Using Data Modules

If you have an application with several forms, you probably find yourself using multiple instances of each table, such as a customer TTable on the customer-maintenance screen, and another on the orders screen to verify customer details. Not only is this procedure time-consuming to implement, it also introduces some maintenance headaches—how do you apply the same business rules across the entire application? You have to call some kind of global routine from each of the event handlers that require common functionality. This solution clearly is not optimal and is precisely the point at which you should investigate a *data module*.

A data module gathers together non-visual components and holds them in one container object. This process allows you to create one instance of the customer table, locate it in the data module, and use it from anywhere within the application.

Creating a Data Module   To create a data module, click File, New Data Module. You then can drop any type of non-visual component on the data module, set its properties, and use it throughout the application. Figure 9.5 shows a data module that holds a TTimer and TOpenDialog object.

FIG. 9.5

Use a data module to group and share your non-visual components.

> **N O T E**   After you finish building your data module, you can add it to the Object Repository for use by another application. Just right-click the data module and select Add to Repository. For more information on the Object Repository, see Chapter 2, "Working with Delphi's IDE." ■

Using a Data Module   Using a data module is just like using a form. Imagine a data module named dmApp, which contains a TTable object named tblCust. This data module is saved in a unit named DM_App. To use dmApp, you need to include the DM_App unit in the uses clause of your unit. The following code displays the record count of the tblCust table stored in dmApp:

```
implementation

uses DM_App;

procedure DisplayRecordCount;
begin
    with dmApp.tblCust do
        ShowMessage(Format('Record count = %d',[RecordCount]));
end;
```

Data Module Events A data module is an instance of the TDataModule class and, as such, is free to provide properties, methods, and events. Because the properties and events aren't particularly interesting, let's concentrate on the two events provided by TDataModule—OnCreate and OnDestroy.

The OnCreate event is triggered when the data module is created. You use this event to initialize the components in the data module, such as logging on to a remote database or setting the Filter property of a TOpenDialog based on user preferences retrieved at application startup. The OnDestroy event is used to clean up resources allocated in OnCreate.

Data-Aware Controls

Chapters 6 and 7, "Using Delphi Components," and, "Using Win32 Common Controls," covered controls—components found in the Visual Component Library that provide commonly used functionality without any real effort on your part. You could use these controls to design a database application and write code to transfer data between the data access components, such as TTable and TQuery, and your interface components (such as TEdit and TStringGrid). This would be exceptionally tedious, and you would probably want to downgrade to Visual Basic just to get rid of some coding. The good news is that Delphi comes with another set of controls that are known as *data aware*. This term means that the control is capable of automatically reading data from the dataset and displaying it on-screen and is intelligent enough to update the data when modifications are made. Data-aware controls are located on the Data Controls page of the component palette.

With data-aware controls, it's possible to create a simple data-entry program without a single scrap of code.

TDataSource

To implement isolation between the dataset interface and the data-aware control interface, Delphi introduces an object known as a *data source*. The data source acts as a pipe of data between the dataset and data-aware control and provides several interesting properties and events.

Properties The TDataSource class exposes the following properties, which you use to manage instances of TDataSource:

- AutoEdit—This property uses a Boolean value to determine whether the dataset is automatically placed into edit mode when you edit a data-aware control bound to this data source. If AutoEdit is True, and you modify the data in the control, it automatically calls the Edit method of the underlying dataset object.

- DataSet—This property indicates the dataset to which this data source component is bound. DataSet may point to a TQuery or TTable.

- State—This property returns the current state of the dataset. For more information on the State property, see the State, TDataSource topic in the online help.

Events   The TDataSource class publishes the following events, which notify you of changes to the data source:

- OnDataChange—This event occurs when one or more fields in the table change as a result of a single-field edit or moving to a new record. The event handler is passed the field that was modified. If the application has moved to a new record, the field argument is Nil, because all fields have changed simultaneously. The OnDataChange event is useful when you want to update non-data–aware controls.

- OnStateChange—This event is triggered when the State property of the data source is changed. This may be from dsBrowse while browsing to dsInactive when the dataset is closed. For more information on OnStateChange and State, see the OnStateChange, TDataSource topic in the online help.

- OnUpdateData—This event is a companion to OnDataChange. OnDataChange notifies your application of when it needs to read updated information from the dataset, while OnUpdateData gives you an opportunity to write data from non-data–aware controls to the dataset.

Overview of Data-Aware Controls

Treating the topic of data-aware controls adequately would require an entire chapter. Only the following two properties need to be set to get you up and running:

- DataSource—This property indicates the TDataSource component to which this data-aware control is connected.

- DataField—This property determines the underlying field of the data-aware control.

Because you are now aware of the two most critical properties, you are free to investigate the usage specifics of these controls at your leisure. To assist you with this task, Table 9.3 gives you a brief introduction to each control.

Table 9.3   Data-Aware Controls

Control	Description
TDBChart	Lets you present information from your database graphically, with very little coding on your part.
TDBGrid	Displays a TTable or TQuery dataset. Also allows insertion, editing, and deletion of records.
TDBNavigator	Lets the user navigate through the dataset and insert, edit, and delete records and post or cancel changes. It usually is used in conjunction with a TDBGrid or a set of data-aware controls, such as TDBEdit and TDBText.
TDBText	Similar to a TLabel control, TDBText displays read-only text.
TDBEdit	Comparable to the TEdit control, TDBEdit allows you to edit single line text. Its use is not restricted to text fields—the control is

Control	Description
	smart enough to validate entry for other field types such as numeric and date.
TDBMemo	An extended version of TDBEdit, TDBMemo lets you edit multiple lines of text and is usually used with the Memo field type.
TDBImage	Displays an image from a BLOB or Graphic field type. You may place a new image into the field by pasting it from the clipboard.
TDBListBox	Provides a scrollable list of values. Selecting a value updates the underlying field value.
TDBComboBox	Similar to TDBListBox, TDBComboBox lets the user select a single value from a drop-down listbox.
TDBCheckBox	Like the TCheckBox control, TDBCheckBox lets you toggle something on or off. Although this control typically is used to store Yes/No or True/False values, you are free to customize the values that represent the checked and unchecked states.
TDBRadioGroup	Use this control when you have more than two possible values for a field.
TDBLookupListBox	This control is an enhanced version of the TDBListBox. In a TDBLookupListBox, the list items are taken from another dataset, rather than specified explicitly in a TStrings property array like TDBListBox.
TDBLookupComboBox	This control is simply a TDBLookupListBox with the form and functionality of a combo-box control.
TDBRichEdit	This control is simply a data-aware version of the TRichEdit control. No more, no less.

Part
III

Ch
9

Advanced Database Programming Techniques

Now that you have a handle on the basics of database programming, let's get down to the good stuff.

Cached Updates

Cached updates are useful when you are simultaneously writing a large batch of records. Rather than posting each record to the table individually, the BDE caches the record writes, and then upon request, performs them in one operation. This dramatically increases the speed of batch operations.

Cached updates are managed with the CachedUpdates property, and the ApplyUpdates method. If you set CachedUpdates to True, the BDE starts caching records. Calling ApplyUpdates writes the cached records to the table in a single operation.

> **CAUTION**
>
> Setting CachedUpdates to False while you have unwritten records will discard them.

The following code uses a cached update to write 50 records to the customer table:

```
var
    iCount : Integer;
begin
    with tblCust do
    begin

        { Turn on cached updates }
        CachedUpdates := True;

        { Write 50 records to the table }
        for iCount := 1 to 50 do
            InsertRecord([iCount]);

        { Write the cached records to the table }
        ApplyUpdates;

    end;
end;
```

Database Exceptions

Exception handling was covered in Chapter 5, "Exception Handling." Delphi also defines the following two exception classes, particular to database programming:

- EDatabaseError—This exception occurs when a component from the VCL detects a database error. It contains a simple text message that indicates the problem and is just like any other exception, such as EDivByZero or EAccessViolation.

- EDBEngineError—This exception is generated when an error occurs in the BDE. Because the exception may stem from several errors, the EDBEngineError class defines two additional properties—ErrorCount and Errors. The following code adds the list of messages from a EDBEngineError object to a TListBox control for display:

```
var
    iCount : Integer;
begin

    try

        { Something }

    except

        { Check what type of exception was generated }
        on E:EDBEngineError do

            { Iterate through the Errors array }
```

```
      for iCount := 0 to E.ErrorCount-1 do

          { Add the error text to the list box }
          lbMsgs.Items.Add(E.Errors[iCount].Message);

    end;
end;
```

Transactions

Transaction processing is used when database integrity is critical. A typical example is the updating of a general ledger (GL) system. You usually need to write to a minimum of two tables—the ledger account table and the transaction table. The ledger account table stores the current balance for each GL account in the system and will have a minimum of two record updates processed against it—one for each account affected by the GL transaction. The transaction table lists every transaction passing through the GL system and will have at least two new records created—one for each part of the GL transaction.

The concept of a database transaction is similar to a GL transaction. A database transaction is simply a group of operations across several datasets. Each of these operations must succeed before the entire database transaction is considered successful. If an operation fails, a database transaction allows your program to back out all previous operations and leave the database in its original state.

Without database transactions, failure and error correction in the GL system is a complete nightmare. If you need to back out the transaction manually, you will have to delete the new transaction records from the transaction table, restore the next transaction number counter, and restore the original account balances in the ledger account table.

The logic behind this quickly becomes complex, especially when you consider that other users may have been creating transactions at the same time. Thankfully, the BDE can perform this horrible work for you, with just three methods of the TDatabase class—StartTransaction, Commit, and Rollback.

The StartTransaction method initiates the recording of a transaction. All operations such as deletes, inserts, and edits are recorded. After you finish your processing, you call Commit to write all modifications to the database. If you detect an error, call Rollback to back out all modifications to the database. The following code implements a single account update for the GL update example previously discussed. It uses a TDatabase object named dbGL.

```
dblTranVal := 100;

{ Start the transaction }
dbGL.StartTransaction;

try

    { Locate the bank GL account }
    if not tblGLAcc.FindKey(['100.100']) then
        raise Exception.Create('Unable to locate bank account');
```

```
{ Modify the balance }
tblGLAcc.Edit;
tblGLAcc.FieldByName('Balance').AsFloat :=
    tblGLAcc.FieldByName('Balance').AsFloat - dblTranVal;
tblGLAcc.Post;

{ Commit the changes }
dbGL.Commit;

except

{ Rollback modifications }
dbGL.Rollback;

{ Reraise the exception }
raise;

end;
```

Note the use of the exception handler to trap any exceptions and rollback the transaction.

TSession and Threaded Database Operations

The advent of Win32 means that you can now write true multithreaded applications with ease. A multithreaded application appears to several things simultaneously, such as spell checking a document while printing another. Chapter 24, "Working with Threads," covers programming threads in detail, but we need to discuss the impact that using threads has on database operations.

Like any other component, data-access components are not safe to share across multiple threads. If you try to use a single TTable object with multiple threads, you may generate Access Violations, corrupt your table, read or write invalid data, and do a great many other undesirable things to your database.

Thankfully, the Delphi VCL provides several classes that make threaded database operations quite painless.

Sessions, TSession, and TSessionList   The BDE already supports multiple applications simultaneously—you may run the Database Desktop at the same time as Delphi. This functionality is supported by the concept of a *session*—simply a unique connection to a database, used by an application or thread.

The TSession class encapsulates the functionality of a session, with an instance named Session automatically created at runtime and destroyed at program termination. The Session object provides a default session for use by the main thread of your application. TSession provides many properties and methods, but the SessionName property is of primary concern—it must contain a string which uniquely identifies this database session.

The TSessionList class encapsulates the list of currently active BDE sessions. You will never need to create an instance of the TSessionList class—Delphi creates the Sessions variable at runtime and frees it at termination.

Creating a New Session The creation of a new session is handled by the OpenSession method of the TSessionList class. OpenSession takes the unique identifier (SessionName) of a session as a parameter and searches the global Sessions variable for a matching TSession object. If it cannot find a match, OpenSession creates and returns a new instance of TSession. The following code creates a session with a TestSession name, and then closes it:

```
var
    ssnTemp : TSession;
begin

    { Open the session }
    ssnTemp := Sessions.OpenSession('TestSession');

    { Close the session }
    ssnTemp.Free;

end;
```

Using a New Session After you have created the new session, you need to create your data-access components and connect them to the session. The data-access components, TTable, TQuery, and TStoredProc, all possess the SessionName property, which is obviously set to the SessionName property of the TSession instance returned by the OpenSession method.

That's it. All the knowledge you need to create a multithreaded database application. To give you a workable example, the code in Listing 9.1 is taken from the UTESTTHREAD.PAS example on this book's companion CD-ROM:

On the CD

Listing 9.1   \UDELPHI3\CHP9\UTESTTHREAD.PAS—Example of a Database-Oriented Thread

```
procedure TTestThread.Execute;
var
   ssnLocal : TSession;
   tblTest : TTable;
begin

   { Set ourselves to the lowest priority }
   Priority := tpLowest;

   try
       { Create a unique session object }
       ssnLocal := Sessions.OpenSession(ExtractFileName(Application.EXEName)
                   +IntToStr(GetTickCount));

       { Create the local table object }
       tblTest := TTable.Create(Nil);
       with tblTest do
       begin
           { Connect this table to the new session }
           SessionName    := ssnLocal.SessionName;

           { Initialize the database and table name properties }
           DatabaseName   := 'DBDEMOS';
```

continues

Listing 9.1   Continued

```
        TableName       := 'Items';

        { Open the table }
        Open;
    end;

    { Loop while the thread has not been terminated }
    while not Terminated do
        { Insert your threaded database code here }
        ;

finally
    { Close the table }
    tblTest.Free;

    { Close the session }
    ssnLocal.Free;
end;

end;
```

Putting It All Together

This chapter contained quite a bit of theory. Let's quickly recap to fit together all these jigsaw pieces, without forcing them into place and wrecking the puzzle! We began by introducing the concepts of a database, table, record, and field. Hopefully, you remember that a database is a collection of tables and that a table is simply a grid, in which the columns are fields and the rows are records.

With the basics down pat, you learned about the types of local databases natively supported by the BDE—Paradox and dBASE. We covered the advantages, disadvantages, and specifics of each format, and decided on Paradox for pretty much all situations.

The data access components provided by the VCL were next in line. You learned about the properties, methods, and events common to both TTable and TQuery and then about the properties and methods specific to the TTable class and those specific to TQuery.

This chapter then moved on to cover centralization of data access components with the TDataModule class, with you learning how to create and use a data module.

The next segment covered the set of data-aware controls supplied with the VCL. Rather than connecting directly to a dataset, these controls use a TDataSource component as a conduit for data. We documented the most interesting properties and events of the TDataSource class and then presented a simple table that introduced each data-aware control, and gave you some direction in selecting the correct control for the task at hand.

To complete the chapter, we walked you to the edge of the pool and threw you in the deep end by jumping into some advanced database-programming techniques. We covered cached updates, database-specific exceptions, transactions, and multithreaded database operations. ●

CHAPTER 10

Working with SQL Databases

by Mark Pritchard and Bill Curtis

Although Delphi's data access components (TTable and TQuery) allow you to treat a remote SQL database in exactly the same way as a local database, there are additional issues that affect the performance and feature set of your application.

SQL databases add a host of new features, such as triggers, stored procedures, implicit transaction processing, and a stack of headaches. Like Chapter 9, we could easily spend the entire book discussing the different implementations of SQL databases and Delphi's SQL database support, but I think my fellow authors would have a serious problem with that! It also would be a complete waste of your time—you most likely will choose one SQL server platform and stick with it. Why do you want to read about the functionality of XYZ SQL server when you are using Acme SQL Server, which by strange coincidence just happened to be written by the boss' nephew? ■

So what is a SQL database?

This section introduces you to the concept of a SQL database and its advantages and disadvantages.

BDE support for SQL databases

In this section, you learn how the BDE supports SQL databases—its limitations and its features.

Delphi's specific SQL functionality

This segment covers the SQL-specific functionality of the TTable and TQuery component and introduces you to several of the SQL-only components such as TStoredProc and TUpdateSQL.

SQL server type specifics

This section discusses the most important BDE settings for each SQL database type.

What Are SQL Databases?

The most important question to ask yourself now is do you actually care about Delphi's support for SQL databases? If you don't, jump straight to Chapter 12, "Using Quick Reports," for the lowdown on components in the Visual Component Library that allow you to easily use reams of paper to print reports from a database, pleasing the accountants among you immensely.

If you are still reading at this point, let's get down to business and define just what the term *SQL database* means. SQL generally is considered an acronym for Structured Query Language—a set of statements and syntax that is divided into two subsets:

- **Data Definition Language**—*Data Definition Language* (*DDL*) is a superlative example of computer jargon because it's merely the set of SQL statements that you use to define and maintain the structure of your database. DDL covers the creation, modification, and deletion of databases, tables, and fields—use it to maintain *how* your data is stored.

- **Data Manipulation Language**—The *Data Manipulation Language* (*DML*) subset of SQL handles the actual data in the database. You use it to add, modify, and remove data in the database's set of tables.

N O T E   If you are interested in the origins of SQL, find a database guru who is not wearing a suit, buy him or her a beer and pizza, and then listen to them wax lyrical for hours. ▪

With the SQL language defined, we can now make the staggeringly obvious deduction that a SQL database is a database with which you interact via the SQL language. Let's carry this a little further. Because the database and its data are defined by a language interpreted at run-time, the SQL server must possess the intelligence to work out what the SQL statement you executed actually does, and then go away and do it. This extra intelligence leads to several benefits:

- **Local File Implementation Ignorance**—You do not need to know anything about the server's database file format. For all you care, the server may store its data in one huge spreadsheet.

- **Data Transmission Efficiency**—The set of physical data transferred between your application and the server is extremely efficient—you send a SQL statement request to the server, it's processed, and the server returns only the data in which you are interested. This is useful for Wide Area Network (WAN) environments, where the client application may be connected via a slow dial-up link.

- **Speed, Speed, and More Speed**—You often will find that the response time of a SQL server is quicker than a local database hosted on a file server. The reason is simple and can be explained with an example. Imagine that you want to update the mileage of a car on your company's fleet. If you were using a local database, the file server would transmit the index file of the vehicle table to your workstation, which then would be processed, to locate the record that contains the car in which you are interested. Your application will then transmit a request to lock the portion of the table that holds the car record, send the new data, and then send a notification to unlock the record. With a SQL database, you merely send a single SQL statement of around 100 bytes, and the remainder of the process is internal to the server.

A Taste of SQL

You may be wondering what this mysterious SQL language looks like. This section provides an example that uses the sample InterBase database included in your Delphi installation. For the moment, leave the Delphi IDE alone—we will use the Database Desktop, which lets you execute queries, restructure tables, and do all kinds of database-oriented functions.

Opening a SQL Table   Follow these steps to load Database Desktop and open a table in the sample InterBase database:

1. Double-click the Database Desktop icon in your Borland Delphi 3.0 folder. The Database Desktop is displayed, as shown in Figure 10.1.

FIG. 10.1
Use the Database Desktop to play with your data outside of Delphi.

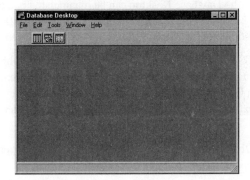

2. Click File, Open, Table. The Open Table dialog box shown in Figure 10.2 is displayed.

 TIP   To open a table, you also can click the Open Table SpeedButton, located to the left of the SpeedBar.

FIG. 10.2
The Open Table dialog box lets you specify which table to open.

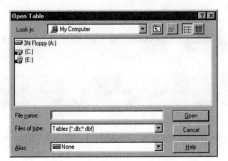

3. Select IBLOCAL: from the <u>A</u>lias drop-down list. The Database Information dialog box, shown in Figure 10.3, is displayed.

FIG. 10.3

The Database Information dialog box lets you log into a SQL server database.

4. Enter your user name and password. If you want to log in as SYSDBA, the password is **masterkey**.
5. Select the employee table, and click <u>O</u>pen. The employee table is displayed.

A SQL table displayed in the Database Desktop can be manipulated in exactly the same way as a local table—it may be browsed, edited, and restructured. The only difference that you may notice is the mouse cursor changing to a SQL hourglass as the BDE sends or fetches data.

SQL via a QBE Query   Now that you are familiar with the employee table, let's build a SQL query. The easiest way to do this is to have Database Desktop generate the SQL language, from a Query By Example (QBE) query. Follow these steps to create a QBE query on the employee table which extracts the first and last names of all employees who have a job grade of 3:

1. Click <u>F</u>ile, <u>N</u>ew, QBE Query. The Select File dialog box is displayed, which looks remarkably like the Open Table dialog box shown in Figure 10.2.

You also can right-click the Query SpeedButton and select <u>N</u>ew from the pop-up menu.

2. Select IBLOCAL: from the Alias list.
3. Select the employee table from the list and click <u>O</u>pen. A new QBE form is displayed, as shown in Figure 10.4.

FIG. 10.4

QBE lets you easily execute simple queries against your database.

4. Click the small white rectangles under the FIRST_NAME and LAST_NAME fields. The QBE window displays tick marks to indicate that these fields will be included in the result table.

5. Click in the JOB_GRADE field. Enter **3**.

6. Click Query, Run Query to execute the QBE query. The Database Desktop displays a table that contains the 14 records matching your query, as shown in Figure 10.5.

FIG. 10.5
Query results are
returned in the form of
another table.

The preceding example was trivial, but it shows how easily QBE queries are constructed.

SQL from QBE   After you prepare your QBE query, you can convert it to a SQL statement with a couple of mouse clicks. Select the window that contains your QBE query, and click Query, Show SQL. The SQL Editor window, shown in Figure 10.6, is displayed.

FIG. 10.6
You can easily generate
SQL from a QBE query.

As you can see, SQL is quite straightforward but still imposes a learning curve. Unfortunately, there are as many flavors of SQL as there are SQL servers. This book couldn't possibly cover all the variations of the language, so you are on your own when learning the SQL language. There are plenty of books on SQL, and your SQL server should come with copious volumes on its implementation of the language. Delphi also ships with a help file titled *Local SQL Help*, which documents the basics of the SQL language.

TTable, TQuery, and SQL Databases

These basic data access components are able to access SQL tables in the same manner as local tables, but warrant further discussion on their SQL-specific functionality.

When to Use *TTable* and *TQuery*

TTable and TQuery interact with the SQL server in a different manner, and each should be used in certain circumstances.

You should use a TTable when you:

- Want to use live data (allow editing) in a non-intensive manner, such as data entry
- Don't want to mess with SQL, database connections, and parameters and are not concerned by the slight performance penalty

Alternatively, the TQuery component should be used when you:

- Perform bulk updates, deletes, simple live queries, and complex non-live queries
- Execute a Data Definition Language (DDL) statement to modify the structure of a table

Additional SQL Functionality

Both TTable and TQuery support the SQL-specific property of UpdateMode. UpdateMode establishes how the BDE identifies the record being updated in a multiuser environment. This is a concern when another user may update the record you are changing before you can commit your modifications. UpdateMode may take one of three values:

- upWhereAll—The upWhereAll value is the strictest option and offers the greatest protection. Before applying your update to the table, the BDE compares all fields in the table record with the record held in your computer's record buffer. If the fields differ, another user has modified the record in the time it took your application to read the record and attempt to apply its modifications. In this case, the BDE will not allow your application to write the modified record to the table.
- upWhereKeyOnly—This value is the least restrictive and least secure. It causes the BDE to check whether only key fields have changed. If they have remained constant, the modification is allowed to proceed.
- upWhereChanged—Fitting somewhere between upWhereAll and upWhereKeyOnly, upWhereChanged makes the BDE check only those fields that you have when determining whether the modification should proceed. If another user has changed a field you are attempting to modify, your update will fail.

Increasing the Speed of *TTable* and *TQuery*

The size of the result table from your SQL statement is the most basic factor that determines the speed of your SQL statements. It is determined by multiplying the number of fields you request by the number of rows that match your query. Both items are subject to optimization, although the method differs, depending on whether you use a TTable or a TQuery.

Reducing the Number of Fields   Reducing the number of fields in your result table often boosts performance by the greatest margin, especially when dealing with a TTable component.

***Field Reduction with* TTable**   By default, a TTable returns all fields in a table. Use the Field Editor to include only fields in which you are interested. To display the Field Editor, double-click the TTable component in the Form Designer. To add fields to the Field Editor, right-click anywhere on the Field Editor and select Add Fields from the pop-up menu. This pop-up menu also gives you access to a multitude of functions, each of which is, sadly, beyond the scope of this chapter.

***Field Reduction with* TQuery**   Reducing the number of fields returned by a TQuery is easy and occurs by default—because you had to type the SQL language to select the fields, you probably have included only the fields that you require. One point: Avoid the use of SELECT *. It's easy to type, but quite inefficient because it is unlikely you will ever require all fields to be returned.

Reducing the Number of Records   Reducing the number of records in the result table is often more difficult than reducing the field count.

***Record Reduction with* TTable**   A TTable returns all records in a table by default. To restrict the set of records, apply a filter with the Filter, Filtered, and FilterOptions properties, the OnFilter event, or the SetRange method. The online help covers these items adequately, and an example of SetRange is provided in Chapter 9, "Working with Local Databases" under the "TTable Specifics" section.

***Record Reduction with* TQuery**   A TQuery is easier to restrict—simply make your selection criteria more stringent. The tighter you can make your result set, the less data your server needs to send over the network, and the more responsive it is for other users.

Data Access Components

Delphi provides several components which implement the additional functionality provided by SQL databases.

TDatabase

The TDatabase component gives you additional control over your connection to the SQL database through the provision of various properties, methods, and events.

TDatabase Properties   The TDatabase component provides several useful properties that let you customize its behavior.

AliasName *and* DatabaseName   These properties identify the database to which the TDatabase component is connected. Use AliasName to specify an existing BDE database alias, and DatabaseName to specify a temporary, application-specific alias. The following code sets up a connection to the IBLOCAL database and creates an application-specific alias named employee. It uses a TDatabase component named dbTest:

```
with dbTest do
begin
    { Ensure the database is closed }
    Close;
```

```
    { Set the new alias and database name }
    AliasName := 'IBLOCAL';
    DatabaseName := 'EMPLOYEE';

    { Open the database }
    Open;
end;
```

KeepConnection   The KeepConnection property uses a Boolean value to determine whether to keep the connection to the server open even when no tables are currently open. If you set KeepConnection to True, the BDE will not force you to enter your user name and password each time it reopens the database.

LoginPrompt *and* Params   The LoginPrompt property specifies whether the BDE will request a user name/password pair each time a connection to the database is established. Setting LoginPrompt to True displays the Database Information dialog box shown in Figure 10.3. If you set LoginPrompt to False, the BDE looks for the user name/password pair in the Params property of the TDatabase component. The following code illustrates this:

```
with dbTest do
begin
    { Add username/password pair to the Params property }
    Params.Add('username=sysdba');
    Params.Add('password=masterkey');

    { Turn off the login prompt }
    LoginPrompt := False;

    { Open the database }
    Open;
end;
```

TransIsolation   The TransIsolation property determines the degree of isolation between transactions executed against the database. It may take one of three values:

- tiDirtyRead—Setting TransIsolation to tiDirtyRead causes the BDE to return the current value of a record, even if the changes have not been committed to disk. While this setting reflects the current state of the database for your application most accurately, it is also the most unreliable—the data you read may change if you call the Rollback method during a transaction.

- tiReadCommitted—This value causes the BDE to return only those changes that have been committed.

- tiRepeatableRead—This value forces the BDE to return the original value for the record throughout the entire transaction.

The following table shows the different points in an explicit transaction where the value for TransIsolation causes the BDE to return the changes to the records:

Transaction Point	Changed Data Accessible
Begin Transaction	-
Modify Record	`tiDirtyRead`
Commit Record	`tiReadCommitted`
End Transaction	`tiRepeatableRead`

TDatabase Methods   The `TDatabase` component publishes the following methods which let you interact with the database:

- Open and Close—The `Open` and `Close` methods respectively connect to and disconnect from the database. The `Connected` property is `True` when the connection is open, and `False` when it is not.

- CloseDatasets—The `CloseDatasets` method closes all datasets in your application which are currently using the database. This is useful when you are preparing to execute a function which requires exclusive access to the database.

- StartTransaction, Commit, and Rollback—These methods are used to provide explicit transaction control, and are covered in more detail in Chapter 9, "Working with Local Databases," under the "Transactions" section.

TDatabase Events   The `TDatabase` component exposes a single event—`OnLogin`. The `OnLogin` event occurs before a database connection is established, and gives you a chance to update the `Params` property. For an example of `Params` usage, see the previous section, "`LoginPrompt` and `Params`."

Database Editor   The Database Editor, shown in Figure 10.7, lets you configure the `TDatabase` component by completing a nice, intuitive dialog, and is activated by double-clicking the component in the form designer.

FIG. 10.7
Use the Database
Editor to quickly set
up your `TDatabase`
component.

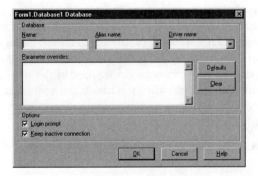

TStoredProc

The `TStoredProc` component is used to execute procedures stored on the SQL server. Stored procedures may return an editable set of data, update a field, modify a table's structure—basically anything you can do with SQL. Storing and executing procedures on the server gives you the following benefits:

- **Centralized Database Logic**—By creating stored procedures, you define the database logic or business rules for your data in the most appropriate place—the database. This means that all applications that require the functionality of the stored procedure may access it from a common place.

- **Security**—Using stored procedures gives you the ability to protect access to sensitive data via your SQL server's security functions.

- **Speed**—Executing a data manipulation routine on the server is simply the quickest place to do it—you have minimal network and interface overheads.

Properties   The `TStoredProc` component provides several properties that let you configure the object and manipulate its state.

DatabaseName *and* **StoredProcName**   These properties identify the stored procedure located on the server. The following code configures a `TStoredProc` component named `spDaily` to run a stored procedure named `DailyProcessing` on a database named `Finance`:

```
with spDaily do
begin
    { Set the database name }
    DatabaseName := 'Finance';

    { Set the name of the stored procedure }
    StoredProcName := 'DailyProcessing';
end;
```

Params, ParamCount, ParamByName, *and* **ParamBindMode**   These properties are used to pass parameters between your Delphi application and the stored procedure. `Params`, `ParamCount`, and `ParamByName` are similar to those published by the `TQuery` component, and are documented in Chapter 9, "Working with Local Databases," under the section titled "`TQuery` Specifics."

The `ParamBindMode` property determines how your parameters are connected to those expected by the stored procedure. If you set `ParamBindMode` to `pbByName`, the BDE uses the parameter names supplied in the `TStoredProc` when matching those defined in the stored procedure. This is useful when you specify parameters in an alternative order to the order anticipated by the stored procedure. If you set `ParamBindMode` to `pbByNumber`, the BDE uses the index number of the parameters to connect items supplied by the `TStoredProc` to those defined by the stored procedure. This is useful when you have taken a parameter list from another source that has defined different names for the same set of parameters (such as via the `CopyParams` method).

TStoredProc Methods   The `TStoredProc` component publishes several methods that you use to manipulate the object at runtime.

Prepare, ExecProc, Open, *and* **Close**   These methods control the basic state of the stored procedure. The `Prepare` method readies the stored procedure for execution by either `ExecProc` or `Open`. Use `ExecProc` when the procedure will return a single record result set, and `Open` when it will return a multi-record result set. The `Close` method simply closes the `TStoredProc` and sets its `State` property to `dsInactive`. The following code executes a stored procedure named `DailyProcessing` against a database named `Finance`:

```
with spDaily do
begin
    { Set database and stored procedure names }
    DatabaseName := 'Finance';
    StoredProcName := 'DailyProcessing';

    { Prepare the stored procedure for execution }
    Prepare;

    { Execute the stored procedure }
    ExecProc;
end;
```

Events   The TStoredProc component publishes the same set of events as TTable and TQuery. See the section, "TTable and TQuery," in Chapter 9, "Working with Local Databases."

TUpdateSQL

You use the TUpdateSQL component to apply cached updates to a SQL dataset. A typical use is to allow modification of a read-only dataset which doesn't conform to live query constraints. TUpdateSQL also may be used to provide additional security when applying updates to a table accessed via a TTable component.

The UpdateObject property of a TTable or TQuery component connects it to the TUpdateSQL component that modifies the underlying dataset. TUpdateSQL implements this functionality through the provision of several properties and methods.

Properties   The properties of interest are DeleteSQL, InsertSQL, and ModifySQL, which hold the SQL statements to apply deletions, insertions, and modifications to the dataset, respectively.

The SQL property adds a three-item enumerated index to separate the three SQL statements. The enumeration values are ukDelete, ukInsert, and ukModify, which correspond to the DeleteSQL, InsertSQL, and ModifySQL properties, respectively. For example, both of the following code examples assign the same TStrings list to a TListBox named lbSQL:

```
{ Assign the SQL statement used for deletion to the TListBox }
lbSQL.Clear;
lbSQL.Items.Assign(usCust.DeleteSQL);
```

and

```
{ Perform the same assignment with the SQL property }
lbSQL.Clear;
lbSQL.Items.Assign(usCust.SQL[ukDelete]);
```

The preceding code uses a TUpdateSQL component named usCust.

Methods   TUpdateSQL publishes three methods of interest:

- SetParams—This method replaces the parameters specified in the SQL statement with those to be used in the update.

- `ExecSQL`—This method executes the SQL statement that updates the dataset.
- `Apply`—This method first calls `SetParams` to set up the SQL statement, and then executes it by calling `ExecSQL`.

Additional Topics

This section presents some supplemental material and some tips on increasing the performance of your SQL server.

Transactions on SQL databases

Chapter 9, "Working with Local Databases," introduced the concept of a transaction—a method of guaranteeing database integrity in the event of failure. This concept expressed an explicit transaction by using the `StartTransaction`, `Commit`, and `Rollback` methods of the `TDatabase` component.

SQL servers introduce the implicit transaction—every SQL statement you execute is surrounded by protection that restores the database in the event of a failure. This requires no coding on your behalf, although explicit transaction control is generally more flexible.

Using Parameters with SQL

A SQL statement allows you to define parameters—special placeholders in the statement whose value will not be known until runtime.

Imagine a program that retrieves the order numbers for all orders placed after a date entered by the user. Without parameters, you would have to create the SQL statements at runtime, with code that looked something like this:

```
procedure SearchForOrders(dtSearch : TDateTime);
var
    sDate : String;
begin

    { SQL requires dates in mm/dd/yyyy order }
    sDate := FormatDateTime('mm/dd/yyyy',dtSearch);

    with qrySearch do
    begin
        { Clear the current SQL statement }
        SQL.Clear;

        { Add the new SQL statement }
        SQL.Add('select OrderNum from STOCK');
        SQL.Add(Format('where OrderDate'' > %s''',[sDate]));

        { Execute the query }
        Open;
    end;
end;
```

Not only is this code unnecessary, it's also quite hard to maintain across the scope of your application. Using parameters, you may construct your SQL statement at design time, and then supply the date value as a parameter at runtime. To define a parameter, you simply prefix the parameter name with a colon, as the following SQL statement shows:

```
select OrderNum from STOCK where OrderDate > :P_OrderDate
```

N O T E As a matter of convention only, you may choose to prefix your parameter identifiers with a sequence of characters, such as P_. This ensures that your parameter names do not clash with field names, and provides your code with additional internal documentation. ■

After you have entered your SQL statement into the SQL property of the TQuery object, Delphi populates the Params property array with the names of your parameters, and sets ParamCount to the number of items in the array. However, before you may assign a value to a parameter, you should nominate its type. To do this, edit the Params property of the TQuery object in the Object Inspector. This displays the Parameters dialog box, shown in Figure 10.8.

FIG. 10.8
Use the Parameters
dialog box to set
parameter types at
design time.

Now that you have named your parameters, and indicated their type, you are free to give them values at runtime. The following code uses parameters to implement the previous order search example:

```
procedure SearchForOrders(dtSearch : TDateTime);
begin
    with qrySearch do
    begin
        { Assign the parameter value }
        ParamByName('P_OrderDate').AsDateTime := dtSearch;

        { Execute the query }
        Open;
    end;
end;
```

The preceding code assumes that you have defined a parameter named P_OrderDate in your SQL statement and assigned it the DateTime parameter type. You may have noticed the use of the ParamByName method. ParamByName is similar to FieldByName—it lets you specify a parameter by its name, rather than by its index in the Params array.

Part
III

Ch
10

Performance Tips

The performance of a SQL server can be enhanced in several ways.

Performance Through BDE Settings   The BDE Administrator program allows you to set the following options, which will increase the speed of your interaction with the SQL server:

- **Schema Cache**—The schema holds the structure of tables and fields in the database. By caching the schema, you let the BDE concentrate on manipulating your data rather than working out where it is and how it's stored. To enable the schema cache, set `Enable Schema Cache` to `True` and set the `Schema Cache Dir` option to an appropriate folder.

- **Batch Count**—The `Batch Count` setting controls the number of records moved in a single operation when executing a batch move. Increasing this setting improves the speed of your batch operations and the Data Migration tool.

Performance Through Explicit Transaction Control   Not only do explicit transactions give you greater control, they also increase the performance of your processing. To use explicit transaction control, set the `SQLPassThru Mode` option in the BDE Administrator to `Shared NoAutoCommit`.

Putting It All Together

This chapter extended your database knowledge into the realm of SQL. We introduced the SQL language, and defined its two subsets—Data Definition Language (DDL) and Data Manipulation Language (DML). With the SQL language defined, we covered the advantages of using a SQL server—it is fast, efficient, and easier to maintain when compared to a local database.

You learned how to use the Database Desktop to create a simple Query By Example (QBE) query, and then convert it into the equivalent SQL statement.

We then indicated the situations in which you should use `TTable` as opposed to `TQuery`, and moved on to document the SQL-specific functionality provided by each of these classes, and how to maximize their efficiency and speed.

We then covered several components used when programming with SQL databases—`TDatabase`, `TStoredProc`, and `TUpdateSQL`. `TDatabase` is used to manage your global connection to the database; `TStoredProc` encapsulates procedures stored on the server, and `TUpdateSQL` is used to modify the underlying data of a read-only dataset.

We ended this chapter by covering some additional topics—implicit transaction control, parameterized SQL, and how to improve the general speed of your SQL work. ●

Using Delphi's Database Tools

by David Powell

Three main tools are built into Delphi to assist programmers developing database applications. The first tool is the Database Explorer, and it comes with all versions of Delphi. The second tool is the Data Dictionary, and it comes only with the Professional and Client/Server versions of Delphi. The third tool, the SQL Monitor, comes only with the Client/Server version. This chapter examines these three tools and explores their usefulness in developing database applications.

Database Explorer

Learn how to use the Database Explorer to examine and manipulate your databases.

Data Dictionary

Learn what the Data Dictionary is and how to use it to create client-side business rules for your database applications.

SQL Monitor

Examine the SQL Monitor and learn how to use it to debug your database applications.

Database Explorer

The Database Explorer is a fully functional database browser that allows you to both view and edit information on your databases. The database information is presented in a tree-view format, much like the Windows Explorer.

The Database Explorer has different functionality, depending on the version of Delphi you use. The Desktop version of the Database Explorer can only access local databases (Paradox and dBASE tables). The Professional version of Delphi can access local databases, ODBC-compliant databases, and Local InterBase Server databases. The Client/Server version of Delphi has all the functionality of the Professional version, and also native access to SQL databases via SQL Links. The name of the Explorer in the Client/Server product was changed to SQL Explorer to distinguish the SQL-enabled version from the regular one. All figures in this chapter were generated with the Client/Server version of the Explorer, so that I can show the full potential of the tool.

The Explorer has two main panels and is shown in Figure 11.1. The panel on the left shows a graphical representation of the databases that the Borland Database Engine (BDE) knows about, and in this chapter I refer to it as the Browsing panel. The panel on the right, which I will refer to as the Information panel, shows various types of information depending on the item selected in the Browsing panel.

FIG. 11.1

The Database Explorer.

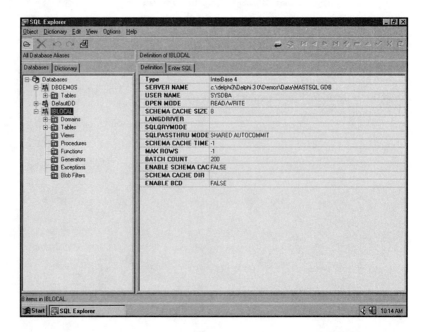

Browsing Panel

The Browsing panel displays a tree-view of all of the BDE alias' configured for the Borland Database Engine. The default databases are: DBDemos, DefaultDD, and IBLocal (with the Professional and Client/Server versions only).

Creating a New Alias　You can create an alias to your database by right-clicking in the Browsing panel and selecting New from the pop-up menu. This brings up a screen where you can select the driver type for your alias. The Database Engine automatically sees the SQL Links drivers that are installed and also any ODBC 2.0 drivers installed on the system. After the driver type is selected, the default values for the connection parameters appear in the information panel, as shown in Figure 11.1. Here, you can set all the information necessary to connect to your database. To save the new alias, right-click in the Browsing panel and select Apply or click the Apply button on the toolbar.

Logging onto a Database　When you expand the database in the Browsing panel, you will be forced to log in to the database if it requires a user name and password (such as when it is a SQL server or ODBC driver). After you are connected to the database, the Explorer will indicate that you are connected by drawing a light-green box around the database icon next to the alias name. In Figure 11.1, notice that an outline shows around the database icon for the DBDemos and IBLocal databases. On your color monitor, this outline appears as a light-green box. The connection will terminate if you close down the Explorer, or select the alias and click Close from the right-click pop-up menu.

Examining the Database　When the Explorer expands your database, it displays information on the database depending on the kind of database it actually is. In Figure 11.1, for example, you see that the DBDemos database has only tables listed under it, but IBLocal has Domains, Tables, Views, Procedures, Functions, Generators, Exceptions, and Blob Filters.

When a local type database is expanded, the Explorer shows all the tables that exist in the database. Each table then can be expanded to show all the attributes of that table. Figure 11.2 shows an expanded view of the ORDERS.DB table, which is part of the standard DBDemos alias. From the expanded view, you can get information on the various fields, indices, validity checks, referential constraints, and so on of the table. Information about each of these aspects is displayed in the Information panel.

Table 11.1 shows the different Database Objects available in the Browsing panel, based on which type of database connection is expanded. The Explorer stores the information for each of the different types of databases to which it knows how to connect, in an INI text file named DBX.DBI in the DELPHI3\BIN folder.

FIG. 11.2

Expanded view of a local table.

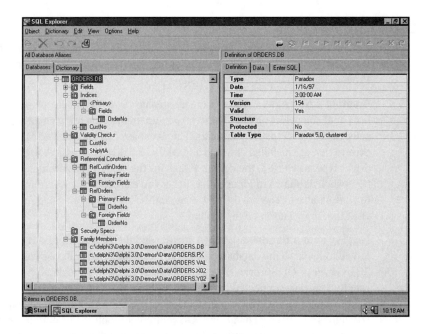

Table 11.1   Available Database Objects per Connection Type

Connection Type	Database Objects
dBASE, Paradox	Tables
DB2	Data Types, Tables, Views, TableSpaces, Aliases, Packages, and Functions
Informix	Tables, Views, Synonyms, and Procedures
InterBase	Domains, Tables, Views, Procedures, Functions, Generators, Exceptions, and Blob Filters
MS Access	Tables
MS SQL	Data Types, Tables, Views, Procedures, Defaults, Rules, Logins, Groups, Users, Segments, and Devices
ODBC	Tables and Procedures
Oracle	Tables, Views, Synonyms, Snapshots, Clusters, TableSpaces, Sequences, Procedures, Functions, and Packages
Sybase	Data Types, Tables, Views, Procedures, Defaults, Rules, Logins, Groups, Users, Segments, and Devices

As mentioned previously, when you expand a SQL server type of database, you receive a listing of all the aspects of your database. The tables in the database are one of these aspects, and when you expand the Tables item, you get a breakdown of the aspects of any particular table. Figure 11.3 shows an expanded view of the PARTS table, which is part of the LIBS database pointed to by the IBLocal alias. Like local tables, you can see all the columns, indices, and referential constraints on the table. The SQL databases, however, also have aspects such as primary keys, check constraints, unique constraints, and triggers, which also are displayed.

FIG. 11.3
Expanded view of a LIBS table.

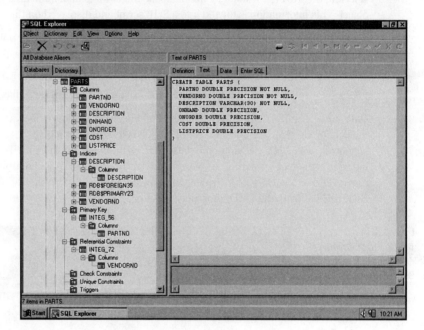

Information Panel

The Information panel displays information about the item selected in the Browsing panel. The Information panel is designed as a Page Control and has four different pages that appear depending on the type of database object that is selected in the Browsing panel. These pages are named Definition, Text, Data, and Enter SQL.

Definition Tab The Definition tab shows the physical characteristics of the item selected in the Browsing panel. The information that is displayed varies broadly, depending on the type of object selected. As shown in Figure 11.1, if a BDE alias is selected, the Definition tab shows all the BDE configuration information for that alias. If a field in a table is selected, the Definition tab will display the field structure information, as shown in Figure 11.2.

For the most part, the information displayed in the Definition tab is not editable. The restructuring of databases, tables, and fields must be performed through the Enter SQL tab or with vendor-provided software. You can edit the BDE configuration information of an alias if you are not connected to that database (in other words, if no green outline box appears around the database icon for the database).

T I P Items on the Definition tab that can be edited appear in plain text (not bold), and items that cannot be edited appear in bold text.

Text Tab   The Text tab is available only in the Client/Server version of the Explorer. When selected, the Text tab will query the database to get meta-data information on the selected object. This information is turned into a SQL script and displayed on the Text tab.

This capability is handy when creating duplicate structures of existing objects. You simply select the original object, copy the SQL script to the clipboard from the Text tab, and then paste it onto the Enter SQL tab.

Figure 11.3 showed the Text tab for the PARTS table for the IBLocal alias.

Data Tab   The Data tab, available in all versions of the Explorer, allows you to browse and edit the data in the selected table. The information is displayed in a grid, but an additional viewing window is available for seeing blob data, such as memos and graphics. To open the blob viewing window, select View, Blob Explorer from the main menu or just double-click the graphic or memo field on the Data tab. Figure 11.4 shows the Data tab with the Blob window open on BIOLIFE.DB from the DBDemos alias.

FIG. 11.4
The Database Explorer, displaying live data with Blob window.

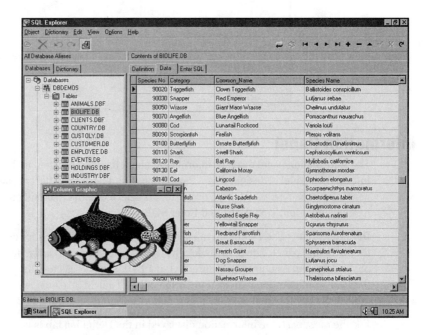

Enter SQL Tab   The Enter SQL tab is available only with the Developer and Client/Server versions of Delphi. The Enter SQL tab allows you to execute SQL statements against the selected database. From this tab, you can drop tables, create tables, grant rights, create triggers, create and execute stored procedures, and so on. To execute a SQL statement, just enter the SQL into the entry window and click the lightning bolt to execute the statement.

When you execute SQL statements that return a result set like a SELECT, the Explorer displays the result set right below the area in which you entered the query. You have the option of making the query result live from the main menu by selecting Options,Query, which brings up a Query Options window. Here, you can select a Live Result set, among other things.

This tab provides an ideal test environment for creating complex queries. Not only do you get immediate results, but the browsing panel also lets you quickly navigate to other database objects to verify things such as field names and indices. Figure 11.5 shows the Enter SQL tab with a simple SELECT statement from the CUSTOMER table of the IBLocal alias.

FIG. 11.5
The Database Explorer, querying live data.

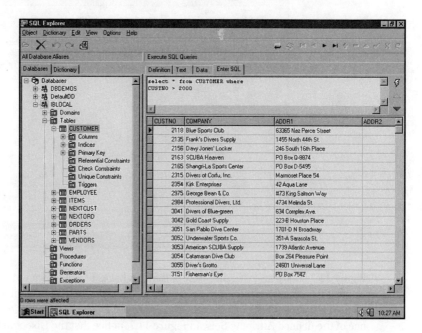

Data Dictionary

The Data Dictionary comes only with the Developer and Client/Server versions of Delphi. You access the Data Dictionary through the Database Explorer by selecting the Dictionary tab in the Browsing panel of the Explorer. The Data Dictionary provides you with the ability to create client-side business rules for your database applications. Most business rules reside on the server, but in some circumstances, you may want the business rules to reside at the client location (such as display and edit formatting). Figures 11.6 and 11.7 show expanded views of the default Data Dictionary. The Data Dictionary consists of two main sections—the Databases and the Attribute Sets.

Databases

The Databases section on the Data Dictionary contains a list of all the BDE aliases, and consequently databases, that are included in the Dictionary. The default Data Dictionary only contains the DBDemos alias. You can add alias to the current Dictionary by selecting the Database entry in the Browsing panel, and then choosing Dictionary, Import from Database. Doing so brings up an Import Database window that allows you to select which BDE alias you want to include into the current Dictionary.

FIG. 11.6

Data Dictionary with expanded table fields.

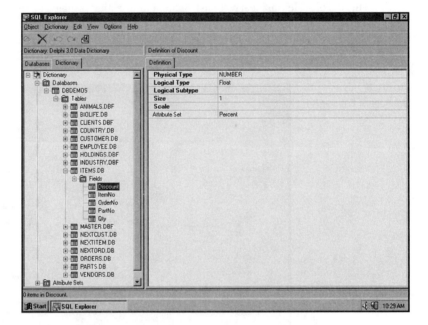

Figure 11.7 shows an expanded view of the Databases object, down to the field level of a table. Notice that the Information panel of the Explorer shows only the Definition tab. The last item on the Definition tab for a field is the Attribute Set. This selection connects a field in a table to one of the defined Attribute Sets. In Figure 11.7, notice that the Discount field of ITEMS is connected to the Percent attribute.

Attribute Sets

The Attribute Sets section on the Data Dictionary contains a list of all the defined *Attributes* in the Dictionary. An Attribute is a collection of information such as formatting, minimum values, maximum values, alignment, precision, and so on that can be applied to a database field.

When you have several database applications that display the information about a specific field the same way, either you can customize the handling of this field in each application, or you can create an Attribute in the Dictionary and associate this field with the appropriate Attribute. Using the Dictionary method makes maintenance easier if the handling of this field should need to be changed on a global level.

Figure 11.7 shows an expanded view of the Attributes Sets object down to the Attribute level. The Definition tab on the Information panel shows all the unique information to the selected attribute. Notice that the last item on the Definition tab is labeled Based On. This selection allows you to base an attribute on an existing attribute, just like inheritance in object-oriented programming. Based On allows you to create a general attribute, and then refine it for individual situations. The TaxRate Attribute, for example, is based on the Percent attribute in the default Dictionary.

FIG. 11.7
The Data Dictionary, with expanded attribute field.

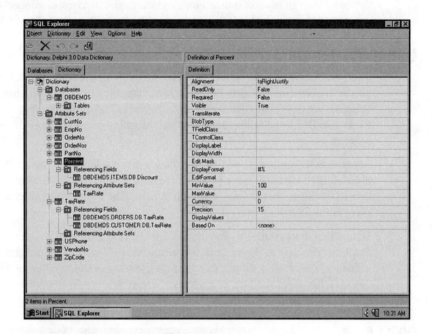

Part
III

Ch
11

Creating New Attributes from the Explorer   New Attributes can be created from within the Database Explorer by selecting the Attribute Sets object in the Browsing panel, and then right-clicking and selecting New or by selecting Object, New.

When you create a new Attribute, you will want to set at least the Alignment, ReadOnly, Required, and Visible properties. You also may want to set the TControlClass to indicate to Delphi what type of data-aware control to drop onto a form when a field with this Attribute is dragged from the Fields Editor onto a form.

Creating and Using Attributes from Delphi   You can create new Attribute sets from within Delphi by customizing a TField component that has been added to a form via the Fields Editor. After you have set all the formatting information for the TField, open the Fields Editor and select the respective field, then right-click the Fields Editor and choose Save attributes from the pop-up menu.

Attribute sets can be associated with a field from within Delphi by selecting a field in the Fields Editor, right-clicking the Fields Editor, and selecting Associate attributes from the pop-up menu. This is not a local association; the association will become part of the Data Dictionary.

SQL Monitor

The SQL Monitor is available only with the Client/Server version of Delphi. The SQL Monitor was first introduced in Delphi 2.0 and is a useful tool when working with back-end databases. The SQL Monitor allows you to trace all the interaction between the BDE and the client DLLs for your database. You can monitor transactions, logins, queries, fetches, disconnects, and so on. You never need to wonder what Delphi is doing with your server when the Monitor is running.

Using the Monitor

The SQL Monitor is not only a powerful tool, it also is easy to use. Using the Monitor is a simple two-step process that consists of launching the actual SQL Monitor program and then selecting the BDE client that you want to trace. You can launch the SQL Monitor from within the Delphi IDE by selecting Database, SQL Monitor or by selecting it from the Delphi 3.0 program group.

After the SQL Monitor is running, the Clients menu selection on the main menu will contain a list of all BDE clients that are currently running. You need to select which BDE client (if multiple BDE clients are running) you want to trace. The Monitor automatically defaults to the first client in the list.

Figure 11.8 shows the SQL Monitor and the resulting trace of the query performed by the Database Explorer in Figure 11.5. The actual SELECT statement is highlighted in the upper window of the Monitor. Notice that the lower window of the Monitor fully displays the selected line from the upper window. This allows you to view an entire statement when it is too long to fit on a single line.

FIG. 11.8

SQL Monitor.

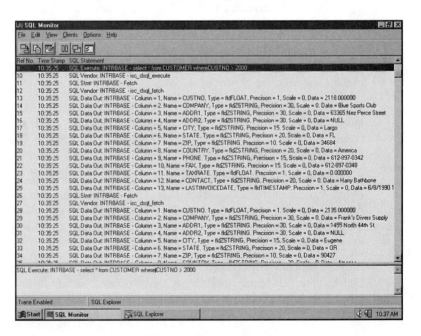

Trace Options

The SQL Monitor has several tracing options available, depending on how detailed a trace you want to perform. The trace shown in Figure 11.8 has all trace options turned on. This trace is more detailed than what usually is required, but it is available when needed. Table 11.2 shows the 11 trace options available for the Monitor. The options can be set by clicking the Trace Options tool button or by selecting Options, Trace Options.

Table 11.2 SQL Monitor Trace Options

Trace Option	Description
Prepared Query Statements	Prepared statements to be sent to the server.
Input Parameters	Parameter information for parameterized queries.
Fetched Data	All data fetched from the server.
Executed Query Statements	Statements to be executed by the server.
Statement Operations	Each operation performed such as ALLOCATE, PREPARE, EXECUTE, and FETCH.
Connect/Disconnect	Operations associated with connecting and disconnecting to databases.
Transactions	Operations associated with transactions.
Blob I/O	Operations on Blob data.
Miscellaneous	All other operations.
Vendor Errors	Error messages returned by the server. The error message may include an error code, depending on the server.
Vendor Calls	API function calls made to the Client DLLs.

Part
III

Ch
11

Parameterized Queries

Parameterized queries are no longer a mystery with the SQL Monitor that ships with Delphi 3. The earlier version of Monitor (the one that shipped with Delphi 2.0) couldn't display parameter information for parameterized queries. The new monitor displays a question mark (?) in the actual SELECT statement but if you look a few lines higher in the trace log, you see where the parameter is being initialized.

Figure 11.9 shows the trace log of a parameterized query from a simple Delphi application that selects all the customers from a table whose customer number is greater than some parameter value, as follows:

```
select * from CUSTOMER where CUSTNO > :p1
```

The parameter was configured to be an integer type with a value of 2000.

FIG. 11.9

The SQL Monitor, showing a parameterized query.

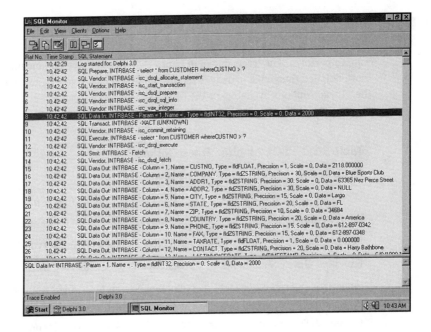

Debugging Applications

The usefulness of this tool in debugging database applications is obvious. You can use it to quickly tell if dynamic queries are being created correctly at runtime. You can use it to fine-tune the performance of your queries against the database. If you experience severe timing problems, the Time Stamp in the trace log can be examined to find out which statements are taking the longest to execute. The trace log also can yield other bits of important information, such as error codes that are returned from the server but not propagated by the BDE back to your application.

Putting It All Together

Delphi provides three powerful database tools to aid the developer of database applications. Among the Database Explorer, the Data Dictionary, and the SQL Monitor you have the capability to create and modify tables, procedures, triggers, packages, indices, and so on; create client-side business rules; and trace the interaction of your application with your database's client DLLs. With a little practice, these tools will quickly become part of your Database Application debugging repertoire. ●

CHAPTER 12

Using Quick Reports

by David Powell

Quick Reports is a powerful report generator that offers programmers the capability to create reports of various degrees of complexity. The 32-bit version of Quick Reports first shipped with Delphi 2.0 and has undergone a complete revision for Delphi 3. This chapter examines each of the different Quick Reports components and shows how to build reports, both manually and automatically.

All versions of Delphi 3 contain a demo project for Quick Reports named QRDemo that is located in your Delphi 3\Demos\QuickRpt directory.

What is Quick Reports?

Quick Reports is Delphi's native VCL banded report generator.

How do I create reports?

In this chapter, you examine each of the Quick Reports components and examine how to put together all the pieces to create a report.

A Quick Reports report is created in three easy steps:

1. Drop a TQuickRep component onto a form.
2. Create the bands necessary for your report.
3. Drop Quick Reports visual controls onto the bands to display the report information.

> **N O T E**   Quick Reports version 1 forms from Delphi 2.0 are not compatible with Quick Reports
> version 2 forms in Delphi 3. If you load a project or a form generated with Delphi 2.0, an
> automatic conversion takes place to make the form compatible with Quick Reports 2. ■

Quick Reports Components

Quick Reports is based on a set of native Delphi controls that are used together to create banded reports. Native VCL components give you a speed, a control, and a flexibility advantage over other report generators that rely on OLE or DDE to communicate between your program and the actual report modules.

There are 18 Quick Reports components that reside on the QReport tab of the component palette. The following section is not intended to be an exhaustive list of each component and its properties. Instead, it briefly covers each component and points out some of the more useful properties and events of each.

TQuickRep

The TQuickRep component is the heart and soul of the Quick Reports package and is the starting place for all reports generated with this package. When a TQuickRep component is dropped onto a form, it aligns itself to the form and expands to a full-page size, which gives you the capability to do a full-page layout of your report.

Bands Property   The Bands property gives you the capability to instantly add the six most common types of bands to your report in their correct visual order by simply clicking in the Object Inspector. The Bands property is a set property with the following values: HasColumnHeader, HasDetail, HasPageFooter, HasPageHeader, HasSummary, and HasTitle. For a description of what each band type is, see Table 12.1.

Table 12.1   BandType Property Values

Value	Description
rbChild	A Child band is linked to another band and prints after the band on which it is linked prints.
rbColumnHeader	A Column Header band is printed at the top of every column in a multiple column report.
rbDetail	A Detail band is printed for every record in your report.

Value	Description
rbGroupFooter	A Group Footer band is printed at the end of a grouping (a master/detail report).
rbGroupHeader	A Group Header band is printed at the beginning of a grouping (a master/detail report).
rbOverlay	An Overlay band is printed from the top-left corner of a page and overlays all other bands on the page.
rbPageFooter	A Page Footer band is printed at the bottom of every page.
rbPageHeader	A Page Header band is printed at the top of every page.
rbSubDetail	A Sub Detail band is used as a Detail band for the detail portion of a master/detail report.
rbSummary	A Summary band is printed only once at the end of the report.
rbTitle	A Title band is printed only once at the beginning of the report.

At designtime, Label appears on each of the bands, indicating what type of band it is so that you can quickly distinguish between the bands as you are adding Quick Report controls to them.

DataSet Property   The DataSet property indicates from which dataset the main report should be getting its values. The dataset can be a TTable or a TQuery. For simple list type reports, you usually will be working with only one dataset but for master/detail reports, the DataSet property of the TQuickRep component should be set to the master dataset. It doesn't matter if the dataset is on the Quick Reports form or on another form or DataModule.

Options Property   The Options property contains five different options for your report. These options include: FirstPageHeader, LastPageFooter, TwoPassReport, MultiThreaded, and Compression. FirstPageHeader and LastPageFooter cause the Page Header band and Page Footer band to print only on the first and last page of the report, respectively. The MultiThreaded option causes Quick Reports to print the report, in a background thread so that your application can continue as normal, without waiting for the report to finish. The TwoPassReport option can be used so that TQRExpr components can contain expressions that calculate values, based on values that are not known until the end of a report. For example, suppose that you create a sales report that displays the percent of total sales per region based on gross national sales, and you do not know the gross national sales until the entire report is run. The two-pass report allows you to overcome this limitation by generating the entire report first and putting off resolving expressions that are invalid on the first pass until the second pass. The Compression option stores the report in a compressed format. The report takes up less room in your program, but takes longer to run. It's a tradeoff between size and speed.

Page Property   The Page property gives you full control over the paper size, margins, page orientation, and so on of your report. Quick Reports queries your system to learn all of the valid options for your currently selected printer.

***PrinterSettings* Property**   The PrinterSettings property allows you to select the number of copies you want to print, whether or not you want duplex printing, and (if supported by your printer) what output bin to print to.

***ReportTitle* Property**   The ReportTitle property is used by the TQRSysData component to display the report title in the Title band.

***ShowProgress* Property**   The ShowProgress property is used to enable the showing of a progress dialog while a report is being prepared and printed. The progress dialog has a Cancel button to allow the user to stop the generation of the report.

***OnNeedData* Event**   The OnNeedData event is used to generate a Quick Reports report from a non-BDE dataset. This event gets triggered when Quick Reports needs data for the next "record." If you are not connected to a BDE dataset, it is your responsibility to fill in the text values for the TQRLabel components in your report. OnNeedData has a Boolean parameter named MoreData that needs to be set to False when the report is done.

TQRSubDetail

The TQRSubDetail component is used to display detail records in a master/detail report. The three main properties for this component are Bands, DataSet, and Master.

***Bands* Property**   The Bands property is a set property with two values—HasFooter and HasHeader. These two values give you the capability to instantly create Group Footer and Group Header bands, respectively.

***DataSet* Property**   The DataSet property indicates from which dataset that components on this band should get their information. You should set this to the Detail dataset of your master/detail relationship.

***Master* Property**   The Master property needs to point to the band that the master data is tied to. This usually is the TQuickRep component. If you are creating a master/detail report, this property would point to the first TQRSubDetail component.

TQRBand

After the TQuickRep component, TQRBand probably is the second most important component in the Quick Reports package. Every report contains TQRBand components of one type or another. When bands are added to a report via the Bands property of the TQuickRep component, Delphi is actually creating TQRBand components. Some bands print automatically, some print every page, and some print only once for the entire report.

***BandType* Property**   As the name implies, the BandType property is used to denote what type of band a TQRBand component is. The band type determines in what position the band will appear in the final report. Table 12.1 lists all of the possible band types, along with a description of where the band will occur in the report.

***ForceNewColumn* Property**   The ForceNewColumn property will cause Quick Reports to create a new column before this band is printed.

***ForceNewPage* Property**   The `ForceNewPage` property will cause Quick Reports to start a new page before the band is printed. In a simple list report, setting this property to True on the Detail band causes only one record per report page to appear. In a master/detail report, setting this property to True for the Detail band forces a new page for each master record in the report, with all the detail records for that master occurring on the same page.

***LinkBand* Property**   When Quick Reports prints a band, it checks the current page to see if there is enough room on it to print the band. The `LinkBand` property is used to force Quick Reports to place the linked band on the same page as the current band. If there is not enough room on the current page to print both the current band and the linked band, Quick Reports starts a new page. Bands are allowed to be chain linked together (band one can link to band two that links to band three, and so on).

TIP   When linking bands, always link in a forward manner. In other words, if band one prints before band two, you can link band one to band two. Linking band two to band one will not produce the desired result because band one already will have been printed before band two is even evaluated.

***BeforePrint* Event**   The `BeforePrint` event is fired before Quick Reports prints a band. A Boolean parameter named `PrintBand` is passed to this event and is used to determine if the band should be printed or not. `PrintBand` is True by default and should be set to False to suppress the printing of the band. This event is frequently used in master/detail reports, where you want to suppress the printing of a Detail and Sub Detail band if there are no detail records for a given master record.

TIP   Code entered in the `BeforePrint` event for a band is not called at designtime when a user right-clicks the report component and chooses Preview from the pop-up menu. The `BeforePrint` event will get called at runtime when the `Preview` method of the report component is called—you will see bands when previewing at designtime that you may not see when actually previewing/printing the report at runtime.

Part
III

Ch
12

TQRChildBand

The `TQRChildBand` component is used to create a band that is associated with another band, much like the relationship between a Detail and Sub-Detail band but without the formality of a master/detail relationship. A Child band can be created by dropping a `TQRChildBand` onto a report or by setting the `HasChild` property of a band to True.

Child bands are commonly used in the situation where a report needs to display memo information in a Detail band followed by some other record information. If you set the `AutoStretch` property of the `QRDBText` component to True, it will expand itself over top of the other controls. The solution is to display the memo information in the Detail band and put the other information in a Child band that is attached to the detail band. This allows the memo information to expand as needed without overwriting the following information.

ParentBand   The ParentBand property is used to associate the Child band with its Parent band. A Child band can be associated with any type of Quick Reports band—even another Child band.

TQRGroup

The TQRGroup component is used to create groupings within a report. Groupings are mainly used for master/detail reports but also can be effectively used in simple list-type reports.

Expression Property   The Expression property is used to create an expression that will indicate when the grouping should break. For example, for a simple list-type report, you can cause a group to break when the first letter of a certain field changes by entering the following expression into the Expression property:

```
copy(fieldname,1,1)
```

Master Property   The Master property is used to indicate from where the TQRGroup component should get its data. This property usually is hooked to the TQuickRep component onto which it was dropped.

TQRLabel

The TQRLabel component is a new component for Quick Reports 2.0 and is used to display static text in reports, much as you would use a TLabel component to display static text values on a form. When I say static values here, I do not mean that you cannot change the value of the text—just that the text value does not change frequently or come from a dataset.

TQRDBText

The TQRDBText component is a data-aware control used to display the values of string fields, numeric fields, date fields, and memo fields. The component is hooked up to a dataset and data field like any other data-aware control, through the DataSet and DataField properties, respectively.

AutoStretch Property   AutoStretch is a Boolean property that indicates whether or not the TQRDBText control needs to stretch vertically to fit the entire contents of a memo field. If TQRDBText is hooked up to a memo field and AutoStretch is false, the memo will be clipped to the size of the TQRDBText control. If AutoStretch is True, the control will display the entire memo, breaking over pages if necessary.

The AutoStretch property will cause a TQRDBText component to resize itself vertically—even over top of other Quick Reports components. If you have a situation where you need to display memo information followed by other record information in the same Detail band, you should print the memo in the Detail band and the other information in a Child band.

TQRExpr

The TQRExpr component allows you to create simple to complex calculations for your reports. This component has undergone great changes since previous versions of Quick Reports and now is very versatile, flexible, and powerful.

Expression Property   The Expression property is the key to this entire component. When you click on the value for the Expression property, you will see the ellipses button (...) that when clicked brings up the Expression Builder property editor (see Figure 12.1). The Expression Builder helps guide you in creating the expression that you need for your report.

FIG. 12.1

The Expression builder.

ResetAfterPrint Property   ResetAfterPrint is a Boolean property that indicates whether or not the value for the TQRExpr component should be set back to its default value every time that it's printed. If you are creating a master/detail type of report where the TQRExpr component is creating some kind of running total, you may want to reset the value under certain situations.

TQRSysData

The TQRSysData component is used to display information about the report and operating system inside your report when it is printed.

Data Property   The Data property indicates the type of information that the TQRSysData component displays. Table 12.2 lists the seven different property values and describes what type of information each displays. It is common to use this component in Header, Footer, and Title bands of a report.

Table 12.2   Data Property Values

Value	Description
qrsDate	Current date
qrsDateTime	Current date and time
qrsDetailCount	Number of records in the report
qrsDetailNo	Current record number
qrsPageNumber	Current page number
qrsReportTitle	Displays ReportTitle property value of the TQuickRep component
qrsTime	Current time

TQRMemo

The TQRMemo component allows you to display non-data-aware memo in your report. This component behaves like a normal TMemo control, and information can be added to it via the Lines property. There is no data-aware memo control. TQRDBText should be used for database memo fields.

TQRRichText

The TQRRichText component allows you to display RTF files in your report. TQRRichEdit has a property named ParentRichEdit that allows you to hook up the TQRRichEdit up to another TRichEdit component. If you do this, the TQRRichEdit will reflect the RTF memo information of the other control.

TQRDBRichText

This is a data-aware version of the TQRRichEdit component.

TQRShape

The TQRShape component is used to draw simple shapes in your report. The shape drawn is dependent upon the Shape property. Table 12.3 lists the different values for the Shape property.

Table 12.3   Shape Property Values

Value	Description
qrsCircle	Draws a circle
qrsHorLine	Draws a horizontal line
qrsRectangle	Draws a rectangle

Value	Description
qrsRightAndLeft	Draws vertical lines on the right and left
qrsTopAndBottom	Draws horizontal lines on the top and bottom
qrsVertLine	Draws a vertical line

TQRImage

The TQRImage component allows you to display static graphic images in your report. You can use this component to add digitized letterhead or logos to your report.

TQRDBImage

The TQRDBImage component is a data-aware control that allows you to add graphics to your report from your database. It is used in the same way as a normal TDBImage control.

TQRCompositeReport

The TQRCompositeReport component gives you the ability to merge multiple reports into a single report. With this component, you can create a large report that contains many different conditional sections, without having to programmatically turn off and on the printing of specific bands. You can simply create the conditional sections as separate reports, and then add only the sections that you want printed to the Composite Report. Reports are added to TQRCompositeReport via the OnAddReports event. In the OnAddReports event, you add the reports to the Reports property as follows:

```
procedure TForm1.QRCompositeReport1AddReports(Sender: TObject);
begin
  with Sender as TQRCompositeReport do begin
    // QuickReport2, QuickReport3 and QuickReport4 are TQuickRep components
    Reports.Add(QuickReport2);
    Reports.Add(QuickReport3);
    Reports.Add(QuickReport4);
  end;
end;
```

TQRPreview

The TQRPreview component allows you to create your own custom preview screen rather than using Quick Reports default one. For more information on creating Custom Preview forms, see the section "Creating Custom Previews" later in this chapter.

TQRChart

The TQRChart component is a Quick Reports customized TChart component that allows you to embed charts into your reports. This component works nicely in TQRGroup band, where you can show graphical summary information for the following detail records.

Part III
Ch 12

Creating Reports

Delphi provides two easy methods to create Quick Report reports—The *QuickReport Wizard* and *Report Templates*. This section shows how to generate reports with both of these methods.

QuickReport Wizard

The Report Wizard is located on the Business page of the Object Repository. It is a quick and easy way of creating a simple list-type report. Figure 12.2 shows how the Report Wizard appears in the Object Repository.

FIG. 12.2

Business page of the Object Repository.

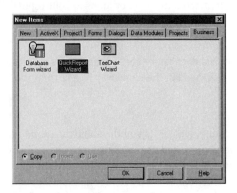

You can create a simple report by using the QuickReport Wizard and the Vendors table in DBDemos:

1. Start a new application in Delphi.
2. Select File, New from Delphi's main menu. This opens the Object Repository.
3. Select the Business tab, and then the QuickReport Wizard.
4. Select the DBDemos alias and the VENDORS.DB table, and then click the Next button.
5. Click the >> button to include all fields in the report, and then click the Next button.
6. Set the Report Title to **UD3 QuickReport Wizard Example** and click the Finish button. This puts you back into the Delphi IDE.
7. Select the Table component on the newly created Quick Reports form, and change its Active property in the Object Inspector to True.
8. Right-click the Quick Reports form and select Preview from the pop-up menu.

You should now see a report similar to that shown in Figure 12.3.

The QuickReport Wizard automatically puts a TTable component onto the form it creates. You could remove that Table component and instead point the DataSet property of the TQuickRep component to a table or query in a DataModule or on another form. If you do this, you also have to change the Expression properties for the TQRExpr components that the Wizard created to point to the same dataset.

FIG. 12.3
QuickReport Wizard-
generated Vendor
report.

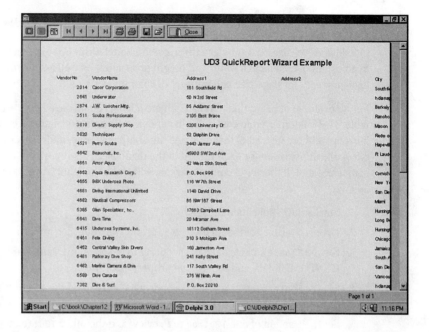

Report Templates

Like the QuickReport Wizard, Report Templates also reside in the Object Repository. The Forms tab holds three Quick Reports templates. Figure 12.4 shows how the Report Templates appear in the Object Repository. Using the Report Templates requires a little more work than using the Wizard, but doing so offers greater flexibility and control. This section shows how to create a report by using the Labels and Master/Detail Templates.

FIG. 12.4
Forms page of the
Object Repository.

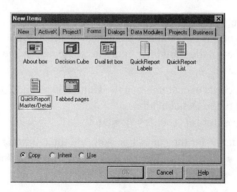

Part
III

Ch
12

Quick Reports List The List Template creates a standard list-style report identical to the one generated by the Report Wizard, minus the automatically generated text controls for each field. In most circumstances, it's quicker and easier to use the Report Wizard for these kinds of reports.

Quick Reports Labels The Labels template creates a Quick Reports report designed to be printed on labels. The report contains only a Detail band that has its width and height set to an individual label size on a standard three-column label form. For different size labels, you have to adjust the Detail band's width and height properties, as well as the TQuickRep component's Page property for page size and number of columns per page.

For an example of using this template, create a label report based on the DBDemos' Customer table. The Customer table contains a list of domestic and international companies. The following steps will create a label that contains the company name, address, city, Zip Code, and contact name information for each record in the database. This report will contain only U.S.-based companies and, if there is a contact person, will make the label "Attn:" to that person, as follows:

1. Start a new application in Delphi.

2. Drop a TTable, TDataSource, TDBGrid, and two TButtons onto the form.

3. Set the TTable's DatabaseName property to DBDemos, the TableName property to CUSTOMER.DB, and the Active property to True.

4. Set the TDataSource's DataSet property to Table1 and the TDBGrid's Datasource property to Datasource1. You now should see data in the Grid.

5. Set the Caption of one TButton to Preview and the other TButton to Print.

6. Select File, New from Delphi's main menu to open the Object Repository. Select the Forms tab and choose the QuickReport Labels form.

7. On the Quick Reports form, set the MasterTable component's DatabaseName property to DBDemos, the TableName property to CUSTOMER.DB, and the Active property to True.

8. Drop seven TQRDBText components onto the Detail band and arrange so that there is one TQRDBText component on the first four lines on the band and three components on the fifth and final line.

9. Set the DataSet property for each of the seven TQRDBText components to MasterTable, and the DataField properties so that Company is on the first line; Contact is on the second line; Addr1 is on the third line; Addr2 is on the fourth line; and City, State, and Zip are on the fifth line.

10. To only print the records of customers in the United States, add the following code to the BeforePrint event of the Detail band:
```
PrintBand := MasterTable['Country'] = 'US';
```

11. To add the attention line for the contact person, add the following code to the OnPrint event of the TQRDBText component that is associated with the Contact field:
```
if Value <> '' then
Value := 'Attn:  ' + Value;
```

12. It is also necessary to manually add a comma after the City field. You can do so by adding the following code to the OnPrint event of the TQRDBText component associated with the City field:
```
Value := Value + ',';
```

13. In the OnClick event for the Preview button, add the following:

    ```
    QRListForm.Report.Preview;
    ```

14. In the OnClick event for the Print button, add the following:

    ```
    QRListForm.Report.Print;
    ```

15. Add Unit2 to the USES section of Unit1.

Listing 12.1 shows the complete code for the Quick Reports form. If this application is run and you click the Preview button, you should see results similar to Figure 12.5. This entire project is located on this book's companion CD-ROM, in the UDELPHI3\CHP12\LABELRPT directory.

Listing 12.1   \UDELPHI3\CHP12\LABELRPT—Label Printing Quick Reports Example

```
{ QuickReport Label template }

unit Unit2;

interface

uses
  Windows, Messages, SysUtils, Classes, Graphics, Controls, Forms, Dialogs,
  Qrctrls, quickrpt, DB, DBTables, ExtCtrls;

type
  TQRListForm = class(TForm)
    Report: TQuickRep;
    MasterTable: TTable;
    DetailBand1: TQRBand;
    QRDBText1: TQRDBText;
    QRDBText2: TQRDBText;
    QRDBText3: TQRDBText;
    QRDBText4: TQRDBText;
    QRDBText5: TQRDBText;
    QRDBText6: TQRDBText;
    QRDBText7: TQRDBText;
    procedure QRDBText3Print(sender: TObject; var Value: String);
    procedure DetailBand1BeforePrint(Sender: TQRCustomBand;
      var PrintBand: Boolean);
    procedure QRDBText6Print(sender: TObject; var Value: String);
  private
    { Private declarations }
  public
    { Public declarations }
  end;

var
  QRListForm: TQRListForm;

implementation
```

continues

Part
III

Ch
12

Listing 12.1   Continued

```
{$R *.DFM}

procedure TQRListForm.QRDBText3Print(sender: TObject; var Value: String);
begin
  Value := Value + ',';
end;

procedure TQRListForm.DetailBand1BeforePrint(Sender: TQRCustomBand;
  var PrintBand: Boolean);
begin
  // Only print customers in the USA
  PrintBand := MasterTable['Country'] = 'US';
end;

procedure TQRListForm.QRDBText6Print(sender: TObject; var Value: String);
begin
  // if there is a contact name add 'Attn:' to the front of it
  if Value <> '' then
    Value := 'Attn:  ' + Value;
end;

end.
```

FIG. 12.5

Quick Reports Label report.

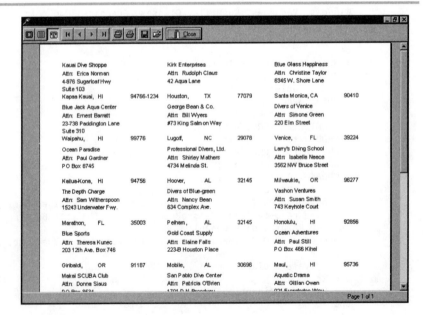

Quick Reports Master/Detail   The Master/Detail Report Template creates a Quick Reports report with Title, Column, Detail, Sub-Detail, and Page Footer bands already linked together on the report in a master/detail relationship. There will be two TTable components named MasterTable and DetailTable on the report form by default, and it is to these tables that the bands are linked.

For an example of using this template, create a report based on the DBDemos' Vendors and Parts tables. The Vendors table contains a list of unique vendor ids, and the Parts table contains a list of unique part numbers and their respective vendor ids. The following steps create a report that contains a list of vendors along with the parts that they produce. If a vendor in the Vendors table has no items in the Parts table, you will not include that vendor in the report. Also, if the vendor is flagged as preferred in the Vendor table, you will indicate this status on the report:

1. Start a new application in Delphi.

2. Select File, New from Delphi's main menu to open the Object Repository. Select the Forms tab and choose the QuickReport Master/Detail form.

3. Select File, New Data Module from Delphi's main menu to create a new Data Module.

4. On the Data Module drop two TTable and two TDataSource components. Name one TTable **MasterTable** and one **DetailTable**. Name one TDataSource **MasterSource** and one **DetailSource**. Set the DataSet properties of the TDataSource components to their respective TTable components. Set the TTable DatabaseName properties to DBDemos. Set the TableName property of the MasterTable to VENDORS and the Active property to True. For the DetailTable, set the TableName property to PARTS, the MasterSource property to MasterSource, the IndexName property to VenderNo, the MasterFields property to VenderNo, and the Active property to True.

5. On the main form of the application (the first form), drop two TDBGrid and two TButton components. Add Unit3 (the Data Module) to the USES section. Set the DataSource property of one TDBGrid to MasterSource and the other TDBGrid to DetailSource. You now should see data in the TDBGrids.

6. On the Quick Reports form remove the two TTable components that were automatically added to the form. Set the DataSet property of the TQuickRep component to MasterTable and the DataSet property of the Sub-Detail band to DetailTable. Create a Group Header band, adding the HasHeader element to the Bands property of the Sub-Detail band.

7. On the Column Header band, add three TQRLabel components for VendorNo, Vendor, and Status.

8. On the Detail band add seven TQRDBText components for the VendorNo, VendorName, Address1, City, State, Zip, and Preferred fields, respectively. Set the ForceNewPage property to True to cause only one vendor to appear on each report page. If you want to see them run together, leave this to its default value of False.

9. On the Group Header band, add three TQRLabel components for PartNo, Description, and Cost.

Part
III

Ch
12

10. On the Sub-Detail band, add three TQRDBText components for PartNo, Description, and Cost fields, respectively.

11. In order to not print a Vendor with no associated Parts, add the following code to the BeforePrint event of the Detail band:

```
PrintBand := DataModule3.DetailTable.RecordCount > 0;
```

12. If a vendor is preferred, show the text "Preferred;" if not, show "Standard." The default text for these fields is True and False because it is a Boolean field. To make this change, add the following code to the OnPrint event of the TQRDBText component associated with the Preferred field:

```
if Value = 'True' then
Value := 'Preferred'
else
Value := 'Standard';
```

13. To format the values in the Cost field to money values instead of float values, add the following code to the OnPrint event of the TQRDBText associated with the Cost field:

```
FmtStr(Value,'%m',[StrToFloat(Value)]);
```

14. In the OnClick event for the Preview button on the main form, add the following:

```
QRListForm.Report.Preview;
```

15. In the OnClick event for the Print button on the main form, add the following:

```
QRListForm.Report.Print;
```

16. Add Unit2 (the Quick Reports form) to the USES section of Unit1 (the main form).

Listing 12.2 shows the complete code for the Quick Reports Master/Detail form. If this application is run and you click the Preview button, you should see results similar to Figure 12.6. This entire project is located on this book's companion CD-ROM in the UDelphi3\Chp12\MDRpt directory.

Listing 12.2   \UDELPHI3\CHP12\MDRPT—Master/Detail Quick Reports Example

```
{ QuickReport master detail template }

unit Unit2;

interface

uses
  Windows, Messages, SysUtils, Classes, Graphics, Controls, Forms, Dialogs,
  Qrctrls, quickrpt, DB, DBTables, ExtCtrls;

type
  TQRListForm = class(TForm)
    Report: TQuickRep;
    DetailBand1: TQRBand;
    PageFooterBand1: TQRBand;
```

```
      TitleBand1: TQRBand;
      ColumnHeaderBand1: TQRBand;
      QRSysData1: TQRSysData;
      QRSysData2: TQRSysData;
      QRSubDetail1: TQRSubDetail;
      QRDBText1: TQRDBText;
      QRDBText2: TQRDBText;
      QRDBText3: TQRDBText;
      QRDBText4: TQRDBText;
      QRDBText5: TQRDBText;
      QRDBText6: TQRDBText;
      QRDBText7: TQRDBText;
      QRDBText9: TQRDBText;
      QRDBText10: TQRDBText;
      QRDBText11: TQRDBText;
      QRLabel1: TQRLabel;
      QRLabel2: TQRLabel;
      QRLabel3: TQRLabel;
      GroupHeaderBand1: TQRBand;
      QRLabel4: TQRLabel;
      QRLabel5: TQRLabel;
      QRLabel6: TQRLabel;
      procedure QRDBText3Print(sender: TObject; var Value: String);
      procedure DetailBand1BeforePrint(Sender: TQRCustomBand;
        var PrintBand: Boolean);
      procedure QRDBText6Print(sender: TObject; var Value: String);
    private
      { Private declarations }
    public
      { Public declarations }
    end;

var
  QRListForm: TQRListForm;

implementation

uses Unit3;

{$R *.DFM}

procedure TQRListForm.QRDBText3Print(sender: TObject; var Value: String);
begin
  // if a preferred customer then print "Preferred" else print "Standard"
  if Value = 'True' then
    Value := 'Preferred'
  else
    Value := 'Standard';
end;

procedure TQRListForm.DetailBand1BeforePrint(Sender: TQRCustomBand;
  var PrintBand: Boolean);
begin
  // Only print the band if there are records in the Detail table
  PrintBand := DataModule3.DetailTable.RecordCount > 0;
end;
```

continues

Listing 12.2   Continued

```
procedure TQRListForm.QRDBText6Print(sender: TObject; var Value: String);
begin
  FmtStr(Value,'%m',[StrToFloat(Value)]);
end;

end.
```

FIG. 12.6

Quick Reports Master/
Detail report.

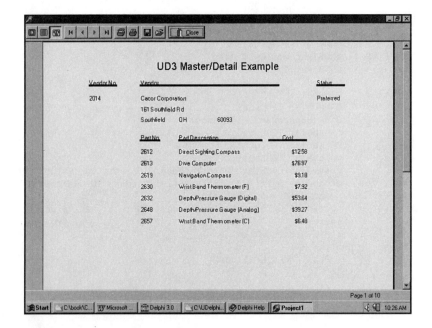

Creating Custom Previews

Custom Previews are easily created in Delphi by using the TQRPreview component. Creating a custom preview consists of the following steps:

1. Create a new form and drop the TQRPreview component on it.

2. Add buttons and menu items to the form that will allow for the navigation, printing, and displaying of the report.

3. Add the following code to the OnPreview event handler for all Reports that will use the custom preview:

    ```
    PrevForm.QRPreview1.QRPrinter := TQRPrinter(Sender);
    ```

    where PrevForm is the name of the Custom Preview form and QRPreview1 is the name of the TQRPreview component.

On the CD

Step 3 is the key step in getting a custom preview to work. It assigns the Printer object of the custom preview to the Printer object of the report. A full example of a Custom Preview is available on this book's companion CD-ROM, in the \UDELPHI3\CHP12\CUSTVIEW directory.

Putting It All Together

Quick Reports is a powerful banded report generator. In this chapter, you examined the many different Quick Reports controls and built three different types of reports, a simple list report, a Master/Detail report, and a Mailing Labels report. You saw that Quick Reports gives you complete control over the positioning of fields, conditional band printing, and even field values at runtime. The built-in Report Wizard and Report Templates help you to quickly create professional-looking reports natively in Delphi. ●

CHAPTER 13

Creating Custom Datasets

by Todd Miller

Until Delphi 3, your choices of data access were to some extent limited. In Delphi 1 and 2, you had three basic ways to access data. You could work with Borland's Paradox and dBASE table types; or if you used Delphi Client/Server, you could connect to the various popular SQL servers. If, however, the data with which you needed to work wasn't one of the supported datasets, the only option you had was to connect via an ODBC driver (which also required the BDE). At times, this was a problem because ODBC drivers are often slow. What if, however, there isn't an ODBC driver that connects to your dataset? Well, prior to Delphi 3, your only option was to write a complete database engine to access your data as well as to create your own data-aware controls to display your data, which could be thousands of lines of code.

Now with Delphi 3 you have another alternative. Delphi 3 made it possible for anyone accessing any data to construct custom datasets that will be able to work with Delphi's fields editor, data repository, and, most important, with the data-aware controls that come with Delphi.

Virtualized datasets

This chapter starts by discussing the benefits of Delphi's new virtual dataset, `TDataSet`. `TDataSet` is not new to Delphi but it was changed so that new custom datasets can be created.

Dataset fundamentals

Next, the implementation of the essential methods that must be overridden to create your own custom dataset are discussed and illustrated.

ASCII Text Driver without the BDE

The example that this chapter uses to illustrate the creation of a custom dataset is a fixed-length ASCII Text Driver that doesn't incorporate the BDE.

To facilitate this, Delphi 3 removed all of the BDE API dependencies from the TDataSet class and moved them into the new TBDEDataSet class. The TBDEDataSet class now provides the core BDE functionality for TTable, TQuery, TStoredProc, and so on. The TDataSet class was re-engineered to have its core functionality virtual so that any custom dataset could be created with it—you can write a custom dataset descending from TDataSet that immediately works with all the data-aware controls that come with Delphi. Minimally, you only need to implement 20+ virtual TDataSet methods and you'll have a custom dataset component.

At this point, I mention that the material covered in this chapter assumes that the reader is familiar with basic component development and has a fundamental understanding of the Object Pascal language. If this isn't the case, you may want to refer to Chapters 16, "Creating Components," and 17, "Writing Advanced Components." I also want to point out that these chapters assume that the reader has a firm understanding of database concepts and behavior. So now, let's look into what virtual datasets are all about. ■

TDataSet, the Heart of Every Custom Dataset

A custom dataset consists of two functional parts: the part you do and the part that TDataSet does. The lesser of the two is the 20+ virtual abstract TDataSet methods that you override. TDataSet is designed to provide the basic functionality that all datasets need, such as navigation and data manipulation. Table 13.1 is a list of the methods and properties that TDataSet provides automatically when its core virtual methods are implemented. TDataSet, however, only knows how to work with records and fields in a generic sense—it doesn't know anything about the actual data with which it's working. Here, the core virtual methods come into play. These methods allow TDataSet to work with your custom data—TDataSet is crucially dependent on its core virtual methods being implemented.

Table 13.1 Default Functionality of *TDataSet* After Implementing Its Virtual Abstract Methods

Category	Properties/Methods
General	Active, Open, Close
Navigation	First, Last, Next, Prior, MoveBy, Refresh, EOF, BOF, and IsEmpty
Editing	Edit, Insert, InsertRecord, Append, AppendRecord, Delete, Post, Cancel, Modified, State, CheckBrowseMode, and SetFields
Bookmark management	BookmarkValid, CompareBookmarks, GotoBookmark, FreeBookmark, GetBookmark, and Bookmark
Data-aware control management	ControlsDisabled, DisableControls, EnableControls, and IsLinkedTo

Category	Properties/Methods
Events	BeforeOpen, AfterOpen, BeforeClose, AfterClose, BeforeInsert, AfterInsert, BeforeEdit, AfterEdit, BeforePost, AfterPost, BeforeCancel, AfterCancel, BeforeDelete, AfterDelete, BeforeScroll, AfterScroll, OnCalcFields, OnDeleteError, OnEditError, OnNewRecord, and OnPostError
Field management	FieldByName, FieldByNumber, FieldDefs, FieldCount, Fields, FieldValues, DefaultFields, FindField, GetFieldList, GetFieldNames, UpdateRecord, and ClearFields
Low-level dataset management	ActiveBuffer, CursorPosChanged, GetCurrentRecord, Translate, and RecordSize

Besides the properties and methods listed in Table 13.1, you can use the Fields Editor to manipulate a custom dataset component on a form to create static fields, calculated fields, and lookup fields just like any other TDataSet descendant. So what part do you have to do? The following list shows the general areas that the 20+ virtual abstract methods encompass:

- Table Opening, Initializing, and Closing routines
- Bookmark management routines
- Record-buffer management routines
- Field management routines
- Navigation management routines
- Exception-handling routine

Writing a Custom ASCII Text Database Driver

Before you get into the nuts and bolts of building a custom dataset, first you need an idea of what data you are trying to access and how to determine what its field layout looks like. To start with, the custom dataset that we are going to build is a simple ASCII text driver that can read in fixed-column text tables. The component, TFixedAsciiDataSet, reads the user-specified test file into a TStringsList whereby each string represents a separate raw text record. The field definition will read from a schema file that is a separate text file that contains a list of field declarations that include the field name, field type, and field size. A schema file's file name is the same name as the text file with an .SCH file extension.

N O T E Besides the example in this chapter, the TBDEDataSet component in the file \SOURCE\VCL\DBTABLES.PAS and the TClientDataSet component in the file \SOURCE\VCL\DATASET.PAS are both solid examples of custom datasets. Both contain a more complete TDataSet implementation of how and why to override the various methods of TDataSet.

Part III
Ch 13

The TFixedAsciiDataSet expected schema format is the same as that documented for the BDE's ASCII text driver; however, only the FIXED field layout is supported; delimited text records are not supported. This means that you can use a text-file dataset with its schema file that was created with the BDE's ASCII driver and use it with the TFixedAsciiDataSet component.

N O T E For a complete description of the BDE schema file format, look in the BDE32.HLP file. A
shortcut to this file exists in the Delphi 3 folder. If you use Windows 95 or Windows NT 4.0,
you can go to your Start menu and select Programs, and then under the Delphi 3 entry, you see the
Borland Delphi 3 folder. ■

In fact, the sample data we will use is an ASCII text file with a schema file that contains the records from Delphi's sample database file EMPLOYEE.DB. This file was created by using Delphi's TBatchMove component. Listing 13.1 shows the schema file that represents our EMPLOYEE.TXT text file. You can find this file on this book's companion CD-ROM.

On the CD

**Listing 13.1   \UDELPHI3\CHP13\EMPLOYEE.SCH—The Schema Field
Definition for the Employee Sample Data**

```
[EMPLOYEE]
Filetype=Fixed
CharSet=ascii
Field1=EmpNo,Long Integer,11,00,00
Field2=FirstName,Char,20,00,11
Field3=LastName,Char,15,00,31
Field4=PhoneExt,Char,04,00,46
Field5=HireDate,TimeStamp,30,00,50
Field6=Salary,Float,20,02,80
```

Notice that a standard schema file starts with a header that is surrounded by square brackets and contains the name of the text file that the field definitions in the schema file represent. Next, you see that the file type is specified. In the BDE's ASCII text driver, both DELIMITED and FIXED are supported, but the example in this chapter supports only fixed columns. So the value following the equal sign must be FIXED. The next item is CharSet and is supported only by the BDE. And then finally you reach the remaining lines, which specify the field definitions of the table's columns. Each field definition line must begin with "Fieldx = ", where x is the field number (such as Field1, Field2, and so on). The rest of each line contains the following comma-delimited items, specifying the following information:

- **Field Name.** Follow the same restrictions as Paradox field names.
- **Data Type.** The field data type. See Table 13.2.
- **Field Size.** The number of characters or units. Must be <= 20 for numeric data types. This also represents the maximum number of characters that a date, time, or timestamp type (date and time) will occupy (including the / and : separators).

■ **Precision**. Number of digits following the decimal (FLOAT only). This value is ignored by the TFixedAsciiDataSet component.

■ **Field Offset**. Number of characters from the beginning of the line where this field's data begins. Used for BDE FIXED format only. This value is ignored by the TFixedAsciiDataSet component because it's calculated from the field size value as the fields are read in from the schema.

The supported data types are listed in Table 13.2. We will see later that these get mapped to compatible data types in Delphi when these values are passed to and from data-aware controls and so on.

Table 13.2 Supported Schema Data Types

Schema Data Type	Description
Char	Character string
Float	64-bit floating-point value
Number	16-bit integer
Long Integer	32-bit long integer
Bool	Boolean (T or F)
7.5	Date field (format specified in Registry)
Time	Time field (format specified in Registry)
Timestamp	Date/Time field (format specified in Registry)

Building the Custom Dataset

Now that you know what we're building, let's roll up our sleeves and start in. The approach taken here to explain the TFixedAsciiDataSet component is to tackle one functional group of methods at a time. For a bird's-eye view of where this is going and what the functional groups are, look at Listing 13.2. Listing 13.2 shows the class definition of TFixedAsciiDataSet which, as you may have guessed by now, is a descendant from TDataSet. So, to start, you need to know what part TDataSet does for you and what you have to do for it.

Part
III

Ch
13

TDataSet's primary function is to manage a group of record buffers. TDataSet doesn't understand what's contained in the buffers, however. The interpretation of information in the buffers is up to the descending class—in this case, TFixedAsciiDataSet. TDataSet also sets no requirements on what is contained in each record buffer. Another significant functionality that TDataSet provides is communication with any data-aware components that are attached to TDataSource components. So what does TDataSet expect from its descendants? It expects the descendant class to implement all functions that directly access the record buffer, which includes creating, populating, interpreting, and freeing the record buffers.

Also, the descendant class must provide *bookmark* capabilities. Bookmarks are used to uniquely identify each record, and are crucial for the correct operation of the internal workings of TDataSet. If you create your own custom dataset and it doesn't have unique identifiers for each record, you need to fabricate your own to have TDataSet work properly with your descendant class. Before going on, also take note of the private variables in the TFixedAsciiDataSet used to track various pieces of information such as the last bookmark assigned, the current record, and the size of the record buffer. For now, you can simply look at the comments in Listing 13.2 to get an idea of their purpose; but as you get into the various functional implementation groups for the custom dataset, they are discussed in greater detail. You can find the file ASCIIDRV.PAS on this book's companion CD-ROM.

> **Listing 13.2 \UDELPHI3\CHP13\ASCIIDRV.PAS—The Class Definition for *TFixedAsciiDataSet* Component as Well as the Required Methods that Must Be Implemented for Any Custom Dataset**

```
TFixedAsciiDataset = class(TDataSet)
  private
    FTextRecords  : TStrings;// Raw records read from the text file
    FFieldInfo    : TList;   // Field offset and size in raw record
    FRawBufSize   : Integer; // Size of the raw data buffer
    FRecBufSize   : Integer; // FRawBufSize + size of TRecInfo record
    FRecInfoOfs   : Integer; // Offset for TRecInfo data in data bufer
    FCurRec       : Integer; // Keep track of the current record
    FFileName     : string;  // File name of the ASCII table
    FLastBookmark : Integer; // Last bookmark
    FSaveChanges  : Boolean; // Determines if data has been modified
    procedure PopulateFieldDefsFromSchema;
  protected
    // Required Dataset methods to be overridden

    // Opening, Initializing and Closing Custom Datasets
    procedure InternalOpen; override;
    procedure InternalInitFieldDefs; override;
    procedure InternalClose; override;
    function  IsCursorOpen: Boolean; override;

    // Dataset bookmark management routines
    procedure GetBookmarkData(Buffer: PChar; Data: Pointer); override;
    procedure SetBookmarkData(Buffer: PChar; Data: Pointer); override;
    function  GetBookmarkFlag(Buffer: PChar): TBookmarkFlag; override;
    procedure SetBookmarkFlag(Buffer: PChar;
              Value: TBookmarkFlag); override;
    procedure InternalSetToRecord(Buffer: PChar); override;
    procedure InternalGotoBookmark(Bookmark: Pointer); override;

    // Dataset record buffer management routines
    function  GetRecordCount: Integer; override;
    function  AllocRecordBuffer: PChar; override;
    procedure FreeRecordBuffer(var Buffer: PChar); override;
    function  GetRecord(Buffer: PChar; GetMode: TGetMode;
              DoCheck: Boolean): TGetResult; override;
```

```
  function  GetRecordSize: Word; override;
  procedure InternalInitRecord(Buffer: PChar); override;
  procedure InternalAddRecord(Buffer: Pointer;
            Append: Boolean); override;
  procedure InternalPost; override;
  procedure InternalDelete; override;

  // Dataset field management routines
  procedure SetFieldData(Field: TField; Buffer: Pointer); override;
  function  GetFieldData(Field: TField;
            Buffer: Pointer): Boolean; override;

  // Dataset navigation management routines
  procedure InternalFirst; override;
  procedure InternalLast; override;

  // Dataset exception handling routine
  procedure InternalHandleException; override;
protected
  procedure SetFileName(Value : String);
published
  property FileName: string read FFileName write SetFileName;
  property Active;
  property BeforeOpen;
  property AfterOpen;
  property BeforeClose;
  property AfterClose;
  property BeforeInsert;
  property AfterInsert;
  property BeforeEdit;
  property AfterEdit;
  property BeforePost;
  property AfterPost;
  property BeforeCancel;
  property AfterCancel;
  property BeforeDelete;
  property AfterDelete;
  property BeforeScroll;
  property AfterScroll;
  property OnCalcFields;
  property OnDeleteError;
  property OnEditError;
  property OnNewRecord;
  property OnPostError;

end;
```

Part III Ch 13

CAUTION

All the methods overridden in the TFixedAsciiDataSet also must be overridden in any custom dataset that you choose to implement. This is because TDataSet is functionally dependent on all these methods at some point or another and if any are missing, you either get a runtime error because TDataSet is calling one of its abstract virtual methods, or you simply don't get the results that you expect.

Opening, Initializing, and Closing Custom Datasets

This functional group is composed of four methods:

- InternalOpen
- InternalInitFieldDefs
- InternalClose
- IsCursorOpen

The implementations of these methods are shown in Listing 13.3.

Let's first look at the InternalOpen method. InternalOpen's purpose is to open the dataset, which entails setting up the field definitions (by calling InternalInitFieldDefs) and initializing crucial internal values such as the record buffer size, the offset of any internally maintained data structure also stored in the record buffer, and initial record position.

In the TFixedAsciiDataset's implementation of InternalOpen, we first check to see if the text file exists and if so, load the entire file into a TStringsList (FTextRecords). Then each record is assigned a unique numeric identifier that will be used as the record's bookmark. Look at the InternalOpen method in Listing 13.3 to see the specific internal variable assignments.

N O T E Regardless of the source of a custom dataset's data, each of its records must be uniquely identified. However, it doesn't have to be a numeric value, as is the case of the example in this chapter. ▪

Next, TDataSet's FieldDefs list must be populated with the field names, types, and sizes of the dataset's fields. This is handled by the InternalInitFieldDefs method, which in turn calls the private PopulateFieldDefsFromSchema method. The PopulateFieldDefsFromSchema method opens the associated .SCH file for the dataset and parses through it to populate TDataSet's FieldDefs list. The schema parsing code is in Listing 13.4.

After the fields are defined and you know the number of bytes that the record occupies (FRawBufSize), you can use it as an offset value for any extra data that you may need to add to the record buffer to track things such as bookmark information. This example *does* add a special record (TRecInfo, discussed later in the section "Record Management") of data at the end of each buffer. Consequently, you need to know where the raw data stops so that you know where TRecInfo starts. We could just use the FRawBufSize variable but to keep things clear in the source a separate variable (FRecInfoOfs) is used to hold the offset value of the TRecInfo data at the end of a buffer. Finally, the BookmarkSize is set to the size of an integer because this is how bookmarks are stored.

The InternalClose method determines if any records have changed and, if so, writes the entire text file back out and then the FTextRecords TStringsList, the dataset's field definitions, and the internal field information list (FFieldInfo list) are freed. The creation of the FFieldInfo list is discussed shortly.

The IsCursorOpen method simply tells TDataSet if the table is open or not, which is determined (in our example) by whether the FTextRecords list variable is assigned.

```
procedure TFixedAsciiDataset.InternalOpen;
//-----------------------------------------------------------------
// Purpose: If the filename exists then load it and associate a
//          unique number to each record which will be used as their
//          internal bookmark value.
//-----------------------------------------------------------------
var
  I: Integer;
begin
  FTextRecords := TStringList.Create;
  try
    // Open the text data file and read in its entire contents.
    if not FileExists(FileName) then Abort;
    FTextRecords.LoadFromFile(FileName);

    //Assign a unique bookmark value to each text record.
    for I := 1 to FTextRecords.Count do
        FTextRecords.Objects[I - 1] := Pointer(I);

    // Initialize our internal position and last bookmark. The
    // internal record numbers range from 0 to FTextRecords.Count - 1,
    // so -1 and FTextRecords.Count are used as BOF and EOF crack
    // values, respectfully.
    FCurRec := -1; // Initially positioned on the BOF crack
    FLastBookmark := FTextRecords.Count;

    // Create the field definition from the schema file and then create
    // the TField objects from the field definition.  And finally
    // bind the fields.
    InternalInitFieldDefs;

    if DefaultFields then CreateFields;
    BindFields(True);

    //Initialize an offset value to find the TRecInfo in each buffer
    FRecInfoOfs := FRawBufSize;

    // Calculate the size of the record buffers (note this is NOT the
    // same as the RecordSize property which only gets the size of the
    // data)
    FRecBufSize := FRecInfoOfs + SizeOf(TRecInfo);

    // Tell TDataSet how big our Bookmarks are (REQUIRED) }
    BookmarkSize := SizeOf(Integer);
  except
    FTextRecords.Free;
    FTextRecords := Nil;
    Active := False;
    Showmessage('Error opening text file: ' + FileName);
    raise;
  end;
end;
```

continues

Listing 13.3 Continued

```
procedure TFixedAsciiDataset.InternalInitFieldDefs;
//-----------------------------------------------------------------
// Purpose: Call schema parse routine to get the FieldDefs list
//          populated with the current table's field definition.
//-----------------------------------------------------------------
begin
  PopulateFieldDefsFromSchema;
end;

procedure TFixedAsciiDataset.InternalClose;
//-----------------------------------------------------------------
// Purpose: When the text table is closed the contents are written
//          out if any changes were made.  The text record string
//          list is freed.  And finally the internal field list's
//          elements are freed and then the field list is freed.
//-----------------------------------------------------------------
var
  I : Integer;
begin
  if FSaveChanges then FTextRecords.SaveToFile(FileName);
  FTextRecords.Free;
  FTextRecords := nil;
  FLastBookmark := 0;
  FCurRec := -1;

  BindFields(False);
  if DefaultFields then DestroyFields;

  // Cleanup the internal fields records
  if Assigned(FFieldInfo) then
  try
    if FFieldInfo.Count > 0 then
      for I := 0 to FFieldInfo.Count - 1 do
        FreeMem(PFieldInfo(FFieldInfo[I]), SizeOf(TFieldInfo));
  finally
    FFieldInfo.Free;  // Remove when inserted into dataset
    FFieldInfo := Nil;
  end;
end;

function TFixedAsciiDataset.IsCursorOpen: Boolean;
//-----------------------------------------------------------------
// Purpose: We need this while opening, this indicates if data is
//          available even though our state is still dsInActive
//-----------------------------------------------------------------
begin
  Result := Assigned(FTextRecords);
end;
```

Before moving to the next functional group, a couple of things need pointing out in the schema parsing routines that are pertinent to later discussions of other methods. Because the `FieldDefs` list doesn't keep track of the relative offsets or size in bytes of the data within the raw record buffer, the schema parsing routine `ProcessField` creates a list of `TFieldInfo` records in the `FFieldInfo` list that track each field's offset and size for use in the field-management methods that are discussed in the "Field Management" section later in this chapter. The `ProcessField` subroutine also maps the various schema data types (see Table 13.2) into one of the following `TDataSet` field types: `ftString`, `ftFloat`, `ftInteger`, `ftBoolean`, `ftDate`, `ftTime`, or `ftDateTime`.

Listing 13.4   \UDELPHI3\CHP13\ASCIIDRV.PAS—The *TFixedAsciiDataSet* Component's Schema Parsing Routines

```
procedure TFixedAsciiDataset.PopulateFieldDefsFromSchema;
//-----------------------------------------------------------------
// Purpose: Parse the schema file associated with the dataset
//          specified in the FileName property.
//
// <Field<#>> = <FieldName>,<Field Type>,<Field Size>,<Precision>,
//              <Offset>
//
// <Field Type> can be one of the following types CHAR, FLOAT,
//              NUMERIC, BOOL, LONG INTEGER, DATE, TIME or
//              TIMESTAMP.
// <Field Size> is the number of characters or units for the field.
//              Total maximum number of characters for date/time
//              field types must include the '/' and ':' separators.
// <Precision>  is the precision supplied for floating point values.
//              This is used when formatting edited floats back into
//              the text file.
// <Offset>     is the relative position within the fixed text record
//              that the specified field starts.  This will be
//              ignored since this can be calculated by the
//              <Filed Size> field.  It is allowed for compatibility
//              with the BDE schema format.
//-----------------------------------------------------------------
var
  SchemaFile : TStrings;
  CalculatedOfset : Integer;
  I : Integer;
const
  ValidFieldTypes : array[1..9] of string = ('CHAR', 'FLOAT',
       'NUMERIC','BOOL', 'LONGINT', 'LONG INTEGER' , 'DATE',
       'TIME','TIMESTAMP');
  FieldTypes: array[1..9] of TFieldType = (ftString, ftFloat,
       ftInteger, ftBoolean, ftInteger, ftInteger, ftDate, ftTime,
       ftDateTime);
```

continues

Listing 13.4 Continued

```
procedure ProcessField(FieldInfo : String);
////----------------------------------------------------------------
// Purpose: This sub-routine processes a field definition string
//          that has the following format:
////----------------------------------------------------------------
var
  FieldName, FieldTypeToken : String;
  FldSize, J : Integer;
  FieldType : TFieldType;
  FieldInfoRec : PFieldInfo;

  function NextToken : String;
  ////--------------------------------------------------------------
  // Purpose: Get the next field text token (i.e. field name, etc.
  ////--------------------------------------------------------------
  var
    DelimPos : Integer;
  begin
    DelimPos := AnsiPos(',', FieldInfo);
    if DelimPos = 0 then
      Result := Trim(FieldInfo)
    else
    begin
      Result := Trim(Copy(FieldInfo, 1, DelimPos - 1));
      FieldInfo := Trim(Copy(FieldInfo, DelimPos + 1, 255));
    end;
  end;

begin
  with FieldDefs do
  try
    FieldName := NextToken;      // Get the field name
    FieldTypeToken := NextToken; // Get the field type

    // Determine the field type index by matching the field type
    // token against the ValidFieldTypes constant string array.
    FieldType := ftUnknown;
    for J := Low(ValidFieldTypes) to High(ValidFieldTypes) do
      if FieldTypeToken = ValidFieldTypes[J] then
      begin
        FieldType := FieldTypes[J];
        Break;
      end;

    FldSize := StrToInt( NextToken ); // Get the field size
    NextToken;                        // Ignore the floating
                                      // point precision
    NextToken;                        // also, eat the field offset

    // Keep track internally of the field offset, size and floating
    // point decimal position if necessary for each field in the
    // schema file.
    GetMem(FieldInfoRec, SizeOf(TFieldInfo));
```

```
      with FieldInfoRec^ do
      begin
        FieldOfs := CalculatedOfset;
        FieldSize := FldSize;
      end;
      FFieldInfo.Add(FieldInfoRec);
      Inc(CalculatedOfset, FldSize);    // Determine next offset pos
      FRawBufSize := CalculatedOfset;   // Reset size of the rec buffer

      // Perform validation and adjustments to field information
      // before adding to the dataset's FieldDefs list.
      if FieldType <> ftString then FldSize := 0;

      // Add schema field information to the dataset's FieldDef list
      // Note: Field numbers must start at 1.
      TFieldDef.Create(FieldDefs, FieldName, FieldType, FldSize,
              False, FieldDefs.Count + 1);
    except
      raise EDatabaseError.Create(
          'Schema Read Error: Error processing field ' + FieldName +
          ' in schema file')
    end;
end;

procedure ProcessTokens(const LeftToken, RightToken : String);
//---------------------------------------------------------------
// Purpose: Process each line of a BDE style schema file.  This
//          dataset supports only FIXED column text tables
//          consequently the DELIMITER and SEPARATOR schema
//          keywords can be ignored.  In addition, this dataset
//          doesn't support language drivers so the CHARSET schema
//          keyword is ignored.  This routine also ignores the
//          [TableName] entry that is valid in a BDE schema. All we
//          really care about is that the table is FIXED and that
//          there is at least one field definition line.
//---------------------------------------------------------------
begin
  // Ignore these keyword tokens
  if Length(LeftToken) > 0 then
  if (LeftToken = 'CHARSET') or
     (LeftToken = 'DELIMITER') or
     (LeftToken = 'SEPARATOR') or
     (LeftToken[1] = '[') then Exit;

  if (LeftToken = 'FILETYPE') and (RightToken <> 'FIXED') then
     Raise Exception.Create(
          'Schema Read Error: FILETYPE must be FIXED');

  // What we really are concerned with are field definitions
  if AnsiPos('FIELD', LeftToken) > 0 then
     ProcessField(RightToken);
end;

function GetSchemaFileName : String;
```

continues

Listing 13.4   Continued

```
//----------------------------------------------------------------
// Purpose: Determine the schema file name based on the text file
//          name.
//----------------------------------------------------------------
begin
  Result := ExtractFileName(FileName);
  Result := Copy(Result, 1, AnsiPos('.', Result) ) + 'SCH';
  Result := ExtractFilePath(FileName) + Result;
end;

var
  LeftStr, RightStr, SchemaFileName : String;
begin
  CalculatedOfset := 1;
  FieldDefs.Clear;
  SchemaFile := TStringList.Create;
  try
    SchemaFileName := GetSchemaFileName;
    if not FileExists(SchemaFileName) then Abort;
    FFieldInfo := TList.Create;
    try
      SchemaFile.LoadFromFile( SchemaFileName );
      for I := 0 to SchemaFile.Count - 1 do
      begin
        LeftStr := AnsiUpperCase(Trim(Copy(SchemaFile[I], 1,
                   AnsiPos('=', SchemaFile[I]) - 1)));
        RightStr := AnsiUpperCase(Trim(Copy(SchemaFile[I],
                   AnsiPos('=', SchemaFile[I]) + 1, 255 )));
        ProcessTokens(LeftStr, RightStr);
      end;
    except
      FFieldInfo.Free;
    end;
  finally
    SchemaFile.Free;
  end;
end;
```

Bookmark Management

What are bookmarks? *Bookmarks* are unique values associated with each record of the custom dataset. Bookmarks can be as simple as a unique four-byte integer or as complex as a user-defined data structure. Also, although TDataSet heavily relies on the existence of bookmarks, it doesn't care what's in the bookmarks; the creation, interpretation, and freeing of bookmarks is delegated to the TDataSet descendant. As far as TDataSet is concerned, it's just passing a pointer around. Bookmarks are used by TDataSet and the user of the TDataSet descendant for record navigation.

In Delphi 1, bookmarks were defined as simply a pointer (shown as follows) that pointed to the unique identity value for the record when a bookmark was requested with the GetBookMark method. This mechanism worked fine but required the developer to free the bookmark when the bookmark was no longer needed by calling the FreeBookmark method.

```
TBookmark = Pointer;
```

TBookmark is still supported in Delphi 3; however, the preferred way of working with bookmarks is to use the Bookmark property, which returns a TBookmarkStr type which is defined as an AnsiString type.

```
TBookmarkStr = string;
```

The advantage of using a TBookmarkStr is that Delphi automatically frees the bookmark when it goes out of scope, as it does with all AnsiStrings. For more information about bookmarks, refer to Delphi's online help.

The bookmark management routines are composed of the following methods:

- GetBookmarkData
- SetBookmarkData
- GetBookmarkFlag
- SetBookmarkFlag
- InternalSetToRecord
- InternalGotoBookmark

As you can see, the custom dataset is responsible for getting and setting bookmark values, getting and setting bookmark flags (discussed shortly), and record repositioning given a valid bookmark value.

Before looking at the TFixedAsciiDataSet's implementation of these methods, you need an understanding of how bookmark values are being associated with each text record. TFixedAsciiDataSet opts for the simple route of using unique integer values for each text record. These integer values are stored in the Object array property of the FTextRecords string list with a value of 1 to *n* records as shown in the following code:

```
for I := 1 to FTextRecords.Count do
        FTextRecords.Objects[I - 1] := Pointer(I);
```

Each time TDataSet requests a particular record from the TDataSet descendant, the record's bookmark value is stored in the TRecInfo structure that is appended to the record buffer passed back. The TRecInfo information is used only by the TDataSet descendant.

The TRecInfo record is shown in the following lines:

```
PRecInfo = ^TRecInfo;
TRecInfo = packed record
  Bookmark: Integer;
  BookmarkFlag: TBookmarkFlag;
end;
```

Part
III

Ch
13

Notice that besides the `Bookmark` field, there also is a `BookmarkFlag` field. This field is mainly used by `TDataSet` indirectly, but your custom dataset needs to implement it for any record buffer that `TDataSet` is currently managing. The record buffer looks something like the following:

```
ActiveBuffer
 ¦
 ¦
 ---------------------------------------------------------------
 ¦          Record Data             ¦ Bookmark ¦ Bookmark Flag ¦
 ---------------------------------------------------------------
        ActiveBuffer + FRecInfoOfs --^
```

N O T E   When a program asks for a bookmark to keep track of the current record, it is indirectly getting the bookmark value out of the `TRecInfo` record in the dataset's active record buffer because, internally, the custom dataset's `GetBookmarkData` method is being called and being passed the active record buffer. ■

You see later that the `GetRecord` method (discussed in the "Record Management" section that follows in this chapter) fills in the `TRecInfo` structure in addition to passing the data record to `TDataSet`, when `TDataSet` requests a specific record.

 T I P   Keep in mind that this is only an example of how the record buffer can be used to store additional information. There is no requirement that `TDataSet` implementations do it this way.

You probably can guess how the `GetBookmarkData`, `SetBookmarkData`, `GetBookmarkFlag`, and `SetBookmarkFlag` routines are used by `TDataSet`. These routines are elementary and are commented in Listing 13.5, so refer to the listing for the specifics of how they work. All four routines are one-liners.

So what is the purpose of `BookmarkFlags`? `TDataSet` uses a record's `BookmarkFlag` to determine if it is the current record, an inserted record, or a record positioned on the beginning (`BOF`) or end of file (`EOF`) "crack." All `BookmarkFlags`, except the current record flag, are assigned internally by `TDataSet`. A record is marked with the current `BookmarkFlag` whenever `TDataSet` calls its overridden `GetRecord` method in the `TDataSet` descendant. `GetRecord` is discussed later in the chapter.

The final point to discuss about bookmarks is how they are used to reposition the current record. The two methods `InternalSetToRecord` and `InternalGotoBookmark` handle this task. These two methods essentially do the same thing—they receive a bookmark value from `TDataSet` in which they attempt to move to the record that corresponds to that bookmark.

Given that the two methods do the same thing and can handle the same raw bookmark data, I simply have `InternalSetToRecord` call `InternalGotoBookmark`. So `InternalGotoBookmark` does all the work. The only real difference between the two methods is the way the bookmark parameters are passed. `InternalSetToRecord` receives the bookmark as a pointer to a null terminated string and `InternalGotoBookmark` receives it as a pointer to a buffer.

In the `TFixedAsciiDataSet` example, the `InternalGotoBookmark` uses the `IndexOfObject` method of the `FTextRecords` `TStringsList` object to search for the bookmark value. If the match is successful, the current record (`FCurRec`) is set to the new record. Otherwise, an error occurs. That is it for the bookmark management routines. Next, on to the record management routines.

Listing 13.5   ASCIIDRV.PAS—Shows the *TFixedAsciiDataSet* Component's Bookmark Management Routines

```
procedure TFixedAsciiDataset.GetBookmarkData(Buffer: PChar;
        Data: Pointer);
//-------------------------------------------------------------------
// Purpose: Return the unique bookmark within the record buffer that
//          TDataSet passing in.  The record's bookmark is stored in
//          the special TRecInfo record placed at the end of the
//          record buffer right after the real data..
//-------------------------------------------------------------------
begin
  PInteger(Data)^ := PRecInfo(Buffer + FRecInfoOfs).Bookmark;
end;

procedure TFixedAsciiDataset.SetBookmarkData(Buffer: PChar;
        Data: Pointer);
//-------------------------------------------------------------------
// Purpose: Set the record's unique bookmark value to the value that
//          TDataSet passed in.  The record's bookmark is stored in
//          the special TRecInfo record placed at the end of the
//          record buffer right after the real data.
//-------------------------------------------------------------------
begin
  PRecInfo(Buffer + FRecInfoOfs).Bookmark := PInteger(Data)^;
end;

function TFixedAsciiDataset.GetBookmarkFlag(Buffer: PChar):
        TBookmarkFlag;
//-------------------------------------------------------------------
// Purpose: Return the BookmarkFlag within the record buffer that
//          TDataSet passed in.  The record's BookmarkFlag is stored
//          in the special TRecInfo record placed at the end of the
//          record buffer right after the real data..
//-------------------------------------------------------------------
begin
  Result := PRecInfo(Buffer + FRecInfoOfs).BookmarkFlag;
end;

procedure TFixedAsciiDataset.SetBookmarkFlag(Buffer: PChar;
        Value: TBookmarkFlag);
//-------------------------------------------------------------------
// Purpose: Set the record's BookmarkFlag value to the value that
//          TDataSet passed in.  The record's BookmarkFlag is stored
//          in the special TRecInfo record placed at the end of the
//          record buffer right after the real data.
//-------------------------------------------------------------------
```

Part
III

Ch

13

continues

Listing 13.5 Continued

```
begin
  PRecInfo(Buffer + FRecInfoOfs).BookmarkFlag := Value;
end;

procedure TFixedAsciiDataset.InternalSetToRecord(Buffer: PChar);
//----------------------------------------------------------------
// Purpose: This function does basically the same thing as
//          InternalGotoBookmark, but takes a record buffer as a
//          parameter instead.
//----------------------------------------------------------------
begin
  InternalGotoBookmark(@PRecInfo(Buffer + FRecInfoOfs).Bookmark);
end;

procedure TFixedAsciiDataset.InternalGotoBookmark(Bookmark: Pointer);
//----------------------------------------------------------------
// Purpose: Move to record that has an integer bookmark that matches
//          the bookmark value passed in.  Otherwise, display an
//          error.
//----------------------------------------------------------------
var
  Index: Integer;
begin
  Index := FTextRecords.IndexOfObject(TObject(PInteger(Bookmark)^));
  if Index <> -1 then
    FCurRec := Index
  else
    DatabaseError('Bookmark not found');
end;
```

Record Management

The record management routines are composed of the following nine methods:

- GetRecordCount
- AllocRecordBuffer
- FreeRecordBuffer
- GetRecordSize
- InternalInitRecord
- InternalAddRecord
- InternalPost
- InternalDelete
- GetRecord

The first four routines do exactly what they imply and are each one line of code, so see Listing 13.6 to see how these methods are implemented.

The `InternalInitRecord` method is called when `TDataSet` needs a record buffer initialized. `TFixedAsciiDataSet`'s implementation of the `InternalInitRecord` method simply fills in the buffer with spaces (ASCII 32).

The `InternalAddRecord` method gets called when records are added implicitly via the `InsertRecord` or `AppendRecord` methods are called. `InternalAddRecord` consequentially receives a record buffer that `TDataSet` has already populated with field data.

In other words, `TDataSet` takes the data passed to the `InsertRecord` or `AppendRecord` methods and calls the custom dataset's `SetFieldData` method for each field in the table to populate the record buffer. The `SetFieldData` method is discussed later in the "Field Management" section. To see how the new record gets inserted or appended to the table, refer to `InternalAddRecord`'s implementation in Listing 13.6.

The `InternalPost` method is called when a record in either `Insert`, `Append`, or `Edit` mode is being saved (or posted). This routine is essentially the same as the `InternalAddRecord` method, so take a look at the few lines of code that handle this routine.

The `InternalDelete` removes the current record and, if it was the last record in the `FTextRecords` `TStringsList`, it decrements the current record (`FCurRec`) by one.

Last (but not least), you have the `GetRecord` method, which basically performs three tasks. The most important of these tasks is to handle requests from `TDataSet` for the current, prior, or next records. Another task is to return a status value (`TGetResult`) that indicates to `TDataSet` the result of its last request. The enumerated type, `TGetResult`, is defined as follows:

```
TGetResult = (grOK, grBOF, grEOF, grError);
```

Finally, `GetRecord` raises an exception if the `DoCheck` flag is `true` and an error has occurred. Next, look at the field management, which is probably the most complex code in the entire custom dataset.

Listing 13.6   ASCIIDRV.PAS—Shows the *TFixedAsciiDataSet* Component's Record Management Routines

```
function TFixedAsciiDataset.GetRecordCount: Longint;
//------------------------------------------------------------
// Purpose: Returns the current number of records in the text file
//          dataset.
//------------------------------------------------------------
begin
  Result := FTextRecords.Count;
end;

function TFixedAsciiDataset.AllocRecordBuffer: PChar;
//------------------------------------------------------------
// Purpose: TDataSet calls this function to allocate the record
//          buffer. Here we use FRecBufSize which is equal to the
//          size of the data plus the size of the TRecInfo structure.
//------------------------------------------------------------
```

Listing 13.6 Continued

```
begin
  Result := StrAlloc(FRecBufSize);
end;

procedure TFixedAsciiDataset.FreeRecordBuffer(var Buffer: PChar);
//------------------------------------------------------------------
// Purpose: Again, TDataSet asks us to free the record buffer.  Make
//          sure the value of FRecBufSize does not change before all
//          allocated buffers are Freed.
//------------------------------------------------------------------
begin
  StrDispose(Buffer);
end;

function TFixedAsciiDataset.GetRecordSize: Word;
//------------------------------------------------------------------
// Purpose: Return the calculated size of the raw data + the size of
//          TRecInfo record structure.
//------------------------------------------------------------------
begin
  Result := FRawBufSize;
end;

procedure TFixedAsciiDataset.InternalInitRecord(Buffer: PChar);
//------------------------------------------------------------------
// Purpose: Called by TDataSet.InitRecord and TDataSet.ClearFields
//          when the buffer needs to be cleared.  Since blank spaces
//          signify Null fields it is essential that the GetFieldData
//          method know how to handle Null fields.
//------------------------------------------------------------------
begin
  FillChar(Buffer^, RecordSize, 32);
end;

procedure TFixedAsciiDataset.InternalAddRecord(Buffer: Pointer;
          Append: Boolean);
//------------------------------------------------------------------
// Purpose: Called indirectly by TDataSet.InsertRecord and
//          TDataSet.AppendRecord.  After incrementing the internal
//          last bookmark, FLastBookmark, then add a string buffer to
//          the text record array along with the object pointer
//          containing the unique bookmark value for this new record.
//------------------------------------------------------------------
begin
  Inc(FLastBookmark);
  if Append then InternalLast;
  FTextRecords.InsertObject(FCurRec, PChar(Buffer), Pointer(FLastBookmark));
  FSaveChanges := True;
end;

procedure TFixedAsciiDataset.InternalPost;
```

```
//------------------------------------------------------------------
// Purpose: Mark that we have changed the data so that it will
//          get saved when the table is closed.  Next we either save
//          the modified contents of an existing record or we are
//          appending a new record.
//------------------------------------------------------------------
begin
  if State = dsEdit then
    FTextRecords[FCurRec] := ActiveBuffer
  else
  begin
    // We are inserting (or appending) so we increment our Bookmark
    // counter and store the data.
    Inc(FLastBookmark);
    FTextRecords.InsertObject(FCurRec, ActiveBuffer,
               Pointer(FLastBookmark));
  end;

  // Set a flag that we need to save changes before closing
  FSaveChanges := True;
end;

procedure TFixedAsciiDataset.InternalDelete;
//------------------------------------------------------------------
// Purpose: Mark that we have changed the data so that it will
//          get saved when the table is closed.  Then delete the
//          record. Also, if the record that was deleted was the last
//          record then decrement the current record bookmark value
//          by 1.
//------------------------------------------------------------------
begin
  FTextRecords.Delete(FCurRec);
  if FCurRec >= FTextRecords.Count then Dec(FCurRec);
  FSaveChanges := True;
end;

function TFixedAsciiDataset.GetRecord(Buffer: PChar;
        GetMode: TGetMode; DoCheck: Boolean): TGetResult;
//------------------------------------------------------------------
// Purpose: This multi-purpose function that does 3 jobs.  It retrieves
//          data for the current, prior, or next record.  It returns
//          the status (TGetResult), and if the DoCheck flag is True
//          and an error occurs an exception is raised.
//------------------------------------------------------------------
begin
  if FTextRecords.Count < 1 then
    Result := grEOF
  else begin
    Result := grOK;
    case GetMode of
      gmNext:
        if FCurRec >= RecordCount - 1 then
          Result := grEOF
        else
```

continues

Part
III

Ch
13

Listing 13.6   Continued

```
              Inc(FCurRec);
          gmPrior:
            if FCurRec <= 0 then
              Result := grBOF
            else
              Dec(FCurRec);
          gmCurrent:
            if (FCurRec < 0) or (FCurRec >= RecordCount) then
              Result := grError;
        end;
        if Result = grOK then
        begin
          StrLCopy(Buffer, PChar(FTextRecords[FCurRec]), FRecBufSize);
          with PRecInfo(Buffer + FRecInfoOfs)^ do
          begin
            BookmarkFlag := bfCurrent;
            Bookmark := Integer(FTextRecords.Objects[FCurRec]);
          end;
        end else
          if (Result = grError) and DoCheck then
              DatabaseError('No Records');
      end;
    end;
```

Field Management

The field management routines are composed of the following two methods—GetFieldData and SetFieldData.

The GetFieldData method is passed a TField object and a buffer pointer. Based on the TField object's FieldNo and DataType values, the GetFieldData method extracts the field's raw data from the current record buffer and passes it back in the provided buffer. When the requested field's data is put in the outgoing buffer, it first must be converted (if necessary) to the universal data format types that are expected by TDataSet and the various TField descendants that represent the data. Table 13.3 shows both the universal formats required by TDataSet but also the text formats that are used by the TFixedAsciiDataSet component.

The SetFieldData method does the opposite task of GetFieldData. It, too, receives a TField object and a buffer pointer. But in this case, the buffer contains data (in the appropriate universal format) to be stored in the current record, based on the specified TField object information. The SetFieldData method converted the buffer data into an appropriate string representation to be inserted into the current record buffer. Again, refer to the universal formats listed in Table 13.3 to understand the conversions. The code also is very enlightening in understanding the conversion process.

NOTE Of all the TDataSet's methods that need overridden, GetFieldData and SetFieldData are the most tricky to get working correctly because of the data conversions that need to take place. Take extra care when writing these methods in your custom dataset. ■

Table 13.3 Universal Data Formats Used by *GetFieldData* and *SetFieldData*

Field Type	Universal Data Format Representation	*TFixedAsciiDataset* String
ftString	PChar string buffer	Extract characters up to nil
ftFloat	Ptr to 8-byte Double	Floating-point string
ftInteger	Ptr to 4-byte Integer	Integer string
ftBoolean	Ptr to 2-byte WordBool False - 0 True - <> 0	T or F string
ftDate	Ptr to 4-byte Integer # Days since 1/1/0001+1	Date string
ftTime	Ptr to 4-byte Integer Milliseconds since midnight	Time string
ftDateTime	Ptr to 8-byte Double	Datetime string Milliseconds since 1/1/0001+1

Listing 13.7 ASCIIDRV.PAS—The *TFixedAsciiDataSet* Component's Field Management Routines

```
function TFixedAsciiDataset.GetFieldData(Field: TField;
        Buffer: Pointer): Boolean;
//-------------------------------------------------------------
// Purpose: Copy the data from the record buffer into a field's
//          buffer.
//-------------------------------------------------------------
var
  FieldAddrInBuffer : Pointer;
  FieldText : String;

  function AsciiDateTimeToDateTime(DateTimeStr : String): Double;
  const
    TimeDelta : Double = 0;
  var
    AM_PM_Pos : Byte;
  begin
    AM_PM_Pos := AnsiPos('M', AnsiUpperCase(DateTimeStr)) - 1;
    if AM_PM_Pos > 0 then
```

continues

Part
III

Ch
13

Listing 13.7   Continued

```
    begin
      if UpCase(DateTimeStr[AM_PM_Pos]) = 'P' then
          TimeDelta := 0.5; // Convert to military time; add 12 hours
        DateTimeStr := Trim(Copy(DateTimeStr, 1, AM_PM_Pos - 1));
      end;
      Result := TimeStampToMSecs(DateTimeToTimeStamp(
                StrToDateTime(DateTimeStr) + TimeDelta));
    end;

begin
  Result := False;
  if IsEmpty or (Field.FieldNo < 1) then Exit;
//if Field.FieldNo = 0 then Showmessage('Field.Name');
  with Field, PFieldInfo(FFieldInfo[FieldNo - 1])^ do
  try
    FieldAddrInBuffer := Pointer(Integer(ActiveBuffer) + FieldOfs - 1);

    // Extract the textual field value from the buffer.
    FieldText := '';
    SetLength(FieldText, FieldSize + 1);
    StrLCopy(PChar(FieldText), FieldAddrInBuffer, FieldSize);
    FieldText := Trim(FieldText);

    if Length(TrimRight(FieldText)) = 0 then Exit;

  // Perform field conversion/transfer to the out going buffer.
    case Field.DataType of
      ftString:   StrLCopy(Buffer, FieldAddrInBuffer, FieldSize);
      ftFloat:    Double(Buffer^) := StrToFloat(FieldText);
      ftInteger:  Longint(Buffer^) := SysUtils.StrToInt(FieldText);
      ftBoolean:  WordBool(Buffer^) := FieldText[1] = 'T';
      ftDate:     Longint(Buffer^) :=
                  DateTimeToTimeStamp(StrToDate(FieldText)).Date;
      ftTime:     Longint(Buffer^) :=
                  DateTimeToTimeStamp(StrToTime(FieldText)).Time;
      ftDateTime: Double(Buffer^) := AsciiDateTimeToDateTime(FieldText);
    end;
  except
    // If a conversion error occurs it is probably due to a blank or
    // corrupt field value in the text file.  In either case Return a
    // value of False to indicate that the field contains a Null
    // value. The Result variable is set to False above.
  end;

  // Everything went OK, so return a result of true.
  Result := True;
end;


procedure TFixedAsciiDataset.SetFieldData(Field: TField;
          Buffer: Pointer);
```

```
//-------------------------------------------------------------------
// Purpose: Copy the data from a field's buffer into the appropriate
//          location within the record buffer.
//-------------------------------------------------------------------

  function RightJustify(const Str : String; Size : Integer): String;
  //-----------------------------------------------------------------
  // Purpose: Pad the given string with sufficient spaces to right
  //          justify it within the result string of the given size.
  //-----------------------------------------------------------------
  begin
    SetLength(Result, Size);
    FillMemory(Pointer(Result), Size, ORD(' '));
    Result := Result + Str;
    Result := Copy(Result, Length(Result) - Size + 1, Size);
  end;

const
  TrueText : PChar = 'T';
  FalseText : PChar = 'F';
var
  FieldAddrInBuffer : Pointer;
  TempStr : String;
  StrSize : Integer;
  TimeStamp :TTimeStamp;
begin
  if Field.FieldNo < 0 then Exit;

  with Field, PFieldInfo(FFieldInfo[FieldNo - 1])^ do
  try
    FieldAddrInBuffer := Pointer(Integer(ActiveBuffer) + FieldOfs - 1);
    FillMemory(FieldAddrInBuffer, FieldSize, ORD(' ')); // Clear field
    case DataType of
      ftString:
        begin
          StrSize := StrLen(Buffer);
          if StrSize > FieldSize then StrSize := FieldSize;
          MoveMemory(FieldAddrInBuffer, Buffer, StrSize);
        end;
      ftBoolean:
        if WordBool(Buffer^) then
          MoveMemory(FieldAddrInBuffer, TrueText, FieldSize)
        else
          MoveMemory(FieldAddrInBuffer, FalseText, FieldSize);
      ftInteger:
        begin
          TempStr := RightJustify(IntToStr(Longint(Buffer^)),
                     FieldSize);
          MoveMemory(FieldAddrInBuffer, Pointer(TempStr), FieldSize);
        end;
      ftFloat:
        begin
          TempStr := RightJustify(FloatToStr(Double(Buffer^)),
                     FieldSize);
```

continues

Listing 13.7   Continued

```
                MoveMemory(FieldAddrInBuffer, Pointer(TempStr), FieldSize);
            end;
        ftDate:
          begin
            TimeStamp.Time := 0;
            TimeStamp.Date := Longint(Buffer^);
            TempStr := DateTimeToStr( TimeStampToDateTime(TimeStamp) );
            MoveMemory(FieldAddrInBuffer, Pointer(TempStr), FieldSize);
          end;
        ftTime:
          begin
            TimeStamp.Time := Longint(Buffer^);
            TimeStamp.Date := 0;
            TempStr := DateTimeToStr( TimeStampToDateTime(TimeStamp) );
            MoveMemory(FieldAddrInBuffer, Pointer(TempStr), FieldSize);
          end;
        ftDateTime:
          begin
            TempStr := FormatDateTime(ShortDateFormat + ' ' +
                       ShortTimeFormat, TimeStampToDateTime(
                       MSecsToTimeStamp(Double(Buffer^))));
            MoveMemory(FieldAddrInBuffer, Pointer(TempStr),
                       Length(TempStr));
          end;
      end;
    except
      Abort;
    end;

    DataEvent(deFieldChange, Longint(Field));
  end;
```

Navigation Management

TDataSet has special needs to go (at times) to the very first or last records in the dataset.
These special navigational routines are called InternalFirst and InternalLast and are shown
in Listing 13.8. The InternalFirst method simply sets the current record value (FCurRec) to
one less than the first record, which is –1. The InternalLast method, on the other hand, sets
the current record value to FTextRecords.Count, which is one more than the last record value.
The reason for this is to simulate what is referred to as *crack behavior*. Cracks are used to
determine when a dataset is at the beginning or end of a file. Crack behavior is accounted
for in the Resync method of TDataSet.

> **Listing 13.8   ASCIIDRV.PAS—The *TFixedAsciiDataSet* Component's Navigation Management Routines**

```
procedure TFixedAsciiDataset.InternalFirst;
//-----------------------------------------------------------------
// Purpose: Crack behavior is required here.  That is we must
//          position to a special place *before* the first record.
//          Otherwise, we will actually end up on the second record
//          after Resync is called.
//-----------------------------------------------------------------
begin
  FCurRec := -1;
end;

procedure TFixedAsciiDataset.InternalLast;
//-----------------------------------------------------------------
// Purpose: Crack behavior required here as above. FTextRecords.Count
//          is one greater than the largest valid value of FCurRec.
//-----------------------------------------------------------------
begin
  FCurRec := FTextRecords.Count;
end;
```

Exception-Handling Routine

The final TDataSet method to look at is InternalHandleException, which is called when an error occurs during the streaming in of the TDataSet component at designtime. The TFixedAsciiDataSet example simply passes the exceptions up to Delphi's default exception handler, as you can see in Listing 13.9.

> **Listing 13.9   ASCIIDRV.PAS—Shows the *TFixedAsciiDataSet* Component's Exception-Handling Routine**

```
procedure TFixedAsciiDataset.InternalHandleException;
begin
  Application.HandleException(Self);
end;
```

Part
III

Ch
13

Putting It All Together

On the CD

Now you have seen everything that makes up a custom dataset in Delphi 3. To see the entire source file for the TFixedAsciiDataSet component, load the file ASCIIDRV.PAS. The only part not discussed yet is how to make TFixedAsciiDataSet a component that you can add to the Delphi Component palette.

First, you need to add a special `Register` procedure that Delphi calls when the component's package is loaded in Delphi. Listing 13.10 shows the Register procedure used in our example.

Listing 13.10 \UDELPHI3\CHP13\ASCIIDRV.PAS—Register Procedure to Add the *TFixedAsciiDataSet* to Delphi's Component Palette

```
procedure Register;

implementation

uses SysUtils, Forms, Dialogs;

procedure Register;
begin
  RegisterComponents('UDelphi3', [Asciidrv.TFixedAsciiDataset]);
end;
```

Now that the Register function is implemented, you can build the component package for the ASCII driver component. Take the following steps to create and install your component package:

1. Select File, Close All, and save any open projects.
2. Select File, New, and then click the Package icon.
3. When the New Package Dialog is displayed, type the path to your Delphi 3 Bin directory (such as \PROGRAM FILES\BORLAND\DELPHI 3\BIN), followed by the following file name, **ASCDRV30**.
4. In the Description edit box, type **UD3 Chapter 13 - Custom DataSet Example**.
5. Select OK.
6. In the next dialog box, press the Add button at the top to add the ASCIIDRV.PAS component file. (The default directory is \UDELPHI3\CHP13\ASCIIDRV.PAS.)
7. Select the Requires Tab and again press the Add button at the top to add a required package. When the dialog appears on-screen, type the following package name, **VCLDB30**. Note: The VCL30 package is installed by default.
8. Select the Install button (the rightmost button).
9. Press Ctrl+F4 to close out of the Package dialog box.

You now should be able to create a new project and go to the **UDelphi3** tab on Delphi's Component Palette and drop a `TFixedAsciiDataSet` component on your form. I also included the test project I used to test the ASCII driver. To see `TFixedAsciiDataSet` in action, load the following project \UDELPHI3\CHP13\CUSTOMDB.DPR into Delphi 3.

Although it seems like a lot of methods to implement to get a custom dataset going, when broken down into their function groups, they are easily digestible. There is more functionality for custom datasets that can be implemented. What was done in this chapter brings to light the bare minimal functionality that must be implemented to get a custom dataset up and running. Now you have a working model to expand as you want for your needs. ●

CHAPTER 14

Building Multi-Tier Applications

by Roland Bouchereau

The growth of COM, OLE, the Internet/intranet, and the synergy between them, has stimulated the Windows development arena. Of particular interest are multi-tier and distributed thin-client database applications. You, like many Windows developers, are looking for ways to exploit or, at least implement, these solutions for yourself or for your customers. Delphi provides three new components that, together with the familiar set of data access components, afford you the means to easily implement thin-client, multi-tier database applications. ■

ClientDataSets

How to populate and track changes made to a ClientDataSet component.

Providers

How to use a Provider component to both furnish data to and apply data received from a ClientDataSet.

RemoteServers

How to use a RemoteServer component to connect ClientDataSets on client applications to Providers on the application server.

Understanding the ClientDataSet, Provider, and RemoteServer Components

The multi-tier application model typically implements three layers: a thin client-side program, an application server, and a DBMS server. This chapter is confined to the creation of programs residing at the first two layers. (How many people do you know write whole DBMS servers for a living?) A thin-client application is one with a small footprint. To better support thin-client applications, the ClientDataSet component was introduced in Delphi 3. If, for example, you create a conventional database application in Delphi using Tables, Queries, and StoredProcs, this application would require the installation and use of the Borland Database Engine (BDE). The dependency on the relatively large footprint BDE is removed when you build an application by using just ClientDataSet components.

In place of the BDE, you only need a single DLL—DBCLIENT.DLL—for a client application to use ClientDataSets. This DLL houses the implementation of the IDSBase and IDSCursor COM interfaces. (All three of the components discussed in this chapter either use or encapsulate COM interfaces.) These two interfaces and another, IProvider, were created expressly for the development of multi-tier database applications. Also, ClientDataSets are stored entirely in memory and have no direct relation to persistent objects such as tables or views. The connection to the originating data is defined by you, either at design time or at runtime.

The ClientDataSet component is a direct descendant of the reworked DataSet component. In many respects, therefore, the functionality of the ClientDataSet component is identical to that of its cousin, the Table component. With some key exceptions, any operation performed against or with a Table can be similarly performed against a ClientDataSet. Moreover, ClientDataSets support a form of in-memory index and the same filtering and searching features as Tables do. A benefit of ClientDataSets is that because all the searching, indexing, and filtering mechanisms operate on data residing in memory, methods such as `AddIndex` and `Locate` and the `Filter` and `Filtered` properties perform quickly.

ClientDataSets are initially empty, void of structure and data. You must provide them with structure and data. You usually accomplish this by using an IProvider interface obtained from the application server. You use a Provider component residing on the application server to furnish this interface. The two programs are connected through the use of the third new component, the RemoteServer, which resides on the client application. Although many ClientDataSets may be needed for the client application, you need use only one RemoteServer component for each application server.

Working with these components requires that you employ a copy-modify-apply methodology, similar to the manner in which the CachedUpdates mechanism operates. First, ClientDataSets are populated with data or metadata from the application server. After changes are made to the ClientDataSet, a small datastream referred to as the *Delta* is sent back to the Provider on the application server, which in turn applies those changes to the originating Table or Query.

Although not a strict requirement, you usually will implement the data transfer mechanism by using OLE Automation. This implementation is relatively simple to accomplish because Automation servers intrinsically support COM/DCOM. If, however, you want to avoid OLE, you can send the data to and from the client application by using any technique you like. Mail slots, named pipes, sockets, and memory-mapped files are all viable transport mechanisms.

Connecting Client Applications to Application Servers

Although RemoteServer components reside on the client application, they provide the conceptual pipeline between which ClientDataSets and Providers transfer data.

```
TRemoteServer = class(TCustomRemoteServer)
...
public
  function GetProvider(const ProviderName: string): IProvider; override;
published
  property ComputerName: string ...;
  property Connected: Boolean ...;
  property ServerName: string ...;
  Beforeproperty AfterConnect: TNotifyEvent ...;
  Beforeproperty AfterDisconnect: TNotifyEvent ...;
end;
```

You connect a RemoteServer component to an application server by specifying the application name and possibly its location. The ServerName property, which is blank by default, identifies the name of the application server. This name typically is the prog ID of an OLE Automation server that will provide access to an IProvider interface. The optional ComputerName property identifies the computer on which the application server resides. Assign a value to this property when the application server actually resides on a separate computer.

After you set ServerName and ComputerName, connect to the application server by assigning True to the Connected property. Once connected, you can obtain an IProvider interface by executing the GetProvider method. GetProvider takes one string argument, ProviderName, that indicates the name of the OLE Automation property that yields an IProvider interface.

Also, the RemoteServer component has two event handlers, OnConnect and OnDisconnect, that fire after connecting and disconnecting with the application server, respectively.

Populating ClientDataSets

As previously mentioned, ClientDataSets are initially void, without structure or content. You must derive the structure (metadata) from a Table or Query, or build it yourself. Either implicitly or explicitly, it is an IProvider interface that obtains a datastream from an application server. The code in Listing 14.1 is a direct excerpt from STDVCL.PAS, the unit in which the IProvider interface is declared.

Part
III

Ch
14

Listing 14.1   Excerpt of STDVCL.PAS—The IProvider Interface Declaration

```
IProvider = interface(IDispatch)
  function Get_Data: OleVariant; safecall;
  function ApplyUpdates(Delta: OleVariant; MaxErrors: Integer;
    out ErrorCount: Integer): OleVariant; safecall;
  function GetMetaData: OleVariant; safecall;
  function GetRecords(Count: Integer; out RecsOut: Integer): OleVariant;
    safecall;
  function DataRequest(Input: OleVariant): OleVariant; safecall;
  function Get_Constraints: WordBool; safecall;
  procedure Set_Constraints(Value: WordBool); safecall;
  procedure Reset; safecall;
  procedure SetParams (Values: OleVariant); safecall;
  property Data: OleVariant read Get_Data;
  property Constraints: WordBool read Get_Constraints write Set_Constraints;
end;
```

Coupling with a RemoteServer Component

By pointing the ClientDataSet's RemoteServer property to an actual RemoteServer component and specifying a ProviderName, you then can populate a ClientDataSet automatically by calling the Open method or setting the Active property to True.

```
TClientDataSet = class(TDataSet)
...
published
  property ProviderName: string ...;
  property RemoteServer: TCustomRemoteServer ...;
...
end;
```

Populating a ClientDataSet in this manner causes the following actions to occur:

1. The associated RemoteServer connects with the application server (if it isn't already connected).

2. An IProvider interface is obtained by invocation of the GetProvider method, with the ClientDataSet's ProviderName property as an argument.

3. The IProvider interface is assigned to the ClientDataSet's Provider property.

4. A datastream is obtained as an OleVariant from the IProvider.GetRecords method.

5. The datastream is placed into the ClientDataSet via AppendData.

Coupling a ClientDataSet with RemoteServer components is the most common manner in which you build and populate a ClientDataSet.

Using the Provider Property Explicitly

The Provider and ClientDataSet components, as well as descendants of DBDataSet, each have an IProvider property, referred to simply as Provider.

```
TClientDataSet = class(TDataSet)
```

```
...
public
  property Provider: IProvider ...;
...
end;

TDBDataSet = class(TBDEDataSet)
...
public
  property Provider: IProvider ...;
...
end;

TProvider = class(TCustomProvider)
...
public
  property Provider: IProvider ...;
...
end;
```

The Provider property on all these components has public access, but is read-only in the case of the Provider component and DBDataSet descendants, such as Tables and Queries. Before the Provider component's Provider property can be used, the component must be associated with a DBDataSet.

```
TProvider = class(TCustomProvider)
...
  published
    property DataSet: TDBDataSet ...;
...
end;
```

To associate a DBDataSet with a Provider, point the Provider's DataSet property to a Table or Query. The following code indicates to Provider1 that Table1 is the source DBDataSet for the datastream:

```
Provider1.DataSet := Table1;
```

While the Provider component implements the IProvider interface, the use of a Provider is not absolutely required. However, you probably will want to make use of one to better control the application server, particularly if you choose COM for your tiered infrastructure.

CAUTION

If you decide to avoid the explicit use of the Provider component in your application server, you must manually include the BDEProv unit in the uses clause of the unit in question. Failing to do so probably will cause your application to cause an access violation because, without this unit, instances of IProvider cannot be manufactured, and any reference to the Provider property of a component will yield nil.

Part
III

Ch
14

After you have obtained and assigned a valid IProvider interface, the ClientDataSet is populated automatically by executing the Open method, just as if a RemoteServer had been connected:

```
ClientDataSet.Provider := Table.Provider;
ClientDataSet.Open;
```

Obtaining an IProvider interface in this manner is the technique employed in many of the code examples accompanying this chapter.

N O T E   Although the Provider and DBDataSet components are intended for use on the application server, many of the samples discussed in this chapter employ them in the same project as the ClientDataSet. This is done in the interest of simplicity. ▪

By default, after you furnish an IProvider interface to a ClientDataSet and open the ClientDataSet, all records from the originating DBDataSet are copied. This may be a prohibitive operation because of table size or narrow bandwidth between the client application and the application server. To alleviate this, you can set a filter or range on the originating DBDataSet. However, using filters and ranges offers an inexact means of governing the number of fetched rows:

```
TClientDataSet = class(TDataSet)
...
public
  function GetNextPacket: Integer;
...
published
  property FetchOnDemand: Boolean ... default True;
  property PacketRecords: Integer ... default -1;
...
end;
```

Use the FetchOnDemand property to determine whether data is fetched automatically. When set to True, the default setting, data is retrieved from the IProvider interface automatically when the ClientDataSet is opened and as you navigate through it. If you want to control when the data is fetched, set FetchOnDemand to False and execute the GetNextPacket method to retrieve unfetched rows. When the last record is fetched from the originating DBDataSet, GetNextPacket will return a value less than the value specified by the PacketRecords property.

Whether done automatically by the component or explicitly by you, the number of rows fetched at a time is governed by the PacketRecords property. Specifying –1 for PacketRecords causes all rows to be fetched into the ClientDataSet. Setting PacketRecords to 0 causes only metadata to be retrieved. This is analogous to calling the IProvider.GetMetaData method. Any positive value will limit the number of rows fetched at a time to the value specified. The sample unit PACKETSAMPLE.PAS illustrates the uses of FetchOnDemand, PacketRecords, and GetNextPacket.

Using the *Data* Property and the *Get_Data* Method

The Data property on both ClientDataSets and IProvider interfaces encapsulates a datastream and is surfaced as an OleVariant type, as follows:

```
TClientDataSet = class(TDataSet)
...
public
    property Data: OleVariant ...;
...
end;

TProvider = class(TCustomProvider)
...
public
  property Data: OleVariant ...;
...
end;
```

You can populate ClientDataSets by assigning a value to the Data property provided the value assigned represents a valid datastream. This method retrieves all records from the dataset, regardless of the current value of PacketRecords. You can populate a ClientDataSet by simply assigning to its Data property, as in the following example:

```
ClientDataSet.Data := Table.Provider.Data;
```

Additionally, by assigning Null to the Data property, you can restore a ClientDataSet to its unpopulated or "virgin" state. For Provider components, accessing the Data property is identical to calling the IProvider.Get_Data method. The Provider component also implements a Get_Data method, but it is hidden in the protected section of its definition.

Fetching Groups of Rows from a DBDataSet

At the heart of all the record-fetching routines, the IProvider interface implements the GetRecords method, as shown in the following example:

```
TProvider = class(TCustomProvider)
...
public
  function GetRecords(Count: Integer; out RecsOut: Integer):
  ➡              OleVariant; override;
  procedure Reset; ...
...
end;
```

Taking two simple arguments (a *count* parameter, specifying the number of rows to fetch, and an *out* parameter, used to indicate the actual number of records fetched), GetRecords returns an OleVariant that contains, at most, the number of rows requested. You can pass a zero for the count parameter to fetch a datastream that contains only metadata. This is the exact manner in which the IProvider.GetMetaData method operates. The GetData method does the

Part

III

Ch

14

same, but with a count parameter of –1. This, of course, causes all rows to be retrieved. If you use the GetRecords method directly, use the ClientDataSet.AppendData method in the client application to append the newly retrieved rows. This is essentially the way in which the GetNextPacket method functions. The AppendData method is declared as follows:

```
TClientDataSet = class(TDataSet)
...
public
  procedure AppendData(Data: OleVariant; HitEOF: Boolean);
...
end;
```

GetRecord's second parameter, HitEOF, informs the ClientDataSet that the last group of records has been appended—that EOF has been reached, in a manner of speaking. Note that if you assign the datastream OleVariant to the ClientDataSet's Data property, you will replace, rather than add, any rows already in the ClientDataSet. Finally, use the Reset method to cause the Provider to restart its fetching from the first record of the associated DBDataSet.

In response to any attempt to retrieve data from the Provider, an OnGetData event is executed, if present. The following excerpt shows the declaration of OnGetData event in the Provider component:

```
TProviderDataEvent = procedure(DataSet: TClientDataSet) of object;
TProvider = class(TCustomProvider)
...
published
  property OnGetData: TProviderDataEvent ...;
end;
```

Whether invoked explicitly or indirectly, the GetRecords method will invoke the OnGetData event handler just after successful retrieval of the requested records.

Implementing a Custom Retrieval Technique by Using the *DataRequest* Method

The DataRequest method is implemented in both the IProvider interface and the Provider component. DataRequest is intended to be used as a somewhat generic method for communicating with the Provider component on the application server. In response to the invocation of the DataRequest method, the Provider's OnDataRequest event handler is fired. No action other than to invoke the event handler is taken.

```
TDataRequestEvent = function(Sender: TObject; Input: OleVariant):
    OleVariant of object;
TProvider = class(TCustomProvider)
...
published
  property OnDataRequest: TDataRequestEvent ...;
end;
```

NOTE   The OnDataRequest event handler is peculiar in that it is one of only two VCL events that
        is implemented as a function. This does violate the contractless programming rule upon
which the VCL event mechanism is based. This is an important point to remember! If you decide to
specify your own OnDataRequest event handler, you *must* return a value. ■

Besides the ubiquitous Sender parameter, the OnDataRequest event handler receives an
OleVariant parameter, aptly named Input. What is contained in this parameter is solely up to
you. Likewise, you decide on the content of the return value. If a return value is meaningless in
your implementation, return Null.

Using Streams and Files

ClientDataSets implement methods mirroring the loading and saving routines that have always
been available to the TStrings class. With the methods LoadFromFile, LoadFromStream,
SaveToFile, and SaveToStream you now can save and load ClientDataSet datastreams to and
from files and streams in the familiar fashion:

```
TClientDataSet = class(TDataSet)
...
public
    procedure LoadFromFile(const FileName: string);
    procedure LoadFromStream(Stream: TStream);
    procedure SaveToFile(const FileName: string);
    procedure SaveToStream(Stream: TStream);
...
end;
```

The Load methods operate directly on the OleVariant ClientDataSet.Data property. Internally,
they create an empty variant array, lock it via the VarArrayLock function, read the stream (or
file) into the resulting byte array, and finally unlock the variant array.

Listing 14.2, extracted from LOADSAVESAMPLE.PAS, makes use of both the SaveToFile and
LoadFromFile methods.

**Listing 14.2   LOADSAVESAMPLE.PAS—Saving and Loading a ClientDataSet
Datastream with *SaveToFile* and *LoadFromFile***

```
procedure TLoadSaveSampleForm.SaveItemClick(Sender: TObject);
begin
  if SaveDialog.Execute then begin
    ClientDataSet.SaveToFile(SaveDialog.FileName);
    ClientDataSet.Data := Null;
    ClientDataSet.IndexName := '';
    SaveItem.Enabled := False;
    LoadItem.Enabled := True
  end
end;

procedure TLoadSaveSampleForm.LoadItemClick(Sender: TObject);
```

Part
III

Ch
14

continues

Listing 14.2   Continued

```
begin
  with ClientDataSet do begin
    LoadFromFile(SaveDialog.FileName);
    AddIndex('CustNo', 'CustNo', [ixPrimary]);
    AddIndex('ByCompany', 'Company', [ixCaseInsensitive]);
    IndexName := 'ByCompany'
  end;
  SaveItem.Enabled := True;
  LoadItem.Enabled := False
end;
```

Note that in the preceding code the IndexName property is cleared after saving the datastream to file and the indices re-created after reloading the datastream. This is necessary because these properties are not written to the file or stream. Before populating a ClientDataSet, make sure that references to entities such as fields and indices are removed. Otherwise, errors that complain of the unknown item will trigger when the ClientDataSet is made active.

> **CAUTION**
>
> Don't confuse the use of a file in the save and load routines with the writing and reading of a table that resides on disk. The format of the datastream used by ClientDataSets is proprietary and completely undocumented. SaveToFile and LoadFromFile are intended for simple uses such as a "Save Work in Progress" feature, certainly not for repeated access to the destination file as is the case with conventional tables.

Although not intended to perform like a Table in this respect, the Load and Save methods afford you a powerful means for transferring datastreams. The LoadFromStream and SaveToStream methods can load and save data using any kind of stream, including streams you create as descendants of the TStream class. With custom stream classes, ClientDataSets can be built and populated with data from across various mediums. For example, a stream type that supports writing and reading to and from a particular URL over a secure connection on the Web could be implemented by overriding as few as four TStream methods.

Using the *CreateDataSet* Method

By using the FieldDefs property, or by creating field components, you can create the structure of a ClientDataSet where none previously existed. After the fields are defined, you only need to call the CreateDataSet method, which is declared as follows:

```
TClientDataSet = class(TDataSet)
...
public
   procedure CreateDataSet;
...
end;
```

Similarly, by building the list of IndexDefs, you also can create indices at the same time. The simplest technique is to first create the field components at design time, and then call the CreateDataSet method early enough to suit your needs. You can create field components at runtime to achieve the same outcome. On this book's companion CD-ROM, the units CREATESAMPLE1.PAS, CREATESAMPLE2.PAS, CREATESAMPLE3.PAS, and their associated form files use these techniques to build a functional ClientDataSet from scratch. Listing 14.3, from CREATESAMPLE3.PAS, illustrates both the creation of fields with FieldDefs and indices with IndexDefs.

Listing 14.3 \UDELPHI\CHP14\CREATESAMPLE3.PAS—Defining a ClientDataSet and Indices with the *FieldDefs* and *IndexDefs* Properties

```
procedure TCreationSampleForm.FormCreate(Sender: TObject);
begin
  with ClientDataSet.FieldDefs do begin
    Add('CustNo', ftFloat, 0, False);
    Add('Company', ftString, 30, False);
    Add('Addr1', ftString, 30, False);
    Add('Addr2', ftString, 30, False);
    Add('City', ftString, 15, False);
    Add('State', ftString, 20, False);
    Add('Zip', ftString, 10, False);
    Add('Country', ftString, 20, False);
    Add('Phone', ftString, 15, False);
    Add('FAX', ftString, 15, False);
    Add('TaxRate', ftFloat, 0, False);
    Add('Contact', ftString, 20, False);
    Add('LastInvoiceDate', ftDateTime, 0, False)
  end;
  with ClientDataSet.IndexDefs do begin
    Add('CustNo', 'CustNo', [ixPrimary]);
    Add('ByCompany', 'Company', [ixCaseInsensitive])
  end;
  ClientDataSet.IndexName := 'CustNo';
  ClientDataSet.CreateDataSet
end;
```

Handling Changes to ClientDataSets

After the ClientDataSet is populated, the client application updates (or permits the user to update) the received data and posts these changes back to the application server. To permit you to track and possibly undo changes, the ClientDataSet component surfaces a number of methods and properties. All the change-tracking features discussed in this section are implemented in the file CHANGETRACKINGSAMPLE.PAS.

Part

III

Ch

14

Tracking Changes

As previously mentioned, changes made to the ClientDataSet are logged to another internal datastream referred to as the delta. You collectively retrieve these changes via the `Delta` property.

```
TUpdateStatus = (usUnmodified, usModified, usInserted, usDeleted);

TClientDataSet = class(TDataSet)
...
public
  function UpdateStatus: TUpdateStatus;
  property ChangeCount: Integer ...;
  property Delta: OleVariant ...;
  property LogChanges: Boolean ...;
...
end;
```

This logging of changes takes place automatically and is active by default. You can turn off logging by setting the `LogChanges` property to False, although doing so obviates the use of the ClientDataSet for real data update. To determine the number of records that have changed, use the `ChangeCount` property.

> **CAUTION**
>
> If you make three separate changes to a record, the ClientDataSet still counts this as one changed record. An insertion or a deletion also counts as only one changed record, regardless of the number of later modifications to the record.

Figure 14.1 shows a ClientDataSet data copy of the Customer.DB table before any modification.

FIG. 14.1

The ClientDataSet copy of Customer.DB, before changes.

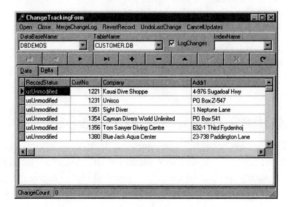

The UpdateStatus method returns an enumeration value of type TUpdateStatus. (This is the same type used to indicate the update status of records when CachedUpdates is active on DBDataSets.) With UpdateStatus, every record in a ClientDataSet can be easily identified as unmodified, modified, or inserted. Although removed from the visible row set, deleted rows do have an UpdateStatus value. You may examine the deleted rows, however, by either copying the delta to another ClientDataSet or by activating a special built-in index. Figure 14.2 illustrates the same ClientDataSet after a single deletion, single insertion, and a single modification. Note the UpdateStatus column, indicating the state of visibly modified rows.

FIG. 14.2
Same ClientDataSet after one insertion, one modification, and one deletion.

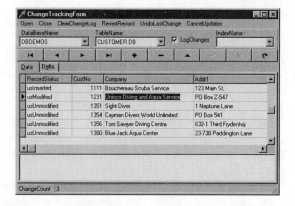

After populating a ClientDataSet, two built-in indices are automatically instantiated. The first index, CHANGEINDEX, allows you to view only records that have changed in some manner. When this index is active, the original version of each changed record appears, as well as a version of that record as it appeared after each change. Again, setting the active index to CHANGEINDEX is the only means you have to inspect records whose UpdateStatus is usDeleted. The other index, DEFAULT_ORDER, yields a normal view of the record set, with the latest changes and in natural order. Figure 14.3 shows the same ClientDataSet as before, but with the CHANGEINDEX index active.

FIG. 14.3
The same ClientDataSet, with the CHANGEINDEX index active.

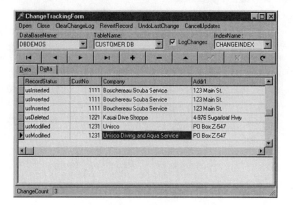

Restoring Changes

Three methods exist for the purpose of restoring changes made to ClientDataSet. These are CancelUpdates, RevertRecord, and UndoLastChange. An excerpt from DBCLIENT.PAS follows, which declares each of these methods:

```
TClientDataSet = class(TDataSet)
...
public
  procedure CancelUpdates;
  procedure RevertRecord;
  function UndoLastChange(FollowChange: Boolean): Boolean;
...
end;
```

Using these methods (or making them available to the user) is particularly important because retrieving a "clean" row set from the application server is a comparatively costly operation in terms of cycles and possibly bandwidth. You can undo the last change to the most recently modified record by calling the UndoLastChange method. Canceling the last change in this manner doesn't necessarily restore a record to its initial condition, but to its condition before the most recent change. For example, if a record is inserted into a ClientDataSet and this record is later deleted, calling UndoLastChange once restores the record, and calling it a second time removes it, because it initially did not exist. The effect on records that were modified multiple times is similar. With each call, UndoLastChange removes the last version of a record and replaces it with the next most recent version. Therefore, you can implement a simple historical undo feature for your client application. UndoLastChange takes a single Boolean parameter, FollowChange, which determines whether the record pointer is moved to the record that is being restored.

You also can restore the original versions of records with the RevertRecord and CancelUpdates methods. CancelUpdates undoes all changes to all records whose changes have been logged. RevertRecord, as the name implies, undoes all changes, but only to the current record. In doing so, the RevertRecord method removes all versions of a changed record from the change log. Also, RevertRecord does nothing to restore deleted records because you cannot position the record pointer to a deleted record.

> **CAUTION**
>
> Turning off LogChanges after modifications are already made has an odd side effect. Further changes go unlogged, as you expect, but the UndoLastChange and CancelUpdates methods do not recognize the changes made, even before LogChanges was turned off. Undoing changes to these records requires that you navigate to each record and execute the RevertRecord method.

Handling Changes

Everything to this point has been preparation. Of the three major steps involved in making a multi-tier system work, only one is left—the actual update of the source data with changes from the client application. Fortunately, this task has been made particularly simple. In the course of the update operation, errors can occur. When they do, you must handle them in some fashion. Again, both the ClientDataSet and Provider components furnish you with methods and events that allow you to govern the actions taken when an update error occurs.

Using the *ApplyUpdates* Method

Although intended to apply ClientDataSet changes, the ClientDataSet and Provider components each implements a different version of the ApplyUpdates method, as follows:

```
TProvider = class(TCustomProvider)
...
public
  function ApplyUpdates(Delta: OleVariant; MaxErrors: Integer;
    out ErrorCount: Integer): OleVariant;
...
end;

TClientDataSet = class(TDataSet)
...
public
  function ApplyUpdates(MaxErrors: Integer): Integer;
  procedure MergeChangeLog;
  function Reconcile(Results: OleVariant): Boolean;
...
end;
```

Examining the Provider's ApplyUpdates method first, the key argument is the Delta parameter. This is that same Delta obtained from the ClientDataSet. The second integer parameter, MaxErrors, indicates to the Provider the maximum number of errors permitted before aborting the update. The third parameter, ErrorCount, is assigned the actual numbers that occurred before ApplyUpdates returned. Finally, ApplyUpdates returns a subset of the submitted Delta, containing just the records that caused an update error.

Use the ClientDataSet's ApplyUpdates method only if an IProvider interface was assigned to its Provider property. You may have accomplished this explicitly via direct assignment or by connecting the ClientDataSet to a RemoteServer component. The ClientDataSet.ApplyUpdates method ultimately invokes the Provider's ApplyUpdates through its IProvider interface. Also, the ClientDataSet's ApplyUpdates method simply takes only one argument (which in turn is passed to the IProvider's method) and returns the number of records that caused update errors.

Part
III

Ch

14

Other than the difference in arguments and return types, a key difference exists between the manner in which the two versions of ApplyUpdates operate. Executing ClientDataSet's ApplyUpdates automatically invokes the ClientDataSet.Reconcile method. If no errors occurred during the execution of ApplyUpdates, then Reconcile calls the ClearChangeLog method to empty the ClientDataSet's delta. Errors are bound to occur sometime.

Handling Update Errors with *OnUpdateError*

You have two opportunities to handle update failures (if a record modified via the ClientDataSet has been otherwise altered or deleted in the interim, for example). The first is on the application server, using the Provider component's OnUpdateError event, as follows:

```
TUpdateKind = (ukModify, ukInsert, ukDelete);
TResolverResponse = (rrSkip, rrAbort, rrMerge, rrApply, rrIgnore);
TResolverErrorEvent = procedure(DataSet: TClientDataSet; E: EUpdateError;
  UpdateKind: TUpdateKind; var Response: TResolverResponse) of object;
TProvider = class(TCustomProvider)
...
published
  property OnUpdateError: TResolverErrorEvent ...;
...
end;
```

Use an OnUpdateError event handler if you want control at the moment that an update problem is encountered. This event fires once for each record that causes an update failure. The event handler is passed four parameters. The first, ClientDataSet, refers to a ClientDataSet that contains as many as three images of the errant record. Access the record's original values by using each field's OldValue property, the current conflicting value by using the CurValue, and the values retrieved from the client application by using NewValue.

The second parameter passed to the OnUpdateError event handler is a reference to the exception that occurred when the update was attempted. The third parameter indicates the type of update attempted. With the last parameter, you can instruct the Provider what action to take in response to the error. Do this by assigning one of five values to the var parameter Response.

Table 14.1—Possible Values for Response Parameter

Response Value	Effect
rrSkip	The problem record is bypassed; record processing continues. The changed record remains in the Delta.
rrAbort	The entire update operation is canceled with no records processed further. All unprocessed records remain in the Delta.
rrMerge	The changed record is merged with the record in the destination table and removed from the Delta.

Response Value	Effect
rrApply	The current record is overwritten with new values. The changed record is removed from the `Delta`.
rrIgnore	The problem record is bypassed; record processing continues. The changed record is removed from the Delta.

Upon entry to `OnUpdateError`, `Response` will have a preset value of rrAbort if the `ApplyUpdates` MaxErrors parameter was 0, and a value of rrSkip if MaxErrors is greater than zero.

After updates are complete, or aborted, the client application should completely validate or invalidate the ClientDataSet datastream. If you want to retain the changes made to the ClientDataSet, then call its `MergeChangeLog` method. Doing so will set ChangeCount to zero and empty the ClientDataSet's delta datastream, but leaves the data otherwise untouched. As previously mentioned, assigning `Null` to the `ClientDataSet.Data` property will empty the ClientDataSet of data and structure. You may do this, and later repopulate the ClientDataSet with a new datastream from the application server.

Handling Update Errors with *OnReconcileError*

Your second opportunity to handle update errors is when the `Reconcile` method is invoked in the client application. You may assign an event handler to the ClientDataSet's `OnReconcileError` event property, as follows:

```
TReconcileAction = (raSkip, raAbort, raMerge, raCorrect, raCancel, raRefresh);
TReconcileErrorEvent = procedure(DataSet: TClientDataSet; E: EReconcileError;
  UpdateKind: TUpdateKind; var Action: TReconcileAction) of object;
TClientDataSet = class(TDataSet)
...
published
  property OnReconcileError: TReconcileErrorEvent ...;
...
end;
```

This event fires once for each record that was not posted on the application server. The parameters closely mirror those in the `Provider.OnUpdateError` event. Similarly, the `Action` parameter can receive one of six possible values, as shown in Table 14.2.

Table 14.2 Possible Values for the Action Parameter

Response Value	Effect
raSkip	The problem record is bypassed; record processing continues. The changed record remains in the Delta.
raAbort	Aborts the Reconcile operation. All unprocessed records remain in the Delta.

continues

Table 14.2 Continued

Response Value	Effect
raMerge	The changed record is merged with the original record image and removed from the Delta.
raCorrect	The changed record is overwritten with new values and removed from the Delta.
raCancel	No change is made to the original record. The changed record is removed from the Delta.
raRefresh	The original record is restored. The changed record is removed from the Delta.

Upon entry to OnReconcileError, Action will have a value of raAbort if the ApplyUpdates method was aborted, and a value of raSkip otherwise. The Reconcile method returns a True value if all records were either posted, reconciled, or both. Also, the ChangeCount has a value of zero and Delta has a value of Null.

Summary

This chapter introduced you to multi-tier application development with Delphi. You learned how to populate a ClientDataSet, both with and without the interaction of an IProvider interface. You saw how to identify, capture, and undo changes made to a ClientDataSet. You also learned how to apply and reconcile these changes in both the client and server applications. These are the ABCs to writing multi-tier applications in Delphi.

Finally, you should examine the sample projects CLNTPROJ.DPR and SERVER.DPR that ship with Delphi. These two projects implement both the client and application server layers in a simple multi-tier application. Together, they form the rudiments for a COM/OLE Automation-based multi-tier implementation. ●

Component Development

CHAPTER 15

Working with Packages

by Eric Uber

I f you've been around computers long enough to have
written MS-DOS programs (remember MS-DOS?), you
know that although DOS provides basic services for accessing disks, the video display, and so on, that's about
the extent of the support that you get for your applications. If you want to write a DOS application with pop-up
menus, for example, you either have to write the menu
code or get it from another programmer. In either case,
this code becomes part of the application; if you later
write another application using the same user interface,
you also have to include the code in that application.
Wouldn't it be nice if you could somehow share the code
among applications? At least, it would reduce the disk
space occupied by your software.

Even if you could share the code among your applications,
what about other programs? The menu interface in *your*
application is probably at least a little different from the
menu interface in *my* application, and the subtle differences between the two probably will drive someone up
the wall who tries to use both applications.

The Windows environment addresses both of these diffi-
culties. First, most of the functionality for menus and
other user interface features, as well as system-related
operations, is built into the system, so you don't have to
redundantly include the same code over and over again in
your applications. Second, because only one copy of the
basic user interface code exists in the system, all

Using packages

Learn what packages are all about
and whether or not they're right for
your application.

Installing packages

Install components and other packages to extend and customize both
the Delphi environment and the
applications you write.

Building packages

Build your own packages, for use in
your applications or to distribute to
other Delphi developers.

applications using this code can present a common, standardized interface to the user. (Of course, many applications don't follow the rules—Windows doesn't *force* a developer to comply with its standard user interface.)

In order to provide this common functionality to multiple applications, Windows uses *Dynamic Link Libraries* (DLLs). These files are code modules that can be shared by different applications running at the same time. Besides making use of the DLLs comprising the basic Windows operating system functions, application developers have the ability to create specialized DLLs to be used by their own applications.

Like other application development environments, early versions of Delphi provided developers with the ability to write their own DLLs. However, there were significant limitations—the biggest was that the standard VCL components were not designed to be accessible across module boundaries. In other words, code in the main application module could not safely access the fields and methods of a component instantiated in a DLL, and vice versa. Another important limitation was that the VCL framework code, which adds 100–200 kilobytes to the size of a Delphi application, would be included in the DLL as well as the main application module, which negates the size reductions gained by placing some of the code in a shared DLL.

In Delphi 3, these limitations are completely gone. Delphi 3 introduces the concept of *packages*. A package is a DLL containing objects, such as VCL components, along with additional information that allows code to be shared among multiple Delphi applications. In this chapter, you learn how to use the standard packages provided with Delphi 3.0 and third-party component vendors in your applications, and also how to create and use your own packages. ■

Why Use Packages?

Why should you consider using packages? Packages have several advantages, but some disadvantages, too. There are no hard and fast rules that apply in every situation, so you have to evaluate the impact of using packages in your applications on a case-by-case basis. Using packages is much like using conventional DLLs, so many of the same considerations apply.

Eliminating Redundant Code

The principal reason for using packages is to reduce the size of your applications by eliminating redundant code. If your application is large and lends itself to partitioning into a number of separate or semi-separate modules, it may make sense to deliver these modules as individual EXEs or DLLs. By compiling the modules to use packages, only one copy of the basic VCL framework (contained in the VCL30 package) needs to be distributed, no matter how many modules the application contains.

The individual modules will be smaller, of course, because the common code isn't duplicated, which can make it easier to distribute your applications. Also, when the time comes to upgrade one of the modules, the amount of new code you need to send to your users is less, reducing distribution costs.

If you distribute applications electronically (over the Internet or World Wide Web, for example), using packages can drastically reduce the amount of time spent by your users to download your applications. They will have to download a given package only once; after it is installed, it's available to *all* their Delphi 3 applications (including applications obtained from other vendors).

A combination of conventional and electronic distribution can give the best of both worlds: First-time users obtain your application, including all necessary packages, on CD-ROM or floppy disk. They then can download new modules electronically to upgrade their applications to the latest version. By using packages, you can make these modules smaller than they otherwise would be.

Partitioning an application into modules and packages has its downside, however. You have to take special care to ensure that different versions of your modules and packages all work together. The best way to do this is to ensure that all versions of your packages are backward-compatible (the code in a newer version of a package should support being called by an application that is familiar only with an older version). This aspect of using packages is discussed in more detail in the following section, "Maintaining Package Versions.")

Also, take care to ensure that when your application is uninstalled, the uninstallation program doesn't inadvertently delete packages still in use by other applications. (Commercial installation toolkits, such as the InstallShield Express utility included with Delphi, should handle this detail automatically, but it pays to be aware of the potential problems.

VCL Components

In Delphi 3, components that will be installed on the component palette in the IDE must be packaged. Therefore, if you plan on creating and distributing components, you have to learn how to build packages. A complete discussion of component creation and packaging is given in Chapter 16, "Creating Components," but the general concepts that you need to know are covered in this chapter.

When *Not* to Use Packages

If you include the sizes of the package files, an application that uses packages is always larger than an application that combines all the code into a single EXE. Therefore, it doesn't make sense to use a package unless the package will be shared among several applications, or you can be sure that your end users will already have the package installed on their systems.

For example, consider a small, simple Delphi application. A nonpackage version of the EXE file might be about 200K in size, while a version using packages would only be 30K. The 170K savings looks good until you remember that all package-enabled Delphi EXEs require the VCL30 package, which is over 1M. A simple-minded analysis shows that using packages doesn't pay off in terms of total disk space consumed until you have at least six modules (EXEs or DLLs) that use VCL30. The exact numbers vary, depending on the applications and the particular selection of packages they require, but the message should be clear: Don't use packages for applications just because they're there; consider the implications from the end user point of view.

Installing and Using Packages

Unless you're a hermit and do your Delphi development in a cave, you eventually will acquire packages written by other programmers. Before you can use them, however, you have to install these packages on your system.

There are two basic categories of packages, *runtime* and *design-time*. Runtime packages are used by a Delphi application; these packages contain code that implements a portion of the functionality of the application. If you distribute an application that uses runtime packages, you also must distribute copies of these packages (unless you can be certain that the packages are already installed on the target machines).

In contrast, design-time packages contain code that is used only during the design phase of application development; design-time code is executed by the Delphi IDE. As a Delphi developer, you use design-time packages to build applications, but you never need to ship a design-time package as part of a finished application. (On the other hand, if your end product is a Delphi component, you need to encapsulate this component into a design-time package so that your users—other Delphi developers—can install it.)

Installing Runtime Packages

If you obtain a runtime package as part of a VCL component, the package usually will install automatically when you install the component. Occasionally, however, you may need to explicitly install a runtime package, which probably will happen if the package consists of a collection of utility functions, rather than components.

Installing a runtime package is a simple two-step process. You first copy the package DLL to a directory where the Windows loader can find it at runtime, and then you modify your Delphi project options so that the compiler knows that the package is available. That's all there is to it.

Packages are *implicitly-linked* DLLs (the Windows loader searches for and loads any packages required by an application before loading the application itself). Because the packages are loaded *before* the application that uses them, you cannot include any path information for locating the packages within the application itself. Rather, you must rely on Windows' capability to find the packages.

A detailed discussion of where to install package DLLs is given in "Deploying Packages" at the end of this chapter. This information is important when you're deciding how to distribute your applications to your users. For your development machine, however, you probably just want to put runtime packages in the Windows system directory (usually, \WINDOWS\SYSTEM or \WINDOWS\SYSTEM32), with the standard VCL runtime packages. Remember that if you use another directory, you probably will have to add the name of this directory to your system path so that the Windows loader can locate the packages.

 TIP If you are like me, you hate adding files to your Windows system directory. Considering the alternatives, however, this probably is the best approach for your development machine.

To make a runtime package available for use in your projects, you need to let the IDE know that the package exists. From the IDE main menu, select Component, Install Packages. This brings up the Packages page of the Project Options dialog box, as shown in Figure 15.1. (Note that you can get exactly the same dialog box by selecting Project, Options, and clicking the Packages tab.)

Part

IV

Ch

15

FIG. 15.1

Use the Project Options dialog box to make runtime packages available for use by your projects.

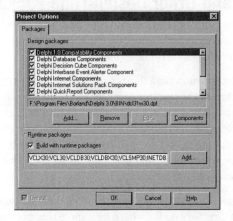

 TIP If you open the Project Options dialog box while no project is currently open in the IDE, any changes you make will become the defaults—they will be applied to *all* new projects. On the other hand, if you make changes to the Project Options while a project is open in the IDE, the changes will apply only to that project, unless you check the Default check box in the lower left corner of the dialog box.

To add a runtime package to the list of available packages, click the Add button in the Runtime packages group box (not the one in the Design packages group box). This brings up the Add Runtime Package dialog box shown in Figure 15.2. You can either type the name of the package to be added or use the browse button (the one labeled with an ...) to locate the package. I recommend that you always use the browse button because doing so also ensures that the search path is set correctly.

FIG. 15.2

Use the Add Runtime Package dialog box to install a runtime package.

The Browse button in the Add Package dialog box brings up a standard Open File dialog box, which you can use to navigate through your directories to find the package file. After you locate the package and select it, click OK to copy the file name to the Package name field of the Add Package dialog box, and then click OK again to add the package to the list of available runtime packages in the Project Options dialog box. At this point, you can add more packages, or you can click OK to close the Project Options dialog box and accept your changes.

After following the preceding steps, your newly added runtime packages are available for use in your applications. Note that it doesn't hurt to add packages to the list of available runtime packages—if your application uses none of the units contained in a particular package, there will be no reference to this package in the final EXE.

Installing Components and Other Design-Time Packages

Design-time packages, as the name implies, contain code that is executed at design time by the IDE. Usually, this means component and property editors, experts, and so on. You will never link code from design-time packages into your applications.

When you receive a VCL component from a third party, two packages typically are included—a runtime package that implements the runtime behavior of the component (some of which may also be applicable at design time) and a design-time package that implements the behavior applicable *only* at design time, such as a property editor. (A simple component that requires no component or property editors might fold the runtime and design-time functionality into a single package.) A wizard, on the other hand, usually consists only of design-time code, so there will not be an accompanying runtime package.

Installing design-time packages is analogous to installing runtime packages. You first need to copy the package DLLs to a directory on your hard disk (note that package files use the extension .DPL, rather than the .DLL used by ordinary DLLs). Here, you want to copy the package DLLs to your Delphi 3.0\BIN directory because the DLLs are specific to the Delphi IDE. Then, go to the main menu in the Delphi IDE and select Component, Install Packages, which brings up the Packages page of the Project Options dialog box (refer to Figure 15.1).

Click the Add button in the Design packages group. This brings up the Add Design Package dialog box, which is just a standard open file dialog box (see Figure 15.3). Navigate through the directories to locate the package you want to add, select the file, and then click OK. The package is added to the list of available design-time packages.

FIG. 15.3

Use the Open Package dialog box to select a design-time package to be installed.

As with runtime packages, you can include design-time packages on a project-by-project basis. All changes you make to the list of design-time packages affect only the current project, unless the Default check box in the lower-left corner of the dialog box is checked.

TIP After a design-time package is installed, you can highlight the package name in the list box in the Project Options dialog box, and then click the Components button to see a list of the components contained within this package.

Notice that there is a check box to the left of each package listed in the Design packages list box. These check boxes provide a convenient means for quickly enabling and disabling different packages for each of your projects. If, for example, your current project doesn't involve the Internet, you can disable the Delphi Internet Components and Delphi Internet Solutions Pack Components packages and reduce the clutter in your Component Palette. If you want to *completely* remove a package, use the Remove button. This action deletes the package from the list of available packages; you have to use the Add button if you want to get it back later.

When you disable design-time packages, you probably will see a dialog box like the one shown in Figure 15.4. Usually, you can safely respond with Yes. However, if for some reason you want to disable a design-time component package yet still use the associated runtime package, respond with No. The only reason why you might want to do this (and I have to admit that it's quite a stretch) is if you want to avoid using a component at design-time, but still have the ability to instantiate it at runtime.

FIG. 15.4
When disabling a design-time package, you might receive a query like this one.

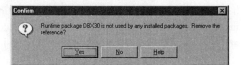

The capability to selectively enable component packages is a great new feature in Delphi 3.0. In previous versions of Delphi, if you wanted to make different sets of components available to different projects, you had to manually load different Component Libraries before loading those projects. Now, you simply modify the project options. To top it off, if you used Delphi 2.0, you know how long rebuilding your component palette can take. In Delphi 3, it's nearly instantaneous.

Using Packages in Your Applications and DLLs

Delphi 3 projects are not *package-enabled* by default, so your Delphi applications will not use packages unless you modify your project options.

You can globally control the use of packages in the Project Options dialog box (refer to Figure 15.1). By checking the Build with runtime packages check box, all available packages will be used in building the project; if any of the units used in the project is contained in a package, the EXE or DLL will be compiled so that it calls on the code in the package, and the compiler will not include that code in the executable. By unchecking the check box, *no* packages will be used in building the project.

You also can selectively disable the use of a particular package by eliminating it from the list of runtime packages. In the Project Options dialog box shown in Figure 15.5, for example, only units included in the VCL30, VCLX30, and VCLOCX30 packages will take advantage of packages because these are the only runtime packages listed. All other units in the project are compiled directly into the EXE or DLL.

FIG. 15.5

Use the runtime packages edit box in the Project Options dialog box to control which units in the project use packages.

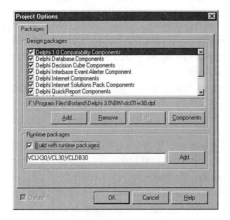

Using packages in DLLs is really no different from using them in EXEs. However, there is an additional consideration: If the DLL will be used only by Delphi applications, you may want to make it into a package instead. In this way, the application has direct access to any classes and functions defined in the package. You only need to add the unit or units included in the package to your application's uses lists, and you can use the package as though it were linked directly into your project.

However, if you're building a DLL that will be used by applications written in other languages, you cannot turn it into a package because other languages don't understand the package format. (Of course, as long as the DLL is written with Delphi, it can still use packages internally, even if it will be called from applications written in other languages.)

Using packages in applications and DLLs can drastically reduce the sizes of the resulting EXE and DLL files. As long as the package DLLs themselves don't need to be updated, this can greatly simplify the process of distributing updates, and also reduce costs.

Building Your Own Packages

Delphi 3 delivers all the tools you need for creating both runtime and design-time packages. The Delphi IDE includes a package editor that makes the process nearly painless. Still, planning goes a long way toward maintaining your sanity. You should build and test all the units that you want to place in a package as conventional units before packaging them. After they're in a package, you can make no modifications to them except by rebuilding the package, which takes longer and requires more effort than just modifying a conventional unit.

When a particular unit is incorporated into a package, the package is said to *contain* that unit. If the package relies on the existence of another package, it is said to *require* that other package. The concepts of "contains" and "requires" are similar to that of the concept of "uses" in a conventional Delphi project, but there are some differences:

If a unit is listed in the uses list in a Delphi project, all the code defined in the unit is available to the project. When the project is built, only the code that is actually used is linked into the EXE. If a unit is contained in a package, however, *all* the code in the unit will be linked into the package.

If a Delphi project uses packages, the corresponding package DLLs will be referenced in the EXE, and the EXE won't run if these package DLLs are not available at runtime. If a package in the EXE requires another package, that other package also will be referenced in the EXE, even if the code in the EXE never directly refers to the other package. So, if your application uses package A, and package A in turn requires package B, the application won't run unless both packages A and B are available at runtime, regardless of whether or not your code explicitly uses any of the units in package B.

TIP   Usually, all code that is valid in a conventional unit also is valid in a package. One exception, however, exists: Design-time packages should not contain exit procedures. A design-time package may be dynamically loaded and unloaded by the IDE; when this occurs, all initialization sections in the units in the package will be called when it is loaded, and all finalization sections will be called when it is unloaded. However, exit procedures are *not* called when the package is unloaded. If you have an existing unit that contains an exit procedure, you should convert this exit procedure to a finalization section before you incorporate the unit into a design-time package.

When you're ready to build your package, go to the main menu in the IDE and select File, New. This brings up the New items dialog box. Select the Package icon on the New page and click OK. This brings up the New Package dialog box, shown in Figure 15.6. Enter a name for your package, which will be the name used throughout the IDE to refer to the package. It also will be used as the name for the package DLL, so it must be a valid filename. For design-time packages, you also should enter a *description* (the text that is displayed in the list of design packages in the Project Options dialog in the IDE). You also can enter a description for runtime packages, but the description isn't used by the IDE.

Click OK to close the New Package dialog box. This brings up the Package Editor, shown in Figure 15.7. The bulk of the window is occupied by a two-page view of the units contained in the package and the other packages required by this package. Click the tabs to switch from one set to the other. Notice that the VCL30 package, which is required by all packages, is listed on the Requires page by default.

FIG. 15.6

Use the New Package dialog box to give your package a name and description.

FIG. 15.7

Use the package editor to create your package.

You can use the row of buttons across the top of the Package Editor to modify the contents of your package. Taking the buttons from left to right, they are as follows:

- **Build/Save package**—Pressing this button saves and compiles the package, creating the package source (.DPK) file, the compiled package (.DCP) file (both of these are described in following paragraphs), and the package DLL, which is given an extension of .DPL to distinguish it from ordinary DLLs.

- **Add unit/Add package**—If the Contains tab is selected, use this button to add a unit to the list of units contained in this package. If the Requires tab is selected, use this button to add a package to the list of packages required by this package.

- **Remove unit/Remove package**—This button has the opposite effect of the previous button. To remove a unit or package, highlight its name in the Contains or Requires list, and then press this button.

- **View unit/View package**—Selecting a unit in the Contains list and pressing this button displays the source code of that unit in the code editor (assuming that the IDE can locate the source code). Selecting a package in the Requires list and pressing this button displays a second Package Editor, showing the contents of the selected package.

- **Package options**—Pressing this button displays the Package Options dialog box (see Figure 15.8). On the Description page of the dialog box, you can modify the package description and set the package attributes. You can mark the package for runtime or design-time use (or both), and you can determine how the package will be rebuilt. If Rebuild as needed is selected, the IDE rebuilds the package whenever it determines that it needs to be updated (if, for example, one of the contained units changes). If Explicit build is selected, the IDE will not rebuild the package, unless you explicitly tell it to by pressing the Build/Save package button in the Package Editor. Most settings on the Build page of the dialog box are analogous to settings on the Compiler and Linker pages of the Project Options dialog box.

- **Install package**—Use this button to install the package into the IDE, if it is a component or other design-time package.
- **Update from source**—Use this button to refresh the package code if you selected Explicit rebuild in your package options.

FIG. 15.8

Use the Package Options dialog box to control how a package is built.

As you can see, the process of building a package is straightforward. Just follow these steps:

1. To the Contains list, add the units that will be contained in the package.
2. To the Requires list, add the packages that are required by the package.
3. Modify the package options, if necessary.
4. Press the Build/Save package button to create the package.
5. (Optional) Press the Install package button to install the package in the IDE.

N O T E You can get into a peculiar situation if your current project includes a unit that also is contained in a package used by the project. If you make a change in this unit, the IDE tries to update the package, provided the package has the Rebuild as needed option. If the IDE can locate the appropriate source files, it recompiles the package, giving you an updated package DLL. If it cannot find the source files, it links the unit code directly into your project, rather than use the package.

The situation gets more complicated if the unit is used indirectly (for example, project A uses package B, which requires package C, which contains unit D, which also is part of project A). When you factor in the possibility that some packages may have the Rebuild as needed option while others have Explicit rebuild, it can become difficult to predict exactly what happens if you make a change in the unit. Therefore, you're better off not trying to modify a packaged unit in a project which uses that unit. Rather, modify the unit and update all your packages first, and then load and build the project. ■

If the process of building the package is successful, three new files are created in the package directory (besides any .DCU files associated with the units in the package), as follows:

- **The .DPK file**—This is the source code for the overall package, and is analogous to the .DPR file in an ordinary Delphi project. Although it is an ordinary text file and may be edited in the Delphi code editor, do so with caution. Refer to the Delphi documentation for detailed information on the format of this file; you will not need to do so unless you plan to compile your packages by using the command-line compiler.

- **The .DCP file**—This is the compiled package file. It consists of all the symbol information from the various .DCU files that make up the package, plus additional header information required by the IDE. The IDE needs to have access to this file to build projects which use the corresponding package.

- **The .DPL file**—This is the actual package DLL, which you distribute with applications that use the package.

After a package is created, you can load it into the IDE for editing by selecting File, Open from the main menu. Click the down-arrow next to the Files of type combo box in the Open dialog box, and click the Delphi package source (*.DPK) item to display all the Delphi packages in the current directory.

After you select the package file and click OK, the package editor opens with your package loaded. You can use the methods discussed previously to edit it.

Package Syntax

There are several new package-related compiler directives that you can use to control the way in which units are packaged. Some of the directives are used in a unit file; the others are used in the package's .DPK file.

The following directives can be used in units that are to be packaged. Place them at the top of the unit source file:

- $G-, $IMPORTEDDATA OFF, or $DENYPACKAGEUNIT ON. All three of these directives have the same effect from the point of view of packages; they prevent the unit from being contained in a package. You may want to use these directives in special cases, where it's important that the code be contained in the EXE and not in a separate DLL.

- $WEAKPACKAGEUNIT ON. A unit that contains this directive will be *weakly packaged*. The concept of weak packaging is somewhat obscure and difficult to understand, and you'll rarely (if ever) need to use it, so I defer discussion of it to the sidebar, "The $WEAKPACKAGEUNIT Directive."

The following directives can be used in the package's .DPK file:

- $DESIGNONLY ON. This directive marks the package as design-time only, and is equivalent to unmarking the Runtime package check box in the Package Options dialog box.

- $RUNONLY ON. This directive marks the package as runtime only, and is equivalent to unmarking the Design package check box in the Package Options dialog box.

■ $IMPLICITBUILD OFF. This directive prevents a package from being implicitly recompiled, and is equivalent to selecting the Explicit rebuild option in the Package Options dialog box.

You need to be concerned about the $DESIGNONLY, $RUNONLY, and $IMPLICITBUILD directives only if you plan on creating or editing .DPK files. Otherwise, the package editor handles inserting these directives as necessary.

The $WEAKPACKAGEUNIT Directive

The $WEAKPACKAGEUNIT directive was introduced by the Delphi architects to cope with a specific problem they had when implementing packages in Delphi 3. They wanted to provide access to all the standard Windows DLLs in the core VCL30 package. This access, however, posed a dilemma because some "standard" Windows DLLs are in fact specialized, and not present on all computers (PENWIN.DLL, installed with Pen Windows, is one example). If they included the PenWin unit, which has implicit references to PENWIN.DLL, in the VCL30 package, an application that used VCL30 wouldn't run on any systems that didn't have PENWIN.DLL installed, which means that it doesn't run on over 99 percent of the Windows systems in the world.

You may think there's a simple solution: Don't reference PENWIN.DLL in the VCL30 package. This certainly is one way to handle the problem, but it leads to another difficulty. Suppose that you obtained a component from Vendor A, and that component implicitly references PENWIN.DLL. You also obtained a different component from Vendor B, which again references PENWIN.DLL. In the pre-Delphi 3 world, using both components in the same application wouldn't be a problem. Both references eventually would be folded into a single implicit reference to PENWIN.DLL in the final EXE. With packages, however, the situation changes. If the two components are implemented in separate runtime packages, each package DLL contains an implicit reference to PENWIN.DLL, so it will load twice when the application that uses the two components is loaded. This can cause problems with initialization order and references to global variables in the DLL, leading to a situation that Borland wanted to avoid, where an application built using packages will behave differently from the same application built without packages.

Enter weakly packaged units. What makes a unit weakly packaged? A unit whose source code includes the $WEAKPACKAGEUNIT ON directive is contained in the package, but its code isn't present in the package DLL. This is obviously somewhat contradictory. Although the code isn't contained in the DLL, it *is* contained in the package's .DCP file. If an application uses a weakly packaged unit, the code is obtained from the .DCP file and directly linked into the EXE. In this way, Borland was able to include PenWin and other units in VCL30, avoiding the problems with multiply loaded DLLs, while still allowing applications that use VCL30 to run on machines that don't have PENWIN.DLL installed.

So you almost never need to use $WEAKPACKAGEUNIT. There really are only two reasons to use $WEAKPACKAGEUNIT. The first reason is the one that induced Borland to implement weak packaging in the first place: If you plan to distribute a DLL that you expect Delphi component developers to use in the packages that they distribute to other Delphi users, you want to weakly package the DLL's interface unit so that the users of the packages encounter no conflicts when two or more components reference the same interface unit.

continues

continued

> The second reason is to ensure that code is linked directly into an application's EXE. If you distribute a package for other Delphi developers to use, it may contain code that for some reason must be linked into the application's EXE and not the package DLL (for example, a utility function optimized for speed—the overhead of making a DLL function call may slow it down unacceptably). By using a weakly packaged unit, you also save having to ship a separate .DCU file for the code that is to be directly compiled into the EXE.
>
> A final point about $WEAKPACKAGEUNIT: Weakly packaged units cannot contain global variables in their interface sections and cannot contain initialization or finalization sections.

Maintaining Package Versions

One overriding consideration that you need to remember when you create runtime packages to distribute to users of your code: Sooner or later, you will release an updated version of this package, and you must be sure that doing so doesn't break all the existing applications that use the earlier version(s) of the package.

The three most important steps you can take to help ensure that the process of updating a package goes smoothly are as follows:

1. Include an accurate VERSIONINFO resource in the package.
2. Include an accurate VERSIONINFO resource in the package.
3. Include an accurate VERSIONINFO resource in the package.

Have I made my point clear? The number one reason for application A to stop working when application B is installed is that application B's installation program overwrote, with an out-of-date or incompatible version, a critical file used by application A. The only way you can avoid this is to include accurate version information in the common files, and to use an installation program smart enough not to overwrite a newer version of a file with an older version (most commercial installation utilities are sufficiently smart).

The options dialog in the packages editor includes a VersionInfo tab, which works just like the VersionInfo tab in Project Options. Use it. For more information about VersionInfo, refer to Chapter 8, "Creating Applications," in the "VersionInfo" section.

It's also worthwhile to make your updated packages as backward-compatible as possible. For example, if the original version of a package included a function Foo, which computed the average of an array of integers, it isn't a good idea to redefine Foo to return the hard disk capacity in an updated version of the package. Also, if a package declares a class, *any* modification to the class declaration renders the new version of the package unusable by applications designed to work with the original package. Period.

If you do need to make a backward-incompatible change to a package, give the updated package a new name. For example, the fundamental Delphi 3 packages have names such as VCL30. If Borland decides to release new, incompatible versions, they will be given names such as

VCL31, VCL35, or VCL40. In this way, both old and new packages can coexist on a single system, and applications that require one or the other still will function correctly.

The safe updating of shared files was one of the biggest bugaboos to plague Windows and other operating systems ever since the concept of shared files was first conceived. Make an effort to ensure that your packages are as backward-compatible as possible and contain accurate version information, and you'll save both you and your users considerable headaches.

Deploying Packages

When you deploy an application that uses packages, you also have to deploy the runtime package DLLs used by the application, unless you can be sure that the users already have the needed packages installed on their machines. It's usually a good idea to include all the packages in the distribution, and let the installation program take care of verifying whether or not packages are already installed, comparing version numbers to determine whether an existing package should be overwritten, and so on. If a needed package DLL is not installed or not located where the Windows loader can find it, Windows displays an error message box when the application is started (see Figure 15.9).

FIG. 15.9

A typical error message displayed by Windows when it can't find a required DLL.

In what directories should packages be installed? There are three general categories of runtime packages, and the directory to use depends on the category:

1. *System packages.* These are packages common to all or nearly all Delphi applications. The runtime packages shipped with Delphi (VCL30 and so on) fall into this category. These packages should be installed in the Windows system directory, where all package-enabled applications can find them.

2. *Common packages.* These are packages common to a number of applications delivered by the same vendor, such as in an application suite. You can create a vendor-specific "Common Files" directory and place these packages there. Because this directory will not be on the system path, you need to set up an application-specific path in the system registry. Suppose that you're the head programmer for SlamDunk Corporation, and your new WhizBang application is going to use \PROGRAM FILES\SLAMDUNK\WHIZBANG\ as its default installation directory, with packages and other common files located in \PROGRAM FILES\SLAMDUNK\COMMON FILES\. The required registry entries would look like Figure 15.10. As you can see, the entries are listed under the HKEY_LOCAL_MACHINE\SOFTWARE\MICROSOFT\WINDOWS\CURRENTVERSION\ APP PATHS\ key, using the name of the application as the subkey (WHIZBANG.EXE in this example). You need two values: the Default value contains the fully qualified path name of the application, while the Path value contains the directory or directories to be appended to the system path each time this application is executed.

Most installation programs allow you to make custom registry entries. Hopefully, Delphi-specific application programs eventually will include the capability to set up application-specific path information semiautomatically.

FIG. 15.10

Creating an application-specific path in the system registry.

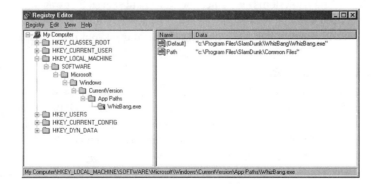

3. *Other packages.* Placing a package in the same directory as the EXEs and DLLs that use it makes sense if multiple modules will use the package. Remember, if your application contains only a few modules that require a given package, you're probably better off linking the code into the modules and not using the package.

If you're building an OLE server DLL, any DLLs it uses—including package DLLs—must be placed in the Windows system directory. This is required because of a limitation of the search algorithm used by the Windows NT module loader. For more information about OLE, see Chapter 18, "Working with OLE, Document Servers, and ActiveX Controls."

If you follow the preceding guidelines, you should have no difficulty getting your package-enabled applications installed and running.

If you distribute packages to other Delphi developers for use in their projects, you need to include, at a minimum, the .DCP and .DPL files. The .DCP files contain the information used by the IDE to generate links to the package DLLs (and also the code for any weakly packaged units), while the .DPL files contain the actual runtime package code.

If your product consists of a number of packages and associated files, distribution can become rather complicated. To deal with this problem, you can use the Package Collection Editor (PCE.EXE), a stand-alone utility included with Delphi 3. The Package Collection Editor allows you to combine all the files associated with your packages (.DPL, .DCP, and so on) into a *package collection*, a single file that has a .DPC extension. Your users can install this file into their copy of the Delphi 3 IDE, and the various constituent files will automatically be extracted and installed.

For detailed instructions on using the Package Collection Editor, refer to the Delphi documentation. You may want to add PCE.EXE to the Tools menu in the Delphi 3 IDE so that it is easily accessible while you work with Delphi.

Putting It All Together

This chapter has described packages, a completely new feature in Delphi 3. Packages allow you to group common code and objects into shared modules to reduce the overall size of your applications. Packages are also the means by which VCL components are distributed and installed in the Delphi 3 IDE. The information provided in this chapter gives you everything you need to know to use packages provided with Delphi or from third-party vendors in your applications, and to create packages of your own. ●

CHAPTER 16

Creating Components

by David Powell

Components are the building blocks for most Delphi applications. The ability to click on components and drop them onto a "form" is not unique among visual-development environments; however, few languages provide the capability to create custom components from within the same environment and in the same language. Delphi is one of those few. From a user's point of view, a component is a "black box." Users don't care how a component performs its tasks, only that it does what they expect. From a component writer's point of view, a component is an instance of a class. You may find yourself wanting to use the term component and class interchangeably; this is not totally correct. A component is an entity that can be dropped onto a form and manipulated from inside the Delphi IDE. Although a class is an object structure that exists as part of the Object Pascal language, all components are classes but not all classes are components.

Delphi's component palette contains over 130 components that cover a wide range of applications. At some point, however, you will reach a situation where either no component exists that does what you want, or there is a component that does mostly what you want but needs to be modified for your specific needs. When you reach this point, it's time to create a custom component.

What are custom components?

First, you look at an overview of the component-writing process.

Choosing the correct ancestor

Depending on what you need, you can inherit from existing controls or one of Delphi's base component classes.

Component framework

You look at a component's structure and how to add properties, methods, and events.

Finishing touches

You look at debugging components, creating custom icons, and installing components.

The component-creation process consists of the following steps:

1. Choose an ancestor class.
2. Create the component framework.
3. Test the component.
4. Create an icon for the component.
5. Add the component to the Component Palette.

 T I P The source code for Delphi's Visual Component Library is an invaluable resource and is a resource often overlooked by beginning component writers. If you ever ask yourself how a component does what it does, you can crack open the source code and find out. If you don't have the VCL source code, get it from Borland.

Choosing the Correct Ancestor

When creating a custom component, the most important step—and thus the first step—is to choose the correct component class to derive your component from. Delphi allows you to derive your component from any class that it knows about (such as classes already defined in the system library or classes that were added to the Component Palette via custom components).

You can take either of two routes when choosing an ancestor class. If you are creating a totally new component, you will have to descend from a "base" component class. If you just need to change the functionality of an existing component, you can derive the component from an existing component class.

Base Component Classes

Delphi provides five standard base classes from which you can derive your custom component. Table 16.1 shows these five classes and describes what they have to offer to your component.

Table 16.1 Delphi's Base Component Classes

VCL Base Class	Description
TObject	TObject is not a component; however, it is the base class for all Delphi classes. You can use TObject as the base class for a component that doesn't need to be interacted with at design time. Components of this type aren't streamable in the IDE.
TComponent	A good starting point for non-visual components. Components of this type are streamable in the IDE.

VCL Base Class	Description
TGraphicControl	Introduces a `Paint()` method and draws on its parent's Client area. Doesn't have a window handle, so it cannot receive focus.
TWinControl	The base class for all windowed components. Introduces a window handle and can receive focus.
TCustomControl	A blend between `TGraphicControl` and `TWinControl`. Maintains a window handle and a custom `Paint()` method. Most visual custom components are derived from this class.

TComponent introduces the following properties: `Owner`, `Name`, `Tag`, `ComponentState`, and `Components`. The `Components` property is an array containing a list of all the components owned by that component. The default destructor for *TComponent* goes through this list and frees all the components it owns. `TComponent` also knows how to stream itself (save its property values) to the DFM file when a project is closed or saved.

TControl is not listed in Table 16.1 because it is not commonly inherited *from*. `TGraphicControl` and `TWinControl` both descend directly from `TControl`. `TControl` introduces many properties in its protected section that are made more public or implemented in descendant classes. The properties introduced are: `Left`, `Top`, `Width`, `Height`, `Align`, `Visible`, `Enabled`, `Cursor`, `OnClick`, and so on. For a complete listing, examine the VCL source code or look in the Object Browser.

TGraphicControl introduces a virtual `Paint()` method as well as the `Canvas` property. It is used mainly for components that need to display information or graphics but do not need the overhead of a window's handle.

TWinControl introduces properties that are needed for a windowed control, such as: `Handle`, `TabOrder`, `TabStop`, `Ctl3D`, `OnEnter`, and so on. For a complete listing, examine the VCL source code or look in the Object Browser.

TCustomControl merges the painting abilities of *TGraphicControl* with the windowed control aspects of *TWinControl*. This is the class from which we will derive our example custom component.

Customizing Existing Components

If Delphi provides a component that does mostly what you want, you may elect to derive your component from that control rather than starting from scratch. When deriving from an existing control you have two options. You can derive the component either directly from the existing control or you can derive from the existing control's immediate ancestor. You could derive your component, for example, from `TEdit` or from `TCustomEdit`. All the functionality of `TEdit` is actually implemented in `TCustomEdit`, and `TEdit` merely publishes many of the properties declared in its ancestor. There is no hard-and-fast rule about which class you should inherit from. A good rule is to inherit from the control if you want to add functionality and inherit from the immediate ancestor if you want to remove functionality. When in doubt, a quick look at the VCL source code can help you to figure out which class to inherit from.

Using Component Templates

If you want to create a custom control to simply change the default setting of an existing control (such as the size, color, font, and so on) or to add a default event handler, you should consider using *Component Templates* instead of creating a custom component. Component Templates are created by selecting one or more components on a form, and then selecting Component, Create Component Template from Delphi's Main Menu. This adds the components and all of the code associated with them, via Event Handlers, to be stored as part of the Component Palette. Component Templates are stored in a binary file named DELPHI32.DCT, which is located in your Delphi3\BIN directory. When you select a Component Template and drop it on a form, Delphi inserts the stored template information into your form and resolves any naming conflicts that may occur with existing code and components.

Creating the Component Framework

The component framework consists of a unit with a class definition that describes the characteristics of your custom component. The Component Expert (see Figure 16.1) is the easiest way to create this starting unit. The Component Expert is available from Delphi's main menu by selecting File, New, which brings up the Object Repository, and then selecting Component or by selecting Component, New Component from the main menu.

FIG. 16.1

Delphi's Component Expert.

The Component Expert has five areas to fill in before it creates the basic component framework. First, you must indicate from which ancestor class your component is to derive itself. Second, you must enter a class name for your component. Delphi's naming convention specifies that class names should start with the letter T. Third, you must indicate which tab on the Component Palette you want to place your custom control. You can specify an existing palette page, or you can enter the name for a new palette page. Fourth, you must specify a unit file name for your component. Finally, you can modify the Component Palette's search path to include the directory path to your component, if it is not already listed.

After the basic framework is created by the Component Expert, your component has all the inherited functionality of its ancestor class, but you wouldn't be creating a custom component if you only wanted the inherit functionality, would you? Now, it's time to roll up your sleeves and add some custom properties, methods, and events to turn this framework into the component that you envisioned.

On the CD

For demonstration purposes, we will create for you a custom component called TEverything, which will be derived from the class TCustomControl. We will place the component on the "Using Delphi" palette page of the Component Library. If you put the preceding entries into the Component Expert, it will create the code shown in Listing 16.1. You can find this file on this book's companion CD-ROM.

Listing 16.1   \UDELPHI3\CHP16\LIST16-1—The Basic Component Framework for *TEverything*

```
unit EvryThng;

interface

uses
  Windows, Messages, SysUtils, Classes, Graphics, Controls, Forms, Dialogs;

type
  TEverything = class(TCustomControl)
  private
    { Private declarations }
  protected
    { Protected declarations }
  public
    { Public declarations }
  published
    { Published declarations }
  end;

procedure Register;

implementation

procedure Register;
begin
  RegisterComponents('UD3', [TEverything]);
end;

end.
```

Creating Properties

Properties provide an interface into the internal data fields of your component. Properties are used to read and write values to and from the internal data fields without necessarily giving the component user direct access to the internal data fields. For purposes of information hiding, most internal data fields are declared in a component's private section.

TIP

Internal data fields are usually declared in the private section of a component and start with the letter F. For example, a property named Color might access an internal data field named FColor.

Types of Properties   Properties can be created from several data types. These types include Simple, Enumerated, Set, Object, and Array types. Each property type shows up differently in the Object Inspector and has its own unique property editor. A full discussion of property editors follows in the next chapter, but for now, think of a property editor as the mechanism that allows the user to change the values of a property in the Object Inspector.

You can increase the visibility of existing properties in a component by redeclaring them in the public or published sections of the component.

Creating Simple Properties   *Simple properties* consist of numeric, character, and string data types. Simple properties are displayed in the Object Inspector and can be changed without using a special property editor. Delphi components already frequently use Integer and string properties. Properties such as Top, Left, Height, and Width are properties of type integer and properties such as Caption, Text, and Name are properties of type string.

On the CD

Listing 16.2 adds three properties to our component, one for each of the simple types, and puts them into the published section of the class so that they show up in the Object Inspector. You can find this file on this book's companion CD-ROM.

Listing 16.2   \UDELPHI3\CHP16\LIST16-2—*TEverything* with Simple Property Types

```
TEverything = class(TCustomControl)
  private
    { Private declarations }
    FNumber : integer;
    FChar   : char;
    FString : string;
  protected
    { Protected declarations }
  public
    { Public declarations }
  published
    { Published declarations }
    property NumberProp: integer read FNumber write FNumber;
    property CharProp: char read FChar write FChar;
    property StringProp: string read FString write FString;
  end;
```

The properties NumberProp, CharProp, and StringProp now show up in the Object Inspector with the default values of 0, #0, and an empty string, respectively. Because default values for each of the properties weren't specified, they take on a default value of nothing. For an integer this is zero, for a character this is a null or #0, and for a string it is an empty string. How to give a property a default value is discussed in the following section. The properties access internal data fields for each of their data types. If this component were added to the Component Palette at this time, it would look like Figure 16.2.

FIG. 16.2

TEverything with inherited and simple properties.

Creating Enumerated Properties *Enumerated properties* consist of predefined enumerated types, Boolean types, and user-defined enumerated types. Enumerated properties are characterized in the Object Inspector by a drop-down listbox. The user can cycle through the different values in the set by double-clicking the value shown in the Object Inspector or by clicking the drop-down arrow and selecting the value directly from the list. Delphi uses enumerated properties for properties such as `Color`, `BorderStyle`, `FormStyle`, and `Cursor`.

By convention, most enumerated sets in Delphi have their elements prefaced with a two-letter prefix that indicates to which enumerated type the elements belongs. Table 16.2 shows these four enumerated type properties, along with some of their possible values.

Table 16.2 Delphi's Enumerated Type Properties

Enumerated Type	Values
Color	clBlack, clYellow, clMenu, clWindow, clBtnFace, just to name a few. See GRAPHICS.PAS for a complete listing.
Cursor	crDefault, crNone, crArrow, crNo, crAppStart, crHelp. See CONTROLS.PAS for a complete listing.
BorderStyle	bsNone, bsSingle, bsSizeable, bsDialog, bsToolWindow, bsSizeToolWin.
FormStyle	fsNormal, fsMDIChild, fsMDIForm, fsStayOnTop.

Before you can add some enumerated properties to TEverything, you must declare your own custom enumerated type. This section will define TEnumProp, which will be an enumerated type that consists of six elements. This is done as follows:

```
TEnumProp = (epZero, epOne, epTwo, epThree, epFour, epFive);
```

Now, add three enumerated properties to TEverything, one predefined type, one Boolean type, and one user-defined type. Call them ColorProp, BooleanProp, and EnumProp, respectively. TEverything will now look like Listing 16.3. You can find this file on this book's companion CD-ROM.

Listing 16.3   \UDELPHI3\CHP16\LIST16-3—*TEverything* with Enumerated Property Types

```
TEnumProp = (epZero, epOne, epTwo, epThree, epFour, epFive);

TEverything = class(TCustomControl)
private
  { Private declarations }
  FColor   : TColor;
  FBoolean : boolean;
  FEnumProp: TEnumProp;
protected
  { Protected declarations }
public
  { Public declarations }
published
  { Published declarations }
  property ColorProp: TColor read FColor write FColor;
  property BooleanProp: boolean read FBoolean write FBoolean;
  property EnumProp: TEnumProp read FEnumProp write FEnumProp;
end;
```

If TEverything were added to the Component Palette, it would look like Figure 16.3 in the Object Inspector. Notice that the drop-down list box in the Object Inspector lists the enumerated values in alphabetical order, not the order in which the elements of the type were defined.

FIG. 16.3

TEverything with Enumerated properties.

Creating Set Properties   *Set properties* consist of Pascal style sets. Set properties are characterized in the Object Inspector by putting the elements contained in the set inside square brackets ([ ]) and by a plus sign (+) to the left of the property name. The user can modify the values in the set by directly editing the values between the square brackets or by clicking the property name. Clicking the property name causes it to expand in the Object Inspector and list all the elements in the set along with a true or false value that indicates whether or not it should be included in the set. Delphi uses Set properties for properties such as `BorderIcons` and `Options`. By convention, elements in a set are named the same as enumerated types.

Part

IV

Ch

16

In order to create your own custom set property, you first need to create a custom set. You can take the enumerated type created in the preceding paragraphs and turn it into a set, like this:

```
TEnumProp = (epZero, epOne, epTwo, epThree, epFour, epFive);

TSetProp = set of TEnumProp;
```

You now can create your own Set property to `TEverything` named `SetProp`. `TEverything` will now look like Listing 16.4.

Listing 16.4   \UDELPHI3\CHP16\LIST16-4—*TEverything* with Set Property Types

```
TEnumProp = (epZero, epOne, epTwo, epThree, epFour, epFive);

TSetProp = set of TEnumProp;

TEverything = class(TCustomControl)
private
  { Private declarations }
  FSetProp : TSetProp;
protected
  { Protected declarations }
public
  { Public declarations }
published
  { Published declarations }
  property SetProp: TSetProp read FSetProp write FSetProp;
end;
```

If `TEverything` were added to the Component Palette, it would look like Figure 16.4.

TIP   Published set properties are limited in size to 32 elements. If you try to publish a set with greater than 32 elements, you see `Error(38): Size of published set 'property name' is >4 bytes`. If you need to create a set with more than 32 elements, you have to create a runtime-only property.

FIG. 16.4

TEverything with
a Set property.

Creating Object Properties   *Object properties* consist of individual classes and objects that are actual properties of other components. Object properties are characterized in the Object Inspector by a plus sign (+) to the left of the property name, or an ellipses (...) button in the property value column. When an object property is expanded in the Object Inspector, Delphi shows a list of all the published properties that belong to that object property's class. Clicking the triple ellipses button brings up a custom property editor for that object property type. An object property must be a descendant of TPersistent for the streaming to and from the Object Inspector to work. Delphi uses Object Properties for properties such as Font, HorzScrollBar, and VertScrollBar.

In order to create a custom object property for TEverything, you first need to create a class that descends either directly from TPersistent or from a class derived from TPersistent. For simplicity, you derive your class directly from TPersistent, as shown in Listing 16.5.

Listing 16.5   \UDELPHI3\CHP16\LIST16-5—*TObjectProp* Declaration

```
TObjectProp = class(TPersistent)
  private
    FMyInt1 : integer;
    FMyInt2 : integer;
    FMyInt3 : integer;
  public
    property MyProp3: integer read FMyInt3 write FMyInt3;
  published
    property MyProp1: integer read FMyInt1 write FMyInt1;
    property MyProp2: integer read FMyInt2 write FMyInt2;
end;
```

TObjectProp has two published integer properties, which will show up in the Object Inspector, and one public integer property, which will not. Because TObjectProp is an object property, the internal data field that holds the value of this property must be instantiated at the component-creation time in order to hold a valid object reference. You can instantiate

TObjectProp by overriding the constructor to TEverything and instantiating TObjectProp after the inherited constructor is called. You need to call the inherited Create first, so that TEverything will be correctly initialized before you start manipulating it, as follows:

```
constructor TEverything.Create(AOwner: TComponent);
begin
  inherited Create(AOwner);
  FObjectProp := TObjectProp.Create;
end;
```

If you create a TObjectProp in your Create constructor, you must find some way of freeing it when TEverything is destroyed. You can dispose of the object that you instantiated in the constructor by overriding the destructor Destroy. You need to free your object property before the inherited Destroy is called because after Destroy is called, TEverything is no longer a valid object.

```
destructor TEverything.Destroy;
begin
  FObjectProp.Free;
  inherited Destroy;
end;
```

Listing 16.6 shows the type declaration for TEverything with an object property and a defined constructor and destructor.

Listing 16.6   \UDELPHI3\CHP16\LIST16-6—Creating Object Properties

```
TObjectProp = class(TPersistent)
private
  FMyInt1 : integer;
  FMyInt2 : integer;
  FMyInt3 : integer;
public
  property MyProp3: integer read FMyInt3 write FMyInt3;
published
  property MyProp1: integer read FMyInt1 write FMyInt1;
  property MyProp2: integer read FMyInt2 write FMyInt2;
end;

TEverything = class(TCustomControl)
private
  { Private declarations }
  FObjectProp: TObjectProp;
protected
  { Protected declarations }
public
  { Public declarations }
  constructor Create(AOwner: TComponent); override;
  destructor Destroy; override;
published
  { Published declarations }
  property ObjectProp: TObjectProp read FObjectProp write FObjectProp;
end;
```

If you were to add TEverything to the Component Palette at this point, it would look like Figure 16.5 in the Object Inspector. Notice that, as expected, the two published properties MyProp1 and MyProp2 are listed in the expanded ObjectProp property and the public property MyProp3 is not. Also, there is no triple ellipses button in the value field for ObjectProp because there is no property editor register for the class TObjectProp.

FIG. 16.5

TEverything with an object property.

Creating Array Properties   *Array properties* are properties that can be accessed as if they were Object Pascal arrays. Array properties can be arrays of any Object Pascal type. Array properties are different from Object Pascal arrays, though, in two major ways:

- Object Pascal arrays can have only an integer index value, while array properties can have non-integer index values (you can index off of a string value).

- Object Pascal array elements are stored in consecutive order in memory; therefore, you can easily "walk" an array with a pointer by changing the position in memory to which the pointer points. Array properties can be accessed only one element at a time.

Array properties are characterized in the Object Inspector by a triple ellipses button (...) in the property value column. Delphi uses array properties for properties such as Lines, Items, and Sections. Published array properties cannot be directly edited from within the Object Inspector. They require using a custom property editor.

Property editors are covered in the following chapter; therefore, we need to create runtime array properties to demonstrate this property type. First, we need to create TArrayProp, which is an array from one to five of type string.

```
TArrayProp = array [1..5] of string[7];
```

Next, we need to create an internal data field named FArrayProp that is of type TArrayProp. We will initialize the string values for this property in the Create constructor of TEverything with the values of: one, two, three, four, and five. Finally, we will create a property named ArrayPropInt, which is an array property that has an integer index value. ArrayPropInt accesses the FArrayProp array via an *access method* and returns the string value of its integer index. Access methods are covered later in the section, "Creating Get and Set Procedures." We also create a property named ArrayPropStr, which is an array type property that has a string index value. ArrayPropStr also will make use of FArrayProp via an access method and return the integer value of its string index if it is defined, as follows:

```
property ArrayPropInt[Index: integer]: string read GetArrayPropInt;
property ArrayPropStr[Index: string]: integer read GetArrayPropStr;
```

Listing 16.7 shows the complete TEverything component with array properties. Notice that ArrayPropInt and ArrayPropStr are listed in the public section of the class. You also should note the overridden Create constructor in which the FArrayProp strings are initialized. Why GetArrayPropInt and GetArrayPropStr are written as they are is discussed later, but for now, you should notice that they behave as indicated previously.

Part

IV

Ch

16

Listing 16.7 \UDELPHI3\CHP16\LIST16-7—*TEverything* with Array Properties

```
unit EvryThng;

interface

uses
  Windows, Messages, SysUtils, Classes, Graphics, Controls, Forms, Dialogs;

type
  TArrayProp = array [1..5] of string[7];

  TEverything = class(TCustomControl)
  private
    { Private declarations }
    FArrayProp : TArrayProp;
    function GetArrayPropInt(pIndex: integer): string;
    function GetArrayPropStr(pIndex: string): integer;
  protected
    { Protected declarations }
  public
    { Public declarations }
    constructor Create(AOwner: TComponent); override;
    property ArrayPropInt[Index: integer]: string read GetArrayPropInt;
    property ArrayPropStr[Index: string]: integer read GetArrayPropStr;
  published
    { Published declarations }
  end;

procedure Register;

implementation

constructor TEverything.Create(AOwner: TComponent);
begin
```

continues

Listing 16.7 Continued

```
  // initialize the string values for FArrayProp
  FArrayProp[1] := 'one';
  FArrayProp[2] := 'two';
  FArrayProp[3] := 'three';
  FArrayProp[4] := 'four';
  FArrayProp[5] := 'five';
end;

function TEverything.GetArrayPropInt(pIndex: integer): string;
begin
  result := 'unknown';
  // if pIndex is defined in FArrayProp, set the result to the string value
  if pIndex in [1..5] then
    result := FArrayProp[pIndex];
end;

function TEverything.GetArrayPropStr(pIndex: string): integer;
var
  x : integer;
begin
  result := -1;
  // loop through FArrayProp and search for pIndex
  for x := 1 to 5 do
    // Use Uppercase to remove case sensitivity
    if UpperCase(FArrayProp[x]) = UpperCase(pIndex) then
    begin
      result := x;
      // drop out of the FOR loop
      exit;
    end;
end;

procedure Register;
begin
  RegisterComponents('UD3', [TEverything]);
end;

end.
```

Property Directives *Property directives* are commands that appear in code along with the property declaration and indicate to the compiler to treat the property in a certain way. All six property directives in Delphi are covered. They are as follows:

- Default
- NoDefault
- Default array property
- Stored
- Index
- Dispid

Default *Directive*   When you create properties, they initially have a zero value. Integer properties have a zero value, string properties an empty string, char properties a #0, set properties an empty set, and so on. When Delphi stores property values to a form file (*.DFM), it compares the current value of the property to its Default value. If they are different, it stores the value and if it is the same, it doesn't. For example:

```
property NumberProp: integer read FNumber write Fnumber default 5;
property EnumProp: TEnumProp read FEnumProp write FEnumProp default epOne;
property SetProp: TSetProp read FSetProp write FSetProp default [epOne];
```

If the property value of NumberProp is equal to 5, Delphi doesn't store a value for NumberProp.

CAUTION

The Default directive doesn't set a default value for a property in the Object Inspector. It is used only to determine if a value is stored or not when the property is streamed to the DFM file.

If no Default value is indicated for a property, Delphi always saves the value.

NoDefault *Directive*   The NoDefault property directive is used to tell Delphi that no default value exists for this property. This directive is commonly used on inherited properties that had a default value specified. By redeclaring the inherited property with the NoDefault directive, it forces Delphi to treat the property as if it had no default value. For example:

```
property NumberProp NoDefault;
```

If NumberProp were an inherited property with a default value, there now would be no default value.

Default *Directive for Array Properties*   The Default directive also can be used in conjunction with array properties. When you put the Default directive on an array property, you indicate to Delphi that this array is the default array property for the component. If you take the ArrayPropInt array property of TEverything and add the Default directive to it, as in the following code line,

```
property ArrayPropInt[Index: integer]: string read GetArrayPropInt; default;
```

and declare a variable named Everything of type TEverything, then we can access the variable Everything like this:

```
Caption := Everything[3];
```

This sets the caption equal to the string "three." A component can have only one default array property.

Stored *Directive*   The Stored property directive is used to indicate to Delphi whether or not to store a property value. The Stored directive can be followed by a true, a false, or a function that returns a Boolean value. By default, Delphi stores the values of all published properties. For example:

```
property NumberProp1: integer read FNum1 write FNum1 stored true;
property NumberProp2: integer read FNum2 write FNum2 stored false;
property NumberProp3: integer read FNum3 write FNum3 stored Func1;
```

The value of NumberProp1 is always stored, NumberProp2 is never stored, and NumberProp3 is stored only if the function Func1 returns a true value.

Index Directive   The Index directive is used in relation to the access methods of a property. This directive is covered in the following section, "Creating Get and Set Procedures."

Dispid Directive   The Dispid directive is used to assign a Dispatch ID to a property and is covered in Chapter 20, "Working with OLE Automation."

Reading and Writing Property Values

As you previously saw, properties provide an interface to internal data fields. As part of this interface, you need to be able to read or write to these internal fields. Delphi provides the capability to define the interaction with your internal data fields through the key words Read and Write. You can read and write directly to the internal data field, or you can create access methods to get and set the values of the internal data field.

You can create read-only and write-only properties by declaring a property with only a Read method or only a Write method, respectively.

Direct to Private Variables   Reading and writing directly to the internal data fields is the simplest method of changing the value of a property. In Listing 16.2, you saw the three simple property types defined as follows:

```
property NumberProp: integer read FNumber write FNumber;
property CharProp: char read FChar write FChar;
property StringProp: string read FString write FString;
```

Each of the three properties directly manipulates the internal data fields of TEverything by reading and writing to the private variables. Giving your component user direct access to the internal data fields, however, isn't always what is desired. Some property values may depend on other internal data field values or upon the state of the component at any given time. These types of properties need to have access methods.

Creating Get and Set Procedures   *Access methods* are functions and procedures that allow you to read from and write to property values. Functions are used to read from a property value and, by convention, start with the word "Get." Read functions take no parameters and return a value of the same type as the property. Procedures are used to write a property value and, by convention, start with the word "Set." Write procedures have one parameter of the same type as the property. The parameter can be passed by reference or by value, and it will contain the new value for that property. To illustrate this, we will create a property that has a read and a write access method, as follows:

```
Property BooleanProp: boolean read GetBooleanProp write SetBooleanProp;
```

The Read function might look something like the following:

```
function TEverything.GetBooleanProp: boolean;
begin
```

```
    result := false;
    if (FState = 0) then
      result := true;
end;
```

The Write procedure might look something like this:

```
procedure TEverything.SetBooleanProp(var pBool: Boolean);
begin
  if pBool then
    FState := 0
  else
    FState := 1;
end;
```

In the preceding example, BooleanProp is used to set an internal data field that is not a Boolean type. In fact, you do not even need to have a private FBooleanProp variable because the BooleanProp gets its value from FState.

There are two exceptions to the rule that Read functions have no parameters. The two exceptions are array properties and the Index property directive.

Array properties must use access methods to manipulate their internal data fields. For array properties the Read and Write methods both have parameters equal to—and in the same order as—their index types. In other words, if the array property has an integer index, the access methods will both have one integer parameter. If the array property has an integer index followed by a string index, the access methods will have two parameters, first an integer, then a string, and so on. For an example of this, see the access methods declared previously in Listing 16.7.

The Index property directive causes Read functions to have an integer parameter equal to the integer value that follows the Index directive on the property definition. Take, for example, the following:

```
property IntProp1: integer index 1 read GetIntProp write SetIntProp;
property IntProp2: integer index 2 read GetIntProp write SetIntProp;
```

Notice that both properties use the same access methods. If these were ordinary access methods, you would be left wondering how the access methods tell which property they are supposed to be accessing. Here, the magic of the Index directive comes into play. An integer parameter is added to each method to indicate which property is being accessed. The access methods GetIntProp and SetIntProp are defined as follows:

```
function TEverything.GetPropInt(pIndex: integer): integer;
begin
  case pIndex of
    1: result := FIntProp1;
    2: result := FIntProp2;
  end;
end;

procedure TEverything.SetPropInt(pIndex : integer; pValue: integer);
begin
```

```
    case pIndex of
      1: FIntProp1 := pValue;
      2: FIntProp2 := pValue;
    end;
end;
```

Initializing Values   There are two methods available for initializing internal data fields. The first method is to override the Create constructor, and the second method is to override the Loaded method.

Overriding the Create Constructor   Overriding the Create constructor provides you with an opportunity to initialize internal data fields to the default value that you want them to have. Unlike using the Default property directive, initializing values in the Create constructor actually sets the value of the internal data field. Previously, in the section, "Creating Object Properties," you saw an example of overriding the Create constructor to instantiate an object property. A good rule when overriding the Create constructor is to call the inherited Create constructor first, before doing any of your own initialization. Very rarely do you need to initialize something before the inherited behavior takes place.

Overriding the Loaded Method   Overriding the Loaded method provides you with an opportunity to initialize internal data fields after your component was created but before it is shown on a form. To understand the significance of the Loaded method, it is necessary to understand the sequence of events when your component is streamed in from a DFM file, which is shown in the following steps:

1. The component is instantiated.

2. Internal data fields are initialized to zero or the value specified in an overridden Create constructor.

3. Stored component data is read in from the DFM file.

4. The Loaded method is called.

5. The component is shown.

> **CAUTION**
>
> When overriding the Loaded method, always call the inherited Loaded method first to ensure that all inherited properties are initialized correctly.

To demonstrate this, the following example overrides the Loaded method of TEverything and sets its Color property equal to clRed if the value "5" was stored in the IntegerProp property and set its color to clGreen if it is any other value. This action cannot be done in the Create constructor because, in the constructor, the value stored in DFM file for the IntegerProp property is unavailable. This code is shown in Listing 16.8. You can find this file on this book's companion CD-ROM.

**Listing 16.8   \UDELPHI3\CHP16\LIST16-8—*TEverything* with an
Overridden Loaded Method**

```
unit EvryThng;

interface

uses
  Windows, Messages, SysUtils, Classes, Graphics, Controls, Forms, Dialogs;

type
  TEverything = class(TCustomControl)
  private
    { Private declarations }
    FInteger  : integer;
  protected
    { Protected declarations }
    procedure Loaded; override;
  public
    { Public declarations }
  published
    { Published declarations }
    property IntegerProp: integer read FInteger write FInteger;
  end;

procedure Register;

implementation

procedure TEverything.Loaded;
begin
  inherited Loaded;
  if IntegerProp = 5 then
    Color := clRed
  else
    Color := clGreen;
end;

procedure Register;
begin
  RegisterComponents('UD3', [TEverything]);
end;

end.
```

Creating Methods

Methods are procedures and functions belonging to the component class definition. You need to give as much thought to creating methods to interface your component as properties. Although properties provide an interface to the characteristics of your component, methods provide a way for the component user to request that your component perform some action. For simplicity and good component design, keep method names simple and intuitive, and try to remove or minimize any interdependencies among your methods.

Types of Methods   Component methods are no different than regular Object Pascal methods. You can create one of five types of methods: standard, virtual, dynamic, message, and abstract. Standard and dynamic methods are covered in Chapter 4, "Object Pascal: Advanced Concepts," and message methods are covered in the following chapter. Here, Virtual and Abstract methods as they relate to component building are covered.

Creating Virtual Methods   Virtual methods add to the extensibility of your component. Just as you occasionally want to inherit from one of Delphi's VCL components, someone may want to inherit from yours. Only virtual and dynamic methods can be overridden, so you should make as many virtual methods available to your users without giving them the capability to change the intent of your component. Who knows, you may end up deriving a component from one of your own custom components!

Creating Abstract Methods   Abstract methods are commonly found in "base class" components and serve as placeholders for methods that must be implemented in descendant components. Calling an abstract method is a surefire way of generating a runtime error 210, as in the following example:

```
type
  TCustomGrid = class(TCustomControl)
...
  protected
    procedure DrawCell(ACol, ARow: Longint; ARect: TRect;
                       AState: TGridDrawState); virtual; abstract;
...
  end;
```

TCustomGrid, the base class from which all grids in Delphi are derived, declares a virtual abstract method DrawCell. DrawCell is a method that is called by the Paint method to draw every cell in a grid. TCustomGrid doesn't implement the DrawCell method so that classes derived from it can draw their cells in their own unique manner. TDrawGrid and TStringGrid are good examples of this: Both are derived from TCustomGrid, and override and implement this method in their respective classes.

N O T E   The Delphi compiler displays a warning message if you try to instantiate a class that contains abstract methods. However, this doesn't prohibit you from creating the instance of the class. Calling an abstract method generates a runtime error 210. ■

Method Visibility   The visibility of methods depends on which section in the class declaration they are declared in. Methods declared in the private section of a component are only available from within the Unit that contains the class declaration. Methods declared in the protected section of a component can be seen only by the class in which they are declared, as well as in derived classes. Methods declared in the public section of a component can be seen by anyone using the component. It's customary to put access methods in the `private` section, base class methods in the `protected` section, and basic functionality methods (methods that all instances of this component need for functionality) to which you want all users to have access in the `public` section. You cannot put methods in the `published` section of a component—only properties.

You can increase the visibility of existing methods in the `protected` section of a component by redeclaring them in the public section of the component.

Creating Events

An event occurs in your application and in your components as a result of the operating system sending a message that some action has taken place. These actions can be a direct result of user interaction, such as a button click or a key press, or they can be the result of a system action, such as the palette was changed or a timer was fired. From a user's point of view, they can hook into these events by creating an *event handler* off of the Events page in the Object Inspector. What the component user doesn't see is that for every event handler, there is an *event dispatch method.* The event dispatch method is what is actually notified that an event occurred. The event dispatch method then processes the event and checks to see if the user has assigned an event handler; if they have, the event dispatch method calls the event handler.

By convention, event handler names are prefixed with `On`, and event dispatch methods are of the same name minus the `On`. A good example of this is the `Click` event dispatch method and the `OnClick` event handler.

Event Structure Event dispatch methods are procedural methods that are called when your component receives a message that an event that affects your component has occurred. Most dispatch methods are declared as virtual and protected so that they can be overridden in descendant components, but not by the user. Event handlers, or event properties (as they are sometimes called), are properties that read and write to method pointers. Event handlers usually are declared in the published section of a component so that they are available in the Object Inspector except for base classes that declare them in the protected section, so that descendant classes can make them available to the user as needed. Examine the following code snippet from `TControl` in the VCL source code:

```
TMouseEvent = procedure(Sender: TObject; Button: TMouseButton;
    Shift: TShiftState; X, Y: Integer) of object;
TMouseMoveEvent = procedure(Sender: TObject; Shift: TShiftState;
    X, Y: Integer) of object;
TNotifyEvent = procedure(Sender: TObject) of object;

TControl = class(TComponent)
private
  ...
  FOnMouseDown: TMouseEvent;
  FOnMouseMove: TMouseMoveEvent;
  FOnMouseUp: TMouseEvent;
  FOnClick: TNotifyEvent;
  FOnDblClick: TNotifyEvent;
  ...
```

Part
IV
Ch
16

```
protected
...
  property OnClick: TNotifyEvent read FOnClick write FOnClick;
  property OnDblClick: TNotifyEvent read FOnDblClick write FOnDblClick;
  property OnMouseDown: TMouseEvent read FOnMouseDown write FOnMouseDown;
  property OnMouseMove: TMouseMoveEvent read FOnMouseMove write FOnMouseMove;
  property OnMouseUp: TMouseEvent read FOnMouseUp write FOnMouseUp;
...
end;
```

When Delphi sees a published property whose type is a method pointer, it automatically puts the property on the Events tab of the Object Inspector. Notice that each event can take only a method pointer, not a function pointer, which is why you cannot assign a standard procedure as an event handler. Each property reads and writes to a private variable of the same method pointer type that the event is declared as.

On the CD

Overriding Standard Events   You may be tempted at first to just create a default event handler and automatically assign it to the event property in order to change the behavior of a component, which definitely changes the behavior of the component, until a user assigns one of his or her own event handlers to the event property. When this situation occurs, your behavior disappears and the default behavior returns. To truly change the behavior of an existing event, you need to override the event dispatch method of the component. By overriding the event dispatch method, you get to determine when the inherited behavior is called and when the event handler is called. For an example of this, create your own button component that changes its caption to the current time when the button is clicked. To do this, you will override the Click event dispatch method, as shown in Listing 16.9. You can find this file on this book's companion CD-ROM.

Listing 16.9   \UDELPHI3\CHP16\LIST16-9—*TTimeButton* with an Overridden Event Dispatch Method

```
TTimeButton = class(TButton)
protected
  procedure Click; override;
end;

Procedure TTimeButton.Click;
begin
  inherited Click;
  Caption := DateTimeToStr(Now);
end;
```

Notice that the inherited Click method is called before the changing of the caption. This means that any event handlers that a user may have attached to the OnClick event will happen before the caption on the button changes. If you wanted your code to occur first, you could have called the inherited method after our code.

Creating Custom Events Creating custom events is a two-part task. First, you must create an event dispatch method that may in turn call an event handler. Then you have to enable your component to respond to the action that you want to trigger your event dispatch method. Most custom events are created to respond to a component receiving a certain message. Handling messages in this fashion is covered in the following chapter. You previously saw how to declare an event property and a private event handler variable. In the following lines, you see the standard code for an event dispatch method:

```
procedure TSomeObject.EventDispatch;
begin
  // Assume FOnEventHandler is of type TNotifyEvent
  // do some code processing here
  if Assigned(FOnEventHandler) then
    FOnEventHandler(Self);
  // do some more code here if needed
end;
```

The preceding code is typical for event dispatch methods. Usually, there is some code processing after an event occurs. Then, if the user has assigned an event handler, it is called. Finally, more code processing may take place. Every event dispatch method differs, depending on the functionality of the event. This is another area in component design where the VCL source code is invaluable. Examining the source code lets you see where in the event handling process the event handler is being called. This helps you determine if you need to create a new event dispatch method or just create an event handler via the Object Inspector.

Testing the Component

Two methods are available to test your component. The first method is to add your custom component to the component palette, and then drop it onto a new application. The second method is to create a small application that instantiates your component at runtime. Both methods have advantages and disadvantages. The first method allows you to test how your component behaves at design-time and runtime and doesn't force you to write code to instantiate and initialize your component. However, the first method forces you to recompile your component's package every time you need to change your component. The second method allows you to test how the component behaves at runtime but cannot be displayed in the Object Inspector.

I tend to use the second method to "rough out" the component and verify that the major functionality works. Then I use the first method to test how the component behaves at design-time from a user's point of view. The first method is covered in a later section, "Registering the Component." The second method is covered here.

A typical application designed to test a component consists of a form with several buttons. One button is used to instantiate the custom component, a second button frees the component, another sets some properties, another triggers some event, and so on. When instantiating components at runtime, it's important to remember to set the Parent property of the component after it is instantiated. If it is a visual control, you also may need to set properties to indicate where and how the control is displayed (Top, Left, Enabled, and Visible). Listing 16.10 shows how a test application might look for TEverything. You can find this file on this book's companion CD-ROM.

Listing 16.10   \UDELPHI3\CHP16\LIST16-10—Test Application for *TEverything*

```
unit Unit1;

interface

uses
  Windows, Messages, SysUtils, Classes, Graphics, Controls, Forms, Dialogs,
  StdCtrls;

type
  TForm1 = class(TForm)
    Button1: TButton;
    Button2: TButton;
    Button3: TButton;
    Button4: TButton;
    procedure Button1Click(Sender: TObject);
    procedure Button2Click(Sender: TObject);
    procedure Button3Click(Sender: TObject);
    procedure Button4Click(Sender: TObject);
  private
    { Private declarations }
  public
    { Public declarations }
  end;

var
  Form1: TForm1;

implementation

uses EvryThng;

{$R *.DFM}

var
  Everything : TEverything;

procedure TForm1.Button1Click(Sender: TObject);
begin
  // Instantiate Everything
  Everything := TEverything.Create(Self);
  // Initialize Everything's values
  with Everything do begin
    Parent := Self;
    Left := 20;
    Top := 20;
```

```
      Height := 40;
      Width := 100;
      Color := clBlue;
      NumberProp := 5;
    end;
end;

procedure TForm1.Button2Click(Sender: TObject);
begin
  if Assigned(Everything) then
    Caption := IntToStr(Everything.NumberProp);
end;

procedure TForm1.Button3Click(Sender: TObject);
begin
  if Assigned(Everything) then
    Everything.color := clRed;
end;

procedure TForm1.Button4Click(Sender: TObject);
begin
  EveryThing.Free;
end;

end.
```

Creating a Component Icon

When Delphi adds your component to the component palette, it looks for an icon in a DCR (Delphi Component Resource) file of the same name as the unit name of your component. A DCR file is simply a RES (Resource) file that was renamed. If Delphi doesn't find the DCR file, it uses a default icon to represent your component on the component palette. Inside the DCR file, you need to create a 16- or 256-color bitmap that is 24×24 pixels in size. It's recommended that you create a 16-color bitmap due to palette issues. A 256-color bitmap looks awful on a machine that runs only 16 colors, and on 256-color machines you are at the mercy of the currently loaded color palette. The bitmap's name must be the same as your component class' name, in uppercase. The following steps show how to create a component icon for TEverything:

1. Open the Image Editor by selecting Tools, Image Editor from the Delphi toolbar.

2. In the Image Editor, select File, New, Delphi Component Resource File.

3. Open the New Bitmap dialog box by selecting Resource, New, Bitmap. This action creates a bitmap named Bitmap1.

4. Set Bitmap1's width and height to 24 and the number of colors to 16 or 256.

5. Double-click Bitmap1 and create your component's bitmap.

6. Rename the bitmap from Bitmap1 to TEVERYTHING.

7. Select File, Save As and enter EvryThng.DCR.

If you didn't save the DCR file to the same location as your component's PAS file, you need to move it there.

TIP When Delphi displays icons on the component palette, it uses the color of the bottom left pixel as the transparent color for your icon. All instances of this color in your bitmap become transparent and are thus "removed" from your bitmap. Delphi uses clOlive for the background and transparent color of all its icons.

Registering the Component

In earlier versions of Delphi, components were installed to the Component Palette by compiling them into the Component Library DLL. In Delphi 3, the Component Library has been replaced by packages, as discussed in Chapter 15, "Working with Packages." In Figure 16.1, you saw Delphi's Component Expert and all the items necessary to create the basic component framework for a custom component. Clicking the Install button on the Component Expert allows you to set which design-time package into which you would like to install your component. If the package that you want does not exist, you can create a new package as shown in Figure 16.6.

FIG. 16.6
The Install Component dialog box.

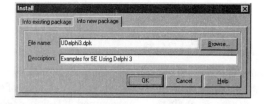

If you do not select a package to install your component into at creation time, you can simply select Component, Install Component from Delphi's Main Menu to accomplish the same result. After you have installed your component into a package, it will automatically appear on the Component Palette, ready to be used.

Putting It All Together

This chapter covered the basics of component writing and laid the foundation for writing custom components in Delphi. You have learned what a component is, the basic VCL class hierarchy, how to choose the correct ancestor, how to create your own properties and events, how to debug your components, and finally how to add your component to Delphi's Component Palette. A firm grasp of these fundamentals is crucial to applying the advanced component-writing techniques discussed in the next chapter.

As an example of the basic techniques learned here, let's create a custom component that encapsulates Delphi's TApplication class. TApplication is an object that gets created behind the scenes as part of every Delphi application. It has numerous properties and events that allow you to control many aspects of your application. Because Delphi doesn't use a visual TApplication component, you are forced to manipulate its properties and event handlers programmatically. This is often accomplished in the OnCreate event for an application's main form.

We will create a non-visual custom component named TApplicationComp that allows you to set these properties and event handlers at design-time. Because this is a non-visual component, we will descend our component from TComponent. We will declare properties and events identical to TApplication class and assign our components properties and events to TApplication's properties and events in the Loaded method. If you do not understand why this must be done in the Loaded method, go back and read the section, "Initializing Values." Using the skills learned in this chapter, you should be able to create the component framework shown in Listing 16.11.

Listing 16.11 \UDELPHI3\CHP16\LIST16-11—*TApplicationComp* Custom Component

```
unit AppCompU;

interface

uses
  Windows, Messages, SysUtils, Classes, Graphics, Controls, Forms, Dialogs;

type
  TApplicationComp = class(TComponent)
  private
    { Private declarations }
    FAllowTesting: Boolean;
    FHint: string;
    FHintColor: TColor;
    FHintPause: Integer;
    FHintShortPause: Integer;
    FHintHidePause: Integer;
    FShowHint: Boolean;
    FShowMainForm: Boolean;
    FUpdateFormatSettings: Boolean;
    FUpdateMetricSettings: Boolean;

    FOnActivate: TNotifyEvent;
    FOnDeactivate: TNotifyEvent;
    FOnException: TExceptionEvent;
    FOnIdle: TIdleEvent;
    FOnHelp: THelpEvent;
    FOnHint: TNotifyEvent;
    FOnMessage: TMessageEvent;
    FOnMinimize: TNotifyEvent;
    FOnRestore: TNotifyEvent;
```

continues

Listing 16.11 Continued

```
    FOnShowHint: TShowHintEvent;
  protected
    { Protected declarations }
    procedure Loaded; override;
  public
    { Public declarations }
  published
    { Published declarations }
    // Properties
    property AllowTesting: Boolean read FAllowTesting write FAllowTesting;
    property Hint: string read FHint write FHint;
    property HintColor: TColor read FHintColor write FHintColor;
    property HintPause: Integer read FHintPause write FHintPause;
    property HintShortPause: Integer read FHintShortPause
                        write FHintShortPause;
    property HintHidePause: Integer read FHintHidePause write FHintHidePause;
    property ShowHint: Boolean read FShowHint write FShowHint;
    property ShowMainForm: Boolean read FShowMainForm write FShowMainForm;
    property UpdateFormatSettings: Boolean read FUpdateFormatSettings
      write FUpdateFormatSettings;
    property UpdateMetricSettings: Boolean read FUpdateMetricSettings
      write FUpdateMetricSettings;

    // Events
    property OnActivate: TNotifyEvent read FOnActivate write FOnActivate;
    property OnDeactivate: TNotifyEvent read FOnDeactivate
                        write FOnDeactivate;
    property OnException: TExceptionEvent read FOnException
                        write FOnException;
    property OnIdle: TIdleEvent read FOnIdle write FOnIdle;
    property OnHelp: THelpEvent read FOnHelp write FOnHelp;
    property OnHint: TNotifyEvent read FOnHint write FOnHint;
    property OnMessage: TMessageEvent read FOnMessage write FOnMessage;
    property OnMinimize: TNotifyEvent read FOnMinimize write FOnMinimize;
    property OnRestore: TNotifyEvent read FOnRestore write FOnRestore;
    property OnShowHint: TShowHintEvent read FOnShowHint write FOnShowHint;
  end;

procedure Register;

implementation

procedure TApplicationComp.Loaded;
begin
  // Assign the Properties
  if FAllowTesting <> Application.AllowTesting then
    Application.AllowTesting := FAllowTesting;
```

```
  if FHint <> '' then
    Application.Hint := FHint;
  if FHintColor <> Application.HintColor then
    Application.HintColor := FHintColor;
  if FHintPause <> Application.HintPause then
    Application.HintPause := FHintPause;
  if FHintShortPause <> Application.HintShortPause then
    Application.HintShortPause := FHintShortPause;
  if FHintHidePause <> Application.HintHidePause then
    Application.HintHidePause := FHintHidePause;
  if FShowHint <> Application.ShowHint then
    Application.ShowHint := FShowHint;
  if FShowMainForm <> Application.ShowMainForm then
    Application.ShowMainForm := FShowMainForm;
  if FUpdateFormatSettings <> Application.UpdateFormatSettings then
    Application.UpdateFormatSettings := FUpdateFormatSettings;
  if FUpdateMetricSettings <> Application.UpdateMetricSettings then
    Application.UpdateMetricSettings := FUpdateMetricSettings;

  // Assign the Events
  if Assigned(FOnActivate)then
    Application.OnActivate := FOnActivate;
  if Assigned(FOnDeactivate)then
    Application.OnDeactivate := FOnDeactivate;
  if Assigned(FOnException)then
    Application.OnException := FOnException;
  if Assigned(FOnIdle)then
    Application.OnIdle := FOnIdle;
  if Assigned(FOnHelp)then
    Application.OnHelp := FOnHelp;
  if Assigned(FOnHint)then
    Application.OnHint := FOnHint;
  if Assigned(FOnMessage)then
    Application.OnMessage := FOnMessage;
  if Assigned(FOnMinimize)then
    Application.OnMinimize := FOnMinimize;
  if Assigned(FOnRestore)then
    Application.OnRestore := FOnRestore;
  if Assigned(FOnShowHint)then
    Application.OnShowHint := FOnShowHint;
end;

procedure Register;
begin
  RegisterComponents('UD3', [TApplicationComp]);
end;

end.
```

Part

IV

Ch

16

CHAPTER 17

Writing Advanced Components

by David Powell

This chapter builds upon the last chapter and covers more useful properties and methods, data-aware controls, message handling, property editors, and component editors. ■

Properties and methods

A continuing look at important properties and methods that are available in the base component classes.

Data-Aware controls

Learn how to database-enable your custom controls.

Messages

Discover how to respond to Windows messages and how to create your own custom messages.

Property editors

Learn how to create property editors.

Component editors

Learn how to create component editors.

More Properties

Besides the properties covered in the last chapter, Delphi's core component classes provide three more key properties that are used in advanced component design. One property indicates the state of a component and the other two are used to determine the state and style of a control.

Examining a Component's State

The base component class TComponent introduces a property named ComponentState. This property is used to indicate the current state of a component. This property can prove to be useful when you want your component to behave in a certain way, depending on what it's doing at a given time.

For example, many component writers release their components as shareware. As a reminder to the component user, they may want to display a registration notification message at design-time or even at runtime. Table 17.1 is an excerpt from Delphi's help file and shows the eight states that your component can be in.

Table 17.1 *ComponentState* **Property Values**

Flag	Component State
csAncestor	Set if the component was introduced in an ancestor form. Only set if csDesigning is also set.
csDesigning	Design mode—it's in a form being manipulated at designtime.
csDestroying	The component is about to be destroyed.
csFixups	Set if the component is linked to a component in another form that has not yet been loaded. This flag is cleared when all pending fixups are resolved.
csLoading	Loading from a filer object.
csReading	Reading its property values from a stream.
csUpdating	The component is being updated to reflect changes in an ancestor form. Only set if csAncestor is also set.
csWriting	Writing its property values to a stream.

To see if your component is in a certain state, you check to see if that state flag is in the ComponentState property set. You would check to see if the component is in design mode as follows:

```
if (csDesigning in ComponentState) then
  ShowMessage('Please register this Component');
```

Examining a Control's State

The base component class TControl introduces a set property that contains the current state of a control at runtime. The ControlState property is defined as follows:

```
TControlState = set of (csLButtonDown, csClicked, csPalette, csReadingState,
                        csAlignmentNeeded, csFocusing, csCreating, csPaintCopy);
```

These state flags are specific to controls (descendants of TControl) and are in addition to the state flags in the ComponentState property. Table 17.2 explains what each state flag means.

Table 17.2 *ControlState* Property Values

Flag	Meaning
csLButtonDown	The left mouse button was clicked and not yet released. This is set for all left button mouse-down events.
csClicked	The same as csLButtonDown, but only set if ControlStyle contains csClickEvents, meaning that left button mouse-down events are interpreted as clicks.
csPalette	A WM_PALETTCHANGED message was received by either the control or one of its parents.
csReadingState	The control is reading its state from a stream.
csAlignmentNeeded	The control needs to realign itself when alignment is re-enabled.
csFocusing	The application is processing messages intended to give the control focus. This doesn't guarantee that the control will receive focus, but prevents recursive calls.
csCreating	The control and/or its owner and subcontrols are being created. This flag clears when all controls have finished creating.
csPaintCopy	The control is being replicated, which means a copy of the control is being painted. The ControlStyle flag csReplicatable must be set for this state to occur.

Setting a Control's Style

The ControlStyle property is a set of control style flags that are used to determine the characteristics of a control. You usually set or alter a control's ControlStyle property in the Create constructor for the component. A control's style is usually fixed after creation time and doesn't change. However, you can programmatically change the control's style at designtime (in a property editor or component editor) or at runtime.

The ControlStyle property is defined as a property of type TControlStyle. TControlStyle is defined as the following:

```
TControlStyle = set of (csAcceptsControls, csCaptureMouse, csDesignInteractive,
            csClickEvents, csFramed, csSetCaption, csOpaque, csDoubleClicks,
            csFixedWidth, csFixedHeight, csNoDesignVisible, csReplicatable,
            csNoStdEvents, DisplayDragImage);
```

The ControlStyle property is introduced in the base class TControl and is initialized in the constructor as containing the following flags:

```
FControlStyle := [csCaptureMouse, csClickEvents, csSetCaption, csDoubleClicks];
```

Table 17.3 examines each of the style flags and describes its effect on appearance and behavior of a control.

Table 17.3 *ControlStyle* Property Values

Flag	Meaning
csAcceptsControls	The control becomes the parent of any controls dropped on it at designtime.
csCaptureMouse	The control captures mouse events when it's clicked.
csDesignInteractive	The control maps right mouse-button clicks at designtime into left-button clicks to manipulate the control.
csClickEvents	The control can receive and respond to mouse clicks.
csFramed	The control has a 3-D frame.
csSetCaption	The control should change its caption to match the Name property if the caption isn't explicitly set to something else.
csOpaque	The control completely fills its client area.
csDoubleClicks	The control can receive and respond to double-click messages. Otherwise, map double-clicks into clicks.
csFixedWidth	The width of the control doesn't vary.
csFixedHeight	The height of the control doesn't vary.
csNoDesignVisible	The control isn't visible at designtime.
csReplicatable	The control can be dropped on a DBCtrlGrid.
csNoStdEvents	Standard events such as mouse, key, and click events are ignored. Use this setting if your code doesn't need to respond to these events, and your application will run faster.
csDisplayDragImage	The control can display an image from an image list when the control is dragged over. Use this setting if your control correctly handles an image list being dragged over it.

T I P If you are subclassing an existing control to surface the `OnClick` or `OnDblClick` events and your control still isn't responding to these events, first check the `ControlStyle` property to see if the `csClickEvents` or `csDoubleClicks` flag has been removed.

Important Methods

Delphi's VCL provides many useful methods that are part of the base component classes. In addition to the methods covered in the last chapter, Delphi's core component classes provide five more key methods that are commonly used in advanced component design.

Loaded Method

Part IV Ch 17

The `Loaded` method was covered in the Chapter 16, "Creating Components," in the section "Initializing Values." The `Loaded` method provides an opportunity in the creation process to examine a component's property values after it has been streamed in from the DFM file and before the component is shown. This is your opportunity to initialize private and public data fields that may depend on the saved value of another property.

Notification Method

The `Notification` method is a virtual method introduced by `TComponent` and is called by the Delphi IDE every time a component is dropped onto a form or removed from a form. The `Notification` method is defined as follows:

```
procedure Notification(AComponent: TComponent; Operation: TOperation); virtual;
```

The `Notification` method has two parameters. The first parameter is the component being added or removed from the form. The second parameter is the operation being performed, either `opInsert` or `opRemove`. This method is important for components that reference other components on the form as one of their properties. Take for example the `Notification` method for `TBatchMove`, as follows:

```
procedure TBatchMove.Notification(AComponent: TComponent;
  Operation: TOperation);
begin
  inherited Notification(AComponent, Operation);
  if Operation = opRemove then
  begin
    if Destination = AComponent then Destination := nil;
    if Source = AComponent then Source := nil;
  end;
end;
```

It calls the inherited `Notification` first, and then checks to see if the operation is an `opRemove`. If so, it checks to see if the component being removed is the same component being used for the `Source` or `Destination` datasets. If so, the respective property is set to `nil`.

FreeNotification Method

The FreeNotification method is a static method introduced by TComponent. FreeNotification takes one parameter of type TComponent. This method is used to ensure that the component passed as the parameter is notified via its Notification method when the called component is freed.

To put it another way, your component calls the FreeNotification method of another component and passes itself as the parameter. When the other component is freed, your component gets notified via its Notification method.

The FreeNotification method is defined as follows:

```
procedure FreeNotification(AComponent: TComponent);
```

The Notification method of your component is automatically called when any component is added or removed from the form on which your component resides. If your component depends on a component that resides on another form, your component will not automatically be notified that the other component was removed, unless you explicitly tell the other component to notify you. This often overlooked scenario commonly comes up when creating data-aware controls where the TDataSource component resides in a DataModule. The "Creating a Data-Aware Control" section, which follows in this chapter, shows an example of using FreeNotification with a data-aware control.

DestroyWnd Method

The DestroyWnd method is first introduced by TWinControl and is part of the destruction process of a component. It is responsible for freeing any device contexts associated with a control and destroying the Window Handle. This is the last place in the destruction sequence that a component's HWnd is valid. This method is called before a component's Destroy destructor. If you keep getting an error message that states "Window has no parent" while executing code in your overridden Destroy destructor, you are doing something that depends on a valid window handle and this code must be done in the DestroyWnd method. When overriding this method, you want to execute your code before calling the inherited DestroyWnd method. For an example of this, take a look at the following code from TCustomEdit:

```
procedure TCustomEdit.DestroyWnd;
begin
  FModified := Modified;
  inherited DestroyWnd;
end;

function TCustomEdit.GetModified: Boolean;
begin
  Result := FModified;
  if HandleAllocated then
    Result := SendMessage(Handle, EM_GETMODIFY, 0, 0) <> 0;
end;
```

The overridden DestroyWnd method sets the internal data field FModified equal to the Modified property. Now GetModified, which is the read method for the Modified property, does a

SendMessage, using the edit control's Window Handle. In this case, it's necessary to perform an action in the destruction sequence where the Window Handle is still valid and the only place that it can be done is in this method.

GetChildren Method

The GetChildren method is a dynamic method that is first introduced in TComponent and is part of the streaming process of a component. GetChildren is defined as follows:

```
procedure GetChildren(Proc: TGetChildProc; Root: TComponent); dynamic;
TGetChildProc = procedure (Child: TComponent) of object;
```

If you are writing a component that descends from one of the base component classes and the component is a container class, you need to override the GetChildren method to have components that are dropped onto your control at designtime saved to the DFM file. The GetChildren method receives two parameters, one named Proc—which in itself is a procedure—and one named Root—which is a TComponent that indicates the "owner" component that GetChildren is looking for Children of. The GetChildren method needs to iterate through every control or component owned by it and call Proc for each child component. The Root parameter is not always used; it depends upon the situation. For an example of this, look at the code for TMenuItem:

```
procedure TMenuItem.GetChildren(Proc: TGetChildProc; Root: TComponent);
var
  I: Integer;
begin
  for I := 0 to Count - 1 do
    Proc(Items[I]);
end;
```

TMenuItem iterates through each element of its Items property and calls the Proc procedure with a parameter of the Item. This causes each element of the Items property to be streamed to the DFM file. In this situation, TMenuItem needs to stream all items in its Items property; so it does not bother to check the owner of each item against the Root parameter because it knows that it is the owner of all of its menu items. If this were a container class, it might have been necessary to check the Owner property of each component against the Root parameter. If you are inheriting from an existing component and not a base class, you rarely need to override this method.

Responding to Messages

Messages are an interface between the Windows environment and your component. Messages indicate to you that some action, somewhere, has taken place. Frequently, it's necessary for a component to respond to Windows messages whether they are standard messages or user defined. Most standard Windows messages are already defined in the WINDOWS.PAS source file. Many standard messages are already implemented in the base component classes. Occasionally, however, you may need to respond to messages that are not already handled or you may need to create your own user-defined messages.

Responding to Windows' Messages

When an application is sent a Windows message, it receives a record that is defined as follows:

```
PMsg = ^TMsg;
TMsg = packed record
  hwnd: HWND;
  message: UINT;
  wParam: WPARAM;
  lParam: LPARAM;
  time: DWORD;
  pt: TPoint;
end;
```

The hwnd field is the window handle of the control that the message is intended for. The message field is a predefined constant value, indicating the message number (these constants are defined in the MESSAGES.PAS source file). The wParam and lParam fields contain message-specific data. The time field indicates the time that Windows dispatched to message, and the pt field indicates the position of the mouse cursor at the time of the message.

Delphi's internal Message Loop grabs messages from the Message Queue and puts them into a generic message type that is defined as follows:

```
PMessage = ^TMessage;
TMessage = record
  Msg: Cardinal;
  case Integer of
    0: (
      WParam: Longint;
      LParam: Longint;
      Result: Longint);
    1: (
      WParamLo: Word;
      WParamHi: Word;
      LParamLo: Word;
      LParamHi: Word;
      ResultLo: Word;
      ResultHi: Word);
end;
```

There are many message-specific records defined in MESSAGES.PAS that are of the same size as TMessage.

In order to respond to a Windows message, you must create a method procedure that takes one parameter of type TMessage (or one of the other TMessage type records mentioned previously). You also must put the keyword message followed by the message constant value at the end of the method declaration. It's standard practice to name the procedure the same name as the message constant without the underscore.

For example, in the interface section, you would declare the following:

```
TEverything = class(TCustomControl)
. . .
public
  procedure WMChar(var Message: TWMChar); message WM_CHAR;
end;
```

In the implementation section, you would declare the following:

```
procedure TEverything.WMChar(var Message: TWMChar);
begin
  MessageBeep(0);
  inherited;
end;
```

Notice that this is much like calling an overridden virtual method because `message WM_CHAR` is actually a dynamic method whose dynamic method table is mapped to the message constants. Unlike virtual methods, you don't need to specify which inherited method needs to be called, nor do you have to specify any parameters. In this instance, `inherited` means "pass the message off to the ancestor's message handler."

Some of Windows' messages expect a result back from the windowed control. This is the purpose of the `Result` field in the `TMessage` record. Simply fill in the `Result` field with the appropriate data.

Responding to User-Defined Messages

At times, it is necessary to define your own custom messages. In Delphi, it's safe to create messages between `wm_User + 151` through `$7FFF` for user-defined messages. Messages should be created only with hard-coded constant values that will be used internally to an application, unless you are absolutely sure that every other Windows application in existence doesn't use the same value. I know this sounds extreme, but when messages are broadcast to windowed controls, they respond to message numbers. Your application could get bogus messages or send bogus messages to other applications.

If you need to send custom messages between applications, you should use the `RegisterWindowMessage` API call to register your custom message with the operating system. The API call returns a message constant to you. Both applications need to make this API call. The first application to run will register the message and the subsequent applications get the registered message number. `RegisterWindowMessage` is defined as follows:

```
UINT RegisterWindowMessage(
    LPCTSTR  lpsz      // address of message string
  );
```

It takes one parameter, which is a null-terminated string that contains the unique message name that you want to register. If Windows doesn't already have this message registered, it registers the message and returns a constant value between `$C000` and `$FFFF`. If it already has the message registered, it just returns the message constant. After a message is registered, it stays registered until the end of the Windows session.

Data-Aware Controls

A data-aware control is created much like other custom components, with the exception of the *data-link object*. The data-link object handles the interaction between the component and a TDataSource. There are several types of data-aware control. Some data-aware controls can only read data from a dataset, others can read and write data, and still others can control multiple records (the DBCtrlGrid). The base class for all data-link objects is TDataLink. Table 17.4 lists the different descendants of the TDataLink class.

Table 17.4   *TDataLink* **Type Classes**

Name	Description
TGridDataLink	Used to specify the dataset for the DBGrid.
TMasterDataLink	Used to specify the master dataset in a master/detail relationship.
TFieldDataLink	Used to specify the dataset for data-aware controls that manipulate only one field.
TNavDataLink	Used to specify the dataset for the TDBNavigator.
TDataSourceLink	Used to specify the dataset for DBLookupComboBox and DBLookupListBox.
TListSourceLink	Used to specify the lookup dataset for DBLookupComboBox and DBLookupListBox.
TDBCtrlGridLink	Used to specify the dataset for the DBCtrlGrid.
TQueryDataLink	Used to specify the dataset of the DataSource property of a TQuery.
THTTPDataLink	Used to specify the dataset in the Internet control TDataSetTableProducer.

Important Properties and Methods of *TDataLink*

TDataLink contains several important public properties and methods inherited by all descendant data-link objects. This section examines these properties and methods.

***UpdateRecord* Method**   The UpdateRecord method is used to notify a data-link object that it needs to update its data values with the values in the associated control. It's up to you, as the component writer, to determine when this should occur to meet your component's specific needs. This method is commonly called when a data-aware control loses focus.

***Active* Property**   The Active property is a read-only property that indicates whether or not the dataset that the data-link object is attached to is active or not.

***ActiveRecord* Property**   The ActiveRecord property is used to get or set the record number of current record in the managed dataset. This isn't the record number of the current record in the database; it applies only to the buffering of the dataset (in a TDBGrid, the managed dataset is the set of visible rows and the ActiveRecord is the row that the current record is on).

***BufferCount* Property**   The BufferCount property is used to get or set the number of records to be buffered together. TDBGrid sets the BufferCount to be the number of fully visible rows in the control. This property is normally used in conjunction with the RecordCount property to see how many records are available versus how many there actually are.

***DataSet* Property**   The DataSet property returns a reference to the TDataSet that the data-link object is attached to via the DataSource property.

***DataSource* Property**   The DataSource property returns a reference to the TDataSource that the data-link object is attached to.

***DataSourceFixed* Property**   The DataSourceFixed property indicates whether or not the DataSource property can be changed.

***Editing* Property**   The Editing property indicates whether or not the DataSource is in Edit mode.

***ReadOnly* Property**   The ReadOnly property indicates whether or not the data-link object can be put into Edit mode.

***RecordCount* Property**   The RecordCount property contains the number of records that are currently being buffered by the data-link object.

Important Properties and Methods of *TFieldDataLink*

TFieldDataLink is the most commonly used data-link object. It descends directly from TDataLink and is defined in the DBCTRLS.PAS source code file. This section looks at some of TFieldDataLink's more significant public properties and methods.

***Edit* Method**   The Edit function is used to put a data field into Edit mode. If the function succeeds, it returns a true, indicating that the field is now or already was in Edit mode. The function fails, and returns a false if the dataset is in read-only mode or if it isn't live data.

***Modified* Method**   The Modified method must be called when a data-aware control changes its data value. Calling the Modified method in turn notifies the TDataSource component that the value of the current record has changed.

***Reset* Method**   The Reset method causes the data-link to refresh its values from the TDataSource. All changes in progress will be lost.

***CanModify* Property**   The CanModify property indicates whether or not the data-link can modify its data values. This property returns false if the data-link object or the dataset are in read-only mode.

***Control* Property**   The Control property links a data-link object back to the data-aware control on the form. This is used by Delphi to set focus to the data-aware control when an error occurs in the program that is related to a field with which the data-aware control is associated.

***Editing* Property**   The `Editing` property indicates whether or not the `DataSource` is in `Edit` mode.

***Field* Property**   The `Field` property is a read-only property that contains a reference to the `TField` component to which the data-link object is bound.

***FieldName* Property**   The `FieldName` property is used to get or set the field name to which the data-link object is bound.

***OnActiveChange* Event**   The `OnActiveChange` event is fired when the `Active` property of the dataset that the data-link object is bound to changes.

***OnDataChange* Event**   The `OnDataChange` event is fired when the data associated to the data link has changed. This event handler is called as a response to the dataset indicating that its data has changed. Your data-aware control should use this event to refresh its values.

***OnEditingChange* Event**   The `OnEditingChange` event gets called when the `DataSource` changes its editing state. This event can be used by your control to toggle on and off a visual editing appearance.

***OnUpdateData* Event**   The `OnUpdateData` event is called when a `DataSource` is ready to post changes to the database. This is your opportunity to ensure that the data value of the data-link object has been updated to reflects the value in the data-aware control.

Creating a Data-Aware Control

There are five steps to follow in creating a data-aware control. They are as follows:

1. Create a custom component.
2. Create a `TDataLink` object as a member of the custom component.
3. Create published properties for the `DataField` and `DataSource`.
4. Respond to the `OnDataChange` and `OnUpdateData` events of the data-link object.
5. Respond to the `cm_GetDataLink` message.

For simplicity, consider a button component that changes its caption to the value of a database field. If the field contains data (or if it is not null), the button is enabled; if not, it is disabled. This example shows how to override the `Create` and `Destroy` methods of `TButton` to instantiate and free the data-link object. Then it shows how to create read and write methods for the published `DataSource` and `DataField` properties. Finally, it shows how to create a `DataChange` method to assign to the `OnDataChange` event. Listing 17.1 shows what this component would look like.

Listing 17.1   \UDELPHI3\CHP17\DBBTN.PAS—A Data-Aware *TButton*

```
unit DBBtn;

interface

uses
  Windows, Messages, SysUtils, Classes, Graphics, Controls, Forms, Dialogs,
```

```
  StdCtrls, DB, DBCtrls;

type
  TDBButton = class(TButton)
  private
    { Private declarations }
    FDataLink : TFieldDataLink;
    function GetDataField: string;
    function GetDataSource: TDataSource;
    procedure SetDataField(const Value: string);
    procedure SetDataSource(Value: TDataSource);
    procedure DataChange(Sender: TObject);
  protected
    { Protected declarations }
  public
    { Public declarations }
    // Don't forget to *override* Create and Destroy!
    constructor Create(AOwner: TComponent); override;
    destructor Destroy; override;
  published
    { Published declarations }
    property DataField: string read GetDataField write SetDataField;
    property DataSource: TDataSource read GetDataSource write SetDataSource;
  end;

procedure Register;

implementation

constructor TDBButton.Create(AOwner: TComponent);
begin
  // Call the inherited Create *first*
  inherited Create(AOwner);
  FDataLink := TFieldDataLink.Create(Self);
  FDataLink.OnDataChange := DataChange;
end;

destructor TDBButton.Destroy;
begin
  // Call the inherited Destroy *last*
  FDataLink.OnDataChange := nil;
  FDataLink.Free;
  inherited Destroy;
end;

function TDBButton.GetDataField: string;
begin
  Result := FDataLink.FieldName;
end;

function TDBButton.GetDataSource: TDataSource;
begin
  Result := FDataLink.DataSource;
end;
```

Part
IV

Ch

17

continues

Listing 17.1 Continued

```
procedure TDBButton.SetDataField(const Value: string);
begin
  FDataLink.FieldName := Value;
end;

procedure TDBButton.SetDataSource(Value: TDataSource);
begin
  FDataLink.DataSource := Value;
end;

procedure TDBButton.DataChange(Sender: TObject);
begin
  if FDataLink.DataSource.State = dsBrowse then
  if FDataLink.Field.AsString <> '' then begin
    Caption := FDataLink.Field.AsString;
    Enabled := true;
  end
  else begin
    Caption := '(Empty)';
    Enabled := false;
  end;
end;

procedure Register;
begin
  RegisterComponents('UD3', [TDBButton]);
end;

end.
```

If you are writing a data-aware control that can edit the values of a data field, you will need to respond to the OnUpdateData event.

TIP The cm_GetDataLink message is an internal component message that returns an instance of the data-link object in the message result. The data-link object reference is only needed if your control is going to be used in a DBCtrlGrid (don't forget to also set the csReplicatable flag in the ControlStyle property).

Writing Property Editors

Property editors provide the designtime interface between your component's properties and the object inspector. When your component is dropped onto a form, Delphi automatically creates a property editor for every published property in your component. When a component user clicks a property of your component in the Object Inspector, Delphi automatically fires off the property editor for the selected property. In keeping with the RAD nature of Delphi, property editors need to be intuitive and easy to use. You have already seen some of Delphi's default property editors in action in the previous chapter, where different property types were discussed. A property editor may be as simple as an editable string, a drop-down combo box, or even a separate dialog box.

There are three steps to creating a property editor, as follows:

1. Choose the correct ancestor.
2. Override the necessary methods.
3. Register the property editor.

Choosing the Correct Ancestor

To create your own property editor, you must first be familiar with default property editors available in Delphi. Most of Delphi's basic default property editors are declared in the DSGNINTF.PAS file, which is located in your \SOURCE\TOOLSAPI directory.

Table 17.5 shows some of the base default property editors that Delphi uses. Several of these editors have been subclassed to meet the specific needs of various properties. For example, a Boolean property is an enumerated type, but rather than use the TEnumProperty editor, Delphi uses a TBoolProperty editor which was derived from TEnumProperty and modified for a Boolean property's specific needs.

Table 17.5 Delphi's Default Property Editors

Class Name	Property Type
TPropertyEditor	The base property editor for all property editors
TIntegerProperty	All integer properties and ranges (Byte, Word, Integer, LongInt, 1..20, and so on)
TCharProperty	All Char properties and ranges of Char (Char, 'A'..'Z', and so on)
TEnumProperty	All enumerated properties
TFloatProperty	All floating point type properties (Float, Single, Double, and so on)
TStringProperty	All strings and subtypes (String, ShortString, String[20], AnsiString, and so on)
TSetProperty	All set properties
TClassProperty	All object properties
TMethodProperty	All method properties
TComponentProperty	All properties of type TComponent

Overriding the Necessary Methods

All property editors are derived from TPropertyEditor and have common virtual methods that were overridden to create a property editor that addresses the unique characteristics of each property type. The GetName and GetValue methods are called to retrieve the name of the property and its simple string value, respectively. SetValue is called when the user changes the value of the property. The Edit method is called when the user double-clicks the property or clicks the triple ellipses button, and the GetValues method (not to be confused with GetValue, this one has an "s") is called when the user drops down the drop-down combo box. GetProperties is called when the user expands the subproperties of a property.

Now look at the methods of a property editor that can, and need to, be overridden to meet the special needs of your component's property.

Activate The Activate method is called every time the property becomes selected in the Object Inspector. This can allow for special initialization that must be done every time the property is selected or to put the component into a certain state while the property is selected. Delphi does require that if your property is going to contain the paMultiSelect and paSubProperties flags of GetAttributes, they must be valid before the Activate method is called (they must be set in the Create constructor).

```
procedure Activate; virtual;
```

AllEqual The AllEqual method is called when a user selects more than one component on a form and only if GetAttributes contains paMultiSelect. If AllEqual returns a True, then GetValue is called; if not, then the property displays a blank value. This method allows you to determine whether or not the value or your property is the same as the values of the other multiselected components.

```
function AllEqual: Boolean; virtual;
```

For an example of this, look at the AllEqual function for the String property editor:

```
function TStringProperty.AllEqual: Boolean;
var
  I: Integer;
  V: string;
begin
  // Default the result to false
  Result := False;
  // If more than 1 component is selected
  if PropCount > 1 then
  begin
    // Get the string value of this property
    V := GetStrValue;
    for I := 1 to PropCount - 1 do
      // Loop through all of the Components and check their string values.
      // If one of the values does not match then exit this method.
      if GetStrValueAt(I) <> V then Exit;
  end;
```

```
    // Made it through the loop therefore, all are equal.
    Result := True;
end;
```

Edit The `Edit` method gets called when the user double-clicks the property or clicks the ellipses button (...) in the Object Inspector. Usually, the `Edit` method invokes some kind of dialog to edit the property (the Font dialog, the Color dialog, and the Picture dialog). By default, the `Edit` method of `TPropertyEditor` changes a property to the next value in the `GetValues` list. If `GetValues` returns nothing, the `Edit` method does nothing.

```
procedure Edit; virtual;
```

For an example, look at the `Edit` method for the `Font` property editor. Notice that the Font dialog is shown inside of a `try...finally` block and freed in the finally section. This is good coding practice that you should follow in your property editor:

```
procedure TFontProperty.Edit;
var
  FontDialog: TFontDialog;
begin
  // Instantiate a Font dialog;
  FontDialog := TFontDialog.Create(Application);
  try
    // Set the font choice in the dialog to the current property value
    FontDialog.Font := TFont(GetOrdValue);
    FontDialog.HelpContext := hcDFontEditor;
    FontDialog.Options := FontDialog.Options + [fdShowHelp, fdForceFontExist];
    if FontDialog.Execute then
      // If the user chose a font change the font property.
      SetOrdValue(Longint(FontDialog.Font));
  finally
    // Free the Font dialog.
    FontDialog.Free;
  end;
end;
```

GetAttributes The `GetAttributes` method returns a set of `TPropertyAttributes` that indicates the characteristics of the property editor. These attribute flags have great control over the appearance of your property in the Object Inspector. They determine if your property will have a drop-down list, if the drop-down list will be sorted, if it can display a property editor dialog, if it can display subproperties, if it can be multiselected, and so on.

```
function GetAttributes: TPropertyAttributes; virtual;
```

`TPropertyAttributes` is declared as a set of values shown in Table 17.6. You may want to override the `GetAttributes` for your property editor to add or remove style flags from the ancestor property editor class. Property editor attributes are not fixed at creation time. You can change the attributes of a property editor whenever you want, with the exception of `paMultiSelect` and `paSubProperties` (refer to the preceding "Activate" section for a discussion on this).

Table 17.6 *TPropertyAttributes* Set Values

Attribute	Meaning
paValueList	Indicates that the property editor can return an enumerated list of values for the property. This flag causes the drop-down button to appear in the Object Inspector.
paSubProperties	Indicates that the property editor has subproperties. The subproperties will be displayed in the Object Inspector in indented form under the main property and in outline format.
paDialog	Indicates that the property editor will bring up an edit dialog when the Edit method is called. This flag causes the ellipses button (...) to appear in the Object Inspector.
paMultiSelect	Indicates that the property can be displayed when multiple components are selected on a form.
paAutoUpdate	Indicates that the SetValue method needs to be called every time the editor changes. This doesn't wait for the user to approve the changes (by tabbing to another property or closing the property editor dialog).
paSortList	Directs the Object Inspector to sort the list returned by GetValues.
paReadOnly	Indicates that the property is read-only.
paRevertable	Indicates that the property can be changed back to its original value.

TIP The paValueList flag causes the drop-down button to appear in the Object Inspector and the paDialog flag causes the triple ellipses button to appear. Both of these buttons cannot be displayed in the Object Inspector at the same time so, if you declare the paValueList and paDialog flags in the same attributes set, Delphi will use the paValueList flag and ignore the paDialog flag.

GetEditLimit   The GetEditLimit method dictates the maximum number of characters a user can enter into the Object Inspector for a given property. By default, the GetEditLimit of TPropertyEditor returns a value of 255.

```
function GetEditLimit: Integer; virtual;
```

GetName   The GetName method returns the property name that appears in the Object Inspector. By default, this value is obtained from the RTTI for the property. Also, by default, underscores in a property name are replaced by spaces. You will rarely need to override this method.

```
function GetName: string; virtual;
```

One situation where the overriding of this method is necessary is in handling subproperties like sets, where you want the name of each subproperty to be the name of the set element rather than the name of the property. For an example of this, look at the GetName method for the TSetElementProperty property editor:

```
function TSetElementProperty.GetName: string;
begin
  Result := GetEnumName(GetTypeData(GetPropType)^.CompType^, FElement);
end;
```

GetProperties   The GetProperties method is called when a user expands a property in the Object Inspector that has subproperties. GetAttributes must contain the paSubProperties flag. This method provides the list of properties and their respective property editors by calling its Proc parameter for each subproperty.

```
procedure GetProperties(Proc: TGetPropEditProc); virtual;
```

For example, look at the GetProperties method of TClassProperty. By default, the Proc parameter is never called, and it's assumed that there are no subproperties:

```
procedure TClassProperty.GetProperties(Proc: TGetPropEditProc);
var
  I: Integer;
  Components: TComponentList;
begin
  // Create a component list
  Components := TComponentList.Create;
  try
    for I := 0 to PropCount - 1 do
      // loop through the properties and add them to the component list
      Components.Add(TComponent(GetOrdValueAt(I)));
    // Call GetComponentProperties with the component list, tell it to list
    // property types, the designer name, and the call-back procedure that
    // was passed to GetProperties
    GetComponentProperties(Components, tkProperties, Designer, Proc);
  finally
    Components.Free;
  end;
end;
```

GetValue   The GetValue method returns the string value of the property being edited. This method has been overridden in all of the default property editors to return a valid string to represent its value.

```
function GetValue: string; virtual;
```

For an example of GetValue, look at the GetValue method of the TStringProperty property editor. By default, the GetValue method of TPropertyEditor returns "(unknown)":

```
function TStringProperty.GetValue: string;
begin
  Result := GetStrValue;
end;
```

GetValues   The GetValues method is used to create the list of values that the Object Inspector displays for a property when the drop-down combo box is clicked. This method is passed a callback procedure that takes one parameter of type string. The callback procedure Proc should be called for every value of the property. GetValues is called only if paValueList is in the GetAttributes set.

```
TGetStrProc = procedure(const S: string) of object;

procedure GetValues(Proc: TGetStrProc); virtual;
```

For an example of this, look at the GetValues method of the TBoolProperty property editor:

```
procedure TBoolProperty.GetValues(Proc: TGetStrProc);
begin
  // Call Proc for each value of the property.
  Proc('False');
  Proc('True');
end;
```

Initialize   The Initialize method is called after the property editor is created but before it's actually used. This allows for any initialization that could not be done in the Create constructor. Unlike the Activate method, this method is called only once. The Initialize method gets called before the Activate method when a property is used for the first time. By default, the Initialize method of TPropertyEditor does nothing.

```
procedure Initialize; virtual;
```

SetValue   The SetValue method is used to assign a value to a property. It receives the new property value as a string and must translate it into whatever data type is necessary to assign it to the property. This method is overridden in all the default property editors to handle each of their own unique data types.

```
procedure SetValue(const Value: string); virtual;
```

If a translation error occurs, it's up to the property editor to raise an exception. The new value can be assigned to the property by calling one of the SetXxxValue methods, which are described in the following section. For an example of this, look at the SetValue method of TBoolProperty property editor:

```
procedure TBoolProperty.SetValue(const Value: string);
var
  I: Integer;
begin
  if CompareText(Value, 'False') = 0 then
    I := 0
  else if CompareText(Value, 'True') = 0 then
    I := -1
  else
    I := StrToInt(Value);
  SetOrdValue(I);
end;
```

Other Properties and Methods of *TPropertyEditor*

TPropertyEditor contains some other important properties and static methods that aid in the creation of your property editor. Although these properties and methods are not considered key elements of TPropertyEditor, in the right situations they are invaluable.

Designer Property   The Designer property contains the form designer object that is being used to edit the current form. This is used as a parameter to GetComponentProperties.

***PrivateDirectory* Property**   The `PrivateDirectory` property specifies a directory where the property editor can write out files. This property is a legacy item from Delphi 1.0, where it was common to use .INI files to store private information for a property editor. You now are encouraged to use the registry to store this information.

***PropCount* Property**   The `PropCount` property indicates how many components were selected in the Object Inspector. This value can be greater than one if a property contains the `paMultiSelect` attribute flag in its property attributes set.

***Value* Property**   The `Value` property is a standard string type property that contains the value of the property being edited. Its read and write methods are `GetValue` and `SetValue`, respectively.

GetComponent   The `GetComponent` method returns an instance of the component specified by the `Index` parameter when multiple components are selected in the Object Inspector. A property editor can refer to multiple components only when `paMultiSelect` is returned from GetAttributes. Use the `PropCount` property to determine how many components are selected.

```
function GetComponent(Index: Integer): TPersistent;
```

GetPropType   The `GetPropType` method is used to return the RTTI information for the property that is currently being edited. For direction on how to use this information, see Chapter 4, "Object Pascal: Advanced Concepts."

```
function GetPropType: PTypeInfo;
```

Modified   The `Modified` method indicates to the `Designer` object—and, therefore, the form that is being edited—that a property has changed. The `SetXxxValue` methods of TPropertyEditor all call this method after they change the value of property being edited. You need to call this method only if you change the value of the property without using the aforementioned `Set` methods.

***Get* and *Set* Methods**   `TPropertyEditor` implements methods to get and set the values of data types listed in Table 17.7. Use these methods when changing the values of a property because they call the `Modified` method after making their changes. If you are working with a data type for which there is no predefined Get or Set method, make sure that you remember to call the `Modified` method after making your changes.

Table 17.7   *Get* and *Set* Methods for *TPropertyEditor*

Data Type	Get Method	Set Method
Float	GetFloatValue	SetFloatValue
Method	GetMethodValue	SetMethodValue
Ordinal	GetOrdValue	SetOrdValue
String	GetStrValue	SetStrValue
Variant	GetVarValue	SetVarValue

Part
IV

Ch
17

Registering the Property Editor

After creating your property editor, you need some way of associating a property of a component with your editor. You register your property editor with the Delphi IDE via the `RegisterPropertyEditor` procedure. The `RegisterPropertyEditor` procedure takes four parameters and is defined as follows:

```
procedure RegisterPropertyEditor(PropertyType: PTypeInfo; ComponentClass: TClass;
        const PropertyName: string; EditorClass: TPropertyEditorClass);
```

PropertyType   This is a pointer to the RTTI information for the property to which the property editor applies. This parameter is obtained by typecasting the property type as `TypeInfo`. Assuming that you have a property of type `TMyPropType`, the syntax would be as follows:

```
TypeInfo(TMyPropertyType)
```

ComponentClass   This is the component type to which this property editor applies. `ComponentClass` can be used to restrict the property editor to a specific component type. If this value is `nil`, the property editor applies to all properties of the first parameter.

PropertyName   This is the name of the property to which this property editor applies. `PropertyName` can be used to restrict the property editor to a specific property name. If this parameter is an empty string, the property editor applies to all properties of the first parameter.

EditorClass   This is the property editor type of the specified property. Delphi uses the last registered property editor, so it's easy to define your own property editors for existing properties.

Writing Component Editors

Component editors are much like property editors in that they provide a way for a component user to change the properties of your component at designtime. Unlike property editors however, a component editor is used to change more than one property of a component at a time. Figure 17.1 shows the component editor for a `TDatabase` component. Notice that most of the properties that you can set in the Object Inspector are shown in the component editor. The component editor provides an easy-to-use interface that helps the user get the "big picture" of the `TDatabase` component rather than the single entry style of the Object Inspector.

FIG. 17.1

TDatabase component editor.

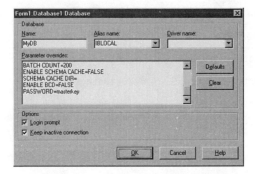

A component editor can be activated in the Forms Editor by double-clicking a component or by right-clicking the component and choosing a pop-up menu option. The base class for all component editors in Delphi is TComponentEditor. From this descends TDefaultEditor, which is the default property editor of all components. In the following section, you learn how to create your own component editor.

TComponentEditor   The TComponentEditor class is the base class for all component editors in Delphi. It contains four key virtual methods besides the Create constructor (well, actually five, but read on). It is defined in DSGNINTF.PAS as follows:

```
TComponentEditor = class
public
  constructor Create(AComponent: TComponent; ADesigner:
                 TFormDesigner); virtual;
  procedure Edit; virtual;
  procedure ExecuteVerb(Index: Integer); virtual;
  function GetVerb(Index: Integer): string; virtual;
  function GetVerbCount: Integer; virtual;
  procedure Copy; virtual;
  property Component: TComponent read FComponent;
  property Designer: TFormDesigner read FDesigner;
end;
```

Now let's take a look at each item in the class declaration.

Create *Constructor*   A component editor is created when a component is selected in the form designer. If you select more than one component, Delphi instantiates a component editor for each component. It receives two parameters—one is the instance of the component that is selected for editing and the other is the instance of the designer object. If you override the Create constructor, it's imperative that you call the inherited Create.

Edit *Method*   The Edit method is called when a user double-clicks a component. TComponentEditor checks to see if GetVerbCount is greater than zero. If so, it calls ExecuteVerb(0), thus calling the first component-defined item on the pop-up menu. TDefaultEditor overrides the Edit method and searches through components published properties for the OnCreate, OnChange, or OnClick event (whichever it finds first) and calls the property editor's Edit method for that event.

GetVerbCount *Method*   The GetVerbCount method is called every time a user right-clicks a component. It returns the number of menu items that need to be added to the pop-up menu of the form editor. You must override this method if you want to add items to the pop-up menu. This value is zero by default.

ExecuteVerb *Method*   The ExecuteVerb method is called when a user selects a component-defined item from the form designer's pop-up menu. It is passed a zero-based Index parameter. This method also is called as the default action to TComponentEditor's Edit method. If you added items to the form designer's pop-up menu, you must override this method to handle the selection choices.

GetVerb *Method* The GetVerb method is called when a user right-clicks a component. It returns the string value that needs to be added to the pop-up menu based upon the Index parameter. The Index parameter assumes a zero-based array, so zero is the first element. You must override this method if you want to add new items to the form designer's pop-up menu.

Copy *Method* The Copy method is never called. According to the documentation, it was intended to be a virtual method that was called when the component was copied to the clipboard. This was to allow you to support different clipboard formats that are not recognized by Delphi (you could copy information to the clipboard, and then pull it back off in another application).

TDefaultEditor The TDefaultEditor is inherited from TComponentEditor and overrides the Edit method. It also introduces a new virtual method named EditProperty. TDefaultEditor is defined as follows:

```
TDefaultEditor = class(TComponentEditor)
protected
  procedure EditProperty(PropertyEditor: TPropertyEditor;
    var Continue, FreeEditor: Boolean); virtual;
public
  procedure Edit; override;
end;
```

Edit *Method* TDefaultEditor overrides the Edit method and loops through the components published properties calling EditProperty for each one. If the property that it was looking for is found, the property's Edit method is called.

EditProperty *Method* The EditProperty method is called by the Edit method for every published property of a component. By default, EditProperty looks for the OnCreate, OnChange, or OnClick event (whichever it finds first). If it finds a match, it saves the instance variable of the property editor in a private variable so that it may be called by the Edit method.

Registering the Component Editor

After creating your component editor, you need some way of associating a component with your editor. You register your component editor with the Delphi IDE via the RegisterComponentEditor procedure. The RegisterComponentEditor procedure takes two parameters and is defined as follows:

```
procedure RegisterComponentEditor(ComponentClass: TComponentClass;
  ComponentEditor: TComponentEditorClass);
```

The first parameter is the Component's class name and the second parameter is the class name of your component editor.

Component Editor Example

To see a component editor in action, consider the TEdit component. A quick search of the source code reveals that it has no component editors registered for it. This means that double-clicking a TEdit brings up either the OnCreate, OnChange, or OnClick event handler, whichever handler Delphi finds first. In this case, Delphi finds the OnChange event.

Suppose that you are building an application that uses many edit fields, and you frequently do validation on the OnExit event. In keeping with the tradition of RAD development, you decide that it would be ideal if double-clicking a TEdit component created an OnExit event instead of an OnChange event. This would save you from having to click the TEdit component on the form, clicking the Object Inspector's Events tab, and double-clicking the OnExit event. Listing 17.2 shows how to create a component editor that creates an OnExit event when double-clicked, and adds the OnExit and OnChange events to the right-click pop-up menu for TEdit.

Listing 17.2   \UDELPHI3\CHP17\TESTCD.PAS—A Component Editor for *TEdit*

```
unit TestCE;

interface

uses
  DsgnIntf, StdCtrls, SysUtils, Classes;

type
  TMyEditEditor = class(TDefaultEditor)
  private
    FIndex : integer;
  public
    constructor Create(AComponent: TComponent;
                       ADesigner: TFormDesigner); override;
    function GetVerbCount: integer; override;
    function GetVerb(Index: integer): string; override;
    procedure ExecuteVerb(Index: integer); override;
    procedure EditProperty(PropertyEditor: TPropertyEditor;
               var Continue, FreeEditor: Boolean); override;
  end;

procedure Register;

implementation

constructor TMyEditEditor.Create(AComponent: TComponent;
                                 ADesigner: TFormDesigner);
begin
  inherited Create(AComponent,ADesigner);
  // Initialize FIndex
  FIndex := -1;
end;

function TMyEditEditor.GetVerbCount: integer;
begin
  // Set GetVerbCount to 2 for the two menu items we will add
  result := 2;
end;

function TMyEditEditor.GetVerb(Index: integer): string;
begin
```

continues

Part
IV

Ch
17

Listing 17.2 Continued

```
  // Return the menu item string
  case Index of
    0: result := 'O&nChange';
    1: result := 'OnE&xit';
  end;
end;

procedure TMyEditEditor.ExecuteVerb(Index: integer);
begin
  // Note a double-click on the Edit control will not make it into
  // here. Only a right-click menu selection will call this method.
  // Set FIndex to Index and then call Edit
  FIndex := Index;
  Edit;
  // Set FIndex back to -1
  FIndex := -1;
  // Call the Modified method of the Designer to indicate that the
  // form has changed.
  if Designer <> nil then
    Designer.Modified;
end;

procedure TMyEditEditor.EditProperty(PropertyEditor: TPropertyEditor;
          var Continue, FreeEditor: Boolean);
begin
  case FIndex of
    // Check FIndex for a right-click menu selection
    0 : begin
          if CompareText(PropertyEditor.GetName, 'OnChange') = 0 then
          begin
            PropertyEditor.Edit;
            Continue := false;
          end;
        end;
    1 : begin
          if CompareText(PropertyEditor.GetName, 'OnExit') = 0 then
          begin
            PropertyEditor.Edit;
            Continue := false;
          end;
        end;
    else
      // Process as normal
      inherited EditProperty(PropertyEditor,Continue,FreeEditor);
  end;
end;

procedure Register;
begin
  // Register TMyEditEditor for the TEdit control
  RegisterComponentEditor(TEdit, TMyEditEditor);
end;
end.
```

Putting It All Together

In this chapter, you learned how to add the polish and shine to your components. You examined how to create data-aware controls, how to create custom property editors, and how to create custom component editors. Using the techniques discussed here and in the previous chapter, you will be able to create professional-looking custom components that stand above and beyond the casual hack. ●

Part
IV

Ch
17

P A R T

V

OLE Development

CHAPTER 18

Working with OLE, Document Servers, and ActiveX Controls

by Quentin J. Sarafinchan

OLE is something that you have probably heard a lot about, but may not have realized that you can take immediate advantage of its power in your own applications. In the past year, hundreds of ActiveX objects have been created taking advantage of the power of OLE. In Delphi, you can easily take advantage of ActiveX components and put them to immediate use, as easily as adding and using a VCL Component.

ActiveX controls is a term that refers to OLE Controls, OLE Servers, and OLE Containers. It has only been in the past year or so that ActiveX technology has really taken off. ActiveX controls have some powerful features that you can take advantage of in Delphi. A technology that has been around for quite a while is the OLE Container. In Delphi, this has been encapsulated in the TOleContainer. The TOleContainer has a lot of capabilities that most people do not realize are at their fingertips. Using OLE Containers and ActiveX controls will be examined in detail so that you can maximize their potential.

Creating OLE containers
At design time and runtime.

Inserting/embedding objects
Various ways to add OLE objects into a container.

Reading and writing
Storing the OLE Objects in a database file on a disk, and as files on a drive.

Overriding built-in OLE container dialogs
An example of how to make your own Custom Insert dialog box.

In-place activation and menu merging
Allow an OLE object to control a form.

OLE verbs
Use OLE verbs from within your application.

Accessing Automation Server
Make method calls to the OLE Server.

Optional parameter passing
Positional versus named arguments.

In Delphi 2, the TOleContainer was radically improved over Delphi 1, and has evolved even more in this release. Most of these changes have been "under the hood," but the capabilities of TOleContainer can be seen through the OLE object that is placed into it. The most notable enhancement is that the TOleContainer now supports Active Documents.

The initial sections of this chapter cover some of the basic ideas behind the OLE technologies. Then it will jump into what you can do to tap this powerful and cool technology, upon which Containers and ActiveX have been built. Many of the concepts discussed are covered more heavily in the upcoming chapters in regard to creating your own objects and containers. We will take pre-existing OLE objects and make the most out of the features that ActiveX OLE Automation objects have on the surface, and some techniques to get to those methods that we cannot directly call. Later chapters discuss the actual creation of these controls. ■

Capitalizing on Existing OLE Technologies

With the advent of more powerful computers and with more programming tools capable of easily creating ActiveX objects, there has been a wave of new OLE-based controls being developed, giving developers quite a selection of tools that they can use to increase productivity and reduce time spent in the development cycle. OLE now is becoming a part of most application development, and it won't be long until operating systems will be built using OLE.

OLE follows a similar paradigm to Delphi, and this is code reusability. If you have an OLE server application that can handle the job for you, you don't need to reinvent the wheel in Delphi; you can just use it to solve the problem at hand.

One of the nicest benefits of OLE is that you can make use of other Application server capabilities. I am sure you will agree with me that it's easier to use the capabilities of a spreadsheet such as Excel, or a word processor such as Word, than it is to actually create these features in your applications.

Delphi allows you to quite easily create many different types of ActiveX components. See Chapter 21, "Creating ActiveX Controls," for more information.

Working with ActiveX controls is quite easy—all you need to do is install them into the VCL (similar to adding a VCL component), and then drop them on a form. Later in this chapter, we walk through a simple example of how to take an ActiveX Control and install it into a package so that it can be used in Delphi.

Delphi comes with an entire page of ActiveX controls on the OCX page, the entire Windows 95 page consists of Windows OLE controls that Delphi has wrapped in a VCL wrapper, and there also are a number of ActiveX components on the Internet page. All you need to do is drop them onto a form and use them as you would use a VCL component. The biggest difference between VCL components and OLE components is that the ones built upon OLE can be used within multiple languages and applications, which means that you can use them with any development tool that supports ActiveX Controls.

OLE Technology in Simple Terms

Well, what is OLE anyway? We have been talking about it, but haven't really said what it is. OLE was originally a standard that allowed Object Linking and Embedding based upon *COM* (Component Object Model). OLE has evolved so much since OLE 1.0 that linking and embedding now are a small subset of its capabilities. Because OLE has evolved so much, today OLE is just a word for the specification; it's no longer an acronym.

COM is an API specification written to allow developers to create COM objects to allow applications to communicate within a language-independent framework. Objects written based on COM are much like VCL components, but they do not have any properties or events.

In the future, COM will be operating system- and possibly even platform-independent, allowing applications and operating systems to carry on interprocess communications. Microsoft is currently working on an operating system that is completely based on OLE, so sometime in the future we will have an OLE operating system. So, a need exists for us, as programmers, to understand OLE, because most programming will be based upon OLE controls.

When an OLE server application is activated, it is activated "inside" a container within your application. In the initial version 1 of the OLE specification, when an OLE object was activated, the server started up in its own window, with your data in it, and ready for editing. Rarely do you find OLE 1 being used today. Because there never will be an OLE version 3, we can drop the 2 when discussing OLE.

Visually, when the OLE server activates, its speed bars and menus will replace or merge with those currently on the form. Also, part of the form will actually become the server application, because the server window will completely take over an area of the form. There are complete examples later in this chapter, RESUME.EXE and OLEDB.EXE, that demonstrate in-place activation.

ActiveX is a name that classifies a large range of OLE technology; you will look at controls that can be dropped into an application. These controls are fast becoming one of the standards for developing Internet applications because of their code reuse between different development systems. In the "Using ActiveX" section, an example program shows how to do a spell check by using the Spell Checking ActiveX control from the ActiveX page on the contents of a DBMemo.

Part

V

Ch

18

Linking and Embedding OLE Objects

Linking occurs when you associate an OLE object file on a drive with an OLE Container. The file object is never stored in the container, but the container will reference the file by a path that is stored in the container. The OLE object file *must* exist before we can link to it.

N O T E A Word document or a BMP file, for example, are not OLE object files; they are just simple data files. To make a document file into an object, you tell the OLE server to write the file to disk as an OLE object. This technique is discussed later in this chapter, in "Linking OLE Objects." ∎

One benefit of linking is that multiple people, OLE server applications, and other OLE container applications can all access the same document. So, the data only needs to exist at one location and is accessible from multiple applications. When the OLE object data is modified, even by other applications, the changes appear in all OLE container applications that contain a link to the file, including your own.

Embedding is the other method that can be used to work with OLE objects. When embedding objects, the actual object is stored in your application, and other OLE Containers have no access to the OLE object. Embedded OLE objects do not exist in files; the OLE object is stored inside the container in the application. This ensures that the OLE data doesn't accidentally get deleted, modified, or corrupted by being stored in an external file.

Embedding has the previously mentioned benefit that the data is part of the application, but the drawback to embedding is that the size of your OLE container application increases by the size of the included OLE data. So, the larger the size is of the OLE object, the larger the size of your application.

At runtime, if changes are made to the data in an OLE object, then to have these changes appear the next time the application is run it is necessary to save the OLE object to a file by using the SaveToFile method.

When should embedding or linking be used? They both have their benefits, but they also have drawbacks. I have compiled a list of issues to look at, to help decide whether linking or embedding will be a better option for your particular scenario.

Linking versus Embedding

Reasons to link:

- You need to have changes to the data reflected in all applications and documents using the object.
- The object file is not going to be moved or deleted.
- The object is large, and you will be distributing it via a network or electronic mail.
- You are limited on disk storage space.

Reasons to embed:

- The changes to the object data are only going to affect one object.
- The object is small.
- The object is large, but the application will not be distributed via a network or electronic mail.

- The object is unlikely to be modified, or will be modified from only one instance of an OLE container application.
- The object file is likely to be moved or deleted.
- Storage of the objects is not an issue; there is plenty of space.

In the section "Using TOleContainer," there are a couple of programs discussed that demonstrate using both linking and embedding.

Using *TOleContainer*

The *TOleContainer* is a container component that accepts OLE servers to be placed inside of it. TOleContainer encapsulates the OLE Container into an easily usable VCL component. These OLE servers can be accessed either by the user directly or programmatically.

> **N O T E** When I started looking into the TOleContainer, I thought this should be a simple section covering a few simple methods, because the TOleContainer didn't seem to be a powerful tool. Well, I have proven myself wrong; it is a very powerful tool. There is really nothing in this world that we cannot do with it. All that is required is to spend a bit of time to understand what's going on, and learn how the TOleContainer works.
>
> I tried to dig as deeply into it as time and the scope of this chapter would allow. You will find some neat and interesting things that can be done with, and to, the TOleContainer in the rest of this chapter. ■

Part V
Ch
18

In Delphi 3, the TOleContainer also has been rewritten to allow active document objects to be dropped into the container. The TOleContainer now accepts active, embedded, and linked documents. You now can insert an active document from Word into the container and edit it at design time, from within the container. The only application currently using active documents is Microsoft Office 7.

Active documents have an interesting feature known as *binders*. A binder is, visually, a panel on the left side of the application, in which many objects are stored as icons. When you click one of the icons, that object is activated in the TOleContainer, as part of the in-place activated server.

The TOleContainer component lets you embed or link OLE objects into your Delphi application. TOleContainer handles many of the complexities of OLE for you. Allowing the user of your application to insert an object is as simple as calling the method InsertObjectDialog (see Figure 18.1). To programmatically add embedded OLE objects to the TOleContainer, you can use the methods CreateObject or CreateLinkToFile or one of the others to create a linked OLE object.

FIG. 18.1

A simple application, showing two TOleContainers on the same form.

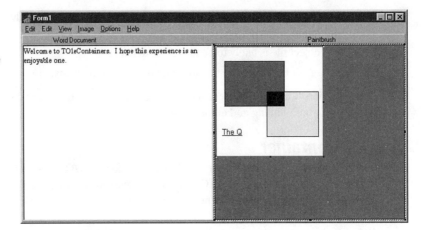

The TOleContainer is very powerful, and over the following sections the topics that will be discussed include:

- What methods and properties the TOleContainer has that we can exploit
- How to embed and link OLE objects
- Cutting and pasting OLE objects to the Windows clipboard
- In-place activation and iconic containers
- Merging of OLE Container menus with your applications' menus
- OLE file streaming
- Making calls to the method DoVerb
- Going "under the hood" and working with the OleObject property as well as making our own InsertDialog box

TOleContainer Class Definition   The TOleContainer class has one new property; the AllowActiveDoc was added to support the ActiveDocument object type. If true, then active document objects can be placed inside the container.

Tables 18.1, 18.2, and 18.3 list all the methods, properties, and events, respectively, that are specific to the TOleContainer or have special purposes when working with the TOleContainer.

Table 18.1   *TOleContainer* Methods

Name	Description
CreateLinkToFile	Creates an OLE object linking it to the physical file.
CreateObject	Creates a new embedded object in the OLE container.

Name	Description
CreateObjectFromFile	Creates an embedded object using the data from the file specified in the OLE container.
CreateObjectFromInfo	Creates an object based on the specifications in a TCreateInfo record.
DestroyObject	Destroys the object and any changes made to it.
DoVerb	Requests the OLE object to perform some action.
GetIconMetaPic	Returns a Global Handle to the icon of the OLE object in a metafile format.
InsertObjectDialog	Executes the built-in Insert OLE Dialog box, which allows you to insert an object either new, embedded, or linked.
ChangeIconDialog	Allows the user to change the icon of the object.
PasteSpecialDialog	Gives the user control over how the contents of the Windows clipboard are pasted into the container.
ObjectPropertiesDialog	Allows the user to see and edit various properties of the OLE object.
LoadFromFile	Loads an OLE object from the specified file.
LoadFromStream	Reads the object from a stream.
SaveToFile	Saves an OLE object to the specified file.
SaveToStream	Writes the object to a stream.
Copy	Copies the object in the container to the windows clipboard.
Paste	Pastes the object in the windows clipboard into the container.
Run	Puts the OLE object into the ovRunning state.
UpdateObject	Rereads the source to ensure that the OLE object has current data.
UpdateVerbs	Refreshes the list of verbs the OLE object currently recognizes.
SourceDoc	The name of the source document for a linked OLE object.
State	The state of the OLE object (osEmpty, osLoaded, osRunning, osOpen, osInPlaceActive, osUIActive).
StorageInterface	The OLE object's IStorage interface.

Part
V

Ch

18

Table 18.2 *TOleContainer* **Properties**

Name	Description
AllowInPlace	If you want the object to always appear in its own window, set this to False.
AllowActiveDoc	If True, TOleContainer automatically creates a pop-up menu that contains the OLE object's verbs.
AutoActivate	This property defines how an object in an OLE container can be activated aaManual, aaGetFocus, aaDoubleClick, AutoVerbMenu.
Align	For in-place activation, set to alClient.
CanPaste	Indicates whether the data in the clipboard can be pasted as an embedded object.
CopyOnSave	If True, an intermediate file is used to write the OLE object, compressing redundant data, thus saving space.
Iconic	If True, an icon is displayed in the container; otherwise, the data from the object will be displayed.
Linked	If True, then the object is linked.
ObjectVerbs	Returns a string list that contains the names of all the verbs the OLE object currently supports.
OleClassName	The class name of the OLE object.
OleObject	Returns an OLE Automation object for the OLE object contained within the TOleContainer.
OleObjectInterface	Returns the IOleObject Interface for the OLE object, which is useful for low-level access to the OLE API.
Modified	If True, the OLE object has been modified, or has been deleted or replaced by another OLE object.
NewInserted	True if the OLE object was newly created via the InsertObjectDialog, rather than pasted in or created as a link to a file.
OldStreamFormat	Stores the OLE object in OLE 1 format, for backward compatibility.
SizeMode	Controls how the OLE object will be sized within the container (smClip, smCenter, smScale, smStretch, or smAutoSize).

Table 18.3 *TOleContainer* Events

Name	Description
OnObjectMove	Fires when the user moves or resizes the OLE object.

OnObjectMove is the only special event that is specific to the TOleContainer: If you want to allow the user to move or resize the container (by moving or sizing the hatched frame around the OLE object), then you must handle this event. At least, the OLE container's BoundsRect must be set to the Bounds parameter of the event handler, or the OLE object won't change its location or size, as in the following example:

```
procedure Tform1.OleContainer1ObjectMove(OleContainer: TOleContainer;
  const Bounds: TRect);
begin
  // Set the container so it can be no smaller than 100 by 100
  with Bounds do begin
    if Left < 100 then Left := 100;
    if Right < 100 then Right := 100;
    end; // with
  OLeContainer1.BoundsRect := Bounds;
end; // Tform1.OleContainer1ObjectMove
```

Embedding New OLE Objects The TOleContainer component lets you embed or link OLE objects in your Delphi application. TOleContainer handles many of the complexities of OLE for you. Allowing the user of your application to insert an object is as simple as calling the method InsertObjectDialog.

Here is a simple, step-by-step example to show what I mean:

1. Start a new Delphi application.
2. Select the TOleContainer component from the System page of the Component Palette.
3. Drop it on your form. Double-click on the component. The InsertObjectDialog opens (see Figure 18.2).

FIG. 18.2
The Insert Object
dialog box.

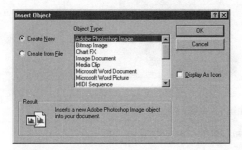

4. From here, select the Bitmap Image for the Object Type. Click OK.

5. Now double-click the container. This time, the container application will activate and the Paint program runs in its own window. Go ahead and draw a little picture (see Figure 18.3). (Your artistic ability is probably better than mine.)

6. Now close the paint program. You should see the same image in the OLE Container. In fact, if you were observant, you noticed that as you made changes to the picture in the Paint application, the image in the container was being updated simultaneously.

FIG. 18.3

Painting a picture in Paintbrush.

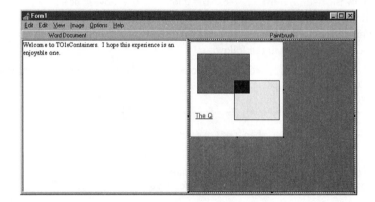

You have now embedded a `Paint` object into an application. The `ObjectPropertiesDialog` can now be used to modify the OLE objects properties, as shown in Figure 18.4. You do this by right-clicking the container and choosing from the displayed list "Object Properties."

FIG. 18.4

The Object Property dialog box for the paint OLE object.

This can be done from within a program, for example:

```
Procedure TForm1.Button1Click(Sender: TObject);
begin
  with OleContainer1 do
    if ObjectPropertiesDialog then
      ShowMessage('OLE objects properties have been changed');
  // we just do not know which properties
end; // TForm1.Button1Click
```

To programmatically add embedded OLE objects to the TOleContainer, you can use the method CreateObject or use the CreateLinkToFile method to create a linked OLE object.

One important item to note is that not just any file can be inserted into a TOleContainer container. You must use a file that the TOleContainer recognizes. If it's a document file, it must have the correct associations set up to load an OLE Server; otherwise, you can use an object file. In the following example, a check is done to see if the object can be inserted; if not, we display a message to the user:

```
Procedure TForm1.Button1Click(Sender: TObject);
begin
  with OleContainer1 do
    if InsertObjectDialog then
      DoVerb(ovShow);
    else
      ShowMessage('An object MUST be specified');
end; // TForm1.Button1Click
```

If you want to create a specific OleObject programmatically, you can. For example, to use the method CreateObject to create a new OLE object you need only specify a ProgId, and whether or not to make the object initially iconized. Two ProgIds that can be used to specify a Paint picture are Paint.Picture and PBrush, both of which can be found in the Registry. These two ProgIds can be used to create a Paint Object. The following line creates a Paint OLE object, and specifies that we want to have the data of the picture image displayed in the container, not displayed as an icon:

```
CreateObject('Paint.Picture', False);
```

ProgIds are values stored in the registry associated with CLSIDs. You also could make your own Insert Dialog if you want. The hardest part is retrieving a list of OLE objects that can be inserted into a container.

There is no way to really access the information in an InsertObjectDialog or ObjectPropertiesDialog. Actually, it's extremely difficult to access the properties for any of the built-in Dialogs. It's far easier to create your own InsertObjectDialog, which can then be customized to suit your needs.

On the CD

Here is the method from the demo program OleDB used to do just that. It retrieves the list of object types and their corresponding ProgIds, from the Registry. You can find the method TdlgInsertableOleObj.GetInsertableObjects, shown in Listing 18.1, in the file InsertableOleObjU.PAS on this book's companion CD-ROM.

Listing 18.1   \UDELPHI3\CHP18\OLEDB\InsertableOleObjU.PAS—Code to Use to Create an *InsertObjectDialog*

```
procedure  TdlgInsertableOleObj.GetInsertableObjects(OLENames,
                               ProgIds : TStrings);
var
  i: integer;
```

continues

Part
V

Ch
18

Listing 18.1   Continued

```
  OleType, CLSID: String;
  KeyNames: TStrings;
begin
  KeyNames := TStringList.Create;

  try
    with TRegistry.Create do
      try
        RootKey := HKEY_CLASSES_ROOT;

        // Go to the CLSIDS, then get a list of them all.
        if not OpenKey('\', False) then exit;

        GetKeyNames(KeyNames);

          // Now we want to find the ones that have a ProgId and a Values
          //   section. For those that have both, add the ProgId to the memo1.
        with KeyNames do
          for i := 0 to count - 1 do begin
            // To go back to RootKey we need to close the key; sounds
            // obvious, but took a bit to realize that. I figured that the
            // Open key always started at root, but it starts from
            // current key position.
            CloseKey;
            RootKey := HKEY_CLASSES_ROOT;
            if OpenKey(Strings[i], False) then begin
              if KeyExists('Insertable') then begin
                OleType := ReadString('');
                OpenKey('CLSID', False);
                CLSID := ReadString('');
                  // Now to go to the CLSID and get the ProgId
                CloseKey;
                if OpenKey('CLSID\' + CLSID, False) then begin
                  OLENames.Add(OleType);
                  if OpenKey('ProgId', False) then
                    ProgIds.Add(ReadString('') )
                  else
                    ProgIds.Add(' [NO PROG ID] ');
                  end; // if CLSID
              end; // if
            end; // for
          end; // with KeyNames
      finally
      Free;
      end; // try
    finally
      KeyNames.Free;
    end; // try
end; //  TdlgInsertableOleObj.GetInsertableObjects
```

The `GetInsertableObjects` method first retrieves a list of all root level key words, and then iteratively examines each one to see if they have a sub-key titled `Insertable`. If one is found it's an object type, and all we need now is the ProgId, which can be found by going to the CLSID that corresponds to the one stored as a sub-key of the object type.

How I Found All the Insertable Objects

During the research to make this method, it took some time to discern the list of OLE object types that are capable of being displayed in the `InsertObjectDialog`. The problem was twofold; first, I knew the information I needed was somewhere in the Registry, but making the `TRegistry` component work for me took time.

I knew from the help that `CreateObject` needed a ProgId, so I set the `RootKey` to HKEY_CLASSES_ROOT, and I expected the `OpenKey` to either work from the root or from the current location along the path. Openkey actually only goes down a path. To reset the path to the root, the `RootKey` must be reset.

My first approach was to initially look at CLSIDs that had a ProgId, and then add verbs as a second condition. This was great: I had a list that was similar to the `InsertObjectDialog` list, but there were a few items in my list not in the `InsertObjectDialog`, and vice versa. I noticed that there was a key named `Insertable` in some of these keys, and by, searching the Registry, I found that I only needed to search all the primary key items off of the `RootKey`, HKEY_CLASSES_ROOT, for the sub-key `Insertable`. Suddenly, my list matched the `InsertObjectDialog`. Then I only needed to use the CLSID from each of these keys, to go to the CLSID and get the ProgId.

For example: doing a search on "insertable" in the Registry gave me the following:

```
Hkey_ClassesRoot
        AVIFile
                CLSID      {00022602-0000-0000-C000-000000000046}
                Compressions
                DefaultIcon
                Extensions
                Insertable
```

Now doing a search for the CLSID, we can find the ProgId, which is an `AVIFile`.

By looking at the extensions, such as BMP and DOC, a list of file types that possibly can be linked or embedded may be found. I have not explored this avenue, but you can!

What you have just looked at is a truly powerful function at your disposal. You can control which objects a user can add to your program, and you can control if you allow linking or embedding. If linking is allowed, you also will know the specific path to the linked file.

Now that we have a method to retrieve the object types and ProgIds, you only need to make a dialog box, like the one shown in Figure 18.5, to allow the user to choose a object type for the container.

FIG. 18.5

The Custom Insert
dialog box.

You can find the following source code in the file InsertableOleObjU.PAS on this book's companion CD-ROM.

Listing 18.2 \UDELPHI3\CHP18\OLEDB\InsertableOleObjU.PAS—Creates and Displays a List of Insertable OLE Objects in a Dialog Window

```
Unit InsertableOleObjU;

interface

uses
  Windows, Messages, SysUtils, Classes, Graphics, Controls, Forms, Dialogs,
  StdCtrls, ExtCtrls, Buttons, Mask, DBCtrls;

type
  TdlgInsertableOleObj = class(TForm)
    Panel1: TPanel;
    ListBox1: TListBox;
    Panel2: TPanel;
    btnCancel: TBitBtn;
    BitBtn3: TBitBtn;
    procedure FormCreate(Sender: TObject);
    procedure ListBox1DblClick(Sender: TObject);
    procedure BtnCancelClick(Sender: TObject);
    procedure FormShow(Sender: TObject);
    procedure GetInsertableObjects(OLENames, ProgId : TStrings);
  private
    ProgIds: TStrings;
  public
    Selected_ProgId : String;

  end;

var
  dlgInsertableOleObj: TdlgInsertableOleObj;

implementation

uses Registry, OLEDBU, OLEu;
```

```
{$R *.DFM}

procedure TdlgInsertableOleObj.GetInsertableObjects(OLENames,
➥ ProgId : TStrings);
var
  i: integer;
  OleType, CLSID: String;
  KeyNames: TStrings;
begin
  // This routine extracts all Object from the Registry that can be
  // inserted into an OLE Container.

  KeyNames:= TStringList.Create;

  try
    with TRegistry.Create do
      try
      RootKey := HKEY_CLASSES_ROOT;

        // Go to the CLSIDS, then get a list of them all.
      if not OpenKey('\', False) then exit;

      GetKeyNames(KeyNames);

        // Now we want to find the ones that have a progID and a Values
        // section. For those that have both, add the prog ID to the memo1.
      with KeyNames do
        for i := 0 to count - 1 do begin
            // To go back to rootkey we need to close the key, sounds
            // obvious, but took a bit to realize that.  I figured that
            // the Open key always started at root, but it starts from
            // current key position.
          CloseKey;
          RootKey := HKEY_CLASSES_ROOT;
          if OpenKey(Strings[i], False) then begin
            if KeyExists('Insertable') then begin
              OleType := ReadString('');
              OpenKey('CLSID', False);
              CLSID := ReadString('');
                // Now to go to the CLSID and get the ProgId
              CloseKey;
              if OpenKey('CLSID\' + CLSID, False) then begin
                OLENames.Add(OleType);
                if OpenKey('ProgId', False) then
                  ProgId.Add(ReadString('') )
                else
                  ProgId.Add(' [NO PROG ID] ');
              end; // if CLSID
            end; // if
          end; // for
        end; // with KeyNames
      finally
      Free;
      end; // try
```

continues

Listing 18.2 Continued

```
     finally
       KeyNames.free;
     end; // try
end; //  TdlgInsertableOleObj.GetInsertableObjects


procedure TdlgInsertableOleObj.FormCreate(Sender: TObject);
begin
  ProgIds := TStringList.Create;
end;

procedure TdlgInsertableOleObj.ListBox1DblClick(Sender: TObject);
begin
  Selected_ProgId := ProgIds[ListBox1.ItemIndex];
  ModalResult := mrOk;
end;

procedure TdlgInsertableOleObj.BtnCancelClick(Sender: TObject);
begin
  Selected_ProgId := '';
  ModalResult := mrCancel;
end;


procedure TdlgInsertableOleObj.FormShow(Sender: TObject);
begin
  Selected_ProgId := '';
  GetInsertableObjects(ListBox1.Items, ProgIds);
end;

end.
```

On the CD

Now, if we wanted to embed a BMP or DOC file, there is a method `CreateObjectFromFile` that allows users to embed objects into the `TOleContainer`. Listing 18.3 shows a method from the OLEDB program that does exactly this, using the `TOpenDialog` and the `CreateObjectFromFile` to add an object to the container. You can find the method `TForm1.LoadEmbedded1Click` shown in Listing 18.3, in the file OLEDBU.PAS on this book's companion CD-ROM.

**Listing 18.3 \UDELPHI3\CHP18\OLEDB\OLEDBU.PAS—Method that
Allows You to Embed Objects into the *TOleContainer***

```
procedure TfrmMain.LoadEmbedded1Click(Sender: TObject);
begin
  if OpenDialog1.Execute then
    Form2.OleContainer1.CreateObjectFromFile(OpenDialog1.FileName,
        IconView1.Checked);
end; // TfrmMain.LoadEmbedded1Click
```

The TOleContainer component lets you embed or link OLE objects in to the Delphi application. TOleContainer handles many of the complexities of OLE. Allowing the user of your application to insert an object is as simple as calling the method InsertObjectDialog. To programmatically add embedded OLE objects to the TOleContainer, you can use the methods CreateObject or use the CreateLinkToFile method to create a linked OLE object.

Linking to OLE Objects   Linking allows multiple users to access the same object, even at the same time, and have any changes made automatically be updated in all applications linked to this file. Just like embedding files, linking also can use the InsertObjectDialog. Here is a simple way to link a BMP into a TOleContainer at design time.

The following shows a simple, step-by-step example to link to a file:

1. Start a new Delphi application.
2. Select the TOleContainer component from the System page of the Component Palette.
3. Drop it on your form, and double-click the container. The InsertObjectDialog appears on-screen (see Figure 18.6).

FIG. 18.6
The Insert Object dialog box.

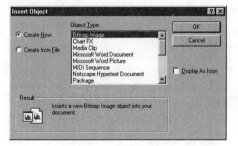

4. From here, select the Create From File check box, and then the Link check box (see Figure 18.7).

FIG. 18.7
The Create from File page of the Insert Object dialog box.

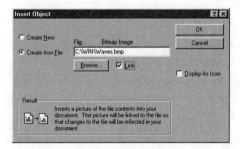

5. Now browse or enter a file name for the file to which you want to link. To keep things simple for this first round, go to the Windows directory and select a bitmap (BMP) file. Click OK. The file you selected should appear in the TOleContainer.

For example, in Figure 18.8, I linked to the file C:\WIN\WAVES.BMP.

FIG. 18.8

The Container at design time, containing WAVES.BMP.

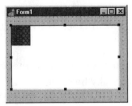

Linking also can be done at runtime. The following method will embed or link to a file and place it into the container. You can find the method TfrmMain.LoadEmbedded1Click, shown in Listing 18.4, in the file OLEDBU.PAS on this book's companion CD-ROM.

Listing 18.4 \UDELPHI3\CHP18\OLEDB\OLEDBU.PAS—Code to Link at Runtime

```
Procedure TfrmMain.LoadDocument(FileName: string; Embedded: Boolean);
begin
    // Loads a Document into a container, including setting the server
  with OleContainer1 do begin
    if Embedded then
      CreateObjectFromFile(FileName, false)
    else
      CreateLinkToFile(FileName, false);
    DoVerb(ovShow);
    end; // with
end; // TfrmMain.LoadDocument
```

In-Place Activation and Iconic Properties   In-place activation is when the OLE object becomes active within the containers. Okay, great. Now, how do we get this in-place activation to occur from within our own applications?

The simplest method is to take these steps:

1. Drop a TOleContainer on a new form, and then set the Align property to alClient. Set the AutoActivate property to aaGetFocus.

2. Double-click the container, select an object type, such as a bitmap image or Word document.

3. Do a little drawing, or enter some text in the Paint program, and then close it.

4. Now run the application. When the application runs, the objects application should be seen inside the container.

    Not all OLE objects can be activated in-place.

You now should see a form that contains an image that resembles the form shown in Figure 18.3.

N O T E The `AutoActivate` property has three possible values: `aaManual`, `aaGetFocus`, and `aaDoubleClick`. The default is `aaDoubleClick`. When `aaDoubleClick` is set, the container will only activate, and show the server, when the mouse is double-clicked on the container.

The `aaGetFocus` value (used in many of the examples in this chapter) has the container automatically come up when it receives focus.

The third method, `aaManual`, is used to allow the server to activate only when some event and specific conditions occur. ■

That was cool, but where was the menu and button bar? Well, we can easily add these to the application. For the menu, just add a `TMainMenu` component from the Standard Page to your form. Now run the program again. You'll see the paint program's menus. See the following section, "Menu Merging," for more details regarding the adding and merging of menus.

For button bars, if the OLE object cannot place its button bar on the form, the button bars may float (as they do in Word), or not appear at all. To allow the OLE object's button bar to become part of your application, a panel is required at the top of the form, aligned to `alTop`. OLE objects that are activated in-place add their servers' toolbars directly into your application's window. Usually, any panels you use for toolbars are replaced by the OLE object's server's toolbars. You can prevent this by setting a panel's locked property to true.

Continued from the previous example:

5. Set `TOleContainer.Aligned = alNone`.

6. Drop two panels onto the form, align one to the top, and one to the bottom of the form.

7. Set the `Panel.Locked` property to true for the panel aligned to `alBottom`.

8. Set `TOleContainer.Aligned = alClient`.

9. Your form now should resemble the form shown in Figure 18.9.

Part

V

Ch

18

FIG. 18.9

The form with two Panels—a menu and an OLE Container.

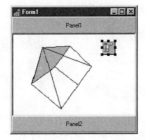

Now run the application, and you should see a form that looks similar to the one shown in Figure 18.10.

FIG. 18.10

A form with two panels: a menu and an OLE container.

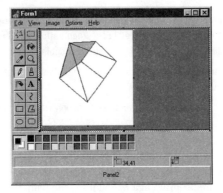

At design time, if we set the `Iconic` property to true, the object in the container appears as an icon. If we were to run the application now, the OLE server will open in its own window when it's activated. Some OLE Container objects are not designed to open in the container and will open in their own window, no matter what the iconic property is set to. Using the object type Sound Objects for the container will use Microsoft's Sound Recorder, which always opens up in its own window.

If you want to allow binders in Active Documents to work, you need to add another panel aligned to `alLeft`.

If desired, you can create a complete OLE container at runtime. Here is an example that demonstrates creating a container, adding an object, allowing it to be auto-activated and in-place, and then displaying it. It also allows menus and button bars to be part of the Form. Just add this to a new application:

```
// add to uses statement : ExtCtrls, Menus

procedure TForm1.FormShow(Sender: TObject);
begin
    // Create the upper panel
  with TPanel.Create(self) do begin
    Parent := self;
    Align := alTop;
    end; // create TPanel

    // Create the Menu
  with TMainMenu.Create(self) do begin
    Parent := self;
    end; // create TMainMenu

    // create the OLE Container
  with TOleContainer.Create(self) do begin
    Parent := self;
    AllowInPlace := True;        // default
```

```
    AutoActivate := aaGetFocus;   // Automatically activates when app is run
    Align := alClient;

      // Even create a default container
    CreateObject('Paint.Picture', false);   // Not iconic
    Iconic := False;   // don't show the icon

      // Give this window focus
    SetFocus;                        // give focus so it will activate
    end; // with TOleContainer create
end; // TForm1.FormShow
```

Menu Merging   When in-place activating a TOleContainer, the menus of the OLE server will integrate into the TMainMenu, if it's on the same form as the TOleContainer. The menu that is on the Form also can *merge* together with the OLE objects menu, which means that if you have a "File" menu item and the OLE server also has a "File" menu item, you can have them merge together so that only one Menu Item "File" appears on the menu bar. The TOleContainer automatically handles the entire process of combining the container form's menu with that of an in-place activated OLE server application.

The menu items property GroupIndex controls how menus are merged. Those main menu items with GroupIndex values of 0, 2, and 4 remain; TOleContainer merges the server application's menus and replaces the main menu items with GroupIndex values of 1, 3, and 5 (if they exist). So, for example, if you had an MDI form with a traditional main menu, you set the menus' GroupIndex properties as shown in Table 18.4.

Table 18.4   Menu Merging and Group Indexes

Menu	Value
File	0
Edit	1
Object	2
Window	4
Help	5

The File, Object, and Window menus will remain, but the Edit and Help menus would be replaced by those of the server application.

Note that there's no menu with a GroupIndex of 3; this isn't a problem.

Figures 18.11 and 18.12 show before and after images of merging of two menus that both contain differing items on the edit item.

Part
V

Ch

18

FIG. 18.11

Before menu merging of a Word document.

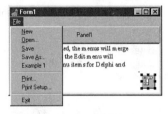

FIG. 18.12

After menu merging of a Word document.

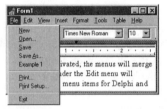

Using the Clipboard to Copy/Paste Existing OLE Objects   Copying and pasting at design time works exactly like copying and pasting anything else in Windows. Copying and pasting also can be done at runtime with the methods Copy, Paste, and PasteSpecialDialog.

Copy and Paste methods work in the same fashion with TOleContainer as they do for all Delphi components. When pasting, the only real difference is that the OLE server first queries the clipboard object to see if it's one that can be inserted into itself. By using the CanPaste method, a check can be done in the code to determine if the container will accept the object.

In the Paste method, a query of the clipboard is done to see if it will accept the paste from the Windows clipboard. Here is an example of using the Paste method:

```
Procedure Tform.DoPaste;
begin
  with OLEContainer1 do
    if CanPaste then
      Paste
    else
      ShowMessage('Can not paste this OLE object from Windows clipboard');
end; // TForm1.DoPaste
```

PasteSpecialDialog gives the user more control over how the contents of the Windows clipboard are pasted into the container (see Figure 18.13). The PasteSpecialDialog box lets the user select the format of the data, whether it should be embedded or linked, and whether to display the OLE object as an icon (and also to be able to choose a different icon).

```
Procedure TForm1.DoPasteSpecial;
begin
  with OLEContainer1 do
    if PasteSpecialDialog then
      ShowMessage('Paste Done');
end; // TForm1.DoPaste
```

FIG. 18.13

The Paste Special dialog box of inserting an Excel spreadsheet.

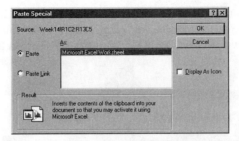

Figure 18.14 shows the Excel spreadsheet pasted into an OLE Container.

FIG. 18.14

An Excel spreadsheet in an OLE Container.

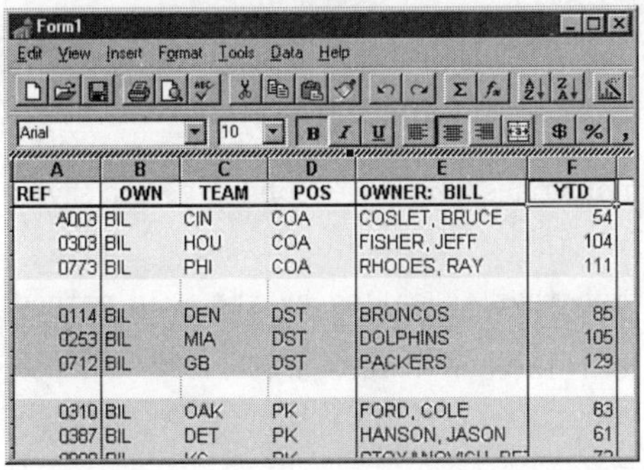

Working with OLE Dialogs   There are four dialog boxes built into the OLE Container, and Delphi surfaces them through the ChangeIconDialog, InsertObjectDialog, ObjectPropertiesDialog, and PasteSpecialDialog methods.

The only dialog box not covered in the preceding sections of this chapter is ChangeIconDialog. This dialog box allows the user to change the icon associated with the OLE object, and is displayed in the TOleContainer. The following code shows a simple example that checks to see if there is an object in the container first, and then allows the icon to be changed:

```
Procedure TForm1.ChangeIcon1Click(Sender: TObject);
begin
with OleContainer1 do
    // Note an object must be in the container first
  if State <> osEmpty then
    if ChangeIconDialog then
      ShowMessage('Icon was Changed');
end; // TForm1.ChangeIcon1Click
```

All of these dialog methods are part of the TOleContainer, they directly modify the OLE object, and have no properties or methods available for you to work with. This means that no way exists of setting any defaults before calling the specific dialog or for querying the dialog afterwards to find out what the user did actually enter.

The ChangeIconDialog can only be accessed at runtime (see Figure 18.15). I have already demonstrated making your own InsertObjectDialog in the section "Embedding New OLE Objects." So here, I'll show how to extract the icon from the OLE object that is in the TOleContainer.

FIG. 18.15

The Change Icon dialog box.

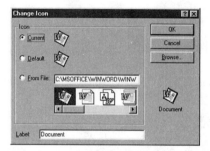

The following example demonstrates taking the Icon Image and saving it to a file in a metafile format:

```
// !!!! This is a function that is called by the main method below !!!!!

function Win32Chk(Win32OK: Integer): Integer;
var
  Buffer: String;
begin
  Result := Win32Ok;
  if Win32OK = 0 then begin
    SetLength(Buffer, ERRORSIZE);
    if FormatMessage(FORMAT_MESSAGE_FROM_SYSTEM,  nil, GetLastError, 0,
                PChar(Buffer), ERRORSIZE, nil) = 0 then
      Buffer := 'Internal Error: Error creating Error String';
    SetLength(Buffer, StrLen(PChar(Buffer)));
    raise EWin32Error.Create(Buffer);
  end;
end; // Win32Ok

Procedure TForm1.ChangeIcon1Click(Sender: TObject);

var
  Hg: HGlobal;
  Mfp: PMetaFilePict; //HMetaFile;
  Hmf: HMetaFile;
  HHH: HMetaFile;

const mfile: pchar = 'c:\test.wmf';
begin
  with OleContainer1 do
      // Note an object must be in the container first
    if State <> osEmpty then
      if ChangeIconDialog then begin
```

```
      Hg := OleContainer1.GetIconMetaPict;
      Hmf := PMetaFilePict(GlobalLock(Hg))^.hMF;
      HHH := CopyMetaFile(hmf, mfile);
      if HHH = 0 then Win32Chk(boolean(HHH));
      GlobalUnLock(Hg);
      end; // if
end; // TForm1.ChangeIcon1Click
```

N O T E So, as you may have noticed, the built-in dialog boxes are quite powerful but lacking the capabilities that we, as developers, require to make the most of them. I have shown some examples throughout this chapter on how to make the dialogs more usable. ■

TOleContainer and File Input/Output

`TOleContainer` allows you to load and save OLE objects via two different methods. The more common of these two methods is to read and write the OLE objects to files.

For example, to load an OLE object:

```
procedure TForm1.LoadObject;
begin
  with OleContainer1 do
    LoadFromFile('c:\udelphi3\chp18\TestFile.bmp');  // NOTE : Object BitMap
end; // TForm1.LoadObject
```

On the CD

The file TESTFILE.BMP can be found at \Udelphi3\Chp18\TestFile.bmp on this book's companion CD-ROM.

N O T E The testfile.bmp is an OLE object file, and not a regular BMP file. The original BMP was 13K in size and the OLE version is about 190K. ■

TForm1.LoadObject loads the OLE object "TESTFILE.BMP". In loading the new object, any object in the container will be discarded, as well as all changes. If the property `OldStreamFormat` is True, `LoadFromFile` loads only files saved with version 1.0 Delphi's `TOleContainer` component.

```
procedure TForm1.SaveObject;
begin
  with TOleContainer1 do
    if State <> osEmpty then
      SaveToFile('c:\udelphi3\chp18\testfile.bmp');  // NOTE : Object BitMap
end; // TForm1.SaveObject
```

Again, The file "testfile.bmp" can be found on this book's companion CD-ROM, in the \Udelphi3\chp18\ folder.

The preceding example will save the object in the OLE container to a file as an OLE object. An OLE object must already be loaded in the container before calling `SaveToFile`. If `OldStreamFormat` is True, `SaveToFile` writes a file compatible with Delphi 1.0's `TOleContainer` component.

Part

V

Ch

18

N O T E   Unless you truly need backward compatibility with existing Delphi 1.0 OLE-formatted files, leave SaveToFile set to False. As in the Delphi 2.0 and later, OLE objects contain extra header information that TOleContainer can use to validate a file or stream. ■

The behavior of the LoadFromStream and SaveToStream methods are exactly like those previously mentioned for the LoadFromFile and SaveToFile methods. The only difference is that streams are being used. The following section demonstrates how an OLE object can be read and written to a database table.

Streaming OLE Objects to a Database   I have seen no examples of reading and writing OLE data to or from a database. So I thought I would create a program that did so, which is how OLEDB.EXE was created. You can find the full source code on this book's companion CD-ROM.

The table has a blob field named OLE_Object and uses the TBlobStream component to read and write this field to the database. You can find the method TfrmMain.LoadFromStreamOLE shown in Listing 18.5, in the file OLEDBU.PAS on this book's companion CD-ROM.

Listing 18.5   \UDELPHI3\CHP18\OLEDB\OLEDBU.PAS—Load an OLE File from a Stream

```
procedure TfrmMain.LoadFromStreamOLE;
var
  BS:  TBlobStream;
begin
  BS := TBlobStream.Create (Table1.FieldByName('OLE_Object') as TBlobField,
bmRead);
  if BS.Size <> 0 then
    try
      with Form2, OLEContainer1 do begin
        LoadFromStream(BS);
        if State <> osEmpty then
          Iconic := True;
        end; //with
    finally
      BS.Free;
    end; // try
end; // TForm1.LoadFromStreamOLE
```

Only after loading the OLE object into the TOleContainer can the method Iconic be set, because it's not valid when working with empty containers.

In the program OLEDB, the LoadFromStreamOLE method is called from the TDataSource.OnDataChanged method so that every time the cursor moves, the OLE object in the TOleContainer also will be changed. You can find the method TfrmMain.WriteToStreamOLE shown in Listing 18.6, which shows an example of writing an OLE object to a table, in the file OLEDBU.PAS on this book's companion CD-ROM.

Listing 18.6   \UDELPHI3\CHP18\OLEDB\OLEDBU.PAS—Write an OLE File from a Stream

```
procedure TForm1.WriteToStreamOLE;
var
  BS:    TBlobStream;
begin
  BS := TBlobStream.Create(
    Table1.FieldByName('OLE_Object') as TBlobField, bmWrite);
  try
    with Form2.OLEContainer1 do
      if State <> osEmpty then
        SaveToStream(BS);
  finally
    BS.Free;
  end; // try
end; // TForm1.WriteToStreamOLE
```

The best place to call this method is from the OnBeforePost event of the TTable. The only problem is knowing when the OLE object has changed, and you can tell by testing the TOleContainer.Modified property. If it's true, the data within the container has been modified.

TOleContainer and Scaling Considerations The TOleContainer allows the OLE object to scale itself within the container in five different ways, which are described in Table 18.5.

Table 18.5   SizeMode

Value	Purpose
smClip	(Default) Displays the OLE object at its normal size, clipping any parts that don't fit within the container.
SmCenter	Displays the OLE object at its normal size, centering it within the container.
SmScale	Scales or shrinks the view of the OLE object to fit within the container, by scaling width and height proportionally.
SmStretch	Scales or shrinks the view of the OLE object to fill the OLE container, without regard to preserving the proportions of the OLE object.
SmAutoSize	Same as smClip, but also automatically resizes the container whenever the size of the OLE object changes.

One little gem I discovered is that the Document doesn't understand its placement in the container correctly (for example, Paint objects or the tick marks in a Word object). To solve this, place the TOleContainer on a TPanel, and set the BorderWidth of the panel to 10, or to whatever is necessary for the object with which you're working. Active documents know that the window is their area of the screen, and display all information correctly. So, for ActiveDocs a panel isn't required to correct this visual problem.

Part
V

Ch

18

N O T E You need to set both the panel and container alignments to `alClient` to get the in-place activation to work. ▇

The following two figures show what I mean regarding the borders. Figure 18.16 is without a border, and Figure 18.17 is with a border.

FIG. 18.16
Without a border.

FIG. 18.17
With a border.

Using OLE Verbs   OLE Containers have a number of verbs that they recognize to perform special actions, as well as being able to pass on OLE object-specific verbs to the object within it. The verbs that each OLE object recognizes vary from object to object, but the standard verbs are consistent. To have a verb action performed, the method `DoVerb` is called, as in the following example:

```
DoVerb(ovShow);
```

This special verb should show the server for the OLE object in the container.

`TOleContainer` contains a number of special verbs. These verbs determine the action to be performed on an OLE Server. Table 18.6 gives a list of special verbs that can be performed by calling `DoVerb`.

Table 18.6   Special OLE Verbs

Verb	Behavior
ovPrimary	Activates the in-place User Interface.
ovOpen	Opens the OLE server as a separate window.
ovShow	Tries to do an `ovPrimary` action; if this fails, the OLE Container does an `ovOpen` action.

Verb	Behavior
ovHide	If in-place activated, this completely deactivates the object; otherwise, hides the server window.
ovUIActivate	Activates the server in-place user interface.
ovInPlaceActivate	Activates the server in-place without the user interface.
ovDiscardUndoState	The server will discard all undo information it's holding.

These verbs are defined by Microsoft, and the server is required to understand them, but the usage of these verbs may vary between applications. The ovShow and ovHide are complementary, the ovShow makes the object visible, and the ovHide makes the object non-visible.

Delphi only uses the ovShow and ovOpen. When ovPrimary is used, then Verb 0 is called. For most servers, this will be the Open verb. If you use the verb ovPrimary, the server is opened in a separate window, but when the Ole Container uses the verb ovPrimary, such as when the user double-clicks the container, the server is displayed within the container.

```
Procedure TFont1.LoadDocumentEmbedded;
begin
    // Embed a document into the Container
  TOC.CreateObjectFromFile('test.doc', false);

  if TOC.State <> osInPlaceActive then
     TOC.DoVerb(ovOpen);  // Loads up Word as a server outside of Delphi
end; // TFont1.LoadDocumentEmbedded
```

Delphi allows you to determine what state the Container is currently in. Table 18.7 lists the possible values as defined by Microsoft.

Table 18.7   OLE Object State Values

State	Description
osEmpty	There is no object in the container.
osLoaded	The in-process object has some of the code loaded into the application space. This doesn't mean that the server has been loaded. The TOleContainer window appears blank.
osRunning	The server for the object is completely loaded and is running. The user interface was created but is not visible to the end user. The OLE server will be running in a separate window. This can be set by calling the method RUN.
osOpen	Activates the user interface.
osInPlaceActive	The object has a window of its own inside the TOleContainer. It can respond directly to mouse clicks and then repaint itself.
osUIActive	The User Interface can be seen, so the OLE server can be accessed via the TOleContainer on the form.

Part V Ch 18

N O T E   *Verbs* are actions that you can have the OLE object perform. The verbs apply to OLE objects that are embedded or linked. Word, for example, has the following two verbs—Open and Edit. So, the verb Open would cause the Word object to activate in the container. You can see all the verbs that belong to an OLE object by running REGEDIT.EXE. If you want to see all the verbs that belong to Paint, then open the entry, HKEY_CLASSES_ROOT/Paint.Picture/StdFileEditing/verb.

You can see that the only verb for Paint is Edit. ■

All the verbs for an OLE object also can be found at runtime. We could add all the verbs to a Main Menu Item "Verbs" as follows:

```
// Note: requires a TOleContainer and TMainMenu on Form1.

function TForm1.AddVerbs;
var
  I: integer;
  Temp: TMenuItem;

begin
    // Check Menu for Verb Menu.
    // Remove all sub items if found.
  With MainMenu1 do begin
    For I := 0 to Items.Count-1 do
      if MainMenu1.Items[I].Caption = 'Verb' then begin
        while Items[I].Count > 0 do begin
          Temp := Items[I].Items[0];
          Items[i].Delete(0);
          Temp.Free;
          end; // while
        end; // if

    // if no verbs then exit
    if OleContainer1.ObjectVerbs.Count = 0 then exit;

    // Create Main Menu Items. This item will appear on the menu bar.
    Temp :=  TMenuItem.create(self);
    Temp.Caption  := 'Verb';
    Items.Add(Temp);
    end; // with

    // Add Verbs as sub items
  With OleContainer1 do
    For I := 0 to ObjectVerbs.Count - 1 do begin
      Temp :=  TMenuItem.create(self);
      Temp.Caption  := ObjectVerbs[I];
      MainMenu1.Items.Items[MainMenu1.Items.Count-1].Add(Temp);
      end; // For
end; // TForm1.AddVerbs
```

Using the *OleObject* Property to Access the Automation Server in an OLE Server   Containers are great for working with other application servers, but there are times when you need to do something programmatically. For example, the Word Document server doesn't allow you to save files or to print them from the menu.

Delphi was designed to allow you to access the automation servers of the container object. Once you have the automation object, you can call all of its methods.

```
procedure TForm1.Button1Click(Sender: TObject);
Var V: Variant;
begin
  // Proper activation of the OleContainer must have already occurred.
  OleContainer1.DoVerb(OLEIVERB_UIACTIVATE);
 V := OleContainer1.OleObject;  // Access the OLE Object
  V := V.Application.WordBasic;  // request the Automation server
  V.Insert('Delphi becomes greater everyday');
end;
```

The line, `Delphi becomes greater everyday`, should be inserted into the OLE container at the cursor's current position in the container.

N O T E The greatest difficulty you may have when working with OLE Automation objects is finding out which methods it supports. Some versions of Word have a wordbasic.hlp file that you can install. Alternatively, you can find a list of all the methods for the wordbasic server in the MSDN. ■

We could have a button create a new document and save it as well, as follows:

```
procedure TForm1.Button1Click(Sender:Tobject);
var v: Variant;
begin
  V := OleContainer1.OleObject.Application.WordBasic;
  V.FileNew;
  V.Insert('Delphi is a temple from ' + #13);
  V.Insert('Greek mythology');
  V.SaveFileAs('DelphiHistory');
end; // TForm1.Button1Click
```

Positional versus Named Arguments   Automation servers allow us to have optional parameters when calling their methods. The following shows the complete method, as specified in the wordbasic.hlp file for the `FormatFont` method:

```
FormatFont [.Points = number] [, .Underline = number] [, .Color = number]
➡ [, .Strikethrough = number] [, .Superscript = number]
➡ [, .Subscript = number] [, .Shadow = number] [, .Hidden = number]
➡ [, .SmallCaps = number] [, .AllCaps = number] [, .Outline = number]
➡ [, .Spacing = number] [, .Position = number or text]
➡ [, .Kerning = number] [, .KerningMin = number or text] [, .Default]
➡ [, .Tab = number] [, .Font = text] [, .Bold = number] [, .Italic = number]
```

There are a lot of optional parameters that you can pass to the `FormatFont` method, a total of 20. It would be a pain if every time you wanted to change the point size of the font, you had to enter all 20 parameters. Well, the Automation object allows you to not have to worry about this. If you want to set the point size of the current font to 12 points, you can do the following:

```
V.FormatFont(12);
```

Part
V

Ch
18

If you want to make the Font really large and underlined, you could use the following:

```
V.FormatFont(40, 1);
```

Both Bold and Underline parameters are Boolean in nature:

- 0OFF
- 1ON

To change the Point Size and make it Bold at the same time, try this:

```
V.FormatFont(12, Bold := 1);
```

The first parameter is set to 12, and Bold is set to 1 (turning it on). Here, the second parameter was passed, by the method referred to as "passing by named arguments." The various methods can be mixed and matched, but you also could do it by using only named arguments:

```
V.FormatFont(Bold := 1, Point := 12);
```

This code does the same thing, but using only named argument passing. The order of named arguments doesn't matter, but when passing arguments in this way, both the name of the parameter and the value must be passed, in an assignment-like fashion, such as Bold := 1.

N O T E   Argument passing by name uses an assignment style that is very Visual Basic in nature. But more important, the order of the named parameters doesn't matter, and you can omit parameters as well.

Delphi passes all these parameters to Word with no type checking, which is why you can get away with not specifying all the parameters because Delphi is a strongly typed language. If Word doesn't like the data that you pass, an exception will be raised. ■

The third and final way of passing parameters is using the position parameters method. When using this method, only the positions that require data have data; the rest are left blank. The following example sets the point size to 13, and turns on Underline and Bold:

```
V.FormatFont(13,1,,,,,,,,,,,,,,,,,1); // uses Position with optional nulls
```

N O T E   When working with Position parameters, only the positions up to the last one in which we are interested need to be comma-delimited. The remainder of the parameters can be ignored, for example:

```
V.FormatFont(13,1,,1); ■
```

The following snippet shows a more elaborate example of setting an edit style, where more than just Font properties are changed:

You can find the function Title shown in Listing 18.7, in the file OLEDBU.PAS on this book's companion CD-ROM.

Listing 18.7 \UDELPHI3\CHP18\RESUME\MAINU.PAS   Editing Style that Adds More than Just Font Properties

```
procedure Title(V: variant);
begin
   // Centre Personal Info
   // Set Font to Bold, 12 point
   V.FormatFont(Bold := 1, Points := 12);      // uses Name Argument passing
   V.CenterPara; // Centre Text
   V.FormatParagraph(0);  // No Indent on Left
end; // Title
```

This snippet is from the program, Resume, which you can find at \UDELPHI3\CHP18\RESUME\MAINU.PAS, on this book's companion CD-ROM.

IStorage Interface   The only really interesting method that hasn't been discussed is the IStorage interface method. IStorage is used to manipulate storages. This interface provides methods for opening and creating streams and sub-storages. You also can enumerate the contents of a storage, and obtain and set element information. The details of how to use this interface are beyond the scope of this chapter. If you're interested in digging into how to use the IStorage interface, I suggest a book on OLE Interfaces, such as *Delphi 2 Unleashed*, Second Edition, Borland Press, 1996.

A Look at the Demo Programs

To demonstrate all the concepts covered so far, two example programs were created. The first one is a simple Resume program that builds a Word Document, using the TOleContainer and a Word OLE object. It demonstrates calling methods of an OLE Word document to build a nicely formatted Word document that then can be used for that upcoming job interview.

Example #1: The Mini-Résumé Builder   The first example is a mini-résumé program that pops up a form you fill in with personal information. Resume.exe then takes this information and places it in the Word Document as formatted text that is contained in a TOleContainer on the main form. Figure 18.18 shows the Résumé Application in progress. Some other features that are demonstrated include the following:

- How to access OLE Automation server to make calls to the document programmatically
- Inserting a Word Document object
- Running with In-Place Activation
- Allowing FilePrint, Save, SaveAs from the Word OLE objects methods
- Using a form in which to enter personal information
- Creating a résumé document from edit boxes and memos
- Formatting Word text
- Allowing Save and Load of Documents as object files

Part
V

Ch

18

FIG. 18.18
The Résumé Application,
demonstrating the
OleObject interface.

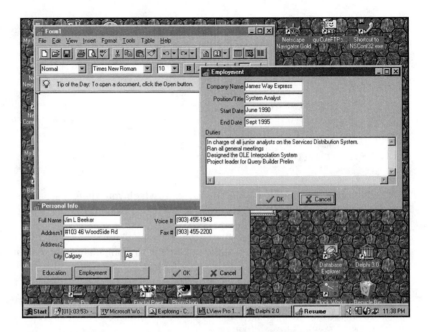

Example #2: OLE Database   The second example, named OLEDB, primarily demonstrates copying OLE objects from and to a database. One good use for this kind of tool is in the creation of this book. All the chapters, their respective figures, and other related material could have been stored in a simple database for easy access and manipulation. Figure 18.19 shows the Résumé Application in progress. Some other features that are demonstrated include the following:

- Reading/Writing OLE Objects with a Database
- Calling the Insert Dialog and Paste Special on a TOleContainer
- Toggling of Iconic and AutoActivate properties to demonstrate their behaviors
- Storing and reading of OleObjects from a Paradox database
- Saving and loading of OleObjects to and from disk
- Creating your own Insert Dialog box
- Reading of Insertable OLE objects types from the Windows Registry

FIG. 18.19
OLE Database application, demonstrating storing OLE objects in a database.

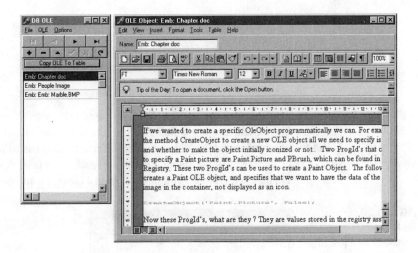

Using ActiveX Controls

ActiveXs are controls that can be used in any development tool, as long as that development tool supports them. As mentioned previously, they are language-independent, so let's look at how we can add them and use them in Delphi.

Adding ActiveX Controls to the Delphi Component Palette

From a user's standpoint, the integrating of controls into Delphi is a snap; only adding the control to the component palette is required. After the ActiveX is added to the palette, you can use it just like any other VCL Component.

Delphi 3 handles the installation of ActiveX differently than previous versions. First, I will give a short list of what is necessary to do to install an ActiveX, and then will go step-by-step through them.

- Register the ActiveX in the Registry.
- Create a wrapper PAS file.
- Add the PAS file to a package.
- Install the package on the component palette.

N O T E If you're interested in learning more about Packages, check out Chapter 15, "Working with Packages." ■

Over the next few pages, we will walk through how to install an ActiveX control. I will use an ActiveX that I found in my \WinNT\System32 directory. The ActiveX you use may or may not be the same.

N O T E This walk-through proceeds as if a package does not already exist, as will usually occur. If you already have a package, then refer to steps 4 through 10 and 13.

Some figures may vary slightly from the ones shown. ▪

Follow these steps to add an ActiveX Control to the Component palette:

1. First, a package needs to be created, and then we add the ActiveX control to it. Select File, New. You should now see a dialog box similar to the one shown in Figure 18.20. Select Package and click OK. A New Package dialog box appears; Figure 18.21 shows what it looks like. For the File name, I entered "Test," and a brief description in the description field. Click OK after you have entered a file name and description.

FIG. 18.20

The New Items dialog window, for selecting an item that you can use as a starting point for your application.

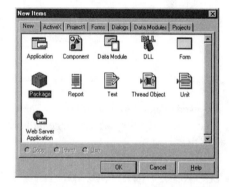

FIG. 18.21

The New Package dialog window, for naming a new package.

2. On clicking OK in the preceding step, a new dialog box appears, which looks like Figure 18.22. We now have an empty package, so let's add our ActiveX to it. Click the Add icon; it's the one with the "+" sign.

FIG. 18.22

The Package mainte-nance dialog window.

3. The "Add Unit" Dialog Window appears (see Figure 18.23). Because we want to Import an ActiveX, click the Import ActiveX tab.

FIG. 18.23

The Add dialog window that you will use to add an ActiveX Control.

4. You now should see a dialog box like the one shown in Figure 18.24. As you can see, the box is divided into two sections. The upper section contains a list of all the controls registered with the system. Here, controls can be added and removed from the system Registry. The bottom portion allows you to customize how the Delphi wrapper for the ActiveX will be created.

FIG. 18.24

The Add window, Import ActiveX page.

5. If you can see the OLE Control that you want to add to the component palette in the upper box, proceed to step 6. If not, you first need to register the control. Click the Add button; the Register OLE Control Dialog should appear, as shown in Figure 18.25. Select the file name for the ActiveX control you want to add and press Open. The control will be registered with the system Registry, and the dialog box will disappear. I installed Hours.Ocx, which may or may not exist on your system.

FIG. 18.25

The Register OLE Control dialog window.

6. Look at the upper portion of the Add Unit Dialog, and select the name of the new ActiveX control you just added to the Registry (see Figure 18.26). Now examine the lower half of the dialog box; here is where modifications can be made to control how the ActiveX will be added to the palette. The Class Names field displays the suggested class names of the OLE controls found in the selected OLE control library. Unless another OLE control library uses the same class names, you should have no reason to change these. If you do make changes, it is strongly suggested that you start each class name with a "T," as is the Delphi convention.

FIG. 18.26

The Add Window - Import ActiveX page (with a selected ActiveX Control).

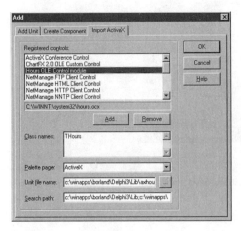

7. The Page Palette field allows you to specify the name of the Component page to which the ActiveX control will be added. The default page is ActiveX, but you can choose any page that already exists, or you can, if you so choose, create a new page.

8. The Unit file name is the path name to the wrapper file that Delphi created so that it can interface to the ActiveX. The path defaults to the directory in which the ActiveX file resides. As you can see, the wrapper name is the same as the control's name, but it has an extension of .PAS.

9. Search Path is the current list of paths that Delphi searches to find the files when compiling.

10. Usually, you rarely need to modify any of the fields in the lower half of the Import ActiveX Control dialog box.

   If you do make any changes, press OK. (If you feel that you have made an error in the adding of the ActiveX, you can press Cancel to back out of the changes you made.)

   Delphi will now create a wrapper for the ActiveX so that it can be used within Delphi applications.

11. You should now be back to the New Package dialog box, as shown in Figure 18.27. Now the package must be saved and built. Click the Build icon, which is the leftmost icon. When this is completed, the next step is to install the package. So click the Install icon. If all went according to plan, you should see a message similar to the one shown in Figure 18.28, saying that your package has been installed.

FIG. 18.27

New Package dialog box, with an ActiveX Control listed.

FIG. 18.28

The Information Dialog message, stating that Package Test.dpl installed correctly.

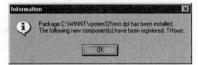

12. If you now double-click the ActiveX in the Package Dialog window (refer to Figure 18.27), the editor will now contain a new file; this is the wrapper PAS file created for the ActiveX, and you should see your ActiveX on the component palette.

In the following section, the wrapper file will be examined.

The OLE Wrapper

The wrapper file for an ActiveX is similar to any unit that you may add to a project. In fact, it is quite similar to a component unit.

The name of the unit, is the same as the name of the ActiveX—in the example, the name is axHours, with ax being a prefix added on because this is a wrapper for an ActiveX.

Near the top of the unit, a comment sometimes may appear containing a group of comments, referred to as the *conversion log*. If any problems occurred in the creation of the wrapper unit, they are placed here. The most common problem to occur is a name conflict between the ActiveX and a reserved word. Delphi automatically modifies the name slightly, and notes the change in the conversion log.

Like all wrappers and components, a class definition is required. All ActiveX control wrappers are inherited from TOleControl. TOleControl is a window-handle bearing component that is a descendant from TWinControl. The purpose of TOleControl is to allow ActiveX controls to act seamlessly in Delphi.

Methods The only method in this unit is InitControlData, which overrides the method defined in the abstract class TOleControl. InitControlData gives the class its unique OLE class and event identification numbers, as well as any other control-specific information. It is a protected member because it has no use outside of the class, only to class members.

This control doesn't have a method exposing an AboutBox, but often one will be exposed. This method usually displays a custom About box for the control. When a method of the wrapper is called, such as the AboutBox, the TOleControl.InvokeMethod of the TOleControl method is called. TOleControl.InvokeMethod doesn't perform a direct function call; instead, it uses OLE automation to call the given function of the ActiveX that is exposed.

Properties The properties of a wrapper can be divided into two sections. The first are the ones having no read or write values specified. These are standard properties, inherited from the TWinControl and TComponent classes.

All the properties belonging to the Control can be found by the fact that they have an index, a get, and a set method specified. These special get and set methods are what allow Delphi to bridge the gap between ActiveX control properties and the Delphi component properties.

There really isn't much to a wrapper file; the most interesting part is the InitControlData. Delphi does a great job of wrapping a complex entity like an ActiveX into something simple and easy to use.

The Wrapper File   The following code shows the PAS wrapper file for the HOURS.OCX ActiveX that we added to the component palette on the ActiveX page, and that was discussed in the preceding section:

```
unit axhours;

interface

uses Ole2I, Classes, Graphics, OleCtrls;

type

  THours = class(TOleControl)
  private
  protected
    procedure InitControlData; override;
  public
  published
    property TabStop;
    property DragCursor;
    property DragMode;
    property ParentShowHint;
    property PopupMenu;
    property ShowHint;
    property TabOrder;
    property Visible;
    property OnDragDrop;
    property OnDragOver;
    property OnEndDrag;
    property OnEnter;
    property OnExit;
    property OnStartDrag;
    property crPermitColor: TColor index 1
        read GetColorProp
        write SetColorProp stored False;
    property crDenyColor: TColor index 2
        read GetColorProp
        write SetColorProp stored False;
    property DateData: Variant index 3
        read GetVariantProp
        write SetVariantProp stored False;
  end;
```

Part

V

Ch

18

```
procedure Register;

implementation

{$J+}

procedure THours.InitControlData;
const
  CControlData: TControlData = (
    ClassID: (
      D1:$A44EA7AD;D2:$9D58;D3:$11CF;D4:($A3,$5F,$00,$AA,$00,$B6,$74,$3B));
    EventIID: (
      D1:$A44EA7AC;D2:$9D58;D3:$11CF;D4:($A3,$5F,$00,$AA,$00,$B6,$74,$3B));
    EventCount: 0;
    EventDispIDs: nil;
    LicenseKey: nil;
    Flags: $00000000);
begin
  ControlData := @CControlData;
end;

procedure Register;
begin
  RegisterComponents('OCX', [THours]);
end;

end.
```

Using ActiveX Controls Within an Application

After the ActiveX control is on the component palette, all the hard work is done. The ActiveX control now acts like a Delphi component, via the wrapper file we previously examined. The ActiveX component has all the properties of a standard Delphi component, plus any that the ActiveX control also has.

Calling Methods

Calling the methods of an ActiveX control is easy. Generally, all ActiveX manufacturers also ship a help file that explains everything you can do with their OLE object. There are ways of getting a listing of these methods and their parameter types via the IDispatch interface, but that is beyond the scope of this chapter.

To call the connect method of the FTP ActiveX component that ships with Delphi, you just call it as you call any other Delphi VCL component.

For example, using the Internet Control Pack, you can call the method Connect by the following:

```
FTP1.Connect(RemoteHost, RemotePort);
```

On the CD

I created an example program showing the use of the ActiveX spelling control, which can be found on the ActiveX page. The program will create questions and answers and store them in a database table. Additionally, it also does a spelling check on the text, using the Spelling control. The application is called QA, and can be found in the \UDELPHI3\CHP18\QA directory.

The routine that does the real work is the SpellCheckDBMemo procedure. A buffer is needed to store the data in when passing to and from the control. First, the buffer is passed to the text property, which is used to set and return the text being checked. The CheckText property then specifies the text to be spell checked and evokes a spell-check session.

The Text property is then used to return the newly checked text, and we put it back into the memo, as shown in Listing 18.8.

Listing 18.8 \UDELPHI3\CHP18\QA\QAEditU.PAS—The *SpellCheckDBMemo* Procedure

```
procedure TDataChangeForm.SpellBtnClick(Sender: TObject);

  procedure SpellCheckDBMemo(var TheDBMemo: TDBMemo);
  var
    buf: PChar;
    SizeOfBuf: word;

  begin
    SizeOfBuf := succ(TheDBMemo.GetTextLen);   {add 1 for the null terminator}

    buf := AllocMem(SizeOfBuf);
    TheDBMemo.GetTextBuf(buf, SizeOfBuf);

    VCSpeller1.Text:= Buf;
    VCSpeller1.CheckText:= Buf;

    TheDBMemo.SetTextBuf(PChar(VCSpeller1.Text));
    FreeMem(buf, SizeOfBuf);
  end;

{ MAIN SpellBtnClick }
begin
  Form1.Table1.Edit;
  SpellCheckDBMemo(DBQues);
  SpellCheckDBMemo(DBAns);

  ShowMessage('Spell Check has Completed.');
end; // TDataChangeForm.SpellBtnClick
```

Part
V

Ch
18

Optional Parameter Passing Some ActiveXs allow you to pass them a variable number of parameters. You still can benefit from this feature in Delphi, although Delphi creates a Pascal wrapper unit around the ActiveX that requires you to fill in the entire parameter list.

To be able to do this, we pass an Unassigned or VT_EMPTY type Variant for the parameters that we are not interested in, as in the following example:

```
var V: Variant;
begin
  V := Unassigned;
  OCX1.Method('Image1.bmp', V, V, V, Read);
end;
```

We could set the variant to VT_EMPTY and call the method like so:

```
var V: Variant;
begin
  TVarRec(V).VType := VT_EMPTY;
  OCX1.Method('Image1.bmp', V, V, V, Read);
end;
```

N O T E Sometimes, the OLE object expects a special variant type such as VT_ERROR, instead of VT_EMPTY or UnAssigned. If so, you can do it the following way:

```
var V: Variant;
begin
  TVarRec(V).VType := VT_ERROR;
  OCX1.Method(21, V, V);
```

Using the *OleObject* Property

Using the OleObject property for ActiveX controls has the same passing methods as does the Variant. To learn more about the OleObject, you can examine the ones shown in these previous sections: "Using the OleObject Property to Access the Automation Server in an OLE Server" and "Positional versus Named Arguments."

```
procedure TForm1.Chart1Click;
var
  V : Variant;
begin
  V := SimpleActiveX.OleObject;
  V.Method('A',,'C');
     .
     .
end; // TForm1.Chart1Click
```

The OleObject returns an IDispatch interface as an automation server, which we can use to make direct calls to the ActiveX, therefore bypassing Delphi's tight type checking.

Distributing an ActiveX Enriched Application

There are many products on the market that allow applications with ActiveX controls to easily be deployed to a customer's site. The tedious part is registering the ActiveXs into the Registry.

Registering ActiveX Controls   To make the deployment of ActiveX controls really easy, you can make use of products such as Installshield and WISE. Both are commercial products, but a version of Installshield is included on the Delphi CD-ROM, to make deploying your applications a breeze.

For those who like to know what is going on, here is a quick overview of the process that is required to deploy an ActiveX control for an application.

First, all the necessary associated files required need to be copied to the target machine. This includes all associated DLLs and a REG file. The runtime license file, LIC, is also required. It contains a license key. Information on when, who, and for how long an ActiveX control can be used can be accessed via the IclassFactory2 interface. Also, the REGSVR32.EXE tool is necessary to add the ActiveX control information to the Registry.

Putting It All Together

On the CD

As previously mentioned, there is a complete example program called QA that can be found in the \UDELPHI3\CHP18\QA directory. It demonstrates how to use the Spell Checking component.

QA is a simple Question and Answer program that shows a question, and then (by pressing a button) shows the answer (see Figure 18.29). You can move forward and backward through the questions, as well as delete, edit, and add new ones. The Edit/Add menu items call a second form that allows new text to be added or modified. There is a button here to do a spell check on the text for both the Question and the Answer, using the spell check control.

Part
V
Ch
18

FIG. 18.29
Question and Answer application, demonstrating using an ActiveX Control.

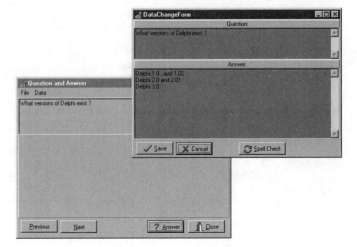

CHAPTER 19

Working with COM Interfaces

by Todd Miller

This chapter focuses on how you can use Delphi 3 to work with component objects and COM interfaces. First, this chapter covers the fundamentals of the Component Object Model (COM) architecture. Then, a discussion of component object servers and clients follows. Then after you have the COM basics down, you get into building a simple COM object server. To get an "under the hood" understanding, we'll first build this simple COM server using Delphi 2 techniques, and then see how easy it is (and how much less coding it takes) by using Delphi 3 techniques. The chapter concludes by showing how to create a Windows shell extension handler. You start by getting an understanding of what COM is all about. ∎

Fundamentals of the Component Object Model (COM)

Discuss the essentials of the COM architecture.

Delphi interfaces

Delphi's new interface language support makes working with COM objects and interfaces extremely easy.

COM server objects

Discusses how to develop COM server objects, register them, and access them from client applications.

Windows shell extensions

Discusses how to develop a shell extensions COM object for Windows 95 and Windows NT 4.

COM Fundamentals

COM, or the *Component Object Model*, is a language-independent, object-based programming specification that defines how *Component Objects* are to be built and made accessible. To help you understand the fundamentals of COM, the following list details the primary concepts of the Component Object Model:

■ A *Component Object* or COM object is a set of one or more services (or interfaces) that are exposed to a client to provide some additional functionality to the client. Think of a component object like a C++ multiple-inheritance object that is a made up of one or more C++ classes. Component objects can be as simple as a Windows 95 shell extension that exposes one or two interfaces (discussed in a following section of this chapter), or as complex as an ActiveX control that uses many interfaces to communicate back and forth with a client application.

■ An *Interface* is both the definition and the identity of an interface object. Fundamentally, an interface is a pure virtual class that defines the methods that will be implemented by an interface object. Each interface also will be uniquely identified so that there is no confusion as to which component object's interface a client is requesting from a server.

■ An *Interface Object* is the implementation of one of the component object's interface(s). Again, the component object may expose more than one interface, so it has to have an interface object implemented for each interface that it supports.

In all, a component object provides a functional solution to a client through one or more interfaces that the component object exposes. Each service or interface object is accessible to the client through the use of an interface, as you will see later.

Understanding Clients and Servers

Where do component objects reside, and how does a client gain access to them? To start with, component objects are contained in a *COM server* that can be either a DLL or an EXE module. They are referred to as *in-process* or *local server*, respectively. The fundamental difference between these two server types is that an in-process (DLL) server will be loaded directly into the client's process memory space as opposed to a local server (EXE), which runs in its own process space separate from the client. This is why local servers are sometimes referred to as "out-of-process" servers. There is also the notion of a "remote" server, which is where the client and server are run on separate machines utilizing Microsoft's new DCOM technology (refer to the note that follows for more information).

The newest term that Microsoft has come up with to refer to all the various types of COM servers generically is *ActiveX*. ActiveX encompasses OLE, ActiveX Controls, and Active Documents, just to name a few. A related term is *DirectX*, which refers to the new COM interfaces that allow direct access to various hardware devices on your system, such as video and sound devices.

Component Object Clients

A component object client is typically an EXE, but it also can be a DLL. It all depends on what the component object(s) are used for within a COM server. With Windows 95 shell extensions, the client is Windows itself or, more specifically, the Windows 95 shell (Explorer.exe). Additionally, clients usually are run independently of the component object server that they might be using. In other words, they don't know where the COM server is located or how to bring it up. The client only knows with which component object it wants to work.

The way in which the client gains access to a particular COM server's component object is by first making a request to Windows to find the desired component object, in which case Windows locates and brings up the server, and then returns the requested interface object (which the client also requests).

So the question is, how does Windows know where to look for the component object's server? Windows accomplishes this task by looking in the Windows Registry database to find the location of the server, which means that the server must have entries made in the Registry that, at minimum, register the location of the server so that Windows can find and load it. Windows first asks the server if it supports the desired component object. If so, Windows then checks to see if the desired component object supports the client's requested interface. If so, it passes a reference to it back to the client. The reference is to the associated interface object created on the server side.

N O T E   COM works only on the immediate machine with either in-process or out-of-process servers. Microsoft, however, recently introduced its Distributed COM technology, which breaks the machine boundary. Distributed COM, or DCOM, was first introduced as a beta in the Professional version of Visual Basic 4. The implementation of DCOM that the authors rely on, however, is that found in Windows NT 4.0. The only advantage to the Visual Basic implementation was that it worked on Windows 95 machines. At the time of this writing, Microsoft was just coming out with its version of DCOM for Windows 95. Another product that enables COM objects to be shared across network boundaries is the OLE Enterprise product that is put out by Open Environment, which is a subsidiary of Borland. OLE Enterprise supports all the Win32 platforms. ■

Finding Component Objects

So now you probably wonder, how does the client know what to tell Windows to look for in order to find the component object that the client wants? The client provides to Windows the globally unique identifier or GUID that is associated with the component object. For a component object, the GUID is known as a *class identifier* or *CLSID*. Besides the client providing the component object's class ID to Windows, it also passes along a request for the initially desired interface to be returned from the server once it is up and running. This also is a GUID but in this case, it refers to a specific interface that the client requests. The GUID associated with a specific interface is known as an *interface identifier* or *IID*.

An interesting thing to note here is that when the client asks for a particular interface object within the requested component object, Windows passes back only the reference to the requested interface—not the component object itself. A component object is merely a container of services—implemented interface(s) or interface object(s)—that make up its functionality. The client must know or be able to make safe assumptions about what interfaces a particular COM server supports.

Getting to Other Interfaces

So then, how can a client obtain one of the other interfaces that a component object may support? Well, as you'll see shortly, the Component Object Model provides a mechanism that allows a client holding a reference to one interface the capability to query or ask for another interface that the component object may support. In other words, a component object is like a broker of interface objects—other than knowing what interfaces that it supports, the component object doesn't have much intelligence. Collectively, the component object's supported interfaces know exactly what to do within the scope and purpose of the component object.

Where Are Interfaces Defined?

The next issue to consider: How does the client know what interfaces it should use? This is where the OLE (Object Linking and Embedding) technology comes into play. OLE, being built on COM, is a predefined set of general purpose interfaces that COM servers use to define their component objects as well as what clients use to access component object's interface objects. The IDataObject interface, for example, is used in many situations to transfer data from an OLE/COM server to a client. You will see this OLE interface used later in this chapter, in the shell extension example. The standard OLE interfaces are only a starting point. You can extend the functionality of any OLE interfaces by creating descendant interfaces. You also can derive entirely new interfaces when the standard OLE interfaces don't fit your needs. The general rule, however, with custom interfaces is that they will, in many cases, require some degree of *data marshaling* (data packaging) set up so that Windows knows how to work with the interfaces. Refer to the note in the following section that discusses marshaling. Windows already knows how to work with OLE interfaces because the marshaling for these interfaces is built into Windows.

COM, the Binary Standard

How does COM facilitate communication across process boundaries? The simple answer is that COM is a binary standard that can be used by any development environment that conforms to this standard, such as Delphi, The binary standard that the Component Object Model employs is essentially the incorporation of a *virtual method table* (or *vtable*) to resolve method calls. This is no different than the VMT mechanism that Delphi employs with virtual class methods. In fact, this is how COM interfaces were defined in Delphi 2. The difference between a COM interface and a Delphi class, however, is that all the methods a COM interface will expose to a client application must be defined as pure virtual methods. A COM interface, therefore, only defines its functionality, which provides a way for a client application to know how an interface works and what methods to call after receiving an interface pointer.

In fact, the client application can receive a reference to an instance of a COM interface object created by another application and know how to operate on it by knowing which entry in the virtual table to call, which is what the COM interface provides to the client application—the knowledge about a COM object. The actual creation of the interface object is handled by the COM server that received a request for a specific interface object via the OLE subsystem in Windows and in turn passes back the reference to the client application. This is where this binary standard comes in, because the client needs to have only a pointer to a virtual method table to call the interface object's methods.

N O T E In Delphi, a pure virtual method is declared as an abstract virtual class. The following class definition illustrates the declaration of class called TPureVirtualClass that has two abstract virtual methods.

```
TPureVirtualClass = class
  public
    procedure Method1; virtual; abstract;
    function Method2: Longint; virtual; abstract;
  end;
```

The purpose of an abstract class is to define the functionality that will be implemented later in a descendant class. ■

In prior versions of Delphi, you could only use classes to define COM interfaces. The focus of this chapter, however, is to discuss how the new Interface language extension in Delphi 3 is used to define COM interfaces.

N O T E The way in which the client applications can access COM objects across process or machine boundaries is through a mechanism known as marshaling. *Marshaling* is the process of packaging the parameters being passed to a method of a particular COM object and sending this information over to the other process or machine, which then will unpackage the parameters and call the method of the COM object. For the marshaling of a particular COM interface to occur, the underlying operating system must have intimate knowledge of the interface that it is processing. Almost all the standard OLE interfaces can be marshaled across process boundaries. It wasn't until Distributed COM (DCOM) was available that these interfaces could be marshaled across the network boundary. The processing of marshaling method calls to COM objects is the most expensive operation in working with COM objects. If your COM server is in a DLL, no marshaling needs to take place, so you simply have the overhead of the virtual table lookup. There are exceptions to this when multithreaded clients are involved, but this topic is beyond the scope of this chapter. ■

Understanding Reference Counting

Another fundamental feature of COM is reference counted interface objects. When an object is first created, it gets an internal reference count of 1. For each additional client that obtains a reference to this interface object, the AddRef method is called to increment the interface object's internal reference count by 1. Conversely, when a client is done with an interface object, it calls the Release method to decrement the interface object's reference count by 1. Each time the Release method is called, it checks to see if the reference count has reached zero—in which case, the Release method causes the interface object to be destroyed.

So, what does reference counting buy? Well, picture this—assume that client A requests an IMalloc interface from a particular server. The server receives the request and determines that the IMalloc interface object doesn't exist, so it creates one, does an AddRef on it to set the initial reference count to one, and then returns a reference to the interface object back to client A. While client A is holding this reference to the IMalloc interface object, client B comes along and also makes a request for an IMalloc interface. The server has two options—it can either create another IMalloc interface object or it could simply return a reference to the existing IMalloc interface object after incrementing the reference count to 2 with a call to the AddRef method. Then when client A is through using its reference to the IMalloc interface object (and the Release method has been called), the IMalloc interface object will still exist because its reference count is not zero yet. When Client B is done with the IMalloc interface object, then it will be destroyed.

The obvious advantage then to reference counted interface objects is that a single object can service several clients simultaneously, which definitely has a direct effect on memory resources. You will see later that you can create both single instance servers (the preceding scenario) or multiple instance servers that create a new component object for each client.

IUnknown, the *TObject* of Interfaces

The AddRef and Release methods are two of the three core methods that all COM objects have in common. The third method is QueryInterface. These three methods constitute the IUnknown interface. The following code shows the Delphi 2 version of the IUnknown interface:

```
IUnknown = class
  public
    function QueryInterface(const iid: TIID; var obj): HResult;
            virtual; stdcall; abstract;
    function AddRef: Longint; virtual; stdcall; abstract;
    function Release: Longint; virtual; stdcall; abstract;
  end;
```

Similar to TObject being the base class to all Delphi objects, IUnknown is the base interface for all COM interfaces, which means that a client holding a reference to an interface object is guaranteed the capability to call QueryInterface, AddRef, and Release. These three methods manage the lifetime of an interfaced object. This chapter already discussed the AddRef and Release methods, so now onto the purpose of the QueryInterface method.

Besides being reference counted, each interface object needs the capability to respond to the question, "Do you support Interface X, or can you get me an interface object that does?" Well, this question is the sole purpose of the QueryInterface method. Notice that it takes an *IID* (an interface ID) and an *object reference* (Obj) variable. The IID is the requested interface and the Obj parameter supplied by the caller is used to return the reference to the interface object that supports the requested interface or, otherwise, a Nil. QueryInterface gives the client the capability to query for any desired interfaces that either the current object supports or one of its aggregate interface objects supports. *Interface Aggregation* is simply a melding of two or more interfaces to provide the desired functionality for a specific component object. As you'll see farther on in this chapter, Delphi makes this easy, so don't let the term concern you.

Although more conceptual material exists than can be discussed, the only real way to begin to grasp COM is to roll up the sleeves and dive into some code.

> **N O T E** To head off some confusion between two units that deal with COM interfaces, I mention them now. In Delphi 2.x, all the OLE interfaces were declared as abstract virtual classes (like IUnknown interface listed previously) in a unit named OLE2. Because Delphi 3 made fundamental changes to the language to facilitate better interface support, the entire set of OLE interfaces must be rewritten and moved into the unit named ACTIVEX. The first example in this chapter will use the older Delphi 2 interfaces to demonstrate the bare-metal coding needed to build a COM server. Then, however, you'll use the new interface extensions and the ACTIVEX unit. ∎

A COM Server from Ground Zero

This section describes how to build a COM server that contains a component object that supports the OLE interface IMalloc. Later in the chapter, after you learn the basics of the new interface extensions, you will see how to write the same IMalloc COM server with the new interface extensions. This section is still important, however, because it shows you all you need to make a fully functional COM server from the ground up. This section will go over each major part of creating the server by pulling excerpts from the full code listing at the end of this section, so that you're not overwhelmed by all the code. You'll find that, after you understand each part, looking at the full source list will make sense.

Creating the Component Object

The first thing a component object needs is a class identifier that uniquely represents the object. In Listing 19.1, you will see the CLSID defined at the top of the listing as a constant with the name of Class_MallocComponentObject. This is based off of the TCLSID type, which is defined as follows:

```
TCLSID = TGUID;
TGUID = record
    D1: Integer;
    D2: Word;
    D3: Word;
    D4: array[0..7] of Byte;
  end;
```

The meaning of TGUID's fields is not important to understand, however, it is important to know that when Windows creates a GUID for you it is statistically guaranteed to be unique. So when do you need to generate a CLSID? This is done once for every component object that you create. In this case, we are placing only one component object in our COM server so only one was required.

Part
V

Ch
19

The next thing to determine is what interface(s) are necessary to fulfill the component object's functionality objectives. In our case we need to be able to allow the client to allocate, reallocate, and free multiple memory blocks. It just so happens that there is an OLE interface, IMalloc, which defines exactly the functionality that we desire. The IMalloc interface is defined in OLE2.PAS as follows:

```
IMalloc = class(IUnknown)
  public
    function Alloc(cb: Longint): Pointer; virtual; stdcall; abstract;
    function Realloc(pv: Pointer; cb: Longint): Pointer; virtual; stdcall;
    abstract; procedure Free(pv: Pointer); virtual; stdcall; abstract;
    function GetSize(pv: Pointer): Longint; virtual; stdcall; abstract;
    function DidAlloc(pv: Pointer): Integer; virtual; stdcall; abstract;
    procedure HeapMinimize; virtual; stdcall; abstract;
  end;
```

For a complete reference of OLE interfaces look at *Inside OLE*, Second Edition, by Kraig Brockschmidt, Microsoft Press.

I want to point out two things about this interface. First, it descends from IUnknown, which is what is expected. Second, this interface is a collection of abstract virtual methods, which means that the implementation is up to you. Of course, this is why you use an interface—so that you can provide the implementation. Also, by using a standard OLE interface, the client can be assured of a certain set of methods being available with a known behavior. So from the perspective of the component object writer, it's imperative that the interface's specification be followed to not break any applications that are making assumptions based on the same interface's specification. The implementation of the IMalloc interface's specific methods is not the focus of this chapter, so I direct you to Listing 19.1 to gain an understanding of the heap functions used to implement the IMalloc interface methods. I do, however, want to focus your attention on the implementation of the IUnknown methods. We start with the AddRef and Release methods listed in the following code:

```
TMallocComponentObject = class(IMalloc)
  private
    FRefCount: Longint;  // Initialized to 0;
...
function TMallocComponentObject.AddRef: Longint;
begin
  Inc(FRefCount);
  Inc(Global_Object_Count);
  Result := FRefCount;
end;

function TMallocComponentObject.Release: Longint;
begin
  Dec(FRefCount);
  Dec(Global_Object_Count);
  Result := FRefCount;
  // check if object is still needed; if not destroy it.
  if FRefCount = 0 then Destroy;
end;
```

The AddRef and Release methods increment and decrement TMallocComponentObject's RefCount, respectively. Additionally, the Release method checks after decrementing to see if RefCount is zero, in which case Release automatically destroys the interface object by calling the Destroy method.

Finally, the incrementing and decrementing of the global variable Global_Object_Count is done by all component objects contained in the COM server. In this case, it's only one. Global_Object_Count is used by the DllCanUnloadNow function discussed in the following section, "Registering the Component Object."

You can find the MALLOC1.PAS, shown in Listing 19.1, on this book's companion CD-ROM.

Listing 19.1   \UDELPHI3\CHP19\MSERVER1\MALLOC1.PAS—Source File that Implements the *IMalloc* Component Object

```
unit Malloc1;

interface

uses Windows, Ole2, SysUtils;

const
  // {0AA17140-310E-11D0-A45E-444553540000}
  Class_MallocComponentObject: TCLSID = (
      D1:$0AA17140; D2:$310E; D3:$11D0; D4:($A4,$5E,$44,$45,$53,$54,$00,$00));

type
  TMallocComponentObject = class(IMalloc)
  private
    FRefCount: Longint;  // Initialized to 0;
    FHeapHandle: THandle;
  public
    Constructor Create;
    Destructor Destroy; override;

    // IUnknown interface methods (IMalloc descends from IUnknown)
    function  QueryInterface(const IID: TGUID;
              var Obj): Integer; override;
    function  AddRef: Integer; override;
    function  Release: Integer; override;

    // IMalloc interface methods
    function  Alloc(cb: Longint): Pointer; override;
    function  Realloc(pv: Pointer; cb: Longint): Pointer; override;
    procedure Free(pv: Pointer); override;
    function  GetSize(pv: Pointer): Longint; override;
    function  DidAlloc(pv: Pointer): Integer; override;
    procedure HeapMinimize; override;
  end;
```

continues

```
var Global_Object_Count: Integer;
// Keep track of currently used objects.  If Global_Object_Count = 0
// there are no component objects being used so the DLL server call
// be unloaded.

implementation

const
  // This is not defined in Delphi 3.0; works with HeapCreate etc.
  HEAP_ZERO_MEMORY = $00000008;

Constructor TMallocComponentObject.Create;
//----------------------------------------------------------------------
// Purpose: Request a 64k block of virtual memory addresses and commit
//          4k of the virtual memory.  Store the heap handle in HeapHandle
//          to be used by the heap related functions in the other
//          methods. if HeapHandle = 0 then the heap functions will fail.
//----------------------------------------------------------------------
begin
  Self.FHeapHandle := Windows.HeapCreate(0, 4096, 65535);
end;

Destructor TMallocComponentObject.Destroy;
//----------------------------------------------------------------------
// Purpose:  Destroy the heap if it was created.
//----------------------------------------------------------------------
begin
  if FHeapHandle > 0 then
     HeapDestroy(FHeapHandle);

  Inherited Destroy;
end;

//======================================================================
// TMallocComponentObject's IUnknown interface methods
//======================================================================

function TMallocComponentObject.QueryInterface(const IID: TGUID;
➡ var Obj): Integer; stdcall;
//----------------------------------------------------------------------
// Purpose: Determine if this interface object supports the client
//          requested interface?  If so return a reference to the
//          requested interface object.
//----------------------------------------------------------------------
begin
  // Always initialize "out" parameters to Nil
  Pointer(obj) := Nil;
  Result := E_NOINTERFACE; // Default to interface not supported

  // We support IUnknown and IClassFactory
  if IsEqualCLSID(iid, IID_IUnknown) or
     IsEqualCLSID(iid, IID_IMalloc) then
```

```
begin
    // We do support the client requested interface so Incrementing
    // our RefCcount and pass back a reference to ourselves.
    TMallocComponentObject(obj) := Self;
    TMallocComponentObject(obj).AddRef;
    Result := S_OK;
  end;
end;

function TMallocComponentObject.AddRef: Longint;
//-------------------------------------------------------------------------
// Purpose: Increment the interface object's reference count and return
//          its new value. Bump up the global object count.
//-------------------------------------------------------------------------
begin
  Inc(FRefCount);
  Inc(Global_Object_Count);
  Result := FRefCount;
end;

function TMallocComponentObject.Release: Longint;
//-------------------------------------------------------------------------
// Purpose: Decrement the interface object's reference count and return
//          its new value.  If the reference count is equal to 0 then
//          the client is done with the object so free it.  Also,
//          decrement up the global object count.
//-------------------------------------------------------------------------
begin
  Dec(FRefCount);
  Dec(Global_Object_Count);
  Result := FRefCount;

  // check if object is still needed; if not destroy it.
  if FRefCount = 0 then Destroy;
end;

//=========================================================================
// TMallocComponentObject's IMalloc interface methods
//=========================================================================

function TMallocComponentObject.Alloc(cb: Longint): Pointer;
//-------------------------------------------------------------------------
// Purpose: Allocates a block of memory.
//-------------------------------------------------------------------------
begin
  Result := HeapAlloc(FHeapHandle, HEAP_ZERO_MEMORY, cb) ;
end;

function TMallocComponentObject.Realloc(pv: Pointer; cb: Longint): Pointer;
//-------------------------------------------------------------------------
// Purpose: Changes the size of a previously allocated memory block.
//-------------------------------------------------------------------------
begin
  Result := HeapReAlloc(FHeapHandle, HEAP_ZERO_MEMORY, pv, cb) ;
end;
```

Part
V

Ch
19

continues

Listing 19.1 Continued

```pascal
procedure TMallocComponentObject.Free(pv: Pointer);
//----------------------------------------------------------------------
// Purpose: Frees a previously allocated block of memory.
//----------------------------------------------------------------------
begin
  HeapFree(FHeapHandle, 0, pv) ;
end;

function TMallocComponentObject.GetSize(pv: Pointer): Longint;
//----------------------------------------------------------------------
// Purpose: Returns the size (in bytes) of the previously allocated
//          memory block previously allocated with Alloc or Realloc.
//----------------------------------------------------------------------
begin
  Result := HeapSize(FHeapHandle, 0, pv);
end;

function TMallocComponentObject.DidAlloc(pv: Pointer): Integer;
//----------------------------------------------------------------------
// Purpose: Enumerate the memory blocks in this object's heap.
//----------------------------------------------------------------------
var
  phe: TProcessHeapEntry;
begin
  Result := -1;   // -1 - unsupported

  // Fail if a Nil pointerr is passed
  if pv = Nil then Exit;

  // Can not determine request because Windows 95 doesn't support HeapWalk
  if Win32Platform = VER_PLATFORM_WIN32_WINDOWS then Exit;

  Result := 0; // 0 - failed
  ZeroMemory(@phe, sizeof(TProcessHeapEntry)) ;

  // Set Result to 1 if successful
  while HeapWalk(FHeapHandle, phe) do
    if phe.lpData = pv then
      Result := 1;
end;

procedure TMallocComponentObject.HeapMinimize;
//----------------------------------------------------------------------
// Purpose:  Minimizes the heap as much as possible by releasing unused
//           memory to the operating system, coalescing adjacent free
//           blocks and committing free pages.
//----------------------------------------------------------------------
begin
  HeapCompact(FHeapHandle, 0)
end;

initialization
  Global_Object_Count := 0;
end.
```

Registering the Component Object

A completely functional COM server would have two special functions, `DllRegisterServer` and `DllUnregisterServer`, exported in the DLL or EXE server. These two functions usually are called by program installers such as InstallShield Express, which comes on the Delphi 3 CD-ROM. Developers often use the utility called REGSVR32.EXE that comes with Windows NT 3.51 and 4.0. It doesn't ship with Windows 95. Why Microsoft chose not to ship it with Windows 95, I have no idea! We use these two functions in the shell extension example, shown in a later section of this chapter.

 TIP To view the Windows Registry database, run the program named REGEDIT.EXE on Windows 95 and Windows 4.0. On Windows 3.51, run REGEDT32.EXE.

For the current example, however, I opted to use a Windows REG file for simplicity. Listing 19.2 shows the contents of the MSERVER1.REG file. The hierarchy of the Registry entries that the REG files makes in the Registry database is as follows:

```
HKEY_CLASSES_ROOT
  CLSID
  {0AA17140-310E-11D0-A45E-444553540000} = 'Using Delphi 3 IMalloc Example'
    InProcServer32 = <DLL path>\MServer1.dll
```

To be registered, a component object must have its unique CLSID entered below the HKEY_CLASSES_ROOT\CLSID key in the registration database and then, under the component object's CLSID string, there must be an entry named InProcServer32 that has a string value that points to the correct DLL or EXE that contains the component object. For a client program to access the `IMalloc` server, these entries must be in the Registry. The client and the server don't need to exist to run the REG file. To run the REG file, simply double-click it in Windows Explorer or File Manager depending on your operating system.

You can find MSERVER1.REG shown in Listing 19.2 on this book's companion CD-ROM.

On the CD

Listing 19.2   \UDELPHI3\CHP19\MSERVER1\MSERVER1.REG—The Registration File Used to Register the *IMalloc* Component Object in the MServer1.dll

```
REGEDIT4
[HKEY_CLASSES_ROOT\CLSID\{0AA17140-310E-11D0-A45E-444553540000}]
@="Using Delphi 3 - Malloc Server"
[HKEY_CLASSES_ROOT\CLSID\{0AA17140-310E-11D0-A45E-444553540000}\InProcServer32]
@="C:\\UDelphi3\\Chap19\\MServer1\\MServer1.dll"
```

So at this point, a component object is defined, and the Registry entries are set up for Windows to find the COM server that is being built. But before compiling the project, two basic parts are left to work on. The first issue to resolve is how will Windows know how to communicate with the DLL-based COM server. Second, assuming that Windows is talking to the server, how does the component object get created the first time?

Part
V

Ch
19

How Windows Communicates with the COM Server

The way that Windows will talk to the server is through two additional functions that must be exported for all COM-based servers. The first one (listed in the lines following this paragraph) is the function named DLLCanUnloadNow, which gets called when Windows wants to release the COM server from memory or when the CoFreeUnusedLibraries is called. See Listing 19.3 (later in this section) for the DLLCanUnloadNow function implemented in the MServer1 project file, as follows:

```
function DLLCanUnloadNow: HResult stdcall;
begin
  if Global_Object_Count > 0 then
     Result := S_FALSE
  else
     Result := S_OK;
end;
```

The IMalloc COM server responds to this with an HRESULT of S_OK when the server has no more running objects or an HRESULT of S_FALSE otherwise. This is the primary goal of the variable Global_Object_Count which gets incremented and decremented as AddRef and Release gets called, respectively, to keep track of the current number of running objects.

The second and most important function in the entire COM server is the DllGetClassObject function, which is the first function that Windows calls after loading the server into memory. Listing 19.3 shows the MServer1 project file which contains the DllGetClassObject function. Windows passes the CLSID that the client requested so that the server can determine which component object is to be created. In our case, there is only one component object, so a simple if statement will suffice to check the valid CLSID passed for our component object.

```
if not IsEqualCLSID(CLSID, Class_MallocComponentObject) then
begin
  Result := CLASS_E_CLASSNOTAVAILABLE;
  Exit;
end;
```

If the CLSID is not valid, then return an OLE error code stating that the CLSID requested is not supported in this server. You may be thinking, if there is a valid registry entry in the Registry database that points to our server, why check for the CLSID when the server is loaded? Don't we already know that ours is the correct server being brought up? The issue is simply that some other Registry entries can be inadvertently pointing to our server for whatever reason, but expecting an entirely different component object to be created. In this case, we potentially could be creating the wrong component object for the client. It's simply good code practice to check.

After the server determines that the requested CLSID is valid, it then returns a special interface called IClassFactory that is used exclusively by Windows or by a client to manufacture other interfaces that are supported by the component object. All COM servers support the IClassFactory interface. Listing 19.4 contains the code for our IClassFactory implementation if you want to peek ahead, but I want to finish up on one last point of interest that took me months to fully comprehend. In looking at the following code used to return the requested

IClassFactory interface, you'll notice that although we create the TClassFactory and could easily pass back its reference immediately to Windows, we opted to call its QueryInterface, requesting the IID that Windows passed to us which (when you look at TClassFactory's QueryInterface method), it simply returns Self:

```
with TClassFactory.Create do
try
  AddRef;
  Result := QueryInterface(IID, InterfaceObject);
finally
  Release;
end;
```

Basically, unless an interface reference was obtained through a QueryInterface call, it can only be considered an IUnknown interface. So we create the TClassFactory object and treat it as an IUnknown just long enough to determine through the QueryInterface method whether it supports the requested interface. This becomes more obvious when we discuss component objects that support more than one interface besides the base IUnknown interface. Finally, I want to point out at the end of the project source file in Listing 19.3, you see that we are exporting the two functions, DllGetClassObject and DllCanUnloadNow, that we just finished discussing.

On the CD

You can find MSERVER1.DPR, shown in Listing 19.3 on this book's companion CD-ROM.

Listing 19.3 \UDELPHI3\CHP19\MSERVER1\MSERVER1.DPR—Project File for the *IMalloc* Component Object Server

```
library MServer1;
uses
  Windows, Ole2,
  ClsFact1 in 'ClsFact1.pas',
  Malloc1 in 'Malloc1.pas';
function DllGetClassObject(const CLSID: TGUID; const IID: TIID;
        var InterfaceObject): HResult stdcall;
begin
  Pointer(InterfaceObject) := Nil;
  if not IsEqualCLSID(CLSID, Class_MallocComponentObject) then
  begin
    Result := CLASS_E_CLASSNOTAVAILABLE;
    Exit;
  end;
  try
    with TClassFactory.Create do
    try
      AddRef;
      Result := QueryInterface(IID, InterfaceObject);
    finally
      Release;
    end;
  except
    Result := E_OUTOFMEMORY
```

Part

V

Ch

19

continues

Listing 19.3 Continued

```
    end;
  end;
function DLLCanUnloadNow: HResult stdcall;
begin
  if Global_Object_Count > 0 then
    Result := S_FALSE
  else
    Result := S_OK;
end;
exports
  DllGetClassObject,
  DllCanUnloadNow;
begin
end.
```

IClassFactory, the Component Object Producer

One last source file to look at is shown in Listing 19.4, and then you will be ready to create a client to test your COM server. The TClassFactory object is used by the server to create the supported component object. It does this through the CreateInstance method. After Windows obtains the IClassFactory interface from DllGetClassObject, it then calls its IClassFactory's CreateInstance method passing, finally, the client's requested IID interface, which CreateInstance creates and returns if it's a supported interface.

You can find CLSFACT1.PAS, shown in Listing 19.4, on this book's companion CD-ROM.

Listing 19.4 \UDELPHI3\CHP19\MSERVER1\CLSFACT1.PAS—Source File for the *IClassFactory* Implementation that Is Called into by Windows to Create Other Interfaces

```
unit ClsFact1;

interface

uses
  Windows, SysUtils, Ole2;

type
 TClassFactory = class(IClassFactory)
   private
     FRefCount: Longint;  // Starts out as 0;
   public
     // IUnknown interface methods (IClassFactory descends from IUnknown)
     function QueryInterface(const iid: TIID; var obj): HResult; override;
     function AddRef: Longint; override;
     function Release: Longint; override;

     // IClassFactory interface methods
     function CreateInstance(unkOuter: IUnknown; const iid: TIID;
```

```
            var obj): HResult; override;
      function LockServer(fLock: BOOL): HResult; override;
  end;

implementation

uses Malloc1, dialogs;

//=======================================================================
// TClassFactory's IMalloc interface methods
//=======================================================================
function TClassFactory.QueryInterface(const IID: TGUID;
        var Obj): Integer;
//-----------------------------------------------------------------------
// Purpose: Determine if this interface object supports the client
//          requested interface?  If so, return a reference to the
//          requested interface object.
//-----------------------------------------------------------------------
begin
  // Always initialize "out" parameters to Nil
  Pointer(obj) := Nil;
  Result := E_NOINTERFACE; // Default to interface not supported

  // Supports IUnknown and IClassFactory only
  if IsEqualCLSID(iid, IID_IUnknown) or
     IsEqualCLSID(iid, IID_IClassFactory) then
  begin
    IUnknown(obj) := Self;
    IUnknown(obj).AddRef;
    Result := S_OK;
  end;
end;

function TClassFactory.AddRef: Longint;
//-----------------------------------------------------------------------
// Purpose: Increment the interface object's reference count and return
//          its new value.  Bump up the global object count.
//-----------------------------------------------------------------------
begin
  Inc(FRefCount);
  Inc(Global_Object_Count);
  Result := FRefCount;
end;

function TClassFactory.Release: Longint;
//-----------------------------------------------------------------------
// Purpose: Decrement the interface object's reference count and return
//          its new value.  If the reference count is equal to 0 then
//          the client is done with the object so free it. Also,
//          decrement up the global object count.
//-----------------------------------------------------------------------
begin
  Dec(FRefCount);
  Dec(Global_Object_Count);
  Result := FRefCount;
```

Part
V

Ch
19

continues

Listing 19.4   Continued

```
  // check if object is still needed; if not destroy it.
  if FRefCount = 0 then Destroy;
end;

//=====================================================================
// TClassFactory's IClassFactory interface methods
//=====================================================================

function TClassFactory.CreateInstance(unkOuter: IUnknown;
        const iid: TIID; var obj): HResult;
//---------------------------------------------------------------------
// Purpose: If the client's requested interface (iid) is supported
//          then create the interface object, add one to its reference
//          count and then return the interface pointer to the client.
//---------------------------------------------------------------------
var
  MallocComponentObject: TMallocComponentObject;
begin
  // Always initialize "out" parameters to Nil
  Pointer(Obj):= Nil;

  // We don't support aggregation
  if (UnkOuter <> Nil) then
  begin
    Result := CLASS_E_NOAGGREGATION;
    Exit;
  end;

  // Create memory allocation object
  try
    MallocComponentObject := TMallocComponentObject.Create;
    try
      AddRef;
      // Return the requested interface if supported
      Result := MallocComponentObject.QueryInterface(IID, Obj);
    finally
      Release;
    end;
  except
    // Creation of component object failed
    Result := E_OUTOFMEMORY;
  end;
end;

function TClassFactory.LockServer(fLock: Bool): HResult;
//---------------------------------------------------------------------
// Purpose: If the client wishes to force the server to stay loaded
//          then they call this method.  We increment or decrement
//          the global object count, respectively, for a lock or unlock.
//---------------------------------------------------------------------
```

```
begin
  if fLock then
    Inc(Global_Object_Count)
  else
    Dec(Global_Object_Count);
  Result := NOERROR;
end;

end.
```

We now have covered the essential parts that make up a COM server. In the following section, you look into what it takes to have a client application connect to our COM server. First, however, make sure that the MServer1.dpr has been compiled into a DLL and that the MServer1.reg file was executed. If the book's source is not located in d:\UDELPHI3\..., use Notepad to edit MServer1.reg to change the server's path. Now the server is ready to be used by a client application.

Creating the *IMalloc* Client

Listing 19.5 shows the project file that demonstrates how to obtain the IMalloc interface from the Malloc1 COM server created previously. The client project first calls CoInitialize to load up the COM library, which is required before making COM library function calls, and just before the client finishes, it calls CoUninitialize to unload the COM library.

N O T E Call OleInitialize rather than CoInitialize if the entire OLE library needs to be loaded. Call OleUninitialize when done with the OLE library. ■

After the COM library is loaded, the client calls the COM function CoCreateInstance. CoCreateInstance takes the CLSID of the component object, the type of server to look for, the initial interface desired (IID), and the client side variable that receives a reference to the IMalloc interface object created in the COM server.

```
OleCheck ( CoCreateInstance(Class_MallocComponentObject,
            Nil, CLSCTX_INPROC_SERVER, IID_IMalloc, Malloc) );
```

This single call to CoCreateInstance causes Windows to go through all the steps outlined in the COM server creation section. The call to CoCreateInstance is wrapped by the OleCheck function to handle any COM/OLE error that might occur—in which case an exception is raised.

N O T E The function CoGetClassObject also can be used to create component objects. You usually use CoGetClassObject only when you want to create multiple interface objects through a component object for which there is a CLSID in the system registry. You then would call IClassFactory.CreateInstance to create an uninitialized object. It isn't always necessary to go through this process. To create a single object, use the CoCreateInstance function instead. ■

Part
V

Ch
19

Once the client has a reference to the IMalloc interface object, it can be used just like any other Delphi class-based object, as you can see in the client application. The only difference is that the object was created in the COM server rather than within the client.

When you run the client application, you should see a few message boxes stating the success of the client in using the IMalloc methods. It should be mentioned that the IMalloc.DidAlloc method will fail on Windows 95 because the function HeapWalk that the COM server's DidAlloc method uses isn't supported on Windows 95.

You can find MCLIENT.DPR, shown in Listing 19.5, on this book's companion CD-ROM.

Listing 19.5 \UDELPHI3\CHP19\MCLIENT\MCLIENT.DPR—Project File Used to Test the Registered *IMalloc* Server

```
program MClient;

uses Windows, OLE2, Dialogs, ComObj;
const
  // {0AA17140-310E-11D0-A45E-444553540000}
  Class_MallocComponentObject: TCLSID = (
    D1:$0AA17140; D2:$310E; D3:$11D0; D4:($A4,$5E,$44,$45,$53,$54,$00,$00));

//-------------------------------------------------------------------
// Purpose: Test the IMalloc COM Server
//-------------------------------------------------------------------
var
  Malloc: IMalloc;
  Str: PChar;
begin
  // First make sure that the MS COM services DLL is loaded
  if Succeeded(CoInitialize(Nil)) then
  try
    OleCheck( CoCreateInstance(
              Class_MallocComponentObject,
              Nil,
              CLSCTX_INPROC_SERVER,
              IID_IMalloc,
              Malloc) );
    try
      Str := Malloc.Alloc(4096);
      if Assigned(Str) then
      try
        if Malloc.DidAlloc(Str) = 1 then // Not supported on Windows 95
          ShowMessage('Memory was definately alocated');
        ZeroMemory(Str,4096);
        ShowMessage('4096 bytes allocated and zeroed out.');
        Malloc.ReAlloc(Str, 8192);
        if Assigned(Str) then
        begin
          ZeroMemory(Str, 8192);
          ShowMessage('8192 bytes reallocated and zeroed out.');
        end;
```

```
    finally
      Malloc.Free(Str);
    end;
  finally
    Malloc.Release; // we're finished with the IMalloc interface object
  end;
finally
  CoUnInitialize; // Unload the MS COM services DLL
end;
end.
```

Using the New Delphi Interface Extension

As you may have noticed, it took a lot of code to write a seemingly simple COM server. My whole point of including the first example was to give you an appreciation for what Delphi 3 has done to simplify the steps of creating COM servers. Two basic changes took place in Delphi 3 that are related to COM objects. First, Delphi 3 added new language semantics to support the creation of COM interfaces and to make this creation as easy as creating classes. The second significant addition to Delphi 3 is an entire ActiveX architecture (DAX) that handles much of the boilerplate type tasks, such as referencing counting, registration, component object creation, and so on. To illustrate the ease of COM object development, this section shows how to write the same IMalloc server using the new Delphi 3 interfaces and the DAX architecture. First, look at the definition of interfaces.

Interface Keyword

The definition of the IMalloc interface using the new Delphi 3 interface language extension would look like the following:

```
IMalloc = interface(IUnknown)
  ['{00000002-0000-0000-C000-000000000046}']
  function Alloc(cb: Longint): Pointer; stdcall;
  function Realloc(pv: Pointer; cb: Longint): Pointer; stdcall;
  procedure Free(pv: Pointer); stdcall;
  function GetSize(pv: Pointer): Longint; stdcall;
  function DidAlloc(pv: Pointer): Integer; stdcall;
  procedure HeapMinimize; stdcall;
end;
```

First, note that in this new interface definition, none of the methods have the "abstract; virtual;" following their declaration. This is because all methods in an interface must be pure virtual so this is done for you. The second area to point out is that the associated CLSID is incorporated right into the definition of the interface, allowing for readability, but an even better feature is that it allows the interface name to be used as a Class ID (TCLSID) constant. To do a CLSID comparison, for example, you can do the following with the IsEqualCLSID function:

```
if IsEqualCLSID(iid, IMalloc) then ...
```

Next, look at the IUnknown interface from which IMalloc descends:

```
IUnknown = interface
  ['{00000000-0000-0000-C000-000000000046}']
  function QueryInterface(const IID: TGUID; out Obj): Integer; stdcall;
  function _AddRef: Integer; stdcall;
  function _Release: Integer; stdcall;
end;
```

The declarations of the IUnknown interface (abstract class) that we used in the Malloc1 COM server is defined in the OLE2 unit. The OLE2 unit is shipped with Delphi 3 for backward compatibility. The new Delphi 3 declaration of the IUnknown interface discussed here is defined in the System unit. Although this new declaration of IUnknown is essentially the same as the OLE2 declaration, there is one subtle difference. The AddRef and Release methods are now prefixed with an underscore (_AddRef and _Release). Delphi did this to discourage the use of these two methods. The reason is because Delphi handles automatic calls to AddRef and Release as interface variables come into and go out of scope. For more information on this, refer to Delphi's Object Pascal Language Guide.

N O T E Delphi 3 defines the OLE interfaces using the new `interface` keyword in the ActiveX unit. IUnknown and IDispatch are defined in System unit. ▣

TComObject, Base Delphi ActiveX Architecture Object

A big pain in component object development is the reference counting code that must be associated with every COM interface object. You saw that even the IClassFactory object in the MServer1 COM server had to implement the AddRef and Release methods of IUnknown. You also saw that every time the server was asked for an interface, you also have to implement QueryInterface method of IUnknown. Well, with introduction of the TComObject, which is the foundation class of the DAX architecture, you can forget about IUnknown because it implements these methods for you, which brings up the subject of actually implementing interface objects with Delphi 3. To implement the IMalloc interface, you need to do the following class definition:

```
type
  TMallocComponentObject = class(TComObject, IMalloc)
  private
    FHeapHandle: THandle;
  public
    // TComObject method that is used in place of the Create
    // constructor.
    procedure Initialize; override;
    Destructor Destroy; override;

    // IMalloc interface methods
    function  Alloc(cb: Longint): Pointer; stdcall;
    function  Realloc(pv: Pointer; cb: Longint): Pointer; stdcall;
    procedure Free(pv: Pointer); stdcall;
```

```
    function  GetSize(pv: Pointer): Longint; stdcall;
    function  DidAlloc(pv: Pointer): Integer; stdcall;
    procedure HeapMinimize; stdcall;
  end;
```

On the CD

A couple of things are happening here. First, the ancestor list contains two items. Delphi 3 requires that the first item in the ancestor list be a TObject descendant, but you can list as many interface objects as you want, which makes it easy to support several interfaces at the same time, which is what many clients will expect, as you will see in the ActiveX chapter. Because we are descending from TComObject all of our referencing counting is handled, and no QueryInterface code needs to be written. So, the implementation will be primarily the IMalloc methods, which are no different than before. One more minor detail needs to be pointed out—instead of using a create constructor to the initialization, you do it in the overridden method of TComObject named Initialize because the create constructors were made static because they are used internally by TComObjectFactory (discussed in a following section). Listing 19.6 shows the full implementation of the new TMallocComponentObject object. You can find MALLOC2.PAS, shown in Listing 19.6, on this book's companion CD-ROM.

Listing 19.6   \UDELPHI3\CHP19\MSERVER2\MALLOC2.PAS—Contains the
***IMalloc* Implementation by Using the Delphi ActiveX Architecture**

```
unit Malloc2;

interface

uses Windows, SysUtils, Classes, ActiveX, ComObj, ComServ;

const
  Class_MallocComponentObject:
    TCLSID = '{0AA17140-310E-11D0-A45E-444553540000}';

type
  TMallocComponentObject = class(TComObject, IMalloc)
  private
    FHeapHandle: THandle;
  public
    // TComObject method that is used in place of the Create
    // constructor.
    procedure Initialize; override;
    Destructor Destroy; override;

    // IMalloc interface methods
    function  Alloc(cb: Longint): Pointer; stdcall;
    function  Realloc(pv: Pointer; cb: Longint): Pointer; stdcall;
    procedure Free(pv: Pointer); stdcall;
    function  GetSize(pv: Pointer): Longint; stdcall;
    function  DidAlloc(pv: Pointer): Integer; stdcall;
    procedure HeapMinimize; stdcall;
  end;

implementation
```

continues

Listing 19.6 Continued

```
const
  // This is not defined in Delphi 3.0; works with HeapCreate etc.
  HEAP_ZERO_MEMORY = $00000008;

procedure TMallocComponentObject.Initialize;
//------------------------------------------------------------------------
// Purpose: Request a 64k block of virtual memory addresses and commit
//          4k of the virtual memory.  Store the heap handle in
//          HeapHandle to be used by the heap related functions in
//          the other methods. if HeapHandle = 0 then the heap
//          functions will fail.
//------------------------------------------------------------------------
begin
  FHeapHandle := HeapCreate(0, 4096, 65535);
end;

Destructor TMallocComponentObject.Destroy;
//------------------------------------------------------------------------
// Purpose:  Destroy the heap if it was created.
//------------------------------------------------------------------------
begin
  if FHeapHandle > 0 then HeapDestroy(FHeapHandle);

  Inherited Destroy;
end;

//========================================================================
// TMalloc's IMalloc interface methods
//========================================================================

function TMallocComponentObject.Alloc(cb: Longint): Pointer;
//------------------------------------------------------------------------
// Purpose: Allocates a block of memory.
//------------------------------------------------------------------------
begin
  Result := HeapAlloc(FHeapHandle, HEAP_ZERO_MEMORY, cb);
end;

function TMallocComponentObject.Realloc(pv: Pointer;
        cb: Longint): Pointer;
//------------------------------------------------------------------------
// Purpose: Changes the size of a previously allocated memory block.
//------------------------------------------------------------------------
begin
  Result := HeapReAlloc(FHeapHandle, HEAP_ZERO_MEMORY, pv, cb);
end;

procedure TMallocComponentObject.Free(pv: Pointer);
//------------------------------------------------------------------------
// Purpose: Frees a previously allocated block of memory.
//------------------------------------------------------------------------
```

```
begin
  HeapFree(FHeapHandle, 0, pv);
end;

function TMallocComponentObject.GetSize(pv: Pointer): Longint;
//-------------------------------------------------------------------------
// Purpose: Returns the size (in bytes) of the previously allocated
//          memory block previously allocated with Alloc or Realloc.
//-------------------------------------------------------------------------
begin
  Result := HeapSize(FHeapHandle, 0, pv);
end;

function TMallocComponentObject.DidAlloc(pv: Pointer): Integer;
//-------------------------------------------------------------------------
// Purpose: Enumerates the memory blocks in this object's heap.
//-------------------------------------------------------------------------
var
  phe: TProcessHeapEntry;
begin
  Result := -1;  // -1 - unsupported

  // Fail if a Nil pointerr is passed
  if pv = Nil then Exit;

  // Can not determine request because Windows 95 doesn't support
  // HeapWalk
  if Win32Platform = VER_PLATFORM_WIN32_WINDOWS then Exit;

  Result := 0; // 0 - failed
  ZeroMemory(@phe, sizeof(TProcessHeapEntry)) ;

  // Set Result to 1 if successful
  while HeapWalk(FHeapHandle, phe) do
    if phe.lpData = pv then
        Result := 1;
end;

procedure TMallocComponentObject.HeapMinimize;
//-------------------------------------------------------------------------
// Purpose:  Minimizes the heap as much as possible by releasing unused
//           memory to the operating system, coalescing adjacent free
//           blocks and committing free pages.
//-------------------------------------------------------------------------
begin
  HeapCompact(FHeapHandle, 0)
end;

end.
```

TComObjectFactory and the Delphi COM Server

Up to this point, you saw that the new Delphi 3 interfaces and the DAX object TComObject have saved quite a bit of typing and complexity—but there's more. If you recall in the first example, a whole separate unit of code was needed to handle the IClassFactory machinery to hand out supported interfaces. However, using the DAX object named TComObjectFactory, you don't have to create code for the IClassFactory interface. On top of this, because DAX architecture maintains a COM server object, the component objects now will support the self registration by exporting the two functions DllRegisterServer and DllUnregisterServer. One misnomer with the term *self registration* is that it implies automatic registration, which is not true. Something must call these DLL functions to make it happen. Self registration simply means that when asked, the server knows how to add its own Registry entries. The Putting It All Together section of this chapter shows how to create a context menu-shell extension that allows you to simply right-click a DLL to register or unregister it. The Registry entries that will be made to the Registry database when DllRegisterServer of MServer2 is called will look like the following:

```
HKEY_CLASSES_ROOT
  CLSID
    {0AA17140-310E-11D0-A45E-444553540000} = 'Using Delphi 3 IMalloc Example'
        InProcServer32 = <DLL path>
        ProgID = MSERVER.IMalloc
HKEY_CLASSES_ROOT
  MSERVER.IMalloc = = 'Using Delphi 3 IMalloc Example'
    CLSID = {0AA17140-310E-11D0-A45E-444553540000}
```

For all this to happen, the component object must be registered with the COM Server object (ComServer) that is declared in the ComServ unit. This is done by creating a new instance of TComObjectFactory for every component object that you want exposed. Listing 19.7 shows how this is done for MServer2 in its project source file. Note also that in Listing 19.7, all four of the COM functions are exported. The functions are all declared in the ComServ unit.

N O T E The ProgID put in the Registry is based on the server name that will be the module name of the DLL or EXE and the class name provided when the TComObject is registered with the ComServer by creating a TComObjectFactory object. Consequently, this server creates a ProgID named MSERVER2.IMalloc. ProgID are basically textual cross references to a COM server via the Class ID. ∎

You can find MSERVER2.DPR, shown in Listing 19.7, on this book's companion CD-ROM.

Listing 19.7 \UDELPHI3\CHP19\MSERVER2\MSERVER2.DPR—This File Contains the Project Source File that Registers the *IMalloc* Component Object

```
library MServer2;

uses
```

```
  ComObj, ComServ,
  Malloc2 in 'Malloc2.pas';

exports
  DllGetClassObject,
  DllCanUnloadNow,
  DllRegisterServer,
  DllUnregisterServer;

begin
  TComObjectFactory.Create(
  ComServer,                        // Delphi's COM Server in ComServ.pas
  TMallocComponentObject,           // The TComObject descendant class
  Class_MallocComponentObject,      // The class ID of the component object
  'IMalloc',                        // Second half of the Server's ProgID
  'Using Delphi 3 IMalloc Example', // Component object description
  ciSingleInstance);                // Create a new instance every time
end.
```

Putting It All Together

So far, you looked at the creation of COM servers that are intended for use by user-created client applications, but there are cases where the client can actually be Windows itself. The final example that you will look at is a COM server that is a special handler for a Windows shell extension. Several types of Windows shell extensions exist, but the one that you'll look at is a context menu shell extension. A *context menu* is the pop-up menu that comes up when you right-click a file in a files list. In this section, you see how to write a context menu handler that allows the user to register or unregister a DLL or OCX server by adding a couple of menu items to the right-click context menu. So first, look at the COM server that will accomplish this.

Part
V
Ch
19

Creating the AXReg Context Menu Handler

A context menu handler requires a component object to support two specific interfaces—IShellExtInit and IContextMenu. These two interfaces are defined in the ShlObj unit. The component object, TContextMenu, uses these two interfaces as the following declaration shows:

```
TContextMenu = class(TComObject, IShellExtInit, IContextMenu)
// Private section omitted
public
  // Redeclared for implementation of IContextMenu methods
  function QueryContextMenu(Menu: HMENU; indexMenu, idCmdFirst, idCmdLast,
        uFlags: UINT): HResult; StdCall;
  function InvokeCommand(var lpici: TCMInvokeCommandInfo): HResult; StdCall;
  function GetCommandString(idCmd, uType: UINT; pwReserved: PUINT;
        pszName: LPSTR; cchMax: UINT): HResult; StdCall;
  // Redeclared for implementation of IShellExtInit method
  function Initialize(pidlFolder: PItemIDList; lpdobj: IDataObject;
        hKeyProgID: HKEY): HResult; StdCall;
end;
```

The full listing is in Listing 19.8. Notice here that now two interfaces are listed in the inherits clause of the class, which means that both of these interfaces are supported. Windows will ask for the IShellExtInit interface when it wants to pass the shell extension handler the file(s) that were selected. In this case, you want to handle only single file selections. Whenever the IShellExtInit's Initialize method gets called, you need to store the file name of the selected item so that it is available when the various IContextMenu interface methods get called.

The selected list of file name(s) are passed to the Initialize method by means of an IDataObject interface object created by Windows itself. You then obtain the file names from the IDataObject as a double nil delimited list of file names in order to get to the selected file name. Being passed an interface object from Windows kind of blurs the line of who is the server and who is the client because both sides are producing interface objects.

The IContextMenu interface has three methods: QueryContextMenu, InvokeCommand, and GetCommandString. The QueryContextMenu gets called when Windows needs to know what menu items to add to the right-click context menu. InvokeCommand is called indirectly by Windows when the user selects one of the context menu's menu items that belong to your handler. Also, GetCommandString is called when Windows wants to show a help context string for the context menu item that the user's mouse cursor currently is over. So, besides some special registry entries required for context menu handlers, this is usually all there is to creating a context menu handler.

On the CD

You can find CONTEXTM.PAS, shown in Listing 19.8, on this book's companion CD-ROM.

Listing 19.8 \UDELPHI3\CHP19\AXREG\CONTEXTM.PAS—Definition and Implementation of the ActiveX Server Registration Context Menu Shell Extension

```
unit ContextM;

interface

uses
    Windows, SysUtils, ComObj, ComServ, ShlObj, ActiveX, ShellApi;

Const
  Class_ContextMenu: TGUID = '{A0516FE0-2F5D-11D0-A45E-444553540000}';
  Class_ContextMenuString = '{A0516FE0-2F5D-11D0-A45E-444553540000}';
type
  TContextMenu = class(TComObject, IShellExtInit, IContextMenu)
  private
    szFile: array[0..MAX_PATH] of Char;
    // Static utility method
    function CallActiveXServerProc(ProcName : String): Boolean;
  public
    // Redeclared for implementation of IContextMenu methods
    function QueryContextMenu(Menu: HMENU; indexMenu, idCmdFirst,
            idCmdLast, uFlags: UINT): HResult; StdCall;
    function InvokeCommand(var lpici: TCMInvokeCommandInfo)
            :HResult; StdCall;
```

```
          function GetCommandString(idCmd, uType: UINT; pwReserved: PUINT;
                  pszName: LPSTR; cchMax: UINT): HResult; StdCall;

          // Redeclared for implementation of IShellExtInit method
          // Note: This method hides TComObject's virtual mehtod Initilize.
          function Initialize(pidlFolder: PItemIDList; lpdobj: IDataObject;
                  hKeyProgID: HKEY): HResult; StdCall;
      end;

implementation

const
  ID_REGISTER = 0;
  ID_UNREGISTER = 1;

function TContextMenu.CallActiveXServerProc(ProcName : String): Boolean;
//------------------------------------------------------------------------
// Purpose: Load the selected OCX/DLL and call its DllRegisterServer
//          or DllUnregisterServer function.  If these functions
//          cannot be found then the file is not an ActiveX server.
//------------------------------------------------------------------------
type
  TProcStdCall = procedure; StdCall;
var
  DllHandle : THandle;
  DllProc   : TProcStdCall;
begin
  Result := False;
  try
    DllHandle := LoadLibrary(szFile);
    if DllHandle <> 0 then
      try
        @DllProc := GetProcAddress(DllHandle, PChar(ProcName));
        if @DllProc <> Nil then
        begin
          DllProc;
          Result := True;
        end;
      finally
        FreeLibrary(DllHandle);
      end;
  except
  end;
end;


function TContextMenu.QueryContextMenu(Menu: HMENU; indexMenu,
        idCmdFirst, idCmdLast, uFlags: UINT): HResult;
//------------------------------------------------------------------------
// Purpose: Insert the context menu item(s) and return the number of
//          menu items inserted.
//------------------------------------------------------------------------
begin
  // Add two menu items to the context menu for DLL file types
  InsertMenu (Menu, indexMenu, MF_STRING or MF_BYPOSITION,
```

Part
V

Ch
19

continues

Listing 19.8   Continued

```
                 idCmdFirst + ID_REGISTER, 'Register Active X Server');
    InsertMenu (Menu, indexMenu + 1, MF_STRING or MF_BYPOSITION,
                 idCmdFirst + ID_UNREGISTER, 'Unrregister Active X Server');

  // Return number of menu items added
  Result := 2;
end;

function TContextMenu.InvokeCommand(var lpici: TCMInvokeCommandInfo)
         :HResult;
//--------------------------------------------------------------------
// Purpose: Perform the appropriate operation for the menu item selected
//--------------------------------------------------------------------
const
  SuccessStringTemplate = 'The Active X server was %s successfully.';
  FailStringTemplate =
    'Attempt to register/unregister the selected OCX/DLL server failed.';
var
  MessageString : String;
begin
  // Make sure we are not being called by an application
  if HiWord(Integer(lpici.lpVerb)) <> 0 then
  begin
    Result := E_FAIL;
    Exit;
  end;

  Result := NOERROR;
  // Execute the command specified by lpici.lpVerb.
  MessageString := FailStringTemplate; // Reassigned if successful
  case LoWord(lpici.lpVerb) of
    ID_REGISTER:
      if CallActiveXServerProc('DllRegisterServer') then
        MessageString := Format(SuccessStringTemplate, ['registered'])
      else
        Result := E_FAIL;
    ID_UNREGISTER:
      if CallActiveXServerProc('DllUnregisterServer') then
        MessageString := Format(SuccessStringTemplate, ['unregistered'])
      else
        Result := E_FAIL;
    else
      // we received an invalid argument number
      Result := E_INVALIDARG;
      Exit;
  end;

  if Result = E_FAIL then MessageString := 'Operation failed';

  MessageBox(lpici.hWnd, PChar(MessageString) , 'Information',
             MB_ICONINFORMATION or MB_OK);
end;
```

```
function TContextMenu.GetCommandString(idCmd, uType: UINT; pwReserved: PUINT;
        pszName: LPSTR; cchMax: UINT): HRESULT;
//--------------------------------------------------------------------
// Purpose: Determine and return the help string for menu item selected
//--------------------------------------------------------------------
const
  HelpStringTemplate = '%s an OCX/DLL Active X server';
var
  HelpString : String;
begin
  Result := NOERROR;
  HelpString := '';

  // Determine the help string
  case idCmd of
    ID_REGISTER:   HelpString := Format(HelpStringTemplate, ['Registers']);
    ID_UNREGISTER: HelpString := Format(HelpStringTemplate, ['Unregisters']);
  else
    Result := E_INVALIDARG;
    Exit;
  end;

  strCopy(pszName, PChar(HelpString) );
end;

function TContextMenu.Initialize(pidlFolder: PItemIDList; lpdobj: IDataObject;
        hKeyProgID: HKEY): HResult;
//--------------------------------------------------------------------
// Purpose: Obtain the selected file that user selected from the
//          IDataObject that is passed in.
//--------------------------------------------------------------------
var
  StgMedium: TStgMedium;
  FormatEtc: TFormatEtc;
begin
  // Fail if lpdobj doesn't contain a pointer to an IDataObject object
  if lpdobj = Nil then
  begin
    Result := E_FAIL;
    Exit;
  end;

  with FormatEtc do
  begin
    cfFormat := CF_HDROP;        // Get file names delimited by double nulls
    ptd      := Nil;             // Don't need to provide target device info
    dwAspect := DVASPECT_CONTENT; // Get the content
    lindex   := -1;              // Get all data
    tymed    := TYMED_HGLOBAL;   // Storage medium is a global memory handle
  end;

  // Render the data referenced by the IDataObject into an HGLOBAL
  // storage medium in the CF_HDROP format (double null delimited list).
  Result := lpdobj.GetData(FormatEtc, StgMedium);
  if Succeeded(Result) then
```

Part

V

Ch

19

continues

Listing 19.8   Continued

```
    try
      // If only one file is selected, retrieve the file name and store
      // it in szFile. Otherwise fail the call.
      if DragQueryFile(StgMedium.hGlobal, $FFFFFFFF, Nil, 0) <> 1 then
        Result := E_FAIL
      else
      begin
        DragQueryFile(StgMedium.hGlobal, 0, szFile, SizeOf(szFile));
        Result := NOERROR;
      end;
    finally
      ReleaseStgMedium(StgMedium);
    end;
end;

initialization
  TComObjectFactory.Create(
    ComServer,
    TContextMenu,
    Class_ContextMenu,
    '',
    'Delphi 3.0 ContextMenu Example',
    ciMultiInstance);
end.
```

In Listing 19.9, you see that not much has to happen to put together the AXReg1 project.
AXREG1.DPR, shown in Listing 19.9, is located on this book's companion CD-ROM.

**Listing 19.9   \UDELPHI3\CHP19\AXREG\AXREG1.DPR—Main Project
Source for the ActiveX Server Registration Context Menu Shell Extension**

```
library AXReg1;
uses
  ComObj, ComServ,
  ContextM in 'ContextM.pas';
exports
  DllGetClassObject,     // Found in ComServ unit
  DllCanUnloadNow,       // Found in ComServ unit
  DllRegisterServer,     // Found in ComServ unit
  DllUnregisterServer;   // Found in ComServ unit
begin
  TComObjectFactory.Create(
    ComServer,                              // Delphi's COM Server in ComServ.pas
    TContextMenu,                           // The TComObject descendant class
    Class_ContextMenu,                      // The class ID of the component object
    '',                                     // No ProgID
    'Delphi 3.0 ContextMenu Example',       // Component object description
    ciMultiInstance);                       // Share existing instance
end.
```

Registering the AXReg Context Menu Handler

Registering a context menu shell extension is somewhat different than registering a normal COM server. You do have to do the normal registration entries, as in the following example:

```
HKEY_CLASSES_ROOT
  CLSID
    {A0516FE1-2F5D-11D0-A45E-444553540000} = "Using Delphi 3 - AXReg 1.0"
      InprocServer32 = <Path of AXReg1.dll>
                       "ThreadingModel" = "Apartment"
```

One entry must be present or context menus don't work: the ThreadingModel = Apartment entry, under the InProcServer32 key. Next, you need to set up the entries for OCX files to trigger your context menu so the following entries also must be made:

```
-- Add context menu support for OCX files ----------------------
HKEY_CLASSES_ROOT
  .OCX = "OcxFile"
  OcxFile
    shellex
      ContextMenuHandlers
        {A0516FE1-2F5D-11D0-A45E-444553540000} =""
```

Finally, you need to add yourself to the DllFile entry that more than likely already exists as follows:

```
-- Add context menu support for DLLs ----------------------
HKEY_CLASSES_ROOT
  DllFile
    shellex
      ContextMenuHandlers
        {A0516FE1-2F5D-11D0-A45E-444553540000}
```

Listing 19.10 shows the REG file (AXREG1.REG) that can be executed to add these entries to the Windows Registry database. As a bonus, the author has included a second AXReg project (AXREG2.DPR) on this book's companion CD-ROM that has the self-registration code implemented in the DllRegisterServer and DllUnRegisterServer exported functions. When the DllRegisterServer function is called, it will add the necessary registry entries for Windows to pick it up as a shell extension server.

Listing 19.10 \UDELPHI3\CHP19\AXREG\AXREG1.REG—Contains Registry Entries that Need to Be Made in Order for Windows 95 or NT 4 to Recognize the Server as a Context Menu Shell Extension

```
REGEDIT4
[HKEY_CLASSES_ROOT\DllFile\shellex\ContextMenuHandlers\
{A0516FE0-2F5D-11D0-A45E-444553540000}] =""
[HKEY_CLASSES_ROOT\CLSID\{A0516FE0-2F5D-11D0-A45E-444553540000}]
@="DLL Server Register"
[HKEY_CLASSES_ROOT\CLSID\{A0516FE0-2F5D-11D0-A45E-444553540000}\InProcServer32]
@="C:\\UDelphi3\\Chp19\\AXReg\\AXReg1.dll"
```

Part
V

Ch
19

continues

Listing 19.10   Continued

```
"ThreadingModel"="Apartment"
[HKEY_CLASSES_ROOT\.OCX]
@="OcxFile"
[HKEY_CLASSES_ROOT\OcxFile\shellex\ContextMenuHandlers\
{A0516FE0-2F5D-11D0-A45E-444553540000}] =""
```

N O T E   To register the ActiveX Server (AXREG1.DLL) double-click the AXReg1.reg file, which is the same directory as the AXReg1 project. If you didn't install the book's source to C:\UDelphi3\..., then you need to edit the AXReg1.reg file with a text editor so that you can change the path to reflect the correct path to the ...\AXReg directory. ▓

This chapter covered the underworkings of COM. It discussed the relationship between a component object, an interface, and an interface object. It also discussed the mechanism that Windows uses to find and connect to COM-based servers using the Windows Registry database. Finally, you got an introduction to creating a Windows context menu server, which illustrated the development of a component object that supported more than one interface.

In the following chapter, you see how easy Delphi makes it to create automation servers. ●

CHAPTER 20

Working with OLE Automation

by Todd Miller

In Microsoft's endeavors to enhance the Windows environment, Microsoft was faced with a challenge to come up with a technology that would make it easy for applications to use objects that are housed separately from the application itself. In other words, an application had to be able to access an external object's properties and methods in a manner no different than if the object were part of the application. Additionally, the objects needed to be language independent and accessible, not only across process boundaries (EXE to EXE), but also across machine boundaries.

Microsoft's answer to the cross-process and cross-machine boundaries issue was to incorporate the Component Object Model (COM and Distributed COM) into the Windows operating system. Fundamentally, the COM subsystem manages all communication between applications and COM-based component objects.

To facilitate the sharing of objects across process and machine boundaries, Microsoft developed OLE Automation, which is built using the Component Object Model. The focus of this chapter is to discuss Microsoft's OLE Automation technology and how easy Delphi makes it to use and create automation objects. ■

- **Understanding OLE Automation**

  Discusses the nature of using OLE Automation.

- **Using automation objects**

  Discusses how to access automation objects using Delphi.

- **Creating automation objects**

  Demonstrates how to create out-of-process and in-process automation servers using the new Delphi 3 Delphi ActiveX (DAX) framework.

- **Type libraries**

  Demonstrates how type libraries and the Delphi Type Library Editor are used in the creation of automation servers.

This chapter covers the following topics:

- OLE Automation in general
- Automation objects
- Automation controllers
- Accessing automation objects
- The `OleVariant` type and variant arrays
- Creating automation objects
- Type Information
- Type Libraries

Understanding OLE Automation

We start by nailing down some terminology. *OLE Automation*, or just *automation*, is a cross-application programming paradigm that enables an EXE or DLL to expose automation object(s) to an automation controller or client.

An *automation object*, like a Delphi class, is a collection of properties and methods that collectively provides a specific functionality useful in some way to an automation controller.

An *automation controller* or client is an application or DLL that wants to connect to and control an automation object.

N O T E   The mechanism that clients use to connect to automation objects boils down to the automation object (which really is a COM object), supporting the `IDispatch` interface and the automation controller knowing how to use the `IDispatch` interface. The `IDispatch` interface allows the client to access the properties and methods of any automation object. Fortunately, you don't have to know how to work with the `IDispatch` interface directly because Delphi encapsulated it entirely for you. As you will see shortly, accessing an automation object is not much different than working with a Delphi class. ■

An *automation server* houses one or more automation object(s). Because of this relationship, the term "connecting to an automation server" is used interchangeably with "connecting to an automation object."

Server Types

There are two types of automation servers:

- In-process
- Out-of-process (or local)

Out-of-Process Servers

Out-of-process servers are applications (EXEs) that expose one or more automation objects. The term out-of-process comes into play because the automation controller will always be in another process memory space. Out-of-process servers usually are full applications that can be controlled externally by another application. Microsoft's Word for Windows software application is an example of an out-of-process server. You will see an example accessing Word for Windows later in this chapter.

> **NOTE** Automation objects, being driven by an external application, are sometimes referred to as *programmable objects*. Applications such as Microsoft Word that can be controlled through automation are also referred to as programmable. ■

In-Process Servers

In-process servers house their automation objects within DLLs. Consequentially, in-process servers will be mapped directly into the automation controller's process memory space. The advantage of in-process servers is speed. In-process servers require nowhere near as much marshaling to convert property and method data to and from the server as do out-of-process servers. If an in-process server is being accessed directly through its interfaces, generally no marshaling occurs at all.

Now that you have an idea of what automation is and how it works, let's move on to the actual process of using an automation object.

Using Automation Objects

Before you can start using an automation object, you need to know what properties and methods that the automation object contains. In the case of methods, you also need to know what their parameters are. So where is this information? Well, hopefully the vendor of the automation object that you are using supplied some documentation, but I wouldn't rely on it. So, where else can you get information about an automation server? Besides calling up the vendor and asking, the most obvious place to look is in the automation server's type information!

What Is Type Information?

Type information is an electronic form of documentation for OCXs, ActiveX controls, and automation servers. Type information is mainly used by interrupted environments such as Visual Basic to do syntax and type checking, and with Delphi's Type Library Editor. Type information can become a great source of documentation about the automation objects contained within an automation server. It is important to point out, however, that not all automation servers have type information.

N O T E In the following chapter, you see how Delphi uses an ActiveX control's type information to create a class wrapper source file that Delphi uses to do compile-time syntax and type checking. ▆

Type information stored within a type library can contain any of the following elements:

- Information about enumeration data types.
- Descriptions of one or more objects, such as an interface, dispinterface, or component object class (CoClass).
- References to type descriptions from other type libraries.

Type information can be stored in either a Type Library file (.TLB), an Object Type Library file (.OLB), a resource linked into the server's EXE or DLL, or—in rare situations—within an OLE compound document. By default, Delphi creates a .TLB file at design-time that is then linked in as a resource at compile-time.

To view an automation server's type information, do the following:

1. Select File, Open.
2. Set the File of type drop-down to Type Library.
3. Navigate through your system's directories to find the desired type library file.
4. Select the Open button which will bring up the Delphi Type Library Editor with the type library's information displayed.

Delphi doesn't require type information to access automation servers. This means, however, that Delphi won't be able to do compile-time (or early binding) syntax checking on code being used to access the automation objects. This means that Delphi won't do type checking against an automation object's properties and methods at compile-time. The type checking occurs at runtime, when the methods and properties are invoked on the server. We'll see later how Delphi knows which code is for automation objects and which is not.

Accessing an Automation Object

Delphi makes accessing automation objects easy. As you will see shortly, it is not a lot different than using a Delphi class object. The difference is that the automation client doesn't actually create the automation object; it simply requests access to the object by calling the Delphi wrapper function, CreateOleObject.

The CreateOleObject function takes one parameter that is a *program identifier* (Prog ID) associated with an automation object and it returns an IDispatch interface reference to that object. A Prog ID is a unique string identifier that acts like an alias to the automation object. The following code snippet calls CreateOleObject to connect to Microsoft Word's internal automation object, using its Prog ID, Word.Basic, and inserts some text into the active Word document.

```
uses ComObj;

var
  WordBasicObject : OleVariant;

procedure TForm1.Button1Click(Sender: TObject);
begin
  WordBasicObject := CreateOleObject('Word.Basic');
  WordBasicObject.Insert('inserting text into Word via Automation');
end;
```

Although it doesn't look like much, a lot is going on here. First, to be able to call the CreateOleObject function, we needed to add the ComObj unit to the uses clause. Next, notice that we declare the WordBasicObject variable as type OleVariant. The OleVariant type is the primary type used in OLE Automation because it can assume the identity of many other data types. In this case, it will be holding a reference to an IDispatch interface object, which is the core interface of OLE Automation.

N O T E The CreateOleObject is not doing any compiler magic to make this work. In fact, it doesn't do a whole lot. It first calls the Windows CLSIDFromProgID function with the Prog ID passed, to get the associated automation object's Class ID (CLSID). Then the Windows function CoCreateInstance is called with the CLSID, requesting the automation object's IDispatch interface object. The Result value is the IDispatch reference to the automation object requested. Here's the implementation of the CreateOleObject function:

```
function CreateOleObject(const ClassName: string): IDispatch;
var
  ClassID: TCLSID;
begin
  ClassID := ProgIDToClassID(ClassName);
  OleCheck(CoCreateInstance(ClassID, nil, CLSCTX_INPROC_SERVER or
    CLSCTX_LOCAL_SERVER, IDispatch, Result));
end;
```

If you recall from the previous chapter, Class IDs and Prog IDs, along with other information about COM servers, are stored in the Windows Registry database.

To access remote DCOM automation servers, use the CreateRemoteComObject function also defined in the ComObj unit. ■

Then, after we receive a reference to the Word.Basic automation object, we are free to call any of its properties and methods. Here, we are simply calling Word Basic's Insert method with a string that we want to insert into the active Word document. Notice that when you run this code, it actually brings up Word (if it is not already running). To learn more about the properties and methods of Word Basic, look in Word for Windows online help. This help information may not have been installed by default.

Part

V

Ch

20

T I P What is the lifetime of an automation object? As we learned in the previous chapter, COM objects (which include automation objects) are reference counted and when their reference count becomes zero, the object is destroyed. With this in mind, notice in the preceding example that the WordBasicObject variable is defined globally rather than locally within the Button1Click method itself. This was done so that the lifetime of the automation object (once created) will not be affected by the lifetime of a local variable. This is due to the fact that when an OleVariant type variable goes out of scope, Delphi automatically decrements the reference count of IDispatch interface object referenced within the OleVariant. This will most likely cause Word to shut down. So by making the WordBasicObject variable global, we are guaranteed that the lifetime of the IDispatch interface object will be the same as the application.

I mentioned previously that I would explain how Delphi knows which code is for automation objects and which is not. Delphi uses OleVariant variable types to differentiate between the two. Delphi knows that OleVariants are the only late binding mechanism that it uses to talk with automation servers, and it also knows that a period following an OleVariant variable is used only to access properties and methods of an automation object. If at runtime, that OleVariant does not contain an IDispatch interface, your application will raise an exception. The method or property information following the period is stored in your EXE and sent to the automation object on an as-needed basis during the execution of your application.

Working with Automation Properties

Automation properties are almost identical to Delphi class properties. They are used to set and get internal state values of an automation object. For example, the following code snippet sets the Sound property of the Beeper automation object that will be created later in the chapter. Beeper is of type OleVariant.

```
Beeper.Sound := MB_ICONEXCLAMATION;
```

Automation also supports parameterized properties, which are syntactically like array properties within a Delphi class, but in many cases behaves like a method. For example, when using Oracle objects (a database automation server), the code required to connect to the server uses a parameterized property with three parameters. Here is an example of this:

```
var
  DBMSServer : OleVariant;
begin
  ...
  DBMSServer.OpenDatabase['US.borland.com', 'SysAdmin / Password', 0]
  ...
```

Another aspect of an automation object's properties is that they can be read/write, read-only, or write-only. Write-only is extremely rare but it can be done. The following is an example of accessing a read-only property from the beeper object built later in the chapter.

```
Beeper.SoundBeep[MB_ICONEXCLAMATION];
```

It takes one parameter (like a method) and, besides assigning the new sound value, it also plays the sound.

The one fundamental restriction on automation object properties is what types can be passed. The following are the valid types that can be used with both automation object properties and methods:

- ▇ Byte
- ▇ Integer
- ▇ SmallInt
- ▇ Currency
- ▇ Double
- ▇ Single
- ▇ WideString
- ▇ TDateTime
- ▇ WordBool
- ▇ OleVariant

This limitation is not imposed by Delphi; it is imposed by the OLE Automation architecture because OLE Automation requires that all property values, method parameters, and return values (if any) get passed as variants (`OleVariant`). So, part of the issue is the architecture of variants, and the other is because of the issues involved with packaging up data passed from a client to a server and vice versa. There are ways to pass more complicated data structure within the OLE framework (such as `IStorage` and `IDataObject` interface objects) but these mechanisms are not covered in this chapter. There is also the ability to utilize variant arrays (safe arrays) that we discuss later on in the chapter.

Working with Automation Methods

Like automation properties, automation methods have some interesting capabilities that make them flexible to use. Of course, you can call automation methods just like Delphi methods, where you make the call with all the parameters passed, as the following example shows:

```
SomeObject.OpenFile('noname.dat', 'File Description Text');
```

N O T E Delphi has set an arbitrary 64-argument parameter limit for automation methods, which means that if you are calling an automation object's method that requires 65 parameters, your application will fail. The `MaxDispArgs` constant in the `ComObj` unit can be changed to a larger number of parameters. You need to recompile this unit to make the changes take effect. I would be surprised if you needed more than 64! ▇

Method Parameters by Position As an alternative to passing all of a method's parameters, OLE Automation enables an automation object to allow a controller to omit passing some of the parameters to a particular method—if the automation object supports optional parameters to methods. For example, assume that you are working with an automation object that has a `Rectangle` method that takes five optional parameters. The `Rectangle` method's definition would look something like the following, using Basic command-language syntax:

```
Rectangle [.Color = number] [,.Left = number] [,.Top = number]
          [,.Width = number] [,.Height = number]
```

So, given that the automation object will provide default values to any optional parameters, you could call the `Rectangle` method like the following to draw a rectangle at its default position, but with a width and height of 100 and a color of red:

```
SomeObject.Rectangle(clRed, , ,100,100);
```

And the following call will draw a rectangle at position 20, 40 with its default width, height, and color:

```
SomeObject.Rectangle(,20,40);
```

Notice that the last two commas weren't needed because commas are used between parameter values only to specify the position of the parameter.

Method Parameters by Name   The final type of parameter passing in OLE Automation is that of passing by name, which means that you can forgo the filler commas needed with positional parameter passing and just specify the names of the parameter that you want to set. For example, to do the preceding example where we wanted to set the color, width, and height but not the left and top positions, we could do the following:

```
SomeObject.Rectangle(Color = clRed, Width = 100, Height = 100);
```

This code is a little wordy but easier to understand.

To this point, we covered the basics of working with an automation object.

To see a simple automation client in action, take a look at Listing 20.1, which demonstrates how to connect to the `Word.Basic` automation object within Word for Windows (Version 7) to copy the contents of a `TMemo` over to a Word document and print it. Figure 20.1 shows the Client application.

FIG. 20.1

Client application that automates Word for Windows.

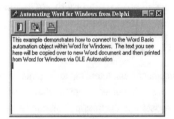

Listing 20.1   \UDELPHI3\CHP20\WORDCLNT\CLIENTFM.PAS—Demonstrate How to Connect to the *Word.Basic* Automation Object Within Word for Windows

```
unit ClientFm;

interface
```

```
uses
  Windows, Messages, SysUtils, Classes, Graphics, Controls, Forms, Dialogs,
  Buttons, StdCtrls, ExtCtrls;

type
  TWordClinetForm = class(TForm)
    Panel1: TPanel;
    Panel2: TPanel;
    Memo1: TMemo;
    CloseButton: TSpeedButton;
    CopyButton: TSpeedButton;
    PrintButton: TSpeedButton;
    procedure CopyButtonClick(Sender: TObject);
    procedure CloseButtonClick(Sender: TObject);
    procedure PrintButtonClick(Sender: TObject);
  private
    { Private declarations }
  public
    WordBasicObject : OleVariant;
  end;

var
  WordClinetForm: TWordClinetForm;

implementation

{$R *.DFM}

uses ComObj;


function HandleException(E : Exception): Boolean;
//------------------------------------------------------------
// Purpose: Centralized OLE Automation error routine.
//------------------------------------------------------------
const
  WordError = 'Error connecting to Word for Windows - ';
begin
  Result := True;
  if (E is EOleError) or (E is EOleSysError) or
     (E is EOleException) then
    ShowMessage(WordError + E.Message)
  else
    Result := False;  // Exception wasn't handled
end;

procedure TWordClinetForm.CopyButtonClick(Sender: TObject);
//------------------------------------------------------------
// Purpose: Establish a connection to Word for Windows and
//          copy the contents of Memo1 to a newly created
//          Word document.
//------------------------------------------------------------
var
  I : Integer;
begin
  try
```

continues

Listing 20.1   Continued

```
    // Have we already connected to Word for Windows?  If not, do so.
    if VarType(WordBasicObject) <> varDispatch then
       WordBasicObject := CreateOleObject('Word.Basic');

    WordBasicObject.FileNew;
    for I := 0 to Memo1.Lines.Count - 1 do
       WordBasicObject.Insert( Memo1.Lines[I] );
  except
    on E : Exception do
       if not HandleException(E) then Raise;
  end;
end;

procedure TWordClinetForm.CloseButtonClick(Sender: TObject);
//-------------------------------------------------------------
// Purpose: Closes the active Word document, if we created it
//          without saving it and then the client form is
//          closed. The link between the client and Word
//          is broken when the application closes.
//-------------------------------------------------------------
begin
  try
    // Was a connect to Word for Windows made?  If so, close the
    // document that we created.
    if VarType(WordBasicObject) = varDispatch then
       WordBasicObject.FileClose(2);  // 1) Save/Close, 2) Close only

    Close;
  except
    on E : Exception do
       if not HandleException(E) then Raise;
  end;
end;

procedure TWordClinetForm.PrintButtonClick(Sender: TObject);
//-------------------------------------------------------------
// Purpose: Print the active Word document if an automation
//          link to Word for Windows has been established.
//-------------------------------------------------------------
begin
  try
    // Was a connection to Word for Windows made?  If not show error.
    if VarType(WordBasicObject) <> varDispatch then
       raise EOleError.Create('No connection established');

    WordBasicObject.FilePrint;
  except
    on E : Exception do
       if not HandleException(E) then Raise;
  end;
end;

end.
```

N O T E   To learn more about the properties and methods of the Word.Basic automation object, refer to the Word for Windows online documentation. You may need to install the Word Basic macro language help file from the Word for Windows installation disks. ▣

Advanced Automation Topics

This section covers some advanced parameter-passing issues and also discusses variants (OleVariant) as they relate to automation. First, you need to get an idea of how variants work.

Variants and OLE Automation   The OleVariant type is one of the most complex data types (more specifically, data structures) in Delphi. The format of an OleVariant type is defined by the 16-byte TVarData structure which is defined in the System unit, as follows:

```
TVarData = record
   VType: Word;
   Reserved1, Reserved2, Reserved3: Word;
   case Integer of
     varSmallint: (VSmallint: Smallint);
     varInteger:  (VInteger: Integer);
     varSingle:   (VSingle: Single);
     varDouble:   (VDouble: Double);
     varCurrency: (VCurrency: Currency);
     varDate:     (VDate: Double);
     varOleStr:   (VOleStr: PWideChar);
     varDispatch: (VDispatch: Pointer);
     varError:    (VError: Integer);
     varBoolean:  (VBoolean: WordBool);
     varUnknown:  (VUnknown: Pointer);
     varByte:     (VByte: Byte);
     varString:   (VString: Pointer);
     varArray:    (VArray: PVarArray);
     varByRef:    (VPointer: Pointer);
   end;
```

Why Are Variants in Delphi?

Variants (the OleVariant type) are in Delphi purely because of OLE Automation. OLE Automation uses variants because Microsoft's Visual Basic's interpreted environment required such a data type to allow non-declared variables to be assigned any valid data type at any time. So, as you can imagine, this data type goes against the entire concept of strong type checking as we find in Delphi. The general rule is to not use variants unless you're working with OLE Automation, and even then, there are few times that you actually need variants because Delphi does all the parameter conversions to variants when you are accessing an automation object's properties and methods. Variants are both costly in size and speed when compared to other Delphi data types.

Part
V

Ch
20

As you can see, a variant is broken up into two parts—the data type that is being stored and the actual data (or a reference to it). So there are now two ways to assign an OleVariant a value. One is to allow Delphi to do the assignment, as follows:

```
V := 25;
```

Alternatively, *you* can do the work by typecasting the variant variable, as follows:

```
TVarData(V).VType := varInteger;
TVarData(V).VInteger := 25;
```

Now, of course, it would be silly to do this extra work but in some cases, you may have to package up your own variant to satisfy some automation object's method parameter requirements. For example, some automation servers will want an optional parameter to come in as an error parameter rather than an empty or null parameter. To do so, you would simply do the following:

```
TVarData(V).VType := varError;
// Don't need to assign a data value for varError
ServerObject.Method(V);
```

Table 20.1 shows variant types codes that are used to represent all the various data types that a variant can hold.

Table 20.1   *OleVariant* Type Codes Defined in the System Unit

Variant Type Code	Description	Delphi Type
varEmpty	The variant is Unassigned.	N/A
varNull	The variant is Null.	N/A
varByte	8-bit signed integer.	Byte
varSmallint	16-bit signed integer.	Smallint
varInteger	32-bit signed integer.	Integer
varSingle	Single-precision floating-point value.	Single
varDouble	Double-precision floating-point value.	Double
varCurrency	Currency floating-point value.	Currency
varDate	Date and time value.	TDateTime
varOleStr	Reference to a dynamically allocated UNICODE string.	WideString

Variant Type Code	Description	Delphi Type
varString	Reference to a dynamically allocated Pascal string.	AnsiString
varDispatch	Reference to an OLE automation object.	IDispatch interface pointer
varError	Operating system error code.	N/A
varBoolean varVariant	16-bit Boolean.	WordBool
varUnknown	Reference to an unknown OLE object.	IUnknown interface pointer

Variants Holding Nothing Most of the types are obvious data types, but some are not so obvious. The varEmpty represents that the variant was not assigned a value. In comparison, varNull represents a variant that was once assigned but no longer has a value. Because these values are commonly used, Delphi has defined two global variables—Null and Unassigned—that are varNull and varEmpty type variants, respectively.

Variants Holding Strings OLE uses a varOleStr to pass strings around. The OLE string type (or UNICODE string) differs from Delphi's default AnsiString type in that each character occupies two bytes rather than one. Consequently, the OLE system doesn't understand Delphi's AnsiString type represented by the varString variant type. This is an additional type that Delphi has added as a variant type code to support AnsiStrings within variants. The varString type code is understood only within Delphi applications. If you have a varString type variant and you are passing it to an automation object, Delphi automatically converts it into a varOleStr string type.

Variants Holding Interfaces The varDispatch type represents a variant that holds an IDispatch interface pointer. Delphi knows to handle a variant that holds a varDispatch as a reference to an automation object. The varUnknown type represents a variant that contains an arbitrary IUnknown interface pointer that the client can use to access other interfaces via the interface's QueryInterface method.

Variants Type Code Flags Table 20.2 lists the type code flags used to further define what a variant is holding. You see these flags in the next couple of sections.

Part
V

Ch
20

Table 20.2   Variant Type Code Flags Defined in the System Unit

VType	Description
varTypeMask	Bit mask ($0FFF) for extracting a variant's type code
varArray	Bit indicating whether a variant is a variant array or not
varByRef	Bit indicating whether a variant contains a pointer to the indicated data or to the data itself

Variants Holding Data by Reference   Occasionally, a data value will be passed by reference rather than having its value put in the variant's 16-byte structure. In these cases, the varByRef will be ORed into the VType along with the actual type. If you want to determine the variant's type code, you can AND the variant's VType with the varTypeMask constant as follows:

```
if (TVarData(V).VType and varTypeMask) = varDispatch then ...
```

Variants Holding Variants   The types varVariant and varArray work hand-in-hand. The varVariant is used exclusively to pass around an array of variants. If the varArray type is ORed in with any of the data types that represent data (including varVariant), the variant represents an array of that type. For example, if the following condition is true, the variant V holds an array of integer values:

```
if TVarData(V).VType = (varInteger and varArray) then ...
```

The following section looks into working with variant arrays.

Variant Support Routines   Table 20.3 lists all the variant support functions and procedures defined in the System unit to manipulate variants. After the table, I demonstrate a couple of the more commonly used routines.

Table 20.3   Delphi Variant Support Procedures and Functions in the System Unit

Helper Routines	Description
VarClear	Makes a variant have a value of Unassigned.
VarCopy	Copies the content of the source variant into a destination variant.
VarCast	Converts a source variant into the specified varXXXX type and stores the resulting variant into a destination variant. The varXXXX type cannot include the varArray or varByRef bits.
VarType	This function returns the varXXXX type code of the given variant. The lower 12 bits of a variant type code define the type of the variant. The value returned by VarType corresponds to the VType field of a TVarData record.

Helper Routines	Description
VarAsType	Converts the source variant to the specified varXXXX variant type code, and then returns the converted variant. The specified variant type cannot include the varArray or varByRef bits.
VarIsEmpty	Returns True if the specified variant contains the value Unassigned (varEmpty).
VarIsNull	Returns True if the specified variant contains the value Null (varNull).
VarToStr	Converts integer, floating point, logical, and string data in a variant to a string. This is no different than directly assigning a variant to a string (MyString := SomeVariant).
VarFromDateTime	Returns a variant that contains the specified TDateTime value. The type code of the resulting variant is varDate.
VarToDateTime	Converts the specified variant to a TDateTime value.

First, look at the VarType function. Rather than using the TVarData structure to determine the variant's type, you can use the VarType function. In the previous Word.Basic example, I used VarType to determine if the automation connection had been established by checking for the varDispatch data type, as follows:

```
if VarType(WordBasicObject) = varDispatch then
     WordBasicObject.FileClose(2);  // 1) Save/Close, 2) Close only
```

Of course, I also could have used the VarIsEmpty helper function because Delphi always initializes variants to varEmpty.

```
if not VarIsEmpty(WordBasicObject) then
     WordBasicObject.FileClose(2);  // 1) Save/Close, 2) Close only
```

Variant Arrays (Safe-Arrays)   One final type that can be used with Automation is variant array. A *variant array* is essentially a variant variable that contains as its data a pointer to a block of memory that is an array of 16-byte variant records, with each element of the array being a variant that can hold any of the possible variant values discussed so far. Obviously, most developers won't want to use variant arrays too often because of the excessive memory usage, but because interpreted environments, such as Visual Basic, optimized data structures were not an option when OLE Automation was being designed. So when passing arrays of data to an automation object, a variant array is about as good as it gets. To declare a variant array, use either the VarArrayCreate function that follows:

```
function VarArrayCreate(const Bounds: array of Integer; VarType: Integer):
Variant;
```

or the VarArrayOf function defined, as follows:

```
function VarArrayOf(const Values: array of Variant): Variant;
```

Part
V

Ch
20

The `VarArrayCreate` function indirectly allocates the memory for the variant array elements based on the array bounds passed in as well as initializes each element to the specified variant type code, and then returns a variant that points to the variant array. The following is an example of creating and assigning values to a variant array:

```
procedure TForm1.VarArrayCreateButtonClick(Sender: TObject);
var
  V: OleVariant;
begin
  V := VarArrayCreate([0, 4], varVariant);
  V[0] := 1;
  V[1] := 1234.5678;
  V[2] := 'Using Delphi 3';
  V[3] := True;
  ShowMessage(V[2]);   // displays 'Using Delphi 3'
end;
```

The `VarArrayOf` function is simply a wrapper around the `VarArrayCreate` function. It allows you to create and assign the variant array all at once, with a variable number of elements. The following is an example of using the `VarArrayOf` function to create a variant array:

```
procedure TForm1.VarArrayOfButtonClick(Sender: TObject);
var
  V: OleVariant;
begin
  V := VarArrayOf([1, 10, 100, 1000]);
  ShowMessage(V[2]);   // displays 100
end;
```

If you find that you need to pass a multidimensional variant array to an automation object, you can take advantage of the fact that a variant array element, being a variant, can itself contain a reference to a variant array. The following example demonstrates this by creating a two-element variant array in which each element is a variant array itself:

```
procedure TForm1.MultiDimensionVariantArrayButtonClick(Sender: TObject);
var
  V: OleVariant;
begin
  V := VarArrayCreate([1, 2], varVariant);
  V[1] := VarArrayOf([1, 10, 100, 1000]);
  V[2] := VarArrayOf([1, 20, 200, 2000]);
  ShowMessage(V[2][3]);   // displays 2000
end;
```

Table 20.4 lists additional support functions that Delphi provides to work with variant arrays.

Table 20.4 Variant Array Support Procedures and Functions Defined in the System Unit

Support Routine	Description
VarArrayRedim	Resizes a variant array by changing its high-bound dimension to the new high-bound value. Existing elements of the array are preserved, and new elements are set to zero or empty.
VarArrayDimCount	Returns the number of dimensions a variant array has.
VarArrayLowBound	Returns the low bound of a particular dimension in variant array.
VarArrayHighBound	Returns the high bound of a particular dimension in variant array.
VarArrayLock	Returns a pointer to the raw data buffer of a variant array after locking it. Once locked, a variant array must later be unlocked using the VarArrayUnlock procedure.
VarArrayUnlock	Unlocks a variant array that previously was locked by VarArrayLock.
VarArrayRef	Returns a variant that refers to the specified variant array by reference, using the varByRef flag.
VarIsArray	Returns True if the specified variant is a variant array (varArray).

Next you look into the creation of an automation object in Delphi.

Creating OLE Automation Servers

Creating automation servers is nothing new to Delphi 3, but the process of creating one is quite different than in Delphi 2. In Delphi 2, you essentially added your automation object's properties and methods to the automated section of an Object Pascal class, which was a descendant of TAutoObject. Although this code still compiles in Delphi 3, it isn't how Delphi 3 automation objects are constructed.

With Delphi 3, the entire interfacing with the Windows ActiveX architecture was revamped, creating the *Delphi ActiveX framework* (DAX), which makes programming COM, OLE, and ActiveX easier than ever before. There is an all-new TAutoObject class defined in the ComObj unit that is built by the DAX framework. Additionally, the DAX framework also incorporates seamless access to type libraries, which are useful for automation objects and essential for ActiveX controls. As you see in the rest of this chapter, the creation of automation objects is surrounded by the creation of an automation object's type information in a type library.

So, to get an idea of how an automation object is created in Delphi 3, I outlined the basic steps as follows:

1. First, you need to determine whether you want to create an *in-process* (DLL) or *out-of-process* (EXE) automation server. For an *out-of-process* server, select File, New Application. For an *in-process* server, select File, New, ActiveX, ActiveX Library.

2. Select File, New, ActiveX, Automation Object to create the automation object. You will then be prompted for a Class Name. The class name entered must follow the rules for Delphi identifiers.

3. In the Type Library Editor that appears, enter the automation object's properties and methods.

4. In the automation object's unit, fill in the code stubs generated by the Type Library Editor.

5. Finally, you must register the automation server. This first requires an error-free compilation of the server (Ctrl+F9). Then to register an *out-of-process* server, simply run the application (F9). And to register an *in-process* server, select Run, Register ActiveX Server.

Creating an Out-of-Process Automation Server

As you can see, the process to creating an automation object is simple. Probably the most difficult part to this process is to understand what goes into the type library to define an automation object. The best way to discuss this is through an example, so we're going to go through the initial steps of creating an automation server and then I'll point you to the full source once you have an idea of what is going on.

The automation object that you will create will have the following characteristics:

- Play the five possible sounds of the MessageBeep function.
- Store the current sound value internally.
- Have a Sound property that can be used to set or get the current sound value.
- Have a Beep method to play the current sound.
- Have a SoundBeep property that receives a new sound value that will be assigned as the current sound value and also be played immediately.
- Log every action taken by the automation controller.

First select File, New Application. Then to create our automation object, select File, New, ActiveX Page. Figure 20.2 shows the ActiveX page in the Object Repository.

Next, double-click the Automation Object icon that you see highlighted in Figure 20.2. Doing so brings up the Automation Object Wizard (see Figure 20.3).

Type **Beeper** for the class name and leave the instancing value set to Multiple Instance. Multiple Instance means that a new instance of the automation object will be created every time a controller requests the automation object. In contrast, Single instance means that all controllers will access the first created automation object. The internal value means that the automation object will be used by the same application and doesn't require registration in the Windows Registry.

FIG. 20.2
To create a new automation object, select File, New, ActiveX, Automation Object.

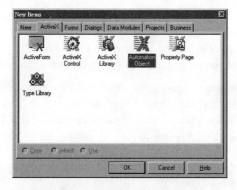

FIG. 20.3
Enter the Class Name and the Instancing type in the Automation Object Wizard to begin creating the automation object.

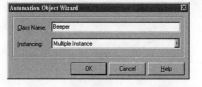

After you select OK in the Automation Object Wizard, Delphi creates a type library with the same name as the project (PROJECT1.TLB), and brings it up in the Type Library Editor (see Figure 20.4).

FIG. 20.4
Edit the project's type information in the Type Library Editor.

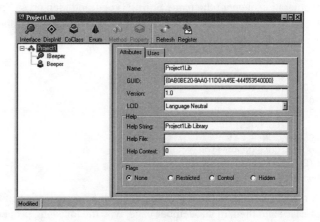

As you can see in Figure 20.4, a type library minimally consists of three elements for an automation server. The first element of the type library is the library's name, information, and attributes. At this point, let's just change the name of the type library to **BeepLib**.

The next element (IBeeper) is of primary interest because it defines the properties and methods of the Beeper automation object. The IBeeper interface is based on the IDispatch interface. We're not going to do anything with this interface just yet.

The final section is the Beeper component object class (coclass). A *component object*, or *coclass*, is a container of interface objects. If you click the Beeper coclass and then select its Members page, you see the IBeeper interface listed. Automation objects need to expose only one IDispatch-based interface to be automatable. In this case, it's the IBeeper interface.

There is one other core element of type libraries and that is enumeration. For this example, we are going to create an enumeration to represent our automation object's supported sound types. To do this, right-click the type libraries tree view and select New, Enum (see Figure 20.5). You can also select the Enum button in the type Library Editor's toolbar.

FIG. 20.5
Adding Sound Type enumerations.

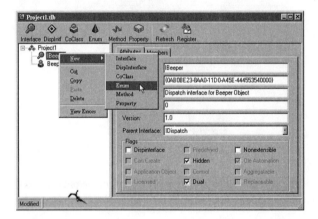

Give the enumeration element the name **SoundTypes**, and then press Enter. To add our enumeration types, select the Members page (if it's not already selected), and enter the following enumerations and their corresponding help strings (see Figure 20.6).

```
MB_Ok = 0;
helpstring = 'Ok sound';
MB_ICONHAND = 16;
helpstring = 'ICONHAND sound';
MB_ICONQUESTION = 32;
helpstring = 'ICONQUESTION sound';
MB_ICONEXCLAMATION = 64;
helpstring = 'ICONEXCLAMATION sound';
MB_ICONASTERISK = 128;
helpstring = 'ICONASTERISK sound';
```

You're now ready to define the Beeper automation object's properties and methods. Select the IBeeper interface and then, in its Member page, type the following property and method definitions along with their unique dispatch identifiers or simply DispIDs (see Figure 20.7):

```
property Sound: SoundTypes; dispid 1;
property SoundBeep[SoundType: SoundTypes]: SoundTypes; readonly; dispid 2;
procedure Beep; dispid 3;
```

FIG. 20.6

To add a new interface, coclass, or enumeration, right-click the Type Library's tree view and select New.

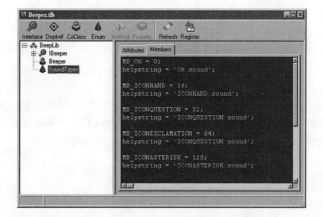

In addition to having to go back and forth from the Type Library Editor (View, Type Library) to add new properties and methods to an automation object, Delphi provides an alternative way of doing this. If you want to add a new property or method while editing an automation object's unit file, you can select Edit, Add To Interface which will bring up the Add to Interface dialog box. Any new properties or methods that are added via the Add to Interface dialog are automatically reflected in the server's type library. ∎

Notice that you can use the SoundTypes enumeration as a type in the property definitions. This is why the SoundTypes enumeration was created first.

FIG. 20.7

The Type Library Editor, after the IBeeper's properties and methods have been entered.

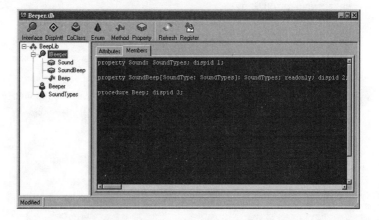

Part

V

Ch

20

Now we defined the Beeper automation object, and we're ready to code up the server's functionality, and then we're done. Before looking at the source code for the finished product, first see what code is generated from our efforts with the type library.

First of all, Delphi will create a source file that has the same name as the project with a "_TLB" appended (for example, Project_TLB). In our case, we used the BeepLib name. Listing 20.2 shows the generated BeepLib unit that contains the enumeration, interface, and coclass information that the project's type library contains.

Listing 20.2   \UDELPHI3\CHP20\BEEPER1\BEEPLIB.PAS—*BeepLib* Unit Generated from the Type Library that Contains the *IBeeper* Interface Definition Using Delphi's New COM Interface Technology

```
unit BeepLib;

{ Project1Lib Library }
{ Version 1.0 }

interface

uses Windows, ActiveX, Classes, Graphics, OleCtrls, StdVCL;

const
  LIBID_BeepLib: TGUID = '{12CFDC67-5519-11D0-A45E-444553540000}';

const

{ SoundTypes }

  MB_Ok = 0;
  MB_ICONHAND = 16;
  MB_ICONQUESTION = 32;
  MB_ICONEXCLAMATION = 64;
  MB_ICONASTERISK = 128;

const

{ Component class GUIDs }
  Class_Beeper: TGUID = '{12CFDC69-5519-11D0-A45E-444553540000}';

type

{ Forward declarations }
  IBeeper = interface;
  DBeeper_ = dispinterface;

  Beeper = IBeeper;

  SoundTypes = TOleEnum;

{ Dispatch interface for Beeper Object }

  IBeeper = interface(IDispatch)
    ['{12CFDC68-5519-11D0-A45E-444553540000}']
    function Get_Sound: SoundTypes; safecall;
    procedure Set_Sound(Value: SoundTypes); safecall;
    function Get_SoundBeep(SoundType: SoundTypes): SoundTypes; safecall;
    procedure Beep; safecall;
```

```
    property Sound: SoundTypes read Get_Sound write Set_Sound;
    property SoundBeep[SoundType: SoundTypes]: SoundTypes read Get_SoundBeep;
  end;

{ DispInterface declaration for Dual Interface IBeeper }

  DBeeper_ = dispinterface
    ['{12CFDC68-5519-11D0-A45E-444553540000}']
    property Sound: SoundTypes dispid 1;
    property SoundBeep[SoundType: SoundTypes]: SoundTypes readonly dispid 2;
    procedure Beep; dispid 3;
  end;

{ BeeperObject }

  CoBeeper = class
    class function Create: IBeeper;
    class function CreateRemote(const MachineName: string): IBeeper;
  end;

implementation

uses ComObj;

class function CoBeeper.Create: IBeeper;
begin
  Result := CreateComObject(Class_Beeper) as IBeeper;
end;

class function CoBeeper.CreateRemote(const MachineName: string): IBeeper;
begin
  Result := CreateRemoteComObject(MachineName, Class_Beeper) as IBeeper;
end;

end.
```

The BeepLib unit defines the IBeeper interface but doesn't implement it. This is done in an-other unit that you will see was added to your project. It should be named UNIT2.PAS, if you started with a new project. As you can see in Listing 20.3, Delphi not only generated the class definition to implement the IBeeper interface, it also created the method stubs for you to sim-ply write the automation object's code.

Listing 20.3   UNIT2.PAS—The Delphi-Generated Implementation for the *IBeeper* Interface

```
unit Unit2;

interface

uses
  ComObj, Project1_TLB;
```

continues

Listing 20.3   Continued

```
type
  TBeeper = class(TAutoObject, IBeeper)
  protected
    function Get_Sound: SoundTypes; safecall;
    function Get_SoundBeep: SoundTypes; safecall;
    procedure Beep; safecall;
    procedure Set_Sound(Value: SoundTypes); safecall;
  end;

implementation

uses ComServ;

function TBeeper.Get_Sound: SoundTypes;
begin

end;

function TBeeper.Get_SoundBeep: SoundTypes;
begin

end;

procedure TBeeper.Beep;
begin

end;

procedure TBeeper.Set_Sound(Value: SoundTypes);
begin

end;

initialization
  TAutoObjectFactory.Create(ComServer, TBeeper, Class_Beeper, ciMultiInstance);
end.
```

There are a couple of things to point out here with this code before looking at the automation object's full implementation. The TBeeper class is using the new COM interface technology to incorporate the functionality of the DAX TAutoObject object, which knows how to make the TBeeper object behave as an automation object within an automation server. You also see in the TBeeper class definition that it supports the IBeeper interface, which requires implementation of the IBeeper interface's virtual methods.

Notice also that each method is using the safecall calling convention. This is the same as the FastCall calling convention, but its real purpose is to catch any unhandled exceptions within the method and propagate them as an OLE exception up to the automation controller.

The true magic of this project is performed by the line of code in the initialization section of UNIT2, as follows:

```
TAutoObjectFactory.Create(ComServer, TBeeper, Class_Beeper, ciMultiInstance);
```

The `TAutoObjectFactory` class is also part of the DAX architecture. The creation of the `TAutoObjectFactory` accomplishes three primary things, shown in the following list:

- The Beeper automation object is registered with Delphi's COM Server object.
- The Windows Registry is updated with the Beeper object's Beeper ClassID and a Prog ID of <Internal Type Library Name>.<Coclass name>. In our example, it is **BeepLib.Beeper**.
- Handles all the `IClassFactory` duties internally, so that the developer doesn't have to code this boilerplate-type code every time a new automation object needs to be created.

We're now ready to look at the full implementation of the Beeper automation server. To look at the Beeper project, load BEEPER.DPR in the \UDELPHI3\CHP20\BEEPER1\ folder. Listing 20.4 shows the `BeepAuto` unit that implements all the functionality of the Beeper automation object. The implementation of the Beeper automation server is fairly straightforward, so examine the `BeepAuto` unit's source listing to understand the Beeper object's implementation. It simply implements the specifications that were outlined previously.

Listing 20.4 \UDELPHI3\CHP20\BEEPER1\BEEPAUTO.PAS—The *BeepAuto* Unit Contains the Full Implementation of the Beeper Automation Object

```
unit BeepAuto;

interface

uses
  ComObj, BeepLib;

type
  TBeeper = class(TAutoObject, IBeeper)
  private
    FSound : Integer;
  protected
    function Get_Sound: SoundTypes; safecall;
    function Get_SoundBeep(SoundType: SoundTypes): SoundTypes; safecall;
    procedure Beep; safecall;
    procedure Set_Sound(Value: SoundTypes); safecall;
  end;

implementation

uses ComServ, Windows, BeepForm, SysUtils;

function TBeeper.Get_Sound: SoundTypes;
begin
  BeeperLogForm.AddActionToLog('Get Sound value: ' + IntToStr(FSound));
  Result := FSound;
end;

function TBeeper.Get_SoundBeep(SoundType: SoundTypes): SoundTypes; safecall;
```

continues

Listing 20.4 Continued

```
begin
  BeeperLogForm.AddActionToLog('Get SoundBeep');
  Set_Sound(SoundType);
  Beep;
  Result := FSound;
end;

procedure TBeeper.Beep;
begin
  BeeperLogForm.AddActionToLog('Beep method called');
  MessageBeep(FSound);
end;

procedure TBeeper.Set_Sound(Value: SoundTypes);
const
  InvalidSound = 'Invalid Sound property parameter. ' +
      'The possible values are: MB_OK(0), MB_ICONHAND(16) , ' +
      'MB_ICONQUESTION(32), MB_ICONEXCLAMATION(64) ' +
      'and MB_ICONASTERISK(128)';
begin
  BeeperLogForm.AddActionToLog('Set Sound value to ' + IntToStr(Value));

  if not (Value in [MB_OK, MB_ICONHAND, MB_ICONQUESTION,
     MB_ICONEXCLAMATION, MB_ICONASTERISK]) then
     Raise EOleError.Create(InValidSound); //Exit;

  if FSound <> Value then FSound := Value;
end;

initialization
  TAutoObjectFactory.Create(ComServer, TBeeper, Class_Beeper, ciMultiInstance);
end.
```

N O T E A Delphi project has an associated type library, the type library file is compiled directly into the EXE or DLL as a resource. If you look at a project's source file (by selecting View, Project Source), you will see that there are two resource types linked in now using the $R compiler directive.

```
{$R *.RES}
{$R *.TLB}
```

In some situations where the type information is too large, you may want to distribute the type library as a separate file (.TLB) rather than as a linked-in resource. ■

On the CD

To demonstrate the Beeper automation object, I created an automation controller project by using the steps outlined previously in this chapter. Before loading the controller, make sure that you run the Beeper automation server project at least once to make sure that it's registered in the Windows Registry. To see the automation controller in action, load and run the

CLIENT.DPR project in the \UDELPHI3\CHP20\BEEPCTRL\ folder. Listing 20.5 shows the core functionality of the client project. Figure 20.8 shows the controller and automation server in action.

FIG. 20.8

Here, you see the automation controller working with the Beeper automation server.

Listing 20.5   \UDELPHI3\CHP20\BEEPCTRL\CLIENTFM.PAS—Shows Code Needed to Connect to and Manipulate the Beeper Automation Object

```
unit ClientFm;

interface

uses
  Windows, Classes, Controls, Forms, Dialogs, ComCtrls,
  StdCtrls, ExtCtrls;

type
  TAutomationController = class(TForm)
    SoundTypes: TRadioGroup;
    ConnectButton: TButton;
    SetSoundButton: TButton;
    BeepButton: TButton;
    SoundBeepButton: TButton;
    DisconnectButton: TButton;
    procedure ConnectButtonClick(Sender: TObject);
    procedure SoundBeepButtonClick(Sender: TObject);
    procedure BeepButtonClick(Sender: TObject);
    procedure SetSoundButtonClick(Sender: TObject);
    procedure DisconnectButtonClick(Sender: TObject);
  private
    BeeperObject : OleVariant;
    function GetMBSoundType : Byte;
  end;

var
  AutomationController: TAutomationController;

implementation

{$R *.DFM}

uses ComObj;

const
```

continues

> **Listing 20.5 Continued**

```
    NotConnectedMsg = 'Please connect to the Beeper automation object first';
    ConnectFailMsg = 'Make sure automation object is registered';

function TAutomationController.GetMBSoundType : Byte;
//--------------------------------------------------------------
// Purpose: Return the Sound Type value that corresponds to
//          user selected sound type index.
//--------------------------------------------------------------
const
  SoundTypes : array[0..4] of Integer = (MB_Ok, MB_ICONHAND,
    MB_ICONQUESTION, MB_ICONEXCLAMATION, MB_ICONASTERISK);
begin
  Result := SoundTypes[Self.SoundTypes.ItemIndex];
end;

procedure TAutomationController.ConnectButtonClick(Sender: TObject);
//--------------------------------------------------------------
// Purpose: Connect to the Beeper automation object.  The
//          CreateOleObject function returns an IDispatch
//          interface that we are assigning to a Delphi
//          OleVariant which is what Delphi uses to do
//          Automation.
//--------------------------------------------------------------
begin
  if VarIsEmpty(BeeperObject) then
  try
    BeeperObject := CreateOleObject('BeepLib.Beeper');
  except
    ShowMessage(ConnectFailMsg);
  end;
end;

procedure TAutomationController.SoundBeepButtonClick(Sender: TObject);
//--------------------------------------------------------------
// Purpose: Assign the user selected sound to the Beeper
//          automation object's SoundBeep property.
//          Internally, the Beeper automation object will
//          play the sound too.
//--------------------------------------------------------------
begin
  if VarIsEmpty(BeeperObject) then
    ShowMessage(NotConnectedMsg)
  else
  BeeperObject.SoundBeep[GetMBSoundType];
end;

procedure TAutomationController.BeepButtonClick(Sender: TObject);
//--------------------------------------------------------------
// Purpose: Invoke the Beeper automation object's Beep method.
//--------------------------------------------------------------
begin
  if VarIsEmpty(BeeperObject) then
    ShowMessage(NotConnectedMsg)
  else
```

```
      BeeperObject.Beep;
end;

procedure TAutomationController.SetSoundButtonClick(Sender: TObject);
//-------------------------------------------------------------
// Purpose: Assign the user selected sound to the Beeper
//          automation object's Sound property.
//-------------------------------------------------------------
begin
  if VarIsEmpty(BeeperObject) then
    ShowMessage(NotConnectedMsg)
  else
  BeeperObject.Sound := GetMBSoundType;
end;

procedure TAutomationController.DisconnectButtonClick(Sender: TObject);
//-------------------------------------------------------------
// Purpose: Release our connection to the Beeper automation
//          object.  Whenever an OleVariant gets assigned a new
//          value, Delphi first checks to see if the OleVariant
//          is currently referencing an automation object and if
//          so the underlying IDispatch interface's Release
//          method is called before the new assignment occurs.
//          Consequentially, if we're the only client with a
//          reference to the Beeper automation object then
//          the Automation server will be shutdown.
//-------------------------------------------------------------
begin
  BeeperObject := Unassigned;
end;

end.
```

Creating an In-Process Automation Server

On the CD

Creating an in-process server is essentially no different than creating an out-of-process server, which we did in the preceding section, except that it is in a DLL. So rather than selecting File, New Application, you select File, New, ActiveX, ActiveX Library, and then proceed to create your automation server, following the steps outlined in the previous section. Listing 20.6 shows the project file for the in-process Beeper automation server, which you can find on this book's companion CD-ROM.

Part
V

Ch
20

Listing 20.6   \UDELPHI3\CHP20\BEEPER2\BEEPER.DPR—Example of How an In-Process Automation Server's Project File Needs to Be Set Up

```
library Beeper;

uses
  ComServ,
  Forms,
  BeepAuto in 'BeepAuto.pas' {Beeper: CoClass},
  BeepLib in 'BeepLib.pas',
```

continues

Listing 20.6   Continued

```
  BeepForm in 'BeepForm.pas' {BeeperLogForm};

{$R *.RES}

{$R *.TLB}

exports
  DllGetClassObject,
  DllCanUnloadNow,
  DllRegisterServer,
  DllUnregisterServer;

begin
  Application.Initialize;
end.
```

To demonstrate the in-process Beeper automation server, you can use the Client project that you used for the out-of-process server. First, however, you need to register the in-process server. Because it's a DLL, you cannot just run it like you could with the out-of-process Beeper automation server. The following five ways that an in-process COM server can be registered are shown in the list (but none are elegant for deployment):

- Select <u>R</u>un, Register <u>A</u>ctiveX Server within the Delphi IDE.

- Use Microsoft's REGSVR32, along with the DLL name. Unfortunately, this utility comes only with Windows NT as well as the MSDN CD-ROMs.

- Invoke an .REG file that contains the necessary Registry entries, including hard-coded paths.

- If installed, you can employ the Register/Unregister ActiveX server context menu example from the COM interfaces chapter.

- Write a program that loads the server DLL and calls the exported DllRegisterServer function.

The full source to the in-process Beeper automation server is on this book's companion CD-ROM, in the \UDELPHI3\CHP20\BEEPER2\ folder. To register the server, double-click the BEEPER.REG file in the project directory.

Putting It All Together

It is worth noting here that we covered automation only within the context of a single machine. Automation also is well suited for distributed objects across machine boundaries. There are two technologies that support distributed COM objects. The first is Microsoft's DCOM technology, which works on Windows NT 4 only. At the time of this writing, Microsoft was working on DCOM for Windows 95. The other technology is OLE Enterprise by Open Environment Corporation (a Borland-owned company) that supports COM objects on both Windows 95 and NT 4. This product is easy to use and is included in the Delphi Client/Server product. OLE

Enterprise and related technologies also support the capability to load-balance client requests of automation objects across multiple server machines so that, if one automation object is overburdened or is not working, OLE Enterprise can get the automation object from another server. This functionality is seamless to the client application.

In the following chapter, you will see that automation is not just to create stand-alone functionality, but is a fundamental element within ActiveX Controls to handle properties, methods, and events. ●

CHAPTER 21

Creating ActiveX Controls

by Todd Miller

When most people hear the term *ActiveX*, they immediately think of OCX controls with a new marketing spin from Microsoft. Part of this thinking is correct; Microsoft uses the term ActiveX to describe its COM-based technologies. The OLE acronym just didn't cut it. Microsoft pushed its definition of Object Linking and Embedding so much that developers had a hard time thinking of its related technologies as something separate from OLE. Therefore, the term ActiveX was invented to encompass the current COM-based technologies and any that Microsoft creates in the future. ActiveX currently encompasses the following technologies:

Delphi ActiveX (DAX) Framework

A discussion of the Delphi ActiveX VCL framework, which facilitates the creation of ActiveX Controls, ActiveForms, as well as supporting OLE Automation with Delphi 3.

Type Library Elements

A discussion of the Interface, DispInterface, Enum, and CoClass elements of a type library, which can be edited within the Delphi Type Library Editor.

ActiveX Control Creation

Demonstrates how to create an ActiveX Control, using Delphi's ActiveX Control Wizard.

ActiveForm Creation

Demonstrates the creation of a multiple component ActiveForm using Delphi's ActiveForm Wizard.

Web Deployment of ActiveX Controls and ActiveForms

Discusses how ActiveX Controls and ActiveForms can enhance your Web pages, as well as how to use Delphi Web deployment features.

■ ActiveX libraries (In-process servers)

■ Automation servers (In-process and out-of-process servers)

■ ActiveX controls

■ ActiveForms (a multiple component ActiveX Control)

■ Property pages ■

Understanding the Delphi ActiveX Framework

To make it easier for Delphi developers to create ActiveX-based technologies, a well-planned and thought-out framework needed to be constructed to encapsulate the many intricacies of the many interfaces and functions of ActiveX and OLE. Now, it's neither here nor there whether or not you're aware of how difficult ActiveX development is because Delphi made ActiveX developing as easy as it gets. The Delphi designers didn't stop at easy, however; they also made it so that you can take any existing TWinControl-based control and make it into an ActiveX control. You can leverage many of your existing VCL-based controls and make them into ActiveX controls that can be used in other development environments such as Visual Basic.

To facilitate this conversion process, the designers of Delphi developed the *Delphi ActiveX (DAX) Framework*. The DAX framework facilitates the development of COM servers, typed COM objects, Automation servers, ActiveX controls, ActiveForms, and property pages. Let's take a closer look at the DAX framework.

DAX ActiveX Objects

The DAX classes that support COM objects, typed COM objects, automation objects, ActiveX controls, and ActiveForms follow, in descending order:

```
TComObject
   TTypedComObject
      TAutoObject
         TActiveXControl

TCustomForm
   TActiveForm
```

The reason that TCustomForm, a new class in Delphi 3, is used as the ancestor class for TActiveForm instead of TForm is because the TCustomForm class publishes only the pertinent properties and events for an ActiveX Form.

DAX Property Pages

Another part of the DAX framework is *property pages*, which are used by various programming environments to change a control's properties values at design time. Often, property pages are obsolete because most development environments have some kind of object or property inspector to modify design-time properties. Having said that, though, you should always include property page(s) for your ActiveX controls. If not for anything else, property pages provide you with a way to create custom property-editing screens for your control's more complex properties. Creating a property page is easy in Delphi, as you will see later. The object's hierarchy to support ActiveX property pages follows, in descending order:

```
TCustomForm
  TPropertyPage
    TActiveXPropertyPage
  [TMyPropertyPage]
```

When you create a new property page, it will descend from the TPropertyPage class.

DAX Object Factories

Delphi exposes COM server objects to clients/controllers through the use of factory objects that get registered with Delphi's global COM Server (ComServer), which is defined in the ComServ unit. Delphi's COM server handles all requests for COM objects and creates the requested object, if registered. The class factory objects used to support COM objects, typed COM objects, Automation objects, and ActiveX controls follows, in descending order:

```
TComObjectFactory
  TActiveXPropertyPageFactory
  TTypedComObjectFactory
    TAutoObjectFactory
      TActiveXControlFactory
        TActiveFormFactory
```

The TActiveXControlFactory and TActiveFormFactory classes are used in this chapter to register ActiveX controls and ActiveForms. The TComObjectFactory class is used to register custom COM objects which are discussed in Chapter 18, "Working with OLE, Document Servers, and ActiveX Controls," and the TAutoObject class is used to register automation objects, which are discussed in Chapter 20, "Working with OLE Automation."

So what do object factories do? These objects encapsulate the IClassFactory interface, which is used to manufacture their associated object each time a client application makes a request for that object. These class factory objects are also responsible for making the appropriate Registry entries in the Windows Registry, based on the class factory type. For example, a TActiveXControlFactory class is responsible for making Registry entries for the ActiveX control COM server and its type library.

Now that we have an idea of how Delphi supports the ActiveX technology, we need to take a look at the tools that Delphi provides to create ActiveX objects. Surprisingly, you don't just start coding away. You actually start with the documentation—more specifically, you start by creating the type library information, which Delphi then uses to generate the DAX-based code into which you then fill in the code stubs and compile, register, and so on. So, before getting into the creation of ActiveX controls, you need to understand what type information is and how to use the Delphi Type Library Editor. Both of these issues are covered in the following section. If you're already familiar with type information, you may want to skip right to "Creating ActiveX Controls," and then come back to the "Type Libraries" section for reference.

Part

V

Ch

21

Type Libraries

Type libraries are OLE compound document files that contain information for COM objects, ActiveX controls, and automation objects such as enumeration data types and interface properties and methods.

The purpose of a type library is to provide information about the component objects it contains to other applications and programming tools. When developing an ActiveX control or automation object, Delphi stores the type library information in a .TLB file, and then at compile time the type library is linked into the DLL or EXE as a resource.

The next couple of sections will briefly go over the various high points of the Delphi Type Library Editor and the types of information it exposes for ActiveX controls, ActiveForms, automation objects, and so on.

Type Library Editor

Delphi's Type Library Editor is used to view or modify type libraries. Its interface is driven by the Object List pane (see Figure 21.1), which allows the user to add, modify, and delete the various elements of a type library. These elements include component classes, interface properties and methods, and enumerations types. The Object List pane is an expandable hierarchical tree where members (discussed in a following section) of a particular element, such as an interface, appear as child nodes. Depending on which element type you selected in the Object List pane, different tab pages appear on the left side of the Type Library Editor. The possible tabs are Attributes, Uses, and Members.

To edit the current project's type library select View, Type Library. To view a type library that is not part of the current project, select File, Open. Then change the File of type combobox to type library to show all the file types that can contain type information.

Now look at the each element of a type library in a little more detail, starting with the type library information.

Type Library Information

Every type library has a section just for describing itself—the type library element. When the type library element is selected in the Object List Pane (see Figure 21.1), the Attributes page and Uses page become available. The following two sections describe the purpose of the Attributes and Uses pages for the type library information element.

Type Library Attributes   The Attributes page contains the general information and characteristics about the type library. The following attributes and flags appear on the Attributes page when a type library is selected in the Object List Pane (see Figure 21.1). Table 21.1 lists the possible type library attributes, and Table 21.2 lists the possible type library flags.

FIG. 21.1
Editing type library
information.

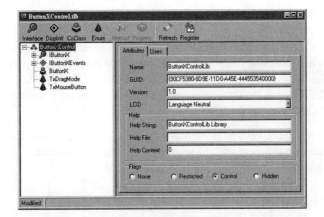

Table 21.1 Type Information Attributes

Attribute	Description
Name	The name of the type library.
GUID	The globally unique 128-bit identifier of the type library.
Version	The type library version is a two-part number with a format of *n.m*, where *n* is the major version number and *m* is the minor version number. A single integer also can be used; it represents the major version number. Both major and minor values can range from 0 to 65535.
LCID	The locale identifier that describes the single national language used for all text strings in the type library and elements.
Help String	A short description of the library. It is strongly recommended that you provide a help string.
Help File	The name of the help file associated with the type library.
Help Context	The Help context ID of the library.

Table 21.2 Type Information Flags

Flags	Description
None	No flags.
Restricted	Prevents the library from being used by a macro programming environment such as Visual Basic.
Control	Indicates that the library represents a control from which a container site will derive additional type libraries or component classes (CoClasses).
Hidden	Indicates that the library exists but should not be displayed in a user-oriented browser.

Type Library Uses Page   The Uses page lists all the type libraries referenced by the current type library. By referencing other type libraries, you can borrow element definitions such as enumerations or interface definitions to help define your own interfaces in your type library. An automation server's primary interface, for example, is derived from the IDispatch interface but, so that you don't have to reinvent the wheel, Delphi adds a reference to the STDOLE32.TLB type library because it already has IDispatch interface defined. STDOLE32.TLB is a standard Windows library file.

For each entry in the Uses page there are two pieces of information. The first is the name of the referenced type library and the second is the GUID that identifies that type library in the Windows registry.

Type Library Enumerations (Enum)

A *type library enumeration* is not much different from an Object Pascal enumeration. A type library enumeration is a collection of related constants used as data types that can be used elsewhere in the type library to define properties and methods. Also, depending on the environment in which your ActiveX objects are used, the enumeration type constants also may be accessible from within that environment for use with the ActiveX object. The following two sections describe the purpose of the Attributes and Member pages for type library enumerations elements.

Enumeration Attributes   Figure 21.2 shows an enumeration type (Enum) element selected within Delphi's Type Library Editor, with its Attributes page showing. Table 21.3 lists the possible attributes that are associated with type library enumeration.

FIG. 21.2
Editing a type library enumeration.

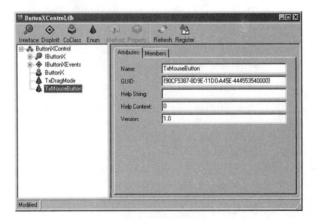

Table 21.3   Type Library Enumeration Attributes

Attribute	Description
Name	The name of the enumeration type.
GUID	The globally unique 128-bit identifier of the enumeration type.

Attribute	Description
Help String	A short description of the enumeration type.
Help Context	The Help context ID of the enumeration type. It's strongly recommended that you provide a help string for your enumerations.
Version	The enumeration version number is a two-part number with a format of *n.m*, where *n* is the major version number and *m* is the minor version number. A single integer also can be used; it represents the major version number. Both major and minor values can range from 0 to 65535.

Enumeration Members The Member page is where the actual enumeration constants are defined. The format for defining these constants is as follows:

```
<Constant Name> = <Constant Value>;
helpstring = 'Descriptive Help String';
```

It's strongly recommended that you provide a help string for your enumerations because applications that may be using your COM object may depend on a help string. Figure 21.3 shows the Member page for an enumeration type element.

FIG. 21.3
Editing the members of a type library enumeration.

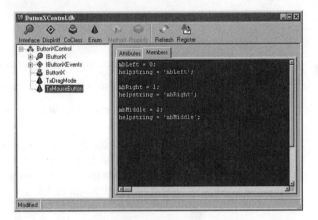

Type Library Interfaces (and DispInterfaces)

A type library interface is a collection of property and method definitions. A client can programmatically access interfaces either through virtual table (`vtable`) method calls or through the use of the special OLE `IDispatch` interface that allows the properties and methods to be invoked via a unique number or DispID. A *DispInterface* refers to an interface that is accessed exclusively through the `IDispatch` interface. A *Dual interface* is one that can be accessed both through virtual table calls and via the `IDispatch` interface. The following two sections describe the purpose of the Attributes and Member pages for type library interface elements.

Part
V

Ch
21

Interface Attributes   Figure 12.4 shows an interface element selected within Delphi's Type Library Editor, with its Attributes page showing. Table 21.4 lists the possible attributes that are associated with a type library interface, and Table 21.5 lists the possible flags.

FIG. 21.4

Editing the attributes of a type library interface.

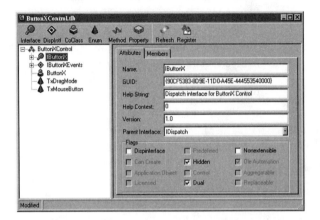

Table 21.4   Type Library Interface Attributes

Attribute	Description
Name	The name of the interface or dispinterface.
GUID	The globally unique 128-bit identifier of the interface or dispinterface.
Help String	A short description of the interface or dispinterface.
Help Context	The Help context ID of the interface or dispinterface. It's strongly recommended that you provide a help string for your enumerations.
Version	The interface or dispinterface version number is a two-part number with a format of *n.m*, where *n* is the major version number and *m* is the minor version number. A single integer also can be used; it represents the major version number. Both major and minor values can range from 0 to 65535.
Parent Interface	The name of the interface that is the base class for the associated interface element. This is not applicable for dispinterfaces.

Table 21.5   Type Library Interface Flags

Flags	Description
DispInterface	The interface describes the methods and properties for an object that must be accessed through the IDispatch Invoke method.
Hidden	Indicates that the interface exists but should not be displayed in a user-oriented browser.

Flags	Description
Nonextensible	Indicates that the IDispatch implementation includes only the properties and methods listed in the interface description.
Dual	Identifies an interface that exposes properties and methods through IDispatch and directly through the virtual table.
OLE Automation	Indicates that an interface can use only Automation-compatible types. Not allowed on a dispinterface because it is Automation-compatible by definition.

Interface Members   The Member page for interfaces is where the interface's properties and method are defined. The syntax for an interface's properties and method is, except for a few minor additions, exactly like an Object Pascal. First, every property and method will be followed by a unique dispatch identifier or DispID. Usually, DispIDs start with a value of 1 and progress with an incremented value of 1. The other addition is the keywords readonly and writeonly to allow properties to be read-only and write-only, respectively. The following are examples of interface properties and methods:

```
property FrameCount: Integer; readonly; dispid 1;

procedure Play(FromFrame, ToFrame: Smallint; Count: Integer); dispid 2;

property OpenDatabase[DatabaseName, TableName, UserName,
        Password : WideString]: WordBool; readonly; dispid 3;
```

The last definition is a read-only parameterized property. I point this out not only to expose you to this type of property, but also because some ActiveX servers choose to use this approach in place of functions. Figure 21.5 shows the Members page for an interface element in the Delphi Type Library Editor.

FIG. 21.5
Editing the members of a type library interface.

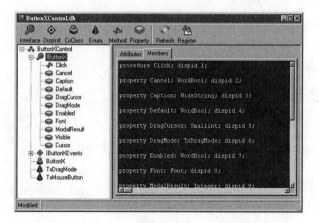

N O T E If an interface's *DispInterface* or *OLE Automation* attributes are checked, and then the data type used in property and method definitions are restricted to OLE Automation-compatible types. The OLE Automation types are: Byte, Smallint, Integer, Single, Double, Currency, TDateTime, WideString, WordBool, and OleVariant. To pass multidimensional data structures, you can utilize variant arrays, discussed in Chapter 20. ■

Property and Method Attributes   Figure 21.6 shows an interface property element selected within Delphi's Type Library Editor, with its Attributes page showing. Table 21.6 lists the possible attributes associated with a type library interface member elements, and Table 21.7 lists the possible flags.

FIG. 21.6
Editing the attributes of a type library interface property.

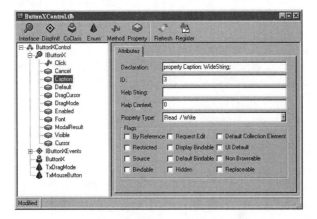

Table 21.6   Type Library Interface Member Attributes

Attribute	Description
Declaration	The declaration of the property or method
ID	Dispatch ID
Help String	A description of the property or method
Help Context	Identifies the Help context ID of the property or method

Table 21.7   Type Library Interface Member Flags

Flags	Description
Restricted	Prevents the property or method from being used by a macro programming language
Source	Indicates that the member returns an object or VARIANT that is a source of events

Flags	Description
Bindable	Indicates that the property supports data binding
Request Edit	Indicates that the property supports the OnRequestEdit notification
Display Bindable	Indicates a property that should be displayed to the user as bindable
Default Bindable	Indicates the single, bindable property that best represents the object
Hidden	Indicates that the property exists but should not be displayed in a user-oriented browser

Type Library Component Class (CoClass)

A *type library's component class* (or CoClass) represents the entire ActiveX control, automation object, or custom COM object. It houses the interfaces and dispinterfaces that get exposed to the client application. The following two sections describe the purpose of the Attributes and Member pages of a type library component class.

Component Class Attributes   Table 21.8 lists the attributes associated with a component class. Table 21.9 lists the flags associated with a type library component class.

Table 21.8   Type Library Component Class Attributes

Attribute	Description
Name	The name of the component class (CoClass).
GUID	The globally unique 128-bit identifier of the component class (CoClass).
Help String	A short description of the component class.
Help Context	The Help context ID of the component class. It is strongly recommended that you provide a help string for your enumerations.
Version	The component class version number is a two-part number with a format of *n.m*, where *n* is the major version number and *m* is the minor version number. A single integer also can be used; it represents the major version number. Both major and minor values can range from 0 to 65535.

Part

V

Ch

21

Table 21.9 Type Library Component Class Flags

Flags	Description
Licensed	Indicates that a design-time and runtime license is required. This usually is used only in conjunction with ActiveX Controls.
Control	Specifies that the component class is a control.
Application Object	Indicates that the component class is contained in an out-of-process server (EXE). This is exclusively for automation servers.

Component Class Members   The members page for component class is where you add and remove the interfaces and enumerations that make up the COM class. The information on this page consists of the following:

- The name of each interface or dispinterface that the COM class implements.
- The GUID of each interface or dispinterface that the COM class implements.
- Specifies whether an interface or dispinterface is a source of events.
- Specifies whether an interface or dispinterface represents the default programmable interface which is used by macro languages such as Word Basic, Visual Basic, Delphi, Object PAL, and Excel Basic.
- Specifies whether an interface or dispinterface is restricted from being used by macro languages such as Word Basic, Visual Basic, Delphi, Object PAL, and Excel Basic.

To insert or remove interfaces from the component class, simply right-click the Member page window to bring up the SpeedMenu, and then choose either Insert Interface or Remove Interface. The Source, Default, and Restricted flags also can be set by using the right-click SpeedMenu in the Member page. When inserting interfaces, you can choose interfaces defined in the current type library or those defined in any type libraries that the current type library references.

ActiveX Controls

We're finally ready to do the fun stuff—creating ActiveX controls. The following sections discuss the steps necessary to build an ActiveX control. But before getting into this, let's first take a look at what ActiveX is and what it provides over and above Delphi's VCL-based controls.

Microsoft's ActiveX technology is fundamentally a revamped OCX technology that makes it possible to pass around controls across the Internet, but primarily across the World Wide Web. I'm sure that you're saying, "Well, this is good, but how will ActiveX help me?" Well, wouldn't it be nice to create controls that not only work in Delphi but also in environments such as Borland C++ Builder, Visual C++, or Visual Basic? ActiveX controls provide this functionality.

To facilitate this functionality, Delphi allows you to wrap any `TWinControl` descendant into an ActiveX control by using the DAX framework. The targeted platforms on which Delphi's ActiveX controls are certified to run are the following:

- Borland Delphi 2 and 3
- Borland C++Builder
- Borland Paradox 8
- Borland IntraBuilder
- Microsoft Visual C++
- Microsoft Visual Basic 4 and 5
- Microsoft Internet Explorer 3.01
- Microsoft ActiveX Control Pad
- Microsoft FrontPage

The general process of creating an ActiveX control is as follows:

1. You must have the desired VCL control that you want to make into an ActiveX control on the Delphi component palette, and it must be a `TWinControl` descendant. If you want to make an ActiveX Control out of a `TGraphicControl` descendant, then in most cases you need to change only the base class to `TCustomControl`. We use this technique in the ActiveX example coming up shortly.

2. Run the ActiveX Control Wizard by selecting <u>F</u>ile, <u>N</u>ew, ActiveX, ActiveX Control. In the wizard you select your VCL component to wrap, determine the new ActiveX name, turn licensing on or off, turn version information on or off, and so on. After selecting OK, Delphi creates a type library with all the public and published properties, methods, and events. In addition, two source files are created—one for the Delphi Type Library information (such as interfaces, dispinterfaces, and so on), and the other is used to implement the interface methods defined in the first.

3. During the creation of the type library, Delphi may not have been able to translate everything, either because it doesn't make sense to translate it or because Delphi just didn't understand how to perform the conversion. No matter the reason, you can easily add any custom properties, methods, or events. To do this, open the type library (<u>V</u>iew, <u>T</u>ype Library) and make any desired additions, select the Refresh button at the top, and let Delphi create the wrapper code for your additions. An example of something that won't translate is component sub-properties.

4. Write any code for `Get` and `Set` methods that are either incomplete for the functionality desired or are blank due to additions to the type library. This also applies to any custom event handlers.

5. After the ActiveX control's functionality is complete, you probably will want to create one or more property pages to allow the user of your control the ability to right-click your control in environments that don't support the notion of an object inspector to change property values. There should at least be a general properties page. Delphi provides four standard property pages for colors, fonts, picture, and Delphi string lists.

6. Compile and register the control.

7. You can now import the new OCX file into any of the support environments in which a Delphi ActiveX Control can be used.

Part
V

Ch
21

Creating an ActiveX Control—PieX

The best way to understand ActiveX development is to build one. So, this section walks you through building an ActiveX control with Delphi's sample TPie component. If you are familiar with the TPie component, you may recall that it's a TGraphicControl descendant and, therefore, disqualified to be used as an ActiveX control. This is correct, as long as it stays a TGraphicControl descendant. If, however, you modify the source and change the TGraphicControl class name to TCustomControl, it is now a prime-time ActiveX control candidate.

Go ahead and modify the PIES.PAS file in the \DEMOS\PROPEDIT\ folder to change its descendant class to TCustomControl. If you don't do this step, the TPie component will not show up in the ActiveX Control Wizard.

Next, you need to add the full path to the PIES.PAS unit to your project options search path (Project, Options, Directories/Conditionals, Search Path).

What is required, next, is to install the TPie component to the component palette before we can wrap it into an ActiveX Control. To do this, select File, Open and set the File of type drop-down to Delphi package source. Then, navigate to the ..\DEMOS\PROPEDIT\ folder and double-click the PIELIB.DPK file name, which brings up the Delphi Package Editor dialog box.

Select the Install button, and then close the dialog box. The TPie component will now be installed on the Samples tab of the component palette. If you are unfamiliar with this component, you may want to play with it a bit before continuing. Specifically, double-click it when it is on the form to see how its component editor works.

Using the ActiveX Control Wizard

Now, the stage is set so let's create an ActiveX control! To launch the ActiveX Control Wizard, simply select File, New, ActiveX, ActiveX Control (see Figure 21.7).

FIG. 21.7
Launching the ActiveX
Control Wizard.

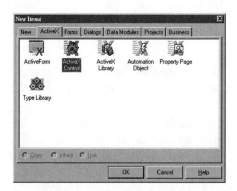

The first field in the wizard is requesting the name of the actual VCL control to wrap into an ActiveX control. Select the VCL Class Name drop-down and pick the TPie component (see Figure 21.8).

FIG. 21.8
Select the TPie
component in the
ActiveX Control Wizard
to make it into an
ActiveX control.

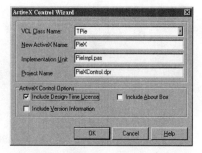

If the TPie component doesn't appear in the drop-down list, you either didn't change the PIES.PAS (discussed previously) or didn't install the PIELIB.DPK package. Just leave the rest of the edit boxes in the wizard to their default values, but note their file names because you'll be looking at them shortly. Also check the Include Design-Time License check box, which is discussed in following sections.

Select OK, and Delphi creates a type library with all TPie's public and published properties, methods, and events. The Brush and Pen properties did not get added because they are sub-properties. Additionally, Delphi creates a project file (PieXControl.dpr), an implementation unit (PieXImpl.pas), a type library file (PieXControl.tlb), and a license file (PieXControl.lic). There also is an in-memory unit that Delphi maintains that corresponds to the contents of the type library information (PieXControlLib.pas). This unit will be included in the uses clause on every implementation unit within the ActiveX Library project.

Checking Type Information

Let's first take a quick look at what's in the PieXControl's associated type library. Unlike working with automation server projects, the Type Library Editor doesn't come up immediately, so you need to select the View, Type Library menu option. Figure 21.9 shows the type library elements for the PieXControl ActiveX control project.

Table 21.10 briefly describes each of the elements in the PieXControl project's type library.

Table 21.10   Elements in the PieXControl Project's Type Library

Element Name	Description
PieXControlLib	Information pertinent to the entire type library
IPieX	An interface that defines the exposed TPie component's properties and methods
IPieXEvents	A dispinterface that defines the exposed TPie component events
PieX	The component class (CoClass) that exposed the IPieX and IPieXEvents interfaces
TxMouseButton	An enumerated type that defines the possible mouse buttons

Part

V

Ch

21

FIG. 21.9

The type library created for the PieXControl project.

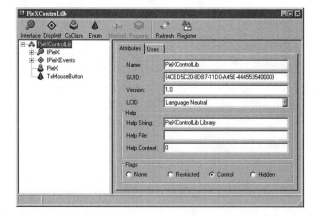

If you select the Members page for the IPieX interface element in the type library, notice that not all the TPie component's properties are exposed. Primarily, the component sub-properties are not exposed. To demonstrate how to add properties and methods in the Type Library Editor, we'll add two properties to allow us to expose these subproperties.

Adding Properties and Methods

Before starting, make sure that you have the Members page of the IPieX interface element showing in the type library. There are four member entries—one procedure and three properties. At the end of the list, add the following four additional member elements:

```
property EndAngle: Integer; dispid 5;

property StartAngle: Integer; dispid 6;

property BrushColor: Integer; dispid 7;

property PenColor: Integer; dispid 8;
```

By adding these member properties, you will be able to expose the TPie component's `Angle.StartAngle`, `Angle.EndAngle`, `Brush.Color`, and `Pen.Color` sub-properties. Notice that I added the `dispid` identifiers in sequence, starting with 5. You must provide a unique identifier for every property and method member of an interface.

> **CAUTION**
> You always must use positive `dispids` with interface members. Negative dispids are reserved by Windows.

After typing these member entries, select the Refresh button in the Type Library Editor to update the PieImpl.pas file.

Now look at the two source files Delphi created for the PieXControl project (not including the project file). The first file to look at is the PIEXCONTROLLIB.PAS file. First, notice that its name is identical to the type library's internal name. The .TLB file that Delphi creates has the same name as the project source file. The PieXControlLib.pas file primarily reflects what is defined in the project's type library (see Listing 21.1).

Listing 21.1   \UDELPHI3\CHP21\PIEXCONTROLLIB.PAS—Reflects the Definitions of the Project's Type Library, Using Delphi's DAX Framework

```
unit PieXControlLib;

{ PieXControlLib Library }
{ Version 1.0 }

interface

uses Windows, ActiveX, Classes, Graphics, OleCtrls, StdVCL;

const
  LIBID_PieXControlLib: TGUID = '{88DAF8E0-5AA5-11D0-A45E-444553540000}';

const

{ MouseButton }

  mbLeft = 0;
  mbRight = 1;
  mbMiddle = 2;

const

{ Component class GUIDs }
  Class_PieX: TGUID = '{88DAF8E3-5AA5-11D0-A45E-444553540000}';

type

{ Forward declarations }
  IPieX = interface;
  DPieX_ = dispinterface;
  IPieXEvents = dispinterface;

  PieX = IPieX;

  MouseButton = TOleEnum;

{ Dispatch interface for PieX Control }

  IPieX = interface(IDispatch)
    ['{88DAF8E1-5AA5-11D0-A45E-444553540000}']
    procedure Paint; safecall;
    function Get_Visible: WordBool; safecall;
    procedure Set_Visible(Value: WordBool); safecall;
    function Get_Enabled: WordBool; safecall;
    procedure Set_Enabled(Value: WordBool); safecall;
    function Get_Cursor: Smallint; safecall;
    procedure Set_Cursor(Value: Smallint); safecall;
    function Get_EndAngle: Integer; safecall;
```

continues

Listing 21.1 Continued

```
    procedure Set_EndAngle(Value: Integer); safecall;
    function Get_StartAngle: Integer; safecall;
    procedure Set_StartAngle(Value: Integer); safecall;
    function Get_BrushColor: Integer; safecall;
    procedure Set_BrushColor(Value: Integer); safecall;
    function Get_PenColor: Integer; safecall;
    procedure Set_PenColor(Value: Integer); safecall;
    property Visible: WordBool read Get_Visible write Set_Visible;
    property Enabled: WordBool read Get_Enabled write Set_Enabled;
    property Cursor: Smallint read Get_Cursor write Set_Cursor;
    property EndAngle: Integer read Get_EndAngle write Set_EndAngle;
    property StartAngle: Integer read Get_StartAngle write Set_StartAngle;
    property BrushColor: Integer read Get_BrushColor write Set_BrushColor;
    property PenColor: Integer read Get_PenColor write Set_PenColor;
  end;

{ DispInterface declaration for Dual Interface IPieX }

  DPieX_ = dispinterface
    ['{88DAF8E1-5AA5-11D0-A45E-444553540000}']
    procedure Paint; dispid 1;
    property Visible: WordBool dispid 2;
    property Enabled: WordBool dispid 3;
    property Cursor: Smallint dispid 4;
    property EndAngle: Integer dispid 5;
    property StartAngle: Integer dispid 6;
    property BrushColor: Integer dispid 7;
    property PenColor: Integer dispid 8;
  end;

{ Events interface for PieX Control }

  IPieXEvents = dispinterface
    ['{88DAF8E2-5AA5-11D0-A45E-444553540000}']
    procedure OnClick; dispid 1;
    procedure OnDblClick; dispid 2;
  end;

{ PieXControl }

  TPieX = class(TOleControl)
  private
    FOnClick: TNotifyEvent;
    FOnDblClick: TNotifyEvent;
    FIntf: IPieX;
  protected
    procedure InitControlData; override;
    procedure InitControlInterface(const Obj: IUnknown); override;
  public
    procedure Paint;
    property ControlInterface: IPieX read FIntf;
  published
    property TabStop;
    property Align;
```

```
      property DragCursor;
      property DragMode;
      property ParentShowHint;
      property PopupMenu;
      property ShowHint;
      property TabOrder;
      property OnDragDrop;
      property OnDragOver;
      property OnEndDrag;
      property OnEnter;
      property OnExit;
      property OnStartDrag;
      property Visible: WordBool index 2 read GetWordBoolProp
                   write SetWordBoolProp stored False;
      property Enabled: WordBool index 3 read GetWordBoolProp
                   write SetWordBoolProp stored False;
      property Cursor: Smallint index 4 read GetSmallintProp
                   write SetSmallintProp stored False;
      property EndAngle: Integer index 5 read GetIntegerProp
                   write SetIntegerProp stored False;
      property StartAngle: Integer index 6 read GetIntegerProp
                   write SetIntegerProp stored False;
      property BrushColor: Integer index 7 read GetIntegerProp
                   write SetIntegerProp stored False;
      property PenColor: Integer index 8 read GetIntegerProp
                   write SetIntegerProp stored False;
    property OnClick: TNotifyEvent read FOnClick write FOnClick;
    property OnDblClick: TNotifyEvent read FOnDblClick write FOnDblClick;
  end;

procedure Register;

implementation

uses ComObj;

procedure TPieX.InitControlData;
const
  CEventDispIDs: array[0..1] of Integer = (
    $00000001, $00000002);
  CLicenseKey: array[0..38] of Word = (
    $007B, $0038, $0038, $0044, $0041, $0046, $0038, $0045, $0035, $002D,
    $0035, $0041, $0041, $0035, $002D, $0031, $0031, $0044, $0030, $002D,
    $0041, $0034, $0035, $0045, $002D, $0034, $0034, $0034, $0035, $0035,
    $0033, $0035, $0034, $0030, $0030, $0030, $0030, $007D, $0000);
  CControlData: TControlData = (
    ClassID: '{88DAF8E3-5AA5-11D0-A45E-444553540000}';
    EventIID: '{88DAF8E2-5AA5-11D0-A45E-444553540000}';
    EventCount: 2;
    EventDispIDs: @CEventDispIDs;
    LicenseKey: @CLicenseKey;
    Flags: $00000000;
    Version: 300;
    FontCount: 0;
    FontIDs: nil);
```

Part

V

Ch

21

continues

Listing 21.1 Continued

```
begin
  ControlData := @CControlData;
end;

procedure TPieX.InitControlInterface(const Obj: IUnknown);
begin
  FIntf := Obj as IPieX;
end;

procedure TPieX.Paint;
begin
  ControlInterface.Paint;
end;


procedure Register;
begin
  RegisterComponents('ActiveX', [TPieX]);
  RegisterNonActiveX([TPieX]);
end;

end.    property Enabled: WordBool read Get_Enabled write Set_Enabled;

    property Cursor: Smallint read Get_Cursor write Set_Cursor;
    property EndAngle: Integer read Get_EndAngle write Set_EndAngle;
    property StartAngle: Integer read Get_StartAngle write Set_StartAngle;
    property BrushColor: Integer read Get_BrushColor write Set_BrushColor;
    property PenColor: Integer read Get_PenColor write Set_PenColor;
  end;

{ Events interface for PieX Control }

  IPieXEvents = dispinterface
    ['{88DAF8E2-5AA5-11D0-A45E-444553540000}']
    procedure OnClick; dispid 1;
    procedure OnDblClick; dispid 2;
  end;

{ PieXControl }

  PieX = IPieX;

  CoPieX = class
    class function Create: IPieX;
  end;

const

{ Component class GUIDs }

  Class_PieX: TGUID = '{88DAF8E3-5AA5-11D0-A45E-444553540000}';

implementation

uses ComObj;
```

```
class function CoPieX.Create: IPieX;
begin
  Result := CreateComObject(Class_PieX) as IPieX;
end;

end.
```

The first information you see in the file is the declaration of the MouseButton enumeration type and constants. Then you see the IPieX interface that defines the ActiveX control's properties and methods. Notice that the Delphi definition of the properties has Get and Set methods defined for each. Next in the file you see the definition of the IPieXEvents dispinterface. Events are defined as a dispinterface because they are always invoked by their DispID values triggering events in the client container.

The complete implementation of the ActiveX control's library file in the PieImpl.pas file (see Listing 21.2). The Get and Set method needed to implement to make the new properties work are listed as follows:

```
function TPieX.Get_EndAngle: Integer; safecall;
begin
  Result := FDelphiControl.Angles.EndAngle;;
end;

procedure TPieX.Set_EndAngle(Value: Integer); safecall;
begin
  FDelphiControl.Angles.EndAngle := Value;
end;

function TPieX.Get_StartAngle: Integer; safecall;
begin
  Result := FDelphiControl.Angles.StartAngle;
end;

procedure TPieX.Set_StartAngle(Value: Integer); safecall;
begin
  FDelphiControl.Angles.StartAngle := Value;
end;

function TPieX.Get_BrushColor: Integer; safecall;
begin
  Result := FDelphiControl.Brush.Color;
end;

procedure TPieX.Set_BrushColor(Value: Integer); safecall;
begin
  FDelphiControl.Brush.Color := Value;
end;

function TPieX.Get_PenColor: Integer;
safecall;
begin
  result := FDelphiControl.Pen.Color;
end;
```

Part
V

Ch
21

```
procedure TPieX.Set_PenColor(Value: Integer);
safecall;
begin
  FDelphiControl.Pen.Color := Value;
end;
```

Listing 21.2 \UDELPHI3\CHP21\PIEIMPL.PAS—Implements the Interface
Methods and Property *Set* and *Get* Methods Defined in PIEXCONTROLLIB.PAS

```
unit PieImpl;

interface

uses
  Windows, ActiveX, Classes, Controls, Graphics, Menus, Forms, StdCtrls,
  ComServ, AxCtrls, PieXControlLib, Pies;

type
  TPieX = class(TActiveXControl, IPieX)
  private
    { Private declarations }
    FDelphiControl: TPie;
    FEvents: IPieXEvents;
    procedure ClickEvent(Sender: TObject);
    procedure DblClickEvent(Sender: TObject);
  protected
    { Protected declarations }
    procedure InitializeControl; override;
    procedure EventSinkChanged(const EventSink: IUnknown); override;
    procedure DefinePropertyPages(
            DefinePropertyPage: TDefinePropertyPage); override;
    function Get_BrushColor: Integer; safecall;
    function Get_Cursor: Smallint; safecall;
    function Get_Enabled: WordBool; safecall;
    function Get_StartAngle: Integer; safecall;
    function Get_EndAngle: Integer; safecall;
    function Get_Visible: WordBool; safecall;
    function Get_PenColor: Integer; safecall;
    procedure Paint; safecall;
    procedure Set_BrushColor(Value: Integer); safecall;
    procedure Set_Cursor(Value: Smallint); safecall;
    procedure Set_Enabled(Value: WordBool); safecall;
    procedure Set_EndAngle(Value: Integer); safecall;
    procedure Set_StartAngle(Value: Integer); safecall;
    procedure Set_PenColor(Value: Integer); safecall;
    procedure Set_Visible(Value: WordBool); safecall;
  end;

implementation

uses PieAngle, PieColors;

{ TPieX }

procedure TPieX.InitializeControl;
begin
```

```
    FDelphiControl := Control as TPie;
    FDelphiControl.OnClick := ClickEvent;
    FDelphiControl.OnDblClick := DblClickEvent;
end;

procedure TPieX.EventSinkChanged(const EventSink: IUnknown);
begin
  FEvents := EventSink as IPieXEvents;
end;

procedure TPieX.DefinePropertyPages(
          DefinePropertyPage: TDefinePropertyPage);
begin
  { Define property pages here.  Propery pages are defined
    by calling DefinePropertyPage with the class id of the
    page.  For example, DefinePropertyPage(Class_PieXPage); }
  DefinePropertyPage( Class_PieGeneralPropertyPage );
  DefinePropertyPage( Class_PieColorPropertyPage );
end;

function TPieX.Get_EndAngle: Integer; safecall;
begin
  Result := FDelphiControl.Angles.EndAngle;;
end;

procedure TPieX.Set_EndAngle(Value: Integer); safecall;
begin
  FDelphiControl.Angles.EndAngle := Value;
end;

function TPieX.Get_BrushColor: Integer; safecall;
begin
  Result := FDelphiControl.Brush.Color;
end;

procedure TPieX.Set_BrushColor(Value: Integer); safecall;
begin
  FDelphiControl.Brush.Color := Value;
end;

function TPieX.Get_PenColor: Integer; safecall;
begin
  Result := FDelphiControl.Pen.Color;
end;

procedure TPieX.Set_PenColor(Value: Integer); safecall;
begin
  FDelphiControl.Pen.Color := Value;
end;

function TPieX.Get_Cursor: Smallint;
begin
  Result := Smallint(FDelphiControl.Cursor);
end;
```

Part

V

Ch

21

continues

Listing 21.2   Continued

```
function TPieX.Get_Enabled: WordBool;
begin
  Result := FDelphiControl.Enabled;
end;

function TPieX.Get_Visible: WordBool;
begin
  Result := FDelphiControl.Visible;
end;

procedure TPieX.Paint;
begin
  FDelphiControl.Paint;
end;

procedure TPieX.Set_Cursor(Value: Smallint);
begin
  FDelphiControl.Cursor := TCursor(Value);
end;

procedure TPieX.Set_Enabled(Value: WordBool);
begin
  FDelphiControl.Enabled := Value;
end;

procedure TPieX.Set_Visible(Value: WordBool);
begin
  FDelphiControl.Visible := Value;
end;

procedure TPieX.ClickEvent(Sender: TObject);
begin
  if FEvents <> nil then FEvents.OnClick;
end;

procedure TPieX.DblClickEvent(Sender: TObject);
begin
  if FEvents <> nil then FEvents.OnDblClick;
end;

function TPieX.Get_StartAngle: Integer;
begin
  Result := FDelphiControl.Angles.StartAngle;
end;

procedure TPieX.Set_StartAngle(Value: Integer);
begin
  FDelphiControl.Angles.StartAngle := Value;
end;

initialization
  TActiveXControlFactory.Create(
    ComServer,
    TPieX,
```

```
        TPie,
        Class_PieX,
        1,
        '{88DAF8E5-5AA5-11D0-A45E-444553540000}');
    end.
```

There are several other important things going in the implementation code. The `InitializeControl` method is overridden to both set up the Delphi VCL control that this ActiveX control is supporting and also delegates an event method to each of the exposed event handlers within the ActiveX implementation file.

```
procedure TPieX.InitializeControl;
begin
  FDelphiControl := Control as TPie;
  FDelphiControl.OnClick := ClickEvent;
  FDelphiControl.OnDblClick := DblClickEvent;
end;
```

This event is a good place to put any special startup code that you want the ActiveX control to have.

Speaking of events, any custom dispinterface events need to be assigned to the container's EventSink when the `EventSinkChanged` method is called, as follows:

```
procedure TPieX.EventSinkChanged(const EventSink: IUnknown);
begin
  FEvents := EventSink as IPieXEvents;
end;
```

At the bottom of the PieImpl.pas file, you see a special class creation for the `TActiveXControlFactory` DAX framework class. Upon creation, this class registers the ActiveX control with Delphi's global ComServer object. In this registration process the ComServer object is given the ActiveX control's unique Class ID (CLSID) and the class reference, so it knows what to create upon a request for the CLSID, as follows:

```
initialization
  TActiveXControlFactory.Create(
    ComServer,
    TPieX,
    TPie,
    Class_PieX,
    1,
    '{88DAF8E5-5AA5-11D0-A45E-444553540000}');
end.
```

The GUID value you see as the last parameter to the TActiveXControlFactory.Create constructor is used as the license key value. You are welcome to change the license key value, but you must also change its value in the <Project Name>.lic file, which is created to differentiate between design-time and runtime licensing of the ActiveX control. We are actually done with the creation of the ActiveX control, but before testing it, let's create an Angle and Color property page for it.

Part

V

Ch

21

Creating Property Pages

Each property page for an ActiveX control is an independent form that can be used by the user of the ActiveX control to modify properties and see the changes reflected at design time. Property pages are defined by calling DefinePropertyPage method for each property page passing it the Class ID of each property page. This is done within the overridden DefinePropertyPages method in the ActiveX control's implementation file. Because we will define two property pages, we make two calls to the DefinePropertyPage method, as follows:

```
procedure TPieX.DefinePropertyPages(DefinePropertyPage: TDefinePropertyPage);
begin
  DefinePropertyPage( Class_PieGeneralPropertyPage );
  DefinePropertyPage( Class_PieColorPropertyPage );
end;

Class_DColorPropPage
Class_DFontPropPage
Class_DPicturePropPage
Class_DStringPropPage
```

To create a new property page, you select File, New, ActiveX, Property Page. Rather than walk you through creating these property pages, I will direct you to open the PIEXCONTROL.DPR project in the \UDELPHI3\CHP21\ folder. The two units in which you're interested are PieAngle and PieColors. Each of these units has a property page form already laid out. What you need to look at is the mechanism in which the property page gets the properties from the control and *vice versa*. This is accomplished by overriding the two special methods— UpdatePropertyPage and UpdateObject.

```
procedure TPieGeneralPropertyPage.UpdatePropertyPage;
begin
  { Update your controls from OleObject }
  StartAngleTrackBar.Position := OleObject.StartAngle;
  EndAngleTrackBar.Position := OleObject.EndAngle;
end;

procedure TPieGeneralPropertyPage.UpdateObject;
begin
  { Update OleObject from your controls }
  OleObject.StartAngle := StartAngleTrackBar.Position;
  OleObject.EndAngle := EndAngleTrackBar.Position;
end;
```

Registering and Installing ActiveX Controls

Registering an ActiveX is a simple matter of using some utility or application that calls the ActiveX control's exported DllRegisterServer function, which knows how to add the necessary registry entries in the Windows registry database—based on all the factory objects that are registered in Delphi global ComServer object. We looked only at the one for the ActiveX control, but each property page also has a factory object.

To register the PieXControl ActiveX control, use the Run, Register ActiveX Server menu option. To test your new ActiveX Control, you will need to install the ActiveX control by selecting the Component, Install ActiveX control menu option to bring up the Import ActiveX control dialog box (see Figure 21.10).

If you don't already see the PieXControlLib library in the registered controls list, select the New button to add the PieXControl.dll. After you select OK, Delphi automatically calls the DllRegisterServer function so that it now is in the list of registered controls. Select it in the list, and press the Add to package button; you can either create a new one or add the ActiveX control to an existing package. I suggest adding it to the PieLib.dpk, and then you have to rebuild only the package because it is already installed.

You now should have an ActiveX palette page with the PieX control. That's all there is to creating, registering, and installing ActiveX controls in Delphi. Other development environments handle the registering and installing differently, so check with that product documentation for instructions.

FIG. 21.10
The Import ActiveX control dialog box.

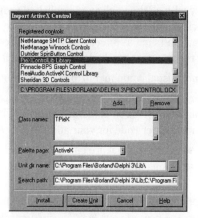

Creating ActiveForms

An *ActiveForm* is a set of one or more visual and non-visual components hooked together on a form in order to create a hybrid ActiveX Control. In other words, you can put together one or more visual controls to make a simple composite control or you can make entire single form applications that are distributed as one ActiveForm.

The fact that you can add non-visual controls means that you can create ActiveForms that use the BDE, or better yet, Delphi's new Data Broker technology that is specifically designed for distrusted datasets across network boundaries, such as the Internet.

Part
V

Ch
21

As for what you can do on the ActiveForm itself, there really aren't any restrictions. One important distinction about ActiveForms is that only the properties, methods, and events associated with the ActiveForm itself are exposed. This means that none of the properties, methods, and events of the VCL components on the ActiveForm will be exposed. They are technically internal to the ActiveForm.

When you want to expose the functionality of the ActiveForm's internal components, you can add new properties and methods to the ActiveForm in the Type Library Editor just as you would with an ActiveX Control. Except in this case, the Get and Set methods of a property would be accessing the internal components rather than the main VCL control.

The steps to create an ActiveForm are almost identical to creating an ActiveX Control but for completeness, they are presented in the following sequence:

1. Run the ActiveForm Wizard by selecting File, New, ActiveX, ActiveForm. In the wizard, you see that an ActiveForm always wraps the TActiveForm VCL control, so you only need to determine the ActiveX name, implementation unit name, project name, turn licensing on or off, turn version information on or off, and so on. After selecting OK, Delphi creates a type library with all the public and published properties, methods, and events of the TActiveForm class. Additionally, two source files are created—one for the Delphi Type Library information (such as interfaces, dispinterfaces, and so on), and the other is used to implement the interface methods defined in the first.

2. Add one or more visual or non-visual components to the ActiveForm.

3. Now add any custom properties, methods, or events. To do so, open up the type library (View, Type Library) and make any desired additions, select the Refresh button at the top, and let Delphi create the wrapper code for your additions.

4. Write any code for Get and Set methods that are either incomplete for the functionality desired or are blank due to additions to the type library. This also applies to any custom event handlers.

5. After the ActiveForm's functionality is complete, you probably will want to create one or more property pages to allow the user of your ActiveForm control the ability to right-click your control in environments that don't support the notion of an object inspector to change property values. There should at least be a general properties page. Delphi provides four standard property pages for colors, fonts, picture, and Delphi string lists.

6. Compile and register the control.

7. You can now import the new OCX file into any of the support environments in which a Delphi ActiveX Control can be used.

On the CD

Because the creation of an ActiveForm is so similar to that of an ActiveX Control, I am not going to walk through the creation of an ActiveForm. However, I have included on this book's companion CD-ROM an ActiveForm project that simply combines a TDBChart, a TTable, and a TCheckbox on an ActiveForm. The TDBChart control is connected to the Country sample table. The check box is simply to toggle the TDBChart control legend on or off.

This project is a simplistic example of how an ActiveForm can be used as entire single form application. The ActiveFormXControl project is in the \UDELPHI3\CHP21\ACTIVECHARTFORM folder of this book's companion CD-ROM. Simply load the project, compile it, and register it by selecting Run, Register ActiveX Server.

Web Deployment of ActiveX Controls and ActiveForms

After you have finished designing an ActiveX Control or ActiveForm, you can deploy it to your Web server. In order to deploy the ActiveX project, Web deployment compiler options must be set appropriately, and the project must be compiled. The general steps are outlined as follows:

1. Select Project, Web Deployment Options.

2. Set the Target Dir to the location on the Web server where the ActiveX Control or ActiveForm (.OCX) is to be placed. This can be a standard path name or a UNC path (such as \\SERVERMACHINE\OCX_FILES\ or S:\OCX_FILES\).

3. Set the Target URL to the location where a browser will need to look for the Active Control or ActiveForm (.OCX) file. This must be a valid Uniform Resource Locator (URL) that refers to your Web server (such as http://ServerMachine/). Don't include the name of the OCX itself.

4. Set the HTML Dir to the location where you want Delphi to put the test HTML file that contains a reference to the ActiveX Control or ActiveForm (.OCX). This can be a standard path name or a UNC path. This path usually is the same as the Target Dir path, unless the OCX files are kept in a different location on the Web server than the HTML files. Also, if you don't have a Web server, you can create a test directory and point to it by using the following format for the URL: **file:///c:\TestRoot**.

5. Choose OK.

6. Choose Project, Build All. This creates the ActiveX library (.OCX) that contains the ActiveX Control or ActiveForm.

7. Choose Project, Web Deploy. The ActiveX library (.OCX) is placed in the Target Dir of step 2. The HTML file is the same name as the project file but with an .HTM extension, and it is created in the HTML Dir of step 4. The HTML file contains an URL reference to the OCX at the location specified in step 3.

8. Invoke your Web browser and view the created HTML page.

When this HTML page is viewed in the Web browser, your form is displayed and runs as an embedded application within the browser.

Besides the preceding basic deployment issues, let's briefly cover some of the other deployment options.

Part
V

Ch
21

Using Runtime Packages

The most important of these is the deployment of runtime packages. If your ActiveX Control or ActiveForm uses packages, you will want to mark the Deploy required packages check box.

Using CAB Compression

Next you have the Use CAB file compression check box, which allows you to compress your ActiveX Control or ActiveForm and any additional required files, such as package DPLs or license files (.LIC). This is supported only on Internet Explorer 3.01. Currently, Netscape Navigator does support CAB files. By default, the ActiveX Control or ActiveForm, the packages (if any), and the additional files (again, if any) are compressed as three separate CAB files. It is possible to compress them all into one CAB file but this is not recommended. By having the CAB files separate, it prevents unnecessary downloads of files that are already on the browser's system.

Using Code Signing

If you want to code sign your ActiveX Control or ActiveForm project, you first must check the Code sign project check box, and then on the Code Signing tab of the Web Deployment Options dialog box:

```
have obtained a Software Publishing Certification file (.SPC)
    Private Key (.PVK)
```

N O T E   What is Code Signing? Microsoft's Internet Explorer 3.x has a technology incorporated into it known as Authenticode™ that allows Internet Explorer to show the user a software certificate of authenticity message when downloading executable code such as Internet install programs, ActiveX controls, and ActiveForms rather than the standard warning about using the software. Code signing is the process of getting a Digital ID from the VeriSign company (**www.verisign.com**) to get a custom Software Publishing Certification and a Private Key that are used to code sign all executables that your company distributes. By code signing, a software publisher can provide customers with the information and assurance they need when downloading software from the Internet.

There is no requirement that software publishers need to code sign their executables, but it promotes a more reliable way to have users download software from the Internet. For more information on obtaining a VeriSign Software Publisher Digital ID, visit VeriSign's Web site at **http://www.verisign.com**.

Important: Please note that enrollment is machine-specific. This means that you must register for your Authenticode Digital ID, pick up the Digital ID, and use the Digital ID on the same computer, using the same copy of Internet Explorer. If you want to use more than one machine for your Authenticode services, you need more than one Digital ID. If you install a new copy of Internet Explorer, you will need to re-enroll. ■

Putting It All Together

This chapter examined how Delphi 3 has made it easy for developers to create ActiveX Controls from existing VCL controls (`TWinControl` descendants). We also saw how `TGraphicControl` descendants can be made into ActiveX Controls as well.

In the first example, the PieX ActiveX Control, we covered the creation of property pages, which are especially useful for editing complex and/or non-exposed properties.

We then covered ActiveForms, which allow the developer a means to put together multiple visual and non-visual controls on a form in order to create a hybrid ActiveX Control. Finally, we wrap up with a discussion of how ActiveX Controls can be embedded within Web pages (currently supported only in Internet Explorer).

After reading this chapter, you will come to realize that there is no limit to what you can do with the Microsoft's ActiveX technology and the ease with which Delphi makes it to develop ActiveX. Almost every other technology in Delphi can be used within ActiveX Controls and ActiveForms. ●

Part
V

Ch
21

Advanced Topics

CHAPTER 22

Working with Graphics

by Joe C. Hecht

Back in the old DOS days, you were either limited to text output or had to go to great lengths to support graphics on a wide range of devices. Microsoft Windows made this job simpler by implementing an almost device-independent interface to the hardware. This interface is known as the Windows GDI, or Graphic Device Interface. The GDI is composed of graphic objects such as pens, brushes and fonts, and graphic functions to use these objects. Before Delphi and the VCL, a programmer had to deal with creating, using, and destroying those GDI objects. Often, programmers would forget to free some of these objects, leading to resource leaks that at times brought Windows to its knees. ∎

How to work with the *TCanvas* and *TPen* objects

These sections cover, respectively, using TCanvas and every aspect of creating standard, custom, and geometric Pens for your project.

How to work with the *TBrush* object

How to create brushes for your canvas.

How to work with the *TFont* object

Everything you ever wanted to know about using fonts under Windows, from simple assignments to creating custom fonts and learning how to set text like a pro.

How to work with the *TImage*, *TPicture*, and *TBitmap* object

This section covers working with images, including direct manipulation of the bitmap bits.

Advanced Windows graphics

Here, advanced graphic topics such as regions, metafiles, mapping modes, and threads are covered.

Working with *TCanvas* and *TPen* Objects

Delphi's TCanvas object encapsulates most GDI objects and drawing commands that your application will need for graphic output, making life a lot simpler. Although it is still possible to program the GDI directly in Delphi, most applications will be able to use the properties and methods of TPrinter to produce graphic output without ever having to deal directly with the GDI.

The TCanvas object is a property of most all graphic components in Delphi. The canvas is considered to be a drawing surface. This drawing surface has additional objects like pens, brushes and fonts to control the current drawing attributes, and methods to accomplish the actual output.

The most important properties of the TCanvas object are discussed in the following sections.

Handle

This is the handle to the Windows *Device context* (or *Dc*) of the surface on which you are drawing, and can be used whenever an HDC is required. This handle property is provided so you can directly call Windows GDI functions whenever you want to extend the drawing capabilities of TCanvas or to retrieve additional information about the canvas Dc. A quick example of where using this handle may be useful is to check to see if the device to which you are drawing is a color or monochrome device, as follows:

```
If GetDeviceCaps(Canvas.Handle, BITSPIXEL) *
   GetDeviceCaps(Canvas.Handle, NUMPLANES) > 1 then
  ThisIsAColorDevice = True;
```

Another good example of using the Canvas.Handle property is when you need to call a GDI function to draw something that is not supported by the supplied methods of the TCanvas. An example would be the Windows PolyPolygon() function. PolyPolygon means "many polygons" and is used to draw a single shape object consisting of many polygons put together. The real power of PolyPolygon() is its capability to have parts of the shape drawn transparently. One example of what this may be used for is rendering text shapes. Consider the letter "O," which is drawn as one shape, but by using two polygons. One polygon describes the outside of the "O," and the other describes the inside (or the hole). The inside of the "O" should be rendered transparently, something you cannot do by rendering the shape as two separate polygons, filling the outside polygon with black, and filling the inside polygon with white.

Here is an example of using the PolyPolygon() function to draw a hollow box:

```
procedure DrawPolyPolygon(Canvas : TCanvas);
var
  ptArray : array[0..9] of TPOINT;
  PtCounts : array[0..1] of integer;
begin
  PtArray[0] := Point(0,   0);
  PtArray[1] := Point(0,   40);
  PtArray[2] := Point(40,  40);
  PtArray[3] := Point(40,  0);
  PtArray[4] := Point(0,   0);
  PtCounts[0] := 5;
  PtArray[5] := Point(10, 10);
  PtArray[6] := Point(10, 30);
```

```
   PtArray[7] := Point(30, 30);
   PtArray[8] := Point(30, 10);
   PtArray[9] := Point(10, 10);
   PtCounts[1] := 5;
   Windows.PolyPolygon(Canvas.Handle,
                       PtArray,
                       PtCounts,
                       2);
end;


procedure TForm1.Button1Click(Sender: TObject);
begin
  DrawPolyPolygon(Form1.Canvas);
end;
```

We called the DrawPolyPolygon, passing the form's canvas to draw on to. The
DrawPolyPolygon() function then fills an array of points with the coordinates of the two polygons we want to fill, and an array of point counts, so the Windows PolyPolygon() function
knows how many elements in the point array belong to each polygon. We then call the Windows PolyPolygon() function passing the canvas's handle, the array of points, the array of
point counts, and the number of polygons. The resulting figure drawn will be a hollow box.

TPen

The Canvas.Pen property controls how shapes are outlined and lines are drawn. For each pen,
you may choose different widths, colors, styles, and drawing modes. Width is the most basic
setting and is used as follows:

```
Pen.Width := 10;
```

This code creates a pen that has a width of 10 units. Using Delphi's default mapping mode,
each unit translates to one pixel. You can set the width of a pen to zero, meaning the smallest
line that the device is capable of producing. This is useful when you are using other mapping
modes, where a width of 1 might translate into any arbitrary size the mapping mode allows.
Be aware that standard pen styles do not allow the width to scale arbitrarily in the x and y
direction.

The Canvas.Color property controls the color that a pen will use. You can use one of the predefined colors or assign your own color. It's worth noting that a pen's color will map to the
nearest pure color available on the system, unless the pen has the psInsideFrame style and is
more than one pixel wide.

Here are three examples of setting the pen's color:

```
Pen.Color := clRed;
```

```
Pen.Color := clInactiveCaption;
```

```
Pen.Color := TColor(RGB(133, 24, 83));
```

The first example uses one of the predefined colors. Delphi's predefined colors consist of the basic pure colors and the predefined Windows system colors that a user can set through the Windows Control Panel. The second example uses a user-defined system color to set the pen's color to the same color used on inactive window caption titles. The third example uses an *RGB* color. An RGB color is a mix of red, green, and blue. Each color value can range from 0 to 255, giving you a total of 16,777,216 colors you can mix. If the device supports the color you mixed, you will get it. If the device doesn't support the color, it will be mapped to the nearest pure color available, unless you have set the pen's style to be psInsideFrame and the pen's width is greater than one, in which case you get a dithered color where a pattern of red, green, and blue dots are combined to create the illusion of the requested color. You can test to see the nearest pure color to which a given color will map by using the Windows function GetNearestColor(). GetNearestColor() takes in an HDC and an RGB color, and then returns the nearest RGB color in the system's palette. You can call the function as follows:

```
var AColor : TColorRef;
begin
 AColor := GetNearestColor(Form1.Canvas.Handle,
                           RGB(133, 64, 22));
 Shape1.Pen.Color := TColor(AColor);
end;
```

There are several color conversion functions available from the Windows GDI. Some of the more useful include functions to retrieve the Red, Green, and Blue components of an RGB color: GetRValue(), GetGValue(), and GetBValue() and color conversion functions to get the RGB color of a palette index. Delphi also has some useful conversion functions such as ColorToRgb(), used to retrieve the RGB value of one of Delphi's predefined colors.

Changing the pen's style to psInsideFrame can affect the way the pen's color is rendered. There also are other pen styles you can use: The default style is psSolid, where the pen draws a solid line. The psClear style is the same as a Windows NULL_PEN, where the pen will make no marks. This can be useful for drawing shapes, where both the pen and the brush are used, and you want no outline. Other styles include patterns of dashes and dots, as shown in the following table:

Style	Result
psDash	The pen draws a line made up of a series of dashes.
psDot	The pen draws a line made up of a series of dots.
psDashDot	The pen draws a line made up of dashes and dots.
psDashDotDot	The pen draws a line made up of dash-dot-dot patterns.

The dash/dot patterns are defined by the driver and its resolution. The pattern you get on one device may not be the same on another. You may see drastic differences when you go to print. If you want complete consistency, you will need to roll up your sleeves and draw the patterns yourself.

The `psInsideFrame` style is worth revisiting. Like its name specifies, this style will draw an outline that is completely inside the shape you are drawing rather than on the edge of the shape. This setting closely emulates the way lines are rendered on Adobe PostScript printers.

The pen's `Mode` property specifies how both lines and fill patterns are combined with the drawing surface, and corresponds with the Windows ROP codes (Raster Operations). There are 16 predefined ROP codes available for non-bitmap graphic objects, as shown in the following table:

Style	Result
pmBlack	Always black
pmWhite	Always white
pmNop	Invisible
pmNot	Inverse of the underlying screen color
pmCopy	Color specified in the pen's color property
pmNotCopy	Inverse of pen color
pmMergePenNot	Combines pen color and inverse of screen
pmMaskPenNot	Combines colors common to both pen and inverse of screen
pmMergeNotPen	Combines screen color and inverse of pen color
pmMaskNotPen	Combines colors common to both screen and inverse of pen
pmMerge	Combines pen color and screen color
pmNotMerge	Inverse of pmMerge
pmMask	Combines colors common to both pen and screen
pmNotMask	Inverse of pmMask
pmXor	Combination of colors in either pen or screen, but not both
pmNotXor	Inverse of pmXor

The following code shows an example of using ROP codes. We will create a program that allows the user to draw a series of ellipses. We will set the pen's mode so as the user drags the mouse, a "rubber band" outline is created, showing the user what the ellipse will look like when he or she releases the mouse button. Due to the pen mode we have chosen (`pmNot`), the "rubber band" outline will erase itself at the last place it was drawn, and redraw itself as the mouse is moved around the screen. The "rubber band" outline will always be visible, no matter what the color is below, because the pen will draw in the inverse color of whatever is below it. This also allows you to quickly erase your "rubber band" by drawing over it a second time, because this will inverse what we already inversed, which gives you back your original image.

```
var
  StartPt : TPoint;
  EndPt   : TPoint;
  Capture : bool;
```

```
procedure TForm1.FormMouseDown(Sender: TObject; Button: TMouseButton;
  Shift: TShiftState; X, Y: Integer);
begin
  StartPt.X := X;
  StartPt.Y := Y;
  EndPt := StartPt;
  SetCapture(Form1.Handle);
  Capture := True;
  with Canvas do begin
    Pen.Mode := pmNot;
    Pen.Color := clBlack;
    Brush.Style := bsClear;
  end;
end;

procedure TForm1.FormMouseMove(Sender: TObject;
                               Shift: TShiftState;
                               X, Y: Integer);
begin
  if (Capture) and ((EndPt.X <> X) or (EndPt.Y <> Y)) then begin
    Canvas.Ellipse(StartPt.X, StartPt.Y, EndPt.X, EndPt.Y);
    Canvas.Ellipse(StartPt.X, StartPt.Y, X, Y);
    EndPt.X := X;
    EndPt.Y := Y;
  end;
end;

procedure TForm1.FormMouseUp(Sender: TObject;
                             Button: TMouseButton;
                             Shift: TShiftState;
                             X, Y: Integer);
begin
  ReleaseCapture;
  Capture := False;
  with Canvas do begin
    Ellipse(StartPt.X, StartPt.Y, EndPt.X, EndPt.Y);
    Pen.Mode := pmCopy;
    Brush.Color := clBlue;
    Brush.Style := bsSolid;
    Ellipse(StartPt.X, StartPt.Y, X, Y);
  end;
end;
```

The program logic works like this: When the user presses the mouse button, we captured all mouse input and remembered the x,y coordinate of the mouse in a variable named StartP, and initialize our EndPt variable. We then set the Pen and brush color so it draws an outline of our shape, and we set the pen's mode to pmNot so the pen would draw in the inverse of the colors below it. Now, whenever the mouse is moved (and we are capturing mouse input), we drew the shape twice: once in the old location to erase our "rubber band" outline and once to show our "rubber band" outline in its new location. We then remembered our new location by inputting the mouse's current x,y position in the EndPt variable. Finally, when the user releases the mouse button, we ended the mouse capture, erased the last "rubber band," and drew our shape in its final color.

Changing and Copying Pens   Don't make the mistake of incorrectly assigning Delphi's graphic objects by making statements like `ThisPen := ThatPen`. Although this statement may look okay, it's not. Instead, you should use the `Assign()` method as follows:

```
ThisPen.Assign(ThatPen)
```

Creating Extended Pens   `TPen` and its properties go a long way in assuring that you have the tools you need to easily program a great graphics application. If you need even more graphic horsepower, `TPen`'s handle property allows you to use any pen style that Windows is capable of using. Take the "Geometric" pens, for example, that are available under Win32. Unlike cosmetic pens, Geometric pens allow you to create pen styles with additional attributes not found in previous Windows versions, or through the attributes available from Delphi's `TPen` object. Examples of some of the additional attributes include setting the way lines join together and the way in which the ends of lines are finished off (capped). To use these new features, you need to create a Windows pen from scratch and assign the newly created pen's handle to the handle property of the canvas's pen.

The following code snippet demonstrates the difference between cosmetic and geometric pens:

```
procedure TForm1.Button1Click(Sender: TObject);
var
  lb : TLogBrush;
begin
  with Form1.Canvas do begin
   {draw a triangle with a cosmetic pen}
    Pen.Width := 10;
    Pen.Color := clRed;
    MoveTo(50, 50);
    LineTo(150, 50);
    LineTo(100, 150);
    LineTo(50, 50);
   {draw a triangle with a geometric pen}
    lb.lbStyle := BS_SOLID;
    lb.lbColor := RGB(255, 0, 0);
    lb.lbHatch := 0;
    Pen.Handle := ExtCreatePen(PS_GEOMETRIC or
                       PS_INSIDEFRAME or
                       PS_ENDCAP_SQUARE or
                       PS_JOIN_MITER,
                       10,
                       lb,
                       0,
                       nil);
    BeginPath(Handle);
    MoveTo(200, 50);
    LineTo(300, 50);
    LineTo(250, 150);
    LineTo(200, 50);
    CloseFigure(Handle);
    EndPath(Handle);
    StrokePath(Handle);
   {reset to a cosmetic pen}
```

```
      Pen.Width := 1;
      Pen.Color := clBlack;
    end;
  end;
```

In this example, we drew two triangles on the form's canvas. The first triangle is drawn with a normal (cosmetic) pen with a pen width of 10. The second triangle is drawn by using a geometric pen. When you run the program, notice that the first triangle's lines are connected with rounded edges, and the second triangle's lines are connected with mitered edges. Rounded edges are the default method that Windows uses for standard pens. The only way to change this behavior is to use geometric pens. To create a geometric pen, we first had to define a brush structure for the pen. Geometric pens are allowed to have a brush for a filling attribute for the line that is drawn. We called the Win32 ExtCreatePen() function, passing in our parameters for our requested pen, and assigning the function's result (an HPen) to the canvas's Pen.Handle property. We requested a pen style that includes the PS_ENDCAP_SQUARE and PS_JOIN_MITER styles. These styles request that all lines drawn will have square ends, and to create a miter joint where lines connect.

To use a geometric pen, you must use a path *sandwich*. Paths are available only under 32-bit windows, unless you are using a third-party library that supports paths under 16-bit Windows. To use paths, you must make a call to the Windows BeginPath() function before you draw anything, and then call the Windows EndPath() when you are finished describing a path. Then you make a stroke (outline), fill, or even fill and stroke your path. To make a closed shape connect correctly with your linejoin style, you need to call the Windows CloseFigure() function. This ensures that the shape will be closed using the linejoin style, rather than using the linecap style.

Note that not all drawing functions are available when using paths under Windows 95, and not all of Delphi's drawing methods will work when using paths under any 32-bit platform. You may want to look at the documentation for the Windows BeginPath() function for an up-to-date listing of compatible functions.

After you are finished using a Geometric pen, you should set the Canvas's pen back to a cosmetic pen.

TBrush

Delphi's TBrush object encapsulates a standard Windows brush object, and is used for filling solid shapes such as rectangles and polygons. Brushes come in four varieties: hollow, solid, hatched, and bitmap. Hollow brushes are equivalent to a Windows NULL_BRUSH and allow the shape to fill transparently, rendering only the outline of the shape with the chosen pen. Solid brushes fill the shape in a solid color, and hatched brushes fill the shape with a hatching pattern. Finally, bitmap brushes fill the shape with repeating patterns by using the bitmap that you supply.

As previously mentioned, solid brushes take in a color, and setting this property is as easy as setting the color property of a pen:

```
Brush.Color := clRed;
```

or

```
Brush.Color := TColor(RGB(255, 0, 0));
```

Using a hatched brush is almost as easy, as follows:

```
Brush.Style := bsBDiagonal;
```

There are six predefined hatch styles:

Style	Result
bsHorizontal	Horizontal hatching pattern
bsVertical	Vertical hatching pattern
bsFDiagonal	45-degree upward left-to-right hatching pattern
bsBDiagonal	45-degree downward left-to-right hatching pattern
bsCross	Horizontal and vertical crosshatch pattern
bsDiagCross	45-degree crosshatch pattern

Note that the hatching pattern's background is transparent, which means that anything located under what you are drawing will show through. You can change this by setting the background color to the color between the hatch marks, and setting the background mode from transparent to opaque, as follows:

```
procedure TForm1.FormPaint(Sender: TObject);
begin
  with Canvas do begin
    Brush.Style := bsHorizontal;
    Brush.Color := clRed;
    SetBkColor(Handle, RGB(0, 0, 255));
    SetBkMode(Handle, OPAQUE);
    Rectangle(0, 0, Form1.Width, Form1.Height);
  end;
end;
```

In this example, we requested a horizontal hatching pattern to be drawn in red. We set the background color to blue, and the background mode to opaque so the GDI would use the background color. We then paint the background of our form with our brush.

Hatched brushes are made from 8-by-8 pixel bitmaps, so it makes sense that you should be able to create your own brush from a bitmap, and you can! Just try the following code, substituting the correct path to your bitmap in the line that contains the `Bitmap.LoadFromFile()` method, as follows:

```
procedure TForm1.FormPaint(Sender: TObject);
var
  Bitmap: TBitmap;
begin
```

```
    Bitmap := TBitmap.Create;
    try
      Bitmap.LoadFromFile('c:\Borland\Delphi2.0\
                              Images\Icons\Earth16.bmp');
      Form1.Canvas.Brush.Bitmap := Bitmap;
      Form1.Canvas.FillRect(Rect(0, 0, Form1.Width, Form1.Height));
    finally
      Form1.Canvas.Brush.Bitmap := nil;
      Bitmap.Free;
    end;
end;
```

In this example, we create a bitmap object, and attempt to load a bitmap from a file. We assign the bitmap to the Brush's bitmap property, and then fill the form with the repeating pattern. When we are done, we set the brush's bitmap property to nil, and free the bitmap. It is necessary to do this because Delphi will not free this resource for you. Note that only the first eight pixels of the first eight rows of a given bitmap will be used. It's also worth noting that an 8-by-8 pattern may look great on a low resolution monitor, but will turn into an indistinguishable blob at the higher resolutions used by printers.

You also may create a brush by using Windows GDI functions and assign the handle of the newly created brush to the `Canvas.Brush.Handle` property, as follows:

```
procedure TForm1.Button1Click(Sender: TObject);
begin
  with Form1.Canvas do begin
    Form1.Canvas.Brush.Handle :=
        CreateHatchBrush(HS_BDIAGONAL,
                           RGB(255, 0, 0));
    Rectangle(0, 0, Form1.Width, Form1.Height);
  end;
end;
```

Although this example is more difficult than simply setting the brush's style, it illustrates how to use one of the many brush creation functions available under Windows.

It's worth noting that brushes are aligned to the client area of a given Window. If you do not like the alignment of a pattern, you are free to change the brush's origin by calling the Windows function `SetBrushOrgEx()` right before you set your font handle. Note that setting the brush origin with a Delphi brush is not supported. You will need to create your own brush and assign the handle to the `Canvas.Brush.Handle` property to make this happen.

Here is an example of changing the origin of a hatched brush:

```
procedure TForm1.Button1Click(Sender: TObject);
var
  org : TPoint;
begin
  with form1.canvas do begin
    Form1.Canvas.Brush.Handle :=
        CreateHatchBrush(HS_BDIAGONAL,
                           RGB(255, 0, 0));
    Rectangle(0, 0, Form1.Width div 2, Form1.Height);
    SetBrushOrgEx(Handle, 0, 6, Org);
```

```
    Form1.Canvas.Brush.Handle :=
       CreateHatchBrush(HS_BDIAGONAL,
                             RGB(255, 0, 0));
    Rectangle(Form1.Width div 2, 0, Form1.Width, Form1.Height);
  end;
end;
```

We start by creating a hatched brush and drawing a rectangle that fills half the form. We then change the brush origin, and now must create a second brush that will have the new pattern at the given offset. You may move a brush's origin in both the x and y direction by up to seven pixels. It's worth noting that brush patterns on child windows may not align properly to their parent under Windows 95, and you may want to account for this. Luckily, this problem doesn't exist under Windows NT, where the system automatically adjusts all brush origins.

TFont

Working with fonts used to be a major headache before the developers of Delphi made font selection so easy with the TFont object. You will find the TFont class neatly encapsulated into the properties of many visual controls and the TCanvas object. Changing the attributes of a font has never been easier, and selecting fonts is a snap with TFontDialog.

Here is an example of using the TFontDialog component to select the font used in a button caption:

```
procedure TForm1.Button1Click(Sender: TObject);
begin
  FontDialog1.Font.Assign(Button1.Font);
  if FontDialog1.Execute then
    Button1.Font.Assign(FontDialog1.Font);
end;
```

In the first line, we assign the FontDialog's font property to equal the button's font, so the FontDialog will display the current font. If the FontDialog successfully executes, and the user doesn't press Cancel, we assign the font returned by the FontDialog to the Button.Font.

TFontDialog has several interesting option properties, which are described in Table 22.1.

Table 22.1 *TFontDialog* Option Properties

Value	Meaning
fdAnsiOnly	Displays fonts with the Ansi Charset only.
FdApplyButton	Displays an Apply button in the dialog box. This button will automatically appear if the OnApply event has been assigned.
FdEffects	Displays the Color list box in the dialog box, and allows the user to select strikeout or underlined text attributes.

continues

Table 22.1   Continued

Value	Meaning
FdFixedPitchOnly	Displays only monospaced (fixed-width) fonts.
FdForceFontExist	Allows the user to enter only valid font names in the dialog's edit box.
FdLimitSize	The dialog box uses the MinFontSize and MaxFontSize properties to select fonts and sizes.
FdNoFaceSel	The dialog box will not automatically select the font name in the dialog's Font combo box when the dialog box appears.
FdNoOEMFonts	The dialog box does not display vector fonts.
FdScalableOnly	The dialog box displays only scalable fonts.
FdNoSimulations	The dialog box will not display simulated font styles.
FdNoSizeSel	The dialog box will not automatically select the size in the dialog's Size combo box.
FdNoStyleSel	The dialog box will not automatically select the style in the dialog's Style combo box.
FdNoVectorFonts	Same as fdNoOEMFonts.
FdShowHelp	A help button appears in the dialog box.
FdTrueTypeOnly	The dialog box only displays TrueType fonts.
FdWysiwyg	The dialog box displays only the fonts that are available to both the printer and the screen.

It's worth noting that like the fdWysiwyg option, the TFontDialog's device property also specifies if the FontDialog should display a font for the screen, for the printer, or both. As of this writing, none of the options for specifying printer fonts works under Delphi. If you want the dialog box to list printer fonts, you need to call the Windows ChooseFont common dialog box yourself, rather than using Delphi's wrapper. Please note that if the printer supports graphics at all, selecting the fdTrueTypeOnly option should always work, providing the user didn't disable TrueType fonts.

You can check to see if TrueType fonts are available on the system by making a call to the Windows GetRasterizerCaps() function, as follows:

```
procedure TForm1.Button1Click(Sender: TObject);
var
  rs : TRasterizerStatus;
begin
  if GetRasterizerCaps(rs, sizeof(rs)) then
    if ((rs.wFlags and TT_AVAILABLE = TT_AVAILABLE) and
```

```
        (rs.wFlags and TT_ENABLED = TT_ENABLED)) then
      ShowMessage('TrueType is available on this system');
end;
```

If you want, you can also create your own font dialog box, and populate a listbox of font names using the `Screen.Fonts` or `Printer.Fonts` string lists, or both, as follows:

```
ListBox1.Items := Screen.Fonts;
```

You also could preset a list of sizes from which the user can choose. Traditionally, type sizes are measured in printer points. In today's time, printer points are defined as 1/72", as measured by the "EM" square of the font. An "EM" square comes from the days when type was set by hand and was made from blocks of lead, and is the size of the block that would enclose a capital letter "M." The block is a little bigger than the "M," but doesn't include any additional line spacing, and doesn't take into account descending letters such as a lowercase "j." This is why when you measure a font's point size against a capital letter, it doesn't exactly match the size you specify, but still, it is the correct size.

Traditionally, line spacing is called "leading" (pronounced like the metal lead), and was the term used when strips of lead where placed between the lines of type to increase the space between lines. Delphi has two different properties to set the size of a font: `Font.Size` and `Font.Height`. If you specify the font's size using the `Font.Size` property, the font is scaled to match the size you specify in printer points. If you use the `Font.Height` property, the font is scaled in pixels. If you specify the height as a positive value, the font's external leading is included in the calculation. If you specify a negative value, the font's external leading is not included in the calculation. Note that it is possible that either the height or size property of the font may be returned as a negative value. You can always use the "absolute" function `Abs()` to turn any given number to a positive value. In other words, if the font's height is –15, then `Abs(Font.Height)` will return 15, and if the font's height is 15, then `Abs(Font.Height)` will also return 15.

If you are interested in how to set the font's height property to reflect points, you can use the following code to do this:

```
FontSizeInPoints := 72;
Font.Height := -Round((GetDeviceCaps(Form1.Canvas.Handle,
                                     LOGPIXELSY) / 72) * FontSizeInPoints);
```

This formula is handy when you want to create a font yourself, and set the font's height in points, something we will do a little later in the chapter. Other font properties include those shown in the following paragraphs.

Font.Color This property sets the font's color, and can be set like any other VCL color property. Note that like pens, font colors map to the nearest pure color, and the background color and background mode affects text in how the text is shown. When you set the canvas's background mode to opaque, the background color is used. If you set the background mode to transparent, the background color is ignored.

Here is an example of setting the background color and mode of a TCanvas:

```
with Form1.Canvas do begin
  SetBkColor(Handle, RGB(0,255,0));
  SetBkMode(Handle, OPAQUE);
  TextOut(50, 50, 'Hello');
end;
```

Font.Name   You are free to assign the font's name property, as follows:

```
Font.Name := 'Arial';
```

Font.Style   With this property, you get your chance to assign bold, italic, underline, and strikeout attributes to the font. If the font doesn't support one of the attributes, the GDI may be able to synthesize the attribute; otherwise, the GDI may substitute a different font. Here is an example of setting the font to have all the attributes possible:

```
Font.Style := [fsBold, fsItalic, fsUnderline, fsStrikeout];
```

If desired, you can leave out the attributes you do not want.

Font.Pitch   This property allows you to select a monospaced or a variable-width font. A monospaced font has characters that all have the same width, and are handy for aligning columns of data. The Courier font family is a good example of a monospaced font, and the Times family is a good example of a variable-width font. The different attributes possible are described in the following table:

Attribute	Description
fpDefault	The pitch is set to the default value.
fpFixed	The pitch is fixed. All characters in the font will have the same width.
fpVariable	The pitch is variable. The characters in the font will have variable widths.

Again, if the font does not support the attribute you choose, then the GDI may substitute a different font in its place.

Font.Charset   This property is new in Delphi 3.0, and it is easy enough to use. You may assign the Charset property to any valid Windows character set as follows:

```
Font.Charset := ANSI_CHARSET;
```

> **CAUTION**
> Beware: The font mapper may decide to substitute a different font if the character set you assign is not available for the font you specify.

Font.Handle   Here is your chance to go really nuts in specifying the exact attributes of a font. You can specify almost any attribute you want, including font rotation. The idea here is to use one of the Windows GDI commands to create a font to your liking, and then assign the font handle to the `TFonts.Handle` property. To do this, you need to fill out a `TLogFont` structure and call the Windows `CreateFontIndirect()` function.

If you want to use the current font as a starting place, you can retrieve a `TLogFont` structure from the current font, using the Windows `GetObject()` function, make your desired changes to the structure, and then create your new font. It's worth noting that simply replacing the font's handle on a VCL component doesn't always work well. It's much better to create a new `TFont` that isn't currently associated with a control, make your changes, and then assign the font to the control.

Here is an example of creating a font that is rotated 45 degrees:

```
procedure TForm1.Button1Click(Sender: TObject);
var
  lf : TLogFont;
  tf : TFont;
begin
  tf := TFont.Create;
  tf.Assign(Button1.Font);
  GetObject(tf.Handle, sizeof(lf), @lf);
  lf.lfEscapement := 450;
  lf.lfOrientation := 450;
  tf.Handle := CreateFontIndirect(lf);
  Button1.ParentFont := false;
  Button1.Font.Assign(tf);
  tf.Free;
end;
```

In this example, we create a new `TFont` and assign the current font of the button to the new `TFont`. This copies all the font attributes of the button's font to the new `TFont`. We then call the Windows `GetObject()` function to retrieve the logical font structure of the new `TFont`. Then we change the escapement and orientation members of the logical font structure to rotate the font 45 degrees, by specifying the angles in 1/10 of a degree.

Now we create a new font based on the logical font structure by using the Windows GDI command `CreateFontIndirect()`. The value passed back will be a Windows font handle that we assign to our `TFont`. Finally, we set the button's ParentFont to False, so the button will no longer inherit its font property from the form's font, and assign our new `TFont` to the Button's font, and free our `TFont`. Be aware that the font you choose to rotate must be "rotatable," and not all are. I suggest using a TrueType font because they can always be rotated.

There are many attributes to choose from when creating your own fonts. You can find a long list of available attributes by searching the Delphi Help system for `LogFont`. Be aware that the Windows font mapper will not always choose a font that matches your request because the font mapper chooses a font based on a weighted average of the attributes that you specify. Some attributes will be more important than others when the font mapper is considering your request.

Getting More Font Information

When rendering text, one of the most important bits of information you need to know is how much space a given string will require in a given font. Delphi has two methods to return this information to you at runtime: `Canvas.TextWidth` and `Canvas.TextHeight`. Both of these methods are wrappers to the Windows function `GetTextExtentPoint()`.

If you really want a lot of information about a given font, try the Windows `GetTextMetrics()` function. With `GetTextMetrics()`, you can get the valid range of characters in the font, the font type (TrueType, Device, Vector, and so on), and even the default break character the font uses.

If you plan to do a lot of calculations based on the character widths of a font and speed is important, you may want to try the Windows `GetCharWidth()` function to retrieve an array of character widths for the font, rather than calling the Canvas's `TextWidth` method. Note that there may be other factors involved in calculating the width of a given string, including extra character spacing, kerning pairs, and justification values. If you plan to go this route, you may want to carefully set each character's placement by using the Windows `ExtTextOut()` function. This handy "all-purpose" text-setting function allows you to supply an array that contains the relative x coordinates of each letter in the string.

Here is an example of retrieving both the text metrics and character widths for the form's currently selected font, and outputting the list of character codes and their associated widths to a memo component. Additionally, the example sets a line of text on the form's canvas, using an additional 10 units of spacing between each character.

```
type TIntArray = array[0..0] of integer;

procedure TForm1.Button1Click(Sender: TObject);
var
  tm : TTextMetric;
  widths : Array[0..255] of integer;
  PNewWidths : ^TIntArray;
  i : integer;
begin
  if GetTextMetrics(Form1.Canvas.Handle, tm) then begin
    GetCharWidth(Form1.Canvas.Handle,
                 0,
                 255,
                 widths);
    for i := ord(tm.tmFirstChar) to ord(tm.tmLastChar) do
      Memo1.Lines.Add( IntToStr(i) + ' ' + IntToStr(widths[i]));
  end;
  if Length(Edit1.Text) > 0 then begin
    GetMem(PNewWidths, sizeof(integer) * length(Edit1.Text));
    for i := 0 to (length(Edit1.Text)-1) do
      PNewWidths^[i] := Widths[ord(pchar(Edit1.Text)[i])] + 10;
    Windows.ExtTextOut(Form1.Canvas.Handle,
                       100,
                       200,
                       0,
                       nil,
```

```
                  pchar(Edit1.Text),
                  length(Edit1.Text),
                  @PNewWidths^[0]);
    FreeMem(PNewWidths, sizeof(integer) * length(Edit1.Text));
  end;
end;
```

In this example, we first declare a new array type named TIntArray that has enough room to hold one integer. We do this to allow us to dynamically allocate an array of integers at runtime, and access all the array's elements without knowing at compile time how many elements really exist. This bit of "magic" is necessary to trick the compiler into allowing access to the additional elements of the array, without generating a compile-time error, something that "C" programmers take for granted. For this trick to work, you must satisfy the following three requirements:

1. The array must be accessed through a pointer variable.
2. Range checking must be turned off.
3. You must access array indices through a variable.

If the last requirement is not clear to you, consider the following line of code:

```
MyIntegerArray^[2] := 10;
```

This line of code will not compile because our array is clearly defined as having only one element starting at an index of zero, and the compiler will catch the error. On the other hand, if you access the index through a variable, the compiler will be happy:

```
i := 2;
MyIntegerArray^[i] := 10;
```

The only gotchas to watch for here to make sure that you allocated enough memory so that the element you are accessing really exists; otherwise, your program may crash, and range checking must be turned off or you will get a runtime error. Finally, you must access the array through a pointer variable, or the compiler will definitely give you an error.

In the var section of the code, we declared a TTextMetric structure, an array of integers to hold the character widths, a pointer to an integer array to hold the new widths used to set our string, and a loop variable named i.

We then call the GetTextMetrics() function to retrieve the font's text metrics, and the GetCharWidth() function to retrieve the font's character widths. Notice how we ask for the entire range of characters, possibly even requesting invalid characters. Note that each font has a default character that gets substituted whenever an invalid character is requested. The GetCharWidth() function will fill in the widths of invalid characters with the width of the default character. We then use the tm.tmFirstChar and the tm.tmLastChar members of the text metric structure to display all the valid character codes of the font along with their associated widths in a memo component.

Now, for the fun part. We will use the Windows function ExtTextOut() to image a string from an Edit control onto the form's canvas, using 10 extra units of space between each character.

Although I chose to add 10 units of additional space between characters, you can use any formula you want to achieve the desired results.

In this section of code, we first check to make sure that the edit control is not empty. If there are characters in the edit control, we proceed to dynamically allocate enough memory to hold our new widths: one element for each character. We then loop through the characters in the edit control, retrieving the correct width for each letter, adding 10, and assigning the result back to our dynamically allocated array. Finally, we can make a call to the Windows ExtTextOut() function, passing the form's Canvas.Handle property, the x and y positions to set the text, the string to set, and our new array of character widths. Last but not least, we free the memory that we allocated for the new array.

This example demonstrated a brute force technique to control each character's exact placement, without having to incur the overhead of setting each character separately. If this seems like too much trouble, there are many other Windows functions available for you to use to get information and perform changes to the orientation, alignment, and spacing of your output string. Here is a list of some of the more useful functions:

```
DrawText()

GetKerningPairs()

GetTextAlign()

SetTextAlign()

GetTextCharacterExtra()

SetTextCharacterExtra()

SetTextJustification()

TabbedTextOut()
```

These functions are well-documented in the Win32 section of Delphi's help system, and can be a real lifesaver when you need the ultimate in controlling text settings. An example of using the SetTextAlign() function also can be found in the printing chapter, shown later in the book. Finally, if you want a really simple method to set text into a rectangular area, complete with word breaks, and you don't mind losing a little control in the process, you can use the Windows function DrawText().

Here is an example:

```
procedure TForm1.Button1Click(Sender: TObject);
var
  r : TRect;
begin
  if length(Edit1.Text) = 0 then exit;
  r.Top := 50;
  r.Left := 50;
  r.Right := 150;
  r.Bottom := 150;
  DrawText(Form1.Canvas.Handle,
```

```
        pChar(Edit1.Text),
        length(Edit1.Text),
        r,
        DT_WordBreak or DT_Left);
end;
```

In this example, we will set the text contained in the exit control onto the form's canvas using the Windows `DrawText()` function. If the edit control is empty, we will exit out of the procedure, else we will define a format rectangle to set the text into, and call the `DrawText()` function, requesting that the text be left-justified, and that new lines are inserted at word boundaries as necessary for the text to fit into the left and right boundaries of the format rectangle.

Many additional options are available that can be passed to the `DrawText()` function, making it one of the more useful text-setting functions available in Windows. One of my favorites is DT_CALCRECT. This option comes in handy when you want to know the size of the rectangle required to display the text in the requested style, without actually setting the text, making it very easy to calculate the required space for a text block.

TImage

If a picture is worth a thousand words, then Delphi's implementation of images is worth an entire book. Fortunately, the designers of Delphi made dealing with images so easy, the subject is covered in a small section of a chapter!

Back in the days before Delphi, working with images was a struggle that required the use of study guides and tutorials from Microsoft just to reliably load and save a bitmapped image to and from the disk. Back in those days, a good, reliable image unit might have required a thousand lines of code or more to achieve what the designers of Delphi have reduced to two simple methods—`LoadFromFile()` and `SaveToFile()`.

Here is an example of using the `TImage` component to load a bitmap from a file, draw to it, and then save the image back out to the disk:

```
begin
  Image1.Picture.LoadFromFile('c:\somepath\some.bmp');
  Image1.Canvas.Ellipse(0, 0, 50, 50);
  Image1.Picture.SaveToFile('c:\somepath\some.bmp');
end;
```

The `Image` component has several interesting properties, such as a canvas to draw on, an Autosize property that will cause the image component to resize itself to fit the picture, a stretch property to cause the picture to resize itself to the image component, and a center property to cause the picture to be displayed in the center of the image component. The most important property of the `TImage` component is the `Picture` property.

TPicture

A TPicture object can contain a bitmap, metafile, icon, or even encapsulate a user-defined graphic object. This component makes short work of loading and saving graphic objects to disk and clipboard. It's worth noting that saving a graphic to the clipboard once was a chore. Now, you simply need to add two lines of code to your application, and you are done!

Here is an example of saving a graphic to the clipboard:

```
uses Clipbrd;

procedure TForm1.Button1Click(Sender: TObject);
begin
  Clipboard.Assign(Image1.Picture);
end;
```

Here is an example of loading a graphic from the clipboard:

```
procedure TForm1.Button1Click(Sender: TObject);
begin
  Image1.Picture.Assign(Clipboard);
end;
```

You also can pass the Graphic property of a TPicture as a parameter to a canvas's Draw() or StretchDraw() method to render the picture onto a canvas as follows:

```
procedure TForm1.Button1Click(Sender: TObject);
begin
  Form1.Canvas.Draw(300, 100, Image1.Picture.Graphic);
end;
```

TBitmap

The TBitmap component encapsulates both a Windows bitmap object and its associated palette, if it has one. Like the TPicture component, TBitmap also has methods for loading and saving a bitmap to and from the disk and clipboard. In fact, TPicture calls these methods in TBitmap to load and store the bitmapped image. Another great place to store bitmaps is in a resource file. Resource files get linked in with your application at compile time, and will embed the bitmap into your application's executable file, making it a snap to deploy your application, because you don't have to worry about shipping and installing additional files.

You can build a resource file with the Borland Resource Workshop, which ships with Borland's RAD pack, or you can use the Borland Resource Command Line Compiler (BRCC32) that ships with Delphi. The Resource Workshop is a full-blown resource editor, capable of creating, editing, and embedding both 16- and 32-bit resource files from a number of sources, including .RC files, executables, DLLs, drivers, vbxes, cpls, fonts, bitmaps, icons, cursors, user-defined resources, and so on. Although most of the RAD pack is geared to 16-bit development, the Resource Workshop 4.5 that ships with the RAD Pack makes this tool a wise investment for anyone who wants to work with resources.

The next example is using BRCC32.EXE, the command-line resource compiler that ships with Delphi. You can find the executable located in Delphi's \Bin directory.

First, create an ASCII text named **TEST.RC** in your project directory, containing the following single line:

```
MYBITMAP BITMAP "c:\download\some.bmp"
```

Here we are telling the resource compiler that we want to create a bitmap resource that contains the bitmap from the file test.bmp, and we want to refer to the bitmap resource by the name, MYBITMAP.

Now, create a bitmap file, and name it **SOME.BMP**.

Finally, compile the .RC file by giving the complete path to both the command-line compiler and the .rc file in your project directory (substituting the correct paths for your system):

```
c:\borland\delphi\bin\brcc32.exe c:\download\test.rc
```

If all goes well, you now should have a new binary file named TEST.RES in your project's directory that you can link into your program by adding one simple line to your code:

```
{$R TEST.RES}
```

You can locate this line of code almost anywhere in your program, but I prefer to place it right under the line {$R *.DFM}, located in the implementation section of a given unit. It's worth noting that, unlike other declarations in the implementation section, resources will be "visible" from anywhere in your program.

Now for the fun part. To use your new resource, simply call the LoadFromResource() method of the TBitmap object, as follows:

```
procedure TForm1.Button1Click(Sender: TObject);
begin
  Image1.Picture.Bitmap.LoadFromResourceName(hInstance, 'MYBITMAP');
end;
```

Wasn't that easy? Notice how we passed our instance variable hInstance to the LoadFromResourceName method. This is to identify the module from which to load the resource. Resources can be loaded from a number of sources, including dynamic link libraries (DLLs). In fact, many dynamic link libraries contain only resources, making it a snap to localize applications for a given market, simply by installing a different DLL. A good example of a resource-only DLL is the MORICONS.DLL file that ships with Windows. This DLL is chock full of great little icons you can use to customize your desktop.

There are many useful properties and methods associated with the TBitmap object, the Create method being one of the most useful.

A good example of where you may want to create a bitmap on-the-fly is to save a canvas object to the disk. Although many components have a canvas property, few have a SaveToDisk() method. The TPaintBox component is one such component. Although TPaintBox goes a long way in helping you add a painting window to your application, it has no method to save the output to a file. Here is a great opportunity to create a new bitmap, transfer the user's output on the PaintBox canvas to the bitmap, and save it to disk. Here is an example of a form with a paintbox that allows the user to "doodle" with his or her mouse. When the user presses the button on the form, we will save the "doodle" to the disk:

```
procedure TForm1.PaintBox1MouseMove(Sender: TObject;
Shift: TShiftState;
X, Y: Integer);
begin
  if ssLeft in Shift then
    Paintbox1.Canvas.Pixels[x,y] := clBlack;
end;

procedure TForm1.Button1Click(Sender: TObject);
var
  Bitmap : TBitmap;
  r : TRect;
begin
  r.Left := 0;
  r.Top := 0;
  r.Right := PaintBox1.Width;
  r.Bottom := PaintBox1.Height;
  Bitmap := TBitmap.Create;
  Bitmap.Width := r.Right;
  Bitmap.Height := r.Bottom;
  Bitmap.Canvas.CopyRect(r, Paintbox1.Canvas, r);
  Bitmap.SaveToFile('c:\download\paintbox.bmp');
  Bitmap.Free;
end;
```

All that was required for this simple paint program was to attach some code to the PaintBox's MouseMove event that paints black dots in the paintbox if the left mouse button is pressed. To save the painting, we simply define a rectangle to be the size of the PaintBox, create a bitmap on-the-fly, size the bitmap, and use the CopyRect() method to copy the image from the PaintBox's canvas to the bitmap's canvas. Finally, we save the image to the disk and free the bitmap.

DIB Bits and Direct Access

Delphi 3 has added a great new property to the TBitmap object: a pointer to the bitmap bits. Although previous versions of Delphi used *device-dependent bitmaps* (DDBs), Delphi 3 uses *device-independent bitmaps* (DIBs). Getting the pointer to the DIB bits is easy, just access the Bitmap.DibMemory property. Here is an example for accessing the DIB memory, and changing the pixels of the first scan line to be equal to the first color in the palette. Note: This code is designed for a 256-color bitmap with a palette. For other formats, you need to adapt your code to deal with differing numbers of bits per pixel, palettes, compression, and so on.

```
Type TByteArray = Array[0..0] of byte;

procedure TForm1.Button1Click(Sender: TObject);
var
```

```
  p : ^TByteArray;
  i : integer;
begin
  Image1.Picture.LoadFromFile('C:\DOWNLOAD\TEST.BMP');
  p := Image1.Picture.Bitmap.DibMemory;
  for i := 0 to (Image1.Picture.Bitmap.Width -1) do
    p^[i] := 0;
end;
```

In this example, we define a byte array type, a pointer variable to a `ByteArray`, and a looping variable called `i`. We then load a bitmap from the disk, and retrieve the pointer to the `DibMemory`. Finally, we loop through the first scan line of the DIB Memory, changing the color to equal the first color in the DIB's palette.

DIBs versus DDBs   As previously mentioned, earlier versions of Delphi used device-dependent bitmaps (DDBs) to store bitmaps in memory. Delphi 3 is capable of storing the bitmap in memory using either DDBs or Device-Independent Bitmaps (DIBs). Delphi 3 uses DIBs as a default, but you are free to convert back and forth by setting the `Bitmap.HandleType` property to either bmDIB or bmDDB. Note that some color information may be lost during the conversion.

Transparency   The Windows 95 system has made it so easy to deal with transparent images through the `TImageList` component that it's hardly worth mentioning, except to point you in the right direction. Although you are still free to use lower-level Windows functions and ROP Codes, using the `TImageList` component is such a breeze, it's hardly worth the bother. In fact, even the `Cavas.Brush` copy method is provided only for backward compatibility.

Regions

The Windows GDI has certainly come a long way in the area of regions (no pun intended). Regions allow you to create a clipping area in almost any shape you can imagine; then, anything you draw will get clipped (or masked) to that area. Under 16-bit Windows, regions commonly caused many hard-to-trace problems related to the Windows GDI heap, overflowing as the shapes where scan converted to line segments. Running under Windows 95, this problem has been drastically reduced and under Windows NT this problem has all but disappeared. Although Delphi doesn't have any methods related to setting clipping regions, you are still able to create them using the Windows GDI. Here is an example of creating an elliptic region using GDI commands:

```
procedure TForm1.Button1Click(Sender: TObject);
var
  MyRgn : hRgn;
  OldRgn : hRgn;
begin
  MyRgn := CreateEllipticRgn(0,0,100,100);
  OldRgn := SelectObject(Form1.Canvas.Handle, MyRgn);
  PatBlt(Form1.Canvas.Handle,
```

```
            0,0,
            Form1.Width,
            Form1.Height,
            blackness);
    SelectObject(Form1.Canvas.Handle, OldRgn);
    DeleteObject(MyRgn);
end;
```

In this example, we first define two region variables—one to hold the handle to the region we will create, and the other to hold the handle to the form's region we are replacing, because we will want to restore it when we are done. We start the code by creating an elliptic region, and selecting it into the form's canvas. Select object returns a handle to the previously selected region for us to store back for later use. To "prove" our elliptic region really works, we draw a back square that covers the entire form; however, only the ellipse will paint. Finally, we select the old region back into the canvas, and destroy the region we created.

Regions are handy, and when combined with paths, give you all the power you need to create some spectacular effects. There are many region functions available for performing all kinds of operations, from turning a path into a region, to checking if a point exists inside of a region (useful for hit testing).

Metafiles

The Windows metafile is a collection of Windows GDI output functions that can be saved to the disk or clipboard, and quickly replayed to a canvas. Because metafiles store actual GDI output calls, they usually are much smaller than a bitmap; they can also be scaled to almost any size without losing the details. Although the Windows metafile goes a long way toward device independence, there are a few things to watch out for:

- Clipping regions do not always scale well in a metafile.
- Text doesn't always scale or align well in a metafile.
- A metafile canvas does not always return canvas information correctly.

The TMetafile component encapsulates a Windows Metafile. As of this writing, there are three metafile formats used in Windows: Standard, Aldus, and Enhanced. The standard Windows metafile was the original and it had a problem that, when you loaded the metafile from the disk, there was no information on how to scale it without reading through the entire metafile record by record, and calculating whatever scaling factors would be necessary to display the image. The Aldus metafile helped solve this problem, by adding a 22-byte header to the file, containing the information needed to accurately display the image. Many programs now export metafiles using the Aldus header, and most programs, including Delphi, refuse to load a metafile that doesn't contain this header information. Finally, there is the Enhanced metafile format (EMF) that contains both internal scaling information, and supports the additional drawing functions available under Windows NT. It's worth noting that not all drawing functions available under Windows NT are available under Windows 95; however, Windows 95 is documented as being able to accurately render any metafile created under Windows NT. Go figure!

Displaying a metafile is quite easy with Delphi. You can simply drop a TImage component onto your form, and either load the metafile through the object inspector, or load it dynamically by using the TImage.LoadFromFile() method.

Drawing with the TMetafile is a little different than drawing to a TBitmap canvas. You first must create a metafile object, and then you must create a MetafileCanvas before drawing to the metafile. When you are through drawing, you must free the MetafileCanvas and only then can you save your drawing to a file, the clipboard, or play it to another canvas.

Here is an example:

```
procedure TForm1.Button1Click(Sender: TObject);
var
  MyMeta : TMetafile;
  MyMetaCanvas : TMetafileCanvas;
begin
  MyMeta := TMetafile.Create;
  MyMeta.Width := 100;
  MyMeta.Height := 100;
  MyMetaCanvas := TMetafileCanvas.Create(MyMeta, 0);
  MyMetaCanvas.Ellipse(0, 0, 100, 100);
  MyMetaCanvas.Free;
  Form1.Canvas.Draw(0, 0, MyMeta);
  MyMeta.Free;
end;
```

In this example, we declare a TMetafile, and a TMetafileCanvas. We then create our metafile and set its width and height before creating the metafile canvas. After we create the metafile canvas, we can finally do some drawing. We then free the metafile canvas, allowing us to then use the metafile. In this example, we have imaged the metafile to the form's canvas, but at this point, you also can save the metafile out to the disk or clipboard. Finally, we free the metafile object.

Mapping Modes

So far, we have been using the standard Windows mapping mode, MM_TEXT. In this mode, all drawing coordinates are expressed in pixels as measured from top left side of the canvas (origin), positive x values increase to the right, and positive y values increase downward.

Windows has several mapping modes available:

Mode	Description
MM_TEXT	Each unit is mapped to 1 pixel. (Positive y increases going down.)
MM_LOMETRIC	Each unit is mapped to 0.1 millimeter. (Positive y increases going up.)

continues

continued

Mode	Description
MM_HIMETRIC	Each unit is mapped to 0.01 millimeter. (Positive y increases going up.)
MM_LOENGLISH	Each logical unit is mapped to 0.01 inch. (Positive y increases going up.)
MM_HIENGLISH	Each logical unit is mapped to 0.001 inch. (Positive y increases going up.)
MM_TWIPS	Each logical unit is mapped to 1/20 of a point (1/1440 inch). (Positive y increases going up.)
MM_ISOTROPIC	Each unit is mapped to an arbitrary unit with equally scaled axes. Use `SetWindowExtEx` and `SetViewportExtEx` to specify the units and the orientation of the axes that you want. The GDI makes small adjustments as necessary to ensure that the x and y units remain the same size. (Positive y defaults to increase going down and can be changed.)
MM_ANISOTROPIC	Each unit is mapped to an arbitrary unit with arbitrarily scaled axes. Use `SetWindowExtEx` and `SetViewportExtEx` to specify the units, the orientation, and scaling that you want. (Positive y defaults to increase going down and can be changed.)

For all mapping modes, the default origin (where the 0,0 coordinate is located), is the upper left corner of the canvas. Note that measurements should be exact on a printer, but will vary on a display because the number of pixels available on any mode doesn't change, but the size of the monitor will. The motto is: "Don't count on being able to hold up a ruler to the display and get accurate results."

When using mapping modes, you use several functions to control the transformations, and to map coordinates back and forth. The functions that you use to control the transformations all return the previous setting, and it is best if you save these settings to a temporary variable, do your work, then reset them. You always should restore the settings in the opposite order that you originally specified. The most important settings are as follows:

Setting	Description
SetMapMode	Sets the mapping mode.
SetWindowOrgEx	Sets the origin. This is where the 0,0 coordinate is located.

`SetWindowExtEx`	Sets the logical units. This is the size of the unit that you want to use. Applies only to MM_ISOTROPIC and MM_ANISOTROPIC modes.
`SetViewportExtEx`	Set the device units. This is the size of the unit that a logical unit maps to. Applies only to MM_ISOTROPIC and MM_ANISOTROPIC modes.

Although the `SetMapMode()` function is easy enough to understand, the other functions may need some clarity. The `SetWindowOrgEx()` function allows you to change where the point 0,0 is located at, and believe me, you will use it. Consider the MM_LOENGLISH mapping mode, where positive y values increase in a upwardly direction. Because the default origin starts at the top of a canvas, unless you draw in negative y coordinates, you will need to move the origin down, or you will be drawing off the top of the canvas. The `SetWindowExtEx()` and `SetViewportExtEx()` functions work together to define how you want to scale your drawing when working in MM_ISOTROPIC and MM_ANISOTROPIC modes. Suppose that you want to make a drawing where you want every two units that you specify in your drawing to equal five units on the device. Simple: You tell the `SetWindowExtEx()` function to use two units, and tell the `SetViewportExtEx()` function to use five units. You can even change the direction that the x and y coordinates increase, by passing negative values to these functions.

Here is an example of using the MM_LOENGLISH mapping mode to draw an ellipse that is one inch in diameter:

```
procedure TForm1.Button1Click(Sender: TObject);
var
  OldMapMode : integer;
  OldOrigin : TPoint;
begin
  OldMapMode := SetMapMode(Form1.Canvas.Handle,
                           MM_LOENGLISH);
  SetWindowOrgEx(Form1.Canvas.Handle,
                 0,
                 100,
                 @OldOrigin);
  Form1.Canvas.Ellipse(0, 0, 100, 100);
  SetWindowOrgEx(Form1.Canvas.Handle,
                 OldOrigin.x,
                 OldOrigin.y,
                 nil);
  SetMapMode(Form1.Canvas.Handle, OldMapMode);
end;
```

Notice how we "remembered" the old mapping mode and window origin, and set them back in reverse order. Also notice how we moved the origin down by 100 units; otherwise, our ellipse would have been drawn above the top of the canvas.

Here is an example of using the MM_ANISOTROPIC mode to draw an ellipse. We specify the ellipse with equal sides that usually would result in a circle, but because we are specifying our scaling factor in the x direction to map to two device units for every unit we input, the ellipse will actually image out to be twice as wide as it is high.

```
procedure TForm1.Button2Click(Sender: TObject);
var
  OldMapMode : integer;
  OldOrigin : TSize;
  OldWindowExtent : TSize;
  OldViewPortExtent : TSize;
begin
  OldMapMode := SetMapMode(Form1.Canvas.Handle,
                           MM_ANISOTROPIC);
  SetWindowExtEx(Form1.Canvas.Handle,
                 100,
                 100,
                 @OldWindowExtent);
  SetViewportExtEx(Form1.Canvas.Handle,
                   200,
                   100,
                   @OldViewPortExtent);
  SetWindowOrgEx(Form1.Canvas.Handle,
                 0,
                 -100,
                 @OldOrigin);

  Form1.Canvas.Ellipse(0, 0, 100, 100);

  SetWindowOrgEx(Form1.Canvas.Handle,
                 OldOrigin.cx,
                 OldOrigin.cy,
                 nil);
  SetViewportExtEx(Form1.Canvas.Handle,
                   OldViewPortExtent.cx,
                   OldViewPortExtent.cy,
                   nil);
  SetWindowExtEx(Form1.Canvas.Handle,
                 OldWindowExtent.cx,
                 OldWindowExtent.cy,
                 nil);
  SetMapMode(Form1.Canvas.Handle,
             OldMapMode);
end;
```

In this example, we also adjusted the windows origin, although it wasn't necessary, because y coordinates increase in a downward direction when using MM_ANISOTROPIC mode. Again, we saved out all the settings as we changed them, and restored the settings in the opposite order of our changes.

Finally, if you need to transform a point from logical units to device units, or from device units to logical units, check out the following Windows functions DPtoLP() and LPtoDP(). These functions will convert a point or group of points back and forth from "user space" to "device space."

Threads

I am happy to report that thread-safe support has been added to Delphi's graphic classes. TCanvas now has two methods for dealing with threads—Lock and Unlock. The Lock method assures exclusive access to a canvas, and the Unlock method releases exclusive access. Note that TBitmaps have implicit thread locks only during the Assign method. If you have multiple threads writing to the same bitmap, you should lock the bitmap's canvas to synchronize access.

Putting It All Together

The developers of Delphi have gone to great lengths to make graphics programming easy, fast, and fun when using Delphi. They also left the full power of the operating system available for your use, allowing you to exploit every last erg of horsepower the GDI has to offer. From here, I suggest you also read Chapter 23, "Printing in Delphi," because it also contains many ideas, workarounds, code snippets, and helpful hints to make your code more robust and portable to other devices. ●

Printing in Delphi

by Joe C. Hecht

In the beginning, there were TTY terminals and text-only printers. Printing in those days was easy. With the advent of graphical displays and graphic printers, every program had to have a specialized device interface for each printer that it supported. In the days before Microsoft Windows, the programmer had to roll up his or her sleeves and become an expert at controlling a wide range of printers. Often, designing the printer interfaces for a program was one of your single biggest issues in delivering a shipping product.

One of the original objectives of Microsoft Windows was to allow programs to share a common interface to the hardware. Life seems easier now because we no longer have to worry about writing code for every printer under the sun, but we still spend far too much time trying to get applications to work with the print drivers over which we now have far too little control. ■

Print drivers

You learn about print drivers, and the problems you may encounter when using them.

Fonts and Dcs

How to work with fonts, printer Dcs, complex polygons, complex regions, 16- and 32-bit print drivers, bogus information, and handling abort procedures.

***Tprinter*, *Writeln*, and the Printer's canvas**

Use TPrinter, Delphi's encapsulation of the Windows printing system, to make producing a shipping application easier; learn how to make printing easy with Writeln; and learn more about the printer's canvas.

Changing printers and settings

Learn how to use GetDevCaps and DeviceCapabilities, printer escapes, and how to work with TPrinter's canvas.

Printing forms

In this section, you learn more about printing forms.

Bypassing *TPrinter*

Finally, you learn how to bypass TPrinter and to use banding for more efficient results.

What's covered in this chapter:

- How print drivers work and problems you will encounter
- Working with color
- Fonts
- Printer Dcs
- Things to watch for
- Complex polygons
- Complex regions
- 16- and 32-Bit print drivers
- Bogus printer information
- Abort procedures
- Using Tprinter
- Using Writeln
- Using the printer's canvas
- Changing printers and settings
- Printer settings: GetDevCaps and DeviceCapabilities
- Using DeviceCapabilities
- Printer escapes
- Working with TPrinter's canvas
- What might not work
- Printing forms
- Bypassing TPrinter

How Print Drivers Work

The *Windows GDI* (Graphic Device Interface) is the layer that allows your application to talk to graphical output devices in a somewhat device-independent manner. The GDI supplies applications with a handle to either a *display context* (Dc) or an *information context* (Ic). The handle to a Dc allows you to make GDI calls to draw to a given device context (rectangles, shapes, text, and so on), while a handle to an Ic enables your application to get information about a given device (pixels per inch, page size, and so on). Although you sometimes can get device information from a Dc, you can never draw to an Ic. Information contexts are handy for extracting information about a device without incurring the overhead of initializing the device for drawing.

Delphi encapsulates many of the drawing and information calls through the properties and methods of the TPrinter object. The TPrinter object then calls the Widows GDI for you. The Windows GDI queries the driver to see its capabilities in order to perform a given operation. If the driver supports the operation directly, GDI passes the request to the driver. If the driver doesn't support the operation, then the GDI queries the driver to see what operations it can perform at lower levels to accomplish the given result, and then the GDI simulates the operation with the lower-level calls.

A good example of this is a call to draw a rectangle. If the driver doesn't directly support drawing a rectangle, the GDI might ask the driver if it can draw patterned lines. If it cannot draw patterned lines, the GDI might ask if the driver can draw pixels. If so, the GDI will produce the rectangle by drawing a bitmap and sending the pixels to the driver. Often, printer drivers report that they can support a given function, and then call back to the GDI to do the dirty work. At this point, the GDI may query the video driver to see if it can perform the operation. And if so, the operation is performed by using the video driver, which in turn may perform the operation in software—directly in its specialized hardware—or it may still be passed back to a GDI support function. This point is important: Printing not only relies on the printer driver, it also can be dependent on the video driver!

A good debugging technique to use when your application fails to print properly is to switch both video and print drivers. The generic drivers that ship with Microsoft Windows are the best drivers to try. If you change your video driver and the application prints correctly, you can suggest to customers that they try to get an updated video driver. If this doesn't remedy the situation, you also can try installing an updated or generic printer driver.

Many times, manufacturers ship custom drivers for use with their printers. Often enough, changing back to the standard drivers that ship with Microsoft Windows fixes many printing problems. Occasionally, changing to a driver that works with a similar printer model also fixes a given printing problem.

Problems You Will Encounter

Although the Microsoft Windows printing system has greatly simplified the task of printing, you cannot expect that everything that works on the display will print correctly on paper.

One of the first considerations is that the printer probably will have a different resolution than the display. A rectangle drawn on the display at 10 pixels high will look tiny when printed on a 600-dpi laser printer. As of this writing, printer resolutions vary from around 75 dpi (dots per inch), all the way up to 4000 dpi. If your application uses a pen that has a width equal to one, it may look good on the display and, perhaps, even look acceptable on a 300 dpi laser printer. However, you may need a microscope to see the line if you print it on a high-resolution Linotronic Imagesetter, where your line now has a width of less than 1/3500 of an inch!

Always consider that the end user may want to have the final output of your program printed *en masse* on an offset printing press. Today, many printing presses can accept a print job electronically, and they produce the printing plates automatically, right at the press! Consider that the final output for solid lines may start "breaking up" under offset printing, somewhere around 1/288 of an inch, and screen patterns may begin to look bad when there are more than 65 dots per inch in the screen pattern.

This difference brings us right to the point. Always scale your output to look good on the device to which you are printing. You can easily do so by adjusting the final output coordinates by using constant measurements such as inches rather than pixels.

You can get this information directly from the GDI with a simple call to the Windows `GetDeviceCaps()` function call:

```
HorizontalInch := GetDeviceCaps(Printer.Canvas.Handle, LOGPIXELSX);
VerticalInch := GetDeviceCaps(Printer.Canvas.Handle, LOGPIXELSY);
```

It's worth noting that, traditionally, printed measurements are expressed in printer points. In today's time, a printer's point is considered to be 1/72 inch. You can extract a lot of control in the placement of your graphic output by using points. You do this by declaring a couple of variables in your program, as follows:

```
var PointsX : double;
var PointsY : double;
```

and then initializing these variables to the following:

```
PointsX := GetDeviceCaps(Printer.Canvas.Handle, LOGPIXELSX) / 72;
PointsY:= GetDeviceCaps(Printer.Canvas.Handle, LOGPIXELSX) / 72;
```

Now, when you want to draw something, you can use printer points as a measurement, and your output will scale correctly on any device!

An example of drawing a rectangle two inches wide, three inches high, and located one inch from the top left corner of the page (not accounting for the printer margin) would look like the following:

```
with Printer.Canvas do
   Rectangle( Round ( PointsX * 72 ),
                  Round ( PointsY * 72 ),
                  Round ( PointsX *  216 ),
                  Round ( PointsY * 288 ));
```

The only time that this doesn't work is when scaling fonts on some devices on which the printer has a different resolution in one direction than the other, and the device doesn't account for the difference. It's always good to test your output, and a good device to test it on is a Fax Printer. Some faxes have an "extra fine" setting, where the horizontal and vertical resolutions differ.

Working with Color

Now, you may want to fill that rectangle with one of the nifty colors available under Windows. If your printer supports color, you probably will get something close to what you expect. If the device can handle a wide range of color, you may get the exact color; if not, you will get a dithered color.

Dithered colors are produced on the video display by printing patterns of red, green, and blue dots closely together to produce an effect that is supposed to fool the eye. At lower resolutions, the pattern is quite noticeable; at higher resolutions, the pattern is less noticeable.

Printing color on paper is far different than displaying color on a video display. On video displays, various amounts of red, green, and blue (RGB) are projected onto phosphors that light the screen. With no light (color), the display is black (the same color as the display when it is turned off), and with combined intensity of red, green, and blue, the display shows white.

When printing on paper, the driver uses the exact opposite of RGB. Printing inks are designed to be somewhat transparent. Where no color is printed, the paper shows through (white), and where there is total color, you see black (the paper doesn't show through the ink). The colors of the ink are also the opposite of red, green, and blue.

When printing, various amounts of cyan, magenta, and yellow (CMY) are combined to produce the desired color. Because printing inks are not pure, printing cyan, magenta, and yellow over one another to produce black often results in a muddy brown. Higher quality color printers use black (CMYK) to reduce the amount of ink used and to produce sharper colors. Under this system, equal amounts of cyan, magenta, and yellow are removed, and black is added in their place. Because the GDI expects colors to be presented in amounts of red, green, and blue, the printer driver is responsible for the conversion to the CMYK color model. If exact color output is important to your application, you can license a color-matching system such as the Pantone® or FocalTone® color-matching system that can make additional color adjustments for the final output.

If the printer is a monochrome device, your color gets converted to a dithered monochrome pattern. A lot of room exists for mistakes here because not all drivers handle this conversion equally. Ideally, you can help out the driver by doing part of the conversion up-front, by using the same formula used on black-and-white televisions to display a color signal.

Set the RGB color values to equal, as follows:

```
Red := Round( ( 0.3 * red ) + ( 0.59 * green ) + ( 0.11 * blue ) );
Green := Red;
Blue := Red;
```

This formula converts a given red, green, and blue value to an equal mix of red, green, and blue. This equal mix produces a gray that will simulate a color. All that is left is a hope that the printer driver will produce a dithered pattern for simulating a gray that looks fairly good.

●

If the printer supports palettes, you can avoid dithering by creating a palette and using your predefined colors. Most printers do not support palettes. Rather, they print by using either full color or monochrome.

You can tell if the printer is a color printer and if it supports palettes by calling GetDeviceCaps(), as in the following:

```
if ( GetDeviceCaps( Printer.Canvas.Handle, BITSPIXEL ) *
     GetDeviceCaps( Printer.Canvas.Handle, BITSPIXEL ) ) > 1 then
  ItsAColorPrinter := true;
if GetDeviceCaps( Printer.Canvas.Handle, RASTERCAPS)  and RC_PALETTE =
RC_PALETTE then
    ThePritnerSupportsPalettes := true;
```

Pen colors do not dither unless you use the PSINSIDEFRAME pen style and the pen width is greater than one pixel. Using the PSINSIDEFRAME pen style results in shapes that have their outlines painted totally inside the shape. If the pen is not a dithered pen, its color is mapped to the nearest pure color. This can lead to unexpected results. You can use the Windows function GetNearestColor() to find the nearest pure color to which your pen will map.

Brushes, however, do support dithering. The only "gotcha" in regard to brushes is related to gray and patterned brushes. Dark gray values usually do not look nearly as good on paper as they do on-screen, which has much to do with the dithering pattern used. The patterns appear smaller, and the human eye tends to see more black than white. Pattern brushes also exhibit this effect. A brush pattern is defined as an 8-by-8-pixel bitmap. This pattern may look fine on-screen, but to the eye, it looks like solid black at the higher resolutions used by printers. The only way around this is to manually draw the patterns, accounting for the device's resolution along the way.

Fonts

If you plan to produce text, there are a few things to watch for. Most important is that the printer may not support the same font set that the display supports. This means that unless you're careful, what you see on-screen may not be what you get on the printer.

One way around this problem is to allow your user to choose only TrueType fonts. TrueType fonts look good both on the printer and on-screen, and unlike GDI fonts, they can be scaled to almost any size. The end user, however, may have invested a bundle in Adobe ATM fonts and may not be too happy about not using them with your application. You can tell the FontDialog in Delphi to use only TrueType fonts by selecting fdTrueTypeOnly in the Font dialog box's options property. I have seen problems with setting the Font dialog box to show printer fonts. Most high-end applications opt to populate a toolbar with a drop-down menu that contains a list of fonts that exist on both the printer and the screen. You can create this list by comparing the fonts listed in the Fonts property of the TScreen and TPrinter object and only displaying fonts that match.

The main "gotcha" concerning printing and fonts with Delphi seems to be a small problem with the fonts' dot-per-inch property not always getting initialized properly. This was a bigger problem under Delphi 1.0 and only occasionally under Delphi 2.0. The problem seems to have disappeared under Delphi 3. Because I like to write code that is portable, I suggest that you add the following line of code whenever you change fonts while printing:

```
Printer.Canvas.Font.PixelsPerInch := GetDeviceCaps(Printer.Canvas.Handle,
LOGPIXELSY);
```

This property is used to scale the font to the correct size when you use the size property. Note that the size property produces fonts of a given point size (remember printer points?), and the height property sets the fonts height in pixels. Both the size and height property can be negative because the GDI can measure a font in different ways. If the font's height is negative, the measurement is based on the height of an *EM* square (the typographically correct way to measure a font), where a positive height denotes having the font's absolute size scaled. If you're printing and also presenting a choice of sizes to a user, it's best to present the numbers in printer points.

To space your lines correctly, a good rule is to add 20 percent to the point size. Traditionally, spacing for forms is done in increments of 6 points. To make a form that works well with a typewriter or line printer, use 10-point type and 12 points of line spacing.

The alignment of your text is important. The typographically correct way to align text is by using the *baseline* rather than the top of the text block (which is the default). To understand the baseline of a font, you first must understand ascenders and descenders. Let's look at descenders first. When you look at the word "Away," notice how the first three letters align at the bottom, and the fourth letter, "y," descends below this mark. This letter has a *descender*.

Ascenders work in the same way in which descenders work. Many foreign character sets have accent marks above some characters. These marks are ascenders. If you choose the default text alignment (align to top), your lines of text may not always align correctly. The correct way to align text is on the baseline. In this way, all lines align correctly, no matter what characters or fonts you intermix on a line. To do so, call the Windows GDI function SetTextAlign().

The SetTextAlign() function enables you to choose both the vertical and horizontal alignment. Several settings are available that can be combined. The most common vertical settings are TA_BASELINE, TA_BOTTOM, and TA_TOP, and the most common horizontal settings are TA_CENTER, TA_LEFT, and TA_RIGHT. Two other settings affect how the current point is updated—TA_UPDATECP and TA_NOUPDATECP. The default is TA_NOUPDATECP, where you are responsible for setting the x,y coordinates of where you want the text output to be placed. Before changing the settings, you will want to declare a variable to hold the old settings, so you can change the settings back after you are done setting your text.

The following code is an example of changing the text alignment to align text to the left and on the baseline, and not to update the current point:

```
var OldTextAlign : integer;
begin
   OldTextAlign := SetTextAlign(Printer.Canvas.Handle,
        TA_LEFT or TA_BASELINE or TA_NOUPDATECP);
Set some text here....
   SetTextAlign(Printer.Canvas.Handle, OldTextAlign);
end;
```

Printer Dcs

It's interesting to note that a printer Dc is far different than its display (screen) counterpart. Although it's common to transfer bitmaps between Dcs based on the display, it's almost impossible to do the same between printer Dcs. First, consider that after an image is printed on the paper, it is impossible to transfer the image back to another Dc. You just cannot get those dots back off the paper (without first scanning the image). The same is true for multiple BitBlts() (*image transfers*) with different *ROP codes*. ROP codes (*raster operations*) enable you to combine one or more images to obtain special effects, such as transparency. Many print drivers support only SRCCOPY (*direct image copy*), WHITENESS (*fill with white*), and BLACKNESS (*fill with black*). Remember: After you transfer an image to the printer, that's it. Also, some print drivers do not support the creation of more than one Dc at a time. If you plan to use multiple printer Dcs, be careful! Blitting a bitmap from a screen Dc to a printer Dc also is a bad idea because under Windows, blitting between devices isn't allowed. Monochrome images are supposed to work across devices, but blitting across devices usually works only by the graces of a well-written print driver.

A final note: Often, the printer Dc you get is actually a metafile Dc that is later spooled to the printer driver. Metafile Dcs are "read only"—you cannot depend on any function that returns information. It is best to get the information you need (text widths and so on) through an Information Context before you print, by using the Windows CreateIc() function.

Other Things to Watch For...

What may seem like a good idea may not always pan out when printing under Windows. There are several abnormalities you need to watch for, which are covered in the following sections.

Complex Polygons   Some print drivers do not support more than 750 points in a polygon. Although the 32-bit GDI should step in and simulate the correct output, this doesn't always work as planned. The lesson: Keep your polygons as simple as possible.

Complex Regions   Under 16-bit Windows, complex regions caused quite a headache. The problem seemed related to the way in which Windows stored the regions on the GDI heap as scan lines. Really complex regions, or large regions combined with the higher printer resolutions, would cause the GDI heap to overflow.

With Windows 95, this limit was increased, and under NT, it is almost eliminated. At any rate, complex clipping is best handled by you and your application, especially if you produce both 16- and 32-bit versions of your application.

16- and 32-Bit Print Drivers   If you produce both 16- and 32-bit versions of your program, watch out—and even if you are not, consider that Windows 95 allows the use of both 16- and 32-bit print drivers through a great deal of "thunking magic," where 32-bit applications can use 16-bit print drivers, and 16-bit applications can use 32-bit print drivers. Loading a 32-bit print driver directly by using the Windows function LoadLibrary() is no longer allowed. For backward compatibility, 16-bit applications can use LoadLibrary on a 32-bit print driver. Because a print driver is a Windows dynamic link library (DLL), a lot of magic goes on behind the scenes to make this happen. For this reason, many printing problems that existed in 16-bit Windows still exist under 32-bit Windows.

Bogus Printer Information   Although many print drivers perform as you may expect, a few out there do not. The printer-driver manufacturer isn't always to blame, either. The Microsoft documentation and source code have a lot to be desired when it comes to building print drivers. There are many places where the manufacturer had to guess about what to do under certain circumstances—for example, when you change the orientation of the page from portrait to landscape. Should the print driver swap the values it reports as the horizontal and vertical resolutions of the printer? There are two arguments—the first is that you cannot physically change the horizontal and vertical resolutions of a printer, and that only the orientation setting should change. The other side of the argument is that applications may expect the numbers to change. The truth is that some drivers will, and some will not, swap the horizontal and vertical resolutions when you change the orientation. In the past, I coded a lot of tests to check what really goes on at runtime, and I adjusted my output accordingly. A reasonable test might look like the following:

```
Get the vertical and horizontal resolution of the printer.
Change the page orientation
Get the vertical and horizontal resolution again.
If the vertical and horizontal resolution changed then
   use what was reported else
   swap my variable's x and y resolution value and use it.
```

Abort Procedures   Many print drivers fail if you do not set an abort procedure. Although Delphi's TPrinter object automatically sets an abort procedure for you, if you plan to handle printing, you need to set up your own abort procedure. I recommend that it is set early in the game.

Down to the Nuts and Bolts: *TPrinter*

TPrinter is Delphi's encapsulation of the Windows printing system, and like most VCL components, can greatly reduce the amount of work needed to produce a shipping application.

Printing under Windows once was one of the largest headaches a programmer faced. It used to be that you had to parse the WIN.INI file for devices, and handle every part of the process of selecting a printer and creating a printer Dc. Even with the advent of the Windows 3.1 common printer dialog box, getting printed output required trial and error, and a lot of confusing code. Delphi's TPrinter solves all this and more by providing your application with the easiest and most powerful path to printing in the industry!

Using *TPrinter*

To use TPrinter in your application, simply add Printers to the uses clause of any unit from which you want to print. There are at least three ways to use the TPrinter unit: You can use TPrinter to produce simple line printer-style output with the Writeln() procedure. You also can use TPrinter with the print methods of the VCL components. Finally, you can opt to make direct Windows GDI commands.

Using *Writeln()*

The easiest way to print is to use the Writeln() procedure. The Writeln() procedure is a holdover from the DOS days, where you would output a line to the teletype, line printer, or output file. The developers of Delphi have graciously enhanced Writeln() to work in the world of Windows, where it is improper or even impossible for an application to open a printer port directly.

Using Writeln() to print a line of text to the printer is as easy as it was under DOS—perhaps easier, considering that you can change fonts and such without ever hard-coding an escape sequence!

You use Writeln() in the same way you did back in the old DOS days: by assigning a text file variable, opening the file, writing some lines, and then closing the file. Unlike the old DOS days, what you write doesn't directly go to the printer. In fact, when you use Writeln() to output a line to the printer, the Printers unit calls the Windows GDI TextOut() command. The good news is that you change fonts and output graphics easily enough; the bad news is that you cannot send your own escape codes—well, at least not easily. For what it's worth, you cannot just send raw data to the printer by using Writeln().

The following is an example of using Writeln() to print a line of text to the printer, and then to advance to the next line:

```
uses Printers;

var
  MyFile: TextFile;
begin
  AssignPrn(MyFile);
  Rewrite(MyFile);
  Writeln(MyFile, 'Hello World!');
  System.CloseFile(MyFile);
end;
```

If you want, you also can change the font and size that Writeln() will use by adding just a few lines of code:

```
Printer.Canvas.Font.Name := 'Courier New';
Printer.Canvas.Font.Style := [fsBold];
Printer.Canvas.Font.PixelsPerInch:=
  GetDeviceCaps(Printer.Canvas.Handle, LOGPIXELSY);
Writeln(MyFile, 'Hello World!');
```

Each time you call `Writeln()`, the text string is output in the current font, and the current point is advanced to the first column in the next line. If the length of the text exceeds the page's width, then the line is automatically continued on the next line. When the end of the page is reached, the page ejects and a new page starts. You can avoid advancing to the next line by using the `Write()` procedure in place of `Writeln()`. `Write()` will write the line of text, but doesn't advance to the next line unless the text length exceeds the page's width. You even can change the font between words by using the `Write()` command.

When using `Write()` and `Writeln()`, `TPrinter` keeps track of setting the x- and y- coordinates of the current point and automatically ejects the page.

For this reason, you shouldn't directly cause the page to be ejected by calling the `TPrinter`'s `NewPage` method. You also have no control with the space between the lines. There is a way to easily hack `TPrinter` and get access to the x and y properties of the current line by declaring a structure named `PrnRec`, as follows:

```
type
  PrnRec = record
    case Integer of
      1: (
        Cur: TPoint;
        Finish: TPoint;
        Height: Integer);
      2: (
        Tmp: array[1..(sizeof(integer)*8)] of Char);
  end;
```

Then, casting the file variable, as in the following:

```
PrnRec(TTextRec(MyFile).UserData).Cur.x := SomeXValue;
PrnRec(TTextRec(MyFile).UserData).Cur.y := SomeYValue;
```

You can even call `TPrinter`'s `NewPage` method (just don't forget to zero out `Cur.x` and `Cur.y`).

As you probably have already guessed, the `Cur` member of the `PrnRec` structure is used to hold the current point on the page. The `Finish` member holds the end of the printable area of the page, and the `Height` member holds the amount of line spacing to use. If `Height` is zero, `Writeln()` will reassign the height member to the height of the current font.

Remember, hacking may not always be portable to the future, so you probably are better off creating a substitute for `Write()` and `Writeln()`, and this creation is easy enough to do. Just use the `TextOut` method of the Printer canvas and keep track of the x and y position as you go along! To do so, you also need to use the `BeginDoc`, `NewPage`, and `EndDoc` methods of `TPrinter`.

Using the Printer's Canvas

To directly control printing under Delphi, you need to handle setting up and shutting down the print job by using the `BeginDoc` and `EndDoc` methods of `TPrinter`. When you want to eject a page, just call the `NewPage` method. The `EndDoc` method will eject the last page for you. The code sandwich looks like the following:

```
Printer.BeginDoc;
Printer.Canvas.TextOut(20, 20, 'A line of text - page 1');
Printer.NewPage;
Printer.Canvas.TextOut(20, 20, 'A line of text - page 2');
Printer.EndDoc;
```

Primer: Changing Printers and Settings

You are free to change the selected printer whenever you aren't currently printing. The list of available printers is available from the string list contained in the `Printer.Printers` property, and the index of the currently selected printer is contained in the `Printer.PrinterIndex` property. You can set the current printer to any of the available printers in the list by changing the `Printer.PrinterIndex` property, and you can change the current printer to the default Windows printer by setting the `Printer.PrinterIndex` property to –1.

The following is an example of filling a `ListBox` component with a listing of the available printers, and selecting the current printer in the `ListBox`:

```
ListBox1.Items := Printer.Printers;
ListBox1.ItemIndex := Printer.PrinterIndex;
```

You also can use the `TPrinterDialog`, and `PrinterSetupDialog` components to change both the printer and the currently selected printer settings, as in the following:

```
PrintDialog1.Execute;
```

or

```
PrinterSetupDialog1.Execute;
```

Take your pick as to the one you want to use. `TPrinterDialog` is more useful if you need to print a page range, where the `PrinterSetupDialog` is more useful for changing paper bins and the like. Both printer dialog boxes allow the user to select the printer's properties directly from either dialog box.

`TPrinter` also has two other methods for getting and setting the printer—`GetPrinter` and `SetPrinter`. Both of these methods are not recommended or well-documented. I highly recommend that if you really want to get down to the metal and start selecting printer devices, driver files, and port settings, that you get a good book on low-level Windows programming, and take on the full task of controlling the printing operation from start to finish. The only other reason for using these methods is to access the printer's `DevMode` structure to change printer settings such as the paper bin, number of copies, and so on. Following sections will present a much better way to control these settings but for now, here is an example of using the `GetPrinter` method:

```
var
  Device : array[0..cchDeviceName-1] of Char;
  Driver : array[0..(MAX_PATH-1)] of Char;
  Port : array[0..32] of Char;
  hDMode : THandle;
begin
```

```
Printer.GetPrinter(Device,
                   Driver,
                   Port,
                   hDMode);
  Label1.Caption := Device;
  Label2.Caption := Driver;
  Label3.Caption := Port;
end;
```

This chapter started out declaring variables to hold the device name, driver name, port name, and a handle to the printer's DevMode structure. After making the call to GetPrinter(), you set the label's captions to show the results. Commonly, the driver will be returned as a blank string.

If you know the device name, driver name, and port name you want to use, you can call the SetPrinter method, as follows:

```
Printer.SetPrinter('HPLJ-IID',
                   'HPPCL',
                   'FILE:',
                   0);
```

Notice that a handle wasn't sent to a DevMode structure. If you have a handle to a valid DevMode structure, you can use it in the fourth parameter. You also can add a new printer that hasn't been installed in Windows to the TPrinter's printer's list by filling in the parameters with the proper data, as in the following:

```
Printer.SetPrinter('SOMEDRV',
                   'C:\SOMEDIR\SOMEDRV',
                   'FILE:',
                   0);
```

Usually, this isn't a good idea because most printer drivers must be installed by Windows to work correctly. In some cases, however, this can be useful. This feature also can be used to change the port that a given driver will use.

To control printer settings in code, you need to work with the printer's DevMode structure. The DevMode structure of the currently selected printer can be retrieved with the GetPrinter method of TPrinter. When you have a handle to the DevMode structure, you can call the Windows GlobalLock() function to retrieve a pointer to the structure, and then make changes to the device-independent portion of the structure.

The DevMode structure is unique for each printer. The first section of the DevMode structure is common to all printers, and the second section is strictly for the drivers' use. You can query the DevMode.dmSize member to find the size of the public part of the driver's DevMode structure, and you can query the DevMode.dmDriverExtra member to find the size of the private part of the driver's devMode structure. If you want to copy and save a complete DevMode structure, you need to allocate and copy (DevMode.dmSize + DevMode.dmDriverExtra) bytes.

The most basic DevMode structure is defined as having the following public members:

dmDeviceName: {the name of the device}

dmSpecVersion: {the minimum Windows version required for the driver}

dmDriverVersion: {the driver's version number}

dmSize: {the size of the public portion of the DevMode}

dmDriverExtra: {the size of the private portion of the DevMode}

dmFields: {flags-initialized portions of the DevMode}

dmOrientation: {page orientation}

dmPaperSize: {predefined paper size or zero if custom size}

dmPaperLength: {used for custom page size only}

dmPaperWidth: {used for custom page size only}

dmScale: {print scale}

dmCopies: {number of copies desired}

dmDefaultSource: {must be zero}

dmPrintQuality: {predefined or printer's x resolution}

dmColor: {if color printing is desired}

dmDuplex: {if two-sided printing is desired}

dmYResolution: {zero, or printer's y resolution if dmPrintQuality > 0 }

Both 16- and 32-bit Windows define some additional flags for the DeviceMode public section that may not apply to all printers. Unless you know the printer you are using supports these additional settings, it's best not to use them.

You can change the members of the DevMode structure by assigning a value to the appropriate member, and then setting the appropriate bit of the dmFields member to let the driver know the member has been initialized, as in the following:

```
DevMode.dmPaperSize := DMPAPER_LEGAL;
DevMode.dmFields := DevMode.dmFields or DM_PAPERSIZE;
```

The following is a complete example of changing a printer's DevMode structure:

```
var
  Device : array[0..cchDeviceName-1] of Char;
  Driver : array[0..(MAX_PATH-1)] of Char;
  Port : array[0..32] of Char;
  hDMode : THandle;
  pDMode : PDevMode;
begin
  Printer.PrinterIndex := Printer.PrinterIndex;
  Printer.GetPrinter(Device, Driver, Port, hDMode);
  if hDMode <> 0 then begin
    pDMode := GlobalLock(hDMode);
    if pDMode <> nil then begin
      pDMode^.dmCopies := 5;
      pDMode^.dmFields := pDMode^.dmFields or DM_COPIES;
```

```
      GlobalUnlock(hDMode);
      Printer.PrinterIndex := Printer.PrinterIndex;
    end;
  end;
  Printer.BeginDoc;
  Printer.Canvas.TextOut(100,100, 'Test 1');
  Printer.EndDoc;
end;
```

We started out by declaring variables to hold the device name, driver name, port name, and both a handle and a pointer to the printer's DevMode structure. The first line of code resets the printer. After making the call to GetPrinter, you check to see if a valid handle to the DevMode structure exists, and if so, you lock it down and make the change. You then unlock the handle and reset the printer. Note that this change can be made only before a print job starts. Also note that not all changes will be supported on all printers.

About now, you're probably thinking that all this is really cool, but you want to be able to change the printer settings in mid-print job. Well, you have two choices—break the job up into a single print job for each page or totally patch TPrinter. The second option is preferred because it can give you a lot of control and doesn't overload the Print Manager with a ton of different jobs, unless necessary. This method works on print drivers designed to run under Windows versions 3.1 and later, and should cause no problems on drivers built for previous versions, because the driver should simply return an error to the Windows GDI if the driver doesn't support changing the DevMode in mid-job. The patch will make a test to see if this error is returned, and if so, you will break up the job by printing each page as a separate job.

To patch TPrinter, you must first have a copy of Delphi's VCL source code. If you're porting code between 16- and 32-bit versions, the 16-bit version of the VCL source code ships with the RAD pack, a separate package available from Borland. If you are porting from Delphi 2.0, the VCL source is included with Delphi 2.0 Developer and the Delphi 2.0 Client/Server Suite.

The patch is rather easy to make: What is really wanted is a new event that gets fired right before every new page is created, and uses the Windows GDI function ResetDc() to change the print settings. The ResetDc() function must be called between pages, and Delphi has no event to do this. Although it normally would be easy to create a new component, TPrinter is special. First, you want a patch that works on all versions of Delphi, and you want the patch to work with all components that already use TPrinter. Another problem: TPrinter seems to keep a printer loaded and ready to go at all times, and we don't want multiple instances of printers going. In fact, some drivers do not even support multiple instances. The final problem is to avoid breaking other VCL components by changing the interface portion of TPrinter.

This is a tall order—adding an event to the TPrinter object without changing TPrinter's interface section, class declaration, or sub-classing.

The idea of overcoming this obstacle came to me one Friday while standing in line at the bank. Create a unit with a single-function pointer, initialized to be nil. Add a uses clause to the implementation section of TPrinter to point to the new unit, so the function pointer can be called from TPrinter, and add a uses clause to the implementation section of the application unit so you can assign your event. Now this is a slick work-around that works across the board!

You need to do the following:

First, create a new directory under Delphi's \SOURCE\ directory and name it **PATCHED**. Copy the file PRINTERS.PAS from Delphi's SOURCE\VCL directory to the SOURCE\PATCHED\ directory.

Now add a new unit in Delphi's SOURCE\PATCHED\ directory named **PRNPAGE.PAS**. The unit's code should look like the following:

- -

```
unit PrnPage;

interface

{$IFDEF Win32}
 uses Windows;
{$ELSE}
 uses WinTypes;
 const MAX_PATH = 144;
{$ENDIF}

procedure JobStart;

var PageProc : procedure(DC : HDC;
                         DeviceMode : THandle);

implementation

uses Printers;

procedure JobStart;
var
  Device : array[0..cchDeviceName-1] of Char;
  Driver : array[0..(MAX_PATH-1)] of Char;
  Port : array[0..32] of Char;
  hDMode : THandle;
begin
  if @PageProc = nil then exit;
  Printer.PrinterIndex := Printer.PrinterIndex;
  Printer.GetPrinter(Device, Driver, Port, hDMode);
  if hDMode <> 0 then begin
    PageProc(0, hDMode);
    Printer.PrinterIndex := Printer.PrinterIndex;
  end;
end;

begin
  @PageProc := nil;
end.
```

- -

This simple unit contains a procedure variable that you will use to interface the application's page event to TPrinter. The PageProc procedure variable is initialized to nil when the unit is first loaded, so if you ever decide not to assign an event, the code will not crash.

The unit also has a procedure named JobStart() that you will call at the beginning of each print job whenever you want to change the printer's DevMode structure before a document is started, and to allow for changes with printers that do not support changing the printer's DevMode structure between pages.

Now you need to patch TPrinter to use the PrnPage unit. Open the PRINTERS.PAS unit in Delphi's \SOURCE\PATCHED\ directory. Add PrnPage to the uses clause in the implementation section of the PRINTERS.PAS file, as follows:

```
...
implementation

uses Consts, PrnPage;
...
```

Now, search out the two places in PRINTERS.PAS that have the line:

```
StartPage(DC);
```

Insert the following critical code just before any lines that start with StartPage(Dc) in the PRINTERS.PAS file, as follows:

```
if @PrnPage.PageProc <> nil then
  PrnPage.PageProc(DC, DeviceMode);
```

The two places you insert the code are contained in TPrinter's BeginDoc and NewPage methods. The code that you added will allow TPrinter to "callback" to your application just before every page is started, allowing your application to make changes to the printer's DevMode structure.

Finally, you need to add the complete path to Delphi's SOURCE\PATCHED directory to the library search path by selecting Tools, Options from Delphi's menu. Turn to the Library page and add the following line to the beginning of the Library Path (substituting the correct path to your Delphi's directory):

```
C:\Borland\Delphi 2.0\Source\Patched;
```

Then select OK and restart Delphi.

Make sure that you do not to forget to do a "build all" when you recompile your project.

Now, whenever you want to print, add the PrnPage unit right after the Printers unit to the uses clause in the implementation section of the unit you are printing from in your application:

```
implementation

{$IFDEF Win32}
 uses Printers, PrnPage;
{$ELSE}
 uses Print, Printers, PrnPage;
{$ENDIF}
```

Now, add the following procedure in your unit's code, making modifications to the settings that you want to change:

```
procedure ThePageProc(DC : HDC;
                      hDMode : THandle);
var
  pDMode : PDevMode;
begin
  if hDMode = 0 then exit;
  pdMode := GlobalLock(hDMode);
  if pdMode = nil then exit;
  pDMode^.dmCopies := 3;
  pDMode^.dmPaperSize := DMPAPER_LEGAL;
  pDMode^.dmFields := pDMode^.dmFields or DM_COPIES;
  pDMode^.dmFields := pDMode^.dmFields or DM_PAPERSIZE;
  if DC <> 0 then
{$IFDEF Win32}
    ResetDc(DC, pDMode^);
{$ELSE}
    ResetDc(DC, pDMode);
{$ENDIF}
  GlobalUnlock(hDMode);
end;
```

Now when you want to print, and change the settings between pages, just assign the `PageProc` variable in the `PrnPage` unit to point to your procedure that will do the changes. The following assignment does the trick:

```
@PrnPage.PageProc := @ThePageProc;
```

Now print, knowing that `TPrinter` will now call your `PageProc` every time a new job and a new page is started.

A quick example would look like the following:

```
@PrnPage.PageProc := @ThePageProc;
JobStart;
Printer.BeginDoc;
Windows.TextOut(Printer.Canvas.Handle,
                100, 100,
                'Test',
                4);
Printer.EndDoc;
@PrnPage.PageProc := nil;
```

Notice when you are done printing, you should set the `PrnPage`'s `PageProc` variable back to `nil`.

Ready for a more complete example? Here is a great example, which shows how to use your new printing system to print several pages and change the device settings between pages reliably, even if the device doesn't support changing the device settings between pages!

```
implementation

{$IFDEF Win32}
 uses Printers, PrnPage;
{$ELSE}
 uses Print, Printers, PrnPage;
 type ShortString = string;
{$ENDIF}

var
  PrintSeparatePages : bool;
  CurrentPage : integer;
  LastPage : integer;

procedure ThePageProc(DC : HDC;
                      hDMode : THandle);
                      {$IFNDEF Win32}
                      far;
                      {$ENDIF}
var
  pDMode : PDevMode;
begin
  if hDMode = 0 then exit;
  pdMode := GlobalLock(hDMode);
  if pdMode = nil then exit;

  if odd(CurrentPage) then begin
    pDMode^.dmCopies := 3;
    pDMode^.dmPaperSize := DMPAPER_LEGAL;
  end else begin
    pDMode^.dmCopies := 2;
    pDMode^.dmPaperSize := DMPAPER_LETTER;
  end;
  pDMode^.dmFields := pDMode^.dmFields or DM_COPIES;
  pDMode^.dmFields := pDMode^.dmFields or DM_PAPERSIZE;

  if DC <> 0 then
{$IFDEF Win32}
    if ResetDc(DC, pDMode^) <> 0 then
{$ELSE}
    if ResetDc(DC, pDMode) <> 0 then
{$ENDIF}
      PrintSeparatePages := false;
  GlobalUnlock(hDMode);
end;

procedure TForm1.Button1Click(Sender: TObject);
var
  s : ShortString;
begin
  PrintSeparatePages := True;
  CurrentPage := 1;
  LastPage := 3;
```

```
@PrnPage.PageProc := @ThePageProc;
while CurrentPage <= LastPage do begin
  if PrintSeparatePages then begin
    JobStart;
    Printer.BeginDoc;
  end;
  Str(CurrentPage, s);
  s := 'Printing Page ' + s;
  s[Length(s) + 1] := #0;
  TextOut(Printer.Canvas.Handle,
          100, 100,
          @s[1],
          Length(s));
  Inc(CurrentPage);
  if CurrentPage <= LastPage then begin
    if PrintSeparatePages then
      Printer.EndDoc
    else
      Printer.NewPage;
  end;
end;
Printer.EndDoc;
@PrnPage.PageProc := nil;
end;
```

- -

This example prints two copies of each odd page on legal-size paper, and two copies of each even page on letter-size paper. The example also handles changing the printer settings between pages on printers that don't support resetting the device, by breaking the job into several print jobs, if necessary. Be aware that some VCL components may not expect device settings to change on-the-fly. Test your code well, and prepare to use Windows GDI calls where needed. Finally, make sure that you set your canvas objects (pens, brushes, and so on) back to the way they were at the beginning of the print job before resetting the device.

Printer Settings: *GetDevCaps()* and *DeviceCapabilities()*

You already used the windows function GetDeviceCaps() to retrieve information about the printer. You can look up GetDeviceCaps() in the Win32 section of Delphi's help system for the different queries that are available. If you are porting code between 16- and 32-bit Windows, be aware that not all 32-bit queries are available under 16-bit versions of Windows. Also be aware that some queries don't always reflect seemingly accurate information. Just because the number of pens reported back is zero, it doesn't mean that the device cannot use pens, and if the device reports the number of fonts as zero or even – 1, then you cannot output text. Some references even suggest that, if the technology reported is not RASTERPRINTER, the device cannot do bitmaps, and if RasterCaps reports that the device is (for example) incapable of StretchBlt, StrechDIB, or producing polygons then you cannot use these functions. This simply is untrue because even vector plotters can draw bitmaps by making lots of little lines, and if the device is incapable of stretching bitmaps, using device-independent bitmaps, or producing polygons, the GDI will step in and simulate the function.

One very important capability will affect your ability to print graphics. If the printer doesn't support graphics at all (such as a TTY line printer), you are out of luck if you plan to use graphics. Many published references are incorrect in documenting to query against RC_BITBLT to test for graphics support. The correct way to test if a given printer can provide graphic output is to query RASTERCAPS against RC_NONE (0x0000) like the following:

```
if (GetDeviceCaps(Printer.Canvas.Handle, RASTERCAPS) and
    RC_NONE) = RC_NONE then
 This_Is_A_Text_Only_Printer := true;
```

Another great way to get information from a printer device is to query the printer's `DeviceCapabilities` function. Although the `DeviceCapabilities` function is correctly declared in Delphi 1.0 and in Delphi 3, in Delphi 2.0—due to confusing documentation from the Microsoft MSDN Knowledgebase and in the Win32 help file from Microsoft—the function was declared incorrectly. Because the MS documentation is incorrect, this book takes on the subject.

First, the documentation suggests that you should call the function `DeviceCapabilitiesEx()`. This is incorrect. Call the `DeviceCapabilities()` function. If you are still using Delphi 2.0, you need to redeclare the three `DeviceCapabilities()` functions to work correctly. If you have the VCL source code, the best way to make the correction is to patch the WINDOWS.PAS file. I prefer the method as listed in the preceding section, where you patched `TPrinter`. Copy the file WINDOWS.PAS from Delphi's \SOURCE\RTL\WIN\ directory to the SOURCE\PATCHED\ directory and make these changes:

Find the following three function declarations in the implementation section of the WINDOWS.PAS file located in the SOURCE\PATCHED\ directory:

```
function DeviceCapabilitiesA; external gdi32 name 'DeviceCapabilitiesA';
function DeviceCapabilitiesW; external gdi32 name 'DeviceCapabilitiesW';
function DeviceCapabilities; external gdi32 name 'DeviceCapabilitiesA';
```

Change them to look like the following:

```
function DeviceCapabilitiesA; external 'winspool.drv'
➥       name 'DeviceCapabilitiesA';
function DeviceCapabilitiesW; external 'winspool.drv'
➥       name 'DeviceCapabilitiesW';
function DeviceCapabilities; external 'winspool.drv' name 'DeviceCapabilitiesA';
```

Using *DeviceCapabilities()*

You will use the `DeviceCapabilities()` function to retrieve the number of copies the current device can produce from a single page description. Here is an example:

```
var
  Device : array[0..cchDeviceName-1] of Char;
  Driver : array[0..(MAX_PATH-1)] of Char;
  Port : array[0..32] of Char;
  hDMode : THandle;
```

```
    pDMode : PDevMode;
    NumOfCopiesPossible : integer;
begin
    Printer.GetPrinter(Device, Driver, Port, hDMode);
    if hDMode <> 0 then begin
      pDMode := GlobalLock(hDMode);
      if pDMode <> nil then begin
        NumOfCopiesPossible :=
          DeviceCapabilities(Device, Port, DC_COPIES, nil, pDMode);
        GlobalUnlock(hDMode);
      end;
    end;
end;
```

There are many different settings you can query the printer for using the
DeviceCapabilities() function. When possible, you always should verify a device's capabilities before requesting a change in the device. You can get a list of the supported queries by
checking in the Win32 section of the Delphi help system. There, you find queries for everything from the paper size supported to the name of each paper bin that a given printer supports. Often, you need to call the DeviceCapabilities() function twice for a given query. The
first time to get the size of the structure needed for the query, and the second time to get the
actual data. An example is the DC_PAPERNAMES query. The first time you call
DeviceCapabilities(), you will pass nil in the fourth parameter, and DeviceCapabilities()
will return the number of paper names that the printer supports. You will then allocate a structure large enough to hold all the paper names, and call DeviceCapabilities() again, only this
time you will pass a pointer to your allocated memory block in the fourth parameter.

Here is an example:

```
type TPaperName = array[0..63] of char;
type TPaperNames = array[0..0] of TPaperName;
type PPaperNames = ^TPaperNames;

procedure TForm1.Button1Click(Sender: TObject);
var
  Device : array[0..cchDeviceName-1] of Char;
  Driver : array[0..(MAX_PATH-1)] of Char;
  Port : array[0..32] of Char;
  hDMode : THandle;
  pDMode : PDevMode;
  pPapers : PPaperNames;
  NumPapers : integer;
  i : integer;
begin
  Printer.GetPrinter(Device, Driver, Port, hDMode);
  if hDMode <> 0 then begin
    pDMode := GlobalLock(hDMode);
    if pDMode <> nil then begin
      NumPapers :=
        DeviceCapabilities(Device, Port, DC_PAPERNAMES, nil, pDMode);
      if NumPapers > 0 then begin
        GetMem(pPapers, NumPapers * sizeof(TPaperName));
        DeviceCapabilities(Device, Port, DC_PAPERNAMES, PCHAR(pPapers), pDMode);
```

```
        for i := 0 to (NumPapers - 1) do
          Memo1.Lines.Add(pPapers^[i]);
        FreeMem(pPapers, NumPapers * sizeof(TPaperName));
      end;
      GlobalUnlock(hDMode);
    end;
  end;
end;
```

In this example, a new type named TPaperName was declared that can hold a null-terminated string with 63 characters plus space for the null terminator. Then a new type called TPaperNames was declared that is an array of TPaperName elements. The TPaperName array is declared to be capable of holding only one PaperName. This is used for a useful trick to play on the compiler to access additional elements of a dynamically allocated array at runtime. Finally, a type of pointer to the array of PaperName named PPaperNames was declared.

When you initially call the DeviceCapabilities() function, you leave the fourth parameter as nil so the function will return the number of paper names. You now know how much memory to allocate. You then allocate enough memory to hold the paper names, and call the DeviceCapabilities() function again to retrieve the paper names by passing the pointer to your memory block in the fourth parameter cast as a PChar to make the compiler happy.

The next bit of code provides the magic necessary to trick the compiler into assessing the array elements to fill in your memo component with the paper names. When you declared the array, you initially gave it a size of one element, but you allocated enough memory for perhaps several elements. Because you are accessing the array index with a variable, the compiler will not complain that the index is out of range. For this trick to work at runtime, range checking must be turned off, and you must not overstep the array, or you will either trash other variables or cause a protection fault. Finally, you release the memory you allocated and clean up.

A final porting note: If you port code from 16-bit windows, and you were using LoadLibrary to get the handle to the printer driver, don't expect this to work under 32-bit versions of Windows. Use the preceding code instead because it's portable. You can no longer use LoadLibrary because Windows 95 allows 32-bit applications to print using 16-bit print drivers, and you cannot directly load a 16-bit DLL from a 32-bit application. Windows now provides this magic automatically. Windows also intercepts LoadLibrary calls on 32-bit print drivers made from 16-bit applications and provides the necessary "up-thunk" to allow older 16-bit applications to work · with 32-bit print drivers.

Printer Escapes

In the early days of Windows, printer escapes were used to control the printer when a low-level call to the driver was needed. Mostly, these calls consisted of starting a job, setting the abort proc, ejecting a new page, and ending the print job. From the application side, all of the basic escapes were replaced with GDI function calls that are wrappers to the old escapes. You still can call the escape functions, and if you really want the ultimate in controlling your print job, you will want to do so.

Aside from the minimum escapes a print driver should support (SETABORTPROC, STARTDOC, NEWFRAME, ENDDOC, and ABORTDOC), many print drivers support additional escapes. Some of these additional escapes are considered standard and are available on most print drivers, and many escapes are available only on specific printers. All drivers should support the QUERYESCSUPPORT escape, which is used to query if a given escape is supported.

When you call the Windows GDI `Escape()` function, the GDI translates the call to the print driver's internal `Control()` function providing any thunking magic needed. Occasionally, the GDI steps in and "hijacks" the call, never letting the call through to the driver. Sometimes, the GDI returns correct information, and other times it doesn't. A good example of this behavior is querying against the NEWFRAME escape. In 32-bit Windows, the GDI returns "this escape is not supported," although it is.

The thunking magic that the GDI provides encompasses far more than just the function call. Both inbound and outbound data also must be thunked and translated. The following is an example of calling the `Escape` function to query if the driver supports getting the printing offset (page margin). If the escape is successful, then you will retrieve the printing offset.

```
var
   TestInt : integer;
   PageMargin : TPOINT;
begin
  PageMargin.x := 0;
  PageMargin.y := 0;
  TestInt := GETPRINTINGOFFSET;
  if Escape(Printer.Canvas.Handle,
                QUERYESCSUPPORT,
                sizeof(testint),
                @TestInt,
                nil) = 0 then
     ShowMessage('Escape is not implemented')
  else begin
     if Escape(Printer.Canvas.Handle,
                 GETPRINTINGOFFSET,
                 0,
                 nil,
                 @PageMargin) <= 0 then begin
        PageMargin.x := 0;
        PageMargin.y := 0;
     end;
  end;
end;
```

A final note: 32-bit Windows defines a new function, `ExtEscape()`. The `ExtEscape()` function allows you to bypass most of GDI's intervention when sending an `Escape`. The Windows GDI still performs most of the thunking magic needed for the call, and if the GDI recognizes the `Escape`, it will thunk and convert any of the buffers you are passing as parameters (if necessary). If the `Escape` is unrecognized by the GDI, the pointers passed are thunked if necessary, but no conversion of the data is provided. This means (for example) if you call a 16-bit driver from a 32-bit application and the driver expects an integer, you need to send a 16-bit integer type. This also means that if you are sending a pointer to a structure that contains a pointer in the structure, you are out of luck! Although the GDI will thunk the pointer to the structure, it doesn't thunk the pointer in the structure. If you are sending an unrecognized Escape, you may need to know if the driver is 16-bit or 32-bit before making the call. Although the ExtEscape() call can be useful, don't take it for granted. Always test your planned Escape well before assuming that it will work properly.

Primer: Working with *TPrinter*'s Canvas

Although the Printer's Canvas property provides a good selection of methods to handle most of your graphic needs, you will be happy to know that you can use any Windows GDI calls or link up with most any third-party graphics library. The key to the magic is TPrinter's Canvas.Handle property. This handle is a standard Windows printer Dc, and you can use it wherever a Dc handle is required. Be aware that you must call the Printer's BeginDoc method (or use AssignPrn and Rewrite the file) before using the handle.

What Might Not Work

Most TPrinter's basic properties and methods work well and greatly simplify printing under Windows. In a few places, your graphic strategy may need to be changed because the printer's canvas may not yield the same great results that you see on-screen.

Consider this scenario: Your application is happily printing along, when the user has the nerve to abort the print job. The printer's Dc has just been destroyed, and you are still outputting to its canvas. Your application may have just reduced a fine operating system like Windows to rubble. Always check to see if the user has aborted the print job by checking the printer's Aborted method. This also can allow the system to timeslice more efficiently.

Another scenario where you may need to change strategy is when working with a canvas method that doesn't work well on a printer device. Most image methods fall into this category because they were designed to work with screen Dcs. If you were sharing the same code to draw to the screen and the printer, you can check the printer's Printing property to determine if any special processing is needed for a given piece of code.

A good example is when transferring bitmaps. You never should transfer a bitmap based on a screen Dc to a printer Dc. Instead, you should get the image as a device-independent bitmap (DIB) and then transfer the DIB to the printer. You will see an example of doing this later in the chapter. You also may need to provide special processing for some of the VCL components. Memo and grid components come to mind because you will need to roll up your sleeves and do the dirty work if you want printed output.

Printing Forms

Although each form has a print method, *you* may want to handle this task, if you want to increase your chances of a successful print on a wide range of devices.

Getting a bitmap to print successfully on a wide range of printers can be one of the most difficult tasks to pull off under Windows. Unless you take on the task from start to finish, you eventually will have to rely on the video and print driver for the conversion. Although the solution presented in the MANUALS.TXT file (which ships with Delphi) goes a long way in the right direction, it has two fatal flaws that keep it from going the additional mile. You must select any palette used into all the Dcs that you use along the way during the conversion, and you cannot always rely on a video driver to correctly fill in the palette information on a DIB.

An example of how this is done is capturing a screen shot of the form as it appears on-screen. If the video driver is a palette device, you will grab a copy of the current system palette and select it into any of the Dcs used during the conversion. If the video driver's mode currently supports more than 256 colors, you request a 24-bit DIB; otherwise, you request a 256-color DIB. If both the printer and the video driver support palettes, you will select the palette into the printer's Dc during the operation. Finally, you scale the output to fill the page in the correct proportion (taking into account the printer's margin), and center the output on the page. A final note: Your form must be the topmost window, and completely visible on-screen. If not, you get a good print of the portion currently showing. If you are firing the print event from a button or if you pop up the Print dialog box, you may want to add some calls to `Application.ProcessMessages` to allow the button and window to repaint before making the screen shot.

```
uses Printers;

procedure TForm1.Button1Click(Sender: TObject);
var
  dc: HDC;
  isSrcDcPalDevice : BOOL;
  isPrnDcPalDevice : BOOL;
  MemDc :hdc;
  MemBitmap : hBitmap;
  OldMemBitmap : hBitmap;
  hDibHeader : Thandle;
  pDibHeader : pointer;
  hBits : Thandle;
  pBits : pointer;
  TestInt : integer;
  PageWidth : integer;
  PageHeight : integer;
  PageMargin : TPoint;
  ImagablePageWidth : integer;
  ImagablePageHeight : integer;
  OffsetX : integer;
  OffsetY : integer;
  ScaleX : integer;
  ScaleY : integer;
  ppal : PLOGPALETTE;
  pal : hPalette;
```

```
  Oldpal : hPalette;
  i : integer;
begin

{Allow the button to repaint}
 Application.ProcessMessages;

{Get the screen dc for screenshot and conversion}
 dc := GetDc(0);

{Create a compatible dc}
 MemDc := CreateCompatibleDc(dc);

{Create a compatible bitmap}
 MemBitmap := CreateCompatibleBitmap(Dc,
                                      form1.width,
                                      form1.height);

{select the bitmap into the memory dc}
 OldMemBitmap := SelectObject(MemDc, MemBitmap);

{Get the system palette if necessary}
 pPal := nil;
 Pal := 0;
 OldPal := 0;
 isSrcDcPalDevice := false;
 if GetDeviceCaps(dc, RASTERCAPS) and
    RC_PALETTE = RC_PALETTE then begin
   GetMem(pPal, sizeof(TLOGPALETTE) +
     (255 * sizeof(TPALETTEENTRY)));
   FillChar(pPal^, sizeof(TLOGPALETTE) +
     (255 * sizeof(TPALETTEENTRY)), #0);
   pPal^.palVersion := $300;
   pPal^.palNumEntries :=
     GetSystemPaletteEntries(dc,
                             0,
                             256,
                             pPal^.palPalEntry);
   if pPal^.PalNumEntries <> 0 then begin
     pal := CreatePalette(pPal^);
     oldPal := SelectPalette(MemDc, Pal, false);
     isSrcDcPalDevice := true
   end else
   FreeMem(pPal, sizeof(TLOGPALETTE) +
           (255 * sizeof(TPALETTEENTRY)));
 end;

{Copy from the screen to the memory dc}
 BitBlt(MemDc,
        0, 0,
        form1.width, form1.height,
        Dc,
        form1.left, form1.top,
        SrcCopy);
```

```
  if isSrcDcPalDevice = true then
    SelectPalette(MemDc, OldPal, false);

{Unselect the bitmap from the memory dc}
 SelectObject(MemDc, OldMemBitmap);

{Delete the memory dc}
 DeleteDc(MemDc);

{Allocate memory for a DIB structure}
 hDibHeader := GlobalAlloc(GHND,
                           sizeof(TBITMAPINFO) +
                           (sizeof(TRGBQUAD) * 256));

{Get a pointer to memory block}
 pDibHeader := GlobalLock(hDibHeader);

{Fill in the dib header with the way we want the DIB}
 FillChar(pDibHeader^,
          sizeof(TBITMAPINFO) + (sizeof(TRGBQUAD) * 256),
          #0);
 PBITMAPINFOHEADER(pDibHeader)^.biSize :=
   sizeof(TBITMAPINFOHEADER);
 PBITMAPINFOHEADER(pDibHeader)^.biPlanes := 1;
 if isSrcDcPalDevice then
   PBITMAPINFOHEADER(pDibHeader)^.biBitCount := 8 else
   PBITMAPINFOHEADER(pDibHeader)^.biBitCount := 24;
 PBITMAPINFOHEADER(pDibHeader)^.biWidth := form1.width;
 PBITMAPINFOHEADER(pDibHeader)^.biHeight := form1.height;
 PBITMAPINFOHEADER(pDibHeader)^.biCompression := BI_RGB;

{Find out how much memory is required for the bits}
 GetDIBits(dc,
           MemBitmap,
           0,
           form1.height,
           nil,
           TBitmapInfo(pDibHeader^),
           DIB_RGB_COLORS);

{Allocate memory for the bits}
 hBits := GlobalAlloc(GHND,
                      PBitmapInfoHeader(pDibHeader)^.BiSizeImage);
{Get a pointer to the memory block}
 pBits := GlobalLock(hBits);

{Get the bits}
 GetDIBits(dc,
           MemBitmap,
           0,
           form1.height,
           pBits,
           PBitmapInfo(pDibHeader)^,
           DIB_RGB_COLORS);
```

```
{If the video is a palette device the fill in the DIB Palette}
 if isSrcDcPalDevice = true then begin
   for i := 0 to (pPal^.PalNumEntries - 1) do begin
     PBitmapInfo(pDibHeader)^.bmiColors[i].rgbRed :=
       pPal^.palPalEntry[i].peRed;
     PBitmapInfo(pDibHeader)^.bmiColors[i].rgbGreen :=
       pPal^.palPalEntry[i].peGreen;
     PBitmapInfo(pDibHeader)^.bmiColors[i].rgbBlue :=
       pPal^.palPalEntry[i].peBlue;
   end;
   FreeMem(pPal, sizeof(TLOGPALETTE) +
           (255 * sizeof(TPALETTEENTRY)));
 end;

{Release the screen dc}
 ReleaseDc(0, dc);

{Delete the memory bitmap}
 DeleteObject(MemBitmap);

{Start print job}
 Printer.BeginDoc;

{If the printer is a palette device then use the palette}
 isPrnDcPalDevice := false;
 if ((isSrcDcPalDevice = true) and
     (GetDeviceCaps(Printer.Canvas.Handle, RASTERCAPS) and
      RC_PALETTE = RC_PALETTE)) then begin
   oldPal := SelectPalette(Printer.Canvas.Handle, Pal, false);
   isPrnDcPalDevice := true
 end;

{Get the page size direct from the printer}
 PageWidth := GetDeviceCaps(Printer.Canvas.Handle, HORZRES);
 PageHeight := GetDeviceCaps(Printer.Canvas.Handle, VERTRES);

{Get the page margin}
 PageMargin.x := 0;
 PageMargin.y := 0;
 TestInt := GETPRINTINGOFFSET;
 if Escape(Printer.Canvas.Handle,
           QUERYESCSUPPORT,
           sizeof(testint),
           @TestInt,
           nil) <> 0 then begin
   if Escape(Printer.Canvas.Handle,
             GETPRINTINGOFFSET,
             0,
             nil,
             @PageMargin) <= 0 then begin
     PageMargin.x := 0;
     PageMargin.y := 0;
   end;
 end;
```

```
{Calculate the imagable area}
 ImagablePageWidth := PageWidth - (2 * PageMargin.x);
 ImagablePageHeight :=  PageHeight - (2 * PageMargin.y);

{Scale the printout size}
 if (((ImagablePageWidth <= ImagablePageHeight) and
     (Form1.width >= Form1.Height)) or
    ((ImagablePageWidth > ImagablePageHeight) and
     (Form1.Height < Form1.Width))) then begin
   ScaleX := ImagablePageWidth;
   ScaleY := Trunc(Form1.Height * (ImagablePageWidth / Form1.Width));
   OffsetX := PageMargin.x;
   OffsetY := (PageHeight div 2) - (ScaleY div 2);
 end else begin
   ScaleX := Trunc(Form1.Width * (ImagablePageHeight / Form1.Height));
   ScaleY := ImagablePageHeight;
   OffsetX := (PageWidth div 2) - (ScaleX div 2);
   OffsetY := PageMargin.y;
 end;

{Send the DIB to the printer}
 StretchDiBits(Printer.Canvas.Handle,
               OffsetX,
               OffsetY,
               ScaleX,
               ScaleY,
               0, 0,
               Form1.Width,
               Form1.Height,
               pBits,
               PBitmapInfo(pDibHeader)^,
               DIB_RGB_COLORS,
               SRCCOPY);

{If the printer is a palette device then delete the palette}
 if isPrnDcPalDevice = true then
   SelectPalette(Printer.Canvas.Handle, oldPal, false);

 if isSrcDcPalDevice = true then
   DeleteObject(Pal);

{Clean up allocated memory}
 GlobalUnlock(hBits);
 GlobalFree(hBits);
 GlobalUnlock(hDibHeader);
 GlobalFree(hDibHeader);

{End the print job}
 Printer.EndDoc;

end;
```

Finally, if you are interested in printing other images besides the form image, you can adapt the preceding code to do this. Just remember that the bitmap cannot be selected into a Dc during the conversion, and you must use the screen Dc to do the conversion rather than using a canvas or memory Dc.

Bypassing *TPrinter*

It was previously mentioned that it's possible that when you print, a read-only Windows metafile may be created. It can be much faster to draw directly to the printer driver and have the Print Manager skip the intermediate step of creating a metafile. You can do so by using a technique known as *banding*. Banding was designed back in the days when a printer lacked enough memory to hold a full page of graphics in memory at one time. The application asks the driver to supply the coordinates for a band (or rectangular section of the page) in which to draw.

The application then draws the correct output for that section, and continues to request more bands until the page is completed. Further, some printers have both a text and a graphic mode; they cannot do graphics when in text mode, and vice versa. To accommodate these printers, you will receive a *TextBand*, where you output only text, and a *GraphicsBand*, where you output only graphics. The main reason for using banding is that you get a real printer Dc with which to work rather than a read-only metafile Dc, which can make a big difference when you need the "real McCoy" to do some direct imaging.

Often, some GDI calls fail or do not work correctly when supplied a metafile Dc, and banding may be the only way around the problem. Finally, banding is incompatible with the `TPrinter` unit, so if you want to implement banding, you need to take on the complete task of printing from start to finish.

Putting It All Together

Well, now that you have the complete list of secrets for successful printing, you need to put this newfound knowledge to work. Although the art of printing has changed a great deal over the years, remember that it's not only how you print, but it's what you print. Plan your printouts. If you're not fully versed with a typography background, look at a quality-printed document before you decide how to lay it out, and then ask a professional for his or her opinion.

Other helpful hints along the way would include not mixing more than three fonts on a page, and choosing your typeface well, based on readability. Don't make the mistake of using all capital letters, even in headlines. Over 99 percent of everything your eye ever reads is printed in lowercase, and I assure you that your eye can interpret lowercase characters much better than uppercase.

Finally, if you want your document to be easy to read, design it so the reader can read it easily! ●

CHAPTER 24

Working with Threads

by Julian Bucknall

One of the most impressive power tools that programming for Windows 95 and Windows NT gives you is threads. Programmers have heard about them (usually how difficult they are to use), and are either anxious to try them or try to forget them entirely. Threads exploit the operating system to its fullest and their use permeates most Windows applications for the 32-bit environment. For example, the cute flying paper animation that you see when you copy a file in Windows 95 or Windows NT 4.0 is displayed by a worker thread while the main copy process gets on with copying data between the old file and the new file.

Threads allow applications to do many things at once; or rather, give the appearance of doing several things at once. Unless you are very lucky (and I'm not!), your PC has a single processor and can only do one thing at a time; you are limited by the Von Neumann serial CPU architecture. However, most processors are (generally) fast and can give the appearance of doing many things at once by using the magical task-switching code in the 32-bit operating system. In reality, it's all smoke and mirrors, with the operating system valiantly switching between different processes and threads, suspending the running task and then reviving the next, in a never-ending merry-go-round. It just goes so quickly that we're fooled.

Terminology

Understanding thread terminology is vital to comprehending this chapter.

Overview

Here, you delve into what threads are, how they are created, how they run, and how they stop.

Synchronization objects

Here, we discuss the different synchronization objects that Windows gives to help threads work together: We shall explore events, mutexes, and semaphores.

Thread local storage

This section shows how to write threaded code that accesses global data, and yet each thread "sees" different values.

The Delphi *TThread* class

Using our newfound knowledge, we'll pull apart the TThread class that Borland provided and look at its internals.

This chapter's intent is to give you a deep appreciation of threads and how to use them and to give you a flavor of the fascination of threads and the paraphernalia that accompanies them. Really, there's nothing so exhilarating as the first time your threaded application runs properly. (Certainly, I admit that there are a few other exhilarating things, but threads are up there, too!) Unfortunately, it's the nature of the beast that this chapter has to be very technical and may seem very dry in places. After all, threads aren't snazzy visual components, and I cannot just show another bitmap when the going gets tough. However, I do promise to be as accurate as possible and to go to a greater depth about threads than other Delphi books have done. You definitely will learn about some things that are taught nowhere else. ■

Thread Terminology

Like it or not, we need to define a few terms immediately—and be explicit about using them. If we don't, you'll be lost.

The first term is *Win32*, a term which will be used a great deal. By Win32, I mean either Windows 95 or Windows NT (or both), the 32-bit Windows operating systems (and no, I will not argue here whether or not it's correct to call Windows 95 a 32-bit operating system because some of it is still implemented with 16-bit DLLs). If I refer to something specific to one or the other operating system, I will say so. Also, when I refer to a routine as being a *Win32 routine*, I mean that it is declared in the Delphi Windows unit (the source file being WINDOWS.PAS).

The next term is *process*. A process is an application or program that has been loaded by Win32 into memory. Win32 also creates the virtual address space for the application. Some authors also use the words *task*, *application*, or *program*; however, Microsoft's Win32 SDK (Software Development Kit) usually uses process.

The last term is *thread*, the stuff about which this chapter is written. A thread is a Win32 object that runs code. When Win32 creates a new process (an application that has been loaded), a thread is created for this process to start running the actual program code. This thread is the *primary thread*. Any thread can create one or more other threads for the same process, and these threads all use the same virtual address space. The address space is provided by the process, which makes it easy—and also difficult, as you will see—to share data between threads. Each thread can be executing the same code or separate threads can execute separate code blocks. When the primary thread terminates, the process is unloaded from the system, and the application terminates.

To reiterate: threads, not processes, execute code. Processes define the data, resources, and address space that will be used by the threads that run inside the process.

Overview of Threads

The power of threads begins to be realized when you notice that your primary thread can create other threads, and those threads can create others, and so on. All threads for a process execute simultaneously. Win32 switches between the threads in a process automatically, without your doing anything about it or, conversely, having any real control over when and where the switch occurs. This is an important point that will be covered again later. Indeed, on some multiprocessor machines, different threads *will* be executing at the same time, but on different physical CPUs. Usually, however, your application will be running on a single processor machine and, in this case, Win32 will preemptively multitask your threads so that they get equal amounts of processor time. (Note that this last statement is oversimplified, because the amount of processor time allocated to each thread depends on factors such as the priority of the thread, whether the thread is waiting for a synchronization object to be signaled, and so on. You return to this a little further on in this chapter.)

Each thread executes in the process' memory space. Therefore, each thread can see all the same global data that the rest of the application sees. All of these threads also can change the same global data in this process, and therein lies the main problem with threads: the so-called race condition. Imagine that thread A and thread B are going to alter a global variable and then use it in a calculation. Thread A executes and increments the variable ready for the calculation. Before it can continue, Win32 does its multitasking magic and Thread A is put to sleep, and then Thread B starts executing. It increments the same global variable, and then completes its calculation. One more wave of the multitasking wand, and Thread A starts up again. It starts its calculation, but with the *wrong value of the variable*. A later section will discuss thread local variables and also the Win32 synchronization objects that enable you to alter and read global variables and structures without being preemptively multitasked.

Assuming that you are a guru adept at writing threaded code, where can you use threads in applications? Well, you can throw in threads *ad nauseam* into your code, and write fabulous synchronization code to tie them all together and let Win32 take care of the rest. However, I guarantee that the result will be a four-dimensional version of spaghetti and will move as sluggishly. (An aside: an old girlfriend of mine used to test whether spaghetti was cooked by throwing a strand at the wall—if it stuck, it was done. Threaded code can look like the wall after a few Bolognese dinners). Turn the question on its head: You should not write threaded code because you know you can; you must write threaded code because without it, the user would view the application as "slow." All too often we, as programmers, forget that we are writing applications for end users. One criterion upon which your application will be judged will be its responsiveness to user actions such as typing or mouse-clicking.

Another consideration: suppose that you have a certain amount of work to do in a routine, and you are wondering whether you can profitably use threads to "speed it up." If the work doesn't involve some kind of I/O, then generally the routine will not be made to execute faster by splitting it into threads. Suppose that the work uses quicksort to order an in-memory array. In this case, splitting up the quicksort to sort partitions in different threads makes the whole routine *slower*. You are just adding the overhead of switching between threads to the execution time of your quicksort. Instead, suppose that the work the routine is doing is sorting a large file. Here, it's conceivable that having several threads performing quicksorts on different parts of the file may be faster because, while one thread is waiting for the next block to be read from the file (a long operation), another thread can be sorting the block it has just read.

So, imagine that you are writing a memo editor with a spell check. At the end of every word the user types, you want to spell check that word and highlight it in some way if it is wrongly spelled (much as Word 7 is doing as I type this chapter). Now, you can spell check in your main code as the user types, but that probably is too slow for the average-to-fast typist. The user might perceive the memo editor falling asleep momentarily after each word. Here, a thread could shine: it would only have to spell check words. The main thread would be responsible for managing the displayed text and converting keystrokes into letters, and so on. Win32 takes care of the multitasking, and you could juggle the priorities of the foreground thread against that of the spell check thread.

Let's look at another example. You are writing a statistical application that reads in a set of data and then does some intensive computations on the data. These calculations can take a long time. However, the calculations do vary in complexity, and you want to show the user the simpler results as you go along. Perhaps the data is also shown and can be altered by the user for a what-if type view. It makes sense for the calculation to be done in a worker thread in the background, and it could signal the main thread when some results change. The main thread also could signal the calculator thread that the data had changed and that it must abandon its current calculation and start again. The user will perceive this route as responsive because he doesn't have to wait for all the calculations to complete before trying the next what-if scenario. Now, you can actually build all this "responsiveness" code into one thread (as was done in the old days in DOS), but that isn't the point. Threads make coding this kind of work easier because each new thread has a well-defined purpose and this is all it does. The operating system is responsible for switching between threads and generally making things run smoothly.

N O T E Another point to consider about threads. Although the Win32 operating systems are adept at task switching, it still takes a small amount of time. Usually, Windows NT is better at task switching than Windows 95. So, if you overload your application with threads that all run at the same time, your application appears sluggish to the user because a significant time is spent switching between threads and not in executing the application's code. ▪

Starting and Stopping Threads

Well, then, how do you start a thread and how do you stop one? At the lowest level, a thread is created by calling the Win32 routine `CreateThread`. In Delphi, however, it is a Bad Thing for programs to call this routine directly because `CreateThread` is much too low-level for Delphi applications to call. Not enough is done by calling it to ensure that the Delphi runtime library is aware of the new thread. There are two problems. First, a global variable named `IsMultiThread` (it's in the System unit) is not set to True when you call `CreateThread` directly. The Delphi heap manager uses this variable to know when multiple threads are running in the process; in knowing this, it can protect its internal structures from being updated by several threads at once. Second, `BeginThread` sets up an exception frame for the new thread, while `CreateThread` does not.

> **CAUTION**
>
> Never use `CreateThread` directly to create threads. It doesn't set up the new thread safely, as far as the Delphi runtime library is concerned.

The System unit provides a `CreateThread` replacement named `BeginThread`, and you should use this routine at all times in preference to the bare-bones Win32 routine:

```
function BeginThread(SecurityAttributes: Pointer; StackSize: Integer;
                ThreadFunc: TThreadFunc; Parameter: Pointer;
                CreationFlags: Integer; var ThreadId: Integer): Integer;
```

`SecurityAttributes` is a record structure to define the access rights of the new thread (its definition and use go beyond the scope of this chapter; refer to your Win32 help file). `StackSize` is the total size of the stack for the new thread; if you specify 0 here, the system uses Delphi's default of 1M. `ThreadFunc` is the Delphi function that the new thread will execute. It is of type `TThreadFunc`:

```
TThreadFunc = function(Parameter: Pointer): Integer;
```

The `Parameter` parameter is the same value as that passed to `BeginThread`, and usually this is either Nil (you don't want to pass any data to the thread) or a pointer to a record structure (if you want to pass data to the thread). You also can typecast a long integer to a pointer and thereby pass a numeric value to the thread.

You cannot initialize a data structure, call `BeginThread` passing the address of that structure as Parameter, alter the structure, and call `BeginThread` again for another thread. Even if you make a local copy of the data structure as your first action in the thread function, this *does not* work in the way you may expect. The thread function doesn't (or rather, probably won't) start executing immediately, and so this "quick" copy as its initial task still won't help you. You should allocate separate copies of the structure for each thread on the heap, for example, as an array of structures. Pass the relevant element of the array as Parameter in the relevant `BeginThread` call.

Back to `BeginThread`'s parameters. `CreationFlags` defines the state in which the thread will start: If this state is 0, the thread starts executing immediately (or rather, when the system gives it a time slice, which *may* be immediately). If it is CREATE_SUSPENDED, the thread is created, but is immediately suspended and does not execute any code until you call the Win32 `ResumeThread` routine. The `ThreadId` parameter is a numeric identifier (and is unique system-wide) for the new thread and is returned after the call to `BeginThread` completes.

The `BeginThread` function result is a thread handle (if it is 0, an error occurred and you will have to call the standard Win32 `GetLastError` routine to find the cause of the error). Note that the `BeginThread` function result is *not* the result of the thread function: The thread will not have executed at this point. The only thing that happened is that the thread kernel object was created, and it's ready to go.

Part
VI

Ch
24

On the other hand, the function result of the thread function is the exit code for the thread. You can query this by using the following Win32 `GetExitCodeThread` routine:

```
function GetExitCodeThread(hThread: THandle; var lpExitCode: DWORD): BOOL;
```

A thread either terminates when the thread function terminates (the thread function executes to its final "end;" statement) or when the Win32 `ExitThread` routine is called. However, you should use `EndThread` from the SYSTEM unit rather than `ExitThread` from the Win32 API to get a thread to terminate itself immediately, as follows:

```
procedure EndThread(ExitCode: Integer);
```

The `ExitCode` parameter is the value of the exit code for the thread.

When you create a thread by calling `BeginThread`, Win32 creates a thread kernel object, associates your thread function with it, and passes a thread handle back to you. When your thread function terminates (either by completely executing to the final "end;" statement, or by calling `EndThread`), Win32 makes a note of the exit code and marks the thread kernel object status as terminated. It does *not* destroy the thread kernel object. The object in fact remains allocated and its state is just marked as terminated. (The object is also signaled, and you can wait for this signal with the Win32 routines `WaitForSingleObject` and `WaitForMultipleObjects`. See "Synchronized Mechanisms" later in this chapter.) In the terminated state, there isn't a lot you can do to the thread apart from query its exit code. You certainly cannot "restart" it, for example. Only when you call the Win32 routine `CloseHandle` in your code, passing the thread handle, that the thread kernel object is finally destroyed.

```
function CloseHandle(hObject: THandle): BOOL;
```

The `hObject` parameter is the handle to the thread, and the function result is True if the call succeeded (and the thread object was destroyed) or False otherwise.

TIP
To avoid memory and resource leaks in your code, you *must* call `CloseHandle` when you have finished with a terminated thread.

CAUTION
If you call `CloseHandle` by using the handle of an executing thread, it is terminated immediately. Note that, in particular, all resources allocated by the thread are *not* freed if you do this. The thread is cut short and destroyed exactly at the point it has reached when the `CloseHandle` call was made.

When a thread is created, Win32 allocates a new stack for the thread from the process' address space (threads do not share stacks, they each have a different one). A corollary of this is that local variables within routines called by a thread are thread-safe: The only thread that can "see" them is the thread that is running the routine. Other threads running the same routine will have different local variables. The size of a thread's stack is 1M of which 16K is committed.

This is the default stack size for Delphi, but it can be changed by choosing Print, Options, and then altering Min Stack Size and Max Stack Size in the Linker dialog box. These two values affect all threads created by the application; you can supply different stack sizes for different threads if you want, but usually it's not worth the bother—after all, the stack is not completely committed at once anyway.

Thread Priorities

When the user loads an application and Win32 creates the process and the primary thread, the process is given a *priority class*, a value that defines how important the process is to the user and to the system. From this priority class the system derives a priority value to assign to the process' threads when they are created. The system will schedule the threads in all the processes in order of priority, and it is only when no executable threads remain at a high-priority level that threads at a lower level are scheduled and executed. If several threads have the same priority, they are scheduled one after the other in a round-robin fashion.

The priority calculated from the process' priority class is known as the *base priority* because all threads created for the process are given priorities that are *relative* to the process' base priority. In other words, to set a priority to a thread, you don't have to query the primary thread's priority and then calculate the priority you want to give your thread; you just tell the system that you want the thread to have the same, a slightly higher, or lower priority than the base priority and the system handles the rest.

When you create a process explicitly (rather than, for example, just executing a program from the desktop), you declare the priority class for the new process. Listed in Table 24.1, the four priority classes you can use (in ascending order of importance) are the idle class, the normal class, the high class, and the real-time class.

Table 24.1 The Base Priorities for the Allowed Priority Classes

Priority Class	Base Priority
IDLE_PRIORITY_CLASS	4
NORMAL_PRIORITY_CLASS	7 (background) or 9 (foreground)
HIGH_PRIORITY_CLASS	13
REALTIME_PRIORITY_CLASS	24

You also can use the Win32 routine SetPriorityClass to set the priority class of any process. Programs you execute from the desktop are run with normal class.

NOTE The normal priority class actually defines two priorities—the normal foreground class and the normal background class. If the window for a process is in the foreground, its threads' priorities are automatically boosted relative to processes that are executing in the background.

All very well, but what about threads? After all, that's why we're here in this chapter. When you create a new thread, it's given a priority equal to the base priority of the process. You can boost or lower a thread's priority by calling the Win32 `SetThreadPriority` routine:

```
function SetThreadPriority(hThread: THandle; nPriority: Integer): BOOL;
```

In this routine, `hThread` is the handle of the thread whose priority you want to change. `nPribority` is a value that describes a relative change to the process' base priority. It can have one of seven values, which are defined in Delphi's WINDOWS.PAS, and these are defined in Table 24.2.

Table 24.2 Relative Priority Constants Allowed by *SetThreadPriority*

Win32 Constant	Assigned Priority
THREAD_PRIORITY_ABOVE_NORMAL	1 point above base priority
THREAD_PRIORITY_BELOW_NORMAL	1 point below base priority
THREAD_PRIORITY_HIGHEST	2 points above base priority
THREAD_PRIORITY_IDLE	For a process with real time priority class, a priority of 16; all other priority classes, a priority of 1
THREAD_PRIORITY_LOWEST	2 points below base priority
THREAD_PRIORITY_NORMAL	Base priority
THREAD_PRIORITY_TIME_CRITICAL	For a process with real time priority class, a priority of 31; all other priority classes, a priority of 15

To find out the relative priority of a thread, you can call the complementary function to `SetThreadPriority`, `GetThreadPriority`:

```
function GetThreadPriority(hThread: THandle): Integer;
```

`hThread` is again the handle of the thread and the function result is one of the values used by `SetThreadPriority`, described in Table 24.2.

Before leaving the fascinating field of prioritization, I must raise a couple of notes. The first and foremost is: don't go wild and boost all your threads to THREAD_PRIORITY_TIME_CRITICAL to make them execute in preference to anything else on the system. If you do, depending on what you are doing in your threads, the whole system will become sluggish. I know I curse when the Windows 95 virtual memory compactor kicks in, and if you write your application with boosted-to-the-max threads, it feels like this all the time.

The second note is that you must try to keep priority boosts to threads that need it. Sometimes, writing Windows programs is a question of cooperation. If other programmers don't boost their threads to the detriment of other applications on the machine, then neither should you. Boost threads where needed (usually, this involves some kind of time-critical I/O), but don't go overboard. Just as in the old days of Windows 3.x, when you didn't write intensive loop code without a message yield type call to allow other Windows programs to execute, today you don't write code with artificially boosted threads.

> **CAUTION**
>
> Whatever you do, don't write code assuming that Win32 will execute your equal-priority threads in a particular order. Don't assume that just because you created thread 1 before thread 2 that thread 1 will execute first. Maybe it will, maybe it won't. *Always* make the assumption that threads are executed at the same time, as if your machine was infinitely parallel with a myriad of Pentium processors. If you don't, you'll be found out. If you have a thread waiting for an event, for example, and you signal that event from another thread, don't assume that the first thread will execute immediately and thereby preempt the thread that woke it up, or even *vice versa*. You'll be right some of the time and wrong the rest of the time. You may be right on Windows 95 but wrong on Windows NT (or *vice versa*; or only when you run Word 7.0; or only on Tuesdays). So please, don't assume anything. Thread bugs are bad enough to track down without making it more difficult from the start.

Thread Safety

To quote Larry Olivier in Marathon Man: "Is it safe?" Recall that threads all share the same memory space: the memory space of the owning process. They all have access to the same global variables. Local variables are safe; they are found on the stack and each thread has a separate stack. But global variables? Well…

The classic example of what happens with global variables and many threads is a linked list. Without going into detail, I'm sure that you have a visualization of what happens when nodes are added to and deleted from the list; all those pointer links being broken and remade. Now, imagine a global linked list with several threads adding and deleting nodes at the same time. The resulting mess would be a sight to behold.

To be *thread-safe* means that all access to global variables is made in a protected manner. The thread code must "lock" access to the global data it wants to read or update, do its access, and then unlock the global data again. The lock can only be granted to one thread at a time. Imagine that the threads are like runners in a relay race. They must grab hold of the baton before they can run on the track; after they turn over the baton to another thread, they must stop. Windows 95 and Windows NT come with a few different "batons" (they're really known as *synchronization objects*), which will be discussed in following sections.

Now imagine that you had such a lock mechanism with your global linked list. The first thread gets the lock, and then goes ahead to add or delete a node. When the operation is complete (and the linked list is whole again), the thread releases the lock. All the other threads that were waiting for the lock now can try to get it, but only one will succeed. This winning thread then can do *its* linked list update and release the lock. Again there's a mad scramble for the lock, and the whole process repeats. (Note that I just bestowed anthropomorphic traits to threads but in reality, it's the system that decides which thread should "win"; there is no discernible rule you can apply.)

An important thing to remember is that the VCL is not thread-safe. If you want to update a window, such as a list box or a button from a thread, while other threads are doing the same thing, you'll rapidly get into trouble. This is why Borland designed and wrote the TThread class (which will be discussed shortly); it has a specific mechanism used to enable the primary thread to update the display on behalf of all other threads, rather than allowing each thread access to the VCL internals.

On the other hand, the heap manager *is* thread-safe. Multiple threads can allocate and deallocate memory at the same time by using GetMem and FreeMem, and creating and destroying instances of classes. The heap manager keeps all requests sorted out and does not allow its (global) internal data structures to be trashed.

The Borland Database Engine also is thread-safe. You can have many threads accessing tables at the same time without the BDE getting confused. The mechanism for this is by having a different session per thread; however, this is not delved into here.

Critical Sections

Before moving on to thread synchronization mechanisms proper, it's best to have a look at the most popular method of making code and data thread-safe—the *critical section*. The critical section object also is used differently from the other synchronization objects, so it makes sense to treat it individually.

The name implies its usage. The critical section object is employed in making sure that a certain piece of code in a thread executes without interference from other threads in the same process: a "critical section" of code.

Using a critical section is the simplest and fastest way of serializing access to a global resource or data structure from many threads. A critical section is a special Win32 variable (actually a record structure) that allows a section of code to execute exclusively without interference from other threads. Suppose that a thread wants to update some global structure while other threads can access the same structure. Also suppose that the update involves many changes, for example adding an item to a linked list. If another thread were to read the structure while it was partially updated, it can be a disaster because not all the links have been updated. To *serialize access* to this structure (a grand way of saying "ensuring that the threads access the structure one at a time"), all the threads will go through the same type of code:

1. Lock the critical section object.
2. Read or update or manipulate the global structure.
3. Unlock the critical section object.

Suppose that you have two threads, A and B, each performing this code. Thread A locks the critical section object (the Win32 SDK calls this "entering the critical section"). Thread B gets preemptively multitasked and starts to run and tries to lock the critical section. The operating system puts Thread B to sleep because the critical section is already locked, and Thread A gets control again. It performs the data update, and then unlocks the critical section (the Win32

SDK calls this "leaving the critical section"). The operating system notes that Thread B is waiting for the critical section to become unlocked and gives the thread control so that it can lock the critical section, and then do its own update.

Critical sections are efficient. Entering one when no other threads are trying to do the same is very fast. Essentially, it is equivalent to setting a couple of values in the critical section data structure. Critical sections also are simple to use. There are drawbacks to using them: They can only be used within one process (threads in different processes cannot access a critical section in another process); and there is no timeout associated with critical sections. The latter drawback means that, if a thread is waiting to enter a critical section and the thread that already entered the critical section doesn't leave it, the first thread is blocked from running forever (or at least until the application is terminated). One Win32 synchronization object, the mutex, gets over these two drawbacks, which will be discussed in a following section. Note that mutexes have their own drawbacks, the principal one being that using a mutex is slower than using a critical section. So, use mutexes only if you want a locking mechanism across several processes or if you need that timeout.

On the CD

For a properly debugged program, critical sections are extremely useful—so much so that it's worth encapsulating the critical section functionality into a class so that it can be more easily used. Listing 24.1 shows one such encapsulation named TsePadlock. You can find the source, PADLOCK.PAS (as well as all other code listings that show paths in their descriptions), on this book's companion CD-ROM.

Listing 24.1   \UDELPHI3\CHP24\PADLOCK.PAS—The Padlock Class, an Encapsulation of Critical Sections

```
unit Padlock;

interface

uses
  Windows;

type
  TsePadlock = class
    private
      FCritSect : TRTLCriticalSection;
    protected
      procedure SetLocked(L : boolean);
    public
      constructor Create;
      destructor Destroy; override;
      property Locked : boolean write SetLocked;
  end;

implementation

constructor TsePadlock.Create;
begin
```

continues

Part
VI

Ch
24

Listing 24.1   Continued

```
    InitializeCriticalSection(FCritSect);
end;

destructor TsePadlock.Destroy;
begin
    DeleteCriticalSection(FCritSect);
end;

procedure TsePadlock.SetLocked(L : boolean);
begin
    if L then
        EnterCriticalSection(FCritSect)
    else
        LeaveCriticalSection(FCritSect);
end;

end.
```

The Create constructor initializes the internal critical section; the Destroy destructor deletes it. To enter the critical section, you set the Locked property to True; to leave it, you set the Locked property to False. That's it.

To test the encapsulation of a critical section, Listing 24.2 serializes access to the console window for two separate threads, both trying to write to it at the same time. One thread writes line numbers in English, the other in French. If you undefine the UsePadlock compiler define, you see that both threads interfere with each other, resulting in nonsense being written to the console.

Listing 24.2   \UDELPHI3\CHP24\TESTPADLOCK.PAS—Testing the Padlock Class

```
program TestPadlock;

{$APPTYPE CONSOLE}

// undefine this compiler define (by placing a period before the $) to
// see what happens when a padlock is not used when writing to the
// console screen
{$DEFINE UsePadlock}

uses
    SysUtils,
    Windows,
    Padlock;

var
    ConsolePadlock : TsePadlock;

procedure SafeWriteLn(const S : string);
begin
```

```pascal
  {$IFDEF UsePadlock}
  ConsolePadlock.Locked := true;
  try
    writeln(S);
  finally
    ConsolePadlock.Locked := false;
  end;
  {$ELSE}
  writeln(S);
  {$ENDIF}
end;

function EnglishThreadRoutine(P : pointer) : integer;
var
  ThreadID : integer;
  i        : integer;
begin
  Result := 0;
  ThreadID := GetCurrentThreadID;
  for i := 1 to 20 do
    SafeWriteLn(Format('[%x] current line: %d', [ThreadID, i]));
end;

function FrenchThreadRoutine(P : pointer) : integer;
var
  ThreadID : integer;
  i        : integer;
begin
  Result := 0;
  ThreadID := GetCurrentThreadID;
  for i := 1 to 20 do
    SafeWriteLn(Format('[%x] ligne courant: %d', [ThreadID, i]));
end;

var
  Handles : array [0..1] of integer;
  ThreadID : integer;

begin
  FillChar(Handles, sizeof(Handles), 0);
  ConsolePadlock := TsePadlock.Create;
  try
    Handles[0] := BeginThread(nil, 0, EnglishThreadRoutine, nil, 0, ThreadID);
    Handles[1] := BeginThread(nil, 0, FrenchThreadRoutine, nil, 0, ThreadID);
    WaitForMultipleObjects(2, @Handles, True, INFINITE);
  finally
    if (Handles[0] <> 0) then
      CloseHandle(Handles[0]);
    if (Handles[1] <> 0) then
      CloseHandle(Handles[1]);
    ConsolePadlock.Free;
  end;

  writeln('Press <Enter> to close...');
  readln;
end.
```

First, the console Padlock is created. Then the two threads that will write to the console window are created: The first thread executes the `EnglishThreadRoutine` function to write English sentences to the window, the second executes the `FrenchThreadRoutine` function to write French sentences to the console. The primary thread then waits for both threads to terminate before performing its cleanup. In each thread function, the routine `SafeWriteLn` is used to write a string to the console. It does this by obtaining the console Padlock, writing the string, and then releasing the console Padlock. In this manner, the complete string is written to the console without another thread preemptively multitasking the current thread and writing its own string (and thereby corrupting the original).

To use a Padlock, you create it at some point in your application, usually right at the start. Obviously, you create it before any of the threads that will use it are created! Similarly, you destroy it at the end of the program after all the threads apart from the primary one have terminated. You create a Padlock at most for every global data structure you need to access in your application. Suppose that you have two data structures that you are manipulating from several threads. Create two Padlocks, one for each structure. When you want to access the first structure, lock the first Padlock, access the structure, and unlock the Padlock when you are done. Repeat this for the second structure.

Note that you must be *very* careful about deadlocks when using multiple Padlocks (or critical sections). Suppose that there are two Padlocks and two threads. To do some particular data manipulation, the threads must lock both Padlocks. If thread A locks Padlock 1 followed by Padlock 2, whereas thread B locks Padlock 2 followed by Padlock 1, then it's entirely possible for thread A to lock Padlock 1, be preemptively multitasked in favor of thread B, which then locks Padlock 2. Now, neither thread A nor B can proceed because the next Padlock they both want to lock was already locked by the other thread. Both threads are blocked forever, each waiting for the other to release the lock on the Padlock it wants: the deadlock situation. Be very careful with the order you lock Padlocks in your threads. Always lock them in the same order in all your threads.

Miscellaneous Routines

So now you have threads running (and stopping), you can clean up after them, you prioritized them, and you made your data thread-safe by using a critical section. You can do a few other things to threads, or you can find more information about them.

```
function GetCurrentThread: THandle;
```

This routine returns a pseudo-handle to the currently running thread. It's called a pseudo-handle because it is just a reference handle to the thread. Unlike standard handles, you don't have to close it when you finish with it (in fact, `CloseHandle` ignores a request to close a pseudo-handle). The pseudo-handle can be used only by the thread that called `GetCurrentThread`; it cannot be used by other threads to refer to this one. You can create a "real" handle to the thread by calling the Win32 routine `DuplicateHandle` (this duplicated handle must be closed properly). Personally, I think `GetCurrentThread` is pretty daft: Rather than use the routine, I would save the returned handle when I create a thread.

```
function GetCurrentThreadID: DWORD;
```

This routine returns the unique ID of the current thread.

```
function TerminateThread(hThread: THandle; dwExitCode: DWORD): BOOL;
```

This routine terminates the thread given by the hThread handle and sets its exit code to dwExitCode. For many of the same reasons that you shouldn't call the basic CreateThread and ExitThread, you really shouldn't call TerminateThread. No resource cleanup is done, for example. It's far better to set a flag that the thread is continually polling (or to signal a Win32 event) and to let the thread routine clean up and terminate. Use TerminateThread only in emergencies.

```
function SuspendThread(hThread: THandle): DWORD;
```

This routine suspends the thread defined by the hThread handle. The thread stays suspended until a corresponding call to ResumeThread is made.

```
function ResumeThread(hThread: THandle): DWORD;
```

This routine resumes the suspended thread defined by the hThread handle. The thread resumes from the point where it was suspended by the call to SuspendThread. Note that ResumeThread has no effect on threads that wait for a kernel object to be signaled (discussed in following sections) or for a critical section to become available.

Synchronization Mechanisms

Synchronization, in terms of Win32 threads, means putting threads to sleep (thereby releasing their CPU timeslice) until some event occurs. For example, a worker thread goes to sleep until a file I/O thread has completed reading a buffer from a file for the original thread to process. You also can do this by polling some global variable (the file I/O thread sets a global Boolean True when it's finished so that the worker thread "knows" when the buffer is full; the worker thread goes into a tight loop, reading the Boolean until it becomes True), but this is frowned upon in Win32 because of its massive inefficiency. Also, if the worker thread were a higher priority thread, it would lock out the file I/O thread because of the tight loop; no data would be read, so the worker thread would never process anything. The application would grind to a halt.

Altogether, polling is a Bad Thing. Luckily, there are two ways to put a thread to sleep until an event happens—by calling the Win32 routines WaitForSingleObject and WaitForMultipleObjects. Before discussing them, you need a little background.

Several kernel objects can be *signaled*. Ah, another term! One way to visualize what signaled means is to consider the object as being your clothes dryer. When the dryer finishes drying a batch of clothes, a buzzer goes off to (a) scare you out of your wits (the house is usually empty and quiet and you're reading a Dan Simmons horror novel), and (b) inform you that it's time to empty the dryer. The buzzer "signals" that the dryer has finished (the dryer moves into a signaled state); until then the buzzer is quiet (the dryer is in a non-signaled state).

Objects get signaled by various means, and these means depend on the nature of the object. For example, previously in this chapter I said that when a thread terminates, the thread kernel object gets signaled. You can wait for this signal to know when the thread terminates. You look for this signal by using the Win32 `WaitForSingleObject` and `WaitForMultipleObjects` routines. Briefly, the former routine allows you to put a thread to sleep until a given kernel object becomes signaled, the latter allows you to put a thread to sleep until either at least one of several objects become signaled, or until they all do.

```
function WaitForSingleObject(hHandle: THandle; dwMilliseconds: DWORD): DWORD;
function WaitForMultipleObjects(nCount: DWORD; lpHandles: PWOHandleArray;
                          bWaitAll: BOOL; dwMilliseconds: DWORD): DWORD;
```

In the `WaitForSingleObject` routine, the `hHandle` parameter is the handle of the kernel object that you want to wait to be signaled; `dwMilliseconds` is how long you want to wait (you can pass the constant INFINITE here to force the call to wait forever). The return value is either the constant WAIT_FAILED, or it will be WAIT_OBJECT_0.

N O T E   There is a case with a mutex where the result of calling `WaitForSingleObject` may be WAIT_ABANDONED. This value is returned when the thread that previously owned the mutex terminated before releasing the mutex. The mutex is described as abandoned. ■

In the `WaitForMultipleObjects` routine, the `nCount` parameter is the number of kernel object handles you want to wait on and `lpHandles` is a pointer to an array of their handles. `bWaitAll` is True if you want to wait for *all* the handles to become signaled, or False if you want the call to finish when at least one of the handles becomes signaled. `dwMilliseconds` is as defined by `WaitForSingleObject`. The return value is again either WAIT_FAILED, or is an indication of which handle was signaled. If `bWaitAll` was True in the original call and the wait did not time-out, all the handles were signaled, and you cannot infer anything from the return value (apart from it not being WAIT_FAILED). If, however, `bWaitAll` was False in the original call and the wait did not time-out, the return value indicates the index of the handle that was signaled. Subtract the return value from WAIT_OBJECT_0 to calculate the index of the handle. If two or more handles became signaled at the same time, the value returned indicates the handle with the smallest index.

The kernel objects that can be signaled are: processes, threads (as previously intimated), files, console input, file change notifications, mutexes, semaphores, and events. Processes and threads become signaled when they terminate. This chapter doesn't go into files, console input, or file change notifications here. Mutexes, semaphores, and events are covered in the following sections.

For an example of waiting for objects to become notified, return to the Padlock test program discussed when I was talking about critical sections. At the time, I glossed over the main routine where `WaitForMultipleObjects` is called. Looking back at it, you will see that the main routine is waiting for both of the threads to terminate (and therefore to become signaled) before it continues with its cleanup exercises.

Deadlock Holiday

When I was talking about critical sections, I brought up the problem of deadlocks. It bears repeating at this juncture that when using synchronization objects you must be very aware of the possibility of deadlocks.

If a thread is waiting on a synchronization object having exclusively obtained another (such as a critical section), and another thread tries to exclusively obtain that same critical section before signaling the first synchronization object, the two threads are deadlocked. The second thread cannot proceed until it gets the critical section; the first thread cannot proceed until the second signals the object on which it is waiting.

To get around deadlocks, you must use care when you use your application's synchronization objects. Try to use them in the same order each time. For example, to obtain two critical sections before continuing with some processing, always obtain them in the same order, the first followed by the second.

Part

VI

Ch

24

If you do get deadlocks, it should be obvious that your threads are no longer doing any work. If so, you need to debug your thread code, concentrating especially on when you call one of the WaitForSingleObject or WaitForMultipleObjects methods. Possibly the best way to debug your thread code is to desk-check it: Thread code is notorious for not failing while you use the debugger. Pretend that you are running a particular thread and follow the code until you get to a Wait method. Assume that the thread will wait on it. Move onto another thread and do the same. Some threads will unblock others. Eventually, you find that a particular thread is continuously blocked, because another also is blocked. At this point, you can decide how to correct the situation. Try to apply the same hands-off reasoning that I argued at various points throughout this chapter when I pointed out problems with threaded code.

If it gets too difficult to desk-check your application, your thread code probably is too convoluted and may possibly need to be redesigned.

Events

Events are simple synchronization mechanisms. They provide a way for one thread to inform one or more other threads that an event has occurred or some processing has been completed. Note that Win32 events have nothing to do with Delphi events—the former are synchronization objects, and the latter are methods usually triggered by window messages being received by a form.

An event has two states—signaled and non-signaled. A thread calls WaitForSingleObject (or alternatively, WaitForMultipleObjects) with the event handle. If the event is non-signaled, the thread waits until another thread causes the event to be signaled (this is known as *setting the event*), at which time the system resumes the thread's execution.

There are two types of events—auto-reset events and manual reset events. With auto-reset events, after the event is signaled and a thread that was waiting for this to happen resumes execution, the event is automatically reset (set to the non-signaled state). With manual reset events, the event must be reset to non-signaled by calling the appropriate Win32 routine.

The main difference is when you have several threads waiting on the same event. With an auto-reset event, only one thread is released from its wait when you set the event (after the one thread is released the event is reset, so other threads cannot be released). With a manual reset event, all the waiting threads are released.

You can perform one more operation on an event (the others are setting the event and resetting the event): You can pulse the event. This is useful only with manual reset events. When you pulse a manual reset event, you set the event, release all the threads waiting for that signal, and then reset the event—all with one call. For auto-reset events pulsing the event is equivalent to setting the event; at most one thread is released, and then the event is reset.

Listing 24.3 is an encapsulation of a Win32 event, the `TseWin32Event` class (the source is found in WIN32EVENT.PAS on the CD-ROM).

Listing 24.3   \UDELPHI3\CHP24\WIN32EVENT.PAS—The *Win32Event* Class, an Encapsulation of Win32 Events

```
unit Win32Event;

interface

uses
  SysUtils,
  Windows;

type
  EWin32EventError = class(Exception)
    private
      FErrorCode : integer;
    public
      constructor Create(aErrorCode : integer);
      property ErrorCode : integer read FErrorCode;
  end;

  TEventResetType = (erAuto, erManual);

  TseWin32Event = class
    private
      FEvent     : THandle;
    protected
      procedure SetReady(R : boolean);
    public
      constructor Create(const aEventName : string;
                         aResetType : TEventResetType;
                         aInitiallySignaled : boolean);
      destructor Destroy; override;
      procedure Pulse;
      function WaitForEvent(TimeOut : integer) : boolean;
      property Handle : THandle read FEvent;
      property Ready : boolean write SetReady;
  end;
```

```
implementation

constructor EWin32EventError.Create(aErrorCode : integer);
begin
  FErrorCode := aErrorCode;
  inherited Create(Format('Win32 event error: %d', [aErrorCode]));
end;

constructor TseWin32Event.Create(const aEventName : string;
                                        aResetType : TEventResetType;
                                        aInitiallySignaled : boolean);
begin
  FEvent := CreateEvent(nil, (aResetType = erManual),
                        aInitiallySignaled, PChar(aEventName));
  if (FEvent = 0) then
    raise EWin32EventError.Create(GetLastError);
end;

destructor TseWin32Event.Destroy;
begin
  if (FEvent <> 0) then
    CloseHandle(FEvent);
end;

procedure TseWin32Event.Pulse;
begin
  PulseEvent(FEvent);
end;

procedure TseWin32Event.SetReady(R : boolean);
begin
  if R then
    SetEvent(FEvent)
  else
    ResetEvent(FEvent);
end;

function TseWin32Event.WaitForEvent(TimeOut : integer) : boolean;
begin
  Result := WaitForSingleObject(FEvent, TimeOut) <> WAIT_FAILED;
end;

end.
```

The Create constructor creates the event handle. You specify the event's name, the type of event you want to create (auto-reset or manual reset), and whether or not the event is to be initially signaled. The Destroy destructor closes the event handle. The WaitForEvent method enables you to get a thread to wait for the event to be signaled. The TimeOut parameter defines how long you want to wait; you can pass INFINITE in this parameter to disable the timeout. The Pulse method pulses the event. The Ready property can only be written to, setting it to True causes the event to be signaled, setting it to False causes the event to be non-signaled.

To help, I declared a new exception class to track any errors that could be returned by the Win32 `CreateEvent` call. The exception object stores the error code that was reported by the Win32 `GetLastError` routine if `CreateEvent` fails.

The name that you pass to the `Create` constructor is used to name the event. This name will be global to the system so that all threads in the system, even those belonging to other processes, "see" this name. This may cause a problem: If the name already exists when you call the `Create` constructor, you will not create a new event object. Rather, you get the handle of the pre-existing event object (the open count of the object's handle gets incremented, so that the handle can get closed twice). If the event is in use by another process for a completely different reason, your thread synchronization will function erratically, to put it mildly. So, name your events with care.

The program `TestWin32Event` on the CD-ROM exercises the event class.

Having defined the Win32 event class, we can turn to another typical multithreaded problem that is fairly complex and sophisticated. Usually, when you want to share a global data structure between threads, you will find that the threads will separate themselves into readers and writers. The technique I've shown you so far is to create a Padlock for the data structure. Whenever you want to access the data structure, whether it's for a read or a write operation, you lock the Padlock, do the access, and then unlock the Padlock. If most of the time threads will just be reading the data structure, it's a waste of resources because all the threads could access the data at the same time. We are assuming here that the structure, or the values in the structure, will not change because of the threads reading the data. Note that certain structures such as splay trees rearrange themselves when a data item is read from the structure: We will ignore these types of use-optimization structures in this argument. The only problem occurs when a thread wants to update the data structure; at this point, the structure must be locked so that all the data can be updated in a single atomic operation. No other threads should be able to read or write the data structure during this operation.

So we want to have some kind of synchronization object that will allow many reader threads to access a global data structure simultaneously. This same object will only allow one writer thread to update the structure at a time, locking out all other threads (readers and writers) while it does so. There also is another problem; there could be so many reader threads active that a writer thread finds that it is continually locked out, waiting for all reading access to cease. So the synchronization object must implement queuing of reading and writing threads.

The `TseGatekeeper` class (in unit GATEKEEPER.PAS) defines this synchronization object, so called because it can monitor and organize who can access the data through the "gate," either hordes of readers or just a single maintenance writer at a time. I originally called it a gatekeeper because I had this visualization of the gatekeepers at Kew Gardens in London, letting in tourists until some maintenance had to be done (see Listing 24.4).

**Listing 24.4   \UDELPHI3\CHP24\GATEKEEPER.PAS—The Gatekeeper
Class, a Solution to the Many Readers/Many Writers Problem**

```
unit Gatekeeper;

interface

uses
  Windows,
  Padlock,
  Win32Event;

type
  TseGatekeeper = class
    private
      Padlock            : TsePadlock;
      WaitingReaderCount : integer;
      RunningReaderCount : integer;
      ReaderCanStart     : TseWin32Event;
      RunningWriterCount : integer;
      WaitingWriterCount : integer;
      WriterCanStart     : TseWin32Event;
    public
      constructor Create(aGateName : string);
      destructor Destroy; override;
      procedure StartReading;
      procedure StartWriting;
      procedure StopReading;
      procedure StopWriting;
  end;

implementation

constructor TseGatekeeper.Create(aGateName : string);
begin
  Padlock := TsePadlock.Create;
  ReaderCanStart := TseWin32Event.Create(aGateName+'Read', erAuto, false);
  WriterCanStart := TseWin32Event.Create(aGateName+'Write', erAuto, false);
end;

destructor TseGatekeeper.Destroy;
begin
  WriterCanStart.Free;
  ReaderCanStart.Free;
  Padlock.Free;
end;

procedure TseGatekeeper.StartReading;
begin
  Padlock.Locked := true;
  if (RunningWriterCount > 0) or (WaitingWriterCount > 0) then begin
    inc(WaitingReaderCount);
    Padlock.Locked := false;
    ReaderCanStart.WaitForEvent(INFINITE);
```

continues

Listing 24.4   Continued

```
    end
  else begin
    inc(RunningReaderCount);
    Padlock.Locked := false;
  end;
end;

procedure TseGatekeeper.StartWriting;
begin
  Padlock.Locked := true;
  if (RunningWriterCount > 0) or (RunningReaderCount > 0) then begin
    inc(WaitingWriterCount);
    Padlock.Locked := false;
    WriterCanStart.WaitForEvent(INFINITE);
  end
  else begin
    inc(RunningWriterCount);
    Padlock.Locked := false;
  end;
end;

procedure TseGatekeeper.StopReading;
begin
  Padlock.Locked := true;
  dec(RunningReaderCount);
  if (RunningReaderCount = 0) and (WaitingWriterCount > 0) then begin
    dec(WaitingWriterCount);
    inc(RunningWriterCount);
    WriterCanStart.Ready := true;
  end;
  Padlock.Locked := false;
end;

procedure TseGatekeeper.StopWriting;
begin
  Padlock.Locked := true;
  dec(RunningWriterCount);
  if (WaitingReaderCount > 0) then begin
    while (WaitingReaderCount > 0) do begin
      dec(WaitingReaderCount);
      inc(RunningReaderCount);
      ReaderCanStart.Ready := true;
    end;
  end
  else begin
    dec(WaitingWriterCount);
    inc(RunningWriterCount);
    WriterCanStart.Ready := true;
  end;
  Padlock.Locked := false;
end;

end.
```

The `TseGatekeeper` class defines four methods: `StartReading`, `StartWriting`, `StopReading`, and `StopWriting`. Internally, it uses a Padlock and two Win32Events to maintain two queues and to serialize reader and writer access.

Now look at using the class from the viewpoint of a reader thread. To access the data structure the gatekeeper is protecting, we first call the `StartReading` method. This method checks whether any writer threads are waiting to run or are currently running. If so, the thread joins the queue of waiting reader threads and waits for the `ReaderCanStart` event to be signaled. If no writer threads are waiting or running, the method assumes that the reader thread can proceed unhindered. After the thread has finished its reading operation, it calls the `StopReading` method. This checks to see if any more reader threads are running. If not, it checks to see if any writer threads are waiting. If so, it signals the `WriterCanStart` event. This in turn causes one (and only one) writer thread to be released and to start running.

Now look at the class from the viewpoint of a writer thread. To access the data structure ready for updating it, the thread calls the `StartWriting` method. This method checks whether any reader or writer threads are still running. If so, the thread adds itself to the queue of writer threads by waiting for the `WriterCanStart` event to be signaled. If no other threads are running, the thread continues execution. After the thread has finished updating, it must call the `StopWriting` method. This method first checks to see whether any reader threads are waiting to start. If so, the method releases them all by signaling the `ReaderCanStart` event once for each waiting reader thread. If no reader threads are waiting, the method checks for waiting writer threads. If any of these are present, one is released by signaling the `WriterCanStart` event.

The internal Padlock is used to serialize access to the internal counters for waiting and running reader or writer threads.

As you can see, the gatekeeper class makes the implementation of the many readers/single writer scenario easy. The class manages the readers and writers in their own queues (note that the queues are *not* FIFO queues because we have no knowledge of which thread the system will release first; all we know is that one of them will be). The algorithm embodied in the class makes sure that first a bunch of reader threads have a go at the protected data, then a single writer thread (if there is one waiting), then a bunch of reader threads, and then a writer thread, and so on.

There's an interesting anecdote to relate at this point. The moral is that being overly clever where multiple threads are concerned sometimes doesn't work. Look at the `StopWriting` method again. If there are waiting reader threads, it releases them all by signaling the `ReaderCanStart` event once for each waiting thread in a simple `while` loop. All well and good, but I thought I could go one better. Make the `ReaderCanStart` event a manual reset event and pulse the event. All the waiting threads would be released at once. Sound good? Well, think a little about it before reading on.

My altered code looked like this:

```
if (WaitingReaderCount > 0) then begin
  RunningReaderCount := WaitingReaderCount;
  WaitingReaderCount := 0;
  ReaderCanStart.Pulse;
end
```

Sounds good, looks good. Now look at the `StartReading` method. If it determines that the thread should wait, it increments the count of waiting reader threads, unlocks the Padlock, and waits on the `ReaderCanStart` event. So? The point is that the method can be preemptively multitasked after the unlocking of the Padlock and before entering the wait. At this point, the count of waiting threads has been incremented. Suppose that the thread that gets control runs my "improved" code. All the reader threads (apart from our hypothetical one) will be released from their wait, but the gatekeeper now believes that there is one more running thread than there actually is. If you look at the other code in the class, you'll see that waiting writer threads will never, ever, gain control again, even if all the reader threads terminate (the gatekeeper will always think that there is at least one reader thread running). When our hypothetical reader thread gets control again, it will execute until it starts waiting for the `ReaderCanStart` event. At this point, it will be blocked forever because that event is only signaled by a writer thread calling `StopWriting`, and I've just shown that all writer threads are blocked. Bad news indeed, especially for such a simple "improvement."

Note that in the correct code it doesn't matter that the reader thread could get preemptively multitasked before it starts waiting, because the event gets signaled anyway and stays signaled until the reader thread waits on it. The effect is that there would be no wait.

Mutexes

Mutexes (MUTual EXclusions) are like grown-up critical sections and function in the same manner, with three important differences. The first difference is that mutexes are global to the system and can be "seen" across all processes; the second is that you can wait for them to be signaled with a time-out (critical sections have no time-out when waiting for them to become available); the third is possibly most important: Using a mutex is much slower than using a critical section. Taking these differences into account should make it easier to decide if you want to use a mutex or a critical section. If you feel the need for speed and are only concerned with a single process, go for a critical section. If you want to serialize data across many threads from many processes, you have no choice but to use a mutex.

I won't be going too much into mutexes in this chapter (mainly because in my time working with threads, I still have yet to use a mutex in connection with them), and shall just introduce my standard class encapsulation in Listing 24.5.

Listing 24.5   \UDELPHI3\CHP24\MUTEX.PAS—The Mutex Class, an Encapsulation of Mutexes

```pascal
unit Mutex;

interface

uses
  SysUtils,
  Windows;

type
  EMutexError = class(Exception)
    private
      FErrorCode : integer;
    public
      constructor Create(aErrorCode : integer);
      property ErrorCode : integer read FErrorCode;
  end;

  TseMutex = class
    private
      FHandle : THandle;
    protected
    public
      constructor Create(aName : string);
      destructor Destroy; override;
      function Lock(aTimeOut : integer) : boolean;
      procedure Unlock;
      property Handle : THandle read FHandle;
  end;

implementation

constructor EMutexError.Create(aErrorCode : integer);
begin
  FErrorCode := aErrorCode;
  inherited Create(Format('Win32 mutex error: %d', [aErrorCode]));
end;

constructor TseMutex.Create(aName : string);
begin
  FHandle := CreateMutex(nil, false, PChar(aName));
  if (FHandle = 0) then
    raise EMutexError.Create(GetLastError);
end;

destructor TseMutex.Destroy;
begin
  if (FHandle <> 0) then
    CloseHandle(FHandle);
end;
```

continues

Part
VI

Ch

24

Listing 24.5   Continued

```
function TseMutex.Lock(aTimeOut : integer) : boolean;
begin
  Result := (WaitForSingleObject(FHandle, aTimeOut) <> WAIT_FAILED);
end;

procedure TseMutex.Unlock;
begin
  ReleaseMutex(FHandle);
end;

end.
```

Just like events, Mutex names are global to the system. If you create a mutex object with a name that already exists somewhere on the system, you will be returned a handle to that pre-existing mutex, not a new one.

Semaphores

Semaphores are Win32 synchronization objects that allow a predetermined number of threads concurrent access to a resource or data. The semaphore has a count associated with it. If the count is greater than zero, the semaphore is in a signaled state and, hence, a wait operation will succeed immediately. When a wait operation succeeds, the count is decremented. When the count reaches zero, the semaphore switches to a non-signaled state and wait operations from a thread will do exactly that, wait. They will wait until the count becomes positive again, in which case the system selects a thread to be released and the count is decremented once more. The count is incremented by a call to a Win32 routine. Unfortunately, you cannot read the count's value: Win32 does not expose it.

Imagine a multiuser game, played over a network, in which the number of players must be limited to four. The game runs on a single machine on the network and uses some kind of protocol, like NetBIOS, to send messages around the network to other workstations that are playing. For each player, it creates a thread to monitor the network traffic from that workstation and to update the internal game play. To limit the number of players, it can create a semaphore with an initial count of 4. The first four threads the game creates will be able to wait on the semaphore and succeed. The semaphore count is reduced to zero and the semaphore is non-signaled. The next player thread that is created will wait on the semaphore, until one of the other players leaves the game and increments the semaphore count. (Of course, in practice, the wait would have a timeout on it so that the player has the choice to try again later.)

Semaphores, like events and mutexes, are global to the system and must be named appropriately to ensure that they are individual. Note also that it is fairly simple to implement a semaphore by use of mutexes and events; I leave it as an exercise for the reader to do so (as my mathematics lecturers used to say at university).

Listing 24.6 is an encapsulation of a semaphore:

Listing 24.6   \UDELPHI3\CHP24\SEMAPHORE.PAS—Encapsulation of the Win32 Semaphore Routines

```
unit Semaphore;

interface

uses
  SysUtils,
  Windows;

type
  ESemaphoreError = class(Exception)
    private
      FErrorCode : integer;
    public
      constructor Create(aErrorCode : integer);
      property ErrorCode : integer read FErrorCode;
  end;

  TseSemaphore = class
    private
      FHandle : THandle;
    protected
    public
      constructor Create(aName : string;
                         aInitialCount : integer;
                         aMaximumCount : integer);
      destructor Destroy; override;
      function DecCount(aTimeOut : integer) : boolean;
      procedure IncCount;
      property Handle : THandle read FHandle;
  end;

implementation

constructor ESemaphoreError.Create(aErrorCode : integer);
begin
  FErrorCode := aErrorCode;
  inherited Create(Format('Win32 semaphore error: %d', [aErrorCode]));
end;

constructor TseSemaphore.Create(aName : string;
                aInitialCount : integer;
                aMaximumCount : integer);
begin
  FHandle := CreateSemaphore(nil, aInitialCount, aMaximumCount, PChar(aName));
  if (FHandle = 0) then
    raise ESemaphoreError.Create(GetLastError);
end;

destructor TseSemaphore.Destroy;
begin
```

continues

Listing 24.6   Continued

```
  if (FHandle <> 0) then
    CloseHandle(FHandle);
end;

function TseSemaphore.DecCount(aTimeOut : integer) : boolean;
begin
  Result := (WaitForSingleObject(FHandle, aTimeOut) <> WAIT_FAILED);
end;

procedure TseSemaphore.IncCount;
begin
  ReleaseSemaphore(FHandle, 1, nil);
end;

end.
```

As you can see, it is a very simple class. Once created, you can either decrement the semaphore count (with a timeout if required), or increment it. The DecCount method will return True if it successfully decremented the semaphore count; otherwise, it returns False, and the assumption is that the timeout expired before it could decrement the count.

Data Local to Threads: TLS and *Threadvar*

If you write threaded code by using the bare BeginThread and EndThread routines, there may come a point when you really have to have a global variable that is local to each thread. Now the problem is that all global variables are visible to all threads, so you'd have to declare somehow an array of such variables (how many elements?) and define an index for each thread you create (how?), so that that thread will only look at and modify the element at that index. There must be an easier way, and there is: thread local storage.

Thread Local Storage (known as TLS) is a method whereby Win32 provides global data that is different for each thread. TLS is easy to describe (there are only four routines to understand), but can be confusing at first glance. I should know: I was confused at first glance(!), and I carried around a false perception of TLS until I really had to research it (which led, incidentally, to the idea for this chapter).

Win32 defines a bit array of 64 bits. Every time a thread is created, Win32 creates an array of 64 pointers on the thread's stack and sets them all to zero. You can only access this array by using the TLS routines. Each bit in the bit array is for one element in each pointer array. All's well so far. Say you want to have a pointer that has a different value for each thread and yet is global. Generally, the pointer would be a pointer to some kind of global data structure. First, you call the Win32 TlsAlloc routine to allocate yourself an index into the TLS pointer array, as follows:

```
function TlsAlloc: DWORD;
```

Win32 searches its array of bits, looking for one that isn't set yet. If it finds one, it sets it and returns the index of that bit (if it doesn't find one, it returns an error code: TLS_OUT_OF_INDEXES). Store that index in a global variable (which obviously all threads can "see"). This index refers to an element of the pointer array that is private to each thread. For example, if TlsAlloc returned 15 as the index, each thread would then refer to index 15 in its own private array to store and retrieve its data.

When you want to save a value to this element of the hidden TLS pointer array, you would call TlsSetValue, as follows:

```
function TlsSetValue(dwTlsIndex: DWORD; lpTlsValue: Pointer): BOOL;
```

You would pass the index you have previously stored (dwTlsIndex) and the pointer value you want to store (lpTlsValue) and Win32 would store the value in that element of the private array given by the index. If another thread wanted to store a different value, it would call the same routine but this time the value would be stored in its copy of the TLS array on its stack.

To get the item back from TLS, call TlsGetValue, as follows:

```
function TlsGetValue(dwTlsIndex: DWORD): Pointer;
```

You'd pass that same index you stored after calling the TlsAlloc routine as the dwTlsIndex parameter. Again, the routine would act on the private array to each thread; different threads would receive data local to themselves.

Finally, when all is done, you call TlsFree to return the index to the pool (to set the bit off in the bit array).

```
function TlsFree(dwTlsIndex: DWORD): BOOL;
```

Again, the dwTlsIndex parameter is the index value you stored earlier.

Because the data you are storing in the TLS is a pointer, you usually would define a large data structure to hold all the global data that you want private and individual to each thread, allocate it on the heap, and then store the pointer to it in the TLS. If you define things properly, you should only be using one of these TLS indexes so that the fact that there are only 64 indexes shouldn't impact you too much.

Enough theory; Listing 24.7 shows a small example program that uses TLS through the Win32 interface.

Listing 24.7 \UDELPHI3\CHP24\TestTLSRoutines.DPR—Testing the Win32 TLS Routines

```
program TestTLSRoutines;

{$APPTYPE CONSOLE}

uses
```

continues

Listing 24.7 Continued

```
  SysUtils,
  Windows,
  Padlock;

var
  ConsolePadlock : TsePadlock;
  OurTlsIndex    : integer;

type
  PThreadLocalData = ^TThreadLocalData;
  TThreadLocalData = record
    Number : integer;
    ID     : integer;
  end;

procedure SafeWriteLn(const S : string);
begin
  ConsolePadlock.Locked := true;
  try
    writeln(S);
  finally
    ConsolePadlock.Locked := false;
  end;
end;

procedure WriteThreadNumber;
var
  TLD : PThreadLocalData;
begin
  TLD := TlsGetValue(OurTlsIndex);
  SafeWriteLn(Format('Thread ID %x is number %d', [TLD.ID, TLD.Number]));
end;

function MyThreadFunction(Parameter : pointer) : integer;
var
  TLD : PThreadLocalData;
begin
  Result := 0;
  New(TLD);
  try
    TLD.Number := longint(Parameter);
    TLD.ID := GetCurrentThreadID;
    TlsSetValue(OurTlsIndex, TLD);
    WriteThreadNumber;
  finally
    Dispose(TLD);
  end;
end;

const
  NumHandles = 20;

var
```

```
    Handles : array [0..pred(NumHandles)] of integer;
    ThreadID : integer;
    i : integer;

begin
  OurTlsIndex := -1;
  FillChar(Handles, sizeof(Handles), 0);
  ConsolePadlock := nil;
  try
    OurTlsIndex := TlsAlloc;
    ConsolePadlock := TsePadlock.Create;
    for i := 0 to pred(NumHandles) do
      Handles[i] := BeginThread(nil, 0, MyThreadFunction, pointer(i), 0,
                               ThreadID);
    WaitForMultipleObjects(NumHandles, @Handles, true, INFINITE);
  finally
    for i := 0 to pred(NumHandles) do
      if (Handles[i] <> 0) then
        CloseHandle(Handles[i]);
    if (OurTlsIndex <> -1) then
      TlsFree(OurTlsIndex);
    ConsolePadlock.Free;
  end;

  writeln('Press <Enter> to close...');
  readln;
end.
```

The main routine allocates a TLS index by calling TlsAlloc. This index is stored in a global variable, OurTlsIndex. 20 threads are then created and each thread routine stores some information (the thread ID and the creation number of the thread) in a record allocated on the heap. The pointer to the record is stored in the correct index of the TLS array by calling TlsSetValue and passing the OurTlsIndex value for the index. A routine called WriteThreadNumber is then called. This routine can be called by many threads at once, and its purpose is to report the values held in the record that each thread initialized. So it finds out the data by calling TlsGetValue and passing the correct TLS index stored in OurTlsIndex.

Having said all this, you can now ignore the TLS routines insofar as you may need to use them. The reason? The threadvar reserved word. Borland recognized that people would be using thread local variables and so made it easy in Delphi to declare them and use them. The threadvar reserved word works much in the same way as var does when applied to global variables, with the sole exception that variables declared in a threadvar block are local to each thread.

That's it. *Morçeau de gâteau.*

You don't have to worry about calling TlsAlloc, TlsSetValue, and so on; the compiler inserts code for you to do just that. The linker also gets into the act: It calculates the total size of all the threadvar variables, and hard-codes a variable in the System unit to that value so that a memory block can be sized and allocated at runtime to hold them all. For each reference to a `threadvar` variable the linker calculates the offset of that variable in this runtime memory block and hard-codes it into the final EXE file (or DLL file for that matter). When the program is loaded, the primary thread executes an initialization routine that allocates a TLS index for you, allocates a block of memory to hold all the threadvar variables, and sets it to zero.

All this happens without any work on your part. You just get to enjoy using `threadvar` variables just as you would use any global variable.

 TIP Do note, however, that it is more expensive in terms of time to read or write a `threadvar` variable than a local variable or a standard global variable (after all, under the hood the compiler has inserted code that calls `TlsGetValue` or `TlsSetValue`). Therefore, if you are using `threadvars` in tight loops (or even several times in the same piece of code), consider making a local copy of the value at the start of the loop.

Listing 24.8 shows the original TLS routine test program described earlier, rewritten to use `threadvar` variables (with the parts that are unimportant to our discussion omitted). All references to TLS have been excised.

Listing 24.8   \UDELPHI3\CHP24\TESTTHREADVAR.PAS—Showing How Much Simpler *threadvars* Are to Use than the TLS Routines

```
threadvar
  OurNumber : integer;
  OurID     : integer;

// code omitted

procedure WriteThreadNumber;
begin
  SafeWriteLn(Format('Thread ID %x is number %d', [OurID, OurNumber]));
end;

function MyThreadFunction(P : pointer) : integer;
begin
  Result := 0;
  OurNumber := longint(P);
  OurID := GetCurrentThreadID;
  WriteThreadNumber;
end;
```

That's it. I'm sure you agree that it's pretty simple stuff.

So where's the catch?

Ah, there is one of course; it's remote, but still present. Win32 defines the TLS bit array to be 64 bits; in other words a process can only allocate 64 indexes by calling `TlsAlloc` in its threads. So what? I hear you say, if I declare a `threadvar` (or several) variables in my application, the Delphi compiler and linker acting in concert make sure that only one TLS index is used.

Correct, but the same thing also applies to Delphi DLLs. Delphi DLLs have their own `threadvar` block (there are at least two variables in it: They are declared in the System unit). DLLs, when loaded, form part of the calling process and they will use up a TLS index in their initialization. So if your app loads over 63 DLLs at once, you will be in trouble. The 64th `threadvar` block allocation will fail (that is, assuming no other routine in your app is using TLS allocations explicitly). DLLs built using other compilers may (and probably do) use other schemes for allocating their static thread local storage, but the problem remains.

Delphi's *TThread* Class

After this chapter's journey so far in the discovery of the threadbare essentials, we suddenly arrive at Delphi's `TThread` class, a class that encapsulates threads. Recalling what we've learned on our journey will enable us to make a light snack of most of the class, leaving the rather meatier entrée for its `Execute` and `Synchronize` methods.

The `TThread` class was designed to alleviate the problem of many threads trying to access the VCL (especially the visual components and controls) at the same time. Succinctly, the VCL is not thread-safe. If you have several threads updating a form at the same time, you will rapidly get a mess and quite probably coax some Access Violations out of it as well. Rather than spending a great deal of time making the VCL thread-safe, Borland decided to document the fact that it is definitely not thread-safe and then to provide a way so that you could almost pretend that it was.

Essentially, the trick is that the primary thread is solely responsible for updating the screen. When a thread declared with a `TThread` instance wants to update the screen, it calls a routine (the `Synchronize` method) that signals to the main thread that a screen update is pending, and then the primary thread does the actual work. We'll discuss the methodology that `TThread` uses in fuller detail in following sections.

TThread Declarations—The Snack

Here's the `TThread` class as defined in the VCL's Classes unit (omitting the private section of the class declaration):

```
TThread = class
  private
    // declarations omitted
  protected
    procedure DoTerminate; virtual;
    procedure Execute; virtual; abstract;
    procedure Synchronize(Method: TThreadMethod);
    property ReturnValue: Integer read FReturnValue write FReturnValue;
    property Terminated: Boolean read FTerminated;
  public
    constructor Create(CreateSuspended: Boolean);
    destructor Destroy; override;
    procedure Resume;
    procedure Suspend;
    procedure Terminate;
```

```
    function WaitFor: Integer;
    property FreeOnTerminate: Boolean read FFreeOnTerminate write
FFreeOnTerminate;
    property Handle: THandle read FHandle;
    property Priority: TThreadPriority read GetPriority write SetPriority;
    property Suspended: Boolean read FSuspended write SetSuspended;
    property ThreadID: THandle read FThreadID;
    property OnTerminate: TNotifyEvent read FOnTerminate write FOnTerminate;
  end;
```

***TThread* Public**   Nibbling smartly through the public section first.

The `Create` *Constructor*   This constructor creates the `TThread` instance. It increments an internal thread count (a global variable), sets a couple of internal fields of the object, and then calls `BeginThread`. The thread is created in a suspended state if the `CreateSuspended` parameter is true.

The `Destroy` *Destructor*   This destructor destroys the `TThread` instance. If the thread is still running, it is terminated by calling the `Terminate` method. The thread's complete termination is waited for by using the `WaitFor` method. The thread's handle is closed by calling `CloseHandle`. `Destroy` then decrements an internal thread count.

The `Resume` *Method*   This method resumes a suspended thread by calling `ResumeThread`.

The `Suspend` *Method*   This method suspends a running thread by calling `SuspendThread`.

The `Terminate` *Method*   This method sets an internal flag to indicate that the thread is to be terminated at the earliest opportunity. The flag is defined by the protected `Terminated` property. It is up to the `Execute` method to periodically check this flag while it's running and to bail out as soon as it sees the flag go True. If the `Execute` method does *not* check this flag, this method has no discernible effect (and certainly, the thread will not terminate no matter how many times you call this method!).

The `FreeOnTerminate` *Property*   This read/write property defines whether the `TThread` object is automatically freed when the thread itself terminates.

The `Handle` *Property*   This read-only property is the handle of the thread as returned by `BeginThread`.

The `Priority` *Property*   This read/write property is the relative priority of the thread as set by `SetThreadPriority` and as returned by `GetThreadPriority`. Incidentally, the read method for this property implements a `for` loop to convert the returned Win32 value into the Delphi `TThreadPriority` enumerated type. After the Win32 value has been recognized and the conversion has been made the loop is *not* exited, and instead the `for` loop is allowed to continue. A small trivial enhancement would be coding a break statement after the `Result` value has been set. However, this is minor compared with a bug we'll be discussing later.

The `Suspended` *Property*   This read/write property defines whether the thread is suspended. Setting the property results in either the `Suspend` or the `Resume` method being called.

The `ThreadID` *Property*   This read-only property is the unique ID of the thread as returned by `BeginThread`.

The OnTerminate *Event*   This event is called after the Execute method has completed, but before the TThread object has been destroyed. It's actually called before EndThread is called for the thread and the OnTerminate event is running as part of the thread itself. To avoid any possible VCL problems, the OnTerminate event handler is called via the Synchronize method.

TThread **Protected**   Now for a positive guzzling through the protected section (avoiding the Execute and Synchronize methods for now).

The DoTerminate *Property*   Calls the OnTerminate event handler via the Synchronize method.

The ReturnValue *Property*   The exit code for the thread. EndThread will be called with this value as its parameter.

The Terminated *Property*   This read-only property is true if the thread is to be terminated at the earliest opportunity. It's up to the Execute method to periodically check this flag and to terminate the thread cleanly when it turns true. The flag is set by the Terminate method.

TThread Declarations—The Entrée

Now we will discuss arguably the most important methods—the Execute and Synchronize methods of the TThread class.

Execute   This method performs the actual processing of the thread. In the TThread class it is defined as virtual and abstract. In other words, TThread is an abstract class, and you cannot create an instance of a TThread and expect it to work. It won't. (You'll get a runtime error.) This, in turn, means that you must create a descendant class from TThread that overrides Execute and create an instance of that class instead whenever you want to use the functionality of the TThread class. Execute will run inside the thread that the Create constructor creates.

Synchronize   This method notifies the primary thread that there is something to update on the screen, and passes the address of a method (the display method) the primary thread can call to get the work done. The notification process is *serialized* (the primary thread will receive notifications one at a time and will be able to complete one update fully before it gets the next notification). The actual algorithm uses a message queue, and notifications are just messages that get sent to that queue. Because the notification message is sent (compare with posted) using the Win32 routine SendMessage, Synchronize waits for the display method to be called. The effect is that the thread will freeze until the display method has completed (the display method runs inside the primary thread). This is not optimal, but at least it means that you don't have to use Padlocks or similar to serialize access to the fields inside your thread object.

Enough theory—it's time to design a small example TThread descendant class that shows how to use Execute and Synchronize. The work that the threads will do is to compress/decompress files by using the splay tree method. I do not discuss this particular compression algorithm other than to say that it is fairly simple and doesn't compress as much as Zip or LZW (text files get compressed to about 66 percent of their original size, for example). Besides this, of course, it is irrelevant to our topic of discussion in this chapter. For more details see the article by

Douglas W. Jones, "Application of Splay Trees to Data Compression," in *Communications of the ACM*, August 1988, page 996. I'm using a variation of the Pascal code originally written by Kim Kokkonen of TurboPower Software, and you can download the original SPLAY.LZH from TurboPower's Web site at **http://www.turbopower.com**.

Anyway, back to the thread code. Each thread will compress or decompress a file. It will report its progress by updating a progress bar on the main form. The Execute method will do the actual compressing/decompressing whereas the Synchronize method will do the updating.

To create the basic application, follow these steps:

1. Create a new project.

2. Drop a button (TButton, on the Standard palette) onto the form and three progress bars (TProgressBar, on the Win95 palette). Set the caption of the button to **Start**, and its name to **StartButton**. Also drop three labels (TLabel) onto the form, to label each of the progress bars. Arrange at will (see Figure 24.1). We shall be running three threads simultaneously, and each of these progress bars will show the progress of one of the threads.

FIG. 24.1

The TThread example form.

3. Create a new thread object (select File, New and select Thread Object from the icon list). Name the class TSplayCompressThread. Save the project (select File, Save All), naming the Unit1 unit as **Main**, the Unit2 unit as **SplayCompressThread**, the Project1 project file as **DemoTThread**.

4. Time for some code. In the SplayCompressThread unit, alter the definition of the TSplayCompressThread class to include some new fields, properties, and methods:

```
TSplayCompressThread = class(TThread)
  private
    { Private declarations }
    FInFileName  : string;
    FOutFileName : string;
    FDoCompress  : boolean;
    FPercentDone : integer;
    FProgressBar : TProgressBar;
  protected
    procedure PercentDoneNotify(Percent : integer);
    procedure DisplayPercentDone;
  public
    constructor Create(InFileName, OutFileName : string; DoCompress :
boolean);
```

```
procedure Execute; override;
property PercentDone : integer
  read FPercentDone;
property ProgressBar : TProgressBar
  write FProgressBar;
end;
```

5. Code the implementation of the Create constructor in the same unit:

```
constructor TSplayCompressThread.Create(InFileName, OutFileName : string;
➥                                       DoCompress : boolean);
begin
  inherited Create(True);
  FInFileName := InFileName;
  FOutFileName := OutFileName;
  FDoCompress := DoCompress;
  FPercentDone := 0;
end;
```

Nothing too interesting here. All the parameters are saved in internal fields. The ancestor's Create method is called with the CreateSuspended parameter as True; in other words, the thread will be created in a suspended state.

6. Code the implementation of the Execute method:

```
procedure TSplayCompressThread.Execute;
var
  SCE : TSplayCompressionEngine;
begin
  SCE := TSplayCompressionEngine.Create(FInFileName, FOutFileName);
  SCE.PercentDone := PercentDoneNotify;
  if FDoCompress then
    SCE.Compress
  else
    SCE.Expand;
  SCE.Free;
end;
```

The method creates an instance of the TSplayCompressionEngine class. It sets the PercentDone property of that class to its own PercentDoneNotify method. What will happen is that the compression engine object will call this event whenever the percentage of the file processed changes. So PercentDoneNotify will be called 101 times, once for every percentage point between 0 and 100 percent, inclusively. The Execute method then calls on the engine to compress or expand the input file. Finally, the compression engine object is destroyed.

7. Code the implementation of the PercentDoneNotify protected method:

```
procedure TSplayCompressThread.PercentDoneNotify(Percent : integer);
begin
  FPercentDone := Percent;
  Synchronize(DisplayPercentDone);
end;
```

This method gets called by the compression engine whenever the percentage of the file that has been compressed (or decompressed) has changed. It calls the Synchronize method passing the DisplayPercentDone method to it. Internally, Synchronize will post a message to a hidden window with this method as parameter. After the message gets retrieved by the primary thread, the method gets called. Hence, eventually, DisplayPercentDone gets called.

8. Code the implementation of the DisplayPercentDone protected method:

```
procedure TSplayCompressThread.DisplayPercentDone;
begin
  FProgressBar.Position := FPercentDone;
end;
```

As you can see, this code only updates the progress bar associated with the thread.

By this point, we have created our descendant thread class, and you can already see how the Execute and Synchronize methods work. The Execute method creates and runs the compression engine object, freeing it after all the work is done. The Synchronize method will get called whenever the progress bar needs updating, and the method that actually does that is the DisplayPercentDone method.

Let us flesh out the TForm1 class in the Main unit.

9. In the private section of the TForm1 class add the following fields:

```
TerminatedCount : integer;
Thread1 : TSplayCompressThread;
Thread2 : TSplayCompressThread;
Thread3 : TSplayCompressThread;
```

10. Add the following method definition to the public section of the same form class:

```
        procedure ThreadTerminated(Sender : TObject);
```

11. Here's the implementation of that ThreadTerminated method:

```
procedure TForm1.ThreadTerminated(Sender : TObject);
begin
  inc(TerminatedCount);
  if (TerminatedCount = 3) then begin
    StartButton.Enabled := true;
    ProgressBar1.Position := 0;
    ProgressBar2.Position := 0;
    ProgressBar3.Position := 0;
  end;
end;
```

As you can see, it counts the numbers of threads that have terminated and after all have done so, it re-enables the Start button and resets the progress bars.

12. Now, create an OnClick event handler for the Start button (double-click it):

```
procedure TForm1.StartButtonClick(Sender: TObject);
begin
  StartButton.Enabled := false;
  TerminatedCount := 0;
  Thread1 := TSplayCompressThread.Create('\8-73.HTML', 'Test1.SCF', true);
```

```
      Thread2 := TSplayCompressThread.Create('\8-73.HTML', 'Test2.SCF', true);;
      Thread3 := TSplayCompressThread.Create('\8-73.HTML', 'Test3.SCF', true);;
      Thread1.ProgressBar := ProgressBar1;
      Thread2.ProgressBar := ProgressBar2;
      Thread3.ProgressBar := ProgressBar3;
      Thread1.FreeOnTerminate := true;
      Thread2.FreeOnTerminate := true;
      Thread3.FreeOnTerminate := true;
      Thread1.OnTerminate := ThreadTerminated;
      Thread2.OnTerminate := ThreadTerminated;
      Thread3.OnTerminate := ThreadTerminated;
      Thread1.Resume;
      Thread2.Resume;
      Thread3.Resume;
    end;
```

The method disables the button, sets the count of terminated threads to zero, and then starts creating the threads. There are three threads and they are all going to compress a large text file each to a different file. (This large text file happens to be called "\8-73.HTML" because that was available on my home machine when I was testing this; use any file name you like, the larger the better to be able see the threads all working simultaneously.) Each thread object is given its own individual progress bar, they are each forced to destroy themselves when they terminate, and just before they do, they'll each call the ThreadTerminated method of this form. Finally, each thread is resumed (remember the thread is created suspended).

13. Compile and run. Press the Start button and watch the threads compress the data and update their own progress bars.

TThread—The Drawbacks

Drawbacks? What's this? Yes, I'm afraid it's true. The programmer at Borland who designed TThread fumbled a catch. Here it is.

When an instance of a TThread is created, an internal routine is run to perform some housekeeping. This routine keeps count of the number of TThread instances active. If this is the first TThread instance, a window handle is created so that the Synchronize method can have somewhere to send messages to. Similarly, when the last TThread instance is destroyed, this window is destroyed. Neither of these two routines protect the global data variables they use with a critical section. The creation routine looks like this:

```
if ThreadCount = 0 then
  ThreadWindow := AllocateWindow;
Inc(ThreadCount);
```

The destruction routine looks like this:

```
Dec(ThreadCount);
if ThreadCount = 0 then DestroyWindow(ThreadWindow);
```

Part

VI

Ch

24

Putting on our thinking caps, we see the following problem. Suppose that a thread is created by first principles, using `BeginThread`. Both this thread and the primary thread can create `TThread` instances. It is easy to see that it is possible to have the final `TThread` instance being destroyed in one thread, just as a new `TThread` instance is being created in the other. With the right multitasking switch at just the right time, a new window handle could be created (displacing the old one, making it an orphan), and a flick of the multitasking wand later, be destroyed. (Imagine the removal routine in the first thread decrementing the thread count to zero; Win32 switching to the addition routine running in the other thread, which then creates a new window; Win32 switching to the removal routine again, which then destroys the window just created; and Win32 switching back to the addition routine to complete incrementing the thread count.) Even if only one switch occurred, you would get an orphan window, reducing resources. A little far-fetched, but possible. It certainly could have been prevented with a judicious critical section, or by documenting that if you use `TThread` objects, don't create threads with `BeginThread` as well.

If you learn nothing else from this chapter, far-fetched things can happen with threaded code.

Eventually.

And generally, only at the client site: You won't be able to duplicate it on your machine.

Other Topics for Research

In this chapter, we glossed over some items and haven't even mentioned others. The main reason for this is that I have a limited amount of space for this chapter and, to do full justice to multithreaded programming techniques, it would require a book on its own.

In no particular order, here are a couple of items for you to research and maybe use:

- **Win32 supports Asynchronous File I/O.** This enables an application to request that the operating system read (or write for that matter) some information from a file handle and continue doing some processing while the operating system performs the file I/O. Generally, you would create a thread to do the file access and let the thread wait for the data to be read; the file handle becomes signaled when the I/O operation has completed. Asynchronous File I/O is most often used for serial communications. In fact, Microsoft recommends that this technique be used in that situation.

- **Windows NT 4.0 introduced a new object: a fiber.** A *fiber* (as may be guessed) is something a little less than a thread. Fibers are lightweight threads, just as threads might be termed lightweight processes. Threads incur a certain amount of overhead and take an appreciable amount of time to switch between them, whereas fibers are individual strands of execution within a single thread and have been devised because they do not have a lot of overhead. Fibers have their own stack and a little context information, but that's about it. Windows NT 4.0 does not preemptively multitask down at the fiber level; only threads are still multitasked. This limits the applicability of fibers because it is up to the thread code to "manually" switch from fiber to fiber. The third edition of Jeffrey Richter's *Advanced Windows* (Microsoft Press) has a section on fibers.

Summary

In this chapter, we talked about threads. Threads enable an application to become more responsive by giving the appearance of doing several things at once. With this ability comes a responsibility for us to make sure that using threads makes an application more responsive and that we are not using threads just because we know how and just because we are gonzo programmers with no fear.

We have seen how to create and use threads. We have seen how to synchronize the threads that we do create, how to make sure that they access data in a controlled manner to eliminate any risks, and why this is important. To help us with this goal, we have defined some synchronization classes to serialize access to global data, culminating with a sophisticated many-readers/many-writers synchronization class. We have touched on the thread deadlock problem.

We have seen why Delphi has the TThread class, and using our knowledge of "raw" thread routines, we have examined its implementation and have touched on its drawbacks.

All in all, threads are fun. The reason: It takes some thought and planning on your behalf, and when the plan comes together, it's impressive.

Very impressive. ●

Part
VI

Ch
24

DLL Programming:
An Introduction

by Eric Uber

DLL is an acronym for *Dynamic Link Library*. This name is appropriate because it describes both function and implementation. DLLs are natively compiled and executable libraries that are linked into a program or larger system at runtime. They provide the benefit of localizing related pieces of code, data, and resources that can be shared between applications. DLLs can be written in a language-independent fashion that allows, for example, a C++ application to use various features available in Delphi.

The capability to share a single DLL module between applications enables the programmer to create a single set of *Application Program Interfaces* (*API*) that reduces the overall footprint of an application's EXE, opposed to statically linking essentially the same code into every application's EXE. Because the code is shared in the form of an executable library, updates to the DLL (such as bug fixes) update all applications that share the DLL.

DLLs can optionally be loaded and unloaded upon demand. This capability gives an application complete control over the amount of memory and resources it uses at any given time. Suppose that an application uses several code- and resource-intensive forms. The forms can be moved into a DLL that you load when you need the forms, and then unload when you're done.

■ **Win32 concepts in DLL programming**

Learn about Delphi's implementation of Win32 concepts in DLL programming.

■ **DLL-based applications**

Acquire the knowledge needed to build faster and more efficient DLL-based applications.

■ **DLLs in project design**

Understand how to design your programs for maintainability and with the least amount of redundancy.

■ **DLL internals**

Gain the insight that will make troubleshooting simpler and less time-consuming.

Note that two of the biggest features in the Delphi 3 release include robust ActiveX support and a *packaged*-based Visual Component Library (VCL). Both of these fantastic features on the lower levels rely on DLL programming technologies and exist in a DLL-based architecture. ■

DLLs and Their Role in Win32

Architecturally, all versions of Windows—including WinNT and Win95—use DLLs in the foundation of their framework. A DLL-based programming model modularizes all aspects of the system. This modularization allows the operating system to support a more dynamic and open interface for the programmer. Consider all of the following places you see DLLs used today:

- CPL files (Control Panel Applets)
- The Win95 and WinNT Shell Extensions
- The Win32 core files such as KERNEL32 and GDI32
- Device drivers such as COMM.DRV
- Creation and Implementation of Thunk layers
- NT System Services
- Process injection for Hooks and sub-classing of window procedures
- OLE in-process automation servers

The list, by far, doesn't stop here. With the release of Win95 and NT 4.0 came not only a better-looking operating system, but also an overall turn in the road of development techniques. Win95 and NT are extremely *COM*-centric, which isn't to be taken lightly because COM is the absolute backbone to the current and future versions of the Windows operating systems. Aspects of COM can be implemented by using in-process servers that are contained within DLLs. Because they are contained in DLLs, the principles discussed in this chapter are an applicable prerequisite to the topic.

For more information about COM and In-process servers, see Chapter 20, "Working with OLE Automation."

Porting from 16-Bit Windows

If you're like most Windows application developers, your personal operating system is WinNT or Win95. If you used Delphi before, you probably already own Delphi 1.0, 2.0, and now 3. The flip side of this is that your customer base probably is still using Windows 3.x or has only recently begun the transition. 16-bit applications seem to run rather well under WinNT and Win95, but it is important to remember these applications do not take advantage of any aspect of the Win32 feature set. Given this, the transition to the world of flat memory and thread-based processing may not always go as smoothly as a simple recompile.

T I P Although Borland claims forward compatibility, this compatibility is in the context of what is realistic. If the operating system removes a feature or changes its internal workings, even a tool as cool as Delphi won't be able to compensate for it.

DLLs in Win16

In direct context to DLL programming, Win32 has made changes to the architecture that cause applications written by following a certain model to simply fail. If your current 16-bit applications share a single DLL, smooth portability to Win32 will be questionable; therefore, this section of the chapter is for you.

The architectural change under Win32 is a result of the removal of the segmented memory model and inclusion of the flat memory process model. In 16-bit Windows, a DLL was perceived to be a globally accessible library that cleanly integrated into the operating system, thus it was sharable by multiple applications.

16-bit DLLs used the stack of the loading application; however, they maintained their own 64K data segment in memory. DLLs also were loaded only once during the initial call to LoadLibrary by the application or operating system. Subsequent calls to LoadLibrary simply incremented a reference count maintained by Windows. When an application was done with the DLL, it called FreeLibrary. FreeLibrary decremented the reference count by 1 for each call until it reached 0, in which case the DLL was physically unloaded.

Part
VI

Ch

25

Huge Memory Allocations

Pascal never supported the huge pointers on which C++ programmers came to depend. Because of the segmented memory model used in 16-bit Windows, a standard 4-byte pointer was actually composed of two parts. The high WORD of the pointer value was a selector which addressed a 64k segment of memory. The low WORD value of the pointer was an offset within this segment.

The OS honored requests for memory blocks larger than 64K, but the programmer was responsible for accessing each piece of the data across segment boundaries. To retrieve the value of a 100K block spread over two segments, you had to read in all the data up to the segment boundary (often one byte at a time). Then you had to increment the selector portion of the pointer's value. After the selector part of the pointer was addressing the next segment, the rest of the data could be retrieved. Then all the data could be reassembled into something meaningful.

Win32 doesn't have the 64K segment limitation found in 16-bit Windows. If you're porting to Win32 and you use routines or classes that manipulate selectors and manage huge memory blocks, this code must be removed. Under Win32, pointers still are 4 bytes, but the value is all offset. If you increment what used to be the selector portion of the pointer, you will really be changing where the offset points into the addressable process space. Where you end up is completely random.

Programmers quickly took advantage of this architecture because they could use a single DLL to share data between applications. Because DLLs had their own data segment, global variables and constants could be used as flags for communication between applications. An application could even ask the DLL to allocate a memory block from the global heap and then pass off the pointer to another application for direct use.

Existing programs that follow this design are now in trouble, or at least will require more work to port. Under Win32, an application and all the DLLs it uses are encapsulated in their own address space. Multiple instances of a single application or the running of two applications that use the same DLL are oblivious to each other.

DLLs in Win32

Under Win32 each application is completely self-contained. When the operating system is notified to load an application, it creates a kernel process object, simply referred to as a *process*. A process houses a virtual 4G of addressable memory in which your application operates. A region of memory from the system paging file is allocated to maintain the addressing. Following the creation of the process, another object is created known as a *kernel file-mapping object*, which maps the executable file into the address space of the process. The executable file is literally mapped from its location on the hard disk, thus eliminating the need to load the entire image into RAM or copy it to the paging file, which ultimately lives on the hard disk anyway.

> **CAUTION**
>
> DLLs usually export functions for use by EXEs or other DLLs within the application. If you recompile your existing DLL from 16-bit, be aware that the default calling convention is no longer Pascal. See "Calling Conventions," a subsequent section of this chapter.

After the executable file is mapped into memory, the operating system moves to an offset within the image to retrieve the names of all DLLs required for use by the EXE. Using a particular search scheme, the required DLLs are sought out within the system and mapped into the same process as the EXE. A kernel file-mapping object is created for each DLL mapped into the region. If any DLLs require the use of other DLLs, they are mapped into the application address space in a similar fashion. This pattern of mappings continues until every piece of the application is in place.

N O T E   There is actually more occurring than discussed here, such as the creation of a primary thread, calling of each DLL's entry point, the resolving of function references, loading at preferred base addresses, relocations, and so on. The intent here is to clarify the bounds of the framework in which your application and its associated DLLs are running. ■

When the application terminates, each DLL file mapped into the address space is unmapped, and the associated file-mapping object is destroyed. This process continues until the EXE is unmapped and the kernel process object gets destroyed, taking with it everything left in the process space—including memory allocations made by the application.

Under Win32, DLLs still can be shared by multiple applications or even multiple instances of the same application. Each application maps the DLL into its own process space. DLLs in Win32 still have their own heap, but the heap is allocated and addressed in context to the loading process. If a 32-bit DLL makes memory allocations in a way that, under 16-bit Windows was said to be from the *Global Heap*, under Win32, this memory also is allocated in the context of the loading process. This is why the sharing model changes and may require some redesign of your application. Now look at some ways to get around this change.

Solving the Porting Problem

Win32 provides several alternatives to the issue of sharing data across process boundaries. All of these alternatives require modifications to your existing code base. Most of these mechanisms are covered in this book. They are as follows:

- **Sending of `wm_CopyData` message**—Use this message to send a data structure from one application to another, thus eliminating the need for the intermediate DLL. (For more information about `wm_CopyData`, see Chapter 32, "Thunking in Delphi.")

- **Implementation of a thunk layer**—Use your existing 16-bit DLL as part of the application. This action should be regarded as only a temporary fix. (For more information about implementation of thunk layers, see Chapter 32.)

- **Kernel file-mapping objects**—Modify the DLL to initialize a kernel `FileMapping` object for each `dll_Process_Attach`. (For more information about kernel file-mapping objects, see Chapter 26, "DLL Programming: Advanced Concepts.")

- **Use of OLE Automation server**—Create an automation server that maintains a single instance of the data. (For more information about OLE Automation servers, see Chapter 20, "Working with OLE Automation.")

This section of the chapter discusses what I believe is the biggest change for DLL programmers moving to Win32. Many more issues pop up in very unexpected places. Throughout this chapter, I point out significant issues as the information applies, so make sure that you check out the various notes and tips as you continue.

Creating the Project

Delphi provides a simple facility for creating a DLL project. A new DLL project consists of a single DPR file. No default form or additional units are provided. To add forms and units to the project, select File, New from Delphi's main menu as needed.

If you like, create a new DLL project. Select File, New from Delphi's main menu. The dialog box shown in Figure 25.1 is displayed.

FIG. 25.1

Delphi's New Items dialog box gives you access to create many elements besides DLL projects.

When the New Items dialog box appears, select the DLL icon, and then click OK. This action results in the project shown in Listing 25.1. You can find BAREBONES.DPR on this book's companion CD-ROM.

Listing 25.1 \DLPHI3\CHP25\BAREBONES.DPR—The BareBones Project, As Its Name Suggests, Has Sparse Content

```
library BareBones;
{ Important note about DLL memory management: ShareMem must be the
  first unit in your library's USES clause AND your project's (select
  View-Project Source) USES clause if your DLL exports any procedures or
  functions that pass strings as parameters or function results. This
  applies to all strings passed to and from your DLL—even those that
  are nested in records and classes. ShareMem is the interface unit to
  the DELPHIMM.DLL shared memory manager, which must be deployed along
  with your DLL. To avoid using DELPHIMM.DLL, pass string information
  using PChar or ShortString parameters. }
uses
  SysUtils,
  Classes;
begin
end.
```

Most of Listing 25.1 comes in the form of a comment generated by the DLL expert. The comment, briefly, is provided as a note in context to redeployment of the DELPHIMM.DLL along with your DLL. Delphi wraps the interface functions to DELPHIMM with an interface unit named ShareMem. By including the ShareMem unit in your project, you give your DLL the capability to pass and receive Delphi's AnsiString data type from your DLL to the loading EXE (or another DLL) and vice versa.

AnsiStrings

Delphi introduced the `AnsiString` (or Long String) in version 2. It differs from the traditional Pascal string because it isn't a fixed length. Rather, it's a pointer to a #0 terminated string. The string is preceded by a 12-byte structure. So, the beginning of the structure is at an offset 12 bytes prior to the beginning of the string data. The pointer points to the beginning of the string data. If you simply dereference the pointer, only the #0 terminated data will be accessible. For this reason, the compiler allows you to typecast an `AnsiString` to a `PChar` and you can support it.

The 12-byte structure portion of an `AnsiString` contains fields for allocation size, reference counting, and the actual data length. These fields are used for the automatic garbage collection and copy-on-write optimization. In context to DLL programming, the seemingly magical string-handling and sharing functionality must be managed by code contained in DELPHIMM.DLL.

After the DLL project is generated, you can save and build it. The result is a bare-bones DLL that does nothing. You can add code, resources, and data to the project as needed and access it all, external to the DLL, but within the bounds of the application process. Now look at the entry point (or initialization code) for your DLL.

The *DLLMain* Entry Point

In a Delphi project, the entry point for a DLL is between the first "begin" and ending "end." in the DPR file. When the loader code executes, all statements in this section of the DPR execute first. This section is a good place for initialization routines or memory instantiations to occur. If you want your DLL to execute some form of batch processing from the moment it is loaded, the code also can be called from here. This capability enables you to give the DLL functionality without ever explicitly calling functions within the DLL itself.

N O T E   DLLMain (discussed in a few paragraphs) is specifically a Win32 and C++ implementation. A fundamental problem for implementation of Win32-specific programming techniques in Delphi is lack of Pascal-based documentation. There is plenty to know and many resources to extract from places like the Microsoft Developers Network (MSDN) and related SDK-oriented magazines and newsgroups. The problem is that the information is always in C or C++, which means that you must translate any examples for use in your own code. Often there are language elements that simply do not translate or are not supported: Multiple Inheritance, for example. ▪

Our concern here is the inclusion of the `DLLEntryPoint`, often referred to as `DLLMain`. All Win32 documentation discusses this topic in the context of C++. In summary, it specifies that the C runtime startup code looks for the optional export of the function `DLLEntryPoint`. If it exists, the function is called each time a process or thread attaches. Similarly, the function is called whenever a thread or process detaches. Most languages also have a provision in the linker to specify any name for the function. The function acts as a single-entry/single-exit routine for the DLL, usually for performing initialization and cleanup tasks. In C++, the declaration of DLLEntryPoint appears as follows:

```
BOOL WINAPI DLLEntryPoint(HINSTANCE hInst, DWORD dwReason, LPVOID lpvReserved);
```

In Delphi, you can export this function (using Pascal syntax); however, the Pascal startup code will never call it. Rather, the initialization code between the begin and end. in the DPR file executes. It executes only once, when the first process maps in the DLL module.

Delphi's Implementation of *DLLMain*

Delphi *does* provide a mechanism to force your DLLMain routine to execute similar to how DLLMain does in C++, but it requires a couple of extra steps. Look at DLLMain in context to Delphi in Listing 25.2.

Listing 25.2   DLLMAIN—Implementation of *DLLMain* in Delphi Is Completely Optional, but Here's How

```
library DLLEntry;
uses
  ShareMem,
  Windows,
  SysUtils,
  Classes;
procedure DLLMain(dwReason: DWORD);
begin
  case dwReason of
    dll_Process_Attach : {Statements here};
    dll_Process_Detach : {Statements here};
    dll_Thread_Attach  : {Statements here};
    dll_Thread_Detach  : {Statements here};
  end;
end;
begin
  DLLProc := @DLLMain;
  DLLMain(dll_Process_Attach);
end.
```

Listing 25.2 begins with the removal of the comment that pertains to the ShareMem unit and DELPHIMM.DLL. The uses section of the unit added ShareMem (as recommended in the comment) along with Windows. The Windows unit is necessary as it contains the declarations for the dll_ constants. Following the uses is the inclusion of the DLLMain entry procedure.

Delphi's implementation of DLLMain requires a single-integer parameter here named dwReason. When the function is called, dwReason contains a value that will be in the range of 0-3. The Windows unit provides the declarations for four constants that represent each of the values. Table 25.1 shows each constant, its value, and its meaning (or reason it is passed).

Table 25.1   Constants Used in *DLLMain*

Constant Name	Value	Reason	Usage
dll_Process_Attach	1	A process has mapped the DLL into its address space. Called only once per process.	*Initialize global objects or variables when the DLL loads, or execute batch processing.*
dll_Thread_Attach	2	A process has created a child thread. (This message is not used for the primary thread.)	*Perform special processing when subsequent threads attach.*
dll_Thread_Detach	3	A thread in the loading process has terminated.	*If the DLL incorporated special processing when a thread was created, allocations can be freed and any flag and counters reset.*
dll_Process_Detach	0	The DLL is being detached from at least one of the processes into which it is mapped.	*Release any global objects, close files, or ports opened or initialized during* dll_Process_Attach.

Although your DLLMain procedure can be called many times, it is called only for one to four reasons, as shown in Table 25.1. Each time an application initially maps your DLL into its address space, DLLMain is called passing dll_Process_Attach. Similarly, when the DLL is finally unmapped by an application, DLLMain is called passing dll_Process_Detach.

Part
VI

Ch
25

N O T E   A process can load a DLL multiple times from any of its threads. The DLL is mapped into the address space only during the initial call. Subsequent calls just increment a reference count whose scope is local to the process. DLLMain will only be called with dll_Process_Attach for the initial call that results in the actual mapping, not each time the same process loads it.

If a process loads a DLL three times, by three threads, the DLL is not actually unmapped from its address space until the third (usually the primary) thread unloads it or the process terminates. Only during the final unload (when the reference count reaches 0), is DLLMain called with dll_Process_Detach.

If multiple processes load the DLL, dll_Process_Attach is called once for each process upon initial mapping and once for each process upon the reference count reaching 0. ■

DLLMain is called passing dll_Thread_Attach each time a thread in the loading process is created. Similarly, DLLMain is called passing dll_Thread_Detach each time a thread terminates within the loading process. If multiple processes use the DLL and one of the processes destroys a child thread, DLLMain is called passing dll_Thread_Detach only in context to the process destroying the thread. The DLL, in context to the other process, does not receive the dll_Thread_Detach notification.

> **CAUTION**
>
> You cannot assume that DLLMain will be called with dll_Thread_Detach once for every call passing dll_Thread_Attach. It's possible for a process to create several threads before loading the DLL.
>
> Suppose that a Process creates two child threads and then loads your DLL. When the process terminates, DLLMain will be called passing dll_Thread_Detach for each thread, even though it never received any calls passing dll_Thread_Attach.

The *DllProc* Assignment

Listing 25.2 demonstrated the modification needed to incorporate a DLLMain procedure in your DLL. I discussed the modifications to the uses section, and the declaration and definition of the DLLMain procedure itself. I also pointed out that DLLMain is not automatically called, as noted in most C or C++ documentation. So how do you convince Delphi to use your DLLMain function? The answer lies in the DLLProc variable.

Delphi implicitly includes all of the functionality defined in the SYSTEM unit. Part of this functionality is the Pascal startup code. The SYSTEM unit declares and defines an assembly language function named _StartLib. This routine is important for several reasons. In context to DLLMain, it's important because it is responsible for executing all code assigned to a system level variable called DLLProc. The DLLProc variable is a pointer that by default is nil. In the initialization code of your DLL, you can assign the address of your DLLMain function to this variable. Your DLLMain function is now automatically called. Take a closer look at the initialization code:

```
...
begin
  DLLProc := @DLLMain;
  DLLMain(dll_Process_Attach);
end.
```

The initialization code is called once per process. In the previous code fragment, the globally accessible DLLProc variable is assigned the address of the previously defined DLLMain procedure. In Delphi, the calling of the initialization code in the DPR of a DLL project is the equivalent of the receipt of the dll_Process_Attach notification. Given this, for your DLLMain to process dll_Process_Attach, you must call it explicitly as shown in the fragment. All subsequent notifications are automatic after the assignment to DLLProc is done.

Using *DLLMain* in Your DLL

Using DLLMain in your DLL project is completely optional but extremely useful. A fundamental application of DLLMain is to initialize global variables and instantiate objects used during the life of the DLL's usage. Listing 25.3 shows a standard use of DLLMain to create an application's global exception handler.

Listing 25.3   DLLEXCEPT.DPR—Standard Initialization Using *DLLMain*

```
library DLLExcept;
uses
  ShareMem,
  Windows,
  SysUtils,
  Forms,
  Classes;
type
  TAppHandler = class
    procedure HandlerProc(Sender: TObject; E: Exception);
  end;
  procedure TAppHandler.HandlerProc(Sender: TObject; E: Exception);
  begin
    {Global error handling code here. }
  end;
var
  AppHandler: TAppHandler;
procedure DLLMain(dwReason: DWORD);
begin
  case dwReason of
    dll_Process_Attach :
    begin
      AppHandler := TAppHandler.Create;
      Application.OnException := AppHandler.HandlerProc;
    end;
    dll_Process_Detach :
    begin
```

continues

Listing 25.3   Continued

```
        Application.OnException := nil;
        AppHandler.Free;
      end;
      dll_Thread_Attach   : {Statements here};
      dll_Thread_Detach   : {Statements here};
    end;
  end;
begin
  DLLProc := @DLLMain;
  DLLMain(dll_Process_Attach);
end.
```

Listing 25.3 provides several modifications beyond those incorporated in Listing 25.2. The first modification is the inclusion of yet another unit named FORMS.PAS. The Forms unit supplies the global `Application` object. The `Application` object is automatically instantiated by including the Forms unit in your program. The `Application` object has an event handler named `OnException`. All exceptions that are not explicitly handled by using `try...except` constructs are raised to the `Application` object `OnException` handler (if assigned). If code is assigned to the `OnException` handler, it is executed. The `OnException` handler gives the programmer a mechanism to handle errors, no matter what the source.

For more information about the `Application` object and `OnException`, see Chapter 5, "Exception Handling."

Listing 25.3 adds a `type` section following the `uses` section. In this section, a class named `TAppHandler` is declared. `TAppHandler` has a single method named `HandlerProc`. Following the declaration of `TAppHandler` is the definition of the `HandlerProc` method. In the example, `HandlerProc` does nothing. You can add any processing you want to occur when an exception is raised inside of the `HandlerProc` method.

The definition of `HandlerProc` is followed by the `var` declaration of the global variable `AppHandler`. `AppHandler` is of type `TAppHandler` and will contain the `object` instance of the `TAppHandler` class. The instantiation and cleanup for the `AppHandler` variable occurs in the `DLLMain` procedure.

Notice the `case` for `dll_Process_Attach` instantiates `AppHandler`. After instantiation, the `HandlerProc` method is assigned to `Application.OnException`. Notice the `case` for `dll_Process_Detach` simply assigns `nil` to `Application.OnException`, and then frees the `AppHandler` object instance. `DLLMain` makes for clean, readable, single-entry, single-exit DLL programming.

Calling Conventions

A *calling convention* defines the protocol for the passing of variables to a method or function. Each calling convention differs; therefore, programmers must be very specific and fully aware of the calling convention they are using. The calling convention specifies the order in which parameters get passed to functions. The calling convention also specifies whether or not to use the CPU registers to pass parameters. Finally, the calling convention specifies who is responsible for cleaning up the stack—the caller or the called function.

Table 25.2 shows each calling convention supported by Delphi, the parameter ordering, and who is responsible for stack cleanup.

Table 25.2 Delphi Supported Calling Conventions

Convention	Ordering	Stack Cleanup
Fast-Call (Register)	Left to Right	Called Routine
StdCall	Right to Left	Called Routine
Pascal	Left to Right	Called Routine
Cdecl	Right to Left	Calling Routine
Safecall	Right to Left	Called Routine

The Default calling convention used by Delphi changed in Delphi version 2 to Fast-Call from Pascal in 16-bit Delphi 1.0. Fast-Call is the most efficient of the protocols. It uses extended CPU registers to pass the first three parameters that fit; therefore, it's fast (as the name implies). The remaining parameters (if any) are passed, following the Pascal calling convention.

Part
VI
Ch
25

CAUTION

Fast-Call (also known as Register) is supported by Borland's Delphi and C++ compilers as well as compilers made by some of Borland's competitors. However, Borland's implementation of Fast-Call is unique to Borland and should be used only where language and compiler independence are unnecessary. You should neither export functions from your DLL using Fast-Call nor use Fast-Call routines for Windows callbacks when language and compiler independence are necessary. Your safest bet is to simply use Fast-Call only within native Delphi code.

Like Delphi version 1, Windows 3.x used Pascal as the calling convention for most of its APIs. Pascal was the standard for any functions exported by a DLL. Win32 changed the standard calling convention to StdCall. Delphi, of course, changed its default to Fast-Call, which ultimately resulted in much confusion.

N O T E In Table 25.2, you may have noticed that all the calling conventions (except Cdecl) result in the called routine cleaning up the stack. Given this, you might question how the return value gets back to the calling routine. If the size of the return value is 32 bits or less, it's placed in the CPU's EAX register and is therefore unaffected when the called routine does the stack cleanup. If the return value is > (greater than) 32 bits, an intermediate storage area is created. The address of this storage area is put on the stack by the caller prior to pushing the parameters. The called routine will pop off only the parameters, leaving the result intact. ■

One of the most common errors made by DLL programmers is forgetting to use the correct calling convention in their application. Most 16-bit Delphi applications never specified any convention; therefore, the default Pascal calling convention was used. When these applications are recompiled under Delphi 2.0 or 3, the routines that don't explicitly specify a calling convention automatically are using Fast-Call, not Pascal. Unless you know the issues up front, your application may simply stop working when using Windows callbacks, third-party DLLs, or your own C++ DLLs.

When troubleshooting DLL programs, start with the calling conventions. The compiler can't warn about incompatibilities, so you're forced to know what you're looking for up-front. If you call a function in a DLL by using StdCall, but the called function is using Pascal, the call probably will be successful. However, the parameters will be received by the called function backward. Operations on those parameters can have very unexpected results.

If your function is using StdCall, and if the function you are calling is Cdecl written in C++, the call itself may fail if the program was compiled with the option for generating underbars, not using *extern "C,"* case sensitivity, or even variable parameters. If you did manage to get the call to work, you will have other problems because the called function will pop (remove) the parameters on the stack. When the routine returns, your calling routine will again try to pop the parameters on the stack. You can imagine the problems this situation can cause.

N O T E   Although Delphi supports the Cdecl calling convention, it doesn't support passing variable parameters. Even if the Cdecl function doesn't use variable parameters, Delphi cannot resolve the reference unless name mangling is disabled. For more information on Cdecl and Name Mangling, see Chapter 30, " Delphi and C++ Synergy."

Always be aware of the calling convention in use. Always exactly match conventions between *caller* and *called*. To ensure Win32 compatibility, standardize on StdCall and avoid using Fast-Call outside of native Delphi code.

Exporting

When the linker writes a DLL to disk, it writes the name of all exported routines and their relative virtual offsets to the file image. At runtime, when your DLL is mapped into the loading process address space, the loader moves within the DLL file image to find the names and addresses of all routines required by the loading EXE (or DLL) to execute properly. If the expected routine doesn't exist, the load of your DLL will fail.

A DLL exports routines for use by the operating system, an EXE, or another DLL. The exported routines are an interface for manipulating objects within the DLL or can be simple flat functions that perform useful processing. The simplest use of exporting in DLLs is to package a set of related functions for generic use by one or more applications. Listing 25.4 demonstrates this attack.

Declaring an export function in Delphi is a simple three-step process. The first step is to declare the function in the `interface` section of a unit. The second step is to list the function in the `exports` section of the unit. The third step is to define the body of the function in the `implementation` section of the unit. Listing 25.4 shows EXPORTU1.PAS, which completes each of these steps.

Listing 25.4 \DLPHI3\CHP25\EXPORTSU1.PAS—*ExportsU1* Is Part of Exporting.dpr and It Makes Several Functions Available to Loading Applications

```
unit EXPORTSU1;
interface
uses
   Sysutils, Windows;
procedure ExSetVolumeLabel(pcName: PChar); StdCall;
exports
    ExSetVolumeLabel;
implementation

procedure ExSetVolumeLabel(pcName: PChar);
begin
  if not Assigned(pcName) then
    Raise Exception.Create('Name passed to LabelDiskVolume is nil');
  if not SetVolumeLabel(nil,pcName) then
    Raise Exception.Create('Cant set volum label. GetLastError reports '+
                        IntToStr(GetLastError));
end;
end.
```

Many Win32 functions are Boolean; so they return True if the objective of the function executes without error and False upon failure. Suppose that you want a library of Delphi routines that wrap each of the Boolean Win32 functions so that they use exception handling. If the function is successful, processing continues. If the function fails, an exception is raised to which you can respond by using `try...except` constructs. Listing 25.4 does exactly this as it wraps the Win32 function `SetVolumeLabel` in an exported function named `ExSetVolumeLabel`.

Notice that `ExSetVolumeLabel` is declared in the interface section of the unit. Because this function is being exported, it should use a standard calling convention, which, of course, would be `StdCall`, which is specified by appending the `StdCall` directive to the end of the declaration. It's unnecessary to specify `StdCall` when defining the body of the function in the implementation section.

N O T E   If you're porting from Delphi 1.0, you may have expected the use of the `far` and `export` directives at the end of the function declaration. Delphi no longer requires either directive. The compiler will not complain if you include either directive because the language supports them for backward compatibility. You may decide to include the `export` directive for readability purposes to indicate which interface routines are actually exported for external use. ■

Part
VI

Ch
25

Following the declaration of ExSetVolumeLabel, the exports section is added, which lists the ExSetVolumeName function. It isn't necessary to list the parameters or return values (if any) for a routine in the exports list.

TIP It isn't required to place the exports list in the interface section of the unit exporting the function. In fact, Delphi 1.0 required the exports list to be in the DPR file. By including it in the unit immediately following the declarations for your routines, however, it reminds you to add the routine name to the list. Failure to include your functions in the exports list results in the functions not being exported.

You can optionally assign an ordinal value to your function in the exports section for faster lookups when the function is imported. In this example, the following modification needs to be made:

```
...
exports
    ExSetVolumeLabel index 1;
...
```

When importing the routine for use by your EXE, you can specify the ordinal value assigned to the routine when it was exported (in this case, 1). Although it's faster to look up the function by ordinal, it isn't recommended because it's more difficult to maintain large programs that look up by ordinals. It's also more difficult to debug. Additionally, some people believe Microsoft recommends not using ordinals because support for them might not exist or function as expected in future versions of the operating system.

NOTE If you're porting an application from Delphi 1.0, you may be familiar with the Resident directive. If you include the Resident directive in your exports list under Win32, it is simply ignored because it exists only for backward compatibility.

In Win16, the New Executable (NE) file format supports a resident and non-resident name table. All routines exported by using the Resident directive resulted in the names being cached in memory, which made the resolving of these routines at runtime very fast, with the penalty of sacrificing a small amount of memory.

The Portable Executable (PE) File format doesn't have a Resident or Non-Resident name table and it is not needed under the process/thread model. Instead, every function your DLL exports is written to the .edata section of the file image. For more information on the sections of a file image or the (PE) File format, see Chapter 26, " DLL Programming: Advanced Concepts." ■

Following the implementation directive, the definition of ExSetVolumeLabel is shown. The routine itself is rather basic and defines a small addition in functionality to the Win32 SetVolumeLabel function. ExSetVolumeLabel checks to see if the name for the volume passed in the pcName parameter is nil. If so, an exception is raised; thus, execution of the function terminates immediately, raising the exception to the calling routine.

N O T E   If you're moving to Delphi 3 directly from 16-bit Delphi 1.0, note that the EXE calling the routine in your DLL can now wrap this call in a try...except or try...finally construct with successful results. This has been possible since Delphi 2.0 because Win32 provides built-in exception-handling facilities that Delphi takes advantage of. These facilities were not available in the 16-bit version of the Windows operating system. ■

If the pcName parameter is not nil, a call is made to the Win32 SetVolumeLabel function. If the call is successful, ExSetVolumeLabel simply returns. Otherwise, an exception is raised, returning the code from GetLastError as part of the message text in the exception object.

When your program incorrectly interacts with your DLL, or totally fails to interact with it, first look at the calling convention being used. When your DLL and loading module are using the same calling convention, the second step is to verify that the functions are actually being exported. Chapter 26, "DLL Programming: Advanced Concepts," discusses the Turbo Dump utility, which can be used to determine if your DLL has successfully exported a function, as well as other useful pieces of information.

For more examples and advanced uses of DLL exporting, see Chapter 26. For more information about exception handling, see Chapter 5, "Exception Handling." For more information about the Turbo Dump utility, see Chapter 26.

Part
VI

Ch
25

Loading and Unloading DLLs from Your Application

In order to use your DLL, it must be mapped into the address space of your application's process. You accomplish this by calling the Win32 API function LoadLibrary or LoadLibraryEx. LoadLibrary is forwarded (and slightly modified) from 16-bit Windows. LoadLibraryEx is available only as a 32-bit call and is an extension to LoadLibrary.

Although DLLs are loaded by calling one of the LoadLibrary*X* functions, this doesn't mean you have to call LoadLibrary yourself. Delphi supports both *explicit* and *implicit* runtime linking. Implicit linking is a mechanism that you can use to have Delphi handle the calls to LoadLibrary and FreeLibrary (discussed later) automatically. Explicit and implicit linking techniques are discussed a little later in this chapter.

Delphi imports LoadLibrary and LoadLibraryEx in the Windows unit. The declaration for LoadLibrary is as follows:

```
function LoadLibrary(LibFileName: PChar): HMODULE; stdcall;
```

LoadLibrary is a simple function to use. It takes a single PChar parameter specifying the name of the DLL file to load. You can omit the .DLL extension from the filename and it will be assumed. The LibFileName parameter can optionally specify a fully qualified path to the DLL. If no path is specified, the function searches for the DLL, using the following order:

1. The directory from where the application is loaded.
2. The current directory.

3. The \WINDOWS\SYSTEM directory (or \Windows\system32 directory followed by the 16-bit \system directory if under NT).

4. The \WINDOWS directory.

5. All directories set in the PATH environment variable (usually set up in the autoexec.bat file).

If the DLL cannot be found, the function returns 0. The Win32 function GetLastError can be called to determine why the function failed. GetLastError returns an error code that can be used to identify the reason the call failed.

TIP

GetLastError can return one of any number of possible values. Usually, the possible error return codes for a specific function are listed in the online documentation for this function. If, for some reason, the values aren't specified, you can look in the \DELPHI 3\SOURCE\RTL\WIN directory for the file, Windows.pas. This file contains all the values and an associated constant. For example, if a Win32 call fails, and then a call to GetLastError returns 15, you can search for 15 in Windows.pas. For this example, you find the following:

```
{ The system cannot find the drive specified. }
  ERROR_INVALID_DRIVE = 15;
```

The constant name may be descriptive enough to help you determine the meaning of the error code; if not, a comment usually associated with the constant does.

Finally, the Sysutils unit implements a routine named SysErrorMessage. This routine returns a string that describes the meaning of the error code passed in its only integer parameter. However, the returned string is usually about as descriptive as the comments associated with the error constants in Windows.pas.

The LoadLibraryEx function works similar to LoadLibrary with a few added twists. The Windows unit imports LoadLibraryEx as follows:

```
function LoadLibraryEx(LibFileName: PChar; hFile:
➥                    THandle; dwFlags: DWORD): HMODULE; stdcall;
```

Like LoadLibrary, LoadLibraryEx takes the name of the DLL file in the first parameter. Again, the DLL file extension is assumed. Optionally, you can specify a fully qualified path to the file as part of the LibFileName parameter. LoadLibraryEx follows the same search pattern as LoadLibrary (by default) if no path is specified, and also returns 0 if the file cannot be loaded (in which case, you can use GetLastError to determine why).

LoadLibraryEx adds two additional parameters to its parameter list. The first parameter, LibFileName, was previously discussed for LoadLibrary. The second parameter always requires a value of 0. It is reserved for future use. The third parameter is a DWORD value, which specifies one of the three available flags.

The *Dont_Resolve_DLL_References* Flag

The Dont_Resolve_DLL_References flag can be specified as the third parameter to LoadLibraryEx. This flag currently is specific to the WinNT operating system. Don't use this flag if you're compiling a single version of your application for use on Win95 and WinNT.

The Dont_Resolve_DLL_References flag prevents the following three actions that occur when the DLL is loaded normally (or just using LoadLibrary):

1. The DLLMain function, if it exists, is not called.
2. The DLL is not checked for dependencies on additional DLLs, which normally results in each of them also being mapped into the process and each of their DLL dependencies resolved.
3. Functions imported by the DLL from other DLLs (external references) are not resolved.

The DLL is otherwise loaded as it usually would be. Aside from how the system sets page-protection attributes for executable code (which a DLL usually contains), this flag is not much different than specifying the Load_Library_As_DataFile flag discussed in the following section. You should use the Load_Library_As_DataFile flag rather than the Dont_Resolve_DLL_References flags whenever possible because it is compatible with both Win95 and WinNT.

Part
VI
Ch
25

The *Load_Library_As_DataFile* Flag

The Load_Library_As_DataFile flag can be specified as the third parameter to LoadLibraryEx. When this flag is specified, the module is mapped into the process address space, just as a file of any type is mapped in, using Kernel File-mapping objects. No special page-protection attributes are applied to the code, DLLMain isn't called, and external references are not resolved. The return value from LoadLibraryEx is still useful when this flag is specified. You can use it to load resources, such as bitmaps and icons.

 You can use this flag if you want a program to extract resources such as an icon from a user-specified DLL or EXE. You can pass the return value from LoadLibraryEx to LoadResource to retrieve the icon handle. Pass the handle to LockResource, copy the data by using the returned pointer, and write it out to an ICO file. All this can be accomplished without ever worrying that LoadLibrary will fail due to dependencies on other modules or failed initialization in DLLMain.

When the Load_Library_As_DataFile flag is specified, you can load a regular EXE file rather than a DLL. LoadLibrary itself couldn't do this because an attempt would be made to call the _StartLib procedure and then DLLMain; both functions of which EXEs don't use or contain. Because Load_Library_As_DataFile doesn't result in a call to the entry point code for the EXE, the EXE file is simply mapped into the process, providing you with access to its data and resources.

The *Load_With_Altered_Search_Path* Flag

The `Load_With_Altered_Search_Path` flag can be specified as the third parameter to `LoadLibraryEx`. This flag tells `LoadLibraryEx` to use a search pattern different from the default used when no path is explicitly specified in the `LibFileName` parameter. The following search pattern is used when this flag is specified:

1. The directory explicitly specified in the `LibFileName` parameter.
2. The current directory.
3. The \Windows\system directory (or \Windows\system32 directory, followed by the 16-bit \system directory if under NT).
4. The \Windows directory.
5. All directories in the PATH environment variable (usually set up in the autoexec.bat file).

When you load a single DLL, it often results in several more DLLs being mapped into the process space, possibly unknown to you. For the mapping to succeed, all the modules must be found. If a module then depends on another module, all of these must be found in the same fashion. `Load_With_Altered_Search_Path` is useful for fine-tuning how the system seeks the dependent DLLs, not the DLL you are loading specifically. For the use of `Load_With_Altered_Search_Path` to serve any purpose, the path of the DLL you're loading must be known in advance and specified in the `LibFileName` parameter. If not, the default search pattern is used.

Module Instance Handle and *FreeLibrary*

Both `LoadLibrary` and `LoadLibraryEx` return a value of type `HModule`. `HModule` is a synonym type for a `THandle`. If either function fails, the return value is `0`. Many of the Windows APIs require the handle to a module to operate on this module or retrieve data, resources, or other information from it. Here are just a few examples:

- EnumResourceNames
- LoadResource
- EnumResTypeProc
- FreeLibraryAndExitThread
- FindResourceEx
- GetProcAddress
- FreeLibrary

The module handle is maintained by the system. When a process maps a DLL into its address space, `LoadLibrary` returns a valid `HMODULE` value. If child threads try to again map the DLL into the process by using `LoadLibrary`, they receive a copy of the `HMODULE` value returned during the initial mapping. The DLL isn't mapped into the process again. Instead, the system maintains a process-specific reference count that gets incremented by 1 each time `LoadLibrary` or `LoadLibraryEx` is called within a process. After the initial mapping in a single process, each additional attempt to load the DLL only causes the reference count to increment.

A DLL is unmapped from a process when its reference count within this process is decremented back to 0. You will usually decrement the reference count to 0 when the DLL is no longer needed. Win32 provides a function named FreeLibrary to serve this purpose. FreeLibrary decrements the reference count of a DLL by 1 (per call) in context to the process in which it is used. If a call to FreeLibrary results in the reference count reaching 0, the file is unmapped from the process. The Windows unit imports FreeLibrary with the following declaration:

```
function FreeLibrary(hLibModule: HMODULE): BOOL; stdcall;
```

FreeLibrary takes a single parameter of type HMODULE. This, of course, would be the return value from LoadLibrary or LoadLibraryEx. If FreeLibrary is successful, it returns True; otherwise, it returns False. If FreeLibrary returns False, you can use the *Win32* GetLastError function to find out why.

Now you know how LoadLibrary is used to load a DLL and how FreeLibrary is used to unload a DLL. However, if the DLL contains code you need to reach, this information isn't enough. The next step is to import the functions exported from the DLL. Read on!

Importing

After you create a DLL and export some functions, to use your work, it's necessary to load the DLL. After the DLL is loaded, your code can call the exported routines; it's this easy—well... almost. If the EXE that uses the DLL tries to simply call one of the exported routines by name, at compile time the compiler does not recognize the symbol and generates an error because the compiler knows nothing of the contents of the DLL. Given this, it's necessary to provide a declaration for each of the exported functions in the DLL so the compiler will recognize the calls without error.

It takes more, however, than just a declaration to get your application built. At link time, the linker will attempt to resolve all declarations; if it cannot, it reports an error. So there must be a way to declare a function for the compiler and flag it as an external reference to the linker, but at the same time be able to resolve the external reference at runtime. It sounds confusing; I'll start by simplifying how to refer to this entire process by giving it the name *importing*.

In Delphi, there are two methods for loading and importing routines from a DLL:

- Implicit—Statically load the DLL when the application loads by specifying the function declarations, using a special Delphi-specific declaration.

- Explicit—Dynamically load the DLL on demand by using LoadLibrary, and then retrieving the exported function addresses by using GetProcAddress.

Most people find using the implicit method much friendlier than the explicit method because less coding is required. However, with the friendliness comes a lack of control and the sacrifice of one of the greatest advantages for using DLLs in the first place—dynamic usage. On the other hand, implicit loading is fast, reliable, and automatically terminates the application upon failure. Take a closer look at each method, starting with the simpler and more commonly used of the two methods: implicit.

Part VI
Ch
25

Implicit

A prior section of this chapter discussed using the *Win32* routines LoadLibrary and LoadLibraryEx for loading a DLL and FreeLibrary to unload it. Delphi supports a special syntax that results in the calls to LoadLibrary and FreeLibrary to occur at runtime automatically.

It isn't Delphi that calls LoadLibrary; it is functionality built into the operating system. By using special declarations, Delphi's linker writes the names of the functions to import and the names of the DLLs that contain them to a particular offset within the EXE file image. When you launch the EXE and it gets mapped into the application's process, Windows moves to a special offset within the EXE file image. From this offset, Windows extracts the names of any DLL modules required for use by the EXE. It also extracts the names of all the functions used by the EXE that are supposed to be exported from each DLL.

When Windows determines that your application relies on a particular DLL, it calls LoadLibrary. LoadLibrary searches for the DLL by using a specific search pattern and, if not found, unloads the entire application. If the DLL is found, it's mapped into the application's process. Windows then moves within the DLL file image to a particular offset from which it extracts the names of all the functions the DLL exports. If the DLL doesn't export even one of the functions the loading EXE expects, the DLL is unmapped from the process and the application terminates.

N O T E   The *Portable Executable* (PE) file specification currently predefines nine generic objects known as *Sections* for use in a 32-bit executable (EXE or DLL) module. These Sections exist within the file image, in addition to the various headers. Each Section is located at a retrievable offset and contains information needed by the operating system to run your application. Section information includes code, data, debug info, and more.

One predefined section (usually named .edata) contains the names, relative addresses, and ordinal values for each function the module exports. Another section (usually named .iData) contains the names of each DLL used by the application and each function within the DLL required by the application.

The OS finds the Sections and information in these Sections by locating a series of addresses at particular offsets within the module file image. Eventually, the desired section and information is found and can be retrieved.

For more information on Sections and the PE file format, see Chapter 26, "DLL Programming: Advanced Concepts." ■

To state it simply, the names of all the functions exported by a DLL are written to a specific offset within the DLL file. The names of all the functions imported (required) by an EXE are written to a specific offset within the EXE file, along with the name of each DLL in which the functions are expected to reside. When Windows loads the EXE, it checks to ensure that each required DLL exists and exports the needed routines. If not, the application will not start.

The importing process occurs in a rather recursive fashion. Your EXE is using more DLLs than you may know. Delphi's Visual Components Library (VCL) makes calls to the Win32 API all the time, which means that the Windows core files Kernel32.dll, user32.dll, and Gdi32.dll, and so on, are being implicitly included in your application. If you're using packages, the package DLLs are also implicitly included. Each package uses the core files, too, and even other package DLLs. Many DLLs in your application can use one another. The result is a vicious circle of sorts. This point is summarized in Figure 25.2.

FIG. 25.2
A single application uses many DLLs, in addition to any you create yourself. Each DLL can depend on another DLL, or two DLLs can even depend on each other.

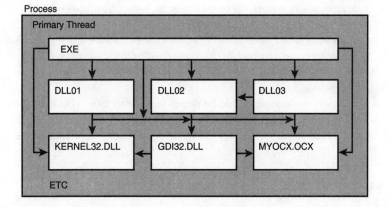

The following declaration implicitly imports a function called `GetNetUserID` from a DLL called NETTOOLS.DLL:

```
function GetNetUserID(sUserName: string): longint; StdCall;
                         external 'NetTools.dll' Name 'GetNetUserIDA';
```

Note that `GetNetUserID` is just a hypothetical function. The declaration starts just as the declaration for any other routine starts. It can be either a procedure or a function. The name of the function is specified next—in this case, `GetNetUserID`. You can actually call the function anything you want, as long as you use its real name (following the `name` directive at the end of the declaration). Following the name is the parameter list and return value (assuming that you're importing a function, not a procedure). Now you can specify the calling convention of the function as it is exported from the DLL. If you don't know what calling convention was used when the exported routine was exported, find out. Mismatches in calling conventions can have negative results that are difficult to troubleshoot. By Win32 standards, all functions exported from a *Win32* DLL should have been exported as `StdCall`.

The `external` directive follows the routine description and calling convention. Don't forget to include `external` because it's used to specify the name of the DLL that contains the function. You should specify the *.DLL* extension for readability; but otherwise, it is assumed.

Following the `external` directive and module name is the optional `name` directive. The `name` directive is needed only if the name used in the function declaration (immediately following the

Part
VI

Ch
25

word `function` or `procedure`) is different than the name the DLL used when it exported the function. In the example, the function description states `GetNetUserID`, but the actual name is `GetNetUserIDA`. In the EXE code, all calls are made by using `GetNetUserID`.

N O T E The Win32 API exports two versions of many of its functions. `MessageBoxA` and `MessageBoxW` is an example. The ending 'A' character means Ansi. The ending 'W' character means Wide (Wide Char). If you look in the `Windows` unit, you find the following import statements:

```
function MessageBoxA; external user32 name 'MessageBoxA';
function MessageBoxW; external user32 name 'MessageBoxW';
function MessageBox; external user32 name 'MessageBoxA';
```

Here, the same routine was imported with three different names. Notice that the documented name `MessageBox` is assuming the Ansi call. To use the Wide character version of the function, you have to explicitly call `MessageBoxW`. ▨

The import declaration should be placed in the interface section of a unit. Optionally, the portion of the declaration that satisfies the compiler can be placed in the interface section, and the portion that satisfies the linker can be placed in the implementation section as follows:

```
...
var
  Form1: TForm1;
function GetNetUserID(sUserName: string): longint; StdCall;
implementation
{$R *.DFM}
function GetNetUserID; external 'NetTools.dll' name 'GetNetUserIDA';
...
end.
```

Another way to import a routine is by ordinal. Consider the following modifications to the import declaration of the `GetNetUserID` routine:

```
function GetNetUserID(sUserName: string): longint; StdCall;
      external 'NetTools.dll' index 25;
```

N O T E Although it's faster to look up the function by ordinal, it isn't recommended because it's more difficult to maintain large programs that look up by ordinals. It's also more difficult to debug. Additionally, some people believe that Microsoft recommends not using ordinals because support for them may not exist or function as expected in future versions of the operating system. ▨

This time the optional `name` directive is not used. You know that this routine is actually exported as `GetNetUserIDA` not `GetNetUserID`, so how can it be found? When the `index` directive is used, the name is not used to look up the routine. Instead, its ordinal value is looked up from within the exports list in the DLL. In this case, the ordinal value specified is 25. For the function call to work, the DLL better have exported `GetNetUserIDA` with an ordinal value of 25. If not, then whatever function *is* exported as 25 will be used instead. You can imagine the results of this! If no routine is exported with an ordinal value of 25, the import will fail.

By using the discussed import declarations, there is no need to call LoadLibrary, LoadLibraryEx, or FreeLibrary. The declared routines and names of required DLLs will be written to the imports table in the EXE, and the operating system takes care of the rest. This kind of automated use of DLLs comes with a price. A huge advantage of using DLLs in your application is to load and unload them on call. Using the discussed implicit load mechanism, all DLLs are loaded when the application loads (resulting in slower application load time) and stay mapped into your application's process for the lifetime of the application, whether or not they are needed, which adds unneeded overhead to the application and drains system resources.

Explicit

On the CD

You can *explicitly* import a routine by using the Win32 API call GetProcAddress along with programmatic calls to LoadLibrary, LoadLibraryEx, and FreeLibrary. An *explicit* load and *import* is a more dynamic and programmatic way to use DLLs in your application. Programmers often avoid this method because it requires more coding. New Pascal programmers often find the syntax confusing; in combination with poor documentation, it's just easier to go the *implicit* way. Now, dive right into the code shown in Listing 25.5. You can find EXPORTING.DLL on this book's companion CD-ROM.

Part
VI

Ch
25

Listing 25.5 \DLPHI3\CHP25\LOADERU1.PAS—The *LoaderEXE* Uses EXPORTING.DLL

```
unit LoaderU1;
interface
uses
  Windows, Messages, SysUtils, Classes, Graphics, Controls, Forms, Dialogs,
  StdCtrls;
type
  TExSetVolumeLabel = procedure(pcName: PChar); StdCall;
  TForm1 = class(TForm)
    Button1: TButton;
    procedure Button1Click(Sender: TObject);
  private
    { Private declarations }
  public
    { Public declarations }
  end;
var
  Form1: TForm1;
implementation
{$R *.DFM}
procedure TForm1.Button1Click(Sender: TObject);
var ExSetVolumeLabel: TExSetVolumeLabel;
    hDllInst: THandle;
begin
  hDllInst := LoadLibrary('Exporting.dll');
  if hDllInst <= 0 then
    Raise Exception.Create('[LoadLibrary Fail] GetLastError reports: '+
```

continues

Listing 25.5   Continued

```
                                  IntToStr(GetLastError));
  try
    @ExSetVolumeLabel := GetProcAddress(hDllInst,'ExSetVolumeLabel');
    if not Assigned(ExSetVolumeLabel) then
      Raise Exception.Create('[GetProcAddress Fail] GetLastError reports: '+
                              IntToStr(GetLastError));
    ExSetVolumeLabel('BOOT DRIVE');
  finally
    FreeLibrary(hDllInst);
  end;
end;
end.
```

Almost all of the `interface` section of the unit shown in Listing 25.5 is automatically generated by Delphi when a new application is opened. The only exception is the statement immediately following the `type` directive:

```
TExSetVolumeLabel = procedure(pcName: PChar); StdCall;
```

This statement is a declaration of a new type named `TExSetVolumeLabel`. `TExSetVolumeLabel` is a `StdCall` procedure that accepts a single `PChar` parameter. `TExSetVolumeLabel` matches the format of the `ExSetVolumeLabel` routine that is exported in the Exporting.dll module. The function changes the volume label for the drive of the current directory. If successful, the new volume name will be the same as the value passed for the `pcName` parameter.

N O T E   If you read this chapter from the beginning, you recall that in Listing 25.4 a DLL that exported a function called `ExSetVolumeLabel` was created. Listing 25.4 showed the function declared and defined in a unit named ExportU1.pas. The ExportU1.pas unit is part of a project named Exporting that, when built, results in the creation of the Exporting.Dll module. The source code to Exporting.dll and all the listings in this chapter are on this book's companion CD-ROM. ■

It's the implementation section that is the workhorse in this example. All the steps for loading the DLL, importing the `ExSetVolumeLabel` function from the `EXPORTING.DLL`.dll module, and the unloading of the Exporting.dll module are done in the single `TForm1.Button1Click` procedure.

The procedure begins by declaring the following two variables:

```
var ExSetVolumeLabel: TExSetVolumeLabel;
    hDllInst: THandle;
```

Notice that the variable `ExSetVolumeLabel` is of type `TExSetVolumeLabel`. `ExSetVolumeLabel` is the symbol to use when it's time to call the function in the DLL. The `hDllInst` variable is used to store the result of the call to `LoadLibrary`, as follows:

```
hDllInst := LoadLibrary('Exporting.dll');
  if hDllInst = 0 then
    Raise Exception.Create('[LoadLibrary Fail] GetLastError reports: '+
                           IntToStr(GetLastError));
```

LoadLibrary is then called. Passed to it is the path to the location of the Exporting.dll module that exports the ExSetVolumeName routine. Under *Win32*, LoadLibrary returns 0 if the DLL cannot be loaded. The next statement checks the return from LoadLibrary. If the hDllInst variable has a value of 0, an exception is raised. The message portion of the exception receives some text plus the error code, as retrieved from the *Win32* GetLastError function.

If the DLL is loaded successfully, GetProcAddress is called in an attempt to get a pointer to the address of the ExSetVolumeLabel function exported from the Exporting.dll module:

```
@ExSetVolumeLabel := GetProcAddress(hDllInst,'ExSetVolumeLabel');
if not Assigned(ExSetVolumeLabel) then
  Raise Exception.Create('[GetProcAddress Fail] GetLastError reports: '+
                    IntToStr(GetLastError));
```

The ExSetVolumeLabel variable isn't a pointer so the @ character is used on the left side of the variable to specify that the address returned from GetProcAddress becomes the address of the ExSetVolumeLabel variable. GetProcAddress is passed the instance handle returned from LoadLibrary in the first parameter and the name of the function as exported from the DLL in the second parameter. The ExSetVolumeLabel variable is nil if GetProcAddress fails.

The Assigned function is used to check if the ExSetVolumeLabel is nil. If so, an exception is raised, passing some text plus the error code as returned from the Win32 GetLastError function. If the ExSetVolumeLabel variable isn't nil, ExSetVolumeLabel is called. In the example, the text "BOOT DRIVE" is passed, as follows:

```
ExSetVolumeLabel('BOOT DRIVE');
```

Immediately following the call to ExSetVolumeLabel, FreeLibrary is called, which will unmap the no-longer-needed Exporting.dll from the application:

```
FreeLibrary(hDllInst);
```

The example in Listing 25.5 really demonstrates the dynamics of using the implicit loading technique. However, like the implicit technique, it has drawbacks. Consider if the TForm1.Button1Click method were called in a loop. The performance would be terrible. Ultimately, it's up to you where to take a hit in performance. Do you want slow initialization all at once and up-front? Do you want small delays throughout your application due to use of LoadLibrary and FreeLibrary? It all depends on the application and, in most cases, you will find that a mix is in order.

Summary

This chapter discussed the basic principles and the precautions needed to integrate DLLs into your programs. It also discussed issues related to porting your existing 16-bit DLL-based programs to Win32. Finally, it discussed calling conventions and various issues related to memory allocation. Next, Chapter 26 takes the foundational information discussed here and puts it to good use. ●

DLL Programming: Advanced Concepts

by Eric Uber

Delphi provides a DLL programming architecture that nicely complements the requirements for the *Win32* operating system. This architecture and how it ties into Win32 were discussed in Chapter 25, "DLL Programming: An Introduction." The basic issues covered were syntax, importing and exporting routines, loading and unloading DLLs, portability, and the various "gotchas" you encounter when programming a DLL-based application. This chapter takes you to the next level, which is using DLLs in a productive fashion and looking at some advanced aspects of the topic.

Your real power with Delphi is in its use of objects. Many of the objects are visual, such as forms, and many useful objects are non-visual, such as lists and streams. You will find that sometimes it makes sense to move related objects into logical groups compiled into independent DLL modules.

Chapter 25 discussed the exporting of flat functions that perform some kind of library routine processing. Although this use is typical of DLLs, it's not their only purpose. You can place actual class declarations in a DLL and use these classes from a loading EXE almost as though the classes were local to the EXE. You can access virtual methods of a class in a DLL directly, or you can use flat

Flat functions

Using flat functions to access objects and their methods

Storing and accessing forms

How to store and access both modal and non-modal forms in DLLs

Sharing objects

Discussion of directly accessing objects through the VMT and sharing classes between a DLL and an EXE

Sharing data

Breaking the process boundaries and moving data between applications

DLL file internals

Using the Turbo Dump utility to find useful information in the PE file structure functions to wrap the class methods. The following section looks at the simplest scenario, which is wrapping a non-visual class by using flat functions. ∎

Wrapping Classes by Using Flat Functions

If you have a class or even an entire hierarchy of classes, you can compile them into one reusable DLL module. It may be obvious to you how to compile the classes into the DLL, but how do you use the classes after they're contained? One answer is to define flat functions that wrap the class. This technique requires that you export a function to instantiate an instance of the class. You also should export a function to release the class instance when you're done with it. For every method and property that you want accessible outside the DLL, you must create and export a function that directly operates on the method or property and particular instance.

This technique is powerful because you can provide another layer of padding between the exported function interface and the object instances. With this power comes a small hit in performance because your calling routines must turn around and call routines in the class. A cost also comes in the form of maintainability. If you change a method in a class, the flat function also may need to change. If you add a method to the class, a flat function will need to be added. If you remove a method from a class, the associated flat function needs to be removed. You will find that class wrapping is a technique most useful if your intent is to package a set of already existing classes that either are finalized or are unlikely to change their programmer interface.

On the CD

Look at a DLL project that contains a single class and exports flat functions to access it. The project is named ClassWrap and is on the CD-ROM accompanying this book.

Listing 26.1   \UDELPHI3\CHP26\CLASSWRAP.DPR—This Project Doesn't Need to Implement a DLLMain; There Is Nothing to Initialize or Free on Exit

```
library ClassWrap;

uses
  NumAccum in 'NumAccum.pas',
  wraplib in 'wraplib.pas';

end.
```

The DPR file in this project is rather sparse. It simply implements a `uses` section that lists the two pas files included in this project. The NumAccum pas file contains the declaration and definition of the example class. The wraplib pas file contains the flat functions that wrap the example class. This wraplib file also includes the `exports` list and function declarations.

N O T E   Chapter 25, "DLL Programming: An Introduction," discusses how to create a DLL project in Delphi. It also describes exporting through the use of the `exports` directive. ∎

Implementing the Class in the DLL

After your DLL project is created, you can add the units that contain the classes you want to include in the project. The example class for the ClassWrap DLL project is declared and defined, as shown in Listing 26.2.

Listing 26.2   \UDELPHI3\CHP26\NUMACCUM.PAS—Token Example Class; Your Project Will Contain Classes of Substantial Value

```
unit NumAccum;

interface

type
  TOrdAccum = class
  private
    FNumber: integer;
  protected
    procedure SetAdd(i: integer); virtual;
    procedure SetSubtract(i: integer); virtual;
    procedure SetDivide(i: integer); virtual;
    procedure SetMultiply(i: integer); virtual;
  public
    constructor Create(InitalValue: integer); virtual;
    property Add: integer read FNumber write SetAdd;
    property Subtract: integer read FNumber write SetSubtract;
    property Divide: integer read FNumber write SetDivide;
    property Multiply: integer read FNumber write SetMultiply;
  end;

var
  NoAccum: TOrdAccum;

implementation

constructor TOrdAccum.Create(InitalValue: integer);
begin
  FNumber := InitalValue;
end;

procedure TOrdAccum.SetAdd(i: integer);
begin
  FNumber := FNumber + i;
end;

procedure TOrdAccum.SetSubtract(i: integer);
begin
  FNumber := FNumber - i;
end;

procedure TOrdAccum.SetDivide(i: integer);
begin
  FNumber := FNumber div i;
```

Part

VI

Ch

26

continues

Listing 26.2 Continued

```
end;

procedure TOrdAccum.SetMultiply(i: integer);
begin
  FNumber := FNumber * i;
end;

end.
```

Listing 26.2 shows the contents of the NUMACCUM.PAS unit. This unit declares a class type named TOrdAccum. The TOrdAccum class contains a single data field called FNumber of type integer. All the methods in the class operate on FNumber. The interface to the class is a set of readable and "writable" properties. The ordinal math operation for each property occurs upon assignment to the property that implicitly calls the appropriate set method. The new value can be retrieved by reading the property immediately after assignment.

The class is initialized to a starting value passed as a parameter to the Create constructor. So if an instance of TOrdAccum is instantiated passing 1 to the constructor, FNumber has an initial value of 1. Suppose that you assign the value 2 to the Add property. If you then read the Add property (or any of the others), the value returned is 3. If you then assign the value 4 to the Multiply property, and then read it again, the value returned is 12. If you then assign the value 3 to the Divide property, and then read it again, Divide returns the value 4. So you see, the class works as kind of an accumulator because each operation always uses the current value of the FNumber object field, and FNumber always retains the result of the last operation.

Certainly, there are more practical and robust classes you can include in your DLL. I choose TOrdAccum as an example because it is small, thus (hopefully) doesn't distort the point of how to wrap a class by using flat functions. After the class is compiled into the DLL project, it still isn't accessible to a loading EXE. The class still must be wrapped with flat functions, and these functions must be exported for external use, which can be accomplished by creating an export unit.

Defining the Flat Functions in the Export Unit

Listing 26.3 shows the code for the WRAPLIB.PAS unit in the CLASSWRAP DLL project. This unit exports six functions. Notice that each routine exported from the WRAPLIB.PAS unit uses the StdCall directive at the end of the routine declaration. This convention is the standard calling convention for use under Win32. You should use StdCall to ensure compatibility and consistency with the WinNT and Win95 operating systems and to maintain language independence in your DLL modules. For more information on calling conventions, see Chapter 25, "DLL Programming: An Introduction."

Listing 26.3 \UDELPHI3\CHP26\WRAPLIB.PAS—This Export Unit Contains Both the Declaration and Definition for Each Function to Export

```pascal
unit wraplib;

interface

uses NumAccum;

procedure FreeOrdAccumInst(Inst: TOrdAccum); stdcall;
function  GetOrdAccumInst(InitialVal: integer): TOrdAccum; stdcall;
function  OrdAdd(Inst: TOrdAccum; iVal: integer): integer; stdcall;
function  OrdDivide(Inst: TOrdAccum; iVal: integer): integer; stdcall;
function  OrdMultiply(Inst: TOrdAccum; iVal: integer): integer; stdcall;
function  OrdSubtract(Inst: TOrdAccum; iVal: integer): integer; stdcall;

exports
  FreeOrdAccumInst,
  GetOrdAccumInst,
  OrdAdd,
  OrdDivide,
  OrdMultiply,
  OrdSubtract;

implementation

function GetOrdAccumInst(InitialVal: integer): TOrdAccum;
begin
  result := TOrdAccum.Create(InitialVal);
end;

procedure FreeOrdAccumInst(Inst: TOrdAccum);
begin
  Inst.Free;
end;

function OrdAdd(Inst: TOrdAccum; iVal: integer): integer;
begin
  Inst.Add := iVal;
  result := Inst.Add;
end;

function OrdSubtract(Inst: TOrdAccum; iVal: integer): integer;
begin
  Inst.Subtract := iVal;
  result := Inst.Subtract;
end;

function OrdDivide(Inst: TOrdAccum; iVal: integer): integer;
begin
  Inst.Divide := iVal;
  result := Inst.Divide;
end;
```

Part

VI

Ch

26

continues

Listing 26.3   Continued

```
function OrdMultiply(Inst: TOrdAccum; iVal: integer): integer;
begin
  Inst.Multiply := iVal;
  result := Inst.Multiply;
end;

end.
```

One of the functions this unit exports is named GetOrdAccumInst, as follows:

```
function  GetOrdAccumInst(InitialVal: integer): TOrdAccum; stdcall;
```

GetOrdAccumInst takes a single integer parameter, the initial value to pass to the constructor of the TOrdAccum class. The return value is a living instance of TOrdAccum. An EXE can call this function multiple times and get a new instance of TOrdAccum for each call. When the EXE is done with an instance, this instance must be released from memory. WRAPLIB.PAS exports another routine named FreeOrdAccumInst. This routine frees the instance passed in its only parameter, as follows:

```
procedure FreeOrdAccumInst(Inst: TOrdAccum); stdcall;
```

On the loading side of the application, each instance received from GetOrdAccum should be saved. Each instance is freed independently by passing them to FreeOrdAccumInst. So if you call GetOrdAccum five times, you also will call FreeOrdAccumInst five times.

N O T E   When you import the GetOrdAccumInst routine, you can declare the routine as returning a THandle rather than a TOrdAccum. If you think about it, you'll realize that the EXE will not know what a TOrdAccum is, nor should it have to. A THandle is the same size (32 bits) as the address of an instance of TOrdAccum. So on the using side, the difference between THandle and TOrdAccum is only in interpretation.

Similarly, you can declare the Inst parameter of FreeOrdAccumInst as type THandle in your import unit. Using THandles in the import unit provides a typical convention for maintaining instances without having to sort out the concept of instance addresses. The user of your DLL considers the handle as a reference to an instance but, in reality, they are maintaining the actual pointers to the instance data itself. ■

WRAPLIB.PAS exports four more routines as follows:

```
function  OrdAdd(Inst: TOrdAccum; iVal: integer): integer; stdcall;
function  OrdDivide(Inst: TOrdAccum; iVal: integer): integer; stdcall;
function  OrdMultiply(Inst: TOrdAccum; iVal: integer): integer; stdcall;
function  OrdSubtract(Inst: TOrdAccum; iVal: integer): integer; stdcall;
```

These routines operate on the appropriate property of the TOrdAccum instance passed in the first parameter. The value passed as the second parameter is assigned to the appropriate property of the TOrdAccum instance. Each routine returns the value of the appropriate property after the assignment is made.

Following the declaration of each routine in the unit is the exports list. It appears as follows:

```
exports
  FreeOrdAccumInst,
  GetOrdAccumInst,
  OrdAdd,
  OrdDivide,
  OrdMultiply,
  OrdSubtract;
```

The function names in this list are written to a special section of the DLL file image. An EXE or another DLL that uses your DLL calls LoadLibrary (directly or indirectly), which looks in the special section of the DLL file image for each of these functions. If the functions exist, they can be called, otherwise LoadLibrary fails. See Chapter 25 for more information on LoadLibrary and exporting.

On the CD

The rest of the WRAPLIB.PAS simply contains the definitions for each exported routine. Again, this example is simple, and the definitions are self-explanatory, as shown, and in actual source files included on this book's companion CD-ROM.

Modal Forms in DLLs

It isn't unusual to standardize on a consistent appearance in User Interface (UI) elements for your applications or applets. You can define your look for dialogs and other forms, and the forms that you can use generically can be compiled into a DLL library. Rather than re-creating the same dialog and re-linking the same code into every application, you can distribute your own dialog control pack of sorts in the form of a DLL. This section discusses the storing of *Modal* dialogs in DLLs. Later sections discuss storing *non-Modal* forms in DLLs.

Looking at the Problems Forms in DLLs Will Solve

Now, start by looking at what putting your modal dialogs in a DLL does for you and your application. Suppose that you're contracting for a company named Tyler's Toys. This company wants you to write a series of software applications. One application is an online catalog, accessible via a TCP/IP link over the Internet. A similar version of the catalog program must be created for customers who are not on the Internet. This version is distributed through direct mail. The main forms and programming logic used for each application are quite different, because one application is a communications-based program and the other is a stand-alone program. Nevertheless, each version of the catalog application must support a user interface that both looks and feels similar.

You can minimize code duplication and simplify maintenance tasks by moving into a single DLL the code and forms that both applications have in common. Each version of the catalog program can use the same DLL and from this DLL use some of the same forms. Examine the forms that the two applications may have in common in Figures 26.1 through 26.4.

FIG. 26.1
Splash Screen—this non-modal form is discussed in the next section of this chapter.

FIG. 26.2
About Box—Modal form displays copyright information and software version number.

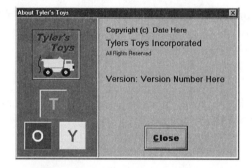

FIG. 26.3
Generic Information Message Box—Modal form displays any given text.

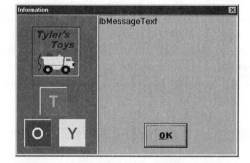

FIG. 26.4
Generic Input Box—Modal form retrieves text from user while displaying generic message prompt.

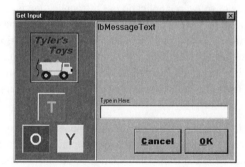

The forms shown in Figures 26.1 through 26.4 are typical UI elements found in almost every Windows GUI-based application. If the forms are created in a generic fashion with variable text displays and input prompts, there is no reason that each program Tyler's Toys asks you to develop cannot use the same DLL.

Here's where the true benefit comes in. Suppose that the Internet-based application downloads to the client machine the DLL that contains these standard forms. When the Internet application needs to display a dialog, it appears quickly because it is actually being loaded on the client side of the connection. Obviously, the first time a user accesses the catalog from the Internet, it takes time for the DLL to download, but it needs to occur only once upon first access.

Now suppose that a bug pops up in one of the dialogs—perhaps the form is too big to display at 640×480 resolution. If the broken form is in a DLL shared by both the Internet-based and the stand-alone applications, you have to fix the problem only once. Rather than sending out a new recompiled version of the stand-alone application to your customers, simply send them the updated DLL.

Creating Access Routines

To access any of the modal forms in your DLL, you have to create and then export an *access* routine. The loading executable calls the access routines, which in turn instantiates the form class instance variable and displays the form modally. If the form receives input data or the user has options such as OK, Cancel, Abort, and so on, the access routine can return this information.

Listing 26.4 shows the access routine for a simple modal message dialog box, like the one shown back in Figure 26.3.

Listing 26.4 \UDELPHI3\CHP26\EXPORTU.PAS—Access Function for Displaying the *TToyInfoDlg* Form in a Modal Fashion

```
procedure ShowToyInfoDlgModal(AppHand: THandle; Prompt: PChar);
begin
  Application.Handle := AppHand;
  with TToyInfoDlg.Create(Application) do
  try
    SetPrompt(Prompt);
    ShowModal;
  finally
    Free;
  end;
end;
```

The ShowToyInfoDlgModal routine literally creates, displays, and frees an instance of the TToyInfoDlg. The AppHand parameter is the handle of the application's main window. If the calling program is a Delphi application, you pass Application.Handle for this parameter. On the receiving side, ShowToyInfoDlgModal assigns AppHand to the local instance of the global Application object. In this way, if the user minimizes the TToyInfoDlg, the entire application is minimized because the dialog box is associated with the main window from which it was spawned. If the loading program doesn't have a main window, 0 can be passed without side effects.

The `Prompt` parameter is passed to the `SetPrompt` method of the new `TToyInfoDlg` instance. `SetPrompt` simply assigns the text `Prompt` points at to the `Caption` property of a local `TLabel` object on the form. Because you can specify the text that `TToyInfoDlg` displays, `TToyInfoDlg` is generic and useful in more than one application.

N O T E   Figure 26.2 shows a generic about box for Tyler's Toys. The access routine for this about box dialog looks almost like the access routine shown in Listing 26.4, but more parameters need to be added to accommodate multiple field values, copyright date, and version number. ■

In summary, the `ShowToyInfoDlgModal` routine creates an instance of `TToyInfoDlg` that specifies the local `Application` object as the owner. `ShowToyInfoDlgModal` then sets the text the dialog will display. `ShowToyInfoDlgModal` calls `TToyInfoDlg`'s `ShowModal` routine to display the dialog. `ShowToyInfoDlgModal` then frees the dialog from memory. There is no reason to return a value from `ShowToyInfoDlgModal` routine because the user input is limited to clicking OK.

Figure 26.4 shows an input dialog box. The access routine for this input box is more complicated than the routine that was used for the message box or the about box because not only can the user input text your program needs to get to, but the user also can decide to cancel the entire operation. Listing 26.5 shows how to handle this kind of dialog box.

Listing 26.5   \UDELPHI3\CHP26\EXPORTU.PAS—User Can Cancel or Continue After Inputting the Necessary Text

```
function ShowToyInputDlgModal(AppHand: THandle; Prompt, pBuf: PChar;
                                             Length: integer): Integer;
begin
  result := -1;
  Application.Handle := AppHand;
  with TToyInputDlg.Create(Application) do
  try
    SetPrompt(Prompt);
    result := ShowModal;
    StrLCopy(pBuf, GetInputBuf, Length)
  finally
    Free;
  end;
end;
```

The handling and assignment of the `AppHand` parameter in Listing 26.5 works just as it did in Listing 26.4. `ShowToyInputDlgModal` also has `Prompt` parameter to display runtime-assignable text again to keep the use of the dialog box generic. `ShowToyInputDlgModal` has a `pBuf` parameter. The `pBuf` parameter expects a pre-allocated `PChar` buffer in which to place to user-input text. The `pBuf` parameter is assumed to be the size specified in the `Length` parameter. Note also that ShowToyInputDlgModal is a function, not a procedure. The actual dialog that is displayed allows the user to select OK or Cancel. This value can be retrieved by and returned from ShowToyInputDlgModal.

After the TToyInputDlg instance is created, the TToyInputDlg SetPrompt method is called, which sets the local lbMessageText TLabel control's Caption property. The ShowModal method then is called, which shows the form modally. The user then can enter text, and then select OK or Cancel. If the user selects OK, ShowModal returns a value of 1. If the user selects Cancel, ShowModal returns 2. The value returned from ShowModal ultimately is returned from ShowToyInputDlgModal.

After the form is displayed and then closed, a method named GetInputBuf is called. Like SetPrompt, GetInputBuf is a public method local to the TToyInputDlg instance. GetInputBuf returns the text that the user inputs into the local edInputEdit TEdit component. The RTL function StrLCopy copies the number of bytes specified in the Length parameter from the buffer returned from GetInputBuf into the pBuf pointer that is passed to the ShowToyInputDlgModal function. The TToyInputDlg instance then is freed from memory with a call to the Free method.

Before ending this discussion, take a quick look at the interface section of the unit that declares, exports, and defines the two access methods discussed in this section of the chapter.

On the CD

Listing 26.6 shows the typical interface section of a unit that exports access routine in a DLL. Each routine is declared publicly and uses the StdCall calling convention. After the declarations, the name of each function is listed in the exports section. The actual definitions of the exported routines should follow the implementation directive in the unit. Declarations, calling conventions, and the exports section are discussed in detail in Chapter 25, "DLL Programming: An Introduction."

Part
VI

Ch
26

Listing 26.6 \UDELPHI3\CHP26\EXPORTU.PAS—Interface to the Export Unit for the FormsLib DLL Project

```
...
interface

uses
  Forms, SysUtils, WinTypes, TTInfoDlg,TTAboutDlg,TTInputDlg,TTSplashDlg;

procedure ShowToyInfoDlgModal(AppHand: THandle; Prompt: PChar); StdCall;
function ShowToyInputDlgModal(AppHand: THandle; Prompt, pBuf: PChar;
                              Length: integer): Integer; StdCall;
exports
  ShowToyInfoDlgModal,
  ShowToyInputDlgModal;

implementation
...
```

Non-Modal Forms in DLLs

Non-Modal forms in DLLs are implemented in a fashion similar to Modal forms, but require a single flat function to create and show the form and another flat function to hide and free the form. This is because processing continues immediately after the call is made to the Show method. With Modal forms, processing doesn't continue after the call to ShowModal until the Modal form is closed. The Modal form examples called Free shortly after calling ShowModal to release the form from memory. Consider if the same code were used for a Non-Modal form. Processing continues immediately after a call to Show. Free will be called, the form destroyed, and you would be lucky to even see the form display on-screen. You solve this by dividing these actions into separate routines.

Start with the declaration of two routines in the interface section of the unit, as follows:

```
function OpenToySplashDlg(AppHand: THandle): THandle; StdCall;
procedure CloseToySplashDlg(hSplashInst: THandle); StdCall;
```

Each routine is declared by using the StdCall calling convention. The function names must be added to the export section of the unit or project. This ensures that each function is properly exported from the DLL.

Creating and Opening the Non-Modal Form

The OpenToySplashDlg routine creates and displays an instance of the TToySplashDlg. This form is simple, doesn't accept user input, and should be closed in code by calling CloseToySplashDlg. A splash screen example is a nice use because your main program can call OpenToySplashDlg; process and initialize other areas of the application; and then call CloseToySplashDlg when complete. The definition (implementation) of the OpenToySplashDlg routine is shown in Listing 26.7.

> **Listing 26.7   \UDELPHI3\CHP26\EXPORTU.PAS—This Example is Part of the Same Project as the Modal Form Examples Discussed Previously**

```
function OpenToySplashDlg(AppHand: THandle): THandle;
begin
  Application.Handle := AppHand;
  result := THandle(TToySplashDlg.Create(Application));
  with TToySplashDlg(result) do
  try
    Show;
  except
    Free;
    Result := 0;
    Raise;
  end;
end;
```

The OpenToySplashDlg routine shown in Listing 26.7 begins by assigning the AppHand parameter to the local Application object's handle data member. AppHand is the *handle* to the window to which the TToySplashDlg instance should be associated. This action is important if your form can be minimized. Minimizing the main form should result in all forms in the application being minimized. Making this assignment completes the association.

The result variable then gets the instance returned from a call to the TToySplashDlg Create constructor. The instance must be *typecast* to a THandle because this is the data type of the result variable. This typecast operation is safe as an instance variable and THandle are both 32 bits long.

After the TToySplashDlg instance is constructed, result is used to call the Show method that will display the TToySplashDlg form. The call to Show returns immediately (unlike a call to ShowModal). If for any reason an attempt to show the form results in an exception being raised, the except statements will execute. This example immediately calls the Free method, sets the result variable to 0, and then re-raises the exception.

Closing and Freeing the Non-Modal Form

The application that calls OpenToySplashDlg needs to retain the THandle return value. This handle value is actually the object instance and is used by the CloseToySplashDlg routine to close and free the instance. The implementation of CloseToySplashDlg is shown in Listing 26.8.

> **Listing 26.8   \UDELPHI3\CHP26\EXPORTU.PAS—Raises an Exception upon Failure, So Be Sure to Wrap the Call in a *try...except* Construct**

```
procedure CloseToySplashDlg(hSplashInst: THandle);
begin
  if hSplashInst < 1 then Raise Exception.Create('hSplashInst is not valid');
  with TToySplashDlg(hSplashInst) do
  begin
    Close;
  Free;
  end;
end;
```

The handle returned from OpenToySplashDlg is passed to CloseToySplashDlg as the hSplashInst parameter. The routine begins with error checking that makes sure that hSplashInst is not 0. There is no surefire way to know if hSplashInst will be valid, but if its value is 0, it's guaranteed not to be 0, in which case an exception stating so is raised.

The routine continues by casting hSplashInst as a TToySplashDlg instance. From this instance the Close method is called. Following Close, the Free method is called. If the hSplashInst is not valid, the call to Close will raise an exception, causing execution to bail out of the CloseToySplashDlg and return to the calling module.

Virtual Method Table

Delphi objects created by using the Object Pascal syntax internally are data structures with an identifiable format. The internal format of an Object Pascal object is compatible with the object format as defined in Microsoft's Component Object Model (COM) specification. Using this object format, Delphi objects can directly support interfaces compatible with COM objects.

Because Delphi and Borland C++ share essentially the same compiler back end, their objects also are compatible. The standardization and unification of object formats makes for easier development of language-independent code. The benefits of this level of development flexibility are obvious.

The COM Object Format

The COM-compatible portion of Delphi's object format is rather simple. The instance received after a call to the class constructor is merely a pointer to a block of memory. The memory block holds the address of a pointer to the Virtual Method Table as its first field. The next field in the memory block is the address of the first data member declared in the base class. In contrast, the last field is the last data member declared in the class from which the instance was instantiated. So, the addresses of data members appear as fields in the instance memory block sequentially, in order of declaration, throughout the class hierarchy.

> **N O T E**   The Virtual Method Table is a name used specifically in the Delphi language, which doesn't mean that Delphi is the only language that uses a Virtual Method Table; it only means Delphi is the one language that calls it this.
>
> The commonly known names are the Virtual Table (VT) or VTable (VT). These names are important to know when you read COM or C++ documentation. It's safe to assume that text that references the Virtual Table (VT) or VTable for other languages talks about the same thing discussed here when using VMT. Keep in mind that it is the positioning of the VMT within the overall layout of an object that deems an object COM-compatible. ■

The Virtual Method Table (VMT) is an array of method addresses. Each address is that of a virtual method declared in the class hierarchy. This relationship is better illustrated in Figure 26.5.

FIG. 26.5

The COM-compatible format of Object Pascal objects.

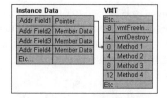

The addresses of the Virtual methods in the VMT are position oriented. They exist sequentially, in the order of declaration, throughout the class hierarchy. Overridden methods are included in the VMT, which is how the authors can support the use of the inherited directive.

Delphi-Specific Object Format

Delphi's object format is actually more robust than the format that is required exclusively for COM. Object Pascal supports additional features, such as dynamic methods, Run Time Type Information (RTTI), and other elements that require pointers to various types of in-memory structures. Because the object structure is defined by the COM specification, you need a way to attach the Delphi-specific information to an instance of an object. This is accomplished by storing pointers to each piece of information at negative offsets from where the VMT pointer points. Table 26.1 shows several constants that represent the offsets to the Delphi-specific object data. This information is further documented in code in System.pas located in the \DELPHI 3\SOURCE\RTL\SYS directory.

Table 26.1   Virtual Method Table Entries

VMT Entry	OffSet
vmtDestroy	−4
vmtFreeInstance	−8
vmtNewInstance	−12
vmtDefaultHandler	−16
vmtSafeCallException	−20
vmtParent	−24
vmtInstanceSize	−28
vmtClassName	−32
vmtDynamicTable	−36
vmtMethodTable	−40
vmtFieldTable	−44
vmtTypeInfo	−48
vmtInitTable	−52
vmtAutoTable	−56
vmtIntfTable	−60
vmtSelfPtr	−64

Part
VI

Ch
26

VMT and DLL Programming

The information discussed here about the VMT was never really important on the surface in Delphi 1.0 and isn't vital knowledge for programming in Delphi 2.0 or Delphi 3. It's significant only in the context of understanding one side of a dual interface in COM and class sharing in DLL programming. Both of these issues recently became hot topics. Microsoft has successfully solidified the need for COM-based DLLs with their release of the ActiveX specifications. C++ programmers have latched onto the idea of developing their GUIs in Delphi for quick application turnaround time, but they still needed a way to use their existing C++ code. Also do not forget third-party product developers that want to develop libraries for use in multiple languages that use a single code base.

With Borland's most recent release of C++ Builder, the need to share code between languages becomes even more significant. The key to sharing code in a language-independent fashion is to make sure that each language can access the key methods in a class declaration. These sharable methods in a class declaration are those that are declared as virtual and exist in the VMT. The following section discusses object sharing by using the VMT in greater detail.

DLL Object Sharing with Virtual Classes

Throughout this chapter, the benefits of DLL-based applications—and more important, what they can contain—were discussed. You learned how flat functions and access routines are exported to manipulate generic objects and Delphi Forms. This section and the following section discuss a more direct approach to using objects stashed away in DLLs.

It's both theoretically and practically possible to access certain methods of the instance of an object stored in a DLL. There are five main limitations involved in using the technique in this discussion, as follows:

- The instance must be instantiated in the DLL.
- Only Virtual methods can be accessed external to the DLL.
- The order of declaration of the Virtual methods in the DLL must be consistent in the EXE.
- The calling convention used in declaration of the Virtual methods in the DLL must be consistent in the EXE.
- Code in the EXE can not descend from the class declared in the DLL.

Each of these limitations is discussed as applicable throughout this section of the chapter. You now can start by looking at a simple communications example. You can use this example to send debug strings to a second computer or can even use it as a phone dialer.

The *TCommDebug* Class

Suppose that during development of your application, you want to send debug strings to track program execution. Often, programmers throw together a group of routines that stream debug information out to a console window. The only problem with using a console window is that it usually ends up behind the main windows in the program that you want to debug. Using the TCommDebug class, you can stream debug messages out the communications port, across a null-modem cable into another system, and read the strings by using any ASCII terminal program.

N O T E   This example demonstrates class sharing by using an example communications program. The example is not a robust communications program. It supports no particular protocol, nor does it have receiver capabilities.

The class is, however, generic. The class doesn't know or care if the data it sends to the port goes to a modem or to another computer. It's used here in context to send out debug strings to a second computer. If you do not have a second computer and still want to run the example, use it as is as a phone dialer class. Simply use the class to open the port that your modem uses, and pass the string 'ATDT'+555-5555 (replacing *555-5555* with the number that you want to dial) to the StringOut method. This will be pointed out again where applicable in the example, so read on! ■

First, look at the source code in the SHAREU1.PAS file in Listing 26.9.

Listing 26.9   \UDELPHI3\CHP26\SHAREU1.PAS—This Class Uses the Win32 Communications API

```
unit shareu1;

interface

uses
  Windows, Messages, SysUtils, Classes, Graphics, Controls, Forms, Dialogs,
  Menus, StdCtrls, Mask, ComCtrls, Buttons, ExtCtrls;

type
  TCommDebug = class(TObject)
  private
    FhPort: THandle;
  public
    procedure   StringOut(sValue: string); virtual; Stdcall;
    constructor Connect(sComPort: String);
    destructor  Destroy; override;
  end;

function GetComDebugInstance(iComPort: integer): TCommDebug; StdCall;

exports
  GetComDebugInstance;

implementation

function GetComDebugInstance(iComPort: integer): TCommDebug;
begin
  result := TCommDebug.Connect(Format('COM%d',[iComPort+1]));
end;
```

continues

Part
VI

Ch
26

Listing 26.9   Continued

```
procedure TCommDebug.StringOut(sValue: string);
var
  wCtr,wLen,wOffset : word;
  TxBuf : array[0..255] of byte;
  dwSent: DWord;
begin
  if strlen(PChar(sValue)) > 255 then
    Raise Exception.Create('Value passed to TCommDebug.StringOut exceeds 255 '+
                           'byte limit');
  dwSent   := 0;
  wOffset := 0;

  if LongBool(Length(sValue))  then
  begin
    wLen := Length( sValue );
    if wLen > 0 then
    begin
      for wCtr := 0 to wLen-1 do
      begin
        TxBuf[ wCtr ] := ord( sValue[ wCtr + 1] );
        wOffset := wCtr;
      end;

      TxBuf[ wOffset+1 ] := Ord(#13);
      TxBuf[ wOffset+2 ] := Ord(#10);
      TxBuf[ wOffset+3 ] := Ord(#0);

      WriteFile( FhPort, TxBuf, wLen+2, dwSent, nil );
    end;
  end;
end;

constructor TCommDebug.Connect(sComPort: String);
var DCB: TDCB;
begin
  inherited Create;

  if Length(sComPort) = 0 then
    Raise Exception.Create('Could not retrieve port settings.');

  FhPort := CreateFile(PChar(sComPort+':'),(Generic_Read + Generic_Write),
                0{expected},nil{expected}, Open_Existing{expected},
                0, 0{expected});

  if FhPort = INVALID_HANDLE_VALUE then
  begin
    FhPort := 0;
    Raise Exception.Create('Open Failed')
  end;

  GetCommState(FhPort,DCB);
  with DCB do
  begin
```

```
   BaudRate   := 9600;
   ByteSize   := 8; // Databits : 4-8
   Parity     := 0; // Parity   : 0-4 = none,odd,even,mark,space
   StopBits   := 0; // StopBits : 0,1,2 = 1, 1.5, 2
 end;

 if not SetCommState( FhPort, DCB ) then
   Raise Exception.Create('SetState ERROR :'+IntToStr( GetLastError() ) );
end;

destructor TCommDebug.Destroy;
begin
  if FhPort <> 0 then CloseHandle(FhPort);
  inherited Destroy;
end;

end.
```

The interface section of SHAREU1.PAS has a uses sections and a type section. The type section declares the TCommDebug class. TCommDebug declares a private member FhPort, which holds the *handle* of the communications port after it is opened. TCommDebug also declares a single *virtual* function, as follows:

```
procedure StringOut(sValue: string); virtual; Stdcall;
```

After an instance of TCommDebug exists and is connected to the port, StringOut is the routine that writes the data specified in the sValue parameter to the port. TCommDebug also declares a new *constructor* named Connect.

```
constructor Connect(sComPort: String);
```

Connect requires the sComPort parameter to specify which COM port to open. The format of the string is COM*n*. The *n* should be replaced by the numeric value that represents the port number, for example:

```
Inst := TCommDebug.Connect('Com2'); //Connects to communications port 2
```

Finally, TCommDebug declares and *overrides* the default Destroy *destructor*, as follows:

```
destructor  Destroy; override;
```

Because SHAREU1.PAS will be linked into a DLL project, the DLL will have to *export* a routine that *instantiates* the TCommDebug instance. To serve this purpose, SHAREU1.PAS *exports*, as follows:

```
function GetComDebugInstance(iComPort: integer): TCommDebug; StdCall;
```

To avoid having to pass a literal string or PChar to the DLL, GetComDebugInstance expects a numeric value in its iComPort parameter. The value 0 represents COM1, 1 represents COM2, and so on. GetComDebugInstance converts the iComPort parameter to the appropriate string, as required by the TCommDebug *constructor*.

Part VI

Ch 26

N O T E The implementation of the Shareu1.pas unit shown in Listing 26.9 is fairly straightforward. The communications aspects of the code may not be familiar; however, it's rather simple to use. Dedicated Win32 communications simply use the standard Win32 file I/O APIs. If you're not already familiar with the Win32 file I/O APIs, see the Win32 API online help reference. ▨

Using the *TCommDebug* Class

After the TCommDebug class and Shareu1.pas unit is built into a DLL project, the class can be used from another DLL or EXE. At this point you may wonder what's the big deal because, so far, nothing different was done other than what you typically do in any DLL project. So a class was created and a routine that returns an instance of the class was exported. Well... so what?

Here is where things get interesting. You may have noticed that the StringOut routine was declared in TCommDebug, using the virtual directive, as follows:

```
procedure StringOut(sValue: string); virtual; Stdcall;
```

This wasn't done specifically so TCommDebug could be descended from and StringOut overridden. It was done so that the address of StringOut would appear as an entry (the first entry) in the VMT after an instance of TCommDebug is created.

When the loading application calls the *exported* GetComDebugInstance function, it returns an instance of TCommDebug. This instance is actually a pointer to the memory block that makes up the instance of the class. If you recall from previous discussion, the first field in the memory block is the address of a pointer. The pointer points to the VMT. In this case, the first entry in the VMT is the address of the StringOut method.

Implicit Instance Parameter

Theoretically, as an alternative way to use an object external to a DLL, you can cast the return value of GetComDebugInstance to a generic pointer. You then could dereference the pointer, cast its value as a pointer, and dereference it to get the runtime address of the StringOut function in the VMT. You then could use this address to make the call to StringOut.

One of the semantical issues of this approach is you then have to declare a function variable (Delphi can call only functions or procedures, not generic addresses) that takes two parameters. The instance returned from GetComDebugInstance is passed as the first parameter and your debug string as the second parameter, which is necessary because all methods in a class have an implicit Self parameter passed first, which is the class instance (or data). With this technique, the method is being called as a flat function so that the magic passing of Self must be done manually. If this technique sounds obscure, it is. You go this route only if you're using the DLL and class in a language that doesn't support the Delphi (or COM) object model.

So far, you have a DLL that exports a routine named GetComDebugInstance that returns an instance of a class. The receiver of the instance (assuming an EXE) then can use the instance to call methods of the object. But wait, the TCommDebug class is declared in the DLL, so the EXE knows nothing about it. When you import the GetComDebugInstance function, the compiler will complain about the TCommDebug return value because the compiler knows nothing about it.

```
function GetComDebugInstance(iComPort: integer):
            TCommDebug; StdCall; external 'Shareit.DLL'
```

You handle this by redeclaring the class in the calling EXE, but the method(s) (in this case, StringOut) are declared as abstract. By making StringOut abstract, the EXE can be compiled without error. The compiler won't error because it's perfectly legal to call abstract methods as long as their implementation is valid.

NOTE When redeclaring the virtual portion of a class in an EXE as demonstrated in this example, the class name and method names used in the redeclaration are not important. They should, however, match the original declarations by convention, for maintainability and readability.

Remember that it's vitally important to redeclare the methods in exactly the same order as declared in the class in the DLL. The method calls made in the EXE are position-oriented and, therefore, are not resolved by name at runtime.

The example TCommDebug class is a simple class that directly descends from TObject, so you are guaranteed that StringOut will be the first virtual method in the VMT. However, the VMT stores the addresses of the virtual methods in parenting classes (if any), in order of declaration, as well as the addresses of any methods you may have overridden.

So, if TCommDebug descended from a class named TCustomComm, and TCustomComm implements four virtual methods of its own, the StringOut method of TCommDebug will end up being the fifth entry in the VMT instead of the first. ■

The instance returned from GetComDebugInstance has a valid VMT that contains a valid address to the implementation of StringOut so it works out all right. Look at the unit in the EXE example shown in Listing 26.10, which demonstrates these principles.

The interface section of LoadComu1.pas in Listing 26.10 redeclares the TCommDebug class. Notice, however, the FhPort data member, the Connect *constructor*, and *overridden* Destroy *destructor* are not declared. They do not need to be declared in the EXE. They all exist in the actual instance, and the implementation of the class in the DLL knows how to access them. The TCommDebug declaration exists in the EXE only so the compiler will not complain about the return type from the GetComDebugInstance import declaration and to be able to resolve the call to the StringOut function when it is used.

Listing 26.10 \UDELPHI3\CHP26\LOADCOMU1.PAS—Form Associated with This Unit Contains Only a Single Control of Type *TButton*; the *Button1Click* Method Calls the *StringOut* Function

```
unit LoadComu1;

interface

uses
  Windows, Messages, SysUtils, Classes, Graphics, Controls, Forms, Dialogs,
  StdCtrls;
```

continues

Listing 26.10   Continued

```
type
  TForm1 = class(TForm)
    Button1: TButton;
    procedure Button1Click(Sender: TObject);
  private
    { Private declarations }
  public
    { Public declarations }
  end;

  TCommDebug = class(TObject)
  public
    procedure StringOut(sValue: string); virtual; Stdcall; abstract;
  end;

var
  Form1: TForm1;

function GetComDebugInstance(iComPort: integer): TCommDebug; StdCall;
                                                external 'Shareit.DLL'
implementation

{$R *.DFM}

procedure TForm1.Button1Click(Sender: TObject);
var CommDebug: TCommDebug;
begin
  CommDebug := GetComDebugInstance(2);
  try
  {^$define PhoneDialer} //remove ^ to use as dialer.
  {$ifdef PhoneDialer}
    //String below dials, pauses, thens hangs up.
    CommDebug.StringOut('ATDT5555555,,ATH');
  {$else}
    //Assumes you have a second system writing to the port.
    CommDebug.StringOut('This could be a debug string');
  {$endif}
  finally
    CommDebug.Free;
  end;

end.
```

The implementation shown in Listing 26.10 contains a single method that is the button-click handler for the Button1 component on the associated form. Button1Click declares a local CommDebug variable of type TCommDebug. CommDebug then is assigned the return value from the imported GetComDebugInstance function. The next line of executable code is the call to StringOut wrapped in a try...finally construct, passing the string to write to the communications port.

NOTE The example uses the `ifdef` compiler directives to determine which one of the calls to `StringOut` to use in the project. Two ways are included to use this example; as a phone dialer or as a tool to send debug messages to a second computer.

If you don't have a second computer but do have a modem, you should use the `StringOut` example that includes the ATDT text. The ATDT portion of the text indicates a modem command to dial the phone number that follows. Replace the *5555555* portion of the string with something appropriate. The ,, means to pause and the ATH is a modem command to hang up. During testing, I used my own phone modem number so the number is dialed, a pause occurs to wait for the busy signal (I'm on the phone obviously), and then it hangs up so that the line isn't tied up. ◼

After the string is output to the port, the `Free` method is called, which in turn calls the destructor of the `TCommDebug` instance. The destructor's existence is implicit in the object instance and will be called correctly even in context to the EXE although it is overridden in the class declaration in the DLL.

The Object Sharing Process Summarized

We just discussed a highly desirable functionality that isn't well-documented or commonly known and understood. Given this, a quick summary is in order, as shown in the following steps:

1. You created a class named `TCommDebug` with a single virtual method named `StringOut`. `StringOut` writes a string to the communications port for debugging or dialing.

2. The `TCommDebug` class is compiled into a DLL project.

3. The DLL exports a single function named `GetComDebugInstance`, which calls the `TCommDebug Connect` constructor and returns the instance to the caller (probably an EXE).

4. An EXE redeclares the `TCommDebug` class but includes only the virtual `StringOut` method.

5. The EXE imports `GetComDebugInstance` from the DLL.

6. The `Button1Click` method in the EXE calls `GetComDebugInstance` to retrieve an instance of `TCommDebug` in the DLL.

7. Using the instance, the `StringOut` method is called and then the instance is released by calling `Free`.

This still leaves one question unanswered. How does the EXE know where the `StringOut` function is in memory? Simple, the compiler knows `StringOut` is the first entry in the VMT because you declared it as so in the redeclaration of the class in the EXE. At runtime when the call is made, the compiler-generated code knows how to find the pointer to the VMT in the instance returned from `GetComDebugInstance`. After it has the pointer to the VMT, it moves to the first address entry and executes that call address.

Part

VI

Ch

26

Sharing Data

Chapter 25 discussed the issue of portability from Win16. The biggest change in the Win32 DLL architecture is that a DLL's data segment exists in context to the process it is mapped into. This means if process A loads a DLL, the global and heap-allocated data and pointers are not accessible or usable to process B if it chooses to load an instance of the same DLL at the same time. Although this architecture is logical, it is contrary to the architecture in Win16.

Under Win16, each DLL has its own data segment that was in global scope. Task A can allocate and initialize memory, and Task B can use the same pointers to access it. Programmers quickly and commonly used this Win16 feature as a medium to share data between applications.

Under Win32 there still are several ways to share data across the process boundaries, but none of them require the use of DLLs. If your Win16 DLL existed only for data sharing, under Win32 the new techniques may make your design obsolete. On the other hand, you will find that (in some cases) the code for data sharing under Win32 is duplicated in each process, so it then does make sense to put your data-sharing code into a DLL after all. Now, look at an easy way to allocate globally accessible memory within the system paging file. This technique is followed up by including it in a DLL project and creating a loader to access and demonstrate its use.

Using a Kernel File-Mapping Object

At the core of the Win32 memory architecture exists the system paging file. This file resides on your hard disk and is used in conjunction with physical RAM. Using a combination of physical RAM and hard disk space allows the OS and applications to allocate physical storage beyond that which is available only as RAM.

When an application runs, only a small region of memory need be allocated in the system paging file. This region holds a table of addresses that map to an EXE file and each dependent DLL on your hard disk. Windows Kernel provides a Kernel File-Mapping Object to manage the mapping of files from their current location on the hard disk into your applications' addressable memory region.

In context to sharing data between applications, you probably are thinking that this book will suggest the obvious—to create a file-mapping object that is backed by some named data file out in the file system, write the data to it in one application, and then map the file into another application to read the data. Well, not exactly. Instead, you can create a file-mapping object that is backed directly by the system paging file. You can specify how much address space is needed and even how much must be immediately backed by physical storage. You then can map a portion of the file into view of your application and thus read from it and write to it directly.

The file-mapping object can manipulate the system paging file that is global to the system. The data written to it can be accessed by any number of applications and isn't required to observe process boundaries limitations.

Creating the File-Mapping Object To create a file-mapping object, you call
CreateFileMapping as follows:

```
function CreateFileMapping(hFile: THandle;
            lpFileMappingAttributes: PSecurityAttributes;
            flProtect, dwMaximumSizeHigh, dwMaximumSizeLow: DWORD;
            lpName: PChar): THandle; stdcall;
```

The hFile parameter specifies the name of the file to associate with the object. Because we are using the system paging file, the magic value of $FFFFFFFF (the same value as the MAXDWORD constant in WINDOWS.PAS) is required. The lpFileMappingAttributes parameter can be set to nil, which causes the default security attributes to be applied. The flProtect parameter specifies the protection attributes to use when the file is mapped into view. This example uses PAGE_READWRITE. The dwMaximumSizeHigh and dwMaximumSizeLow parameters represent the high DWORD and low DWORD parts of a total 64-bit numeric value that specifies the maximum size of the file to map. When mapping from the system paging file, you can look at these parameters as how many bytes of memory to allocate.

The lpName parameter is a unique user-provided name employed to obtain a reference to the file-mapping object from processes other than the one that initially called CreateFileMapping. So if process A calls CreateFileMapping passing the string _GMem and process B calls CreateFileMapping also passing the string _GMem, both processes will effectively look at the region of memory. This is how the sharing aspects are accomplished. CreateFileMapping returns a handle to the file-mapping object if successful; otherwise, it returns 0.

Mapping the File into View After the File-Mapping object is created, a portion of the memory can be mapped into view for use by your application. This is accomplished with a call to MapViewOfFile, as follows:

```
function MapViewOfFile(hFileMappingObject: THandle;
                dwDesiredAccess: DWORD;
                dwFileOffsetHigh, dwFileOffsetLow,
                dwNumberOfBytesToMap: DWORD): Pointer; stdcall;
```

The hFileMappingObject parameter is the handle returned from CreateFileMapping. The dwDesiredAccess parameter is used to specify the kind of access to be used for accessing the view. This example uses FILE_MAP_WRITE. The dwFileOffsetHigh and dwFileOffsetLow parameters are combined together to make up a single 64-bit numeric value that specifies the OffSet into the file from where the mapping should begin. Because you're working specifically with the system paging file, both of these will be 0. The dwNumberOfBytesToMap parameter specifies how many bytes should be mapped into view.

> **CAUTION**
>
> If 0 is passed to the dwNumberOfBytesToMap parameter, MapViewOfFile tries to map into view all the memory as specified by the dwMaximumSizeHigh and dwMaximumSizeLow parameters in the call to CreateFileMapping. These numbers can be quite large; if so, MapViewOfFile probably will fail. When the amount of memory to map into view isn't known up front, you should pass 1 to the dwNumberOfBytesToMap parameter.

`MapViewOfFile` returns the starting address of the mapped view if it is successful; otherwise, it returns nil. The starting address is a generic pointer that can be written to and read from directly.

UN-Mapping the File and Releasing the File-Mapping Object   After a view of the file is mapped into memory, and you have finished manipulating it, you should UN-map the view then close the handle associated with the File-Mapping object. To UN-map the view of the file, use the API function `UnmapViewOfFile`. WINDOWS.PAS declares `UnmapViewOfFile` as follows:

```
function UnmapViewOfFile(lpBaseAddress: Pointer): BOOL; stdcall;
```

The `lpBaseAddress` parameter is the pointer returned from a successful call to `MapViewOfFile`. If `UnmapViewOfFile` is successful, it returns True. After the view is UN-mapped, the handle of the associated File-Mapping object should be closed. This is accomplished with a call to `CloseHandle` declared in the Windows.pas unit as follows:

```
function CloseHandle(hObject: THandle): BOOL; stdcall;
```

The `hObject` parameter is the parameter returned from a successful call to `CreateFileMapping`. If `CloseHandle` is successful, it returns True.

Using the Object in Context to a DLL

Suppose that you want to create a DLL that allocates a shared block of memory from the system paging file that can be manipulated by multiple applications. The DLL can allocate a large chunk of memory initially, and then manually maintain its own suballocation scheme. The applications that use the DLL can request memory blocks of various sizes all maintained in code by the DLL.

Now, look at a simple example that uses the File-Mapping APIs to allocate some space in the system paging file. The DLL will export a single function that returns a pointer to the global memory. Look at Listing 26.11.

Listing 26.11   \UDELPHI3\CHP26\ShareHeap.DPR—Initializes and Deinitializes the File-Mapping Object by Incorporating a DllMain

```
library ShareHeap;

uses
  Forms,
  SysUtils,
  Windows;

const Key: String = '_GMem';
      MaxSize = $FFFF;

var
  hObjHand: THandle;
  pGMem: pointer;

procedure UnmapMemory;
```

```
begin
  if Assigned(pGMem) then
  begin
    UnMapViewOfFile(pGMem);
    pGMem := nil;
  end;

  if hObjHand > 0 then
    CloseHandle(hObjHand);

  hObjHand := 0;
end;

procedure MapMemory(dwAllocSize: DWORD);
begin
  hObjHand := CreateFileMapping(MAXDWORD,nil,PAGE_READWRITE,
                               0,dwAllocSize,PChar(Key));

  if (hObjHand = 0) then
    Raise Exception.Create('Could not create file-mapping object');

  pGMem := MapViewOfFile(hObjHand,FILE_MAP_WRITE, 0,0,1);
  if not Assigned(pGMem) then
  begin
    UnmapMemory;
    Raise Exception.Create('Could not map file');
  end;
end;

procedure DLLMain(dwReason: DWORD);
begin
  case dwReason of
  dll_Process_Attach:
    begin
      pGMem := nil;
      hObjHand := 0;
      MapMemory(MaxSize);
    end;
  dll_Process_Detach:
    UnmapMemory;
  end;
end;

function GetGBlock: Pointer; StdCall;
begin
  result := pGMem;
end;

exports
  GetGBlock;

begin
  DLLProc := @DLLMain;
  DLLMain(dll_Process_Attach)
end.
```

Part VI
Ch 26

The initialization code at the bottom of Listing 26.11 assigns the address of a local routine named DLLMain to the global DLLProc variable, which is done so the DLL is notified each time a process attaches or detaches from the DLL. DLLMain then is called manually, passing the dll_Process_Attach constant. If you're not already familiar with Delphi's implementation of DLLMain, read Chapter 25 before attempting to decipher this code.

The DLLMain procedure evaluates the dwReason parameter in a case...of construct. If the value is dll_Process_Attach, a new application is using the DLL. The dll_Process_Attach statements initialize two global variables that call the local MapMemory function (described shortly).

If dwReason evaluates to dll_Process_Detach, then the DLL is being unloaded so any memory, including memory allocated to File-Mapping objects, should be released. In the example, this is accomplished with a call to the local UnmapMemory procedure.

So, what is happening here? The functionality of the DLL is to know how to allocate and map into view some memory from the system paging file. In the example, this mapping occurs upon load of the DLL. When the DLL is unloaded, the view is UN-mapped and the local File-Mapping object is destroyed. Although there is only one DLL, this same sequence of events must occur every time the DLL is used in a different process.

Ultimately, a pointer is returned to the loading EXE when it calls the exported GetGBlock function. If process A loads the DLL and calls GetGBlock, the pointer is to a view mapped into process A address space. If process B then loads the same DLL and calls GetGBlock, the pointer is returned in context to the view mapped into process B. Theoretically, the views can exist at different offsets in each process, which is the way the view must be mapped in each time the DLL is newly loaded.

Accessing the Global Memory

Using the SHAREHEAP.DLL (discussed previously), you can allocate a block of memory from the system paging file, and then call the exported GetGBlock routine to retrieve a pointer to it. Multiple applications can load SHAREHEAP.DLL after the initial load. When they call GetGBlock, they get a pointer back to the same memory block as initially allocated. The pointer addresses may be different in each application as the view of the memory block is remapped into view in context to the process accessing it.

Listing 26.12 demonstrates a simple EXE program that uses the SHAREHEAP.DLL.

Listing 26.12   \UDELPHI3\CHP26\LoadShareHeapU1.PAS—Loader Program Uses a *TButton* and *TTimer* to Demonstrate Use of SHAREHEAP.DLL

```
unit LoadShareHeapU1;

interface

uses
  Windows, Messages, SysUtils, Classes, Graphics, Controls, Forms, Dialogs,
  StdCtrls, ExtCtrls;
```

```
type
  TForm1 = class(TForm)
    Memo1: TMemo;
    GroupBox1: TGroupBox;
    WriteButton: TButton;
    Edit1: TEdit;
    Timer1: TTimer;
    procedure FormCreate(Sender: TObject);
    procedure WriteButtonClick(Sender: TObject);
    procedure Timer1Timer(Sender: TObject);
  private
    { Private declarations }
  public
    { Public declarations }
  end;

var
  Form1: TForm1;
  pcBuf: PChar;

function GetGBlock: Pointer; StdCall; external 'SHAREHEAP.DLL'

implementation

{$R *.DFM}

procedure TForm1.FormCreate(Sender: TObject);
begin
  pcBuf := GetGBlock;
end;

procedure TForm1.WriteButtonClick(Sender: TObject);
begin
  Edit1.GetTextBuf(pcBuf,Length(Edit1.Text)+1);
end;

procedure TForm1.Timer1Timer(Sender: TObject);
begin
  Memo1.SetTextBuf(pcBuf);
end;

end.
```

When the main form is created, the SHAREHEAP.DLL's GetGBlock function is called that returns a pointer to sharable memory allocated from the system paging file. The pointer is stored to a global variable named pcBuf.

After the form is displayed, you can type into the provided edit control. After entering data, click the Write button, which executes the WriteButton1Click method. WriteButton1Click retrieves the data from the edit controls and writes it to the sharable memory pointed to by pcBuf. Moments after clicking the Write button, the test you typed shows up in the provided memo control. This is accomplished because the application uses a TTimer component that calls the Timer1Timer method every 1,000 milliseconds. Timer1Timer simply sets the memo text buffer to be that of the shared memory pointed to by pcBuf.

To see the across process sharing in action, load and build the `LoadShareHeap` project, which uses the LOADSHAREHEAPU1.PAS file. Then load and build the SHAREHEAP DLL project. Then run two instances of LoadShareHeap. You can type into the edit control in instance A, click `Write`, and the data appears in the memo control in both instances A and B. You then can type into the edit control in instance B, click `Write`, and the data again appears in the memo in both instances A and B.

PE File Structures

Executable modules for the Win32 platforms are known as *Portable Executables* (PE). PE is a file-format specification composed of various structures that have meaning to both the application and operating system. What you see as a DLL or EXE is viewed by the operating system as virtually the same entity. In fact, concerning file format, the only difference between a DLL and an EXE is the value of a 2-byte flag written to a magic OffSet within the file image.

Knowledge of the internal format of an executable module (from here on, referring to a DLL or EXE) will not necessarily make you a more productive Delphi developer. It does, however, help put into perspective and remove the mystique of the effects certain switches, compiler directives, and project options that you set or are set by default in your projects. The information in this section also is prerequisite to the discussion of the powerful Turbo Dump utility discussed at the end of the chapter.

Headers

PE files are written to disk by the linker in a binary format that contains much more than just machine code. Structures of retrievable data exist that contain information valuable to the application and operating system.

An executable module (EXE or DLL), when loaded, is mapped into the address space for a particular process beginning at the first byte in the file image.

> **N O T E** EXE and DLL modules are mapped into the address space for the loading process, using the File-Mapping facilities of the operating system. This chapter previously discussed the APIs for these facilities. If you recall, we created a Kernel File-Mapping Object, and then mapped a portion of the file to which it refers (system paging file, in this case) into memory. When the OS maps your EXE or DLL into memory, it always starts with the first byte in the image. The location within the process in which the EXE or DLL is mapped at runtime is referred to as the *Image Base* or *Image Base Address*. Don't forget this term: It is used (rather loosely) throughout the remaining text. ■

Beginning with the first byte in an executable file image is what is known as the *DOS header* (or *MZ header*). The DOS header is the first structure in the PE file, because it describes the DOS stub that follows it. The DOS Stub is a small real-mode DOS program that usually only provides the user with a message, telling him or her the module must be run in Microsoft Windows.

Following the DOS stub is the PE file signature. This DWORD value is used to validate the intended target operating system. The value can specify that the file is intended to run under

DOS, NT/Win95, or even OS/2. All these platforms use a similar file format, so this field can be used to reliably determine if the module can be executed under NT or Win95. The alternative to having such a field is to just assume that the file is the correct format, execute, and let it crash if it is not.

Following the PE file signature is another structure known as the *PE File Header*. The PE File Header is a structure that contains fields with information such as the Machine type, Time and Date stamps, address of symbol table, debug characteristics, and more. The PE File Header then is followed by another structure named the *Optional Header*.

The Optional Header is not really optional; it contains some of the most important information for an executable module. The Optional Header contains information on linker versions, sizes of initialized and UN-initialized data, code size, the address of the application's entry point, Loader flags, and so on. One of the most important fields in this structure is named *Image Base*. Image Base is a DWORD value and is the tenth field in the structure.

The Image Base is actually the linker-specified *preferred base address* to where the module image should be mapped within the loading process. The linker can perform some special link time optimizations if the Image Base is known up front. However, there is no guarantee that the linker-specified Image Base is where the file will be mapped at runtime.

N O T E   The actual Image Base is determined at runtime and is the address of where in the process's address space a module's file mapping begins. When you call LoadLibrary or LoadLibraryEx, a variable of type THandle, commonly known as the hInstance, is returned. Generically, in Win32, this is referred to as an instance handle. The instance handle for a module in Win32 happens to be the runtime *Image Base* address. ■

The default *preferred Image Base* used in Delphi is $00400000. At runtime, this value is retrieved and used for the mapping of the file image. If the file cannot be mapped to the *preferred* location (perhaps, it's already in use by the EXE or another DLL), the file will be mapped somewhere else, thus causing relocation of other pieces of data, such as addresses used by certain instructions. When relocations occur, the application ultimately takes a load time performance hit. Fortunately, the performance degradation is minimal.

N O T E   In Delphi, you can specify both the (*preferred*) *Image Base* and the minimum and maximum stack sizes on the Linker page of the Project Options dialog box. This dialog box is accessible from the Project menu Options command. ■

Along with the Image Base, the Optional Header contains fields for the minimum and maximum application level (primary thread) stack sizes. The default maximum stack size for an application is 1M. Under Win32, a maximum stack size is used to intentionally trigger a stack overflow (by the OS) in the event of endless recursion. Consider if your program is stuck in an endless loop, eventually the 1M limit is hit, causing an exception to be raised. If the maximum stack size were limited only by virtual memory, the recursive loop would execute until all the virtual memory was consumed, probably resulting in complete loss of system resources and total lockup.

Sections

Following the primary headers in the PE file format discussed so far is a table of image section headers that contain information about the raw data contained within an executable module's particular section. Sections in the PE file format can be compared to segments in the 16-bit file format. Understand that raw data that comprises a module's code is neatly packaged into one section in the file image. The raw data that composes a modules resources is packaged into another section. The raw data that makes up a module's data is in another section, and so on.

The image section headers contain information about the raw data for a given section, such as where it is located relative to the *Image Base* and the characteristics (section attributes) for each section.

N O T E In 16-bit Delphi, it was possible to specify the characteristics (attributes) of a code segment by using the $C compiler directive. You could specify PRELOAD for example, and this attribute was stored in the segment table for that segment. When the module was loaded into memory, segments flagged as PRELOAD would load first. There are still attributes applied to sections under the PE file format; however, PRELOAD isn't one of them, nor can you specify attributes on your own. ▨

Section characteristics in a PE executable typically are flagged with a combination of one or more of the following attributes:

- ▨ $00000020: Contains code
- ▨ $20000000: Executable
- ▨ $00000040: Contains initialized data
- ▨ $40000000: Readable
- ▨ $10000000: Sharable
- ▨ $80000000: Writable

Probably the most interesting attribute listed is $10000000 (sharable). By specifying this attribute to the linker, the OS maps the file in such a way that the information is accessible in a process-independent fashion. Unfortunately, Delphi doesn't provide a user directive for flagging a section as shared.

N O T E If you recall from Chapter 25, the LoadLibraryEx function excepted a flag named Load_Library_As_Datafile. When this flag is specified, an executable module is mapped into the process address space, as is any typical data file. To manipulate sections of an executable file image at runtime (without actually executing it) that are otherwise flagged as read only, you can call LoadLibraryEx passing the Load_Library_As_Datafile. The return value will be an hInstance that is the *Image Base Address*. ▨

Generically (if the language you're using permits), an executable module can contain any number of programmer defined sections with virtually any name or combination of attributes applied to them. Delphi, however, isn't this flexible and doesn't currently permit you to generate your own sections. The sections you usually will see generated for you by Delphi's linker are as follows:

- **CODE**—(Microsoft linker usually calls this `.text`) This is your application's code. In Win16, each unit comprised its own code segment. Under Win32, the code for all units is combined and written to this section.

- **BSS**—(Microsoft linker usually calls this `.bss`) This is a data section which contains only UN-initialized data.

- **DATA**—(Microsoft linker usually calls this `.data`) This is a data section that contains global variables.

- **.rsrc**—This is a resource section that contains resources such as String Tables, bitmaps, and icons.

- **.idata**—This section contains the listing of implicitly loaded module names and names of the functions used in each module.

- **.edata**—This section contains the listing of function names and ordinal values exported by the module.

- **.reloc**—Some of the addresses for variables and instructions are assumed to exist at an OffSet relative to the preferred *Image Base*. If the module cannot be loaded at the preferred *Image Base*, the information in this section is used to determine which addresses must be relocated at runtime.

You can view the names and attributes of any section in an executable module by using the Turbo Dump utility discussed in the following section. The most useful sections to view, in context to DLL programming, are `.idata` and `.edata`. View these sections to troubleshoot function import and export dependencies (which are discussed in the next section).

Another useful reason to become familiar with section information (but less common) is to write tools similar to Turbo Dump or Microsoft's Quick View utility. You can even write a resource explorer as was done in the ResXplor demo that comes with Delphi. However, such tasks are accomplished only by knowing the specifics of the PE file format.

For specific header structures, offset, and detailed documentation on the PE file format, query on the string "Portable Executable" in the Microsoft Developer Network (MSDN) library. There also is some information available (at the time of this writing) directly from Microsoft's Web page. If your interest is only to extract resource information or to generally hack around the files on your hard disk, look at the ResXplor demo in the \Delphi 3.0\Demos\ResXplor directory. This demo reads some of its information directly from the file image.

Turbo Dump

All versions of Delphi and Borland C++ ship with a small command-line utility named Turbo Dump. Turbo Dump is a DOS command-line executable and is located in the \bin directory with the name, TDUMP.EXE. The current version of Turbo Dump (at the time of this writing) is 4.2.15.2.

Part
VI

Ch
26

The Turbo Dump utility (named TDump, after its physical file name on disk) knows how to read several binary file formats and display the appropriate information they contain in an organized fashion. TDump can read files of the following formats:

■ DOS Executable files

■ New Executable (NE) files

■ Linear Executable files

■ Portable Executable files (PE)

■ OMF files (.OBJ & .LIB)

■ COFF files (.OBJ & .LIB)

■ Borland & Microsoft symbolic debug information

If you're unfamiliar with all the file types TDump supports, don't worry; here, you are concerned only about Portable Executable files (PE)—specifically, DLLs.

TDump supports several command-line options. To see a complete listing of TDump command-line options, simply type TDump at the command prompt then press enter. The simplest command line for TDump is as follows:

```
TDUMP MyFile.exe [PRESS ENTER]
```

MyFile.exe should be replaced with the name of the file you're interested in dumping. If command-line options are to be specified, they should be passed as the first command-line argument, as follows:

```
TDUMP -h c:\Win95\System\GDI32.DLL [PRESS ENTER]
```

There are three simple command-line options worth noting in this chapter; you can pursue the rest by looking at the listing TDump provides as default output. The first is -e, which forces an executable file display. The second is -a, which forces an ASCII file display. The third is -h, which forces a hexadecimal file display.

By default, TDump tries to output a report of the executable file format when applied against an EXE or DLL. If the file is simply text or binary, TDUMP shows the contents by using a hexadecimal output. This feature is handy but sometimes you want to see the information in a format other than that which TDump chooses to use by default. This is, of course, where the command-line options previously mentioned kick in.

So, what is the problem in relation to DLL programming that Turbo Dump can solve? There is one primary issue that comes up time and again in relation to DLL programming. Your application EXE is trying to link to a function in a DLL, but the operating system (or GetProcAddress) complains that the function cannot be found. This occurs for one reason: *The function name specified in the EXE is not valid.*

Although this issue is merely a single problem, the reasoning for the problem can occur for many more reasons. For example:

- The DLL doesn't have an exports section; therefore, the function is not exported.
- The name specified in the EXE is different than the actual exported function name because of a typographical error.
- The name of the function specified in the EXE is EXACTLY the same name as the function exported in the DLL, but the DLL is in C++ and the function name was exported mangled.
- The name of the function specified in the EXE is EXACTLY the same as the name of the function exported in the DLL, but the DLL is in C++ and the function was exported by using the _cdecl calling convention and the generation of underbars for exported routines wasn't disabled.

Although four scenarios are listed, there are probably more. Each scenario is not too hard to track down if you're thinking extremely clearly (in which case, you wouldn't have erred in the first place). TDump only tracks it down faster with usually less frustration. A frustration-elimination tool such as TDump is worth a bundle!

If you recall from previous discussion, the PE file format contains sections. The two sections that contain information important here are .idata and .edata. As soon as you fail to link one module to another, you can TDump the calling module and look at the names of the modules and functions it imports by reading the .idata section. You then can TDump the destination module and read its .edata section. The .edata section contains the names of all the routines (if any) the module exports.

Listing 26.13 shows the .idata section TDump output for the core file GDI32.DLL in the \WINDOWS\SYSTEM directory.

Listing 26.13 GDI32.TXT—TDump Reports Infomation in a Top-Down Fashion

```
Imports from KERNEL32.dll
    SMapLS_IP_EBP_24(hint = 01ee)
    38
    89
    FT_Exit12(hint = 0076)
    FT_Exit20(hint = 0078)
...
    GetSystemDefaultLCID(hint = 012b)
    HeapCreate(hint = 0168)
    GetOEMCP(hint = 0102)
    RtlUnwind(hint = 01e8)

Imports from ADVAPI32.dll
    RegCreateKeyExA(hint = 0082)
    RegQueryInfoKeyA(hint = 0098)
    RegDeleteKeyA(hint = 0085)
...
    RegSetValueExA(hint = 00a9)
    RegQueryValueExA(hint = 009d)
    RegCloseKey(hint = 007e)
    RegOpenKeyA(hint = 0094)
```

Note that Listing 26.13 shows only partial output. Listing 26.13 starts with the name of function Imports from KERNEL32.DLL and ends with the name of function Imports from ADVAPI32.DLL. If GDI32.DLL tried to implicitly load KERNEL32.DLL, and even one function listed is spelled wrong, mangled, or completely omitted, the load attempt will fail. On the flip side of this, consider that GDI32.DLL is a DLL and, therefore, likely exports some routines used by other modules. The following Listing 26.14 shows the .edata section TDump output for the core file GDI32.DLL in the \WINDOWS\SYSTEM directory.

Listing 26.14   GDI32.TXT—TDump Reports the Assigned Ordinal Value that Should Be Added to the Ordinal Base; the Relative Virtual Offset and Exported Symbol Names Are Also Listed

```
Exports from GDI32.dll
  330 exported name(s), 335 export addresse(s).  Ordinal base is 100.
    Ordinal RVA         Name
    ------- ---------   ----
    0005    000027a0    AbortDoc
    0006    00002837    AbortPath
    0007    000027dc    AddFontResourceA
    0008    0000282f    AddFontResourceW
...
    0324    0000107e    TextOutW
    0325    00002477    TranslateCharsetInfo
    0326    0000247b    UnrealizeObject
    0327    0000750e    UpdateColors
    0328    000021a9    UpdateICMRegKey
    0331    00002493    WidenPath
    0332    0000210c    gdiPlaySpoolStream
    0333    000088ba    pfnRealizePalette
    0334    000088a1    pfnSelectPalette
```

GDI32.DLL actually exports over 300 functions. Only a handful of these functions are displayed in the listing. So, the quickest way to ensure that a DLL exports exactly what the EXE expects, TDump the EXE and look at the .idata information. Then TDump the DLL and look at the .edata section. Compare the .edata in the DLL to what is expected in the .idata in the EXE. The function names must match perfectly.

N O T E TDump sends its vast amounts of output to the screen faster than it can be read as it scrolls by. You can capture the output to a text file by using the following DOS command line, and then use a simple text editor such as Windows Notepad to open and read it:

TDUMP -e GDI32.DLL > GDI32.TXT

TDump is a neat utility that can save a great deal of time if used when problems start. TDump displays a lot of information in its PE file output. If the previous section in the chapter on the PE File Format piqued your curiosity to what is actually in your DLL, TDump is the tool you can use to find out. Listing 26.15 shows the report that TDump generates when applied against the Windows core file GDI32.DLL. Note that the listing is incomplete; it was cut off at the beginning of the imports information, which you already looked at, and to preserve paper—even then, the listing is still rather verbose.

Listing 26.15   \UDELPHI3\CHP26\GDI32.TXT—TDump Displays Much of the Information This Chapter Discusses in Context to the PE File Format

```
Turbo Dump  Version 4.2.15.2 Copyright (c) 1988, 1996 Borland International
            Display of File C:\WINDOWS\SYSTEM\GDI32.DLL

Old Executable Header

DOS File Size                                    20000h  (131072. )
Load Image Size                                    450h  (  1104. )
Relocation Table entry count                      0000h  (     0. )
Relocation Table address                          0040h  (    64. )
Size of header record       (in paragraphs)       0004h  (     4. )
Minimum Memory Requirement  (in paragraphs)       0000h  (     0. )
Maximum Memory Requirement  (in paragraphs)       FFFFh  ( 65535. )
File load checksum                                0000h  (     0. )
Overlay Number                                    0000h  (     0. )


Initial Stack Segment   (SS:SP)           0000:00B8
Program Entry Point     (CS:IP)           0000:0000


Portable Executable (PE) File

Header base: 00000080

CPU type              80386
Flags                 210E [ executable backwards 32bit library ]
DLL flags             0000 [ ]
Linker Version        2.32
Time stamp            2FF383BC
O/S Version           1.0
User Version          0.0
Subsystem Version     4.0
Subsystem             0002 [ Windows GUI ]
Object count          00000007
Symbols offset        00000000
Symbols count         00000000
Optional header size  00E0
Magic #               10B
Code size             00019600
Init Data size        00006600
Uninit Data size      00000000
Entry RVA             00002B6C
Image base            BFF30000
Code base             00001000
Data base             0001B000
Object/File align     00001000/00000200
Reserved              00000000
Image size            00025000
```

Part **VI**

Ch **26**

continues

Listing 26.15 Continued

```
Header size                 00000400
Checksum                    0002CB01
Stack reserve/commit        00100000/00001000
Heap reserve/commit         00100000/00001000
Number interesting RVAs     00000010
Name                 RVA        Size
------------------   --------   --------
Exports              0001E000   00002099
Imports              0001D000   00000A40
Resources            00022000   00000394
Exceptions           00000000   00000000
Security             00000000   00000000
Fixups               00023000   000016B4
Debug                00000000   00000000
Description          00000000   00000000
TLS                  00000000   00000000
Callbacks            00000000   00000000
reserved             00000000   00000000
reserved             00000000   00000000
reserved             00000000   00000000
reserved             00000000   00000000
reserved             00000000   00000000

Object table:
#    Name      VirtSize   RVA        PhysSize   Phys off   Flags
--   --------  --------   --------   --------   --------   --------
01   .text     00019580   00001000   00019600   00000400   60000020 [CER]
02   .data     00001910   0001B000   00001A00   00019A00   D0000040 [ISRW]
03   .idata    00000A40   0001D000   00000C00   0001B400   50000040 [ISR]
04   .edata    00002099   0001E000   00002200   0001C000   40000040 [IR]
05   _GPFIX    0000011C   00021000   00000200   0001E200   D0000040 [ISRW]
06   .rsrc     00000394   00022000   00000400   0001E400   40000040 [IR]
07   .reloc    000017F0   00023000   00001800   0001E800   42000040 [IDR]

Key to section flags:
  C - contains code
  D - discardable
  E - executable
  I - contains initialized data
  R - readable
  S - sharable
  W - writable

Imports from KERNEL32.dll
    SMapLS_IP_EBP_24(hint = 01ee)
    38
Turbo Dump  Version 4.2.15.2 Copyright (c) 1988, 1996 Borland International
            Display of File C:\WINDOWS\SYSTEM\GDI32.DLL

Old Executable Header

DOS File Size                              20000h  (131072. )
Load Image Size                              450h  (  1104. )
```

```
Relocation Table entry count                        0000h  (     0. )
Relocation Table address                            0040h  (    64. )
Size of header record       (in paragraphs)         0004h  (     4. )
Minimum Memory Requirement (in paragraphs)          0000h  (     0. )
Maximum Memory Requirement (in paragraphs)          FFFFh  ( 65535. )
File load checksum                                  0000h  (     0. )
Overlay Number                                      0000h  (     0. )


Initial Stack Segment   (SS:SP)            0000:00B8
Program Entry Point     (CS:IP)            0000:0000



Portable Executable (PE) File

Header base: 00000080


CPU type                 80386
Flags                    210E [ executable backwards 32bit library ]
DLL flags                0000 [ ]
Linker Version           2.32
Time stamp               2FF383BC
O/S Version              1.0
User Version             0.0
Subsystem Version        4.0
Subsystem                0002 [ Windows GUI ]
Object count             00000007
Symbols offset           00000000
Symbols count            00000000
Optional header size     00E0
Magic #                  10B
Code size                00019600
Init Data size           00006600
Uninit Data size         00000000
Entry RVA                00002B6C
Image base               BFF30000
Code base                00001000
Data base                0001B000
Object/File align        00001000/00000200
Reserved                 00000000
Image size               00025000
Header size              00000400
Checksum                 0002CB01
Stack reserve/commit     00100000/00001000
Heap reserve/commit      00100000/00001000
Number interesting RVAs  00000010
Name             RVA       Size
---------------  --------  --------
Exports          0001E000  00002099
Imports          0001D000  00000A40
Resources        00022000  00000394
Exceptions       00000000  00000000
Security         00000000  00000000
Fixups           00023000  000016B4
Debug            00000000  00000000
Description      00000000  00000000
```

Part

VI

Ch

26

continues

Listing 26.15   Continued

```
TLS                    00000000  00000000
Callbacks              00000000  00000000
reserved               00000000  00000000
reserved               00000000  00000000
reserved               00000000  00000000
reserved               00000000  00000000
reserved               00000000  00000000
```

Object table:

#	Name	VirtSize	RVA	PhysSize	Phys off	Flags	
01	.text	00019580	00001000	00019600	00000400	60000020	[CER]
02	.data	00001910	0001B000	00001A00	00019A00	D0000040	[ISRW]
03	.idata	00000A40	0001D000	00000C00	0001B400	50000040	[ISR]
04	.edata	00002099	0001E000	00002200	0001C000	40000040	[IR]
05	_GPFIX	0000011C	00021000	00000200	0001E200	D0000040	[ISRW]
06	.rsrc	00000394	00022000	00000400	0001E400	40000040	[IR]
07	.reloc	000017F0	00023000	00001800	0001E800	42000040	[IDR]

```
Key to section flags:
  C - contains code
  D - discardable
  E - executable
  I - contains initialized data
  R - readable
  S - sharable
  W - writable

Imports from KERNEL32.dll
    SMapLS_IP_EBP_24(hint = 01ee)
    38
Turbo Dump  Version 4.2.15.2 Copyright (c) 1988, 1996 Borland International
            Display of File C:\WINDOWS\SYSTEM\GDI32.DLL


Old Executable Header

DOS File Size                                 20000h  (131072. )
Load Image Size                                 450h  (  1104. )
Relocation Table entry count                   0000h  (     0. )
Relocation Table address                       0040h  (    64. )
Size of header record       (in paragraphs)    0004h  (     4. )
Minimum Memory Requirement  (in paragraphs)    0000h  (     0. )
Maximum Memory Requirement  (in paragraphs)    FFFFh  ( 65535. )
File load checksum                             0000h  (     0. )
Overlay Number                                 0000h  (     0. )


Initial Stack Segment  (SS:SP)            0000:00B8
Program Entry Point    (CS:IP)            0000:0000


Portable Executable (PE) File

Header base: 00000080
```

```
CPU type                80386
Flags                   210E [ executable backwards 32bit library ]
DLL flags               0000 [ ]
Linker Version          2.32
Time stamp              2FF383BC
O/S Version             1.0
User Version            0.0
Subsystem Version       4.0
Subsystem               0002 [ Windows GUI ]
Object count            00000007
Symbols offset          00000000
Symbols count           00000000
Optional header size    00E0
Magic #                 10B
Code size               00019600
Init Data size          00006600
Uninit Data size        00000000
Entry RVA               00002B6C
Image base              BFF30000
Code base               00001000
Data base               0001B000
Object/File align       00001000/00000200
Reserved                00000000
Image size              00025000
Header size             00000400
Checksum                0002CB01
Stack reserve/commit    00100000/00001000
Heap reserve/commit     00100000/00001000
Number interesting RVAs 00000010
Name                    RVA        Size
----------------        --------   --------
Exports                 0001E000   00002099
Imports                 0001D000   00000A40
Resources               00022000   00000394
Exceptions              00000000   00000000
Security                00000000   00000000
Fixups                  00023000   000016B4
Debug                   00000000   00000000
Description             00000000   00000000
TLS                     00000000   00000000
Callbacks               00000000   00000000
reserved                00000000   00000000
reserved                00000000   00000000
reserved                00000000   00000000
reserved                00000000   00000000
reserved                00000000   00000000

Object table:
#   Name      VirtSize   RVA        PhysSize   Phys off   Flags
--  --------  --------   --------   --------   --------   --------
01  .text     00019580   00001000   00019600   00000400   60000020 [CER]
02  .data     00001910   0001B000   00001A00   00019A00   D0000040 [ISRW]
03  .idata    00000A40   0001D000   00000C00   0001B400   50000040 [ISR]
04  .edata    00002099   0001E000   00002200   0001C000   40000040 [IR]
05  _GPFIX    0000011C   00021000   00000200   0001E200   D0000040 [ISRW]
```

continues

Listing 26.15   Continued

```
06  .rsrc    00000394  00022000  00000400  0001E400  40000040 [IR]
07  .reloc   000017F0  00023000  00001800  0001E800  42000040 [IDR]

Key to section flags:
  C - contains code
  D - discardable
  E - executable
  I - contains initialized data
  R - readable
  S - sharable
  W - writable

Imports from KERNEL32.dll
    SMapLS_IP_EBP_24(hint = 01ee)
    38
...
Etc.
...
```

Summary

This chapter covered a vast array of technical issues, with an emphasis on using objects in DLL modules. This approach is appropriate, considering Delphi's object-based environment and component library.

The following list quickly recaps the issues discussed in this chapter:

1. You started by compiling a class into a DLL, and exporting flat functions to access it.

2. In a similar fashion, you moved to compiling form classes into a DLL and provided access functions to display the forms in modal and non-modal fashions.

3. You then dug into the internals of Delphi objects, with an emphasis on the Virtual Method Table.

   The VMT information is the backbone to the discussion, regarding the sharing of objects by using virtual classes.

4. Next you learned about sharing memory across process boundaries by using a File-Mapping object. You also learned how to create the object so that it accessed the process-independent system paging file.

5. For a crystalline internal understanding of DLLs, the relevant portions of the PE File Format, including imports, exports, code, and data were discussed.

6. You used what you learned about the PE File Format to better understand the Turbo Dump (TDump) utility. The section on TDump showed you how to debug DLL programming problems and save time in doing so. ●

CHAPTER 27

Testing and Debugging

by Steve Schafer

As a Windows user, you've almost certainly had the experience of being annoyed when an application you're using doesn't work properly. Now, as an application developer, the shoe is on the other foot.

You've just put the finishing touches on your masterpiece, the application that will blow away the competition and bring you fame and glory. It's truly a work of art, but there's this one little problem: It doesn't seem to work quite right. It sometimes gives the wrong answers, and it occasionally crashes with a disturbing Access `Violation` error message. Even worse is the nagging suspicion that the problems are probably your own fault. What do you do?

You're using Delphi, so you're in luck. The Delphi integrated development environment (IDE) includes a variety of features that simplify the task of testing and debugging your application. In this chapter, you'll learn how to use these features to help ensure that your masterpiece works as you intended, and doesn't present you or your users with nasty surprises. ■

Testing your application

Design your application for testability by making use of Delphi's conditional compilation and assertion features.

Using the Delphi integrated debugger

Learn how to set breakpoints, step through code, and use Delphi's other advanced debugging capabilities.

Brute-force debugging

Sometimes you can get more information by using some simple coding techniques instead of the debugger.

Stalking wild bugs

Debugging can be difficult work. This section provides tips on how to handle tricky debugging situations.

Testing

Testing and debugging go hand-in-hand, so much so that most programmers don't consider them independent activities. However, you will have greater success if you keep them separate in your mind as you develop an application. Although it's true that you'll often find yourself jumping back and forth (figuratively, if not literally) between test mode and debug mode, try to remember that the purpose of testing is *to determine the existence (or non-existence) of bugs*, while the purpose of debugging is *to locate and eradicate bugs*. The tools that you use, and the approaches that you take, are different for these two tasks.

Build a Robust Application

The best way to eliminate bugs from your application, of course, is to prevent them from occurring in the first place. A robust application is one that was designed from the beginning to be easy to test, debug, and maintain. Here are some general guidelines you can follow to help reduce the number of bugs in your applications:

■ *Keep your application well-organized and modular*. Divide the application into clearly defined modules, each of which plays a specific role. If the code that generates a report, for example, is spread out over 10 procedures in six units, you'll have a hard time finding a bug lurking somewhere in the middle of the mess—you will spend all your time jumping around in the code and trying to remember where you are. It's certainly all right to *call* procedures, functions, and object methods in other units, but you should design these procedures so that they perform single, well-defined operations, and then return to the caller. Calling one procedure to perform the first half of an operation and another to finish up just doesn't make sense.

■ *Program defensively*. If a procedure can fail catastrophically when you pass it bad data, consider including some code at the beginning of the procedure to verify the integrity of the data. Don't go overboard, however, with defensive programming. Too much integrity-checking code slows your application. Even worse, it may mask bugs that are occurring in other parts of the program.

■ *Maintain a test/debug version of your application*. A debug version of your application contains a considerable amount of code whose only purpose is to ensure that the application is running correctly, and to make the application easier to debug. This concept is covered in greater detail in the following section.

Maintain "Ship" and "Debug" Versions of Your Code

If you've ever participated in the field test (sometimes known as a *beta test*) of a commercial application, you probably noticed that early test versions of the application often are ponderously slow, and quite a bit larger than the final version. Is the size because the developers do a poor job at first, but clean up their act before shipping the product? Well, this may be part of the reason, but the main reason is usually that the test versions of the product contain extensive test and debug code. This code is used by the developers to verify that the application is operating correctly.

With Delphi, you can easily incorporate test and debug code in your applications. For example, you may be building a database application, and you want to use a fast but tricky-to-implement algorithm for sorting database records. How can you be sure that you implement the sorting algorithm correctly? One way is to include *two* algorithms: a "quick-but-tricky" algorithm to use during both testing and in the final product, and a "slow-and-steady" algorithm to use only during testing. In the test version of your application, you sort the records by using *both* algorithms, and compare the results to verify that the quick-but-tricky algorithm is working. In the final version, you will only use the quick (but now debugged) algorithm.

You can write a program that executes different code during testing and production by using *conditional compilation*. You can define a symbol (I usually use Debug, but you can call it anything you want) to distinguish between your debug version and your shipping version, and then use the $IFDEF, $IFNDEF, $ELSE, and $ENDIF directives to control which code is included in each version. For example, to include the slow sorting algorithm I mentioned in the previous paragraph in your debug version, you'd do something like the following:

```
DataSet := GetData;  // get the data to be sorted
{$ifdef Debug}
TestResultSet := Sort_Tortoise(DataSet);  // sort records using slow-and-steady
{$endif}
ResultSet := Sort_Hare(DataSet);  // sort records using quick-but-tricky
{$ifdef Debug}
if not CompareData(ResultSet, TestResultSet) then  // are results the same?
  raise Exception.Create('Sort failure in DataSorting module!');  // nope
{$endif}
```

If the Debug symbol is defined, the code in the $IFDEF..$ENDIF blocks is included in the compilation, so the resulting code looks like the following example:

```
DataSet := GetData;  // get the data to be sorted
TestResultSet := Sort_Tortoise(DataSet);  // sort records using slow-and-steady
ResultSet := Sort_Hare(DataSet);  // sort records using quick-but-tricky
if not CompareData(ResultSet, TestResultSet) then  // are results the same?
  raise Exception.Create('Sort failure in DataSorting module!');  // nope
```

If the Debug symbol is not defined, the code in the $IFDEF..$ENDIF blocks is not included in the compilation, so the resulting code looks like this:

```
DataSet := GetData;  // get the data to be sorted
ResultSet := Sort_Hare(DataSet);  // sort the records using quick-but-tricky
```

Part
VI

Ch
27

As you see, using conditional compilation is a simple way to generate both debug and shipping versions of your application. You can define a conditional compilation symbol in either of two ways. The first method, appropriate for a symbol that is to be applied globally, is to define the symbol in your project options. From the main menu, select Project, Options to display the Project Options dialog box. Go to the Directories/Conditionals page of the dialog box and enter the symbols to be defined in the Conditional defines edit box. Figure 27.1 shows what the dialog box looks like when the symbols Debug and Alpha are being defined. Press the OK button to close the dialog box and accept your changes.

FIG. 27.1

Use the Directories/
Conditionals page of the
Project Options dialog
box to define condi-
tional compilation
symbols.

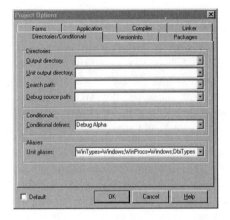

 Whenever you modify the definition of conditional compilation symbols in your project options, you
need to recompile the project by using Project, Build All from the main menu in order for your changes
to take effect.

The other method for defining conditional compilation symbols is to insert a $DEFINE directive
directly into your source code:

```
{$define Debug}
```

You probably won't want to do this with the Debug symbol because it generally makes more
sense to enable or disable it globally. You may, however, want to turn it off in a particular unit,
even in your debug version, if you're certain that the unit is bug-free (sure it is). You can do
this by using the $UNDEF directive:

```
{$undef Debug}
```

This directive will undefine the Debug symbol from this point until a corresponding $DEFINE
directive is found or until the compiler reaches the end of the unit, whichever comes first.
Of course, you can define and undefine a symbol as often as you want within a unit.

Besides conditional compilation directives, there are a number of other directives that may be
applicable to the debug version of your application. I say "may be applicable" because these
directives can introduce subtle differences between your ship and debug versions that are not
apparent from looking at the code. In other words, you may find that your test version is testing
code that doesn't exist in the same form in your ship version. Therefore, modify these settings
with caution. The options are listed on the Compiler page of the Project Options dialog box
(see Figure 27.2). They are as follows:

FIG. 27.2

Use the Compiler page of the Project Options dialog box to modify debugging-related compiler options.

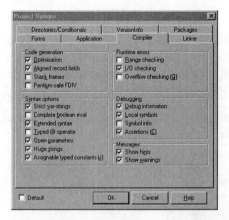

- *Optimization*. This setting controls the optimizing compiler. I recommend that you leave this setting enabled and turn it off only if you suspect that the optimizer is itself introducing a bug into your code. You can locally control the generation of optimized code by using the $O+ directive to turn on the optimizer and the $O- directive to turn it off.

- *Stack Frames*. If this setting is enabled, the compiler includes code that generates a stack frame for each procedure and function, even if this code doesn't need to use the stack. Like the Optimization directive, you should rarely need to change this setting. You can use $W+ to enable stack frames and $W- to disable them.

- *Range Checking*. Range checking can catch errors that otherwise may go undetected by including runtime code that verifies that all array and string subscripts are within appropriate bounds. The additional code slows your application's operation, however, so you probably want to turn off range checking in your ship version. In your source code, use $R+ to turn on range checking, and $R- to turn it off.

- *Assertions (C)*. Assertions are a debugging aid that is discussed in more detail in the next section. The use of assertions allows you to quickly and easily add a variety of validity checks to your code. You'll want to have assertions enabled during testing and debugging, but disabled in the ship version of your application. In your source code, use $C+ to enable assertions and $C- to disable them.

- *Overflow checking (Q)*. Overflow checking ensures that you don't try to store the result of an integer operation in a location too small to hold the value. Like range checking, overflow checking can help in your debug version but it adds size to your application and slows it, so you want to turn it off in your ship version. Use $Q+ to turn on overflow checking, and $Q- to turn it off.

The debug version of your code probably will be much slower and larger than the ship version. Figure on a factor of two (or even more) of size increase and speed decrease. Just don't ship the debug version to your end users by mistake!

Part
VI

Ch
27

Using Assertions

Assertions are new to Delphi 3. An *assertion* is really just a Boolean true/false test. When you use an assertion, you *assert* that the Boolean condition is true; if at runtime it turns out to be false, the assertion code will raise an exception. The syntax for using assertions is simple:

```
Assert(<boolean expression>);
```

You may use an assertion at the beginning of a procedure—for example, to verify that a parameter passed to the procedure is within a given range, as follows:

```
procedure Foo(Count: Cardinal);
begin
Assert(Count < SizeOf(Word));
...
end;
```

If it's not within the given range, you see an error message similar to the one shown in Figure 27.3.

FIG. 27.3

An Assertion
failure error message.

You may ask, "What's the big deal? What advantage does an assertion have over a conventional `if..then` statement?" The difference between an assertion and an `if..then` statement is that you can easily control whether or not assertion code is generated, simply by using a compiler directive. To enable assertions, use $ASSERTIONS ON or $C+; to turn them off, use $ASSERTIONS OFF or $C-. When assertions are disabled, any calls to `Assert` are ignored by the compiler, and don't generate any code. Another advantage of assertions is that the file name and line number where an assertion failure has occurred are automatically displayed in the error message.

Because you'll want to turn on assertions in your debug version and turn them off in your ship version, you can use code that looks like the following:

```
{$ifdef Debug}
{$ASSERTIONS ON}
{$else}
{$ASSERTIONS OFF}
{$endif}
```

What kind of expression can be used in an assertion? Any expression that has a boolean value can be used. However, you generally will want to avoid expressions that include function calls because a function call can have side effects. A *side effect* occurs when the act of calling a function causes the state of something else in the system to change. For example, the following function keeps track of how many times it's been called:

```
function CountMe: Integer;
const
  ReferenceCount: Integer = 0;
```

```
begin
  Inc(ReferenceCount);
  Result := ReferenceCount;
end;
```

This obviously is a contrived example, but it points out the potential for problems. If you include this function in an assertion expression, the function is called more often when assertions are enabled than when they are disabled, leading to an inaccurate reference count.

Feel free to use assertions liberally in your code. Consider them "sanity checks" that ensure that variables contain what they're supposed to contain at every stage of execution. In fact, think of assertions as a generalization of the range checking and related compiler options. By using assertions, you can incorporate your own custom state checking code anywhere you want.

Unit Testing

The subject of unit testing is so broad—entire books are devoted to the topic—that I can say only a few words here. (Note: The word *unit* as used here has no relation to the concept of a Delphi unit, and refers to a function, subsystem, or other well-defined program module.) Briefly, the idea behind *unit testing* is to break your application into functional units, and to thoroughly test each of these units independently of the others. This often means writing one or more auxiliary applications whose sole purpose is to act as a "test harness" for the unit under test. The idea is to exhaustively exercise all the paths of execution within the unit. For example, an `if..then` statement has two (or more) paths of execution; you want to provide your unit with test data that ensures that both paths are taken during the test.

A simple procedure that contains only a few lines of code isn't a likely candidate for a unit test, because you probably can test the code as thoroughly by going over it by hand. On the other hand, a complex function that performs a high-end financial calculation, for example, probably should be subjected to unit testing to verify its accuracy.

Finally, the error messages that are displayed when something goes wrong are useful while testing and debugging, but they have no place in the final version of your application. You should strive to handle *every* exception and error in a meaningful way in the version of the application you give to your users. You know how frustrating it is when an application you're using crashes or pops up a meaningless error message. Your users feel the same way; to them, an error message that is displayed while they're using your application is equivalent to the one shown in Figure 27.4.

Part
VI

Ch
27

FIG. 27.4
What your users think about you when your application crashes with an error message.

If you do a good job testing your application, you probably will reveal some bugs. Even the best commercial applications contain bugs, and the goal of a careful testing program is to find as many of them as possible so that they can be fixed before the application gets into the hands of users. After you determine that a bug exists, you have to find where in your application the bug is occurring, and figure out what you must do to fix it. The following section of this chapter describes the tools Delphi provides for locating and repairing bugs.

Delphi's Integrated Debugger

Back in the ancient history of computing (around 20 years ago), debugging a program meant sitting down with a stack of source code and output listings (along with a pot of coffee and, probably, some aspirin), and going over the code by hand, a line at a time, trying to see where things went wrong. In contrast, modern software-development environments such as Delphi include numerous features that enhance and simplify the debugging process. Nobody likes to debug a program, and anything the development environment can do to make the job easier and faster is naturally welcome.

The Delphi integrated debugger has many features, and learning how to use them may at first seem daunting. However, using the Delphi debugger really is a piece of cake. In fact, if you've compiled and run a program from within the Delphi IDE, you probably already used the debugger without knowing it. As with most software products, 90 percent of the tasks you may need to perform can be accomplished by using only 10 percent of the features, so you can quickly start debugging your application and master the more advanced features later as the need arises.

Configuring the IDE for Debugging

Several options are available in the Delphi 3 IDE that control the overall operation of the integrated debugger. Usually, you can leave them at their default settings. If you do need to change them, select Tools, Options from the main menu to display the Environment Options dialog box. The debugger-related settings are located on the Preferences page of the dialog box, shown in Figure 27.5.

FIG. 27.5

Use the Preferences page of the Environment Options dialog box to configure the Delphi integrated debugger.

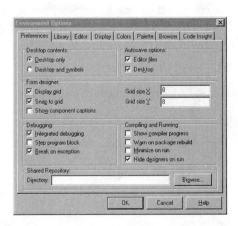

The effect of each setting is as follows:

- *Integrated Debugging.* This option enables and disables the integrated debugger. As you may guess, you have to turn on this option to use the integrated debugger. If you disable this option, the debugging commands in the Run menu are grayed and the corresponding hot keys are ineffective.

T I P
If you have trouble running your application in the IDE, there may be a conflict between the integrated debugger and some other software running on your system. Try temporarily turning off Integrated Debugging. If this fixes the problem and allows your program to run, you can be sure that other software is fighting with the debugger for control of your application. When this happens, the best action is to reboot your system and load only applications, drivers, and so on that are absolutely required before debugging your Delphi application.

- *Step Program Block.* This option controls whether or not the debugger pauses at the beginning of the application's main `begin..end` block when you trace into the program by using the stepping commands described later in this chapter. Usually, you can leave this option off. You need it only if you've explicitly added some code to the main program block, or if you're debugging a console application.

- *Hide Designers on Run.* When enabled, this option causes the Object Inspector and design-time forms to close before your application begins execution. Turning it off seems to cause the application to start up more quickly, but the effect is minor. Whether or not you leave it enabled is a matter of personal preference.

- *Break on Exception.* When this option is enabled, the IDE pauses execution and displays an exception message box whenever code within your application raises an exception, even if this exception is handled in a `try..except` block. Enabling this option can help while debugging because it gives you an error message that is more informative than the message provided by the default application exception handler (compare Figure 27.6 to Figure 27.7). Also, the IDE brings the code editor window to the front and highlights the line of code that raised the exception so you can see exactly where it occurred.

T I P
Although Break on Exception is useful, its behavior also can be confusing if you're new to Delphi, and if you expect exceptions handled by a `try..except` block not to result in the display of an error message. You can either turn off Break on Exception or run your application outside of the IDE to avoid the message box and see how the application appears to your users.

Part
VI

Ch
27

- *Minimize on Run.* This option causes the main IDE window to minimize while your application runs. Similar to the Hide Designers on Run option, this choice is mostly a matter of personal preference. While your application is paused, the IDE window is displayed regardless of this option's setting, which is done so that you have immediate access to the various debugging commands.

FIG. 27.6

The exception message box displayed by the IDE when Break on Exception is enabled.

FIG. 27.7

The exception message box displayed by the default application exception handler.

Another setting you will want to turn on is found on the Display page of the Environment Options dialog box—the Visible Gutter option. The gutter is displayed as a gray vertical bar on the left side of the editor window (see Figure 27.8). A variety of small glyphs are displayed in the gutter during debugging to convey information about each line of code. These glyphs are described in the following sections.

FIG. 27.8

A code editor window, showing the gutter along the left side, which contains several informative glyphs.

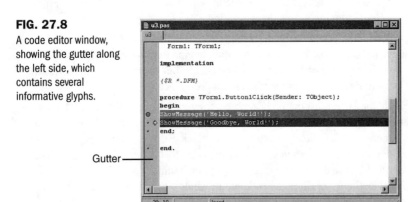

Gutter

Including Debugging Information in Your Code

Before you can begin debugging your application, you need to ensure that it was compiled with debugging information enabled. Delphi allows you to include debugging information on a unit-by-unit basis, which can be useful if you have some units that are well-tested and previously were thoroughly debugged. By turning off debugging information for these units, you can avoid tracing into them while you're stepping through code.

To compile your project with debugging information, use the Project Options dialog box. Select Project, Options from the main menu and go to the Compiler page (see Figure 27.9).

FIG. 27.9

The Compiler page of the Project Options dialog box.

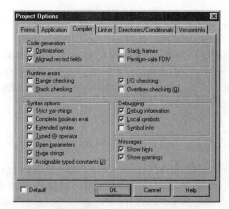

The following three settings control the inclusion of debugging information on a project-wide basis:

- *Debug Information*. This option controls the inclusion of debugging information. If disabled, you cannot trace through the code or set breakpoints in any units. This option is equivalent to the `$D` or `$DEBUGINFO` compiler directives.

- *Local Symbols*. This option controls the inclusion of local symbol information. *Local symbols* are those declared in the implementation section of a unit, as well as local variables in functions and procedures. This option is ignored unless Debug Information is enabled, and you rarely have any reason to turn off this option. This option is equivalent to the `$L` or `$LOCALSYMBOLS` compiler directives.

- *Symbol Info*. This option isn't strictly a debugging option because it affects the object browser rather than the integrated debugger. When this object is enabled, the object browser can display symbol definition and reference information for symbols defined in a unit. This option is ignored unless both Debug Information and Local Symbols are enabled. This option is equivalent to the `$Y` or `$REFERENCEINFO` compiler directives.

You usually will want to leave the Debug Information and Local Symbols options enabled for your project, so that you can step through the code in your application. As mentioned previously, however, you may want to disable debugging information for certain units. You can do so by inserting a `$D-` or `$DEBUGINFO OFF` compiler directive at the top of the unit:

```
unit MyUnit;
{$D-}
interface
...
```

Note that using `$D-` automatically turns off Local Symbols and Symbol Info, so you don't need to disable these two options separately.

Part
VI

Ch

27

T I P   If you distribute Delphi units as .DCU files (VCL components, for example), and you don't provide the corresponding source code (.PAS files), make sure that you compile the units with $D– so that debugging information is *not* included. Otherwise, when your users try to debug applications that use your units, their Delphi debugger will complain about the missing .PAS files if they try to step into those units. The debugger will automatically step over code in units that contain no debugging information, sparing your users an unfriendly error message.

Stepping Through Code

One of the most frequent tasks you need to perform as a part of debugging is to step through your code a line at a time to verify that the statements are being executed properly and in the order you expect them. While stepping through code, the debugger displays the currently executing code in the editor window. The *execution point*, which shows which statement will execute next, is indicated by a green arrow glyph in the gutter.

N O T E   After a unit is successfully compiled, the gutter displays a small blue circle at every source line that contributes code to the unit's .DCU file. If a line of source code exists that isn't marked by a blue dot, the corresponding executable code was stripped out by the optimizer. Because no code exists for these lines, the execution point never can land on one of them. You will see a message after Linking is Completed if anything was taken out by the Smart Linker. ▪

The Delphi integrated debugger offers several commands with which you can step through code. All these commands are available on the Run menu (see Figure 27.10). These commands are:

FIG. 27.10

Use the Run menu in the Delphi IDE to execute debugging commands.

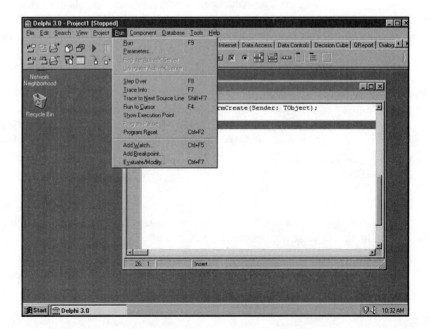

■ *Run*. Selecting this command causes the application to run normally. You can use this command to begin execution of the application, and you also use it to resume normal execution if the program is paused for any reason, such as at a breakpoint. If Break on Exception is enabled, you need to use Run to resume execution after an exception has been raised.

■ *Step Over*. When the execution point is at a line of code that contains a function or procedure call, using the Step Over command executes the line and all embedded function or procedure calls in a single step, without stepping through individual lines of code in the called function or procedure. The execution point then moves to the next line of code.

■ *Trace Into*. Unlike Step Over, Trace Into *will* step into function or procedure calls. Therefore, if the execution point is positioned at a statement that contains a call to function Foo, selecting Trace Into moves the execution point to the first line of code in Foo. If the execution point is at a line of code that contains no function or procedure calls, Trace Into and Step Over have the same effect.

 T I P Use care when tracing into OnPaint event handlers. Because an OnPaint event handler is invoked whenever a window needs to be repainted, it's easy to get into an infinite loop: You step into the OnPaint event handler, causing the code editor window to appear on top of the window being painted, which means that the window must be repainted on the next execution step, which causes you to enter the OnPaint handler again, which causes the code editor window to once again appear on top...

To avoid this problem, make sure that the code editor window and the window whose OnPaint event handler you're debugging don't overlap on-screen.

■ *Trace to Next Source Line*. Occasionally, a line of code indirectly causes other code in your application to run. This can happen, for example, if you call a function that triggers an event handler, or you call a Windows API function that in turn invokes a callback function in your code. Because they are indirect, the debugger doesn't normally "see" these calls and steps over the code in the indirectly called function. However, by using Trace to Next Source Line, you place the debugger into a "heightened state of awareness," and it pauses execution at the first line of an indirectly invoked function or procedure.

■ *Run to Cursor*. Often, you have a good idea of the location of a bug, and you don't want to waste time stepping through code to get to this point. To avoid having to repeatedly Step Over or Trace Into, you can place the cursor in the code editor window (strictly speaking, it's the *caret*, not the cursor) on the line of code where you want execution to pause, and then select Run to Cursor. Doing so is equivalent to temporarily placing a breakpoint on the selected line; the IDE executes the program to this point, and then pauses. This feature can be useful when you try to narrow down the location of a bug. If you position the cursor on a line that contains no debugging information and then select Run to Cursor, you receive the error message shown in Figure 27.11 because the debugger cannot pause on a line of code that it doesn't know about. Run to Cursor also is useful if you accidentally trace into a function or procedure you meant to step over. Place the cursor on the final end and then Run to Cursor. Now you're at the end of the routine, and stepping once more will take you back to the calling routine.

FIG. 27.11

This is what you see if you select Run to Cursor after placing the cursor on a line of code that contains no debugging information.

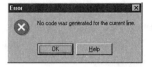

- *Show Execution Point.* This command causes the IDE to open the code editor window and bring the line of code that contains the current execution point to the front. You need to use this command only if you closed or minimized the code editor window because the debugger normally will display the execution point automatically.

- *Program Pause.* Selecting Program Pause immediately pauses execution of the program. I find this command most useful when I inadvertently get myself into an infinite loop.

- *Program Reset.* If at any time while you use the debugger you decide that you've had enough and want to quit without running the application to its normal exit, use the Program Reset command. Doing so halts execution of the application and returns you to the IDE.

Many menu items have associated hot keys (for example, Run is F9). However, the hot key assignments vary, depending on the keymapping you selected on the Editor page of your Environment Options dialog box. Step Over is F8 when using the default keymapping, but becomes Ctrl+F11 when using the BRIEF keymapping, and so on. You can see which hot keys are in effect for the keymapping you're using by selecting Run from the main menu—the assigned hot keys are listed beside each command.

Speed buttons for the Run, Step Over, Trace Into, and Program Pause commands are provided on the default toolbar. You can add to or remove these speed buttons by right-clicking the toolbar and selecting Properties from the pop-up menu.

Watching Variables

While stepping through code in the debugger, you undoubtedly will want to examine the contents of some of the variables in your application. To do so, you can use either the Watch List window (which provides a passive view of one or more variables), or the Evaluate/Modify dialog box (which shows you only one variable at a time, but allows you to change as well as inspect its value).

To watch a variable, select Run, Add Watch from the main menu, or position the cursor on the variable in the code editor window, right-click to pop up the local menu, and select Add Watch at Cursor. This action pops up the Watch Properties dialog box shown in Figure 27.12. If you use Run, Add Watch, enter the name of the variable to watch in the Expression edit box (if you use the local menu technique, the name of the variable is entered for you). Note that you can watch an expression, such as (X + 3 * Y) / Z, as well as a simple variable. The only restriction is that the expression can contain no function calls because of the possibility of side effects that were mentioned previously. You also can watch records, arrays, and other structured variables.

FIG. 27.12

Use the Watch Properties dialog box to add or modify an entry in the Watch window.

Repeat Count is useful if you have a large array and want to look at only part of it. Suppose that you want to watch elements 826 through 833 of the following large array:

```
var
  BigArray: array[1..1000] of Integer;
```

You can't just put a watch on BigArray, because all 1,000 elements don't fit in the Watch List window (besides, counting through the first 825 elements to locate the ones in which you're interested would be a bit tedious). Instead, you can watch BigArray[826], and set Repeat Count to 8. This way, only the values of BigArray[826] through BigArray[833] are displayed.

Use the Digits edit box to specify the number of significant digits to display when watching floating-point values.

The Enabled field, if unchecked, disables display of the watch, but the IDE will still remember all the settings for the watch. This way, you can temporarily remove a watch from the Watch List window to reduce clutter, yet quickly get it back if you need it, without entering all the settings again. Also, disabling watches in which you're not currently interested speeds up the debugger because it doesn't have to constantly evaluate the watched expressions.

As you can see in the Watch Properties dialog box, a number of options control the display of the watched expression. Most of these are self-explanatory. The Default display mode (which is the default, naturally) lets the IDE decide how best to display the data, but you can override its decision by specifying one of the other options. The Memory Dump option formats the display so that the information is shown as a series of bytes, which is useful to look at the internal representation of a variable.

After you set up a few watches, they are displayed in the Watch List window and look something like Figure 27.13. This figure also shows some of the messages that are displayed when the debugger cannot display a watch.

Part

VI

Ch

27

FIG. 27.13

Viewing variables in the Watch window.

The reasons for these messages are as follows:

- `Variable 'Foo' inaccessible here due to optimization`. The variable cannot be evaluated at this point in the execution because no storage location was allocated for it. The variable possibly may be visible at some other point in the code.

- `Symbol was eliminated by linker`. The variable was stripped out by the Smart Linker because it's never referenced by any other code.

The debugger also will display an error message if a syntax error exists in your watch expression. For example, `Foo[2]` is not a valid expression if `Foo` is not an array or string.

N O T E If you watch an object property in the Watch window, the displayed value may make no sense. Remember what was said previously about functions having side effects? Many properties, although they *look* like simple variables, are implemented as function calls. The debugger will not execute a function to display a property value because the function may have undesirable side effects. Therefore, you cannot count on the value of a property to display correctly in a watch.

The solution is to assign the property to a variable, and to watch the variable rather than the property. This technique has its own problems, however, because the optimizer will notice that the assignment has no bearing on the operation of the program and strip it out of the compiled code. To get around this second problem, use a *global variable* (one declared outside of a function or procedure). The debugger will always correctly display the value of a global variable. ■

The Evaluate/Modify Dialog Box

To display the Evaluate/Modify dialog box, from the main menu select Run, Evaluate/Modify (see Figure 27.14). You also can position the cursor in the code editor window on the variable you want to inspect, and then right-click to bring up the local menu. Select Evaluate/Modify.

FIG. 27.14

Use the Evaluate/ Modify dialog box to inspect and modify (or both) a single variable.

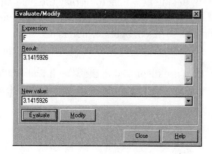

Enter an expression in the Expression edit box, just as you did in the Watch Properties dialog box previously (refer to Figure 27.12), then click the Evaluate button to display the value of the expression in the Result box. If the expression consists of the name of a simple variable (not an array or other structure), you also can enter a new value for this variable in the New Value edit box, and then click the Modify button to record the change. You may want to do so if you're in the middle of a debugging session, and you realize there's a bug that's causing a certain variable to have the wrong value. Rather than stopping to fix the bug now, you may want to verify that the rest of the code works properly if the value of the variable is corrected. You can modify the variable to "patch" the bug, continue with your testing, and then repair the bug later.

 TIP The Evaluate/Modify dialog box is a non-modal dialog box, which means you can leave it up while you trace through code. Unlike the Watch List window, however, the Result field of the Evaluate/Modify dialog box is *not* updated as the value changes. You need to click the Evaluate button each time you want to update the display.

As with the Watch List window, the Result box in the Evaluate/Modify dialog box may display an error message if the debugger cannot evaluate the given expression. And, as is also the case with the Watch List window, the Evaluate/Modify dialog box cannot evaluate an expression that contains a function call.

As you can see, the Watch List window and Evaluate/Modify dialog boxes have similar functions and capabilities but in some situations, each has advantages over the other. One other difference exists between the two that you may want to remember: Because the Evaluate/Modify dialog box displays the evaluation result in a multi-line edit box, it's often easier to view the contents of large structures, such as records and objects, by using Evaluate/Modify rather than the Watch List window.

The Fly-By Evaluator

Delphi 3 contains a new feature that makes the Watch window nearly obsolete. While the program you're debugging is paused, just move the mouse cursor so that it points at the identifier whose value you want to see. Up pops a small window, displaying the value. What could be easier? Of course, you still want to use the Watch List if you're interested in watching the values of several variables simultaneously, but if you want a quick check, you can't beat the Fly-By Evaluator.

Setting Breakpoints

A *breakpoint* acts like a stop sign to the debugger (a breakpoint is, in fact, signified in the code editor by a small red glyph shaped like a stop sign). When your application is running in the debugger, it will pause execution as soon as it reaches a line of code that contains a breakpoint. A breakpoint can be either *unconditional* or *conditional*. The debugger always stops at an unconditional breakpoint but stops at a conditional breakpoint only if the breakpoint's *stop condition* is satisfied. The Delphi integrated debugger supports two kinds of stop conditions: Boolean conditions and pass counts. These two types of conditional breakpoints are described in a following part of this section.

There are two ways to set a breakpoint, as follows:

1. Place the code-editor cursor on the desired line of code, and then press the Toggle Breakpoint hot key (F5 in the default editor keymapping) to set or clear the breakpoint. You can perform the same task by using the code editor's Local menu. Click the desired line of code in the editor window, then right-click to bring up the local menu. Select Toggle Breakpoint to set or clear the breakpoint.

2. Select Run, Add Breakpoint. This action brings up the Edit breakpoint dialog box (see Figure 27.15). To set a simple breakpoint, just click the New button. You also can use the Filename and Line Number fields to set a breakpoint in a location other than the current location of the editor cursor. (The Condition and Pass Count fields are used for conditional breakpoints, as mentioned previously.)

FIG. 27.15

Use the Edit breakpoint dialog box to add a new breakpoint.

After you set one or more breakpoints, you can use the Breakpoint list window to manage the breakpoints. To display the Breakpoint list window, select View, Breakpoints from the main menu (see Figure 27.16). You can select one of the displayed breakpoints, and then right-click to bring up the local menu. You can enable and disable breakpoints using the Enabled menu item, or delete a breakpoint entirely with the Delete command. The View Source and Edit Source commands display the location of the selected breakpoint in the code editor; the Edit Source command also moves the editor cursor to the line that contains the breakpoint. The Properties command displays the Edit breakpoint dialog box (refer to Figure 27.15), which you can use to modify the breakpoint's settings.

FIG. 27.16

Use the Breakpoint list window to manage your breakpoints.

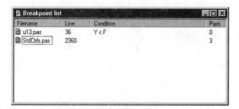

If you right-click the Breakpoint List window with no breakpoint selected, a different local menu is displayed. The Add command allows you to add a new breakpoint (by displaying the Edit Breakpoint dialog box). The Delete All command deletes all breakpoints (be careful with this one!). The Disable All and Enable All commands disable or enable all the breakpoints, respectively.

To convert an unconditional breakpoint into a conditional one, you need to bring up the Edit Breakpoint dialog box for this breakpoint (refer to Figure 27.15), and enter a condition expression or pass count into the appropriate fields.

A condition expression, entered into the Condition field, can be any Boolean expression. Each time the debugger reaches the breakpoint, it evaluates the expression. If the expression evaluates to false, the debugger continues execution. If the expression evaluates to true, the debugger pauses execution at the breakpoint. As always, the expression cannot include a function call. This kind of conditional breakpoint is useful when the breakpoint can be reached in many different ways, and you want the debugger to pause execution only when a certain condition is met.

A non-zero pass count entered into the Pass Count field tells the debugger to continue execution through a breakpoint a number of times before pausing. Each time the debugger arrives at a breakpoint, it decreases the pass count. When the pass count reaches zero, the debugger pauses execution. This procedure is especially useful when you're debugging code that contains a loop, and you know that the error you want to locate occurs somewhere in the middle of the sequence of loop iterations. You can first set the pass count to a high number and run the program. When the error occurs and execution pauses, you can look at the remaining pass count to see how many times the breakpoint was reached. You then can reset the program and set the pass count to a number slightly smaller than the number of passes required to trigger the error, and then run the program again. This time, when you reach the pass count, the error will not have occurred yet, and you can trace through the code a line at a time to determine exactly where the error is happening.

N O T E Now that you have learned basic debugging commands and techniques, you may want to pause at a mental breakpoint of your own and try them out in your applications, or perhaps in one of the demo applications included with Delphi. Using the debugger to trace through an existing application is a great way to learn how that application works. Because you don't modify code when you set breakpoints, watch variables, or step and trace, you can experiment as much as you want with no danger of "damaging" the application. ■

Debugging DLLs

In previous versions of Delphi, you needed to use an external debugger (Turbo Debugger for Windows) to debug DLLs. Delphi 3.0 now adds DLL debugging to its list of capabilities. Windows cannot load a DLL without first loading an EXE that uses this DLL, so you need to specify the EXE you want to use for this purpose. In the main menu, select Run, Parameters to display the Run Parameters dialog box. If the active project is a DLL (the .DPR file starts with the library keyword, rather than with the program keyword), the Host Application edit box will be enabled. You can either type the name of an executable application directly or use the Browse button to select one.

After you select a host application, running and debugging the DLL is virtually the same as running and debugging an ordinary executable. You can set breakpoints, step through code, and so on in the DLL, just as you do in an application.

You can debug ActiveX Components and OLE Automation objects in the same way. As with DLLs, select Run, Parameters to enter the name of a host application, and you'll be able to step through all of the code in your component or automation object.

The CPU Window (Disassembly View)

The CPU window gives you a view into the detailed inner workings of your application, at the assembly language level. If you've ever used Borland's stand-alone Turbo Debugger for Windows, you probably already are familiar with the layout and functions of the CPU window. Effective use of the CPU window requires knowledge of Intel x86 assembly language and processor architecture, so if you're unfamiliar with these topics, you probably want to skip over this section.

You rarely need to use the CPU window, but when you do need it, you *really* need it. Think of it as providing the final word on exactly what's happening inside your application and the rest of the system. If you find yourself against a wall, with confounding debugging results that just make no sense, stepping through your code in the CPU window may shed some light.

Before you can use the CPU window, you need to enable it (it's disabled by default). To do this, you need to use the RegEdit program included with Windows 95 and Windows NT. Start RegEdit and navigate through the hierarchy of folders in the lefthand tree view. Start by clicking the + box to the left of HKEY_CURRENT_USER. This action opens a list of subfolders. Using the same technique, open the Software folder, then the Borland folder under that, the Delphi folder under that, and finally the 3 folder under that. Whew!

One of the folders under 3 is named Debugging. Click it and when it opens, you see a list of name/data pairs displayed in the righthand view. You need to add a new value with a name of **EnableCPU** and data equal to **1**.

To do add the new value, select Edit, New, String Value. This action inserts a new item in the righthand view. Next, type the name of the value **EnableCPU**, and then press Enter. Now select Edit, Modify and enter **1** in the Value Data edit box. Click OK and close RegEdit. The next time you start Delphi, you will see a new menu item titled CPU Window on the View menu.

To display the CPU window, from the main menu select View, CPU Window. As shown in Figure 27.17, the CPU window is divided into five panes. You can resize the panes by clicking and dragging the bars that separate the panes.

FIG. 27.17

The CPU window (DisassemblyView).

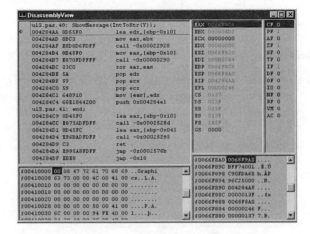

Clockwise, from the upper left, the panes are as follows:

- *Code pane.* The code pane presents a disassembled view of the code in the vicinity of the current execution point. (If you're not currently debugging an application, the code pane will be mostly empty.) The code pane also displays the source code lines that correspond to the assembly language instructions. As in the code editor, the execution point is indicated by a small green arrow glyph. As you step through the code in either the CPU window or the code editor, the two execution point indicators move in synchrony.

- *Register pane.* The register pane displays the contents of the 16 CPU registers. Registers whose values have changed as the result of the most recent step or trace are shown highlighted in red.

- *Flags pane.* The flags pane displays the states of the 14 CPU flags. A set flag is indicated by a 1, a cleared flag by a 0. Note that depending on which CPU you have in your system (486, Pentium, and so on), some of the flags may not be applicable.

- *Stack pane.* The stack pane displays the contents of the application's stack. You can change the display mode by right-clicking the pane to bring up the local menu. Select Display As from the menu; this brings up a submenu with several display choices.

- *Data pane.* By default, the data pane displays the contents of the application's global data segment. As with the stack pane, you can change the way in which the data are displayed by right-clicking the pane and selecting Display As from the local menu.

Each of the panes in the CPU window has its own local menu. You may want to experiment with the menu items to get a feel for how you can manipulate your view of the CPU and memory.

Part

VI

Ch

27

The Thread Status Window

The Thread Status, Modules, and Call Stack windows provide additional information that can be helpful while you're debugging.

The Thread Status window lists all currently active threads in the current process (your application). To see which threads are running in your application, select View, Threads from the main menu, which displays the Thread Status window (see Figure 27.18). Listed in this window are entries for each active thread in your application. (Unless you are debugging a multi-threaded application, only one thread is shown.)

FIG. 27.18

Use the Thread Status window to display the active threads in your application.

The four columns in the window contain the following information:

■ *Thread ID*. The unique identification number for the thread, assigned by the operating system. No two threads in the system ever have the same thread ID.

■ *State*. The state of a thread is normally either Running or Stopped. If your application is running but waiting for user input, the state is displayed as Runnable.

■ *Status*. The status of a thread can be any of four values. Breakpoint indicates that the thread is stopped at a breakpoint, Stepped means the thread is stopped after successfully executing a step or trace, Faulted means the thread is stopped because of an exception, and Unknown means the status of the thread is unknown because it isn't the current thread.

■ *Location*. The location column displays the source code line that corresponds to the current execution point of the thread. If the debugger cannot determine the source code line (this may be true for threads other than the current thread), a 32-bit address is displayed instead.

If you have a multithreaded application and you want to debug a thread other than the main thread, you can make a different thread the current thread by using the Thread Status window. Select a thread to make the thread current by clicking the Thread ID, and then right-click to bring up the local menu. Select Make Current to make this thread the current thread. The execution point in the code editor jumps to the execution point in the selected thread. You now can step or trace in this thread, just as you do in the main thread.

The Thread Status window local menu has two other commands: View Source and Go to Source. These commands are useful to see where the execution point of another thread is located without having to make the thread the current thread.

The Modules Window

The Modules window lists all modules (your application's EXE file and all DLLs) currently mapped into your application's process address space. This includes any DLLs that you loaded implicitly or explicitly, and the system DLLs implicitly loaded by the operating system. To display a list of the modules in an application, from the main menu select View, Modules. The Modules window is shown in Figure 27.19. The three columns of information are *Name*, the name of the module; *Address*, the load address of the module (the address at which the module's code begins); and *Path*, the fully qualified path of the directory from which the module was loaded. You can use the Path information to double-check that a module is loaded from the correct directory (which can be important if you're working with a DLL and you have different versions of the DLL in different directories). You can use the Address information in conjunction with the CPU window to display and trace through the code in a module.

FIG. 27.19

Use the Modules window to display the list of modules used by your application.

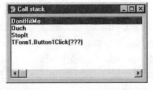

The Call Stack Window

The Call Stack window displays a list of all of the function and procedure calls that brought the execution point to the statement at which execution is currently paused. To display the Call Stack window, select View, Call Stack from the main menu (see Figure 27.20).

FIG. 27.20

Use the Call Stack window to determine what function and procedure calls brought the application to the current execution point.

The top line in the Call Stack window displays the name of the current procedure (DontHitMe in this example). The next line shows the name of the procedure that called the current procedure (Ouch). The line after that shows the name of the procedure that called this procedure (StopIt), and so on. You can use the list of procedures to help you determine how you reached any given breakpoint in your code.

Although the procedure names are helpful, it's possible that a procedure calls a second procedure in more than one place. The Call Stack window doesn't tell you which of these calls got you where you are. For this information, you can use the Call Stack window's local menu by selecting the procedure you want to look at and then right-clicking to bring up the local menu. The View Source command displays a highlight bar on the source code line that shows where the procedure will return to (this is the statement *after* the one that led to the function or procedure call). The Edit Source command is similar but moves the edit cursor to the source line as well.

Tracing into VCL Source Code

If you use the Developer, Client/Server, or Enterprise editions of Delphi 3, a copy of the VCL (Visual Component Library) source code is included in the package. As delivered, the VCL is compiled without debugging information, which means that if you try to step into VCL code while debugging, the debugger steps over it instead. Usually, you want this because you can assume that bugs are probably in your code rather than in the VCL. Occasionally, however, you may need to trace into the VCL code, either to determine if a bug in your application is actually being caused by a bug in the VCL, or because you need to determine exactly how a function call is being processed.

To trace into the VCL code, you need to recompile the units you want to trace into with debugging information enabled. To do this, copy the source code for these units to your project directory. Next, from the Delphi main menu, select Project, Options and verify that the debugging options are set on the Compiler page. Finally, select Project, Build All. Your project, along with the VCL units you copied to your project directory, are now ready for debugging.

 Some of the standard VCL units require that Overflow Checking be disabled to work properly. If you recompile any VCL units with debugging information included, make sure that the Overflow Checking option is turned off in your project's compiler options.

After you finish tracing into the VCL units, simply delete the corresponding .PAS and .DCU files from your project directory, and you're back to normal.

Brute-Force Debugging

During development, you frequently are faced with situations in which you need to extract only a bit of information from an application so that you can verify that the program is working the way you think it is. (I often get in this situation when I work with an unfamiliar API function or object method whose documentation is ambiguous or incomplete, and I need to experiment to determine whether or not the function works in the way I think it does.)

In these cases, it's often simpler to forego the debugger and insert a few lines of code to display the information directly. There are a number of ways to do this, and I collected some of the more popular ones here.

CAUTION

A word of warning, however: Most of these techniques definitely fall into the category of "quick-and-dirty," and I don't recommend them as substitutes for the robust application design, testing, and debugging techniques previously described.

Displaying Debugging Information on a Form

One way to display such information is to write it directly onto the surface of a form. Rather than write on the form's canvas, it's usually better to drop a TLabel or similar component onto the form and write to it. The advantage of using a component is that the information will persist, even if the form is repainted.

Look at the ExtractFileDir and ExtractFilePath documentation in the Delphi 3 online help. I cannot tell for sure from the documentation exactly what the difference is between these two functions. Well, there's one sure way to determine this. Start a new application in Delphi (select File, New Application from the main menu), and then drop a TButton and two TLabels on the main form. The form should look like Figure 27.21.

FIG. 27.21

Displaying debugging information by using a TLabel.

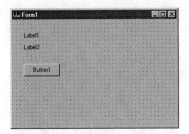

Double-click the TButton and add this code to the skeleton OnClick event handler generated by Delphi, as follows:

```
procedure TForm1.Button1Click(Sender: TObject);
begin
  Label1.Caption := ExtractFileDir(Application.ExeName);
  Label2.Caption := ExtractFilePath(Application.ExeName);
end;
```

(Note that Application.ExeName returns the fully qualified path name of the application.) Press F9 to compile and run the application, and then click the button. It now should be obvious how the two functions differ. (You don't think I'm going to give you the answer here, do you?)

Recently, I ran into a predicament while using a third-party DLL whose source code I didn't have. From my testing, I was fairly confident that the DLL was allocating but not freeing a large chunk of virtual memory every time it loaded. I came up with the idea to put a button on the main form of the application, and every time I pressed the button, it would tell me how much virtual memory was still available. In this case, I wanted to preserve the results of the previous button clicks, so I used a TMemo rather than a TLabel, and simply added the latest virtual memory measurement to the existing list.

To see how I did this, start another new application and drop a TMemo and a TButton on the main form. You also want to set the TMemo.ScrollBars property to ssVertical. Your form will look similar to Figure 27.22.

Part
VI

Ch
27

FIG. 27.22

Displaying debugging information in a TMemo.

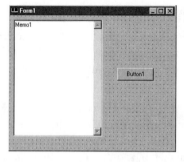

In the button's OnClick event handler, add the following code:

```
procedure TForm1.Button1Click(Sender: TObject);
var
  MemStat: TMemoryStatus;
begin
  VirtualAlloc(nil, 1000000, MEM_RESERVE, PAGE_READWRITE);   // line 1
  MemStat.dwLength := SizeOf(TMemoryStatus);                 // line 2
  GlobalMemoryStatus(MemStat);                               // line 3
  Memo1.Lines.Add(IntToStr(MemStat.dwAvailVirtual));         // line 4
end;
```

Don't worry too much about the details of the call to the VirtualAlloc API function in line 1. As used here, it tells the operating system to reserve 1 million bytes of memory for later use. The GlobalMemoryStatus API function returns information about the memory consumption of the current application and the system as a whole. This information is returned in the MemStat variable, which is a record of type TMemoryStatus (to see the definition of TMemoryStatus in the online help, look under MEMORYSTATUS). Before calling GlobalMemoryStatus, you need to tell the operating system how big the TMemoryStatus record is. You do so by setting the dwLength field appropriately, as shown in line 2. Next, you make the actual call to GlobalMemoryStatus in line 3. Finally, you display the value of the dwAvailVirtual field in the TMemo in line 4.

Compile and run this program, and then click the button a few times. You see the available virtual memory drop by about 1M every time you press the button, as expected. Figure 27.23 shows what the form looks like after the button has been clicked five times.

FIG. 27.23

Displaying available virtual memory in a TMemo.

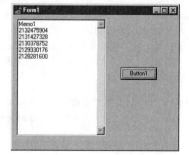

When I used this code in my test application (without the call to VirtualAlloc, of course), I discovered that the DLL indeed allocated 60M (!) of virtual memory every time it was loaded, and didn't free the memory when it was unloaded. Even though Windows 95 provides each application with a 2G virtual address space, a loss of 60M a shot was not something I could ignore.

ShowMessage

Rather than displaying the debugging information on a form, you may want to use a modal dialog box. The principal difference is that a modal dialog box stops the program in its tracks until you dismiss the dialog box. This action has advantages when the information you want to see is normally transient, and you need the ability to "freeze" the program long enough to read and record the information.

The ShowMessage procedure (in the Dialogs unit) is ideal for this purpose. It allows you to display a string of essentially unlimited length in a simple modal dialog box. To use it, just pass the desired string as the only parameter to the procedure. (You also can use MessageDlg, but it has extra bells and whistles that usually are more trouble than they're worth when you just want to display a few pieces of information on-screen.)

ShowMessage expects a single string, but most of the time you'll want to display other kinds of information. Therefore, you need to convert this information into a string before you can display it. My favorite function for this purpose is Format, which is both flexible and easy to use.

Let's put together another simple example application to show how all this works. I'll use the GlobalMemoryStatus function once again but this time, I display all the information it returns, using a ShowMessage dialog box.

Start a new application and drop a single TButton on the main form. The button's OnClick event handler should look like the following:

```
procedure TForm1.Button1Click(Sender: TObject);
var
  MemStat: TMemoryStatus;
begin
  MemStat.dwLength := SizeOf(TMemoryStatus);
  GlobalMemoryStatus(MemStat);
  with MemStat do ShowMessage(Format('Memory load: %d%%'#13 +
    'Total physical: %d'#13 + 'Available physical: %d'#13 +
    'Total page file: %d'#13 + 'Available page file: %d'#13 +
    'Total virtual: %d'#13 + 'Available virtual: %d',
    [dwMemoryLoad, dwTotalPhys, dwAvailPhys, dwTotalPageFile,
    dwAvailPageFile, dwTotalVirtual, dwAvailVirtual]));
end;
```

Notice how I inserted several #13 characters (ASCII carriage returns) into the format string. These become line breaks when the string is displayed by ShowMessage. As mentioned previously, the string displayed by ShowMessage is practically unlimited in length, but that's not too useful if it's all on one line; the line breaks make the display much easier to read. Figure 27.24 shows what you get when you run the program and click the button.

FIG. 27.24

Using ShowMessage to display debugging information.

The Memory Load and Available Physical numbers suggest that maybe I should take advantage of low DRAM prices and invest in more main memory!

Writing to the Console

Yet another way to display debugging information is by writing it to a console window, using the Write and WriteLn procedures. You can turn your project into a console application either by selecting the appropriate project option (Project, Options, go to the Linker page, and select Generate Console Application), or by inserting an $APPTYPE CONSOLE directive into the project's main .DPR file. Assuming that your application is primarily graphical and you only want to use the console for debugging, you can wrap the $APPTYPE directive in a conditional define like the following example:

```
{$ifdef Debug}
{$APPTYPE CONSOLE}
{$endif}
```

The console will be present only when you run your debug version.

TIP If you try to use Write or WriteLn to display information in a console window and you receive an I/O Error 103, you forgot to make your project a console application.

Now, use the same code as in the previous example, but send the output to a console window instead of a ShowMessage dialog box. You need to ensure that your project is compiled as a console application, and to change the procedure used in the button's OnClick event handler from one ShowMessage statement to seven WriteLn statements, as shown here:

```
procedure TForm1.Button1Click(Sender: TObject);
var
  MemStat: TMemoryStatus;
begin
  MemStat.dwLength := SizeOf(TMemoryStatus);
  GlobalMemoryStatus(MemStat);
  with MemStat do
    begin
    WriteLn(Format('Memory load: %d%%', [dwMemoryLoad]));
    WriteLn(Format('Total physical: %d', [dwTotalPhys]));
    WriteLn(Format('Available physical: %d', [dwAvailPhys]));
    WriteLn(Format('Total page file: %d', [dwTotalPageFile]));
    WriteLn(Format('Available page file: %d', [dwAvailPageFile]));
    WriteLn(Format('Total virtual: %d', [dwTotalVirtual]));
```

```
    WriteLn(Format('Available virtual: %d', [dwAvailVirtual]));
    end;
end;
```

Figure 27.25 shows the result.

FIG. 27.25
Using the console
window to display
debugging information.

N O T E Old-time Pascal users will notice that I used Format when I didn't really need to—
WriteLn has its own formatting capabilities. However, I try to get into the habit of using
Format for just about everything. Format is flexible and powerful, but most important, by using
Format exclusively, I have to remember only one set of rules for formatting my strings. ■

Writing to a Log File

Writing debugging information to a log file is a bit different from the previous three approaches because it doesn't qualify as quick-and-dirty. In fact, using a log file is an excellent technique that is appropriate to any application.

Writing to a log file is essentially the same as writing to a console window; the only difference is that rather than WriteLn(...), you use WriteLn(LogFile, ...), where LogFile is the name of the log file variable, of type TextFile. You also have to take care of opening the log file at the beginning of program execution and closing it when the program ends, which is most easily accomplished by putting the logging code in its own unit, one that is conditionally included in your project. I put together a simple logging unit named ULOG.PAS, shown in Listing 27.1 and included on this book's companion CD-ROM. You can use this unit to add logging capabilities to your own applications.

**Listing 27.1   \UDelphi3\Chp27\ULOG.PAS—The *uLog* Debug Information
Logging Unit**

```
unit uLog;
interface
procedure Log(S: String);
implementation
```

continues

Listing 27.1   Continued

```
uses
  Windows, SysUtils;
var
  LogFile: TextFile;
  LogCriticalSection: TRtlCriticalSection;
procedure Log(S: String);
var
  SystemTime: TSystemTime;
  FileTime: TFileTime;
begin
  GetSystemTime(SystemTime);
  SystemTimeToFileTime(SystemTime, FileTime);
  EnterCriticalSection(LogCriticalSection);
  WriteLn(LogFile, Format('%s %.8x%.8x %s',
    [FormatDateTime('yy.mm.dd hh.mm.ss', Now),
    FileTime.dwHighDateTime, FileTime.dwLowDateTime, S]));
  LeaveCriticalSection(LogCriticalSection);
end;
procedure Startup;
var
  FileName: String;
begin
  InitializeCriticalSection(LogCriticalSection);
  FileName := Format('Log file for %s at %s.txt',
    [ParamStr(0), DateTimeToStr(Now)]);
  while Pos(':', FileName) > 0 do FileName[Pos(':', FileName)] := '.';
  while Pos('/', FileName) > 0 do FileName[Pos('/', FileName)] := '-';
  while Pos('\', FileName) > 0 do FileName[Pos('\', FileName)] := '.';
  AssignFile(LogFile, FileName);
  Rewrite(LogFile);
end;
procedure Shutdown;
begin
  CloseFile(LogFile);
  DeleteCriticalSection(LogCriticalSection);
end;
initialization
  Startup;
finalization
  Shutdown;
end
```

This unit handles the housekeeping details of creating and opening the log file, and then closing it at program termination. The log file's name is derived from the name of the application and the current date and time, so there's no chance of accidentally overwriting a previous log file. To use the unit, conditionally include it in your application's units like this:

```
unit MyUnit;
interface
uses
  {ifdef Debug} uLog, {$endif}
  Windows, Messages, SysUtils, Classes, Graphics, Controls, Forms, Dialogs,
  StdCtrls;
  ...
```

Then call the `Log` function when you want to send a string to the log file, as follows:

```
{$ifdef Debug}
Log(Format('entering the Foo procedure; Bar = %d', [Bar]));
{$endif}
```

Don't forget to wrap every call to `Log` in `{$ifdef Debug}..{$endif}` directives, or you will receive a compile error when you try to compile the ship version of your application.

The `uLog` unit has two other features that add to its usefulness. First, besides writing the passed string to the log file, the `Log` function also stamps each string with the current date and time, along with a hexadecimal integer that corresponds to the current system time in milliseconds. This information can be useful when trying to figure out the sequence of events in your application. Second, the unit uses a *critical section*, which ensures that only one thread can access the log file at a time. In this way, if your application uses multiple threads, two threads trying to log information at the same time won't turn your log file into a hopeless mishmash. Figure 27.26 shows a typical log file, displayed in Windows Notepad. For more information about critical sections, refer to Chapter 24, "Working with Threads."

FIG. 27.26

A sample debug log file.

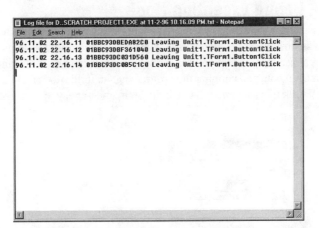

How should you use a log file? What information should you put in it? There are different schools of thought, ranging from one extreme (log *everything*) to the other (only log data associated with the procedures or functions you're currently debugging). By logging every imaginable bit of data, you can be pretty certain that everything you may need to debug a problem will be there. The downside is that the log file is probably going to be huge, and you'll have to wade through it all to find records of problems. I personally tend to take a middle-of-the-road approach, leaning somewhat towards the "log everything" end of the spectrum.

Stalking Wild Bugs

Before embarking on a bug-hunting expedition, it's best to heed the words of Henry David Thoreau: "Simplify, simplify." The process of debugging frequently becomes a search for a needle in a haystack. This is always easier if you make the haystack as small as possible.

Part VI

Ch

27

If you have a good idea where the bug is occurring, you can concentrate your efforts in that area. It's almost always worthwhile to take time to strip out (or at least comment out) any code not related to the bug. Because this may mean making major modifications to your program, it's often a good idea to copy your entire project to a new directory before chopping away at the code. After you locate the bug, you can apply the fix to your original code and delete the entire directory that contains the hacked-up copy. Make sure that you test the fixed code to ensure that the bug is gone before you delete the copied project directory!

Don't be too overzealous in the application of this divide-and-conquer philosophy—if you're not careful, you may find that you wiped out the code that contains the bug, and you'll have to start over. Comment out a little at a time, and test the program frequently to verify that the bug still exists in the remaining code.

There are certain "hard-to-debug" situations that may occur while you debug your application. I listed a few of these situations in the following paragraphs, and provided some tips that may help you get past the hurdles they represent.

Error Setting Debug Exception Hook

If you ever see this error message displayed (see Figure 27.27), it indicates that the debugger was left in an unstable state, which usually happens when the application you're debugging terminates abnormally. Often, you can fix the problem simply by selecting Run, Program Reset from the main menu, and running the program again. If this doesn't do the trick, try Program, Build All. If even this isn't enough to eliminate the message, you may need to exit the IDE and restart it.

FIG. 27.27

The Error setting debug exception hook message.

Access Violations

Access violations are the bane of software developers. The most difficult aspect of access violations is that they frequently lie dormant, ticking time bombs triggered by coding errors occurring hundreds of lines from the point where they finally explode. By the time access violations show themselves, any information that may have led to their detection is often long gone.

In reality, an *access violation* is a simple error that means your application attempted to access a section of memory that doesn't belong to it. When you receive an access violation error message (see Figure 27.28), make a note of both numbers displayed. The first number (00405E81 in this example) gives the address in your code of the instruction that violated the system's security, while the second number (0096B43F in this example) gives the address of the location that this instruction attempted to read or write.

FIG. 27.28
An Access Violation
error message.

Back in the IDE, go to the main menu and select Search, Find Error. Enter the code error address (the first number) into the edit box and click OK. If you're lucky, the IDE will locate the error and take you to the line of code that caused the access violation. More often than not, however, the IDE won't find the error address, almost always because the actual error occurred in the VCL or runtime library, which are not compiled with debugging information enabled. You probably passed a bad pointer or other memory address to a library function, and the problem didn't surface until the function tried to use the pointer.

This is where compiling the VCL units with debugging information may come in handy. Even if you don't trace into these units, compiling a unit with debugging information allows the debugger to locate an error address in the unit. After you determine in which function the error occurred, you have a good clue as to where in your code the problem originated.

Stack Overflows

Stack overflows are far less common in 32-bit applications than in 16-bit applications because the available stack space is much larger. About the only way to get a stack overflow in a Delphi 3.0 application is through infinite recursion. For example, calling the following function leads to a stack overflow:

```
function BlowTheStack(I: Integer): Integer;
var
  J: Integer;
begin
  J := 2;
  Result := BlowTheStack(I * J);
end;
```

Every time the function calls itself recursively, space for the local variable J must be allocated on the stack. Because the function calls itself repeatedly with no means of terminating the recursion, the stack eventually overflows.

Of course, not all infinitely recursive code is this obvious. However, if you ever receive a stack overflow error, infinite recursion is the first thing to check.

External Exceptions

An External exception error message (see Figure 27.29) can occur if your application causes an exception to be raised in another, non-Delphi module (a DLL). The error codes are defined in the WINDOWS.PAS file included with Delphi; their symbolic names are all of the form STATUS_xxxx. For example, the exception shown here, C000001D, is a STATUS_ILLEGAL_ INSTRUCTION exception. Although this gives some information about the kind of exception that occurred, there is no indication of *where* it occurred, so your only recourse is to use the divide-and-conquer approach to try to narrow down what in your application is leading to the exception.

FIG. 27.29

An External exception error message.

Using the Stand-Alone Debugger (TD32.EXE)

Eventually, despite the features available in the Delphi debugger, you may be faced with a completely intractable bug. If this situation ever happens, you have my sympathies. You may want to try Borland's stand-alone debugger, TD32.EXE, available as part of the Turbo Assembler and C++ packages. In addition to a set of features that correspond to those in the Delphi 3 integrated debugger, TD32 can do a few things that the integrated debugger cannot. In particular, TD32 provides hardware breakpoint capability, which means that you can trigger a breakpoint, for example, when a certain I/O port is accessed. This is heady stuff, and I want to emphasize that you should consider it only as a last resort. If the Delphi integrated debugger can't help, you probably will need to really get your hands dirty. Debugging in this regime requires intimate knowledge of the details of both hardware and system software.

Putting It All Together

In this chapter, you learned how to design your applications so that they're easier to test and debug, how to use the many features of the Delphi integrated debugger, and what to do when the standard debugging techniques don't work. This was a long chapter to read, and you're probably a little dazed by now. Don't worry, though. You don't have to use everything I talked about all at once. Each technique can stand pretty much on its own, so take your time and familiarize yourself with them one at a time. It won't be long before it all becomes second nature. ●

CHAPTER 28

Creating Web Server Applications

by Chaim Krause

I strongly suggest that you don't tell anyone that you've read this chapter. If you do, prepare to answer questions—a lot of them. A key problem with knowing about the Internet is that anyone who discovers that you understand the beast will bombard you with questions. Everyone has heard much about what the WWW can do, but hardly anyone outside of the Webmaster clan has a solid understanding of the technologies behind the Internet.

Some of you may be reading this chapter out of desperation. Perhaps you ran into the boss in the cafeteria and struck up a conversation, and then made the mistake of mentioning the new Internet components in the latest version of Delphi. By the time the conversation was over, you promised your boss that you would develop a fully Internet-enabled application for the international traveling sales force by the end of the quarter. Now you need to find out if your company even owns a WWW server.

Some of you are here because of your ego. You didn't run into the boss in the cafeteria; you ran into an eccentric graphic artist type from the Committee Assigned to SomeHow Compete On the Web (CASHCOW), which was formed overnight by management to catch up with every other Tom, Dick, and Harry, Inc. with a home page on the WWW. The artist type mentioned that he had created 101

■ **Create an application to return static HTML pages**

Learn how to develop server-side extensions that enable your WWW server to provide static pages.

■ **Extend the application to return dynamic pages**

Learn how to develop server-side extensions that enable your WWW server to provide dynamic pages based on user input.

■ **Add database connectivity**

Extend your applications to have the capability to include data from a TTable or TQuery in the returned HTML page.

graphics-filled HTML pages for the Web site, but couldn't figure out a way to get the pages to display the current time.

To prove the superiority of the analytical mind of the programmer over the abstract mind of the artist, you began to spew all the wonderful things you can do with your extensive set of development tools, acquired at this year's Coders Almost Found Facing Extinction In the Net Explosion Conference (CAFFEINE-Con). You didn't mention that this extensive array of tools was a single copy of Delphi Client/Server Suite. The artist explained that everything was under control and that CASHCOW had already set up the Web server and created all the necessary pages, complete with animated graphics and a few ActiveX controls. He explained that you only need to write a simple server-side extension to facilitate the use of a few dynamic pieces of information. He asked if you could do it. "Sure," you replied. "No problem. I'll get it to you by Friday." On your way back to your cubicle you ran into John from IS. "John, remember that Web server application session you attended while I went to the one on Rendering 3-D Worlds That Could Only Exist in a Video Game? Did they mention what a server-side extension was?"

In the second case, you're in luck. You don't have to deal with the myriad of technologies that must be combined to create a fully functional dynamic Web site today. You only need to know that a *server-side extension* is simply an ISAPI application. Think of this as a simple DLL that takes a few parameters as input, processes them, and spits out a string as the return value.

Those of you super-troopers who promised the boss the world on a silver home page need to know that it's going to take a lot more than Delphi to get you a functional Web server application and a corresponding pat on the back: It takes more than just eggs to bake a cake, and it takes more than just Delphi to make a complete Web server application. Delphi does provide most of the necessary tools, however, and most other aspects of the task are relatively simple to tackle. For your sake, this chapter presents a number of tips, notes, and sidebars to bring you up to speed on all the other items that need to be in place for a Web server application to be functional in the real world. Many of these items do not concern Delphi, but they are necessary either for your server-side extension to function or to provide you with ways to spruce up the HTML page that can act as the GUI front end for your ISAPI application.

CAUTION

To develop and deploy Web server applications, you need to already have implemented a few things. The main items required are a WWW browser and a functional WWW server that allows the use of ISAPI-compliant server-side extensions. Both items can reside on the development platform—you don't need a network. You also need to have the BDE and its associated drivers installed on the server if your Web server will be connecting to a database.

N O T E If you lack a WWW server or browser, don't panic. You have plenty of existing ones from which to choose, as well as the ability to build these with Delphi.

You already may have these items and not know it. Windows NT 4.0 Workstation ships with Peer Web Services and Internet Explorer (IE). IE is a WWW browser and Peer Web Services provides an ISAPI-compliant WWW server, along with FTP and Gopher servers. Many other alternatives are freely available from a multitude of sources. WWW browsers and servers can be easily obtained from the Internet, online services such as CompuServe or America Online, and also from many books.

You can employ the Client and Server Winsock Socket VCL components in Delphi 3 to build your own WWW server and browser from scratch. You also can use the IE ActiveX control to speed the development of your browser. ■

Prerequisites for Web Server Application Development

Before you fire up Delphi, a few things need to be covered in at least a cursory manner so that you understand the environment in which Web server applications function. Some of these items are as follows:

- **HTTP**—This is an acronym for *Hypertext Transfer Protocol*, an application-level protocol used to transmit various forms of data across the Internet.
- **HTML**—This is an acronym for *Hypertext Markup Language*, a mutated subset of *Standard Generalized Markup Language (SGML)*. HTML is used to describe the formatting of text through a series of tags.
- **URI & URL**—A *Universal Resource Identifier/Locator* is used to identify a specific entity on the Internet.
- **CGI**—The *Common Gateway Interface* was the first attempt at integrating WWW servers and stand-akō‡e progqã s; CGI pr ograms can be either compiled or scripted.
- **Win-CGI**—The Windows flavor of CGI is named Win-CGI.
- **Web scripting languages**—These include, but are not limited to, the following: Java, JavaScript, JScript, and VBScript.
- **ActiveX**—For a description of ActiveX technologies, see Chapter 21, "Creating ActiveX Controls."
- **ISAPI**—The *Internet Server API* was originally the Microsoft-specific *Information Server API*, but since its inception, it has been submitted to committee as an open standard.
- **NSAPI**—The *Netscape Server API* is used to interact with server products from Netscape.

   There may soon be no need to learn two separate APIs. As this chapter is being written, Netscape has announced that it intends to adopt the ISAPI standard.

Intranet

Most people understand the concept of the Internet yet are unsure of the meaning of *intranet*. This is odd because the Internet is an intangible entity, while an intranet is an easily defined network environment that's limited in scope.

Most businesses today have a corporate LAN or WAN. An intranet is simply the extension of a conventional LAN or WAN through the use of technologies and standards developed for use on the Internet. Some people refer to a LAN that uses Internet technologies as an intranet and refer to a WAN using Internet technologies as an extranet.

Part VI
Ch 28

HTTP versus HTML

HTTP stands for *Hypertext Transfer Protocol*, and *HTML* stands for *Hypertext Markup Language*. Although these acronyms may seem similar and are often misunderstood as synonymous, the words "protocol" and "language" should make it apparent to programmers that these terms describe separate concepts.

HTTP is an application-level protocol that works on top of TCP/IP. (*Transmission Control Protocol/Internet Protocol* consists of two separate protocols that are so related they're usually referred to with a single term, *TCP/IP*.) HTTP is just one of many protocols that ride on TCP/IP. Others include *File Transfer Protocol* (FTP), *Post Office Protocol* (POP), and *Simple Mail Transfer Protocol* (SMTP). The purpose of HTTP is to transmit data, which can take many forms. The most popular form is textual data formatted in HTML.

The HTTP 1.1 specification describes HTTP as a "generic, stateless, object-oriented protocol which can be used for many tasks." This means that HTTP is not exclusively for HTML document transmission. Other items, such as graphical images or audio files, also may be transmitted. The client and server applications can differentiate between document types through the use of HTTP's request methods.

HTML uses a series of tags to describe the format of the text between them, or in some cases, after them. For example, `<H1>` and `</H1>` are used to bracket a section of text that the author wants to have presented as a header with the greatest level of superiority. When the `<B>` and `</B>` tags surround a word, the author is asking that the word be displayed in a bold font. The `<LI>` tag denotes a list item.

How do these concepts relate to your Web server applications? First, your application most likely will use these two standards to obtain input and present output. Second, knowledge of these concepts brings the realization that your Delphi-developed Web server applications are not limited to the mundane world of ASCII text.

Learning More About HTTP and HTML

Due to limits on the size of this chapter, as well as the tremendous amount of information available elsewhere on these two topics, I won't cover them in detail. If you are unfamiliar with the specifics of these two open standards, however, this sidebar conveys what I feel are the most important aspects of these items.

HTTP

Gaining further knowledge of the specifics of HTTP allows you to extend your Web server applications beyond what is covered in this chapter. This is not difficult, because only three methods are currently supported in HTTP version 1.0 (finalized in RFC 1945):

- GET is used to retrieve an entity specified by a URI.
- HEAD is used to request only the header information on the entity. This differs from GET, which requests both the header and body of the entity.
- POST is a request for the contacted server to accept an entity from the client.

HTML

Learning HTML is extremely easy for any Delphi programmer. The number of HTML tags is minuscule compared to the daunting number of reserved words, functions, methods, and properties with which you deal in Delphi.

The easiest way to learn the basics of HTML is to view the source code of existing HTML pages. Most WWW browsers provide this capability.

The main thing to understand is that the tags bracketing, or preceding, a section of text describe the intended format for that text.

Consider the following example:

```
<H1>Welcome To My Home Page</H1>
```

This HTML tells the browser that the text "Welcome To My Home Page" is a heading of the highest priority. This usually causes the browser to render the text in a bold font larger than the "normal" text in the document.

For more information on HTTP and HTML, check out **http://www.w3.org**, the home of the World Wide Web Consortium (W3C). W3C is an international industry consortium founded in 1994 to develop common standards for the evolution of the WWW.

A Web Browser as the User Interface

When developing a Web server application, keep in mind that your application doesn't have a front end. Standard applications in today's world provide a GUI *front end* with which the program interacts with the real world. These front ends, or *user interfaces* (*UIs*), enable the program to obtain input from an end user, and also to present feedback to the user through some form of visible output.

While you are developing Web server applications, however, you don't have this luxury. Usually, you need to rely on a WWW browser to provide a means of interacting with your Web server application's end user. The remaining topics to be covered before plunging into actual Delphi code should be of great interest, because they are critical to the ease of use of your application and, therefore, the acceptance of your Web server application by its end user. Web programming/scripting languages and ActiveX provide you increased control over the "appearance" of your Web server application.

ActiveX ActiveX is more powerful and versatile than straight HTML. Leveraging this technology allows you to provide an interface that's closer to what usually is understood as a GUI front end for a standard application than a standard HTML page.

See "Creating an ActiveX Control—PieX" in Chapter 21 for more information about developing ActiveX forms and components for use with your Web server applications.

Web Programming/Scripting Languages You may wonder why Web programming and scripting languages should concern a Delphi programmer. Although Delphi is a great language for development of stand-alone executables, it's useless when it comes to controlling the display of text in documents by a WWW browser. HTML provides the means necessary to control the format of your Web page.

Java, JavaScript, JScript, and VBScript give you, the Web server application developer, even greater control over the appearance of your output, and extend your ability to gather input. These languages have been created for the purpose of manipulating the appearance of HTML content and providing Web pages with rudimentary capabilities such as looping, testing, event handling, and other tasks taken for granted in the world of conventional programming.

Server APIs

Although NSAPI, Netscape's version of a server API, was around before ISAPI, Netscape has announced that they also are adopting the ISAPI standard. In my opinion, most or all of NSAPI will rot on the vine because there is no impetus to develop two versions of a Web server application when a developer can adhere to a single standard and have the application work across platforms. This chapter, therefore, is devoted to discussing only the ISAPI standard.

N O T E The developers at Borland took a similar approach with the elements in Delphi related to server APIs. Borland provided a DLL to, in effect, translate between ISAPI and NSAPI. This allows Delphi developers to develop a single server-side extension conforming to the ISAPI standard, and then deploy the "translator" DLL alongside it. This cuts down on development time and lessens the need to learn and understand two competing APIs. ■

ISAPI was recently presented as an open standard to W3C, so an abundance of documentation is available on the subject. I leave it up to you to learn about the general nature of ISAPI from sources like Microsoft's and W3C's WWW sites. This chapter focuses instead on how to use ISAPI to develop Web server applications in Delphi that work on the increasing number of ISAPI-compliant servers.

The Big Three

The rest of this chapter demonstrates how to build ISAPI DLLs. When creating your first ISAPI DLL in the following example, you see a New Web Application dialog box where you choose ISAPI/NSAPI Dynamic Link Library. You also can choose CGI or Win-CGI at that time. The initial projects will differ in minor ways but beyond this, you code all four types of Web server applications in the same way.

Using Delphi to Write ISAPI DLLs

At the time of this writing, ISAPI server-side extensions are the *de facto* standard for the Windows world. Because you are programming in Delphi, it's safe to assume that you're programming your Web server applications to function under Windows. The two standard bearers in the Windows WWW server market are Microsoft and Netscape. Both companies have accepted the ISAPI standard, so you can avoid the problems and limitations that accompany both CGI and Win-CGI.

At this point, you should have a good understanding of the concepts behind the development of Web server applications. It's time now to use the tools that Delphi provides to implement some of these ideas and create an ISAPI DLL that responds to a client's request with some valid HTML pages. To start off simply, you learn how to get your server-side extension to return a standard HTML page—this page will be the same every time it is requested. The purpose of this is to show the mechanics of getting a simple HTML page back to the client through a Web server application as compared to the standard request-respond process of the HTTP server.

Returning a Static HTML Page

Beginning the creation of an ISAPI DLL is similar to the development of other standard DLLs. You start by beginning a new project as shown in the following list:

1. From the main menu, choose File, New. This brings up the New Items dialog box as shown in Figure 28.1.

FIG. 28.1
The New Items dialog box.

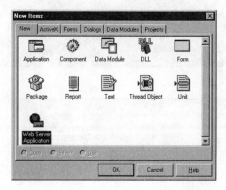

2. Click to select Web Server Application, then click OK. This brings up the New Web Server Application dialog box (see Figure 28.2).

3. ISAPI/NSAPI Dynamic Link Library is the default choice, so click OK.

   At this point, you have the framework in place to develop an ISAPI server-side extension. Notice that this project includes a WebModule(see Figure 28.3)—this isn't much different from a standard DataModule. It allows you to drop down components and work with them interactively. As you will see later in the chapter, this includes database components. This simplifies development by taking advantage of the Delphi IDE.

   Just as you can develop standard DLLs to export several functions, you also can do so with ISAPI DLLs. This is done through the use of WebDispatcher ActionItems.

Part

VI

Ch

28

FIG. 28.2
The New Web Server
Application dialog box.

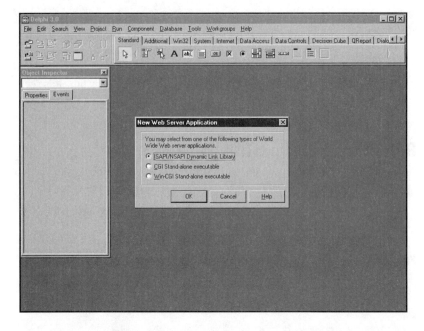

FIG. 28.3
A blank Web server
application, with your
empty WebModule.

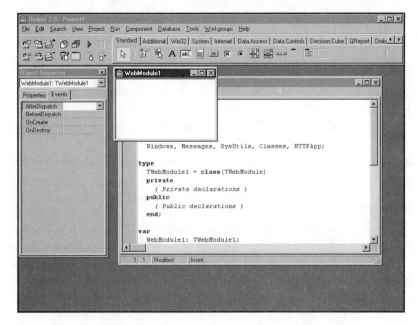

Each WebModule contains a default WebDispatcher. The WebDispatcher is the traffic cop of
your Web server application. Each time you request the ISAPI DLL from your Web browser,
WebDispatcher determines which ActionItem to perform. WebDispatcher does this by keeping

track of all the ActionItems available, checking their properties, and determining if an ActionItem's OnAction event should be carried out. To better see how this works, create an ActionItem to facilitate the return of your first static HTML page.

To create an ActionItem, you must bring up the Action Editor. As with many property editors in Delphi, you can do this in one of three ways:

- Double-click the Web Module.
- Right-click the WebModule, and then choose Action Editor.
- Click the Actions property in the Object Inspector while the WebModule has focus. This presents an ellipses (...) in the Object Inspector. Click the ellipses to bring up the Action Editor.

After bringing up the Action Editor, follow these steps:

1. With the Action Editor displayed, click Add to create the first ActionItem.
2. Click the ActionItem (WebActionItem1) in the Action Editor to highlight it. Its properties become available in the Object Inspector to edit.
3. Give the ActionItem a relevant name by changing the Name property to something like **aiStatic**.
4. Next, you need to bind the ActionItem with a URI. Use **HelloWorld** in the PathInfo property for this one.

At this point, your project should look like the one pictured in Figure 28.4.

FIG. 28.4
Delphi's Action Editor with one ActionItem added and the Object Inspector after its properties have been altered.

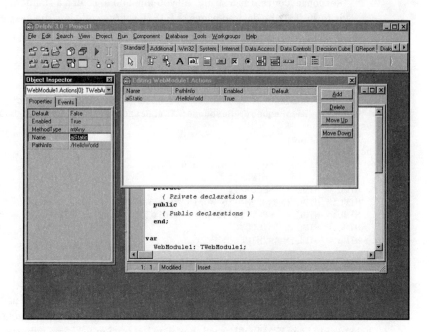

Assigning the URI to the ActionItem is like naming a method. Think of it in terms of YourDll.HelloWorld. Give your DLL a name as well. Do this in the usual manner—the name of the project determines the name of the DLL. Naming the unit doesn't matter much under these circumstances, so Unit1 suffices as well as any other name.

1. Save the project as **WEBDEMO.DPR**. This names your ISAPI DLL **WEBDEMO.DLL.**

2. Next, you need to put some code behind the ActionItem. Select the Events tab of the Object Inspector. You see that ActionItems has only one event, OnAction, exposed.

3. Double-click the OnAction event in the Object Inspector to have Delphi generate the procedure template.

   Delphi generates the following code:

```
procedure TWebModule1.WebModule1Actions0Action(Sender: TObject;
  Request: TWebRequest; Response: TWebResponse; var Handled: Boolean);
begin

end;
```

   Don't worry about most of this for now. The only parameter you're concerned with when returning a static page is the Response parameter. You use this TWebResponse object to return your HTML page; this object has a Content property that serves the purpose. As you may recall, an HTTP server responds to a browser's request with two entities, the header and the content. Delphi creates the header for you based on defaults, so you only need to worry about the content.

   Response.Content is a string. All you must do to return a standard static HTML page is to stuff all the desired pages of HTML source code into the Response.Content parameter.

4. Add HTML to the Content property of the Response object.

Here is the code to add to the procedure:

```
procedure TWebModule1.WebModule1Actions0Action(Sender: TObject;
  Request: TWebRequest; Response: TWebResponse; var Handled: Boolean);
var
  HTML: string;
begin
  // These few lines use standard HTML.
  HTML:=          '<HTML>';
  HTML:= HTML + '<BODY>';
  HTML:= HTML + '<H1>Hello World Wide Web</H1>';
  HTML:= HTML + '<P>This is an example of a static HTML page.</P>';
  HTML:= HTML + '</BODY>';
  HTML:= HTML + '</HTML>';

  Response.Content := HTML;
end;
```

Congratulations! You have your first Web server application. Go ahead and compile it. If you know how to test it, go ahead and do so, and then feel free to skip the next section. If you need help testing your ISAPI DLL, read the following section for some pointers.

Deploying/Testing Your ISAPI DLL

Much of the way you test your DLL depends on your individual setup, but a few general things apply to all situations. As you know by now, ISAPI DLLs currently work on only a few Windows WWW servers. You must have an ISAPI-compliant HTTP server to use these server-side extensions. If your HTTP server supports ISAPI, then it probably created a directory specifically for these DLLs during setup. With Microsoft's Personal Web Server for Windows 95, this directory is named `scripts`. The WWW server is configured within the server's administrator application to allow DLLs to be executed from this directory. You need to determine which directory this is on your machine.

Next, you need to know the URL needed to invoke the appropriate ActionItem within the DLL. For example, if your server is at **www.server.com** and the directory for your ISAPI extensions is `scripts` and is directly off the server's root directory, then the correct URL is as follows:

> **http://www.server.com/scripts/WebDemo.dll/HelloWorld**

When you enter this in your WWW browser, you get back something that resembles Figure 28.5.

FIG. 28.5
The browser here shows the results of calling the new ISAPI extension.

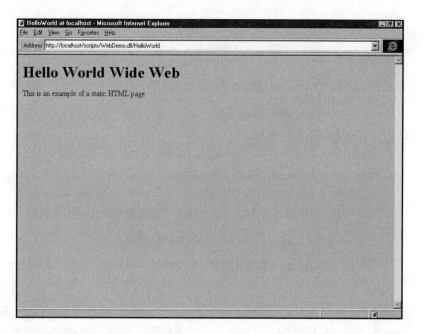

Returning a Dynamic HTML Page

Now that you can send a static page back to a browser, alter the extension slightly to return a page that changes each time it's requested. For this example, include the date and time that the page is created. If you take a moment to review how you created the static page, you should be able to figure out the dynamic version on your own.

The key to producing this type of page is that no input is required from the client. The date and time are dynamic, but not dependent on any interaction with the requester. Thus, all that's necessary is to include the system date and time in your HTML. Instead of altering your existing ActionItem, add a second ActionItem to the project and have that item return the current date and time. Here are the steps:

1. If you haven't done so already, load the existing WebDemo project into Delphi's IDE.
2. Bring up the Action Editor and add a second ActionItem.
3. Change the name of the second ActionItem to **aiDynamic** and the `PathInfo` to **/DateTime**.
4. Double-click the `OnAction` event for the second ActionItem, then add the following code:

```
procedure TWebModule1.WebModule1Actions1Action(Sender: TObject;
  Request: TWebRequest; Response: TWebResponse; var Handled: Boolean);
var
  HTML: string;
begin
  // These few lines use standard HTML.
  HTML :=         '<HTML>';
  HTML := HTML + '<BODY>';
  HTML := HTML + '<H1>The Current Date and Time is...</H1>';
  HTML := HTML + DateTimeToStr(Now);
  HTML := HTML + '</BODY>';
  HTML := HTML + '</HTML>';

  Response.Content := HTML;
end;
```

All that you're doing in this procedure is including the current date and time. This is obtained through the system clock of the server via Delphi's Now function. The resulting DateTime variable is converted to a string and added to your HTML source.

Compile and test the expanded ISAPI DLL. To get to the new ActionItem, you need to alter the URL that you request. In keeping with the earlier example, the new URL is as follows:

http://www.server.com/scripts/WebDemo.dll/DateTime

The returned page should resemble Figure 28.6.

You're ready now to take things a bit farther and base your dynamic page on some input from the client.

 TIP If you ran `WebDemo.dll/HelloWorld` earlier, it may still be in your server's memory. You may want to review your server's documentation on how to flush the DLL to allow you to overwrite it with a new DLL. If all else fails, you usually can achieve this by restarting the WWW server.

FIG. 28.6
The browser shows the returned page, displaying the current date and time.

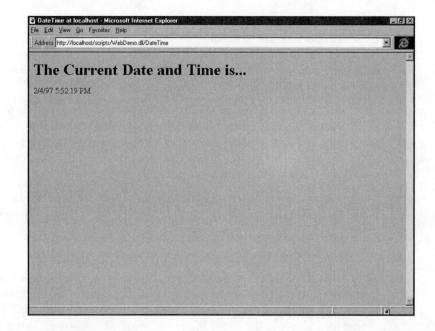

Using User Input Parameters

At this point, you should look at the rest of the parameters in the OnAction event that were ignored to this point. Here's how the OnAction event looks:

```
procedure TWebModule1.WebModule1Actions1Action(Sender: TObject;
  Request: TWebRequest; Response: TWebResponse; var Handled: Boolean);
begin

end;
```

The parameter that gives you access to the user's input is the Request parameter. The TWebRequest object has four properties, defined in the following table, of interest at this time:

Property	Definition
Query	A string of all the parameters obtained through a GET request
QueryFields	A parsed form of Query
Content	A string of all the parameters obtained through a POST request
ContentFields	A parsed form of Content

We have no choice but to put Delphi aside for a moment and talk about GET, POST, and the formation of an URL through the use of HTML forms.

Part
VI

Ch
28

GET* and *POST   GET and POST are the methods used by HTTP clients to request information from HTTP servers. The GET method attempts to retrieve a document from the server by reading a page. The POST method requests the opportunity to write to the server, at which point most servers provide a return page in response. The information that is requested is sent to the server through the request. The easiest example is a simple GET.

You may have noticed the use of the GET method while working with any of the popular search engines available on the Internet these days. The URI your browser requests after you fill out a search form and hit the submit button is a longer-than-usual URL that has some extra stuff after the "normal" URL you're used to. These extra characters are an encoded form of the information on the HTML form you've just filled out.

The format for these parameters is simple enough. At the end of a standard URL, a question mark (?) is added. The parameters are then tacked on in the format *name=value*. For example, assume that the URI of the page being requested is as follows:

> **http://www.server.com/search/results.dll?keyword=Delphi**

This means that there's only one parameter, named keyword, which holds the value Delphi. If there were more than one parameter, they would be separated by an ampersand (&). If any of the values contained spaces, the spaces will be replaced by the plus sign (+). For example, if a subject parameter with the value Web server applications were added to the preceding example, the following URI would result:

> **http://www.server.com/search/results.dll?keyword=Delphi&subject=web+server+applications**

The Use of HTML Forms   Typing such URIs by hand can result in many typos. You can solve this by hard-coding the URIs into links on an HTML page, but this requires a separate link for each variation in the URI. A more practical approach is to use HTML forms to create the URIs on-the-fly. Although this chapter doesn't go into depth on the use of HTML forms, you see a sample HTML page using a form, and learn how it can be used to simplify your next ISAPI DLL. Listing 28.1 shows the HTML code, which you can find on this book's companion CD-ROM.

Listing 28.1   \UDELPHI3\CHP28\FORM01.HTM—A Web Page, Containing Two Forms for Input

```
<html>

<head>
<title>Web Server Applications</title>
</head>

<body>

<h1 align="center">Web Server Applications</h1>
```

```
<h2>Parsed HTML File</h2>

<p>This example shows how an ISAPI DLL is used to parse a
standard HTML page and replace TTags with data
determined at run time.</p>

<p>To see this example, fill out the following form and
submit.</p>

<hr>
<p>This form uses the GET method</p>

<form action="../scripts/WebDemo.dll/ParseFile" method="GET">
<p>Name: <input type="text" size="20" name="Name"></p>
<p>Address: <input type="text" size="20" name="Address"></p>
<p>Phone: <input type="text" size="20" name="Phone"></p>
<p>E-mail: <input type="text" size="20" name="email"></p>
<p><input type="submit"><input type="reset"></p>
</form>

<hr>
<p>This form uses the POST method</p>

<form action="../scripts/WebDemo.dll/ParseFile" method="POST">
<p>Name: <input type="text" size="20" name="Name"></p>
<p>Address: <input type="text" size="20" name="Address"></p>
<p>Phone: <input type="text" size="20" name="Phone"></p>
<p>E-mail: <input type="text" size="20" name="email"></p>
<p><input type="submit"><input type="reset"></p>
</form>

</body>
</html>
```

The page in Listing 28.1 actually contains two forms. Each form is bracketed by the <FORM> and </FORM> tags. Each form has two buttons, one to reset the form (<INPUT TYPE="reset">) and one to submit the form (<INPUT TYPE="submit">). When the submit button is clicked, it performs some action; this action is described in the line with the <FORM> tag. For the first form on this page, the action is your WebDemo ISAPI DLL and the action item you're about to create. Notice that the first form uses the GET method and the second form uses the POST method.

When this page is loaded into the browser, it presents several edit boxes to the user via the <INPUT TYPE="text"> tags. Each edit box has an associated name and its value is determined by what the user enters in the edit box. When the submit button is clicked, the browser does all the work of formatting the requested URI.

To better understand how this all works, you can add an ActionItem to WEBDEMO.DLL that will use the input from this form.

Part
VI

Ch
28

The TPageProducer Component   Now's the time to take advantage of another of the new Internet components, TPageProducer, included with Delphi 3. TPageProducer assists you through the use of templates that can be parsed by this component to create your dynamic HTML output. The component works by taking either a text file or TStrings as input, parsing the input for special TTags, and replacing those tags with data determined at runtime. TPageProducer then returns a completed HTML page for the server to send to the browser.

On the CD

In the sample project, you will take the information gathered from your form and present the user with a Thank You page that repeats the information the user provided and tells him that he'll be contacted soon. Since this page will be the same every time—with the exception of the input data—you can use a template for the page. Listing 28.2 shows the code for this template, which you can find on this book's companion CD-ROM.

Listing 28.2   \UDELPHI3\CHP28\THANKYOU.HTM—Template for the Thank You Page

```
<html>

<head>
<title>Thank You</title>
</head>

<body>

<h1>Thank you for filling out our survey.</h1>

<h3>The following is a copy of the information that we received.</h3>

<table border="0">
    <tr>
        <td>Name:</td>
        <td><#Name></td>
    </tr>
    <tr>
        <td>Address:</td>
        <td><#Address></td>
    </tr>
    <tr>
        <td>Phone:</td>
        <td><#Phone></td>
    </tr>
    <tr>
        <td>E-mail:</td>
        <td><#email></td>
    </tr>
</table>

<h5>We will be contacting you shortly.</h5>
</body>
</html>
```

What you should notice about this file are the *TTags* (these are tags such as <#NAME> and <#EMAIL>). When TPageProducer processes this template, it triggers an OnHTMLTag event for each tag it encounters. The procedure for the OnHTMLTag event is your chance to determine which TTag has triggered the event, then tell TPageProducer what to substitute for that TTag. You need to follow these steps:

1. Put a copy of the HTML template on your server and note its full path.
2. If you haven't done so already, load the existing WebDemo project into Delphi's IDE.
3. Drop down a TPageProducer component from the Internet tab.
4. Set the HTMLFile property of TPageProducer to point to the HTML template. (Note: UNC paths/filenames are acceptable and, in many cases, will be safer than hard-coded drive letters and paths.)
5. Select the Events tab in the Object Inspector and double-click the OnHTMLTag event to add code to it (see Figure 28.7).

CAUTION

Make sure that you use the correct path to the template. This must be the path to the file on the server, not on the development machine (if they're different machines).

FIG. 28.7
The WebDemo project now has the TPageProducer component added.

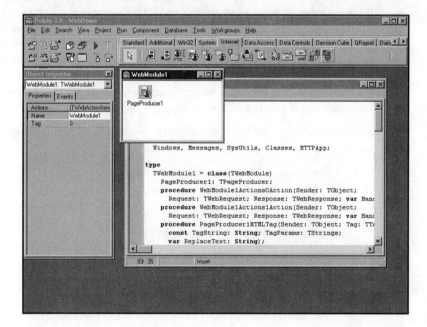

Although this procedure requires little code, the code that's there accomplishes a great deal:

```
procedure TWebModule1.PageProducer1HTMLTag(Sender: TObject; Tag: TTag;
  const TagString: String; TagParams: TStrings; var ReplaceText: String);
var
  Data : TStrings;
begin
  Data:= nil;
  with Request do begin
    case MethodType of
      mtPost: Data:= ContentFields;
      mtGet : Data:= QueryFields;
    end;
    ReplaceText := Data.Values[TagString];
  end;
end;
```

The most confusing part is getting access to the input parameters sent from the browser. Although the Request object is not passed as a parameter directly to this procedure, it still is accessible. After you get access to the Request property, you must check MethodType because the parameters passed from the browser are stored in different properties, based upon the method used. If MethodType is mtGet, the parameters are stored in QueryFields; if the method is mtPost, the parameters are stored in ContentFields.

The next step is to determine which TTag caused the event to fire and replace it with the appropriate value from the input parameters. In this example, the <#EMAIL> TTag gets replaced with the value from the e-mail input box on the form. You use the Values method to do this. Values is a useful method that allows you to access everything to the right of the equal sign (=) by telling the method what's to the left. This is possible because you're using the ContentFields or QueryFields property instead of the Content or Query property. The ContentFields or QueryFields property automatically parses the input string and separates each *name=value* pair into a TStrings object.

All that remains is to set up an ActionItem to perform the action (see Figure 28.8), which is shown in the following steps:

1. Add a new ActionItem to your WebDemo project.

2. Set the name to **aiParseFile** and the PathInfo to **/ParseFile**.

3. For the OnAction event, add the following code:

```
Response.Content := PageProducer1.Content;
```

4. Compile WebDemo again with the changes you made, and put the new DLL in your HTTP server's script directory.

5. Put Form01.htm on your WWW server. Make sure that the action in your forms points properly to WebDemo.dll.

6. Put the HTML template ThankYou.htm in the location you specified in the PageProducer1.HTMLFile property.

7. Request Form01.htm with your WWW browser.

8. Fill out the top form and click its submit button.

   Check the URL in your browser. Notice the passed URI, which should be complete with the parameters and values you entered in the form.

   Return to the form page.

9. Fill out the bottom form and click its submit button.

   Notice that, because you've used the POST method, the parameters do not appear in the passed URI. This is valuable when passing passwords!

FIG. 28.8
Form in browser.

You can see the results of GET and POST in Figures 28.9 and 28.10, respectively.

FIG. 28.9

Results of GET.

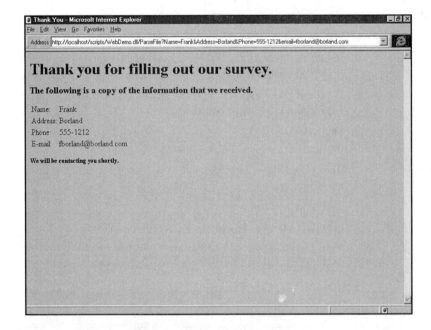

FIG. 28.10

Results of POST.

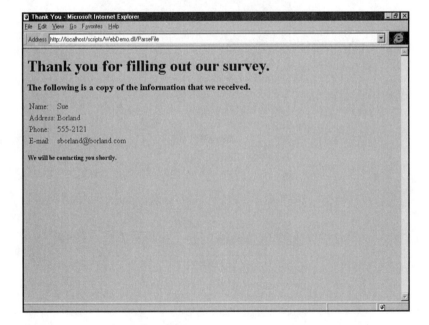

Adding Database Connectivity

So far, you've returned static pages and pages based on user input. In this section, you use existing databases to determine what to return to the client. To do so, you need a few more of the new Internet components included with Delphi 3.

The TDataSetTableProducer produces output in the form of a standard HTML table based on a standard dataset object. This dataset object can be a TTable, a TQuery, or one of the new datasets available in Delphi 3. TQueryTableProducer differs from TDataSetTableProducer in that it works with queries that have parameters (TParams) in the SQL.

As usual, the best way to learn is through doing, so try adding some functionality to WebDemo.dll by using the new components and taking the following steps:

1. If you haven't done so already, load the existing WebDemo project into Delphi's IDE.
2. Drop down a TSession component from the Data Access tab.
3. Set the AutoSessionName property of the TSession to True.
4. Drop down a TDataSetTableProducer from the Internet tab.
5. Drop down a TTable from the Data Access tab.
6. Set the Table1.Database name to **DBDEMOS**.
7. Set Table1.TableName to **CUSTOMER.DB**.
8. Set TDataSetTableProducer1.DataSet to **Table1**.
9. Set TDataSetTableProducer1.MaxRows to **200**.

You've now added a TSession component to handle the administrative details of allowing multiple connections to the database. Don't forget that we are creating a DLL and, as such, multiple instances of it can be running simultaneously. Each of these must maintain its own session. The TTable was pointed to the dataset in which you're interested, and TDataSetTableProducer is set to base the table it produces on whatever's in the TTable. The MaxRows property tells TDataSetTableProducer to limit a table to no more than 200 rows of data. Because TDataSetTableProducer sends back the whole table, you should limit it to a few fields in this example, using the standard method of limiting which fields appear in a table:

1. Right-click the TTable component and choose the Fields Editor.
2. Right-click within the Fields Editor and choose Add Fields.
3. Select only the CustNo, Company, City, State, and Phone fields.

Okay, you've installed the plumbing to produce an HTML-formatted table that can be read by a WWW browser, but the table lacks context. Only raw data from the dataset is returned at this point. Fortunately, TDataSetTableProducer also provides Header and Footer properties to give the table some context. Header and Footer are both TStrings, so can add additional HTML code as you previously did in Delphi with other properties of type TStrings. You can set these properties through the Object Inspector.

You should add the following HTML to the Header and Footer properties of the TDataSetTableProducer in your project.

DataSetTableProducer1.Header :=

```
<html>

<head>
<title>For Internal Use Only</title>
</head>

<!-- Note: You will need to change the image source
     to reflect the true location of the image
     on your system -->

<body>

<center>
<h1><font color="#FF0000">For Internal Use Only</font></h1>
<p><img src="http://localhost/Warning.gif" width="28" height="28"></p>
</center>

<!-- Header.htm ends here -->
```

TDataSetTableProducer.Footer :=

```
<!-- Footer.htm begins here -->

<hr>
<p>Send any corrections to
<a href="mailto:jsmith@company.com">John Smith</a>

</body>
</html>
```

The properties have been set, so we need to put some code behind it.

1. Add another ActionItem to your DLL. Set the name to **aiDataSet** and the PathInfo to **/ShowTable**.

2. Add appropriate code to the OnAction event for the new ActionItem.
   ```
   procedure TWebModule1.WebModule1Actions3Action(Sender: TObject;
     Request: TWebRequest; Response: TWebResponse; var Handled: Boolean);
   begin
     with DataSetTableProducer1 do begin
       // Set Caption
       Caption:= '<H1>Phone List</H1>';
       // Set Caption Alignment [caBottom, caDefault, caTop]
       CaptionAlignment:= caTop;

       // Open DataSet
       DataSet.Open;
       // Respond with table
       Response.Content := DataSetTableProducer1.Content;
   ```

```
    // Close DataSet
    DataSet.Close;
  end; // for with
end;
```

3. Put the image (`warning.gif`) on the server, and alter the HTML in the `Header` property to point to the location of this image (see Figure 28.11).

4. Compile the DLL, move it to the server, and test it.

FIG. 28.11

WebDemo now has database connectivity components added.

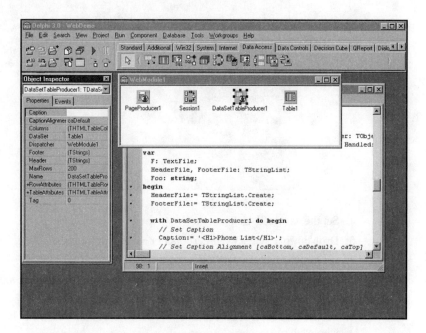

Taking Advantage of Added Features in TQueryTableProducer The last ActionItem added to your Web server application takes advantage of the added database connectivity inherent in TDataSetTableProducer. TQueryTableProducer goes even further—this component parses the input parameters for you and inserts them into the proper location in a SQL statement with TParams embedded. You only need set up the TQuery component in the standard fashion, and TQueryTableProducer does the rest (see Figure 28.12). The following steps show what you do:

1. Drop down a standard TQuery component from the Data Access tab.

2. Set the `DatabaseName` property to **DBDEMOS**.

3. Set the `SQL` property to:
```
SELECT MASTER."SYMBOL" AS Symbol, MASTER."RCMNDATION" AS Recommend,
➥ INDUSTRY."IND_NAME" AS Industry
FROM "MASTER.DBF" MASTER , "INDUSTRY.DBF" INDUSTRY
WHERE ( MASTER.INDUSTRY = INDUSTRY.IND_CODE ) AND
( ( MASTER."RISK" =:Risk ) AND ( MASTER."RATING" =:Rate ) )
ORDER BY INDUSTRY."IND_NAME"
```

Part
VI

Ch

28

FIG. 28.12

This is how the table is returned in the browser.

4. Set the Rate and Risk parameters to the strings data type.

5. Drop down a TQueryTableProducer component from the Internet tab.

6. Set its Query property to **Query1**.

7. Set the RowAttributes.Align property to **haCenter** to center-align the data in the table's cells.

8. Set the TableAttributes.Border property to **1**. This puts a thin border around the whole table.

You now have set up the TQuery and have pointed TQueryTableProducer at it. When you call the ActionItem associated with this component, it passes parameters (in the same format as always) through the URI and the Request object. These parameters match the TParams inserted in the SQL statement, and TQueryTableProducer (see Figure 28.13) sets them in the same manner in which they would be used in a standard database application.

You continue by adding another ActionItem to your project. Set the name to **aiQueryTable** and the PathInfo to **/Query**. Then, add code to the OnAction event as explained in the following paragraph and code.

FIG. 28.13
WebDemo now has
TQueryTableProducer
added.

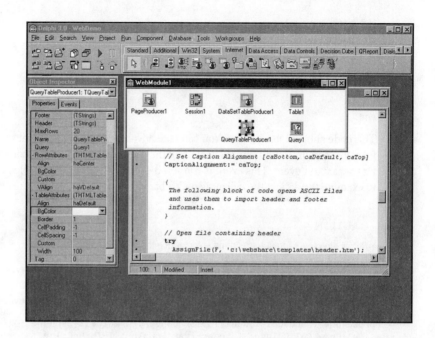

TQueryTableProducer has Header and Footer properties just like TDataSetTableProducer. The following code uses these properties, along with the Caption property, to produce the desired output:

```
procedure TWebModule1.WebModule1Actions4Action(Sender: TObject;
  Request: TWebRequest; Response: TWebResponse; var Handled: Boolean);
begin
  with QueryTableProducer1 do begin

    Caption:= 'Stock Recommendations';

    Header.Add('<HTML>');
    Header.Add('<BODY>');

    Footer.Add('</BODY>');
    Footer.Add('</HTML>');

    // Establish Link
    Query := Query1;

    // Open Query
    Query.Open;
```

Part
VI

Ch

28

```
    // Return Results
    Response.Content := QueryTableProducer1.Content;

    // Close Query
    Query.Close;

  end;
end;
```

This code should look familiar. You can take advantage of another event to add some meaning-ful color to your ActionItem. Inspection of the TQueryTableProducer component reveals the OnFormatCell event. This event is triggered each time the cell of a table is formatted. Use this to examine the data in the cell and apply a background color to make the cell stand out better.

CAUTION

Not all browsers support background colors within the cells of a table. This does work correctly, however, in Internet Explorer 3.x.

You can accomplish this with the following code for the OnFormatCell event:

```
procedure TWebModule1.QueryTableProducer1FormatCell(Sender: TObject;
  CellRow, CellColumn: Integer; var BgColor: THTMLBgColor;
  var Align: THTMLAlign; var VAlign: THTMLVAlign; var CustomAttrs,
  CellData: String);
begin
  If      CellData = 'BUY'   then BgColor:= 'Green'
  else if CellData = 'SELL'  then BgColor:= 'Red'
  else if CellData = 'HOLD'  then BgColor:= 'White';
end;
```

You can see that this event exposes several useful things. You could look at CellRow, for ex-ample, and alternate shading rows by varying BgColor. You also could change the horizontal and vertical alignment.

On the CD

Compile the project again with the newest ActionItem. Use the HTML page in Listing 28.3 to test the revised project (see Figures 28.14 and 28.15), which you can find on this book's com-panion CD-ROM.

Listing 28.3   /UDELPHI3/CHP28/FORM02.HTM—Form for Testing the *aiQueryTable* ActionItem

```
<html>

<head>
<title>Web Server Applications</title>
</head>

<body bgcolor="#FFFFFF">
```

```
<h1 align="center">Web Server Applications</h1>

<h2>Show Table From Query</h2>

    <p>This example shows how an ISAPI DLL is used to return a
    standard HTML page containing a table based on a Query.</p>
    <form action="../scripts/WebDemo.dll/Query" method="POST">
        <p>Rate: <select name="Rate" size="1">
            <option>A</option>
            <option>B</option>
            <option>C</option>
        </select></p>
        <p>Risk: <select name="Risk" size="1">
            <option>LOW</option>
            <option>MED</option>
            <option>HIGH</option>
        </select></p>
        <p><input type="submit"><input type="reset"></p>
    </form>

</body>
 </html>
```

FIG. 28.14

Form02.htm, with values chosen.

Part

VI

Ch

28

FIG. 28.15

The query shown in Figure 28.14 leads to these results.

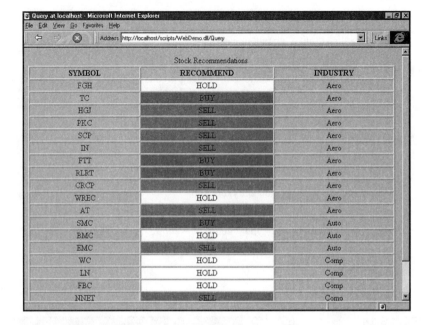

Putting It All Together

Now that you created your first ISAPI DLL in Delphi 3, you realize how simple it really is. The main concerns are learning how to get access to the input parameters sent from the form and learning how to return HTML to the browser.

The major thing to remember at this point is that you aren't very limited in what you can do. You know how to create tables based on TTable and TQuery objects, and the possibilities for what you can do with these tools are endless.

Your mind is probably already racing, thinking up new and creative ways to take advantage of Web server applications. You undoubtedly will want more control over the appearance of the forms that serve as your interface with the end user, and will want to create spectacular output based on your results. This is where scripting languages, ActiveX controls, and the other technologies outside of Delphi that I previously mentioned come into play. ●

CHAPTER 29

Working with Delphi's Open Tools API

by Todd Miller

Have you ever wished that the Delphi IDE did more than it currently does? For example, wouldn't it be nice if the IDE allowed you to move entire projects from one folder to another, or allowed you to search the VCL source code for keywords, and then load a source file directly into the code editor? (These were some of the enhancements on my personal wish list.) Well, with Delphi's Open Tools API, it's easy to add to the IDE's functionality. You can create any add-on tools you want to enhance the Delphi environment. This chapter focuses on Delphi's Open Tools API and the process of creating Delphi experts.

You may have noticed while working with the built-in Delphi experts that they are called "Wizards." The TeeChart Wizard and the QuickReports are two examples. This is merely a marketing change by Borland. In this chapter, I continue to refer to experts as "Experts" because the key elements of the Open Tools API use this term throughout what little documentation is found in the source code; I use this term so that I don't confuse the issue. ■

Delphi's Open Tools API

Learn about the various services that Delphi's Open Tools API provides.

Delphi experts

Find out how to create and register the four types of IDE experts.

ToolServices, the gateway to Delphi

Examine the core Open Tools API interface, `ToolServices`, which is used to directly manipulate the Delphi IDE.

The *Open Tools API* is a set of class interfaces that allow you to perform many of the same tasks as the Delphi IDE itself. Within an IDE expert, the Open Tools API can be used to perform many services, including the following:

- Obtain project information
- Obtain unit and form information
- Manipulate project modules (open, add, close, create, and so on)
- Manipulate project resources (icons, bitmaps, cursors, and so on)
- Manipulate Delphi menus
- Provide project-change notifications
- Provide module-change notifications

The Open Tools API is accessible only from code running as part of the Delphi IDE. This is where *experts* come into play. Experts are special component-like programs that, when registered, can work directly with the Delphi IDE to do the tasks just listed, and more.

In this chapter, you learn how to create and register experts, and then you examine the `ToolServices` interface used to directly manipulate the Delphi IDE and projects in particular. Finally, you look at some specific services that the Open Tools API provides, such as menu and editor management.

N O T E This chapter covers the Open Tools API as it's defined in Delphi 3. The experts written in this chapter may not work in Delphi 1 due to numerous subsequent changes in the Open Tools API. This chapter doesn't discuss the differences between Delphi versions 1, 2 and 3, so if you need to write experts that can be used on earlier Delphi platforms, consult Ray Lischner's *Secrets of Delphi 2* (Waite Group Press). ■

Creating a Delphi Expert

To create a new expert, you simply derive a new class from the `TIExpert` class, overriding particular methods that are required (based on the expert style) to tell Delphi about your expert. `TIExpert` is defined as an *abstract virtual class*, which means that its functionality is defined but not implemented. The methods of the `TIExpert` class are designed to provide information to the Delphi IDE about your expert so that the IDE knows what to do with your expert, plus critical details such as how the expert will be activated.

Expert Styles

Before exploring the various `TIExpert` methods, review the types of experts that Delphi allows you to create. The four expert styles are *standard*, *add-in*, *form*, and *project*. Table 29.1 describes how each style of expert is invoked by the user within the Delphi IDE.

Table 29.1 The Four Delphi Expert Styles

Style	How It Is Invoked
Standard	Menu item added to the Delphi Help menu
Add-in	Menu item added to an expert-specified Delphi menu
Form	Expert icon added to the File, New, Forms page of the New Items dialog box
Project	Expert icon added to the File, New, Projects page of the New Items dialog box

The primary difference between various expert styles is how the user invokes the expert from within the Delphi IDE. In other words, the style of the expert has no effect on how and when an expert can work with the Open Tools API. Of course, the style of expert you choose does imply the expert's purpose to the user, after the expert has been registered in the Delphi IDE. (Registration of experts is covered in a following section of this chapter.)

Standard experts are the simplest to design because you only have to provide the menu text that will be added to the Delphi Help menu, and specify whether or not the new help menu item is enabled. Though standard experts are the easiest to set up, most professional experts are add-in experts, because then the expert's menu items can be added almost anywhere on the Delphi IDE's menu. Form and project experts are designed to be invoked when a user wants to create specialized forms or projects. Form and project experts tend to use the module-management services of the Open Tools API more extensively than standard or add-in experts.

N O T E The Open Tools API source code is available only in the Delphi Developer and Client Server products. The compiled units, however, are available in all Delphi products. The source code is located in the ..\DELPHI 3\SOURCE\TOOLSAPI folder. ■

Implementing *TIExpert*

As many as ten methods may need to be overridden in a new expert descending from the TIExpert class interface. The particular methods you need to override are determined by the style of expert you choose. Listing 29.1 shows the abstract class definition for TIExpert.

Listing 29.1 EXPTINTF.PAS—Abstract Class Definition of *TIExpert*

```
TIExpert = class(TInterface)
  public
    { Expert UI strings }
    function GetName: string; virtual; stdcall; abstract;
    function GetAuthor: string; virtual; stdcall; abstract;
    function GetComment: string; virtual; stdcall; abstract;
```

continues

Listing 29.1 Continued

```
    function GetPage: string; virtual; stdcall; abstract;
    function GetGlyph: HICON; virtual; stdcall; abstract;
    function GetStyle: TExpertStyle; virtual; stdcall; abstract;
    function GetState: TExpertState; virtual; stdcall; abstract;
    function GetIDString: string; virtual; stdcall; abstract;
    function GetMenuText: string; virtual; stdcall; abstract;
    procedure Execute; virtual; stdcall; abstract;
  end;
```

The following sections take a closer look at the `TIExpert` methods to show when and why you would override particular methods when creating an expert. What you see as you read about each of the `TIExpert`'s methods is that each is intended to return a particular attribute about the expert to the Delphi IDE. Consequently, each method will consist of a Result := *something>* line, which you will see shortly.

The *GetStyle* Method   As mentioned previously in this chapter, every expert has a specified style. The four possible styles are standard, add-in, form, and project (`esStandard`, `esAddin`, `esForm`, and `esProject`). To specify a standard expert, you would return the `esStandard` constant as follows.

```
Result := esStandard;
```

If `GetStyle` returns `esStandard`, the IDE treats the expert as a simple Help menu expert. If `GetStyle` returns `esAddin`, the IDE assumes that the expert will add its own menu item(s) to the IDE. (How this is done with the Open Tools menu interface is discussed in a following section of this chapter.) If `GetStyle` returns `esForm` or `esProject`, the IDE treats the expert like a form or project expert that will show up on the Forms or Projects tabs in the Net Items dialog, respectively.

The *GetIDString* Method   `GetIDString` must be overridden by all experts. This simply is a text string that uniquely identifies the expert as different from any other registered expert. Borland recommends the following format for the ID string:

> *CompanyName.ExpertFunction*

Here's an example of returning a unique text ID for a project information expert that, in this case, combines a shortened version of the book title and the purpose of the expert itself:

```
Result := 'UDelphi3.ProjectInfoExpert';
```

If you ever decide to copy an existing expert to create a new one, make sure that you change this value to something different because Delphi doesn't like two experts with the same ID string.

The *GetName* Method   The `GetName` method also is a required method that must be overridden. This method needs to return a short descriptive name for the expert you're writing.

Here's an example of returning the display name of a project information expert:

```
Result := 'Project Information Expert'
```

If you write a Form or Project expert, then this name will show up under the expert's icon in the New Items dialog box in the Delphi IDE.

The *GetMenuText* Method   This method is required only for standard (esStandard style) experts. It returns the menu text that will be inserted into the Delphi IDE's Help menu to allow the user to invoke the expert.

> **N O T E** This method will be called every time the Help menu is opened, so it's possible for your expert to be context-sensitive. ∎

Here's an example of returning the menu text for a project information expert:

```
Result := 'UD3 Project Information Expert...'
```

The *GetState* Method   This method, which is required only for standard experts, is called by the IDE to determine if the Help menu expert is to be enabled or checked. The possible values that can be returned are esEnabled and esChecked.

> **N O T E** Like GetMenuText, GetState is called every time the Help menu is opened, so it's possible for your expert to be context-sensitive. ∎

Here's an example of returning the esEnabled set value—indicating to the Delphi IDE that the expert's menu text is to be enabled on the IDE's Help menu:

```
Result := [esEnabled]
```

The *Execute* Method   This method is required for standard, form, and project experts. Execute is called whenever the user selects the Help menu item for the expert (or selects the expert icon on the Forms or Projects page of the New Items dialog box). An add-in expert doesn't invoke the Execute method, because it has its own click event handler if it has added a menu item to the Delphi IDE.

The Execute method usually is responsible for bringing up the expert dialog box. The following code shows a typical Execute method:

```
procedure TProjectInfoExpert.Execute;
begin
  if not Assigned(ProjectInfoForm) then
    ProjectInfoForm := TProjectInfoForm.Create(Application);
  ProjectInfoForm.Show;
  ProjectInfoForm.SetFocus
end;
```

This code first checks to see if the expert dialog box has already been created. If not, the code dynamically creates the dialog box. After this dialog box is created, the code displays it and sets the focus to it.

It's the programmer's responsibility to destroy all dialog boxes created by an expert when the expert's unit is unloaded. This destruction usually is done in the Finalization section of a unit.

The *GetPage* Method   This method is required for form and project experts. It returns the name of the page to which the form or project expert is to be added in the New Items dialog box.

Here's an example:

```
Result := 'Projects';
```

The *GetGlyph* Method   This method is required for form and project experts. GetGlyph returns a handle to an icon to be displayed in the form (or project) list boxes and dialog boxes. If 0 is returned, the default icon is displayed.

Here's an example:

```
Result := LoadIcon(Hinstance, 'MYICON');
```

The *GetAuthor* Method   This method is required for form and project experts. It returns the author's or company's name who created the expert. The author of a form or project expert appears in the New Items dialog box when a user views the list in Detail mode.

Here's an example:

```
Result := 'Todd Miller';
```

The *GetComment* Method   This method is required for form and project experts. GetComment returns a one- or two-sentence description of the form or project expert. Form or project expert comments appear in the Object Repository when a user views the list in Detail mode.

Here's an example:

```
Result := 'DLL project expert.  Write Delphi 1 style DLLs';
```

Because it isn't always easy to remember which TIExpert methods need to be overridden, Table 29.2 summarizes the methods that need to be overridden for the various expert styles.

Table 29.2   *TIExpert* Methods to Override for Each Expert Style

Method Name	Standard	Add-In	Form	Project
GetStyle	✔	✔	✔	✔
GetIDString	✔	✔	✔	✔
GetName	✔	✔	✔	✔
Execute	✔		✔	✔
GetPage			✔	✔
GetGlyph			✔	✔

Method Name	Standard	Add-In	Form	Project
GetAuthor			✔	✔
GetComment			✔	✔
GetMenuText	✔			
GetState	✔			

You're now ready to start building an expert, a fairly straightforward process. Create a standard Delphi form (for the expert dialog box), then add the definition of the derived expert class to the source file's interface section. Next, add the implementation of the expert's derived methods to the source file's implementation section. That's it!

Listing 29.2 shows the source code for a generic expert that you can use as your first expert to register.

Listing 29.2   COMPEXPT.PAS—Generic Form and Expert Definition

```
unit compexpt;

interface

uses
  Windows, Messages, SysUtils, Classes, Graphics, Controls, Forms,
  Dialogs, ExptIntf, ToolIntf;

type
  TGenericComponentDialog = class(TForm)
    procedure FormCreate(Sender: TObject);
  private
    { Private declarations }
  public
    { Public declarations }
  end;

Type
  // Note: Not all of the TIExpert's methods are required to be
  // overridden.  They are all here for completeness.
  TGenericExpert = class(TIExpert)
  public
    function GetIDString: string; Override;
    function GetStyle: TExpertStyle; Override;
    function GetState: TExpertState; Override;
    function GetMenuText: string; Override;
    function GetPage: string; Override;
    function GetName: string; Override;
    function GetAuthor: string; Override;
    function GetComment: string; Override;
    function GetGlyph: HICON; Override;
    procedure Execute; Override;
  end;
```

continues

Listing 29.2 Continued

```
var
  GenericComponentDialog: TGenericComponentDialog;

implementation

{$R *.DFM}

//======================================================================
// TGenericExpert Implementation
//======================================================================

function TGenericExpert.GetIDString: String;
begin
  Result := 'UDelphi3.GenericComponentExpert';
end;

function TGenericExpert.GetStyle: TExpertStyle;
begin
  Result := esStandard; // Help menu expert
end;

function TGenericExpert.GetState: TExpertState;
begin
  Result := [esEnabled] // Our menu item will always be enabled
end;

function TGenericExpert.GetMenuText: String;
begin
  Result := 'UD3 Generic Component Expert...'
end;

function TGenericExpert.GetName: String;
begin
  Result := 'Generic Component Expert'
end;

function TGenericExpert.GetPage: string;
begin
  Result := ''; // Required only for esForm and esProject style experts
end;

function TGenericExpert.GetAuthor: string;
begin
  Result := ''; // Required only for esForm and esProject style experts
end;

function TGenericExpert.GetComment: String;
begin
  Result := ''; // Required only for esForm and esProject style experts
end;
```

```
function TGenericExpert.GetGlyph: HICON;
begin
  Result := 0; // Required only for esForm and esProject style experts
end;

procedure TGenericExpert.Execute;
begin
  if not Assigned(GenericComponentDialog) then
     GenericComponentDialog := TGenericComponentDialog.Create(Application);
  GenericComponentDialog.Show;
  GenericComponentDialog.SetFocus;
end;

//========================================================================
// TTestDialog Implementation
//========================================================================

procedure TGenericComponentDialog.FormCreate(Sender: TObject);
begin
  if not Assigned(ToolServices) then Exit;

  // Setup the expert dialog
end;

end.
```

Although every method of the TIExpert class is overridden, not all are actually used. This generic expert is a standard expert, so only the GetIDString, GetStyle, GetState, and GetMenuText methods are implemented with the proper result values. The others are shown only to drive home the point that not all TIExpert methods need to be overridden (because some will never get called by the IDE).

 TIP Notice that the TGenericExpert class is added to the expert dialog box's source file. This is by no means necessary, but is done for convenience.

Now that you have the expert defined, the following section explains how to add it to the Delphi IDE.

Registering an Expert

After you define the type and behavior of your expert, you must register it with the IDE. There are two ways to do this. The first way is to install the expert like a component by calling the RegisterLibraryExpert procedure from within the Register procedure used by Delphi to install components. (This method is primarily used throughout the rest of this chapter.)

The second way is to create a DLL expert wherein the Delphi IDE calls a specific initialization function in the DLL that requests the expert interface object as one of its parameters. Delphi knows to load the DLL expert in the first place by looking in the Windows Registry under Delphi's special Experts section.

N O T E   The main advantage of using component experts over DLL experts is that you don't need to get out of Delphi to reinstall your expert—you simply rebuild the package that contains the component expert. ■

Registering a Component Expert

To register an expert as a component, you must complete two steps. The first step is to add the special `Register` procedure to your expert's unit file. The following `Register` implementation is taken from the generic expert's unit file:

```
procedure Register;

implementation

{$R *.DFM}

procedure Register;
begin
  RegisterLibraryExpert(TGenericExpert.Create);
end;
```

This `Register` procedure is called whenever a source file is added to a Delphi package that's installed in the Delphi IDE. Delphi calls this function so that components and experts can be registered as part of the IDE. In the generic example, you call the `RegisterLibraryExpert` procedure and pass it an instance of the expert definition so that it becomes part of the IDE.

On the CD

The second step, of course, is to add the expert's unit file to a package that gets installed in the IDE. To install the generic expert discussed here, and also all the other example component experts in this chapter, install the UD3EXPRTS package located in the \UDELPHI3\CHP29\ folder on this book's companion CD-ROM. See Chapter 15, "Working with Packages," for more information on installing packages.

After the generic expert is installed, a new menu option for this expert appears on the Delphi Help menu (see Figure 29.1).

Registering a DLL Expert

You must take two steps to register an expert as a DLL. The first step is to create a new DLL project. Listing 29.3 shows the Delphi project used to create the generic DLL expert.

FIG. 29.1

The menu text for the generic expert appears on the Help menu in Delphi.

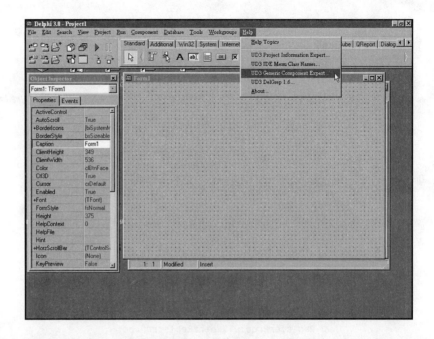

Listing 29.3   \UDELPHI3\CHP29\DLLEXPRT.DPR—Library Project to Create the Generic DLL Expert

```
library DllExprt;

uses
  ExptIntf,
  dllexpt in 'dllexpt.pas' {GenericDLLDialog};

{$R *.RES}

exports
  InitExpert name ExpertEntryPoint;

begin
end.
```

Notice that the function InitExpert is exported with the special export constant ExpertEntryPoint that Delphi has defined for all DLL-based experts. InitExpert acts in the same manner the Register procedure does in component-based experts. Listing 29.4 shows the implementation of the InitExpert function.

T I P When compiling a DLL expert, make sure that packages options is turned off in the DLL's project options. At the time of this writing, this functionality was not available.

Listing 29.4   \UDELPHI3\CHP29\DLLEXPT.PAS—*InitExpert* Implementation from the Generic DLL Expert

```
function InitExpert(ToolServices: TIToolServices;
                    RegisterProc: TExpertRegisterProc;
                    var Terminate: TExpertTerminateProc): Boolean;
                    export; stdcall;

implementation

{$R *.DFM}

procedure TerminateExpert;
begin
  // Expert is being terminated
end;

function InitExpert(ToolServices: TIToolServices;
        RegisterProc: TExpertRegisterProc;
        var Terminate: TExpertTerminateProc): Boolean;
        export; stdcall;
begin
  Result := False;

  // Make sure we're the first and only instance
  if (ToolServices = nil) or Assigned(ExptIntf.ToolServices) then Exit;

  // Assign the IDE's ToolServices pointer to ours
  ExptIntf.ToolServices := ToolServices;

  // Assign the IDE's Parent Window Handle to ours
  Application.Handle := ToolServices.GetParentHandle;

  // Setup the terminate routine
  Terminate := TerminateExpert;

  // register the expert(s)
  RegisterProc(TGenericExpert.Create);

  { Everything went okay }
  Result := True;
end;
```

`InitExpert` has two main purposes—to receive the all important `ToolServices` object reference that needs to be stored for later use and to call the `RegisterProc` procedure to register the expert by creating an instance of the expert and passing it back to the IDE. If needed, you can set a termination procedure. After the DLL expert's entry point is implemented, simply compile the project into a DLL, and then add the proper Registry entry so that Delphi knows to load and register the DLL expert.

To register the generic expert, for example, run the REGEDIT program (REGEDT32 on Windows NT) and add the following entry to the Registry:

```
HKEY_CURRENT_USER
  Software
  Borland
  Delphi
    3.0
      Experts
       TestExpert= C:\UDELPHI3\CHAP29\GENERIC\AS_DLL\DLLEXPRT.DLL
```

> **CAUTION**
>
> You must exit and restart Delphi to see the DLL expert that was added to the Help menu. I usually don't use DLL experts because of the inconvenience of exiting Delphi each time I want to make a change.

Handling Exceptions

It's recommended that the code for your experts handle all exceptions that are raised. For any unhandled exceptions, you should call the `RaiseException` method of the `TIToolServices` interface (discussed in a following section of this chapter). `RaiseException` usually is passed the result of the `ReleaseException` procedure found in the `VirtIntf` unit. `ReleaseException` destroys the exception object and returns the exception message string. Of course, you also use `RaiseException` to raise your own error messages. Here's an example:

```
procedure HandleException;
begin
  if Assigned(ToolServices) then
     ToolServices.RaiseException(ReleaseException)
end;
```

Open Tools API Interfaces

All the Open Tools API interfaces are contained in the following eight units: `ToolsIntf`, `EditIntf`, `ExptIntf`, `FileIntf`, `VcsIntf`, `DsgnIntf`, `VirtIntf`, and `IStreams`. Table 29.3 lists all these interfaces and shows the units in which they're defined.

Table 29.3   Overview of Delphi's Open Tools API Interfaces

Interface	Description
***ToolIntf* Unit**	
TIToolServices	As the primary Open Tools API interface, it provides access to most of the IDE-created interfaces. Provides access to the component library interfaces, the virtual file system interfaces, the editor interfaces, the menu interfaces, and so on. Additionally, provides the functionality to manage files and projects.
TIMainMenuIntf	Provides the capability to find and obtain an interface to a particular menu item with the Delphi IDE. This interface is obtained via the TIToolServices interface.
TIMenuItemIntf	Provides the capability to manipulate various attributes of a menu item, such as the item's caption text. It also allows the developer to hook into the OnClick event of the menu item. This interface is obtained via the TIMainMenuIntf interface.
TIAddInNotifier	Provides the capability to capture notifications of events such as the opening and closing of projects and files. This interface is obtained via the TIToolServices interface.
***EditIntf* Unit**	
TIModuleInterface	Provides access to a particular module (file, or file and form). Later in this chapter, you see how to insert code by using this interface to gain access to the editor buffer of the file currently being edited. This interface is obtained via the TIToolServices interface.
TIEditorInterface	Allows access to a particular editor's buffer through the TIEditReader, TIEditWriter, and TIEditView interfaces. This interface is obtained via the TIModuleInterface interface.
TIEditReader	Provides read-only access to a particular module with which it has been associated. This interface is obtained via the TIEditorInterface interface.
TIEditWriter	Provides write-only access to a particular module with which it has been associated. This interface is obtained via the TIEditorInterface interface.
TIEditView	Provides the capability to get and set the cursor position for the particular view of the module with which it has been associated. The Delphi IDE provides the means to show multiple views of a

Interface	Description
	module by choosing View, New Edit Window. This interface is obtained via the TIEditorInterface interface.
TIFormInterface	Provides the capability to create or find components on a particular form or data module. This interface is obtained via the TIModuleInterface interface.
TIComponentInterface	Provides the capability to directly manipulate a component of a form or data module. This interface is obtained via the TIModuleInterface interface.
TIResourceFile	Provides the capability to create, find, or delete resource entries in the project's resource file (PROJECT1.RES). This interface is obtained via the TIModuleInterface interface.
TIResourceEntry	Provides the capability to directly access information on a particular resource in the project's resource file. This interface is obtained via the TIResourceFile interface.

ExptIntf Unit

TIExpert	Provides the base class that is overridden to define how the new expert will be integrated into the Delphi IDE. An instance of the new interface will be passed to the IDE during the registration of the expert via the RegisterLibraryExpert function (for a component expert) or as a parameter in the ExpertEntryPoint function (for a DLL expert).

VcsIntf Unit

TIVCSClient	Provides the base class that is overridden to define how a new version control add-in tool will be integrated into the Delphi IDE. An instance of the new interface will be passed to the IDE during the registration of the add-in tool as a parameter in the VCSManagerInitProc function in the version control DLL. The VCSManagerInitProc function is of type T_VCSManagerInitProc, which also is defined in the VcsIntf unit.

FileIntf Unit

TIVirtualFileSystem	Provides the base virtual file system class that is overridden to define a new file system that can be used by experts, VCS managers, property editors, and component editors within the Delphi IDE. This allows for redirection of file operations to the editor and form/data module designer.

continues

Table 29.3 Continued

Interface	Description
***DsgnIntf* Unit**	
TPropertyEditor	The base abstract class type for all property editors. TPropertyEditor defines the properties and methods used or overridden by all useful property editors. Property editors are registered with the RegisterPropertyEditor function (also in the DsgnIntf unit) called from within the Register function of a component unit.
TComponentEditor	The base abstract class type for all component editors. TComponentEditor does not actually edit components. The default component editor is TDefaultEditor, a descendent of TComponentEditor, which implements a working Edit method. Component editors are registered with the RegisterComponentEditor function (also in the DsgnIntf unit) called from within the Register function of a component unit.
TFormDesigner	The abstract class type that Delphi's form designer descends. This object, when obtained from the IDE, allows a property or component editor to do tasks such as creating event handlers in the code editor or finding components on the form. This object is obtained through the TPropertyEditor, TComponentEditor, and TDesignWindow (in the DsgnWnds unit) objects.
***VirtIntf* Unit**	
TInterface	The base class from which most of the Open Tools API descends. It provides the reference-count mechanism that makes Open Tools API objects behave like COM interfaces.
TIStream	The base abstract class from which TIMemoryStream and TIFileStream descend. They both are implementations of TStream-based objects but are reference-counted as COM objects.
***IStreams* unit**	
TIFileStream	A reference-counted version of a TFileStream.
TIMemoryStream	A reference-counted version of a TMemoryStream.
TVirtualStream	An object that can work with both TIFileStream and TIMemoryStream.

The following sections discuss several important aspects of the Open Tools API.

ToolServices, the Heart of Delphi's Open Tools API

ToolServices is a global variable that is defined in the ToolIntf unit along with its class definition, TIToolServices. When you start Delphi, it creates an instance of TIToolServices and assigns the reference to the ToolServices variable. Experts use the ToolServices variable to gain access to and manipulate projects. All Open Tools API services are directly or indirectly obtained through the ToolServices object. The remainder of this section discusses the immediate functionality that the ToolServices object provides. Rather than list the entire class definition for TIToolServices, Table 29.4 condenses the services provided by TIToolServices into functional categories.

Table 29.4   Services Provided by *ToolServices*

Functional Category	*ToolServices* Interface Methods
Action interfaces	CloseProject, OpenProject, OpenProjectInfo, SaveProject, CloseFile, SaveFile, OpenFile, ReloadFile, ModalDialogBox, CreateModule, and CreateModuleEx
Project/UI information	GetParentHandle, GetProjectName, GetUnitCount, GetUnitName, EnumProjectUnits, GetFormCount, GetFormName, GetCurrentFile, IsFileOpen, and GetNewModuleName
Component library interfaces	GetModuleCount, GetModuleName, GetComponentCount, and GetComponentName
Virtual File System interfaces	RegisterFileSystem, UnRegisterFileSystem, and GetFileSystem
Editor interfaces	GetModuleInterface and GetFormModuleInterface
Menu interfaces	GetMainMenu
Notification registration	AddNotifier and RemoveNotifier
Pascal string-handling functions	NewPascalString, FreePascalString, ReferencePascalString, and AssignPascalString
Error handling	RaiseException
Configuration access	GetBaseRegistryKey

For an explanation of the purpose of each method, pull up the TOOLINTF.PAS unit and step through the documentation in the source code. Our focus with the ToolServices interface here is how to use it within an expert. Listing 29.5 shows the source listing for the Project Information Expert.

**Listing 29.5 PROJINFO.PAS—Source Listing for the Project Information
Expert**

```
unit ProjInfo;

interface

uses
  Windows, Messages, Classes, Forms, StdCtrls, Controls,
  Buttons, ExtCtrls, ComCtrls, ToolWin, ExptIntf, ToolIntf;

type
  TProjectInfoForm = class(TForm)
    UnitsList: TListBox;
    UnitsLabel: TLabel;
    FormsList: TListBox;
    FormsLabel: TLabel;
    ToolBar1: TToolBar;
    ToolButton1: TToolButton;
    ToolButton2: TToolButton;
    ImageList1: TImageList;
    Panel1: TPanel;
    CurrentFileNameLabel: TLabel;
    Label2: TLabel;
    Label1: TLabel;
    ProjectNameLabel: TLabel;
    ToolButton3: TToolButton;
    procedure FormShow(Sender: TObject);
    procedure CloseClick(Sender: TObject);
    procedure CopyProjectClick(Sender: TObject);
    procedure MoveProjectClick(Sender: TObject);
  end;

type
  TProjectInfoExpert = class(TIExpert)
  public
    function GetIDString: string; Override;
    function GetStyle: TExpertStyle; Override;
    function GetState: TExpertState; Override;
    function GetMenuText: string; Override;
    function GetName: string; Override;
    procedure Execute; Override;
  end;

var
  ProjectInfoForm: TProjectInfoForm;

procedure Register;

implementation

uses FileCtrl, Dialogs, SysUtils, OTUtils;

{$R *.DFM}
```

```
procedure Register;
begin
  RegisterLibraryExpert(TProjectInfoExpert.Create);
end;

//=========================================================================
// TProjectInfoExpert Implementation
//=========================================================================

function TProjectInfoExpert.GetIDString: String;
begin
  Result := 'UDelphi3.ProjectInfoExpert';
end;

function TProjectInfoExpert.GetStyle: TExpertStyle;
begin
  Result := esStandard; // Help menu expert
end;

function TProjectInfoExpert.GetState: TExpertState;
begin
  Result := [esEnabled] // Our menu item will always be enabled
end;

function TProjectInfoExpert.GetMenuText: String;
begin
  Result := 'UD3 Project Information Expert...'
end;

function TProjectInfoExpert.GetName: String;
begin
  Result := 'Project Information Expert'
end;

procedure TProjectInfoExpert.Execute;
begin
  // Only execute if we are running as a Delphi IDE Expert.
  if not Assigned(ToolServices) then Exit;

  if not Assigned(ProjectInfoForm) then
    ProjectInfoForm := TProjectInfoForm.Create(Application);
  ProjectInfoForm.Show;
  ProjectInfoForm.SetFocus
end;

//=========================================================================
// TProjectInfoForm Implementation
//=========================================================================

procedure TProjectInfoForm.CloseClick(Sender: TObject);
begin
  Close;
end;

procedure TProjectInfoForm.FormShow(Sender: TObject);
```

continues

Listing 29.5   Continued

```
//---------------------------------------------------------------
// Purpose: Populate the project Information expert dialog box with
//          information about the current project.  This information is
//          obtained from Delphi's ToolServices IDE object.
//---------------------------------------------------------------
var
  I : integer;

  procedure AddModule(List : TStrings; const ModuleName : String);
  //---------------------------------------------------------------
  // Purpose: This helper procedure adds the specified module name to
  //          the specified TStrings object indicating whether it is
  //          open or not.
  //---------------------------------------------------------------
  begin
    if ToolServices.IsFileOpen(ModuleName) then
      List.Add(ModuleName + ' - Open')
    else
      List.Add(ModuleName + ' - Closed');
  end;

begin
  // Only execute if we are running as a Delphi IDE Expert.
  if not Assigned(ToolServices) then Exit;

  with ToolServices do
  begin
    ProjectNameLabel.Caption := GetProjectName;
    CurrentFileNameLabel.Caption := ToolServices.GetCurrentFile;
    UnitsLabel.Caption := IntToStr(GetUnitCount) + ' Unit(s)';
    FormsLabel.Caption := IntToStr(GetFormCount) + ' Form(s)';

    // Populate the unit file list box with DPR, RES, PAS and DOF files.
    UnitsList.Clear;
    for I := 0 to GetUnitCount - 1 do
      AddModule(UnitsList.Items, GetUnitName(I));

    // Populate the form files list box with DFM files.
    FormsList.Clear;
    for I := 0 to GetFormCount - 1 do
      AddModule(FormsList.Items, GetFormName(I));

  end; // with ToolServices do
end;

procedure TProjectInfoForm.CopyProjectClick(Sender: TObject);
//---------------------------------------------------------------
// Purpose: Copy project files to a new destination
//---------------------------------------------------------------
begin
```

```
    TransferProjectFiles(True);
end;

procedure TProjectInfoForm.MoveProjectClick(Sender: TObject);
//-----------------------------------------------------------------
// Purpose: Move project files to a new destination
//-----------------------------------------------------------------
begin
  TransferProjectFiles(False); // Move
end;

initialization
  ProjectInfoForm := nil;
end.
```

This expert's initial functionality is obtaining project information for the currently loaded project. The unit file is composed of a form definition designed to show information about the current project. It's a standard Help menu expert, and because it's a component expert, it contains the Register procedure to register the expert. So far, there's nothing new.

The interesting code begins in the expert dialog box's FormShow event handler. The FormShow routine uses the ToolServices interface to obtain the project name, current module name, number of units and forms, and a listing of the project's units and forms specifying whether each one is open or closed.

This information is nice, but what can you really do with it? I found myself asking this question, so I came up with a handy utility that I use quite often. It's a general purpose routine that allows an expert to copy or move a project. Listing 29.6 shows the source code for the TransferProjectFiles procedure. This routine employs many of the common ToolServices routines to copy or move projects. The comments in Listing 29.1 describe how the code actually works.

Listing 29.6   OTUTILS.PAS—*TransferProjectFiles* Procedure from the *OTUtils* Unit

```
procedure TransferProjectFiles(CopyOnly : Boolean);
//-----------------------------------------------------------------
// Purpose: Move or copy the current project's unit and form files to
//          the user specified path.  If the CopyOnly Flag is set to
//          True then the files are not removed from their original
//          location.  On the other hand, if CopyOnly is False then
//          once the move is complete then the current project is
//          closed and then the project in its new location is
//          reopened.  Regardless of whether a move or copy is
//          performed the current project is always saved to ensure
//          that what is on disk is up to date.
//
// Notes:   This routine also copies any files in the project's
//          subdirectories maintaining the sub-tree structure,
//          however, if the project contains files that are in other
```

continues

Listing 29.6 Continued

```
//            parallel or higher subdirectories the files are copied
//            to the root directory of the new project's destination.
//------------------------------------------------------------------
var
  ProjSrcPath, ProjectName : String;
  DestPath, DestFile : String;
  SrcPath, SrcFile : String;
  I : Integer;

  function MakeDestFile: String;
  //----------------------------------------------------------------
  // Purpose: This helper function determines if the current source
  //          file is in a subdirectory and if so reconstructs the
  //          subdirectory under the project's destination path.
  //          The return value will be the source file prefixed with
  //          its destination path (with subdirectory if applicable).
  //----------------------------------------------------------------
  var SubPath : String;
  begin
    if Length(SrcPath) > Length(ProjSrcPath) then
      begin
        SubPath := Copy(SrcPath, Length(ProjSrcPath), Length(SrcPath));
        Result := DestPath + SubPath;
        // Do we need to make any subdirectories
        if not DirectoryExists(Result) then Mkdir(Result);
        Result := Result + SrcFile;
      end
    else
      // If not a subdir of the source path then put in DestPath
      Result := DestPath + '\' + SrcFile;
  end;

  procedure TransferFile(const SourceFile : String);
  //----------------------------------------------------------------
  // Purpose: This helper procedure primarily determines if the current
  //          source file is to be moved or copied based on the
  //          CopyOnly flag parameter. The function, MakeDestFile, is
  //          called for copy/move of a file because the destination
  //          path may vary based on whether the source file is in
  //          a subdirectory or not.
  //----------------------------------------------------------------
  begin
    SrcPath := ExtractFilePath(SourceFile);
    SrcFile := ExtractFileName(SourceFile);
    DestFile := MakeDestFile;

    if CopyOnly then
    begin
      if not CopyFile(PChar(SourceFile), PChar(DestFile), False) then
        RaiseLastWin32Error;
```

```
            end
        else
            if not MoveFile(PChar(SourceFile), PChar(DestFile)) then
                RaiseLastWin32Error;
        end;

begin
    // Only execute if we are running as a Delphi IDE Expert.
    if not assigned(ToolServices) then Exit;

    with ToolServices do
    try
        // Save all module file, but leave the project open so that all
        // the project files are accessible.
        if not SaveProject then Exit;

        // Get the destination path from the user.
        if not SelectDirectory(DestPath, [sdAllowCreate,
            sdPerformCreate, sdPrompt], 0) then Exit;

        ProjSrcPath := ExtractFilePath(GetProjectName);

        // Copy the unit file(s) (e.g. DPR, RES, PAS, DOF files)
        for I := 0 to GetUnitCount - 1 do TransferFile(GetUnitName(I));

        // Copy the form file(s) (e.g. DFM files)
        for I := 0 to GetFormCount - 1 do TransferFile(GetFormName(I));

        // In the case of a move close and reopen the project in its
        // new location.
        if not CopyOnly then
        begin
            ProjectName := ExtractFileName(GetProjectName);
            CloseProject;
            OpenProject(DestPath + '\' + ProjectName);
        end;

    except
        RaiseException('Project copy failed with message: '
            + Exception(ExceptObject).Message);
    end;
end;
```

On the CD

To install the Project Information Expert, install the UD3EXPRTS package in the \UDELPHI3\CHP29\ folder on this book's companion CD-ROM. See Chapter 15, "Working with Packages," if you need more information on installing packages.

Now that you've worked with some ToolServices properties and methods, the following sections introduce some other interfaces that can be accessed through the ToolServices interface.

Open Tools Menu Interfaces

The purpose of the Open Tools menu interfaces is to allow an expert to add and manipulate menu items. There are two menu interfaces, TIMainMenuIntf and TIMenuItemIntf. These are defined in the EditIntf unit. To access the Delphi main menu, you call the GetMainMenu method from ToolServices, which returns a TIMainMenuIntf interface. This interface gives you access to the rest of the menu items in the IDE. The menu interface is usually used only by add-in experts. Recall that an add-in expert implies to the Delphi IDE that the expert will take care of making an interface for the user to invoke the expert. An expert does this through the menu interfaces. Listing 29.7 shows the InsertMenu function, which allows an expert to add a menu item to the Delphi IDE in a particular position on a certain menu.

Listing 29.7   OTUTILS.PAS—*InsertMenu* Function from the *OTUtils* Unit

```
function AddMenuItem(MenuBarName, NewMenuText, ComponentName : String;
        ShortCut : TShortCut; Position : Integer;
        OnClick : TIMenuClickEvent): TIMenuItemIntf;
var
  IDE_MainMenu : TIMainMenuIntf;
  IDE_MenuItem : TIMenuItemIntf;
begin
  Result := Nil;

  if Assigned(ToolServices) then
  try
    IDE_MainMenu := ToolServices.GetMainMenu;
    if Assigned(IDE_MainMenu) then { we've got the main menu }
    try
      IDE_MenuItem := IDE_MainMenu.FindMenuItem(MenuBarName);
      if Assigned(IDE_MenuItem) then
      try
        Result := IDE_MenuItem.InsertItem(Position, NewMenuText,
                  ComponentName,'', ShortCut, 0, 0,
                  [mfEnabled, mfVisible], OnClick);
        // Note: Inserting under the separator on the tools menu
        // appears to ignore/fail if Delphi created dynamic tool menus
        // items.
      finally
        IDE_MenuItem.Release
      end
    finally
      IDE_MainMenu.Release;
    end
  except
    HandleException
  end
end;
```

You also can pass a keyboard accelerator for the user to use to invoke the add-in expert. Keep in mind that many combinations won't work because Delphi already has accelerators defined for these combinations.

Finally, the expert must provide a special `OnClick` method that's called whenever the user invokes the add-in expert. This replaces the `Execute` method used with the other three types of experts.

Listing 29.8 shows the source code for the Project Copy Expert, which adds two menu items to the Tools menu in the Delphi IDE to copy and move a project, respectively.

Listing 29.8 PROJCOPY.PAS—Source Code for the Project Copy Add-In Expert

```
unit ProjCopy;

interface

uses
  Windows, Classes, ExptIntf, ToolIntf;

type
TProjectTransferExpert = class(TIExpert)
  public
    function GetIDString: string; Override;
    function GetStyle: TExpertStyle; Override;
    function GetName: string; Override;

    constructor Create;
    destructor Destroy; Override;
  private
    CopyProjectMenuItem: TIMenuItemIntf;
    MoveProjectMenuItem: TIMenuItemIntf;
    procedure CopyProjectClick(Sender: TIMenuItemIntf);
    procedure MoveProjectClick(Sender: TIMenuItemIntf);
  end;

procedure Register;

implementation

uses FileCtrl, Dialogs, SysUtils, Menus, OTUtils;

procedure Register;
begin
  RegisterLibraryExpert(TProjectTransferExpert.Create);
end;

//=====================================================================
// TProjectTransferExpert Implementation
//=====================================================================

function TProjectTransferExpert.GetIDString: String;
begin
  Result := 'UDelphi3.ProjectTransferAddinExpert';
end;
```

continues

Listing 29.8 Continued

```
function TProjectTransferExpert.GetStyle: TExpertStyle;
begin
  Result := esAddin // Help menu expert
end;

function TProjectTransferExpert.GetName: String;
begin
  Result := 'Project Copy and Move Expert'
end;

constructor TProjectTransferExpert.Create;
begin
  inherited Create;
    MoveProjectMenuItem :=
      AddMenuItem('ToolsMenu', 'Move Project...', 'ToolsMoveProject',
        ShortCut(Ord('M'),[ssCtrl]), 0, MoveProjectClick);

    CopyProjectMenuItem :=
      AddMenuItem('ToolsMenu', 'Copy Project...', 'ToolsCopyProject',
        ShortCut(Ord('D'),[ssCtrl]), 0, CopyProjectClick);
end;

destructor TProjectTransferExpert.Destroy;
begin
  try
    if Assigned(CopyProjectMenuItem) then
      CopyProjectMenuItem.Release;

    if Assigned(MoveProjectMenuItem) then
      MoveProjectMenuItem.Release;

    inherited Destroy
  except
    HandleException
  end
end;

procedure TProjectTransferExpert.CopyProjectClick(Sender: TIMenuItemIntf);
begin
  TransferProjectFiles(True);
end;

procedure TProjectTransferExpert.MoveProjectClick(Sender: TIMenuItemIntf);
begin
  TransferProjectFiles(False);
end;

end.
```

The first thing to notice about the Project Copy Expert is that it's defined as an add-in expert. Next, notice that the expert has a `Create` constructor and a `Destroy` destructor. Also in the definition are two member fields to store the menu interfaces that reference the two menus this expert adds to the Delphi menu. Finally, there are two methods to serve as the `OnClick` event handlers that you will pass to the IDE when you create the menu items for this expert.

After you add the `OTUtils` unit to the `uses` clause to gain access to the `InsertMenu` function, you have fully set the stage for the Project Copy Expert to add its own menus. As you may have guessed, the `Create` constructor calls the `InsertMenu` function twice to add Copy and Move menus to the Delphi IDE. Notice that the Delphi `ShortCut` utility function is used to construct a shortcut for each menu item. The expert's `Destroy` destructor is used to release the menu interfaces if they're created.

You also should take note of the first parameter passed to the `InsertMenu` function. This parameter is the class name of the menu on which you want the additions placed. Table 29.5 lists the top-level menu items' class names.

Table 29.5   Class Names for Top-Level Menu Items

Menu Name	Class Name
File menu	`FileMenu`
Edit menu	`EditMenu`
Search menu	`SearchMenu`
View menu	`ViewMenu`
Project menu	`ProjectMenu`
Run menu	`RunMenu`
Component menu	`ComponentMenu`
Database menu	Inaccessible
Tools menu	`ToolsMenu`
WorkGroups menu	Inaccessible
Help menu	Inaccessible

N O T E   As a bonus, this book's companion CD-ROM contains an expert that shows all the Delphi IDE menu class names that are required to insert new menu items. The source code for this IDE Menus Expert is found in \UDELPHI3\CHP29\MENUS\IDEMENUS.PAS. ▦

Open Tools Editor Interfaces

The Open Tools editor interfaces allow an expert to read from and write to the Delphi source code editor. The four editor interfaces are: TIEditorInterface, TIEditView, TIEditReader, and TIEditWriter. To gain access to a particular unit's source code, you must have a TIModuleInterface interface to it so that you can call the GetEditorInterface method. This method returns a TIEditorInterface to the source file, which you can use to get a TIEditView, TIEditReader, or TIEditWriter interface. The OTUtils unit contains an InsertIntoEditor procedure that inserts a given text string into the active text buffer. The procedure's code is too lengthy to present here, but you can find the entire OTUtils unit on this book's companion CD-ROM, in the UDELPHI3\CHP29\OTUTILS folder.

> **N O T E**   When you're done with an Open Tools API interface that has been provided by the Delphi
> IDE, you need to call the Release method rather than the Free method, because the
> Open Tools API interfaces are COM-like objects and, therefore, are reference-counted. ■

Putting It All Together

You now have seen many facets of Delphi's Open Tools API, and you've learned that the ToolServices interface is the heart of this API. With ToolServices you can directly manipulate projects and gain access to many other Open Tools API interfaces to manipulate the Delphi IDE or project in various ways. As an added bonus, the accompanying CD contains a GREP/ Source Search Expert for you to explore on your own to gain more insight into Delphi experts. The source files are DELGREP.DPR and FINDEXP.PAS in the \UDELPHI3\CHP29\DELGREP\ folder. ●

CHAPTER 30

Delphi and C++ Synergy

by Eric Uber

Object Pascal and C++ are languages with remarkable similarity in capability. This is especially true of Borland C++ (BC5.x and C++ Builder) and Delphi because the back end to the compilers are essentially the same. With this compiler unity come other similarities, including the in-memory format of objects and use of a *Virtual Table* (VT in C++, VMT in Delphi speak). Although there are many "behind-the-scenes" similarities between these products, productive CO-implementation of elements between these languages is not immediately obvious. The purpose of this chapter is to discuss ways to use Delphi and C++ together in a productive fashion.

So why would you want to mix the use of languages? The answer is simple: maximum code reuse and a wider range of feature availability. Consider the scenario of having an existing code base in C++. Delphi moves into the picture with a rich set of *COM* and *WEB* features. Also, do not forget about its database support, including the use of the TClientDataSet component. Delphi is tempting, perhaps, but the thought of porting all that C++ code isn't a reasonable alternative.

Mixing both C++ and Delphi languages simply makes sense. Consider that maintaining a single code base written in one language, that can be used with two languages,

Using C++ and Delphi classes together

In this section, you learn about ways to share compiled code between C++ and Delphi, thus allowing you to harness the strengths of both languages.

The Virtual Table in class sharing

Perhaps the most difficult concept to understand, you learn how to interface with an object whose definition resides in a module external to your EXE.

Understanding module information by looking at the PE file layout

By becoming familiar with the contents of portable executable files, you better understand windows interaction with your applications, which makes for better program design.

Obtaining module information by using Turbo Dump

You learn how to employ Turbo Dump to extract PE file information, a useful technique to debug imported and exported symbols.

is more cost effective for third-party product developers and expands their target market at the same time. Depending on your situation, you may be in the same boat. So, raise sails! ▪

> **N O T E** This chapter assumes that you have read Chapters 25 and 26 and have experience programming in both Object Pascal and Borland C++.

In an effort to avoid being arrested by the C++ language police, and for simplicity, the C++ code in this chapter uses the simplest of types, directives, and declarations. For example, I use __stdcall rather than WINAPI in my function declarations. ▪

Mixing It Up

There are several ways to mix the use of Pascal and C++ code, and all of them have limitations. Usually, some ways work well and some don't. Ultimately, the correct route depends on the application.

Middle Ware

One technique of using multiple languages in a single application is to compile each code base into a separate executable module. One of the modules could use `CreateProcess` to spawn the other. Communication and manipulation of common data can be performed through the implementation of a middle layer or socket of sorts. The middle layer could be as simple as the use of the OS messaging system. Each executable could pass data to another, using the `wm_CopyData` message (discussed in Chapter 32, "Thunking in Delphi"). Another way is through use of *kernel file-mapping* objects (or memory-mapped files). Data is written to a disk file or the system paging file by one executable and read in by the other. You can even use the BDE in both applications to access tables of common data.

The use of a middle or an "out-of-process communication" layer is not a clean implementation but is often resorted to (perhaps, out of frustration) because it can be put in place quickly and usually doesn't require much trial-and-error programming. It seems, however, that most people are not content with this technique for the reasons stated and because it would seem that a cleaner way exists. Actually, there is; it's through the use of the `Component Object Model` (`COM`) in automation.

`COM` is a binary specification that describes an object's format and a way for objects to behave and communicate with each other in a language-independent fashion. This is still a middle-layer implementation with a number of drawbacks (performance is the most obvious); however, it works well in most cases and, lately, it's the hottest topic. `COM` is totally viable because Microsoft supports it as the way of the future. For more information on `COM`, see Chapter 19, "Working with COM Interfaces."

OBJ Files

Delphi supports the use of OBJ files generated in the *Intel relocatable object file* format. This is the format of the OBJ file produced by Borland C++ and Delphi (when the option to generate OBJ files is on, the default in Delphi is to generate DCU files), but it isn't the format produced from Visual C++, which uses the *COFF* format. COFF is a different specification that is most similar to the (PE) *portable executable* format, with a few twists.

After reading the last paragraph, you might think your prayers are answered with OBJ support. However, as I mentioned previously, each technique has some limitations. In fact, limitations are especially great in the support for using C++ OBJs in your Delphi programs, as you will see in later discussion.

DLLs

Use of DLLs is by far the most powerful and flexible way to mix C++ and Delphi code into a single application. DLLs can be generated with both C++ and Delphi in a common and even language-independent fashion. Functions that reside in a DLL written in one language can be called by another DLL or EXE written in the other language. C++ can even use Delphi classes and vice versa—to a point.

Because of the flexibility DLLs provide, this chapter puts most of the emphasis on them. Use of a middle ware layer between multiple EXEs is not very clean, and the use of OBJs is extremely limited. DLLs seem to pull together the strengths in both techniques and then add more functionality of their own.

Calling Conventions

When discussing the mixing up of languages, no conversation is complete without starting the discussion with *calling conventions*. A calling convention is a protocol that specifies how parameters are passed and maintained by routines. Although both C++ and Delphi support common calling conventions, their defaults are different. Before getting into the details, look at the calling conventions supported by Delphi and Borland C++, shown in Table 30.1.

Table 30.1   The Common Calling Conventions

Name	C++ Symbol	Delphi Symbol	Default
C-Decl	cdecl	cdecl	C++
Pascal	pascal	pascal	Delphi 1.0 and Windows 3.x
StdCall	stdcall	stdcall	Win95 and WinNT
SafeCall	<NONE>	safecall	Delphi only!
Fast-call	__fastcall	register	Delphi 2.0, 3

N O T E   The Name column in Table 30.1 is how I refer to each convention in the text discussion throughout this chapter.

The C++ Symbol column shows the directive used to specify the calling convention in the C++ language. Similarly, the Delphi Symbol column shows the directive used to specify the calling convention in the Delphi language.

The Default column specifies which language, or OS, defaults to which calling convention. ▨

You probably notice that Delphi and C++ have different default calling conventions. When declaring a routine that resides in an external module, make sure that you specify the calling convention that the routine uses. Failure to correctly match calling conventions will have disastrous results.

Table 30.1 shows that Delphi uses the Fast-call convention by default and C++ uses the C-Decl convention by default. Because the conventions must exactly match in both languages, you may wonder which language to use. Usually, neither! Code written in a language-independent fashion should declare publicly-accessible routines to use the StdCall calling convention. This rule forces all your code to be consistent with the calling convention the OS uses (which is StdCall). If everyone simply agrees to always follow this rule, there will be much more re-usable code in today's marketplace.

How to Be a Conformist

One problem with not standardizing on a single calling convention is that not all languages support all calling conventions. Even when they do, the support is sometimes limited (such as the case of C-Decl), or the implementation is different (such is the case of Fast-call). The problem becomes obvious when trying to use code that comes from out-of-house.

A third-party vendor often produces a DLL library (that does whatever) written in C++ that exports all its functions mangled and using C-Decl. Worse, these vendors often don't even know what calling conventions are or why it's important to document them.

I personally take the stance that, if a vendor doesn't document the calling convention they're using and the calling convention is not StdCall, then that vendor is not concerned about producing quality software. Therefore, I will not buy from such vendors. Although this may seem limiting—it saves hours of trial-and-error coding and the frustration of talking to vendors' technical support departments.

N O T E   Chapter 26, "DLL Programming: Advanced Concepts," goes into more specific details about calling conventions and their effects on parameters, return values, stack maintenance, and register usage. ▨

Although most of the calling conventions are rather well-discussed in Chapter 26, the C-Decl convention deserves some particular notation. It's possible you don't agree with my insistence on using the StdCall calling convention, so I want to at least give you some warnings about C-Decl.

Delphi's implementation of C-Decl is limited. This is because C-Decl is case-sensitive (where StdCall converts all symbols to uppercase), and changes the way the symbol is exported. By default, an underscore character is added to the front of the symbol (this option can be turned off; however, it is the default). Programmers often export routines as C-Decl in C++, but when they try to use them in Delphi, the reference is unresolved. Suppose that a DLL exports a routine called GetHeartRate. The symbol will actually export as _GetHeartRate. In your Delphi code, your import statements need to use the underscore character explicitly; otherwise, the loader deems the reference to be unresolved.

By default, the name of a C++ function will be *mangled*—the types in the parameter list of a function are converted to special symbolic characters and appended to the end of the function name. This occurs to allow C++ to support *function overloading*, which is a feature of the C++ language that isn't supported by Delphi and is not affected by specifying alternative calling conventions. You can declare Pascal routines as C-Decl all day and function overloading still will not work. This also is true of support for the passing of variable parameters. Pascal simply doesn't support it.

Name mangling can (and *should* for all exports) be disabled by using the extern "C" directive. A C++ DLL, for example, would export a routine (that supports language independence) as follows:

```
extern "C" int __stdcall SomeFunction(int)
```

The extern "C" portion of the statement disables name mangling. The return value is declared as int. The __stdcall directive states the routine is to use the StdCall calling convention. SomeFunction is the function name that takes a single parameter of type int.

Using OBJs to Combine C++ and Object Pascal Code

C++ generates OBJ files (machine code modules written by following a precise specification) that can be linked into Delphi by using the following compiler directive:

```
{$L Filename}
```

The L means to link in the specified file. The file extension is assumed to be .OBJ, unless specified otherwise. At link time, Delphi's linker will bind the module into the resulting executable module. This binding process is commonly known as a *static link*. Because the link is in fact static, the OBJ becomes part of the executable, which makes for a larger overall footprint.

Using a C++ OBJ in Delphi

You link an OBJ into a Delphi program to access the functions that it contains. Look at Listing 30.1, which you can also find on this book's companion CD-ROM.

Listing 30.1 \UDELPHI\CHP30\SAMP1.CPP—SAMP1.CPP Is Compiled into the SAMP1.OBJ File Used in the Next Example

```
int iGlobal = 0;


int __stdcall SetGlobalValue(int iValue)
{ int iTmp = iGlobal;
  iGlobal = iValue;
  return iTmp;
}

int __stdcall GetGlobalValue()
{ return iGlobal;
}
```

Listing 30.1 is a rather simplistic example. A global integer variable iGlobal is declared and initialized to zero. Two functions are declared by using the __stdcall calling convention. SetGlobalValue assigns the value passed in its iValue parameter to the global iGlobal variable and then returns the previous value. GetGlobalValue returns the current value of iGlobal. Listing 30.2 demonstrates how you can use these functions from Delphi.

Listing 30.2 USEOBJU1.PAS—A Partial Listing of the Unit's Content; the Rest Is on the CD-ROM Accompanying This Book

```
...

var
  Form1: TForm1;

implementation

{$R *.DFM}

{$L SAMP1} //Here's the include of SAMP1.OBJ!

function SetGlobalValue(iValue: integer): integer; stdcall; external;
function GetGlobalValue: integer; stdcall; external;

procedure TForm1.Button1Click(Sender: TObject);
begin
  SetGlobalValue(10); //Set variable in OBJ to 10.
  ShowMessage(Format('Variable in OBJ contains %d',[GetGlobalValue]));
end;

end.
```

Following the implementation directive in Listing 30.2, the compiler directive shown in the following line is used to include the OBJ generated from the SAMP1.CPP file shown in Listing 30.1:

```
{$L SAMP1} //Here's the include of SAMP1.OBJ!
```

After the `$L` directive is the declaration of the `SetGlobalValue` and `GetGlobalValue` functions. Notice the external directive appended to the end of the declaration. This directive flags the linker that the definition of these routines is in an external module—here, SAMP1.OBJ.

The `Button1Click` method serves as proof-of-concept. The `SetGlobalValue` call sets the `iGlobal` variable in SAMP1.OBJ to the value `10`. The `ShowMessage` call displays the return value of `GetGlobalValue` in a message box. The displayed value will, of course, be `10`.

But why such a simplistic example? How about using C++ classes in the OBJ? How about calling into the C++ RTL (Runtime library)? How about accessing some global system variables such as `errno`? As mentioned previously, use of OBJ files is extremely limited. I showed you, largely, the extent of what you can do in this single example.

You can access routines in your OBJ, but if the routines in the OBJ file access routines in other modules (such as RTL or Windows API routines), Delphi's linker simply fails. Your C++ OBJ file cannot contain C++ class declarations either. Like the C++ RTL, the class support in C++ is implicitly dependent on external modules of which Delphi's linker will be unaware; again, the link process will fail.

> **NOTE** If you cannot really stop using some of the C++ RTL or Windows API routines in your OBJ, you can get around the link errors in another way. Suppose that your C++ OBJ needs to call the `MessageBox` API routine. You can redefine `MessageBox` in the OBJ after the inclusion of Windows.h (if you're using it). This gives `MessageBox` local scope, but you can use the `extern` directive to specify that the definition is in another module:
>
> ```
> extern "C" int __stdcall MessageBox(long, char*, char*, long);
> ```
>
> Delphi's linker sees the declaration and that it is external and, therefore, searches the other modules and finds the call in context to Delphi, not C++. Although this is a clever technique, it can get messy. ▪

Your first inclination may be to include the library OBJs for all of C++, but the downfall (if it could be done) is that your Delphi EXE would seriously bloat. Unfortunately, even if this isn't an issue, it cannot be done anyway because much of what you want is actually stored in LIB files. LIB files are kind of a combination of OBJ files and cannot be linked into a Delphi program.

Just a final point: Delphi's linker doesn't let you access global variables in a C++ OBJ file. However, as I showed in my example, you can still declare and use them in your OBJ, so you (usually) only need to create a function to retrieve and set their values, and then use those from your Delphi code rather than accessing them directly.

Using a Delphi OBJ in C++

Like C++, Delphi also can generate OBJ files that then can be used in your C++ programs. In fact, Borland's C++ Builder uses an OBJ version of the actual Delphi 2.0 VCL library. (Yes, you read this correctly!) The C++ team added a special switch to the DCC32 compiler (this switch is available only in the version of DCC32 that ships with C++ Builder and BC5.02) that compiles Pascal source to generate OBJ files as well as C++ header files. Your C++ code includes the header file in the project and the OBJ(s) in the MAK file and poof—instant VCL support.

Using Delphi OBJs in C++ has the advantage that the C++ linker knows how to access global Delphi variables. Remember that this isn't true in the reverse scenario.

Suppose that your Pascal OBJ declares the following global variable:

```
var iGlobal: integer;
```

You can access iGlobal in your C++ code directly but you must first redeclare iGlobal using the extern directive, as follows:

```
extern int iGlobal;
```

Delphi doesn't generate OBJ files by default. You can instruct Delphi to generate OBJ files by selecting the Generate Object Files radio button on the Linker page of the Project Options dialog box. This dialog box is accessible from Project, Options.

Using DLLs to Combine C++ and Object Pascal Code

Perhaps the simplest and most logical way to combine your C++ and Object Pascal sources is by using DLLs. DLLs offer a plug-and-play architecture that, when properly used, make for solid, standard, reusable, and language-independent libraries. I will not spend much time in this chapter restating what was already said, so if you haven't read Chapters 26 and 27, do so before continuing in this chapter.

In simple summary, there are basically three ways to cleanly reuse your Delphi and C++ objects, using a DLL-based architecture:

- Using in-process COM server
- Using Flat functions, which wrap the methods of an exported class or just call library functions
- Exporting a class's virtual interface

The first item, in-process COM server, is a truly language-independent way to mix your Delphi and C++ code. In-process automation has the disadvantage of carrying the overhead of the OS's OLE subsystem, and there is a small learning curve for any practical implementation.

However, considering the popularity of intranet, networks, and client/server applications, using this architecture up-front better lends itself to scaling to a Distributed COM application architecture later, if the need arises.

It's also rumored that future versions of Microsoft's WinX operating system(s) will provide strong support of the COM implementations.

The next two items, flat functions and library routines, are discussed in greater detail, so read on!

Flat Functions

A *flat function* (or Access Routine) is only a routine that is exported from a DLL. The DLL can be loaded by an EXE or another DLL implicitly by using special declarations or explicitly by using LoadLibrary (or LoadLibraryEx) and GetProcAddress. Flat functions generally do one of two things. They usually directly contain useful processing code (or call other routines that contain useful processing code), which will make the flat function simply a library routine. Flat functions also can be used as a wrapper around an existing class. Perhaps exported Function1 instantiates an instance of TFoo. Maybe exported Function2 calls TFoo's Method1. Maybe exported Function3 releases the object instance created by Function1. Get it? This technique is class wrapping. Now, take a closer look at these techniques.

Library Routines   Suppose that your C++ program is working with comma-delimited ASCII data. Delphi's TStringList object can easily sort the fields of such a data record by using its Sorted property. Listing 30.3 shows a DLL project that exports a single function named CDSort, which does just that.

Listing 30.3   \UDELPHI3\CHP30\SDFMOD.DPR—This Example Uses the *CommaText* Property of the *TStringList* Object

```
library SDFMod;

uses
  SysUtils,
  Dialogs,
  Classes;

procedure CDSort(pStrings: PChar); stdcall;
begin
  if not Assigned(pStrings) then Raise
    EInvalidPointer.Create('Buffer is nil');

  with TStringList.Create do
  try
    CommaText := pStrings;
    Sorted := True;
    StrCopy(pStrings,PChar(CommaText));
  finally
    Free;
  end;
end;

exports
  CDSort;

begin
end.
```

The CDSort procedure is an example of a simple flat function or library routine that performs some useful type of processing. You could implement many routines of this type in an Object

Pascal DLL and use them from your C++ code. Listing 30.4 shows how the CDSort routine exported from the SDFMOD.DLL can be used in your C++ code.

Listing 30.4   \UDELPHI3\CHP30\USELIB.CPP—SDFMOD.DLL Is Loaded Dynamically and the *CDSort* Routine Is Imported Using *GetProcAddress*

```cpp
#include <windows.h>
#include <string.h>

#define C_STRING "\"CString\",\"DString\",\"BString\",\"AString\""

void (__stdcall *CDSort)(char*) = NULL;

#pragma argsused
int WINAPI WinMain(HINSTANCE hCurInstance, HINSTANCE hPrevInstance,
                   LPSTR lpCmdLine, int nCmdShow)
{   char* pBuf = new char[256];
    strcpy(pBuf,C_STRING);

    MessageBox(0,pBuf,"Before",MB_OK);
    HINSTANCE hInst = LoadLibrary("SDFMod.dll");

    if (hInst) {
     (FARPROC)CDSort = GetProcAddress(hInst,"CDSort");
     if (CDSort) CDSort(pBuf);
        MessageBox(0,pBuf,"After",MB_OK);
    }

    delete pBuf;
    return 1;
}
```

In Listing 30.4, note the line void (__stdcall *CDSort)(char*) = NULL;" This statement declares a variable named CDSort, which is a function pointer. The CDSort variable will later hold the address of the entry point of the CDSort routine exported from the SDFMOD.DLL. Notice that the StdCall calling convention is explicitly specified by using the __stdcall directive as part of the declaration. This is a match to how CDSort is actually exported in SDFMOD.

The Address of CDSort is obtained from the call to GetProcAddress, which is passed the return value from LoadLibrary in the first parameter. The second parameter is the name of the exported function. The return value is the runtime address of the CDSort function.

```cpp
(FARPROC)CDSort = GetProcAddress(hInst,"CDSort");
```

Assuming that GetProcAddress succeeds, CDSort can be called passing the pBuf variable that contains the comma-delimited string to sort. The data in the memory to which pBuf points will be altered by the code in the DLL. The following call to MessageBox acts as a simple as proof-of-concept.

Another more obvious use of a flat function is to create and display a Delphi form from your C++ program. The function exported from the Delphi DLL could be simple, as follows:

```
function ShowModalForm(hMainWnd: THandle): integer; stdcall;
begin
  Application.Handle := hMainWnd;
  with TForm1.Create(Application) do
  try
    result := ShowModal;
  finally
    Free;
  end;
end;
```

The C++ code to access such a routine mechanically doesn't differ much from what I showed in Listing 30.4. The main change would be to the function pointer declaration, as follows:

```
int (__stdcall *ShowModalForm)(HWND) = NULL;
```

Of course, the call is different because the parameter changed. It also could appear similar, as follows:

```
...
if (hInst) {
  (FARPROC)ShowModalForm = GetProcAddress(hInst,"ShowModalForm");
  if (ShowModalForm) ShowModalForm(0);
...
```

Now, look at another scenario that exports a flat function to access the methods of a class. This time, the DLL will be written in C++, and then used by your Delphi EXE.

Class Wrapping   Suppose that you have an existing code base written in C++ or that you simply want to access an instance of an existing C++ container class. You can do so by exporting a function that creates and gets an instance of the desired class. You then could export one function per public class member. Each of these functions directly accesses the public class members. Finally, you could export a function that also frees the class instance.

Let's look at implementing such functionality in Listing 30.5.

Listing 30.5   \UDELPHI3\CHP30\CWRAP.CPP—Functions Are Exported to Access *TCharQue* Members

```
#include <windows.h>
#include <queues.h>

typedef TQueue <char> TCharQue;

extern "C" {
    //Returns an instance of TCharQue
    HANDLE _stdcall _export QueLoadQueueInst(int iSize)
{ TCharQue* CharQue =
  new TCharQue(( iSize ? iSize : DEFAULT_QUEUE_SIZE));
  return (HANDLE)CharQue;
}
//Releases an instance of TCharQue
void _stdcall _export QueFreeQueueInst(TCharQue* CharQue)
{ delete CharQue;
```

continues

Listing 30.5   Continued

```
}
void _stdcall _export QueFlush(TCharQue* CharQue)
{ CharQue->Flush();
}
int _stdcall _export QueIsEmpty(TCharQue* CharQue)
{ return CharQue->IsEmpty();
}
int _stdcall _export QueIsFull(TCharQue* CharQue)
{ return CharQue->IsFull();
}
void _stdcall _export QuePut( TCharQue* CharQue, char t )
{ CharQue->Put(t);
}
char _stdcall _export QueGet(TCharQue* CharQue)
{ return CharQue->Get();
}
int  _stdcall _export QueGetItemsInContainer(TCharQue* CharQue)
{ return CharQue->GetItemsInContainer();
}
}
```

Cwrap.cpp shown in Listing 30.5 exports eight routines. These eight routines know how to operate on an instance of the TCharQue type. TCharQue is actually of type TQueue, which is template class and part of the container class library. TCharQue is declared in such a way that the datatype on which it expects to operate will be characters.

N O T E   The TQueue container class accepts input by way of a call to its Put method. Put adds the passed data to the tail of the queue. The Get method retrieves whatever data is sitting at the head of the queue. Data is added and retrieved in a first-in, first-out (FIFO) fashion.

The TQueue class is useful in situations where data or objects are retrieved faster than they can be processed, which may be the case in reading bytes off the COM port or if you implemented your own print-spooling mechanisms. ■

The QueLoadQueueInst routine returns an instance of the TCharQue class to the caller. The caller will be treating the received instance as a handle that gets passed back to the other exported functions. The caller must retain this instance because it is unique for each call to QueLoadQueueInst. The instance also should be retained and passed to the QueFreeQueueInst routine which simply calls delete to free the instance from memory.

Take a look at the flip side of all this, which is using the class from your Delphi EXE program. The example code shown in Listing 30.6 imports each routine implicitly in the interface section. Note that some of the data types in the import declarations appear differently than what are actually exported from the DLL.

Listing 30.6 \UDELPHI3\CHP30\CWAPU1.CPP—Uses the CWRAP.DLL, which Exports Access Functions to Operate on an Instance of *TCharQue*

```pascal
unit cwrapu1;

interface

uses
  Windows, Messages, SysUtils, Classes, Graphics, Controls, Forms, Dialogs,
  StdCtrls;

type
  TForm1 = class(TForm)
    Button1: TButton;
    procedure Button1Click(Sender: TObject);
  private
    { Private declarations }
  public
    { Public declarations }
  end;

var
  Form1: TForm1;

  const
    CWRAP = 'C:\BOOKS\DELPHI30\CHAPT30\CODE\CWRAP.DLL';

  function  QueLoadQueueInst(iSize: integer): THandle; stdcall; external CWRAP;
  procedure QueFreeQueueInst(hCharQue: THandle); stdcall; external CWRAP;
  procedure QueFlush(hCharQue: THandle); stdcall; external CWRAP;
  function  QueIsEmpty(hCharQue: THandle): longbool; stdcall; external CWRAP;
  function  QueIsFull(hCharQue: THandle): longbool; stdcall; external CWRAP;
  procedure QuePut( hCharQue: THandle; t: char ); stdcall; external CWRAP;
  function  QueGet(hCharQue: THandle): char; stdcall; external CWRAP;
  function  QueGetItemsInContainer(hCharQue: THandle): integer;
                                          stdcall; external CWRAP;

implementation

{$R *.DFM}

procedure TForm1.Button1Click(Sender: TObject);
var
  hInst: THandle;
begin
  hInst := QueLoadQueueInst(0);

  if QueIsEmpty(hInst) then
    ShowMessage('IsEmpty = TRUE');

  QuePut( hInst, 'H' );
  QuePut( hInst, 'E' );
  QuePut( hInst, 'L' );
  QuePut( hInst, 'L' );
  QuePut( hInst, 'O' );
```

continues

Listing 30.6 Continued

```
  if not QueIsEmpty(hInst) then
    ShowMessage(IntToStr(QueGetItemsInContainer(hInst)));

  ShowMessage(Format('%s%s%s%s%s',
                      [ QueGet(hInst),QueGet(hInst),
                        QueGet(hInst),QueGet(hInst),
                        QueGet(hInst)
                      ]));
  QueFreeQueueInst(hInst);
end;

end.
```

The export declarations for QueIsEmpty and QueIsFull specify a return value of type integer. In the import declarations, the type is changed to Longbool so that you can use the routines in logical operations without having to typecast or otherwise translate a 0 return value as False and Positive return value as True. Because the Pascal Longbool is the same size as the C++ integer type, the redeclaration is secure.

Interfacing with the Virtual Table

Another way to mix up Delphi and C++ code in DLLs is by making the virtual interface to your objects exportable. On the DLL side, you do this by exporting a single routine that returns the object instance to the caller (probably an EXE). The source can be either a C++ or Pascal DLL—both languages support this technique. The caller can be from any language that supports the COM object format and can load and access routines exported from DLLs.

N O T E The main example for this topic uses a C++ DLL, which is accessed from a Pascal EXE. Chapter 26, "DLL Programming: Advanced Concepts," already discusses the details of this topic as well as shows the reverse scenario. The reverse scenario is using a Pascal DLL. ■

The Virtual Class in C++ Previously, this chapter discussed exporting flat routines to access an instance of the C++ container class TQueue. The routines manipulated the instance by calling its member functions. Listing 30.7 is the main CPP in the CClass project, which gives your Pascal code access to an instance or TQueue another way. This technique involves creating a wrapper class for TQueue whose public member functions are virtual. Because the member functions are virtual, their addresses will reside in the VT (Virtual Table) of the resulting object instance after instantiation.

Listing 30.7 \UDELPHI3\CHP30\CCLASS.CPP—*GetQueue* Returns an Instance of *TCharQueue*; *TCharQueue* Type Is Declared in CHARQUE.H

```
#include <windows.h>
#include <queues.h>
#include <stdio.h>
#include "charque.h"
```

```
extern "C" TCharQueue* _stdcall _export GetQueue(int iMax)
{       return new TCharQueue(iMax);
}
```

The GetQueue function exported in CClass.cpp excepts a single integer parameter which specifies the maximum size of the queue. The return value is a pointer to an instance of the TCharQueue class, which is the wrapper class to the TQueue container class. The declaration of the TCharQueue class is shown in Listing 30.8.

Listing 30.8   \UDELPHI3\CHP30\CHARQUE.H—The *TQueue* Template Class Is Type Defined to Hold the *char* Type

```
#ifndef charque_h
#define charque_h

#include <queues.h>

typedef TQueue <char> TCharQue;

class TCharQueue {
public:
  TCharQueue(int i = 0);
  ~TCharQueue();
private:
  TCharQue* FCharQue;
public:
  virtual char _stdcall Get();
  virtual void _stdcall Put( char t );
  virtual int  _stdcall IsEmpty();
  virtual int  _stdcall IsFull();
  virtual int  _stdcall GetItemsInContainer();
  virtual void _stdcall Flush();
  virtual void _stdcall Delete();
};

#endif
```

Listing 30.8 shows the CharQue.h header file. It begins by type defining the TQueue container class with a new name TCharQue. Because TQueue is a *template* class, the data type must be identified—for simplicity, the example uses the char type.

The TCharQueue wrapper is extremely simple, and it should be. It exists only as a vehicle to export the functionality of the TCharQue class type. It isn't written with the intention of being descended from, or even directly manipulated.

TCharQueue has a private data member that holds the pointer to the instance of TCharQue. The instance is initialized in the constructor, as you will later see. The public interface to this class is most important. The first notable thing about the public method declarations is that all are declared as virtual. As mentioned previously, this is necessary for our purposes to ensure that the method addresses end up in the VT of our instance. Only the virtual methods of a class can be accessed external to the DLL from Delphi. The second notable thing about the declarations of the public methods is they all use the StdCall calling convention (by including the __stdcall directive). You should do this for any routine that is to be available in a language-independent fashion.

Listing 30.9 is the CHARQUE.CPP source file that defines the implementation of the TCharQueue class.

Listing 30.9   \UDELPHI3\CH30\CHARQUE.CPP—Contains the Code that Operates on the *TCharQueue* Instance

```
#include "charque.h"

TCharQueue::TCharQueue(int i)
{  FCharQue = NULL;
   FCharQue = ( !i ? new TCharQueue : new TCharQueue(i) );
   if (!FCharQue) throw;
}

TCharQueue::~TCharQueue()
{  if (FCharQue) delete FCharQue;
}

char _stdcall TCharQueue::Get()
{  return FCharQue->Get();
}

void _stdcall TCharQueue::Put(char t )
{  FCharQue->Put(t);
}

int _stdcall TCharQueue::IsEmpty()
{  return FCharQue->IsEmpty();
}

int _stdcall TCharQueue::IsFull()
{  return FCharQue->IsFull();
}

int _stdcall TCharQueue::GetItemsInContainer()
{  return FCharQue->GetItemsInContainer();
}

void _stdcall TCharQueue::Flush()
{  FCharQue->Flush();
}

void _stdcall TCharQueue::Delete()
{  ::delete this;
}
```

The definition of each method of the class isn't totally important for the point of this information. Generally, each method simply turns around and calls one of the methods of the TQueue class. See your C++ class library online reference for more information on the TQueue class.

There are a couple methods worth pointing out. The following constructor initializes the private FCharQue data member:

```
TCharQueue::TCharQueue(int i)
```

If the value passed in the i parameter is 0, FCharQue is constructed by using its default maximum size. Otherwise, it is constructed by using the maximum size you specify. Of course, FCharQue is heap allocated, so it must be released from memory in the destructor when the object is destroyed.

Recall in Listing 30.7 that the exported routine for use by a loading executable appeared as follows:

```
extern "C" TCharQueue* _stdcall _export GetQueue(int iMax)
```

This routine returns a pointer to an instance of TCharQueue. How do you release this instance when you're through? You could export another function that you pass the instance back to, so delete can be called to release the memory. Here, however, I added a virtual Delete method to the actual TCharQueue class:

```
void _stdcall TCharQueue::Delete()
{   ::delete this;
}
```

This method can be invoked from the loading executable. It calls delete on this, which is the current instance. The call to delete results in the destructor being called, which is important so that private member FCharQue also gets deleted from memory.

Using the Virtual Class in Delphi   Compilation of CClass.ide results in the creation of a 32-bit DLL named CCLASS.DLL that exports a single routine named GetQueue. GetQueue returns an instance of the TCharQueue class (which is a wrapper class for the C++ TQueue container class). The interface section of Loadu1.pas shown in Listing 30.10, pretty much sums up how to get at your TCharQueue instance.

Listing 30.10   \UDELPHI3\CHP30\LOADU1.PAS—The Loader Code in Object Pascal

```
unit loadu1;

interface

uses
  Windows, Messages, SysUtils, Classes, Graphics, Controls, Forms, Dialogs,
  StdCtrls;

type
  TForm1 = class(TForm)
    GroupBox1: TGroupBox;
```

continues

Listing 30.10   Continued

```
    Button3: TButton;
    procedure Button3Click(Sender: TObject);
  private
    { Private declarations }
  public
    { Public declarations }
  end;

  TCharQueue = class
  public
    function    Get: char                          stdcall; virtual; abstract;
    procedure   Put( t: char )                     stdcall; virtual; abstract;
    function    IsEmpty: longbool                  stdcall; virtual; abstract;
    function    IsFull: longbool                   stdcall; virtual; abstract;
    function    GetItemsInContainer: integer       stdcall; virtual; abstract;
    procedure   Flush                              stdcall; virtual; abstract;
    procedure   Delete                             stdcall; virtual; abstract;
  end;

var
  Form1: TForm1;

function GetQueue(iMax: integer): TCharQueue; stdcall; external 'CClass';

implementation

{$R *.DFM}

procedure TForm1.Button3Click(Sender: TObject);
begin
  with GetQueue(5) do
  try
    Put('H');
    Put('E');
    Put('L');
    Put('L');
    Put('O');

    if IsFull() then
      ShowMessage(Format('There are %d characters in Queue',
              [GetItemsInContainer()]));

    ShowMessage( Format('%s%s%s%s%s',
              [ Get(),
                Get(),
                Get(),
                Get(),
                Get() ] ));

    if IsEmpty() then
      ShowMessage(Format('There are %d characters in Queue',
              [GetItemsInContainer()]));
  finally
    Delete;
```

```
    end;
  end;

  end.
```

The last part of the interface section attempts to implicitly load the CCLASS DLL and import the GetQueue function:

```
function GetQueue(iMax: integer): TCharQueue; stdcall; external 'CClass';
```

Of course, for this code to compile, TCharQueue first must be declared. The type section (contained in the interface section) of the unit declares the TCharQueue class exactly as it is declared in the C++ DLL, with one exception. The methods in the pascal declarations are abstract. By declaring the class in this way, the compiler cannot complain about references to TCharQueue, and the linker will not try to resolve the references at design time. Instead, the binding occurs at runtime, using the instance provided as a return from the call to GetQueue.

N O T E Note that in the abstract declaration, the methods do not need the same name that they need in the DLL. The functions are not resolved by name. They are actually resolved by offset into the Virtual Table (VT)—the position is relevant. Be certain to declare the methods in the exact same order as they are declared in the DLL. Although consistent naming is optional, it makes for readability and maintainability.

The implementation section defines the TForm1.Button3Click method of TForm1. The method doesn't do anything significant other than exercise some of methods of the TCharQueue instance returned from GetQueue. GetQueue is called passing the value 5. The most characters this queue can hold is five. If you put more than five, the first characters in will be popped out of the queue.

The example puts the characters that, as a whole, spell "Hello" into the TQueue instance. Then, a message box is displayed that specifies how many characters are in the queue (five). Another message box is then shown which displays the *Hello* text. Then yet another message box is shown that again specifies how many characters are in the queue (zero).

Type Conversion Table

Table 30.2 shows many common Delphi data types and the synonym C++ language data type, that is, the C++ type equivalence that would not result otherwise in a type conversion. To make the list realistically useful, I mixed the native intrinsic, generic, fundamental, and user-defined types (UDT) into a single reference.

Table 30.2   Delphi and C++ Conversion

Delphi	C++
Ordinal Types	
ShortInt	short
Smallint	unsigned short
Byte	BYTE
char	unsigned short
Cardinal	unsigned int
Integer	int
Word	unsigned int
LongInt	long
DWORD	unsigned long
DWORD	UINT
Float Types	
Double	double
Extended	long double
Comp	unsigned long
Real	<None>
Single	float
Character and String Types	
Char	char
String (AnsiString)	<None: String classes are available however>
ShortString	<None>
WChar	wchar_t
PChar	char*, LPSTR
Logical Types	
Boolean	<any single byte type: BYTE, Char, enum>
Bool	bool

Logical Types

WordBool	unsigned int
LongBool	long

Other Types

pointer	void*
PInteger	int*
Variant	\<None\>
Currency	\<None\>
Set	\<None\>

Table 30.2 shows many types that you're likely to encounter in Delphi that you may need a C++ equivalent for. Considering that I included some common UDTs, the table is nowhere near complete. My intention here is to mention what I feel raises the most obvious question or is most commonly used.

One point I didn't reflect in the chart is *enumerated types*. An enumerated type in Delphi is an unsigned byte (one byte) by default and C++ is usually an unsigned short (two bytes) by default. Both languages provide options for changing the default enumeration type. Typically, you want to increase the enumeration size in Delphi to be compatible with your C++ type (it's safer to go too large than too small). Delphi provides two compiler directives for modifying the size of enumerated types.

```
{ $Z }, { $MINENUMSIZE }
```

The use of const in Delphi works about the same as in C++. Consider if a C++ function, Foo, is declared using the unnamed type T prefix with const, as follows:

```
int __stdcall _export Foo(const T tVar);
```

then the Delphi equivalent declaration would be

```
function Foo(const tVar: T): integer; stdcall;
```

Use of function pointers also are of interest. In C++, you can create a *User Defined Type* (*UDT*) that is a function pointer by using a typedef, as follows:

```
typedef int (__stdcall *TMyProc)(char* c);
```

You then would create a variable of type TMyProc, as follows:

```
TMyProc MyProc;
```

The following code shows the same function pointer UDT declaration, but this time in Pascal:

```
type  TMyProc = function(c: PChar): integer; stdcall;
```

In Pascal, you then would create a variable of type TMyProc, as follows:

```
var MyProc: TMyProc;
```

You can declare a variable as a function pointer without first declaring a type. The following shows this in both C++ and Delphi:

```
var MyProc: function(c: PChar): integer; stdcall; //The Pascal Way
int (__stdcall *MyProc)(char* c); //The C++ Way
```

So you see, Delphi and C++ are not only similar in capability, and object format—they also share similarities in their available data types. This includes enumerations and function pointers.

Summary

This chapter touched various issues related to using Delphi and C++ together. It really all comes down to four techniques:

- EXE interacts another EXE
- Language 1 uses OBJ from Language 2
- DLL exports routines
- DLL exports object instance

EXEs interacting with one another doesn't reflect a tightly integrated application (unless, of course, the application is distributed). Use of OBJs is so extremely limited and complicated to implement, this technique might as well not be supported.

By far, the best implementation is using DLLs to modularize your applications. The DLLs must be written in a language-independent fashion. This means that exports shouldn't be name mangled, and the StdCall calling convention should be used.

Various techniques are available for exporting from a DLL. If your functions are basic library routines, you can simply directly export them as such. You also could export a series of routines that know how to retrieve, free, and otherwise manipulate an object of a particular type. You also could export a single return that returns an instance of an object declared in the DLL. You then can redeclare the object as abstract in the loading executable and use the instance as if it were local.

So you see, a lot of functionality can be incorporated between the languages. One of the biggest drawbacks is that most people know both C++ and Delphi, but they usually know one language significantly better than the other. This chapter also provided you with a data type conversion chart that will help those of you who fall into this category. ●

CHAPTER 31

Working with the Windows API

by Joe C. Hecht

In the early days of the PC, every program executed in its own code space. At the time, this was no big deal because under DOS, you could only run one program at a time anyway. Back in those days, the average PC had 256K of RAM and two floppy drives. Today, it's hard to imagine that the first version of Microsoft Windows was designed to run on such a system. The architects of Windows had a lot of code and data to "shoehorn" into that 256K of RAM and two floppy drives, and they worked hard to devise ways to pull off this trick. One of the first things they noticed was that quite a bit of a program's bulk was spent on common tasks such as menuing systems, dialog boxes, and so on. Creating a single code library that could provide these common services to multiple programs would save a lot of disk space and speed development time. Thus, the Windows Dynamic Link Library was born.

Almost all of Windows' system is built up of dynamic link libraries. Dynamic link libraries (or DLLs) allow applications to share both a common code base and resources. In fact, the MORICONS.DLL file that ships with Windows is a "resource only" DLL that contains a variety of colorful icons. It's worth noting that a dynamic link library doesn't need to end with the .DLL extension. Many parts of the Windows system are made up of DLLs that have extensions such as .DRV (drivers), .FON (fonts), and even .EXE (although they are not executable).

Dynamic linking and function prototyping

Learn about Windows dynamic link libraries, and creating function prototypes for interfacing to the Windows API functions.

Calling conventions

In this section, we discuss the various calling conventions used with Windows API functions.

Unsigned 32-bit integers

Here we present a work-around for dealing with 32-bit unsigned integers in Delphi.

Callback functions

After reading this section, you will be able to take on Windows Callback functions with complete confidence!

Hook functions

Here we cover the Windows Hook functions in preparation for the next section, where we will build a DLL that uses hook functions.

Sending keyboard and mouse input to any window

In this section, we build a full-featured Windows Macro player PlayKeys, which allows you to send mouse and keyboard input to any active Windows control!

The functions that make up a DLL can be used by many applications at any given time. Furthermore, only the portions of code and resources that are currently called need to be in memory at any given time, and they are freed when no longer in use.

There also are other advantages of using DLLs to hold code and resources. You can reduce your deployment if you have several executables that can share code and resources and, if you ever want to upgrade a portion of an application, you can trade out DLLs rather than shipping out new executables. Finally, placing code and resources in a dynamic link library can give your application the capability to load different code and resources based on conditions at runtime, by loading up different sets of DLLs. This can be useful for deploying international applications, where you might want to place localized dialog boxes, menu items, and string lists in a DLL, and load the appropriate DLL for the language in effect at runtime. Finally, the ability to load DLLs at runtime can help you extend your application with after-market "plug-ins."

If you plan to access the Windows API, you need to know how to work with DLLs, because almost all of the Windows system is built from dynamic link libraries. ■

Dynamic Linking and Function Prototyping

The developers of Delphi put a lot of work into making the Windows API available to your application. There are literally thousands of type declarations, constants, functions, and procedure calls defined in the WINDOWS.PAS file that ships with Delphi. If you're lucky enough to have the Windows API library interface source code (located in Delphi's \SOURCE\RTL\WIN folder), you will find the declarations for all the Windows API units included with Delphi.

Calling a predefined Windows API function is easy, as follows:

```
var NumTicks : LongInt;
begin
    NumTicks := GetTickCount;
end;
```

This example makes a call to the Windows API function GetTickCount(), returning the number of milliseconds since Windows was started. Note that under Delphi, this value goes negative after the 24th day because Delphi doesn't support true unsigned 32-bit integers, and under any system will wrap around to zero sometime on the 49th day Windows is left running. Note that a solution exists to the unsigned 32-bit integer problem, listed in the section "Unsigned 32-Bit Integers" later in this chapter.

Linking to a dynamic link library whose entry point is predeclared is known as *static linking*. Usually, DLL function declarations are put into their own unit so the function can be called from many different units in your application. Here is a short version of WINDOWS.PAS, containing the function declaration for GetTickCount():

```
unit Windows;

interface
```

```
type  DWORD = Integer;

function GetTickCount: DWORD; stdcall;

implementation

function GetTickCount; external 'kernel32.dll' name 'GetTickCount';

end.
```

Notice how the interface section declares a type called DWORD that is simply an integer type, along with the function prototype for GetTickCount(). The function prototype also includes the key word stdcall to let the compiler know how to make the call. There are four different types of calling conventions available in Delphi that will be discussed later in this chapter but for now, we can say that most all Windows functions use the standard calling convention. In the implementation section, we declared that the GetTickCount() function is external to the program, and is located in kernel32 DLL module. Finally, we declare that the function should be located by looking up the name GetTickCount in the module. As was mentioned previously, this method of linking is called "static" linking because we defined the function entry point at design time. When you have a statically linked DLL function, the DLL must exist either in the program's directory, the WINDOWS or \WINDOWS\SYSTEM directory, or somewhere in the search path of the system. If the DLL you are statically linking to isn't found at runtime or if the function doesn't exist, your program will fail to load.

You are also free to remap the name of an imported function, as follows:

```
function GetTimerTicks; external 'kernel32.dll' name 'GetTickCount';
```

Notice how the name that will be used was changed to GetTimerTicks(), although the function still points to the GetTickCount() function. This technique is used quite often in the Windows interface units to map a given function to use the equivalent ANSI or wide haracter function when compiling your application for international markets. To drive the point home, look at the implementation declarations for the Windows function lstrlen(). This function takes in a pointer to a character array, and returns the number of characters in the string. Some international versions of Windows use wide character sets, where a character's size may consist of more than a byte. The good folks at Borland made it easy to rebuild your application for these markets by exporting two different versions of each Windows function that expects strings— one for the ANSI characters and one for wide characters. Here are the implementation declarations for the lstrlen() functions:

```
function lstrlenA; external kernel32 name 'lstrlenA';
function lstrlenW; external kernel32 name 'lstrlenW';
function lstrlen; external kernel32 name 'lstrlenA';
```

The first declaration lstrlenA points to the ANSI version, and the second declaration lstrlenW points to the wide version. Finally, the third declaration lstrlen points to the ANSI character version. If you were using one of the international versions of Delphi that support wide characters, the third declaration would be mapped to 'lstrlenW'. This allows you to simply recompile your project for international markets, without having to keep two different sets of code.

Although it is certainly advisable to try to keep your imported function declarations in a separate unit, occasionally you may want to import a function directly without having to make a separate unit. Simply place the complete prototype declaration in the implementation section of the unit you want to use the function from. Here is an example of doing just that:

```
procedure SomeProc(l : LongInt);
{$IFDEF Win32} stdcall; {$ELSE} far; {$ENDIF}
 external 'TESTDLL' index 1;
```

Notice how this procedure was defined to work with both 16- and 32-bit versions of Delphi by using the $IFDEF compiler directive, and the function also was imported by ordinal number instead of by name. Importing by ordinal number is faster than importing by name, but is recommended only when you know the export index of the function will never change.

Although it's convenient to be able to statically link to a dynamic link library at designtime, dynamically linking to a DLL at runtime can save a lot of memory by reducing the number of modules that are mapped to your application at any time and also can provide your application the capability to extend itself with aftermarket plug-ins. With dynamic linking, you first load the library, and search out the address of the function you want to call "on-the-fly" at runtime. When you no longer need to use the function, you simply unload the library.

I once wrote an application that could apply special effects to bitmap images. One requirement for the application was that each effect should be a plug-in module. At runtime, I made a list of all the DLL files available in the applications directory, and loaded each one, looking for a specific function named GetPlugInEffectName(). If the function was found in the DLL, I knew that the DLL was one of my plug-in modules, and simply recorded the DLL's name, and the name of the effect in a list. When the user selected an effect, I simply loaded the DLL, searched out the ApplyEffect() function, and then called the function passing a handle to the bitmap to which I wanted to apply the effect. Finally, when the function returned, I would unload the DLL.

The following is an example of loading a DLL, searching out a procedure address, calling the procedure, and then unloading the DLL:

```
{$IFDEF Win32}
    const BadDllLoad = 0;
{$ELSE}
    const BadDllLoad = 32;
{$ENDIF}

procedure DoEffect(TheBitmap : HBitmap;
                   DllName : pChar);
var
  DllHandle: THandle;
  EffectProc: procedure(TheBitmap : HBitmap);
 {$IFDEF Win32} stdcall; {$ENDIF}
begin
  DllHandle := LoadLibrary(DllName);
  if DllHandle >= BadDllLoad then begin
    @EffectProc := GetProcAddress(DllHandle, 'ApplyEffect');
    if @EffectProc <> nil then
```

```
      EffectProc(TheBitmap);
    FreeLibrary(DllHandle);
  end;
end;
```

Notice that this example was written to be compatible with both 16- and 32-bit versions of Delphi and Windows. We start by defining a constant value for the error code returned when a DLL doesn't load correctly. We defined a procedure named DoEffect() that takes in a handle to a bitmap, and the name of the DLL that contains the effect we want to apply.

Inside the procedure, we declare a DllHandle of type THandle, and a procedure variable called EffectProc that is prototyped identically to the procedure contained in the DLL. In the procedure code, we load the DLL, and check to make sure that no error occurred. If the DLL loaded successfully, we search for the address for the ApplyEffect() procedure in the DLL, and assign the address to our EffectProc procedure variable. If the address of our EffectProc variable is valid, we call the procedure, passing the handle to our bitmap. Finally, we clean up by freeing the library.

As you see, dynamic linking can be a powerful tool to enhance your application and your pocketbook, well after you ship your product!

Calling Conventions

Making a function call to a DLL is much like two jugglers passing bowling pins back and forth. It works only if both jugglers know how they will pass the pins back and forth. The "agreement" forged between the application and the DLL is known as a *calling convention*, and it specifies how parameters are to be passed to the function or procedure, how functions return results, and who is responsible for cleaning up the stack. If you make a call to a function and use the wrong calling convention, the function certainly will not work correctly, and your application will most likely crash.

In the preceding examples, we made an additional declaration for 32-bit DLL functions to use the stdcall (or standard call) calling convention where in 16-bit Windows, all functions defaulted to the pascal convention, unless otherwise specified. Four different calling conventions are commonly used in Windows, and you will be happy to know that 32-bit Delphi supports all four: stdcall, pascal, cdecl, register (also known as fastcall), and safecall. Note that 16-bit Delphi only supported the pascal and cdecl calling conventions, unless you dropped down to assembler level, and handled all the aspects of making the call yourself.

Just in case you're curious (and we know you are), here is the rundown on the five calling conventions and how they work.

cdecl   Parameters are passed on the stack in right to left order and the caller is responsible for cleaning up the stack. Advantage: Functions and procedures can accept a variable number of parameters.

pascal   Parameters are passed on the stack in left to right order, and the function is responsible for cleaning up the stack. Advantage: Up to 20 percent faster than cdecl.

stdcall   Parameters are passed on the stack in right to left, and the function is responsible for cleaning up the stack. The stdcall convention combines some of the advantages of cdecl and the pascal convention.

register   This convention is also known as fastcall. Up to the first three parameters are passed in left to right order though the EAX, EDX, and ECX CPU registers, and all additional parameters are passed on the stack, also in left to right order. The function is responsible for cleaning up the stack. Advantage: Combines the speed of the pascal calling convention with the additional speed of passing parameters through the CPU registers. Real types and method pointers are never passed through the CPU registers.

Note that 32-bit Windows defaults to using the stdcall convention and for performance reasons, 32-bit Delphi defaults to using the faster register convention. In 16-bit land, both Windows and Delphi default to using the pascal calling convention.

safecall   Same as stdcall, but this call is enclosed in a try/except block and is used with OLE Automation.

Function Results

Most of the conventions for returning values are fairly standard, except for the way floating-point types are returned. Historically, Borland has always returned floating-point types on the math coprocessor's top-of-stack register ($ST(0)$), where Microsoft tends to return a pointer to the floating-point value. In 16-bit Windows, this pointer sometimes will be a near pointer, wreaking havoc for the calling application. If you plan on writing a dynamic link library that returns floating-point values and you want the functions to work across the board, I suggest that, rather than passing the floating-point value back as a function result, you pass the floating-point result as a variable parameter, thus eliminating any confusion.

Patching WINDOWS.PAS

With the thousands of constants, types, functions, procedures, and macros included in the Windows API, creating the interface files for the Windows system certainly must have been a daunting task for the developers of Delphi. Although most of the functions and types are declared correctly, there may be occasions where the declaration may be incorrect. If you have the VCL source code (located in Delphi's \SOURCE\RTL\WIN folder), you can peek at the source code for the unit in question to see if the declaration is correct. You can suspect any function or procedure that was not declared as using the stdcall convention. You are free to make the change to the unit's source code, and then rebuild the unit by adding the path to the unit to the library path contained on the library page of the Options dialog box, accessible from the Tools menu option. You need to restart Delphi after adding the path, and then do a complete rebuild on your project. After you are satisfied that your code is working correctly, you can remove the path to the RTL\WIN folder, shut down Delphi, and copy the rebuilt unit to Delphi's Lib directory, which prevents Delphi from performing the time-consuming task of rebuilding the RTL source every time you rebuild your project.

When the chips are really down and you have examined all other possibilities, you may want a look at all type declarations to ensure that they are correct. Sometimes, changing a record declaration to have the "packed" attribute may help. Finally, make sure that the function is mapped to the correct dynamic link library. Occasionally, functions of the same name are declared in more than one Windows system DLL. This is usually done to accommodate "thunking" between 16- and 32-bit programs and the supporting system DLLs. Once in a while, confusing MSDN documentation results in the function getting mapped to the incorrect DLL.

Occasionally, you may find that function parameter or record structure is incorrectly prototyped, or a function prototype does not fit your needs. This is usually not a difficult problem to fix, but be forewarned that making these types of changes may result in breaking a VCL component. In this case, you must choose between fixing up the VCL source or making a local declaration to the function or record structure in the unit you are calling the function from. If the function is truly prototyped incorrectly, you probably are better off fixing up any VCL code that depends on it. If the function prototype is correct, but you need to change the prototype to fit your needs (such as changing a var parameter to a pointer), you may be better off declaring a local version of the function that doesn't affect the VCL. The Windows GetSystemPaletteEntries() function is a good example of a function that is prototyped in a way that may not always suit your needs, yet the VCL components and many third-party components will break if you change it. Here is the current prototype:

Part
VI

Ch
31

```
function GetSystemPaletteEntries(DC: HDC;
                        StartIndex, NumEntries: UINT;
                        var PaletteEntries): UINT; stdcall;
```

Notice that the last parameter, PaletteEntries, is declared as an untyped var parameter. This means you are allowed to pass any variable, hopefully an uninitialized array of PaletteEntries. When you pass a var parameter, the compiler substitutes the address (or a pointer to the variable). Suppose that you want to dynamically allocate this array and pass the pointer to your dynamically created array. The compiler will not complain, but instead sends a pointer to your pointer, and your program probably will crash, or you will, at least, lose quite a few of your program's variables. One way around this problem is to declare a local version of the GetSystemPaletteEntries() function in the implementation section of your unit that accepts a pointer as the final parameter like this:

```
function GetSystemPaletteEntries(DC: HDC;
                        StartIndex, NumEntries: UINT;
                        PaletteEntries : pointer): UINT;
{$IFDEF Win32} stdcall; {$ELSE} far; {$ENDIF}
 external 'gdi32.dll' name 'GetSystemPaletteEntries';
```

Now you can safely pass a pointer as the last parameter to the function without breaking the VCL or losing your variables as follows:

```
procedure TForm1.Button1Click(Sender: TObject);
var
  dc : hdc;
  p : pointer;
```

```
begin
  Dc := GetDc(0);
  GetMem(p, 256 * sizeof(TPaletteEntry));
  GetSystemPaletteEntries(dc, 0, 256, p);
 {Do something here with the palette entries}
  FreeMem(p, 256 * sizeof(TPaletteEntry));
  ReleaseDc(0, dc);
end;
```

In this example, we first get the desktop's Dc, and allocate an array large enough to hold 256 palette entries. Then we make the call to the GetSystemPaletteEntries() function, and finally clean up by freeing the allocated memory block, and release the Dc back to the system.

A final note: If you do find an error in the Windows interface files, the best thing to do is be a "good neighbor" and promptly submit a complete bug report to Borland. This is best done through Borland's Web site or tech-fax service. Although you can always call the bug into the good folks at Borland's Developer Support group, if you directly submit the report, the QA and R&D departments will have your phone number if they need to get in touch with you directly.

Unsigned 32-Bit Integers

Another problem you may eventually run into is Delphi's lack of support for true 32-bit unsigned integers. You have several ways around the problem, including dropping off into assembler. I prefer to convert incoming 32-bit unsigned integers to doubles, work with them, and convert back as necessary. It's a little slower, especially on older machines that have no math coprocessor, but converting to doubles is far more convenient because you can directly work with the value.

Remember that functions such as Windows.GetTickCount() are declared in Delphi to return a longint because Delphi has no native unsigned 32-bit integer. If the value returned from one of these functions exceeds 2,147,483,647, the high bit of the longint gets set, causing the number to be treated by Delphi as a negative number.

Here we present two functions to help you along the way—UIntToDouble() and DoubleToUInt().

The UIntToDouble() function will take in an unsigned 32-bit integer disguised as a longint and return a double that contains the correct positive value. The DoubleToUInt() function provides the reciprocal function, converting a double to a unsigned 32-bit value disguised as a longint. Note that the range of a 32-bit unsigned integer goes up from zero, all the way to 4,294,967,295, where the range of a longint is –2,147,483,648 to +2,147,483,647.

```
{$IFOPT Q+}
  {$DEFINE CKOVERFLOW}
  {$Q-}
{$ENDIF}

function UIntToDouble(u : longint) : double;
var
  d : double;
begin
```

```
    if u >= 0 then
      d := u else
    if u = -1 then begin
      d := $7FFFFFFF;
      d := d + d + 1;
    end else
    begin
      d := $7FFFFFFF;
      d := d + abs($7FFFFFFF - u);
    end;
    result := d;
end;

function DoubleToUInt(d : double) : longint;
var
  n : double;
begin
  if d < 0 then d := Abs;
  d := Int;
  n := $7FFFFFFF;
  n := n + n + 2;
  while d >= n do
    d := d - n;
  if d = (n - 1) then
    result := -1 else
  if d > $7FFFFFFF then
    result := not ($80000000 - trunc(d - $7FFFFFFF)) else
    result := Trunc;
end;

{$IFDEF CKOVERFLOW}
  {$UNDEF CKOVERFLOW}
  {$Q+}
{$ENDIF}

procedure TForm1.Button1Click(Sender: TObject);
var
  NumTicks : longint;
  RealNumTicks : double;
begin
 {NumTicks may be negative!}
  NumTicks := GetTickCount;

 {Whew! Now we will be ok}
  RealNumTicks := UIntToDouble(NumTicks);

 {Change it back!}
  NumTicks := DoubleToUInt(RealNumTicks);
end;
```

In this example, we sandwiched the two functions with the $IFOPT and $IFDEF statements. We did this to turn off overflow checking if it is currently enabled, and then turn it back on (if the option was originally enabled) after we are done. We did this to avoid runtime errors because we will purposely (and safely) overflow some of our values along the way. Numbers greater than hex $7FFFFFFF (2,147,483,647) are interpreted as negative longints, even when assigned to a type that can safely hold the value (like a `double`). Note that the `DoubleToUInt()` function tests to see if the number contained in the `double` is beyond the range of a 32-bit unsigned integer. If so, we simulate a "wrap," by repeatedly subtracting 4,294,967,296 until the number is in range (less than 4,294,967,296). When you turn off range checking, numbers that overflow "wrap around" back to the lowest value the number can hold. An example would be if you tried to assign 4,294,967,295+1 to an unsigned `int`. Because the integer can only hold 4,294,967,295, the integer would simply "wrap around" to zero.

The example ends by using the `UIntToDouble()` function to return the correct positive tick count since Windows was started, and then convert the value back to the value from which we originally started.

Callback Functions

Callbacks are one of the most useful things you can do with a function under Windows. Simply put, you define a function in your application to perform some sort of "work," and then pass a pointer to that function to a second function. The second function then can "callback" to the first function, passing information for the function to work with.

A good example of where you may want to use a callback function is when enumerating system fonts. Suppose that you have a form in your application that contains a listbox that you want to fill with the names of all the available fonts on the system. You create a function in the application that accepts information about the font as a parameter and adds the font name to the listbox. You then can call one of the system font enumeration functions, passing the address of your function that will process the font information. The system's function will then callback to the function in your application for each font found on the system, passing it data about that font. Your function then adds the font's name to the listbox and returns `true` if you want more font names, or `false` if you want the enumeration to stop.

Note that the last parameter usually passed to a Windows callback function is defined as a "user-application defined data" parameter. It usually is called `lparam` and takes a 32-bit application-defined value (you are free to define what that value will be). This `lparam` value will be passed back to the callback function that you defined in your application. What you use this parameter for is your own business, but usually you want to pass a pointer to something in your application.

Suppose that you have several forms in your application that display font information in a listbox. You could define a separate callback function for each form, but instead, you want to use a single callback function that will work with all the forms. The easy way to do so is to pass a pointer to the listbox as the `lparam` to the Windows callback. This way, the callback function in your application will know which listbox to fill. Here is an example:

```
function FillFontList(lpelf : PEnumLogFont;
                      lpntm : PNewTextMetric;
                      FontType : integer;
                      Param : pointer) : integer
{$IFDEF Win32} stdcall; {$ELSE} ; export; {$ENDIF}
begin
```

```
    TListBox(param^).Items.Add(lpelf^.elfLogFont.lfFaceName);
    FillFontList := 1;
end;


procedure TForm1.Button1Click(Sender: TObject);
var
  dc : hdc;
  fn : pointer;
begin
  dc := GetDc(0);
  fn := MakeProcInstance(@FillFontList, hInstance);
  EnumFontFamilies(dc,
                   nil,
                   fn,
                   {$IFDEF Win32}
                   longint(@ListBox1));
                   {$ELSE}
                   @ListBox1);
                   {$ENDIF}
  FreeProcInstance(fn);
  ReleaseDc(0, dc);
end;
```

We begin this example by declaring our callback function `FillFontList`. We have declared the function to be compatible with both 16- and 32-bit versions of Windows by using the `$IFDEF` compiler directive. If we are compiling under 32-bit Delphi, we want the callback function to use the stdcall calling convention. If we are compiling under 16-bit Delphi, we want the function marked as exported. This is unnecessary under Win32 because a DLL is automatically mapped into the application address space. The `FillFontList()` function simply casts the `param` parameter as a pointer to a listbox, adds the font's face name to the listbox, and returns 1 (True) to indicate we want more font names to be enumerated.

In our `ButtonClick` event, we declare two variables—an `hdc` and a `pointer`. We then get the `Dc` of the desktop, and initialize the pointer to the "procedure instance" of our `FillFontList()` function by calling the Windows `MakeProcInstance()` function. In 32-bit Windows, this is unnecessary because the DLL will be automatically mapped into the application's address space; but under 16-bit Windows, the `MakeProcInstance()` function is the "glue" that binds the callback function back to its application because the data segment pointer normally would still point to the data segment of the DLL. In 32-bit Windows, `MakeProcInstance()` is still safe to call, and simply returns a pointer to the function. If you are not porting between 16- and 32-bit Windows, you may omit the step of calling the `MakeProcInstance()` and `FreeProcInstance()` functions, and simply pass `@FillFontList` in the place of `fn` where needed. Finally, we call the `EnumFontFamilies()` function, passing the `dc` for which we want the fonts listed, a `nil` parameter to let the function know we want all the font families, the procedure address of our callback function, and a pointer to the listbox we want filled. Under 32-bit Delphi, we must cast this address to a `longint` because the prototype has changed from 16-bit versions of Delphi. Finally, we are able to clean up by calling `FreeProcInstance()` and releasing the screen's `Dc`.

As you can see, callbacks are a great way to pass information back and forth between functions.

Hook Functions

A *hook* is a callback function that is installed into the Windows message system to access messages before other processes receive them. Usually, there will be other hooks already installed on the system. Installing a hook function is much like stealing an interrupt from back in the old DOS days. When you install your hook function, you probably want to do some processing on the message, and then call the next hook in the *hook chain* to allow the message to filter down through the system.

When you install a Windows hook function by using the Windows API function SetWindowsHookEx(), you receive a 32-bit handle to identify your hook to the system. Unlike most Windows handles, this handle is 32 bits wide in both 16- and 32-bit Windows. You need this handle to call the next hook installed in the hook chain using the Windows CallNextHookEx() function (unless you plan to "swallow" the message and not pass it on down the chain). You also need this handle when you want to remove your hook from the system when calling the UnHookWindowsHookEx(). Note that all the HookEx() functions are available under both 16- and 32-bit Windows.

The Windows Hooks

Windows defines the following hook types.

WH_CALLWNDPROC

A window procedure hook called when the SendMessage() function is called allowing for modification of the message.

WH_CALLWNDPROCRET

A window procedure hook called after the SendMessage() function returns. Available under Windows 95 only.

WH_CBT

A computer-based training hook called before activating, creating, destroying, minimizing, maximizing, moving, or sizing a window; before completing a system command; before removing a mouse or keyboard event; before setting input focus; and before synchronizing the system message queue.

WH_DEBUG

A debugging hook. Called before any other filtering hook is called.

WH_GETMESSAGE

A message hook called when the GetMessage() function has retrieved a message from an application queue.

WH_HARDWARE

A hardware message hook called when the application calls the `GetMessage()` or `PeekMessage()` function and there is a nonstandard hardware event (other than a mouse or keyboard event).

WH_JOURNALRECORD

A recording hook called when the system removes messages from the system message queue.

WH_JOURNALPLAYBACK

A playback hook used to insert keyboard and mouse messages into the system message queue.

WH_KEYBOARD

A keyboard hook called when the application calls the `GetMessage()` or `PeekMessage()` function and there is a `WM_KEYDOWN` or `WM_KEYUP` keyboard message waiting to be processed.

WH_MOUSE

A mouse message hook called when the application calls the `GetMessage()` or `PeekMessage()` function and there is a mouse message waiting to be processed.

WH_MSGFILTER

An application message hook called after a dialog box, message box, or menu has retrieved a message, but before the message is actually processed.

WH_SHELL

A hook used by shell applications to receive notification messages from the system.

WH_SYSMSGFILTER

A system-wide message hook called after a dialog box, message box, or menu retrieves a message, but before the message is processed.

Additional Notes on Hooks

Application-specific hooks may reside either in an application or a dynamic link library, while system-wide hooks require that the hook function reside in a dynamic link library. Also, debugging a Windows hook can be a difficult and time-consuming task. The documentation for Windows hooks isn't always correct and doesn't always reflect any quirks that different versions of Windows may have. A good source for additional documentation is Microsoft's KnowledgeBase, available both online and on the MSDN CD. Finally, if your system-wide hook manages to lock up the system, try pressing Ctrl+Esc or Ctrl+Alt+Del. This should remove any system-wide hooks that are installed.

Sending Keyboard and Mouse Input to Any Window

There are so few examples of using Windows hooks in the real world that this chapter simply would not be complete without one. Here we present a worthy item for any programmer's toolbox: The capability to send keyboard and mouse input to any window from your application. You may wonder why you cannot simply use the Windows `SendMessage()` function to accomplish the same goal. Well, the Windows message queue is a limited resource that can handle only so many messages at a time, so you risk overflowing the buffer every time you add a new message to the queue. The correct work-around is to create a JournalPlayback Windows hook, and let Windows decide when to allow new messages to be posted. In the presented example, we will create a dynamic link library that contains the JournalPlayback hook and its supporting functions, along with an application to demonstrate using our new DLL. Because many of you probably develop for both 16- and 32-bit platforms, I added a few lines of code to make the example portable.

The playback logic works like this: We create a message buffer that will contain the messages we want to play. The message buffer will start with a header record that contains pointers to both the first and last message item in the buffer. Each message item will contain the message we want to send, and a `pointer` to the next `MsgItem` record. This is known as a *linked list*. We added several support functions to make it easy to create a message list from your application, and then "play" the keyboard and mouse messages back to the window controls of your choice.

CreateMsgBuff

This creates a new message buffer.

IsPlaying

This returns the status of the playout.

AddKeyString

This adds a string of keystrokes to be played.

AddMouseMessage

This adds a mouse message to be played.

AddVkMessage

This adds a virtual key message to be played.

AddVkMsgPair

This adds a keypair to be played (KeyUp/KeyDown).

PlayMouseKeys

This plays the messages in the buffer.

DeleteMsgBuff

This deletes the message buffer.

As you can see, we covered all our bases. This industrial-strength DLL has the capability to send strings, mouse messages, and even virtual key combinations such as Shift+Ctrl+F2 to any window that accepts input, and gives you the ability to combine any virtual key sequence in any combination.

Because JournalPlayback functions are considered to be "system-wide" functions, by definition they should be located in a dynamic link library.

On the CD

You will need to load and compile the PlayKeys DLL project. You can find PLAYKEYS.DPR on this book's companion CD-ROM. Listing 31.1 shows the code for the PLAYKEYS DLL.

Part
VI
Ch
31

Listing 31.1   \DLPHI3\CHP31\BAREBONES.DPR—The BareBones Project Is Just That Because Its Content Is Sparse

```
{$C FIXED PRELOAD PERMANENT}

library PLAYKEYS;

{$IFDEF Win32}
 uses Windows, Messages;
 type
   TwMessage = LongInt;
   TwParameter = LongInt;
   TlParameter = LongInt;
{$ELSE}
 uses WinTypes, WinProcs, Messages;
 type
   TwMessage = Word;
   TwParameter = Word;
   TlParameter = LongInt;
{$ENDIF}

type PMsgItem = ^TMsgItem;
  TMsgItem = record
    Event : TEventMsg;
    Next  : PMsgItem;
  end;

type PMsgHeader = ^TMsgHeader;
  TMsgHeader = record
    First : PMsgItem;
    Last  : PMsgItem;
  end;
```

continues

Listing 31.1   Continued

```
var
  Playing     : LongBool;
  lpMsg       : pMsgItem;
  HookHandle : HHook;

function PlaybackProc(Code: Integer;
                      wParam: TwParameter;
                      lParam: TlParameter): LongInt;
{$IFDEF Win32} stdcall; {$ELSE} export; {$ENDIF}
begin
  PlaybackProc := 0;
  case Code of

    HC_SKIP : begin
     {fetch the next message}
      lpMsg := lpMsg^.Next;
     {are we done?}
      if lpMsg = nil then
        if UnHookWindowsHookEx(HookHandle) then
          Playing := false;
      exit;
    end;

    HC_GETNEXT : begin
     {play the current message}
      PEventMsg(lParam)^ := lpMsg^.Event;
      PEventMsg(lParam)^.Time := GetTickCount;
      exit;
    end;

    HC_SYSMODALON : begin
     {system error - let the next hook know about it}
      CallNextHookEx(HookHandle, Code, wParam, lParam);
      exit;
    end;

    HC_SYSMODALOFF : begin
     {system error - let the next hook know about it}
     {note : our hook has been canceled by the system}
      CallNextHookEx(HookHandle, Code, wParam, lParam);
      exit;
    end;

  end;
 {request to call the next hook}
  if code < 0  then
    PlaybackProc := CallNextHookEx(HookHandle,
                                   Code,
                                   wParam,
                                   lParam);
end;
```

```
function PlayMouseKeys(lpMessages : PMsgHeader): LongBool;
{$IFDEF Win32} stdcall; {$ELSE} export; {$ENDIF}
begin
  PlayMouseKeys := false;

 {avoid data segment corruption}
  if Playing then exit;

  Playing := true;

 {is the buffer a valid pointer?}
  if lpMessages = nil then begin
    Playing := false;
    exit;
  end;

 {are there messages to play?}
  if lpMessages^.First = nil then begin
    Playing := false;
    exit;
  end;

 {get the first message}
  lpMsg := lpMessages^.First;
 {set the hook}
  HookHandle := SetWindowsHookEx(WH_JOURNALPLAYBACK,
                                 PlayBackProc,
                                 hInstance,
                                 0);

 {was there an error setting the hook?}
  if HookHandle = 0 then begin
    Playing := false;
    exit;
  end;

 {everything is ok!}
  PlayMouseKeys := true;
end;

function IsPlaying : LongBool;
{$IFDEF Win32} stdcall; {$ELSE} export; {$ENDIF}
begin
  IsPlaying := Playing;
end;

procedure CreateMsgBuff(var lpMessages : PMsgHeader);
{$IFDEF Win32} stdcall; {$ELSE} export; {$ENDIF}
begin
 {create and the message buffer }
  GetMem(lpMessages, sizeof(TMsgHeader));

 {Was there an error?}
  if lpMessages = nil then exit;
```

continues

Listing 31.1   Continued

```
  {initialize the message buffer}
   lpMessages^.First := nil;
   lpMessages^.Last := nil;
end;

procedure DeleteMsgBuff(var lpMessages : PMsgHeader);
{$IFDEF Win32} stdcall; {$ELSE} export; {$ENDIF}
var
  Next : PMsgItem;
  Temp : PMsgItem;
begin

  {is the buffer pointer valid?}
   if lpMessages = nil then exit;

  {loop though buffer and destroy items}
   Next := lpMessages^.First;
   while Next <> nil do begin
     Temp := Next^.Next;
     FreeMem(Next, sizeof(TMsgItem));
     Next := Temp;
   end;

  {destroy the header record}
   FreeMem(lpMessages, sizeof(TMsgHeader));

  {invalidate the message buffer}
   lpMessages := nil;
end;

procedure CreateNextMsgItem(lpMessages : PMsgHeader);
begin
  {is the buffer pointer valid?}
   if lpMessages = nil then exit;

  {is this the first item?}
   if lpMessages^.First = nil then begin
     GetMem(lpMessages^.First, sizeof(TMsgItem));
     lpMessages^.Last := lpMessages^.First;
   end else begin
     GetMem(lpMessages^.Last^.Next, sizeof(TMsgItem));
     lpMessages^.Last := lpMessages^.Last^.Next;
   end;

  {was there an error?}
   if lpMessages^.Last = nil then exit;

  {initialize the new item with zeros}
   FillChar(lpMessages^.Last^, sizeof(TMsgItem), #0);
end;

function AddVkMessage(lpMessages : PMsgHeader;
                      TheMsg : Word;
                      TheVkKey : Word) : LongBool;
```

```
{$IFDEF Win32} stdcall; {$ELSE} export; {$ENDIF}
begin
  AddVkMessage := false;

 {is the buffer pointer valid?}
  if lpMessages = nil then exit;

 {create a new message item}
  CreateNextMsgItem(lpMessages);

 {was there an error?}
  if lpMessages^.Last = nil then exit;

 {fill in the new message item}
  lpMessages^.Last^.Event.Message := TheMsg;
  lpMessages^.Last^.Event.ParamL := TheVkKey;
  lpMessages^.Last^.Event.ParamH :=
    MapVirtualKey(lpMessages^.Last^.Event.ParamL, 0);
  AddVkMessage := true;
end;

function AddVkMsgPair(lpMessages : PMsgHeader;
                      The1stMsg : Word;
                      The2ndMsg : Word;
                      TheVkKey : Word) : LongBool;
{$IFDEF Win32} stdcall; {$ELSE} export; {$ENDIF}
begin
  AddVkMsgPair := false;
 {add the first message}
  if AddVkMessage(lpMessages,
                  The1stMsg,
                  TheVkKey) = false then exit;
 {add the second message}
  if AddVkMessage(lpMessages,
                  The2ndMsg,
                  TheVkKey) = false then exit;
  AddVkMsgPair := true;
end;

function AddKeyString(lpMessages : PMsgHeader;
                      lpBuffer : PChar) : LongBool;
{$IFDEF Win32} stdcall; {$ELSE} export; {$ENDIF}
var
  i : integer;
  VkCode : word;
begin
  AddKeyString := false;
  i := 0;

 {is the character buffer valid?}
  if lpBuffer = nil then exit;

 {loop through the character buffer}
  while lpBuffer[i] <> #0 do begin
```

continues

Part
VI

Ch

31

Listing 31.1   Continued

```
  {get the characters vkKeyCode and shift state}
  {$IFDEF Win32}
    VkCode := VkKeyScan(lpBuffer[i]);
  {$ELSE}
    VkCode := VkKeyScan(ord(lpBuffer[i]));
  {$ENDIF}

  {does the character require a shift key down?}
   if (HiByte(VkCode) and 1) = 1 then
     if not AddVkMessage(lpMessages,
                         WM_KEYDOWN,
                         VK_SHIFT) then exit;

  {make the character message}
   if not AddVkMsgPair(lpMessages,
                       WM_KEYDOWN,
                       WM_KEYUP,
                       vkCode) then exit;

  {does the character require a shift key up?}
   if (HiByte(VkCode) and 1) = 1 then
     if not AddVkMessage(lpMessages,
                         WM_KEYUP,
                         VK_SHIFT) then exit;

   {point to the next character}
    Inc(i);
  end;
  AddKeyString := true;
end;

function AddMouseMessage(lpMessages : PMsgHeader;
                         Msg : integer;
                         x : SmallInt;
                         y : SmallInt) : LongBool;
{$IFDEF Win32} stdcall; {$ELSE} export; {$ENDIF}
begin
  AddMouseMessage := false;

 {is the buffer pointer valid?}
  if lpMessages = nil then exit;

 {create next message}
  CreateNextMsgItem(lpMessages);

 {was there an error?}
  if lpMessages^.Last = nil then exit;

 {fill in the message}
  lpMessages^.Last^.Event.Message := Msg;
  lpMessages^.Last^.Event.ParamL := x;
  lpMessages^.Last^.Event.ParamH := y;
  AddMouseMessage := true;
end;
```

```
exports
  PlayBackProc index 1 name 'PLAYBACKPROC' resident,
  PlayMouseKeys index 2 name 'PLAYMOUSEKEYS' resident,
  IsPlaying index 3 name 'ISPLAYING' resident,
  CreateMsgBuff index 4 name 'CREATEMSGBUFF' resident,
  DeleteMsgBuff index 5 name 'DELETEMSGBUFF' resident,
  AddVkMessage index 6 name 'ADDVKMESSAGE' resident,
  AddVkMsgPair index 7 name 'ADDVKMSGPAIR' resident,
  AddKeyString index 8 name 'ADDKEYSTRING' resident,
  AddMouseMessage index 9 name 'ADDMOUSEMESSAGE' resident;

begin
  Playing := false;
end.
```

The first line of the code sets the code segment to be a preloaded, permanent segment that doesn't move around in memory on 16-bit platforms, and is just ignored under the Win32 platform. The next few lines define the correct function parameters for the needed playback hook function under both 16- and 32-bit platforms. We then prototype the two necessary structures for our message buffer—TMsgItem and TMsgHeader. Finally, we declare three global variables, as shown in the following list:

- Playing—A flag denoting if a macro is currently playing.
- lpMsg—The pointer to the current message buffer.
- TheHook—The handle to our hook function.

We then declare our playback hook function and process four types of requests, as shown in the following list:

- HC_SKIP—Get the next message. If no more messages exist, then we end the playout and unhook our function.
- HC_GETNEXT—Play the current message.
- HC_SYSMODALON—A system error occurred, and we need to call the next hook in the chain to let the hooks further down the chain know about the error.
- HC_SYSMODALOFF—The system is removing all hooks due to an error. We will call the next hook in the chain to let the hooks further down the chain know their hook also is getting removed.

We return zero from our hook function unless we receive any other request code types. If we receive a request that we are not handling, we simply need to call the next hook in the chain, and return the value passed back from the call.

The next function to declare, PlayMouseKeys(), installs our hook function. This function accepts a pointer to the message list to play, and installs the hook only if the buffer is valid and we are not currently playing another macro. If the hook gets installed, we return true for success. It may not be apparent that the SetWindowsHookEx() function returns immediately, and the hook will start playing at some future time.

Part VI Ch 31

The IsPlaying() function simply returns true if the player is currently playing a macro, so you can have your application wait for the macro to finish before allowing your application to accept additional input, or requesting another macro to play. Because you need to allow the system to continue execution while you wait, your application should go into a loop as follows:

```
while IsPlaying do
   Application.ProcessMessages;
```

The next two procedures, CreateMsgBuff() and DeleteMsgBuff, create and destroy the message buffer, respectively. The CreateMsgBuff() procedure passes back a nil pointer if an error occurred, and the DeleteMsgBuff returns a nil pointer if the deletion is successful.

Our CreateNextMsgItem() procedure will add a new message item node to the message list if successful, and initialize the new message by zeroing out all the members. You can test for any failures to add the next message by checking to see if lpMessages^.Last = nil. Although this procedure is not exported from the DLL, you can always change the declaration to provide this functionality if you want.

The next two functions, AddVkMessage() and AddVkMsgPair(), add virtual key messages to the message buffer. The AddVkMsgPair() function is simply a wrapper to AddVkMessage(), making it convenient to add pairs of key sequences such as WM_KEYDOWN and WM_KEYUP with a single call. This function returns True for success.

The AddKeyString() function creates a series of WM_KEYDOWN and WM_KEYUP messages for each character in a null-terminated string, taking into account the shift status of the key. This function returns True for success.

The last function, AddMouseMessage(), will add a MouseMessage to the message list. This function returns True for success.

Finally, we export the functions by both index and name, and initialize the Playing variable to False.

Interfacing to the PlayKeys DLL

On the CD

The easy way to interface to the PlayKeys library is to create an interface unit. In this way, when you want to use PlayKeys in an application, you simply add the name of the interface unit to the uses clause in the unit from which you want to use it. Here is the code for a unit named KeyImp that allows you to easily import the functions in the PlayKeys DLL (see Listing 31.2). The unit file is on the book's companion CD-ROM, located in the same directory as the PLAYKEYS.DLL project.

Listing 31.2   \DLPHI3\CHP31\KEYIMP—Dummy Interface Unit

```
unit keyimp;

interface
```

```
function PlayMouseKeys(lpMessages : pointer): LongBool;
{$IFDEF Win32} stdcall; {$ELSE} far; {$ENDIF}

function IsPlaying : LongBool;
{$IFDEF Win32} stdcall; {$ELSE} far; {$ENDIF}

procedure CreateMsgBuff(var lpMessages : pointer);
{$IFDEF Win32} stdcall; {$ELSE} far; {$ENDIF}

procedure DeleteMsgBuff(var lpMessages : pointer);
{$IFDEF Win32} stdcall; {$ELSE} far; {$ENDIF}

function AddVkMessage(lpMessages : pointer;
                      TheMsg : Word;
                      TheVkKey : Word) : LongBool;
{$IFDEF Win32} stdcall; {$ELSE} far; {$ENDIF}

function AddVkMsgPair(lpMessages : pointer;
                      The1stMsg : Word;
                      The2ndMsg : Word;
                      TheVkKey : Word) : LongBool;
{$IFDEF Win32} stdcall; {$ELSE} far; {$ENDIF}

function AddKeyString(lpMessages : pointer;
                      lpBuffer : PChar) : LongBool;
{$IFDEF Win32} stdcall; {$ELSE} far; {$ENDIF}

function AddMouseMessage(lpMessages : pointer;
                         Msg : integer;
                         x : SmallInt;
                         y : SmallInt) : LongBool;
{$IFDEF Win32} stdcall; {$ELSE} far; {$ENDIF}


implementation

function PlayMouseKeys; external 'PLAYKEYS' index 2;

function IsPlaying; external 'PLAYKEYS' index 3;

procedure CreateMsgBuff; external 'PLAYKEYS' index 4;

procedure DeleteMsgBuff; external 'PLAYKEYS' index 5;

function AddVkMessage; external 'PLAYKEYS' index 6;

function AddVkMsgPair; external 'PLAYKEYS' index 7;

function AddKeyString; external 'PLAYKEYS' index 8;

function AddMouseMessage; external 'PLAYKEYS' index 9;

end.
```

Part

VI

Ch

31

Notice how we declared the function prototypes in the interface section, and the actual pointers to the DLL indices in the implementation section. Now, every time you want to use PlayKeys, just add the word KeyImp to the uses clause in the unit in which you want to use it, and you will have instant access to the functions. Just don't forget to deploy the PlayKeys DLL with your application when you ship your project.

Using PlayKeys

Using PlayKeys to send a string of keystrokes to a windowed control is easy. First, you must set the focus to the receiving control or window. If you are sending keystrokes to a VCL component, simply call its setfocus method. If you want to send input to a window, you can use the Windows FindWindow() function to get the handle to the receiving window and use the Windows BringWindowToTop() function to make the window active. Regardless of the method that you use, you should make a call to Application.ProcessMessages to allow the control or window time to get focus before you start playing messages. Now that the receiving window has focus, you can call the CreateMsgBuff() function passing it a pointer to be initialized and start adding messages to the buffer. After you have your messages constructed, you are ready to play them. First, you should verify that no messages are currently playing by calling the IsPlaying() function. If there are no messages playing, you may safely make your call to PlayMouseKeys(); otherwise, you should "wait in line" until it's your turn by calling Application.ProcessMessages. After you have called PlayMouseKeys(), you should "wait around" until all your messages finish playing by calling Application.ProcessMessages until IsPlaying() returns false. Finally, you should make a call to the DeleteMsgBuff() function to dispose of your buffer.

Here is an example of playing a string of characters to a memo component:

```
procedure TForm1.Button1Click(Sender: TObject);
var
  p : pointer;
begin

  {Set the Focus to the control to receive input}
  Memo1.SetFocus;

  {Allow time for the control to get focus}
  Application.ProcessMessages;

  {Create a message buffer}
  CreateMsgBuff(p);

  {Add a string to the message buffer}
  AddKeyString(p, 'Now Is The Time!');

  {wait if any messages are currently playing}
  while IsPlaying do
    Application.ProcessMessages;

  {Start playing our message}
  PlayMouseKeys(p);
```

```
{wait for our messages to be played}
  while IsPlaying do
    Application.ProcessMessages;

{Delete our message buffer}
  DeleteMsgBuff(p);
end;
```

Although this example probably seems a little extreme for adding text to a memo component, remember that the real power of the PlayKeys library is the capability to send any combination of keystrokes and mouse input to any window control in any running application. This includes sending "system keys" such as Alt+Ctrl+Shift+Key combinations, PrintScreen, and function keys. Usually, you will want to send WM_KEYDOWN - WM_KEYUP and WM_SYSKEYDOWN - WM_SYSKEYUP combinations. There are many virtual keys available to send, and you can find the declarations for these keys in the WINDOWS.PAS file located in Delphi's SOURCE\RTL\WIN directory. Simply search for the word "vk_" to be presented with the complete list of keys. After you know the keys you want to send, you can use the AddVkMessage() and AddVkMsgPair() functions to add those keys of your choice, in any combination, to the list.

The following example shows how to create a group of messages that will activate Delphi's menu, select the help menu, choose the about box, and then type **TEAM** while holding down the Alt key. This little piece of code reveals an "Easter egg" that displays the team members who contributed to the product. You need to use the FindWindow() and BringWindowToTop() functions to get Delphi's main window to accept the input from your application:

```
{Activate the menu by pressing and releasing the alt key}
AddVkMsgPair(p, WM_SYSKEYDOWN,WM_SYSKEYUP, VK_MENU);

{type in "H" for the help menu, and "A" to bring up the about box}
AddKeyString(p, 'HA');

{Hold the alt key down}
AddVkMessage(p, WM_SYSKEYDOWN, VK_MENU);

{type "team"}
AddKeyString(p, 'team');

{release the alt key}
AddVkMessage(p, WM_SYSKEYUP, VK_MENU);
```

Now that you have a firm grasp of sending keystrokes, we wrap up by sending a few mouse messages. In this final example, we move the mouse to the center of a second button component and click the button with the mouse:

```
procedure TForm1.Button1Click(Sender: TObject);
var
  pt : TPoint;
  p : pointer;
begin
 {Create the message buffer}
  CreateMsgBuff(p);
```

```
{get the location of the middle of the button}
 pt.x := Button2.Left + (Button2.Width div 2);
 pt.y := Button2.Top + (Button2.Height div 2);

{get the screen coordinates}
 pt := ClientToScreen(Pt);
{add the mouse messages}
 AddMouseMessage(p,
                 WM_MOUSEMOVE,
                 pt.x,
                 pt.y);

 AddMouseMessage(p,
                 WM_LBUTTONDOWN,
                 pt.x,
                 pt.y);

 AddMouseMessage(p,
                 WM_LBUTTONUP,
                 pt.x,
                 pt.y);

{wait if someone else is playing}
 while IsPlaying do
   Application.ProcessMessages;

{play our macro}
 PlayMouseKeys(p);

{wait till the macro plays}
 while IsPlaying do
   Application.ProcessMessages;

{delete the message buffer}
 DeleteMsgBuff(p);
end;
```

In this example, we had to get the screen coordinates for the button component because mouse messages are played out relative to the top of the screen, not the form. Note that there are several useful functions for receiving the handle of a control in another application, and converting its window-relative coordinates to screen coordinates listed in the Windows API help file.

Summary

We have covered a lot in this chapter, everything from DLL basics and patching the VCL interfaces file to building a full-featured Windows macro player capable of sending mouse and keyboard input to any Windows control. With the material you have just covered, you can go on to conquer almost any Windows API function prototype with confidence! ●

CHAPTER 32

Thunking in Delphi

by David Powell

When migrating code to a 32-bit platform, programmers frequently run into situations where their software depends on 16-bit DLLs that are unavailable in a 32-bit form. This often arises from the use of third-party library DLLs or legacy code that time doesn't permit converting to 32-bit code. This situation also can occur when writing 32-bit library DLLs that need to be used by both 16-bit and 32-bit applications. When faced with this situation, the only option available is to create a mechanism to *thunk* to the DLLs. ■

What is thunking?

Find out what thunking is and if your application needs to do it.

Types of thunking

Examine the three different types of thunking and learn what platforms support them.

Example of thunking

A sample application that thunks from a 32-bit application down to a 16-bit DLL. Complete source code is written in Delphi only.

Types of Thunks

Thunking is the process of a 16-bit application calling into a 32-bit DLL or vice versa. A *thunking layer* is the actual piece of code that implements one of the three thunking methods available. Table 32.1 shows the three thunking methods and their availability on the three different implementations of the Win32 specification.

Table 32.1   Supported Thunking Methods

	Universal Thunk		Generic Thunk		Flat Thunk	
Platform	16->32	32->16	16->32	32->16	16->32	32->16
Win32s	Y*	Y	N	N	N	N
Windows NT	N	N	Y	N	N	N
Windows 95	N	N	Y	N	Y	Y

* Not officially supported

Universal Thunk

The *Universal thunk* is supported only under Win32s, which makes it quite "non-universal." Under Win32s all applications, 16-bit and 32-bit, run under the same address space and may communicate back and forth across the 16-32-bit boundary via Universal thunk. The two main API calls involved in the Universal thunk are UTRegister and UTUnRegister, which are exported by KERNEL32. Because Delphi 3.0 isn't designed to work under the Win32s platform, this chapter doesn't cover this thunking method.

Generic Thunk

The *Generic thunk* provides support for 16-bit applications to call into 32-bit DLLs on both the Windows 95 and Windows NT platforms. Unfortunately, Generic thunking doesn't provide a way for 32-bit apps to call into 16-bit DLLs. Not only can this method be used to access 32-bit library DLLs, as mentioned previously, it can be used to allow your 16-bit applications to access the Win32 API. The Win32 API offers many new API calls and also provides an avenue to use the new Common Controls in Windows 95 and NT 4.0. Conceivably, you can use the Status Bar, Header control, and so on in your 16-bit application. Generic thunking was documented in many Delphi books and magazines since the release of Delphi 2.0. Due to the abundance of information on this thunking method as well as its limited application (it is mainly used in developing 16-bit applications), I will not cover this method in any detail.

Flat Thunk

The *Flat thunk* provides support for 16-bit applications to call into 32-bit DLLs as well as support for 32-bit applications to call into 16-bit DLLs. It is a dream come true... well, almost. Two things turn this dream into a nightmare. First of all, Flat thunking is currently supported only on the Windows 95 platform. And second, according to the Microsoft documentation, Flat thunking requires the use of a Thunk Compiler. The Thunk Compiler, called THUNK.EXE, takes a thunking script that you manually generate, along with the EXE and DLL, and recompiles both, with the necessary modifications to allow them to work together. The 16-bit DLL still has to be further modified to be marked as a Windows 4.0 DLL and a DllEntryPoint must be created.

Fortunately, there is an undocumented way of doing Flat thunks that doesn't require using the Thunk Compiler. Matt Pietrek, in his book, *Windows 95 System Programming Secrets*, IDG Books, 1995, documents the QT_Thunk API call. This API call is actually what is used by the code generated from the Thunk Compiler. If you need to access a 16-bit DLL from a 32-bit program and you do not have to run on Windows NT machines, this is probably the method for you. A full example of using QT_Thunk is given in a following section of this chapter.

What About Windows NT?

Windows NT does not support any thunking method from 32-bit applications to 16-bit DLLs. However, there is some hope to be had in the form of a windows message called WM_COPYDATA. This doesn't provide a true thunking method in that you cannot call a procedure or function in a 16-bit DLL and pass its parameters as you can using one of the previously mentioned thunking methods. You can, however, pass binary data from the 32-bit application to the 16-bit DLL. Now most DLLs are not written to accept only binary data (records or similar structures), so you have to create a 16-bit DLL that accepts the binary data via WM_COPYDATA, processes it, calls the desired 16-bit DLL, gets the result, and sends the result back to the 32-bit application. This involves an extra DLL, but it is the only way to transfer data between 32-bit and 16-bit applications under Windows NT. A full example of doing this is shown in the following section.

Using *WM_COPYDATA*

WM_COPYDATA allows you to pass data from one process to another. The processes can be 32- or 16-bit; it doesn't matter. The sending application passes its window handle in the wparam and a pointer to a TCopyDataStruct in the lparam. The receiving application can access the data, and then send a WM_COPYDATA message back to the calling application if needed. Windows takes care of converting the 0:32 pointer to a 16:16 pointer, and vice versa. TCopyDataStruct is defined as follows:

```
PCopyDataStruct = ^TCopyDataStruct;
TCopyDataStruct = packed record
  dwData: DWORD;
  cbData: DWORD;
  lpData: Pointer;
end;
```

The dwData parameter can be used for user-defined data. The cbData parameter contains a DWORD that indicates the size (in bytes) of the binary data. The lpData parameter is the pointer to the binary data.

TIP When sending the WM_COPYDATA message, you must use SendMessage, not PostMessage, because you want your program to stop execution until the SendMessage call returns.

For an example of this, consider a 32-bit application that needs to send a record to a 16-bit application. The record will contain three different type fields that can be changed by the 32-bit sending program. The 16-bit receiving program then will display these fields correctly. In a real-life scenario, the 16-bit receiving program might take the record structure and call another 16-bit DLL with the record elements as parameters to some desired procedure or function call. Listing 32.1 shows what the sending application will look like. You can find the code in this listing as well as the code in subsequent listings in this chapter, on this book's companion CD-ROM.

Listing 32.1 \UDELPHI3\CHP32\WMCOPYDATA\CPYDAT32.PAS—32-Bit Sending Application

```
unit CpyDat32;

interface

uses
  Windows, Messages, SysUtils, Classes, Graphics, Controls, Forms, Dialogs,
  StdCtrls;

type
  TCopy32 = class(TForm)
    Label1: TLabel;
    Label2: TLabel;
    Label3: TLabel;
    Send: TButton;
    Edit1: TEdit;
    Edit2: TEdit;
    Edit3: TEdit;
    procedure SendClick(Sender: TObject);
  private
    { Private declarations }
  public
    { Public declarations }
  end;

var
  Copy32: TCopy32;

implementation

{$R *.DFM}

type
  TMyRec = packed record
    F1 : SmallInt;    // Integer in 16-bit
    F2 : Double;
    F3 : String[20];
```

```
  end;

procedure TCopy32.SendClick(Sender: TObject);
var
  RecSize: integer;
  MyRec: TMyRec;
  CopyDataStruct: TCopyDataStruct;
  TargetWnd: hWnd;
begin
  // Note: no error checking is done when moving values from the Edit boxes
  // into the record fields.  If this were an actual application, error
  // checking should be added.

  // Get the hWnd of the 16-bit application
  TargetWnd := FindWindow(nil,'16-bit Receiving Application');

  // Fill the Data Structure
  RecSize := SizeOf(TMyRec);
  with CopyDataStruct, MyRec do begin
    F1 := StrToInt(Edit1.Text);
    F2 := StrToFloat(Edit2.Text);
    F3 := Edit3.Text;
    dwData := 5;  // put whatever DWORD value you want here.
    cbData := RecSize;
    lpData := @MyRec;
  end;

  // Send the Message WM_CopyData
  SendMessage(TargetWnd, WM_COPYDATA, Handle, Longint(@CopyDataStruct));
end;

end.
```

In Delphi 1.0, both the WM_COPYDATA message and the TCopyDataStruct are available to 16-bit applications running under Win32 but are not defined in WINPROCS or WINTYPES, so they need to be defined in the application. Listing 32.2 shows what the receiving application will look like.

Listing 32.2 \UDELPHI3\CHP32\WMCOPYDATA\CPYDAT16.PAS—16-Bit Receiving Application

```
unit Cpydat16;

interface

uses
  SysUtils, WinTypes, WinProcs, Messages, Classes, Graphics, Controls,
  Forms, Dialogs, StdCtrls;

const
  {Define the message constant for WM_COPYDATA}
  WM_COPYDATA = $004A;
```

continues

Listing 32.2   Continued

```delphi
type
  TCopy16 = class(TForm)
    Edit1: TEdit;
    Edit2: TEdit;
    Edit3: TEdit;
    Label1: TLabel;
    Label2: TLabel;
    Label3: TLabel;
    Edit4: TEdit;
    Label4: TLabel;
  private
    { Private declarations }
    procedure WMCopyData(var M: TMessage); message WM_COPYDATA;
  public
    { Public declarations }
  end;

var
  Copy16: TCopy16;

implementation

{$R *.DFM}

type
  PMyRec = ^TMyRec;
  TMyRec = packed record
    F1 : Integer;   {SmallInt in 32-bit}
    F2 : Double;
    F3 : String[20];
  end;

  {Define the structure for WM_COPYDATA}
  PCopyDataStruct = ^TCopyDataStruct;
  TCopyDataStruct = packed record
    dwData: LongInt;   {DWORD in 32-bit}
    cbData: LongInt;   {DWORD in 32-bit}
    lpData: Pointer;
  end;

procedure TCopy16.WMCopyData(var M: TMessage);
var
  MyRec: TMyRec;
begin
  MyRec := PMyRec(PCopyDataStruct(M.lParam)^.lpData)^;
  Edit1.Text := IntToStr(MyRec.F1);
  Edit2.Text := FloatToStr(MyRec.F2);
  Edit3.Text := MyRec.F3;
  Edit4.Text := IntToStr(PCopyDataStruct(M.lParam)^.dwData)
end;

end.
```

Figure 32.1 shows what these two programs look like when running side-by-side. When changes are made in the 32-bit application and the Send button is clicked, the 16-bit receiving application reflects these changes.

FIG. 32.1

WM_COPYDATA example programs.

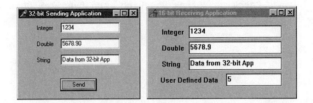

If the receiving application needed to modify the data and send it back, it needs to copy the record to a local variable and then send it back to the calling application in the same way that it was sent (in other words, reverse the process). The handle of the calling application was passed in the wparam of the WM_COPYDATA message.

Quick Thunking with *QT_Thunk*

QT_Thunk is an undocumented API call that provides an easy way of doing Flat thunking without the use of the dreaded Thunk Compiler and is supported only on Windows 95. When QT_Thunk is called, it takes the value in the EDX register, assumes that it is a 16-bit address, and tries to jump to that location. Notice that I call QT_Thunk inside an asm block to ensure that the value in the EDX register is what I want it to be when the API call is made.

Theoretically, I could move the 16:16 address of the procedure into the EDX register via an asm block, and then call the QT_Thunk API in regular Pascal code. This method assumes that the compiler will preserve the value that I moved into the register when the API call is made. And that is not a bet that I would be willing to make!

There are several necessary steps that you must take when using QT_Thunk. The order in which you take these steps is unimportant. They are as follows:

- The procedure or function in the calling application that makes the QT_Thunk call must have a stack frame set up. This can be accomplished via the $W+ compiler directive.
- Reserve at least $3C bytes on the calling stack so that QT_Thunk can set up its own peculiar stack frame.
- Load the 16-bit DLL, get the procedure address, and free the 16-bit DLL via the undocumented API calls: LoadLibrary16, GetProcAddress16, and FreeLibrary16.
- Do not create any local variables in the calling procedure. Experience has shown that QT_Thunk may overwrite them.

Listing 32.3 shows a unit that contains the declaration of QT_Thunk as well as several other useful API calls that can be used when thunking.

Part
VI

Ch
32

Listing 32.3 \UDELPHI3\CHP32\QT_THUNK\QTTHUNKU.PAS—A Unit Declaring API Calls Used for *QT_Thunk*

```
unit QTThunkU;
//Turn off Range Checking, Stack Checking, and Overflow Checking
{$R-,S-,Q-}

interface

uses
  Windows;

type
  //Declare a 16 bit handle, in Delphi 3.0 THandle is 32 bits
  TShortHandle = Word;

//API calls declared in WOW32.DLL
function  WOWGetVDMPointer(vp, dwBytes: DWord;
                           fProtectedMode: Bool): Pointer; stdcall;
function  WOWGetVDMPointerFix(vp, dwBytes: DWord;
                             fProtectedMode: Bool): Pointer; stdcall;
procedure WOWGetVDMPointerUnfix(vp: DWord); stdcall;

//Undocumented Windows 95 API calls declared in Kernel32.DLL
function  GlobalAlloc16(Flags: Integer; Bytes: Longint): TShortHandle; stdcall;
function  GlobalLock16(Mem: TShortHandle): Pointer; stdcall;
function  GlobalUnLock16(Mem: TShortHandle): WordBool; stdcall;
function  GlobalFree16(Mem: TShortHandle): TShortHandle; stdcall;

function  LoadLibrary16(LibFileName: PChar): THandle; stdcall;
function  GetProcAddress16(Module: HModule; ProcName: PChar): TFarProc; stdcall;
procedure FreeLibrary16(LibModule: THandle); stdcall;

procedure QT_Thunk;


implementation

uses
  SysUtils, Classes;

type
  EVersionError = class(Exception);

//Exported API calls from WOW32.DLL
function  WOWGetVDMPointer;      external 'wow32.dll';
function  WOWGetVDMPointerFix;   external 'wow32.dll';
procedure WOWGetVDMPointerUnfix; external 'wow32.dll';

//Exported API calls from Kernel32.DLL
function  GlobalAlloc16;     external 'kernel32.dll' index 24;
function  GlobalLock16;      external 'kernel32.dll' index 25;
function  GlobalUnLock16;    external 'kernel32.dll' index 26;
function  GlobalFree16;      external 'kernel32.dll' index 31;

function  LoadLibrary16;     external 'kernel32.dll' index 35;
```

```
procedure FreeLibrary16;     external 'kernel32.dll' index 36;
function  GetProcAddress16; external 'kernel32.dll' index 37;

procedure QT_Thunk;          external 'kernel32.dll' index 559;

initialization
  //Check for Win32 under Windows 95
  if Win32Platform <> Ver_Platform_Win32_Windows then
    raise EVersionError.Create('QT_Thunk only works under Windows 95!'+#13#10+
                               'For Windows NT use the WM_COPYDATA technique.');

end.
```

In order to examine QT_Thunk, I will create a 32-bit application that calls two Pascal-type procedures and one C-type function contained in a 16-bit DLL. The first Pascal-type procedure has no parameters and the second passes two long integers, one by value and one by reference. The parameter passed by reference will be modified by the 16-bit DLL and passed back to the 32-bit application. The C-type function will take two long integer parameters and return the sum of the parameters. Listing 32.4 shows the 32-bit calling application.

Listing 32.4 \UDELPHI3\CHP32\QT_THUNK\QT_TESTU.PAS—32-Bit Calling Application

```
unit QT_TestU;

interface

uses
  Windows, Messages, SysUtils, Classes, Graphics, Controls, Forms, Dialogs,
  StdCtrls, ExtCtrls;

type
  TCall32 = class(TForm)
    PasProcNoParam: TButton;
    PasProc2Param: TButton;
    CFunc2Param: TButton;
    procedure PasProcNoParamClick(Sender: TObject);
    procedure PasProc2ParamClick(Sender: TObject);
    procedure CFunc2ParamClick(Sender: TObject);
  private
    { Private declarations }
  public
    { Public declarations }
  end;

var
  Call32: TCall32;

implementation

{$R *.DFM}
```

Part
VI

Ch

32

continues

Listing 32.4 Continued

```
// Turn on Stack Frames, This is *required* for QT_Thunk
{$W+}

uses
  QTThunkU;

//Declare all variables as global not local, so that QT_Thunk
//won't trash them!
var
  Dll16Handle : THandle;
  Proc16Addr : Pointer;
  IntParam1 : integer;
  IntParam2 : integer;
  PIntParam32 : ^integer;
  PIntParam16 : ^integer;
  Return : integer;

function Lock16Pointer(var P32: Pointer; Size: integer): Pointer;
begin
  result := nil;
  // Allocate memory in a 16-bit address range and get a 16-bit pointer to it
  LongRec(result).Hi := GlobalAlloc16(GMEM_FIXED or GMEM_ZEROINIT, Size);
  // Convert the 16-bit address to a 32-bit address
  P32 := WOWGetVDMPointer(DWORD(Result), 0, True);
end;

procedure UnLock16Pointer(P: Pointer);
begin
  GlobalFree16(LongRec(P).Hi);
end;

procedure TCall32.PasProcNoParamClick(Sender: TObject);
var
  QT_Stack_Space : String[$3C];
begin
  //Use QT_Stack_Space so that it won't be optimized out
  QT_Stack_Space := '';

  // Load the 16-bit library DLL
  Dll16Handle := LoadLibrary16('Lib16DLL.DLL');
  Proc16Addr := GetProcAddress16(Dll16Handle, 'PasProcNoParam');
  if Assigned(Proc16Addr) then
    asm
      mov edx, Proc16Addr
      call QT_Thunk
    end;
  FreeLibrary16(Dll16Handle);
end;

procedure TCall32.PasProc2ParamClick(Sender: TObject);
// This procedure passes two integer parameters, one by value
// and one by reference.
var
  QT_Stack_Space : String[$3C];
begin
```

```
  //Use QT_Stack_Space so that it won't be optimized out
  QT_Stack_Space := '';

  // Load the 16-bit library DLL
  Dll16Handle := LoadLibrary16('Lib16DLL.DLL');
  Proc16Addr := GetProcAddress16(Dll16Handle, 'PasProc2Params');
  if Assigned(Proc16Addr) then begin
    IntParam1 := 100;
    IntParam2 := 200;
    //Allocate memory some memory in 16-bit land
    PIntParam16 := Lock16Pointer(Pointer(PIntParam32), SizeOf(IntParam2));
    //Move IntParam2 into the new buffer pointed to by PIntParam32
    Move(IntParam2, PIntParam32^, sizeof(IntParam2));
    asm
      push IntParam1
      push PIntParam16
      mov edx, Proc16Addr
      call QT_Thunk
    end;
    ShowMessage('IntParam2 was 200 now it is '+ IntToStr(PIntParam32^));
    UnLock16Pointer(PIntParam16);
  end;
  FreeLibrary16(Dll16Handle);
end;

procedure TCall32.CFunc2ParamClick(Sender: TObject);
// This procedure passes two integer parameters to a C
// function that returns the sum of the two values.
var
  QT_Stack_Space : String[$3C];
begin
  //Use QT_Stack_Space so that it won't be optimized out
  QT_Stack_Space := '';

  // Load the 16-bit library DLL
  Dll16Handle := LoadLibrary16('Lib16DLL.DLL');
  Proc16Addr := GetProcAddress16(Dll16Handle, 'CFunc2Params');
  if Assigned(Proc16Addr) then begin
    IntParam1 := 100;
    IntParam2 := 200;
    // This is a C function so push the parameters from right to left
    // and clean up the stack when done.
    asm
      push IntParam2
      push IntParam1
      mov edx, Proc16Addr
      call QT_Thunk
      //Clean up the stack
      add esp, 2 * 4  // Two LongInts, four bytes each
      mov Return.Word.2, dx
      mov Return.Word.0, ax
    end;
    ShowMessage(Format('%d + %d = %d', [IntParam1,IntParam2,Return]));
  end;
  FreeLibrary16(Dll16Handle);
```

continues

Listing 32.4 Continued

```
end;

end.
```

The 16-bit DLL is created just like any other DLL—nothing special needs to be done. Listing 32.5 shows the 16-bit DLL that implements the procedures and functions described in Listing 32.4.

Listing 32.5 \UDELPHI3\CHP32\QT_THUNK\LIB16DLL.DPR—16-Bit DLL for *QT_Thunk* Example

```
library Lib16DLL;

uses
  Dialogs,
  SysUtils;

procedure PasProcNoParam; export;
begin
  ShowMessage('Pascal procedure called with no parameters');
end;

procedure PasProc2Params(p1: LongInt; var p2: LongInt); export;
begin
  ShowMessage(Format('Pascal procedure called with parameters %d and %d',
                     [p1, p2]));
  p2 := p2 * 5;
end;

function CFunc2Params(p1, p2: LongInt): LongInt; cdecl; export;
begin
  ShowMessage(Format('C Function called with parameters %d and %d',
                     [p1, p2]));
  CFunc2Params := p1 + p2;
end;

exports
  PasProcNoParam,
  PasProc2Params,
  CFunc2Params;

begin
end.
```

Putting It All Together

Thunking provides a method for processes to cross the 16-32-bit boundary. This chapter covered the three thunking methods that are available on the different Win32 platforms as well as a way of transferring data via a Windows message. You may never need to do thunking but if you do, this chapter should serve as a handy reference for Flat thunking via QT_Thunk and binary data transfer via WM_COPYDATA. ●

Index

G

M

S

Safecall convention, 785

Samples page (Component Palette), 31

Save command (File menu), 21

SaveToFile method, datastreams, ClientDataSet, 433-434

SaveToStream method, datastreams, ClientDataSet, 433-434

saving OLE objects, 547-548

Scale command (Speedmenu), 42

scaling OLE objects (TOleContainer class), 549-550

schema data types, 399

scoping identifiers, 93

scoping directives (classes)
private members, 103
protected members, 103
public members, 103
published members, 103-104

SCRCAP1.PAS, Image List source code, 217-219

SDFMOD.DPR, flat functions source code, 941

SDI (Single Document Interface)
applications, creating, 288-292
Application templates, 305-306
codes, writing, 291
defined, 287-288
EgSDIApp project overview, 288-292

Search menu commands
Browse Symbol, 24
Find Error, 23, 876

searching text (RichEdit), 241-242

SECCRT1.PAS, Header Control source code, 211-212

SECDRW1.PAS, Header Control source code, 212

sections (Portable Executables)
attributes, 832-833
viewing, 833

security, digital certificates, 664

SELATR1.PAS, RichEdit source code, 235-236

Select All command (Edit menu), 22

selecting
component ancestor class, 464
debugging information settings, 852-854
exceptions, 137-138
property editors, corrector ancestors, 507
TCheckBox control, 168

selection events
OnClick, 159-160
OnDblClick, 159-160
OnMouseDown, 159-160
OnMouseUp, 159-160

SEMAPHORE.PAS source code, 757-758

semaphores
defined, 756-763
source codes, SEMAPHORE.PAS, 757-758

sending keystroke strings (PlayKeys DLL), 978-980

servers (COM)
component object clients, 571
DLL modules, 570
DllRegisterServer function, 581
DllUnregisterServer function, 581
EXE modules, 570
OLE interfaces, 572
Windows communication process, 582-584
DLLCanUnloadNow function, 582-584
DLLGetClassObject function, 582-584

sessions, creating databases, 347-348

Set method (TPropertyEditor class), 513

set procedures, creating property values, 478-480

set property components, 471

set property editor (Object Inspector), 34-35

set types
ordinal values, 76-77
structured data type functions, 76-77

SetBookmarkData method (TDataSet class), 409-412

SetBookmarkFlag method (TDataSet class), 409-412

SetFieldData method (TDataSet class), 416-420

SetLength(s,newlen) function, 73

SetParams method (TUpdateSQL class), 359-360

SetPrinter method (TPrinter object), 710-718

SetRange method (TTable class), 338-339

SetString function, 73

SETTCK2.PAS, TrackBar source code, 187-189

setting
breakpoints in source codes, 859-861
SQL Monitor trace options, 373
thread priorities, 737-739

settings
modifying
print drivers, 711-718
printers, 710-718
querying in printers, 718-729

SetValue method (TPropertyEditor class), 512

Shape property (TQRShape class), 382-383

shared event handlers, creating, 317

shared repository, storing form templates, 283-284

ShareHeap.DPR source code, 826-827

SHAREU1.PAS, virtual class source code, 817-819